D1265739

Dictionary of Literary Biography

1 *The American Renaissance in New England,* edited by Joel Myerson (1978)

2 *American Novelists Since World War II,* edited by Jeffrey Helterman and Richard Layman (1978)

3 *Antebellum Writers in New York and the South,* edited by Joel Myerson (1979)

4 *American Writers in Paris, 1920–1939,* edited by Karen Lane Rood (1980)

5 *American Poets Since World War II,* 2 parts, edited by Donald J. Greiner (1980)

6 *American Novelists Since World War II, Second Series,* edited by James E. Kibler Jr. (1980)

7 *Twentieth-Century American Dramatists,* 2 parts, edited by John MacNicholas (1981)

8 *Twentieth-Century American Science-Fiction Writers,* 2 parts, edited by David Cowart and Thomas L. Wymer (1981)

9 *American Novelists, 1910–1945,* 3 parts, edited by James J. Martine (1981)

10 *Modern British Dramatists, 1900–1945,* 2 parts, edited by Stanley Weintraub (1982)

11 *American Humorists, 1800–1950,* 2 parts, edited by Stanley Trachtenberg (1982)

12 *American Realists and Naturalists,* edited by Donald Pizer and Earl N. Harbert (1982)

13 *British Dramatists Since World War II,* 2 parts, edited by Stanley Weintraub (1982)

14 *British Novelists Since 1960,* 2 parts, edited by Jay L. Halio (1983)

15 *British Novelists, 1930–1959,* 2 parts, edited by Bernard Oldsey (1983)

16 *The Beats: Literary Bohemians in Postwar America,* 2 parts, edited by Ann Charters (1983)

17 *Twentieth-Century American Historians,* edited by Clyde N. Wilson (1983)

18 *Victorian Novelists After 1885,* edited by Ira B. Nadel and William E. Fredeman (1983)

19 *British Poets, 1880–1914,* edited by Donald E. Stanford (1983)

20 *British Poets, 1914–1945,* edited by Donald E. Stanford (1983)

21 *Victorian Novelists Before 1885,* edited by Ira B. Nadel and William E. Fredeman (1983)

22 *American Writers for Children, 1900–1960,* edited by John Cech (1983)

23 *American Newspaper Journalists, 1873–1900,* edited by Perry J. Ashley (1983)

24 *American Colonial Writers, 1606–1734,* edited by Emory Elliott (1984)

25 *American Newspaper Journalists, 1901–1925,* edited by Perry J. Ashley (1984)

26 *American Screenwriters,* edited by Robert E. Morsberger, Stephen O. Lesser, and Randall Clark (1984)

27 *Poets of Great Britain and Ireland, 1945–1960,* edited by Vincent B. Sherry Jr. (1984)

28 *Twentieth-Century American-Jewish Fiction Writers,* edited by Daniel Walden (1984)

29 *American Newspaper Journalists, 1926–1950,* edited by Perry J. Ashley (1984)

30 *American Historians, 1607–1865,* edited by Clyde N. Wilson (1984)

31 *American Colonial Writers, 1735–1781,* edited by Emory Elliott (1984)

32 *Victorian Poets Before 1850,* edited by William E. Fredeman and Ira B. Nadel (1984)

33 *Afro-American Fiction Writers After 1955,* edited by Thadious M. Davis and Trudier Harris (1984)

34 *British Novelists, 1890–1929: Traditionalists,* edited by Thomas F. Staley (1985)

35 *Victorian Poets After 1850,* edited by William E. Fredeman and Ira B. Nadel (1985)

36 *British Novelists, 1890–1929: Modernists,* edited by Thomas F. Staley (1985)

37 *American Writers of the Early Republic,* edited by Emory Elliott (1985)

38 *Afro-American Writers After 1955: Dramatists and Prose Writers,* edited by Thadious M. Davis and Trudier Harris (1985)

39 *British Novelists, 1660–1800,* 2 parts, edited by Martin C. Battestin (1985)

40 *Poets of Great Britain and Ireland Since 1960,* 2 parts, edited by Vincent B. Sherry Jr. (1985)

41 *Afro-American Poets Since 1955,* edited by Trudier Harris and Thadious M. Davis (1985)

42 *American Writers for Children Before 1900,* edited by Glenn E. Estes (1985)

43 *American Newspaper Journalists, 1690–1872,* edited by Perry J. Ashley (1986)

44 *American Screenwriters, Second Series,* edited by Randall Clark, Robert E. Morsberger, and Stephen O. Lesser (1986)

45 *American Poets, 1880–1945, First Series,* edited by Peter Quartermain (1986)

46 *American Literary Publishing Houses, 1900–1980: Trade and Paperback,* edited by Peter Dzwonkoski (1986)

47 *American Historians, 1866–1912,* edited by Clyde N. Wilson (1986)

48 *American Poets, 1880–1945, Second Series,* edited by Peter Quartermain (1986)

49 *American Literary Publishing Houses, 1638–1899,* 2 parts, edited by Peter Dzwonkoski (1986)

50 *Afro-American Writers Before the Harlem Renaissance,* edited by Trudier Harris (1986)

51 *Afro-American Writers from the Harlem Renaissance to 1940,* edited by Trudier Harris (1987)

52 *American Writers for Children Since 1960: Fiction,* edited by Glenn E. Estes (1986)

53 *Canadian Writers Since 1960, First Series,* edited by W. H. New (1986)

54 *American Poets, 1880–1945, Third Series,* 2 parts, edited by Peter Quartermain (1987)

55 *Victorian Prose Writers Before 1867,* edited by William B. Thesing (1987)

56 *German Fiction Writers, 1914–1945,* edited by James Hardin (1987)

57 *Victorian Prose Writers After 1867,* edited by William B. Thesing (1987)

58 *Jacobean and Caroline Dramatists,* edited by Fredson Bowers (1987)

59 *American Literary Critics and Scholars, 1800–1850,* edited by John W. Rathbun and Monica M. Grecu (1987)

60 *Canadian Writers Since 1960, Second Series,* edited by W. H. New (1987)

61 *American Writers for Children Since 1960: Poets, Illustrators, and Nonfiction Authors,* edited by Glenn E. Estes (1987)

62 *Elizabethan Dramatists,* edited by Fredson Bowers (1987)

63 *Modern American Critics, 1920–1955,* edited by Gregory S. Jay (1988)

64 *American Literary Critics and Scholars, 1850–1880,* edited by John W. Rathbun and Monica M. Grecu (1988)

65 *French Novelists, 1900–1930,* edited by Catharine Savage Brosman (1988)

66 *German Fiction Writers, 1885–1913,* 2 parts, edited by James Hardin (1988)

67 *Modern American Critics Since 1955,* edited by Gregory S. Jay (1988)

68 *Canadian Writers, 1920–1959, First Series,* edited by W. H. New (1988)

69 *Contemporary German Fiction Writers, First Series,* edited by Wolfgang D. Elfe and James Hardin (1988)

70 *British Mystery Writers, 1860–1919,* edited by Bernard Benstock and Thomas F. Staley (1988)

71 *American Literary Critics and Scholars, 1880–1900,* edited by John W. Rathbun and Monica M. Grecu (1988)

72 *French Novelists, 1930–1960,* edited by Catharine Savage Brosman (1988)

73 *American Magazine Journalists, 1741–1850,* edited by Sam G. Riley (1988)

74 *American Short-Story Writers Before 1880,* edited by Bobby Ellen Kimbel, with the assistance of William E. Grant (1988)

75 *Contemporary German Fiction Writers, Second Series,* edited by Wolfgang D. Elfe and James Hardin (1988)

76 *Afro-American Writers, 1940–1955,* edited by Trudier Harris (1988)

77 *British Mystery Writers, 1920–1939,* edited by Bernard Benstock and Thomas F. Staley (1988)

78 *American Short-Story Writers, 1880–1910,* edited by Bobby Ellen Kimbel, with the assistance of William E. Grant (1988)

79 *American Magazine Journalists, 1850–1900,* edited by Sam G. Riley (1988)

80 *Restoration and Eighteenth-Century Dramatists, First Series,* edited by Paula R. Backscheider (1989)

81 *Austrian Fiction Writers, 1875–1913,* edited by James Hardin and Donald G. Daviau (1989)

82 *Chicano Writers, First Series,* edited by Francisco A. Lomelí and Carl R. Shirley (1989)

83 *French Novelists Since 1960,* edited by Catharine Savage Brosman (1989)

84 *Restoration and Eighteenth-Century Dramatists, Second Series,* edited by Paula R. Backscheider (1989)

85 *Austrian Fiction Writers After 1914,* edited by James Hardin and Donald G. Daviau (1989)

86 *American Short-Story Writers, 1910–1945, First Series,* edited by Bobby Ellen Kimbel (1989)

87 *British Mystery and Thriller Writers Since 1940, First Series,* edited by Bernard Benstock and Thomas F. Staley (1989)

88 *Canadian Writers, 1920–1959, Second Series,* edited by W. H. New (1989)

89 *Restoration and Eighteenth-Century Dramatists, Third Series,* edited by Paula R. Backscheider (1989)

90 *German Writers in the Age of Goethe, 1789–1832,* edited by James Hardin and Christoph E. Schweitzer (1989)

91 *American Magazine Journalists, 1900–1960, First Series,* edited by Sam G. Riley (1990)

92 *Canadian Writers, 1890–1920,* edited by W. H. New (1990)

93 *British Romantic Poets, 1789–1832, First Series,* edited by John R. Greenfield (1990)

94 *German Writers in the Age of Goethe: Sturm und Drang to Classicism,* edited by James Hardin and Christoph E. Schweitzer (1990)

95 *Eighteenth-Century British Poets, First Series,* edited by John Sitter (1990)

96 *British Romantic Poets, 1789–1832, Second Series,* edited by John R. Greenfield (1990)

97 *German Writers from the Enlightenment to Sturm und Drang, 1720–1764,* edited by James Hardin and Christoph E. Schweitzer (1990)

98 *Modern British Essayists, First Series,* edited by Robert Beum (1990)

99 *Canadian Writers Before 1890,* edited by W. H. New (1990)

100 *Modern British Essayists, Second Series,* edited by Robert Beum (1990)

101 *British Prose Writers, 1660–1800, First Series,* edited by Donald T. Siebert (1991)

102 *American Short-Story Writers, 1910–1945, Second Series,* edited by Bobby Ellen Kimbel (1991)

103 *American Literary Biographers, First Series,* edited by Steven Serafin (1991)

104 *British Prose Writers, 1660–1800, Second Series,* edited by Donald T. Siebert (1991)

105 *American Poets Since World War II, Second Series,* edited by R. S. Gwynn (1991)

106 *British Literary Publishing Houses, 1820–1880,* edited by Patricia J. Anderson and Jonathan Rose (1991)

107 *British Romantic Prose Writers, 1789–1832, First Series,* edited by John R. Greenfield (1991)

108 *Twentieth-Century Spanish Poets, First Series,* edited by Michael L. Perna (1991)

109 *Eighteenth-Century British Poets, Second Series,* edited by John Sitter (1991)

110 *British Romantic Prose Writers, 1789–1832, Second Series,* edited by John R. Greenfield (1991)

111 *American Literary Biographers, Second Series,* edited by Steven Serafin (1991)

112 *British Literary Publishing Houses, 1881–1965,* edited by Jonathan Rose and Patricia J. Anderson (1991)

113 *Modern Latin-American Fiction Writers, First Series,* edited by William Luis (1992)

114 *Twentieth-Century Italian Poets, First Series,* edited by Giovanna Wedel De Stasio, Glauco Cambon, and Antonio Illiano (1992)

115 *Medieval Philosophers,* edited by Jeremiah Hackett (1992)

116 *British Romantic Novelists, 1789–1832,* edited by Bradford K. Mudge (1992)

117 *Twentieth-Century Caribbean and Black African Writers, First Series,* edited by Bernth Lindfors and Reinhard Sander (1992)

118 *Twentieth-Century German Dramatists, 1889–1918,* edited by Wolfgang D. Elfe and James Hardin (1992)

119 *Nineteenth-Century French Fiction Writers: Romanticism and Realism, 1800–1860,* edited by Catharine Savage Brosman (1992)

120 *American Poets Since World War II, Third Series,* edited by R. S. Gwynn (1992)

121 *Seventeenth-Century British Nondramatic Poets, First Series,* edited by M. Thomas Hester (1992)

122 *Chicano Writers, Second Series,* edited by Francisco A. Lomelí and Carl R. Shirley (1992)

123 *Nineteenth-Century French Fiction Writers: Naturalism and Beyond, 1860–1900,* edited by Catharine Savage Brosman (1992)

124 *Twentieth-Century German Dramatists, 1919–1992,* edited by Wolfgang D. Elfe and James Hardin (1992)

125 *Twentieth-Century Caribbean and Black African Writers, Second Series,* edited by Bernth Lindfors and Reinhard Sander (1993)

126 *Seventeenth-Century British Nondramatic Poets, Second Series,* edited by M. Thomas Hester (1993)

127 *American Newspaper Publishers, 1950–1990,* edited by Perry J. Ashley (1993)

128 *Twentieth-Century Italian Poets, Second Series,* edited by Giovanna Wedel De Stasio, Glauco Cambon, and Antonio Illiano (1993)

129 *Nineteenth-Century German Writers, 1841–1900,* edited by James Hardin and Siegfried Mews (1993)

130 *American Short-Story Writers Since World War II,* edited by Patrick Meanor (1993)

131 *Seventeenth-Century British Nondramatic Poets, Third Series,* edited by M. Thomas Hester (1993)

132 *Sixteenth-Century British Nondramatic Writers, First Series,* edited by David A. Richardson (1993)

133 *Nineteenth-Century German Writers to 1840,* edited by James Hardin and Siegfried Mews (1993)

134 *Twentieth-Century Spanish Poets, Second Series,* edited by Jerry Phillips Winfield (1994)

135 *British Short-Fiction Writers, 1880–1914: The Realist Tradition,* edited by William B. Thesing (1994)

136 *Sixteenth-Century British Nondramatic Writers, Second Series,* edited by David A. Richardson (1994)

137 *American Magazine Journalists, 1900–1960, Second Series,* edited by Sam G. Riley (1994)

138 *German Writers and Works of the High Middle Ages: 1170–1280,* edited by James Hardin and Will Hasty (1994)

139 *British Short-Fiction Writers, 1945–1980,* edited by Dean Baldwin (1994)

140 *American Book-Collectors and Bibliographers, First Series,* edited by Joseph Rosenblum (1994)

141 *British Children's Writers, 1880–1914,* edited by Laura M. Zaidman (1994)

142 *Eighteenth-Century British Literary Biographers,* edited by Steven Serafin (1994)

143 *American Novelists Since World War II, Third Series,* edited by James R. Giles and Wanda H. Giles (1994)

144 *Nineteenth-Century British Literary Biographers,* edited by Steven Serafin (1994)

145 *Modern Latin-American Fiction Writers, Second Series,* edited by William Luis and Ann González (1994)

146 *Old and Middle English Literature,* edited by Jeffrey Helterman and Jerome Mitchell (1994)

147 *South Slavic Writers Before World War II,* edited by Vasa D. Mihailovich (1994)

148 *German Writers and Works of the Early Middle Ages: 800–1170,* edited by Will Hasty and James Hardin (1994)

149 *Late Nineteenth- and Early Twentieth-Century British Literary Biographers,* edited by Steven Serafin (1995)

150 *Early Modern Russian Writers, Late Seventeenth and Eighteenth Centuries,* edited by Marcus C. Levitt (1995)

151 *British Prose Writers of the Early Seventeenth Century,* edited by Clayton D. Lein (1995)

152 *American Novelists Since World War II, Fourth Series,* edited by James R. Giles and Wanda H. Giles (1995)

153 *Late-Victorian and Edwardian British Novelists, First Series,* edited by George M. Johnson (1995)

154 *The British Literary Book Trade, 1700–1820,* edited by James K. Bracken and Joel Silver (1995)

155 *Twentieth-Century British Literary Biographers,* edited by Steven Serafin (1995)

156 *British Short-Fiction Writers, 1880–1914: The Romantic Tradition,* edited by William F. Naufftus (1995)

157 *Twentieth-Century Caribbean and Black African Writers, Third Series,* edited by Bernth Lindfors and Reinhard Sander (1995)

158 *British Reform Writers, 1789–1832,* edited by Gary Kelly and Edd Applegate (1995)

159 *British Short-Fiction Writers, 1800–1880,* edited by John R. Greenfield (1996)

160 *British Children's Writers, 1914–1960,* edited by Donald R. Hettinga and Gary D. Schmidt (1996)

161 *British Children's Writers Since 1960, First Series,* edited by Caroline Hunt (1996)

162 *British Short-Fiction Writers, 1915–1945,* edited by John H. Rogers (1996)

163 *British Children's Writers, 1800–1880,* edited by Meena Khorana (1996)

164 *German Baroque Writers, 1580–1660,* edited by James Hardin (1996)

165 *American Poets Since World War II, Fourth Series,* edited by Joseph Conte (1996)

166 *British Travel Writers, 1837–1875,* edited by Barbara Brothers and Julia Gergits (1996)

167 *Sixteenth-Century British Nondramatic Writers, Third Series,* edited by David A. Richardson (1996)

168 *German Baroque Writers, 1661–1730,* edited by James Hardin (1996)

169 *American Poets Since World War II, Fifth Series,* edited by Joseph Conte (1996)

170 *The British Literary Book Trade, 1475–1700,* edited by James K. Bracken and Joel Silver (1996)

171 *Twentieth-Century American Sportswriters,* edited by Richard Orodenker (1996)

172 *Sixteenth-Century British Nondramatic Writers, Fourth Series,* edited by David A. Richardson (1996)

173 *American Novelists Since World War II, Fifth Series,* edited by James R. Giles and Wanda H. Giles (1996)

174 *British Travel Writers, 1876–1909,* edited by Barbara Brothers and Julia Gergits (1997)

175 *Native American Writers of the United States,* edited by Kenneth M. Roemer (1997)

176 *Ancient Greek Authors,* edited by Ward W. Briggs (1997)

177 *Italian Novelists Since World War II, 1945–1965,* edited by Augustus Pallotta (1997)

178 *British Fantasy and Science-Fiction Writers Before World War I,* edited by Darren Harris-Fain (1997)

179 *German Writers of the Renaissance and Reformation, 1280–1580,* edited by James Hardin and Max Reinhart (1997)

180 *Japanese Fiction Writers, 1868–1945,* edited by Van C. Gessel (1997)

181 *South Slavic Writers Since World War II,* edited by Vasa D. Mihailovich (1997)

182 *Japanese Fiction Writers Since World War II,* edited by Van C. Gessel (1997)

183 *American Travel Writers, 1776–1864,* edited by James J. Schramer and Donald Ross (1997)

184 *Nineteenth-Century British Book-Collectors and Bibliographers,* edited by William Baker and Kenneth Womack (1997)

185 *American Literary Journalists, 1945–1995, First Series,* edited by Arthur J. Kaul (1998)

186 *Nineteenth-Century American Western Writers,* edited by Robert L. Gale (1998)

187 *American Book Collectors and Bibliographers, Second Series,* edited by Joseph Rosenblum (1998)

188 *American Book and Magazine Illustrators to 1920,* edited by Steven E. Smith, Catherine A. Hastedt, and Donald H. Dyal (1998)

189 *American Travel Writers, 1850–1915,* edited by Donald Ross and James J. Schramer (1998)

190 *British Reform Writers, 1832–1914,* edited by Gary Kelly and Edd Applegate (1998)

191 *British Novelists Between the Wars,* edited by George M. Johnson (1998)

192 *French Dramatists, 1789–1914,* edited by Barbara T. Cooper (1998)

193 *American Poets Since World War II, Sixth Series,* edited by Joseph Conte (1998)

194 *British Novelists Since 1960, Second Series,* edited by Merritt Moseley (1998)

195 *British Travel Writers, 1910–1939,* edited by Barbara Brothers and Julia Gergits (1998)

196 *Italian Novelists Since World War II, 1965–1995,* edited by Augustus Pallotta (1999)

197 *Late-Victorian and Edwardian British Novelists, Second Series,* edited by George M. Johnson (1999)

198 *Russian Literature in the Age of Pushkin and Gogol: Prose,* edited by Christine A. Rydel (1999)

199 *Victorian Women Poets,* edited by William B. Thesing (1999)

200 *American Women Prose Writers to 1820,* edited by Carla J. Mulford, with Angela Vietto and Amy E. Winans (1999)

201 *Twentieth-Century British Book Collectors and Bibliographers,* edited by William Baker and Kenneth Womack (1999)

202 *Nineteenth-Century American Fiction Writers,* edited by Kent P. Ljungquist (1999)

203 *Medieval Japanese Writers,* edited by Steven D. Carter (1999)

204 *British Travel Writers, 1940–1997,* edited by Barbara Brothers and Julia M. Gergits (1999)

205 *Russian Literature in the Age of Pushkin and Gogol: Poetry and Drama,* edited by Christine A. Rydel (1999)

206 *Twentieth-Century American Western Writers, First Series,* edited by Richard H. Cracroft (1999)

207 *British Novelists Since 1960, Third Series,* edited by Merritt Moseley (1999)

208 *Literature of the French and Occitan Middle Ages: Eleventh to Fifteenth Centuries,* edited by Deborah Sinnreich-Levi and Ian S. Laurie (1999)

209 *Chicano Writers, Third Series,* edited by Francisco A. Lomelí and Carl R. Shirley (1999)

210 *Ernest Hemingway: A Documentary Volume,* edited by Robert W. Trogdon (1999)

211 *Ancient Roman Writers,* edited by Ward W. Briggs (1999)

212 *Twentieth-Century American Western Writers, Second Series,* edited by Richard H. Cracroft (1999)

213 *Pre-Nineteenth-Century British Book Collectors and Bibliographers,* edited by William Baker and Kenneth Womack (1999)

214 *Twentieth-Century Danish Writers,* edited by Marianne Stecher-Hansen (1999)

215 *Twentieth-Century Eastern European Writers, First Series,* edited by Steven Serafin (1999)

216 *British Poets of the Great War: Brooke, Rosenberg, Thomas. A Documentary Volume,* edited by Patrick Quinn (2000)

217 *Nineteenth-Century French Poets,* edited by Robert Beum (2000)

218 *American Short-Story Writers Since World War II, Second Series,* edited by Patrick Meanor and Gwen Crane (2000)

219 *F. Scott Fitzgerald's* The Great Gatsby: *A Documentary Volume,* edited by Matthew J. Bruccoli (2000)

220 *Twentieth-Century Eastern European Writers, Second Series,* edited by Steven Serafin (2000)

221 *American Women Prose Writers, 1870–1920,* edited by Sharon M. Harris, with the assistance of Heidi L. M. Jacobs and Jennifer Putzi (2000)

222 *H. L. Mencken: A Documentary Volume,* edited by Richard J. Schrader (2000)

223 *The American Renaissance in New England, Second Series,* edited by Wesley T. Mott (2000)

224 *Walt Whitman: A Documentary Volume,* edited by Joel Myerson (2000)

225 *South African Writers,* edited by Paul A. Scanlon (2000)

226 *American Hard-Boiled Crime Writers,* edited by George Parker Anderson and Julie B. Anderson (2000)

227 *American Novelists Since World War II, Sixth Series,* edited by James R. Giles and Wanda H. Giles (2000)

228 *Twentieth-Century American Dramatists, Second Series,* edited by Christopher J. Wheatley (2000)

229 *Thomas Wolfe: A Documentary Volume,* edited by Ted Mitchell (2001)

230 *Australian Literature, 1788–1914,* edited by Selina Samuels (2001)

231 *British Novelists Since 1960, Fourth Series,* edited by Merritt Moseley (2001)

232 *Twentieth-Century Eastern European Writers, Third Series,* edited by Steven Serafin (2001)

233 *British and Irish Dramatists Since World War II, Second Series,* edited by John Bull (2001)

234 *American Short-Story Writers Since World War II, Third Series,* edited by Patrick Meanor and Richard E. Lee (2001)

235 *The American Renaissance in New England, Third Series,* edited by Wesley T. Mott (2001)

236 *British Rhetoricians and Logicians, 1500–1660,* edited by Edward A. Malone (2001)

237 *The Beats: A Documentary Volume,* edited by Matt Theado (2001)

238 *Russian Novelists in the Age of Tolstoy and Dostoevsky,* edited by J. Alexander Ogden and Judith E. Kalb (2001)

239 *American Women Prose Writers: 1820–1870,* edited by Amy E. Hudock and Katharine Rodier (2001)

240 *Late Nineteenth- and Early Twentieth-Century British Women Poets,* edited by William B. Thesing (2001)

241 *American Sportswriters and Writers on Sport,* edited by Richard Orodenker (2001)

242 *Twentieth-Century European Cultural Theorists, First Series,* edited by Paul Hansom (2001)

243 *The American Renaissance in New England, Fourth Series,* edited by Wesley T. Mott (2001)

244 *American Short-Story Writers Since World War II, Fourth Series,* edited by Patrick Meanor and Joseph McNicholas (2001)

245 *British and Irish Dramatists Since World War II, Third Series,* edited by John Bull (2001)

246 *Twentieth-Century American Cultural Theorists,* edited by Paul Hansom (2001)

247 *James Joyce: A Documentary Volume,* edited by A. Nicholas Fargnoli (2001)

248 *Antebellum Writers in the South, Second Series,* edited by Kent Ljungquist (2001)

249 *Twentieth-Century American Dramatists, Third Series,* edited by Christopher Wheatley (2002)

250 *Antebellum Writers in New York, Second Series,* edited by Kent Ljungquist (2002)

251 *Canadian Fantasy and Science-Fiction Writers,* edited by Douglas Ivison (2002)

252 *British Philosophers, 1500–1799,* edited by Philip B. Dematteis and Peter S. Fosl (2002)

253 *Raymond Chandler: A Documentary Volume,* edited by Robert Moss (2002)

254 *The House of Putnam, 1837–1872: A Documentary Volume,* edited by Ezra Greenspan (2002)

255 *British Fantasy and Science-Fiction Writers, 1918–1960,* edited by Darren Harris-Fain (2002)

256 *Twentieth-Century American Western Writers, Third Series,* edited by Richard H. Cracroft (2002)

257 *Twentieth-Century Swedish Writers After World War II,* edited by Ann-Charlotte Gavel Adams (2002)

258 *Modern French Poets,* edited by Jean-François Leroux (2002)

259 *Twentieth-Century Swedish Writers Before World War II,* edited by Ann-Charlotte Gavel Adams (2002)

260 *Australian Writers, 1915–1950,* edited by Selina Samuels (2002)

261 *British Fantasy and Science-Fiction Writers Since 1960,* edited by Darren Harris-Fain (2002)

262 *British Philosophers, 1800–2000,* edited by Peter S. Fosl and Leemon B. McHenry (2002)

263 *William Shakespeare: A Documentary Volume,* edited by Catherine Loomis (2002)

264 *Italian Prose Writers, 1900–1945,* edited by Luca Somigli and Rocco Capozzi (2002)

265 *American Song Lyricists, 1920–1960,* edited by Philip Furia (2002)

266 *Twentieth-Century American Dramatists, Fourth Series,* edited by Christopher J. Wheatley (2002)

267 *Twenty-First-Century British and Irish Novelists,* edited by Michael R. Molino (2002)

268 *Seventeenth-Century French Writers,* edited by Françoise Jaouën (2002)

269 *Nathaniel Hawthorne: A Documentary Volume,* edited by Benjamin Franklin V (2002)

270 *American Philosophers Before 1950,* edited by Philip B. Dematteis and Leemon B. McHenry (2002)

271 *British and Irish Novelists Since 1960,* edited by Merritt Moseley (2002)

272 *Russian Prose Writers Between the World Wars,* edited by Christine Rydel (2003)

273 *F. Scott Fitzgerald's* Tender Is the Night: *A Documentary Volume,* edited by Matthew J. Bruccoli and George Parker Anderson (2003)

274 *John Dos Passos's* U.S.A.: *A Documentary Volume,* edited by Donald Pizer (2003)

275 *Twentieth-Century American Nature Writers: Prose,* edited by Roger Thompson and J. Scott Bryson (2003)

276 *British Mystery and Thriller Writers Since 1960,* edited by Gina Macdonald (2003)

277 *Russian Literature in the Age of Realism,* edited by Alyssa Dinega Gillespie (2003)

278 *American Novelists Since World War II, Seventh Series,* edited by James R. Giles and Wanda H. Giles (2003)

279 *American Philosophers, 1950–2000,* edited by Philip B. Dematteis and Leemon B. McHenry (2003)

280 *Dashiell Hammett's* The Maltese Falcon: *A Documentary Volume,* edited by Richard Layman (2003)

281 *British Rhetoricians and Logicians, 1500–1660, Second Series,* edited by Edward A. Malone (2003)

282 *New Formalist Poets,* edited by Jonathan N. Barron and Bruce Meyer (2003)

283 *Modern Spanish American Poets, First Series,* edited by María A. Salgado (2003)

284 *The House of Holt, 1866–1946: A Documentary Volume,* edited by Ellen D. Gilbert (2003)

285 *Russian Writers Since 1980,* edited by Marina Balina and Mark Lipovetsky (2004)

286 *Castilian Writers, 1400–1500,* edited by Frank A. Domínguez and George D. Greenia (2004)

287 *Portuguese Writers,* edited by Monica Rector and Fred M. Clark (2004)

288 *The House of Boni & Liveright, 1917–1933: A Documentary Volume,* edited by Charles Egleston (2004)

289 *Australian Writers, 1950–1975,* edited by Selina Samuels (2004)

290 *Modern Spanish American Poets, Second Series,* edited by María A. Salgado (2004)

291 *The Hoosier House: Bobbs-Merrill and Its Predecessors, 1850–1985: A Documentary Volume,* edited by Richard J. Schrader (2004)

292 *Twenty-First-Century American Novelists,* edited by Lisa Abney and Suzanne Disheroon-Green (2004)

293 *Icelandic Writers,* edited by Patrick J. Stevens (2004)

294 *James Gould Cozzens: A Documentary Volume,* edited by Matthew J. Bruccoli (2004)

295 *Russian Writers of the Silver Age, 1890–1925,* edited by Judith E. Kalb and J. Alexander Ogden with the collaboration of I. G. Vishnevetsky (2004)

296 *Twentieth-Century European Cultural Theorists, Second Series,* edited by Paul Hansom (2004)

297 *Twentieth-Century Norwegian Writers,* edited by Tanya Thresher (2004)

298 *Henry David Thoreau: A Documentary Volume,* edited by Richard J. Schneider (2004)

299 *Holocaust Novelists,* edited by Efraim Sicher (2004)

300 *Danish Writers from the Reformation to Decadence, 1550–1900,* edited by Marianne Stecher-Hansen (2004)

Dictionary of Literary Biography Documentary Series

1 *Sherwood Anderson, Willa Cather, John Dos Passos, Theodore Dreiser, F. Scott Fitzgerald, Ernest Hemingway, Sinclair Lewis,* edited by Margaret A. Van Antwerp (1982)

2 *James Gould Cozzens, James T. Farrell, William Faulkner, John O'Hara, John Steinbeck, Thomas Wolfe, Richard Wright,* edited by Margaret A. Van Antwerp (1982)

3 *Saul Bellow, Jack Kerouac, Norman Mailer, Vladimir Nabokov, John Updike, Kurt Vonnegut,* edited by Mary Bruccoli (1983)

4 *Tennessee Williams,* edited by Margaret A. Van Antwerp and Sally Johns (1984)

5 *American Transcendentalists,* edited by Joel Myerson (1988)

6 *Hardboiled Mystery Writers: Raymond Chandler, Dashiell Hammett, Ross Macdonald,* edited by Matthew J. Bruccoli and Richard Layman (1989)

7 *Modern American Poets: James Dickey, Robert Frost, Marianne Moore,* edited by Karen L. Rood (1989)

8 *The Black Aesthetic Movement,* edited by Jeffrey Louis Decker (1991)

9 *American Writers of the Vietnam War: W. D. Ehrhart, Larry Heinemann, Tim O'Brien, Walter McDonald, John M. Del Vecchio,* edited by Ronald Baughman (1991)

10 *The Bloomsbury Group,* edited by Edward L. Bishop (1992)

11 *American Proletarian Culture: The Twenties and The Thirties,* edited by Jon Christian Suggs (1993)

12 *Southern Women Writers: Flannery O'Connor, Katherine Anne Porter, Eudora Welty,* edited by Mary Ann Wimsatt and Karen L. Rood (1994)

13 *The House of Scribner, 1846–1904,* edited by John Delaney (1996)

14 *Four Women Writers for Children, 1868–1918,* edited by Caroline C. Hunt (1996)

15 *American Expatriate Writers: Paris in the Twenties,* edited by Matthew J. Bruccoli and Robert W. Trogdon (1997)

16 *The House of Scribner, 1905–1930,* edited by John Delaney (1997)

17 *The House of Scribner, 1931–1984,* edited by John Delaney (1998)

18 *British Poets of The Great War: Sassoon, Graves, Owen,* edited by Patrick Quinn (1999)

19 *James Dickey,* edited by Judith S. Baughman (1999)

See also DLB 210, 216, 219, 222, 224, 229, 237, 247, 253, 254, 263, 269, 273, 274, 280, 284, 288, 291, 294, 298

Dictionary of Literary Biography Yearbooks

1980 edited by Karen L. Rood, Jean W. Ross, and Richard Ziegfeld (1981)

1981 edited by Karen L. Rood, Jean W. Ross, and Richard Ziegfeld (1982)

1982 edited by Richard Ziegfeld; associate editors: Jean W. Ross and Lynne C. Zeigler (1983)

1983 edited by Mary Bruccoli and Jean W. Ross; associate editor Richard Ziegfeld (1984)

1984 edited by Jean W. Ross (1985)

1985 edited by Jean W. Ross (1986)

1986 edited by J. M. Brook (1987)

1987 edited by J. M. Brook (1988)

1988 edited by J. M. Brook (1989)

1989 edited by J. M. Brook (1990)

1990 edited by James W. Hipp (1991)

1991 edited by James W. Hipp (1992)

1992 edited by James W. Hipp (1993)

1993 edited by James W. Hipp, contributing editor George Garrett (1994)

1994 edited by James W. Hipp, contributing editor George Garrett (1995)

1995 edited by James W. Hipp, contributing editor George Garrett (1996)

1996 edited by Samuel W. Bruce and L. Kay Webster, contributing editor George Garrett (1997)

1997 edited by Matthew J. Bruccoli and George Garrett, with the assistance of L. Kay Webster (1998)

1998 edited by Matthew J. Bruccoli, contributing editor George Garrett, with the assistance of D. W. Thomas (1999)

1999 edited by Matthew J. Bruccoli, contributing editor George Garrett, with the assistance of D. W. Thomas (2000)

2000 edited by Matthew J. Bruccoli, contributing editor George Garrett, with the assistance of George Parker Anderson (2001)

2001 edited by Matthew J. Bruccoli, contributing editor George Garrett, with the assistance of George Parker Anderson (2002)

2002 edited by Matthew J. Bruccoli and George Garrett; George Parker Anderson, Assistant Editor (2003)

Concise Series

Concise Dictionary of American Literary Biography, 7 volumes (1988–1999): *The New Consciousness, 1941–1968; Colonization to the American Renaissance, 1640–1865; Realism, Naturalism, and Local Color, 1865–1917; The Twenties, 1917–1929; The Age of Maturity, 1929–1941; Broadening Views, 1968–1988; Supplement: Modern Writers, 1900–1998.*

Concise Dictionary of British Literary Biography, 8 volumes (1991–1992): *Writers of the Middle Ages and Renaissance Before 1660; Writers of the Restoration and Eighteenth Century, 1660–1789; Writers of the Romantic Period, 1789–1832; Victorian Writers, 1832–1890; Late-Victorian and Edwardian Writers, 1890–1914; Modern Writers, 1914–1945; Writers After World War II, 1945–1960; Contemporary Writers, 1960 to Present.*

Concise Dictionary of World Literary Biography, 4 volumes (1999–2000): *Ancient Greek and Roman Writers; German Writers; African, Caribbean, and Latin American Writers; South Slavic and Eastern European Writers.*

Dictionary of Literary Biography® • Volume Three Hundred

Danish Writers from the Reformation to Decadence, 1550–1900

Dictionary of Literary Biography® • Volume Three Hundred

Danish Writers from the Reformation to Decadence, 1550–1900

Edited by
Marianne Stecher-Hansen
University of Washington

A Bruccoli Clark Layman Book

Detroit • New York • San Francisco • San Diego • New Haven, Conn. • Waterville, Maine • London • Munich

Dictionary of Literary Biography
Volume 300: Danish Writers from the Reformation to Decadence, 1550–1900
Marianne Stecher-Hansen

For more information, contact
Thomson Gale
27500 Drake Rd.
Farmington Hills, MI 48331-3535
Or you can visit our Internet site at http://www.gale.com

LIBRARY OF CONGRESS CATALOGING-IN-PUBLICATION DATA

Danish writers from the Reformation to decadence, 1550–1900 / edited by Marianne Stecher-Hansen.
p. cm. — (Dictionary of literary biography ; v. 300)
"A Bruccoli Clark Layman Book."
Includes bibliographical references and index.
ISBN 0-7876-6837-0 (hardcover: alk. paper)
1. Danish literature—16th century—Bio-bibliography. 2. Danish literature—17th century—Bio-bibliography. 3. Danish literature—18th century—Bio-bibliography. 4. Danish literature—19th century—Bio-bibliography. I. Stecher-Hansen, Marianne, 1957– . II. Series.

Z5271.D36 2004
[PT7663]
016.83981'09—dc22 2004010068

Printed in the United States of America
10 9 8 7 6 5 4 3 2 1

In loving memory of my father,
Knud Poul Stecher
(1921–2000)

Contents

Plan of the Series

. . . Almost the most prodigious asset of a country, and perhaps its most precious possession, is its native literary product–when that product is fine and noble and enduring.

Mark Twain*

The advisory board, the editors, and the publisher of the *Dictionary of Literary Biography* are joined in endorsing Mark Twain's declaration. The literature of a nation provides an inexhaustible resource of permanent worth. Our purpose is to make literature and its creators better understood and more accessible to students and the reading public, while satisfying the needs of teachers and researchers.

To meet these requirements, *literary biography* has been construed in terms of the author's achievement. The most important thing about a writer is his writing. Accordingly, the entries in *DLB* are career biographies, tracing the development of the author's canon and the evolution of his reputation.

The purpose of *DLB* is not only to provide reliable information in a usable format but also to place the figures in the larger perspective of literary history and to offer appraisals of their accomplishments by qualified scholars.

The publication plan for *DLB* resulted from two years of preparation. The project was proposed to Bruccoli Clark by Frederick G. Ruffner, president of the Gale Research Company, in November 1975. After specimen entries were prepared and typeset, an advisory board was formed to refine the entry format and develop the series rationale. In meetings held during 1976, the publisher, series editors, and advisory board approved the scheme for a comprehensive biographical dictionary of persons who contributed to literature. Editorial work on the first volume began in January 1977, and it was published in 1978. In order to make *DLB* more than a dictionary and to compile volumes that individually have claim to status as literary history, it was decided to organize volumes by topic, period, or genre. Each of these freestanding volumes provides a biographical-bibliographical guide and overview for a particular area of literature. We are convinced that this organization–as opposed to a single alphabet method–constitutes a valuable innovation in the presentation of reference material. The volume plan necessarily requires many decisions for the placement and treatment of authors. Certain figures will be included in separate volumes, but with different entries emphasizing the aspect of his career appropriate to each volume. Ernest Hemingway, for example, is represented in *American Writers in Paris, 1920–1939* by an entry focusing on his expatriate apprenticeship; he is also in *American Novelists, 1910–1945* with an entry surveying his entire career, as well as in *American Short-Story Writers, 1910–1945, Second Series* with an entry concentrating on his short fiction. Each volume includes a cumulative index of the subject authors and articles.

Between 1981 and 2002 the series was augmented and updated by the *DLB Yearbooks*. There have also been nineteen *DLB Documentary Series* volumes, which provide illustrations, facsimiles, and biographical and critical source materials for figures, works, or groups judged to have particular interest for students. In 1999 the *Documentary Series* was incorporated into the *DLB* volume numbering system beginning with *DLB 210: Ernest Hemingway*.

We define literature as the *intellectual commerce of a nation:* not merely as belles lettres but as that ample and complex process by which ideas are generated, shaped, and transmitted. *DLB* entries are not limited to "creative writers" but extend to other figures who in their time and in their way influenced the mind of a people. Thus the series encompasses historians, journalists, publishers, book collectors, and screenwriters. By this means readers of *DLB* may be aided to perceive literature not as cult scripture in the keeping of intellectual high priests but firmly positioned at the center of a nation's life.

DLB includes the major writers appropriate to each volume and those standing in the ranks behind them. Scholarly and critical counsel has been sought in deciding which minor figures to include and how full their entries should be. Wherever possible, useful refer-

**From an unpublished section of Mark Twain's autobiography, copyright by the Mark Twain Company* ences are made to figures who do not warrant separate entries.

Each *DLB* volume has an expert volume editor responsible for planning the volume, selecting the figures for inclusion, and assigning the entries. Volume editors are also responsible for preparing, where appropriate, appendices surveying the major periodicals and literary and intellectual movements for their volumes, as well as lists of further readings. Work on the series as a whole is coordinated at the Bruccoli Clark Layman editorial center in Columbia, South Carolina, where the editorial staff is responsible for accuracy and utility of the published volumes.

One feature that distinguishes *DLB* is the illustration policy–its concern with the iconography of literature. Just as an author is influenced by his surroundings, so is the reader's understanding of the author enhanced by a knowledge of his environment. Therefore *DLB* volumes include not only drawings, paintings, and photographs of authors, often depicting them at various stages in their careers, but also illustrations of their families and places where they lived. Title pages are regularly reproduced in facsimile along with dust jackets for modern authors. The dust jackets are a special feature of *DLB* because they often document better than anything else the way in which an author's work was perceived in its own time. Specimens of the writers' manuscripts and letters are included when feasible.

Samuel Johnson rightly decreed that "The chief glory of every people arises from its authors." The purpose of the *Dictionary of Literary Biography* is to compile literary history in the surest way available to us–by accurate and comprehensive treatment of the lives and work of those who contributed to it.

The *DLB* Advisory Board

Introduction

In the broad context of world literatures, Danish literature is relatively young. If the runic inscription on the Jellinge stone (erected 983–987 by King Harald Bluetooth, who claims to have "won all Denmark and Norway and made the Danes Christian") marks the inception of a national literature, then Danish literature is about a thousand years old. Yet, the true flowering of a printed literature produced by individuals writing in the Danish language occurred in the sixteenth century. Danish literature of the Middle Ages was almost exclusively a Latin literature, adhering to classical models. The single most significant medieval work is Saxo Grammaticus's *Gesta Danorum* (The Deeds of the Danes, circa 1200), which depicts the feats of ancient Danish kings. Composed in dignified Silver Age Latin, Saxo's work was first translated and published in Danish in 1579. The greatest Danish literary heritage of the Middle Ages, however, is not a written literature; it is the folk ballad, which flourished in an oral tradition. This treasury of ballads, which eventually reached more than six hundred songs in scholarly editions, was first recorded in the late sixteenth century: a manuscript collection known as "Hjertebogen" (The Heart Book) dates from 1553–1555, and the first published collection of a selection of folk ballads dates from 1591, the work of Renaissance scholar Anders Sørensen Vedel.

Thus, this volume is loosely framed by the 350-year period 1550–1900, which encompasses the lives of the literary and historical figures who, acting as "modern" individuals with diverse motivations and backgrounds, produced the canon that today is recognized as Danish literature. The selection in this volume presents dramatists, poets, and prose writers who produced literary texts that shaped literary development during this period of language, poetic form, narrative style, and genre. The volume also features those creative writers who broke with literary conventions and rebelled against established trends, as well as figures whose extraordinary work as critics or translators of classical and European literatures had immense influence on the formation of Danish letters. By virtue of its lexical structure and design, this volume does not seek to offer a master narrative or a history of Danish literature delineating homogeneous centuries and coherent literary movements. Instead, it describes the contributions of distinct individuals who engendered the revolutions in language, form, and representation that became the seeds of new literary developments.

The literature of Denmark, at one time a vast maritime empire at the northern periphery of Europe, bears the mark of its more powerful neighbors–especially Germany, France, and England–countries that during various periods over the centuries dominated the intellectual life of Europe. Nevertheless, Danish literature can be distinguished from the literatures of other small language-communities by many impressive and outstanding contributions to world literature. In addition to the aforementioned folk-ballad heritage, the work of the intellectual giants of Denmark during its Golden Age (1800–1850), philosopher Søren Kierkegaard and theologian and poet N. F. S. Grundtvig, exercised considerable influence well beyond the borders of Denmark. Their contemporary, Hans Christian Andersen, produced fairy tales that revolutionized that literary genre and became part of everyday vocabularies the world over. Further, Danish literature of these approximately three and a half centuries presents an extremely rich and varied tradition, often mirroring or reacting to predominant European literary trends and intellectual life but always from a distinctly localized Danish perspective. The Danes as a people are outstanding cultural mediators, people who readily adopt foreign words, customs, and ideas, but not without first adapting and reinventing them to suit local tastes and sensibilities. The same tendency may be seen in the literary work of the nation. Much inspiration may be traced to foreign literary sources, but little direct imitation.

For several reasons, the Danish Reformation of 1535 marks the inception of a distinct Danish literary tradition. Most obvious are the implications of the Lutheran principle that people should read the Bible in their own language. In Denmark, as in other Protestant countries of this period, Bible translation is a milepost in the history of the national language and literature. The first official Danish translation of the Bible, which was commissioned by the king, is the so-called Christian III's Bible of 1550. The translation, by humanist scholar and publisher Christiern Pedersen, was closely based on Martin Luther's translation of the Bible. (The first publication of Saxo's Latin manuscript in 1514 is also credited to Pedersen.) Despite the flow of German loanwords that accompanied the Reformation, Pedersen's translation is remarkably free of Germanisms and is distinctly Danish in style. In addition to religious reform, the Reformation initiated a period of linguistic reform during which Danish as a written language began to undergo standardization that eventually led to its modern form. The introduction of the first printing presses in Denmark in 1482 served as a catalyst to the initial phase of this orthographical reform implemented by the typesetters and reformers who adopted consistent rules of orthography.

The Lutheran Reformation also brought about the creation of devotional literature and hymnology in the Danish language. A Danish hymnal in the mother tongue was an important goal for such early reformers as the "Danish Luther," Hans Tausen (1494–1561). While Hans Thomissøn (1532–1573) compiled the first Danish hymnal, *Den danske Psalmebog* (The Danish Hymnal, 1569), consisting of translations of Martin Luther's hymns as well as hymns by various Danes, pastor and poet Hans Christensen Sthen was the first original writer of hymns in Denmark. Sthen's *En liden Vandrebog* (A Little Traveling Book, 1589), which includes the majority of Sthen's original hymns, is the first significant collection of Danish hymns and marks the birth date of an indigenous hymn tradition.

Following the upheaval of the early Reformation period, theater took on a modest role as part of an anti-Catholic polemic, often in the satirical genre. Luther, in fact, made the recommendation that grammar schools produce dramas (both classical and original) in order to train pupils in Latin as well as in the mother tongue; a Danish Church Ordinance of 1537 encouraged schools to perform plays in Latin and in Danish. By the late sixteenth century, when the religious-political crisis of the early part of the century had subsided, four centers of school drama arose in Denmark–Elsinore, Ribe, Viborg, and Randers. The masterpiece of Danish secular drama of this period is the work of Hieronymus Justesen Ranch; his comedy *Karrig Niding* (Nithing the Niggard, 1664) was probably first performed at the University of Copenhagen in 1597. In the classical tradition of Plautus and Terence, *Karrig Niding* depicts the foibles of a miserly husband; it continues to be performed with success to modern audiences and is regarded as the most important drama prior to the Enlightenment comedies of Ludvig Holberg.

Another aspect of sixteenth-century Danish literature is the blossoming of New Latin poetry in the spirit of Renaissance humanism. While the Reformation prompted the use of the vernacular in such literary genres as hymnology and drama, humanism simultaneously fostered a knowledge and cultivation of the literature and languages of classical antiquity. From the Middle Ages through the Reformation and Renaissance (which in Denmark extends into the seventeenth century), Danish literature continued to develop as a bilingual literature. This volume features the superb poetry of world-famous Renaissance scientist and astronomer Tycho Brahe, who in the late twentieth century was finally recognized as one of the most prominent neo-Latin poets of Renaissance Denmark. Brahe's six-hundred-verse heroid, *Urania Titani* (Urania to Titan, 1994), composed in 1594, develops a literary genre derived from Ovid's *Heroides*.

The close of the sixteenth century marked the consolidation of the relationship between the Lutheran Church and the monarchy. Humanistic scholarship remained a strong influence in the shaping of Danish letters. The translations and scholarship of Vedel (who served as the tutor of the young Brahe in the 1560s), particularly his Danish translation of Saxo's *Den Danske Krønicke* (The Danish Chronicle, 1575) and his important collection of Danish folk ballads, *It Hundrede vduaalde Danske Viser* (One Hundred Selected Danish Ballads, 1591), demonstrate the epochal interest in preserving and mediating the treasures of the national past.

The seventeenth century may be described as a literary epoch characterized by baroque poetry, Lutheran orthodoxy, and Renaissance scholarship. Like the previous century, the literary developments of the 1600s evince strong ties between literary production and the Lutheran-monarchical state. The impetus for poetic expression is often closely related to religious devotion, biblical interpretation, or service to the Crown. The greatest literary achievement of the early part of the century is the metrical reform of poetic versification carried out by Anders Arrebo. Inspired by classical, as well as French and Italian Renaissance models, Arrebo broke with the versification practices that had been employed in Denmark since the Middle Ages and introduced a sophisticated principle, regular alternation between stressed and unstressed syllables. Arrebo's translation of the Book of Psalms (1623) is the first work of Danish poetry composed consistently on the basis of modern prosody and anticipating the canonical work of German literature, Martin Opitz's *Buch von der deutschen Poeterey* (Book on German Poetics, 1624). Arrebo's *Hexaëmeron* (The Six-Day Work, 1666), an original literary work about the first six days of Creation, is inspired by the Book of Genesis as well as by classical Latin and contemporary French models. Composed variously in hexameters and alexandrines, and informed by an encyclopedic knowledge of Nordic Renaissance scholarship, *Hexaëmeron* is the magnum opus of Danish baroque poetry.

The work of Arrebo was completed during the tempestuous reign of the most renowned Renaissance king of Denmark, Christian IV (1588–1648). This period was characterized by impressive architectural construction, ambitious foreign campaigns (particularly against Sweden), and involvement in the devastating European Thirty Years' War (1618–1648), a military engagement that eventually weakened the twin kingdom of Denmark-Norway. Concurrent with Renaissance-inspired scientific research and learning, monarchical power grew during the seventeenth century and resulted in Protestant zealousness and witch persecutions. (The last witch burning in Denmark took place in 1693.) In September 1660 the rights of the nobility were abolished under King Frederik III (1648–1670), and the absolute hereditary monarchy was established, the form of government that endured in Denmark until 1849. Under absolutist monarch Frederik III, occasional poet Anders Bording found himself employed in the service of the royal government. From 1666 until his death in 1677, Bording composed in flowing alexandrines the monthly "newspaper" *Den danske Mercurius* (The Danish Mercury), which served as the mouthpiece of the government and played an important role in shaping public opinion on foreign wars, public policy, and the royal court.

Thomas Kingo is the major baroque poet of Denmark and the earliest of the four most widely recognized Danish hymnists (followed by Hans Adolph Brorson in the eighteenth century and by Grundtvig and B. S. Ingemann in the nineteenth century). Kingo is the earliest Danish poet who is widely known in Denmark today; his hymns are still sung in Danish churches and schools. Bishop Kingo's work embodies a personal expression of the crosscurrents of the century–Lutheran orthodoxy and Renaissance secularism–two conflicting views of human existence, which are expressed in dialogic exchange between such various poetic texts as "Far, Verden, Farvel" (Fare, World, Farewell) and "Hver har sin Skæbne" (Everyone Has His Destiny). Kingo achieved the reinvention of both the private devotional lyric and the church hymn, often using secular melodies for religious songs. His widely acclaimed "Chrysillis" demonstrates his mastery of the private love poem. In 1699, Kingo compiled *Den forordnede ny kirke Psalmebog* (The Ordained New Church Hymnal) for the Danish Lutheran Church; replacing Thomissøn's hymnal of 1569, it became widely known as "Kingo's hymnal."

The most important prose work written in Danish in the seventeenth century is *Jammers Minde* (Memories of Woe, 1869; translated as *Memoirs of Leonora Christina,* 1872), the memoir of Leonora Christina Ulfeldt, a daughter of Christian IV and his morganatic wife, Kirsten Munk. This eloquent memoir depicting a learned noblewoman's imprisonment in the Blue Tower of Copenhagen Castle for nearly twenty-two years (1663–1685) is a remarkable document unparalleled in seventeenth-century European literature. The prose style ranges from formal baroque rhetoric to an intimate colloquial style; the author's literary genius was finally recognized in the late nineteenth century after the manuscript (which had remained in the family's possession) was published in 1869; it has since become a classic in Scandinavian literature. Another noble and *femina docta,* or learned woman, of this century is Birgitte Thott, whose foremost contribution to secular learning of intellectual humanism in Denmark is her monumental translation of the works of Roman philosopher Seneca (*Seneca Lucci Annæi Senecæ . . . Skrifter,* 1658), one of the most eminent books of the seventeenth century. In a noteworthy preface to the translation, written decades before the Enlightenment, Thott argues that women should have access to education. Handwritten transcripts of Thott's principal original work in Danish, "Om Weyen till et Lycksalligt Liff" (About the Way to a Happy Life, circa 1659–1660), a secular treatise on moral philosophy, circulated among scholars and intellectuals in the seventeenth century; however, this work remained unpublished, likely because it could not pass the censorship of the Church fathers.

In Europe, the eighteenth century is widely identified as the Enlightenment, the Age of Reason, *Aufklarung, Le Siècle des Lumières,* or the neoclassical period. The names suggest democratic political and social reforms accompanied by a secular and socially conscious literature. While this perception applies to some aspects of cultural and literary developments in Denmark–primarily to the work of the central figure of the century, Holberg–significant crosscurrents to Enlightenment ideas and values in Denmark indicate "Den brogede oplysning" (The Multifaceted Enlightenment), to use the title of Thomas Bredsdorff's 2003 study of eighteenth-century Denmark. The dual kingdom of Denmark-Norway remained an absolutist monarchy during this century (actually a complex union of Norway, Iceland, and the unruly duchies of Slesvig and Holsten under the kingdom of Denmark), ruled by a lineage of increasingly weak or senile hereditary monarchs. At the opening of the century, Denmark was still a powerful empire of the North (despite significant territorial losses to Sweden brought about by the war of 1675–1679). In the 1730s, the country came strongly under the sway of German Pietism (a Protestant evangelical reform movement), which inspired such sects as the Moravian Brethren. King Christian VI (1730–1746) became an ardent convert to Pietism, a movement that soon took hold in Denmark as the unofficial state religion. As a result, censorship of the press and theater occurred (although it eased with the death of the king in 1746). A brief social experiment in Enlightenment political ideology (lifting press censorship and enacting many social reforms) under the unofficial "reign" in 1771–1772 of Minister Johan F. Struensee (the royal physician of mad King Christian VII [1766–1808]) ended with the execution of Struensee and a coup d'état by the reactionary members of the king's cabinet. Hence, a Danish revolution inspired by French Enlightenment ideology was curtailed at the outset, and the absolutist monarchy remained the form of government in Denmark until the mid nineteenth century.

Copenhagen was the center of Danish intellectual and literary activity in the eighteenth century. The first theater performing plays in Danish opened its doors in Copenhagen in September 1722 with performances of Holberg's comedies; drama soon became the foremost literary genre of the century. Although secular literature in the vernacular flourished in the eighteenth century, church hymns continued to be the primary form of literature that reached the largely rural population of the kingdom; at the same time, a marked increase in the circulation and production of chapbooks (which included poems, ballads, and popular stories) is indicative of an overall rise in literacy during this time. The folk ballad and folktale continued to flourish in an oral tradition during the eighteenth century.

The contributions to Danish letters and intellectual life of the Dano-Norwegian Holberg are of great importance. Holberg's satirical comedies written for the Danish stage of the 1720s and 1730s particularly demonstrated that a socially oriented and nonreligious literature could appeal to a broad populace. As historian, dramatist, critic, essayist, and travel writer, Holberg integrated a strong European orientation into his work (since he had traveled widely in the Netherlands, England, France, Italy, and Germany), creating a Danish literature that was distinctly national in character and humor but not at all provincial in ideological perspective. Inspired by classical genres–satire, comic epic, epigram, fable, and comedy–Holberg published prolifically in many literary genres. In addition to his popular comedies in the Danish language, he also contributed literary works in Latin in order to reach a learned audience. With the philosophical science-fiction novel *Nicolai Klimii iter subterraneum* (1741; translated as *A Journey to the World Under-Ground by Nicholas Klimius,* 1742), inspired by contemporary works such as Jonathan Swift's *Gulliver's Travels* (1726), Holberg subversively criticized the strict Pietistic reign of Christian VI.

The hymns and religious poetry of Bishop Brorson represent the finest influence of eighteenth-century Pietism on Danish literature. In contrast to the worldliness of Holberg's literary production, Brorson's poetry reminds readers that the religious experience of the Pietists centered on a deeply personal and intimate relationship to God; Brorson's work was a strong source of inspiration to Kierkegaard's philosophy. Brorson's *Troens Rare Klenodie* (Rare Jewel of Faith, 1739), many editions of which were published during his lifetime, is a major contribution to Danish hymnology. The sophisticated style of *Svane-Sang* (Swan-Song, 1765) recalls the piety of the Danish baroque lyric; its deeply private and profound religious sentiment ensures it a central position in Danish devotional literature. The original lyrical poetry of Brorson's contemporary and humble neighbor in Ribe, Ambrosius Stub, the author of occasional and religious poems, is unconventional in musicality and linguistic vigor. Although not recognized in his lifetime, Stub's work earned him canonical status posthumously.

In the second half of the eighteenth century (after the death of Christian VI), the Danish theater continued to gain momentum. The enlightened successor to Holberg was the most gifted woman writer of the century, Charlotta Dorothea Biehl. Known for her important work as a translator of European literatures (particularly her 1776–1777 translation of Miguel de Cervantes's *Don Quixote,* 1605, 1615), Biehl was the foremost writer of comedies for the Danish stage from 1764 to 1772 and later of ballad operas. Biehl was also an innovator in a popular genre of eighteenth-century Europe, the epistolary novel. She is recognized as a talented prose writer for her autobiographical *Mit ubetydelige Levnets Løb* (The Course of My Insignificant Life, written in 1787; published in 1909; revised, 1986), the only autobiography written by an eighteenth-century Danish woman.

One could argue that the first "modern" poets entered Danish literature in the late eighteenth century. Jens Baggesen and Johannes Ewald are conventionally regarded as transitional figures whose literary work reflects both neoclassical trends and early Romanticism. Their innovative, autobiographical prose works–Baggesen's *Labyrinten* (The Labyrinth, 1792, 1793) and Ewald's *Levnet og Meeninger* (Life and Opinions, published posthumously in 1804, 1805)–were inspired by a new conception of the individual in the modern world. By means of subjective first-person narration and stylistic experimentation, these sophisticated literary texts anticipated developments in nineteenth- and even twentieth-century literary aesthetics. Ewald also wrote successfully for the Danish stage; his ballad opera, the tragedy *Balders Død* (1775; translated as *The Death of Balder,* 1886), for example, was performed in January 1779 at the Royal Theater in celebration of the birthday of King Christian VII; its blend of Nordic mythology, English Restoration drama, and democratic humanism marks it as a work ahead of its time. Another enduring classic of the eighteenth-century Danish stage is the work of a Norwegian-Dane, Johan Herman Wessel; written in witty alexandrines, his parodic comedy *Kierlighed uden Strømper* (Love without Stockings, 1772; first produced, 1773) still entertains modern audiences. Wessel also crafted versified "comic tales" that continue to be anthologized. An ironist with a specialty in absurd humor, Wessel stands as the most amusing rhyme smith of Denmark.

The Golden Age or Romantic period of Danish literature is best understood in a broad cultural and political context framed by particular historical events as well as by a wider European context. During the first years of the nineteenth century, the kingdom of Denmark-Norway suffered the consequences of the Napoleonic Wars: an ill-fated alliance with France, a national bankruptcy in 1813, the cession of Norway to Sweden in 1814, and an ensuing economic depression. The British had interpreted the 1794 Armed Neutrality Pact of Denmark and Sweden as an act of hostility. The English navy attacked Copenhagen in 1801 (the Battle of Copenhagen) and again in 1807 by bombarding the Danish capital and seizing the naval fleet of Denmark. The weakened kingdom of Denmark-Norway entered the war as an ally of the French, an alliance that eventually brought about the series of national catastrophes. Yet, the strong blows to national morale also served as a catalyst to a countermovement, a Golden Age of arts and letters and a revival of Nordic and national cultural heritage. In Denmark, as in many European nations, the early and mid nineteenth century were marked by conscious efforts at constructing and defining a national culture and identity based on a relatively modern concept of a homogeneous state defined by linguistic and political parameters; parallel cultural and literary developments in Finland, Germany, and Norway also prompted the first collections and editions of indigenous literature, especially folktales and folk ballads.

Adam Oehlenschläger's *Digte* (Poems) was published in 1803 after a pivotal meeting with Danish philosopher Henrich Steffens (1773–1845), who introduced the young poet to German Romantic philosophy. The collection included "Guldhornene" (translated as *The Gold Horns,* 1913), a poem that became one of the best known in Danish literature. It relates the discovery and subsequent loss of the Gallehus horns, two golden fifth-century (circa 400–450) drinking horns inscribed with primitive runes. Found in southern Jutland in the seventeenth and eighteenth centuries, these treasures were stolen from Christiansborg Castle and melted down in 1802. The symbols employed in Oehlenschläger's "Guldhornene" offered new poetic idioms for the next generation of Danish poets and also articulated a plea for a greater appreciation of the indigenous national past. The position in Danish letters of Romantic poet Schack Staffeldt–conventionally considered merely an imitator of Oehlenschläger–has recently been reassessed in Denmark with the publication of new scholarly editions of Staffeldt's work.

Other major figures associated with the early decades of Romanticism in Denmark (called *Romantikken* in Danish literary history) include Grundtvig and Ingemann. Grundtvig's contributions as a sophisticated poet and prolific hymnist are difficult to separate from his immense influence on Danish culture and intellectual life in his roles as clergyman, critic, educational reformer, philosopher, philologist, politician, scholar, and theologian–for example, Grundtvig retranslated Saxo's Latin chronicles into colloquial Danish. In terms of volume, Grundtvig's oeuvre constitutes the single largest authorship in Danish literature; the entry in this volume focuses on Grundtvig's literary production, including his immeasurable contributions to Danish hymnology. While Ingemann's hymns have been criticized by clergymen and theologians for their lack of Christian dogma, his morning and evening songs celebrating nature and evincing a naive religious sensibility are well known and loved in Denmark. Between 1824 and 1836 Ingemann published a series of historical novels (based on the models of Sir Walter Scott) that depict the Danish monarchs of the Middle Ages; the past of Denmark was a favored motif in the wave of nationalism that engulfed much of Europe following the Napoleonic Wars. Ingemann's historical novels remained popular classics well into the mid twentieth century. He recently has been most highly regarded for his fine contributions to short prose, a genre that made its breakthrough in Denmark in the 1820s.

A breakthrough in early prose realism in Danish literature occurred specifically in 1824, a year that marks the beginning of "poetic realism," as it came to be known and defined by such writers as Steen Steensen Blicher and Poul Martin Møller, as well as Thomasine Gyllembourg and Carsten Hauch. The works of poetic realism (also a term used to describe the idyllic Danish paintings of this period) tended to find poetic motifs in everyday life. Rather than the distant mythological or medieval settings favored by the early Romantic poets, these literary works are framed by the contemporary and familiar, recognizable Danish landscapes and social milieus. In 1824 Møller (who became Kierkegaard's mentor) read aloud chapters of his fragmentary novel *En dansk Students Eventyr* (The Tale of a Danish Student, 1843) to fellow students in Copenhagen. That same year Blicher published *En Lands-*

bydegns Dagbog (translated as *The Journal of a Parish Clerk,* 1945), a modern novella in diary form featuring an unreliable narrator. In his stories, Blicher captured the heather-covered moors of northern Jutland peopled by peasants, gypsies, and lonely hunters. His use of sophisticated narrative devices, his ear for dialect, and his eye for local color came to have considerable influence on the development of nineteenth-century Danish literature, particularly late-nineteenth-century realism.

Gyllembourg's novellas, such as *En Hverdags-Historie* (A Story of Everyday Life, 1828), offer a picture of the marriages and manners of the Copenhagen bourgeoisie. Behind the idyllic facade of Biedermeier society, the reader glimpses the oppressive lives of early-nineteenth-century women in Gyllembourg's comic-satirical depictions. Gyllembourg's son, Johan Ludvig Heiberg, together with his wife, Johanne Luise Heiberg–the prima donna of the Danish stage–became the foremost arbiter of literary taste during the Romantic period in Denmark. As a remarkably prolific and influential literary critic, dramatist, scholar, translator, and eventually director of the Royal Theater, as well as professor of aesthetics, Johan Ludvig Heiberg came to define a new type of literary aesthetics, "the Heiberg School." His adaptations of French theatrical works to the Danish stage, as well as his own original works (particularly vaudevilles), transformed the repertoire of the Danish Royal Theater. Johan Ludvig Heiberg may also be credited with introducing a formalist approach to literary criticism (influenced by a system invented by German philosopher Georg Wilhelm Friedrich Hegel) to Danish literature. One Romantic poet who emulated Heibergian aesthetics is Frederik Paludan-Müller, best known for his epic poem *Adam Homo* (1841–1848).

The flourishing cultural and literary climate of Golden Age Copenhagen provided fertile groundwork for the emergence of the two nineteenth-century geniuses Andersen and Kierkegaard. Andersen, who is internationally recognized as a writer of fairy tales, revolutionized Danish prose in 1835 with the publication of a slim pamphlet, *Eventyr, fortalte for Børn* (Fairy Tales, Told for Children), his first collection of fairy tales and stories, which have made his name immortal. During his own lifetime, Andersen was best known in Denmark as a writer of adult fiction and celebrated in Europe and the United States for his novels, travel books, and popular autobiography, as well as for his tales and stories. The literary fairy tale was not a concept invented by Andersen; he learned much from his Danish mentors, Oehlenschläger and Ingemann, as well as from such German Romantic writers as E. T. A. Hoffmann and Ludwig Tieck. Yet, Andersen succeeded in reinventing the genre by means of a lively colloquial style derived from his firsthand knowledge of oral narrative tradition. Although Andersen's masterpieces of the late 1830s through the 1850s reflect the tendencies of late Danish Romanticism, his work lies far from the Heiberg school of literary aesthetics. (In fact, Heiberg and his thinking are the butt of Andersen's satire in such well-known tales as "Nattergalen" [The Nightingale, 1843].) Andersen was truly an innovator of prose. His dark and philosophical tales, such as "Skyggen" (The Shadow, 1847) and "Tante Tandpine" (Auntie Toothache, 1872), reveal him as a sophisticated literary modernist whose experimentations with narrative techniques and literary forms point forward to such early-twentieth-century modernists as Franz Kafka.

Kierkegaard, who published his principal philosophical writings in a carefully orchestrated series of works between 1843 and his death in 1855, may be regarded in a philosophical context as Andersen's diametrical opposite. One of the most scathing critiques of Andersen's literary work was written by Kierkegaard, a literary review that appeared in 1838 (actually, Kierkegaard's first book), *Af en endnu Levendes Papirer* (translated as "From the Papers of One Still Living," 1990). In it Kierkegaard carried out a systematic analysis of Andersen's third novel, *Kun en Spillemand* (1837; translated as *Only a Fiddler,* 1845), according to the Heiberg school of literary criticism, attacking Andersen's novel as lacking ideological and aesthetic coherence. Kierkegaard is most widely regarded, however, as the father of modern existentialism. His body of work has had profound influence on the theology, philosophy, and literature of Europe (although it was not available in English translation until the 1930s). While in an international context he is most often regarded as a philosopher, his works had significant influence on the development of Danish and Scandinavian prose. As an ironist, rhetorician, and prose stylist, Kierkegaard is unsurpassed. His works dealing with aesthetic, ethical, and religious questions have influenced the direction of critical inquiry and literary concerns in Scandinavia for more than a century.

Poet and doctor Emil Aarestrup spent his visits to the capital city strolling with Kierkegaard, his preferred author. With the exception of one work, Aarestrup's poetry, however, was published only posthumously, in 1863, seven years after his death, by his friend Christian Winther. Aarestrup's explicitly erotic language initially alienated critics, but over time he has come to be highly regarded as a modern poet, a source of inspiration for many Danish poets. His friend and contemporary Winther (the stepbrother of Møller) is a more conventional poet. Winther's works have remained Danish classics; his poetic epic *Hjortens Flugt* (The Flight of the Stag, 1855) is generally considered the last great work of Danish Romanticism.

The mid nineteenth century was a turning point in Danish culture, history, and literature. Following the revolutionary year 1848 in Europe, Denmark experienced a peaceful transformation of government, which was solidified on 5 June 1849 with the granting of a democratic constitution under King Frederik VII. After 190 years, the absolute monarchy was finally abolished. About the same time, the first Dano-Prussian War (1848–1851) erupted over the Slesvig-Holsten question. This conflict over the duchies continued a decade later, with Denmark facing the combined Austro-Prussian army. The second war ended in a crushing defeat for the Danes in 1864 and enormous territorial losses to Germany (which were partially recovered by the plebiscite of 1920). The Dano-Prussian wars and the defeat of 1864 resulted in a common experience of loss and national humiliation evident in the work of many late-nineteenth-century Danish writers.

Three prose writers of the mid nineteenth century–Mathilde Fibiger, Meïr Goldschmidt, and Hans Egede Schack–may be regarded as transitional figures, who bridge the decades between Romanticism and the new realism that emerged in the 1870s. With epistolary novels and essays, Fibiger addressed questions of women's emancipation two decades before the establishment of the first Danish women's movement in 1871. Goldschmidt was not only the first author to address the matter of Jewish identity in nineteenth-century Danish society, but he also contributed substantial prose works that integrated a psychological realism with Romantic idealism. Schack's name is nearly synonymous with the "Fantast" or dreamer motif in Danish literature–novels dealing with the problematic of an idealistic daydreamer or irresolute protagonist paralyzed by his own idealism–a theme cultivated subsequently by many Danish writers. Schack is known exclusively for his only completed novel, *Phantasterne* (The Fantasts, 1857), a work that is defined in literary history as breaking with Romanticism and at the same time heralding realism. The "Fantast" motif came to resonate decades later with such significant writers of the Modern Breakthrough as J. P. Jacobsen and Norwegian playwright Henrik Ibsen, who made renunciation of dreams and delusions a central theme in their works.

Much has been written about Georg Brandes as a catalyst for the so-called Modern Breakthrough in Scandinavian letters. His lectures at the University of Copenhagen in 1871 set into motion new forms of literary discourse not only in Denmark but also in Norway and Sweden. He called for Danish writers to awake from their Romantic stupor and to write a new literature that would "sætte Problemer under Debat" (put problems to debate), as he wrote in the oft-quoted introduction to his *Hovedstrømninger i det nittende Aarhundredes Litteratur* (Main Currents in Nineteenth-Century Literature, 1872). Brandes's influence on the development of Scandinavian literature is profound. Few literary critics can claim to have a movement named because of them: Brandes is associated with two synonymous terms, the Modern Breakthrough and "Brandesianism." As a biographer, literary critic (the first modern comparatist), cultural mediator, scholar, and translator, he reached a broad international audience. Brandes may be credited as the first critic to recognize the innovative nature of Ibsen's work (1898) and the first to write an academic essay on the work of Andersen (1869). Two decades after he had called for a socially engaged and realistic literature, Brandes also introduced Friedrich Nietzsche and the concept of "Aristokratisk Radikalisme" (Aristocratic Radicalism), the title of his 1889 essay, to Scandinavian letters.

All of the Danish writers who debuted during the last three decades of the nineteenth century may be discussed in relation to or as part of a countermovement to the Modern Breakthrough and the currents initiated by Brandes. Despite Brandes's enormous prestige and influence, the relationships between him and his Danish contemporaries were often complex and conflict-ridden. Few devoted disciples of Brandes are to be found among the major Danish writers of this period. Poet Holger Drachmann was the most widely read and popular writer of this period. For nearly four decades, until his death in 1908, Drachmann was considered the national poet of Denmark; his literary production is voluminous, exceeded only in size by the oeuvres of Andersen, Grundtvig, and Kierkegaard. Although Drachmann still holds a place in Danish literary history, his status has declined rapidly in the twentieth century. On the other hand, the work of conservative writer Vilhelm Topsøe, whose prose was admired by Norwegian writer Knut Hamsun and who was generally considered Brandes's ideological foe, continues to warrant critical assessment. Jacobsen's influential historical novel *Fru Marie Grubbe* (1876; translated as *Marie Grubbe. A Lady of the Seventeenth Century,* 1917), about a noblewoman's sensuality and social decline, is regarded as the first naturalistic novel of Denmark, but it is more directly indebted to Emile Zola than to Brandes. Jacobsen's prose, particularly his masterpiece, *Niels Lyhne* (1880; translated in 1896), was lauded by Thomas Mann, James Joyce, August Strindberg, and Rainer Maria Rilke.

Drachmann's sister, Erna Juel-Hansen, was one of the most prolific and professionally successful of the Danish women writers of the Modern Breakthrough; she was inspired by one of Brandes's lectures in the early 1870s. Her oeuvre was rediscovered in the 1980s with the publication of Pil Dahlerup's study *Det moderne gennembruds kvinder* (The Women of the Modern Breakthrough, 1983), a work that sought to challenge the exclusively male canon established one hundred years earlier by Brandes's *Det Moderne Gjennembruds Mænd* (The Men of the Modern Breakthrough, 1883). The few published works of Adda Ravnkilde demonstrate potential artistic talent, which might have developed had not a meeting with Brandes precipitated her suicide; Brandes wrote the foreword to Ravnkilde's posthumously published novel, *Judith Fürste* (1884). Undoubtedly, the most significant Scandinavian woman writer of this period is Norwegian naturalist Amalie Skram, who wrote and published much of her work in Denmark and whose husband, Erik Skram, was a disciple of Brandes. However, as Amalie Skram is today claimed by Norwegian literary historians, she has not been included in this volume on Danish writers.

In addition to Jacobsen, two of Denmark's finest prose writers emerged in the 1880s in the wake of the Modern Breakthrough–Herman Bang and Henrik Pontoppidan. As a literary critic, Bang countered Brandes with his own work, *Realisme og Realister* (Realism and Realists, 1879). Bang was later (in 1883) cruelly attacked by Brandes as a writer with a "woman's mediocre intelligence." As the world's first "literary impressionist," to use the words of Claude Monet, Bang was widely recognized in Europe, especially in Germany, where his work was held in high esteem by Mann, Rilke, and Hugo von Hofmannsthal. Bang's public persona and his art embody the tendencies of literary "decadence," which are evident in much of the fin de siècle literature of Europe. His novels *Ved Vejen* (1886; translated as *Katinka,* 1990), *Tine* (1889; translated as *Tina,* 1984), and *Ludvigsbakke* (1896; translated as *Ida Brandt,* 1928) are among the finest and most memorable masterpieces of Danish literature. Although not stylistically as innovative or sophisticated as Bang's works, the voluminous novels of Pontoppidan offer a comprehensive illustration of Danish society in the transition from a rural, agrarian culture to a modern, industrialized, urban country. His significant multivolume novels *Det forjættede Land* (1892; translated as *The Promised Land,* 1896), *Lykke Per* (Lucky Per, 1898–1904), and *De Dødes Rige* (The Realm of the Dead, 1917) earned him a Nobel Prize in literature, which he shared with Karl Gjellerup in 1917.

The last decade of the nineteenth century belongs to the Danish symbolist poets, who initiated a literary movement that challenged the Brandesian program of the Modern Breakthrough. With the avant-garde literary journal *Taarnet* (The Tower, 1893–1894), inspired by French symbolist poetry, Sophus Claussen, Johannes Jørgensen, and Viggo Stuckenberg formulated a new aesthetic that moved away from the demands of prose realism and cultivated spirituality and religion, subjectivity, and irrationality in lyrical poetry. The influence of Nietzsche's works on Scandinavian literature of this period is quite significant. Of these three poets who debuted in the 1890s, posterity has valued Claussen's innovative contributions most highly. His work remains a model and source of inspiration for many contemporary Danish poets.

Finally, this *DLB* volume includes a handful of writers–Harald Kidde, Jakob Knudsen, Thøger Larsen, and Gustav Wied–who made their literary debuts around the turn of the twentieth century. Although they published work well into the twentieth century, their literary contributions build strongly on nineteenth-century traditions and literary conventions. The true innovators and leaders of the next generation of writers that emerged around 1900, such as Johannes V. Jensen and Martin Andersen Nexø, are included in *DLB 214: Twentieth-Century Danish Writers.*

–*Marianne Stecher-Hansen*

Acknowledgments

This book was produced by Bruccoli Clark Layman, Inc. Penelope M. Hope and R. Bland Lawson were the in-house editors. They were assisted by C. Bryan Love and Philip B. Dematteis.

Production manager is Philip B. Dematteis.

Administrative support was provided by Ann M. Cheschi and Carol A. Cheschi.

Accountant is Ann-Marie Holland.

Copyediting supervisor is Sally R. Evans. The copyediting staff includes Phyllis A. Avant, Caryl Brown, Melissa D. Hinton, Philip I. Jones, Rebecca Mayo, Nadirah Rahimah Shabazz, and Nancy E. Smith.

Pipeline manager is James F. Tidd Jr.

Editorial associates are Joshua M. Robinson and Joshua Shaw.

In-house prevetter is Catherine M. Polit.

Permissions editor is Amber L. Coker.

Layout and graphics supervisor is Janet E. Hill. The graphics staff includes Zoe R. Cook and Sydney E. Hammock.

Office manager is Kathy Lawler Merlette.

Photography editors are Mark J. McEwan and Walter W. Ross.

Digital photographic copy work was performed by Joseph M. Bruccoli.

Systems manager is Donald Kevin Starling.

Typesetting supervisor is Kathleen M. Flanagan. The typesetting staff includes Patricia Marie Flanagan and Pamela D. Norton.

Walter W. Ross is library researcher. He was assisted by the following librarians at the Thomas

Cooper Library of the University of South Carolina: Jo Cottingham, interlibrary loan department; circulation department head Tucker Taylor; reference department head Virginia W. Weathers; reference department staff Laurel Baker, Marilee Birchfield, Kate Boyd, Paul Cammarata, Joshua Garris, Gary Geer, Tom Marcil, Rose Marshall, and Sharon Verba; interlibrary loan department head Marna Hostetler; and interlibrary loan staff Bill Fetty, Nelson Rivera, and Cedric Rose.

The volume editor offers heartfelt thanks to the Danish Royal Library for permissions; the Danish Literature Center and the Department of Scandinavian Studies, University of Washington for translation subsidies; Tiina Nunnally and Steven Murray of Oso Books for translations and invaluable advice; Mark Mussari for translations and helpful editorial assistance; and Inger Tranberg, Kirsten and Michael Stecher, as well as my husband and sons, for assistance and moral support. Finally, I am most grateful to my many colleagues in the field of Danish literature–in North America and Europe–for their outstanding contributions to this volume.

Dictionary of Literary Biography® • Volume Three Hundred

Danish Writers from the Reformation to Decadence, 1550–1900

Dictionary of Literary Biography

Emil Aarestrup

(4 December 1800 – 21 July 1856)

Keld Zeruneith
University of Copenhagen

(Translated by Mark Mussari)

BOOKS: *Digte* (Copenhagen: C. A. Reitzel, 1838);
Efterladte Digte, edited by Christian Winther and F. L. Liebenberg (Copenhagen: Thieles Bogtrykkeri, 1863).

Editions and Collections: *Samlede Digte,* edited by F. L. Liebenberg, with a biographical sketch by Georg Brandes (Copenhagen: C. A. Reitzel, 1877);
Digte, 2 volumes, with an introduction and notes by Oluf Friis (Copenhagen: M. P. Madsen, 1918; second edition, Copenhagen: Hans Reitzel, 1962);
Samlede Skrifter, edited by Hans Brix and Palle Raunkjær (5 volumes, Copenhagen: Det danske Sprog- og Litteraturselskab/Henrik Koppels Forlag, 1922–1925; reprinted photographically, with minor additions, 6 volumes, Copenhagen: C. A. Reitzel, 1976);
Udvalgte digte, edited by Dan Ringgaard (Copenhagen: Det danske Sprog- og Litteraturselskab/Borgen, 1998).

TRANSLATIONS: *Samlede Skrifter,* volume 5, edited by Hans Brix and Palle Raunkjær (Copenhagen: Det danske Sprog- og Litteraturselskab/Henrik Koppels Forlag, 1925)–comprises a comprehensive collection of Aarestrup's translations of selected poetry.

Emil Aarestrup (daguerrotype, circa 1855; courtesy of the Danish Royal Library, Copenhagen)

Emil Aarestrup was a poet unappreciated in his own time. During his lifetime he published only one collection–*Digte* (Poems, 1838). Any hope for the success of the book was shattered by the critics' silence, and only forty copies were sold. In 1863, seven years after his death, his friend poet Christian Winther published Aarestrup's *Efterladte Digte* (Posthumous Poems). The collection comprises poems written before 1838 as well as the relatively few he wrote thereafter. Aarestrup's openly erotic use of language particularly repulsed the arbiters of taste. Peter Andreas Heiberg, a prominent critic, privately referred to Aarestrup's book as "svineri" (filth). Aarestrup achieved some redress when the scholar P. L. Møller, in his *Kritiske Skizzer* (Critical Sketches, 1847), wrote the first introduction to Aarestrup's work. Georg Brandes, however, was the first critic to place Aarestrup in a literary-historical context–even though Aarestrup continued to be devalued as an "offensive" writer.

By championing Aarestrup's natural sensuality, Møller and Brandes used his poetry in their own ideological war against bourgeois morality. Thus, they became the progenitors of the later myth that Aarestrup was a zealous and naive poet. In this sense they distorted Aarestrup's notion of the nothingness of existence, a notion he expressed intensely in his poetry as a tension between his cultivation of the erotic and the aesthetic. By insisting on this naiveté, critics hid his true talent as a thoughtful stylist. Aarestrup's tension between the world of urges and his radical use of language made him the first truly modern Danish poet.

Aarestrup's father, Jørgen Voigt Aarestrup, came from Jutland and was employed as a clerk in the customhouse in the Østerbro district of Copenhagen. Aarestrup's mother, Sophie Charlotte Aagaard, was the daughter of a successful tea and porcelain merchant, and the entire family lived in her father's house in Store Kongensgade in Copenhagen. Although their firstborn died as a child, the couple soon had Carl Ludvig Emil and Frederik Christian Wilhelm. The brothers became orphans at an early age, however, when their parents died within a month of each other in 1808 after having separated the year before. Emil Aarestrup was placed with a former chambermaid at court. After his maternal grandfather's death, he inherited a small fortune, making him economically independent. He matriculated in 1819 and began to study medicine at the University of Copenhagen.

Throughout his authorship Aarestrup returned to the experience of being orphaned; he proffered, according to the circumstances of his life, various evaluations of its relevance. For example, in letters to his fiancée and cousin, Caroline Frederikke Aagaard, to whom he became engaged in the summer of 1824, he viewed the loss as a fortunate circumstance of fate. Being orphaned, he felt, made him independent of outer authorities and free to become himself. Slowly, however, as life wore him down, he could no longer hold onto this optimistic interpretation. By age thirty-five he viewed his life as a search for the identity and wholeness that the memory of his parents now represented. At the sight of a child crying because he lost his parents among the crowd at an amusement park outside of Copenhagen, Aarestrup wrote, "Selv misted jeg min Fader og Moder, som du / En syvaarig Stakkel, og jeg leder endnu" (I too lost my father and mother, like you / A poor seven-year-old, and I am still searching).

Poems written when Aarestrup was in his mid teens disclose that the loss of his parents held two important meanings for him. First he viewed this time as Edenic, a lost harmonious existence for which he continued to long. This longing lies, perhaps, at the heart of his poetic search for beauty. He reinforced this view in his poem "Om min Muse" (About My Muse, written circa 1817; published in 1922), in which he illustrates how the inspiration of poetry filled the emotional void left by his parents.

As the world of desire took form in his burgeoning sexuality, Aarestrup was initially dominated by the Christian, middle-class notion of sin. Plagued with anger over the temptations of the flesh–which he claimed appeared to him in serpentine images–he prayed to the Savior to free him. The decisive break in his consciousness, life, and writing surfaces in his 1820 poem "Sonett" (Sonnet). Aarestrup no longer threatens the serpent; instead, he begins to identify with it and its forbidden sensuousness. This covenant with the natural world may explain Aarestrup's decision to become a doctor. At the same time, his lyrical production mostly ceased over the next fourteen years. By choosing this heretical approach, symbolized by the snake (or Lucifer), he created a reality free from the pangs of conscience and far beyond any bourgeois moral code.

In addition, his choice opened Aarestrup's eyes to a previously unknown world of the senses, one that characterized his later poetry. A surprising example occurs in his letter to his cousin Caroline. During an autopsy exercise with a cadaver, Aarestrup discovered a striking beauty, which he described to his eighteen-year-old cousin:

> Hvor stygt er ikke Cadaveret, saaledes som vi faaer det, smudsigt, hentæret, uskjønt; men naar Huden er borte, naar de enkelte Dele betragtes hver for sig; de røde, friske Kjødtrevler med deres fine, gjennemsigtige Hinder; Senerne, blanke som Sølv; Brusket paa Ledemodene, snehvide, glatte; det uendelige fine Net af Aarer, Pulsaarer og Nerver; og den beundringsværdige Sammenhæng, Forstanden kan opdage deri–o Caroline! et dødt Legeme indeholder en Skat af den høieste Skjønhed; man maa tabe sig i Beundring derover, som om man stod over for fuldendeste Værk i Naturen.

> (The cadaver is truly ugly when we first get it–grimy, withered, and unsightly; but when we have removed the skin, when the separate parts are viewed, each on its own, the fresh, red shreds of flesh with their fine, transparent membranes; the sinews, shiny as silver; the cartilage on the joints, snow-white, shiny; the endless, fine network of veins, arteries, and nerves; and

the amazing connection the intellect can discover therein–Oh, Caroline! A dead body possesses a treasure of the highest beauty. You can lose yourself in wonder over it–as if you stood over the most perfect work in Nature.)

The doctor's gaze merges with the poet's lyrical eye, an eye that, without religious undertones, can resuscitate beauty even in the dead. He described the same wondrous sense of resurrection many years later in his poem "I en Landsbykirke" (In a Village Church, 1838). The decay the narrative voice sees in the surroundings of the church, an image of the disintegration of the world of faith, inspires a contradictory aesthetical movement in which he regains the lost metaphysic in the sheer joy of his beloved's body.

The linguistic activity whereby Aarestrup, in his first youthful poems, sought to orient himself to existence is redirected in his letters to his lover during their engagement. She was staying among relatives in the provincial town of Præstø. Aarestrup's lengthy, well-written letters constitute a protracted attempt at talking his beloved out of a bourgeois sense of virtue and into the erotic world of desire–a world he had achieved entrée to through his identification with the snake. He proffered much advice to his lover to behave naturally–to loosen her corset, breathe out, and surrender to him. Along the way he ridicules middle-class Christianity. One can discern from her reaction, garnered from his answers and new demands, that his educational project failed. She reacted at first with a strong headache, obviously initiated by his radical thinking; she also held fast to the rules she believed were necessary for a proper girl's behavior.

Following his medical examinations in 1827, Aarestrup married Caroline. In his poem "Var det Synd?" (Was It a Pity? 1838) he describes their wedding as an erotic union in nature–without the participation of the clergy. Only the "unge Gud for Kjærlighed" (young god of love) was present. Shortly after the wedding, the couple moved to the small market town of Nysted, on the island of Lolland, but they became like two distant satellites. While she focused all her energies on their children–twelve in all–he attended to his medical duties and was frequently in a bad mood. A poem to his wife, "Gunløde" (the title character of the poem, 1838), appears at first to be an homage to her attentiveness: she waits on him and feeds his children, but then he says, "Med Tiden hun sætter / Mig Urnen paa Graven" (In time she will place / The urn on my grave). When one compares this poem to the wedding poem, however, "Gunløde" seems an ambivalent homage. The bride of nature has turned into a provincial matron; she has become one with their monotonous and petty surroundings and, implicitly, sucks life out of him. The monotonous rhythm of the poem underscores his view of life as dull.

Aarestrup's traveling chest (from Hans Henrik Jacobsen, Emil Aarestrup. Stiftsfysikus i Odense 1849–1856, *1975; Main Library, University of Illinois at Urbana-Champaign, 1975)*

During these years Aarestrup took refuge in his visits to the many manor homes of the area, especially the nearby castle of Aalholm, and in the delicacies and news sent from Copenhagen by his good friend, merchant Christian Pedersen (with whom he maintained a lifelong correspondence). The letters constitute a sarcastic, running commentary on Aarestrup's dissatisfaction with life as a country doctor. Bored with his marriage and with traversing country roads, he wondered whether he was actually curing his patients or killing them. In Kierkegaardian terms, he felt like one of the living dead.

An important link in Aarestrup's poetic development was his journey as a doctor to the spa at Karlsbad in 1832. He accompanied a sick young noblewoman from Aalholm, Amalie Raben, who died in Dresden on the way home. The trip sparked an infatuation for the young woman that Aarestrup reworked poetically into an intense sexual longing for his wife. While in Dresden, he expressed this emotional experience in a poem to his wife:

Du! Du! Du Søde!
Du Smekkre! Hvide!
Du Længselsvarme!

Som ved min Side,
Som tidt i mine Arme
Med kjælne Øielaage,
Med Blik
Slukt af en salig Taage,
Forstummende af Lykke,
Og kysforgiftet, næsten døde–
O jeg forsmægter!
Jeg kan Din runde Hals ei trykke!
Jeg tørster efter
Din Aandes Blomsterdrik,
Din Arms Omfavningskræfter,
Din slangebygte Ryg,
Din Tunges sagte Kys, Din Munds–
Ha, hvad mig Skjæbnen nægter!–
Ak, følte jeg dog kuns
Din Haands, Din lille Fingers Tryk!

(You! You! Gentle one!
You Supple! Pale!
Of longing passionate!
By my Side,
Often in my Embrace
With Eyes of Love,
With Gaze
Eclipsed by sacred Mist,
And by Ecstasy muted,
Poisoned by Kiss, almost dead--
O, I perish!
Your curved Neck I cannot grasp!
I thirst for
Your Nectar Breath,
The Strength of your Embrace,
Your serpentine Back,
Your gentle Kiss, your Tongue, your Mouth–
What Destiny denies me!–
Oh, if only I could feel
Your Hand's–your little Finger's–Touch!)
(Translation by Elizabeth Stokkebye)

The content of the poem drives expression, so that the poem rhythmically, almost mimetically, communicates the silent embrace. Aarestrup once again unites sexual activity with the image of the snake in the description of her back as serpentine. That the poem is only a fantasy results, ultimately, in its lament. This pattern functions as a recurring motif in his poetry. Aarestrup returned to his old life in Nysted. During his journey, though, he experienced a splendor he had never known. Foreign landscapes, especially the mountains, now functioned as an important motif in his poetry.

Only a few years later did Aarestrup feel the actual impulse to return to his writing. On New Year's Day, 1834, he invited Winther to lunch, and afterward in his study Aarestrup read his poetry to Winther. Winther was overwhelmed; he expressed his feelings in a letter: "Den prægtige Mand forelæsde os en Mængde saa fortræffelige, orignale, kraftige characteristiske, snurrige og alvorlige, dybttænkte og lette poetiske Productioner, at jeg i 2–3 Timer sad og hørte derpaa som en Billedstøtte. Han kan! Han skriver os andre smaa Poeter rent sønder og sammen" (This glorious man read to us a number of splendid, original, strong, characteristic, droll and serious, deep and light poetic productions that for two–three hours I sat listening like a statue. He can do it! He is writing us other small poets into a cocked hat).

Winther's admiration called Aarestrup back to the world of poetry. During the following three years Aarestrup wrote most of the important poems that became the backbone of *Digte.* One possibly more important cause of this inspiration was that Winther's lover, Sophie Hansen, spent these years living near Nysted; she soon became the object of Aarestrup's passionate worship. Through her, he developed the poetic phenomenon he referred to as "erotisk Videnskab" (erotic science), apparent in the poem "Nordexpeditionen" (Northern Expedition, 1838). The most famous of Aarestrup's poems to Hansen is "Til en Veninde" (To a Girlfriend, 1838); the first and last stanzas read,

Der er en Trolddom paa din Læbe,
Der er en Afgrund i dit Blik,
Der er i Lyden af din Stemme
En Drøms ætheriske Musik.
. . . .
Der er en Verden i dit Indre,
En sværmerisk, chaotisk Vaar–
Som jeg umulig kan forglemme,
Som jeg tilbeder og forstaaer.

(There is Sorcery on your Lips,
There is Abyss in your Gaze,
There is in the Sound of your Voice
Music of an ethereal Dream.
. . . .
There is a World within you,
A fluttering, chaotic Spring–
Impossible for me to forget,
That I worship and comprehend.)
(Translation by Elizabeth Stokkebye)

In this poem, Aarestrup succeeds, in a highly evocative mode, at uniting the physical and the spiritual. The poem does not possess a concrete narrative; instead, Aarestrup places himself and the woman in a musical, thoroughly erotic atmosphere. At the same time, serpentine imagery lurks behind such words as "Trolddom" (magic) and "Afgrund" (abyss).

Aarestrup's erotic poetry is, thus, characterized by an atmospheric enjoyment of female beauty. He develops his notion of "woman" in fragments, focusing his sensual intensity on such features as lips, eyes, hair, and beauty marks. By isolating these impressions of beauty, he is able to impart to each of them all the power that would otherwise be disseminated in a broader and more typically complete experience. Even the breaking down of wholeness strengthens sense perception, as it acquires its radiance in the linguistic richness of each isolated experience.

Several factors affected Aarestrup's attempt to control this form of sense impression. For example, he does not respect–nor is he bound to–thinking in broad terms that might reveal a Christian view of creation as their basis. He creates, instead, on his own subjective terms and manages to individualize the rhythmic pattern and meter of his poetry. Thus, expression corresponds to the feelings he attempts to give aesthetic form and durability.

Aarestrup's need for beauty relates also to another conflicting side of his writing–the poetry in which he expresses, in parallel fashion, his spleen. It is an almost nihilistic emotional basis as he experiences existence as empty, a nothingness that wakens his longing for death. He expresses this thought in his characteristic poem "Hør, Dødens Klokker kime" (Hear Death's Bell Toll, 1863), directed to a funeral procession; the final stanza reads,

Hvo venter ei–nedhugget
Lemlæstet og forblødet–
I Kamp mod Livets Qvalet
Med Længsel Naadestødet?

(Who yearns not–cut down,
damaged, and bleeding–
In the fight against Life is pain
For the final Stab of Mercy?)
(Translation by Elizabeth Stokkebye)

The end of all searching is "det store Intet" (the great nothingness), an allusion to Georg Wilhelm Friedrich Hegel that Aarestrup refers to in a letter. Whereas negation for Hegel leads, logically, to a still higher, synthesizing recognition, Aarestrup is unable to unite his daily existence and his poetry.

This disparity results in his irony and the cultivation of beauty in his poetry, particularly activated by erotic tension set up against the gloom of everyday living. He can now utilize his surroundings, whether the "plumbe Grønhed" (coarse greenery) of Denmark or "Alpesneens Hvidhed" (the whiteness of the Alps), to describe female beauty, while nothingness suddenly becomes the rubric through which fantasy can actually run free.

An extreme example of this nihilistic sense appears in Aarestrup's carnival or demonic poetry. In these poems he turns the world upside down by cultivating the dark sides of existence, the sides usually repressed by the bourgeoisie. The door was, therefore,

Aarestrup's wife, Caroline Frederikke, née Aagaard, circa 1830 (artist unknown; courtesy of the Danish Royal Library, Copenhagen)

opened to a coarse sensuousness that could only be viewed by his contemporaries as offensive (and which saw no counterpart until the demonic poems of Sophus Claussen). In a poem with the telling title "Fortvivlelse" (Despair, 1863) Aarestrup describes a psychological split. As his beloved, like a goddess or dream lover, vanishes upward into the heavens, he descends in a state of ironic audacity and damnation with the words "Jeg er den sorte, faldne Dæmon" (I am the black, fallen demon). The poem concludes,

Jeg vælter mig i mine Flammer,
Og har det–saavidt–ganske godt
Jeg har endnu min gamle Latter
Min Djævlefrækhed, og min Spot.

(I welter deep within my Flames,
And find–so far–I'm not forlorn
I still possess my old Laughter
My devilry, and my Scorn.)
(Translation by Elizabeth Stokkebye)

The poem, with roots in his previous serpentine identification, implies that virtue is an obstacle to erotic happiness. He presses the notion not only that virtue creates demons but also that penetration into this forbidden subconscious world releases strong creative forces. He assumes this view of reality in his pursuit of purely demonic scenarios, as in "Paa Maskeraden" (At the Masquerade, 1863):

> Ved alle Tisler, alle sorte Slanger!
> Jeg elsker dig, skjønt du er grim og styg;
> Det Ideal, min barske Sjæl forlanger,
> Er i din Pukkel og din skjæve Ryg.
>
> (By all Thistles, by all black Serpents!
> I love you, though you are ugly and foul;
> The Ideal, that my coarse Soul craves,
> Is in your hump and bent Spine.)
> (Translation by Elizabeth Stokkebye)

Aarestrup did not include this poem in his *Digte*–just as he excluded many others he felt the public would find unpleasant. Therefore, his only published collection of poetry failed to offer the full range of his tension and potential. Despite the omissions to *Digte,* traces of his general source of inspiration still exist.

Aarestrup concludes his *Digte* with a poem cycle, *Erotiske Situationer* (Erotic Situations), consisting of fifty-one poems, many of which constitute his most important work. Research has previously indicated that Aarestrup made an unsuccessful attempt to create a poetic short story, a genre then developed by such authors as Frederik Paludan-Müller and Winther. Compared to their poetic short stories, with their epic forerunners, Aarestrup's attempts in this genre were a failure.

A specific epic influence on *Erotiske Situationer* is difficult to locate. Aarestrup's own notes indicate, though, that he viewed his poem cycle as one short story; he envisioned the poems as a total composition. If they are, the work also indicates that the concept of a short story and its composition must be viewed in a manner different from his contemporaries' use of these terms. Whereas their works are epic in nature, Aarestrup's poetic short story characteristically creates a dreamworld and an aesthetic alternative to the moral world of the bourgeoisie. Thus, his "short story" loses any general interpretive environment and consists, instead, of situations–erotic moments experienced as particularly tense and insightful.

In his notes, Aarestrup offered the formula "legende, drømmende, sværmende, elskende, døende, digtende" (playing, dreaming, swooning, loving, dying, writing) as the structure for the poetic "short story." The poems follow this rhythm in their depiction of a romantic relationship between the *you* of the poem–the woman–and the male narrator. From this perspective the reader can see a tripartite construction.

Aarestrup, in the cycle's first phase, describes a romance with many similarities to his own betrothal. The poetic narrator struggles to emancipate his beloved from the moral obstructions that lie both in her subconscious and in the morality of her milieu and that interfere with their relationship. Unlike his own betrothal story, the narrator, now recalling the events, succeeds in separating the woman from her mores and convinces her to surrender. The second phase deals with her sickness and death, while the final phase describes how the narrator, by writing, preserves the memory of their relationship and immortalizes it in his poetry. Aarestrup anticipates this process in "En Middag" (A Supper, 1838), in which he describes how death can be transformed into art. Therefore, *Erotiske Situationer* functions, as a whole, as an aesthetic counterpoint to Aarestrup's experience of the mutability of life.

In his writing, Aarestrup attempted to manifest those moments of erotic beauty and power that his memory concentrated upon and to immortalize them. When poetry substitutes for the idleness of everyday living, however, and replaces faith in eternal life, the poetic expression must still create its own metaphysical existence. The poet must, therefore, master his art to near perfection.

This relationship explains why Aarestrup developed an artistry unparalleled in Danish poetry. He struggled not to create art for art's sake, although that thought was evident to him. On the contrary, he sought–through his optimal artistic ability–to create a counterprocess to death, a process by which his highly developed aesthetic reflection could fill the emptiness he had felt in his life since he was orphaned and later in his marriage. Through the beauty of a poem, the feeling of pleasure in an erotic dreamworld, he found a reply to nothingness and death.

In many poems, Aarestrup recognized, however, the limits of poetic transformation from life to death. In one of the erotic situations, "Paa Sneen" (On the Snow, 1838), the narrator follows the object of his desire through the snow-covered city. He describes how he can feel himself inside her, feel her breath, how he can–by identifying with her muff–touch her hands, hear how the smooth silk "skriger" (screams) around her knees. Through his fantasy and senses he can completely envelop her–although separated from her. The shadow functions as his stand-in; his heightened senses search for release as his shadow on the moonlit snowy blanket–in a phantom copulation–unites with her shadow:

> De svulmede–Canova
> Ei bedre Grupper skabte–
> Imellem blev de borte,

Naar Maanens Lys sig tabte.
Og kom igjen tilsyne
I Stillinger–o Lykke,
Mit Kjød og Blod maa savne,
Men opnaaes af min Skygge!

(The voluptuous–Canova
No better Groups created–
In between they dissolved,
As Light of Moon abated.
And once more appeared
In Postures–o Bliss,
My Flesh and Blood without,
What my Shadow thus attained!)
(Translation by Elizabeth Stokkebye)

In these final verses a wistful dichotomy exists between life and fantasy. Despite the aesthetic beauty Aarestrup creates around the erotic situation, the poem ultimately cannot replace the satisfaction that lies in a real embrace. Thus, he becomes merely an observer of desire, transformed into poetry and thereby immortalized. Writing supplants the very instinct on which it feeds.

Through his poetry, Aarestrup struggled to sustain his erotic experiences so that they could be recalled with all their momentary fullness. Ostensibly, this attempt demanded that he be capable, linguistically, of conveying the sensual character of experience and of giving it its individual quality (as in "Du! Du! Du Søde!" and "Paa Sneen"). He often employs the sonnet form, and he manages to bend it rhythmically to his own purpose. His skill is apparent in such sonnets as "Tag dette Kys, og tusind til, du Søde" (Take This Kiss, and a Thousand More, Oh Sweet One, 1863). In the closing terza rima he reflects on the demands of the form, calling it "reen og plastisk" (pure and malleable) and "ret elastisk" (truly elastic). As the "fire of love" drives his poetic form, he finds himself in the erotic situation, enjoys it, but at the same time distances himself from it in the aesthetic role of observer.

Aarestrup also broke with the metric norms of his time. He appeared in contemporary educational books as an example of a poet committing a breach of the given ground rules of poetry. Such breaks with rhythm and meter imply a hidden revolt against the accepted order, which the narrator replaces with his or her own poetic musicality. Consequently, Aarestrup's poetry awakened resistance–not only because of its erotic license but also as a consequence of its lyrical being. The break with the established order also explains why, in retrospect, Aarestrup has come to be regarded as the most modern lyricist of his time.

A special characteristic of Aarestrup's meter is his use of enjambment. (This effect occurs when the meaning of a line stretches beyond it.) Thus, he breaks with classical meter, in which meaning and line unite in regularity. In this break with order from within the poem, Aarestrup creates a tension in the reading: the reader partly wants to stop at the end of each line of verse and partly is drawn further to grasp meaning. Aarestrup can then inscribe his sensations in long, rhythmic movements–for example, those constructed around his fascination with a woman's singular body parts, as in "Paa Sneen."

Aarestrup in 1847 (lithograph after a drawing by A. Schiøtt; courtesy of the Danish Royal Library, Copenhagen)

He also possesses a sense for arresting perspectives of both sight and sound. He composes in rhyming couplets of foreign words, such as "Bajadere" (Bayadere) and "Cavaliere," or with colorific words, such as "glimmerhvide" (glimmering white), "glødende purpurrøde" (burning scarlet), and "rødtskummende" (foaming red).

One group of Aarestrup's poems consists of the three-lined ritornello, which originated in Asia but which he discovered in the writings of German poet Friedrich Rückert. Aarestrup rapidly developed its simple, basic form and thus was able to vary the short verses in all possible modes (for example, with the help of brief dialogues). In a short period he produced more than two hundred ritornellos; in this abbreviated form,

Headstone of Aarestrup and his wife in Assistenskirkegarden Odense (from Hans Henrik Jacobsen, Emil Aarestrup. Stiftsfysikus i Odense 1849–1856, *1975; Main Library, University of Illinois at Urbana-Champaign)*

he discovered a poetic form that answered his episodic view of experience. He calls his ritornellos "winged" and "lovely," because within them he can craft beauty in a sudden, euphoric moment lifted out of everyday drabness, as in "Lægen" (The Doctor, 1922):

Hans Blik er naglede til Loftets Planker,
Hans Haand til Ninas Arm, hvor Pulsen banker,
Men under Teppet finder du hans Tanker.

(His gaze is nailed to the ceiling beams,
His hand to Nina's arm, where her pulse beats,
But under the covers you'll find his dreams.)
(Translation by Mark Mussari)

Aarestrup's *Digte* was published in 1838. His letters to Winther reveal that long before the publication of the collection, Aarestrup waited anxiously for the response to his first–and only–book. He asked, for example, what Winther thought of the manuscript. He waited in vain, however, for the book was never reviewed and only sold a few copies. He believed he had given the public "En Drøms ætheriske Musik" (The Music of an Ethereal Dream) but that the public had only found filth and materialism.

As a consequence of the suppression of his work, Aarestrup wrote satirical verses on the ridiculous and petty state of criticism in Denmark. He viewed the critics as mere puppets of the masses–the morality police. He also loathed the young celebrated poet H. P. Holst, who ascended to the place Aarestrup believed was his. Aarestrup once again began to long for death, as evidenced in his poem "Kom, Gudsengel, stille Død" (Come, God's Angel, Silent Death, 1863), written at this time.

Meanwhile, Aarestrup tried to procure a new, livelier existence by moving to the larger town of Sakskøbing in 1838. Although his duties took on greater meaning during the eleven years he lived there, the distance from Nysted was short enough that the move did not constitute the hoped-for rejuvenation. Thus, he searched for years after new posts. He finally succeeded in 1849 when he was named county medical officer for Fyn, with residence in Odense, where he remained until his death. He continued his education in Copenhagen, which for years had represented the avatar of art and joie de vivre. He organized his yearly visits to the capital with strict exactitude. He usually spent the final day walking with Søren Kierkegaard: this activity represented the culmination of his visit. As a youth, Aarestrup knew and admired Adam Gottlob Oehlenschläger, but Kierkegaard had become his preferred author. Aarestrup praised the philosopher's "gadestrygende Genius" (street-smart genius) and "enorme penneførende Færdighed" (enormous authorial proficiency). Aarestrup's copious, excellent translations also indicate those writers in whom he discovered a spiritual affinity: Johann Wolfgang von Goethe; Heinrich Heine; George Gordon, Lord Byron; Victor Hugo; and Thomas Moore.

Following the disappointing response to *Digte,* Aarestrup applied his poetic talents chiefly to *pièces d'occasion* (occasional pieces), whose high quality indicates that his poetic powers remained strong. Of special note is his commemorative poem to Amalie Raben, from 1844: "O hvor smukt dette Landskabs Form i sit dæmrende Mørke" (Oh, the Beauty of the Form of this Landscape in the Encroaching Darkness). The poem includes a highly evocative meeting with the departed woman, who now functions as a kind of Beatrice for him. His faith in the natural world underscores his belief that he must always be able to touch the earth if he is ever to understand the heavenly body.

Aarestrup also wrote many political poems. He enjoyed visiting the large manor houses and being waited on, and his sparkling wit made him a welcome guest. Politically he was liberal, with sympathies for workers, but he also had little faith in the people's judgment, as demonstrated in his poem "Den stakkels Blindebuk" (The Pitiable Blind-Man's Bluff). He viewed election to the Constituent Assembly in 1848 as a game of blindman's bluff.

On the occasion of their silver wedding anniversary in 1852 Aarestrup, in many letters, attempted once again to write his wife into the erotic abandon and solidarity he had hoped for during their engagement. As he had predicted in his poem "Gunløde," shee placed his urn on his grave: he died on 21 July 1856, and she survived him by forty years. Today they rest together in the cemetery in Odense. Emil Aarestrup, once ignored, is today counted among the most important Danish authors of the Romantic period. He has inspired such important poets as Sophus Claussen, Jørgen Sonne, and Pia Tafdrup, and his words frequently surface in hidden references in Karen Blixen's work.

Letters:

Emil Aarestrup. Breve fra Emil Aarestrup til Caroline Aarestrup, volume 2, edited by Hans Brix (Copenhagen: Gyldendal, 1952);

Emil Aarestrups breve til Christian Pedersen, edited by Morten Borup (Copenhagen: Gyldendal, 1957).

Biographies:

Hans Brix, *Emil Aarestrup. Digteren og Doktoren,* volume 1 (Copenhagen: Gyldendal, 1952);

Keld Zeruneith, *Den frigjorte. Emil Aarestrup i digtning og samtid. En biografi* (Copenhagen: Gyldendal, 1981).

References:

Søren Baggensen, "Om Emil Aarestrup," in *Seks sonderinger i den panerotiske linje i dansk lyrik* (Odense: Odense University Press, 1997), pp. 43–83;

Georg Brandes, "Emil Aarestrup," in *Samlede Skrifter,* volume 2 (Copenhagen: Gyldendal, 1899), pp. 61–90;

Hans Henrik Jacobsen, *Emil Aarestrup. Stiftsfysikus i Odense 1849–1856* (Odense: University of Odense Press, 1975);

P. L. Møller, "Emil Aarestrup," in *Kritiske Skizzer fra Aarene 1840–47,* volume 2 (Copenhagen: P. G. Philipsen, 1847);

Jørgen Sonne, "I rimets hvidskende egne," *Kritik,* 116 (1995): 41–43;

Frederik Stjernfelt, "Emaljens mørke hieroglypher. Emil Aarestrup: Digte," in *Læsninger i dansk litteratur,* volume 2 (Odense: University of Odense Press, 1998), pp. 86–101.

Papers:

Emil Aarestrup's papers and letters are at the Danish Royal Library in Copenhagen.

Hans Christian Andersen

(2 April 1805 - 4 August 1875)

Johan de Mylius
University of Southern Denmark, Odense

(Translated by Tiina Nunnally)

BOOKS: *Ungdoms-Forsøg,* as Villiam Christian Walter (Copenhagen: Privately printed, 1822);

Fodreise fra Holmens Canal til Østpynten af Amager i Aarene 1828 og 1829 (Copenhagen: Privately printed, 1829);

Kjærlighed paa Nicolai Taarn eller Hvad siger Parterret? Heroisk Vaudeville i 1 Act (Copenhagen: C. A. Reitzel, 1829);

Digte (Copenhagen: Privately printed, 1830);

Phantasier og Skizzer (Copenhagen: Privately printed, 1831);

Skyggebilleder af en Reise til Harzen og det sachsiske Schweiz . . . i Sommeren 1831 (Copenhagen: C. A. Reitzel, 1831); translated by Charles Beckwith Lohmeyer as *Rambles in the Romantic Regions of the Hartz Mountains, Saxon Switzerland . . .* (London: Richard Bentley, 1848);

Skibet, Vaudeville i een Act. Bearbejdet efter Scribes og Mazeres "La Quarantaine" (Copenhagen: C. A. Reitzel, 1831);

Vignetter til danske Digtere (Copenhagen: C. A. Reitzel, 1831);

Bruden fra Lammermoor. Originalt romantisk Syngestykke i fire Acter (Copenhagen: F. Prinzlau, 1832);

Ravnen eller Broderprøven. Trylle-Opera i tre Acter (efter Gozzis tragicomiske Eventyr) (Copenhagen: Schubothske Boghandel, 1832); revised as *Ravnen: Eventyr-Opera i fire Acter* (Copenhagen: C. A. Reitzel, 1865);

Aarets tolv Maaneder, Tegnede med Blæk og Pen (Copenhagen: C. A. Reitzel, 1832);

Dronningen paa 16 Aar. Drama i to Acter, oversat efter Bayards "La reine de seize ans," Det Kongelige Theaters Repertoire, no. 47 (Copenhagen: Schubothske Boghandel, 1833);

Samlede Digte (Copenhagen: C. A. Reitzel, 1833);

Agnete og Havmanden. Dramatisk Digt (Copenhagen: Privately printed, 1833);

Hans Christian Andersen (painting by Christian Albrecht Jensen, 1847; Hans Christian Andersen Museum, Odense)

Improvisatoren. Original Roman i to Dele (Copenhagen: C. A. Reitzel, 1835); translated (from German) by Mary Howitt as *The Improvisatore; or, Life in Italy,* 2 volumes (London: Richard Bentley, 1845; New York: Harper, 1845);

Eventyr, fortalte for Børn, 2 volumes (Copenhagen: C. A. Reitzel, 1835)–volume 1 comprises "Fyrtøiet," "Lille Claus og store Claus," "Prindsessen paa Ærten," and "Den lille Idas Blomster"; volume 2 comprises "Tommelise," "Den uartige Dreng," and "Reisekammeraten";

Sangene i Festen paa Kenilworth (Copenhagen: C. A. Reitzel, 1836);

Skilles og mødes, Det Kongelige Theaters Repertoire, no. 76 (Copenhagen: J. H. Schubothes Boghandling, 1836);

O.T. (Copenhagen: C. A. Reitzel, 1836); translated (from German) by Howitt as *O.T.*, in *Only a Fiddler and O.T.; or, Life in Denmark* (London: Richard Bentley, 1845; New York: Harper, 1845);

Eventyr, fortalte for Børn, Tredie Hefte (Copenhagen: C. A. Reitzel, 1837)–includes "Den lille Havfrue" and "Keiserens nye Klæder";

Kun en Spillemand, 3 volumes (Copenhagen: C. A. Reitzel, 1837); translated (from German) by Howitt as *Only a Fiddler,* in *Only a Fiddler and O.T.; or, Life in Denmark* (London: Richard Bentley, 1845; New York: Harper, 1845);

Tre Digtninger (Copenhagen: C. A. Reitzel, 1838)–includes *Lykkens Kalosker, En rigtig Soldat, Det har Zombien gjort;*

Eventyr, fortalte for Børn. Ny Samling. Første Hefte (Copenhagen: C. A. Reitzel, 1838)–comprises "Gaaseurten," "Den standhaftige Tinsoldat," and "De vilde Svaner";

Eventyr, fortalte for Børn. Ny Samling. Andet Hefte (Copenhagen: C. A. Reitzel, 1839)–comprises "Paradisets Have," "Den flyvende Kuffert," and "Storkene";

Den Usynlige paa Sprogø. Dramatisk Spøg, i een Act, med Chor og Sange, Det Kongelige Theaters Repertoire, no. 113 (Copenhagen: J. H. Schubothes Boghandling, 1839);

Billedbog uden Billeder (Copenhagen: C. A. Reitzel, 1840 [i.e., 1839]); translated by Meta Taylor as *A Picture-Book Without Pictures: From the German Translation of De la Motte Fouqué* (London: David Bogue, 1847);

Mulatten. Originalt romantisk Drama i fem Akter (Copenhagen: Privately printed, 1840);

En Comedie i det Grønne. Vaudeville i een Akt efter det gamle Lystspil. "Skuespilleren imod sin Villie," Det Kongelige Theaters Repertoire, no. 124 (Copenhagen: J. H. Schubothes Boghandling, 1840);

Maurerpigen. Original Tragedie i fem Akter (Copenhagen: Privately printed, 1840);

Eventyr, fortalte for Børn. Ny Samling. Tredie Hefte (Copenhagen: C. A. Reitzel, 1841)–includes "Ole Lukøie," "Rosen-Alfen," "Svinedrengen," and "Boghveden";

En Digters Bazar (Copenhagen: C. A. Reitzel, 1842); translated by Lohmeyer as *A Poet's Bazaar* (London: Richard Bentley, 1846);

Nye Eventyr (Copenhagen: C. A. Reitzel, 1843)–includes "Engelen," "Nattergalen," "Kjærestefolkene," and "Den grimme Ælling";

Kongen drømmer. Originalt romantisk Drama i een Act, anonymous (Copenhagen: C. A. Reitzel, 1844);

Nye Eventyr. Anden Samling (Copenhagen: C. A. Reitzel, 1844);

Lykkens Blomst. Eventyr–Comedie i to Acter (Copenhagen: C. A. Reitzel, 1845);

Nye Eventyr: Tredie Samling (Copenhagen: C. A. Reitzel, 1845)–includes "Elverhøi," "De røde Skoe," "Springfyrene," "Hyrdinden og Skorsteensfeieren," and "Holger Danske";

Liden Kirsten, originalt, romantisk Syngestykke i een Act (Copenhagen: Privately printed, 1846);

A Christmas Greeting to My English Friends, translated by Lohmeyer (London: Richard Bentley, 1847)–includes five new stories originally published in England;

Das Märchen meines Lebens ohne Dichtung, in *Gesammelte Werke* (Leipzig: Carl B. Lorck, 1847); translated by Howitt as *The True Story of My Life* (London: Longman, Brown, Green & Longmans, 1847; Boston: J. Munroe, 1847); published in Danish as *Mit eget Eventyr uden Digtning,* edited by H. Topsøe-Jensen (Copenhagen: Nordisk/Arnold Busck, 1942);

Digte, gamle og nye (Copenhagen: C. A. Reitzel, 1847 [i.e., 1846]);

Nye Eventyr. Andet Bind. Første Samling (Copenhagen: C. A. Reitzel, 1847)–includes "Den gamle Gadeløgte," "Nabofamilierne," "Stoppenaalen," "Lille Tuk," and "Skyggen";

Ahasverus (Copenhagen: C. A. Reitzel, 1848);

Nye Eventyr. Andet Bind. Anden Samling (Copenhagen: C. A. Reitzel, 1848)–includes "Det gamle Huus," "Vanddraaben," "Den lille Pige med Svovlstikkerne," "Den lykkelige Familie," "Historien om en Moder," and "Flipperne";

Kunstens Dannevirke. Forspil ved det kongelige danske Theaters hundredeaars Fest 1848 (Copenhagen: C. A. Reitzel, 1848);

The Two Baronesses, translated by Lohmeyer (London: Richard Bentley, 1848); Danish version published as *De to Baronesser. Roman i tre Dele* (Copenhagen: C. A. Reitzel, 1848);

Brylluppet ved Como-Søen. Opera i tre Acter. Stoffet er taget af nogle Capitler i Manzonis Roman. "I promessi sposi" (Copenhagen: C. A. Reitzel, 1849);

H. C. Andersen's Eventyr. Med 125 Illustrationer efter Originaltegninger af V. Pedersen, skaarne i Træ af Ed. Kretzschmar (Copenhagen: C. A. Reitzel, 1849);

Meer end Perler og Guld Eventyr. Comedie i fire Acter. Fri Bearbeidelse efter F. Raimund og "Tusinde og een Nat" (Copenhagen: C. A. Reitzel, 1849);

6 Characteerstykker componerede som Studier for Pianoforte, af J. P. E. Hartmann, 1-2 Hæfte, opus 50 (Copenhagen: C. C. Lose & Delbanco, 1849)–introductory verse by Andersen to each piano piece;

Den nye Barselstue. Originalt Lystspil i een Act (Copenhagen: C. A. Reitzel, 1850);

En Nat i Roeskilde. Vaudeville-Spøg i een Act. Bearbeidet efter Warin og Lefèvre's "une chambre à deux lits" (Copenhagen: C. A. Reitzel, 1850);

Julehilsen til Store og Smaae fra danske Componister (Copenhagen: C. C. Lose & Delbanco, 1850)–includes six short verses by Andersen serving as introductions to each of the six piano compositions by Niels W. Gade, J. P. E. Hartmann, Eduard Helsted, Emil Hornemann den Ældre, H. S. Paulli, and Anton Rée;

Ole Lukøie. Eventyr-Comedie i tre Acter (Copenhagen: C. A. Reitzel, 1850);

Fædrelandske Vers og Sange under Krigen: Udgivne samlede til Indtægt for de Saarede og Faldnes Efterladte (Copenhagen: C.A. Reitzel, 1851);

Hyldemoer. Phantasiespil i een Act (Copenhagen: C. A. Reitzel, 1851);

I Sverrig (Copenhagen: C. A. Reitzel, 1851); translated by Lohmeyer as *Pictures of Sweden* (London: Richard Bentley, 1851);

Historier (Copenhagen: C. A. Reitzel, 1852)–includes "Aarets Historie," "Verdens deiligste Rose," "Et Billede fra Castelsvolden," "Paa den yderste Dag," "Det er ganske vist!" "Svanereden," and "Et godt Humeur";

Historier. Anden Samling (Copenhagen: C. A. Reitzel, 1852)–includes "Hjertesorg," "'Alt paa sin rette Plads!'" "Nissen hos Spekhøkeren," "Om Aartusinder," and "Under Piletræet";

Nøkken. Opera i een Act (Copenhagen: C. A. Reitzel, 1853);

En Landsbyhistorie. Folke-Skuespil i fem Acter efter S. H. Mosenthals "der Sonnenwendhof" med tildigtede Chor og Sange (Copenhagen: C. A. Reitzel, 1855);

Mit Livs Eventyr (Copenhagen: C. A. Reitzel, 1855); translated by Howitt as *The True Story of My Life* (London: Longman, Brown, Green & Longmans, 1847; Boston: J. Munroe, 1847);

Novellette i sex Smaastykker for Pianoforte af J. P. E. Hartmann (Copenhagen: C. C. Lose & Delbanco, 1855)–introductory verses by Andersen to each of the six piano pieces;

"At være eller ikke være." Roman i tre Dele. "To be, or not to be: that is the question." Shakspeare, in *Samlede Skrifter,* volume 23 (Copenhagen: C. A. Reitzel, 1857); translated by Anne Bushby as *To Be or Not to Be?* (London: Richard Bentley, 1857);

Nye Eventyr og Historier (Copenhagen: C. A. Reitzel, 1858)–includes "Suppe paa en Pølsepind," "Flaskehalsen," "Pebersvendens Nathue," "Noget," "Det gamle Egetræes sidste Drøm (Et Jule-Eventyr)," and "Abc-Bogen";

Nye Eventyr og Historier. Anden Samling (Copenhagen: C. A. Reitzel, 1858)–includes "Dynd-Kongens Datter," "Hurtigløberne," and "Klokkedybet";

Nye Eventyr og Historier. Tredie Samling (Copenhagen: C. A. Reitzel, 1859)–includes "Vinden fortæller om Valdemar Daae og hans Døttre," "Pigen, som traadte paa Brødet," "Taarnvægteren Ole," "Anne Lisbeth," "Børnesnak," and "Et Stykke Perlesnor";

Nye Eventyr og Historier. Fjerde Samling (Copenhagen: C. A. Reitzel, 1859)–includes "Pen og Blækhuus," "Barnet i Graven," "Gaardhanen og Veirhanen," "Deilig!" and "En Historie fra Klitterne";

Nye Eventyr og Historier. Anden Række (Copenhagen: C. A. Reitzel, 1861)–includes "Tolv med Posten," "Skarnbassen," "Hvad Fatter gjør, det er altid det Rigtige," "De Vises Steen," "Sneemanden," "I Andegaarden," and "Det nye Aarhundredes Musa";

Nye Eventyr og Historier. Anden Række. Anden Samling (Copenhagen: C. A. Reitzel, 1862)–includes "Iisjomfruen," "Sommerfuglen," "Psychen," and "Sneglen og Rosenhækken";

I Spanien (Copenhagen: C. A. Reitzel, 1863)–also published as volume 24 of *Samlede Skrifter;* translated by Bushby as *In Spain* (London: Richard Bentley, 1864);

Paa Langebro, Folkekomedie med Chor og Sange i fire Acter [not identical with *Langebro,* written in 1837 for the Student League but never printed]; *Efter Musæus* [Musäus] *og Kotzebue; (Eventyret "Den stumme Kjærlighed")* (Copenhagen: C. A. Reitzel, 1864);

Han er ikke født, originalt Lystspil i to Acter (Copenhagen: C. A. Reitzel, 1864);

Da Spanierne var her. Originalt romantisk Lystspil i tre Acter (Copenhagen: C. A. Reitzel, 1865);

Nye Eventyr og Historier. Anden Række. Tredie Samling (Copenhagen: C. A. Reitzel, 1865)–includes "Lygtemændene ere i Byen, sagde Mosekonen," "Veirmøllen," "Sølvskillingen," "Bispen paa Børglum og hans Frænde," "I Børnestuen," "Guldskat," and "Stormen flytter Skilt";

Nye Eventyr og Historier. Anden Række. Fjerde Samling (Copenhagen: C. A. Reitzel, 1866)–includes "Gjemt er ikke glemt," "Portnerens Søn," "Flyttedagen," "Sommergjækken," "Moster," and "Skrubtudsen";

Femten Eventyr og Historier af H. C. Andersen. Ny Udgave. Med Illustrationer af Lorenz Frølich (Copenhagen: C. A. Reitzel, 1867);

Kjendte og glemte Digte (1823–1867) (Copenhagen: C. A. Reitzel, 1867);

Et Besøg i Portugal, printed together with many smaller travel sketches and two biographical essays about B. S. Ingemann and J. P. E. Hartmann in volume 28 of *Samlede Skrifter* under the common title *Reiseskizzer og Pennetegninger* (Copenhagen: C. A. Reitzel, 1868); translated, with an introduction, by Thornton as *A Visit to Portugal 1866* (London: Peter Owen, 1972);

Dryaden. Et Eventyr fra Udstillingstiden i Paris 1867 (Copenhagen: C. A. Reitzel, 1868);

Tre nye Eventyr og Historier (Copenhagen: C. A. Reitzel, 1870)–includes "Hønse-Grethes Familie," "Hvad Tidselen oplevede," and "Hvad man kan hitte paa";

Supplement to The Story of My Life–printed as a supplement to Horace E. Scudder's new translation of Andersen's memoirs, published as *Hans Christian Andersen. Author's Edition* (New York: Hurd & Houghton, 1870);

Lykke-Peer (Copenhagen: C. A. Reitzel, 1870); translated by Scudder as *Lykke-Peer, Scribner's Monthly* (January, February, March, and April 1871);

Eventyr og Historier. Ny Samling (Copenhagen: C. A. Reitzel, 1872)–includes "Kometen," "Ugedagene," "Solskins-Historier," "Oldefa'er," "Hvem var den Lykkeligste?" "Lysene," "Det Utroligste," "Hvad hele Familien sagde," "'Dandse, dandse Dukke min!'" "'Spørg Amagermo'er!'" "Den store Søslange," and "Gartneren og Herskabet";

Nye Eventyr og Historier: Tredie Række. Anden Samling (Copenhagen: C. A. Reitzel, 1872)–includes "Hvad gamle Johanne fortalte," "Portnøglen," "Krøblingen," and "Tante Tandpine";

Mit Livs Eventyr. Fortsættelse (1855–1867), edited by Jonas Collin (Copenhagen: C. A. Reitzel, 1877);

Levnedsbogen, edited by Hans Brix (Copenhagen: Aschehoug, 1926)–incomplete autobiography, written in 1832;

Mit eget Eventyr uden Digtning, edited by H. Topsøe-Jensen (Copenhagen: Nyt Nordisk Forlag/Arnold Busck, 1942)–the original Danish manuscript for *Das Märchen meines Lebens ohne Dichtung,* 1847, and *The True Story of My Life,* 1847;

H. C. Andersens Dagbøger 1825–1875, 12 volumes, edited by Kirsten Vang Lauridsen, Tue Gad, and Kirsten Weber (Copenhagen: Gad, 1971–1976);

H. C. Andersens Almanakker, edited by Vang Lauridsen and Weber (Copenhagen: Gad, 1990).

Editions: *Samlede Skrifter* (33 volumes, Copenhagen: C. A. Reitzel, 1854 [i.e., 1853]–1879; 15 volumes, second edition, 1876–1880);

Historien om en Moder i Femten Sprog, published by Jean Pio and Vilhelm Thomsen (London: Williams & Norgate / Copenhagen: C. A. Reitzel / Leipzig: Brockhaus, 1875);

Romaner og Rejseskildringer, 7 volumes, edited by H. Topsøe-Jensen (Copenhagen: Gyldendal, 1943–1944);

H. C. Andersens Eventyr. Kritisk udgivet efter de originale Eventyrhæfter, 7 volumes, edited by Erik Dal and Flemming Hovmann (Copenhagen: Dansk Sprog- og Litteraturselskab & Hans Reitzel, 1963–1990);

Samlede digte, edited by Johan de Mylius (Copenhagen: Aschehoug, 2000);

H.C. Andersen's samlede værker, edited by Klaus P. Mortensen (Copenhagen: Gyldendal/Danske Sprog og Litteraturselskab, 2003–).

Editions in English: *Wonderful Stories for Children,* translated by Mary Howitt (London: Chapman & Hall, 1846);

A Danish Story-Book, translated by Charles Boner, illustrated by Count Pocci (London: Joseph Cundall, 1846);

Danish Fairy Legends and Tales, translated by Caroline Peachy (London: William Pickering, 1846; enlarged, 1853);

The Nightingale, and Other Tales, translated by Boner, illustrated by Pocci (London: Joseph Cundall, 1846);

The Shoes of Fortune, and Other Tales, translated by Boner, with four drawings by Otto Speckter, and other illustrations (London: Chapman & Hall, 1847);

Tales for the Young (London: James Burns, 1847);

The Dream of Little Tuk, and Other Tales, translated by Boner, illustrated by Pocci (London: Grant & Griffith, 1848; Boston & Cambridge: J. Munroe, 1848);

A Poet's Day Dreams, translated by Anne Bushby (London: Richard Bentley, 1853);

Stories and Tales by Hans C. Andersen, translated by H. W. Dulcken, illustrated by A. W. Bayes (London: Routledge, Warne & Routledge, 1865);

Later Tales: Published during 1867 and 1868, translated by Peachy, Augusta Plesner, and Henry Ward, illustrated by Otto Speckter, A. W. Cooper, and others (London: Bell & Daldy, 1868);

Hans Christian Andersen Author's Edition, 10 volumes, published by Horace E. Scudder (New York: Hurd & Houghton/Riverside Press, 1869–1871)–comprises volume 1: *The Improvisatore;* 2: *The Two Bar-*

onesses; 3: *Wonder Stories, Told for Children;* 4: *In Spain and Portugal;* 5: *O.T.;* 6: *Only a Fiddler;* 7: *The Story of My Life;* 8: *Stories and Tales;* 9: *A Poet's Bazar;* and 10: *In the Hartz Mountains;*

Fairy Tales and Sketches, translated by Peachy, Plesner, Ward, and others, illustrated by Otto Speckter, Cooper, Bayes, and others (London: Bell & Daldy, 1870);

The Complete Andersen; All of the 168 stories by Hans Christian Andersen, 6 volumes, translated by Jean Hersholt, illustrated by Fritz Kredel (New York: Limited Editions Club, 1949);

Seven Poems, translated by Keigwin (Odense: H. C. Andersens Hus, 1955);

The Complete Fairy Tales and Stories, translated by Erik Christian Haugaard (Garden City, N.Y.: Doubleday, 1974; London: Gollancz, 1974);

Tales and Stories, translated, with an introduction, by Patricia L. Conroy and Sven H. Rossel (Seattle: University of Washington Press, 1980);

Fairy Tales, 4 volumes, translated by R. P. Keigwin (Copenhagen: Hans Reitzel, 1986);

The Diaries of Hans Christian Andersen, selected and translated by Conroy and Rossel (Seattle & London: University of Washington Press, 1990);

Brothers, Very Far Away and Other Poems, translated by Paula Hostrup-Jessen, edited, with an afterword, by Rossel (Seattle: Mermaid Press, 1991);

Fairy Tales, translated by Tiina Nunnally, introduction and notes by Jackie Wullschlager (London: Penguin/Allen Lane, 2004; New York: Viking, 2005).

PLAY PRODUCTIONS: *Kjærlighed paa Nicolai Taarn eller Hvad siger Parterret?* Copenhagen, Royal Theater, 25 April 1829;

Skibet, Copenhagen, Royal Theater, 5 October 1831;

Bruden fra Lammermoor, with music by I. Bredal, Copenhagen, Royal Theater, 5 May 1832;

Ravnen, with music by J. P. E. Hartmann, Copenhagen, Royal Theater, 29 October 1832; revised, Copenhagen, Royal Theater, 23 April 1865;

Dronningen paa 16 Aar, Copenhagen, Royal Theater, 29 March 1833;

Festen paa Kenilworth, with music by C. E. F. Weyse, Copenhagen, Royal Theater, 6 January 1836;

Skilles og mødes, Copenhagen, Royal Theater, 16 April 1836;

Souffleurens Benefice (vaudeville), Copenhagen, Royal Theater, 24 December 1836;

Langebro, Copenhagen, Studenterforeningen, December 1837;

Den Usynlige paa Sprogø, Copenhagen, Royal Theater, 15 June 1839;

Mulatten, Copenhagen, Royal Theater, 3 February 1840; produced again, Stockholm, Royal Theatre, 22 March 1841;

Mikkels Kjærlighedshistorier i Paris, Copenhagen, Royal Theater, 11 March 1840;

En Comedie i det Grønne, with music by Edvard Helsted, Copenhagen, Royal Theater, 13 May 1840;

Maurerpigen, with music by Hartmann, Copenhagen, Royal Theater, 18 December 1840;

Studenterforeningens Muser, et Maaneeventyr med tilhørende stort allegorisk-pantomimisk Billede i een Akt med Musik af berømte Komponister og 7 à 8 Blik ind i Fremtiden, conceived by Andersen, revised by H. P. Holst, Copenhagen, Hofteatret, 8 April 1841;

Vandring gjennem Opera-Galleriet, declamatorisk Ramme for en Scene-Række af ældre og nyere Componisters Arbeider paa den danske Scene, Copenhagen, Royal Theater, 19 December 1841;

Fuglen i Pæretræet, dramatisk Spøg i 1 Akt med Chor og Sange, with music by Helsted, Copenhagen, Royal Theater, 4 July 1842;

Agnete og Havmanden, with music by Niels W. Gade, Copenhagen, Royal Theater, 20 April 1843;

Kongen drømmer, anonymous, with music by H. Rung, Copenhagen, Royal Theater, 14 February 1844;

Lykkens Blomst, with music by Rung, Copenhagen, Royal Theater, 16 February 1845;

Den nye Barselstue, Copenhagen, Royal Theater, 26 March 1845;

Hr. Rasmussen, Copenhagen, Royal Theater, 19 March 1846;

Liden Kirsten, with music by Hartmann, choreographed first by P. Larcher and then by August Bournonville, Copenhagen, Royal Theater, 12 May 1846; produced again as *Klein Karin,* Weimar Theater, 17 January 1856;

Kunstens Dannevirke. Forspil ved Royal Theaters hundredeaars Fest 1848, with music by Rung, Copenhagen, Royal Theater, 18 December 1848;

Brylluppet ved Como-Søen, with music by F. Glæser, ballet choreographed by Bournonville, Copenhagen, Casino, 29 February 1849;

En Nat i Roeskilde, Copenhagen, Casino, 6 May 1849;

Meer end Perler og Guld, Copenhagen, Casino, 3 October 1849;

Ole Lukøie, Copenhagen, Casino, 1 March 1850;

Hyldemoer, Copenhagen, Casino, 1 December 1851;

Nøkken, with music by Glæser, Copenhagen, Royal Theater, 12 February 1853;

En Landsbyhistorie, Copenhagen, Casino, 17 January 1855;

The house in Odense where Andersen lived from 1807 until 1819 (gouache by J. H. T. Hanck, 1836; Hans Christian Andersen Museum, Odense)

I Maaneskin. Alpescener fra de Tyrolske Bjerge, with music by Ignaz Lachner (after Kobell og Seidl, *Letzte Fensterl'n* and *Drei Jahre*), Copenhagen, Casino, 2 June 1855;

Paa Langebro, Copenhagen, Casino, 9 March 1864;

Han er ikke født, Copenhagen, Royal Theater, 27 April 1864;

Da Spanierne var her, Copenhagen, Royal Theater, 6 April 1865.

During his lifetime, Hans Christian Andersen was well known in both Europe and the United States for his novels, fairy tales, and stories, as well as for his literary travel books and autobiography. Some of his poems and plays were also translated into German and English. In Russia, readers were familiar with his tales and one of his novels. Today he is known the world over for his fairy tales, which are particularly popular in China and Japan, but few readers outside of Europe know his other works.

Andersen was recognized by his contemporaries as an author of adult fiction, with an adult sensibility inherent in his fairy tales and stories. This recognition was especially evident in both Germany and France. Today Andersen's works have been translated into more than 150 languages, but his worldwide acclaim is based largely on the mistaken perception that he is primarily a children's author. Andersen has, indeed, won a place in the literary world because he revitalized children's literature by creating a fairy-tale form and narrative style that was all his own.

Many forerunners to the fairy-tale side of his literary production existed; the long tradition of fairy tales includes *A Thousand and One Nights* (first mentioned in the ninth century), which stood on the bookshelf of his impoverished childhood home. Andersen also heard folktales recounted by the poor women of Odense, and he later renewed acquaintance with these stories by reading *Kinder- und Hausmärchen* (Child and Household Tales, 1812–1815) by Jacob Grimm and Wilhelm

Grimm as well as the Danish counterpart, *Danske Folkeeventyr* (Danish Folk Tales, 1822), collected by Mathias Winther. Andersen was also influenced by the German tales known as "Kunstmärchen," written by Ludwig Tieck, E. T. A. Hoffman, Adelbert von Chamisso, and Friedrich de la Motte Fouqué. In Denmark early fairy-tale writers included Adam Oehlenschläger and B. S. Ingemann.

Only 7 of the 156 fairy tales and stories that Andersen published in his lifetime are retellings, in his own style, of folktales. Some of the others, such as "Den lille Havfrue" (The Little Mermaid, 1837) and "Skyggen" (The Shadow, 1847), have literary origins, while a few of the tales are based on legends or historical material. But the majority of Andersen's stories are completely original.

Andersen wrote the story of his life three times. He wrote the first account in 1832 when he was twenty-seven years old and about to embark on a grand cultural tour of Europe. This autobiography remained unfinished and was not published until 1926, when it was discovered by Hans Brix, professor of Danish literature at the University of Copenhagen, who published it then under the title *Levnedsbogen* (Autobiography). Andersen's first official autobiography was written for inclusion in the German edition of his collected works published beginning in 1847 as volumes one and two under the title *Das Märchen meines Lebens ohne Dichtung* (and the same year in English as *The True Story of My Life*). The Danish version of his autobiography, *Mit Livs Eventyr,* an edited and expanded edition of the German, was published in 1855 as part of his *Samlede Skrifter* (Collected Works, 1854–1879). In connection with the ten-volume American "Author's Edition" of his works (1869–1871), Andersen updated his autobiography (volume seven in the collection) to include events up until 1867.

Andersen himself stated in the German version that his life provides the best key to understanding his work. When the French critic Xavier Marmier heard the details of Andersen's life from the author himself and asked whether he might be allowed to tell the story to the rest of the world, Andersen replied, "My life belongs to the world."

This attitude can be explained in two ways. First, Andersen belongs to those modern authors whose lives and work are closely intertwined. Second, the nature of Andersen's life reached far beyond his personal sphere and took on a universal quality. This truth is apparent in the Danish title of his autobiography, translated literally as "The Fairy Tale of My Life." Thus, the genre that made him well known becomes an interpretative model for the course of his life.

The story of Andersen's life is one of unparalleled social and artistic success, rising as he did from the lowest and poorest layer of society to achieve not only the acceptance but the utter devotion of the highest social groups, the artistic elite and royal houses of many European countries. Outwardly, his story was a tremendous success–but he achieved it at great personal and psychological cost.

In spite of several fanciful theories concerning Andersen's origins, what seems most likely is that Andersen's biological father was the impoverished cobbler Hans Andersen who married Hans Christian's mother, Anne Marie Andersdatter, on 2 February 1805. Anne Marie was probably about ten years older than her husband, although her exact date of birth is unknown. At the time of her marriage, Anne Marie had a daughter, Karen Marie, who was born out of wedlock in 1799 and who died in Copenhagen in 1846.

Andersen was born on 2 April 1805 in Odense, on Fyn, the second-largest island in Denmark. As he was growing up, he presumably had little or nothing to do with his half sister, because she was sent away at his birth, apparently to her maternal grandmother, and thus did not share his childhood home. Hans Christian was closer to his father's side of the family and had a strong emotional bond with his paternal grandmother.

The Andersen family moved several times during the boy's first two years; presumably, for her son's birth Anne Marie went to stay with an aunt of Andersen's father, who in 1805 occupied one room of the corner house on Hans Jensensstræde. In accordance with the popularly accepted tradition that this was the birthplace of Andersen, Odense Municipality acquired the house in 1905 and made it the center of the present-day Hans Christian Andersen Museum. The house has since become an Andersen icon and is probably the best-known Danish building. But whether it was actually the site of the author's birth cannot be confirmed.

Not until 1807 did the family have a real home, when they rented one room plus a kitchen in a small house on Munkemøllestræde near the Odense River. The house was occupied by two other families as well, each with children, so that twelve people lived together in close quarters under one roof. This house, which today serves as a minor museum to the author's life, was Andersen's childhood home until 1819, when his family moved to another house on the same narrow street but closer to the river. By that time his father was dead, and his mother had remarried.

In his memoirs Andersen says of his mother that she was a pious but superstitious woman and that she could neither read nor write. He gives the impression that she was the stable force in the home and rather overprotective toward her son. His father was inclined toward book learning, but he had been forced into the shoemaker trade by his own father, who was a shoemaker of meager means and former smallholder. Andersen's father was unhappy in the profession that had been thrust upon him, and he dreamed of going out into the world to become something quite different. In Andersen's mind his father's sense of discontent and yearning became coupled with his paternal grandmother's claim that she was a descendant of a prominent German family in Kassel, a claim which had no basis. Both helped to shape the boy's ambitions, which led him to flee Odense and the poverty of his childhood to spend the rest of his life striving for fame and recognition.

Andersen's father owned several books, from which he read aloud to the boy, including *A Thousand and One Nights* and the comedies of the Dano-Norwegian playwright Ludvig Holberg. The Bible also stood on the bookshelf of their humble home, even though his father, in keeping with the spirit of the eighteenth century, declared himself to be a freethinker and, much to his wife's dismay, insisted on regarding Jesus as a great man, but not the son of God. As an adult, his son also accepted this understanding of who Jesus was. Of great significance was that Andersen's childhood reading included the works of Holberg, who was also an historian and philosopher of morals, who is considered the founder of the Danish theater tradition, and whose comedies continue to entertain Danish audiences today. During the eighteenth century Holberg's plays were also performed in German and eastern European theaters. His humor is regarded as quintessentially Danish, and one may draw a direct line between Holberg's humor and Andersen's, which is also considered typically Danish. As an adult, Andersen even wrote a satirical comedy blatantly reminiscent of Holberg, called *Den nye Barselstue* (The New Receiving Room, first performed 26 March 1845; first published, 1850).

When Andersen was growing up, Odense, with six thousand residents, was the second-largest city in Denmark. Today it is the third-largest, while Copenhagen, which now has more than a million citizens, was then a city of about a hundred thousand. Even though Odense was a small provincial town, it had ambitions. The city was, and remains today, a bishopric with a thirteenth-century cathedral and several other imposing medieval churches. It had a garrison and a castle, both of which house municipal offices today; Prince Christian Frederik took up residence there as governor of Fyn in 1816. Whenever Andersen's mother was hired to do washing in the castle cellars, she took her son along and let him play in the courtyard. There he sometimes played with little Prince Fritz, who later reigned as Frederik VII from 1849 to 1863.

Most important of all, Odense had its own theater, built in 1795. At the time Copenhagen could boast of only two theaters–the small Court Theater, which in Andersen's day mostly presented Italian operas; and the Royal Theater, established in 1748, which was licensed to present serious Danish dramas. Other than Copenhagen, Odense was the only town in Denmark with a theater, and it could seat an audience of four hundred. During Andersen's childhood a German theater troupe leased the theater for its performances, and in the summer touring actors from Copenhagen's Royal Theater occasionally appeared.

From an early age Andersen was fascinated by the theater world, and once in a while his parents would take him to a performance. He also helped out by delivering theater posters around the city and in return was allowed to keep some of them. At home he stared at the posters, letting his imagination dream up his own comedies, based on the titles of the plays. He also managed to gain admittance to the theater and sometimes even won permission to be an extra in a play–for example, taking the role of the page in *Cendrillon* (Cinderella, 1812). When Andersen was quite young, his father made him a little puppet theater, and the boy sewed costumes from leftover scraps of fabric.

The theater represented a tangible world of the imagination that could provide an outlet for Andersen's dreams. This world was separate from and elevated above the impoverished working-class daily life that he knew. In it he met actors from Copenhagen whose stories about the Royal Theater lent his dreams direction and gave him the courage to leave Odense at an early age to seek his fortune at the theater in the capital. Andersen maintained a lifelong connection to the theater as a translator, adapter, and author of plays. He was also a devoted theatergoer, often attending performances on a daily basis, both in Copenhagen and abroad. He became extraordinarily knowledgeable about the world of the theater. Perhaps his fairy tales would never have acquired the scenic-dramatic form that they have if Andersen had not literally grown up with the theater.

Andersen's father died in 1816, before the boy turned eleven. At the time, Denmark was involved in the Napoleonic Wars, siding with the French. In 1801 and again in 1807 Copenhagen came under British attack. In the second, decisive battle, the English armada shelled Copenhagen and captured the Danish navy, thus ending a half century of progress and middle-class prosperity built on overseas trade. When peace was declared in 1814, Denmark was forced to cede Norway to Sweden, which had acquired the renegade French general Bernadotte as king. The Norwegians had elected the Danish-born Christian Frederik to be their

The home of Andersen's patron, Jonas Collin, in Copenhagen (Hans Christian Andersen Museum, Odense)

king, but that same year the Swedes ousted him from power just after he managed to grant Norway a free constitution. Christian Frederik later became King Christian VIII of Denmark.

Thus, Andersen's childhood years were marked by great catastrophes in Denmark and the beginning of a lengthy recession. Oddly enough, however, this period was followed by a cultural explosion that has never been equaled, either before or since. It is known as the Golden Age of Denmark.

The effects of the war were felt in Odense, where Spanish mercenaries occupied the garrison. In 1812 Andersen's father enlisted as a musketeer and joined a contingent of soldiers being sent to Germany in support of Napoleon. In those days military conscription was mandatory only for sons of farmers, while young men living inside the city walls were exempt. A prosperous farmer paid Andersen's father to take the place of his son. A similar episode described in Andersen's third novel, *Kun en Spillemand* (1837; translated as *Only a Fiddler,* 1845), suggests that his father was paid 1,000 Rigsdaler, or the equivalent of approximately $15,000 today–quite a fortune for the shoemaker's family. As a result of the disastrous war efforts, however, the Danish government declared bankruptcy in January 1813, and the krone subsequently lost nine-tenths of its value. The family's hopes of a brighter future were crushed.

Andersen's father did not take an active part in the war, since his regiment only reached Holsten. When the soldiers set up camp there, he fell ill and returned home in January 1814, a broken man. He died exactly two years later.

Although affiliation of Denmark with Napoleon represented both a national catastrophe and a great misfortune for the Andersen family, the general public in Denmark as well as the Danish literary circles continued to embrace Napoleon with enthusiasm for many years. In the beginning of his writing career, Andersen also sang the praises of Napoleon, particularly in his early poetry. Napoleon was romanticized as a man of the people who, by virtue of his genius, catapulted himself to the position of the ruler of Europe, only to become a tragic victim of his own greatness and the guile of the British.

The death of Andersen's father brought even worse misery to his wife and son. Anne Marie took in laundry, which she washed in the river, standing barelegged in the cold water. Andersen went to a school for the poor children of Odense, though his attendance was apparently irregular, and he never learned to spell correctly, a fault that plagued him all his life. Not until late in his career did the critics stop hounding him about this shortcoming.

But the theater was not the only spur to Andersen's dreams of a different and better life. Until he entered puberty, he had a beautiful voice, and he often sang outdoors so that more prosperous families would hear him and invite him inside to sing for them. He became known as the "little nightingale from Fyn." Thus, the roots of his fairy tale "Nattergalen" (The Nightingale, in *Nye Eventyr*) from 1843 can be found in his early childhood.

Even as a boy he had the ability to attract attention and win the favor of people who might help him achieve his goals. In spite of his awkward manner and far-from-handsome appearance, at a young age Andersen exhibited a talent for enchanting people. He possessed a charisma that he retained all his life and that opened many doors. His stubborn determination in the face of countless disappointments, setbacks, and defeats, along with his irresistible charm, prompted his departure from Odense and his breakthrough as a writer–not, as sometimes is suggested, protection from the Royals to the illegitimate son of a prince (which he was not).

During the years he lived in Odense, Andersen made many contacts that proved beneficial later on, even in Copenhagen. The garrison commander, Colonel Christian Høegh-Guldberg, took a special interest in the boy. One day he took Andersen to see Prince Christian Frederik to seek help for the boy's future. Andersen was full of dreams about the theater, but the sober-minded prince advised him instead to learn a useful trade. In spite of this less-than-encouraging experience, Andersen's contact with Høegh-Guldberg turned out to be valuable. The colonel's brother, who lived in Copenhagen, was a poet, a teacher at the artillery cadet school, and a titular professor. He became one of Andersen's benefactors during those first difficult years in Copenhagen.

In July 1818 Anne Marie remarried. Her new husband was also a shoemaker and twelve or thirteen years younger than his wife. After being overprotected by his mother and the only male in the house for a few years after his father's death, Andersen was now directly exposed to his mother's intimate life in their cramped one-room living quarters. For a boy who lived so much in his imagination, this circumstance no doubt contributed to his decision to leave Odense. It also had a long-lasting psychological effect on his own vexed and confused relationship to sexuality. It was a factor in his constant state of homelessness and flight, his perpetual dream of release and death, and transformation and rebirth–issues that deeply impacted his life and permeated his writings.

About six months after his mother's marriage, Andersen and his family left their home and moved to another small house on the same street. These two events, along with one other milepost–his confirmation at St. Knud's Cathedral on 18 April 1819–marked the end of Andersen's childhood.

An additional reason that young Andersen began thinking about leaving home was that his mother had several times tried to place him in a factory or to apprentice him to a skilled worker. Andersen now seized upon the idea of realizing his old dreams of a theater career. He had saved 13 Rigsdaler, and he persuaded his mother to let him travel to Copenhagen to seek his fortune in the theater. He managed to get a letter of introduction from Christian H. Iversen, a printer and publisher of one of two newspapers in Odense. Iversen's immediate family, and in particular his daughter's family, later had close ties to Andersen in his hometown. The letter was addressed to ballet dancer Madame Schall at the Royal Theater, even though Iversen had never even met her. On 4 September, Andersen traveled by mail coach from Odense to Copenhagen, arriving two days later in the midst of the persecution of the Jews. For years Andersen mistakenly remembered his arrival date as 5 September, and he celebrated that date as his Copenhagen birthday.

When he appeared before Madame Schall and performed for her a dance of his own composition, she dismissed him at once. The theater director did the same, saying that he had absolutely no use for Andersen as an actor. Andersen, however, received help from the contacts he had made while still in Odense. Colonel Guldberg's brother, Frederik Høegh-Guldberg, a professor, gave Andersen a little money and arranged lessons for him. A young woman named Laura Tønder-Lund, who had attended confirmation class with Andersen in Odense and was now living in Copenhagen, also gave him money and paved the way for him to enter the finer social circles in Copenhagen. Andersen himself opened several doors. Until his voice changed, Andersen sought out Italian choirmaster Giuseppe Siboni and became a constant visitor in his home and school. As a result of his visits to Siboni,

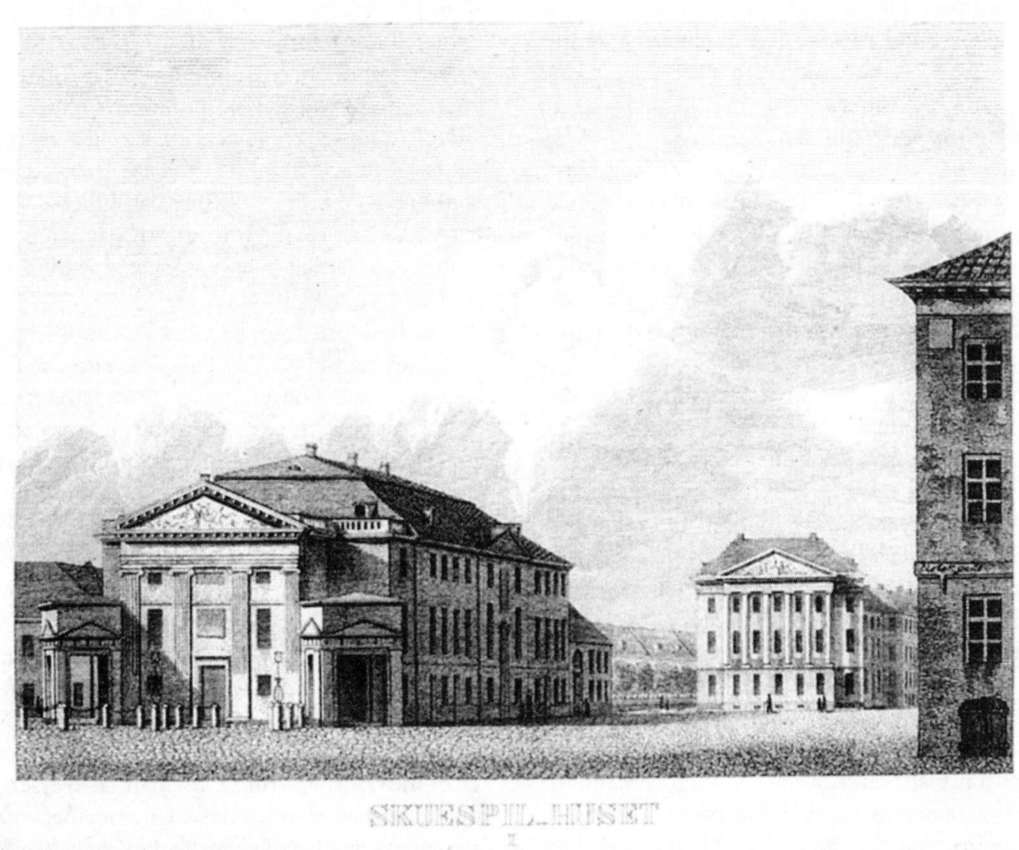

The Royal Theater in Copenhagen, where Andersen's first play, the student farce Kjærlighed paa Nicolai Taarn eller Hvad siger Parterret? *(Love at Nicolai Tower, or What Does the Gallery Say?), was produced in 1829 (Hans Christian Andersen Museum, Odense)*

Andersen also met composer C. E. F. Weyse, who collected money from his friends for the young boy.

Andersen had no intention of giving up and returning to Odense, even though he could not find work in the theater as an actor, a ballet dancer, or a singer. For three years he lived in Copenhagen on a bare subsistence level, taking lodgings for a time in one of the infamous prostitute districts of the city. He sought help from his mother's sister without realizing that she ran a bordello. The only work he managed to find in Copenhagen from 1819 to 1822 was as an extra in the theater, although occasionally he did have a minor role in a play. One high point occurred in April 1821 when his name appeared on a theater poster for the ballet *Armida* (1821), composed by Carl Dahlén. The list of minor roles included: "A Troll–Mr. Andersen." The same poster announced that the part of Cupid was played by "Johanne Petcher," or rather Johanne Pätges, who later became Johanne Luise Heiberg, the greatest Danish actress of the nineteenth century. She later appeared in several of Andersen's plays.

In 1822 Andersen seemed to have exhausted all hope of a theater career; he set about writing a couple of plays and then submitted them, in the hopes of seeing them performed. The first was a "patriotic tragedy" titled "Røverne i Vissenberg" (The Robbers of Vissenberg), set in a small village west of Odense. The play was rejected with the comment that it lacked any basis in fact, including "basic skills in the Danish language," although the critique did note that there was an "unmistakable trace of artistry" to the drama. The second play, which he submitted immediately after the first was returned, was titled "Alfsol." It met with an equally harsh reception: it was rejected as unsuitable for the theater.

Before learning of the fate of his second play, Andersen tried to launch his literary debut by publishing "Alfsol" along with an autobiographical prologue and a short story that was little more than a Sir Walter Scott pastiche. The title of this volume was *Ungdoms-Forsøg* (Youthful Attempts, 1822). He did not use his own name but took the pseudonym Villiam (referring to William Shakespeare) Christian (referring to himself) Walter (referring to Sir Walter Scott). The book did not sell at all. The printer, whom Andersen had persuaded to produce the book, later tried to sell the volume with a new cover, but without success. In the end almost all of the copies were shredded; consequently, today it is a costly antiquarian collectible.

The theater manager had asked critic Knud Lyne Rahbek to contribute a literary evaluation, and even though it was negative, Rahbek pointed to traces of potential talent and recommended that the author be given proper training. Andersen was duly summoned to a meeting with the theater managers, who gave him an ultimatum: Either he would accept their offer to attend school and acquire the necessary basic education, or else they were going to wash their hands of him for good. The school was a grammar school in the provincial town of Slagelse on Zealand, and he would have to start at the beginning, along with much younger boys. But the state would pay the cost of his education through a grant from the royal foundation in support of art and education, *ad usus publicos* (for the public use). Finance councillor Jonas Collin, who was one of the three board members of the theater, was secretary of this foundation. Andersen accepted the offer.

In 1822 Andersen entered Slagelse Grammar School. The headmaster was Simon Meisling, a classical philologist, whose heavy-handed treatment of the boy soon gave rise to conflict. Nevertheless, in accordance with Meisling's wishes, Andersen moved in with the headmaster's family in October 1825. Meisling, who was in dire need of money, received payment for Andersen's room and board. In May 1826 Meisling was transferred to the grammar school in Helsingør, and Andersen followed him, still taking lodgings with the Meisling family. After Andersen complained bitterly about the headmaster's mistreatment of him, Collin took him out of Meisling's school in April 1827 and allowed him to move to Copenhagen. There Andersen was privately tutored until he passed his final exams.

The period in Slagelse had a profound impact on Andersen, however, because he spent his weekends and holidays in the town of Sorø, about 14 kilometers away, visiting the Ingemann family. Romantic poet B. S. Ingemann proved to be a literary and personal mentor for young Andersen as well as a lifelong friend. In 1822 Ingemann was hired as a lecturer at Sorø Academy, where Andersen made two friends–Carl Bagger, who later became a writer and editor for the Odense newspaper *Fyens Stiftstidende,* and Fritz Petit, who later immigrated to Germany and ended up translating some of Andersen's works into German and writing one of the early German biographies of Andersen.

In Helsingør, Andersen met Rudolph Schley, who was on his way to Libau in East Prussia. Schley took an interest in Andersen and translated into German Andersen's poem "Det døende Barn" (The Dying Child), written in 1826. Schley took the translation along to Libau and had it published there. This work was Andersen's first German-language publication. On 25 September 1827 Andersen had the Danish original and Schley's translation printed side by side in A. P. Liunge's newspaper *Kiøbenhavnsposten.*

In October of the following year Andersen took his final exams, which were held at the University of Copenhagen. One of the examiners, physicist H. C. Ørsted, was known throughout Europe. He had become personally acquainted with Andersen and later served as an important spiritual mentor for the author. The dean who signed Andersen's certificate was Oehlenschläger, professor of aesthetics at the University of Copenhagen and Andersen's lifelong literary idol. Oehlenschläger's drama *Aladdin* (1805) became practically a model for understanding the story of Andersen's life and significant facets of his work.

During his student days in Copenhagen, Andersen continued his friendship with Bagger and Petit. Through the latter he met Orla Lehmann, who later became a leader of the liberal students. Along with Bagger and Petit, Andersen became an enthusiastic devotee of the work of Hoffmann, and from Lehmann he learned to appreciate Heinrich Heine. Both authors became important models for Andersen's own writings. Traces of Hoffmann's work can be found in *Fodreise fra Holmens Canal til Østpynten af Amager i Aarene 1828 og 1829* (Walking Tour from Holmen's Canal to the Eastern Point of Amager, 1829) and in such fairy tales as "Den lille Idas Blomster" (Little Ida's Flowers), collected in his *Eventyr, fortalte for Børn* (Fairy Tales, Told for Children, 1835). Heine had an especially strong influence on Andersen's youthful poetry. Even as a student, Andersen, along with his classmate Frederik Paludan-Müller, was singled out by the other students as a promising literary talent.

A few days after passing his final exams, Andersen entered the second company of the Royal Guard. Military service in this regiment was compulsory for all students at that time. In 1830 his fellow soldiers elected him corporal, although he resigned from this position the following year. At his own request he was removed from the roster in 1833–1834 because of his lengthy travels abroad.

On 2 January 1829 Andersen made his real literary debut with *Fodreise fra Holmens Canal til Østpynten af Amager,* a self-published fantasy work heavily influenced by Hoffmann. Advance interest in the book was assured because several excerpts had been published in 1827–1828 in *Kjøbenhavns flyvende Post,* Johan Ludvig Heiberg's prominent journal. Heiberg himself wrote a positive review of the book, which Andersen included in the third printing when it appeared in December 1839 (although the copyright page listed 1840 as the publication date). The second printing appeared only three months after the first, this time under the imprint of C. A. Reitzel, the foremost publisher of the Golden Age.

Andersen's dramatic debut was a student farce in the style of a Heiberg vaudeville. Titled *Kjærlighed paa Nicolai Taarn eller Hvad siger Parterret?* (Love at Nicolai Tower, or What Does the Gallery Say? 1829), the play was performed three times at the Royal Theater in April of the same year.

The vaudeville is of interest only in that it signifies an adherence to a particular genre and tone that were typical of Heiberg, who was the trendsetter and arbiter of theatrical taste at that time. *Fodreise fra Holmens Canal til Østpynten af Amager,* on the other hand, is an important work in Andersen's literary career. It is significant partly because it features some of the themes that Andersen addressed and expanded upon in later works. It also touches on the darker sides of the psyche. In addition, it seems quite modern in the way in which reality dissolves into "script." The final chapter is a purely formal gesture, consisting entirely of such marks as dashes, periods, and exclamation points.

In October and November 1829 Andersen took his entrance exam at the university in philology and philosophy. Although he had already had poems published in various magazines, his first actual poetry collection, *Digte* (Poems), appeared on 2 January 1830. Oehlenschläger had ended his debut poetry collection, *Digte* (1803), with the small drama "Sanct Hansaften-Spil" (A Midsummer Night's Play); Andersen chose a prose piece for the end of his poetry collection. The tale, written in the style of Johann Karl August Musäus, is called "Dødningen" (The Ghost). The author later reworked it into a "proper" fairy tale and renamed it "Reisekammeraten" (The Traveling Companion), which appeared in 1835 in the second volume of *Eventyr, fortalte for Børn.*

Andersen made a summer trip to Jutland and Fyn in 1830. On the island of Fyn he went to Fåborg to pay a visit to his school friend Christian Voigt and the young man's wealthy family. There he met and fell in love with Christian's sister Riborg, although she was already engaged. Andersen's love for Riborg left its mark on his poetry suite "Hjertets Melodier" (Melodies of the Heart), which was printed for the first time in 1831 as part of *Phantasier og Skizzer* (Fantasies and Sketches). Thirty years later Norwegian composer Edvard Grieg set this poetry cycle to music. The work was not merely a matter of feigned poetic posturing, however. Andersen's feelings for the young girl were genuine enough, one may assume, because of the role that the Riborg episode plays in "Kjærestefolkene" (The Sweethearts), which Andersen wrote in 1844 after having met Riborg again, this time with her husband and children. At his death, Andersen ostensibly wore a little leather pouch on a ribbon around his neck–a leather pouch that held Riborg's farewell letter to him. (In accordance with the author's wishes, this letter was burned unread.) Interestingly enough, the Riborg episode marks the culmination, "Katastrofen" (The Catastrophe), of Andersen's unfinished first autobiography, *Levnedsbogen,* while it is mentioned only in passing in *Mit Livs Eventyr.*

The money that Andersen earned with *Fodreise fra Holmens Canal til Østpynten af Amager* enabled him to undertake the first of his nearly thirty trips abroad. His travels took him first to Germany, and his itinerary was planned to correspond more or less with the travels of several people, including Ingemann, who gave him a letter of introduction to Tieck in Dresden, and Henriette Wulff, who had been a pupil of the Norwegian-born painter J. C. Dahl in Dresden. Andersen also based his plans on the ideas of his future foe Christian Molbech, who published a three-volume travel book in 1821–1822 titled *Reise giennem en Deel af Tydskland, Frankrige, England og Italien i Aarene 1819 og 1820* (Travels through Parts of Germany, France, England, and Italy during 1819–1820). Andersen also gleaned advice from his new literary model, Heine, whose *Harzreise* (Harz Journey) appeared in 1826 in the first section of his *Reisebilder* (Travel Sketches).

In Berlin on his homeward journey Andersen made the acquaintance of Romanticist Chamisso, author of *Peter Schlemihl* (The Shadowless Man, 1814), which served as the model for Andersen's story "Skyggen" (The Shadow). Chamisso translated some of Andersen's poems into German, and Robert Schumann later set some of them to music. Only a few months after Andersen returned home in 1831, he was able to present to his readers a travel book titled *Skyggebilleder af en Reise til Harzen og det sachsiske Schweiz . . . i Sommeren 1831* (Shadow Pictures of a Journey to the Harz and the Saxon Switzerland . . . in the Summer of 1831). This book represented a breakthrough in Andersen's writing toward a more painterly prose. It also allowed

The poet Torquato Tasso's house in Sorrento, drawn by Andersen during his stay in Italy in 1833–1834 (Hans Christian Andersen Museum, Odense)

him to express his politically liberal sympathies. In terms of literature, the model for the book was neither Molbech nor Heine but Jens Baggesen's *Labyrinten* (The Labyrinth, 1792, 1793). In the context of Andersen's oeuvre, this travel book is the first prose work in which the author's feeling for nature and, thus, the theme of nature are fully developed, as yhey are in his poetry of the same time period; in *Fodreise fra Holmens Canal til Østpynten af Amager* the central focus was on the city, while nature was virtually absent. With *Skyggebilleder af en Reise til Harzen og det sachsiske Schweiz . . . i Sommeren 1831* nature moves to the foreground in all of Andersen's writing.

Andersen's major work in the first half of the 1830s was the large poetry collection *Phantasier og Skizzer,* in which the influence of Heine's *Buch der Lieder* (Book of Ballads, 1827) is fully realized. Andersen took on many different types of work during these years, including translating, adapting, and writing plays, though not many of them prompted a positive response. His furious output was driven by his perpetual need for money. As a member of the Student Association, he took on the role of actor and also wrote revues. Andersen's dramatic works from the period include his libretto for the opera *Ravnen* (The Raven; first performed and first published, 1832) with music by J. P. E. Hartmann. Andersen's *Levnedsbogen,* written the same year, marks a further development in his prose toward a focus on the "local" (typical of the new realism of the period), the interesting psychological self-portrait, and a painterly style. It is the liveliest of Andersen's autobiographies, full of personal details. Thematically, it is similar to a bildungsroman, which moves toward an ultimate realization of a writer's life and includes the emotional breakthrough that comes with "first love."

Andersen had a fervent desire to escape the growing negative criticism of his theater work, since it was having an unfavorable impact on his other publications. Andersen submitted to King Frederik VI his poetry suite *Aarets tolv Maaneder, Tegnede med Blæk og Pen* (The Year's Twelve Months, Sketched with Pen and Ink, 1832) in an attempt to draw attention to himself as a candidate for a major travel grant from the *ad usus publicos* fund. The king took little notice of the book, but with the intercession of Collin and several others, Andersen did receive a grant for a lengthy cultural tour, although his name remained on a waiting list for some time. His travels took him via Germany to France and Italy, where he stayed for more than six months, mainly in Rome. There he became friends with Danish sculptor Bertel Thorvaldsen, poet Ludvig Bødtcher, and painter Albert Küchler, who painted Andersen's portrait. Andersen also stayed in Naples, where he climbed Mount Vesuvius during an eruption.

During his stays in both Paris and Le Locle, Switzerland, he had poured his heart into the dramatic poem "Agnete og Havmanden" (Agnete and the Merman, 1833), which he sent back to Copenhagen. It was published just before Christmas, and after New Year's Day he received in Rome some harshly critical letters from home, including one from his friend Edvard Collin. This denigration of his work crushed Andersen. Thorvaldsen had to step in and bolster his artistic courage.

Just as Andersen's arrival in Copenhagen on 6 September 1819 was a landmark in his life, his first day in Rome, 18 October 1833, was also significant. Thus, he had three birthdays in his lifetime: his real birthday, his Copenhagen birthday, and his Roman one.

That Andersen's arrival in Rome became a landmark event in his life undoubtedly was tied to his desire to put himself on equal footing with Thorvaldsen, who always celebrated his own Roman birthday. Andersen began viewing the sculptor's life as analogous to his own. Thorvaldsen was an artist who, by virtue of his genius, had worked his way up from impoverished circumstances to European acclaim. References to Thorvaldsen appear many places in Andersen's writings. When the sculptor died in 1844, Andersen wrote both a poem and an article in homage.

In personal terms, Andersen found Italy to be the first suitable counterpart to his own emotional and fiery nature, which was so unlike the generally sedate Danish temperament. The opposition of north and south was a widespread theme of the period and had been ever since Oehlenschläger's *Vaulundurs Saga* and *Aladdin* (collected in his *Poetiske Skrifter* [Poetic Writings, 1805]).

Back home in Denmark, Andersen had claimed that a writer should adopt the methods of a painter (the aesthetic program for *Skyggebilleder af en Reise til Harzen og det sachsiske Schweiz . . . i Sommeren 1831*), but in Italy he truly learned to see with the eye of a painter, a process that can be traced in the sketches from his Italian sojourn.

That Italy set its mark and signaled a personal and artistic new departure for him is evident in the novel that he began writing during his stay, *Improvisatoren* (1835; translated as *The Improvisatore; or, Life in Italy,* 1845). As early as 1830 he had started planning to write an historical novel, a fragment of which, "Christian den Andens Dværg" (Christian II's Dwarf), has survived. The success that Scott and Ingemann had enjoyed with their historical novels invited imitation. But *Improvisatoren* marked Andersen's breakthrough as a writer of contemporary novels, and at the same time he launched the modern novel in earnest in Danish literature.

Although Andersen had put a great deal of effort into the dramatic genres and poetry, by 1835 he realized, as he recounts in a letter, that he wanted to be "den første romanfatter i Danmark" (the foremost novelist in Denmark). Only a few weeks after the Danish publication of *Improvisatoren,* the German edition appeared, so the translation must have been under way simultaneously. The novel was well received in both Denmark and Germany, and it marked a turning point in Andersen's writing career. In personal terms, his return home from Italy also heralded the start of a new phase of his life, with new skills and experiences acquired during his stay abroad.

Improvisatoren is a colorful novel, with an autobiographical strain, about an artist; it depicts the upbringing and development of a poor Italian boy until he makes his breakthrough as a singer and poet, an improviser, who seizes inspiration from the moment and transforms it into art. Life and art–also, love and art–merge into a harmonious whole in the novel. Furthermore, the story embeds the remarkable destiny of the protagonist in vividly colored descriptions of Italian landscapes and cities, with an active Vesuvius and the Blue Grotto in Capri (at that time newly discovered) as the picturesque and symbolic high points. It is the first bildungsroman in Danish literature, a genre that had its birth and prototype in Johann Wolfgang von Goethe's *Wilhelm Meister* (1795–1796), though most Danish examples of this type of novel appear in the 1850s and 1860s. As a bildungsroman, *Improvisatoren* attempts to reconcile dream and reality, art and life, the spiritual and the temporal, the individual and society.

In that same year–1835–two slim, modest-looking books also appeared titled *Eventyr, fortalte for Børn.* The first volume comprised "Fyrtøiet" (The Tinderbox), "Lille Claus og store Claus" (Little Claus and Big Claus), "Prindsessen paa Ærten" (The Princess on the Pea), and "Den lille Idas Blomster." Of these stories the first two were retellings, in Andersen's own style, of folktales he had heard as a child. The second volume, which appeared just before Christmas, comprised "Tommelise" (Thumbelina), "Den uartige Dreng" (The Naughty Boy), and "Reisekammeraten." The first and last of these stories were again retellings of folktales. Until 1841 the fairy-tale collections bore the subtitle "fortalte for Børn." From 1843 on, Andersen omitted the subtitle, and in 1850 he began alternating "fairy tales" with "stories." Originally, Andersen's primary intention with his children's fairy tales had been to earn money. In the late 1820s a growing market arose in Denmark for children's literature. In the mid 1830s Andersen's strongest critic, Molbech, began publishing a series of booklets called *Julegaver for Børn* (Christmas Gifts for Children), to which a female writer named Sille Beyer contributed fairy tales in the sentimental and moralizing spirit that characterized the Biedermeier period in early-nineteenth-century Europe. Andersen wanted to tap this new market, and at first that was the extent of his ambition in this genre. His real literary ambitions were directed at drama and, above all, novels.

After seeing the first fairy tales, Andersen's older friend and mentor, physicist Ørsted, told him that although his novels might make him famous, his fairy tales would make him immortal. Andersen mentioned this in a letter, adding that he did not believe it. For him, the important thing was to make his mark as a novelist.

During the 1830s Andersen published three novels in rapid succession. In 1836 the novel *O.T.* (translated, 1845) appeared, followed in 1837 by *Kun en Spillemand.* With *O.T.* the setting shifts to Denmark, and the novel represents a northern counterpart to *Improvisatoren.* In this new novel the emphasis is on social and psychological themes in the depiction of the main character, Otto Thostrup, whose initials form the title of the work. The initials "O.T." are also a brand on Otto's shoulder, a social brand that shows he was born at Odense Tugthus (Odense Jailhouse). As an adult, Otto tries to conceal this mark, and in one ominous scene he even attempts to scour it off, because it makes him an outcast, socially unacceptable.

Andersen in 1836 (painting by Christian Albrecht Jensen; from Jackie Wullschlager, Hans Christian Andersen: The Life of a Storyteller, *2000; Scandinavian Studies Library, University of Washington)*

In the beginning of the novel Otto is a student, in those days a part of the intellectual elite. At the same time, he has set his sights on the upper echelons of society by falling in love with a young baroness who is the sister of one of his classmates. The novel is not a bildungsroman; rather, it is a progressive unveiling–also for the protagonist–of the dark past and its consequences in the present. The latter has to do with identifying Otto's sister. Is she the bestial, demonic woman named Sidsel or the angelic, poor, and virginal but much-sought-after girl named Eva? In keeping with the aesthetic fascination of the period with what was called "interesting" (meaning what was complex, hidden, demonic, and more or less forbidden), the novel is a study in traumas and social and psychological suppression, in spite of its positive ending. *O.T.* was also translated into several languages, but it did not win the same acclaim and popularity as Andersen's first novel.

An event that gave real impetus to the spread of Andersen's fame abroad was a meeting that took place in 1837. The much-traveled French critic Marmier, who was familiar with Scandinavian literature, was on a visit to Denmark and Sweden when, during his stay in Copenhagen in the spring of 1837, he developed an interest in Andersen after the writer paid him a call. After their meeting, Marmier immediately wrote an article about Andersen titled "La vie d'un poète" (The Life of a Poet) for the journal *Revue de Paris.* The article was accompanied by a translation of Andersen's poem "Det døende Barn." This article has endured in France because it was reprinted, in slightly revised form, as the preface to one of the most widely read French editions of Andersen's fairy tales–*Contes,* translated by D. Soldi. Marmier's essay was also translated into German in 1837 and was used as the basic material for an article about Andersen in the Brockhaus reference work *Conversationslexikon der Gegenwart* (4 volumes, 1838–1841). By 1838 Marmier's essay had appeared in Russian as well, even though at the time not a single line of Andersen's work was available in that language. The story of Andersen's life spread like lightning throughout Europe, attracting as much attention as his books. Although Germany was from the beginning Andersen's biggest market and "second homeland," a Frenchman created the basis for Andersen's European celebrity.

Kun en Spillemand won Andersen enormous success in Germany (1838) but a sharp rebuke in Denmark. The German translator of the novel, a certain Captain von Jenssen, wanted to introduce the German edition with a lengthy biographical essay about the author, and Andersen obligingly sent him the material for it. The novel is a deeply pessimistic story about a poor but talented violinist named Christian who is destroyed partly by his own weakness and partly because his environment, meaning society, refuses to encourage or support him. Another reason for his downfall is that he psychologically never grows up and becomes a man. On the other hand, his female counterpart and childhood sweetheart, a Jewish girl, Naomi, possesses everything that he lacks–independence, sexual power, and a desire to be free. But she, too, is destroyed, in her case by a vacuous upper-class life. After Christian dies, his meager funeral procession has to move over into the ditch to allow an elegant coach to pass. Inside sits the proud and cold Naomi. In the German edition this profoundly melancholy story was coupled with von Jenssen's optimistic portrait of the author under the motto that genuine talent will always find its way, regardless of any obstacles. This combination made the book a huge success in Germany, where both rich and poor wept over the novel and felt edified by the author's life story.

Viewed from a modern perspective, the novel is interesting for several reasons. It is original in form, since it is structured contrapuntally as it moves back and forth between the parallel lives of Christian and Naomi and between their two worlds–the north of Denmark and the south of France and Austria. It is also one of the few novels before the Modern Breakthrough (meaning before the naturalism and realism of the 1870s and 1880s) to ignore the convention that a novel should present an optimistic outlook on life and a positive ending.

Use of this convention was precisely what infuriated a young Danish author whose first book addressed Andersen's third novel. Philosopher Søren Kierkegaard wrote an eighty-page critique of *Kun en Spillemand* and published it under the cryptic title *Af en endnu Levendes Papirer* (From the Papers of One Still Living, 1838). Kierkegaard's concepts were at this stage still heavily influenced by Georg Wilhelm Friedrich Hegel, and at the same time he felt called upon to defend the Goethe-inspired humanistic ideas of "bildung" (education), which were the basis for the Golden Age in Copenhagen. He attacked Andersen for lacking a philosophy of life, for his inability to be objective, and for focusing on the negative, exactly like the "savage" rebellious-critical literature in the rest of contemporary Europe. Kierkegaard's criticism served largely as a bulwark against revolutionary tendencies that might threaten Danish society and its culture. It is basically a political critique disguised as a literary review. Denying the author of *Kun en Spillemand* any talent as a novelist, Kierkegaard's criticism had a crushing effect on Andersen. Ten years passed after the appearance of Kierkegaard's critique before Andersen published another novel.

All his life, Andersen's economic situation remained highly unstable. In the mid 1830s he was still in debt to Collin, who had lent Andersen money to finance his return from Italy. At the same time Andersen had great trouble paying for the barest necessities. The year 1838 brought stability to his situation and thus marked a turning point in his life. Thanks to an enthusiastic reader of *Improvisatoren*–Count Conrad Rantzau-Breitenburg, a minister in Frederik VI's cabinet–Andersen received a government grant with a yearly stipend of 400 Rigsdaler. The grant gave him a solid financial basis. Combined with the earnings from his writing, he now had an annual income comparable to 100,000 kroner today. His income grew steadily during the following years. The government stipend was also increased, first in 1845 to 600 Rigsdaler and again in 1860 to 1,000 Rigsdaler. In those days support for an artist was not a social disbursement but rather a form of acknowledgment that increased in size as the artist's fame (and income) grew.

The two volumes of *Eventyr, fortalte for Børn* were followed by new books with the same title in 1837, 1838, 1839, and 1841. A yearlong trip abroad in 1840–1841 was partially responsible for delaying the final volume. Originally, the fairy tales were only sporadically reviewed and received mostly negative critiques. The criticism was based on the attitude expressed by writer and professor of philosophy Poul Martin Møller, who was also Kierkegaard's admired teacher: to fill a child's imagination with fairy tales is harmful to his or her development. Children should instead be brought up on reality. At the same time, Andersen's tales were thought to be immoral. For example, the dog in "Fyrtøiet" brings the sleeping princess to the soldier's room.

Not even Andersen's colleague Ingemann cared for the fairy tales, although he had written many fairy tales and fantasy stories himself. Yet, in spite of the relatively negative reception, Andersen's fairy tales quickly became popular in Denmark, and the first German translations began appearing in 1839. The first English translations were published in 1846, as well as translations into Dutch. Along with "Fyrtøiet," the fairy-tale collections of the 1830s include stories such as "Den lille Havfrue," "Keiserens nye Klæder" (The Emperor's New Clothes, 1837), "Den standhaftige Tinsoldat" (The Steadfast Tin Soldier, 1838), and "De vilde Svaner" (The Wild Swans, 1838).

From the start, Andersen's deeply original fairy-tale style was fully developed. While the Grimm brothers refined and polished the folktales they had collected to achieve a normalized prose style without any particularly significant characteristics, Andersen took the opposite tack. He created a style and narrative voice that largely stayed close to colloquial speech and thus held a lively appeal for children, whom he had originally targeted as his audience. If one regards Andersen as a children's author (though he was never exclusively writing for children, even in his fairy tales), then his groundbreaking contribution is that he neither addresses children as adults nor talks down to them, as was the custom in literature at the time. On principle, he chose his perspective from below, from the children's level, and thereby seemed to show a solidarity with his audience. For this reason, the language of his fairy tales is not an academically correct prose, full of abstract words and hypotactic sentence structure.

At the time, critics in Denmark, both those who addressed him in private and those who wrote publicly, failed to see the originality of Andersen's language. Instead, they reproached him for not being able to write "proper Danish." They attributed his inability to his having so much faith in his own talent that he did not wish to submit to any kind of serious studies or to learn from the great classical authors. The critics were not prepared to accept or recognize that Andersen was a modern writer who had created a prose based on the premises of a new era. Even his old friend Edvard Collin, who assisted him by copying out and proofing his manuscripts, repeated the criticism in the book he published after the author's death, *H. C. Andersen og det Collinske Huus* (Hans Christian Andersen and the Collin Family, 1882). He also stated that Andersen regrettably lacked all desire or ability to submit to any kind of rigorous course of study.

Although the fairy-tale collections up until 1841 bore the subtitle "fortalte for Børn," certain dualities typical of Andersen were present from the beginning–for example, his ability to tell a story that would appeal to adults and children alike. He accomplished this goal by several methods. Some of the fairy tales, such as "Den lille Havfrue," have a philosophy embedded in a story that children can easily follow and enjoy–a philosophy that is directed solely at an adult reader who has a literary background. These stories include concepts regarding the relationship between nature and spirit; the fundamental urge in human beings and nature that, according to Platonic tradition, is called *eros;* religious ideas about the longing of the soul and the path to immortality or God; the dual nature of love, involving a destructive urge and a vanquishing of the self, or agape; an ascent (for example, socially) and the subsequent costs; the relationship between unrequited love and artistic expression (the mermaid, for example, seems to float as she dances, but each step cuts her feet like a knife); a human life that is wasted and the compensation for it in (artistic) immortality; and the transformation of the soul through death and an "intermediate state" after death.

The concurrent appeal to adult readers is also accomplished through the use of irony and humor, and often satire. Andersen achieves this tone by playing with the sound of words and their meanings. His language and narrative style are full of surprises and secondary meanings. He is a conscious linguistic artist. The previously mentioned common perception that "the childish nature" of his style was an expression of a childishness and naiveté in Andersen himself is far from the truth. Both as a human being and as an artist, Andersen had access to the naive and childish side of himself, but the "childish style" is consciously elaborated. This characteristic is evident in his reworking of "Dødningen" (1830) into "Reisekammeraten" (1835) and the comparable (but not nearly as radical) revising of "Lykkens Kalosker" (The Galoshes of Fortune, 1838 and 1850). It is also evident from his revising and rewriting texts over and over until he found just the right expression, just the right form, as, for example, in "Vinden fortæller om Valdemar Daae og hans Døttre" (The Wind Tells of Valdemar Daae and His Daughters, 1859).

Three additional elements characterize Andersen's fairy tales and distinguish them from the stories of the Grimm brothers. First, except for a few stories based on folktales, the tales have a contemporary setting. Most of them do not take place in a particularly fairy-tale-like milieu; nor does the introductory phrase "once upon a time" occur more than a few times in Andersen's stories. His fairy tales are most often set in his own time and in a world quite familiar to his readers, both young and old. In this way, Andersen moved the fairy tale (meaning poetry or the poetic concept that makes the world into a story of universal significance) from a distant and indeterminate past to his own modern times. In "Dryaden" (The Wood Nymph, 1868), a companion piece to "Den lille Havfrue" that appeared thirty years later, Andersen both begins and ends the story with the sentence "*Our time,* the great, wondrous time of fairy tales." In spite of the influences of Romanticism, Andersen was fundamentally of his time–a "modernist," not a traditionalist.

Second, his fairy tales are often scenically dramatic in form. Andersen's fairy tales have often been adapted to such dramatic formats as cartoons, puppet plays, dramatic performances for adults, ballet, opera, and hybrid productions combining actors and animation. Many of the texts are plays in prose form, as evident in "Det er ganske vist!" (It's Perfectly True, 1852); Andersen's lifelong ties to the theater clearly had a strong influence on the narrative form of his fairy tales.

Third, Andersen's stories typically make inanimate objects come alive–toys such as a spinning top, ball, or tin soldier; or other objects such as a house, a paving tool, rags, or a darning needle. He also anthropomorphizes animals, birds, insects, flowers, trees, and other natural phenomena such as the wind. In this sense Andersen's tales are related to fables, although they do not include the same one-dimensional reference to the human world, nor do they generally possess the clear and instructive moral of fables. Instead, Andersen paints miniature pictures of life: humoresques, satires, and social and psychological snapshots.

Even during the first period of Andersen's fairy-tale production (up until 1841), the tales evince a conscious urge to experiment with form. Hence, Andersen published in 1839 (although the book lists the date as 1840) a collection of interconnected prose sketches or arabesques under the title *Billedbog uden Billeder* (1839; translated as *A Picture-Book Without Pictures,* 1847). Originally, the collection comprised twenty sketches (labeled "evenings"), but the number was increased in later editions to a total of thirty-three. The fictional framework is the notion that the moon appears every evening to recount what it has seen to a poor young painter who lives in a garret room–to narrate or rather *show* visually. The result is a series of brief sketches that are often blatantly lyrical prose pieces from all over the world. The title of the book was clearly influenced by Felix Mendelssohn's *Lieder ohne Worte* (Songs Without Words; completed in 1830), but it also enjoins the reader to perceive the work as a counterpart to *A Thousand and One Nights*. In this instance, however, the poetic images come from far and wide and are situational sketches. The painterly foundation is completely in keeping with Andersen's aesthetic endeavors in the 1830s, a decade that for him was demarcated by *Skyggebilleder af en Reise til Harzen og det sachsiske Schweiz . . . i Sommeren 1831* and *Billedbog uden Billeder*. The book did not attract much attention in Denmark, and even today it is not especially well known among Danish readers. It is rarely reprinted in Denmark along with the fairy tales, even though the later tales include "stories" that are actually similar in nature to the "evenings" in *Billedbog uden Billeder*. The reception of the book was quite different abroad, particularly in Germany, where it was popular, appearing in several translations. It was also reprinted many times, and individual "evenings" were published in various journals and magazines.

Andersen soon also had a major new dramatic work accepted by the Royal Theater, the "romantic drama" *Mulatten* (The Mulatto; first performed and first published, 1840). He received approximately 1,000 Rigsdaler for the work. This sum, combined with the anticipated fee for his next play, *Maurerpigen* (The Moorish Girl; first performed and first published, 1840), made possible a lengthy journey to the Middle East.

The premiere of *Mulatten* was scheduled for December 1839, but the performance was canceled. The theater was closed for two months after the death of King Frederik VI. For this reason the debut of the play occurred in February 1840 when it also appeared in print. It was one of Andersen's greatest dramatic successes, staged twenty-one times at the Royal Theater during his lifetime. The greatest Danish actress of the era, Johanne Luise Heiberg, played one of the leading female roles.

Mulatten was also performed at the Royal Theater in Stockholm, at theaters in Malmö and Odense, as well as throughout Denmark by traveling theater companies. Clearly, Johanne Luise Heiberg was not solely responsible for its success, even though Andersen tended to place great weight on her contribution to its

Andersen paper cutting of a jumping clown carrying a town on a tray. Andersen often made such cuttings for his own amusement; he gave many of them to children of families he visited (Hans Christian Andersen Museum, Odense).

favorable reception. He insisted that she also play the leading role in *Maurerpigen,* but she declined. After a series of setbacks, the tragedy had its premiere in December 1840, but it was a flop. In his memoirs Andersen attributes the failure to his disagreement with Johanne Luise Heiberg. Her husband, Johan Ludvig Heiberg, the professor and writer who had earlier helped Andersen, satirized him in his *Nye Digte* (New Poems, 1841), which includes the satirical play *En Sjæl efter Døden* (A Soul after Death), in which hell has a theater where the condemned are tortured by staging daily performances of Andersen's *Mulatten* and *Maurerpigen.*

Nevertheless, *Mulatten* was an indisputable success. The play is also thematically central to Andersen's writing. The plot, based on a French short story that Andersen had read, involves a slave rebellion on Martinique. The topic was particularly relevant in an age when Denmark had its own overseas colonies, including those in the West Indies (the Virgin Islands). Although Denmark had outlawed the slave trade in 1803, slavery continued in the West Indies until 1848. That same year slavery was abolished by France; England had banned it in 1834.

Slavery provides a framework for the play, rather than its theme. In *Mulatten* Andersen discusses a more general, erotic-psychological and social theme, which in many ways is the dramatic counterpart to the novel *O.T.* It deals with the outsider who has the spiritual qualifications to raise himself up or–in the words of Andersen, and in keeping with the Zeitgeist–spiritual nobility. But he ends up caught between social disparities, between those above and those below, or in this case between the white plantation owners and the black slaves. The mulatto Horatio belongs to neither group–or to both. At the same time Horatio stands at the intersection of spiritual love and dark sexuality, between the world of culture and that of rebellion. The story ends when his beloved (a white woman belonging to the ruling class) buys his freedom at a slave market where he has landed, unjustly, since he is a free man, not a slave.

A mixture of jealousy and oppression brought him there, but then he is bought–for marriage.

Andersen was able to venture out on a second lengthy trip abroad, which took him through Germany, France, and Italy, and then via Malta to Greece and Turkey. From there he returned by way of the perilous route up the Danube, journeying through the turbulent Balkans to Vienna, then on to Prague and Germany and back to Denmark. His travels lasted nearly a year and resulted in the great, colorful travel book *En Digters Bazar* (1842; translated as *A Poet's Bazaar,* 1846).

This travel book includes several purely poetic pieces. Among the better-known chapters of the book are the introductory description of a concert by Franz Liszt in Hamburg and the chapter "Jernbanen" (The Railroad), which testifies to Andersen's fascination with the modern wonders of technology. On this journey Andersen had his first experience traveling by train, on the stretch between Magdeburg and Leipzig, a distance of 110 kilometers. The trip lasted from 7:00 A.M. until 10:30 A.M., so the speed was obviously slow by modern standards, but for Andersen the experience was a mixture of Mephistophelian sorcery and divine revelation–human triumph over nature. Andersen returned to this theme again and again for the rest of his writing career, in keeping with the growing mechanization of transportation and communication, with urbanization, and with the progress of the exact sciences, especially the natural sciences. The theme allowed both praise of progress and, more subtly, a worry about it.

The failure of *Maurerpigen* brought Andersen financial difficulties, since the anticipated fee was supposed to help pay for his lengthy trip to the East. Instead, he had to seek support from the king (once again from the *ad usus publicos* fund); he did receive a grant, although it was not as large as he had hoped.

For Andersen this trip was also a means of placing himself in the "proper" circles, which meant among artists and intellectuals. He made the acquaintance of painters, writers, composers, and publishers. His later friendship with Mendelssohn in Leipzig was particularly propitious. Andersen had heard Liszt play at a concert in Hamburg, and after his return home Andersen heard Liszt again in Copenhagen and met with him in person. Their friendship, which deepened over the succeeding years during Andersen's travels in Germany, came to mean a great deal for the author's musical experience. Liszt sparked Andersen's interest in Richard Wagner, whom Andersen later visited in Switzerland in 1855. Wagner's music, in turn, played an important role in Andersen's last novel, *Lykke-Peer* (Lucky Peer, 1870; translated, 1871).

In 1839 Andersen's fairy tales began appearing in German translations, and their popularity among readers was quickly assured. Throughout the 1840s Andersen's reputation in Europe grew rapidly. By 1843, when he made another European trip that took him to Germany, Belgium, and France, Andersen was able to enjoy the laurels of his celebrity. He also consorted on equal footing with such men as Victor Hugo, Alexandre Dumas *père,* Alphonse de Lamartine, Heine (exiled by then), and sculptor Pierre-Jean David in Paris.

The year was a landmark in Andersen's life for another reason. After returning home from his travels, he heard Jenny Lind (then only twenty-three years old) sing in Copenhagen. She soon delighted audiences in the great opera houses of Europe and became known as the "Swedish Nightingale." Andersen spent a good deal of time with her in private and fell madly in love. In contrast to other, brief, and equally hopeless infatuations after Riborg, Andersen's enchantment with Lind lasted many years. Even in his later years he kept a bust of her next to one of himself in his apartment in the Nyhavn district of Copenhagen. He states in his autobiography that Lind was a major reason behind his ability to lift himself out of the recurrent desperation that can be traced in his letters throughout the 1830s and into the early 1840s. For him she was the incarnation of the union of art and religiosity; at the same time, she represented a counterpart to Andersen in the uniting of humble origins and great success.

Ever since the publication of Hans Brix's dissertation *H. C. Andersens og hans Eventyr* (The Fairy Tales of Hans Christian Andersen, 1907), "Nattergalen" has commonly been accepted as Andersen's declaration of love to Lind. Brix does not, however, provide any proof for this theory, which is based solely on Lind's being known as the "Swedish Nightingale." Yet, this nickname is not mentioned in a review of her performance at the Royal Theater nor in the poems of homage that appeared in the newspaper *Fædrelandet* in September 1843. Presumably, she did not acquire this sobriquet until later, after her breakthrough on the German opera stages. The biographical interpretation of "Nattergalen" as Andersen's declaration of love, therefore, is uncertain.

Six months after Lind's departure, Andersen developed a highly secret but deeply emotional attachment to the young baron Henrik Stampe from Nysø manor, one of the estates where Andersen was often invited as a guest. Similar intense relationships with young men often occurred in Andersen's life at the same time as or alternating with his infatuations with women.

In 1901 Albert Hansen, a Danish critic, published the article "H. C. Andersen–Beweis seiner Homosexualität" (Hans Christian Andersen–Proof of His Homosexuality) in the *Jahrbuch für sexuelle Zwischenstufen* in

Berlin. Since then, claims have frequently been made that Andersen was homosexual, especially among German scholars of Andersen's work. The latest contribution in Germany is Heinrich Detering's *Das offene Geheimnis* (The Open Secret, 1994). This hypothesis has led to interpretations of many of his tales, such as "Den lille Havfrue," as covert accounts of this type of forbidden love. In Denmark this view has not won much sympathy. Two Andersen biographies in English, however, make homosexuality a central thread in Andersen's personal history. They are Alison Prince's *Hans Christian Andersen: The Fan Dancer* (1998) and Jackie Wullschlager's *Hans Christian Andersen: The Life of a Storyteller* (2000).

Edvard Collin's *H. C. Andersen og det Collinske Huus,* which is highly critical of Andersen, does not include any hint that Andersen was gay. Collin mentions with a certain satisfaction that he was familiar with some of Andersen's love affairs (understood to be with women) and was quite pleased with that side of the author's life. The critic Georg Brandes and his younger brother, Edvard, who both knew Andersen, held widely different views of the writer. In an article from 1900, Georg Brandes said that Andersen was not a man–but what this assessment implies remains unclear. Edvard wrote an article about Andersen in 1930 and stated emphatically that Andersen was indeed "a man."

Andersen's letters, diaries, and almanac notes provide evidence that he had strong emotional friendships with men and used language to discuss these feelings that other men would reserve for their relationships with women. The evidence is equally compelling that he was in love with women and felt sexually attracted to–and threatened by–certain types of women.

During the 1840s, Andersen's career was soaring. His fairy tales were a grand success in Germany, while his early novels and *En Digters Bazar* were published in English, including American pirated editions. The fairy tales appeared in Dutch and English, beginning in 1846, with several different English translations. The first illustrated fairy-tale editions were published the same year in German, with illustrations by Otto Speckter, and in English, with illustrations by Count Pocci. Andersen's new fairy-tale books published in Denmark during the 1840s no longer included the subtitle "fortalte for Børn." This omission indicates that Andersen was now much more self-aware as a writer of tales, that he was also writing for adult readers, and that he had attained full artistic mastery of the style and narrative form that were all his own. This decade also marked the publication of key, poetically important texts, such as the–in a Kierkegaardian sense–almost existentialist story "Grantræet" (The Fir Tree); the religious story "Sneedronningen"; the tale about art and nature, "Nattergalen"; the mythologizing, autobiographical story "Den grimme Ælling" (The Ugly Duckling, collected in *Nye Eventyr,* 1843); the Romantic nature text "Klokken" (The Bell); and its desperate counterpart "Skyggen."

In 1844 Andersen was a guest of the Danish royal couple on the North Sea island of Föhr (at the time, a Danish possession, although it became German after 1864). There Christian VIII honored him by celebrating the twenty-fifth anniversary of Andersen's arrival in Copenhagen in 1819. This celebration occurred in September, but earlier in the summer Andersen was in Weimar, where he was received at the court of the grand duke and became fast friends with Carl Alexander, the young heir to the duchy. Carl Alexander had grand plans for including Andersen in the circle of artists with whom he was associated in Weimar. Carl Alexander's intention was to make Andersen for Weimar of the 1840s what Goethe had been for his grandfather's time, the poet king, although Andersen had no desire to move to little Weimar. The friendship between Andersen and Carl Alexander lasted until the Three-Year War of 1848–1850, a conflict over continued possession of Slesvig-Holsten by Denmark. The friendship was renewed later on, although it was more moderate in tone.

For Andersen, the highlight of the decade occurred in 1847. In Leipzig, Carl B. Lorck began publishing Andersen's collected works. (A comparable Danish edition did not begin appearing until six years later.) For this German edition, Andersen had signed a contract to deliver an autobiography (*Das Märchen meines Lebens ohne Dichtung,* 1847), which would comprise the first two volumes. He wrote the autobiography during a European trip that lasted almost a year, although he did not have his diaries at hand to support his memory. He sent the manuscript back in sections to Edvard Collin, who made a clean copy and then sent it to be translated and printed in Leipzig. This method of operation meant that Andersen did not read through the entire text before it was published. Even so, it is an exceedingly well-composed autobiography. The theme is Andersen's laborious but triumphant rise to the zenith of his career, which coincides geographically with the mountains at Vernet, where Andersen stands peering into the land of the future as he sets down the final period. A secondary theme in the middle of this narrative about development and ascent is the human cost, which is formulated as "Sorgen rider med paa Rytterens hest" (the sorrow that shares the horseman's saddle). The triumphant ending in which he, like Moses, beholds the promised land also includes the shadow of an uncertain future.

Eventyr,

fortalte for Børn

af

H. C. Andersen.

Første Hefte.

Kjøbenhavn.
Forlagt af Universitets-Boghandler C. A. Reitzel.
Trykt hos Bianco Luno & Schneider.
1835.

Title page for the first publication in book form of Andersen's fairy tales (British Library)

When the English edition of his autobiography appeared in 1847, Andersen made his first trip to England; he made his second visit in 1857. In London he spent time with Lind, with the heir to the duchy of Weimar, and with his old friend Ludwig Spohr, a German composer. Andersen devoted much time to his publishers and translators, and they reciprocated. He had his portrait painted, and he was feted as the great literary man of the season. He was the celebrated focus of the upper echelons of society. During his stay, Andersen made the acquaintance of Charles Dickens, with whose work he felt a particular kinship. Both authors had written about childhood and the life of children, and both had shown their readers the circumstances of the poor. Andersen's travels also took him to Scotland, which ever since his youth had held a special attraction for him because of his fascination with Scott and his own operatic works that were inspired by Scott's novels. In Scotland, Andersen was delighted to find himself recognized by citizens who had seen his portrait in the newspaper.

During the 1840s Andersen began thinking about writing another novel. In 1843 he conceived of an idea for a book, and his visit to Föhr in 1844 gave his imagination further impetus. But the new novel was not published until 1848–first in English, as *The Two Baronesses* (because of royalty considerations), and then in Danish, as *De to Baronesser.* The only Danish novel from the time that has a female protagonist, it is further distinguished from the contemporary novel genre by its not focusing exclusively on the development and fate of one individual. On the contrary, the story broadens the perspective in space (from Copenhagen in the east across Fyn to the islands of Halligerne in the west) and time (from the emancipation of the peasants in the 1780s up to the present–that is, the early 1840s). The novel is a broad depiction of fates in a society undergoing change. The intent of the book is to find some "meaning," a "red thread" in the midst of a world of chance, in which the "higher justice" consists of allowing nature to take its rightful place in society. Andersen's utopia in this novel concerns an organic interdependence that crosses all class boundaries–a perpetual interchange and mobility.

The book appeared in the year Christian VIII died, and a new era, as well as a new type of society, was heralded. Absolute rule was abolished, and Denmark adopted a constitution on 5 June 1849. Signs of this departure from an old way of life and the advent of a new era were visible everywhere during the following years. By 1843 the Østersø-Jernbane (Baltic Railway) of Christian VIII was opened between Altona and Kiel, and in 1847 railroad connections between Copenhagen and Roskilde were instituted. Andersen greatly admired this modernization of transportation. Sailing ships were replaced by steamships, and the telegraph connected the new world with the old. A telegraph line from Helsingør to Hamburg, via Copenhagen, was opened in 1854.

The theater world was also touched by the new times. Christian VIII had given permission to Georg Carstensen, the founder of Tivoli, to erect the Casino building as a wintertime amusement park on Amaliegade. This venture went bankrupt, and the Casino became instead the site for a theater, which marked the first incursion into the monopoly held by the Royal Theater in Copenhagen. The Casino theater opened in 1848 as the first private theater in the city. At New Year's the theater performed Andersen's vaudeville *En Comedie i det Grønne* (A Comedy in the Open, 1840), which was staged twenty-seven times during Andersen's life. In 1849 Casino showcased works by Andersen that included the vaudeville *En Nat i Roeskilde* (A

Night in Roskilde), a merry play that had forty-six performances. October 3 of the same year marked the debut of Andersen's reworking of *Der Diamant des Geisterkönigs* (The Diamond of the Spirit King, 1824) by Austrian writer Ferdinand Raimund, which in the Danish version was called *Meer end Perler og Guld* (More than Pearls and Gold). The "Wiener-Posse" became a "Fairy Tale-Comedy," as Andersen called it. It was a great success and ran until 1888, with 162 performances. Andersen followed it in 1850 with the romantic comedy *Ole Lukøie* (The Sandman) and in 1851 with the "fantasy drama" *Hyldemoer* (The Elder Tree Mother), all well-known titles from Andersen's fairy tales, although they had no connection to each other. These and many other plays made Andersen the "house playwright" at the Casino theater, which was disparaged by other writers of the day. Andersen also acted as a consultant for the theater and was a member of its board.

The Three-Year War brought changes to Andersen's life as well. For him, as for other Danes with close ties to Germany, this war with Prussia and its allies among the other German states (including the duchy of Weimar) prompted a cooling of relations; for Andersen this meant in particular his connections with Weimar. A European at heart, Andersen was pressured by his fellow Danes to demonstrate his patriotism during the war. He did so in a series of poems; the best-known is the one that is often considered Denmark's "alternative" national song: "I Danmark er jeg født" (In Denmark I was Born). The poem was printed in the collection *Fædrelandske Vers og Sange under Krigen* (Patriotic Verse and Songs During War, 1851), published by Andersen for the benefit of the wounded and the survivors of war victims.

Because of the war, he could not travel in Europe as he usually did. Instead, he undertook a lengthy trip around Sweden, including the Dalar districts north of Uppsala. This journey resulted in a charming, lyrical book called *I Sverrig* (1851; translated as *Pictures of Sweden,* 1851). It is much more than a travel book, since everywhere the author is seeking poetry in reality, even when he encounters modern industrial reality. The book features two chapters that are programmatic in character. The first is the chapter titled "Tro og Virkelighed" (Faith and Reality), with the subtitle "Prædiken i Naturen" (Sermon in Nature), in which Andersen maintains that faith and the natural sciences have one and the same goal–divine truth. The second programmatic chapter is "Poesiens Californien" (The California of Poetry), in which he prophetically points to the poetry of a new era that will turn away from the Romantic devotion to the past and instead seek poetry in the micro- and macrocosm of natural science, what Andersen calls "the infinitely small and the infinitely vast–a definition that word by word recurs approximately twenty years later in Georg Brandes's principles for a new realism.

Andersen had appropriated these ideas from others, particularly from Ørsted, his mentor of many years and by now a close friend. (Ørsted had discovered electromagnetism and was the founder of what is today known as Danmarks Tekniske Universitet [Technical University of Denmark] in Copenhagen.) Ørsted's work of natural philosophy *Aanden i Naturen* (The Spiritual in Nature) was published in 1850, although it consisted primarily of articles that had appeared earlier. Andersen was familiar with the contents from conversations with Ørsted long before the publication of his Sweden book.

Ørsted died in 1851, and Oehlenschläger, who was Andersen's other great model, had died the year before. Thus, in every sense Andersen had entered a new world in the 1850s. In spite of his longtime royalist leanings and his many visits to Danish manors, Andersen was politically liberal-minded and had cultivated a friendship with student leader Lehmann. In 1848 Lehmann gave his great politically incendiary speeches at the Casino, demanding a constitution. But Andersen, like the majority of Danish writers, did not want to get involved in the growing political disputes during the 1840s. After 1848 he turned his back on the struggles for democracy and declared himself above politics. In several texts from this time period, including the story "Alt paa sin rette Plads!" (Everything in Its Proper Place! 1852), Andersen lashes out at the nouveau riche, the middle class, and the power-hungry peasants.

Andersen loved technology, the natural sciences, and progress, and yet he did not clearly foresee the consequences of these things that he so enthusiastically hailed. He did not anticipate that in terms of a philosophy of life they would be accompanied by a rising materialism and secularism. Worried by this development, Andersen attended the lectures of Professor Eschricht at the university in 1855 and there found material for a major polemical novel titled *"At være eller ikke være"* (1857; translated as *To Be or Not to Be?* 1857). In this book he tries to reconcile the realities of modern life with a belief in immortality. The story takes place before and during the Three-Year War and thus uses a time of crisis–in both a philosophical and a nationalistic sense–for its departure point. The emergent industrialism is also evident as a framework, with a side glance at the completely new industrial town of Silkeborg and its paper factory, which Andersen had visited several times. The novel has often been misinterpreted as an attempt to argue in support of religion. On the contrary, the novel acknowledges that the external authority, which had guaranteed a life after death, is powerless. In contrast, Andersen points to a rejuvenation of inner faith in human beings.

The new era prompted Andersen to experiment with new forms of short prose and also to choose a new genre label. In the fall of 1849 a new collection of his tales was published, illustrated by an amateur artist, Vilhelm Pedersen. Published in five volumes from August to December 1849, it was the first illustrated book edition in Denmark. Pedersen's illustrations originally appeared in a German edition, *Gesammelte Märchen. Mit 112 Illustrationen nach Originalzeichnungen von V. Pedersen. Im Holz geschnitten von Ed. Kretzschmar* (1848). This edition marks the end of another epoch in Andersen's fairy-tale production. Pedersen's simple, quiet drawings, done in a typical Biedermeier style, are viewed today as classic Andersen illustrations, along with the more artistic illustrations of his successor, Lorenz Frølich. But Pedersen's drawings, in particular, contributed to making Andersen seem more harmless than he actually is.

From 1852 until 1855 Andersen published a series of books that no longer bore the label "fairy tales" but were then called "Historier" (Stories). Andersen clearly felt the need to indicate a break with the fairy-tale genre, which was tinged with Romanticism. At the same time he wanted to indicate a shift toward greater realism, in keeping with the developments of the day. Finally, he wanted to create a framework within which everything was possible, from the traditional story to regular fairy tales and hybrid forms in between to pure experiments in style and genre, moving toward musical-lyrical texts, rhapsodic hymns, monologues, and satirical sketches. After 1855 and up until the last submission in 1872, Andersen combined the two-time-honored labels and called his books "Nye Eventyr og Historier" (New Fairy Tales and Stories). This title gave him all the freedom he desired, without compromising his international reputation.

The genre was not the only thing undergoing transformation during this period. Andersen's language also changes in "Historier" and "Eventyr og Historier." The simple, "childish," and idiomatic style was replaced by a form of expression that was often more abstract, an abrupt style that seldom had patience for the calm progression of the narrative but was instead a leaping, virtuoso form of writing. Andersen in many ways far surpassed the literature of his day with a series of more-experimental texts, such as "Hjertesorg" (Heartbreak, 1852), "Det nye Aarhundredes Musa" (Muse of the New Century, 1861), "Bispen paa Børglum og hans Frænde" (The Bishop of Børglum and His Kinsman, 1865), "Loppen og Professoren" (The Flea and the Professor, first published in *Folkekalender for Danmark,* 22 [1873]) and "Tante Tandpine" (Auntie Toothache, 1872). He moved into forms that are precursors to the modernism that characterized the twentieth century.

While Andersen found room to experiment in his short prose pieces, he simultaneously continued writing other works along more-traditional lines, especially his work for the theater. Of particular note during these years were his librettos. As early as 1830 Andersen began collaborating with Danish composers to deliver musical pieces and operas to the Royal Theater. For many years he worked on an opera libretto, *Liden Kirsten* (Little Kirsten, 1846), based on material from folk ballads. He persuaded his good friend Hartmann, a major figure in Danish Romantic music, to set the text to music. The first performance was at the Royal Theater in 1846. It was a tremendous success and was performed sixty-five times during Andersen's life. It was also considered the Danish national opera until Carl Nielsen composed his *Maskarade* (Masquerade, 1906), based on a comedy by Holberg. Ten years later Andersen asked his friend Liszt to bring his opera to the theater in Weimar, under the title *Klein Karin.* Andersen also worked with Hartmann on another opera, *Ravnen,* which Schumann praised highly in 1840 in *Neue Zeitschrift für Musik,* lauding Andersen's libretto as well. Yet, the opera was never successfully staged. Hartmann and Andersen decided to rework *Ravnen* in 1865, but the two versions of the opera were performed a total of only ten times during Andersen's life.

As a poet Andersen was tremendously productive in the 1830s, and he won much acclaim. Many of his poems are still well known today, largely because they were set to music and are sung in schools and at all kinds of occasions. In Denmark they are as well known as the most popular of his fairy tales. But after this initial lyrical outpouring, Andersen's poetic vitality diminished noticeably in a sea of lesser verses written for specific occasions. Yet, in his old age, Andersen surprised his readers with a series of colorful and intense poems on the subjects of eroticism and death as well as ironic meditations–in quite modern fashion–on the feeble flame of poetry, the glow of cigarettes, and the futile flare of passion. These poems are included in his great travel book *I Spanien* (1863; translated as *In Spain,* 1864). Andersen had long yearned to see Spain, which at the time was little known to Danish travelers. Not until June 1862, however, could he make the trip, a journey that lasted eight months.

On his travels abroad during this period Andersen often took with him young men of the Collin family, paying their way. Edvard Collin's son, Jonas Collin Jr., went along this time. The trip cost Andersen a fortune, but it was one of the ways in which he could repay his old debts to the family who had taken him in when he was a youngster.

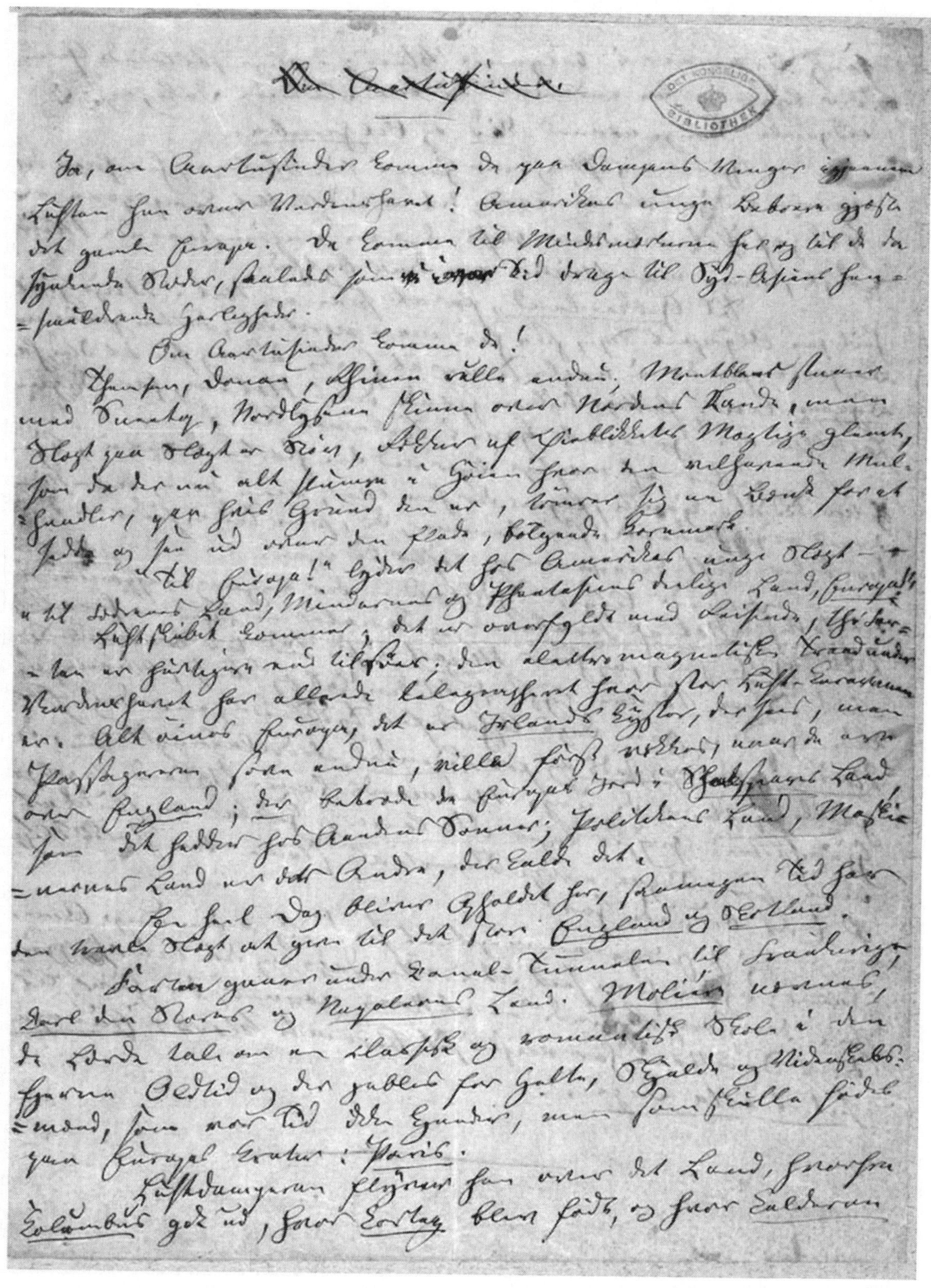

First page of the manuscript for Andersen's satirical tale "Om Aartusinder" (In a Thousand Years' Time), about a group of Americans visiting Europe by airplane. It was first published in his Historier. Anden Samling *(Stories: Second Collection) in 1852 (courtesy of the Danish Royal Library, Copenhagen).*

Andersen's last travel book, *Et Besøg i Portugal* (1868; translated as *A Visit to Portugal 1866,* 1972), which was based on his travels two years earlier, also includes poems, although the lyrical, painterly prose makes a stronger impression. Andersen's last novel appeared in 1870. It was called *Lykke-Peer,* a title later used by realistic Danish novelist Henrik Pontoppidan for his great bildungsroman (1898–1904). Danish author Herman Bang also alludes to Andersen's last novel in his own naturalistic debut work, *Haabløse Slægter* (Hopeless Generations, 1880). *Lykke-Peer,* as a novel about an artist and a semi-fairy tale, is both a summation of Andersen's self-mythologizing and an homage to Oehlenschläger's Romantic masterpiece *Aladdin.* Andersen's interest in music, particularly opera, plays a central role in this short novel. The protagonist is an impoverished boy who, as an artistic genius specially chosen by fate, pulls himself up to make his breakthrough as a singer and the composer of his own opera, titled *Aladdin.* He experiences the eternal dilemma that is typical of Andersen: bourgeois and human happiness, meaning happiness in love, must be sacrificed to achieve artistic success. But this happiness is the same as Andersen described in his German autobiography: sorrow is always sitting on the horse behind the rider.

The end of "Lykkens Kalosker" says that perhaps death was the best gift the galoshes brought with them. In "Den standhaftige Tinsoldat" the ballet dancer and the tin soldier are united in the flames of the stove, as a true highlight of their fate. In "Den lille Pige med Svovlstikkerne" (The Little Match Girl, 1845), the final rising up to the light is equated with death in the dark and cold. In "Det gamle Egetræes sidste Drøm" (The Last Dream of the Old Oak Tree, 1858) the tree's sudden flood of energy as it rises up toward the sunlight is really death, pulled up by the roots as it is on a stormy Christmas Eve. Death and resurrection are one. In "En Historie fra Klitterne" (A Story from the Dunes, 1859) Jørgen is redeemed at the visionary, illuminated moment of his death, buried in the imaginary flying church nave, where he has sought shelter from the sandstorm.

Andersen's second autobiography, published in German, still included hints of these themes, but not his third. His Danish readers knew primarily this latter work, the one titled *Mit Livs Eventyr,* which was published in Denmark as part of Andersen's *Samlede Skrifter* (beginning in 1853). The more widespread second edition of his collected works began appearing immediately after Andersen's death in 1875. *Mit Livs Eventyr* is a broader and more extensively documented presentation of the German autobiography, but it also has a different purpose. It is not as concerned with depicting Andersen's own development and personality as the two previous autobiographies were. Instead, it is composed as both a defensive text and an attack on the disfavor and persecution that Andersen felt in Denmark during the first decades of his writing career. He makes a special point of describing his travails with the censors at the Royal Theater. Conversely, he also provides ample documentation of the admiration and honors that were heaped on him abroad. In the American "Author's Edition" of his works, published in ten volumes in 1869–1871, Andersen brought his autobiography up to 1867, when he was proclaimed an honorary citizen of Odense, his birthplace.

In the archive-based supplement that he wrote for the American version of his autobiography, Andersen mentions an honor from the previous ten to fifteen years: He was invited to read some of his fairy tales at meetings of the newly established Workers Union, an association formed on the initiative of local burghers for the purposes of improving the education of workers. Andersen says that he was the first writer to read for this new social class that had arisen with emerging industrialization. Andersen read at the Workers Union twenty times, each time with an audience of between five hundred and one thousand. Many times he did not ask for payment. He also read for groups of seamstresses. At his death the workers formed an honor guard at the Cathedral (where the royal family was also represented) and then accompanied his coffin to the grave site. Andersen had risen from the poorest ranks of a provincial Danish town to the elite cultural scenes in Europe, becoming an international celebrity in his own lifetime. Yet, he has often been criticized for being snobbish, vain, and a traitor to his class. More accurately, in his later years Andersen tried to realize the ideal he had promoted in his novel *De to Baronesser*–that the top and bottom should be united, since the blood that now flows in the head once flowed in the heel.

Even though the homage and favors from above often went to his head, Andersen never forgot what he saw on his way up. He always had a sharp eye for hypocrisy and inhumanity, wherever he encountered it. His experiences were incorporated into what he wrote, both as a source of inspiration and as something that remained traumatically suppressed. The great breadth of his social experiences and the subsequent breaches in his identity and emotional life created his tremendous sense of humor, his sharp irony, and his enormous capacity for empathy.

Hans Christian Andersen died on 4 August 1875 at the summer residence of the wealthy Jewish Melchior family. The estate, known as Rolighed (Tranquility), was located in Østerbro (today part of Copenhagen, although then the estate lay outside the city). For many years Andersen had been a permanent guest of the Melchiors, and during his final difficult illness Dorothea Melchior tended him. She also wrote down his last diary entries, which he dictated to her. The cause of death was determined to be liver cancer. Andersen was buried in the Collin family plot at Assistens Cemetery in Copenhagen. Several years after Andersen's death, a public debate arose about the way in which the Collin family had treated the author. Consequently, a descendant of the Collins had the family grave marker moved so that today only Andersen's headstone stands at the site.

Letters:

Breve til og fra H. C. Andersen, 3 volumes, edited by C. St. A. Bille and Nikolaj Bøgh (Copenhagen: C. A. Reitzel, 1877–1878);

H. C. Andersens Brevveksling med Edvard og Henriette Collin, 6 volumes, edited by C. Behrend and H. Topsøe-Jensen (Copenhagen: Munksgaard, 1933–1937);

H. C. Andersens Brevveksling med Henriette Hanck 1830–1846, edited by Svend Larsen, in *Anderseniana,* nos. 9–13 (Odense: Odense Bys Museer, 1941–1946);

H. C. Andersen: Brevveksling med Jonas Collin den Ældre og andre Medlemmer af det Collinske Hus, 3 volumes, edited by Topsøe-Jensen (Copenhagen: Levin & Munksgaard, 1945–1948);

H. C. Andersen og Horace E. Scudder: En Brevveksling, edited by Jean Hersholt, with notes by Waldemar Westergaard and an afterword by Topsøe-Jensen (Copenhagen: Gyldendal, 1948); translated as *The Andersen–Scudder Letters: Hans Christian Andersen's Correspondence with Horace Elisha Scudder* (Berkeley & Los Angeles: University of California Press, 1949);

H. C. Andersen og Henriette Wulff: En Brevveksling, 3 volumes, edited by Topsøe-Jensen (Odense: Flensted, 1959–1960);

H. C. Andersens Breve til Carl B. Lorck, edited by Topsøe-Jensen, in *Fynske Studier,* no. 8 (Odense: Odense Bys Museer, 1969);

H. C. Andersens brevveksling med Lucie og B.S. Ingemann, 3 volumes, edited, with an introduction and commentary, by Kirsten Dreyer (Copenhagen: Tusculanum, 1997);

Mein edler, theurer Grossherzog! Briefwechsel zwischen Hans Christian Andersen und Grossherzog Carl Alexander von Sachsen-Weimar-Eisenach, edited by Ivy York Möller-Christensen and Ernst Möller-Christensen (Göttingen: Wallstein, 1998).

Bibliographies:

Birger Frank Nielsen, *H. C. Andersen Bibliografi: Digterens danske Værker 1822–1875* (Copenhagen: Hagerup, 1942);

Elias Bredsdorff, *Danish Literature in English Translation: With a Special Hans Christian Andersen Supplement–A Bibliography* (Copenhagen: Munksgaard, 1950), pp. 121–194;

Bredsdorff, "A Critical Guide to the Literature on Hans Christian Andersen," *Scandinavica,* 6 (1967): 108–125;

Sv. Juel Møller and others, *Bidrag til H. C. Andersens Bibliografi,* 11 volumes (Copenhagen: Det kongelige Bibliotek, 1967–1978);

Aage Jørgensen, *H. C. Andersen litteraturen 1875–1968* (Aarhus: Akademisk Boghandel, 1970);

Ivy York Möller-Christensen, "Tekster på tysk af og om H. C. Andersen 1831–1850," in *Den gyldne trekant: H. C. Andersens gennembrud i Tyskland 1831–1850* (Odense: Odense Universitetsforlag, 1992), pp. 305–401;

Jørgensen, *H. C. Andersen-litteraturen 1969–1994* (Odense: H. C. Andersens Hus, 1995).

Biographies:

Robert Nisbet Bain, *Hans Christian Andersen: A Biography* (London: Lawrence & Bullen / New York: Dodd, Mead, 1895);

Nicolai Bøgh, *Fra H. C. Andersens Barndoms- og Ungdomsliv,* in *Personalhistorisk Tidsskrift,* second series, 5 (Copenhagen, 1905), pp. 58–79;

Signe Toksvig, *The Life of Hans Christian Andersen* (London: Macmillan, 1933);

Fredrik Böök, *H. C. Andersen: En levnadsteckning* (Stockholm: Albert Bonnier, 1938); translated by George C. Schoolfield as *Hans Christian Andersen: A Biography* (Norman: University of Oklahoma Press, 1962);

Rumer Godden, *Hans Christian Andersen* (London: Stratford Library, 1955);

Monica Stirling, *The Wild Swan: The Life and Times of Hans Christian Andersen* (London: Collins, 1965);

Bo Grønbech, *H. C. Andersen: Levnedsløb–Digtning–Personlighed* (Copenhagen: Nyt Nordisk, 1971);

Reginald Spink, *Hans Christian Andersen and His World* (London: Thames & Hudson, 1972);

Elias Bredsdorff, *Hans Christian Andersen: The Story of His Life and Work 1805–1875* (London: Phaidon / New York: Scribner, 1975);

Klaus P. Mortensen, *Svanen og Skyggen: Historien om unge Andersen* (Copenhagen: Gad, 1989);

Alison Prince, *Hans Christian Andersen: The Fan Dancer* (London: Allison & Busby, 1998);

Jackie Wullschlager, *Hans Christian Andersen: The Life of a Storyteller* (London: Allen Lane / New York: Penguin, 2000);

Jens Andersen, *Andersen–en biografi,* 2 volumes (Copenhagen: Gyldendal, 2003); translated by Tiina Nunnally as *Hans Christian Andersen* (New York: Overlook, 2005).

References:

Søren Baggesen, "Individuation eller frelse? Om slutningen på H. C. Andersens eventyr 'Den lille Havfrue,'" *Kritik,* 1 (1967): 50–77;

Georg Brandes, "Andersens Eventyr," *Illustreret Tidende* (1869); reprinted in Elias Bredsdorff, *H. C. Andersen og Georg Brandes* (Copenhagen: Aschehoug, 1994);

Elias Bredsdorff, *H. C. Andersen og Charles Dickens: Et Venskab og dets Opløsning* (Copenhagen: Rosenkilde og Bagger, 1951);

Bredsdorff, *H. C. Andersen og England* (Copenhagen: Rosenkilde og Bagger, 1954);

Hans Brix, *H. C. Andersen og hans Eventyr* (Copenhagen: Det Schubothske Forlag, 1907);

Mogens Brøndsted, "Livsrejsen: Omkring H. C. Andersens 'I Sverrig'" (Copenhagen: Danske Studiert, 1967), pp. 5–45;

Beth Wagner Brust, *The Amazing Paper Cuttings of Hans Christian Andersen,* Books for Young Readers (New York: Ticknor & Fields, 1994);

Edvard Collin, *H. C. Andersen og det Collinske Huus* (Copenhagen: C. A. Reitzel, 1882);

Erik Dal, *Danske H. C. Andersen–illustrationer 1835–1975* (Copenhagen: Forum, 1975);

Dal, *Udenlandske H. C. Andersen-illustrationer: 100 billeder fra 1838 til 1968* (Copenhagen: Det Berlingske Bogtrykkeri, 1969);

Johan de Mylius, *Forvandlingens pris: H. C. Andersen og hans eventyr* (Copenhagen: Høst, 2004);

de Mylius, *H. C. Andersen: Mit Danmark* (Copenhagen: Høst & Søn, 2001);

de Mylius, *H. C. Andersen. Papirklip / Paper Cuts* [bilingual edition] (Copenhagen: Aschehoug, 2000);

de Mylius, *H. C. Andersen-liv og værk. En tidstavle 1805–1875* (Copenhagen: Aschehoug, 1993); revised and enlarged as *H. C. Andersens liv. Dag for dag* (Copenhagen: Aschehoug, 1998);

de Mylius, *Hans Christian Andersen: On Copenhagen* (Copenhagen: Aschehoug, 1997);

de Mylius, *"Hr. Digter Andersen": Liv, digtning, meninger* (Copenhagen: Gad, 1995);

de Mylius, *Myte og roman: H. C. Andersens romaner mellem romantik og realisme: En traditionshistorisk undersøgelse* (Copenhagen: Gyldendal, 1981);

de Mylius, Aage Jørgensen, and Viggo Hjørnager Pedersen, eds., *Andersen og Verden / Andersen and the World. Indlæg fra den første internationale H. C. Andersen-konference: 25.–31. august 1991* (Odense: H. C. Andersen Center / Odense University Press, 1993);

de Mylius, Jørgensen, and Pedersen, eds., *Hans Christian Andersen: A Poet in Time–Papers from the Second International H. C. Andersen Conference 29 July to 2 August, 1996* (Odense: H. C. Andersen Center / Odense University Press, 1999);

Heinrich Detering, "Geistige Amphibien–Hans Christian Andersen," in *Das offene Geheimnis. Zur literarischen Produktivität eines Tabus von Winckelmann bis zu Thomas Mann* (Göttingen: Wallstein, 1994), pp. 175–232;

Arne Duve, *H. C. Andersens hemmelighet* (Oslo: Psychopress, 1969);

Duve, *Symboliken i H. C. Andersens eventyr* (Oslo: Psychopress, 1967);

Bo Grønbech, *H. C. Andersens Eventyrverden* (Copenhagen: Povl Branner, 1945);

Kjeld Heltoft, *H. C. Andersens billedkunst* (Copenhagen: Gyldendal, 1969);

Hjalmar Helweg, *H. C. Andersen. En psykiatrisk Studie* (Copenhagen: H. Hagerup, 1954);

Gustav Hetsch, *H. C. Andersen og Musiken* (Copenhagen: H. Hagerup, 1930);

Tage Høeg, *H. C. Andersens Ungdom* (Copenhagen: Levin & Munksgaard, 1934);

H. St. Holbeck, *H. C. Andersens Religion* (Copenhagen: Det Schønbergske Forlag, 1947);

Elisabeth Hude, *Henriette Hanck og H. C. Andersen. Skribentinden og digteren* (Odense: Flensted, 1958);

Anker Jensen, *Studier over H. C. Andersens Sprog* (Haderslev: Carl Nielsen, 1929);

Jørgen Bonde Jensen, *H. C. Andersen og genrebilledet* (Copenhagen: Babette, 1993);

Søren Kierkegaard, *Af en endnu Levendes Papirer* (Copenhagen: C. A. Reitzel, 1838);

Else Marie Kofod, *De vilde svaner og andre folkeeventyr: Sidestykker til syv af H. C. Andersens eventyr,* Foreningen Danmarks Folkeminders Skrifter, no. 86 (Copenhagen: Forlaget Folkeminder, 1989);

Niels Kofoed, *H. C. Andersen og B. S. Ingemann. Et livsvarigt venskab* (Copenhagen: Reitzel, 1992);

Kofoed, *Studier i H. C. Andersens fortællekunst* (Copenhagen: Munksgaard, 1967);

Wolfgang Lederer, *The Kiss of the Snow Queen: Hans Christian Andersen and Man's Redemption by Woman* (Berkeley, Los Angeles & London: University of California Press, 1986);

Martin Lotz, *Eventyrbroen: Psykoanalytiske essays om H. C. Andersen* (Copenhagen: Gyldendal, 1988);

Tove Barfoed Møller, *Teaterdigteren H. C. Andersen og "Meer end Perler og Guld": En dramaturgisk-musikalsk undersøgelse* (Odense: Odense Universitetsforlag, 1995);

Eigil Nyborg, *Den indre linie i H. C. Andersens eventyr: En psykologisk studie* (Copenhagen: Gyldendal, 1962);

H. G. Olrik, *Hans Christian Andersen: Undersøgelser og Kronikker 1925–1944* (Copenhagen: H. Hagerup, 1945);

Ulrich Horst Petersen, *I H. C. Andersens verden* (Copenhagen: Gyldendal, 1977);

Elith Reumert, *H. C. Andersen og det Melchiorske Hjem* (Copenhagen: H. Hagerup, 1924);

Reumert, *H. C. Andersen som han var* (Copenhagen: H. Hagerup, 1925);

Sven Hakon Rossel, ed., *Hans Christian Andersen: Danish Writer and Citizen of the World* (Amsterdam: Rodopi, 1996);

Paul V. Rubow, *H. C. Andersens Eventyr: Forhistorien–Idé og Form–Sprog og Stil* (Copenhagen: Levin & Munksgaard, 1927);

Steven P. Sondrup, ed., *H. C. Andersen: Old Problems and New Readings* (Odense: H. C. Andersen Center & University of Southern Denmark Press / Provo: Brigham Young University, 2004);

Peer E. Sørensen, *H. C. Andersen & Herskabet: Studier i borgerlig krisebevidsthed* (Grenå: GMT, 1972);

Villy Sørensen, "De djævelske traumer. Om H. C. Andersens romaner," in *Hverken–eller. Kritiske betragtninger* (Copenhagen: Gyldendal, 1961), pp. 136–157;

Sørensen, "Digter og filosof," in his *Digtere og dæmoner: Fortolkninger og vurderinger* (Copenhagen: Gyldendal, 1959), pp. 10–22;

Sørenson, *Sørensen om Andersen,* edited by Torben Broshøm (Copenhagen: Gyldendal, 2004);

Rigmor Stampe, *H. C. Andersen og hans nærmeste Omgang* (Copenhagen: Aschehoug, 1918);

Helge Topsøe-Jensen, *Buket til Andersen: Bemærkninger til femogtyve Eventyr* (Copenhagen: Gad, 1971);

Topsøe-Jensen, *H. C. Andersen og andre Studier* (Odense: Odense Bys Museer, 1966);

Topsøe-Jensen, *Mit eget Eventyr uden Digtning: En Studie over H. C. Andersen som Selvbiograf* (Copenhagen: Gyldendal, 1940);

Topsøe-Jensen, *Omkring Levnedsbogen: En Studie over H. C. Andersen som Selvbiograf 1820–1845* (Copenhagen: Gyldendal, 1943);

Topsøe-Jensen, *Vintergrønt: Nye H. C. Andersen Studier* (Copenhagen: Gad, 1976).

Papers:

Hans Christian Andersen's letters and manuscripts are housed at the Danish Royal Library in Copenhagen (manuscripts, drawings, paper cuttings, editions); the Hans Christian Andersen Museum, Odense (manuscripts, drawings, paper cuttings, editions, personal belongings, and documents); and the Jean Hersholt Collection, Library of Congress, Washington, D.C.

Anders Arrebo

(2 January 1587 – 12 March 1637)

Peer E. Sørensen
University of Aarhus

(Translated by Marianne Stecher-Hansen)

WORKS: *En gantske kort Extract offuer den store Lycke og Seyeruinding, som den Herre Zebaoth moxen paa tre Maanderes tid, haffuer voris allern. Herre oc Konning, Konning Christian den III. Med velsignet udi Smaalandene ved Suerrige i sanguijsz befattet* (Copenhagen, 1611);

En Sørgelig ny Dict om Høyborne Førstindes Salig oc Høyloffllig Ihukommelse, Dronning Annae Catharinae, Fordum Danmarckes, Norges, Wenders oc Gothers etc. Dronning, Hendes Majestetes Christeligste oc Saligste Fredfart aff denne Verden, som skede paa Kiøbenhaffns Slot den 29. Martij vid 1 slet effter M. i Nærværendes Aar 1612 (Copenhagen, 1612);

En ny Dict om de Tegen, som Gud allermæctigste lader dagligen skinne, oc aabenbaris for Mennisken, huilcke der kand vel reegnis blant de Tegen, som skal fremgaa for Menniskens Søns tilkommelsis Dag (Copenhagen, ca. 1618);

Pest-Pulver eller Pestilentz Forgifft, som i denne farlige og megit skrøbelige Tid, seckerligen, i Aanden oc Sandhed, aff alle Guds Børn, inden oc vden Lircken, brugis kand, Pestilentzen der met, enten slet af fordriffue oc forgiffue, eller oc endelig, til en evig Sundhed forvende (Copenhagen, 1618);

K. Davids Psaalter, sangvijz udsat, under hundrede oc nogle Melodier og Toner, som I vore Danske Kirker oc christelige Huse brugelige og velbekante ere (Copenhagen: Printed by Salomon Sartor, 1623); revised as *Davids Psaalter: Anden Edition paa ny offuerseet oc met Noderne forbedret,* published with *Nogle udvalde Bøner, som mand kand bruge om Morgenen oc Aftenen, oc ellers effter Tidsens Leylighed* (Copenhagen: Printed by Henrich Waldkirch, 1627);

Guillaume de Salluste, seigneur du Bartas, *Hexaëmeron rhytmico-danicum. Det er: Verdens første Uges sex Dages præctige og mæctige Gierninger, med den allerhøiste Skaberes alting-formuende Finger paa det allermesterligste skabte og beredde, paa heroiske Riim-maade, af Mose første og andet Capitel* (Copenhagen: Christen Andersen Arrebo, printed by Henrick Gøde, 1661);

Torcular Christi eller Jesu Christi Pinis, Døds oc Begraffvelsis Historia, befattet udi 15 Prædickener nu for Liuset fremstillet af Chr. Andersøn Arrøboe (Copenhagen: Printed by Jørgen Lamprecht, 1670);

Courtesy of the Danish Royal Library, Copenhagen

Ossa rediviva, det er, den underbarlige høytrøstelige oc aandrige Siun om de tørre døde Been, som Propheten Ezechiel paa én aaben Marck hafver seet liggende, oc ved Guds Søns Ord tilhaabe samlet oc lefvende giort, udi XV Prædickner eenfoldigen forklaret oc udlagt, igiennem seet oc til Trycken forferdiget aff Christen Anderssøn Arrøbo (Copenhagen: Printed by Daniel Paulli, 1680).

Collections: *Mester Anders Christensen Arrebos Levnet og Skrifter,* volume 2: *Skrifter i Udvalg,* edited by Holger Frederik Rørdam (Copenhagen: Samfundet til den Danske Literaturs Fremme, 1857);

Samlede Skrifter, 5 volumes, edited by Vagn Lundgaard Simonsen, Henrik Glahn, and Flemming Hovmann (Copenhagen: Danske sprog- og litteraturselskab/Munksgaard, 1965–1984).

The literary achievements of Anders Arrebo heralded a new era in Danish literature, marking the arrival of baroque poetry in Denmark. Arrebo is considered the first important Danish poet to break with the poetic forms of the Middle Ages by mastering and developing a metrical system, which is the norm in Germanic languages. Arrebo created the foundation for modern Danish poetry by consistently applying the accent principle to the construction of poetic stanzas (that is, regular alternation between stressed and unstressed syllables). His break with the traditions of the Middle Ages and late Middle Ages began in 1623 with his translation of the Book of Psalms and was further developed in the revised edition of 1627. This metrical reform departed from the medieval principle of versification, which was based on a common number of stressed syllables in the rhyming lines, filled out at random with the aid of unstressed syllables. With the writing of Arrebo, regular alternation between stressed and unstressed syllables became the principle for versification in Danish poetry. By achieving this reform, Arrebo opened Danish literature to European traditions and poetic forms.

Anders Christensen Arrebo was born on 2 January 1587 in Ærøskøbing, on the isle of Ærø; he was the son of Christen Andersen Arrebo, who died in 1606. Little is known about Arrebo's childhood and youth. In 1608 he became court chaplain at the Palace Church in Copenhagen; in 1610 he was granted the degree of Magister (Master). He married Else Jørgensdatter in 1611 and two years later became court chaplain at Frederiksborg Castle. Beginning in 1612 he wrote occasional poems, including tributes to the royal family. He rose quickly in the church hierarchy and in March 1618 was named bishop of Trondheim in Norway by Christian IV, the Danish king. (At this time Norway was part of Denmark.) As bishop, Arrebo was zealous and authoritative and quickly made enemies. In July 1622 he was removed from his position and charged with lack of respect for the episcopal dignity. He was accused of having loose morals and leading a frivolous life. The king presided at the hearings, but the judgment was not fair, and the charges remained unproven.

Arrebo then lived for several years in Malmö. There he worked on translating the Book of Psalms, which was popular in Europe in the 1600s. In 1620 he published *Trende Psalmer, som han Gud til Ære og sit Huses Opbyggelse daglig haver forlystet sig udi,* a sample of his translation, copies of which are no longer extant. In 1623 he published *K. Davids Psaalter, sangvijz udsat, under hundrede oc nogle Melodier og Toner* (K[ing] David's Psalms, Arranged for Song, with More than a Hundred Melodies and Tunes). The introduction included weighty eulogies by the anatomist Caspar Bartholin and Jesper Rasmussen Brochmand, later bishop of Zealand. The selection of melodies is traditional and orthodox. As a good Lutheran, Arrebo used the old Reformation tunes of the sixteenth century from the hymnal of Hans Thomissøn and the gradual of Niels Jespersen, and not the Calvinistic tunes of Claude Goudimels, which were popular at that time. The translation is modern in form and has no connection with the poetry of Arrebo's youth, which was quite traditional and adhered to the versification principles of the late Middle Ages. Arrebo's efforts to renew Danish literature were especially concentrated on developing a rhetorical style similar to the best international models and on creating a national metrical standard; his work was an extension of the attempts during the Renaissance to convert Latin poetry to the mother tongue. In the preface to his translation he boasts, "Isen i slig Maade første Gang brydes" (In this way the ice is broken for the first time), expressing his pride in the use of the new metrical system. Arrebo was the first Danish poet to create an entire work based on regular stanzas, in which the corresponding lines in the various stanzas have the same number of stressed and unstressed syllables. And he did this a year before Martin Opitz published his *Buch von der deutschen Poeterey* (Book on German Poetics, 1624), which in a similar way revolutionized the metrical system for versification in German.

The ideal for Danish poets at the beginning of the seventeenth century was first and foremost Latin poetry, but also other European poetry. It was not possible to translate Latin verse directly into the national language, partly because only the medieval stanza, with its free and random distribution of unstressed syllables, was known in the Danish language. The classical, regulated system of versification belonged to Latin poetry and to the Romance-language verse of the Renaissance. The desire to introduce the Latin and Romance metrical system bore another complication. The Latin stanza is built on syllable quantity (that is, the difference between long and short syllables), while the Danish stanza is built on quality, or variations in stress. It is Arrebo's insight into this difference that makes his translation so important. He was the first to master the new metrical system and to possess the linguistic prowess to use it convincingly in an entire work of poetry. In addition, he was able to place the syllabic stresses so that the natural intonation of the words was preserved in the stanzas. In this light, Arrebo's translation of the Psalms is a poetic achievement unequaled in the history of Danish literature. In 1624 he received royal privilege for a future edition. The second edition was published in 1627, and in it his poetic technique was further improved.

Despite the earlier judgment against him, Arrebo obtained royal permission to apply for another clerical post in 1625; the following year he was named the parish pastor in Vordingborg on the Danish island of Zealand. Two of the sermons he wrote there were published posthumously by Christian Andersen Arrebo, his son. *Torcular Christi* (Persecution of Christ, 1670) is about the Passion, during which Christ bitterly reflected on his own fate, and *Ossa rediviva* (The Resurrected Bones, 1680) concerns Christ's resurrection from the dead. Both works were written in sonorous baroque prose. The style is characterized by hyperbolic figures of speech, such as parallelisms, antitheses, and tautologies, just as they are pervaded by orthodox thought and orthodox allegories in their sense of the world and the Bible.

At the request of Chancellor Christian Friis, who appreciated his mastery of poetic meter and rhetoric, Arrebo worked in Vordingborg on a Danish interpretation of a French magnum opus about the creation of the world, *La Semaine* (The Week, 1578), by Guillaume de Salluste, seigneur du Bartas. *La Semaine* was in those days admired and translated throughout Europe. Arrebo's version can be considered a part of the effort on Danish soil to create an epic with Christian themes similar to the classical epic, in which the pagan world is replaced for the most part by a Christian world. Considered Arrebo's principal work, it remained incomplete at the time of his death and was published posthumously by his son. Arrebo did not have time to translate the seventh day of the Creation; thus, the title reads *Hexaëmeron rhytmico-danicum. Det er: Verdens første Uges sex Dages præctige og mæctige Gierninger* (The Six-Day Work in Danish Verse. It Is the World's First Week of Six Days of Magnificent and Powerful Deeds, 1661). In his labyrinthine and imaginative composition Arrebo developed an elaborate style that was of crucial importance for Danish baroque poetry until some point in the eighteenth century, when the Classicists suppressed the rhetorical style of the baroque. Yet, Ludvig Holberg praised Arrebo's contribution and pronounced him "en af de største Poeter, ja. Den som allerførst har skreven sirligen i dansk Poesi" (one of the greatest poets, yes, the very first to write meticulous Danish poetry).

Arrebo's free adaptation of style and content in comparison with du Bartas's text makes *Hexaëmeron* an independent literary work that may be read and studied without constant comparisons to its French original. Arrebo attempted to avoid the French alexandrines of *La Semaine,* instead basing his translation on Virgil's hexameter. He renewed this verse form by combining Classical and new prosody and by pairing hexameters with masculine internal rhymes before the caesura and female end rhymes. In this way Arrebo tied the stanzas together two and two. Arrebo invented this double-rhymed hexameter and first used it in the "Fortalen til Skaberen" (Foreword to the Creator) and in the description of the first day. But in the second day of the Creation he retreated to the French alexandrines–although without mastering the presentation of this poetic form. It was Arrebo's intention to use the hexameter again in the concluding seventh song, but he died before reaching that goal. Thus, *Hexaëmeron* is not metrically perfect. It is marked by a restless and indecisive experimentation with the metrical system.

Hexaëmeron is a comprehensive work of scholarship in which Arrebo sought to describe God's entire creation. For this purpose he used several sources not found in du Bartas's text. Throughout the work Arrebo mixes religious dogma with his own scholarly reflections. He describes a multitude of natural phenomena and vital necessities as being suitable for people in making the case that God created the world for human beings. The Danish poet demonstrated independent thinking in his handling of this encyclopedic material. Du Bartas's references to French nature and wildlife are replaced in Arrebo's text by Danish Norwegian representations of entirely different natural environs and wildlife, described for the first time in Danish literature. The Book of Genesis was Arrebo's basic source, but he constantly refers to various works of Moses, David, Aristotle, and many others. He also integrates findings from his own time in the fields of anatomy (Bartholin), cartography, botany, zoology, physiology, and astronomy (Tycho Brahe). Furthermore, Arrebo employs the repertoire of the Classical mythology as poetical-rhetorical subject matter, especially Ovid's *Fasti* (Calendar, A.D. 8) and *Metamorphoses* (A.D. 8). Throughout, theology dominates as the science of sciences. At that time natural science had not yet been singled out as an independent field, and thus it was used for Christian edification.

This encyclopedic learning, its inclusion in the biblical story of the Creation, and Arrebo's theological dogmatism all demonstrate that *Hexaëmeron* represented an important cultural ambition on the part of the chancellor and the author: they wanted to produce a great work of art. The poem is an extension of European Renaissance poetics, specifically an attempt to introduce the works of the Classical epic poets (Homer, Virgil, Ovid, and Hesiod) and their Renaissance imitators (Pierre de Ronsard, Ludovico Ariosto, Torquato Tasso, and Luíz Vaz de Camões) to a Danish context and thereby transform and inspire Danish literature so that it could come up to par with the foremost international works. In the midst of an era of Lutheran orthodoxy, Arrebo's work was inspired by a Renaissance optimism that pointed beyond the horizon of orthodox domestic theologians.

In *Hexaëmeron* the reader follows the story of the Creation from the beginning, the release of the world from chaos on the first day, until the creation of Adam and Eve on the sixth day. The poem moves from the origin of matter and light by way of the creation of sky, water, plants, stars, fish, and birds to the appearance of other animals and the human being. The thematic core is the transition from chaos to cosmos. From first to last the work is saturated with theological notions of the order of things. The world is presented as an expression of the loving care and infinite wisdom of the Creator. For that reason, there is a constant correlation between observation and interpretation. A marginal note at the beginning of the text reads, "Alle Creatur ere kun jdel Bogstafver oc Ord for vore Herre" (All creatures are only letters and words for Our Father). In order to comprehend the world in its abundance, it must be interpreted. What is observed is appreciated based on the theological master science, which constantly demonstrates that the Creator wants the best for mankind. Therefore, observation and interpretation always conclude in eulogy. The text is characterized by allegorical thinking, which still survived in the poetry of the seventeenth century, although Luther had renounced it. Everything in the poem has several deeper meanings *(sensus spiritualis)* of a theological nature that cannot be perceived by the senses but must be interpreted via theological thinking, revealing meanings that exist above and beyond the literal meanings *(sensus litteralis)* of the words. In the beginning was the Word, says Genesis, and God's word has creative power in the poem: "Himlens gandske Hærskare, / koster ickun et Ord" (All of the heavenly flocks, / take only a word). Thus, the poet follows in the footsteps of the Creator and makes himself a contemporary of the creative task. With his words that only approximate the divine Word, the poet re-creates in his poem the actual Creation. God is the original author, and Arrebo recomposes God's work. In this manner Arrebo portrays himself as a typical baroque poet: his work does not create a new world but rather repeats that which is already created. The author is not a creator, but a re-creator. The work of art, in this case *Hexaëmeron,* is a paean to what is already created.

Painting of Arrebo on display at Vor Frue Kirke (Church of Our Lady) in Vordingborg, where he served as pastor from 1626 until his death in 1637 (from P. M. Mitchell, A History of Danish Literature, *1957; Scandinavian Studies Library, University of Washington)*

Anders Arrebo's epic poem was the most ambitious effort in the Danish baroque period to create in the Danish language a work of art to be a match for the works of great epic poetry of the luminous literature of antiquity. Arrebo died in Vordingborg on 12 March 1637, before his epic was completed, but with its later publication by his son, it came to exert crucial stylistic and rhetorical influence on subsequent Danish baroque literature. In fact, several seventeenth-century authors and scholars had access to the manuscript before its publication in 1661. Arrebo's baroque poetry is the most notable milestone in Danish baroque literature.

Biography:

Holger Frederik Rørdam, *Mester Anders Christensen Arrebos Levnet og Skrifter,* volume 1: *Levnet* (Copenhagen: Samfundet til den Danske Literaturs Fremme, 1857).

References:

Gustav Albeck and F. J. Billeskov Jansen, *Dansk litteraturhistorie,* volume 1: *Fra runerne til Johannes Ewald* (Copenhagen: Politiken, 1964), pp. 208–215;

Hans Brix, "Anders Christensen Arrebos *Hexaëmeron,*" in his *Analyser og Problemer,* volume 5 (Copenhagen: Gyldendal, 1933);

Jansen, *Danmarks Digtekunst,* volume 1 (Copenhagen: Munksgaard, 1944);

P. M. Mitchell, *A History of Scandinavian Literature* (Copenhagen: Gyldendal, 1957), pp. 60, 63, 67, 72;

Karl Mortensen, *Studier over ældre dansk Versbygning* (Copenhagen: Det Nordiske forlag, 1901);

Erik A. Nielsen, "Dyrenes betydning–Anders Arrebos muntre teologi," in *Kamp må der til: Festskrift til Ole Jensen,* edited by Niels H. Brønnum and others (Hadsten: Mimer, 1997);

Nielsen, "Lyst-forundret: Anders Arrebo: *Hexaëmeron,*" in *Læsninger i dansk litteratur,* volume 1 (1200–1820), edited by Ulrik Lehrmann and Lise Præstgaard Andersen (Odense: Odense University Press, 1998), pp. 111–127;

Carl S. Petersen and Richard Paulli, *Illustreret dansk Litteraturhistorie,* volume 1: *Den danske Litteratur fra Folkevandringstiden indtil Holberg* (Copenhagen: Gyldendal, 1929), pp. 496–512;

Holger Frederik Rørdam, "Aktstykker og andre Bidrag til hans Historie," *Ny kirkehistoriske Samlinger,* 3 (1864–1866): 642–658;

Rørdam, "Danske Bearbejdelser af Davids Salmer i det 17. Aarhundrede," *Ny kirkehistoriske Samlinger,* 1 (1857–1859): 538–583;

Carl F. Rosenberg, *Nordboernes Aandsliv,* volume 3 (Copenhagen: Samfundet til den Danske Literaturs Fremme, 1885), pp. 509–527;

Vagn Lundgaard Simonsen, *Kildehistoriske studier i Anders Arrebos forfatterskab* (Copenhagen: Munksgaard, 1955);

Peer E. Sørensen, "Reformpoesi og sprogpatriotisme," in *Dansk litteraturhistorie,* edited by Søren Kaspersen and others, volume 3: *Stænderkultur og enevælde, 1620–1746* (Copenhagen: Gyldendal, 1983), pp. 109–113, 126–129;

Eira Storstein and Sørensen, *Den barokke tekst* (Frederiksberg: Dansklærerforeningen, 1999);

Ejnar Thomsen, *Barokken i dansk digtning* (Copenhagen: Munksgaard, 1971), pp. 73–87.

Jens Baggesen

(15 February 1764 - 3 October 1826)

Henrik Blicher
University of Copenhagen

(Translated by Tara F. Chace)

BOOKS: *Comiske Fortællinger* (Copenhagen: A. F. Stein, 1785);

Poesier. Første Samling (Copenhagen: J. F. Schultz, 1785)–includes "Da jeg var lille";

En ny og sandfærdig Historie, om Oprindelsen til Bog-Censur; hvorlunde den blev opfunden af en gammel Borgemester i Kallundborg, som ikke kunde lide, at man 100 Aar i Forveien havde fortalt en meget uskyldig Historie. Efter ringe Evne, paa Riim forfattet af Simon Simonsen uværdig Substitut ibidem. Med den dybsindige Magister Ypsilons sprænglærde Anmærkninger, in Minerva (Copenhagen: J. F. Schultz, 1786);

Holger Danske. Opera i tre Acter (Copenhagen: J. F. Schultz, 1789);

Ungdomsarbeider, 2 volumes (Copenhagen: J. F. Schultz, 1791);

Labyrinten eller Reise giennem Tydskland, Schweitz og Frankerig, 2 volumes (Copenhagen: J. F. Schultz, 1792, 1793); volume 1, revised as *Digtervandringer eller Reiser i Europa i Begyndelsen af det attende og mod Enden af det nittende Aarhundrede* (Copenhagen: F. Brummer, 1807);

Ordene til Concerten, som opføres i Frue Kirke 17. Oct. 1792 (Copenhagen: N. Møller, 1792);

Erik Eiegod. En Oper (Copenhagen: J. F. Morthorst, 1798);

Jens Baggesens Samtlige Værker. Forhen trykte og hidtil utrykte, samlede, sidste Gang rettede og heel igiennem med Anmærkninger forsynede udgivne af ham selv (Copenhagen: F. Brummer, 1801 [i.e., 1800]);

Parthenäis oder Die Alpenreise. Ein idyllisches Epos in neun Gesängen (Hamburg & Mainz: G. Vollmer, 1803); revised and enlarged as *Parthenäis, oder Die Alpenreise. Ein idyllisches Epos in zwölf Gesängen* (Amsterdam: Kunst- und Industrie-Comptoir, 1806); revised in *Jens Baggesen's poetische Werke in deutscher Sprache,* 5 volumes, edited by Carl Baggesen and August Baggesen (Leipzig: F. A. Brockhaus, 1836); translated into Danish by Flemming Dahl as *Parthenaïs eller Alperejsen* (Copenhagen: Borgen, 1965);

Jens Baggesen (lithograph by Tegner & Kittendorf, based on the 1806 pastel by Christian Hornemann; courtesy of the Danish Royal Library, Copenhagen)

Gedichte, 2 volumes (Hamburg: F. Perthes, 1803);

Skiemtsomme Riimbreve (Copenhagen: F. Brummer, 1807 [i.e., 1806]);

Eventyrer og Comiske Fortællinger, 2 volumes (Copenhagen: F. Brummer, 1807 [i.e., 1806, 1807]);

Giengangeren og han selv eller Baggesen over Baggesen ved Forfatteren af Riimbrevene. Med et Tillæg (Copenhagen: F. Brummer, 1807);

Nye Blandede Digte (Copenhagen: F. Brummer, 1807);

Nyeste Blandede Digte (Copenhagen: F. Brummer, 1808);

Heideblumen. Vom Verfasser der Parthenaïs. Nebst einigen Proben der Oceania (Amsterdam: Kunst- und Industrie- Comptoir, 1808); *Oceania* verses translated into Danish by Dahl as *Oceania* (Copenhagen: Strube, 1968);

Prøve af Ny Sange for Danske Sømænd (Copenhagen: F. Brummer, 1808);

Der Karfunkel oder Klingklingel-Almanach. Ein Taschenbuch für vollendete Romantiker und angehende Mystiker, auf das Jahr der Gnade 1810 (Tübingen: J. G. Cotta, 1809); reprinted, with an introduction by Gerhard Schultz, Seltene Texte aus der deutschen Romantik, no. 4 (Bern: Lang, 1978);

Taschenbuch für Liebende (Tübingen: J. G. Cotta, 1810);

Flaskebrev fra Knud Vidfadme, hin Sjællandsfar, til sine Landsmænd, d.d. 28 januar 1808 (Copenhagen: F. Brummer, 1811);

Om Jøderne. En Anmeldelse (Copenhagen: A. Seidelin, 1813);

Poetiske Epistler (Copenhagen: J. R. Thiele, 1814);

Trylle-Harpen. Originalt Syngespil (Copenhagen: B. Brünnich, 1816);

Rosenblade med Et Par Torne (Copenhagen: H. F. Popp, 1819);

Adam und Eva oder die Geschichte des Sündenfalls. Ein humoristisches Epos in zwölf Büchern (Leipzig: G. J. Göschen, 1826);

Fragmente von Jens Baggesen, aus dem literarischen Nachlasse des Verfassers, edited by August Baggesen (Copenhagen: C. A. Reitzel, 1855);

Jens Baggesen's philosophischer Nachlass, 2 volumes, edited by Carl Baggesen (Zurich: F. Schulthess / Copenhagen: C. A. Reitzel, 1858, 1863);

Til Minde om Jens Baggesen paa hans hundredeaarige Fødselsdag d. 15. Febr. 1864, preface by August Baggesen (Copenhagen: Gyldendal, 1864);

Blätter aus dem Stammbuch Jens Baggesen's, 1787–1797, edited by Theodor Baggesen and Eduard Grupe (Marburg: Ehrhardt, 1893);

Reisen til Korsør (Copenhagen: P. Sørensen, 1925).

Editions and Collections: *Jens Baggesens danske Værker,* 12 volumes, edited by Carl Baggesen, August Baggesen, and Caspar Johannes Boye (Copenhagen: A. Seidelin, 1827–1832); second edition, 12 volumes, edited by August Baggesen (Copenhagen: C. A. Reitzel, 1845–1847);

Labyrinthen. Digtervandringer, 4 volumes, edited by Carl Baggesen, August Baggesen, and Boye (Copenhagen: A. Seidelin, 1829–1830);

Jens Baggesen's poetische Werke in deutscher Sprache, 5 volumes, edited by Carl Baggesen and August Baggesen (Leipzig: F. A. Brockhaus, 1836);

Digte, edited by August Baggesen (Copenhagen: C. A. Reitzel, 1857);

Udvalgte Digte, introduction and notes by Kristian Arentzen (Copenhagen: A. F. Høst, 1876);

Udvalgte komiske og satiriske Poesier, introduction and notes by Arentzen (Copenhagen: A. F. Høst, 1878);

Værker, 4 volumes (Copenhagen: Nyt dansk Forlagskonsortium, 1879–1882);

Poetiske Fortællinger (Copenhagen: Nyt dansk Forlagskonsortium, 1884);

Jens Baggesens Poetiske Skrifter, 5 volumes, edited by August Arlaud (Copenhagen: J. H. Schubothe, 1889–1903);

Digte, edited, with an introduction, by Herman Schwanenflügel (Copenhagen: Foreningen "Fremtiden," 1890);

Udvalgte Digtninger (Copenhagen: Gyldendal, 1907)–comprises *Comiske Fortællinger, Skiemtsomme Riimbreve,* and *Blandede Digte;*

Labyrinten eller Reise giennem Tydskland, Schweitz og Frankerig, edited by Torben Brostrøm (Copenhagen: Gyldendal, 1965);

Epigrammatisk Billedbog, edited by Leif Ludwig Albertsen, Baggeseniana, no. 5 (Copenhagen: Lademann, 1974).

OTHER: *Sange til den 26de november 1785,* by Baggesen and others (Copenhagen: N. Møller, 1785);

Ludvig Holberg, *Niels Klims underjordiske Reise,* translated by Baggesen (Copenhagen: J. F. Schultz, 1789);

Benoît Joseph Marsollier des Vivetières, *Adolph og Clara,* adapted by Baggesen (Copenhagen: J. F. Morthorst, 1801);

Alexandre Duval, *Arrestanten eller Et Syngespil i I Act,* adapted by Baggesen (Copenhagen: J. Irgen, 1801);

Forhandlinger ved Festen i Kiøbenhavn d. 11 decemb. 1811, by Baggesen and others (Copenhagen: F. Brummer, 1812);

Sange for Studenterforeningen, by Baggesen and others (Copenhagen: J. R. Thiele, 1822);

Christian Molbech, ed., *Yduns Aarsgave. Udvalgte danske lyriske Digte,* by Baggesen and others (Copenhagen: Gyldendal, 1854).

As a talented young man, Jens Baggesen came into contact with the Danish and Holstenian nobility in Copenhagen. He adapted to the cultural and social conventions of these circles with surprising poise. In fact, one must look to Hans Christian Andersen to find a similar story of successful social climbing. Literary histories categorize Baggesen as a transitional figure whose work fluctuated between cosmopolitan Enlightenment writing and nationalistic Romanticism. The course of his life–with his countless travels, leave-takings, and new beginnings–looks just as erratic as his authorship. Baggesen's recitation piece "Da jeg var lille" (When I Was Little, 1785), which was translated by Henry Wadsworth Longfellow as "Childhood" (1844), has long served as the quintessential example of sentimentalism and of the author himself. The first stanza, and Longfellow's translation, read:

Der var en Tid, da jeg var meget lille,
Min hele Krop var knap en Alen lang:
Sødt, naar jeg den mig tænker, Taarer trille,
Og derfor tænker jeg den mangen Gang.

(There was a time when I was very small,
When my whole frame was but an ell in height;
Sweetly, as I recall it, tears do fall,
And therefore I recall it with delight.)

Baggesen was born on 15 February 1764 in the provincial town of Korsør on the west coast of Sjælland. His father, Bagge Baggesen, worked as a clerk at the town mill, and in this way his clever son picked up an almost calligraphic script, which proved useful. Jens came from a poor home, one that was characterized by his strongly religious mother, Anna Møller Baggesen. Although it was unusual for a child of his background, he was sent to the nearby Slagelse Grammar School in 1777.

In 1782 the poet Christen Pram described the young theology student Baggesen as "en Dreng, som har alle mulige Talenter til at blive en god og stor Digter . . . en underlig, enthusiastisk, melancholsk, ubeskrivelig En" (a boy, who has every possible talent to become a good and important poet . . . a strange, enthusiastic, melancholy, indescribable one). Not long after this time, Baggesen became the latest discovery in Copenhagen's literary circles. He was a regular visitor in Pram's household, which also included Pram's wife, Maria Magdalene Pram, ten years Baggesen's senior. He fell in love with her and extolled her as the chaste moon goddess, Selene.

Baggesen debuted as a classical poet in the middle of the 1780s and tried his hand at a variety of established genres. In his many ardent poems to Selene, the unattainably distant goddess of his love, he developed a Danish elegiac style based on classical foundations. Baggesen's elegies are grounded in the absence of the loved one, which becomes the lover's chance to show the scope of his longing. In a characteristic maneuver in "Savnet. Til Seline" (Longing. For Selene, 1787), the speaker of the poem takes representative delight in the rose in Selene's hair, the chain around her neck, and the lily at her breast, but he laments the fact that those same unfeeling objects have the opportunity of being close to her that he is not in a position to enjoy. Just as Ixion in Greek mythology was tricked into lying with a cloud that resembled Hera, the lover in "Savnet. Til Seline" is rewarded for his fervent advances only with optical illusions and insubstantial embraces. Another characteristic trait in the poem is the speaker's pronounced inability to express the boundless passion Selene has awakened in him.

The most noteworthy of the Selene poems is "Min anden Skabelse" (My Second Creation, 1785). The poem is strictly structured around the contrast between the situation before and after the protagonist's breakthrough as a sentimental lover, which is the truest condition of mankind. Before the breakthrough he exists only as a feeble body absorbed in his study of ancient ruins. After the breakthrough (his second creation)–like Petrarch's vision of Laura–everything is changed from then on. Not only does the change make him receptive to the divine loveliness of nature, but now he can also be touched by others' pain and can cry tears of empathy. The revelation also makes him poetically powerful. Selene is almighty but mortal; he can achieve immortality through his artistic production.

In 1784 Baggesen succeeded in getting as many as 1,175 subscribers for a planned volume called *Comiske Fortællinger* (Comical Tales, 1785). Johan Herman Wessel's mixture of racy comedy and elegant versification was one of the models for Baggesen's jovial tales, but according to the young author, that was only one side of his talent. The public expected more gaieties written in verse.

The verse tales belong to the early phase of Baggesen's authorship. The majority were published and republished before 1807. The often utterly absurd stories are typically set in a distant, indeterminate past, during the age of chivalry or in an Old Norse god's court, inhabited by life-like citizens from Baggesen's day. The tales typically take their point of departure from some relatively familiar story or anecdote. "Poesiens Oprindelse" (The Origin of Poetry) is drawn from Paul Mallet's 1766 French retelling of Snorri Sturluson's myth of the skaldic mead: the colorful story of the disguised Odin's journey to see the giants and bring home the priceless drink of poetry. The Old Norse myth serves, in a joking fashion, to demonstrate that Baggesen's contemporary world was populated by several minor poets and only a few great ones. Baggesen used the sources at his own discretion; the goal of his retelling was not to be true to the Old Norse version of the story but to have a bit of fun with the gods' humanity.

Der var en Tid, da jeg var meget lille,
Min hele Krop var knap en Alen lang;
Sødt, naar jeg den mig tænker, Taarer trille,
Og derfor tænker jeg den mangen Gang.

Jeg spøgede i min ømme Moders Arme,
Og sad til Hest paa bedste Faders Knæ,
Og kiendte Mismod, Uro, Grubler, Harme,
Saa lidt, som Penge, Græsk, og Galathee.

Da syntes mig, vor Jord var meget mindre,
Men og tillige meget mindre slem;
Da saae jeg Stiernerne, som Prikker, tindre,
Og ønskte Vinger, for at fange dem.

Manuscript for Baggesen's "Da jeg var lille" (When I Was Little), published in 1785 (courtesy of the Danish Royal Library, Copenhagen)

Med barnlig Andagt bad min unge Læbe
Den Bön, min fromme Moder lærte mig:
O gode Gud! o lad mig altid stræbe,
At være viis, og god, og lyde Dig!

Saa bad jeg for min Fader, for min Moder,
Og for min Söster, og den hele By;
Og for ukiendte Konge, og den Stodder,
Der gik mig krum og sukkende forbi.

De svandt, de svandt, de glade Barndoms Dage,
Min Rolighed, min Fryd, med dem svandt hen—
Jeg kun Erindringen har nu tilbage;
Gud! lad mig aldrig, aldrig tabe den!

Baggesen

Baggesen frequently imitated and parodied other literature, making his work thoroughly intertextual. For example, he wrote the long title for *En ny og sandfærdig Historie, om Oprindelsen til Bog-Censur* (A New and Truthful History, on the Origins of Book Censorship, 1786; revised as *Kallundborgs Krønike* [Kallundborg's Chronicle, 1791]), in imitation of an early edition of Ludvig Holberg's *Peder Paars* (1720), which in turn shows a dependence on the classical model of Virgil's *Aeneid* as broadside. At times, Baggesen's erudite jesting (or refined intertextuality) also takes the form of references to fictional characters from other of his works.

In his verse tales Baggesen shifted the stress from brief story development and situational comedy (Wessel's forte) to verbal comedy within the framework of a tale in elastic verse. From the popular German writer Christoph Martin Wieland, Baggesen had learned to manage a hodgepodge of disparate styles and to play on the whole gamut of emotions. His diction is by turns parodic, sentimental, and risqué. According to F. J. Billeskov Jansen, from a classical point of view this variability is a sign of decay. For recent scholars such as Marianne Stidsen, the absence of unity in Baggesen's diction is the most interesting aspect of his work because it ties him to such modern authors as Peter Laugesen and Dan Turèll. Finally, one might point out the audience as a neglected rhetorical category, whose presence in the poem the narrator constantly keeps in mind.

Baggesen soon gave up on his theological studies. His friendship with Christen Pram brought him into distinguished circles, especially into the sphere of Holstenian aristocracy. The patronage of powerful individuals such as Count Ernst Schimmelmann and Prince Frederik Christian of Augustenborg then became a convenient alternative to years of study in order to earn his bread and butter. The nobility valued Baggesen's poetry and his unique social talents. Through Schimmelmann and, especially, his wife, Charlotte, Baggesen met agricultural reformer J. L. Reventlow and his wife. A travelogue titled "Indenlandsk Reise 1787–1788," posthumously published in *Jens Baggersens Biograhie* (1843–1856), provides a preview of his later work, *Labyrinten, eller Reise giennem Tydskland, Schweitz og Frankerig* (The Labyrinth; or, A Journey through Germany, Switzerland, and France, 1792, 1793).

The unrhymed ode was another classical form that Baggesen employed. For Johannes Ewald (following Friedrich Gottlieb Klopstock's model) the ode had become synonymous with the most sublime form of lyrical poetry. In his odes Baggesen regularly employs a classical style, but the subjects vary, including tributes to a friend, a literary patron, Napoleon, and God. "Formastelsen. Til Grev Frederik Leopold Stolberg" (The Presumption. For Count Frederik Leopold Stolberg, 1787) is a loyal, perceptive account of the perilous path of inspiration between heaven and earth. Baggesen uses the symbolism of the high-flying Icarus to describe the similarity–but not the equivalence–between erotic temptation and poetic inspiration. Only after a five-stanza-long train of thought does he justify the preceding erotic short story with a bold flight and shy smiles. When contemplated as a theory of poetry, the poem equates the culmination of wet dreams with poetic impotence; that is, silence. It is as if Baggesen is saying that the sacred shall remain sacred, and the tangible shall remain tangible.

There was growing interest in Holberg, and the young Baggesen was entrusted with retelling Holberg's 1741 Latin-language travel account about Niels Klim in modern Danish. In 1789 the result, *Niels Klims underjordiske Reise,* was published in a deluxe edition with illustrations by painter and academy professor Nicolai Abildgaard. But 1789 was also to be a decisive year for Baggesen. A few months before the French Revolution, *Holger Danske* (Holger the Dane), an opera for which he wrote the libretto, was performed at the Royal Theater in Copenhagen. The plot, borrowed from Wieland's verse epic *Oberon* (1780), had relatively little to do with the legendary Danish hero. Instead, it is an oriental Romantic epic about a knight, his beautiful princess, and the many ordeals they face in the service of a higher cause. The collaboration with composer Friedrich Ludwig Aemilius Kunzen worked perfectly for the musically talented Baggesen. Nonetheless, *Holger Danske* was removed from the playbill after only six performances, although it lived on for some time in the form of a heated newspaper polemic, called "the Holger controversy," about the artistic legitimacy of the opera and the right of German immigrants to hold positions of power in the autocratic Danish administration. Baggesen found himself in the middle of the scandal: German culture was his source of inspiration, his patrons were Germans living in Denmark, and he considered himself to be a cosmopolitan man. He left the country on 26 May 1789, before the scandal had reached its full height.

With the support of Prince Frederik Christian of Augustenborg, Baggesen traveled through Holsten, Hamburg, Bad Pyrmont, Göttingen, Hesse, Frankfurt, and Worms, and on to Zurich, St. Gotthard, and Berne–hardly a labyrinthine journey in geographical terms. For the most part, he traveled a straight line south through Europe.

His first destination was Bad Pyrmont, a fashionable spa town, where the illness-plagued Baggesen hoped to regain his health. His course of treatment consisted of taking in the spring water and strolling, but it did not have the dramatic effect he had hoped for. A doctor in Hamburg had prescribed a treatment that Baggesen was still shy enough to hide from his readers and only pointed out more obviously in the revised 1807 version of *Labyrinten,* in which the doctor expressly recommends a more wholesome sex life: "De maa givte Dem!" (You must get married!).

Labyrinten has been at the center of late-twentieth-century metaliterary interest in Baggesen's writing. It is also one of the finest works of literature written in Danish. One must look ahead to Søren Kierkegaard in order to find a similarly stylistic literary tour de force. Henning Fenger calls it "utvivlsomt den bog Kierkegaard stilistisk har lært mest af" (without a doubt the book that Kierkegaard learned the most from stylistically). *Labyrinten* truly does include a digressive catalogue of styles. Opinions are split on whether it is possible to find a compositional unity behind the many side routes, pleasure trips, and excursions. Klaus P. Mortensen considers Baggesen one of the great authors of the Romantic movement and views his work as a continuous elevation and mental transformation of the first-person narrator. Thomas Bredsdorff, on the other hand, cautions against reading Romantic traits into *Labyrinten:* the text consists of a series of coordinated flights of ecstasy and depressions, emotional demonstrations that in their own right were prevalent in eighteenth-century literature.

Baggesen himself is the stated main character. In the preface he distances himself from the many scholarly and quantifying travel accounts of the day: "Man kalde det Automanie, Egoisme, Jegsyge, hvad man vil–heller vil jeg fremstille *mig* i min hele Svaghed end giøre mig skyldig i en virkelig Forbrydelse mod andre" (One can call it automania, egoism, self-centeredness, what you will–I would rather present *myself* in my full weakness than make myself guilty of an actual offense against others). Jean-Jacques Rousseau, whose work was one of Baggesen's sources of inspiration for *Labyrinten,* set a high standard for candor: giving in to the confessional, biographical truth would be a true crime against others.

This narrative program reaches its pithiest expression in the concluding direct address to the reader, in which Baggesen apologizes for the delays to which the work has been subject. The world had become politicized since the revolutionary year of 1789; everyone was being carried away by political obsessions. But Baggesen offers another means of transportation: a "lille Valnødskal, jeg har sat Hiul under" (little walnut shell I put wheels on). The reference has to do with Hamlet's famous exclamation: "O God, I could be bounded in a nutshell and count myself king of infinite space." In this simultaneously constrained and all-encompassing world Baggesen's sensual, subjective journey takes place.

By all accounts, the plan was for a brief spa visit in Bad Pyrmont financed by the infirm young poet's local patrons. By the time Baggesen returned to Copenhagen in October 1790, after a harrowing journalistic and poetic trip through the central part of Europe, he had married the Swiss Sophie von Haller. He also brought back quite a few notebooks, primarily from the latter part of the trip.

In his introduction Baggesen describes the problem he had with a lack of material for the first part of *Labyrinten,* which covers the trip as far as Bad Pyrmont. The lack of his many letters home to his spiritual friend Maria Magdalene Pram (Selene) was palpable, since he had decided to use them in his writing. She had allegedly let more than fifty letters go up in smoke–reputedly annoyed at having been slighted in favor of a Swiss beauty from a good family.

Baggesen set confessional candor as his highest standard. All the same, he was still able to work in a story that came from his first trip to northern Germany in 1787. The overall chronology of the trip was broken up in favor of a boundless fantasy about circumnavigating the globe. Baggesen–along with fellow poet Matthias Claudius and a small group of others–had previously imagined that a trip on a small northern German lake was a trip to the end of the world in the footsteps of Captain James Cook. Baggesen does not hide the fact that this imaginary journey stemmed from an earlier date. He glosses over some facts of his journey because, for example, a coin factory is not a proper subject for his art, and he proceeds instead to tell the tale of the imaginary voyage. In other words, Baggesen turns to his imagination when the facts are too dull to serve his purpose. In this way he admits his debt to Laurence Sterne, who had introduced the digression as a stylistic device of the modern travel account in *A Sentimental Journey* (1768). According to Leif Ludwig Albertsen's 1991 analysis, the voyage around the globe signals that *Labyrinten* is an allegorical work. Baggesen wanted to show that the factual circumstances were secondary to his sovereign interpretation of them. There is no doubt that it is a misreading to insist, as later biographers and critics did, that the work is a straightforward, purely biographical tale.

Baggesen's journey through Germany, Switzerland, and France includes a series of highlights that have become classics: his philosophical wanderings on the heaths outside Lüneburg; his journalistic, wide-eyed depiction of the Jewish neighborhood in Frankfurt; his condensed love-at-first-sight experience in Mainz; his virtuoso reflections on the all-too-ordinary city of Mannheim; and his description of climbing the cathe-

Labyrinten

eller

Reise giennem

Tydskland, Schweitz og Frankerig

ved

Jens Baggesen.

— Pauper veniat quoque gratus ad aras
Et placeat cæso non minus agna bove.
Ovid.

Første Deel.

Kiøbenhavn, 1792.
Trykt hos Johan Frederik Schultz,
Hof- og Universitets-Bogtrykker.

Title page for Baggesen's allegorical travel account (Society of Danish Language and Literature)

dral in Strasbourg. Yet, these incidents are only part of the text. The first volume of *Labyrinten* came out in 1792; the second, the following year. The original edition was more than eight hundred pages long, but at present the work is available only in abridged versions.

Baggesen never gave up on the idea of continuing *Labyrinten.* From time to time he worked, interrupted by other trips, to incorporate his time in Switzerland and later experiences into the travel account. His most monumental effort came in 1807, when he published a second edition called *Digtervandringer eller Reiser i Europa i Begyndelsen af det attende og mod Enden af det nittende Aarhundrede* (Poetic Wanderings, or Travels in Europe at the Beginning of the Eighteenth Century and the End of the Nineteenth). In the preface he promises a total of seven volumes–all as long as the first one–which would have amounted to 3,600 pages. Ultimately, however, there was to be only one abbreviated revision of the original work. The continuation of *Labyrinten* includes Baggesen's description of meeting the twenty-one-year-old Sophie, the grandchild of the famous Swiss German alpine poet Albrecht von Haller. Their marriage became a reality in March 1790, but Baggesen had to wait for financial guarantees from home and used the waiting period for a trip to revolutionary Paris, where on New Year's Day he danced enthusiastically on the ruins of the Bastille. The trip home from Berne was a triumphal procession that brought new friendships: in Weimar it was Wieland, Baggesen's poetic idol, and in Jena it was the philosopher K. L. Reinhold, who introduced him to Immanuel Kant (from whom he adopted the middle name Immanuel), and Friedrich Schiller, whose philosophical writings Baggesen read enthusiastically. In October 1790 the newlyweds arrived in Copenhagen.

Baggesen's next trip, undertaken in the spring of 1793, had several purposes. Sophie had fallen ill after giving birth to her first child, Ernst, in May 1792, and the hope was that the trip would strengthen both mother and child. In addition, the Danish grant-awarding authorities believed that Baggesen was the right man to conduct an investigation of Europe's educational system and pedagogy. For this purpose he received a three-year grant. He was also on a secret mission for Prince Frederik Christian, who wanted information about the secret life of European Masons.

Whereas on his first trip Baggesen had traveled like a bee "for at indsue Sødmen af Blomsterne" (in order to drink in the sweetness of the flowers), he now traveled as a responsible, educated man in order to bring back honey. But the benefits of the trip were just as hard to pin down as the stated mission, and Sophie did not regain her health. She gave birth to another son, Carl, in 1793, but lost her firstborn shortly thereafter. Another son, August, was born in 1795, and in 1797 Sophie died in Kiel after a brief stay in Copenhagen.

Traveling was becoming a way of life for Baggesen. From 1793 until his wife's death, he traveled around Europe expanding his already formidable network of acquaintances. He was gregarious, had a good eye for women who resembled Sophie, and feasted on artistic experiences. For several spells, the family lived in Switzerland, Weimar, Augustenborg, and Kiel. Starting in 1795 Baggesen served as vice dean at the Regensen College of the University of Copenhagen, but he performed his duties poorly. In May 1798 he was again in northern Italy and Switzerland, where–against the backdrop of the expectations raised by the French Revolution–he became politically engaged in Switzerland's transformation into the Helvetic Republic. In terms of literature, Baggesen was busy with his

German epic *Parthenäis oder Die Alpenreise. Ein idyllisches Epos in neun Gesängen* (Parthenäis; or, The Alpine Journey: An Idyllic Epic in Nine Books, 1803). In Paris, thanks to the efforts of his mother-in-law, he became engaged to a beautiful and wealthy French Swiss woman, Françoise "Fanny" Reybaz. They were married in 1799. Fanny's education was irreproachable, but not so her credentials as a housewife.

In November 1798 Baggesen was back in Copenhagen. As codirector of Copenhagen's Royal Theater he had his 1789 opera *Erik Eiegod* (Erik the Kindhearted), with music by Kunzen. His contribution here was limited mostly to his 1807 poem "Theateradministratoriade," in which Baggesen ridiculed both the Royal Theater and his own shortcomings as a public servant. In 1799 the coughing and indisposed Fanny bore him a daughter, Emma. At the end of 1800 he resettled in Paris; before his departure, which his patrons in Copenhagen did not approve of, he returned to work on an old opera, *Trylle-Harpen* (The Magic Harp, performed in 1816), and on an epic about Napoleon.

Among Baggesen's many attempts at longer works, one stands out in that he actually completed it. *Parthenäis* is a tale from the Swiss Alps, an idyllic epic in hexameter about three graceful, pastoral beauties and their outing to Mount Jungfrau under the knowledgeable guidance of a young Scandinavian named Nordfrank. *Parthenäis* takes place in the mountains around Bern, a region that is now a nature preserve but first became popular with travelers in the latter half of the 1700s. Like several of his contemporaries, Baggesen had a lifelong enthusiasm for the Alps. (They did not make much of an impression, however, on the rational Holberg earlier in the eighteenth century. To him the mountains were almost in the way.) The alpine landscape itself plays a central role in the poem; it illustrates the role played by the concept of the scenic, which at that time fell under the term *sublime.* The rugged landscape also requires great physical efforts. Just as in Homeric epics, many gods, as well as more locally specific demons, such as Azeus, the personification of dizziness, are included. The character Nordfrank embodies the battle of conflicting interests within the pantheon—that is to say, the opposing forces within human beings. On one side are Hermes, the god of commerce, and Eros, the lesser god of love; and on the other side, Apollo, the poets' god, and the platonic goddess of love, Venus Urania, who resides on the top of Jungfrau. (*Jungfrau* is German, and *parthenos* is Greek for *virgin.*) The poem includes a long series of risqué scenes with scantily clad girls whose goal is to try the young man's resolve. In the end, Nordfrank achieves the best of both worlds since he runs off with the most beautiful of the three, Myris; obtains her parents' heartfelt consent to their marriage; and, amid the sounds of heavenly music, is initiated into the life of a poet. The fact that there is certainly no biographical basis for the idyll leads Aage Henriksen to call *Parthenäis* "det pinagtigste digt i vor litteratur" (the most agonizing poem in Danish literature). Baggesen revised the work several times; the final version, completed in 1823, was published posthumously in 1836.

Baggesen had received a royal grant for a two-year stay in Paris. Beyond the recovery of Fanny, however, the point of this time in Paris is unclear. In 1802 he traveled across Germany—where his publisher wanted to release two volumes of his poetry—to Denmark in order to extend the grant and then went back to Paris with additional funding. In Paris he was reunited with C. F. Cramer, who had translated *Labyrinten* into German. Baggesen also attended lectures on experimental physics and was introduced to chemistry by H. C. Ørsted. He planned a modern epic, titled "Uranion eller Lysets Helte" (Uranion or Heroes of the Light), and longer poems rooted in the Norse sagas.

An inheritance from Fanny's father enabled the Baggesen family, which had grown with the birth of son Adam Paul in 1804, to buy a small summer cottage in Marly-le-Roi, outside of Paris. In 1805 Baggesen was working on *Oceania,* which he planned as a long epic in German. He described it as "et Heltedigt uden Krig" (an epic without war) about Captain Cook's voyage around the world. Five of the songs from this work were published with *Heideblumen* (Heath Flowers, 1808), but that is as far as the project got.

In June 1806 Baggesen returned to Denmark for what was originally planned as a three-week stay. His reception was quite warm in general, but before his departure a year later, he had managed to turn Copenhagen on its head by falling madly in love with the writer Adam Oehlenschläger's sister Sophie, who was ostensibly happily married to lawyer A. S. Ørsted. The scandal had two crests. The first came with the town gossip, which had ample justification because in November, Baggesen moved in with the Oehlenschlägers to lay siege to Lilia, as he called Sophie. She was at the heart of the social circle responsible for Denmark's Romantic breakthrough and for a brief time managed to win Baggesen over to Johann Wolfgang von Goethe and contemporary poetry. But a married woman's obvious fascination with a married and mercilessly charming Danish exile was the subject of people's curiosity. The second wave of the scandal was unleashed when Baggesen published a series of poems in *Heideblumen* to his "Lilia," with allusions to the Copenhagen affair that were altogether too blatant.

Other circumstances also contributed to making Baggesen into a persona non grata in refined circles. He offered advice and assistance–in the form of the rhyming epistle "Noureddin til Aladdin" (Noureddin to Aladdin, 1806)–to Oehlenschläger, who had distinguished himself as the foremost poet of the new school with his *Digte* (Poems, 1803) and especially his two-volume *Poetiske Skrifter* (Poetic Writings, 1805). Oehlenschläger declined this offer of advice. Baggesen was eager to associate himself with the new school, which is evident from his clashes with the literary establishment in Copenhagen. This attitude is also clear in *Giengangeren og han selv eller Baggesen over Baggesen* (The Ghost and the Man; or, Baggesen on Baggesen, 1807), in which the rejuvenated Baggesen passes judgment on his own ghosts and other outdated characters from before "det aandelige Jordskiælv" (the spiritual earthquake) at the start of the new century.

The rhymed epistle is another genre in which Baggesen wrote throughout his life. He published two collections: *Skiemtsomme Riimbreve* (Merry Rhyming Epistles, 1806) and *Poetiske Epistler* (Poetic Epistles, 1814). But his interest in the genre had already been well established earlier, stemming from his notorious passion for correspondence. In Baggesen's own words, what is striking about the genre is that it is the "letteste, den utvungneste, den skiødesløseste af alle tænkelige" (easiest, the most spontaneous, the most nonchalant of all conceivable forms), while at the same time being about almost nothing at all. Ease is the greatest art. Baggesen brought the matter to a head in the form of a polemic against the solemn Romantic thinking of the day, which he challenged in *Skiemtsomme Riimbreve* with his rhyming epistle "Romerering" (Roaming), his final literary testimonial.

When news of the British bombardment of Copenhagen in 1807 reached Paris, Baggesen became a patriotic poet. He extended his German authorship with the satirical, anti-Romantic *Der Karfunkel oder Klingklingel-Almanach* (The Carbuncle or Ding-Dong Almanac, 1809). After six months in Germany in 1808–1809, he returned to Paris. During this period, he wrote exclusively philosophical and theosophical texts in German.

Out of necessity, Baggesen spent the years 1811–1814 in Kiel as a professor of Danish language and literature. His old friends in Copenhagen had turned their backs on him. The years from 1813 to 1819 were characterized by various polemics culminating in a prolonged and embittered feud with Oehlenschläger and his followers. As a theater critic, Baggesen had offended the new consensus, which held Oehlenschläger to be the infallible national poet. For the most part, posterity has agreed with Baggesen's diagnosis of the mature Oehlenschläger's dramatic abilities, but it has also agreed that Baggesen was wasting his own critical talents. He ended the dispute himself with *Rosenblade med Et Par Torne* (Rose Petals with a Couple of Thorns, 1819), which was to be his last book in Danish.

In his periodicals *Skuddagen* (1814) and *Danfana* (1816), Baggensen published the first nine books of the hexameter epic *Thora,* which was never completed. In his 1961 study of Baggesen's writing, Henriksen devotes considerable space to this poetic fragment. He considers *Thora* to be Baggesen's skillful revision of the whimsical alpine wandering epic *Parthenäis.* This high appraisal can be traced back to Vilhelm Andersen, who found brooding self-knowledge and more of a conceptual grounding in *Thora* than in *Giengangeren og han selv,* the verse narrative "Emma" (1791), or *Parthenäis.*

The first book in *Thora* is a masterfully executed cliff-hanger, written in the style of the Gothic novel. It is set in the sixteenth century, in the remote countryside at Havsgaard in Skåne, where late one evening the vassal Herkuller is reading aloud to his somewhat inattentive daughter Thora. That is where the idyll ends. A charcoal burner named Grim then arrives with his ten sons hidden in a sack of coal, but Herkuller's wily daughter succeeds in holding her own against the red-bearded thief, so that the whole gang is overpowered and put on trial. Grim and his sons are beheaded and their bodies displayed on the gallows hill, but their rough laughter can still be heard when the moon is full, and every eleventh night the words "Jeg kommer igjen!" (I will return!) echo in the ringing of the church bells.

"Skjebnens rædsomme Gang og Uskylds Kamp mod det Onde" (Destiny's Frightful Course and Innocence's Battle Against Evil) continues in light of the first book. In the books that follow, Baggesen unfolds an extensive network of characters, starting with two families engaged in a persistent feud (Thora and her father's family versus the underground Grim family). The situation is complicated by the fact that individual characters sometimes change names or have no knowledge of their actual origins, which is true of Grimkul, who is actually the youngest of the Grim patriarch's sons but has married Thora under the name of Roller. The characters are not what they seem to be, and on several occasions the epic muse is called on to cast a light on the dark goal of his desire. According to Vilhelm Andersen, Roller is one of Baggesen's most sophisticated self-portraits. For Henriksen, *Thora* is Baggesen's most authentic report on the sex life that he, in accordance with the ideals of his day, tried to "tugte . . . op i dens sande, oprindelige skikkelse" (discipline . . . into its true, original form). But the demonization is almost "modernist."

In September 1820 Baggesen left Denmark for the last time with his family. He spent a brief period in debtors' prison because of his persistent financial problems. Fanny died in June 1822, followed later in the year by their son, Adam Paul. Once again, Baggesen intensified his theological studies and left France in 1823 to live in Switzerland, interrupted by visits to spas in Germany. While battling a progressive abdominal disease, he managed to write metaphysical treatises and complete his old plan for a speculative verse tale, *Adam und Eva oder die Geschichte des Sündenfalls* (Adam and Eve; or, The Story of the Fall, 1826). He died on the way to Denmark on 3 October 1826. An autopsy was performed (the cause of death was kidney failure), and Baggesen's body was taken to Kiel, where he was buried by the side of his first wife, Sophie.

On behalf of himself and his brother Carl, August Baggesen memorialized his father in *Jens Baggesens Biographie* (1843–1856) comprising four freely compiled volumes of their father's fictional texts, diaries, and letters. Carl and August's ambition was to humanize their father, to make him mortal and real. One might say that Baggesen's sons–along with *Labyrinten* and, especially, its "continuation," *Labyrinthens Fortsættelse*–raised a monument to their father's healthy, uncomplicated love for their mother.

Shortly after his death Jens Baggesen once again became the subject of a dispute. The critic Peder Hjort had anonymously published a protest against a planned commemoration of Baggesen at the Royal Theater in 1826. This protest provoked one of the most pronounced literary struggles of the decade, which came to underscore the growing influence of Johan Ludvig Heiberg. In his comprehensive review of Oehlenschläger's latest tragedy, Heiberg carried on the criticism of Oehlenschläger where Baggesen had left off. Oehlenschläger and his colleagues from the Sorø Academy took part in the debate, but Heiberg managed to target the outdated forms of tragedy represented by Oehlenschläger and his successors Carsten Hauch and B. S. Ingemann, at the same time preparing the way for his own contemporary brand of drama, the vaudeville. When he later became a professor, Heiberg presented his own writing as a continuation of the works of Holberg, Wessel, and Baggesen. The playwright Henrik Hertz, a close friend of Heiberg, outlined the principal aspects of the dispute, which centered on the difference between a formalistic, French-influenced style and a sentimental German style that did not make sufficient demands on form. Baggesen became associated with the former side of the debate, which held the harmonic fusion of subject and form to be pivotal. In this way he became "en nødvendig ingrediens i heibergianismen" (a neccesary ingredient in Heibergianism), as Fenger put

Parthenaïs oder Die Alpenreise. Ein idyllisches Epos in neun Gesängen

von

IENS BAGGESEN

mit sechs Kupfern nach Schnorr u. Schubert von Schule.

Hamburg und Mainz bei Gottfried Vollmer.

C. Martin fc. Leipzig.

Facsimile af titelbladet af den formentlige første udgave af »Parthenaïs« (A), udkommet enten i december 1802 eller – sandsynligst – i januar 1803. Stærkt forstørret

Title page for Baggesen's allegorical epic poem (1803), written in German, in which a young man and three beautiful women are confronted by Greek gods and goddesses as they travel through the Swiss Alps (from Parthenaïs eller Alperejsen, *translated by Flemming Dahl, 1965; Walter Royal Davis Library, University of North Carolina at Chapel Hill)*

it. Thanks to Heiberg, Baggesen lived on. As late as J. P. Jacobsen's novel *Niels Lyhne* (1880), certain fashionable circles are characterized by the fact that they know Molière better than Holberg and Baggesen better than Oehlenschläger. In a broader sense, Baggesen has not had successors: the epic was abandoned with Romanticism, the lyric epistle was replaced by romances and other forms of less-subjective poetry, and, finally, meter disappeared as a governing poetic principle. Recent scholarly interest in Baggesen has focused on *Labyrinten.* When the postmodern American novelist Thomas Pynchon's *Mason & Dixon* (1997) was to be translated into Danish, *Labyrinten* served as the verbal model.

Letters:

Aus Jens Baggesen's Briefwechsel mit Karl Leonhard Reinhold und Friedrich Heinrich Jacobi, 2 volumes, introduction by Carl Baggesen and August Baggesen (Leipzig: F. A. Brockhaus, 1831);

Louis Bobé, ed., *Efterladte Papirer fra den Reventlowske Familiekreds i Tidsrummet 1770–1827,* volume 6 (Copenhagen: Lehmann & Stage, 1903);

Timoleon und Immanuel. Dokumente einer Freundschaft. Briefwechsel zwischen Friedrich Christian zu Schleswig-Holstein und Jens Baggesen, edited by Hans Schulz (Leipzig: S. Hirzel, 1910).

Bibliographies:

Karl Goedeke, *Grundrisz zur Geschichte der deutschen Dichtung aus den Quellen,* 13 volumes (Dresden: L. Ehlermann, 1884–1953), VI: 161–165; supplementary volume 15, edited by Herbert Jacob and Leopold Magon (Berlin: Akademie-Verlag, 1964), pp. 432–441;

K. F. Plesner, *Baggesen Bibliografi* (Copenhagen: Gyldendal, 1943).

Biographies:

Jens Baggesens Biographie. Udarbeidet fornemmeligen efter hans egne Haandskrifter og efterladte litteraire Arbeider, 4 volumes, edited by August Baggesen (Copenhagen: C. A. Reitzel, 1843–1856);

Julius Clausen, *Jens Baggesen. En litterær-psykologisk Studie* (Copenhagen: Brødrene Salmonsen, 1895).

References:

Leif Ludwig Albertsen, *Immanuel. En bog om Jens Baggesen* (Copenhagen: Rosenkilde & Bagger, 1991);

Albertsen, *Odins mjød. En studie i Baggesens mytiske poetik* (Aarhus: Akademisk Boghandel, 1969);

Vilhelm Andersen, *Illustreret dansk Litteraturhistorie,* edited by Carl S. Petersen and Andersen, volume 2: *Den danske Litteratur i det attende Aarhundrede* (Copenhagen: Gyldendal, 1934), pp. 715–832;

Oskar Bandle, "Baggesens 'Parthenais' im Umfeld deutscher Klassik und Romantik," in *Scandinavian Literature in a Transcultural Context: Papers from the XV IASS Conference,* edited by Sven H. Rossel and Birgitta Steene ([Seattle]: University of Washington, 1986), pp. 83–89;

Thomas Bredsdorff, "The Fox at Ploen: The Idea of Nature in a Major Work of Danish Eighteenth-Century Literature: Jens Baggesen's 'The Labyrinth,'" *Orbis Litterarum,* 22 (1967): 241–251;

Hans Brix, "Til Jens Baggesen: Labyrinten," in his *Analyser og Problemer. Undersøgelser i den ældre danske Litteratur,* 7 volumes (Copenhagen: Gyldendal, 1935–1955), III: 204–232;

Torben Brostrøm, *Labyrint og Arabesk* (Copenhagen: Gyldendal, 1967), pp. 9–22, 23–33, 34–38;

Henning Fenger, *Familjen Heiberg* (Copenhagen: Museum Tusculanum, 1992);

Aage Henriksen, *Den rejsende. Otte kapitler om Baggesen og hans tid* (Copenhagen: Gyldendal, 1961);

F. J. Billeskov Jansen, *Danmarks Digtekunst,* volume 2: *Klassicismen* (Copenhagen: Munksgaard, 1947);

Aage Jørgensen, "Jens Baggesens homeriske alperejse," in his *Kundskaben på ondt og godt. En studiebog* (Aarhus: Akademisk Boghandel, 1968), pp. 21–29;

Jette Lundbo Levy, "Det talende skrammel. Bevægelser rundt i Baggesens labyrint," in *Digternes paryk. Studier i 1700-tallet. Festskrift til Thomas Bredsdorff,* edited by Marianne Alenius and others (Copenhagen: Museum Tusculanum, 1997), pp. 209–221;

P. M. Mitchell, *A History of Danish Literature* (New York: American-Scandinavian Foundation, 1957), pp. 104–105;

Klaus P. Mortensen, *Himmelstormerne. En linje i dansk naturdigtning* (Copenhagen: Gyldendal, 1993), pp. 119–144;

Gert Sautermeister, "Spannweite der Gegensätze, Nähe der Extreme. Zur Unverjährtheit eines Unbekannten. Jens Baggesen: 'Das Labyrinth oder Reise durch Deutschland in die Schweiz 1789,'" in *Europäische Reisen im Zeitalter der Aufklärung,* edited by Hans-Wolf Jäger, Neue Bremer Beiträge, no. 7 (Heidelberg: Winter, 1992), pp. 360–385;

Søren Schou, "Agtet–og upåagtet," *Dansk Noter,* 3 (1991): 20–27;

Marianne Stidsen, "Med og uden paryk–Jens Baggesens forfatterskab i formalistisk belysning," in *Mere Lys! Indblik i oplysningstiden i dansk litteratur og kultur,* edited by Mads Julius Elf and Lasse Horne Kjældgaard (Hellerup: Spring, 2002), pp. 147–174.

Papers:

The main body of Jens Baggesen's papers is at the Danish Royal Library in Copenhagen. See Lauritz Nielsen, *Katalog over danske og norske Digteres Originalmanuskripter i det Kongelige Bibliotek* (Copenhagen: Munksgaard, 1943), pp. 32–38; and Birgitte Possing and Bruno Svindborg, *Det Kongelige Biblioteks Håndskriftafdeling. Erhvervelser, 1924–1987,* volume 1 (Copenhagen: Museum Tusculanum, 1995), p. 75. Other papers are in the Kiel University Library, the Uppsala University Library, the Oslo University Library, the Goethe-Schiller Archive in Weimar, and the Preussische Staatsbibliothek in Berlin.

Herman Bang

(20 April 1857 - 29 January 1912)

George C. Schoolfield
Yale University

Herman Bang (courtesy of the Danish Royal Library, Copenhagen)

BOOKS: *Hverdagskamp og Du og jeg. Komedier* (Copenhagen: Schou, 1878);

Realisme og Realister. Portrætstudier og Aforismer (Copenhagen: Schubothe, 1879);

Haabløse Slægter (Copenhagen: Schubothe, 1880; revised edition, Copenhagen: Schou, 1884; revised again, Cophenhagen: Schubothe, 1905);

Kritiske Studier og Udkast (Copenhagen: Schubothe, 1880);

Tunge Melodier. Studier (Copenhagen: Schou, 1880)–includes "Fortællinger fra Skumringen 1-3," "Fragment," "Fra Kirken 1-2," "Stille Existenser," "Hjemme," "Elsket og Savnet," and "Kvindehistorier 1-2";

Graa vejr. En Akt (Copenhagen: Schubothe, 1881);

Herhjemme og Derude (Copenhagen: Schubothe, 1881);

Inden fire Vægge. En Akt (Copenhagen: Schubothe, 1881);

Præster (Copenhagen: Riemenschneider, 1883)–comprises "Præster," "Livskald," "Ve den, fra hvem Forargelsen kommer," "Genstridige Sind," "En Hyrde," "Kvindefigurer," "Elna," "Célimène," "Danaë," "'Frökenen,'" "En miniature," "Efter Ballet," "Kærlighed," and "25° R.";

Fædra. Brudstykker af et Livs Historie (Copenhagen: Schubothe, 1883);

Excentriske Noveller (Copenhagen: Schou, 1885)–includes "Franz Pander," translated by P. M. Mitchell and Kenneth H. Ober as "Franz Pander," in *The Royal Guest and Other Classical Danish Narratives* (Chicago: University of Chicago, 1977), pp. 197–217; "Fratelli Bedini," and "Charlot Dupont";

Ellen Urne. Skuespil i fire Akter (Copenhagen: Schou, 1885);

Stille Eksistenser. Fire Livsbilleder (Copenhagen: Schubothe, 1886)–includes "Min gamle Kammerat," "Hendes Højhed," "Enkens Søn," and "Ved Vejen"; "Ved Vejen" revised and enlarged as *Ved Vejen* (Copenhagen: Schou, 1898); original version translated by Tiina Nunnally as *Katinka* (Seattle: Fjord Press, 1990);

Stuk (Copenhagen: Schubothe, 1887);

Tine (Copenhagen: Schubothe, 1889); translated by Paul Christophersen, with an introduction by Walter Allen, as *Tina* (London & Dover, N.H.: Athlone, 1984);

Digte (Copenhagen: Schubothe, 1889);

Under Aaget. Noveller (Copenhagen: Schubothe, 1890)–includes "En dejlig Dag," "Fortælling fra en Krog i Livet," and "Irene Holm," translated by Hanna

Astrup Larsen in *Denmark's Best Stories* (New York: American-Scandinavian Foundation/Norton, 1928), pp. 195–214; and "Frøken Caja";

Les quatre diables. Excentrisk Novelle (Copenhagen: Olsen, 1890); translated by Marie Ottilie Hejl as *The Four Devils,* in *Great Short Novels of the World,* edited by Barrett Harper Clark (New York: McBride, 1927), pp. 1059–1088;

To Sørgespil. Brødre, Naar Kærligheden dør (Copenhagen: Schubothe, 1891)–*Brødre* translated by Joseph A. Weingarten as *Brothers,* in *A Play [Brothers] by Herman Bang; & Some Poems by Joseph A. Weingarten* (New York: Weingarten, 1943);

Ti Aar: Erindringer og Hændelser (Copenhagen: Schubothe, 1891)–includes "Udvist af Tyskland," translated by Mitchell and Ober as "Expelled from Germany," in *The Royal Guest and Other Classical Danish Narratives* (Chicago: University of Chicago, 1977), pp. 218–235;

Teatret (Copenhagen: Schubothe, 1892);

Rundt i Norge. Skildringer og Billeder (Kristiania: Aschehoug, 1892);

De fire Djævle. Excentrisk Novelle (Kristiania: Cammermeyer, 1895);

Ludvigsbakke. Roman (Copenhagen: Schubothe, 1896); translated by Arthur Chater as *Ida Brandt* (New York: Knopf, 1928);

Det hvide Hus (Copenhagen: Schubothe, 1898);

Liv og Død (Copenhagen: Schubothe, 1899)–includes "En Fortælling om Lykken," "En Fortælling om Elskov," and "En Fortælling om dem, der skal dø";

Udvalgte Fortællinger (Copenhagen: Schubothe, 1899)–includes the previously uncollected "Gennem Rosenborg Have," translated by J. Wittmer-Hartmann, *American-Scandinavian Review,* 2 (1914): 42; also includes five stories from *Tunge Melodier* under new titles: "Fortællinger fra Skumringen 1" as "Den siste Aften," translated by Henry Steele Commager as "The Last Evening," *American-Scandinavian Review,* 17 (1929): 161–171; "Fortællinger fra Skumringen 3" as "Chopin"; "Fra Kirken 2" as "Foran Alteret"; "Kvindehistorier 2" as "Pernill," translated by E. Gyllich, *American-Scandinavian Review,* 2 (1914): 19–23; and "Stille Existenser" as "Præsten," translated by Commager as "The Pastor," *American-Scandinavian Review,* 15 (1927): 749–753;

Det graa Hus (Copenhagen: Schubothe, 1901);

Ravnene; To Fortællinger (Copenhagen: Gyldendal, 1902)–includes "Ravnene" and "Julegaver";

Sommerglæder (Copenhagen: Gyldendal, 1902);

Mikaël (Copenhagen: Gyldendal, 1904);

De uden Fædreland (Copenhagen: Gyldendal, 1906); translated by Marie Busch and Arthur Chater as *Denied a Country* (New York & London: Knopf, 1927);

Sælsomme Fortællinger (Copenhagen: Gyldendal, 1907)–includes "Barchan er død"; "Men Du skal mindes mig," translated by William O. Makely as "You Shall Remember Me," *American-Scandinavian Review,* 61 (1973): 62–67; and "Stærkest";

Aus der Mappe: Novellen von Herman Bang, translated into German by Julia Koppel (Berlin: S. Fischer, 1908)–includes works not collected in Danish: "Der rumänische Weihnachtsbaum," "Geschlagen," "Eine sonderbare Geschichte," "Die Zaghaften," "Ein Sommernachtstraum," and "Über den Ruhm";

Masker og Mennesker (Copenhagen & Kristiania: Gyldendal, 1910);

Gedanken zum Sexualitätsproblem, edited by Max Wasbutzski (Bonn: Marcus & Weber, 1922);

Helg. Et Fortællingsfragment, edited by Ejnar Thomsen (Copenhagen: Gyldendal, 1935);

Teaterindtryk fra Rusland 1911 (Århus: Arkona, 1979).

Editions and Collections: *Værker i Mindeudgave,* 6 volumes, edited by Johan Knudsen and Peter Nansen (Copenhagen: Gyldendal, 1912);

Gesammelte Werke, 4 volumes (Berlin: S. Fischer, 1919);

"Vekslende themaer, 1879–1883," in *Københavnske Skildringer,* edited by Cai M. Woel (Copenhagen: Gyldendal, 1954);

Fra de unge Aar: Artikler og Skitser 1878–1885, edited by Woel (Copenhagen: Gyldendal, 1956);

Herman Bangs første journalistik, edited by Hans Christian Andersen (Århus: Centrum, 1981);

Reportager, edited by Clæs Kastholm Hansen (Copenhagen: Gyldendal, 1983);

Udenrigspolitisk journalistik, edited by Vivian Greene-Gantzberg (Copenhagen: Gyldendal, 1990).

The work of Herman Bang is little known in the Anglophone world. Two of his novels, *De uden Fædreland* (1906; translated as *Denied a Country,* 1927) and *Ludvigsbakke* (1896; translated as *Ida Brandt,* 1928), were published by Alfred A. Knopf, and a handful of his stories and a play came out in English, as well; but Bang's name is scarcely as familiar to the public as those of his contemporaries Knut Hamsun and Sigrid Undset, both of whom won the Nobel Prize in literature. (Bang's reputation as a decadent would have disqualified him in the eyes of the Swedish Academy.) The publication in English of his short novel *Tine* (1889; translated as *Tina,* 1984), about the Dano-Prussian War of 1864, and his novella "Ved Vejen" (By the Wayside, 1886; translated as *Katinka,* 1990), about a muted human tragedy, attracted little attention.

His obscurity among readers of English should be compared with the reputation he has had, almost from the start of his career, in German-speaking lands. In 1902 Thomas Mann wrote to his fellow novelist Kurt Martens: "I'm reading Bang constantly now, an author to whom I feel deeply related; I recommend *Tine* to you as an essential book." (Bang's texts had appeared in German as early as 1888; but his genuine popularity began when, ten years later, Samuel Fischer–who became Mann's publisher as well–accepted Bang as one of his authors.) Hugo von Hofmannsthal was equally impressed; in his diary for 1905 he noted, "Herman Bang. This Dane puts things in a way that no one else can. This sense of being pressed against the wall–this sense of being weaker. And he sees things to which almost no one else pays attention. The story about waiters." (The last remark alludes to Bang's story "Franz Pander," about a vain and handsome room-service waiter, the spoiled son of a laundress, who is seized by an erotic mania for the exquisite, sweet-smelling female guests in the hotel; realizing he is merely "an object" in their eyes, he kills himself.) Perhaps the most devoted of Bang's admirers was Rainer Maria Rilke; in 1902 Rilke wrote a review of Bang's novelistic memoir *Det hvide Hus* (The White House, 1898), in which he said, "We know the novels of Herman Bang. They all have something deeply sad, hopeless, despairing about them. We remember the people who appear in them as we perhaps remember lost or unhappy existences we knew as a child." (Neither Hofmannsthal nor Rilke was sufficiently aware of Bang's sometimes sly, sometimes cutting humor.) A few months later, reviewing *Tine,* Rilke called Bang "this great artist," an opinion he never abandoned, however much he was put off–as Bang's Danish colleagues frequently were–by Bang's notorious lifestyle. Bang provided more Danish material for Rilke's novel *Die Aufzeichnungen des Malte Laurids Brigge* (The Notebooks of Malte Laurids Brigge, 1910), the journals of a fictive Danish nobleman, than did J. P. Jacobsen.

Paperback cover, with illustration by Cheri O'Brien, for the English translation (1990) of Bang's 1886 novella, "Ved Vejen" (By the Wayside), about a young woman's stifled life in a railway-station town (courtesy of Fjord Press)

Herman Joachim Bang was born on Als–an island just off the east coast of Slesvig, near the present Danish German border–on 20 April 1857, at Asserballe, a village where his father was pastor. That Frederik Ludvig Bang had landed in such an out-of-the-way spot did not mean he was untalented or came from a simple background; he was the son of a distinguished obstetrician, university professor, and society doctor, Olof Lundt Bang, inventor of the universally popular "Bang's stethoscope." Grandfather Bang was a half brother of the bishop, Jakob Peter Mynster, who, postmortem, bore the brunt of Søren Kierkegaard's scorn in *Øjeblikket* (The Moment, 1855), and a cousin of great Danish poet and pedagogical reformer N. F. S. Grundtvig. Pastor Bang was thirty-four when he arrived in Asserballe, having spent years in travel and literary dabbling, at Professor Bang's expense, before he married Thora Elisabeth Salomine Blach in 1850 and belatedly, with his twenty-one-year-old bride, took up his pastorate. When the third of their children, Herman, was four years old, the Bangs moved to Horsens, the old commercial capital of Jutland; yet, Herman Bang claimed throughout his life that he had clear memories of the lush island of his birth. The Horsens stay was the peak of Frederik Bang's career. In 1871, Thora Bang died of tuberculosis–she was only forty-one–and the pastor, who had long been prey to a manic-depressive condition, requested a move to a less taxing parish: he was sent to Tersløse, a hamlet near the academic town of Sorø on Sjælland. He had already been confined to mental asylums for brief periods. On the Sunday after Easter, 1873, his illness burst out during a confirmation service (he began interjecting nursery rhymes into his sermon), and he was taken away to Copenhagen for treatment. He tried to assume his post once more but, worn out, died in November 1875 at the age of fifty-nine.

Herman Bang's fiction suggests that his relationships with his father and mother were different. His devotion to his mother was never-ending. She appears as Stella Høg, the mother in Bang's first and autobiographical novel, *Haabløse Slægter* (Hopeless Generations, 1880), and *Det hvide Hus* nearly two decades later is an extended tribute to her. His father is treated less kindly in Bang's fiction: some of the macabre details of Ludvig Høg's growing disorientation and sudden death in *Haabløse Slægter* may be imaginary, but Bang had a large store of embarrassment and resentment on which to draw. He was a pupil at the venerable Sorø Academy during the latter phases of his father's illness.

Although Bang spoke and wrote German well, and cultivated German publishers, he was largely indifferent to German literature. His roots lay in the Danish Golden Age, and he often displayed his affection for Adam Oehlenschläger, B. S. Ingemann, Frederik Paludan-Müller, and, less openly, Hans Christian Andersen. An enthusiastic reader of his immediate predecessors in Denmark (for example, Vilhelm Topsøe and Jacobsen), he was also an assiduous student of the French novel from Alfred de Musset's *Confession d'un enfant du siècle* (Confession of a Child of the Century, 1836) on. He readily confessed (and perhaps exaggerated) his debt to the impressionism of another Francophile, Jonas Lie, and treasured the Norwegians Lie and Bjørnstjerne Bjørnson as fatherly friends; he was an advocate for Bjørnson's realistic dramas, as he was, in still greater measure, for Henrik Ibsen's.

In Sweden, Bang sometimes acquired unlikely admirers. Parnassian poet Carl Snoilsky devoted his final sonnet cycle to Bang in 1897. At Lund University in southern Sweden, which maintained a long tradition of interest in Danish letters, Ola Hansson, in his "Herman Bang som kritiker" (Herman Bang as Critic, 1883), published in volume three of his *Efterlämnade Skirfiter i Urval* (1928–1932), described young Bang's talents as a critic. Later, the precocious Vilhelm Ekelund, just coming into his own as a connoisseur of fin de siècle literature, ranked Bang with sensational Polish German eroticist Stanislaw Przybyszewski in "the art of nuance." Hjalmar Söderberg's journal of a passive murderer, *Doktor Glas* (1905; translated as *Doctor Glas,* 1963), was plainly indebted to Bang. For the Swedish speakers in Finland, threatened by Russification and by a burgeoning "true Finnish" movement, Bang exerted a poignant appeal. In *Ti Aar* (Ten Years, 1891), Bang detected the resemblance between the language and cultural-struggles in Prague and Helsingfors (Helsinki)–to his mind, struggles between a doomed "aristocratic" minority and a vital "democratic" majority.

If Bang's account in his debut novel is to be believed, the most important memories from his years in Horsens were the capture of the town by Prussian and Austrian troops in 1864; his mother's reading aloud of poetry and drama; the plays he made up and performed with his elder sister and their friends; his poring over tales about the past of Denmark; a chance contact with "the priest's soft whispering, the sound of the altar bells, and the incense of the service" in the little Roman Catholic chapel in the town; and a performance in the theater of the town by a "large foreign ballet troupe" that caused his sexual awakening. At Sorø, Bang was teased by his fellow students because of his dark, "exotic" appearance and his effeminate manner. Evidently, too, he grew conscious of his homoerotic tendencies; Harry Jacobsen proposes in his *Herman Bang: Resignationens Digter* (Poet of Resignation, 1957) that Bang's romantic initiation by the experienced Camilla Falk–with her sensual gait, full figure, and "small, pointed teeth"–in *Haabløse Slægter* is a carefully transposed retelling of his seduction by an unknown member of his own sex: thus, this description was the first of Bang's many confessions made in disguise. Another episode at Sorø confirmed him in his dramatic ambitions: distinguished actor Ludvig Phister visited Sorø to perform the title role in Ludvig Holberg's *Jeppe paa Bjerget* (1723; translated as *Jeppe of the Hill,* 1915) with some of the pupils of the academy. Bang saved the day by improvising when the star's memory failed. The thankful Phister predicted a great future in the theater for the quick-witted boy. Bang tactfully left the story of Phister's lapse out of *Haabløse Slægter*–in which the actor is called "the Professor"–but included it in his 1892 collection of essays, *Teatret* (The Theater).

After finishing at Sorø, Bang joined his grandfather in Copenhagen to attend the university. The physician, despite his years (he was in his late eighties), still maintained a little of his practice. His objections to his grandson's plan of taking acting lessons were overcome after Phister himself interceded on young Bang's behalf. Bang promised to continue his legal studies; however, he abused his grandfather's generosity (and forgetfulness) by wheedling large sums of money out of him to support an existence that already had an air of aestheticizing extravagance about it. The death by rheumatic fever of Bang's younger sister, Stella, in February 1877 was followed in October by his grandfather's passing. Before the grandfather died, however, he gave his charge 1,500 crowns, which Bang quickly spent while trying unsuccessfully to find a position on one of Copenhagen's stages and to write for the theater. Forced to pay his own way, Bang embarked on a career as a journalist, first for the provincial paper *Jyllandsposten,* and then for the major Copenhagen dailies, *Dagbladet* and *Nationaltidende,* becoming the star reporter of the latter and persuading himself that he was in love with the daughter of its owner, Christian Ferslew. (Later, Anna Ferslew-Levin congratulated herself for not having listened to his talk of marriage.) Simultaneously, he was busy on other fronts, translating the works of Honoré de Balzac and writing *Realisme og Realister* (Realism and Realists, 1879), essays on contemporary Danish authors (Topsøe, Holger Drachmann, Sophus Schandorph, J. P. Jacobsen, Karl Gjellerup, and Erik Skram) and Balzac, Alexandre Dumas *fils,* Gustave Droz, and Emile Zola. Its sequel, *Kritiske Studier og Udkast* (Critical Studies and Sketches, 1880), included still more vignettes of French men of letters (Octave Feuillet, Alphonse Daudet, and Balzac again): he admired them because of their psychological refinement and the bravery with which they examined their society. The book was filled out with "dramaturgical pen-and-ink drawings" of actresses and actors he had seen. A third volume of essays, *Herhjemme og Derude* (At Home and Abroad, 1881) followed, including descriptions of poverty and crime in Copenhagen and sketches of members of the royal house. He also brought out a collection of stories, *Tunge Melodier* (Melancholy Melodies, 1880), full of the disappointments and the sadness its title promises. Yet, the main work was *Haabløse Slægter;* when it was done, Bang boasted that he had written "three-hundred pages in six weeks."

By any contemporary standard, *Haabløse Slægter* does not seem shocking; but some of its passages–particularly those about the slave-like behavior (and the manifest impotence) of William Høg, confronted by a middle-aged femme fatale, the Countess Hatzfeldt–transgressed Danish laws concerning pornography, and the book (after most of the copies had been sold) was confiscated, while Bang was threatened with a fine and/or jail sentence. Remarkably, the hints of homoeroticism in the other main male character of the novel, Bernhard Hoff (the initials are Bang's in reverse), went unnoticed: Hoff has a perfumed apartment; keeps a bust of Antinous, the Bithynian boy who was the lover of the Emperor Hadrian, on his mantelpiece; and leads the admiring Høg, for a while, down the path of hedonism. The Danish press made capital of the Bang case, all the more because Bang had already called attention to himself through his public posturing. (The parallels to Oscar Wilde are obvious.) The legal contest ended with Bang having to pay a minimal fine for his "life-story of the last male personality of a physically and spiritually degenerate family," as the judgment of the court said. As a sign of repentance, he brought out a shortened version in 1884, which not only put the Hatzfeldt passages into softer focus but also removed many long-winded diaristic reflections from the work that Danish critic Villy Sørensen later designated (in his introduction to the 1965 reprint of the first edition) the "first Danish novel about puberty." Still, Bang remained an object for cartoonists and columnists, not least in the Danish version of *Punch.* Only later did people realize that, with what he himself called "this chaotic book" (in the introduction to the second version), Bang had made an important contribution, twenty years before Mann's *Buddenbrooks* (1901), to the European tradition of novels about a family's decline. In the 1880 printing of Bang's book, "William Høst" ends as an obscure actor in the provinces; in the later versions (Bang brought out a third in 1905, in which the corrections were almost entirely stylistic) he seems to take his own life–the final weakling member of a heroic line. Bang liked to toy with the idea that he was descended from a Danish clan of the middle ages, the Hvides; William Høg, while still in school, visits the church where the graves of his mighty ancestors lie and walks among them "with mad pride." Subsequently, Bang affected a nobleman's pose, styling himself "de Bang" on his visiting card. (Again, Bang resembles Wilde, in the latter's wholly fabricated tale of descent from "the kings of Ireland," as he does Rilke, who never ceased believing his forebears had belonged to "the ancient nobility of Carinthia.")

Those who knew Bang well realized that the novel was also an effort to work out the problems of sexuality that tormented him; in a kind of literary transvestism, he tried again with *Faedra* (1883), the heroine of which–Ellen Urne, née Maag–is a member of an old noble family. The victim of a high-strung or "eksalteret" (exalted) temperament, she marries the wrong man and falls in love (chastely) with her stepson: she ends her life by sinking "deeper and deeper into morphine's lethargy," like Leo Tolstoy's *Anna Karenina* (1877). The novel–much more moral in tone than *Haabløse Slægter*–was an artistic and a critical failure, and Bang eventually wanted to forget it. At the same time, though, his reputation as a brilliant journalist increased: his gifts in journalism can be compared to those of his contemporaries Rudyard Kipling in British India, Lafcadio Hearn in Cincinnati and New Orleans, and Stephen Crane in New York. Sometimes his articles go abroad for their topics (for example, his terrifying account of the "city of the mad," Gheel, in Belgium), but most are set in Copenhagen, of which he, as a former provincial, could take a fresh view, sometimes dazzled and sometimes horrified. In his feuille-

Bang circa 1889 (photograph by Frederik Riise; courtesy of the Danish Royal Library, Copenhagen)

tons, he ranged easily from the expensive elegance of Magasin du Nord to the wretched tenements into which the poor were crowded. Despite his sybarite's pose and his would-be nobility, Bang entertained strong social sympathies, although he seldom proposed remedies: the very recognition of misery sufficed, and, besides, he had already begun to develop the resigned attitude that marked such later books as *Det hvide Hus:* "Vi lider og–bereder Lidelser.–Mere véd vi ikke . . ." (we suffer and cause suffering, more we do not know).

The best-known of Bang's sketches, perhaps, is about the burning of Christiansborg Castle in October 1884: "Det var, som om selve Luften tændtes i Lue. Alt lyste af Ild. Men Flammerne selv var mere gulhvide, mere 'spillende' end den glødende Luft" (It seemed as though the air itself was ablaze. Everything shone in the fire. Yet, the flames themselves were more yellow and whiter, and more 'flimmering' than the air as it glowed); it is a preview of the "impressionistic style" he later used in his mature narratives. He venerated the old Copenhagen that was going up in smoke. His attitude toward the expanding Copenhagen of the 1870s and 1880s was less friendly, and it informed his novel *Stuk* (Stucco, 1887), in which a large theater-and-restaurant complex–built on a foundation of shady deals–fails, almost pulling the honest (and rather pale) main figure of the novel down with it. The title alludes to the false fronts (of buildings and of the entrepreneurs who slammed them together) in the new metropolis–no longer the solid, cozy, and seemingly idyllic town of Andersen, Kierkegaard, and Christian Winther, that of painters C. W. Eckersberg, Christen Købke, and Johan Thomas Lundbye. Bang meant to emulate the depictions of Parisian life during the gaudy years of Napoleon III's Second Empire, which he had come across in Daudet's *Le Nabab* (1877), Zola's *La Curée* (The Curate, 1872), and Ocatave Feuillet's *Monsieur de Camors* (1867).

Stuk was not written in Copenhagen, however, nor was it written directly after *Faedra.* Even as he reached the peak of his journalistic fame, Bang's vanity received a public blow. In a newspaper article from the summer of 1883, critic Georg Brandes found fault (or so Bang concluded) with *Haabløse Slægter:* Brandes wrote that "certain authors . . . seldom or never sacrifice a section which for one reason or another it was their whim to compose." Remembering what Brandes's brother Edvard had said in a review of *Haabløse Slægter* (to the effect that the book would have been improved by leaving out two-thirds of it), Bang gave a somewhat muddy reply, "Teknik i vor nye Litteratur" (Technique in our Recent Literature), published in *Nationaltidende* on 29 July 1883. Brandes, with an overreaction, said Bang "has a dead point in his head, for he cannot think; I mean that he cannot think scientifically. He has no sense for philosophy, no ability for conceptual thought. . . . His intelligence is a woman's mediocre intelligence. There is no manly progress in his thoughts; plainly, they have never been submitted to the discipline which strengthens and protects against constant stumbling." The attack by Brandes had its kernel of accuracy; Bang was not a systematic thinker.

Brandes's words, however, did not deter Bang from writing novels. (The revision of *Haabløse Slægter* was done, in part, to meet the tastes of critics such as Brandes.) But for the time being he was diverted by other undertakings. He pursued the fata morgana of acting success. (Hoping to emulate Swedish actor August Lindberg, Bang toured Scandinavia as Oswald in Ibsen's *Gengangere* [1881; translated as *Ghosts,* 1885], fascinated by the decadent possibilities of Mrs. Alving's "worm-eaten" son.) More profitably, he began a career as a public reader (of his own works and those of others). His dramatic persona, disruptive in ensemble playing, could at last be brought to bear. But his journalistic career began to crumble: he had written too much, for too many papers, and his main employer, Ferslew, had grown tired of his demands and his independence (and was pained as well by the bad press Bang had received for *Faedra*). Further, the publishers of his second book of stories, *Præster* (Pastors, 1883) and of a weekly newspaper, *Vor Tid* (Our Times), the latter sustained largely by Bang's reputation for trenchant reportage, had resorted to counterfeiting in order to shore up their failing venture: they were seized as they tried to flee the country. Bang was not implicated, except by innuendo, in the scandal (he used the story for the denouement of *Stuk*), yet felt that he was deemed guilty by association. He was glad to leave Copenhagen on another acting tour: in its course, a newspaper in Bergen stated that, as Oswald, Bang was a little Samson, smashing his fist into the proscenium so often that he was on the brink of making the temple of Thalia collapse, a heavy-handed but telling description of his stage manner. Later, in *Ti Aar,* Bang made fun of his own excesses: the actress playing Mrs. Alving got a doctor's excuse from further performances with Bang: "Sagnet gaar, at hun var gul og grøn og mør i sin ganske Krop, saadan havde Osvald i Kampen om Morfinkapslerne haandteret hende" (The story goes that she was black and blue and tender all over her body, a result of the way Oswald had manhandled her in the fight for the morphine capsules). As usual, his public readings went much better; his lecture about Aleksandr Ivenovich Turgenev characterized the Russian as an author whose whole effort was sustained by human sympathy. He might have been speaking of his own work to come.

A restful late-summer stay at Castle Itter in the Tyrol gave Bang a chance to reconsider his life and his prospects; in the autumn he went to Berlin, thinking he would be able to forge a fresh career (once he had improved his German) in the capital of the Wilhelmine Empire. The portents for the Prussian venture were reasonably favorable: two new books of his soon appeared in Denmark. One of them, *Ellen Urne* (1885), was a dramatization of *Faedra,* for which Bang fleetingly held great expectations. The other was *Excentriske Noveller* (Eccentric Tales, 1885), in which Bang's experience of the life of the traveling entertainer was put on display in the bitterly comical "Charlot Dupont," about a child prodigy who is a child no longer. "Fratelli Bedini" (The Bedini Brothers) is about circus performers–a lion tamer and a trick rider–whose fraternal bond is shattered because one of them, the rider, falls passionately in love with a trapeze artist, Miss Alida. The story is one more representation of Bang's own loss of a lover to a rival. "Franz Pander" is also included in this most overtly erotic of Bang's collections.

With remarkable ease, Bang got a foothold in the journalistic world of Berlin. To his friend Peter Nansen, just before Christmas 1885, he boasted that he had made contact with "one of Germany's greatest weeklies" and that "people here say that I have an astounding talent for the language." On the other hand, Bang harbored a curious private aversion to Germans: to Nansen he wrote in 1886, "Nowhere, I assume, is shamelessness greater, make-up more clumsily applied, vice more deprived of grace."

Early in 1886 Bang was visited by the police and given twenty-four hours (the Danish ambassador got them extended to forty-eight) to leave Germany. In October he had sent a "travel letter" to a Bergen newspaper in which he had indulged in disrespectful remarks about photographs of the German imperial family he had seen in a Hamburg shop window. The German consul in Bergen had sent the clipping to Berlin. Bang scurried off to the Duchy of Meiningen, whose duke, Georg II, was celebrated for his theatrical and musical passions, but Bang had to leave this new refuge within the month, again pursued by the police. The same fate awaited him in Munich, where he turned to Ibsen for advice and help. To go on to Vienna, beyond German jurisdiction, seemed wise; since his money was running out, he quickly abandoned his hotel for rooms in the lower-class suburb of Hernals and there finished the text of "Ved Vejen." In "Udvist af Tyskland" (1891; translated as "Expelled from Germany," 1977) he says that his landlady and her six children lived in a kitchen with a pantry. The pantry was always full of men, who, she told him, were her suitors–until the day she confessed that they were detectives stationed there to watch her Danish boarder. Now, he had to leave this imperial capital, too. Before setting out, he wrote the introduction–signed "Vienna, June 1886"–to the quartet of stories, *Stille Eksistenser* (Quiet Existences, 1886), of which "Ved Vejen" is the crown.

The second of the quartet, "Hendes Højhed" (Her Highness)–about performers at a court theater and their blue-blooded audience–is dedicated to Max Eisfeld, an actor Bang had met in Berlin; at Christmas, Eisfeld joined Bang in Prague, the author's next sanctuary. (Eisfeld's real name, Appel, was later bestowed on a likable lieutenant in *Tine.*) In April 1887, Bang wrote to Nansen that "the only person whom I knew, saw, and lived with–Eisfeld–has gone away to an engagement in Berlin . . . and I don't know anyone else. In this isolation I should try to wrestle with my talent–all alone, all alone." At last, he finished *Stuk,* the working title of which had been "Bernhard Hoff and Company," at a spa on the German Bohemian border. By October 1887, Bang was back in Copenhagen; yet, the Prague months stayed with him, and, in *Ti Aar,* as in his poems, he saluted the city (whereas other writers–

Franz Kafka, Fritz Mauthner, Gustav Meyrink, and Rilke–detected the sinister side) for the happiness it had briefly bestowed on him: "Du gav et Menneske, der var ukendt og ene, Arbejdsdage og Haab. Og Du lærte en Fremmed, at hvert Menneske, selv det fattigste, ejer ét: at vie sin Kærlighed–Fædrelandet. Ejer ét at skænke sit Arbejde, selv det ringeste–Fædrelandet. Om Fædrelandskærlighed talte det stolte Hradschin, Stenkongen over alt Bøhmens Land" (You gave a being who was unknown and alone days of work and hope. And you taught a stranger that everyone, even the poorest person, possesses one thing–the dedication of his love to his homeland. He owns one thing on which to bestow his work–even the slightest piece–his homeland. The proud Hradschin speaks of love of the homeland, the Hradschin, the king of stone ruling the whole of the land of Bohemia).

The task Bang undertook after his return to his homeland was the composition of the short novel that earned him Rilke's accolade, *Tine,* published in 1889, on the twenty-fifth anniversary of the Danish defeat in the war of 1864. The book has a connection with *Stuk* in that Herluf Berg (another H.B. in Bang's work), the young man who narrowly escapes financial catastrophe, is present as a child in the first peaceful episodes of the war novel, when he is together with his beloved mother, his kindly father, and the mother's best friend and confidante, Tine Bølling, the daughter of a schoolmaster in the district of Als, where the elder Berg is head forester. The coming of hostilities destroys the little paradise (the chapter in which the assembled and noisy patriots hear that the first line of Danish defense, the Dannevirke, has fallen became one of the parade numbers in Bang's reading performances); mother and son are sent to safety in Copenhagen, and the father, now an officer, engages–out of a kind of desperate lust–in an affair with Tine, who genuinely loves him. Slowly, the Danish troops, trudging back and forth from Als to the front line at Dybbøl, are decimated by the massed Prussian cannon, and Lieutenant Berg is mortally wounded and dies (tended by Tine), calling for his wife and child. Tine drowns herself. The novel became an instant critical success thanks to its crowded scenes, its intimate scenes, its effective compactness, and its plumbing of the degradation caused by war. Today, with "Ved Vejen" and *Ludvigsbakke,* it is ranked as one of Bang's masterpieces.

In the next years Bang moved away from the novel: a cause may be sought in the turmoil of his personal life. His free-verse outpourings in *Digte* (Poems, 1889) provide heartfelt commentaries–poems about jealousy; about the abuses of love, as in "Kærlighed–Aagrerske Du er" (Love, You Are a Usurer); about the emptiness of life; and about self-disgust, as in "Der vaagnede den Morgen" (That Morning There Awoke):

Der vaagnede den Morgen et Lig,
Og det væmmedes selv
ved at Liget spiste,
at det stod op og gik om,
og at Liget talte.

(That morning a corpse awoke,
and itself was sickened
at the fact the corpse ate,
that it arose and walked about,
and that the corpse spoke.)

The reception of this frank (and sometimes maudlin) verse was unfriendly. An anonymous reviewer in the daily *Dagbladet* (21 December 1889) characterized it as "weak-nerved whining." Bang thought of voluntarily entering a mental hospital; he made a halfhearted attempt at suicide; and he traveled–journeys had always seemed to restore him–to Norway again. But he ran out of money (thus repeating a familiar pattern), and friends in Denmark had to help him get home. He wrote fiction for periodicals as a possible alleviation, both financially and emotionally: the novellas, collected under the title *Under Aaget* (Beneath the Yoke, 1890) and introduced by a dedicatory essay to Lie, include "En dejlig Dag" (A Nice Day), about a poor but culturally ambitious family's attempt to entertain a visiting piano star, Madame Simonsen (a portrait of the pianist Sophie Menter, his hostess at Itter, with whom Bang had once been on an abortive tour); the story "Irene Holm," about a provincial dancing teacher–and old maid–who is persuaded to perform the Tarantella and makes a fool of herself; and "Frøken Caja," a tale of the frictions and disappointments that flourish in a shabbily respectable boarding house. Then, separately, Bang published the long story, or novella, *Les quatre diables* (1890; translated as *The Four Devils,* 1927), in which he returned to the circus milieu and to physical passion–this time between the acrobats Fritz and Aimée, a couple whom love, or lust, destroys. When Austrian man of letters Richard Schaukal came across it in 1901, he found it "a tragedy, narrated with a serious artist's astonishing surety of touch" (review collected in *Intérieurs aus dem Leben der Zwanzigjährigen* [1959]), and Count Harry Kessler recommended its "quite special and remarkably strong art, sensual but never smutty" to Hofmannsthal. Ever restless, Bang left Denmark once more, hoping this time to find a niche in the entertainment world of Norway. He failed; the only result was a rather dispirited travel book, *Rundt i Norge* (Roundabout in Norway, 1892). As the director of a literary variety show, he discovered that he was pursued by his Danish detractors, who journeyed to Kristiania (renamed Oslo in 1925) simply to make fun of him.

The latest frantic flight continued; the exposure of a homosexual ring in Copenhagen and the arrest of some of its members made him decide to run farther still; his destination was Paris, where he lived in 1893 and 1894. His activities in Paris were almost entirely in the theater, as a producer at young Aurélien Lugné-Poë's Théâtre de l'Œuvre. His entrance into the Parisian stage world had been prepared for him by Count Maurice Prozor, translator of Ibsen into French; but Ibsen was not the only Nordic dramatist whom Bang helped to bring onto the French stage. Bjørnson's *Over Ævne* (Beyond Human Power, 1883), August Strindberg's *Fordringsägare* (1889; translated as *Creditors,* 1910), and his own–unstageworthy–*Brødre* (Brothers, 1891) were also in actor and theater manager Lugné-Poë's repertoire. Decades later, in his memoirs, Lugné-Poë compared Bang to such master directors as Max Reinhardt, Désiré Porel, André Antoine, and Konstantin Stanislavsky and decided that he outdid them all. Also, Bang coached the distinguished Gabrielle Réjane at Porel's Théâtre du Vaudeville, a major Parisian institution; she recorded that without Bang's aid she could not have created her character Nora in Ibsen's *Et Dukkehjem* (1879; translated as *A Doll's House,* 1880). As usual, Bang's triumphs were counterbalanced by his fits of nerves and his illnesses, psychosomatic and real. Lou Andreas-Salomé, a former friend of Friedrich Nietzsche (and, in future, of Rilke and Sigmund Freud), called on him at Saint-Germain-en-Laye in the summer of 1894, where he had gone to get away from the bustle of the capital. She found Bang (according to her *Lebensrückblick: Grandriß einiger Lebenserinnetungen* [Life's Backward Glance: Sketch of Some Life-Memories, 1951]) "constantly ailing" but "sparkling from within," and he told her how afraid he was to begin a new literary work, saying that "sometimes he would run to the window to see if there were not some helpful diversion outside to keep him from his task."

Following the French sojourn, he took part in the Scandinavian tour of Lugné-Poë's troupe (they performed Ibsen's work in French to Danish, Norwegian, and Swedish audiences) and was gratified to hear Ibsen remark that the visitor's production of *Bygmester Solness* (1892; translated as *The Master Builder,* 1893) gave the play a rebirth. A recuperative stay in Norway during the winter of 1894–1895 improved Bang's outlook. At a favorite hideaway, the resort of Sandviken, southwest of Kristiania, Bang met Claude Monet, who had traveled north to find out how snow actually looked. Even less inclined to theorize than Bang, Monet refused to be pulled into close discussions of painting; the encounter with Monet may have restored Bang's confidence in his own gift. An effort to complete a novel tentatively called "Den sidste Dansker" (The Last Dane) foundered; then, Bang began work on *Ludvigsbakke*–in which, as usual, his personal traumas constituted an underlay without causing any deformation of the artistic objectivity of the novel. Ida Brandt, the heroine (the English translation carries her name), is the only child of an overbearing mother, a sometime servant-girl who manages to marry the overseer of Ludvigsbakke Estate. After her husband's death Mother Brandt and little Ida have to move away, but the widow has laid aside a tidy sum: in her stinginess, she guards it (as the narrator remarks) like a dragon resting on its trove of gold. Liberated by her mother's passing, Ida–a sweet and helpful soul–goes to Copenhagen and takes training to become a nurse; she gets a post at the Municipal Hospital, where Bang had been a "mental patient" for a month in October 1891. The records of the examining physician state that Bang "appeared to enjoy his profound 'Weltschmerz'"; in the novel, Bang is present as the reflective and gentlemanly occupant of "Room A," who spends his nights watching the stars: "Da jeg var ung,

Bang circa 1900 (courtesy of the Danish Royal Library, Copenhagen)

betragtede jeg dem, fordi jeg vilde rive dem ned. Nu ser jeg paa dem for at lære Taalmodighed" (When I was young, I wanted to pull them down. Now, I look at them in order to learn patience). At the hospital, Ida falls in love with and is seduced by an acquaintance from her childhood at Ludvigsbakke, Karl von Eichbaum, the ne'er-do-well scion of the family that had owned (and recently lost) the estate. Having twice failed his engineering examinations, he is employed as a clerk in the hospital office and is constantly in need of money. Ida supports him, succumbs to him, and, at last, is abandoned by him. He then becomes engaged to the daughter of the butter manufacturer who has bought Ludvigsbakke, chopped down its fine old trees, and razed the manor house to make way for a vulgarly splendid mansion. The novel demonstrates that Bang's wonderful eye for detail in the creation of atmosphere–the estate as timid little Ida knew it in childhood; the small town where Ida, belatedly growing up, leads her circumscribed life under her mother's thumb; the hospital with its routines and its nurses' cliques; and the would-be elegant and crowded apartment in Copenhagen, where Karl and his mother cling to the prejudices of their class–makes every episode alive. Against these backgrounds and interwoven with them, Bang's precise chronicle of the exploitation, humiliation, and degradation of Ida gives the book that air of ineluctable defeat that Hofmannsthal perceived as Bang's special quality.

As he completed *Ludvigsbakke,* Bang again found himself involved in one of those attachments that inevitably led to emotional misery; this time, the beloved was Fritz Boesen, a naval cadet with theatrical ambitions, which Bang encouraged. Bang's letters to Boesen show how the author idolized the not-so-gifted young man, how he showered Boesen with gifts, and how his knowledge of Boesen's interest in women tormented him. Boesen eventually married one of Bang's protégées, was divorced, and married again. The literary harvest from the most intense period of the relationship seems not to reflect Bang's predicament or unhappiness until one reads between the lines: the mother in *Det hvide Hus* is gently portrayed, but one is reminded, concomitantly, of the fragile woman's erotic frustration by a husband (the dark figure in the door of his study) who no longer loves her. Further, Bang abruptly introduces the mother's friend, Lady Lipton, near the end of book. Having taken a young lover, she asks, "Er Elskov andet end at føle Begær og at undsé sig derved?" (Is love anything but knowing desire and feeling ashamed that one does?). (The theme of the mother's neglect by her husband is continued in the sequel, *Det graa Hus* [The Gray House, 1901].)

The tales Bang produced in these years, however, are not in the same autobiographical vein, although they deal once more with the many small defeats of life. The long novella *Sommerglæder* (Summer Pleasures, 1902) is a virtuoso performance in which, using less than a hundred pages, Bang introduces some ninety sharply delineated characters crowded into (and around) a country hotel that cannot possibly meet the demands placed on it. (Herman Hesse admired the "enormous technical mastery" of its "almost playfully fine filigree," as he said in a 1915 review later published in his *Gesammelte Werke* [1970].) The three tales in *Liv og Død* (Life and Death, 1899) are wistful, and all are set in the failing world of the nobility. The two in *Ravnene* (The Foxes, 1902) are quietly excruciating. In the title story, the putative heirs–the "little foxes that spoil the vines" in the Song of Solomon–jockey for an old aunt's money, while in its companion, "Julegaver" (Christmas Gifts), a country storekeeper, his wife, and his mother-in-law make an excursion to Copenhagen to see a play they have loved to read aloud, Oehlenschläger's *Aladdin,* only to learn that the program has been changed. When they return to their boardinghouse, they put the cake the wife has brought along–"Aladdin" written across it in large letters–on the table, flanked by wine and candles. At the husband's request, the wife has brought her wedding dress, too. (The mother-in-law has locked herself into her room, where she examines the bedclothes before she spreads out her own sheets that she has packed into her luggage.) The husband says, "Men det er alligevel underligt, sagde han: som det sker, naar et Menneske skal ha'e en Glæde" (But it's really strange . . . what happens when you want to have a happy time).

Bang's grudging acceptance by critics (Brandes greeted the memoiristic novels with backhanded compliments) should have made him a happier man, were it not for his evidently unrequited devotion to Boesen. (For Söderberg in Sweden, *Det hvide Hus* and *Det graa Hus,* "old memories, dreamed in a visionary twilight," were, paradoxically enough, a sign of Bang's rejuvenation.) The burden of his new critical respectability weighed heavily on him. The novel he next undertook, expected to be "monumental," was disappointing. In *Mikaël* (1904) he made the mistake of choosing Paris as a milieu and non-Danes as characters: the great painter from humble beginnings, Claude Zoret, betrayed by his adoptive son; a Czech, Eugene Mikaël, ambitious and grasping (who had sought out the master during Zoret's visit to Prague); and the rest of the large cast, mainly noblemen and noblewomen and the dealers and hangers-on of the art world. Through the glittering society in *Mikaël,* he was trying to reach an international audience and to rival Guy de Maupassant's *Fort comme la mort* (1889; translated as *Strong as Death,* 1950) and *Notre coeur* (1890; translated as *A Woman's Heart,* 1926), but the novel achieved a measured popularity only in Germany and Austria: Robert Musil wrote in 1906 (collected in volume one of his *Tagebücher I* [1955]) that he was impressed by its "stern style."

Two years later, Bang published a second determinedly major book, *De uden Fædreland,* again with some quasi-exotic settings. Joán Ujhazy, son of a Hungarian count and a Danish lady, has been reared on an island in the Danube, near the Iron Gate; he learns early on that he is an outsider (under a curse, he thinks, like the Jews who are despised by the several other nationalities inhabiting this limbo) and that he has no language he can call his own–none he can speak like a native. After boarding school in Paris (from which he is expelled for striking a Hungarian boy who claims that Joán is not his compatriot), he becomes, rather miraculously, a violin virtuoso, yet loses faith in his talent when he meets Jens Lund, a competitor whose ability is greater than his own (a portrait of Johannes V. Jensen, who in 1944 became the recipient of the Nobel Prize in literature). On a sentimental tour in his mother's homeland, Ujhazy visits a dismal little town tight against the territory the Prussians had taken in the war of 1864; he speaks his broken Danish, plays Danish songs in his concert, and believes for a moment that he has found his way to a true home. He even falls in love with Gerda, the shy daughter of the "poison mixer," the powerful owner of the tumbledown Hotel Denmark, where he has his quarters. But he does not belong and never will; in the last pages of the book, he sets out for the island of his birth, "Hvor ingen Kvinde lever" (where there are no women). For all its over-obvious symbolism, the book makes some fascinating revelations: the sense of isolation Bang labored under throughout his life; the doubt he harbored about the value of his gifts; the love and hate he felt for an ungrateful homeland (the audience at his patriotic concert turns against Joán, making fun of his accent and his music); and the passing thought that the love of a good woman could, perhaps, save even the confirmed homosexual from his lot. (At the end, the singing of the song about Olaf Rye, the general who fell defending Fredericia in the Slesvig War of 1849, is another of Bang's recondite games with names; he was presently enamored of a lieutenant named Stellan Rye.)

That Joán Ujhazy was mocked by the same Danes he wanted to please was a self-fulfilling prophecy. Jensen, to whom Bang had paid nervous homage in his *De uden Fædreland,* attacked him in a 30 November 1906 *Politiken* article, "Samfundet og Sædlighedsforbryderen" (Society and the Moral Criminal), taking Bang's militant stance in the question of the defense of Denmark as a springboard. (Bang was presently involved with the lieutenant, as Jensen reminded his readers: there had been another newspaper probe of homosexual circles in Copenhagen.) Once again Bang fled, and once again to Berlin. This incident occurred in 1907, and Bang, who had celebrated his fiftieth birthday in April, planned never to return to Denmark. Eventually, he did so to continue his other careers, as acting coach and occasional journalist and public reader, but his acquaintances noticed that he had aged markedly and seemed more distraught than before. His last collection of stories, *Sælsomme Fortællinger* (Strange Tales, 1907), deals with uncanny demises and premonitions of death. *Masker og Mennesker* (Masks and Men, 1910) which ended his writing about his lifetime passion, the theater, includes brilliant essays on "homeless" actor Josef Kainz, with whom he plainly identified, and forever restless Eleonora Duse. The lecture tours went farther and farther afield. In 1911 Bang journeyed through Norway, Sweden, and Finland (received there "with cold politeness") and then to Russia, thinking he would be accepted as the Anton Chekhov of Denmark, but the audiences (even though his work had appeared in Russian) were thin. In his first review of Bang's work, Rilke in 1902 had singled out "this haste, this feverish inactivity" that so often "lies upon especially refined and sensitive people" (article collected in volume five of Rilke's *Sämtliche Werke* [1965]) as a central theme in Bang's novels; the same empty haste now utterly possessed their author. Returning to the west by way of Berlin (to pay a visit to his psychiatrist, Max Wasbutzski, who–after Bang's death–published his patient's little treatise on his erotic disposition, *Gedanken zum Sexualitätsproblem* [1922]), he went on to Cuxhaven and took ship for America, intending to make a lecture trip around the world. On board the liner *Moltke,* he wrote a letter to actress Betty Nansen, the wife of his sometime confidant Peter Nansen; he told her how he enjoyed the spectacle of a storm at sea; how he had met a young Spaniard, "as handsome as a Hermes"; and how he was approaching the shores of America, the land "where I want to be least of all." He thought that his cabin number, 8, resembled handcuffs.

In New York he told the hotel barber to hide his bald spot before he gave a reading for a circle of Scandinavian admirers; he felt lost, since he spoke little English. He took the train to Chicago and was met by the Danish consul, who had arranged a luncheon in his honor; then, in the evening, Bang was driven to the station, to board the Overland Express for San Francisco. The train left on a Friday; on Saturday, he seemed weak, and a young man named Lowenstein–who spoke German–accompanied him to the diner; the porter had to help him into his bunk that night. At noon on

HERMAN BANG

VÆRKER
I MINDEUDGAVE

SJETTE BIND

KJØBENHAVN OG KRISTIANIA
GYLDENDALSKE BOGHANDEL
NORDISK FORLAG
MDCCCCXII

Title page for the final volume of Bang's collected works, published in the year of his death (courtesy of the Danish Royal Library, Copenhagen)

Sunday, Bang was found unconscious in his compartment, paralyzed on his left side. At Ogden, Utah, he was taken to the Thomas D. Dee Memorial Hospital; he died the next morning, 29 January 1912, without regaining consciousness. The sensational circumstances that had surrounded his life followed him into death: rumors were spread about murder, but his health had been fragile for many years. Some evidence existed that he may have been robbed after his stroke: one of his trouser legs had been cut open; his watch was missing; and he had only a small sum of money on his person. An investigation by the Pullman Company at the behest of the Danish consul in Chicago led to nothing. The stories about foul play never quite subsided; as late as 1950 they were renewed in the posthumous memoirs of Christian Houmark–an actor, author, and intimate of Bang–who asserted that the corpse's neck bore marks of throttling. The source of Houmark's information is unknown, and the tale probably cannot be proven. But a grotesque mischance did take place at Bang's burial in Denmark: his body was placed in the wrong grave and had to be moved after the mourners had departed. Bang might have been amused at the mistake, as at the circumstance that he had died in a Mormon hospital.

When the Swedish author Oscar Levertin met Bang during one of the latter's lecture tours, he was put off at first by Bang's extravagant posing, his carefully combed forelock, his powdered cheeks, and his exquisite dress. But then Levertin noticed that the speech given by this "exotic hothouse flower" betrayed a "melancholy self-irony" and a "remarkably sophisticated naiveté." Deceptively, Bang's works–in this respect like Andersen's–can seem melodramatic or sentimental. Yet, everything he wrote bears the unmistakable mark of his narrative energy and of his ability to suggest full-blown portraits through a few remarks or gestures by his many characters. Bang wrote some unforgettable bravura pieces–for example, the headlong abandonment of Horsens by the crown prince and his troops in *Haabløse Slægter,* as William Høg's baby brother lies dying; the crowds bustling to the variety theater in the first pages of *Stuk;* the day at the fair and the walk through the graveyard in "Ved Vejen"; the interrupted jingoist meeting in *Tine;* the nurses' party and the snobs' dinner in *Ludvigsbakke;* the franticness at the Brasens's hotel in the tragicomic *Sommerglæder;* and the dining car on the Orient Express in *De uden Fædreland.* (A neglected triumph is the Paris get-together of Danish expatriates in *Helg* [Holiday, 1935], which Bang never completed.) Bang is a swift and sure conjurer of moods–for instance, the Christmas, summer, and harvest idylls in *Det hvide Hus;* the autumnal decay of *Det graa Hus;* and the rottenness of the jerry-built border community in *De uden Fædreland* set against the fresh early springtime of Slesvig. Persons, scenes, and atmospheres are swept along by the peculiarly oral nature of Bang's narratives; he allegedly talked to himself incessantly as he paced and wrote. A failure as a playwright, he was a skillful dramatist in his prose, not least in his short stories and novellas: examples are "Fratelli Bedini," "Hendes Højhed," "En dejlig Dag," "Irene Holm," and "Frøken Caja." (*Les quatre diables* was turned into a successful silent movie in 1928 by F. W. Murnau.) Throughout his rather small production, Herman Bang bore witness to his sympathy with humankind, no matter how foolish or deluded or desperate he knew its representatives to be, a quality that makes him a companion to Chekhov or to the James Joyce of "Clay" and "The Dead" in *Dubliners* (1914).

Letters:

Herman Bangs Vandreaar, Fortalt i Breve til Peter Nansen, edited by Lauritz Nielsen (Copenhagen: Koppel, 1918);

Breve til Fritz, edited by Ulla Albeck & Erik Timmermann (Copenhagen: Westermann, 1951);

Min egen ven. Herman Bangs sidste brev til Betty Nansen, edited by Per Busck Nielsen (Copenhagen: Busck, 1974).

Biographies:

P. A. Rosenberg, *Herman Bang* (Copenhagen: Schønberg, 1912);

Louis E. Grandjean, *Herman Bang: Et Essay om Mennesket og Digteren* (Copenhagen: Gyldendal, 1942);

Harry Jacobsen, *Der unge Herman Bang: Mennesket, Digteren, Journalisten og Hans By* (Copenhagen: Hagerup, 1954);

Jacobsen, *Herman Bang: Resignationens Digter* (Copenhagen: Hagerup, 1957);

Jacobsen, *Den miskendte Herman Bang: Aarene der gik tabt* (Copenhagen: Hagerup, 1961);

Jacobsen, *Den tragiske Herman Bang* (Copenhagen: Hagerup, 1966);

Vivian Greene-Gantzberg, *Biography of Danish Literary Impressionist Herman Bang* (Lewiston, Queenston & Lampeter: Edwin Mellen Press, 1997).

References:

Hans Aarsleff, "Rilke, Herman Bang, and Malte," *Proceedings of the IVth Congress of the International Comparative Literature Association* (1966): 628–636;

Knut Ahnlund, "Utanför normen: Herman Bang," in his *Diktarliv i Norden: Litterära essäer* (Stockholm: Bromberg, 1981), pp. 145–221;

Hanne Amsinck, *Sceneinstruktøren Herman Bang og det franske symbolistiske teater* (Copenhagen: Gad, 1972);

Maurice Bigeon, "Arne Garborg et Herman Bang," in his *Les Scandinaves révoltés* (Paris: Grasilier, 1894), pp. 207–234;

Pål Bjørby, "Herman Bang's 'Franz Pander': Narcissism, Self, and the Nature of the Unspoken," *Scandinavian Studies,* 62 (1990): 449–467;

Bjørby, "The Prison House of Sexuality: Homosexuality in Bang Scholarship," *Scandinavian Studies,* 58 (1986): 223–255;

Jørgen Bonde Jensen, "Franz Panders skinvirkelighed," *Vindrosen,* 20, no. 4 (1973): 116–144;

Mette Borg, *Sceneinstruktøren Herman Bang: Teatersyn og metode* (Copenhagen: Busck, 1986);

Thomas Bredsdorff, "At lide af kærlighed: Om Bangs 'Ludvigsbakke,'" in his *Tristans børn: Angående digtning om kærlighed og ægten skab i den borgerlige epoke* (Copenhagen: Gyldendal, 1982), pp. 143–162;

Carl Burchardt, "Herman Bang," in his *J. P. Jacobsen og andre essays* (Oslo: Rambæk, 1947), pp. 51–72;

Georg Christensen, "Herman Bangs teknik," *Edda,* 9 (1918): 57–80;

Beverly Driver Eddy, "Herman Bang's 'Irene Holm' as a Study of Life and Art," *Scandinavica,* 28 (1989): 17–27;

Eddy, "Herman Bang's Prose: The Narrative as Theater," *Mosaic,* 4 (1970): 79–89;

Harald Elovson, "Vilhelm Ekelund och Herman Bang," *Vetenskap-societeten i Lund: Årsbok* (1977): 22–54;

Johannes Fjord Jensen, *Turgenjev i dansk åndsliv* (Copenhagen: Gyldendal, 1961), pp. 252–268;

Annalisa Forsberger, *Eros och speglingar* (Stockholm: Rabén & Sjögren, 1961), pp. 251–322;

Maurice Gravier, "Herman Bang et la peinture," in *Växelverkan mellan skönlitteraturen och andra konstarter: Den sjätte internationella studiekonferensen över nordisk litteratur,* edited by Gunnar Svanfeldt (Uppsala: Litteraturhist. Inst., 1967), pp. 9–29;

Gravier, "Herman Bang et le roman naturaliste français I," *Etudes Germaniques,* 9 (1954): 278–290;

Gravier, "Herman Bang et le roman naturaliste français II: Herman Bang et Guy de Maupassant," *Etudes Germaniques,* 11 (1956): 21–35;

Vivian Greene-Gantzberg, "Herman Bang als Theaterkritiker in Deutschland," *Skandinavistik,* 16, no. 1 (1986): 7–20;

Greene-Gantzberg, *Herman Bang og det fremmede* (Copenhagen: Gyldendal, 1992);

Olav Harsløv, *Omkring Stuk* (Copenhagen: Hans Reitzel, 1977);

Finn Hauberg Mortensen, "Sproglige og fortælletekniske Iakttagelser i Herman Bangs Novelle, 'Irene Holm,'" *Poetik,* 2, no. 1 (1969): 54–83;

Arnold Hending, *Herman Bang paa Film* (Copenhagen: Kandrup & Wunsch, 1957);

Mogens Hermansen, "Herman Bang," *American-Scandinavian Review,* 45 (1957): 170–172;

Sofus E. Hermansen, "Herman Bang: Life and Theme," *Germanic Notes,* 3, no. 5 (1972): 34–37;

Hans Holmberg, "Nordiska kulturförbindelser: August Lindberg och Herman Bang," *Horisont,* 28, no. 6 (1981): 56–60;

Aage Houken, "Thomas Mann og Norden," *Nordisk Tidskrift,* 45 (1969): 213–229;

Christian Houmark, *Timer der blev til Dage. Udgivet efter hans Død af Horatio* (Copenhagen: Thaning & Appel, 1950), pp. 48–160;

Harry Jacobsen, *Herman Bang: Nye Studier* (Copenhagen: Nordisk Bogforlag, 1974);

Astrid Jensen and Jytte Jonker, "The Expectant Text: On Herman Bang's *Det hvide Hus* and *Det graa Hus,*" *Scandinavica,* 6 (1967): 85–94;

John Chr. Jørgensen, "Herman Bang og Georg Brandes mellem positivistisk og kritisk realisme," in his *Den sande kunst: Studier i 1800-tals realisme* (Copenhagen: Borgen, 1980), pp. 289–341;

Josef Kleinheinrich, *Kopenhagener Panoramen um 1900: Varianten der Großstadtapperzeption und der poetischen Transformation von Großstaderlebnissen im journalistischen Œuvre Herman Bangs* (Münster: Hölker, 1986);

Rafael Koskimies, *Der nordische Dekadent* (Helsinki: Suomalaisen Kirjallisuuden Seura, 1968), pp. 37–57;

Ulrich Lauterbach, *Herman Bang: Studien zum dänischen Impressionismus* (Breslau: Maruschke & Berendt, 1937);

Anna Levin, *Fra Herman Bangs Journalistaar ved "Nationaltidende" 1879–84: Minder, samlede omkring Breve til mine Forældre* (Copenhagen: Gyldendalske: Boghandel, Nordisk Forlag, 1932);

Peter Madsen, "Lidens smerte og storbyens atmosfær: Journalisten Herman Bang og hans roman 'Stuk,'" *Poetik,* 6, no. 4 (1974–1975): 7–31;

Leonie Marx, "Herman Bangs Regiekunst in 'Hendes Højhed,'" *Journal of English and Germanic Philology,* 95 (1996): 52–78;

Klaus Matthias, *Thomas Mann und Skandinavien* (Lübeck: Schmidt-Römhild, 1969);

Knud Michelsen, "Storbyen som sjælstilstand: Om Herman Bangs *Stuk,*" *Kritik,* 25 (1973): 32–64;

David Miles, "Hofmannsthals 'Dänischer Schriftsteller' und das Bild des sterbenden Tieres," *Hofmannsthal-Blätter* (1975–1976): 462–463;

Jöran Mjöberg, "*Ved Vejen,*" in his *De sökte sanningen: En studie i fem romaner 1879–1886* (Stockholm: Rabén & Sjögren, 1977);

Jan Mogren, *Herman Bangs Haabløse Slægter* (Lund: Gleerup, 1957);

Sven Møller Kristensen, *Impressionismen i dansk Prosa 1870–1900* (Copenhagen: Gyldendal, 1955);

Klaus P. Mortensen, *Sonderinger i Herman Bangs romaner* (Copenhagen: Vinten, 1973);

Torben Nielsen, "Digter og politisk iagttagere: Herman Bangs Finland 1911," *Historiska och Litteraturhistoriska studier,* 63 (1988): 141–160;

Torbjörn Nilsson, *Impressionisten Herman Bang: Studier i Herman Bangs författarskap till och med 'Tine'* (Stockholm: Norstedt, 1965);

Ib Ostenfeld, "Herman Bang og århundredskiftets degenerationslære," in his *Seks patografiske miniaturer* (Copenhagen: Nyt Nordisk Forlag, 1966), pp. 31–39;

Felix Poppenberg, "Herman Bang," in his *Nordische Porträts aus vier Reichen* (Berlin: Bard Marquardt, 1904): 1–17;

Saladin Schmitt, "Über Herman Bang," *Mitteilungen der Literaturhistorischen Gesellschaft Bonn,* 7 (1912): 207–229;

George C. Schoolfield, "De uden Fædreland," in his *A Baedeker of Decadence: Charting a Literary Fashion* (New Haven & London: Yale University Press, 2003), pp. 305–326;

Schoolfield, "*Die Aufzeichnungen des Malte Laurids Brigge.*" *A Companion to the Works of Rainer Maria Rilke,* edited by Erika Metzger and Michael M. Metzger (Rochester, N.Y. & Woodbridge, U.K.: Camden House [Boydell & Brewer], 2001), pp. 154–187;

Claus Secher, *Sexualitet og samfund i Herman Bangs romaner* (Copenhagen: Borgen, 1973);

Eckart von Sydow, *Die Kultur der Decadenz* (Dresden: Sibyllen-Verlag, 1922), pp. 287–291;

Louise E. Van Wijk, "Notitser om Herman Bang," *Edda,* 47 (1947): 184–203;

Mette Winge, *Omkring Haabløse Slægter* (Copenhagen: Hans Reitzel, 1972);

Raimund Wolfert, "Max Eisfeld–die große Liebe Herman Bangs," *Forum-Homosexualität und Literatur,* 33 (1998): 5–42.

Papers:

Herman Bang's letters and manuscripts are at the Danish Royal Library in Copenhagen.

Charlotta Dorothea Biehl

(2 June 1731 - 17 May 1788)

Marianne Alenius
Museum Tusculanum Press, University of Copenhagen

(Translated by Gaye Kynoch)

BOOKS: *Den kierlige Mand. Comedie udi fem Acter* (Copenhagen: Printed by L. H. Lillie's Widow, 1764; revised edition, Copenhagen: Printed by H. C. Sander & J. F. Morthorst, 1772);

Den forelskede Ven, eller Kiærlighed under Venskabs Navn. Comedie i fem Acter (Copenhagen: Printed by P. H. Höecke, 1765);

Haarkløveren. Comedie udi fem Acter (Copenhagen: Printed by L. H. Lillie's Widow, 1765);

Den listige Optrækkerske. Comedie i fem Acter (Copenhagen: Printed by L. H. Lillie's Widow, 1765);

Melpomenes og Thaliæ Trætte. En Prologus til at opføres paa den Kongel. Danske Skueplads, den 2den Jan. 1765 (Copenhagen: Berlingske Arvinger, [1765]);

Den glædede Thalia, forestillet i en Prologus til at opføres paa den danske Skueplads den 3die Octobr. 1766 (Copenhagen: Printed by N. Møller, 1766);

Tvistigheden eller Critique over den listige Optrækkerske. Comedie i een Act (Copenhagen: Printed by P. H. Höecke, 1766);

Den Ædelmodige. Comedie i fem Acter (Copenhagen: Printed by N. Møller, 1767);

Den alt for lønlige Beiler, eller den som giør Hemmelighed af alle Ting. Comedie udi fem Acter (Copenhagen: Printed by H. C. Sander & J. F. Morthorst, 1772);

Silphen. Et Syngespil i tre Acter (Copenhagen: Printed by N. Møller, 1773);

Kierligheds-Brevene. Et Syngespil i tre Acter (Copenhagen: Printed by N. Møller, 1774);

Den prøvede Troeskab. Et Syngespil i tre Acter (Copenhagen: Printed by N. Møller, 1774);

Euphemia. Tragedie i fem Akter (Copenhagen: Printed by M. Hallager, 1775);

En Tale holden i Kiede-Forsamlingen d. 13de Martii 1778 af Søster B[iehl] (Copenhagen: Privately printed, 1778);

Moralske Fortællinger, 4 volumes (Copenhagen: Printed by H. C. Sander & H. C. Schrøder, 1781-1782);

Brevvexling imellem fortrolige Venner, 3 volumes (Copenhagen: Printed by P. Horrebow, 1783);

Charlotta Dorothea Biehl (miniature by Cornelius Høyer, circa 1775; Museum of National History at Frederiksborg Castle)

Den tavse Pige eller de ved Tavshed avlede Mistanker. En Original Comedie i fem Acter, anonymous (N.p., [1783]);

Til Hans Kongelige Høihed Cronprindsen Den 4 April 1784 (Copenhagen: Printed by N. Møller, [1784]);

Orpheus og Euridice. Et Syngespil i 3 Acter. Poesien er af C. D. Biehl. Musiquen af Hr. Nauman (Copenhagen: Printed by F. W. Thiele, 1786);

Mit ubetydelige Levnetsløb, edited by Louis Bobé (Copenhagen: J. L. Lybecker, 1909); revised and enlarged as *Mit ubetydelige Levnets Løb,* edited by Marianne Alenius (Copenhagen: Museum Tusculanum, 1986; reprinted, 1999).

Editions and Collections: *Lustspiele der Jungfer Charlotta Dorothea Biehl,* translated by Johann Adolph Scheibe (Copenhagen & Leipzig: Mummische Buchhandlung, 1767);
Comedier, 2 volumes (Copenhagen: Typografiske Selskab, 1773);
Den listige Optrækkerske, edited by Leif Nielsen (Aarhus: Arkona/Svalegangen, 1984);
Moralske Fortællinger, 1761–1805, edited by Anne-Marie Mai and Esther Kielberg (Copenhagen: Borgen, 1994).

SELECTED PLAY PRODUCTIONS: *Den kierlige Mand,* Copenhagen, Den Danske Skueplads, 17 October 1764;
Haarkløveren, Copenhagen, Den Danske Skueplads, 16 January 1765;
Den listige Optrækkerske, Copenhagen, Den Danske Skueplads, 16 October 1765;
Den forelskede Ven, Copenhagen, Den Danske Skueplads, 27 November 1765;
Den kierlige Datter, Copenhagen, Den Danske Skueplads, 18 January 1768;
Den Ædelmodige, Copenhagen, Den Danske Skueplads, 2 November 1768;
Den alt for lønlige Beiler, Copenhagen, Den Kongelige Danske Skueplads, 2 December 1771;
Silphen, Copenhagen, Hofteatret, 27 October 1773;
Den prøvede Troeskab, Copenhagen, Den Kongelige Danske Skueplads, 31 January 1774;
Kierligheds-Brevene, Copenhagen, Hofteatret, 22 March 1775;
Den Tavse Pige, Copenhagen, Hofteatret, 2 March 1780;
Orpheus og Euridice, music by Johan Gottlieb Naumann, Copenhagen, Den Kongelige Danske Skueplads, 31 January 1786.

OTHER: *Den kiærlige Daatter. Comedie udi fem Acter,* in *Forsøg i de skiønne og nyttige Videnskaber,* volume 3, part 5 (Copenhagen: Printed by N. Møller, 1766); republished as *Den kierlige Datter. Comedie udi fem Acter* (Copenhagen, 1772);
"Brev fra Waldborg Immers Datter til hendes Veninde," in *Poetiske Samlinger udgivne af et Selskab,* part 1 (Copenhagen: Printed by A. H. Godiche & F. C. Godiche, 1775), pp. 101–126;
"Hovmesterinden. En original Fortælling," in *Bibliothek for det Smukke Kiøn,* volume 4, part 2 (Copenhagen: Gyldendal, printed by F. W. Thiele, 1786), pp. 1–76.

SELECTED TRANSLATIONS: Charles-Simon Favart, *Soliman den Anden. Comoedie udi tre Acter,* anonymous (Sorø: Printed by J. Lindgren, 1763);
Salomon Gessner, *Abels Død oversadt af det Tydske efter H. Gesners Original,* anonymous (Copenhagen: Printed by L. H. Lillie's Widow, 1764);
Françoise d'Isembourg-d'Happoncourt de Grafigny, *Cénie. Comoedie i 5 Acter,* anonymous (Copenhagen: Printed by L. H. Lillie's Widow, 1764);
Antoine Léonard Thomas, *Lovtale over Maximilian de Bethune, Hertug af Sully, Surintendant over Finandserne a. Premier-Minister under Henrik IV,* anonymous (Copenhagen: Printed by N. Møller, 1764);
Charles-Pierre Colardeau, *Caliste. En Tragoedie i fem Acter* (Copenhagen: Berlingske Arvinger, 1765);
Isidoro Bianchi, *Betragtninger over adskillige Puncter af den almindelige og private Lyksalighed* (Copenhagen: A. H. Godiche's Descendants & F. C. Godiche, 1774);
Bianchi, *Belønningerne der tilkomme dydige Indbyggere* (Copenhagen: A. H. Godiche's Descendants & F. C. Godiche, [1775]);
Frimurer-Sange, oversatte af det Tydske ved Ordenes sande Veninde, anonymous (Copenhagen: Printed by N. Møller, 1776);
Miguel de Cervantes Saavedra, *Den sindrige Herremands Don Quixote af Mancha Levnet og Bedrifter* (4 volumes, Copenhagen: Gyldendal, 1776–1777; 2 volumes, revised by F. L. Liebenberg, with illustrations by Wilhelm Marstrand, Copenhagen: F. Wøldike, printed by B. Luno, 1865, 1869);
Nicolas Boindin and Antoine Houdar de La Motte, *Søe-havnen. Comoedie i 1 Act,* anonymous, in *Skuespil til Brug for den Danske Skueplads,* volume 3 (Copenhagen: Gyldendal, 1777);
Sébastien-Roch Nicolas Chamfort, *Den unge Indianerinde. Comoedie i 1 Act,* anonymous, in *Skuespil til Brug for den Danske Skueplads,* volume 3;
Johann Jacob Engel, *Pagen. Comoedie i 1 Act,* anonymous, in *Skuespil til Brug for den Danske Skueplads,* volume 3;
Gotthold Ephraim Lessing, *Emilie Galotti. Tragoedie i 5 Acter,* anonymous, in *Skuespil til Brug for den Danske Skueplads,* volume 3;
Michel-Jean Sedaine, *Kongen og Forpagteren, et Syngestykke i 3 Acter,* anonymous, in *Syngespil for den danske Skueplads,* volume 3 (Copenhagen: Gyldendal, 1778);
Sedaine, *Væddemaalet. Comoedie i 1 Act,* anonymous, in *Skuespil til Brug for den Danske Skueplads,* volume 4 (Copenhagen: Gyldendal, 1778);
Philippe Néricault Destouches, *Den forstilte Taabelige eller Landsbye-Poeten,* anonymous, in *Skuespil til Brug for den Danske Skueplads,* volume 6 (Copenhagen: Gyldendal, 1780);
Destouches, *Det sære Menneske. Comoedie i 5 Acter,* anonymous, in *Skuespil til Brug for den Danske Skueplads,* volume 6;

Cervantes Saavedra, *Lærerige Fortællinger. Oversat af det Spanske efter det i Haag 1739 udgivne Oplag,* 2 volumes (Copenhagen: Printed by N. Møller, 1780, 1781);

Gérard Dudoyer de Gastels, *Laurette. Et Syngestykke i 1 Act,* in *Syngespil for den danske Skueplads,* volume 4 (Copenhagen: Gyldendal, 1781);

Alexandre Frédéric Jacques de Masson, marquis de Pezay, *Rosen-Bruden i Salenci. Et Syngespil i 3 Acter,* in *Syngespil for den danske Skueplads,* volume 4;

Gottlieb Stephanie, *Raptussen, eller Den eene har for meget, den anden for lidet. Komedie i 3 Akter,* anonymous, in *Skuespil til Brug for den Danske Skueplads,* volume 8 (Copenhagen: Gyldendal, 1783);

Joseph Marie Piccini, *Den foregivne Lord. Et Syngestykke i 2 Akter,* in *Syngespil for den danske Skueplads,* anonymous, volume 7 (Copenhagen: Gyldendal, 1785);

August Wilhelm Iffland, *Jægerne. Comoedie i 5 Acter,* anonymous (Copenhagen: Sønnichsen, 1787);

Giovanni Battista Casti, *Trophonii Hule. Et Syngestykke i 2 Akter,* in *Syngespil for den danske Skueplads,* volume 8 (Copenhagen: Gyldendal, 1790).

SELECTED PERIODICAL PUBLICATIONS–UNCOLLECTED: "C. D. Biehls Anekdoter om Christian VI i 2 Breve til Joh. Bülow 1784," in *Dansk Maanedsskrift,* volume 1, edited by M. G. G. Steenstrup (Copenhagen: Gyldendal, 1865), pp. 30–51;

"Charlotte Dorothea Biehls Historiske Breve," edited by J. H. Bang, *Historisk Tidsskrift,* third series, volume 4 (1865–1866): 147–494;

"Regeringsforandringen d. 14. April 1784," edited by Edvard Holm, *Historisk Tidsskrift,* third series, volume 5 (1866–1867): 281–455.

Biehl's father, Christian Æmilius Biehl, secretary of the Royal Academy of Fine Arts (painting by C. G. Pilo, circa 1755; Danmarks Kunstbibliotek, Copenhagen)

Charlotta Dorothea Biehl is the best-known Danish woman writer and translator of the eighteenth century. She stands apart from her female contemporaries in terms of her extensive output in many genres. Most of her works were published during her lifetime, some in two or three editions and in German translations, although part of her literary production was published posthumously. Biehl was especially innovative in her approach to playwriting and the epistolary novel, a genre with widespread appeal across large parts of eighteenth-century Europe. As a dramatist she was Ludvig Holberg's successor in supplying comedies for the Danish stage, and from 1764 to 1772 she was both the most significant and, by and large, the only writer of comedies for the theater in Denmark. She wrote in the new, bourgeois, French-Italian-inspired style, which in the theater was manifested in a genre lying between tragedy and comedy, in Scandinavia called "the sensitive comedy." From 1772 onward Biehl was known for her ballad operas (*syngespil,* or *Singspiel* in German). As a letter writer she made her mark in several fictional epistolary genres, inspired both by French *chroniques scandaleuses* (scandalous chronicles) and British epistolary novels; many thousands of pages of her fictional letters were published. Alongside this achievement, she wrote more or less private letters, both in prose and verse, nearly all of them addressed to Lord Chamberlain Johan von Bülow.

Biehl was interested in other countries, although she never traveled internationally. From her home in the center of Copenhagen, she spent her life studying European culture and taught herself several languages. One of the results of these endeavors was her many translations of works of drama, literature, and moral philosophy from French, German, Italian, and Spanish. A large part of her literary output was published, and many of her plays were staged, while others are preserved in manuscript form. Her proficiency in foreign languages was one of the reasons she was well connected and sought after in intellectual circles and in the European milieu at the Danish court.

Charlotta Dorothea Biehl was born on 2 June 1731 in Copenhagen, where she lived all of her life. Her parents both belonged to the respectable bourgeoisie.

Her father, Christian Æmilius Biehl, was superintendent at Charlottenborg Castle in the center of Copenhagen, and he moved his family into the castle in 1754 when it became Det Kongelige Akademi (The Royal Academy of Fine Arts), of which he was appointed secretary. This job brought his daughter into contact with many artists, of whom two later painted her portrait. Charlotta Dorothea's mother, Sophie Hedevig Brøer, also came from the higher social echelons. Her father, Hans Brøer, *præsident for borgretten* (president of the court for nonroyal employees) at the Danish Royal Court and castle steward at Copenhagen Castle, was the most important person to his granddaughter during her childhood. Charlotta Dorothea lived with her maternal grandparents until her grandfather's death in 1739, when she was seven years old. Brøer had given her a loving upbringing, a Christian ethic, and a taste for study. The faith he placed in her talents and her personality was the foundation from which she drew strength for the next two decades, during which she had to develop intellectually and artistically without any encouragement from her immediate family. In her posthumously published autobiography *Mit ubetydelige Levnets Løb* (The Course of My Insignificant Life, 1909) she explains that her grandfather helped her to learn to read when she was four years old, taught her German, and gave her books. He had promised that she would be allowed to learn Latin, even though he did not understand why she would want to: "Hvad kunde det gavne dig? Sagde han. Du har io ingen Buxer paa og kan ikke Blive Professor" ("How would that help you," he said. "As you do not wear trousers, you cannot be a professor"), he apparently said. Her argument was that without a knowledge of Latin she would be unable to understand Holberg properly: "Ja, men det er dog hæsligt, sagde jeg, at man ikke forstaar en Bog heel" (Yes, but is it not horrible if one does not understand a book completely?). During Biehl's childhood Holberg was the leading author and playwright in Denmark; thanks to her grandfather, she had some of his works on her private bookshelf.

Brøer's death closed the only channel of education open to Biehl, including the possibility of learning Latin. She now received a traditional girls' upbringing: needlework, domestic skills, and a limited instruction in writing. She had to learn the rest herself because, according to Biehl, her father opposed her desire for knowledge to such an extent that, threatening a whipping should he find her with a book in her hand, he impeded her access to learning. She surreptitiously read the books they had at home, however, and gradually procured more from friends of her parents. Her interest in music led her to start learning to play the flute, but even though she quickly reached the stage where she could play to the accompaniment of a piano, she gave up the instrument because of her father's constant mockery. Yet, the foundation had been laid for her later collaborations with composers when working on the librettos for ballad operas and operas.

As an old woman Biehl looked back on the later part of her childhood and most of her teenage years without much fondness. Her younger sister, Lise, died in 1739, and her brother, Carl, with whom she later shared an apartment, does not seem to have played any kind of influential role in her childhood. Her mother was apparently of a kindly disposition but of no help to Biehl in her quarrels with her father.

In 1750 Biehl's interest in theater was awakened when a French troupe of actors visited Copenhagen and performed on a small stage erected for them in the concert hall at Charlottenborg, to which, because of her father's job, she had free access. She was now inspired to learn French; using a grammar and a dictionary borrowed from friends of the family, she worked her way through the text of the play and learned the rules of pronunciation by following the script as she watched the performance. Subsequent hard study of texts and conjugation of verbs, with no formal instruction, soon enabled Biehl to read a novel in French. She then set to work in a similar fashion with Italian and also became accomplished in this language.

During her adolescence and early adulthood, from 1745 until 1755, Biehl was primarily occupied with domestic work, language and literature studies, and conjectures about the nature of love and the attentions of young men. Her father also opposed her in this matter. She was not allowed to marry the man she loved, and she declined to marry another. The quarrel went on for ten years, and Biehl remained unmarried all her life, but she had garnered material for her writing, which was to deal chiefly with the bourgeois family. She established intense and long-lasting friendships with many influential men, but she probably never experienced physical love. Lacking the opportunity to protest against the demands and proscriptions inflicted by her father, on whom she was financially dependent, she formed a pact with herself in her dealings with him: through dutiful politeness she ensured a certain degree of invulnerability.

In 1760 Biehl was one of the motivating forces behind an amateur production of a play in the private apartments at Charlottenborg, where the family now lived. The play came about as pure entertainment for cultural members of the nobility and upper class, but the dynamic and high-quality work with such an influential group of people had radical consequences for Biehl's career. At the direct request of Vilhelm Bornemann, a lawyer who was interested in the theater and

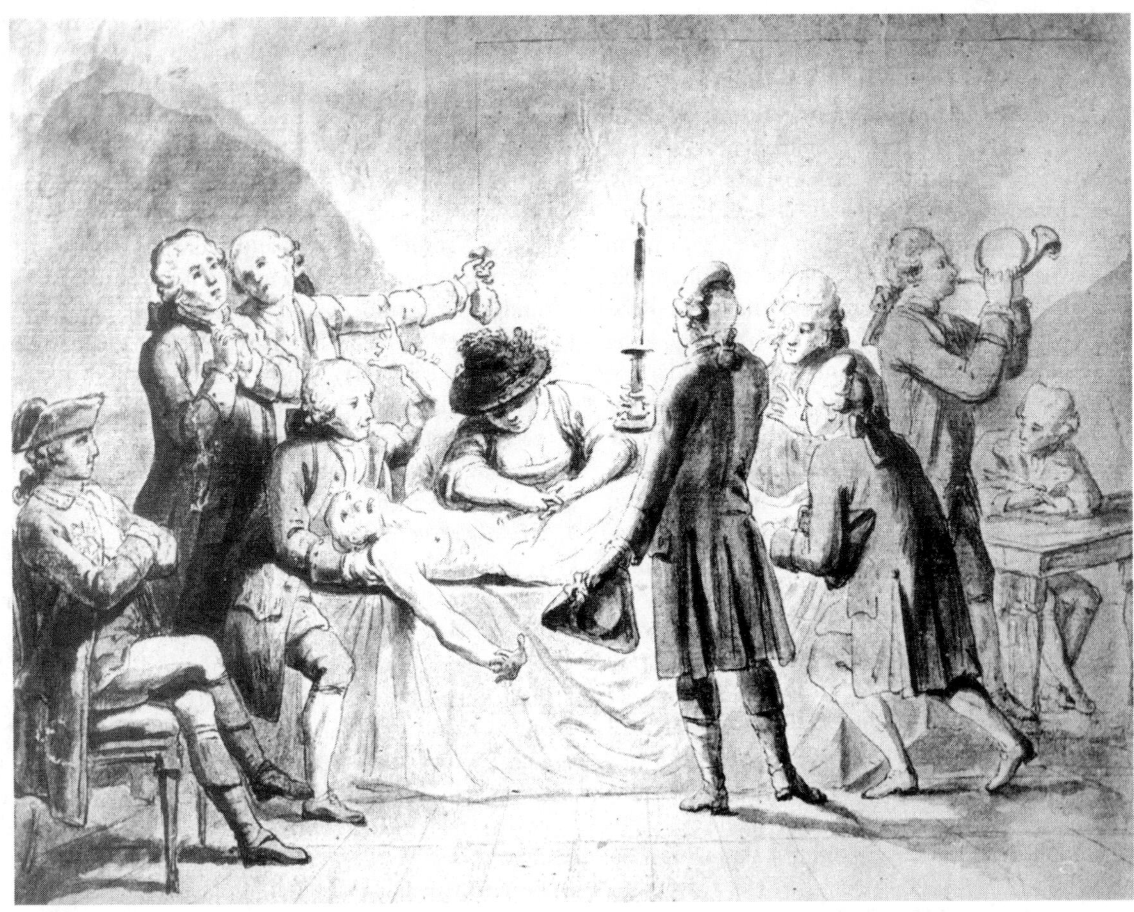

Biehl emasculating Ludvig Holberg, whom she replaced as a popular writer of comedies for the Danish stage (satirical drawing by Cornelius Høyer, 1775; Sorø Academy Library; photograph courtesy of the Danish Royal Library, Copenhagen)

had noticed her talent in her work on the production, she set out to translate plays from French into Danish. Contemporary French comedy, as represented by Philippe Néricault Destouches, was her carefully selected textual foundation for the translation project. The first comedy she translated, *L'Amour usé* (1741), was completed under the guidance of Bornemann in a mutually rewarding collaboration. She later referred to him as her "Ven og Læremester" (friend and mentor) in *Mit ubetydelige Levnets Løb*. The translation of *L'Amour Usé* is lost, but Biehl's work on it is discussed in her autobiography.

Biehl continued translating works by Destouches, and by the early spring of 1761 she was ready to submit two plays to the Royal Theater at Kongens Nytorv (King's New Square) in Copenhagen. The theater immediately accepted *Den forstilte Taabelige eller Landsbye-Poeten,* Biehl's translation of Destouches's *La fausse Agnès, ou Le poete Campagnard* (The False Agnes, or The Country Poet, 1734; first staged, 1759), and it premiered on 13 October 1761. Her translation was not published until 1780, but the play was immediately so successful that people speculated as to the true identity of the translator. These doubts about her ability were, however, groundless, and reports of her talent had already spread throughout the city. Biehl received a request from Crown Prince Christian's tutor, the Swiss Elie Salomon François Reverdil, to translate Charles-Simon Favart's recently published moralizing comedy *Les Trois Sultanes; ou, Soliman second* (The Three Sultans; or, Soliman the Second, 1761). Biehl's translation, *Soliman den Anden,* was published in 1763; it was her first published work, but at her request her name was not listed as translator. *Soliman den Anden* was first performed on 8 October 1770 at the Royal Theater, and six years later it was republished with a highly complimentary introduction, which, although published anonymously, had been written by Jens Schielderup Sneedorff, who at the time represented the intellectual circle at Sorø Academy and was active in the first literary society in Denmark. Sneedorff considered Biehl's translation to be good and interesting because it was not prejudiced by the viewpoint of traditional, rhetorical schooling. It bore the characteristics of having been translated by a woman, as the language was based on common sense, natural good taste, and industrious reading of quality works written in a modern language. Sneedorff found not a female aesthetic but a female style in the translation, "eine anti-intellektualistische, emotiv bestimmte Ästhetik" (an anti-intellectualistic aesthetic determined by emotions), as Wilfried Hauke puts it. Sneedorff was absorbed by the text itself, writing in his introduction that the contrast of the two main figures, Sultan Soliman the Second and the slave Roxelane, threw light on the fact that "En lykkelig Forestilling deraf [nemlig: af handlingen] skulde vist giøre Kiønnet megen Ære. Den skulde viise, hvor meget en fornuftig Brug af dets Yndigheder kunde giøre til at formilde endog den grummeste Despotisme" (a successful staging could certainly pay much honor to the female sex. It should demonstrate how much a reasonable use of female beauty could allay even the most terrible despotism).

Biehl hereafter translated a hotly debated prose work by the Swiss Salomon Gessner, *Der Tod Abels* (The Death of Abel, 1758), as *Abels Død* at the indirect request of Count Adam Gottlob Moltke. She was provided with a French translation to use as a basis for her work, but she rejected it on professional grounds and instead translated from the original German text. The book was published, without crediting Biehl as translator, in 1764.

During this period Danish theater was engaged in a debate on genre, and Sneedorff clearly articulated the evolution of drama as he saw it. A golden middle way between tragedy, about which the British seemed enthusiastic, and festive comedy, as favored by the French, would surely appeal to Danish taste. Sneedorff envisioned the future of Danish comedy in his meticulous *fortale* (foreword) to M. H. Høyer's 1763 Danish translation of Françoise d'Isembourg-d'Happoncourt de Grafigny's *Cénie* (1750), describing "en nye Art af Skuespil, som var en Blanding af Begge, hverken saa alvorlig, som et Sørge-Spil, eller saa latterlig, som en Comedie. Et Skuespil f. Ex., som forestillede en borgerlig Dyd, øvet paa en anstændig og rørende Maade, og kronet med et lykkeligt Udfald . . ." (a new kind of play which was a mixture of both, neither as grave as a tragedy nor as preposterous as a comedy. A play, for instance, presenting a civic virtue observed in a respectable and touching manner, and crowned with a happy outcome . . .). Sneedorff singled out *Cénie* as a model of this new genre, which had yet to find a fixed form and examples of which had no sooner been called "grædende Comedier" (weeping comedies) than they were called "lystige Sørgespil" (merry tragedies).

Biehl made a fresh and less literal translation of *Cénie* in a style more suitable for performance, both in the use of Danish and, indeed, the incorporation of Holbergian humor, as in the portrayal of the servants, which featured an appropriate mixture of gravity and amusement. Her translation was published anonymously in 1764 and is thought to have been the version used for the subsequent theater production. Biehl also took issue with Sneedorff himself. At the request of Johan Samuel Augustin and Henrik Henriksen Hielmstierne, two prominent gentlemen in Danish cultural life and later members of Det Kongelige Danske Videnskabernes Selskab (The Royal Danish Academy of Sciences and Letters) who considered Sneedorff's own style to be tainted with that of the French, she also retranslated Antoine Léonard Thomas's *Eloge de René Duguay Trouin* (Eulogy of René Duguay Trouin, 1761), of which Sneedorff had submitted his own version. In *Mit ubetydelige Levnets Løb* she recalls the honor of being caricatured by Augustin, who chose to substantiate her talent thus: "Pigen ryster tree Professorer af Ærmet" (The girl eats three professors for breakfast).

Encouraged by Augustin and Bornemann, Biehl now began writing her own works for the theater. The new *comédie larmoyante* (tearful comedy) was her chosen genre. Carlo Goldoni's play *La Moglie Saggia* (The Wise Wife, 1755) gave her, as she said, the idea of turning things upside down and writing a drama about a loving husband. The literary source was not Goldoni's play, however, but rather Jean-François Marmontel's "Le bon mari" (The Good Husband), from his *Contes Moraux* (Moral Stories, 1761). Biehl wrote night and day for a fortnight and then submitted her first play to the theater on Kongens Nytorv. *Den kierlige Mand* (The Loving Husband) was immediately published and staged in the autumn of 1764. Its first run lasted for seven performances, and all in all, the play was performed twelve times. At the time, twelve performances was quite a lot, three being the usual maximum. It was the first Danish play since Holberg's day to catch on with the audience, and it stayed in the repertoire for five seasons.

The theme of *Den kierlige Mand* was new to Denmark: a pleasure-seeking wife, Leonora, neglects both spouse and child in her pursuit of merrymaking, while her husband, by means of trust, moral instruction, and love, gently coaxes her back onto the right track. This plot did not involve revolutionary feminism but rather provided a portrait of the new man. He had been heard about, but he had not yet been seen on the Danish stage, and women of the bourgeoisie were beginning to hope that they might meet him: the sensitive husband who loved his wife. After marriages as depicted by Holberg, centered on financial interests and bearing the hallmark of a contract between patriarchs, marriages based on a young couple's respect and feelings for one another had become a debating point, and Biehl wanted to put this issue on the stage. A marriage should be based on "Gemytternes Overensstemmelse" (the concord of temperaments). The moral concept involved was not the chief concern of the debate, but the discussion of the male-female relationship in different contexts was groundbreaking. The new comedies took place in domestic environments, the drawing-room milieu with which the audience was familiar as the public zone of the private home. It was not as if one were out visiting but was more like being at home, and this dramatic setting thus gave a universal validity to the theme of the comedies: marriage and love, genuine as well as cynical sham.

Den kierlige Mand provoked a strong critical reaction, including anonymous articles published in 1764 and 1765 that were traced to members of the Sorø Academy circle, such as Heinrich Wilhelm von Gerstenberg, Christian Fleischer, and Peter Kleen. The critique was meticulous and therefore interesting. These articles constituted the first examples of comparative dramatic analysis in Denmark, comparing the originality of the work with the French and also British comedies of the period, as scenes from *The Provok'd Husband* (1728), a play begun by Sir John Vanbrugh and completed by Colley Cibber, were brought into the discussion. *Den kierlige Mand* was also staged in Sweden. Inspired by the success of the play with Danish audiences, the kapellmeister in Copenhagen, Johann Adolph Scheibe, anonymously published a German translation, *Der zärtliche Ehemann* (1765), which Biehl was swift to criticize for inaccuracies.

Biehl continued to publish translations of plays and her own original works, both complete plays and prologues. A prologue about the rivalry of tragedy and comedy titled *Melpomenes og Thaliæ Trætte* (The Combat of Melpomene and Thalia) was published in 1765, and more comedies followed in quick succession. Even though sensitivity in treatment of theme was now considered important, some of her own early comedies preserved the humorous and satirical tone associated with her predecessor Holberg, such as *Haarkløveren* (The Quibbler, 1765), with its local Copenhagen wit based on current debates about the use of language. Biehl joined in this debate in part by demonstrating her misgivings regarding Sneedorff. The old pedant at the center of *Haarkløveren,* who wants his daughter to marry a young man cut from the same cloth as himself, has obvious similarities to Sneedorff.

Den forelskede Ven (The Enamored Friend, 1765), written and published in the same year as *Haarkløveren,* depicts a much-courted young woman, Leonora, whose widowed mother allows her to choose her own husband. Leonora, however, has no desire to be married, finding friendship with Leander preferable to marriage with one of her suitors. Her younger sister, ten-year-old Lise, is the exact opposite in this respect, and her portrayal is a humorous exposition of this sisterly contrast. Lise is the first child with a speaking role in Danish theater. The play placed the right to remain unmarried center stage as a theme in comedy, and the sensitive man, the friend, was allowed to end up as the husband. *Den forelskede Ven* threw the audience into an uproar, as one of the characters, a German officer called von Prahlendorff, was the object of the dramatist's ridicule. This depiction could be excused as the continuation of a standard comic figure employed from Plautus's *Miles Gloriosus* (The Boastful Soldier, circa 205 B.C.) to Holberg's *Jacob von Tyboe* (1725), but it could also undeniably be seen as a critical analysis of the German elite found in positions of power in the military and other institutions of authority in Copenhagen at the time.

Holbergian humor was prominent in Biehl's most amusing comedy, *Den listige Optrækkerske* (The Cunning Extortionist, 1765), the only one of her comedies to have been staged in the late twentieth century (Aarhus, 1984). The subject of this play is the manner in which a woman of easy virtue exploits men's sexual urges and desire for self-affirmation. The play caused so much offense that it was immediately taken off the bill. In the published text of a one-act play, *Tvistigheden eller Critique over den listige Optrækkerske* (The Dispute or Critique on The Cunning Extortionist, 1766), inspired by Molière's *L'Ecole des femmes* (The School for Wives, 1662), Biehl answered her critics through the hero, Ariste, who is, however, obliged to concede defeat when faced with the uneducated masses. The central character in *Den listige Optrækkerske,* Lucretia, is unmarried and quite uninhibited in her employment of tricks to her own advantage at the expense of men. She is not an out-and-out prostitute; she is a deluxe trickster who exploits male hypocrisy and double morality for her own profit. In defending the right to remain unmarried, she compares the lover with the husband and spells out the difference: "I stedet for de behagelige Ord: Vil min Elskelige forbinde mig derved? vil jeg saa faa en brummende Lyd I Øret af: Kone giør det" (Instead of the agreeable words "Will my beloved thus oblige me?" I will hear a growling sound in my ear of "Wife, do it"). Lucretia enjoys her freedom and healthy financial situation, of which she says, "Ey! Det er en Tidsfordriv, og tillige en inderlig Fornøyelse for mig at kunde trække disse Visdommens indbildte Sønner ligesaa meget ved Næsen, som jeg lyster" (Ah! It is a diversion, and besides a pleasure for me to be able to lead these would-be sons of wisdom as much by the nose as I should so desire). She snares them in their own traps, and, what is more, she is paid for doing so, she boasts.

Biehl circa 1780 (copperplate by J. F. Clemens, circa 1814, based on a miniature by W. A. Müller; courtesy of the Danish Royal Library, Copenhagen)

Even though she is unmasked at the end and loses everything she has, she triumphs optimistically in the final scene and proclaims, "saa længe der er unge Mandfolk til, vil der aldrig fattes mig og mine Liige paa Leylighed til at giøre Lykke" (so long as there are young men, I and my like will never lack the opportunity to make our fortune). As Stig Dalager and Anne-Marie Mai have put it, "Lucretia's misfortune is in point of fact not that she challenges the status quo, but, on the contrary, that she exploits the rules of the patriarchal society to the utmost, and she does it better than the men."

Biehl's next plays in the *comedie larmoyante* genre did not aspire to the comical but rather to a discussion of morality and values. The style was polished and the tone edifying. In 1766 she wrote *Den kiærlige Daatter* (The Loving Daughter), which was awarded a prize by the *Selskabet for de skiønne Videnskaber* (Society for the Fine Arts) and was published that year in *Forsøg i de skiønne og nyttige Videnskaber* (Essays in the Fine and Applied Arts). It is, however, uncertain as to whether the prize was a form of honorary award for her contribution to the arts or was actually intended as a reward for excellence. This play, with which Biehl later expressed great contentment, was not quite to the reviewers' taste; the critic Jakob Baden considered it too anxious to produce a moral, at the expense of plausibility. In his opinion, on stage it was preferable to show vices, warts and all, rather than virtue in all its finery. Biehl's *Den Ædelmodige* (The Noble-Minded Man, 1767) concerns a man who declines to enter into an advantageous marriage because the young woman involved is not in love with him but with another. The moral, as in *Den kiærlige Datter,* is heavy-handed; however, *Den Ædelmodige* presents a relevant protest against the expedient, cold marriage. Biehl had moved the private debate into the public discussion; there was something wrong with the way in which marriage was conducted in Denmark. By means of the theater she had introduced the topic for discussion in the drawing rooms of the higher bourgeoisie, both through her plays and her participation as an unmarried writer in soirée society. Her comedies, in keeping with the French and English dramas of the time, might not have made the audience laugh, but her themes were new and relevant, at least for the females of the bourgeoisie. As an indication of audiences' appreciation of Biehl's relevance, a collected German-language edition of her dramatic works, *Lustspiele der Jungfer Charlotta Dorothea Biehl,* was published in 1767. Scheibe was again responsible for the translation, and he avowed that he had revised *Den kierlige Mand* in response to Biehl's earlier criticism.

Biehl's next comedy, *Den alt for lønlige Beiler* (The Too Retiring Suitor), was first performed in 1771 and published in 1772. The play was a humorous drama of mistaken identity, centered on a hapless and long-winded suitor. The so-called Biehlian period came to an end at the same time as a two-volume collected edition of her works, *Comedier* (Comedies), was published in 1773. In 1772 and 1773 her plays had been savaged by, among others, the first actual theater critic in Denmark, Peder Rosenstand-Goeske, in the theater periodical *Den dramatiske Journal.* The new manager of the Royal Theater, Hans Vilhelm von Warnstedt, made sure that as of 1778 her plays were no longer produced in his theater. With the theater manager against her and (unlike some of her male colleagues) with no steady job at the theater, Biehl was in financial difficulty.

A chance encounter on 16 June 1771 in Kongens Have, the king's park surrounding Rosenborg Castle, with the young first lieutenant Bülow, later lord chamberlain, proved crucial to the quality of the rest of Biehl's life. With him she enjoyed a friendship of the kind she had extolled in her plays: a friendship between a man and a woman, without marriage but with lifelong trust and reciprocal support. Many of the projects that Biehl took on during the following years were commissioned by Bülow, and for several of them she received sorely needed payment, either in the form of payment in kind, such as fruit and flowers, of which she was appreciative, or in the form of nonregistered financial acknowledgment, which undoubtedly enabled her to maintain a reasonable standard of life for her remaining years. Through Bülow she became more closely connected to the court and Danish higher society than she had previously been through her father, and she was relied on as a well-regarded cultural personality who could brighten up cultural events when guests from abroad were staying in Copenhagen. The poet Christian Bie amused himself by ridiculing Biehl's learning in his verse fable *Den lærde Gås* (The Erudite Goose, 1767), making association via her corpulence with stupidity and the intelligence level of a goose.

In bitter recognition that the Royal Theater at Kongens Nytorv had closed its doors to her, Biehl set to work with renewed zest in the new theater genre of ballad opera. By 1773 she had already seen her *Silphen* (The Sylph) staged; it was published in two editions (1773 and 1778) and was performed at Hofteatret (the Court Theater) in Copenhagen. The Royal Theater performed at Hofteatret twice a week, and this platform gave Biehl the opportunity to use her excellent musical talent to prepare rhythmically tailored translations, her own original arias, and whole ballad operas to be performed to music. Her next ballad opera, *Den prøvede Troeskab* (Faithfulness on Trial, 1774), was performed on King Christian VII's birthday. At the same time she had completed translations of two lengthy philosophical-political treatises by the Italian cultural attaché in Copenhagen, Isidoro Bianchi, who had given her to understand that he would like her to take on this assignment. Her translation of his *Meditazioni sù vari punti di Felicità Pubblica e Privata* (Meditations on Several Points of Public and Private Happiness, 1773) was titled *Betragtninger over adskillige Puncter af den almindelige og private Lyksalighed* (1774). Another work of Bianchi, *Del premio devuto ai cittadine virtuosi* (1773), was translated as *Belønninger, der tilkomme dydige Indbyggere* (Rewards Earned by Virtuous Citizens, 1775). Bianchi repaid her by writing admiringly of her talents in journals for Il Café circle, a group of northern Italian intellectuals of which he was a part.

Biehl made one foray into the genre of tragedy with the five-act *Euphemia* (1775). This work was an extension of her 1765 translation of Charles-Pierre Colardeau's *Caliste* (1760) and her translation of Gotthold Ephraim Lessing's 1772 tragedy *Emilia Galotti* as *Emilie Galotti* (1775). The Copenhagen audience was unfamiliar with tragedy and possibly not ready for it, and Biehl did not repeat the experiment. In the audience-pleasing lighter style, her ballad opera *Kierligheds-Brevene* (The Love Letters) was staged at the Hofteatret in 1775 (a year after it was first published), with music by Giuseppe Sarti. Biehl's sociolinguistic awareness of the epistolary genre is clearly demonstrated in the opera, which involves the misunderstandings caused by a mix-up of love letters sent between pairs of lovers from different social classes. In 1775, as Biehl's career as a dramatist was drawing to a close, the finest miniaturist of the period, Cornelius Høyer, made a satirical drawing of her castrating Holberg, who is lying on an operating table surrounded by bewigged, horrified gentlemen. In the same year, Høyer also produced a charming miniature of Biehl, quite likely a prettified commission.

In 1775 Biehl published the first original "heroid" letter written in Danish, "Brev fra Waldborg Immers Datter til hendes Veninde" (Letter from Waldborg Immer's Daughter to her Woman-Friend). The heroid, a literary form used throughout Europe in the 1500s and 1600s, was familiar in Denmark from Tycho Brahe's Latin *Urania Titani* (1594) and from poor translations of some of Ovid's original *Heroides* (Heroines, before 16 B.C.). Biehl found her material in Nordic folklore and reshaped the genre by having the verse letters addressed to a female friend instead of being exchanged between male and female, as was the case in Ovid's *Heroides*.

Biehl's greatest endeavor in 1775 was, however, in a completely new language, Spanish. That year she met the Spanish envoy to Denmark, Emanuel Delitala, who persuaded her that he should teach her Spanish so that she would be able to translate Cervantes into Danish. With the help of her solid foundation in French and Italian, within eighteen months she had learned the language. She translated Cervantes's *Don Quixote de la Mancha* (1605) as *Den sindrige Herremands Don Quixote af Mancha Levnet og Bedrifter* (1776–1777) and his *Novelas Ejemplares* (Moral Tales, 1613) as *Lærerige Fortællinger* (1780–1781). No new Danish translation of *Don Quixote* appeared for the following 225 years, and her translation, with minor revisions, stayed in use for the whole of the intervening period. In 1865–1869 it was republished with drawings by the Danish artist Wilhelm Marstrand.

From 1776 onward Biehl produced a stream of translations of plays and ballad operas, mainly from French and German, of which most were either published or performed. For the new and mysterious brotherhood of Freemasons, she translated a song booklet as *Frimurer-Sange* (Freemason Songs, 1776) and later also wrote some of her own, which survive in manuscript at the Sorø Academy Library. Both Bülow and Biehl's brother, Carl, joined the Nordstjernen (North Star) lodge, and now and then small meetings were held in the flat shared by brother and sister. The Freemasons' social aims and liberal attitude to different religions gave the movement a progressive air. Through Bülow, Biehl became intimately acquainted with the work of the brotherhood. In *Mit ubetydelige Levnets Løb* she states that in 1782 she had felt that Bülow had given her such solid proof of his friendship and respect, by asking her

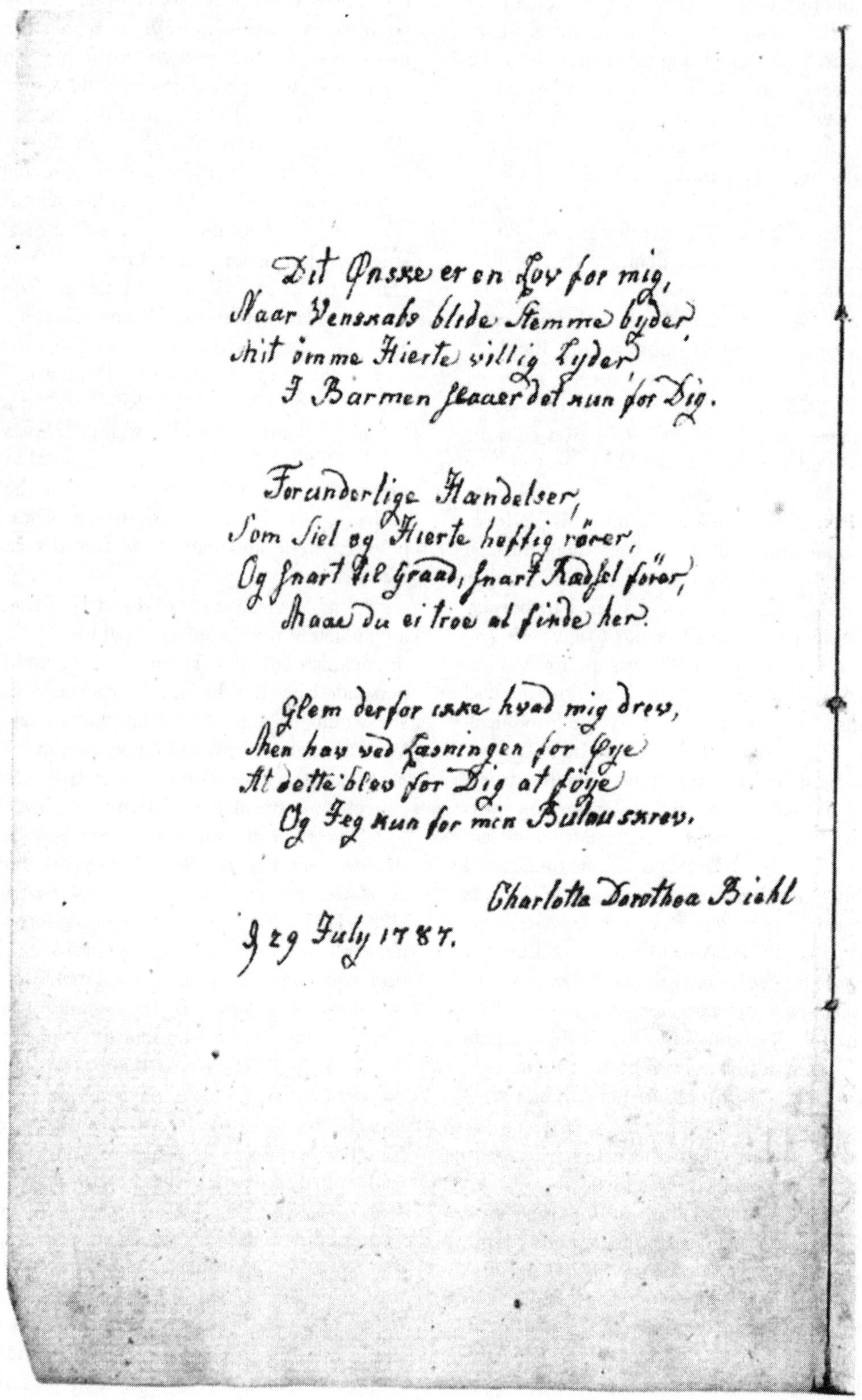

Dit Önske er en Lov for mig,
Naar Venskabs blide Stemme byder,
Mit ömme Hierte villig lyder,
I Barmen slaaer det kun for Dig.

Forunderlige Handelser,
Som Siel og Hierte heftig rörer,
Og snart til Graad, snart Rædsel förer,
Maae du ei troe at finde her.

Glem derfor ikke hvad mig drev,
Men hav ved Læsningen for Öye
At dette blev for Dig at föye
Og Jeg kun for min Bülow skrev.

Charlotta Dorothea Biehl
d 29 July 1787.

Verso of the title page of the manuscript for Biehl's autobiography, "Mit ubetydelige Levnet Sløb" (The Course of My Insignificant Life), with a dedicatory poem to her friend Lord Chamberlain Johan von Bülow. The work was not published until 1909 (courtesy of the Danish Royal Library, Copenhagen).

advice in connection with his admission to the Masonic lodge, that she was willing to sacrifice her life for him. Such declarations of trust motivated Biehl to bestow great love and put in a great deal of hard work for Bülow, unselfishly and often unpaid. He seems to have understood and made use of this character trait in her, and at the same time he discreetly helped her with money from his private funds, which he had in abundance thanks to his wife.

As happy as trust in another could make Biehl, she became just as unhappy and furious if she experienced a breach of trust. Her exclusion from the Royal Theater, which the manager, Warnstedt, continued to uphold and which she continued to find inexplicable, was avenged in her next major work, the four-volume *Moralske Fortællinger* (Moral Tales, 1781–1782). Playing along with the sexual outrage of the day, she exposed Warnstedt in an extremely indelicate way as a homosexual, easily recognizable in the figure of a cardinal, Don Varini, in one of the tales, "Den falske Ven" (The False Friend). Gratified by the good sales figures for *Moralske Fortællinger,* she pointed out this caricature of Warnstedt in her autobiography. "Den falske Ven," like some of Biehl's other works, takes place in a fictional setting abroad–a place she had never been, such as Italy or France. Some tales play on the topical literature of the time; for example, "Den unge Wartvig" (Young Wartvig) was a response to the recently published *Siegwart. Eine Klostergeschichte* (Siegwart: A Monastery Tale, 1776; translated into Danish, 1778), by the German author Johann Martin Miller. "Emilie eller den belønnede Standhaftighed" (Emily or Constancy Rewarded) was clearly influenced by Samuel Richardson's *Pamela; or, Virtue Rewarded* (1740). Some of the tales in *Moralske Fortællinger* have a certain tautness and tension, even though the moral of the story is quickly apparent. The fictional letter is frequently employed as a stylistic device designed to make the tales realistic.

This fictional prose, which had few precedents in Danish literature, set new linguistic challenges, but, rather than being a viable form in itself, it acted as a bridge between didactic comedy for the stage with stylized roles and the later novel with individual characterization. But characterization and stylistic variation could also be created by passing the pen from character to character, and this stylistic sport was now introduced in Denmark. The epistolary genre had long sparkled elsewhere, with Jean de La Bruyère's *Les Caractères* (1688), Marmontel's *Contes Moraux,* Richardson's epistolary novels, and Christian Fürchtegott Gellert's extremely popular *Fabeln und Erzählungen* (Fables and Tales, 1746–1748), translated into Danish by Barthold Johan Lodde as *Fabler og Fortællinger* (1769). No one had as of yet tried his hand at this genre in Denmark, but Biehl was ready to try. Her next original publication was a one-thousand-page work, *Brevvexling imellem fortrolige Venner* (A Correspondence between Confidential Friends, 1783), the first Danish epistolary novel. It is a long and heavy read, with its fretwork of letters going back and forth between the characters, and it is perhaps principally of interest as evidence that this genre too had now reached Denmark.

As a final work in the comedy genre, Biehl published *Den tavse Pige eller de ved Tavshed avlede Mistanker* (The Silent Girl; or, The Suspicions Bred by Silence) in 1783. This play was possibly influenced by her work with the Cervantes translations, with appropriations from his style and subject matter. Biehl brought her theater career to a grand conclusion in 1786 when she participated in the staging of the first large-scale opera in Denmark, the Saxon composer Johan Gottlieb Naumann's *Orpheus og Euridice.* Biehl was given the job of translating the libretto, written by the German court councillor von Lindemann, and worked on the actual production. Von Lindemann's text was not to Biehl's liking, but she made the best she could of it, adding some of her own poetry. At the subsequent celebration, with dinner and dancing, she and Naumann opened the ball. An extant manuscript in the Danish Royal Library in Copenhagen shows that Biehl had previously worked on Raniero Calzabigi's libretto to Christoph Willibald Gluck's opera on the same subject, *Orfeo ed Euridice* (1762), a production of which seems to have been planned.

Biehl's health was failing, and her financial circumstances were wretched. She spent her final five years developing the epistolary genre. At the request of Bülow, who in the meantime had been appointed lord chamberlain, she wrote approximately four hundred letters to him–and possibly, as with many other contemporary European writers, for a later public readership. In the letters she inserted short *versbreve* (verse letters), the first dated 23 June 1783. An unpublished religious collection titled "Morgen- og Aftensange" (Morning and Evening Songs) also survives. The posthumously published "Historiske Breve" (Historical Letters, 1865–1867), made her Denmark's answer to Marie de Rabutin-Chantal, Marquise de Sévigné. Biehl does not herself refer to any model but calls them in a letter of 5 March 1784 "Chronique Scandaleuse" (Scandalous Chronicle), in so doing acknowledging the conscious choice of a genre that had not previously been found in Danish literature. The "Historiske Breve" are well-written descriptions of life at the Danish court of King Frederik IV at the beginning of the eighteenth century. They continue up to the 1784 palace revolution, which overturned the power held at the court of the mad King Christian VII by his stepmother, Juliana; his

Painting of Biehl by Christian Zahrtmann (1874) that was inspired by the publication of her historical letters in the mid 1860s (private collection; photograph courtesy of the Museum of National History at Frederiksborg Castle)

half brother; and the politician Ove Høegh-Guldberg. Power was then turned over to Christian's rightful royal heir, Crown Prince Frederik, who later became Frederik VI. Biehl's letters are, in keeping with the semiofficial *chronique scandaleuse* genre, full of gossip from the royal court and high-society life but also so detailed about actual events that some parts have been read by later historians as an eyewitness narrative with the status of historical source material.

Biehl received her instructions and information from Bülow, who was not only her friend but also the lord chamberlain. Encouraging her to write the letters, which were kept secret during his lifetime, Bülow of course had an interest in her judgments; the manuscripts of Biehl's letters include occasional comments in his handwriting, such as an exclamation regarding her description of the 1784 palace revolution: "Jfr. Biehl! Deres Dom er for haard, for stræng, meget for stræng" (Miss Biehl! Your judgment is too cruel, too severe, far too severe). However biased Bülow might have been, he was a firsthand witness to the events, and Biehl's letters thus should be taken into consideration on equal terms with other letters and diaries from the period. She also offers comments on the life and execution of Christian's physician, Johann Friedrich Struensee, in April 1772. (Through his influence over the king, Struensee had virtually ruled Denmark for the two years preceding his execution.) More-private accounts, such as those of the erotic cherry eating of Frederik V and his bride, Louise, and of Louise's death in childbirth, also make for interesting reading. Biehl was a reliable and experienced chronicler of court life. The "Historiske Breve" could not, however, be published until all those referred to had died. Carefully stored among Bülow's papers, they were found in the mid nineteenth century and published in installments in the Danish historical review *Historisk Tidsskrift;* the choice of this periodical shows that they were read as historical source material rather than as literary works, although they were also the latter. The narratives inspired the artist Christian Zahrtmann to paint two imaginary interiors featuring Biehl with her quill pen in her mouth.

As an eloquent conclusion to a wide-ranging writing career, and again at the request of Bülow, Biehl wrote her autobiography, *Mit ubetydelige Levnets Løb.* She composed it in a small, hand-sewn book, tied with ribbons and dated 29 July 1787, Bülow's thirty-seventh birthday. It is the only substantial autobiography written by a Danish woman during the eighteenth century. In the form of a single long letter, but clearly written with the general public in mind, the forty-seven closely written pages tell her life story as she chose to appraise and present it. The narrative is characterized by restraint, omission, and deliberate falsehood, but in these respects Biehl's autobiography is no different from others in the genre. She does not lack irony, and a talent for observation pervades her account and makes for good reading. Both her private life and her professional activities are presented in a work glowing alternately with joy and anger. *Mit ubetydelige Levnets Løb* is a reliable portrait of a woman who led an interesting and extremely unusual life as a translator, author, and letter writer.

Charlotta Dorothea Biehl died in Copenhagen on 17 May 1788. She was buried in Sct. Petri Kirke (St. Peter's Church), where her grave was hit by a bomb in 1807 during the English bombardment of Copenhagen. In 1988 she was bestowed the honor of figuring as the protagonist in Mette Winge's historical novel *Skriverjomfruen* (Miss Scribbler).

Letters:

Breve om Kong Christian VII, edited by Louis Bobé (Copenhagen: O. B. Wroblewski, 1901);

Interiører fra Kong Frederik den Femtes Hof. Charlotte Dorothea Biehls Breve og Selvbiografi, edited by Bobé (Copenhagen: J. L. Lybecker, 1909);

Brev fra Dorothea. Af Charlotta Dorothea Biehls historiske breve, edited by Svend Cedergreen Bech (Copenhagen: Politiken, 1975).

Bibliography:

Holger Ehrencron-Müller, "Biehl, Charlotte Dorothea," in his *Forfatterlexikon omfattende Danmark, Norge og Island indtil 1814,* volume 1 (Copenhagen: Aschehoug, 1924), pp. 391–397.

References:

Marianne Alenius, "Biehl efter Holberg–eller Enden på komedie(n)," *Kritik,* no. 77 (1986): 59–72;

Alenius, *Brev til eftertiden. Om Charlotta Dorothea Biehls selvbiografi og andre breve* (Copenhagen: Museum Tusculanum, 1987);

Alenius, "Digte og versbreve fra en øm Veninde," in *Digternes paryk. Studier i 1700-tallet,* edited by Alenius and others (Copenhagen: Museum Tusculanum, 1997), pp. 289–302;

Alenius, "Forfatteren bag *Den listige Optrækkerske*" and "Et skandalestykke. Publikums reaktion på *Den listige Optrækkerske* i 1765," in Biehl, *Den listige Optrækkerske,* edited by Leif Nielsen (Aarhus: Arkona/Svalegangen, 1984), pp. 4–9, 61–64;

Alenius, "Portrætter af Charlotta Dorothea Biehl," in Biehl, *Mit ubetydelige Levnets Løb,* edited by Alenius (Copenhagen: Museum Tusculanum, 1986), pp. 198–210;

Alenius, Lisbet Grandjean, Hakon Lund, and Emma Salling, eds., *Den lærde jomfru Biehl. Udstilling 1989 Kunstakademiets Bibliotek* (Copenhagen: Museum Tusculanum, 1989);

John E. Andersen, "Professorer, bachelorer og listige optrækkersker. Charlotta Dorothea Biehl i pragmatikkens lys," in *Digternes paryk. Studier i 1700-tallet,* pp. 119–133;

Louise Arnheim, *Registrant over Johan von Bülows manuskriptsamling i Sorø Akademis bibliotek* (Sorø: Lokalhistorisk Selskab, 1999);

Hans Jørgen Birch, *Billedgallerie for Fruentimmer,* volume 1 (Copenhagen: S. Poulsen, 1793), pp. 163–224;

Louis Bobé, "Charlotte Dorothea Biehl," in his *Fra Renaissance til Empire* (Copenhagen: H. Hagerup, 1916), pp. 79–95;

Pil Dahlerup, *Pigeopdragelse* (Copenhagen: S. Hasselbalch, 1969);

Stig Dalager and Anne-Marie Mai, "Charlotte Dorothea Biehl–Kvinden som dukke, hustru, optrækkerske og tyranniseret forstandsvæsen," in their *Danske kvindelige forfattere,* volume 1 (Copenhagen: Gyldendal, 1982), pp. 97–116;

Mogens Dupont-Petersen, "Den skønne Dorothea," in *Kunst og antikvitets årbogen 1979* (Copenhagen: Thaning & Appel, 1979), pp. 117–120;

Mette Ewald, "Charl. Dor. Biehl. Kvindeemancipation i 1700-tallet eller mandschauvinisme i kvindelig forklædning," *Teaterarbejde,* no. 4 (1979): 41–49;

Johan Fjord Jensen and others, eds., *Dansk litteraturhistorie,* volume 4: *Patriotismens tid 1746–1807* (Copenhagen: Gyldendal, 1983), pp. 119–141;

Christian Fleischer, Heinrich Wilhelm von Gerstenberg, and Peter Kleen, *Samling af adskillige Skrifter til de skiønne Videnskabers og det danske Sprogs Opkomst og Fremtarv,* volume 1, nos. 1–2 (Sorø, 1765); no. 3 (Copenhagen, 1765);

Peter Hansen, *Den danske Skueplads,* volume 1 (Copenhagen: Bojesen, 1889);

Wilfried Hauke, *Von Holberg zu Biehl. Das dänische Aufklärungsdrama, 1747–1773,* Beiträge zur Skandinavistik, no. 10 (Frankfurt & New York: Peter Lang, 1992);

Annegret Heitmann, *Selbst Schreiben. Eine Untersuchung der dänischen Frauenautobiographik,* Beiträge zur Skandinavistik, no. 12 (Frankfurt & New York: Peter Lang, 1994);

Lisbet Holst, "Fra Eva til Lilith. Om dannelsen af en alternativ kvindelig selvbevidsthed. En forelæsning," *Kritik,* no. 71 (1985): 101–114;

Elisabeth Møller Jensen, ed., *I Guds navn, 1000–1800,* Nordisk Kvindelitteraturhistorie (Copenhagen: Rosinante, 1993), I: 370–380, 448–472;

Anna Levin, "Den Biehlske Slægt," *Personalhistorisk Tidsskrift,* series 10, volume 5 (1938): 153–167;

Georg Albrecht Mai, "Die Frauenfiguren im dramatischen Werk der Charlotte Dorothea Biehl. Studien zur Komödienform in Dänemark im 18. Jahrhundert," dissertation, Christian-Albrecht-Universität zu Kiel, 1981;

Johannes Mulvad, "Om Dorotheas Troværdighed," *Personalhistorisk Tidsskrift,* sixteenth series, volume 4 (1976): 179–186;

Niels Åge Nielsen, "Brugen af tiltalepronominer i Charlotta Dorothea Biehls komedier 1764–1772," *Sprog og Kultur,* 16, nos. 1–2 (1948): 121–134;

Thomas Overskou, *Den danske Skueplads,* volumes 1–2 (Copenhagen: Thiele, 1856, 1860);

Knud Frederik Plesner, "En dansk forfatterinde fra det 18. årh. Charlotte Dorothea Biehl," *Edda,* 27, no. 4 (1927): 427–446;

Paul V. Rubow, *Litterære Studier* (Copenhagen: Levin & Munksgaard, 1928), pp. 203–208.

Papers:

Collections of Charlotta Dorothea Biehl's manuscripts and correspondence are at the Sorø Academy Library (includes approximately four hundred private letters to Johan von Bülow) in Sorø; Rigsarkivet (the National Archive) and the Danish Royal Library in Copenhagen; and at Sanderumgaard, Odense.

Steen Steensen Blicher

(11 October 1782 - 26 March 1848)

Niels Ingwersen
University of Wisconsin–Madison

BOOKS: *Digte, Første Deel* (Aarhus: Elmquist, 1814);

Digte. Anden Deel: Jyllandsreise i sex Døgn (Aarhus: Aarhus Stiftsbogtrykkerie, 1817);

Generalprøven i Kragehul (Aarhus: Aarhus Stiftsbogtrykkerie, 1819);

Bautastene (Odense: Hempel, 1823);

Johanne Gray, Tragødie i 5 Acter (Copenhagen: Reitzel, 1825);

Sneklokken (Viborg: Dons, 1826);

Samlede Noveller, 5 volumes (Copenhagen: C. Steen, 1833–1836);

Samlede Digte, 2 volumes (Copenhagen: C. Steen, 1835, 1836);

Svithiod. Efteraarserindringer fra en Sommerreise i Sverrig i Aaret 1836 (Randers: F. Smith, 1837);

Trækfuglene (Randers: F. Smith, 1838)–includes "Præludium," translated by R. P. Kiegwin as "Prelude to 'Birds of Passage,'" in *From the Danish Peninsula* (Copenhagen: Munksgaard, 1957), pp. 24–27;

Kornmodn (Randers: Blicher, printed by Elemenhoff, 1839);

Nyeste Noveller og Digte (Copenhagen: C. Steen, 1839);

Vestlig Profil af den Cimbriske Halvøe, Fra Hamburg til Skagen (Copenhagen: C. Steen, 1839);

Viborg amt (Copenhagen: J. H. Schultz, 1839);

Samlede noveller og digte (Copenhagen: C. Steen, 1840);

Sommerreise i Sverige i 1836 (Randers: Printed by Elmenhoff, 1841);

E Bindstouw (Randers: F. Smith, 1842);

Min Tidsalder (Copenhagen: C. Steen, 1842);

Nye Noveller (Copenhagen: Høst, 1842);

Fem Noveller og to Jydske Sange (Copenhagen: Høst, 1844);

Min Vinterbestilling i 1842 og 1843, Samlede Noveller, volumes 6 and 7 (Randers: N. Schmidt, 1844);

Min Vinterbestilling i 1844 og 1845, Samlede Noveller, volume 8 (Copenhagen: Reitzel, 1845);

Gamle og ny Noveller, 7 volumes, edited by P. L. Møller (Copenhagen: Reitzel, 1846–1847);

Digte, 2 volumes, edited by Møller (Copenhagen: Reitzel, 1847).

Steen Steensen Blicher (pencil drawing by J. Wilhelm Gertner, 1845, signed by Blicher with his place and date of birth; courtesy of the Danish Royal Library, Copenhagen)

Editions and Collections: *Samlede Noveller og Skitser,* edited by Hans Hansen (3 volumes, Copenhagen: Rosenkilde og Bagger, 1905–1907; republished in 5 volumes with illustrations, 1964–1965);

Steen Steensen Blichers Samlede Skrifter, 33 volumes, edited by Jeppe Aakjær and others (Copenhagen: Det Danske Sprog- og Litteraturselskab, 1920–1934);

Erindringer af Steen Steensen Blichers Liv optegnede af ham selv, edited by Søren Vasegaard (Copenhagen: Aschehoug, 1928);

Blichers Noveller i Udvalg, 6 volumes, edited by Vilhelm Andersen, with introductions by Kaj Munk and Andersen (Copenhagen: Carl Aller, 1943);

Digte og Noveller, 2 volumes, edited by Johannes Nørvig (Copenhagen: DSL/Gyldendal, 1964);
Ak! Hvor forandret. Fire noveller, edited by Nørvig and Folmer Jensen (Copenhagen: Dansklærerforeningen/Gyldendal, 1972);
Udvalgte Værker, 4 volumes (Copenhagen: Blicher-Selskabet/Gyldendal, 1983).
Editions in English: *Twelve Stories by Steen Steensen Blicher,* translated by Hanna Astrup Larsen, introduction by Sigrid Undset (Princeton, N.J.: Princeton University Press / New York: American-Scandinavian Foundation, 1945)–includes "The Journal of a Parish Clerk," "The Robbers' Den," "Tardy Awakening," "Alas, How Changed!" "The Parson at Vejlbye," "Gypsy Life," "The Hosier and His Daughter," "Marie," "The Gamekeeper at Aunsbjerg," "An Only Child," "Three Holiday Eves," and "Brass-Jens";
From the Danish Peninsula, translated by Larsen and R. P. Keigwin (Copenhagen: Munksgaard, 1957)–includes "The Parson at Vejlby";
The Diary of a Parish Clerk, translated by Paula Hostrup-Jessen (Copenhagen: Hans Reitzel, 1968; edited by Sven H. Rossel, afterword by Niels Ingwersen, Seattle: Mermaid Press, 1991);
The Diary of a Parish Clerk and Other Stories, translated by Hostrup-Jessen (London & Atlantic Highlands, N.J.: Athlone, 1996);
Tardy Awakening and Other Stories, translated by Paula Brugge and Faith Ingwersen, edited, with an afterword and commentary, by Niels Ingwersen, WITS II, no. 7 (Madison: Department of Scandinavian Studies, University of Wisconsin, 1996)–includes "Tardy Awakening," "The Hosier," "The Three Holiday Eves," and "The Parson of Vejlby."

OTHER: *Nordlyset. Et Tidsskrivt,* edited by Blicher and J. M. Elmenhoff (Randers, 1827–1829);
Diana: Et Tidsskrivt for Jagtelskere, edited by Blicher (Randers, 1832–1836);
"De tre Helligaftener, En jydsk Røverhistorie," in *Dansk Folkekalender for 1841* (Copenhagen, 1841).

TRANSLATIONS: James Macpherson, *Ossians Digte,* 2 volumes (Copenhagen: Reitz, 1807, 1809);
Alexander Pope, *Abeilard og Heloise* (Copenhagen: Brünniche, 1818);
Oliver Goldsmith, *Præsten i Wakefield* (Copenhagen: C. Steen, 1837).

SELECTED PERIODICAL PUBLICATIONS–UNCOLLECTED: "En landsbydegns Dagbog," *Læsefrugter* (1818–1833); edited by A. F. Elmquist, translated by Hanna Astrup Larsen as "The Journal of a Parish Clerk," in *Twelve Stories* (Princeton: Princeton University Press, 1945), pp. 49–78; reprinted in *Anthology of Danish Literature,* edited by F. J. Billeskov Jansen and P. M. Mitchell (Carbondale: Southern Illinois University Press, 1964), pp. 158–213;
"Jydske Røverhistorier" and "Oldsagn paa Alheden," *Harpen* (1824).

In 1890 Dansklærerforeningen (the Danish Teachers' Association) published the first edition of "En Landsbydegns Dagbog" (1824; translated as "The Journal of a Parish Clerk," 1945). That innocuous event foreshadowed the assigning to nearly all future Danish high-school students of Steen Steensen Blicher's account of a melancholy young man who sees all his hopes shattered. That text has made generations of Danish readers aware of Blicher's mastery in spinning narratives that cleverly contrive to make readers become involved in the creative act. Even if Blicher's stories are easily read, he is an author who demands much of his audience.

Blicher's short stories–that is, the best of them–constitute a breakthrough not only in Denmark but in all the Nordic countries, for even if brief narrative forms had become popular at the same time as the novel rose to prominence in Europe during the latter part of the eighteenth century, they were related by an omniscient author, were quite often moralizing, and included characters neither well developed nor complex. Blicher probably did not set out to be innovative, but he was exactly that. Earlier writers of fiction had used first-person narration, but Blicher introduced a narrator who, for various reasons, could not be trusted and thus forced the reader to become a psychological detective and explore texts of uncommon depths. Blicher's contemporaries who wrote short stories did not reach such levels of sophistication, even though the texts by Bernhard Severin Ingemann compete well with those of E. T. A. Hoffmann. Only such younger writers as Hans Christian Andersen and Meïr Aron Goldschmidt managed to transcend the traditional short story and thus, along with Blicher, to foreshadow the golden age of Danish short narratives–the last third of the century, when Jens Peter Jacobsen, Henrik Pontoppidan, and Herman Bang were writing prose.

Blicher's formative years spent in rural Jutland prepared him to be an inventive author of tales. He was exposed to much storytelling and, early on, became intimately acquainted with the dialects of his region; otherwise, he would hardly have been able to compose *E Bindstouw* (In the Knitting Room, 1842), which, besides being written in a regional dialect, reveals the keen sense of narrative joy and of traditions among the rural population. His ventures into the study of folklore (he published two small collections of legends, "Jydske Røverhistorier" and "Oldsagn paa Alheden," in the periodical *Harpen* [The Harp] in 1824) likewise suggest his interest not only in the tales that a curious collector could record but also in the way people told those tales. When stories are narrated, the teller gauges the audience and settles on the way in which the tale should be performed. The approach is one that Blicher used when he sat down to write a story. Just as storytellers wanted their audiences to be spellbound and engaged, Blicher, too, wanted to involve his readers.

The folktale that intrigued Blicher was not the "happily-forever-after" magic tale, but the legend, which might be open to a view of tragic perspectives. Although some critics praise Blicher's technique as modern, he relies on an age-old tradition of legends. Other Romantic authors pretended, as well, that their narratives were "papers" they found and merely passed on, but, unlike Blicher, they scarcely captured the idiom or vernacular of bygone ages. Understandably, however, critics have found that Blicher foreshadowed literary techniques to come, for his tales are told, more often that not, by a first-person narrator and not by the then-reigning omniscient author. When a legend is told, the audience gains a sense of a narrator who should be trusted, but Blicher twists that belief, for he subtly makes the audience aware that the narrator may not be reliable. Blicher's narrators may not deceive on purpose–though some of his characters do–but they often make judgments that, for many reasons, should be met with skepticism. The reader is sent on a hunt for what has been called "the implied author," or the truth about what takes place in the story. As critic Søren Baggesen makes clear, while scrupulously charting Blicher's literary strategies, readers are manipulated into a position that requires that they determine what is really happening in the texts. Baggesen's *Den blicherske novelle* (The Blicher Short Story, 1965), however, finally gave Blicher the position he deserved in the Danish literary canon.

Steen Steensen Blicher was born on 11 October 1782. His father, Niels Blicher, a parson of Vium–a small, impoverished parish in mid-Jutland, not far from Viborg–was an important formative influence on the young boy, for Niels instructed his son in his own rationalistic worldview. Niels felt that he had to fulfill the demands that the Age of Reason made on a minister: he should not only be the shepherd of his flock but also a pragmatic instructor in agricultural economy. Since most farmers were poorly educated, they were in extreme need of assistance to become more productive.

Niels Blicher wrote a topographical account of Vium parish that depicts the region in detail and reveals its author to be a firm and optimistic believer in the ideals of his age. His publication makes clear that ordinary people must become better informed, and he offers practical advice on how education and medical service might be improved. Knud Sørensen, a Blicher biographer, reports that of the 464 inhabitants of the parish, only 16 could read or write. Since the Blichers, father and son, were very attached to each other, Steen Steensen Blicher attempted, in many ways, to emulate his father's educational mission.

The pastor of Vium suffered from the poor economy of this parish, and he was undoubtedly pleased when he was transferred to a parish in a much wealthier part of Jutland. At that point, his son was of an age to enter high school and was sent to Randers, quite a distance from his new home. The mental instability of his mother, Kirstine Marie Blicher, née Curtz, may have been one reason for his being sent so far away.

On his graduation from high school Blicher was sent to the University of Copenhagen, where he followed in his father's footsteps by studying theology. The Copenhagen of 1799 was a city of about one hundred thousand inhabitants with theaters, cafés, and a milieu in which recent literature was discussed. Blicher was poor, but his years in Copenhagen seem to have been pleasant ones. In 1802 he fell ill–perhaps from malnutrition–but he decided to cure himself by going hunting, playing his flute, and eating whatever he enjoyed. His plan worked, it seems, and he then applied to be a tutor on a large farm on the island of Falster.

He was accepted for the job, and he proved to be a good, if nontraditional, tutor. While surrounded by that pleasant, gentle landscape, so different from that of Jutland, in 1801 Blicher came across some poetry of Ossian. These poems were concocted by the Scottish schoolteacher James Macpherson, who cleverly purported to have found the works of Ossian, a melancholy bard who sang about the demise of his clan and his age. Blicher, like Johann Wolfgang von Goethe and many other admirers of Ossian, believed in the authenticity of the poetry and decided to learn English in order to render a competent translation. Solemn Ossianic moods continued to echo in many of Blicher's works, and the melancholy, nostalgia, and sense of loss that permeated Macpherson's accomplished literary fake–which should be respected in its own right–struck a chord in Blicher.

Blicher's translation *Ossians Digte* (The Poems of Ossian, 1807, 1809) was well received by the critics. Blicher also published original works, and clearly he anticipated having a career as a poet. He did, however, complete his degree in theology in 1809 and applied for a position at his old high school in Randers. Blicher got the job, but he fell out with the headmaster. Glimpses of his colleagues are given with a mixture of gentle and

Blicher paa Heden med tre Tatere *(Blicher on the Heath with Three Gypsies); painting by Christen Dalsgaard, 1866 (Museum of National History at Frederiksborg Castle; photograph courtesy of the Danish Royal Library, Copenhagen)*

scathing humor in "Juleferierne" (The Christmas Vacations, 1834). During his short time as a teacher he met his uncle's widow, Ernestine Juliane Berg Blicher, whom he married on 11 June 1810. She was well situated economically, but apparently the couple had a lifestyle that soon depleted their resources; their eight children can be seen as an extenuating factor, however. Financial problems pursued them for the rest of their lives and undoubtedly put a strain on their relationship. Ernestine also is commonly assumed to have been unfaithful to her spouse.

Blicher had to resign from his teaching position in 1811; he worked as the manager of the farm at his father's parsonage until he was appointed in 1819 to the pastorate of the less-than-prosperous Thorning parish, not far from Randers. As Blicher scholar Johannes Nørvig points out, the ambitious poet was probably bitter to realize that he had to settle for the clergy. He published a couple of volumes of poetry and some plays, but he was far away from the literary circles of Copenhagen and was considered–by most critics of Copenhagen–to be a secondary, if gifted, provincial writer. Blicher may not have had high regard for prose, since poetry was deemed to be a higher form, according to the aesthetics of the time, but his financial situation was miserable, so when he was asked, he agreed to submit stories to a provincial magazine, A. F. Elmquist's *Læsefrugter* (Fruits of Reading), which mainly offered sensational or sentimental tales translated from German. Blicher was likely familiar with the kind of stories published by that magazine and knew what would sell–even if improved upon artistically.

Blicher then wrote "En Landsbydegns Dagbog," a novella that records, in diary form, approximately forty years of a man's life. At the age of fifteen, Morten Vinge, whose intelligence has been discovered by the local clergyman, has high hopes of transcending his class by becoming a minister. Morten seems priggish, sanctimonious, and pleased that he is doing better than the minister's son, Jens, with whom he continues to compete, in various ways, for years. On the other hand, Morten is undoubtedly deeply grateful to the minister, who discovered his talent for learning and who is teaching him Latin. The reader listens to a young man who loves knowledge, has high dreams for his future, and is acutely aware of the social hierarchy of his society.

These dreams are shattered when the minister dies and Morten has to settle for becoming a servant at Tjele, a nearby manor house. The flighty, wild Jens is instrumental in securing Morten that position. Morten, who had such high hopes, does not form relationships with people from his own class. His only confidant is his diary, which, the reader realizes, often reveals young Morten's failure to understand himself and others. The theme of limited perception–the inability to understand a situation correctly and the false assumptions that result–is one that Blicher returned to time and again.

Morten is bright, learns fast, becomes a good hunter, switches from learning Latin to learning French, and is soon a valued servant. He has, however, fallen in love–as he discovers from reading Ovid–with Sophie, the daughter of the noble family he is serving. He knows that his love is hopeless and is relieved when he is sent to Copenhagen as a valet to his beloved's brother. Morten's fairly carefree life is brutally interrupted, however, by an epidemic illness that kills his master. For the first time, Morten, who has written religious clichés in his diary, seems to be a true believer in the grip of a bleak Old Testament Christianity. He is twenty years old but sounds like an old man longing for death. He returns home to Tjele, and when Sophie is about to be married to a man far above her in social standing, Morten realizes that his passion for her is still alive, as is that of his rival, Jens, who is equally upset with Sophie's forthcoming arranged marriage.

Blicher's stories deal little with ideas, but rather with experience. They tend to focus on the one event that changes everything. That is what happens to Morten through a typical Blicher intrigue that modern readers may see as somewhat contrived. Jens and Morten switch rooms so that Jens and Sophie can share a bed–something that Morten typically does not grasp. One day Morten, on a whim, takes a nap in his old room, and Sophie comes to him, lies down next to him, and kisses him passionately, but as he declares his love for her, she abruptly leaves. He is ecstatic; he believes that she has loved him secretly, just as he has loved her. He, as a servant, knows that his desire is wrong, but he cannot regret it. Several times Morten seems to break out of his narrow mold, but fate never quite allows that. Shortly afterward, he realizes that when Sophie had embraced and kissed him, she thought she was with Jens. Morten is devastated, and after that moment of recognition his life is changed forever.

Sophie and Jens elope; the sorrow and scandal kill the master of the manor; and Morten is homeless–and masterless. Morten, the servant, needs a master, and he enlists as a soldier to fight for his country but hopes a bullet may end his life. Instead, he ends up as a prisoner in Siberia for twenty-four years. Since Morten no longer has any expectations of life, he has only recorded a few entries in his diary. Finally, he is released and can go back to Denmark; the return seems to be a kind of liberation for this austere and private man who could speak freely only to his diary. He now confides his past troubles to his new master, a wealthy landowner, but then those troubles return with devastating impact. He discovers that Sophie and Jens are lowly employees on the farm; they are both alcoholics and spiritually and physically ruined by the lives they have led. Morten, who had retained a dream of his lady love, is utterly disgusted with life and asks his new master for permission to leave.

Morten returns to Tjele as parish clerk and thinks back on the days when he and Sophie were both innocents. In his last diary entry, Morten, whose life has been filled with many disappointments, thanks the good Lord for being righteous and merciful. His Old Testament fatalism allows him to accept a life that has not been fulfilling. Blicher, however, may be suggesting to the reader that the mindset of Morten's time–with its Lutheran orthodoxy that admonished Christians to serve their masters–curtailed his protagonist from leading a life over which he could have control. Jens and Sophie tried to take charge of their lives but were defeated.

Blicher contributed a few more pieces to *Læsefrugter,* among them the pleasant, if melodramatic, love story "Præsten i Thorning" (The Minister of Thorning, 1824); but since Elmquist refused him a raise, Blicher started, together with a colleague, a magazine called *Nordlyset* (Northern Lights), which was supposed to be somewhat more literary than Elmquist's. Although the magazine lasted for only three years, Blicher published in it several stories that were far ahead of their time and are still among the best short stories in Danish literature.

In 1826 Blicher became pastor of Rentrup, north of Randers. Around this time he began to write poetry in the Jutland dialect, texts that reveal his keen sense of–and respect for–the language of the common people of his region. Poignantly set in Jutland–probably as a protest against the cultural dominance of Copenhagen–the short stories were "Røverstuen" (1827; translated as "The Robbers' Den," 1945) and "Kjeltringliv" (1829; translated as "Gypsy Life," 1945), both of which reveal Blicher's compassion for people who were marginalized by society. In "Røverstuen" he interrupts his tale–a common feature in Blicher's first-person narratives–to size up his relationship to his famous foreign competitors (among them, "W.S." [Sir Walter Scott]); he pays them compliments but makes clear that he is independent of them and has invented his own manner of story-telling.

A modern flashback technique is used in "Sildig Opvaagnen" (1828; translated as "Tardy Awakening," 1945). The setting is a provincial town in Jutland, and the characters are prominent citizens–the doctor, the minister, the officer, and their wives. They meet every Wednesday night and enjoy a merry time together. All seems well, but a "tardy awakening"–an ominous title–is in the offing for them all. After years of the couples' seeming marital harmony, the doctor's wife, Elise, is revealed to have had a long-lasting affair with the officer and has even given birth to his children. The discovery shatters the life of the doctor, who dearly loves his wife, and he commits suicide. The officer's wife, who truly loved her husband, finds her life in tatters as well.

The narrator lets his readers know why he is writing his account: he has recently seen Elise, the adulteress, and that encounter has infuriated him, for while his best friends have died in terrible mental turmoil, she lives on in tranquility. He lashes out at her, calling her a vampire, a soulless being, a person who ruined the happiness of others. His judgment is unambiguous, and when one reads his account, Elise seems to have lured the officer into their illicit relationship; nevertheless, the reader should remember, the affair was not a one-night stand but lasted for many years. Some letters from Elise to her lover, which Blicher cleverly brings into the story, indicate, without a doubt, that no matter how conniving Elise may have been in starting the affair, she is profoundly in love with the officer.

What happens to Elise, then, may be just as tragic as what has happened to her husband. He lost his belief in her, and she lost the man she loved. She lives on, but her life may be without meaning. Elise, who always seemed to conceal her feelings, may even now be hiding behind a mask of cheerfulness. As usual in Blicher's

Lithograph of Blicher by E. Bærentzen & Co. (courtesy of the Danish Royal Library, Copenhagen)

narratives, the reader will never know exactly what some characters feel. Blicher's denial to his readers of complete closure suggests his modernity.

The reader who is alert to Blicher's subtle characterizations may nevertheless realize that the judgmental pastor who lashes out at illicit sexuality is hiding, whether he knows it or not, behind a mask of self-righteousness. In several passages–from the minister's first encounter with Elise on a dance floor to his keen observations of her across the years–he reveals that he is enthralled by her.

The minister, the unambiguous narrator who insists on assigning blame for the tragedy that ruined the lives of three families–his own, strangely, included–may have experienced his own "tardy awakening" as he wrote his account, for it suggests that, for years, he has been profoundly drawn to the woman he is condemning. What if he, and not the officer, had been Elise's lover? "Sildig Opvaagnen" is a remarkably sophisticated text; it is easily read, but it requires much of its reader. Each reading results in a new understanding; the story is a demonstration of Blicher's mastery.

Some of Blicher's characters may seem dour, but they are often counterbalanced by people with a sense of humor, and Blicher wrote several tales that reveal how painfully funny folly can be. For that purpose he invented an alter ego, Peer Spillemand (Peer the Fiddler), who continued to appear in his fiction–for example, in "Baglænds" (Backwards, 1839), "Julianes Giftermaal" (Juliane's Marriage, 1840), and "To paa en Hest" (Two on a Horse, 1842). Peer is not a consistent figure, but he offers Blicher the opportunity to create a distance between himself and his characters. Peer is introduced in "Ak! Hvor Forandret" (1828; translated as "Alas, How Changed!" 1945), in which he makes a fool of himself at a hunt as well as at a party. He becomes enamored of a young woman but fails to understand that he is perceived by others as a ridiculous figure. Years later, Peer returns to the same region and finds that a former friend is married to the woman of his dreams and that both have been transformed into materialistic and scarcely recognizable caricatures of their youthful selves.

How inevitable and dire change is in Blicher's work becomes obvious in "Hosekræmmeren" (1829; translated as "The Hosier and His Daughter," 1945). A wanderer, while crossing the moors, is contemplating the summer skies and making the clouds into romantic images. At the same time, he misanthropically suggests that any human abode will represent a sign of suffering and that he would welcome the absence of humanity in this landscape. The wanderer, whom some critics have equated with Blicher, seems to be a man who feels that life can offer only disillusionment.

But when thirst and hunger set in, he is glad to come upon the home of a wealthy hosier, who receives him with hospitality. He is, then, witness to a quiet drama, for the hosier's daughter, Cecil, is in love with Esben, a young man of meager resources. The hosier, as a good father should, is looking out for his daughter's best interests when he weighs the doubtful prospects of the young man. The hosier is the patriarch, and no one opposes him; still, the young man does ask that Cecil not be married until he returns from a journey abroad that he hopes will make him monetarily acceptable to the hosier.

That scene, observed and narrated by the outsider, is a minute study of people who were otherwise not a part of Danish literature–the rural population of a province that no one in distant Copenhagen knew about. The two young people, Cecil and Esben, hardly exchange a word or a glance, and the calm, if tense, dialogue between the young man and the hosier captures the suspense of a situation that is not allowed to become emotional.

Esben leaves, and the narrator says (to himself and thus to the reader) that he could have intervened and lectured the hosier about the rights of young love. He did not, however, for he has realized that the hosier will never agree with him and, more importantly, that the hosier is likely right. Money–as well as the lack of it–counts in a marriage, and perhaps Esben's love for Cecil is as ephemeral as the smoke that rises from his pipe as he disappears into the distance. The hosier and the narrator seem almost to engage in a silent debate, and the romantic visitor is convinced by the patriarch's firm opinion that money is what matters. Six years later, the wanderer returns and hopes to see an idyllic scene, a happily married couple with a baby, but his expectations are not fulfilled. Blicher returns every so often to the theme of lack of fulfillment, and he does so in this case with a vengeance: outside the house sits the beautiful Cecil with terrifyingly vacant eyes; clearly, she has lost her mind.

The hosier's wife explains what has happened–and with her taking over the narration of the story, Blicher brings into Danish literature the vernacular of the common people, which also found a voice in many of Hans Christian Andersen's tales. Blicher makes a brilliant move in allowing another narrator to relate the second section of "Hosekræmmeren": the wanderer is too reflective and digressive a narrator to render an effective account of the drama that caused Cecil's madness. But the hosier's wife tells the story in her "egen simple og enfoldige stil" (own simple and naive style).

Mads, a well-heeled suitor, showed up and was accepted by the hosier, though he hardly considered Cecil's feelings. When the banns were read in church for the third and last time, Cecil objected by rising and stating that she and Esben were married in Paradise. Her family was scandalized. But there is reason in Cecil's madness, for by escaping into insanity, she has fled from a world ruled by her father's pragmatic ideology into one in which feelings alone rule. The wanderer's previous tacit agreement with the hosier that love has lesser priority than money has reflected an insufficient understanding of Cecil and of the nature of passion. No mouthpiece for the author states that overtly, for typically Blicher lets readers draw such conclusions.

After some months, Esben returns; moreover, he has received an inheritance from a rich uncle, so the monetary obstacle to his marrying his sweetheart has been removed. Cecil, however, is trapped by the world into which she has fled, and she insistently asks, with authority, that Esben die and join her in the afterlife. Esben is grieved by her condition–and even breaks down and cries, a reaction that is most unusual for people in his milieu; then, the hosier asks Esben to stay for the night and adds that all may still turn out well.

Esben's emotional breakdown and Cecil's rebellion against parental authority do not belong in the world of the hosier, nor does what happens next. During a ferocious thunderstorm–Blicher had a weakness for romantic special effects–Cecil slits Esben's throat to be certain that he will join her in Paradise. After that, she regains her sanity but cannot recall what she has done, until her former suitor, Mads, cruelly tells her. From then on, she is incurably insane, forever waiting for Esben to return.

The woman who tells the latter part of the story mentions that her husband, the hosier, stated that whatever happened was God's will. That seems to be his psychological defense against the accusations he has raised against himself, but a man who is used to feeling right about his choices can hardly handle such existential complexity, and before long, he dies. He was a proud, self-assured man who wanted the best for his child. He was thrown into a chaotic world that he could not control, and he realized that his decisions had resulted in insanity and murder. Blicher's title for the story is "The Hosier," as in the 1996 translation, and not, as the older translation has it, the sentimental title "The Hosier and His Daughter" (1945). The hosier's tragedy ought to be added to those of Cecil and Esben.

When the narrator has heard the hosier's wife out, he leaves, and–true to Blicher fashion–the reader gets the last word. The reader will likely react against the wanderer-narrator, who could have intervened but did not. The narrator has seemed uninvolved but perhaps realizes that he should not have been.

Blicher understood that women felt trapped by their roles in Danish society. In "Sildig Opvaagnen," a woman rebels against the rules put down by bourgeois society, which considers the family–ruled by a patriarch–to be at the center of civilization. Elise rebels against those mental shackles, and so, in quite different ways, do Sophie in "En Landsbydegns Dagbog" and Cecil in "Hosekræmmeren." They all free themselves from, or rebel against, those who represent ideological powers that want to restrict their thinking and lives, but these women seem sadly defeated.

The term *defeat* also comes to mind when one reads "Præsten i Vejlbye" (1829; translated as "The Parson at Vejlbye," 1945). Blicher used the true story of a pastor who was accused of having killed his farmhand and who, in 1626, was executed for that crime, but Blicher adds his own unmistakable touch to the tale.

The story is mainly narrated by a young judge and sheriff, Erik Sørensen, who takes up his first position with a sense of pride and humility: he knows that he will serve the Lord and the king well and see to it that justice is done. He is a product of his Lutheran culture. His life has purpose and becomes even fuller when he falls in love with Parson Søren Quist's daughter, Mette. Their marriage, as often was the case then, could have been one of convenience, but Sørensen's

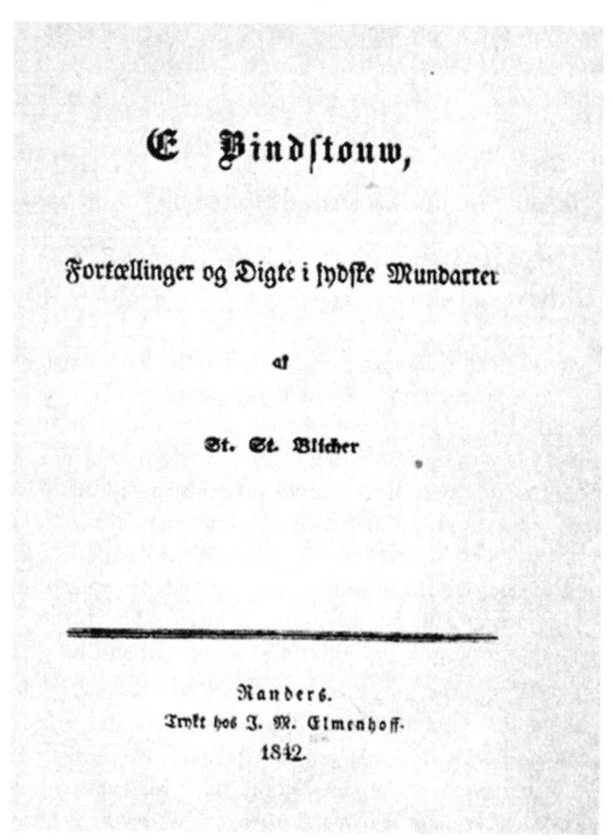

E Bindstouw,

Fortællinger og Digte i jydske Mundarter

af

St. St. Blicher

Randers.
Trykt hos J. M. Elmenhoff.
1842.

Title page for Blicher's collection of stories and ballads that he presents as being told and sung by Jutland farmers at a pre-Christmas gathering (from Knud Sørensen, St. St. Blicher. Digter og samfundsborger, *1984; Alderman Library, University of Virginia)*

journal makes clear that the two young people look forward to a long life of marital bliss.

The minister, his daughter, and Erik Sørensen have all managed, however, to insult a rich farmer, Morten Bruus. He wanted to marry Mette, but she rejected his proposal, even though her father was in favor of her marrying a wealthy man. When her father realized that his daughter had a mind of her own, he supported her wishes and angered Bruus. At a court case, in which Bruus attempts to gain possession of a poor farmer's meadow, Bruus tries to bribe the new judge, but in vain. Bruus is a man of grudges and of no conscience, so he plots a clever conspiracy that is intended to destroy his enemies. His brother Niels, a man with a nasty temper, manages to get hired by Parson Quist, another man with a tempestuous mind, and soon the two fall out. Suddenly Niels disappears, and rumor soon suggests that he has been killed by Quist. Morten Bruus demands an investigation, and what seems to be Niels's body is dug up in the parson's garden. The sheriff has no choice but to arrest Quist.

As the court case unfolds, more and more witnesses seem to suggest that the parson is guilty, and eventually he himself comes to believe so, for he is a sleepwalker, and he surmises that in a somnambulistic state he may have killed Niels. In fact, he is so convinced of his own guilt that he refuses his future son-in-law's offer to close his eyes to a possible escape attempt.

This tortuous story, so far told from Sørensen's point of view, reveals that his world is crumbling. He has to judge the man he thought would be his father-in-law; he will likely lose his beloved; and he has betrayed his oath of office by permitting an attempt to let Quist flee. The young protector of the law who sought meaning in carrying out the duties of his office finds himself in a chaotic world beyond his control. Not surprisingly, he falls gravely ill and desires to die. Quist is condemned to death. The temperamental minister, who has many human weaknesses, grows in maturity as his execution approaches; he fully realizes that he deserves his punishment, and before he is beheaded in public, he gives a rousing sermon in which he admonishes his congregation to learn from his ugly and sinful mistakes.

As in "Hosekræmmeren," Blicher adds a postscript. It is written by the minister who gave Quist the last sacrament. The minister recounts the sinner's last moments and testifies to the condemned man's stature as he prepared to die. Twenty-one years later, an old vagabond who shows up on his doorstep proves to be Niels Bruus, the man whom Quist supposedly beat to death. When the minister tells him what happened in the past, Niels is completely devastated and reveals that Quist was framed by Niels's brother Morten. The body that was supposedly Niels's was that of a suicide; the corpse was dressed in Niels's clothes and its face was smashed.

Sørensen has lived a sad and lonely life but believed that justice was meted out. When Niels, driven by his bad conscience, suddenly appears and tells the truth, Quist's death must seem like a cruel joke. For years Sørensen has thought that he convicted a man who was guilty; now, he realizes that he was a manipulated fool, a tool in the hands of evil. Understandably, both he and Niels die, for those two victims, no matter how different they are, realize how ruthlessly they have been used and to what end. What is chillingly clear about "Præsten i Vejlbye" is that Morten Bruus, who was not inhibited by any sense of ethics or moral qualms, has been victorious. When he had died a few years earlier, he was given an honorable burial. "Præsten i Vejlbye" is perhaps Blicher's darkest story.

Blicher's characters are Christians who have to realize that their lives will not be eased by their beliefs. The Lord seems to be a distant being, one who listens little to their prayers. As Baggesen has pointed out, life seems inscrutable; it is a riddle that will never be fully understood. The ways of the Lord are many, and, like Job, human beings cannot fathom why their destinies take such disastrous turns.

In a sense, Blicher's modern reputation rests on a small foundation–a handful of short stories. Some of his other stories were fine for their time and are worth reading today, but they lack the resonance of those discussed. Those remarkable stories are bleakly pessimistic, for many of their characters have a desire or a dream of happiness that they attempt to realize but cannot. Society or fate or chance prevents the fulfillment of their dreams.

When the literary magazine *Nordlyset* ceased publication, Blicher stopped writing stories for three years. He carried out his duties, wrote a few occasional poems to the king–with whom he could not find fault–and started a magazine, *Diana* (1832–1836), intended for hunters. At the same time, a Copenhagen publisher decided to bring out a volume of Blicher's stories. The result was no fewer than eight volumes of short stories, *Samlede Noveller* (Collected Short Stories, 1833–1836, 1844, and 1845), and two volumes of poetry *Samlede Digte* (Collected Poems, 1835, 1836); most of the texts had been published earlier in periodicals, but the editions included a few new stories, among them "Himmelbjerget" (Sky Mountain, 1833). It is a comedy on the slight side that flirts with tragic themes, but it ends on a most happy note, with young men and women united in engagements.

Baggesen has discussed "Himmelbjerget" in detail, and he has used it to emphasize the masks Blicher's characters wear to pretend to be something they are not. Morten Bruus in "Præsten i Vejlbye" successfully masquerades as the parson to fool the parishioners into believing him guilty of murder. Elise in "Sildig Opvaagnen" pretends to be a docile, happy housewife, and even after her world has crumbled, she seems to be coolly in control of her life. The tragedy in "Sildig Opvaagnen" is initiated at a masquerade, the point of which is to hide one's identity. The narrator of "Sildig Opvaagnen," the minister, hides his true feelings, as well–perhaps even to himself.

The reviews of the first five volumes of *Samlede Noveller* were initially positive, but young Nicolai Madvig, a rising intellectual star in Copenhagen, praised Blicher while lashing out at the immorality of "Sildig Opvaagnen" and generally found that Blicher did not support the idyllic, harmonious view of the bourgeois family then accepted. Madvig was right, and that is one reason that Blicher has superseded many of his contemporaries. Blicher offers what has been called Biedermeier settings and characters–an idyllic and harmonious view of life–but as a rule, he undercuts them severely. Madvig's critique, however, served to pigeonhole Blicher as a provincial author out of step with the taste of his age.

In spite of Blicher's attachment to his region, he wanted to see other parts of the world, and he felt that traveling would offer him new, and badly needed, inspiration. One short trip westward resulted in the story "Marie" (1836), which leans heavily on "Hosekræmmeren" but was inspired by Blicher's encounter with the Danish west coast and the North Sea. The descriptions of nature, rather than the plot, may fascinate the modern reader. Blicher's less-than-fortunate attempt at writing a novel, "Fjorten Dage i Jylland" (Fourteen Days in Jutland, 1836), likewise conjures up the western coast of Jutland.

With the help of an incredibly supportive Copenhagen benefactor, Jonas Collin–who for years also served as Hans Christian Andersen's mentor–Blicher received a grant that enabled him to travel to Sweden to do philological and antiquarian research. For a while he had a traveling companion, critic Christian Molbech, who had recognized Blicher's talent in composing poems in dialect. The men parted ways, and Blicher continued northward toward Stockholm through a forested landscape that had little in common with the heaths and fields of Jutland. Blicher observed that Sweden, unlike Denmark, was still a land of forests with only scattered fields. A travel memoir in verse was published the following year as *Svithiod. Efteraarserindringer fra en Sommerreise i Sverrig i Aaret 1836* (Svithoid. Autumn Memoir from a Summer Journey in Sweden in 1836, 1837), and later a prose version of the memoir appeared, *Sommerreise i Sverige i 1836* (Summer Journey in Sweden in 1836, 1841). The trip lasted five weeks, and it was Blicher's only journey abroad. His Copenhagen peers saw much of Europe; Blicher remained locked within the region he wrote about in text after text.

Back in Denmark, Blicher fell ill. During his illness he composed some of his best poetry, which was published as *Trækfuglene* (Birds of Passage, 1838). In the introductory poem, "Præludium" (translated as "Prelude to 'Birds of Passage,'" 1957), the approach of death is registered without sentimentality as it also is in "Ouverture," in which in the midst of a winter that is icily cold and white, a yearning for spring defies the grip of winter on nature.

In Blicher's later life, his activities, as well as his writings, suggest that he wanted to promote a belief in the ordinary people as resilient, courageous, and patiently stubborn and thus to vouch for the future of Denmark. Blicher had reasons for that trust in the people, for a national collection in his behalf was successful, and most of the contributors were commoners. Blicher's belief in the common people is voiced in "De tre Helligaftener" (1841; translated as "Three Holiday Eves," 1945). It is based on a legend, which the language clearly reveals, for it seems told by a person who has

Graves of Blicher and his wife, Ernestine Juliane, in the Spentrup churchyard (from Knud Sørensen, St. St. Blicher. Digter og samfundsborger, *1984; Alderman Library, University of Virginia)*

heard the story many times. The plot is simple: two young, poor people are in love, but Seier, the young man, is a bit too temperamental for the owner of the manor house from whom the young people would like to rent a farm. Young rebels were not well liked in feudal Denmark, and the outlook for Seier and Maren seems dismal, especially since a wealthy stranger seems interested in Maren. But all ends well: the stranger is a highwayman, and on Christmas Eve, Seier catches him and his companions. Consequently, he is granted the farm that he desires, and the young people can marry. The story has become a beloved tale often read aloud, and it is quite different from Blicher's stories from the 1820s.

As Blicher was composing that happy story, he was planning a festival for ordinary people on Himmelbjerget (Sky Mountain). Located in a hilly, rugged landscape, it had assumed a symbolic significance to the Danish mind. Blicher hoped that all classes would be represented at the festival, the purpose of which was a rejuvenation of the Danish nation. In his speech to the crowds, he compared the event to the Olympic Games in ancient Greece. The first meeting in 1839 was a success. Five meetings took place at Himmelbjerget; Blicher spoke, but apparently he was not a good public speaker, and he was eventually eased out of the festival. Despite that Blicher was a jovial fellow who enjoyed good company, he could be edgy and difficult, especially when he felt that he was being belittled by authority figures–such as his clerical superiors and Copenhagen critics. Although he had been an admirer of the royal house, he became a proponent of a constitution that would abolish the absolute monarchy and institute a parliamentary system. Blicher was, as well, taken with Pan-Scandinavianist ideas of a united North. Consequently, he may have made himself suspect in the eyes of powerful conservatives. Blicher was a man who was always planning new projects, but his enthusiasm often failed to inspire those who were to fund the plans.

Blicher's economic woes continued to plague him, and even though he retained his talent for churning out stories that excited readers, in retrospect he seemed to be repeating himself or getting a bit sloppy as a narrator. His joy in storytelling was replaced by routine. Blicher did, however, pull himself together for another small masterpiece, *E Bindstouw,* which is written entirely in Jutland dialects. In a review, critic P. L. Møller wrote that it was a shame that this little book could only be fully comprehended and enjoyed by people from Jutland, for it comprised some of the best that Blicher–or for that matter, any Danish poet–had written. Møller was a young critic who had admired Blicher for years and who dared go against the generally condescending views that Copenhagen critics held of him. Blicher was profoundly grateful to Møller.

The fictional frame of *E Bindstouw* is a gathering just before Christmas of local farmers to knit and sew. As they work, they tell stories and sing ballads. The small book gave Blicher the opportunity to pull together old and new poems and tales that demonstrate not only his narrative talent but also his profound knowledge of the rural population. Perhaps this book more than any other publication reveals his sense of humor. Some of the tales, however, veer toward the sadness and tragedy that can be found in many oral, formulaic legends and ballads.

In 1842, after Blicher's enemies had forced him out of the committee for planning the Himmelbjerg festivals, he decided to leave his clerical position and settle permanently in Copenhagen. The capital city–the site of his youthful years–apparently continued to fascinate him. After a pitiful existence for half a year, though, he had to return to Jutland. Rumors spread that he was drinking and performing his duties poorly. Nevertheless, stubborn Blicher was not a person to give up: he was planning–and trying to get funds together–for another trip abroad, collecting legends, and trying to revive his Himmelbjerg meetings at another location. With such a rebirth in mind, he wrote a brief, but remarkable, poem in dialect celebrating the Jutland character, "Jyden" (1849, translated as "The Jutlander," 1947). The man from Jutland is strong and stubborn and, therefore, resilient and a survivor.

Blicher was ailing, and he was told to request permission to retire. He resented the suggestion. In 1848 he received his dismissal, and he died in Spentrup on 26 March 1848. His biographers point out that the recently declared war–Slesvig-Holsten intended to secede from Denmark–obscured his death from the Danish public. Blicher may seem a bit of a paradox. He was a minister who often wrote stories expressive of a bleak outlook on existence. One may detect a mellowing, however, as Blicher became more involved with political issues and tried to reach out to the ordinary Dane. Perhaps one could raise the question whether Blicher's gradual involvement in secular, political matters was an escape from the relentlessly tragic view depicted in his best stories. Several of Blicher's biographers have pointed out that he hardly wanted to become a clergyman but merely followed in his father's footsteps, as was expected. He might not have been a traditional minister, but even though he was involved with many issues and events outside his parish, he seemed to be well liked by his flock.

The question has been asked whether or not this clergyman was a believer. In "Sildig Opvaagnen," the minister points out that he cannot spiritually help his agonized friend, the doctor, who has just realized that his entire life has been a sham, for the doctor is a superficial Christian whose belief is too shallow to help him in a time of existential crisis. Curiously, the clergyman, who laments his friend's weak faith, finds no solace through belief and writes his embittered account without any sense of Christian forgiveness. The narrator, of course, is not Blicher, but Blicher did a marvelous job of imagining a minister who does not find spiritual or emotional sustenance in Christian doctrine. Perhaps, Blicher–like Søren Kierkegaard–found the Old Testament, rather than the Gospels, to be his frame of reference. The stories of Job and Jephta make clear that suffering is a part of existence, something that cannot be avoided. The person who expects life to be fair is a fool, and Blicher wrote eloquently about many fools. But that hardly relegates him to a passive fatalism. Although he knew that his secular endeavors might fail, he pursued them anyway, with an optimism and fervor that might seem surprising, and he refused to accept defeat. He seems to be a paradox, but only if he is considered to be a person who looks at life ahistorically. His characters who fail are not the victims of an unchangeable human condition but people who are caught by ideologies and biases that are products of society. The characters themselves do not understand that they are victims of these beliefs, to their detriment, but those who rebel, even if in vain, stake out new paths for those who come after them, the readers of Steen Steensen Blicher's stories.

Letters:

Blicher i breve, edited by Johannes Nørvig (Copenhagen: Blicher-selskabet, 1959).

Bibliographies:

Jørgen K. Berthelsen, *Blicher Bibliografi* (Copenhagen: Boghallens Antikvariat, 1933);

Henrik Denman, *Steen Steensen Blicher litteraturen* (Roskilde: Denman, 1983);

A. Gjedde, *St. St. Blicher. En bibliografi* (Copenhagen, 1993).

Biographies:

Jeppe Aakjær, *Steen Steensen Blichers Livs-Tragedie i Breve og Aktstykker,* 3 volumes (Copenhagen: Gyldendal, 1903-1904);

Johannes Nørvig, *Steen Steensen Blicher. Hans Liv og Værker* (Copenhagen: Munksgaard, 1943);

Dansk Biografisk leksikon, volume 2, third edition, edited by Svend Cedergreen Bech (Copenhagen: Gyldendal, 1979), pp. 221-228;

Knud Sørensen, *St. St. Blicher. Digter og samfundsborger* (Copenhagen: Gyldendal, 1984).

References:

Ulla Albeck, *Stil og Teknik i Blichers Noveller* (Copenhagen: Munksgaard, 1942);

Søren Baggesen, "Blichers masker," in *Himmelbjerget og andre noveller* (Copenhagen: Gyldendal, 1975), pp. 175-213;

Baggesen, *Dansk Litteraturhistorie: Borgerlig enhedskultur 1807-1848,* volume 5 (Copenhagen: Gyldendal, 1984), pp. 424-441;

Baggesen, *Den blicherske novelle* (Copenhagen: Gyldendal, 1965);

Peter Brask, "Den fremmedgjorte Eros," *Poetik* (1969): 13-38;

Brask, *Om en Landsbydegns Dagbog,* 2 volumes (Copenhagen: Gyldendal, 1983);

Thomas Bredsdorff, "De tre virkeligheder. Om Blichers Hosekræmmeren," in *Tristans børn. Angående digtning om kærlighed og ægteskab i den borgerlige epoke* (Copenhagen: Gyldendal, 1982), pp. 98-120;

Hans Brix, *Blicher Studier* (Copenhagen: Gyldendal, 1916);

Erik M. Christensen, "Den blicherske tolkning," *Kritik* (1967): 20-44;

Niels Ingwersen, "Forfatterens mange stemmer i Blichers 'Sildig Opvaagnen,'" *Danske Studier* (1971): 37-57;

Henrik Ljungberg, *Dødens fortællere–om Blichers bedste noveller* (Copenhagen: Gyldendal, 1989);

Felix Nørgaard, ed., *Omkring Blicher 1974* (Copenhagen: Gyldendal, 1974);

Kenneth Olwig, *Nature's Ideological Landscape; A Literary and Geographic Perspective on its Development and Preservation on Denmark's Jutland Heath* (London: Allen & Unwin, 1984);

Tage Skou-Hansen, "Efterskrift," in *Noveller* (Copenhagen: Gyldendal, 1964), pp. 289-304;

Søren Vasegaard, *Til Belysning af Blichers Liv og Digtning 1820-1836* (Copenhagen: Woels Boghandel, 1926).

Papers:

Steen Steensen Blicher's papers and manuscripts are housed at the Danish Royal Library in Copenhagen, at the State Library in Århus, and at the Herning Museum.

Anders Bording

(21 January 1619 - 24 May 1677)

Paul Ries
Darwin College, University of Cambridge

BOOKS: *Disputatio solennis, super Justini sententia instituta, de Ignibus Subterraneis* (Sorø, 1653);

Den berømte og velfortiente M. Anders Bordings Poëtiske skrifter, edited by Friderich Rostgaard and Peder Terpager, with a preface by Hans Gram and a biographical sketch by Terpager (Copenhagen: Kongl. privilegerede Bogtrykkeries Forlag, 1736 [i.e., 1735])–comprises part 1, *Befattende hans adskillige slags Vers, Ære-Digter, Lykynskninger, Brude- og Lüg-Vers, Binde-Breve, lystige Indfald etc. saa og Aandelige Sange og Verdslige Viser;* and part 2, *Indeholdende alle hans Mercurier, eller Maanedlige Tidender paa Vers, Ved Conferentz-Raad Friderich Rostgaards, og Mag. Peder Terpagers, Læsemester i den Hellige Skrift i Ribe, deres Flid og Omhue, for rum Tid siden samlede, og nu endeligen til Trykken befordrede.*

Editions and Collections: *Udvalgte Vers,* edited, with an introduction, by Carl Dumreicher (Copenhagen: Dansk kautionsforsikring, 1955);

Den danske Mercurius 1666–1677, selections edited, with commentaries and afterword, by Paul Ries (Copenhagen: Danske Sprog- og Litteraturselskab/Munksgaard, 1973);

Samlede skrifter, 4 volumes published (Copenhagen: Danske Sprog- og Litteraturselskab/C. A. Reitzel, 1984-)–comprises volume 1, *Digte,* edited by Erik Sønderholm; volume 2, *Kommentar til Anders Bordings digte,* edited by Sønderholm; volume 3, *Den danske Mercurius,* edited by Paul Ries; and volume 4, *Kommentar til Mercurius,* edited by Ries.

Anders Bording (lithograph by E. Bærentzen & Co., based on a painting at Rosenberg Castle, Copenhagen, by an unknown artist; courtesy of the Danish Royal Library, Copenhagen)

Between 1642 and 1677 Anders Bording wrote 44 pastoral, 42 congratulatory, and 37 commemorative poems; 36 hymns; 34 epigrams and improvisations; and 18 political poems, as well as the 14,700 alexandrines that filled his monthly newspaper *Den berømte og velfortiente Den danske Mercurius* (The Danish Mercury, 1666–1677). Popular in its day, Bording's complete oeuvre was seen by his contemporaries as the pinnacle of the Danish literary Parnassus, and more than half a century after his death he became the first Danish poet to have his complete works published in his honor as *Den berømte og velfortiente M. Anders Bordings Poëtiske Skrifter* (The Poetic Works of Anders Bording, 1735). Focusing their studies of Danish Baroque on the religious poetry of Anders Arrebo and Thomas Kingo, literary critics since 1800, however, have tended to emphasize only part of Bording's oeuvre–usually some pastorals and a few poems deemed to be significantly autobiographical–at the expense of his elegies, hymns, and panegyrics, which, with his political poems and the newspaper *Den Danske Mercurius,* have been relegated to a lower order of perfunctory verse typical of what has been seen as the quaint but inconsequential political and religious mindset of a bygone age. In addition, historians and literary critics of the period of National Romanticism launched the myth about Bording as a brave defender during the siege of Copenhagen in 1659, an idea that, together with the equally undocumented myths about his having to eke out an existence by living off the sale of his poems, helped create a romantic image of him as a talented, but wayward, Bohemian that still makes an appearance in standard literary histories. However, as recent research has suggested, Bording was not just a gifted, minor writer of occasional verse between two religious giants, he was something quite different both as a person and as a poet. He was different as a person because in an age when most poets served the church and composed their verse within the boundaries of its strict ideology, he pursued a secular career and engaged with his public by addressing its interests in and concerns about a multitude of aspects of life in seventeenth-century Denmark; and he was different as a poet because unlike his contemporaries, who adopted and excelled in the fashionable Baroque style, Bording, an admirer and imitator of the classics since his schooldays, avoided its excesses and developed a clear, simple, at times even colloquial, poetic diction and style much admired by and aspired to by the foremost poets of the Enlightenment.

Anders Bording was the second of four children born into a prominent, professional family in the cathedral city of Ribe. His father, Christen Bording, a doctor of medicine, had been surgeon to Prince-elect Christian and visited Leipzig, Siena, and Padua as tutor to a young nobleman before his appointment as chief medical officer for the province. His mother, Ingeborg Klyne, was the daughter of a wealthy bourgeois family that also counted among its members such academic luminaries as historians Hans Svaning and Anders Sørensen Vedel, Bishop Peder Hegelund, and politically powerful Archbishop Hans Svane. From 1626 Bording, together with his older brother Laurids, continued his education for eleven years at the prestigious Ribe Cathedral School before they were both admitted to the University of Copenhagen in 1637. Laurids was tutored by the historian Ole Worm, for whose *Monumenta Danica* (1643) he supplied material for the county of Ribe but then chose a conventional career within the Lutheran church and spent the rest of his life as a parish pastor in Western Jutland. By contrast, Anders–whose tutor was linguist, book collector, and university librarian Thomas Bang–left the university after seven years of study without a degree and never took up the offer of assistance with a career, which Worm also extended to him in 1643 and again in 1646. When in 1653 Anders's master's degree qualified him for a post as a vicar or schoolmaster, moreover, he applied for neither, and when forced to accept one of each–in Slagelse (1662) and Ribe (1664)–he mismanaged both so badly that he was replaced.

Instead, Anders Bording took up employment as tutor to the children of various noble families, first in Copenhagen and then in Jutland, and in this environment, he wrote his earliest, datable poems, an epithalamium in Latin on a relative's wedding (1642) and four Latin epigrams on the graduation of some of his university friends (1643). As his pastoral "Daphnis gik for nogle Dage" (As Daphnis One Day Wandered, 1645) shows, however, he had become aware of the programs for the regeneration of vernacular languages as vehicles for poetry that swept through literary Europe at the time. In Germany such programs had been devised and practiced by the members of several literary societies, but the immediate impact of this poetic revolution on Bording clearly came through renowned pastoral poet and hymn writer Johann Rist, who in 1642 had published a small collection of translations, or rather adaptations, of pastorals from Honoré d'Urfé's fashionable pastoral novel *Astree* (1607–1627), titled "Des Daphnis aus Cimbrien Galathee" (The Cimbrian Daphnis and his Galathee). From his parish near Hamburg, Rist also established contact with like-minded poets from the region, among them Gabriel Voigtländer, whose small volume *Allerhand Oden und Lieder* (Diverse Odes and Songs, 1642) also included pastorals in imitation of d'Urfé, and Søren Terkelsen, who in 1645 began the publication of his adaptations of d'Urfé's work. Another member of Rist's circle, Georg Greflinger, later played an important part in Bording's life, but when in 1645 Bording announced that his pastoral was a translation of one of Rist's poems from 1642, he clearly placed himself within the ranks of the literary avant-garde of his day.

In addition to producing a series of fashionable pastorals, Bording turned his hand to religious poetry; his earliest datable hymn was "Ørnen med sin lette Vinger" (The Light-Winged Eagle, 1647). In this poem he followed the traditional pattern for didactic religious verse, in that its twenty-four stanzas are no more than a versification of a multitude of scriptural passages whose precise origins are given in marginal notes. But he equally followed the examples of Rist and Voigtländer, for he wrote the hymn in the same meter as his own pastoral of 1645 and specifically stated that it be sung to the same tune; indeed, according to Hans Gram, at this stage of his career Bording made his mark precisely because he "skrev slige Digter efter fornemme Adels-

Folkes og Fruentimmers Begiering. . . . Og saasom hand forstod Musiken vel, var en god Sanger og skiøn Lutenist, sang og spillede han sine Viser, baade de Aandelige og Verdslige, ret paa de gamle Lyriske Poeters viis" (wrote such poems at the request of distinguished aristocratic gentlemen and ladies. . . . And as he understood music well, was a good singer and an accomplished lute player, he sang and played his songs, spiritual as well as secular, in the manner of the ancient lyrical poets).

During his time as a tutor in Jutland, he also wrote a didactic poem on the topical debate about women's access to education ("Scutum gynaicosophias eller Lærde Kvinders Forsvar," 1647), dedicated to a young lady of the household about to join the royal court at Copenhagen, but, in addition, he was writing poems in genres in the literary canon that he would have to master if he were to engage with a wider public and hope to leave Jutland by catching the eye of influential patrons closer to the capital and the court. Among those poems were some elegies and epithalamia addressed to members of the aristocracy and other prominent persons, and having gained a master's degree in 1653 from Sorø Academy–an educational establishment founded to provide young members of the nobility and the gentry with an education that would enable its graduates to pursue a career within the civil or military administration or at court–he published his first political poem, "Jyllands lykønskende Frydeskrig" (Jutland's Congratulatory Exultation, 1655), in a small run at the Hans Skonning workshop in Aarhus. A panegyric formally hailing the Danish king's nine-year-old son, Christian, as the elective prince at Viborg by the Estates of Jutland, the poem also celebrated the political order of the day, impressing upon the representatives of the four estates–nobility, clergy, bourgeoisie, and peasantry–their specific duties toward the monarchy.

However, being politically "on message" was not his only passport to entry into the political establishment; poets and musicians with sufficient knowledge and learning were often attached to the courts of powerful aristocratic politicians. Voigtländer had played just such a role at the court of the Danish prince-elect, who had also been Bording's father's patron, and Rist's learning and poetry were greatly appreciated at the court in Copenhagen, which also employed an official, though German, court poet. Bording later (1663) applied specifically for the post of Danish court poet, but in the meantime he concentrated on the kind of social networking without which he was unlikely ever to succeed, and by 1655 he was well on the way. His fashionable pastoral poetry was highly acclaimed in aristocratic circles; his hymns demonstrated his unswerving adherence to the strict ideology of the Lutheran church; and his political poem of 1655 confirmed the correctness of his politics. His learning, moreover, was evident from his references to such classical writers as Homer, Pythagoras, Pindar, Plato, Cato, Caesar, Cicero, Virgil, Ovid, and Martial, and to such modern poets as d'Urfé, Rist, Sir Philip Sidney, Martin Opitz, and Jacob Cats, while his thesis on earthquakes and his didactic poem on women's education displayed his ability to debate important questions in religion, modern science, and education.

Though Bording clearly addressed his political poem to the king of Denmark and his men, his next appointment took him not to Copenhagen but to Scania, then part of Denmark, where he joined the court of Tage Thott, an aristocrat and member of the Council of the Realm so powerful that he was known as the king of Scania. In this milieu, Bording, who had been called to Thott's court because he "for sin Lærdom og Riime-Konst bleven meget navnkyndig" (had become famous for his learning and poetry), joined former fellow student Vitus Bering, who had spent five years as tutor for Count Thott's son during his studies in the Netherlands, France, Italy, Switzerland, and Germany. In 1650 Bering had been appointed professor of history and royal historiographer at the University of Copenhagen, but with permission to remain in Count Thott's service, and when he finally left Thott's court, his intention was to write the official account of the siege and relief of Copenhagen during the war with Sweden, (1657–1660). Also present at Count Thott's court was young lawyer Jørgen Fog, who later rose to political power in absolutist Denmark under the auspices of the prime minister, Count Griffenfeld, who was his brother-in-law.

The events that Bering returned to record were followed by a coup d'état in which the king, supported by the representatives of the clergy and the Copenhagen bourgeoisie, ousted the nobility from its former political powers and brought about the transition from elective to hereditary and eventually absolutist, monarchical rule, but no evidence shows that Bording witnessed these events. On the other hand, clearly Bording was aware of the events of those years, for soon after his return from Scania, now part of Sweden, he published his second political poem, "Frydeskrig over Frederik III" (Exultation on Frederik III, 1660), a panegyric in which he not only hailed the king as the savior of the capital against the Swedes but also showed his political astuteness by congratulating the king on the outcome of the bourgeois revolution. The poem was published in Copenhagen by the university printer Christian Jensen Wering.

Den Danske

MERCURIUS

Til den 1. April 1675.

Danmark.

1 Mand store Kongers raad vel bør i løn at dølge:
Men tak och fryde-sang bør offentlig at følge
Paa Guds velgjerninger/ som hand saa kjendelig
J mange maader med formerke lader sig.
Op derfor/ op/ med lyst/ o ædle Cimber Rige/
Lad takkepsalmers klang til Himlens Gud opstige/
Som med sin almagt har vor Daner Dronning ført
Igjennem Dødsens poort/ och Landsens bøner hørt;
At hendes Majestæt blant glade Mødres orden
Nu skrifves kand/ i det hun lykkelig er vorden
Forløst/ och uden meen/ udi sin rette tid/
Et yndigt Herre-Barn har fød til verden hjd.
Tormaanets sjette Dag til tifvende begyndtes/
Der os hans fødsels bud høytidelig forkyndtes
Formedelst ære-skud af Stadens høye vold/
Samt klokkers glade klang/ som hørdes mangefold.
Hærpukkers hule glam och mester slag ey spardes/
Hvor til och af klarin med høye toner svardes.
Ja hver mand priste Gud/ och der til sagde saa:
Velkommen ædle Prinds! gid det dig lykkes maae!
Men baade først och sidst kand Jeg ey nær udbrede/
Hvor høy-fornøyet sig hans Fader Kongen tede.
Der hand fornam/ at det saa vel var gangen af:
Hvorfor hand mangen skenk til budde-løn udgaf.

First page of an issue of the monthly newspaper in verse that Bording published from 1666 to 1677 (courtesy of the Danish Royal Library, Copenhagen)

Bording's expression of loyalty to the new regime did not immediately gain him the hoped-for position at court, so during and after the two unwanted and mismanaged clerical appointments in Ribe and Slagelse, he launched a poetic offensive in which he bombarded certain political grandees of the new regime and members of the royal household with flattering poems and witty supplications in verse. At the same time, he published his third political poem, a vitriolic attack on Corfitz Ulfeldt, the fugitive leader of the defeated aristocratic opposition, who had just been executed in effigy outside the prison in the royal castle, the Blue Tower, in which his spouse, Leonora Christina Ulfeldt, was completing the first of what was to be twenty-three years of imprisonment for her unproven complicity in his plans. No doubt these post-1660 poems played their part in securing Bording's appointment as editor of the monthly newspaper *Den Danske Mercurius,* a task for which he was granted an annual income of 200 Rixdaler from the king's private purse, increased to 250 Rixdaler from 1672, and which he performed without fail until his death in 1677.

Bording's appointment as author and publisher of a newspaper in Danish reflects the complete confidence of the government in his political astuteness, for the broadcasting of news, which had always been under strict state control, was an even more sensitive matter at a time of changes in domestic and foreign policy that did not have universal public support. No instructions about which sources Bording was supposed to use have survived, but analysis of all the news items in his paper has shown that he received his information from two sources: for the Danish news, a government office–presumably the *Danske Kancelli* (Danish Chancellery or Home Office), the principal secretary of which, Peder Schumacher, later Count Griffenfeld, confirmed Bording's privilege as sole editor and publisher–and for international news, three weekly German-language newspapers printed in Hamburg, which regularly arrived at the printing works of the Royal and Principal Printer to the University of Copenhagen, Henrik Gøde, the only printer with permission to print *Den Danske Mercurius.*

As editor, Bording faced a mammoth task, for the Hamburg papers brought no fewer than two hundred and fifty news items every month, and though Gøde printed his own selection from them twice weekly under the title *Ordinaire Post-Zeitung,* Bording clearly made his selection from the more than three thousand news items, which the fuller, original sources reported regularly each year from nearly thirty towns in Europe and beyond. Consequently, *Den Danske Mercurius* served as a monthly summary of all those newspapers, while Gøde increased its circulation and his own business by offering his readers a joint annual subscription of 4.00 Rixdalers for his own paper and Bording's *Mercurius,* which included delivery to their homes.

In Bording's case, however, the work was not completed with the selection of news items, for they had to be translated into Danish and finally rewritten in alexandrines before they could be handed to the printer as close to the end of each month as possible. Newspapers in verse existed in other countries, but in his choice of the alexandrine, Bording followed the example of Hamburg notary Greflinger, a member of Rist's literary society, who had used this meter in a panegyric addressed to Frederik III in 1660 and who, as editor of the twice-weekly newspaper *Nordischer Mercurius,* Bording's principal source for news, had begun the year 1666 with a summary in alexandrines of the state of affairs in Europe. Bording chose precisely this format for his own paper, presenting the news in numbered rubrics headed by the name of the country concerned, and without interruption over the next eleven years he informed his readers about political, economic, and religious affairs throughout the world. In the process he introduced them to nearly six hundred persons–or as he called them, actors on the world stage–including kings, queens, princes, princesses, aristocrats, politicians, merchants, tradesmen, peasants, officers, men on land and at sea, clergy, criminals, and hoaxers. By presenting them in their geographical context, moreover, he acquainted his readers with more than five hundred locations worldwide–cities from Trondheim to Alexandria, Lisbon to Moscow, as well as towns, villages, rivers, waterways, overseas territories in the East and the West, and the high seas separating them.

Naturally, as a monthly publication, *Den Danske Mercurius* could not compete with the volume of news published in the weeklies nor with the speed with which it reached the readers. On the other hand, it had two characteristics that compensated for the late arrival of news already broadcast and that made *Den Danske Mercurius* a truly exceptional seventeenth-century newspaper. One was that almost one-third of the total 14,700 alexandrines in the complete *Den Danske Mercurius* were devoted to news about Danish affairs, while censorship regulations prevented the weeklies from reporting on domestic issues; the other was that whereas the weeklies merely published a myriad of disparate reports ill suited to create an overall picture of world events, Bording was able to link them together and, by means of judiciously placed comments, interpret them in a manner consonant with current government thinking. This talent enabled *Den Danske Mercurius* to report on and interpret events at court; such new economic measures as the foundation of trading companies, import controls, devaluation, value-added tax, and conservation of forests; and the politically sensitive question about the creation of a new class of nobility of equal rank with established aristocratic families. When Danish foreign policy drifted away from a prosperous, armed neutrality based on alliances into a new and disastrous war with Sweden (1675–1679), *Den Danske Mercurius* provided the required mixture of information and propaganda to justify the change. In other words, *Den Danske Mercurius* was not only a source of information for its readers but, in the hands of a trusted royal servant, also a means of influencing public opinion in the direction desired by the government.

Bording's use of the Danish language in *Den Danske Mercurius*–pliable and precise at the same time and peppered with learned references as well as with colloquialisms and more than five hundred proverbs–and his easy mastery of the alexandrine for narrative as well as analytical purposes were, in the opinion of the editors of the 1735 edition, the principal reasons that his newspaper was received "med Fornøjelse hos de Højpriseligste Konger og ald Berømmelse og Yndest hos andre af høj og nedrig Stand, baade da og nu" (with pleasure by the Most Estimable Kings and made him famous and loved among others of high or low estate, both then and now). Their recommendation still stands: whosoever wishes to experience "hans Poetiske Opfinding og Artighed, eller hans Rigdom og Overflødighed i Talen [og] ret agtede at kende hans Styrke" (his poetic invention and decorum, or the riches and abundance of his diction and wishes to appreciate his true strength) should, above all, turn to the pages of *Den Danske Mercurius,* but not, one must add, at the expense of his rich output of secular and spiritual occasional verse, which he continued to write until his death on 24 May 1677; for each of those poems serves as an exploration, or just as a snapshot, of specific events in the full lives of the actors on the stage of seventeenth-century Denmark, which all come together in the rich image of the age created by Bording in *Den Danske Mercurius.*

Biographies:

H. Ehrencron-Müller, *Forfatterlexikon for Danmark, Norge og Island indtil 1814,* 12 volumes (Copenhagen: 1924–1939), I: 514–519;

R. Paulli, "Anders Bording," *Dansk biografisk Leksikon,* edited by Poul Engelstoft and Svend Dahl (Copenhagen: Schultz, 1933–1944), I: 470–473;

Erik Sønderholm, "Anders Bordings levned," in *Samlede Skrifter* (Copenhagen: Danske Sprog- og Litteraturselskab/C. A. Reitzel, 1986), II: 7–47;

Paul Ries, "Anders Bording," in *Arkiv for Dansk Litteratur,* Royal Danish Library (Victoria Laursen) and the Society for Danish Language and Literature (Jørgen Hunosøe) <http://www.adl.dk>.

References:

Pil Dahlerup, "Renæssanceteori og renæssancetekst," in *Hindsgavl Rapport, Litteraturteori i praksis,* edited by Thomas Bredsdorff and Finn Hauberg Mortensen (Odense: Odense University Press, 1995), pp. 27–52;

G. Haastrup, "Anders Bordings forsvar for lærde kvinder," in *Man må studere . . . Festskrift til G. Torresin* (Aarhus: Humanities Faculty, Aarhus University, 1984), pp. 140–145;

J. Hougaard, T. Nielsen, T. V. Rasmussen, A. Rindom, and Per E. Sørensen, *Dansk litteraturhistorie: Stænderkultur og enevælde 1620–1746,* volume 3 (Copenhagen: Gyldendal, 1983);

F. J. Billeskov Jansen, *Dansk litteratur historie: Fra runerne til Thomas Kingo,* volume 1 (Copenhagen: Politiken, 1976);

Christian Kirchhoff-Larsen, *Den danske Presses Historie: 1634–1749,* volume 1 (Copenhagen: Munksgaard, 1942);

Paul Ries, "The Anatomy of a Seventeenth-Century Newspaper. A Contribution towards a Re-definition of the Methods Employed in Newspaper Research, by Way of an Analytical and Comparative Study of Four German-language Newspapers Published in Hamburg and Copenhagen in the Year 1669," *Daphnis,* 6, nos. 1–2 (1977): 171–232;

Ries, "The Politics of Information in Seventeenth-Century Scandinavia," in *The Politics of Information in Early Modern Europe,* edited by B. Dooley and S. Baron (London & New York: Routledge, 2001), pp. 237–273;

Nils Schiørring, *Det 16. og 17. århundredes verdslige danske visesang,* 2 volumes (Copenhagen: Thanning & Appel, 1950);

J. Søllinge and N. Thomsen, *De danske aviser 1634–1989,* volume 1 (Odense: Dagspressens Fond, 1988);

P. M. Stolpe, *Dagspressen i Danmark, dens Vilkaar og Personer indtil Midten af det attende Aarhundrede,* 4 volumes (Copenhagen: Samfundet til den danske Litteraturs Fremme, 1878–1884);

Ejnar Thomsen, *Barokken i dansk digtning* (Copenhagen: Munksgaard, 1971).

Papers:

Anders Bording's manuscripts at the Danish Royal Library in Copenhagen and elsewhere are listed in his *Samlede skrifter,* volume 2: *Kommentar til Anders Bordings digte,* edited by Erik Sønderholm (Copenhagen: Danske Sprog- og Litteraturselskab/C. A. Reitzel, 1986), pp. 326–342.

Tycho Brahe

(14 December 1546 – 24 October 1601)

Peter Zeeberg
Society for Danish Language and Literature

(Translated by Mark Mussari)

BOOKS: *De nova et nullius aevi memoria prius visa stella* (Copenhagen: L. Benedikt, 1573); translated by V. V. S. as *Learned Tico Brahae His Astronomicall Coniectur of the New and Much Admired [Star] Which Appeared in the Year 1572* (London: Printed by B. Alsop & T. Fawcet for Michael Sparke & Samuel Nealand, 1632); translated by Otto Gelsted and Thøger Larsen as *Danskeren Tyge Brahe's Matematiske Betragtning over den ny og aldrig nogensinde før sete Stjerne, nylig for første Gang observeret i November Anno 1572 e. Kr. Kbh., 1573* (Lemvig: Atlantis, 1923);

De mundi aetherei recentioribus phaenomenis (Uraniborg: Privately printed, 1588);

Epistolæ Astronomicæ (Uraniborg: Privately printed, 1596);

Astronomiae Instauratae Mechanica (Wandsbek, Germany: P. von Ohr, 1598); translated by Hans Ræder, Elis Strömgren, and Bengt Strömgren as *Tycho Brahe's Description of His Instruments and Scientific Work, as Given in Astronomiae Instauratae Mechanica* (Copenhagen: Kongelige danske Videnskabernes Selskab/Munksgaard, 1946); revised by Alena Hadravová, Petr Hadrava, and Jole R. Shackelford as *Instruments of the Renewed Astronomy=Astronomiae instauratae mechanica,* Clavis monumentorum litterarum (Regnum Bohemiae), no. 2 (Prague: KLP, 1996);

Astronomiae Instaurandae Progymnasmata (Prague: Privately printed, 1602);

De disciplinis mathematicis oratio. Publice recitata in Academia Hafniensi anno 1574 & nunc primum edita (Copenhagen: H. Waldkirch, 1610);

Tycho Brahes lille skrift om kometen 1577, translated by Jørgen Brager and Niels Henningsen (Copenhagen: E. Eilertsen, 1986);

Tycho Brahes "Urania Titani." Et digt om Sophie Brahe, edited by Peter Zeeberg, Renæssancestudier, no. 7 (Copenhagen: Museum Tusculanum, 1994).

Tycho Brahe, from the title page for the 1602 reprint of Astronomiae instauratae mechanica, first published in 1598 *(Danish Royal Library, Copenhagen)*

Edition and Collection: *Astronomiae instauratae mechanica* (Nuremberg: Levinus Hulsius, 1602);

Tychonis Brahe Dani opera omnia, 15 volumes, edited by J. L. E. Dreyer and Johannes Ræder (Copenhagen: Danske Sprog- og Litteraturselskab/Gyldendal, 1913–1929).

SELECTED BROADSIDES: *Fratri gemello, mortuo in utero* (Copenhagen: M. Vingaard, 1572);

Epitaphium clarissimo et omnigena eruditione vituteque ornatissimo viro D. Johanni Pratensi Aarusiensi, Medicinae Paracelsicae et Galenicae Doctori, ob ingenitam naturæ bonitatem, morumque incomparabilem suavitatem omnibus cuiuscunque status hominibus, et charissimo et desideratissimo. Obiit Ao. 1576 (Uraniborg: Privately printed, 1584);

Nobilitate ingenii generisque viro inprimis conspicuo, D. Jacobo Ulfeldio, domino de Ulfelsholm, amico svo plurimum colendo. s.d. (Uraniborg: Privately printed, 1584);

Magnifico, amplissimo nobilissimoque viro, sapientia, doctrina, omnimodaque virtute praeeminenti, D. Nicolao Kaasio, domino de Taarup, Regiæ Maiestatis Daniæ cancellario et consiliario prudentissimo, utilitatis et tranquillitatis publicæ suasori conservatorique fidelissimo, amico svo inprimis observando (Uraniborg: Privately printed, 1585);

Nobilissimo et amplissimo viro, sapientia, eruditione inprimis excellenti, D. Henrico Ranzovio potentissimi Regis Daniæ in Holsatia vicario et consiliario, præfecto arcis Segebergæ et domino in Bredenberga &c: astrologiæ omniumque liberalium disciplinarum excultori & promotori lavdatissimo, amico svo plurimum colendo (Uraniborg: Privately printed, 1585).

One of the central figures of the modern scientific breakthrough, Tycho Brahe was also a multifaceted cultural personality and a promoter of Renaissance art and culture in Scandinavia. Among his many talents he excelled as a poet writing in Latin. For Brahe, as for all academics of his time, Latin was the preferred mode of written expression, and he wrote almost everything in this language. The only notable exceptions are his letters, written in Latin, German, and Danish, depending on their recipient.

Several weighty astronomical books comprise Brahe's official oeuvre, along with his epistolary *Epistolæ Astronomicæ* (Astronomical Letters, 1596). His Latin poetry served a different purpose, written mainly in regard to his social life and the development of his career. As was common at the time, Brahe's poetry possesses, to a large extent, the quality of occasional verse. Some of his poems appear in his scientific works as programmatic writings, thus providing a more personal tone. Others circulated in handwritten form among his large circle of scientific contacts. A few poems were printed individually but were probably intended primarily for the same readers as those that remained in manuscript. Around one hundred poetic texts by Brahe are extant today, ranging from brief epigrams to a six-hundred-verse heroid (a literary form derived from Ovid's *Heroides*).

Tyge (later Latinized as Tycho) Brahe was born to nobility in the province of Skåne on the manorial estate of Knudstrup (now Knutstorp) on 14 December 1546. The eldest son of Otte Brahe and Beate Bille, he was born into the most prominent circles of the realm. His father and both his paternal and maternal grandfathers were members of the Danish Privy Council and thus held important political positions. Brahe grew up in the house of his uncle Jørgen Brahe, who was married to Ingrid Oxe, sister to the statesman Peder Oxe. Ingrid Oxe was also mistress of the robes to Queen Sophie until Brahe's mother assumed that post.

As the eldest son in such a family, Brahe was educated with an eye toward a future as a statesman. After his initial education at grammar school and at the University of Copenhagen, he was sent to Germany to continue his studies, focusing on law. He started at the university in Leipzig (1562–1565) and went on to Wittenberg (1566), Rostock (1566–1567 and 1568), and Basel (1568–1569). Brahe was accompanied by his tutor, Anders Sørensen Vedel, who was later to become an author and historian. According to Brahe's account in a brief autobiography, he was at this point already involved in astronomy. Despite opposition from his tutor, who had orders from home, he spent a great deal of time studying the subject on his own. During a visit to Augsburg in 1569–1570, Brahe–working with the town mayor, Paul Hainzel, and his brother Johann Baptist–constructed his first astronomical instrument. In Augsburg he also met the controversial philosopher Petrus Rasmus.

After he returned home in 1570 and following his father's death early in 1571, Brahe lived primarily with his uncle Steen Bille at Herrevad Abbey near Knudstrup in Skåne. During this time Brahe devoted much of his attention to the study of chemistry in the tradition of Paracelsus. As Brahe states in his autobiography, chemistry remained throughout his life as important to his research as astronomy, even though, for reasons of secrecy, he never published his chemical results. His interest in chemistry also corresponded with his fundamentally occult worldview, in which heaven and earth, and the human microcosm between them, were bound together by a network of analogies. In Brahe's eyes astronomy and chemistry were mutually analogous systems; therefore, the two disciplines could illuminate each other. This approach was embodied in the mottos *despiciendo suspicio* (by looking down I look up) and *suspisciendo despicio* (by looking up I look down), both of which appear in his scientific works. The same approach lies behind Brahe's fundamentally positive attitude toward astrology. He had no interest, however, in alchemy in the sense of transforming base metals into gold.

In 1572 Brahe published his first work, *Fratri gemello, mortuo in utero,* a Latin epitaph written in verse to his stillborn twin brother. The depiction of the separation between the living but mortal Brahe and the dead but eternally living brother becomes, by implication, a portrait of every mortal's desire to realize the divine, spiritual part of himself. Brahe developed this theme more fully in his scientific debut, *De nova et nullius aevi prius visa stella* (On the New and Never Previously Seen Star, 1573; translated as *Learned Tico Brahae His Astronomicall Coniectur of the New and Much Admired [Star] Which Appeared in the Year 1572,* 1632).

The book is a short treatise on a newly sighted star, a supernova, visible for eighteen months in 1572–1573, which Brahe observed throughout this period. An initial selection of correspondence between Brahe and his close friend the medical professor Johannes Pratensis, in Copenhagen, serves as an apologia: as a nobleman Brahe should not have expressed himself in print on subjects of natural science. He also indicates that he may have to leave the country to devote himself to science. In its consistent reliance on observations, the main section of the book marked a new era in astronomy. Brahe also broke with commonly held views of the universe by stating that the new star existed among the fixed stars. According to traditional astronomical thinking, no changes could occur beyond the sphere of the moon.

If one detects a defensive response toward the demands of the nobility in the introduction to the book, in the epilogue Brahe goes on the counterattack with "Ad Uraniam Elegia Autoris," his great poem to Urania. The poem illustrates how he was called to astronomy: the muse of astronomy, Urania, reveals herself to him, orders him to take responsibility for her science, and points to the new star as the first object of his research. Brahe's answer, which comprises the second half of the poem, depicts his choice of science over the traditional life of a nobleman as a mystical experience in the Neoplatonic tradition. The way of life of the nobility, Brahe explains, is earthly. Everything associated with the noble class–from politics and the running of landed estates to drinking and fornication–is meaningless because it is all transitory. In science, however, the soul separates from the mortal, so that it may unite with the eternal–the divine.

In the plot device of the poet's meeting with a muse, Brahe alludes to Ovid's *Amores* (after 16 B.C.), in which Ovid, in a similar poem, chooses the muse of love poetry over that of epic poetry. For the first time the reader can trace the elective affinity that functions as a leitmotiv throughout all of Brahe's poetry. He obviously felt a kinship with Ovid, a nobleman who became a poet against his family's wishes. Brahe surely realized the irony when, many years later, after his departure from Denmark, he was forced to write poetry "in exile"–as did Ovid.

Around the time that *De nova et nullius aevi memoria prius visa stella* was published Brahe married Kirsten Jørgensdatter, who may have been the daughter of a local minister in Kågerød, near Knudstrup. In any case, she was not of noble birth, which only served to exacerbate the animosity Brahe awakened among noble circles. The couple had six children, two of whom died at a young age.

Following the publication of his book about the new star, Brahe became a respected scientist. In 1574 he was invited to hold a series of lectures at the University of Copenhagen. His introductory lecture on the significance of mathematics, *De disciplinis mathematicis oratio,* has been preserved, although it was not published until 1610, nine years after his death. Nevertheless, Brahe regarded combining his position as a nobleman with a scientific career as impossible in Denmark. Thus, in 1575 he once again traveled abroad, this time primarily to arrange for his emigration. At the time he seems to have had concrete plans for settling down in Basel, Switzerland. But at this point the government in Denmark became aware of the potential value of his talents. Early the following year, King Frederik II offered Brahe the island of Hven (now Ven), located in the Øresund (Sound) between Copenhagen and Helsingör, as a fief for lifetime usage. In exchange Brahe had to agree to serve as the royal mathematician. The opposition between nobility and science dissolved: Brahe was commissioned as a scientist but held the traditionally noble position of a royal lieutenant.

For the next twenty-one years, from 1576 until 1597, Brahe lived and worked on Hven. On the island he built his famous castle, Uraniborg, which–thanks to large grants from the king–became a center for the European scientific community. Scholars from all over Europe visited the island, and young academics collaborated on scientific projects there. The central project of the institute became Brahe's weightiest contribution to the sciences: the systematic and controlled observations of the sky over long periods of time. To this end he developed several new instruments that could take measurements with a previously unknown accuracy. The data gathered during these years became, particularly through the work of Brahe's scientific successor, Johannes Kepler, the basis for the breakthrough of modern astronomy in the seventeenth century.

Uraniborg functioned as much more, however, than a research institute in the modern sense. Indications are that Brahe also viewed it as a counterpart to the contemporary Italian academies, in which nobles and academics cultivated art, literature, and science in a

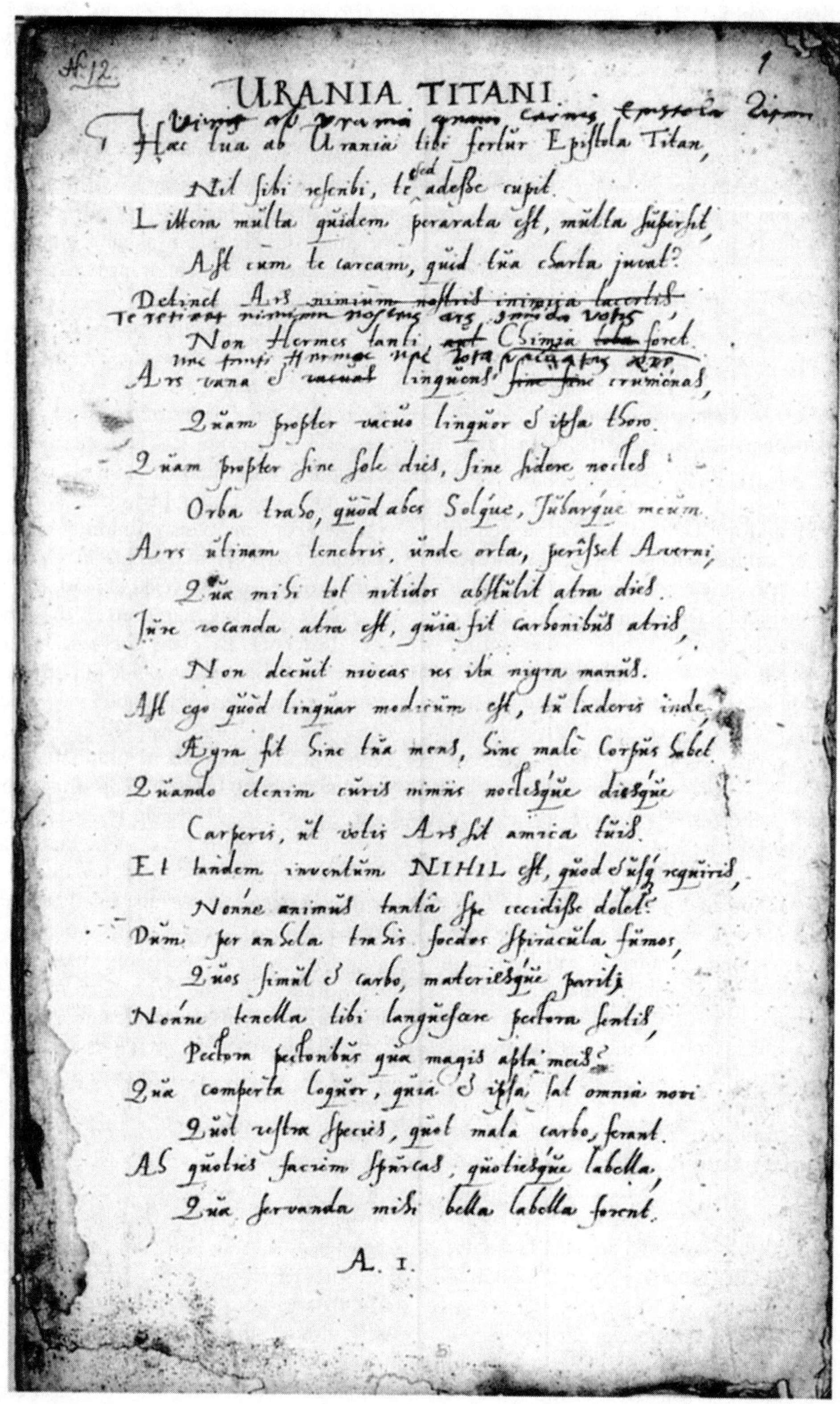

URANIA TITANI.

Haec tua ab Urania tibi fertur Epistola Titan,
Nil sibi rescribi, te sed adesse cupit.
Littera multa quidem perarata est, multa superest,
Ast cum te careat, quid tua charta juvat?
Non Hermes tanti … Chimia … foret.
Ars vana et vacuat linquens crumenas,
Quam propter vacuo linquor et ipsa thoro.
Quam propter sine sole dies, sine sidere noctes
Orba traho, quod abes Solque, Jubarque meum.
Ars utinam tenebris, unde orta, perisset Averni,
Quae mihi tot nitidos abstulit atra dies.
Jure vocanda atra est, quia fit carbonibus atris,
Non decuit niveas res ita nigra manus.
Ast ego quod linquar medicum est, tu laederis inde,
Aegra fit sine tua mens, sine male corpus habet.
Quando etenim curis nimis noctesque diesque
Carperis, ut votis Ars sit amica tuis.
Et tandem inventum NIHIL est, quod denique requiris,
Nonne animus tanta spe cecidisse dolet?
Dum per anhela trahis foedos spiracula fumos,
Quos simul et carbo, materiesque parit,
Nonne tenella tibi languescere pectora sentis,
Pectora pectoribus quae magis apta meis?
Quae comperta loquor, quia et ipsa sat omnia novi
Quot vestra species, quot mala carbo, ferant.
Ad quoties faciem spurcas, quotiesque labella,
Quae servanda mihi bella labella forent.

A. 1.

First and last pages of the manuscript for Brahe's poem Urania Titani *(Urania to Titan), composed in 1594 (Österreichische Nationalbibliotek, Vienna)*

Tunc quae passus eris, mihi denarrabis acerba,
Ipsaque nostra tibi; forte levamen erit.
Quod superest bene vive diu; ut salvusque revisas
Uraniam; ô Titan semper Amate Vale.

Superscriptio Epistolae huius ubi composita
et ab Vrania obsignata fuerit haec erit:

Hanc sexcenteno quae constat Epistola versu,
Accipe, mi Titan, et lege quando vacat.
Tam prolixa ideo est, ne sit responsio prompta,
Ipse sed hanc nobis ore referre velit:

En tibi sexcentos tenuit quos Pagina versus
Sunt ideo multi ne sit responsio prompta.
Haec in Erichsholmi perarata est litora Castro,
Cum geminos Pisces Sol redeundo capit.
[illegible] gemini [illegible] pisces [illegible] Amandos,
Tuque redux Titan, [illegible] Tua ego Urania

sophisticated fashion. It was therefore no accident that a chance meeting at Uraniborg led Queen Sophie to commission Anders Sørensen Vedel to publish the first Danish collection of folk ballads, *It Hundrede vduaalde Danske Viser* (One Hundred Selected Danish Ballads, 1591).

Uraniborg was gradually equipped with all the facilities a researcher needed: observatory, library, chemical laboratory, instrument workshop, printing press, and paper mill. On the occasion of the inauguration of the printing press, Brahe published a series of poems in the half year between the end of 1584 and the beginning of 1585. He published at least six–and possibly more–poems addressed to or in memory of learned friends and patrons in Denmark. The first of these poems, *Et generis et ingenii nobilitate juveni claro Erico Lange* . . . (To the Illustrious Young Erik Lange, Noble in Birth and Character, 1584), of which only a transcript survives, is a stylistic tour de force in which every other line (the pentameter lines in elegiac meter) ends with the word *amor* (love). The poem builds thematically on the Platonic opposition between earthly and spiritual love. Brahe's good friend Erik is in love but should instead be directing his love toward the heavenly–toward science–as they do on Hven. Consequently, the poem may be read as a text of sublimation but equally as a program for Brahe's learned institute on Hven.

The remaining poems in the series are not as philosophically ambitious. Several of them recall Brahe's 1573 elegy to Urania, self-confidently describing Uraniborg as the new sanctuary for Urania, a place where astronomy will be established anew. This claim represents Brahe's personal version of a characteristic Renaissance motif: the transference of the muses, in which the wandering of the muses from country to country becomes a portrait of the gradual dissemination of Renaissance humanism. In Brahe's version this motif develops into a kind of local mythology, one that presents the poet as the savior of astronomy. The same mythological approach appears in the institution of Uraniborg and its architectural decoration. Not only was the castle called Uranienborg (Urania's Castle) in its first years of existence–as opposed to the later form of Uraniborg (Heaven's Castle)–but also its ornamentation was designed to symbolize Helicon, the mountain of the Muses. The castle's weather vane depicted Pegasus, symbol of the poet's art, and directly beneath it, inside the building, stood a fountain representing Hippocrene, the classical spring of inspiration. Similarly, the observatory, Stjerneborg, was designed to resemble Mount Parnassus, also associated with the Muses.

During the 1580s Brahe began to write his masterwork of astronomy, conceived in three parts. The second part, *De mundi aetherei recentioribus phaenomenis* (Concerning the New Phenomena in the Ethereal World, 1588), about a comet sighted in 1577, was published first. The first part, intended to provide the definitive discussion of the new star that was the subject of *De nova et nullius aevi prius visa stella,* was begun at Uraniborg and partially printed there. It was finished in Prague, however, and published posthumously under the title *Astronomiae Instaurandae Progymnasmata* (Introductory Exercise Toward a Restored Astronomy, 1602). This volume also includes a poem in which Brahe proudly exhorts future astronomers to follow in his footsteps–now that he, like another Hercules, has saved the firmament from collapsing. He was never able to begin the third part of the work.

In 1594 Brahe composed his most ambitious poetic work, the Ovidian heroid *Urania Titani* (Urania to Titan). It consists of a six-hundred-verse love letter from "Urania" (Sophie, Brahe's sister) to "Titan" (Sophie's betrothed, Lange). Brahe chose the epistolary genre because Lange, an alchemist, was in Germany on the run from creditors, while Sophie waited for him in Skåne. Details gathered from the preserved manuscript indicate that it was sent as an actual letter to Lange. The poem was not published at that time but circulated, instead, in manuscript form. Depending on the reader, the poem can be perceived as a personal appeal from Brahe and his sister or as a sophisticated literary endeavor. A modern edition was published in 1994.

Urania Titani depicts a love-struck woman's inner struggle between hope and despair. Time and again her hope surges, only to collapse when confronted with the harsh truth. Two "scientific" passages are central to the work: first, an intentionally distorted analysis of the lovers' horoscopes in which Urania repeatedly ignores negative signs in her search to find the positive; and second, a showdown with Titan's alchemy in which the poem, in parodic fashion, misinterprets central alchemical texts to reach the conclusion that the proper alchemy for Titan must be for him to return home and father a child with Urania. Allusions to Ovid's *Heroides* serve as an undercurrent throughout the entire poem. The primary model, which is referred to throughout the poem, is the first *Heroid,* a letter from the loyal Penelope to her husband, Odysseus. Every time doubt resurfaces in Urania's mind, however, allusions are made to Ovid's second *Heroid,* a letter from the despairing Phyllis to her unfaithful lover, Demophoon, who, unlike Odysseus, never returns. *Urania Titani* ends on a note of frail hope.

Woodcut of the brass globe on which Brahe engraved the positions of the stars (from the 1602 edition of Astronomiae instauratae mechanica; *Smithsonian Institution Libraries)*

Urania Titani offers a penetrating psychological study without equal in the Danish literature of its time. An important secondary theme is Urania's (that is, Sophie's) fight for love despite her family's conventional attitudes, a clear parallel to Brahe's own unconventional choice of pursuing his love for science. Brahe's only Danish-language poem, an undated satire about a comic episode at Uraniborg, also involves his sister. It was first published in *Danske Magazin* in 1747.

Epistolæ Astronomicæ, Brahe's publication of his own scientific correspondence, was–like *Astronomiae Instaurandae Progymnasmata*–also conceived as a multivolume work. Only the first volume was published; printed at Uraniborg in 1596, it includes Brahe's correspondence with Count Wilhelm IV of Hesse-Kassel and his astronomer, Christopher Rothmann. The book also provides a detailed description of the institute on Hven, both the buildings and their furnishings. This description includes a great number of verse inscriptions from both Uraniborg and Stjerneborg. For example, both buildings housed portraits of Brahe's most famous astronomical predecessors, each portrait bearing a Latin poem written by Brahe. Preliminary material for the second volume of *Epistolæ astronomicæ* is preserved among Brahe's papers at the Österreichische Nationalbibliothek in Vienna.

The golden years on Hven came to an end in 1597. After the coronation of the new king, Christian IV, in 1596, the institute fell out of favor with the grant-giving authorities. A formal complaint, including dereliction of duty in several areas, was drawn up; although the accusations were undoubtedly well founded, they were not new. Brahe's contempt for rules and obligations was renowned. It is impossible to discern the reasons for the complaint, but presumably both personal and ideological motives were at play. The new king and his government did not feel the same sense of responsibility for Uraniborg as had Christian's father or the interregnum authorities. Apparently, Brahe was convinced that his distribution of free medicine was to blame, believing that it had caused professional jealousy among influential doctors. In any case, Brahe seems to have presented the king with an ultimatum and lost. After spending some time in Copenhagen, he and his entire household moved to Rostock, where he wrote to the king in the hope that the monarch would call him back. Christian viewed the appeal as an affront, however, and the result was a final break. Shortly thereafter Brahe headed for Holstein, where the royal governor, Henrik Rantzau, offered him lodgings at Wandesburg Castle, near Hamburg.

Here, Brahe could once again turn his attention to his astronomical observations, and the occasion gave birth to his elegy to Denmark, "Ad Daniam Elegia," which was entered into his record of observations. It was later published in two different versions in *Tychonis Brahe Dani opera omnia* (1913–1929), edited by J. L. E. Dreyer. The poem is a long and bitter tirade against those forces in Denmark who had opposed him. Although no names are mentioned, Brahe was clearly thinking of one or several specific enemies. During this same period he also made great efforts to convince other poets, among them the German Martin Brasch, to support his case through their poetry, preferably by subscribing to Brahe's own mythology and depicting Urania as once again homeless.

While at Wandesburg, Brahe also completed a catalogue of one thousand fixed stars, which circulated only in manuscript, along with *Astronomiae Instauratae Mechanica* (1598; translated as *Tycho Brahe's Description of His Instruments and Scientific Work, as Given in Astronomiae Instauratae Mechanica,* 1946). The latter is a scientific document of his astronomical instruments and a summary of his work on Hven. In addition to the descriptions of instruments, the book also includes an account of the island and the castle, as well as Brahe's brief autobiography. Both works were sent to princes all over Europe, among them Holy Roman Emperor Rudolf II, in an attempt to secure a new position. This ploy worked: Rudolf summoned Brahe to Prague to serve as imperial astronomer and counselor.

In the fall of 1598 Brahe left Wandesburg and set off for Prague. Along the way he spent seven months in Wittenberg; in the summer of 1599 he reached Bohemia, where the emperor put at Brahe's disposal the castle of Benatky, outside of Prague. Yet, Brahe lived mostly in the city during his two years in Bohemia. His time there was not happy; he never found the peace to work that he longed for, and he encountered constant problems in receiving the money the emperor had granted him. This period was epoch making in the history of science, however, for it was in Prague that Brahe came into contact with Kepler.

Tycho Brahe died on 24 October 1601 and was buried in Teyn Church in Prague. Recent studies of hairs from his beard, exhumed from his grave in 1901, reveal that he died of acute mercurial poisoning. The most likely explanation is that he was treating himself with one of his own medicinal remedies that contained mercury and unwittingly poisoned himself.

Although Brahe counts among the most prominent Danish poets writing in Latin, research into his poetry is a recent phenomenon. His poems were first printed in their entirety in his collected works, *Tychonis Brahe Dani opera omnia* (1913–1929). A few appear in Danish translation, but translations of Brahe's poems into English and other languages, generally speaking, do not exist.

References:

Peter Brask, Karsten Friis-Jensen, and Minna Skafte Jensen, *Dansk litteraturhistorie,* volume 2: *Lærdom og magi, 1480–1620* (Copenhagen: Gyldendal, 1984), pp. 404–412, 464–465, 507–510;

John Robert Christianson, *On Tycho's Island: Tycho Brahe and his Assistants, 1570–1601* (Cambridge & New York: Cambridge University Press, 2000);

J. L. E. Dreyer, *Tycho Brahe: A Picture of Scientific Life and Work in the Sixteenth Century* (Edinburgh: A. & C. Black, 1890; reprinted, New York: Dover, 1963);

Georg Ellinger, "Tycho de Brahe als lateinischer Dichter," in *Festgabe der Gesellschaft für deutsche Literatur: zum siebzigsten Geburtstag ihres Vorsitzenden, Max Herrmann* (Langensalza, Germany: J. Beltz, 1935);

Victor E. Thoren, *The Lord of Uraniborg: A Biography of Tycho Brahe* (Cambridge & New York: Cambridge University Press, 1990);

Peter Zeeberg, "Adel og Lærdom hos Tycho Brahe," in *Latin og Nationalsprog i Norden efter reformationen,* edited by Marianne Alenius, Birger Bergh, and Friis-Jensen, Renæssancestudier, no. 5 (Copenhagen: Museum Tusculanum, 1991), pp. 21–31;

Zeeberg, "Alchemy, Astrology, and Ovid: A Love Poem by Tycho Brahe," in *Acta Conventus Neo-Latini Hafniensis: Proceedings of the Eighth International Congress of Neo-Latin Studies,* edited by Rhoda Schnur and others, Medieval and Renaissance Texts and Studies, no. 120 (Binghamton, N.Y.: Medieval and Renaissance Texts and Studies, 1994), pp. 997–1008;

Zeeberg, "Amor på Hven–Tycho Brahes digt til Erik Lange," in *Renæssancen. Dansk, europæisk, globalt,* edited by Marianne Pade and Jensen, Renæssancestudier, no. 2 (Copenhagen: Museum Tusculanum, 1988), pp. 161–181;

Zeeberg, "The Inscriptions at Tycho Brahe's Uraniborg," in *A History of Nordic Neo-Latin Literature,* edited by Jensen (Odense: Odense University Press, 1995), pp. 251–266;

Zeeberg, "Kemi og Kærlighed–Naturvidenskab i Tycho Brahes latindigtning," in *Litteratur og lærdom. Dansk-svenske nylatindage, April 1985,* edited by Alenius and Zeeberg, Renæssancestudier, no. 1 (Copenhagen: Museum Tusculanum, 1987), pp. 149–161;

Zeeberg, "En muse finder sit hjem. Tycho Brahe set med hans egne øjne," in *Tycho Brahe, Stjärnornas Herre,* edited by Johanna Erlandson (Landskrona, Sweden: Landskrona Kommun, 1996), pp. 67–78;

Zeeberg, "Neo-Latin Poetry in Its Social Context: Some Statistics and Some Examples from Sixteenth Century Denmark," in *Mare Balticum, Mare Nostrum: Latin in the Countries of the Baltic Sea (1500–1800),* edited by Outi Merisalo and Raija Sarasti-Wilenius, Annales Academiae Scientiarum Fennicae, series B, no. 274 (Helsinki: Academia Scientiarum Fennica, 1994), pp. 9–21;

Zeeberg, *Den praktiske Muse. Tycho Brahes brug af latindigtningen,* Studier fra Sprog- og Oldtidsforskning, no. 321 (Copenhagen: Museum Tusculanum, 1993);

Zeeberg, "Renæssancen på Hven," in *Renässans för Skåne 1999,* edited by Camilla Sjöstrand (Hammenhög, Sweden: Renässans för Skåne, 1998), pp. 204–209;

Zeeberg, "Science Versus Secular Life, a Central Theme in the Latin Poems of Tycho Brahe," in *Acta Conventus Neo-Latini Torontoniensis: Proceedings of the Seventh International Congress of Neo-Latin Studies,* edited by Alexander Dalzell, Charles Fantazzi, and Richard J. Schoeck, Medieval and Renaissance Texts and Studies, no. 86 (Binghamton, N.Y.: Medieval and Renaissance Texts and Studies, 1991), pp. 831–838.

Papers:

Tycho Brahe's papers are in the Österreichische Nationalbibliothek, Vienna. His original observational records are at the Danish Royal Library in Copenhagen.

Georg Brandes

(4 February 1842 - 19 February 1927)

Neil Christian Pages
State University of New York, Binghamton

BOOKS: *Dualismen i vor nyeste Philosophie* (Copenhagen: Gyldendal, 1866);

Æsthetiske Studier (Copenhagen: Gyldendal, 1868);

Den franske Æsthetik i vore Dage (Copenhagen: Gyldendal, 1870);

Kritiker og Portraiter (Copenhagen: Gyldendal, 1870);

Forklaring og Forsvar. En Antikritik (Copenhagen: Gyldendal, 1872);

Hovedstrømninger i det nittende Aarhundredes Litteratur, 6 volumes (Copenhagen: Gyldendal, 1872–1890)–comprises volume 1, *Emigrantlitteraturen* (1872); volume 2, *Den romantiske Skole i Tyskland* (1873); volume 3, *Reactionen i Frankrig* (1874); volume 4, *Naturalismen i England. Byron og hans Gruppe* (1875); volume 5, *Den romantiske Skole i Frankrig* (1882); and volume 6, *Det unge Tyskland* (1890); translated as *Main Currents in Nineteenth-Century Literature,* 6 volumes (London: Heinemann / New York: Macmillan, 1901–1905)–comprises volume 1, *The Emigrant Literature,* translated by Diana White and Mary Morison (1901); volume 2, *The Romantic School in Germany,* translated by White and Morison (1902); volume 3, *Reaction in France,* translated by Morison (1903); volume 4, *Naturalism in England,* translated by Morison (1905); volume 5, *The Romantic School in France,* translated by White and Morison (1904); and volume 6, *Young Germany,* translated by Morison (1905);

Danske Digtere. Charakterbilleder (Copenhagen: Gyldendal, 1877);

Ferdinand Lassalle. Ein literarisches Charakterbild (Berlin: F. Duncker, 1877); translated as *Ferdinand Lassalle* (London: Heinemann / New York: Macmillan, 1911);

Søren Kierkegaard. En kritisk Fremstilling i Grundrids (Copenhagen: Gyldendal, 1877);

Esaias Tegnér. En litteratur-psychologisk Studie (Copenhagen: Gyldendal, 1878);

Benjamin Disraëli, Jarl af Beaconsfield. En litterær Charakteristik (Copenhagen: Gyldendal, 1878); translated by Mrs. George Sturge as *Lord Beaconsfield: A Study* (New York: Harper, 1878);

Georg Brandes (photograph by Frederik Riise; courtesy of the Danish Royal Library, Copenhagen)

Det moderne Gjennembruds Mænd. En Række Portræter (Copenhagen: Gyldendal, 1883);

Mennesker og Værker (Copenhagen: Gyldendal, 1883); translated by Rasmus B. Anderson as *Eminent Authors of the Nineteenth Century* (New York: Crowell, 1886);

Ludvig Holberg. Et Festskrift (Copenhagen: Gyldendal, 1884);

Berlin som tysk Rigshovedstad. Erindringer fra et femaarigt Ophold (Copenhagen: Gyldendal, 1884, 1885);

Indtryk fra Polen (Copenhagen: Gyldendal, 1888); translated as *Poland: A Study of the Land, People, and Liter-*

ature (London: Heinemann, 1903; New York: Macmillan, 1903);

Indtryk fra Rusland (Copenhagen: Gyldendal, 1888); translated by Samuel C. Eastman as *Impressions of Russia* (New York: Crowell, 1889; London: Scott, 1889);

Essays. Danske Personligheder (Copenhagen: Gyldendal, 1889);

Essays. Fremmede Personligheder (Copenhagen: Gyldendal, 1889);

Udenlandske Egne og Personligheder (Copenhagen: Gyldendal, 1893);

William Shakespeare, 3 volumes (Copenhagen: Gyldendal, 1895–1896); translated by William Archer, Mary Morison, and Diana White as *William Shakespeare,* 2 volumes (London: Heinemann, 1898; New York: Ungar, 1898);

Heinrich Heine (Copenhagen: Gyldendal, 1897);

Henrik Ibsen (Copenhagen: Gyldendal, 1898); translated by Morison as *Henrik Ibsen, Björnstjerne Björnsen. Critical Studies* (London: Heinemann, 1899; New York: Macmillan, 1899);

Levned, 3 volumes (Copenhagen: Gyldendal, 1905–1908)–comprises volume 1, *Barndom og første Ungdom* (1905); translated as *Recollections of My Childhood and Youth* (London: Heinemann, 1906); republished as *Reminiscences of My Childhood and Youth* (New York: Duffield, 1906); volume 2, *Et Tiaar* (1907); and volume 3, *Snevringer og Horizonter* (1908);

Om Læsning (Copenhagen: Gyldendal, 1908); translated as *On Reading* (New York: Duffield, 1906);

Wolfgang Goethe, 2 volumes (Copenhagen: Gyldendal, 1915); translated by Allen W. Porterfield as *Wolfgang Goethe,* 2 volumes (New York: Brown, 1924);

Verdenskrigen (Copenhagen: Gyldendal, 1916); translated by Catherine D. Groth as *The World at War* (New York: Macmillan, 1917);

François de Voltaire, 2 volumes (Copenhagen: Gyldendal, 1916, 1917); translated by Otto Kruger and Pierce Butler as *Voltaire,* 2 volumes (New York: A. & C. Boni, 1930);

Napoleon og Garibaldi. Medaljer og Rids (Copenhagen: Gyldendal, 1917);

Cajus Julius Cæsar, 2 volumes (Copenhagen: Gyldendal, 1918);

Tragediens anden Del. Fredslutningen (Copenhagen: Gyldendal, 1919);

Homer (Copenhagen: Gyldendal, 1921);

Michelangelo Buonarroti, 2 volumes (Copenhagen: Gyldendal, 1921); translated by Heinz Norden as *Michelangelo. His Life, His Times, His Era* (New York: Ungar, 1963);

Uimodstaaelige. Attende Aarhundrede, Frankrig (Copenhagen: Gyldendal, Nordisk, 1924);

Hellas (Copenhagen: Gyldendal, 1925); translated by Jacob W. Hartmann as *Hellas. Travels in Greece* (New York: Adelphi, 1926);

Sagnet om Jesus (Copenhagen: Gyldendal, 1925); translated by Edwin Björkman as *Jesus. A Myth* (New York: A. & C. Boni, 1926);

Petrus (Copenhagen: Gyldendal, 1926).

Collection: *Samlede Skrifter,* 18 volumes (Copenhagen: Gyldendal, 1899–1910)–comprises volume 1, *Danske Personligheder* (1899); volume 2, *Danske Personligheder* (1899); volume 3, *Danske Personligheder* (1900); volume 4, *Hovedstrømninger i det 19. Aarhundredes Literatur: Emigrantliteratur, Den romantiske Skole i Tydskland* (1900); volume 5, *Hovedstrømninger i det 19. Aarhundredes Literatur: Reaktionen i Frankrig; Naturalismen i England* (1900); volume 6, *Hovedstrømninger i det 19. Aarhundredes Literatur: Den romantiske Skole i Frankrig; Det unge Tydskland* (1900); volume 7, *Franske Personligheder; Tydske Personligheder* (1900); volume 8, *William Shakespeare, første og anden del* (1901); volume 9, *William Shakespeare, tredje del.; Lord Beaconsfield; John Stuart Mill* (1901); volume 10, *Indtryk fra Polen; Indtryk fra Rusland* (1902); volume 11, *Europa og Asien* (1902); volume 12, *Tanker om Liv og Kunst etc.; Navneregister* (1902); volume 13, *Supplement 1: Striden om Tro og Viden; Dualismen i vor nyeste Philosophie; Den franske Æsthetik i vore Dage; Skuespilkritik Sept 1867–Oct 1869* (1903); volume 14, *Supplement 2: Berlin som tysk Rigshovedstad; Julius Lange. Breve fra hans Ungdom* (1904); volume 15, *Supplement 3: Skikkelser og Tanker, 1* (1905); volume 16, *Supplement 4: Skikkelser og Tanker, 2* (1906); volume 17, *Supplement 5: Skikkelser og Tanker, 3* (1906); and volume 18, *Supplement 6: Fra mange Tider og Lande* (1910).

TRANSLATION: John Stuart Mill, *Kvindernes Underkuelse* (Copenhagen, 1869).

SELECTED PERIODICAL PUBLICATION–UNCOLLECTED: "Aristokratisk Radikalisme. En Afhandling om Friedrich Nietzsche," *Tilskueren. Maanedskrift for Literatur, Samfundsspørgsmaal og almenfattelige videnskabelige Skildringer,* 6 (August 1889): 565–613; translated by A. G. Chater as *An Essay on Aristocratic Radicalism* (London: Heinemann, 1914).

On 8 June 1914 *The New York Times* reported on the first visit of Georg Brandes to New York: "One of the most remarkable welcomes ever extended to a foreign lecturer was given to Dr. Georg Brandes, the Danish critic and essayist, last night when he delivered his first lecture in New York at the Comedy Theatre on West Forty-first Street." The article recounted how a crowd of one thousand was turned away at the doors of the sold-out theater and that "it was necessary for the police to take a hand in clearing the street" in front of the building. Brandes had made his first trip to the United States for a series of lectures on William Shakespeare, but his fame had preceded him. The works of Georg Morris Cohen Brandes, prolific Danish literary critic, biographer, autobiographer, and intellectual, had already reached a broad international readership. Initiator of the Modern Breakthrough in Scandinavian literature and inaugurator of crucial changes in literary, philosophical, and political currents, Brandes was equally well versed in a wide range of European literatures. Considered the first modern comparatist, Brandes wrote criticism that transgressed national borders and academic disciplines. Brandes's writings combined art and politics in an astute manner and earned him an international reputation that was fueled by the many translations of his works. (In his capacity as a critic, he discovered figures such as Søren Kierkegaard and Friedrich Nietzsche.) His extensive personal travels and contacts plus a lifelong correspondence with the leading minds of his day only served to increase his fame and fortify his stature as a leading European critic and an arbiter of the literary tastes of the period.

Brandes's critical method was a blend of literary analysis and biography with philosophical, political, and social commentary. His works aim to describe the role literature plays in changing values and social norms. Brandes is perhaps best known for his major project, *Hovedstrømninger i det nittende Aarhundredes Litteratur* (1872–1890; translated as *Main Currents in Nineteenth-Century Literature,* 1901–1905). This magnum opus began as a series of lectures given at the University of Copenhagen between 1871 and 1887 and was published in six volumes between 1872 and 1890. A response to what Brandes saw as a malaise in Danish cultural and intellectual life, which he felt lagged forty years behind the rest of Europe, the lectures that formed the basis for these volumes called for a break from the provincial and reactionary stagnation that marked the cultural milieu of the country. Indeed, Brandes promoted a progressive literary program that aimed to represent and critique the human and social realities of the day. The lectures caused a stir in Denmark and promoted Brandes's reputation as an enfant terrible on the intellectual scene and beyond. In tandem with his work as a lecturer, Brandes's role as a journalist and critic proved large and important; his interests ranged from political and social movements to the latest novels and plays, and he played a key role in introducing Scandinavian audiences to literary trends from the rest of Europe.

Brandes was born in Copenhagen on 4 February 1842 to a cultivated middle-class Jewish family that had lived in Denmark for several generations. He was the eldest son of Herman Cohen Brandes, a cloth merchant, and Emilie Brandes, née Bendix. Brandes's paternal grandmother, Emilie Fränkel, had married twice, first to Moses Israel Cohen, Herman Brandes's father, and later to Joel Israel Brandes, so that her son bore the names of both men, Cohen and Brandes, which were then passed down to his son Georg.

Brandes's parents were part of the small Jewish community in Copenhagen, but they were far from devout. Brandes's mother, in particular, was highly skeptical of religion, and Brandes's depictions of his childhood in his autobiography, *Levned* (Life, 3 volumes, 1905–1908; volume 1 translated as *Reminiscences of My Childhood and Youth,* 1906), attest to the lack of religious devotion at home. Brandes describes his ambivalent relationship to his Jewish roots with an anecdote on his childhood experiences with Judaism: After receiving anti-Semitic taunts from boys on the street, young Brandes asked his mother if he might see a Jew: "Det kan du godt, sagde moder, og løftede mig rask op foran det store ovale spejl, der hang over sofaen. Jeg udstødte et skrig, så moder hurtigt satte mig ned på gulvet, og jeg viste mig så forfærdet, at moder fortrød, hun ikke havde forberedt mig" (Sure you can, said Mother, and promptly lifted me up before the oval mirror that hung over the sofa. I let out a scream, so she quickly put me down on the floor, and I appeared so frightened that she regretted that she had not prepared me).

While Brandes enjoyed a stable home life with a large extended family, the bankruptcy of his father's business in 1861 plunged the family into economic uncertainty. This condition affected the young man's development from then on, requiring him to work as a tutor during his student years and exposing him more intensely to the class and social divisions of Danish society. These inequities had already become apparent to Brandes during his early schooling, which he describes in some detail in his autobiography.

Brandes began his education as a five-year-old with private tutoring and then entered the elite Det von Westenske Institut of Copenhagen in 1849. During these formative years, young Brandes demonstrated impressive intellectual talents and also discovered his love of books. Between the ages of seventeen and twenty-three Brandes kept a diary listing the books he had read. That list comprised 1,217 titles that spanned many European literary traditions. The plays of Greek antiquity, sixteenth-century Spanish literature, the French classicists, the German Romantics, and important Scandinavian authors were only some of the works that Brandes read, with books by great authors such as Shakespeare and Johann Wolfgang von Goethe figuring large in his literary tastes. This immense breadth of reading experience continued throughout Brandes's career as a critic and secured his status as one of the foremost authorities in a broad range of European national literatures.

In 1859 Brandes began his studies at the University of Copenhagen. Following his parents' wishes, he first studied law, but he soon switched to aesthetics, literature, and philosophy. During his early years at the university, Brandes formed close friendships with several young men who became major figures in Danish cultural and political life. One central relationship was with gifted art student Julius Lange, who later, during an excursion to the island of Møn in southern Zealand, attempted to persuade young Brandes to convert to Christianity. Influenced by his Christian friends at school and later at the university, Brandes had read the Bible and the works of Kierkegaard and was intrigued by Christianity and Kierkegaard's critique of religious institutions. Brandes attended Christian religious training at school but nonetheless celebrated his bar mitzvah at the age of fifteen. As a young student, he underwent a religious crisis, but he never converted to Christianity. In the end, Kierkegaard's espousal of a singularly individual relationship to Christian teachings was what fascinated Brandes, whose religious views remained those of a skeptical agnostic, and even an atheist, for all of his life.

At the university Brandes studied with some of the great Danish intellectuals of the day, including philosophers Hans Brøchner and Rasmus Nielsen, and writer Carsten Hauch. As a student of Brøchner, Brandes studied the works of German idealist philosopher Georg Wilhelm Friedrich Hegel, whose philosophy of history and dialectic method, particularly as interpreted by Danish Hegelians such as critic and writer Johan Ludvig Heiberg, were fashionable in Copenhagen at the time. The elder Brøchner also played a pivotal role in Brandes's career, as he considered Brandes the logical successor to Hauch in the chair for aesthetics at the University of Copenhagen. Brandes's studies during the 1860s were for all intents and purposes training for this position, which he received only late in life, in 1902, after he had already established himself as an unaffiliated critic and scholar.

In April 1864, Brandes received his master's degree in aesthetics, as literary study was called at the time, from the University of Copenhagen. The degree was awarded as *admissus cum laude praecipua* (admitted with extraordinary distinction), a rare honor that recognized the exceptional work of this young scholar. In

Brandes as a student at the University of Copenhagen in 1859 (courtesy of the Danish Royal Library, Copenhagen)

1865 Brandes began to write as a reviewer for the influential newspapers *Fædrelandet* (The Fatherland), *Dagbladet* (The Daily), and *Illustreret Tidende* (The Illustrated Times). His articles for these publications focused on contemporary Danish and Scandinavian authors such as Hauch, Frederik Paludan-Müller, Christian Richardt, Magdalene Thoresen, Bjørnstjerne Bjørnson, and Henrik Ibsen. Brandes's position as a critic writing for such prominent periodicals demonstrated his talents as a writer and his exceptional abilities as a literary critic. These early reviews also reveal Brandes's considerable skill as a close reader. His critical method in this early period of his career was still determined by speculative aesthetics, by a separation between art and life, and the aesthetic standpoints in these first reviews exhibit only a little of the critic's later more radical, activist positions. Brandes continued to write articles for journals and newspapers throughout his life, many of which were later published as collections of essays. An essay Brandes wrote on Hans Christian Andersen as a writer of fairy tales, which appeared in *Illustreret Tidende* in July 1869, was the first scholarly treatment of Andersen's work and demonstrated the critic's impressive literary acumen.

In addition to these activities, Brandes was at work on his first major book, *Dualismen i vor nyeste Philosophie* (Dualism in Our Latest Philosophy, 1866), in many ways a precursor to his writings during the period often referred to by literary historians as the Modern Breakthrough of the 1870s. In this debut, Brandes attacks his former university professor Nielsen in a treatise on the conflicts between religion and modern science. Brandes's first substantial book reveals the influences of thinkers such as Ludwig Feuerbach and David Strauss in its critique of Nielsen's views on the relationship between science and religion. Nielsen had attempted to merge the thought of N. F. S. Grundtvig with that of Kierkegaard in an effort to reach a kind of Hegelian unity between knowledge and faith, while Brandes questioned any possibility of believing in the miracles of the Bible while still embracing the advances of modern science. Brandes's debut at the age of twenty-four was brave and bold: the ensuing controversy on "Tro og Viden" (Faith and Knowledge) raged in Danish newspapers and journals between 1866 and 1888. Brandes's critique of Nielsen's philosophy angered many conservatives, particularly among intellectual and ecclesiastical circles, and marked the young critic as an agitator and enemy of orthodoxy.

In November 1866 Brandes embarked on his first extended trip abroad, a journey that began a life of travel and contacts with the leading minds of the day. Brandes went first to Paris, where he remained until January 1867. In the French capital he met philosopher and critic Hippolyte Taine and heard his lectures at the Ecole des Beaux Arts. This period abroad sparked Brandes's interest in the work of other French positivists such as Charles-Augustin Sainte-Beuve and turned the young critic's attention to the novels of Emile Zola and Honoré de Balzac. In addition to the influence of Taine's historical approach and Sainte-Beuve's psychological method, Brandes's perspective was altered by the burgeoning natural sciences, including geography, biology, and the work of Charles Darwin. On the social and political front, Brandes's experiences in France confirmed his assessment of Denmark as a backward and reactionary country isolated from the cultural and political changes sweeping the rest of Europe. These impressions stirred his desire to agitate for cultural reform and renewal in Scandinavia.

Brandes returned to Denmark in 1867 and began studies for a doctoral degree at the University of Copenhagen, which he completed in 1870 with a dissertation on Taine titled *Den franske Æsthetik i vore Dage* (Contemporary French Aesthetics). In this study Brandes explores the links between methods of literary criticism and the growing importance of scientific methods. The opening chapter of the work examines Taine's notion of "faculté maîtresse," or main faculty, in which the critic, functioning as a kind of natural scientist, identifies and explores the major characteristic that has guided an author's work. Brandes found Taine's notion too simplistic and reductive, but it nonetheless proved important for Brandes's later works, particularly those projects that addressed the notion of the great men of culture and other figures of genius. The dissertation also provided Brandes with the opportunity to distance himself farther from the abstraction of Hegelian philosophy and German criticism in general and move toward a more socially engaged view of literary criticism. More importantly, Brandes's dissertation includes a literary-biographical portrait of Taine. This genre became characteristic of his work in later years.

Brandes's aesthetic writings on Taine, Sainte-Beuve, and other French positivists blended well with his early fascination with Kierkegaard, for these thinkers led Brandes toward investigating how an individual author's personality shaped his or her work and its reception. Nonetheless, Brandes's approach, especially in regard to figures of genius, departs somewhat from Taine's method, which was more concerned with commonalties between different epochs of artistic production. Blending Taine's naturalist aesthetics with Sainte-Beuve's literary portraiture and psychological perspective, Brandes's critical method aimed to understand how the artist's personality affects his artistic production. Brandes, however, sought to avoid reducing an author's work to one single character trait that would allow the critic to place him or her in a uniform historical context. The figure of the great individual and his or her role in shaping culture structures many of Brandes's interventions, and in many ways the individual and not the age determines the progress of cultural developments.

In 1868 Brandes published his second book, *Æsthetiske Studier* (Aesthetic Studies). This collection of essays included treatments of Ibsen, Paludan-Müller, and other important authors. Brandes was one of the first critics to recognize the innovative nature of Ibsen's writing and played a key role in popularizing the Norwegian writer in Scandinavia and beyond. In addition, Brandes took an interest in the politics of the day and its related cultural phenomena. He had witnessed the vibrant debates on social and political life during his first stay in Paris. His interests in political reform were reflected in his translation into Danish of John Stuart Mill's *The Subjection of Women* (1869), published in 1869 as *Kvindernes Underkuelse*. Brandes's translation of this important work stimulated heated debate on the position of women in Scandinavian society and further promoted Brandes's growing reputation as an activist critic and radical committed to unmasking bourgeois social constructions of class and matrimony.

In 1870 Brandes embarked on a second and longer trip abroad, which lasted almost a year and a half. The journey took him to France, England, and Italy. As a world traveler for most of his life, Brandes found that his journeys provided him with a European perspective on literature and culture that proved crucial for his understanding of the role of the literary critic in various cultural environments. These journeys also formed the basis for the many descriptive travelogues in Brandes's body of works. In Paris, Brandes visited Taine and made the acquaintance of philosopher and critic Ernest Renan, whose thoughts on the aristocratic individual intrigued Brandes. He also met Mill and later visited the philosopher in London. Brandes noted in his autobiography that Mill was the first intellectual figure who fit his ideal of the great man: "Netop derved traadte mig her for første Gang i mit Liv personligt i Møde med en Skikkelse, der levendegjorde det Ideal, jeg havde dannet mig af det store Menneske. Dette havde to Sider, Begavelsen og Karaktereren, Evnerne og Ubøjeligheden" (Thus in him I met for the first time in my life a figure who embodied the ideal I had formed for myself of the great man. This ideal had two sides; talent and character, great capacities and inflexibility). This crucial contact with Mill brought Brandes closer to pragmatist and utilitarian ideas and helped him to distance himself from more aesthetic influences such as Hegel and Brøchner. It also signaled the beginning of Brandes's infatuation with great figures of culture.

In 1871 Brandes returned to Denmark where, on 3 November, he delivered at the University of Copenhagen the introductory lectures that became the basis for his monumental six-volume work, *Hovedstrømninger i det nittende Aarhundredes Litteratur*. With the experiences of his European travels at hand, Brandes condemned the reactionary elements of the nineteenth century and called for a liberation of the human spirit. He divided his lectures into periods that each traced literary history as it related to movements of revolution and reaction in European society. His manner of comparative analysis focused on descriptions of developments in European literature that were then related in his lectures to the cultural situation in Denmark. The topics of the lectures included émigré literature, Romanticism in Germany, reaction in France, Naturalism in England, the Romantic school in France, and the movement of Young Germany. In the years that followed, Brandes published his lectures as the six volumes of *Hovedstrømninger i det nittende Aarhundredes Litteratur,* which comprises the volume on émigré literature followed by *Den romantiske Skole i Tydskland* (1873; translated as *The Romantic School in Germany,* 1902), *Reactionen i Frankrig* (1874; translated as *Reaction in France,* 1903), *Naturalismen i England. Byron og hans Gruppe* (1875; translated as *Naturalism in England,* 1905), *Den romantiske Skole i Frankrig* (1882; translated as *The Romantic School in France,* 1904), and *Det unge Tydskland* (1890; translated as *Young Germany,* 1905).

The resounding theme of Brandes's *Hovedstrømninger i det nittende Aarhundredes Litteratur* is the manner in which individual authors instigated revolutionary changes in the societies in which they wrote. Taking cues from Hegel's dialectics, Brandes traces the changes and upheavals in European literature from the time of the French Revolution onward, relating these developments to political events and literary tastes of the day—a movement of revolution and reaction that serves as an engine for developments in the European cultural scene. England, France, and Germany during the period between 1789 and 1848 are the major European literatures at the heart of Brandes's project. Its recurring theme is the individual versus society, summarized in Brandes's programmatic statement: "Det, at en Litteratur i vore Dage lever, viser sig i, at den sætter Problemer under Debat" (Literature in our day demonstrates that it is alive by putting problems to debate). This summation of Brandes's views on literature and society accompanies an assessment of the critic's approach, a combination of positivist literary critique and scientific method: "Den, der i Litteraturens Historie bevæger sig fra en Variation af et vist Tidrums Type til en anden, bærer sig tilnærmelsesvis ad som Naturforskeren, der forfølger en og samme Grundforms Omdannelse, f.eks. Armens til Ben, til Pote, til Vinge, til Luf igennem Forskellige Arter i Zoologien" (In the history of literature we move from one variety of epoch-type to another in much the same way as the natural scientist studies the evolution of the same basic form, from, for example, the arm to the leg, to the paw, to the wing, to the webbed foot in different species in zoology).

Thus, literary history attempts to define itself via the scientific methods of criticism. Brandes's first lecture examined what he called "émigré literature," as represented by authors such as Goethe, Vicomte François-René de Chateaubriand, Jean-Jacques Rousseau, Benjamin Constant, and Anne-Louise-Germaine de Staël. In this lecture Brandes explores the revolutionary and reactionary characteristics of authors who emigrated in 1789. From France, Brandes's work moves to Germany and what he views as the rise of reaction during the period of German Romanticism. These reactionary forces emerge victorious in the next volume on France, met by revolution again in the form of George

Brandes's wife, Gerda (née Juliane Louise Henriette Steinhoff), whom he married in 1876 after her divorce from her first husband, Adolf Strodtmann (courtesy of the Danish Royal Library, Copenhagen)

Gordon, Lord Byron, followed then by the Romantic school in France. The revolutionary movements in France eventually spread to the German literature of authors such as Heinrich Heine and Karl Ludwig Börne, which Brandes addresses in his volume on Young Germany. Thus, Brandes created a literary and cultural landscape in which artistic and national interdependencies determine the development of authors and their works.

Brandes's lectures were both a success and a scandal, with packed lecture halls and many commentaries in the newspapers. They also served to galvanize Danish intellectual circles for or against Brandes. Conservatives and theologians were shocked by Brandes's unorthodox approach, and he was castigated for his atheist views, positions many Danes felt insulted the revered institutions and social mores of the country. "Free thinkers" and reform-minded groups, on the other hand, found inspiration in Brandes's critique of Christianity, idealism, and the reigning post-Romantic aesthetics. They saw in Brandes's work an opportunity for a renewal of Danish intellectual and cultural life via his call for a literature that would serve as a vehicle for social and political change, a literature of the Modern Breakthrough.

One of the results of the furor surrounding Brandes's lectures was the rejection of his application for a position at the University of Copenhagen, accompanied by an extensive campaign in the press against his radical brand of criticism. Brandes eventually found himself barred from publishing replies to his critics and was forced to seek other outlets in order to present and defend his views. One of these responses to the press blockade against Brandesianism was a pamphlet titled *Forklaring og Forsvar* (Explanation and Defense, 1872), in which Brandes explained the manner in which his lectures had been misinterpreted. Brandes, together with his younger brother Edvard, also founded a monthly journal of literature and criticism called *Det nittende Aarhundrede* (The Nineteenth Century). The magazine appeared from October 1874 to September 1877 and attracted a small circle of Naturalist writers and other intellectuals whose ideas followed those of Brandes in their liberal-positivist outlook; these writers included Holger Drachmann, Harald Høffding, Jens Peter Jacobsen, Otto Borchsenius, and Christian K. F. Molbech.

Under considerable attack at home, Brandes accepted several invitations, among them one from Ibsen, and left Denmark for Germany on 10 September 1872 for a journey that became an extended period of voluntary exile. In Dresden, Brandes visited Ibsen, a friend and confidant from earlier days. In Berlin Brandes was the guest of his German translator, Adolf Strodtmann, and his young wife, Henriette. The Strodtmanns had wed when Henriette, whom Brandes called Gerda, was nineteen and Adolf thirty-five, and the young woman appears to have been unhappy in her marriage. Brandes and Henriette began a secret relationship. After a difficult divorce from Strodtmann, she married Brandes in a civil ceremony in Berlin on 29 July 1876. Gerda and Georg Brandes had two children, Edith (born 1879) and Astrid (born 1880; died of diphtheria in 1890).

Upon his return to Copenhagen, Brandes gave twelve lectures on German Romanticism at the university. He also published a collection of literary portraits under the title *Danske Digtere. Charakterbilleder* (Danish Writers: Character Portraits, 1877), which included essays on Danish authors such as Hauch, Christian Winther, and Paludan-Müller. These literary portraits served as a precursor to larger literary biographies. Indeed, in 1877 the fruits of a longer research project on German socialist thinker Ferdinand Lassalle appeared under the title *Ferdinand Lassalle. Ein literarisches Charakterbild* (translated as *Ferdinand Lassalle,* 1911). The book was published first in German in 1877 and appeared in Danish in 1881.

In 1876 Brandes began a lecture tour of Sweden and Norway. The subject of these lectures was the Danish philosopher Kierkegaard, on whom Brandes was writing a biography. While Kierkegaard was a well-known figure in Denmark, Brandes's lectures brought his work to a broader audience for the first time. Brandes's early infatuation with Kierkegaard's thought had, in the meantime, developed into a critical stance toward the philosopher's reception in Denmark, particularly toward the appropriation of Kierkegaardian thought by theologians. Nonetheless, Brandes admired Kierkegaard's formidable literary style with its irony and wit, and considered Kierkegaard one of the greatest minds Denmark had ever produced. Brandes maintained that his research into Kierkegaard's thought and biography was a result of a change in perspective. Kierkegaard had inspired Brandes in his youth; Brandes now approached the philosopher more dispassionately and reevaluated earlier conclusions.

Brandes's lecture tour commenced in Sweden and, after a successful presentation in Stockholm, was scheduled to continue in Christiania (Oslo). Once again, however, Brandes's reputation as a radical led conservative university authorities to ban him from the lecture halls and from appearing under official auspices. Brandes did, however, speak in Christiania to the student society at the university. Following this lecture tour, Brandes published his literary biography on Kierkegaard, *Søren Kierkegaard. En kritisk Fremstilling i Grundrids* (Søren Kierkegaard: A Critical Exposition in Outline, 1877), the first scholarly work on Kierkegaard and Brandes's first attempt to treat an author's entire biography and body of work. Although Brandes later wrote in an 11 January 1888 letter to Nietzsche that his book on Kierkegaard was a mere "Streitschrift, geschrieben um seinen Einfluss zu hemmen" (polemic designed to limit his influence), Brandes also admitted that he considered this work "in psycholgischer Hinsicht entschieden das feinste, was ich veröffentlicht habe" (from a psychological standpoint decisively the finest work I have published).

Søren Kierkegaard. En kritisk Fremstilling i Grundrids consists of twenty-eight chapters and an introduction in which Brandes traces the main currents that formed Kierkegaard's personality. The role of Kierkegaard's stern and pious father looms large in Brandes's psychological investigations, as do two fundamental passions, *Pietet* (piety) and *Foragt* (contempt, disdain), which Brandes identifies as the central characteristics guiding Kierkegaard's development. Brandes's treatise on Kierkegaard demonstrates the development of Brandes's critical biographical method, which included political, social, and textual commentary in a literary portrait. Though critical of Kierkegaard's stance on Christianity, the book hails Kierkegaard as an exceptional stylist and psychologist, whose critical assessment of society proved useful for Brandes's activist project. As in all of his writing, Brandes attempts to secure footing for criticism as both a form of art and as a manner of changing existing conditions, a tool for reform. Thus, in tracing the history of Kierkegaard's genius, Brandes returns to Taine's method of localizing central traits in literary and historical figures but closely reads the manner in which Kierkegaard's biography altered his writings. Brandes also completed two other large literary biographies during this period, one on Swedish writer Esaias Tegnér (*Esaias Tegnér. En litteratur-psychologisk Studie,* 1878) and another on British prime minister and writer Benjamin Disraeli (*Benjamin Disraeli, Jarl af Beaconsfield. En litterær Charakteristik,* 1878; translated as *Lord Beaconsfield. A Study,* 1878). Each text compares and contrasts the subject's life and work and seeks to identify those central developments and causalities that formed his great personality.

Facing increased harassment and controversy at home, Brandes chose to settle in Berlin with his German-born wife. The Brandeses moved to Germany in 1877 and lived in the German capital until 1883. In Berlin, Brandes moved in circles of liberal politicians, artists, and intellectuals, but his work found supporters among a broader reading public as well. In Germany, Brandes was counted as a native son, and his works were widely translated and read. In addition to many articles for newspapers and magazines in Germany and Scandinavia, Brandes wrote a larger work on his time in Berlin–*Berlin som tysk Rigshovedstad. Erindringer fra et femaarigt Ophold* (Berlin, Capital of the German Reich: Memories from a Five-Year Stay, 1885). In this work, Brandes describes the capital of the young German Empire and some of its leading political and cultural personalities. In equal parts travelogue, historical survey, and cultural study, Brandes's book on Berlin, comprising essays originally written for Swedish and Norwegian newspapers (since he was banned from the Danish press), was critical of Prince Otto Eduard Leopold von Bismarck's Germany, though also enamored of German culture. The portrait of a city and its leading figures also summarizes the critic's own experience of exile there, underscoring the manner in which the German reading public had supported him and his work, and assisted in securing his status as a respected critic.

Brandes returned to Copenhagen in 1883, supported by a group of donors interested in his presence there, since a professorship at the university was still out of the question. In the meantime, his brother Edvard had been elected to the Danish Parliament. In 1885 the Brandes brothers, together with newspaperman Viggo Hørup, founded the daily newspaper *Politiken,* which remains one of Denmark's leading dailies. Brandes's column "Skikkelser og Tanker" (Personalities and Thoughts) filled a large part of the front page for many years. In his regular contributions, Brandes commented on both cultural and political events and introduced the readers of the newspaper to a vast range of literary, political, and philosophical figures and works.

Among many of Brandes's undertakings upon his return to Denmark after years of exile in Germany was work on a book dedicated to writers of the reform-minded literature that he had long supported and that had once shocked the Scandinavian reading public. The result of this project was a collection of essays titled *Det moderne Gjennembruds Mænd* (The Men of the Modern Breakthrough, 1883). As the title suggests, the subject of the book is the group of Realist and Naturalist writers who had challenged bourgeois conceptions of literature and changed literary tastes during the 1870s and early 1880s. It includes essays on seven authors: Bjørnson, Ibsen, Drachmann, J. P. Jacobsen, Edvard Brandes, Sophus Schandorph, and Erik Skram. In these essays, most of which had appeared earlier as individual articles, Brandes considers these Scandinavian authors as the inaugurating figures of a modern breakthrough in the literature of northern Europe, writers whose works followed Brandes's notion of literature as a reflection of desires for social and political reform. In many ways a polemic manifesto, Brandes's book exhibits his typical type of radicalism with hopes that these new literary currents will continue to bear fruit for Scandinavian culture in general. Brandes knew most of these men personally and carried on an extensive correspondence with Ibsen and Bjørnson that had begun much earlier. Thus, the work reveals an intimate knowledge of the cultural currents that had influenced these authors. Brandes's essays recount how these figures and their works came to alter the face of Scandinavian culture and shape literary currents throughout Europe. In the same year, Brandes published *Mennesker og Værker* (1883; selections translated as *Eminent Authors of the Nineteenth Century,* 1886), a collection of essays on figures such as Renan, Mill, and Ibsen–most of whom Brandes also knew personally.

While the volume on the men of the Modern Breakthrough served as a recapitulation of Brandes's earlier interests, Brandes nonetheless continued to pursue innovative and often contentious projects in the years that followed. In 1886 and 1887 he traveled to Poland and Russia for a series of lectures. The books resulting from these journeys, *Indtryk fra Polen* (1888; translated as *Poland: A Study of the Land, People, and Literature,* 1903) and *Indtyrk fra Rusland* (1888; translated as *Impressions of Russia,* 1889), were two of the first works to introduce Scandinavian and European readers to Slavic literatures. These undertakings were also new areas for Brandes. The two books offer comprehensive assessments of the literature and culture of both countries. In *Indtryk fra Polen* Brandes expresses his sympathy for Poland as a country oppressed by foreign occupation. The volume on Russia addresses works by such major authors as Fyodor Dostoevsky, Leo Tolstoy, and Ivan Turgenev. These early forays into the literature of eastern Europe reflect Brandes's burgeoning interest in and commitment to the literatures of minorities and oppressed peoples, for whom he served not only as a spokesperson but also as a disseminator of their cultural productions, which had been unknown in other parts of Europe. In later years, Brandes's attentions to lesser-known cultures included works on literatures written in Czech, Dutch, Armenian, and Icelandic.

During the same period, Brandes began to read the works of the then-unknown philosopher and philologist Nietzsche. Nietzsche's Leipzig publishers had sent copies of the philosopher's works for Brandes's review, and the result was a long correspondence between Nietzsche and Brandes that ended only with Nietzsche's fall into madness in 1889. As with so many authors, Brandes's interest in Nietzsche brought the philosopher's works to a larger reading public. Contact with Nietzsche, however, also changed Brandes's political and aesthetic views. Nietzsche's individualism and his critique of mass culture and the herd intrigued Brandes, who had already encountered such positions in the works of Renan. Disappointed by the failure of social and political reforms in Denmark, Brandes during this period began to turn away from social engagement and reform projects and toward what he called "Aristokratisk Radicalisme" (aristocratic radicalism), a nebulous term that describes a belief in great figures of culture as central to historical progress. In this notion of aristocratic radicalism, Brandes excavates earlier fascinations with figures of genius such as Kierkegaard and demonstrates the impact of his contacts with thinkers such as Mill and Renan by promoting the great personality as the source of culture.

What became the first critical essay on the philosophy of Nietzsche began with a series of lectures Brandes gave, again at the University of Copenhagen, in 1888. The first article to arise from these presentations appeared in the August 1889 issue of the Danish journal *Tilskueren* (The Spectator) as "Aristokratisk Radikalisme. En Afhandling om Friedrich Nietzsche" (1889; translated as *An Essay on Aristocratic Radicalism,* 1914). Brandes's treatise on Nietzsche combines his growing interest in the phenomena of genius with his political concern about the leveling tendencies of mass culture. A letter to author Schandorph on 1 April 1888 reveals the changes under way in Brandes's thinking:

> I de sidste Tider har jeg kastet en af mine Slanghuder af. Jeg er fra Englændere vendt tilbage til Tyskerne i Filosofien. Den engelske filosofi synes mig at have kulmineret. Men min Ven N. [Nietzsche] har Fremtid for sig. Desuden bliver jeg mere radikal, mindre historisk, og stedse mere aristokratisk i æthetiske og historiske Synsmaader. Jeg troer ikke mere for en Døjt paa at de store Mænd er concentreret Masse, skabes nedefra, er Udtryk for Hoben osv. Alt kommer fra de Store, Alt siver fra dem nedefter.

> (Lately I have shed one of my snakeskins. I have gone from the English back to the Germans in regard to philosophy. For me English philosophy has culminated. But my friend N [Nietzsche] has a future for himself. Furthermore, I have become more radical, less historical, and increasingly more aristocratic in my aesthetic and historical views. I no longer believe the nonsense about great men being concentrations of the masses, formed from below, an expression of the herd, etc. Everything comes from the great ones, everything filters down from them.)

The skin that Brandes shed during this crucial period might be described as his adherence to the utilitarian philosophy of thinkers such as Mill. With this change in critical direction, Brandes rejected the utilitarian motto of the "greatest happiness for the greatest number" and replaced it with a belief in the primacy of great individuals. This transformation in Brandes's literary, political, and philosophical interests determined much of his writing after the 1870s, despite Brandes's later attempts to distance himself from his early enthusiasm for Nietzsche. Indeed, one of the results of Brandes's interest in Nietzsche was a heated dispute over Brandes's political allegiances, this time with Harald Høffding, a professor of philosophy at the University of Copenhagen. In a public debate carried out in the pages of *Tilskueren,* Høffding chastised Brandes for abandoning the critic's activist role in promoting democratic reform and for espousing an elitist stance on culture and politics.

During the 1880s and 1890s, Brandes's criticism and approach changed with social, political, and literary events. With the decline of naturalism and the rise of modernism, Brandes remained a realist but lost his adherence to positivist thinking and utilitarianism. In addition, Brandes's activist stance waned, although his interest in oppressed minorities, his outspoken views in the Dreyfus Affair (the scandal involving Captain Alfred Dreyfus, an officer on the French general staff, who was accused of spying for Germany and persecuted, convicted, and imprisoned largely because he

Brandes on his seventy-fifth birthday (courtesy of the Danish Royal Library, Copenhagen)

was a Jew), and his attention to the oppression of the Danish population in Slesvig (a Danish province [formerly a Duchy] in southern Jutland, under German rule 1864–1920) attest to the remnants of an earlier devotion to political activities. In 1889, the year of the World Exhibition, Brandes traveled once again to Paris, where he renewed longtime friendships and acquaintances and met a new generation of authors, including Paul Bourget and Joris-Karl Huysmanns. The result of this trip was a collection of essays titled *Udenlandske Egne og Personligheder* (Foreign Personalities, 1893). The book includes impressions from Brandes's travels, commentary on literary figures, and a revised version of the essay on Nietzsche.

Brandes's production of essays and criticism continued unabated during the 1890s. A three-volume literary biography of Shakespeare appeared in 1895–1896 and was followed by works on Heine (1897) and Ibsen (1898). One critic called Brandes's work on Shakespeare one of the most brilliant studies of the great writer in any non-English language. In his study Brandes describes the manner in which Shakespeare's genius came to influence generations of readers in a wide range of nations. Brandes emphasizes Shakespeare's role in creating intellectual revolutions and in shaping the spiritual lives of thinkers, writers, and poets, but he also addresses the position of average readers. In an essay titled *Om Læsning* (translated as *On Reading,* 1906)–written in 1899 but not published in an authorized Danish edition until 1908–Brandes restates these themes when he remarks that books "sætter Tanker i Bevægelse" (set thoughts in motion). Books and reading, Brandes contends, inspire readers to "forøge vor Indsigt, aflægge vore Fordomme og blive i stedse højere Grad Personligheder" (increase our insight, shed our prejudices, and become, to an ever higher degree, personalities).

These qualities Brandes finds in the works and biography of Shakespeare and other great figures of culture. Brandes's later writings can be viewed in light of this citation as a search for both the great artist and those readers who would be attracted, captivated, and changed by his or her work. In addition to his autobiography, *Levned,* Brandes published several larger biographies during this period, which included *Wolfgang Goethe* (1915; translated as *Wolfgang Goethe,* 1924), *François de Voltaire* (1916, 1917; translated as *Voltaire,* 1930), *Cajus Julius Cæsar* (1918), and *Michelangelo Buonarroti* (1921; translated as *Michelangelo. His Life, His Times, His Era,* 1963). Brandes's 1925 book *Sagnet om Jesus* (translated as *Jesus. A Myth,* 1926) views Jesus as a myth lacking historical foundation. In all of these works Brandes locates the great artist as the source of culture.

The final political engagement of Brandes's later career involved his stance on World War I, which spelled the end of his friendship with French statesman Georges Clemenceau and other European intellectuals. Brandes took a position that many of his readers viewed as a pacifist stance. Indeed, Brandes saw the conflict as a barbaric competition among the great powers for economic and political spoils, and remained critical of all its players. He did, however, express his understanding for the German position and his appreciation of German culture. Readers looked to Brandes, a critic of international stature, for a position, and his unwillingness to offer complete support to the Entente powers led to scathing public criticism in France and England. In a public debate with William Archer, British critic and translator of Ibsen, Brandes defended his critical assessment of the carnage of World War I. Citing Brandes's unfounded sympathies for Germany, Archer replied by calling Brandes an apologist for Germany. In an open letter to Brandes published in 1917 under the title *Shirking the Issue,* Archer chastises the critic for his naive neutrality and for "displaying the *triste courage* to attack and malign the nations who are pouring out their blood and treasure in defence of the very things which–unless your spirit has become hopelessly Prussianised–you hold most precious for the future of civilization."

Two books, essentially collections of essays and articles, emerged from Brandes's critical engagement with the war, *Verdenskrigen* (1916; translated as *The World at War,* 1917) and *Tragediens anden Del. Fredslutningen* (The Tragedy's Second Part: The Conclusion of the Peace, 1919). These collections of essays demonstrate Brandes's bitter disappointment with the projects of cultural radicalism that he had once promoted and reflect his critical stance toward the manner in which peace was dictated following the armistice. In the end, Brandes concludes that the United States was the only victor in the conflict and that the country would emerge dominant from the war.

Frequent lecture tours and other personal travels marked Brandes's later years as an elder statesman of literary criticism. He continued to demonstrate his critical acumen with essays, commentaries, and reviews that spoke to descriptions Nietzsche had once offered of him as both "ein guter Europäer" and "Kulturmissionär" (a good European and a missionary of culture).

When Georg Brandes died on 19 February 1927, he left a legacy as a prolific critic and an untiring defender of literary innovation. Ibsen had once suggested to Brandes that the two men should share the role of provocateurs: "Ærgr De de danske, så skal jeg ærgre normændene" (You provoke the Danes and I'll stir up the Norwegians). Indeed, much of Brandes's critical energy went toward promoting and popularizing little-known, often controversial authors and in instigating debates on the problems of the day. The controversies surrounding Brandes's positions provoked ire, but they also won him admiration at home and abroad. Despite the contradictions evident in Brandes's many changing allegiances and convictions, his dedication to a comparative and humanist project–to angering just the right people and tracing the newest currents in European cultures–secures his legacy as a crucial figure in the history of criticism.

Letters:

Georg Brandes' Breve til Hjemmet, edited by Alf Hjorth-Moritzen (Copenhagen: H. Hirschsprung, 1938);

Georg og Edv. Brandes' Brevveksling med nordiske Forfattere og Videnskabsmænd, 8 volumes, edited by Morten Borup, Francis Bull, and John Landquist (Copenhagen: Gyldendal, 1939–1942);

Correspondance de Georg Brandes, 3 volumes, edited by Paul Krüger (Copenhagen: Rosenkilde og Bagger, 1952–1966);

Breve til forældrene 1859–71, 3 volumes, edited by Borup (Copenhagen: Det danske Sprog- og Litteraturselskab, 1978);

Georg Brandes. Selected Letters, edited by W. Glyn Jones (Norwich: Norvik Press, 1990).

References:

William Archer, *Shirking the Issue. A Letter to Dr. George Brandes* (London & New York: Hodder & Stoughton, 1917);

Doris R. Asmundsson, *Georg Brandes: Aristocratic Radical* (New York: New York University Press, 1981);

Hans Hertel and Sven Møller Kristensen, *The Activist Critic: A Symposium on the Political Ideas, Literary Methods and International Reception of Georg Brandes,* Orbis Litterarum, no. 5 (Copenhagen: Munksgaard, 1980);

Hertel and Kristensen, eds., *Den politiske Georg Brandes* (Copenhagen: Hans Reitzel, 1973);

Jørgen Knudsen, *Georg Brandes,* 5 volumes (Copenhagen: Gyldendal, 1985–2004)–comprises volume 1, *Frigørelsens vej 1842–1877;* volume 2, *I modsigelsernes tegn 1877–83;* volume 3, *Symbolet og Manden 1883–1895;* volume 4, *Magt og Afmagt 1896–1914;* and volume 5, *Uovervindelig taber 1914–1927*;

Kristiansen, *Georg Brandes. Kritikeren. liberalisten. humanisten* (Copenhagen: Gyldendal, 1980);

Henri Nathansen, *Georg Brandes. Et Portræt* (Copenhagen: Nyt Nordisk Forlag, 1929);

Bertil Nolin, *Georg Brandes* (Boston: Twayne, 1976);

Nolin, *Den goda europén: Studier i Georg Brandes' Idéutveckling 1871–1893* (Stockholm: Bökforlaget Norstedts, 1965);

Neil Christian Pages, "On Aristocratic Radicalism. Singularities of Georg Brandes, Friedrich Nietzsche and Søren Kierkegaard," dissertation, New York University, 1999;

Paul V. Rubow, *Georg Brandes' briller* (Copenhagen: Levin & Munksgaard, 1932).

Papers:

Georg Brandes's letters and manuscripts are at the Danish Royal Library in Copenhagen and at the Brandes Archive at the University of Århus.

Hans Adolph Brorson

(20 June 1694 - 3 June 1764)

Marianne Stecher-Hansen
University of Washington

and

Bo Kampmann Walther
University of Southern Denmark

BOOKS: *Nogle Jule-Psalmer/GUD til Ære og Christne-Siæle/i sær siin elskelige Meenighed til Opmuntring. Til den forestaaende Glædelige Jule-Fest enfoldig og i hast sammenskrevne af H. A. B.* (Tønder, 1732)–includes "Den yndigste Rose er funden" and "Mit Hierte altid vancker"; translated by J. C. Aaberg as "Now Found Is the Fairest of Roses" and "My Heart Remains in Wonder," in *Songs from Denmark,* edited by Peter Balslev-Clausen (Copenhagen: Danish Cultural Institute, 1988), pp. 61–64;

Troens Rare Klenodie (Copenhagen: Frank Christian Mumme, 1739; revised, [ca. 1742, 1747, 1752, 1752–1760, 1760, 1760–1767])–includes "Op! all den ting, som Gud har giort"; translated by A. M. Andersen as "Arise, All Things That God Has Made," in *Songs from Denmark,* edited by Balslev-Clausen (Copenhagen: Danish Cultural Institute, 1988), pp. 37–38;

Lissabons ynkelige Undergang ved Jordskiælv den 1. November 1755 (Copenhagen: Andreas Hartvig Godiche, 1756);

Doct. Hans Adolph Brorsons fordum Biskop over Riber-Stift Svane-Sang, edited by Broder Brorson (Copenhagen: Printed by August Friderich Steins Skrifter, 1765).

Editions and Collections: *Samlede skrifter,* 3 volumes, edited by L. J. Koch (Copenhagen: Danske Sprog- og Litteraturselskab, 1951–1956);

Visitatsberetninger og Breve, edited by Koch (Copenhagen: Danske Sprog- og Litteraturselskab, 1960);

Op! Al den ting som Gud har giort. Udvalgte salmer, edited by Erik Sønderholm, graphic illustrations by Bodil Kaalund (Copenhagen: Brøndum, 1982);

Hans Adolph Brorson (painting by Johan Hörner, 1756; Museum of National History at Frederiksborg Castle; photograph courtesy of the Danish Royal Library, Copenhagen)

Udvalgte salmer og digte, edited, with notes and afterword, by Steffen Arndal (Copenhagen: DSL/Borgen, 1994).

OTHER: "Ved Anna Christina Brorsons begravelse 19. juni 1721," in Nicolai and Broder Brorson,

Sidste Afskeed Med sin . . . Egte-Hustrue Anna Christina Brorson (Flensborg, 1727).

The literary work of Bishop Hans Adolph Brorson represents an enduring Danish tradition of hymnology and religious poetry. His work is strongly influenced by the Pietist movement that emanated from Germany northward through Slesvig and Holsten in the early eighteenth century and came into contact with the official Lutheran Church of Denmark. Brorson is the most gifted religious poet of eighteenth-century Denmark, and he serves as a striking contrast to his contemporary Ludvig Holberg, the greatest secular writer of that century. Brorson eventually gained recognition as one of the four greatest Danish hymn writers alongside Thomas Kingo of the seventeenth century and N. F. S. Grundtvig and B. S. Ingemann of the nineteenth century. His major contributions to Danish hymnology are *Troens Rare Klenodie* (Rare Jewel of Faith, 1739), which includes several hymns known by nearly all Danes today, and a sophisticated collection of religious lyrics from his later years, *Doct. Hans Adolph Brorsons fordum Biskop over Riber-Stift Svane-Sang* (Doctor Hans Adolph Brorson's, former bishop of Ribe Diocese, Swan Song, 1765), known as *Svane-Sang.* In terms of Brorson's influence, his Pietistic poetry served as a strong source of inspiration to the philosopher Søren Kierkegaard.

Brorson was born on 20 June 1694 in Randerup. The small town lies at the heart of rural *Sønderjylland* (North Slesvig), the birthplace of Pietism in Denmark. His parents were the parish pastor Broder Brodersen and Cathrine Margrethe, née Clausen. Hans Adolph was the youngest of three sons; his older brothers Nicolai (born in 1690) and Broder (born in 1692) also assumed prominent positions in the Danish Lutheran Church. After graduating from the Latin school in 1712, Brorson received a scholarship to the University of Copenhagen (with residence at *Borchs kollegium*), where he began a study of theology in 1715. Apparently, he overexerted himself and lay ill for months during the winter of 1716, eventually returning to Randerup as a result of the illness. He recovered later that year. Under the influence of German Pietism, he served as a tutor for a few years at Løgum Abbey only to move back to Copenhagen in order to finish his theological degree in 1721. From 1722 to 1729 he served as a pastor in Randerup, and later in Tønder. In 1732 his career took a further step upward when he was appointed archdeacon of Ribe and, finally in 1741, bishop of Ribe diocese. During his years in Ribe he wrote the hymns collected in his important works, *Troens Rare Klenodie* and *Svane-Sang* (posthumously published by his son Broder Brorson).

Brorson's work contributed to–and in ways came to define–the Pietist movement on Danish soil. Pietism was a widespread Protestant movement in eighteenth-century Germany that stressed emotional piety and the pure Christian life; it is a form of religious revivalism that can be traced back to the mysticism of the Middle Ages as well as to August Hermann Francke of Halle. In his work, Francke sought to regain the individuality and sensuality of the Christian faith, which had been repressed by Lutheran orthodoxy, by stressing the rich, often erotic, imagery of the Bible, especially that found in the Song of Songs. Brorson's verse often includes the emphasis that Pietistic Christianity placed on the individual's illumination of his own religious conversion and faith.

While he was at Løgum Abbey, Brorson began his lifelong enterprise of translating German hymns into Danish. As a translator of German into lyrical Danish, Brorson is highly regarded. The year before his marriage on 26 November 1722 to Catharina Steenbek Clausen, Brorson wrote an elegiac poem for the funeral of his brother Nicolai's young wife, Anna Christina Brorson. This poem, "Ved Anna Christina Brorsons begravelse 19. juni 1721" (At the Funeral of Anna Christina Brorson 19 June 1721), published in 1727 alongside his brothers' poems and funeral sermon in memory of Anna, *Sidste Afskeed Med sin . . . Egte-Hustrue Anna Christina Brorson,* offers the first example of many of his celebrated themes and rhetorical images that flourished later, especially in *Svane-Sang.* In the poem, the deceased sister-in-law is likened to a Christ-like rose: "Sov sødt, Du yndigste udi Din *Rosen*-Dal! / I Ævighedens Vaar Du ævig blomstre skal" (Sleep sweetly, You loveliest one in your Valley of Roses / In the Spring of Eternity you shall forever blossom). In this poem Brorson compares the tomb with paradise and death with life; throughout the poem he uses a strong concentration of contrasting words and meanings, a technique that he inherited not only from the rhetorical masters of antiquity but also from seventeenth-century Baroque poet Thomas Kingo.

In 1730 Brorson was appointed Danish pastor in Tønder, which at that time was under the sway of the Pietists. He gave his morning sermons in Danish, although other church matters, including the singing of hymns, were conducted in German. In 1731 the German-speaking part of southern Jutland received its own hymnal, *Vollständige Gesang-Buch,* known in Danish as "Tønder-salmebogen" (The Tønder Hymnal), which attempted to reconcile orthodox Lutheran hymns with the Pietistic canon. Brorson became immensely inspired by the hymnal, and around Christmas the following year he published a small volume in Danish titled *Nogle Jule-Psalmer/GUD til Ære og Christne-Siæle/i sær siin elskel-*

ige Meenighed til Opmuntring. Til den forestaaende Glædelige Jule-Fest enfoldig og i hast sammenskrevne af H. A. B. (Some Christmas Hymns. To the Glory of GOD and Christian Souls / in particular to cheer his beloved Congregation. For the coming joyous Christmas Celebration, simply and in haste, compiled by H.A.B., 1732). *Nogle Jule-Psalmer* includes "Den yndigste Rose er funden" (1732; translated as "Now Found Is the Fairest of Roses," 1988), which is often sung at Christmastime in Lutheran churches. As a theme for the hymn, Brorson chose a quote from Song of Songs 2: 1: "I am a rose of Sharon." Building upon the allegory of biblical exegesis, Brorson likens Salomon to Jesus and Shulamite to the human spirit or the Church. However, just as there were thorns in the rose garden of Jesus, so there are evil men among true believers. Hereditary sin also signifies this decline of faith, but the miracle of Christ's birth gives hope for those who seek to shelter the sweet rose against worldly threats and dangers, as Brorson suggests in the last verse of "Den yndigste Rose er funden":

Lad Verden mig alting betage
Lad Tornene rive og nage,
Lad Hiertet kun daane og briste,
Min Rose jeg aldrig vil miste.

(The world may of all things bereave me,
Its thorns may annoy and aggrieve me,
The foe may afflictions engender,
My rose I will never surrender.)

Personal identification with the suffering of Christ–found frequently in Pietistic preaching and hymnology–supports the belief in salvation, and the actual singing of the hymn is meant to inspire hope in the hearts of the congregation. The collection *Nogle Jule-Psalmer* also includes other hymns that have remained popular in the Lutheran Church in Denmark and abroad–for example, "Mit Hierte altid vancker" (1732; translated as "My Heart Remains in Wonder," 1988) and "Her kommer dine Arme Smaa" (Here Come Your Poor Little Ones).

The Pietistic notion of a symbiotic relationship between Christ and man is developed in Brorson's major collection *Troens Rare Klenodie.* Between the years 1732 and 1739 Brorson had published a series of hymns in pamphlets; in 1739 he supplemented these works and edited them in order to produce the single collection *Troens Rare Klenodie,* which appeared in six subsequent editions, gradually expanded during Brorson's lifetime. The expanded edition of *Troens Rare Klenodie* includes 274 hymns, out of which 82 are original compositions by Brorson, and 192 are his translations of German hymns. In his arrangement of the hymnal, Brorson employs a traditional liturgical structure–that is, each group of hymns corresponds to significant events in the church year. The first part is titled "Troens Fryde-Fest" (The Joyous Celebration of Faith), followed by "Troens Grund" (The Basis of Faith), "Troens Midler" (The Means of Faith), "Troens Frugt" (The Fruit of Faith), "Troens Kamp og Seyer" (The Battle and Victory of Faith), "Troens Herlighed" (The Greatness of Faith), and finally "Troens Ende" (The Ends of Faith).

In Brorson's canonical hymn "Op! all den ting, som Gud har giort" (1739; translated as "Arise, All Things That God Has Made," 1988) from this collection, the dynamic relation between words and God's transcendence is explored. First, nature is summoned to praise the wonders of God. Second, the hymn turns to the church community so that it may cherish God. Finally, in the last verse, the hymn calls for God, who in his eternal wisdom always remains beyond any attempt to name or conceptualize him:

Hvad skal jeg sige? mine ord
Vil ikke meget sige;
O GUd! hvad er din viisdom stoer;
Din Godhed, Kraft og Rige!

(What shall I say? Weak are my words
And humble my opinion.
How great Thy wisdom, Lord of lords,
Thy might and Thy dominion!)

The culmination of Brorson's career in the church took place on 5 May 1741, when King Christian VI appointed him bishop of Ribe diocese. Shortly before the ordination, Brorson's wife Catharina died in her thirteenth childbirth on 9 June 1741, and the grieving Brorson threatened to give up his promotion–but not for long. He was ordained as bishop on 6 August 1741 in Copenhagen, and the following year, on 29 June 1742, he married Johanna Christiane Riese. They had three children, about whom little is known. Brorson remained bishop of Ribe until his death in 1764.

Brorson sensed that a spiritual as well as an institutional crisis existed in Europe. The Pietistic revivalist movement was gradually being replaced by the rational philosophy of the Enlightenment. For those who could not afford the luxury of philosophy and politics–namely, the impoverished social classes of Denmark and Europe–daily life was marred by deceit, corruption, and amorality. In reaction to the harsh realities of existence in eighteenth-century Europe, Brorson interpreted the earthquake in Lisbon on 1 November 1755 according to his perception of a decline in religious faith. In 1756, in the aftermath of the Lisbon earthquake, Brorson wrote a giant poem, consisting of 380 Alexandrines, titled *Lissabons ynkelige Undergang ved Jord-*

Statue of Brorson outside Ribe Cathedral. Erected in 1911, it is a copy of the 1893 original by August Vilhelm Saabye (courtesy of the Danish Royal Library, Copenhagen).

skiælv den 1. November 1755 (Lisbon's Pitiful Destruction by Earthquake on 1 November 1755). But instead of explaining this natural catastrophe as an apocalyptic sign from God signifying difficult times to be followed by a new holy millennium, the earthquake represents in Brorson's poem a horrible, but justified, punishment of men living in superficial certainty in a kind of false Tower of Babel. He transforms the name of the landscape that surrounds Lisbon, "Estremadura," which literally means "the far away land on the other side of the river Duoro,"–into "dit land Extrema dura"–that is, "extremes that are hard to come to terms with." Across Europe, the Lisbon earthquake was regarded as the radical destruction of the philosopher Leibniz's notion of "the best of all worlds." With the Lisbon catastrophe, modernity seemed to burst forth into the eighteenth-century worldview, and mankind was left with endless questions, especially the one found in the Theodicée: How can God allow evil within the world?

In 1760 Brorson was named doctor of theology and presented a dissertation in Latin titled "De vexillo ecclesiæ" (About the Church's Banners). According to his biograher Steffen Arndal, Brorson was known as a clergyman who was industrious, zealous, and kind. He often accompanied his own songs on a lute. His visitations to his parishioners are recorded in *Visitatsberetninger og Breve* (Accounts of Visitations and Letters), first published in 1960 and demonstrating that the bishop was actively involved in the spiritual life of his parish. The Pietists not only devoted themselves to religious activities, but they also initiated such important social reforms in the eighteenth century as the opening of orphanages, poorhouses, and hospitals. Brorson was himself active in early efforts at public education. Pietist Christianity appealed to a great extent to the poor, the poorly educated, and to women and children; an intimate appeal to the individual and to his experience of faith is evident in many of Brorson's hymns.

The religious lyrics of Brorson's last years, written not for publication but for the spiritual edification of his closest relations, were published the year after his death in 1765 by his son Broder. *Doct. Hans Adolph Brorsons fordum Biskop over Riber-Stift Svane-Sang* consists of seventy original hymns. Unlike *Troens rare Klenodie,* which combines the liturgical traditions with a strong Pietistic revivalism by attacking sin and conventional, habitual Christianity, *Svane-Sang* is artistically more innovative in its language and composition. In this collection, a yearning for eternity and heavenly existence is pronounced. In his later religious poetry, Brorson adapted popular musical forms–such as the aria, the cantata, and the duet–and he experimented with meter and rhetorical figures, making *Svane-Sang* a lyrical zenith in the Danish poetic tradition.

In his arrangement of *Svane-Sang,* Brorson's son only pretended to follow the conventional composition of a hymnal. First is a section in connection with the church year; then one about the baptism and the Trinity; then a longer section about the different aspects of religious life; and, finally, a section dealing with the relationship between the soul and Jesus. These last hymns, especially, use a complicated composition inspired by the Bible. They are often written as explicit dialogues, in which the soul asks questions and Jesus responds, as in "Samtale imellem JEsum og Siælen" (Conversation Between Jesus and the Soul). In this poem, the soul expresses both longing and doubt, and Jesus responds by offering comfort and peace. Although the dialogue is essential to this text, the format might also be considered a psychomachia–that is, a dramatically composed inner spiritual conflict, in which the heart functions as the dramatic stage. The internal rhymes and the run-on lines (enjambment) that tie Jesus' short replies to the soul's iambic pace have the effect of an echo in the mind of the listener. "Naar faaer min Aand bestandig Roe?" (When will my mind have peace?), asks the soul in the second stanza, and Jesus replies, not until "mandig troe" (manly faith) is achieved. In the poem, Brorson also makes use of an image from the Song of Solomon, in which the dove seeks shelter in the crevice of the cliff, an image that can also be expanded to include Noah's dove in search of the window to the ark.

"Samtale imellem JEsum og Siælen" is closely related in style and theme to the three other arias–"Samtale imellem Brudgommen og Bruden" (Conversation Between the Bridegroom and the Bride), "Hvad est du dog skiøn, ja skiøn" (How Beautiful You Are, Yes Beautiful), and "Her vil ties, her vil bies" (Silence Heeded, Waiting Needed)–also published in *Svane-Sang.* These arias have in common a sensual and expectant tone, a titillating combination of wounds and blood with ecstasy and the peace of salvation as well as with the eroticism of the Song of Solomon, in which the meeting of the soul with Jesus is rendered as a mystical union. In "Samtale imellem Brudgommen og Bruden," Jesus gently and playfully guides the apprehensive soul away from the winter cold and toward salvation, which is momentarily hidden. He directs the longing soul toward the gates of the heavenly Jerusalem, where converted souls gather, assume the shape of a shiny white flock, and invoke Zion's Bridegroom in a spherical harmony. The hymn describes in images how spring shall arrive as the savior or the heavenly dove; all the while, the soul of the turtledove is cheered during the long winter by the green buds on Christ's rose.

If Jesus' conciliatory tone in "Samtale imellem Brugommen og Bruden" seems carefree, the tone is far more ecstatic, even imploring, in the aria "Hvad est du dog skiøn, ja skiøn." This hymn includes no explicit dialogue, but the soul speaks in the first two verses of the stanzas, and Jesus in the last two. Inspired by F. J. Billeskov Jansen's discussion of Brorson's *Svane-Sang,* one could call this style "Pietistic Rococo." The erotic vocabulary of Pietism appears here side by side with the rhetorical refinement of Rococo. The syntax moves almost aggressively with its small leaps over the verbs and in this way reinforces the many repetitions–the *exclamatio* (exclamation): "Saa kom Due!" (Come here, dove!); the *chiasmus* (reversed repetition): "Du min Sulamith, Sulamith. Ja mit" (You my Shulamite, Shulamite. Yes mine), with a change in syllabic stress; the *hyperbaton* (reversed word order): "du min skal blive her og hist" (you mine shall be here and yonder); the assonance and alliterations.

In *Svane-Sang* the ornamental and pretentious style of the Rococo seems to force the Pietistic, naive tone of the earlier collection, *Troens rare Klenodie,* into the background. Nevertheless, one sees a connection between the metric and figurative restlessness and the impatient overuse of possessive pronouns in these poems: the language of the soul is distracted, nearly manic, in its emptiness, precisely because the soul has ended up in a place where it can only repeat itself. In this sense the poem also deals with silence. It is speaking in tongues.

"Her vil ties, her vil bies" includes no indication of a dialogue exchange; however, scholars agree that stanzas 1, 3, 5, and 6 represent the voice of Jesus, whereas two and four are expressions of the soul. The poem opens with a prayer for silence and patience, which–given the use of the exclamation mark–may be understood as a hidden imperative:

Her vil ties, her vil bies
Her vil bies, o svage Sind!

(Silence heeded, waiting needed
Waiting needed, o fragile soul!)
(Translation by Steven T. Murray)

The poem is markedly different from "Hvad est du dog skiøn, ja skiøn" in that it depicts the cycle of nature–the transition from winter to summer–and lets it emphasize the divine movement from the "Trange Tider" (difficult times), which "Langsom skrider" (slowly move), over "Forsommers Minde" (the memory of summer) and all the way forward to "Stunden" (the moment), which has "næsten oprunden" (almost arrived). The poem ends, or rather, becomes silent just before Judgment Day and death. Brorson has created silence and patience as the themes for the poem already in the first verse. It may be understood as *vekselsang* (an antiphony) of the soul, not as a harsh doubting of Jesus' words, which make up most of the poem, but on the contrary, as a prophecy of precisely that which the poem cannot produce–silence. In this way the period of waiting is reflected in the lyrical repetition and redundancy of the poem. This idea is also represented in the composition of the hymn, in which the first and third verses are repeated in the second and fourth verses. Thus, by means of these poetic devices, the conclusion of the poem beckons a return to the beginning. The cyclical infinity of the poem on a thematic level creates a redundancy in its stylistic composition; neither the language, nor the soul's longing, nor Nature's wonders can exceed it. Brorson's lyrical masterpiece "Her vil ties, her vil bies" betrays an aesthetic sophistication and an increasingly emotional religious passion. *Svane-Sang* recalls the piety of Danish Baroque lyric, but at the same time its unusual personal religious sentiment ensures it a central position in Danish devotional literature.

Bishop Hans Adolph Brorson died on 3 June 1764; he lies buried inside Ribe Cathedral and is memorialized by a statue by sculptor A. V. Saabye, which stands outside the cathedral. During his lifetime Brorson was considered by his contemporaries as being as important to the eighteenth century as Thomas Kingo had been to the seventeenth century. Many of Brorson's original hymns were included in the official Lutheran hymnal of Denmark, *Den nye Psalme-Bog* (The New Hymnal), edited by Erik Pontoppidan, when it was published in 1740. However, despite that it appeared in seven editions between 1739 and 1767, *Troens Rare Klenodie* never became the official hymnal of the Danish Church. Because it was long the practice to omit the name of the hymn writer, Brorson was for a time after his death nearly forgotten in the Danish Lutheran Church, although his hymns always remained popular in Pietistic circles in Denmark and Norway, and certainly in his native *Sønderjylland.* In approximately 1820 his hymns began to re-emerge in the Danish Church, and from that point on, his national reputation grew steadily. Finally, with the publication of *Den danske salmebog* (The Danish Hymnal) in 1953, which followed the reunification of *Sønderjylland* in 1920 with Denmark and the merging of that region's specific hymn tradition with the established Danish canon, Brorson secured a solid position as one of the greatest hymn writers of Denmark.

Biographies:

Laurids Johannes Koch, *Hans Adolf Brorson* (Copenhagen: Schønberg, 1920);

Koch, *Salmedigteren Brorson. En Mindebog til Tohundredeaaret for Hans Julesalmer* (Copenhagen: Lohse, 1932);

Koch, "Hans Adolph Brorson," in *Dansk biografisk leksikon,* volume 2, edited by Svend Cedergreen Bech (Copenhagen: Gyldendal, 1979–1983), pp. 566–569;

Erik A. Nielsen, "Hans Adolf Brorson," in *Dansk forfatterleksikon: Biografier,* edited by John Christian Jørgensen (Copenhagen: Rosiante, 2001), pp. 64–65.

References:

Vilhelm Andersen, "Den yndigste Rose–Et Omrids af Skønhedsfølelsens Historie i dansk Digtning," *Dansk Tidsskrift* (1902);

Steffen Arndal, *H. A. Brorsons liv og salmedigtning* (Frederiksberg: Religionspædagogisk Center, 1994);

Arndal, "Hans Adolf Brorson: Forfatterportræt," *Arkiv for Dansk Litteratur* <http://www.adl.dk>;

Arndal, *"Den store hvide flok vi see . . ." H. A. Brorson og tysk pietistisk vækkelsessang* (Odense: Odense University Press, 1989);

Arthur Arnholtz, "Brorsons Sangkunst," in his *I Svane-Sangens to-hundredeår* (Aarhus, 1965);

Arnholtz, "Brorsons Svanesang," *Dansk Kirkesangs Aarskrift* (1943): 44–74;

Georg Brandes, "Sønderjyllands Betydning for dansk Kultur," in his *Samlede Skrifter,* volume 7 (Copenhagen: Gyldendal, 1901), pp. 236–252;

Thomas Bredsdorff, *Digternes natur. En idés historie i 1700–tallets danske poesi* (Copenhagen: Gyldendal, 1975);

Hans Brix, *Tonen fra Himlen. Billeder af den kristelige Lyrik* (Copenhagen: Gyldendal, 1912);

Knud Eyvin Bugge and Th. Borup Jensen, *Salmen som lovsang og litteratur,* 2 volumes (Copenhagen: Gyldendal, 1972);

Johan de Mylius, *Anskuelsesformer. Træk af dansk litteraturhistorie,* volume 1 (Odense: Odense University Press, 1991);

Jan Ulrik Dyrkjøb, ed., *Brorson: en bog i 300-året for salmedigterens fødsel* (Frederiksberg: ANIS, 1994);

Jørgen Elbek, "Brorsons jul og påske," in *Fantasiens naturhistorie,* edited by Arndal (Aarhus: Husets Forlag, 1995), pp. 272–282;

Bo Green Jensen, "Den sagte Bevægelses liflige Vind. Om Brorsons rosenbilleder og højsangssymbolik," in *Fra Nexø til Saxo. Een snes essays af gode læsere* (Copenhagen: DSL/C. A. Reitzel, 1986), pp. 124–134;

Laurids Johannes Koch, *Brorson-Studier* (Copenhagen: Lohse, 1936);

Koch, *Hans Adolf Brorson og hans Psalmer* (Copenhagen: Frimodt, 1918);

Anders Malling, *Dansk Salmehistorie,* volume 6 (Copenhagen: Schultz, 1962), pp. 98–125;

Anne Marie Petersen, *Kom min due. Hans Adolph Brorson og hans salmer* (Odense: Odense University Press, 2000);

Dan Ringgaard, "Brorsons lyrik," in *At gå til grunde. Sider af romantikkens litteratur og tænkning,* edited by Anne-Marie Mai and Bo Kampmann Walther (Odense: Odense University Press, 1997), pp. 75–96;

Harald Vilstrup, "Digteren Hans Adolph Brorson," *Vartovbogen* (1952): 88–122;

Bo Kampmann Walther, "Roser og himmelduer. Hans Adolph Brorson: Salmer og digte," in *Læsninger i dansk litteratur,* volume 1, edited by Ulrik Lehrmann and Lise Præstgaard Andersen (Odense: Odense University Press, 1998), pp. 177–193;

Walther, "Stille øjeblikke. Et essay om Kierkegaard, Brorson og forunderlige naturlakuner," *Edda,* 1 (1998): 3–19.

Papers:

Hans Adolph Brorson's papers are at the National Archives in Copenhagen.

Sophus Claussen

(12 September 1865 - 11 April 1931)

Lise Præstgaard Andersen
University of Southern Denmark

(Translated by Gillian Fellows-Jensen)

BOOKS: *Naturbørn* (Copenhagen: Reitzel, 1887);

Unge Bander. Fortællinger fra en Købstad. Med et lyrisk Forspil: "Frk. Regnvejr" (Copenhagen: Kihl & Langkjær, 1894);

Kitty. Lyrisk Fortælling (Copenhagen: Gyldendal, 1895);

Antonius i Paris. Hans Optegnelser ved Sophus Claussen (Copenhagen: Gyldendal, 1896);

Valfart (Copenhagen: Gyldendal, 1896);

Arbejdersken. Skuespil i tre Akter (Copenhagen: Gyldendal, 1898);

Pilefløjter (Copenhagen: Schubothe, 1899)–includes "I en Frugthave," translated by Lee Marshall as "In an Orchard," in *Anthology of Danish Literature,* edited by F. J. Billeskov Jansen and P. M. Mitchell (Carbondale: Southern Illinois University Press, 1964), pp. 577–579;

Mellem to Kyster. Fortællinger og Satirer (Copenhagen: Schubothe, 1899);

Byen. I: Junker Firkløver. Nutidsroman (Copenhagen: Schubothe, 1900);

Trefoden (Copenhagen: Schubothe, 1901);

Mina. Et Digt om Byen (Copenhagen: Schubothe, 1902);

Djævlerier (Copenhagen: Gyldendal, 1904);

Eroter og Fauner. En Række Digte (Copenhagen: Gyldendal, 1910);

Danske Vers (Copenhagen: Gyldendal, 1912)–includes "Imperia," translated by Henry Meyer as "Imperia," in *Anthology of Danish Literature,* edited by Billeskov Jansen and Mitchell (Carbondale: Southern Illinois University Press, 1964), pp. 579–581;

Frøken Regnvejr. Unge Bander. Anden Udgave (Copenhagen: Gyldendal, 1912);

Fabler (Copenhagen: Gyldendal, 1917);

Løvetandsfnug (Copenhagen: Gyldendal, 1918);

Samlede Værker, 7 volumes (Copenhagen: Gyldendal, 1918);

Heroica (Copenhagen: Gyldendal, 1925);

Courtesy of the Danish Royal Library, Copenhagen

Titania holdt Bryllup (Copenhagen: Levin & Munksgaard, 1927);

Foraarstaler (Copenhagen: Gyldendal, 1927);

Fortællingen om Rosen (Copenhagen: Gyldendal, 1927);

Hvededynger (Copenhagen: Gyldendal, 1930).

Editions and Collections: *Udvalgte digte,* selected and edited by Inger Claussen and Carl Bergstrøm-Nielsen (Copenhagen: Gyldendal, 1952);

Jord og sjæl. Erindringer, noveller og litterær journalistik, edited by Stig Krabbe Barfoed (Copenhagen: Gyldendal, 1961);

Pilefløjter (Copenhagen: Gyldendal, 1968);

Det aandelige overskud. Journalistik i udvalg, edited by Lise Brinch Petersen and Mogens Rukov (Copenhagen: Gyldendal, 1971);

Sophus Claussens lyrik, 9 volumes, edited by Jørgen Hunosøe (Copenhagen: Gyldendal, 1982–1984);

Unge Bander. Fortællinger fra en Købstad. Med et lyrisk Forspil: "Frk. Regnvejr," edited by Hunosøe (Copenhagen: DSL/Borgen, 1986);

Antonius i Paris; Valfart, edited by Hunosøe and Esther Kielberg (Copenhagen: DSL/Borgen, 1990);

Notater og skitser, edited by Keld Zeruneith (Copenhagen: Gyldendal, 1993);

Samlede digte, 4 volumes, edited by Hunosøe (Copenhagen: Gyldendal, 2000).

TRANSLATION: *Den følende Blomst: efter Shelley's "The Sensitive Plant"* (Copenhagen: Gyldendal, 1906).

Sophus Claussen, one of the greatest lyricists of Denmark, is widely regarded as the poet who, though a symbolist, nevertheless heralded modernism. But he also tried to retain a romantic view of the poet as an almost prophetic figure who could merge the disparate elements of modernity into a harmonious whole: "Ak giv mig som Afgrunds- / og Himmel-Stormer- / det Greb, som kan knytte de tusinde Former" (Oh give me as Titan of the Abyss / and of the Heavens / that grasp which can unite a thousand forms), he wrote in the poem "Nætter" (Nights, 1901). In a manner similar to that of other fin de siècle poets, he reached to the utmost extremes in his poems, often associating opposites such as life and death, cold and heat, and conflict and love. Many great Danish writers are indebted to him–among them, Tom Kristensen, Karen Blixen, and Thorkild Bjørnvig. Influential professor of Danish literature Aage Henriksen has even made Claussen a kind of key figure in his controversial doctrine of the artist's remarkable talent for sublimation. Another indication of the continuing relevance of Claussen is the consistent scholarly attention to his literary production since the 1980s.

In his youth, Claussen occupied a central position in Danish letters by his association with the circle of lyrical poets–including Johannes Jørgensen and Viggo Stuckenberg, who heralded Danish symbolism with their literary periodical *Taarnet* (The Tower, 1893–1894). The journal opposed the program of Georg Brandes and the Modern Breakthrough of the 1870s, which had encouraged socially relevant topics in prose and drama. Instead, the young editors of *Taarnet* professed an adherence to the irrational, to religion and mysticism, to dreaming and yearning, and to lyrical poetry. Claussen's contribution to Danish literature is first and foremost his erotic poetry, although according to modern tastes, his work is characterized by a conspicuous cultivation of the femme fatale, which he shared with many contemporary artists and authors. Claussen's poetry includes a whole gallery of women, ranging from the cold and dismissive ice queen, conscious of her own power (who sometimes takes the shape of the merciless, chaste huntress Artemis/Diana), to the depraved, beguiling witch and provocative, devil-may-care whore, who apparently represent pure sensuality but somehow have to be coolly calculating as well–and at all events appeal to the desire for barrier-breaking behavior and defiance against respectability. Claussen's praise of women is directed to the apparently powerful woman, who is best worshiped from afar, by no means the ingenue preferred by the Romantics. Thus, he properly considered himself a progressive and modern man, but his poems nevertheless reflect an old-fashioned view of women's liberation (meaning the contemporary radical women's movement fighting for social and intellectual freedom for women) as an expression of disappointed eroticism. For example, in the poem "Kvindebevægelse" (Feminism), in *Fabler* (Fables, 1917): "Hver Gang et Ønske glipped–en Mand slap dem af Hænderne– / de krænkede Kvinder, de ruster sig til tænderne" (Every time a wish was disappointed–a man dropped them / the offended women, they armed themselves to the teeth).

According to Claussen, the woman's role first and foremost is to challenge and arouse the man erotically and poetically. But even if the reader does not especially care for this point of view, one must admit that Claussen's poems reflect a deep and lifelong fascination with womankind.

Sophus Niels Christen Claussen was born on 12 September 1865 in Langeland, a beautiful island to the south of Fuen. He was the son of politician and newspaper owner Rasmus Claussen, who had risen from tenant farmer to member of Parliament, representing the farmer's party, Venstre (Liberal), and who ended up as chairman of the Danish Parliament, and his wife, Hanne Sophie Hendriksen. The family moved to Falster, an island south of Zealand, when Sophus Claussen was five years old, so that his father, who continued his farming activities, could be nearer to his work in the Parliament in Copenhagen. Claussen retained throughout his life traces of the dialect of the southern islands, which does not have the glottal stop so characteristic of standard Danish; this manner of speech gave his reading of his own poems a charming and melodious intonation.

After passing his secondary-school examinations in 1884 and undertaking a journey through Germany, Claussen dutifully began to study law. This course of study, however, was broken off a couple of years later. Of greater significance for his subsequent career was his contact with the literary movement associated with Brandes and the radical *Studentersamfundet* (Student Society). In this context, Claussen also met Jørgensen and Stuckenberg, with whom he struck up a close friendship and intense spiritual fellowship. Stuckenberg's fiancée and later wife, Ingeborg Pamperin, came to function as a muse for the circle of friends.

During his first year at the university, Claussen fell in love with a *caberet* singer named Mary, whose capricious nature–according to him–forced him over into the world of fantasy and poetry. The relationship is reflected in the collection of poems *Naturbørn* (Children of Nature, 1887), which aroused scandal because of the nonchalant, offhand remark that it was better to kiss a hundred girls once than one girl a hundred times. Subsequent relationships repeated the pattern of his love affair with Mary. What went wrong between Claussen and his women, however, is difficult to understand. Were the young women capricious, or did the problems simply reflect that they, reasonably enough, protected their virtue to avoid becoming social outcasts? As a good radical, Claussen was always opposed to the strict sexual morality of his time, but nevertheless he little by little unconsciously became addicted to one of the consequences of this morality–that the coquettishness of the girls led to a power game. For Claussen a woman's coquetry became a prerequisite for his being attracted to or falling in love with her. His enraptured ovations to this type of woman in his poetry, first and foremost, and his biography make this requirement clear. Sometimes he felt that the charming unpredictability of women corresponded to something in himself: The best-known example of this attitude derives from an early poem, "Sang" (Song, 1885), later published in *Danske Vers* (Danish Verses, 1912). In "Sang" the loved one is described as pure and delicate: "Du er som Skummet paa Vandet" (You are like the foam on the water), but she also embodies vampire features: "Jo mere blodfattig Læben, desmere tørster den Blod" (The more anemic the lip is, the more it thirsts for blood). The concluding line includes the paradoxical confession of adherence to "den høje / Foragt i Stemme og Øje / hos én, der er slet, som jeg selv" (The deep / contempt in the voice and eye / of one who is evil as I myself). All the variants of Claussen's femme fatale figures are found in the work of Carl Gustav Jung, who calls these female figures "negative anima-projections" (in contrast to the positive ones: Madonna and Eve)–that is, the offshoots of a man's own inmost femininity.

As a young man, Claussen shared with fellow poets Jørgensen and Stuckenberg an admiration for Brandes and his work, even though these poets later formulated their own aesthetic program in opposition to Brandes. Such admiration for Brandes was common at the time among intellectuals, and Claussen in his own way always retained that feeling. He wrote several small poems in praise of Brandes. One example is "Den skønne Propaganda" (Beautiful Propaganda) in *Antonius i Paris* (Anthony in Paris, 1894). Claussen also maintained ties with the progressive Venstre environment of his childhood in other ways. In the course of time his father built up a considerable fortune through his newspaper business, which supported the Venstre party. This fortune made possible Claussen's travels in Italy and France and gave him his ability to take up residence abroad for long periods. Nevertheless, Claussen continued to work, even if only sporadically, for his father's newspaper empire, and he later ran it in partnership with his brothers-in-law. The newspaper *Lolland-Falsters Folketidende* (The Lolland-Flaster's People's Times) reaped the greatest benefit from Claussen's journalistic efforts, but as a young man he also put considerable effort into *Horsens Folkeblad* (The Horsens People's Paper)–where he was employed in 1886 with the deliberate aim of provoking the conservative citizens of the town–and later on during the years 1888–1891 he was employed by *Nyborg Dagblad* (The Nyborg Daily). Both these periods of employment had far-reaching personal consequences for Claussen.

In Horsens at Christmas of 1886, Claussen announced his engagement to Anna Catherine Christensen. Later in Nyborg, while he tried to recover from the breaking off of this engagement, he experienced an extremely productive period for his lyrical composition. Although Claussen finally married Anna Christensen ten years later, their relationship was plagued from the beginning by quarrels and reconciliation. The story of Claussen's engagement to Christensen is rendered in fictional form in his first novel, *Unge Bander* (Young Gangs, 1894). The work depicts an impetuous young Venstre journalist who gradually forgets his political commitment because of his romantic interests, which are divided between a mature, provocative woman–compared in the text to an alluring mermaid–and a chaste, provincial girl. He associates the chaste girl, Margrete, with the Roman goddess of the hunt, Diana, and he never succeeds in becoming close to her in spite of an official engagement.

After his years working for *Nyborg Dagblad,* Claussen traveled to Paris in 1892. In France he met the

SOPHUS CLAUSSEN

VALFART

KØBENHAVN

GYLDENDALSKE BOGHANDELS FORLAG (F. HEGEL & SØN)

TRYKT HOS J JØRGENSEN & CO. (M. A. HANNOVER)

1896

Title page for the prose work in which Claussen's best-known poem, "Ekbátana," was first published (Suzzallo Library, University of Washington)

French symbolist poets Paul Verlaine and Stéphane Mallarmé; he also became involved in a new love affair, almost identical to the previous ones. As far as the affair can be judged from glimpses in the later prose works *Antonius i Paris* and *Valfart* (Pilgrimage, 1896), the young woman, Karen Topsøe, was willing to be adored and gave Claussen the impression that the two shared a special spiritual bond, but she consistently avoided taking a clear stand on the question of a carnal or civil union. After his frustrating amorous experiences in Paris, Claussen fled to Italy in 1894, where he had a happy love affair with a generous woman named Clara Robinsson. Both Célimène (cover name for Topsøe) and Clara (as she is also called in the novel) are referred to in these early novels as "dronninger" (queens), Claussen's favorite word for describing elegant and dashing ideal women. In contrast to Célimène, Clara is willing and quickly allows the principal male character, Silvio, to take her to bed. Silvio claims to be able to recognize in Clara's face the countenance of the Madonna herself as it appears in Michelangelo's famous sculpture *Pietá,* in which the Virgin Mary, in sublime resignation, accepts her loss and mourns over her crucified son. This image is perhaps not a good omen for a relationship between man and woman in which mind and body are to merge in a synthesis. Such a union is what Silvio is looking for. Although he claims that Clara is able to mix "pure" and "impure" in a magnificent way, she is, however, sacrificed at the end. Silvio abandons her as her insolvent debtor, after the wounds inflicted on him by Célimène have been healed and after he, with Clara's help, "har gjort sin Vilje rede til alt stort" (has prepared his will for everything great).

In reality, the story of Clara's abandonment was even less flattering for Claussen. He allowed himself to be forced by his angry father to abandon Clara, whose surviving letters indicate that she believed that Claussen would return to her. In her letters she also claims to be pregnant. Claussen's replies were evasive, and finally he stopped replying to her letters. Clara probably was not the great love of his life, as some scholars have thought, but the reflection of her figure–the proud, generous, and ruthless woman–either in the form of a queen or in a more deranged form as a witch, appears later in Claussen's poetry, most clearly in *Djævlerier* (Devilries, 1904) but in fact down to the poem "Digteren og Daarskaben" (The Poet and the Folly) from 1916. After this time a kind of reconciliation with the thrilling female figure seems to have taken place, or perhaps simply an abandonment of the attempt to cope with sex between man and woman. Claussen made himself be satisfied with "Fantasia," the poetic creative power that was in him, when the real women were inadequate.

While traveling in Italy, Claussen met the friend of his youth, Jørgensen. In Rapallo they carried on an intense debate for several days about their philosophies of life. Jørgensen, who was in process of conversion to Catholicism, tried to convince his friend that to locate the undogmatic mysticism of their youth in the well-defined Catholic church would be right. Claussen, however, protested with the words "mod min Ven som mod en Voldsmand" (against my friend as against a thug). A significant part of their shared youthful rebellion had been the atheism advocated by Brandes, although they had both considered that Brandes's rationalism was not sufficiently profound. That Jørgensen was now about to commit himself to the Catholic church, however, probably made Claussen look upon his friend as a renegade. This view was later unambiguously expressed by the Stuckenbergs, particularly by the uncompromising Ingeborg. Claussen was perhaps more understanding and tolerant–his poems in hexameters, published later in *Heroica* (1925), about Jørgensen suggest this view. At all events, Claussen refused to allow himself to be pressed into a dogmatic religion, which he considered to be sexually hostile, at least according to Jørgensen's interpretation. Claussen claimed, on the contrary, that earthly love could be the way to a higher spirituality.

After his return from his journey to France and Italy, Claussen was appointed editor of one of his father's newspapers, and on 12 September 1896 he married the woman to whom he had earlier been engaged, Anna Christensen, from Horsens. The marriage soon resulted in the birth of two girls but proved unsatisfying to the restless husband after only a couple of years. Claussen seems to have been in love with the Madonna herself, and no earthly woman could ever satisfy him. Not only was he in love with the Madonna, but he was also infatuated with her demonic counterpart, a more refined and complex female fantasy figure, who as early as 1896 appears in the poem "Valfart" (which has the same title as the prose work), in which are sung the praises of the depraved and thrilling Mylady (from Alexandre Dumas *père*'s *The Three Musketeers* [1844–1845]). At any rate, his wife could not live up to his fantasies, which embodied a complex dream-woman able to heal all the schisms in man and at the same time remain an eternally alluring riddle.

While Claussen may not have been lucky with women in his own life, his poetry flourished in recompense. He described the dilemma as follows: first he loved a girl; then he loved the dream of her, until in the end even the dream was consumed. Some critics have seen Claussen as an example of a poet who devours real life in order to produce art. He would rather write poetry about being in love than possess the girl herself. Henriksen and his disciples are representative adherents of this psychological interpretation of Claussen's work. It is linked with oriental esoteric beliefs, according to which erotic inhibition is supposed to promote inspiration, a belief that Claussen perhaps adapted from contemporary French literary circles during his visits to Paris. That Claussen was not entirely unaffected by the late-nineteenth-century interest in Eastern religions is suggested by his poem "Buddha" in the collection *Pilefløjter* (Willow Pipes, 1899). This poem, however, stands isolated in his production with its longing for Nirvana. That Claussen may not have cared for a too earthbound eroticism is suggested by several poems, including one that remained unpublished in his lifetime but is dated Rome, 5 May 1894, titled "Raad til en Kvinde fra det syttende Aarhundrede" (Advice to a Seventeenth-Century Woman) with the verse: "Svimlende ved Himlens Porte / vil et alt for jordisk Krav / strække os tilintetgjorte / paa vor unge Elskovs Grav" (Floating at the Gate of Heaven / a too earthly demand will leave us / stretched out annihilated / on the grave of our young love).

Alongside his career as a poet, Clausen remained professionally involved with the press, and he even stuck to the radical political views of his youth. As late as 1905–the year of his father's death–he applied for the post of chief editor of the daily newspaper *Politiken,* although without success. Later the same year he was present at the founding of the political party Det radikale Venstre (the Radical Liberal party). This political engagement, which may seem slightly surprising to the readers who know Claussen first and foremost as a symbolist poet, not only earned him his living but was undoubtedly also completely sincere on his part. The discrepancy between politics and soulful poetry must have been obvious to Claussen himself, and throughout his life he attempted to overcome a more fundamental schism by trying to reconcile reality with poetry. One of the manifestations of this view was the drama *Arbejdersken* (The Female Worker, 1898), in which he tried in vain to unite social indignation with a poetical-symbolical form of expression; the drama was a complete failure.

Claussen's undoubted major works are his great volumes of collected poetry. In them he displays himself as one of the foremost lyric poets in Danish literature, particularly in *Pilefløjter, Djævlerier, Danske Vers, Fabler* (Fables, 1917), and *Heroica.* As indicated by the titles, the mood on the whole is lighter and brighter in *Pilefløjter* than in the next major work, *Djævlerier. Pilefløjter* includes such gems as the stanza that forms the motto: "Over mit hoved / slaar Tungsindets Fugl, / dens natbrede Vinger / beskygger min Sjæl, / naar jeg tænker paa, / hun var ung og fin / med et Blik, der beruste / som nygæret Vin" (Over my head the bird of melancholy beats its night-broad wings, shadows my soul, when I consider that she was young and fine with an expression that was as inebriating as newly fermented wine) or "Hvidtjørn" (Hawthorn): "Brune, skumle Kør, som gumle / Aftengræsning efter Regn! / Hvidtjørn, lille vilde Hvidtjørn / dufter I det store Hegn" (Brown, somber cows munching, evening grazing after rain! Mayflower, little wild mayflower, fragrant in the great hedge); the wet and thorny but freshly blooming plant becomes a picture of both the cool but promising Danish summer and the shy girl who in spite of all has bravely turned up for an assignation. The paradoxical metaphors and the contradictory moods apply not only to the woman and love but also to the chilly Danish spring, which at Easter time is nevertheless pervaded by an all-embracing longing: "Paaske–de graablaa Dage, / Vaarsæd og Naaletræer / Bøgeskoven visnet, / isnet af Foraars-Begær!" (Easter–the grey-blue days, / spring corn and coniferous trees, / the beech wood withered, / frozen by the craving for Spring!) as in "Evangelium." The poem concludes, however, with the adjuration: "Med Tiden vil Verden være / saa rig som i mit Begær" (In time the world shall become as rich as in my desire).

The collection *Djævlerier* is more somber and dominated by dark and seductive female figures. One of the more significant poems deals with "Sorte Blomst" (Black Flower), a devil-may-care and inconsiderate prostitute, who turns her bottom to the priest like a horse, an image similar to a contemporary painting by the Austrian artist Gustav Klimt titled *Goldfische.* In Claussen's poem, Black Flower is described as follows: "Hendes blod var vildt som den solviltre Dag / Letsind og Flammer, Ild og Bedrag. / Kul hendes Øje og Kul hendes Skød, / men hendes Attraa var Nellike-rød" (Her blood was as wild as the sun-frisky day / Improvidence and flames, fire and deceit. / Coal her eyes and coal her sex but her lust was carnation-red). Another poem has as its theme the figure of the witch. The title of this widely regarded poem is "Trappen til Helvede" (The Staircase to Hell); the staircase is searched for in vain in the hope of discovering genuine intensity: "Naar en ung og ugudelig Krop faar i Sinde / at elske en hæslig og ældet Kvinde, / hvis bedagede Pragt det er djævelsk at vinde.–er det ofte en yngre Lykke, han vrager / for en Hex, en Sibylle saa benradsmager / som Knokler og Skind og gravlagte Sager" (When a young and ungodly body takes it into its mind to love an ugly and aged woman / whose worn-out splendor it is devilish to win, / there is often a younger delight he abandons for a witch, a sibyl as skeletal / as skin and bones and buried effects). In this context, the paintings of another contemporary Austrian artist, Egon Schiele, come to mind. Although Claussen probably was not familiar with these artists, they share certain decadent artistic tastes of the fin de siècle period.

Danske Vers was published in 1912 after Claussen and his family had lived in Paris from 1902 to 1904 and again from 1906 to 1911, years during which Claussen suffered from a lack of poetic inspiration. In 1903, however, he had met a fellow Danish poet, Helge Rode, and Rode's wife, Edith, while traveling in Italy. Edith Rode assisted Claussen with secretarial help in editing *Danske Vers,* a collection that mainly consists of older works. These works include the incomparable memorial poem to Ingeborg Stuckenberg, the friend of his youth who had committed suicide in New Zealand. Claussen sees in her youthful dreams a parallel to his own dreams. But in the last stanza of the poem to Ingeborg, he concludes that "Der bliver saa fortvivlende lidt af saa meget: / kun Aandemusik" (So desperately little results from so much: / only the music of the spirit). The same collection of poems also includes the sardonic self-portrait "Skizze" (originally written in 1898), which describes how the poet chooses his proudest, most valuable experience with which to tear himself to bits like a rough draft. However, this mad behavior is designed for a higher purpose: "Han vil samle sit liv i et eneste Ord / af Solskin og Fryd–før han jævnes med Jord" (He wants to collect his life in one single word / of sunshine and joy–before he is razed to the ground).

In the collection *Fabler* one finds the splendid poem "Mennesket og Digteren" (The Person and the Poet), in which the art of poetry is first wittily reduced "at sige lidt med mange Ord" (to say a little in many words), but in which the triumphant conclusion says something completely different: "Rødt som Blodet, lyst som Solen, stærkt som Græsset er mit Ord, / let som Fuglen, frit som Folen, spiretungt som Vaarens Jord, duftende som Markens Kløver, vildt som Engens Blomsterrøver / Bien . . . følger mig mit Ord. Jeg har alt, hvad jeg behøver. Jeg er død, men om mit Spor svæver Livets Skaberord" (Red as blood, light as the sun, strong as the grass are my words, / light as the bird, free as the foal, ripe for germination as the earth of Spring, / fragrant as the clover of the field, wild as the flower-robber / the bee . . . my words accompany me. I have everything that I need. / I am dead but around my tracks float the creative words of Life). Claussen had already in 1892 contributed to the contemporary existentialist debate with a double article in the radical newspaper *København,* "Hvad Menneskene tror paa I–II" (What Human Beings Believe In), in which he claims to believe in "Love" and "Genius," which are associated with the heroic (that is, the transcendent) powers that human beings, or perhaps exceptional human beings, are able to mobilize against daily lethargy and conventions so that their lives are filled with greater quality, exuberance, and depth. Claussen was probably inspired by Friedrich Nietzsche, whom Brandes had presented in his lectures in 1888. A Nietzsche-derived inspiration is found in a couple of significant later poems, including "Imperia" (1912; translated as "Imperia," 1964) and "Digteren og Daarskaben," 1916 (The Poet and Folly, published in *Fabler*). An end of the world, at which the slate is wiped clean, is seen as a precondition for the creation of a new and better world–a scene of ruin and resurrection that occurred frequently in European poetry at the time of the outbreak of World War I, as, for example, in Henrik Pontoppidan's great novel *De dødes rige* (The Kingdom of the Dead, 1912–1916). "Imperia" applauds barren, uncultivated Nature, to the innermost poten-

J. F. Willumsen's 1915 painting of himself (center) and the poet Helge Rode listening to Claussen read "Imperia" from Claussen's 1912 volume Danske Vers *(from P. M. Mitchell,* A History of Danish Literature, *1957; Scandinavian Studies Library, University of Washington)*

tially explosive and pitiless core of the earth, which can only be made fertile by fire. A cosmic and catastrophic act of love is set in motion: "Alt er unyttigt undtagen vor Skælven" (Nothing is useful but for our throbbing), states the narrator of the poem, who concludes by acknowledging that "Kongernes Slot har jeg sænket i Havet, / slaaet den fattiges fattige Lykke i Skaar . . ." (Castles of kings I have sunk in the ocean, ruined the paupers' poor happiness, blind to their tears . . .). Imperia (the female ruler) is a gigantic variant of Claussen's powerful women, or perhaps an expression of that which he considered to be the female in himself, in this case the amoral creative potential, which was in possession of tremendous strength but had long lain dormant during a crisis in his production that extended from 1904 through 1917. The poem was first published in the periodical *Tilskueren* together with "Dronningen i Thule" (The Queen in Thule), a poem in praise of a murderess, namely Hamlet's mother, who with sublime consistency poisons her husband when she longs for a new lover. In "Digteren og Daarskaben" the idea of allying himself with destructive powers is exploited once more in order to achieve greater insight. In this poem a female figure, at the same time a "Profetinde og et bedårende Vrag" (Prophetess and an enchanting wreck) offers him all the glories of the world if only he will make love to her but frightens him away when he understands that the indiscriminate murders of the world war are also a reflection of the powers she possesses.

The culmination of the poetry of Claussen's old age is found in *Heroica,* in which his scruples seem to have calmed down. This change probably occurred under the influence of the admiration of young people, including his helpful young lover and assistant Inger Nielsen as well as a few young male poets who gradually came to show him due respect, namely Tom Kristensen and even the young Communists Hans Kirk and

Otto Gelsted. In the hexameters of "Atomernes oprør" (The Atoms' Rebellion) the poet is now in a position to fight chaos and achieve the artistic form that can subjugate all the rebellious atoms, which otherwise seem to be threatening to blow the world into pieces:

Som naar i Pampas en Gaucho med Lasso skal indfange Heste,
Samles fra Pegasus' Ryg de rimløse spand Hexametre,
Let uden skole og Tvang–kun lidt Pudsning af Fødder og Manke!

Rytteren bæres fornøjet af Versets heroiske Gangart,
Følger det følsomme Sexspand og lader det trave og springe.
Hjertet hos den der staar oprejst og snar i Bevægelsens Midte,
Smiler og tror paa Bedrifter fra glemte homeriske Tider.

(As on the prairie when cowboy with lasso must rope in the horses,
So too off Pegasus's back are the rhymeless hexameters herded,
Deftly without force or training [the hooves and the manes get some grooming]!

Pleased at the pace of heroical verses the rider is carried,
After the six frisky horses, and lets them both rear up and canter.
He who stands upright and cool in the midst of the turmoil, in heart he'll
Smile and believe in achievements related of Homer's lost ages.)
(Translation by Thomas Pettitt)

In spite of his central position in the avant-garde of the 1890s, Claussen felt for most of his life that he was misunderstood by the literary critics. They found his poetry difficult, "divided," and "blown to bits," and this opinion offended him deeply, since he actually aimed to make his poetry and his everyday life, dream and reality, consistent with one another, even if he occasionally declared his adherence unambiguously to the dreamworld. An example appears in his best-known poem, "Ekbátana," published in *Valfart.* The title refers to the nonexisting dreamland where human beings, in a state of euphoria, at the same time at rest and in action, can experience the highest and deepest states of happiness, grand passion, and poetry. In this poem, Claussen states that the ability to dream and to yearn is worth more than fulfillment. In the poem "Mennesket og Digteren," published in *Fabler,* he declares that his human Self has died while the poetic Self rises in magnificence over the defeat of reality and even dares to declare proudly that he is in possession of "the creative word" that is practically identical with God's own creating word. Nevertheless, his poetry, essays, notebooks, and private correspondence provide evidence of a lifelong search for unity: life should be filled with poetry, not the opposite of poetry. The expression of this idea is found, for example, in "Venedig" (Venice), published in *Djævlerier,* in which the poet imagines that the many conflicting impressions from the city will sound out together in a single fanfare "on a campaign-day, a feast-day." Similarly, this idea is found in the great hexameter hymns from the end of his career, first and foremost "Atomernes oprør," in which he complains that "alle Atomer forlanger at sættes i Frihed" (all atoms demand to be set free), at a time when Niels Bohr's epoch-making theories on the splitting of the atom were just being published. In this poem he turns against the increasing desire for emancipation during that period and ends by seeing in a vision the heathen god of nature, Pan, and "Gudsmoder og den lidende Kristus" (the Mother of God and the suffering Christ) sitting down at the table together.

Claussen's long marriage to Anna had been disharmonious and marked by travels and prolonged stays abroad, which his wife did not always want to take part in. In 1927, Anna asked for a separation, much to Claussen's amazement. A divorce was granted on 1 April 1931 when Claussen was terminally ill. Not until 10 April was he well enough to fulfill his promise to marry Inger Nielsen, his friend and assistant of many years, whom he had met in 1914. The next day, on 11 April 1931, Claussen died in his home in Gentofte, a northern suburb of Copenhagen.

That Sophus Claussen's works should actually have been found incomprehensible by his contemporaries seems peculiar. His poetry is characterized by paradoxes, composite imagery, and subtle comments, but it is also characterized by humor, roguishness, pathos, elegance, touching expressions of his joy over Denmark's nature, and erotic excitement. Nevertheless, contemporary critics repeatedly complained that his works could not be understood. Claussen did, in fact, have difficulty getting his works published. His major lyrical work *Pilefløjter,* for example, was not published until 1899, after it had first been rejected by Gyldendal, the leading publisher of Denmark–that is, eleven years after he had published his first collection of poems, *Naturbørn.* In the meantime his poems only appeared in periodicals and in his prose works. His literary contemporaries seem to have had a better ear for the religious content of Jørgensen's lyrical poetry and for Stuckenberg's heartfelt heroic lyrics than for Claussen's complex poetics; nevertheless, of the generation of poets who heralded a symbolism in Danish literature in the 1890s, posterity has come to value Claussen's innovative work most highly.

Letters:

Viggo Stuckenberg–Sophus Claussen. En Brevvexling, with introduction and notes by Johannes Brøndum-Nielsen (Copenhagen: Munksgaard, 1963);

Fra Ekbátana til Klareboderne. En brevbog om Sophus Claussen og hans forlæggere, edited by Frans Lasson (Copenhagen: Gyldendal, 1981);

Sophus Claussen og hans kreds. En digters liv i breve, 2 volumes, edited by Lasson (Copenhagen: Gyldendal, 1984);

Sophus Claussen og Inger Nielsen. Breve fra et venskab, edited by Lasson (Viborg: Nørhaven, 1984).

Bibliography:

Sophus Claussen. En bibliografi 1882–1981, edited by Tom Engelbrecht and René Herring, with an introduction by Thorkild Bjørnvig (Copenhagen: Centrum, 1982).

Biography:

Keld Zeruneith, *Fra klodens værksted. En biografi om Sophus Claussen* (Copenhagen: Gyldendal, 1992).

References:

Harry Andersen, *Studier i Sophus Claussens lyrik (Festskrift ugdivet af Københauns Universitet i anledning af universitetets årsfest november 1967)* (Copenhagen: Bianco Luno, 1967);

Lise Præstgaard Andersen, *Sorte Damer. Studier i femme fatale-motivet i dansk digtning fra romantik til århundredeskiftet* (Copenhagen: Gyldendal, 1990);

Søren Baggesen, *Seks sonderinger i den panerotiske linje i dansk lyrik* (Odense: Odense Universitetsforlag, 1997);

Ernst Frandsen, *Sophus Claussen,* 2 volumes (Copenhagen: Gyldendal, 1950);

Søren Hallar, *Sophus Claussen Studier* (Copenhagen: Athenæum, 1943);

Aage Henriksen, "Digtersfinxen. Et portræt af Sophus Claussen," in *Den erindrende faun* (Copenhagen: Fremad, 1968), pp. 179–191;

Henriksen, "Pavens Madonna. Fra Sophus Claussens ungdom," in *Det guddommelige barn og andre essays om Karen Blixen* (Copenhagen: Gyldendal, 1965);

Henriksen, "Svanereden," in *Svanereden. Essays, foredrag, debat* (Copenhagen: Amadeus, 1990);

Jørgen Hunosøe, *Gift med den sidste engel? Om Sophus Claussen* (Copenhagen: Amadeus, 1994);

Bo Hakon Jørgensen, *Maskinen, det heroiske og det gotiske–om Johs. V. Jensen, Sophus Claussen og århundredeskiftet* (Odense: Odense Universitetsforlag, 1977);

Jørgensen, *Symbolismen–eller jegets orfiske forklaring* (Odense: Odense Universitetsforlag, 1993);

Jørgensen and Jan Sand Sørensen, *Sophus Claussen–en studiebog* (Copenhagen: Gyldendal, 1977);

Tom Kristensen, *Sophus Claussen* (Copenhagen: Gyldendal, 1929);

P. M. Mitchell, *A History of Danish Literature* (Copenhagen: Gyldendal, 1957), pp. 200–201, 203–204, 225, 236, 272;

Gunnar Modvig, *Eros, kunst og socialitet. En analyse af de erotiske hovedmotivers udvikling i Sophus Claussens forfatterskab* (Copenhagen: Gyldendal, 1974);

Christian Refsum, *En verden av oversettelse: fransk og dansk symbolisme sett fra Taarnet 1893–94* (Oslo: Universitetsforlaget, 2001);

Christian Rimestad, "Sophus Claussen," in his *Fra Stuckenberg til Seedorff. Den lyriske Renæssance i Danmark,* volume 1 (Copenhagen: Pio, 1922), pp. 78–95;

Dan Ringgaard, *Den poetiske lækage. Sophus Claussens lyrik, rejsebøger og essayistik* (Copenhagen: Museum Tusculanum, 2000);

Helge Rode, "Sophus Claussen," in *Det sjælelige Gennembrud. Udvalgte Kritiker,* volume 2 (Copenhagen: Gyldendal, 1928), pp. 47–59;

Peer E. Sørensen, *Udløb i uendeligheden. Læsninger i Sophus Claussens lyrik* (Copenhagen: Gyldendal, 1997);

Rune Stefansson, "Chiasmens tale. En retorisk analyse af Sophus Claussens tale *Jord og Sjæl,*" *Spring,* 12 (1998): 132–142.

Papers:

Sophus Claussen's papers and manuscripts are at the Danish Royal Library in Copenhagen.

Holger Drachmann

(9 October 1846 - 14 January 1908)

Henk van der Liet
Universiteit van Amsterdam

BOOKS: *Med Kul og Kridt* (Copenhagen: Andr. Schou, 1872);

Digte (Copenhagen: Andr. Schou, 1872);

I Storm og Stille (Copenhagen: P. G. Philipsen, 1874);

Dæmpede Melodier (Copenhagen: Gyldendal, 1875);

En Overkomplet (Copenhagen: Gyldendal, 1876);

Derovre fra Grænsen (Copenhagen: Gyldendal, 1877);

Sange ved Havet–Venezia (Copenhagen: Gyldendal, 1877);

Tannhäuser (Copenhagen: Gyldendal, 1877);

Ungt Blod (Copenhagen: Høst, 1877);

Paa Sømands Tro og Love (Copenhagen: Gyldendal, 1878);

Prinsessen og det halve Kongerige (Copenhagen: Gyldendal, 1878);

Lars Kruse (Copenhagen: Gyldendal, 1879);

Poul og Virginie under nordlig Bredde (Copenhagen: Gyldendal, 1879); translated by Francis F. Browne as *Paul and Virginia of a Northern Zone* (Chicago: Way & Williams, 1895); republished as *Nanna, a Story of Danish Love* (Chicago: McClurg, 1901);

Ranker og Roser (Copenhagen: Gyldendal, 1879);

Ungdom i Digt og Sang (Copenhagen: Gyldendal, 1879);

Østen for Sol og Vesten for Maane (Copenhagen: Gyldendal, 1880);

Peder Tordenskjold (Copenhagen: Gyldendal, 1880);

Gamle Guder og nye, as Svend Trøst (Copenhagen: J. H. Schubothe, 1881);

Vandenes Datter (Copenhagen: Gyldendal, 1881);

Vildt og Tæmmet (Copenhagen: Gyldendal, 1881);

Puppe og Sommerfugl (Copenhagen: Gyldendal, 1882);

Rejsebilleder (Copenhagen: Gyldendal, 1882);

Skyggebilleder fra Rejser i Indland og Udland (Copenhagen: Gyldendal, 1883);

Strandbyfolk (Copenhagen: Gyldendal, 1883);

Dybe Strenge (Copenhagen: Gyldendal, 1884);

Lykken i Arenzano (Copenhagen: Gyldendal, 1884);

Smaa Fortællinger. Ældre og nye (Copenhagen: Gyldendal, 1884);

Danmark leve! (Copenhagen: Gyldendal, 1885);

Fjæld-Sange og Æventyr (Copenhagen: Gyldendal, 1885);

Holger Drachmann (photograph by Atelier Limon, Bad Harzburg; courtesy of the Danish Royal Library, Copenhagen)

Alkibiades eller Grækere i Forfald (Copenhagen: Gyldendal, 1886);

Med den brede Pensel (Copenhagen: Gyldendal, 1887);

Fest-Spil. I Hundredaaret efter de store Landbo-reformer og Stavnsbaandets Løsning (Copenhagen: Gyldendal, 1888);

To dramatiske Digte (Copenhagen: Gyldendal, 1888);

Sangenes Bog (Copenhagen: Gyldendal, 1889);

Tusind og en Nat (Copenhagen: Gyldendal, 1889);

Forskrevet (Copenhagen: Gyldendal, 1890);
Tarvis (Copenhagen: Gyldendal, 1891);
Unge Viser, as Svend Trøst (Copenhagen: J. H. Schubothe, 1892);
Bonifacius-Skæret (Copenhagen: Gyldendal, 1893);
Gøglere (Copenhagen: Gyldendal, 1893);
Renæssance (Copenhagen: Gyldendal, 1894); translated by Lee. M. Hollander as *Renaissance, Poet Lore,* 19, no. 4 (1908): 369–419;
Vølund Smed (Copenhagen: Gyldendal, 1894);
Kitzwalde (Copenhagen: J. H. Schubothe, 1895);
Melodramer (Copenhagen: Gyldendal, 1895);
Sømandshistorier (Copenhagen: Gyldendal, 1896);
Brav-Karl (Copenhagen: Gyldendal, 1897);
Gurre (Copenhagen: Gyldendal, 1898);
Kors og Kaarde (Copenhagen: Gyldendal, 1898);
Ungdomsdigte (Copenhagen: Gyldendal, 1898);
Den hellige Ild (Copenhagen: Gyldendal, 1899);
Dædalus (Copenhagen: Gyldendal, 1900);
Hallfred Vandraadeskjald (Copenhagen: Gyldendal, 1900);
Broget Løv (Copenhagen: Gyldendal, 1901);
Udvalgte Fortællinger (Copenhagen: Gyldendal, 1901);
Det grønne Haab (Copenhagen: Gyldendal, 1902);
Kirke og Orgel (Copenhagen: Gyldendal, 1904);
Den fattige Drengs Æventyr (Copenhagen: Gyldendal, 1905);
Kærlighedsdigte (Copenhagen: Gyldendal, 1905);
Hr. Oluf han rider (Copenhagen: Gyldendal, 1906);
Fortællinger (Copenhagen: Gyldendal, 1908);
Venezias Nat (Copenhagen: Gyldendal, 1909);
Vagabundus (Copenhagen: Gyldendal, 1910).

Editions and Collections: *Samlede poetiske Skrifter,* 12 volumes (Copenhagen: Gyldendal, 1906–1909);
Poetiske Skrifter, 10 volumes (Copenhagen: Gyldendal, 1911–1912);
Digte fra Hjemmet (Copenhagen: Gyldendal, 1921);
Femten Digte 1937, collected by Johannes Ursin, introduction by Paul V. Rubow (Copenhagen: Gyldendal, 1936);
Lyrik i Udvalg, edited by Morten Borup (Copenhagen: Gyldendal, 1938);
Digte og Sange, edited by Rubow (Copenhagen: Gyldendal, 1942);
Cimbrer og Teutoner, collected by Ursin (Copenhagen: Gyldendal, 1962);
Improvisation om bord, collected by Sten Kaalø (Copenhagen: Gyldendal, 1985);
Tag da disse friske sange, collected by Poul Bernth (Copenhagen: Carit Andersen, 1996).

Editions in English: *Sakuntala,* set for voice and orchestra by Frederick Delius (1889), translated by Rolf Kristian Stang (London: Delius Trust, 1993);
The Cruise of the "Wild Duck" and Other Tales, translated by H.C.M. (London: Unwin, 1893);
Byron in Homespun, translated by Jethro Bithell (London: G. G. Harrap, n.d.; New York: Brentano's, 1920);
The Fiddler, translated by Albert van Sand, *American-Scandinavian Review* (1921): 381;
Robert Burns. A Poem, translated by J. Christian Bay (Holstebro: Privately printed, 1925);
A Ship in Church, translated by Henry Commager, in *Denmark's Best Stories,* edited by Hanna Astrup Larsen (New York: American-Scandinavian Foundation/Norton, 1928), pp. 175–194;
The Wild Red Wine, translated by Charles Wharton Stork, *American-Scandinavian Review* (1929): 36;
The Bumble Bee, translated by C. V. Loye, *American-Scandinavian Review* (1932): 417;
Perilous Dreams, translation of "Farlige Drømme," *American-Scandinavian Review* (1946): 112;
Summer Landscape, translated and set for voice and piano by Frederick Delius (New York: Oxford University Press, 1952);
There Was Once, translated by Ellen Arendrup and W. H. Allderdice (N.p.: n.d.).

PLAY PRODUCTIONS: *Nytaarsaften,* by Drachmann and Edvard Brandes, Copenhagen, Kasino, 31 December 1873;
Prinsessen og det halve Kongerige, Oslo, Nationalteatret, 8 April 1880;
Puppe og Sommerfugl, Copenhagen, Det kongelige Teater, 24 September 1882;
Strandby Folk, Copenhagen, Det kongelige Teater, 10 April 1883;
Lykken i Arenzano, Copenhagen, Det kongelige Teater, 8 October 1884;
Der var engang, Copenhagen, Det kongelige Teater, 23 January 1887;
Efter Syndefaldet, Copenhagen, Det kongelige Teater, 30 November 1887;
Esther, Copenhagen, Dagmarteatret, 31 August 1889;
Ved Bosporus, Copenhagen, Det kongelige Teater, 4 December 1891;
Amor triumphans, Copenhagen, Folketeatret, 1 December 1892;
Tusind og en Nat, Copenhagen, Dagmarteatret, 18 December 1892;
Dansen paa Koldinghus, Copenhagen, Dagmarteatret, 24 April 1894;
Snefrid, Mannheim, Hof Theater, 1 September 1895;
Middelalderlig, Copenhagen, Det kongelige Teater, 9 October 1896;
Vølund Smed, Copenhagen, Det kongelige Teater, 13 March 1898;

Naar Klostermuren brydes, Copenhagen, Dagmarteatret, 1 November 1898;
Gurre, Oslo, Nationalteatret, 26 March 1900;
Renæssance, Copenhagen, Dagmarteatret, 9 November 1901;
Brav-Karl, Stuttgart, Hof Theater, 19 October 1903;
Det grønne Haab, Copenhagen, Frederiksberg Teater, 7 October 1904;
Den fattige Drengs Æventyr, Aarhus, Aarhus Teater, 2 April 1905;
Hr. Oluf han rider, Copenhagen, Det kongelige Teater, 9 October 1906;
Hallfred Vandraadeskjald, Copenhagen, Dagmarteatret, 3 November 1906;
Bonifacius-Skæret, Copenhagen, Dagmarteatret, 12 March 1910.

TRANSLATIONS: Jules Barbier and Michel Carré, *Romeo og Julie* (Copenhagen: Kgl. Musikhandel, 1888);
George Gordon, Lord Byron, *Don Juan,* 2 volumes (Copenhagen: J. H. Schubothe, 1902).

Holger Drachmann made his official debut as a writer in 1872 and was a prolific artist until his death in 1908. During most of this period, his contemporaries regarded him, as he himself did, as *the* national Danish poet par excellence. In the eyes of many of his countrymen, Holger Drachmann was the Danish alternative to such famous Scandinavian contemporaries as Bjørnstjerne Bjørnson, Henrik Ibsen, and August Strindberg. But in contrast to these authors, and despite his pursuit of literary fame, Drachmann never was able to gain a level of international recognition that could equal theirs. In his own country, though, Drachmann's renown was undisputed and lasted until his death. The enthusiasm evinced for Drachmann's work by his fellow countrymen during his lifetime turned out to be fleeting, and in the decades succeeding his death, a slow but unstoppable decline in the popularity and recognition of his oeuvre took place.

Nevertheless, Drachmann's name still has a familiar ring to most Danes. This recognition results to some extent from his affiliation with the literary movement of which critic Georg Brandes was the embodiment–the so-called Modern Breakthrough of Scandinavian literature. Other reasons that Drachmann is still remembered and still appeals to the imagination of many contemporary Danes are his once much-discussed, notoriously bohemian lifestyle and his tempestuous love life. In the eyes of the public at large, he was, and still is, perceived as *the* bohemian poet of his time. The tenacious biographical mythology accompanying this image has outlived the author and today overshadows his literary legacy. Only a few of his works have remained popular–a play and a handful of his poems that were set to music and, as songs, belong to the most-treasured in the Danish singing tradition.

Drachmann's body of work is one of the most voluminous in all of Danish nineteenth-century literature, only paralleled by the work of N. F. S. Grundtvig, Hans Christian Andersen, and Søren Kierkegaard. Approximately sixty books and many smaller publications appeared during Drachmann's lifetime; they cover a wide range of genres: poetry, drama, novels, stories, essays, travelogues, journalism, translations, and more. Furthermore, Drachmann was a productive visual artist too. He was a skillful painter and often illustrated his own works.

Reflecting the turbulent atmosphere of the late nineteenth century, Drachmann's work expresses the loss of traditional values, decomposition of genre, and the appearance of new forms of artistic expression and reception. In his prose and poetry, relicts of Romanticism and the first signs of modernity battle each other, just as they did in late-nineteenth-century European society and culture.

Drachmann kept writing feverishly until his death, always in search of new sources of inspiration, often personified by new female acquaintances. Impulsive and endowed with an extremely receptive–and at times "nervous"–mind, he was one of the most sensitive writers in his day. He registered and expressed the turbulence and restlessness that accompanied the transformation of Danish society from relatively rural toward modern and more urban. This atmosphere fitted his dualistic personality, which contemporaries often judged as inconsistent. Later criticism has characterized the ambiguity of Drachmann's work and psyche as a typical mixture of late-nineteenth-century Romanticism and early-twentieth-century modernity. His special position–as an intermediary between epochs and literary paradigms–is the reason for Drachmann's distinctive place in Danish literary history and the key to the fascinating dynamics in his work, as well as to its fall from grace in the twentieth century.

Holger Henrik Herholdt Drachmann was the eldest son of A. G. Drachmann, an energetic and ambitious self-made man who eventually became a highly esteemed professor of orthopedics. In 1844, A. G. Drachmann married his first wife, Vilhelmine Marie Stæhr, with whom he had five children, of whom Holger was the second. Holger's elder sister, Erna Juel-Hansen, also made a literary career. Their mother died when they were in their teens, and in 1859 A. G. Drachmann was married for the second time, to Clara Josephine Sørensen. From this marriage three more

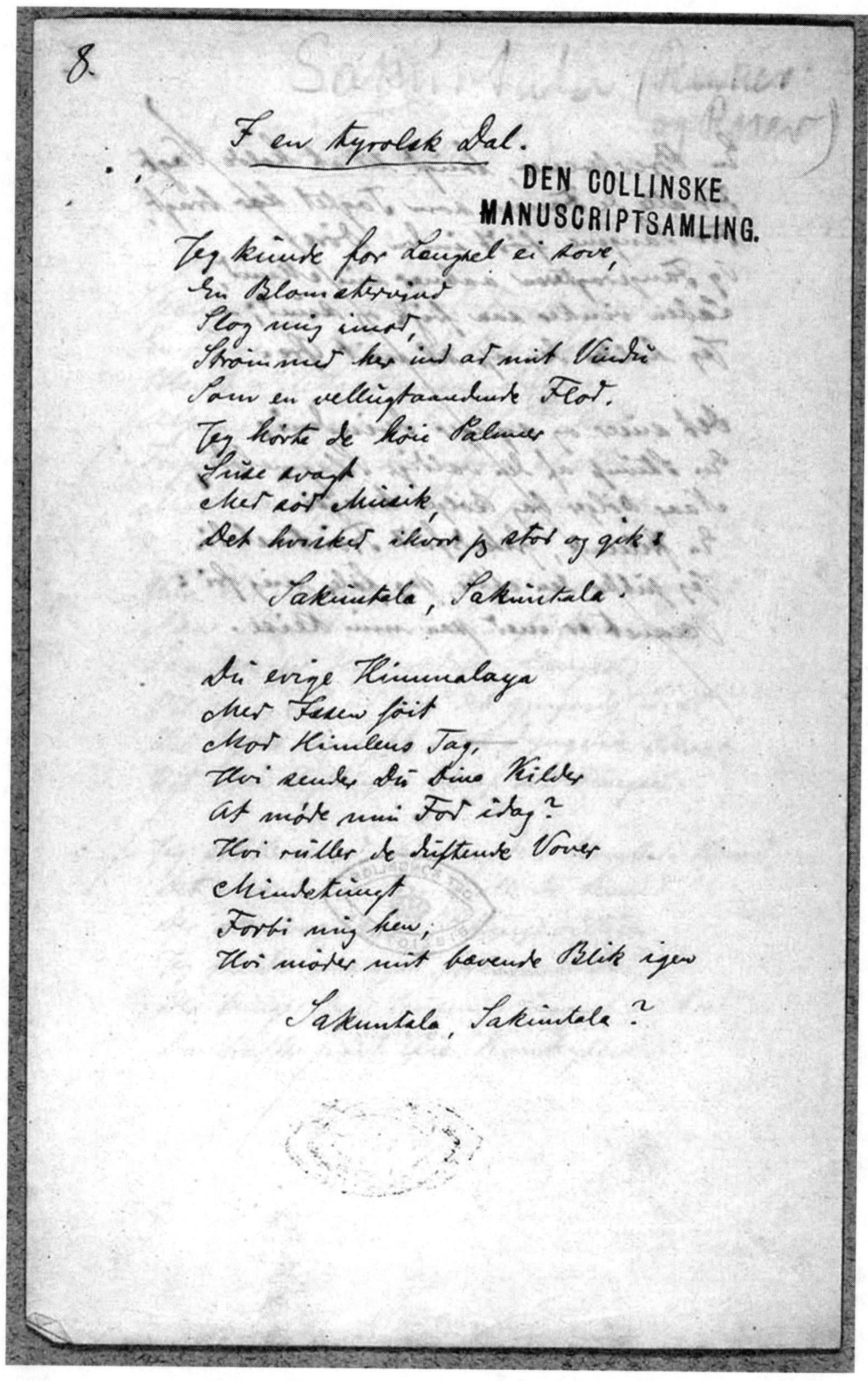

8.

I en tyrolsk Dal.

Jeg kunde for Længsel ei sove,
En Blomstervind
Slog mig imod,
Strömmed her ind af mit Vindu
Som en vellugtaandende Flod.
Jeg hörte de höie Palmer
Suse svagt
Med söd Musik,
Det knirked ikkun jeg stod og gik:

Sakuntala, Sakuntala.

Du evige Himmalaya
Med Fossen föit
Mod Himlens Tag,
Hvi sender Du dine Kilder
At möde mig Fod idag?
Hvi ruller de duftende Vover
Mindeklingt
Forbi mig hen;
Hvi möder mit bævende Blik igen

Sakuntala, Sakuntala?

Manuscript for Drachmann's poem "Sakuntala," written in early 1876 with a title that means "In a Tyrolese Vale" and published in final form in his collection Ranker og Roser *(Vines and Roses) in 1879 (courtesy of the Danish Royal Library, Copenhagen)*

children were born, among them the renowned classical philologist A. B. Drachmann, who became widely known as one of the editors of Kierkegaard's collected works.

Holger Drachmann grew up in the Copenhagen inner city in a family distinguished by liberal attitudes and social mobility. During the summer season, the family tended to reside in the countryside north of Copenhagen, near the royal Fredensborg Castle. The urban bustle of the rapidly expanding city of Copenhagen, on the one hand, and the tranquil natural charms of the surroundings of Fredensborg, on the other, had a lifelong impact on Drachmann's work as an artist. Other profound and lasting sources of inspiration were the maritime milieus that he became acquainted with through the activities of his father and by rummaging the quays and wharves just around the corner from the parental home. Thus, from an early age, Drachmann was familiar with ships, sailors, and life at sea, which became thematic cornerstones in his oeuvre.

Drachmann finished school in 1865, and the next year he was enrolled in the Royal Academy of Fine Arts in Copenhagen. Under the guidance of his professor, C. F. Sørensen, he specialized in marine painting. Drachmann turned out to be a promising young artist, and when his first paintings were exhibited in 1869, his talent was appreciated. Drachmann seemingly had no high academic ambitions, and during his student years, he became a well-known face in Copenhagen bohemian circles. Afraid that his son's dissolute lifestyle would disrupt his career and damage his future, A. G. Drachmann sent Holger on several trips abroad. On one of these early quasi-grand tours, in 1866, Holger Drachmann visited the island of Bornholm, where he met his future wife, Vilhelmine Erichsen. They married on 3 November 1871. In 1871, Drachmann visited the United Kingdom. His stay in London, where he met refugee French communards and witnessed the less attractive sides of the modern industrial age, made a deep impression on the sensitive young artist. During these turbulent years, Drachmann began to write seriously.

By comparison with Britain, Denmark was still a preindustrial society. But, during the last quarter of the nineteenth century, Danish economy, culture, and politics changed fundamentally. The expansion of the city of Copenhagen had been frustrated for decades by the fortifications that surrounded it. When they were demolished in the 1860s, the capital underwent a rapid metamorphosis, transforming into a metropolis. The modernization of Danish society had also been slowed down by the collective trauma inflicted by the Danish-Prussian war of 1864 and the persistent power of the dominant conservative political and ecclesiastical elites. During this era of change–roughly from 1870 to 1900–the political opposition was still frail and badly organized, and the democratization of society depended heavily on intellectuals. Progressive forces gained increasing influence through the expanding new media, primarily newspapers and journals, which disseminated their political views on such issues as general suffrage and equal rights for both sexes. Modern newspapers were established in this period, and the press played a crucial role in the process of modernization of Danish society. Among the most influential papers of the day were *Social-Demokraten* and *Politiken.* The latter became one of the vital mouthpieces of the cultural avant-garde, in which Drachmann's cousin, influential politician Viggo Hørup, and Drachmann's former schoolmate, equally prominent writer-politician Edvard Brandes, were two of the most powerful figures.

In 1871, the year of Drachmann's visit to London, Georg Brandes attracted huge public attention through a series of lectures on European literature at Copenhagen University. Brandes came across Drachmann's newspaper reports about his experiences abroad and felt that he and Drachmann shared the same ideas. Brandes went to see Drachmann after his return and suggested to him that he take up writing instead of pursuing a career as a painter. Drachmann officially made his literary debut in 1872 with a book of brisk short stories titled *Med Kul og Kridt* (With Charcoal and Chalk). Two years later, in 1874, another book in the same popular genre followed–*I Storm og Stille* (During Storm and Calm). These first works are prose sketches–lively, impressionistic fragments about interesting people and milieus. Sometimes they are mere vehicles for folkloristic interest, using the island of Bornholm as local color. These popular stories fill a gap in the evolution of Danish prose: they are a significant contribution to the emancipation and refinement of the modern short story in Danish literary history. In the context of Drachmann's later work, they show the first signs of his vivid style and the scope of his prose.

But Drachmann's real breakthrough as a writer came with *Digte* (Poems, 1872). The title refers, not without a sense of bravura, to the debuts of such renowned predecessors as romanticists Adam Oehlenschläger, B. S. Ingemann, A. W. Schack von Staffeldt, Christian Winther, and Emil Aarestrup. *Digte* includes poems originating from two fundamentally opposing sources of lyrical inspiration–on the one hand, the Romantic tradition and, on the other, modern socially conscious poetry in the vein of Georg Brandes, to whom the book is dedicated. Drachmann took up the kind of issues Brandes had advocated in his lectures the year before. Significantly, though, Drachmann did not express himself in prose, the predominant genre used by those who followed Brandes's plea for a naturalist literature, but in verse.

The best-known poems in *Digte* are "Engelske Socialister" and "King mob," but the collection also includes such lesser-known poems as the love poem "Nyt Liv" (New Life), the elegy "I de lyse Nætter" (In the Light Nights), and the jovial "Skipperen synger" (The Captain Sings) and "Kom muntre Gutter" (Come on Ye Jolly Lads). Thus, already in his first collection of poems, some themes appear that recur in all of Drachmann's work: a bacchanal lust for life and natural beauty, a heartfelt sympathy for ordinary people, and a romantic awareness of the radical metamorphosis of contemporary culture and society. The most remarkable feature of *Digte* is that the book reflects the complexity of the author's mind. *Digte* maps the main lines along which Drachmann's oeuvre unfolded and indicates the richness of his poetic talent. Drachmann was soon recognized as the main poet of the Modern Breakthrough.

Drachmann's marriage to Vilhelmine Erichsen was short-lived. It was dissolved in 1875, the year his second collection of poems, *Dæmpede Melodier* (Subdued Melodies, 1875), was published. Contrary to what the title seems to indicate, the majority of the poems in this book are mostly exuberant and energetically written. In a handful of subdued, nocturne-like poems, though, a new vein in Drachmann's art can be discerned. Fueled by remorse and guilt because of his marital crisis, a plaintive tenderness crops up, resulting in some of the finest poetry he ever wrote, such as the harmonious and reflective "Improvisation ombord" (Improvisation on Board). With *Dæmpede Melodier,* the span of Drachmann's modes of poetic expression reached maturity–juxtaposing extremes in style and matter that drew on the conflicting Apollonian and Dionysian undercurrents in his character.

Similar ambiguities appeared in his prose. A recurrent topos in Drachmann's novels is the doppelgänger motif, which not only reveals a central dichotomy in Drachmann's way of modeling characters but also reflects his own fundamental dual nature. In Drachmann's first major work of prose, *En Overkomplet* (A Supernumerary, 1876), this duality–expressed though the doppelgänger motif–is the backbone of the narrative and of the complex relationship between the two main antagonists.

En Overkomplet depicts, in lively prose, the adolescent friendship between the boys Erik and Adolf, opposites in personality. Although the initial scheme of two contrasting characters is maintained throughout the novel, the opposites eventually trade places. Adolf, a typical romantic dreamer who cannot adjust himself to conventional society, ends up as a "supernumerary"–that is, a lethargic misfit whose only way out of his social decline is to emigrate to America. Erik, the high-spirited narrator who in the beginning of the novel represents positive values–such as lust for life–finally ends as an ordinary, well-adapted member of society. Thus, the "negative," Byronesque bohemian dreamer Adolf, who is unable to adapt himself to the civil demands of everyday life, in effect becomes the positive hero. The opposite applies to Erik, who in the end has sold his soul to mediocrity, gaining in return an average, rather trivial, middle-class existence.

Drachmann circa 1880 (photograph by Christensen and Zahrtmann, Copenhagen; courtesy of the Danish Royal Library, Copenhagen)

In *En Overkomplet,* Drachmann again drew extensively on childhood memories, primarily of the idyllic summer life in the rural Fredensborg district, which must have stood in sharp contrast to his ordinary life as a city schoolboy. Thematically, *En Overkomplet* refers to the novels of his countrymen, Carl Bagger's *Min Broders Levnet* (The Life of My Brother, 1835) and Hans Egede Schack's *Phantasterne* (The Dreamers, 1857). Furthermore, *En Overkomplet* is deeply indebted to the work of Russian novelists Ivan Goncharov and Ivan Turgenev.

Drachmann's next novel, *Tannhäuser* (1877), is closely related to *En Overkomplet.* Although the title refers to a medieval legendary subject matter and Richard Wagner's opera from 1845, Drachmann's *Tannhäuser* is a contemporary love story situated in the natural and picturesque surroundings of Fredensborg. This novel, however, has only one central character, Anton Kolb, an archetypical Drachmannian hero–that is, a man with a fundamentally split personality. Kolb is a representative of modern times who at the same time is subject to atavistic romantic tendencies. In Kolb's psyche, two conflicting forces rule, and every now and then, sudden and unpredictable changes of mood carry him away.

Tannhäuser is a loosely composed novel that mainly serves as a vehicle for several poetic interludes. A striking feature of Drachmann's prose, in particular the early novels *Tannhäuser* and *En Overkomplet,* is the incorporation of lyrical intermezzi. Thus, both form and content reflect the author's psychological complexity, or–as many critics have labeled it–his personal instability and his shortcomings as a novelist. Many of the best poems in *Tannhäuser* and *En Overkomplet* were subsequently incorporated into the poetry collection *Ranker og Roser* (Vines and Roses, 1879). Among the finest are the erotic "Farlige Drømme" (Perilous Dreams) and Drachmann's most famous poem, the exotic-romantic "Sakuntala." The latter had originally appeared in a slightly different shape in *En Overkomplet,* but in *Ranker og Roser* it obviously found its final form and was published with its mysterious title. "Sakuntala" stands out as one of the most euphonious and sensuous poems Drachmann ever created, and it has since been a classic in virtually every anthology of Danish verse. In 1889 the text was set for voice and orchestra by the English composer Frederick Delius.

Drachmann was also a prolific essayist and chronicler, and his first polemic collection of essays, *Derovre fra Grænsen* (From Across the Border, 1877), is one of the best examples of his work in this genre. *Derovre fra Grænsen* includes a handful of impressionistic essays based on a journey in the Danish-German borderland, where the Danish-Prussian war had been fought, and lost, by the Danes in 1864. Drachmann's essays were praised in conservative circles, while they evoked vehement reactions in progressive intellectual circles, especially among the followers of Georg and Edvard Brandes. The outcome of the war still threw dark shadows over Danish society in the 1870s, and therefore the subject matter of *Derovre fra Grænsen* was politically delicate. That Drachmann dared to touch upon the conflict was perceived as an expression of his increasingly nationalistic sympathies. As a result, the friendly relations between Drachmann and the Brandes brothers began to cool off. Notably, his close friendship with Edvard Brandes now turned into an animosity that lasted for the rest of their lives. Notwithstanding their growing political and literary differences of opinion, Georg Brandes always maintained his admiration for Drachmann's work, especially his poetry.

Derovre fra Grænsen clearly demonstrates Drachmann's skills in depicting the lives of ordinary people in a passionate and original way. This ability is related to his "discovery" of the little fishing hamlet Skagen on the northernmost tip of the peninsula Jutland in the early 1870s. There, in this remote corner of Denmark, he encountered peasants, fishermen, and sailors–people he felt were still unaffected by modernity. When he learned, for example, about a local lifeboat sailor who had risked his life in a hazardous rescue operation but had not received a medal of honor because of a minor misdemeanor in his youth, Drachmann denounced this injustice publicly and wrote the novelette *Lars Kruse* (1879) about the matter. As a result of his intervention, Lars Kruse was eventually decorated for his heroic valor.

Soon after, Skagen was discovered by other artists, and it rapidly became a refuge for visual artists from all over Scandinavia. Drachmann often returned to Skagen and used the townsfolk as models in his work–for example, in the play *Strandbyfolk* (Shoreville People, 1883) and in dozens of stories such as those in the collections *Smaa Fortællinger. Ældre og nye* (Minor Stories. Old and New, 1884), *Sømandshistorier* (Sailor's Stories, 1896), *Udvalgte Fortællinger* (Selected Stories, 1901), and *Fortællinger* (Stories, 1908).

In 1876, on his way to Italy, Drachmann paid a visit to Munich, where he met Norwegian playwright Ibsen. Drachmann's interest in drama was sparked by Ibsen, but it took considerable time before he completed his first play, *Puppe og Sommerfugl* (Pupa and Butterfly, 1882), which was strongly influenced by Ibsen's masterpiece, *A Doll's House* (1879). Writing for the stage opened new perspectives for Drachmann, financial as well as creative.

From Munich, Drachmann left for Italy, where he lived for more than a year in the Northern Italian Alps. There he wrote the poems that were collected in *Sange ved Havet–Venezia* (Songs by the Seashore–Venice, 1877). This collection reflects Drachmann's 1877 involvement in a turbulent love affair with Polly Thalbitzer (née Culmsee). Drachmann eventually married Polly's younger sister, Emmy, on 17 May 1879, and the marriage marks a stable and fruitful period in Drachmann's career. The prime examples of the poetry that he produced in these years are found in the collection *Ranker og Roser.*

In the 1880s, Drachmann wrote many plays and other works. During this period his hostile relationship with Edvard and Georg Brandes turned into an open and bitter feud. Drachmann was increasingly looked upon as a renegade from the Brandesian movement who had fallen prey to conservatism. For the Brandes brothers, the essayistic travel book *Skyggebilleder fra Rejser i Indland og Udland* (Silhouettes from Travels at Home and Abroad, 1883) was a particular provocation. The reason for their dismay–as well as the popularity of the volume–was the essay "Ostende-Brügge." In this essay, the lush Belgian seaside resort of Ostende is depicted as the epitome of decadence and modernity, whereas the quiet medieval town of Bruges symbolizes the opposite–timeless traditional values. The dichotomy between the "healthy," full-hearted folklore of the common people of Bruges and the affected, cynical lifestyle in Ostende is a covert, but unmistakable, reference to Georg and Edvard Brandes and their French-inspired radical views on society and art. *Skyggebilleder fra Rejser i Indland og Udland* clearly marked the growing ideological gap between Drachmann and the champions of modern times.

In 1885, Drachmann tried to equal the success of *Skyggebilleder fra Rejser i Inland Udland* with a related work, *Danmark leve!* (Hurray for Denmark). Many works created in this phase of Drachmann's career are traditionalist in form and content and air bourgeois values. Examples of this period are the collection of poetry *Ungdom i Digt og Sang* (Youth in Poetry and Songs, 1879), the substantial "historicized" fairy-tale poems *Prinsessen og det halve Kongerige* (The Princess and Half of the Kingdom, 1878) and *Østen for Sol og Vesten for Maane* (East of the Sun and West of the Moon, 1880), the belligerent national-heroic poem *Peder Tordenskjold* (1880), the novelette *Vandenes Datter* (The Daughter of the Sea, 1881), the short-story collection *Vildt og Tæmmet* (Wild and Tame, 1881), and the classical Greek tragedy *Alkibiades eller Grækere i Forfald* (1886). The joyful vitality and musicality of the 1870s is rarely present in Drachmann's poetic works of the 1880s. The best poems he wrote in this decade were brought together in the collection *Gamle Guder og nye* (Old Gods and New, 1881), published under the pseudonym Svend Trøst. He later used the same pseudonym for the book of poems *Unge Viser* (Youthful Songs, 1892).

Some of the poems collected in *Fjæld-Sange og Æventyr* (Mountain-Songs and Fairytales, 1885), however, include fine poetry, some of which was written while Drachmann was hiking in Norway with composer Edvard Grieg. Grieg not only became an intimate friend of Drachmann but also a sensitive interpreter of his works as well, as many of his compositions to Drachmann's texts clearly show. Above all, *Fjæld-Sange og Æventyr* is remembered because, as a kind of appendix, it includes the romantic fairy-tale comedy *Der var engang* (Once Upon a Time, first performed, 1887). This graceful romance instantly became one of the most popular works in the Danish national theatrical heritage, securing Drachmann his most lasting success and providing him with a Danish royal knighthood as well. *Der var engang* was translated into several languages, and composer P. E. Lange-Müller turned it into a symphony. A substantial share of the enduring success of the play stems from Lange-Müller's splendid mixture of late-Romantic musical idiom and traditional Danish folk music. One of the songs from *Der var engang,* "Midsummer Eve Song," is still one of the Danes' most cherished ballads.

Drachmann circa 1890 (courtesy of the Danish Royal Library, Copenhagen)

In 1887 Drachmann became romantically involved with young cabaret singer Amanda Nilsson, whom he called Edith. For about a decade, until approximately 1897, the relationship with Edith was Drachmann's main source of inspiration. During these years Drachmann mostly lived in Hamburg, Germany, in cumbersome physical and financial circumstances.

The first time Edith's presence is tangible is in the loosely composed artist's novel, *Med den brede Pensel* (With Bold Strokes, 1887), but the novel that immortalized Edith's name was the panegyric *Forskrevet* (Signed Away, 1890). *Forskrevet* is a voluminous, autobiographical novel about two male protagonists–painter Henrik Gerhard and poet Ulf Brynjulfsen–and their mutual love for a young female singer called Edith. But the book also is an ode to modern Copenhagen. Together with the novel *Stuk* (Stucco, 1887) by Drachmann's compatriot Herman Bang, *Forskrevet* is one of the first big city novels in Danish literature.

Although it is a huge novel, the narrative plot essentially describes the inner lives of the three main characters. In the opening scene of *Forskrevet,* Henrik Gerhard has just returned to Copenhagen after a long stay in Paris. On his first night in town, he attends a performance at the Royal Theatre, and afterward he meets "modern" poet Ulf Brynjulfsen, who subsequently becomes Henrik's closest friend and alter ego. Ulf is a Byron-like enfant terrible who becomes a modern bohemian outcast, just as did Adolf in *En Overkomplet.* One night, the two friends visit a cabaret, or *café chantant,* in the Frederiksberg quarter in Copenhagen–one of the places where "modern" entertainment blossomed–and there they both instantly fall in love with young female singer Edith.

The impression that the two men actually represent two sides of one psyche, just as with Erik and Adolf in *En Overkomplet,* becomes increasingly evident in the course of the novel. This psychological merger of two characters is also addressed by the text itself in scenes where Drachmann uses such modern literary techniques as a proto-stream-of-consciousness in which mental images flow together and fragments of discourse are interwoven.

The only way Ulf can avoid rapid social and psychological decline is to create an ultimate piece of art. With the assistance of Henrik, he writes a grandiose historical tragedy. When it is put onstage at the Royal Theatre, it becomes, as expected, a major disaster, symbolizing the ultimate collapse of Ulf's Romantic worldview and his inability to accept modernity.

Finally, Henrik trades places with Ulf, leaving his wife and becoming Edith's lover. Edith is the main heroine and the incorporation of pure femininity. She stands in clear contrast to Annette, Ulf's sister and Henrik's former wife, who is described in purely physical terms. Thus, the married woman is depicted in a negative, hedonistic way, whereas the "public woman," Edith, stands out as the embodiment of higher values and pure, platonic love.

The final scene of *Forskrevet* is surprising and remarkably violent. Without warning, some kind of anonymous enemy force is about to overrun the modern city of Copenhagen, and Armageddon seems imminent. In this melodramatic finale, the city is in ruins, symbolizing the end of traditional culture. Nevertheless, amid all the violence and destruction, the final words of the novel consist of a few snatches of a love song that offer a glimmer of hope for the future–indicating that human love will survive.

The autobiographical content of *Forskrevet* was evident to contemporary readers, who perceived the novel as a roman à clef. Partly because of the weak plot structure and partly because of the unvarnished representation of the artistic coterie in fin de siècle Copenhagen, *Forskrevet* was primarily judged a failure. Recent scholarship has reevaluated the book, and it is now regarded as an example of novelistic impressionism and a sophisticated representation of Copenhagen city life in the 1880s, employing new and experimental aesthetic techniques. Furthermore, *Forskrevet* is now taken as a kind of "missing link" in the literary historical process of transition from analytical naturalism–characterized by Darwinist determinism of the 1870s–to a more spiritually and psychologically oriented impressionism in Danish fiction of the 1890s.

During this so-called Edith period, Drachmann continued to work on plays, especially melodramas and verse dramas. He attempted to repeat the huge success of his earlier play *Der var engang* with *To dramatiske Digte* (Two Dramatic Poems), a book with two romances, or verse dramas, published in 1888. One of the plays is the exotic piece *Tyrkisk Rococo* (Turkish Rococo). The subject matter and erotic atmosphere of the play appealed strongly to Drachmann's imagination and led to a series of poems in the collection *Sangenes Bog* (The Book of Songs, 1889) and more dramatic poems, such as *Tusind og en Nat* (Thousand and One Nights, 1889).

In *Sangenes Bog,* Drachmann tried to revive the poetic intensity of his earlier work. *Sangenes Bog* is dominated by subdued, ponderous poems, which melancholically revisit the days of the author's youth and lament the deterioration of mankind and society.

Tusind og en Nat is a more accurate reflection of Drachmann's work of the Edith period. It is a versified closet drama about the romantic love of the youngsters Suleîma and Osman, set against the exotic backdrop of the Orient. The entire play–covertly–sings the praises of Edith and, through the difficulties the two lovers are confronted with, shows glimpses of the problems Drachmann and his new lover had to cope with because of the secrecy that surrounded their affair. A little less "exotic" than *Tusind og en Nat* are the verse drama *Bonifacius-Skæret* (The Boniface Skerries, 1893),

Drachmann's grave, a Viking-style burial mound by the sea north of Skagen (courtesy of the Danish Royal Library, Copenhagen)

set in an early-nineteenth-century coastal village in Brittany, and *Gøglere* (Buffoons, 1893), a play about a group of mountebanks and circus people. The milieu presented in *Gøglere* reflects Drachmann's growing interest in more popular, and socially marginal, forms of theatrical entertainment–a result of his involvement with vaudeville singer Amanda Nilsson.

The influence of popular entertainment can be seen most clearly in another innovation in Drachmann's oeuvre in the 1890s, his turn to melodrama. The handful of melodramas Drachmann wrote around 1895 were popular–not least as closet dramas–but only two of them found acclaim on the stage: *Vølund Smed* (Wieland the Smith, 1894; first performed, 1898) and *Renæssance* (Renaissance, 1894; first performed, 1901).

Vølund Smed, a verse drama written in an "elevated" style, is historical in flavor, archaic in tone and setting, rather than a truly historical piece. It echoes Viking mythology and is reminiscent of William Shakespeare's *The Tempest* (1611). The play is about goldsmith Vølund, who settles in the realm of King Nidung without his permission. At the place where Vølund has chosen to build his house and workshop, he discovers a sleeping woman and falls in love with her, but she turns out to be a Valkyrie. She belongs partly to humanity and partly to the world of the gods; after having spent some time with Vølund, she suddenly disappears. Then, Vølund is captured by the king, who has him hamstrung to prevent him from fleeing. Thus, the king is able to benefit from Vølund's extraordinary skills as a goldsmith. But Vølund still longs for his Valkyrie and thirsts for revenge on the king and his kin. Finally, when the opportunity arises, Vølund takes revenge, killing the king's sons and raping his daughter. The violent Wagnerian climax of the play takes place on Christmas Eve, when a bloody massacre is set in motion, accompanied by thunder, lightning, and the "mighty sounds of horns in the distance. . . . Everything disintegrates to the accompaniment of deafening screams." The action of the play is rounded off with an epilogue, which, just as in the final scene of *Forskrevet,* indicates a utopian vision of a better future world, which will arise from the ruins of the old.

In *Renæssance,* the action takes place in Venice in the second half of the sixteenth century. It is not a verse drama, as is *Vølund Smed,* and is generally more subtle in its subject matter and tone. The main character is Venetian painter Tintoretto, and its central themes are the relationship between art and love, and the awareness of aging. Just as in *Vølund Smed*–and as Drachmann himself experienced in his love for Edith–the middle-aged painter Tintoretto falls in love with Teresina, a young lower-class girl. In order to paint her, and thus be able to grasp the essence of her female beauty and youth, Tintoretto fills Teresina's glass with a lethal sleeping potion. He is prepared to kill her, but the potion is not strong enough, and she awakens unexpectedly. Notwithstanding the mischief done to her, Teresina is finally convinced of the sincerity of the artist's love for her, and all ends well.

In the melodramas, as well as in almost all of Drachmann's other plays, the historical context is purely ornamental, a more or less exotic framework emphasizing the timelessness and universality of the action and subject matter. Many of Drachmann's melodramas were collected in the volume *Melodramer* (Melodramas, 1895), and apart from *Vølund Smed* and *Renæssance,* they all appear today as antiquated and often unintentionally comic in their sentimentality, violence, and drastic changes of mood. With his choice of the genre of melodrama, Drachmann followed an important trend in late-nineteenth-century popular drama, which at the same time offered him the opportunity to distance himself from mainstream realism and naturalism.

In *Vølund Smed* and *Renæssance,* Drachmann voiced his increasingly pessimistic opinion about the future of civilization–a peculiar mixture of a regressive glorification of the past and a Romantic view of art. Already, in the tragedy *Alkibiades eller Grækere i Forfald,* Drachmann had expressed the idea of art as an antidote to the degeneration of mankind, symbolized by the fall of Athenian democracy, but in his later plays–and especially the melodramas–his pessimism intensified, and increasingly the power of love appeared as the sole option for the salvation of humanity. From this perspective, Drachmann's work is among the earliest signs of fin de siècle decadence in late-nineteenth-century Danish letters. Middle-aged, in a marital crisis, and jeopardizing his fame by entering into an adulterous affair with Amanda Nilsson, Drachmann still adhered to the gospel of love.

The majority of Drachmann's works from the last ten years of his career were considered unsuccessful. Of some interest are the novel of chivalry, *Kitzwalde* (1895), a Sir Walter Scott pastiche; the play *Brav-Karl* (An Honest Fellow, 1897; first performed, 1903); and two historical dramas collected in the volume *Kors og Kaarde* (Cross and Sword, 1898). Time and time again, Drachmann tried in vain to equal the success of *Der var engang,* but all these works are swiftly written trifles–littered with knights, wayfaring wanderers, and troubadours–merely pale shadows of his former literary genius.

In 1897, Drachmann became involved with another vaudeville singer, Norwegian Bokken Lasson. Together, they traveled to the United States in 1898, where he stayed for nearly two years. In New York, Drachmann was welcomed and celebrated in a grand manner by delegations of the large community of Scandinavian American immigrants. He found a more or less permanent base in the fishing hamlet Rosebank on Staten Island. On his extensive tours of the east coast of the United States, Drachmann was feted in Philadelphia, Washington, and elsewhere, finally receiving the acclaim for his work that he had so desperately looked for at home. Nevertheless, after two years he gave up the idea of settling in the United States and returned to Europe. This time, Bokken's sister Soffi followed him, and she became his third wife on 15 June 1903. The couple settled in the picturesque fishing village of Skagen in 1902.

In the final phase of his work, Drachmann strained more and more after effect, often even descending to bombast. This tendency is apparent in the collection *Ungdomsdigte* (Juvenile Poems, 1898), the Viking drama *Hallfred Vandraadeskjald* (1900; first performed, 1906), and all the prose works of this period, such as *Dædalus* (1900) and *Kirke og Orgel* (Church and Organ, 1904). The only works that, in fits and starts, exceed this negative trend and reveal glimpses of Drachmann's former poetic spirit are the collections of poetry *Den hellige Ild* (The Holy Fire, 1899) and *Broget Løv* (Variegated Foliage, 1901). These collections include intense and sincere verse as well as prose fragments, often on themes and motifs recycled from his earlier work.

Instead of stopping with *Broget Løv,* which would have been a powerful finale to one of the most versatile and diverse oeuvres in Danish literary history, Drachmann sought once more to equal *Der var engang,* with the romantic history play *Hr. Oluf han rider* (Squire Oluf Is Riding, 1906). *Hr. Oluf han rider* was written for the occasion of Drachmann's sixtieth birthday, which was celebrated with the premiere of the play at the Royal Theatre on 9 October 1906 and by a range of festivities all over the country. *Hr. Oluf han rider* became the last play Drachmann finished before his death and one of his most devastating fiascoes. Unable to see the uselessness of the enterprise, Drachmann, later that year, went to Stockholm, attempting in vain to enhance his chances for the newly founded Nobel Prize in literature, for which he saw himself to be an obvious candidate.

On 14 January 1908 Drachmann died in a hospital in Hornbæk, a seaside resort north of Copenhagen. His ashes were sailed over to Skagen and found their last resting place in a burial mound by the sea, due north of the town. The design of this most northern grave in Denmark, similar to the grandiose grave of a

Viking warrior, can be interpreted as an ultimate gesture, symbolizing Drachmann's status as a writer and cultural icon of a past era. In 1911 his home in Skagen was opened to the public and is now a museum with rich holdings of Drachmann's paintings, sketchbooks, and memorabilia.

Holger Drachmann was an unusual lyrical talent, and some of his verse is among the most beloved by his countrymen. In Drachmann's poetic idiom, everything is in motion. The absence of stability and clear contours in his art reflects that the best of his prose and poetry was written in moods of imminent change and moments of transgression. He shows a great liking for the shades of dusk and dawn, and prefers spring and autumn to summer and winter.

Drachmann's poetic style, too, is rhythmic and full of contrasts, favoring such radical forms as the oxymoron and antithesis, and using rhythmic variation and surprising breaches, inversions, and repetitions in rhyme and rhythm. Many of his works have been set to music, and he created one of the most popular midsummer-night songs. His play *Der var engang* is among the most frequently performed Danish plays ever. And, finally, Drachmann's novel *Forskrevet* is one of the most versatile prose works of late-nineteenth-century Danish literature and served as an important source of inspiration for Tom Kristensen's now classic novel *Hærværk* (Havoc, 1930).

Letters:

Holger Drachmann i Breve til hans Fædrenehjem, edited by Harriet Bentzon (Copenhagen: Gyldendal, 1932);

Breve fra og til Holger Drachmann, 4 volumes, edited by Morten Borup (Copenhagen: Gyldendal, 1968–1970).

Bibliographies:

Johannes Ursin, *Bibliografi over Holger Drachmanns Forfatterskap* (Copenhagen: Gyldendal, 1956);

Ursin, *Bibliografi over Litteraturen om Holger Drachmann* (Copenhagen: Gyldendal, 1959).

Biographies:

Valdemar Vedel, *Holger Drachmann* (Copenhagen: Det Schønbergske Forlag, 1909);

Paul V. Rubow, *Holger Drachmanns ungdom* (Copenhagen: Ejnar Munksgaards Forlag, 1940);

Rubow, *Holger Drachmann 1878–97* (Copenhagen: Ejnar Munksgaards Forlag, 1945);

Rubow, *Holger Drachmann. Sidste Aar* (Copenhagen: Ejnar Munksgaards Forlag, 1950);

Johannes Ursin, *Holger Drachmann. Liv og Værker I–II* (Copenhagen: Rosenkilde & Bagger, 1953).

References:

Bo Hakon Jørgensen, "En kvindes smil. Holger Drachmann *Forskrevet,*" in *Læsninger i dansk litteratur,* edited by Povl Schmidt and others (Odense: Odense University Press, 1998), II: 266–281;

Henk van der Liet, "'A Fleeting Glimpse of Former Times': Holger Drachmann's Melodramas: *Vølund Smed* and *Renæssance,*" *Scandinavica,* 33, no. 2 (November 1994): 183–199;

Liet, "'French Fungi': Some Snooping in Holger Drachmann's Letters," in *Nordic Letters 1870–1910,* edited by Michael Robinson and Janet Garton (Norwich: Norvik Press, 1999), pp. 201–227;

Liet, "Über Holger Drachmanns Roman *Forskrevet* und die Suche nach einer Ästhetik urbaner Erfahrung," in *Die inszenierte Stadt: Zur Praxis und Theorie kultureller Konstruktionen,* edited by Bernd Henningsen and others (Berlin: Arno Spitz, 2000), pp. 81–104.

Papers:

Holger Drachmann's manuscripts, letters, and other papers are primarily in the Danish Royal Library in Copenhagen.

Johannes Ewald

(18 November 1743 - 17 March 1781)

Peer E. Sørensen
University of Aarhus

(Translated by Tara F. Chace)

BOOKS: *Sørge-Sang i Christianborgs Slots-Kirke 18. Martinus 1766 da Kong Frederik V skulde føres til sit Hvilested,* music by Johann Adolf Scheibe (Copenhagen: Printed by C. & G. C. Berling, 1766);

Cantate som til Kong Christian den Syvendes og Dronning Caroline Mathildes Salvings-Fest den 1. May 1767, music by Scheibe (Copenhagen, 1767);

De poëseos natura et indole (Copenhagen: Printed by A. F. Stein, 1767);

Adam og Ewa eller Den ulykkelige Prøve. Et dramatisk Stykke i fem Handlinger med Mellemsange (Copenhagen: Printed by C. Philibert, 1769);

Passions-Cantata, som i Fasten opføres af det Musicaliske Selskab paa Bryggernes Laugs-Huus, music by Scheibe (Copenhagen, 1769);

Rolf Krage. Et Sørgespil i fem Handlinger (Copenhagen: Printed by N. Møller, 1770);

Philet, en Fortælning (Elhøy, 1770);

De brutale Klappere. Et tragi-comisk Forspil (Copenhagen: Printed by M. Hallager, 1771);

Philets Forslag om Pebersvendene, som vist vil blive iværksat (Copenhagen: Printed by N. Møller, 1771);

Harlequin Patriot eller den uægte Patriotisme. En comisk Comoedie i tre Handlinger paa Vers (Copenhagen: Rothen & Proft, 1772);

Taarer ved Herr Frederik von Arnsbachs Grav (Copenhagen: Printed by N. Møller, 1772);

Pebersvendene. Et Lystspil i fem Handlinger (Copenhagen: Printed by L. N. Svare, 1773);

Balders Død. Et Heroisk Syngespil i Tre Handlinger. En Priisdigt (Copenhagen: Forsøg i de Skiønne og nyttige Videnskaber, 1775); translated by George Borrow as *The Death of Balder* (London: Reeves & Turner, 1886);

Fiskerne. Et Syngespil i tre Handlinger. En Priisdigt (Copenhagen: Forsøg i de Skiønne og nyttige Videnskaber, 1779);

Lithograph based on a painting by Erik Paulsen, 1780 (courtesy of the Danish Royal Library, Copenhagen)

Maria og Johannes. Et Passions-Oratorium, music by J. A. P. Schulz (Copenhagen: S. Sønnichsen, 1789);

De Fremmede (Copenhagen, 1805).

Editions and Collections: *Johannes Ewalds Samtlige Skrifter,* 4 volumes (Copenhagen: C. G. Proft, 1780–1791)–includes "Fortale," volume 1;

Johannes Ewalds Samtlige Skrifter, 8 volumes in 4, edited by Frederik Ludvig Liebenberg (Copenhagen: E. L. Thaarup, 1850–1855)–comprises volume 1, *Sørge-Cantater og aandelige Poesier; Festdigte og Hæderssange til Kongehuset;* volume 2, *Philet; Blandede Digte; Bryllupsdigte Sørgedigte; Fragmenter; Tydske Digte; Tillæg til Sørge-Cantaterne i Første Deel;* volume 3, *Adam og Eva; Rolf Krage;* volume 4, *De brutale Klappere; Philemon og Baucis; Harlequin Patriot; Pebersvendene;* volume 5, *Balders Død; Fiskerne; Dramatiske Fragmenter;* volume 6, *Lykkens Tempel; De Fremmede; Herr Panthakaks Historie;* volume 7, *Dissertationer; Hvorfor en guddommelig Forløb var nødvendig for det menneskelige Kiøn; Philets Forslag om Pebersvendene; Om Almuens Oplysning;* and volume 8, *Forerindring; To Avisartikler; Adskilligt om Joh. Ewalds Levnet og Meninger; Joh. Ewalds Levnet og Meninger; Fortale til Joh. Ewalds samtlige Skrifter. I, 1780; Breve; Efterslæt;*

Udvalgte Digte, introduction by Carsten Hauch (Copenhagen: C. Steen, 1870);

Fiskerne. Et Syngespil i tre Handlinger, edited by Ida Falbe-Hansen (Copenhagen: Gyldendal, 1893);

Johannes Ewalds Levnet og Meninger, edited by Erling Rørdam (Copenhagen: W. Prior, 1899);

Udvalgte Skrifter (Copenhagen: Gyldendal, 1904)–comprises *Balders Død; Fiskerne; Udvalgte Digte; Johannes Ewalds Levnet og Meninger* (fragment); *Fortale til Johannes Ewalds Samtlige Skrifter, Første Bind, 1780;* and *De brutale Klappere;*

Levnet og Meninger. Selvbiografiske Brudstykker og Breve, edited by Louis Bobé (Copenhagen: J. L. Lybecker, 1911);

Samlede Skrifter, 6 volumes, edited by Victor Kuhr, Svend Aage Pallis, and Niels Møller (Copenhagen: Gyldendal, 1914–1924; reprinted, Copenhagen: Gyldendal, 1969);

Philets Forslag og Levnet og Meeninger, edited, with an afterword, by Erik M. Christensen (Copenhagen: Gyldendal, 1964);

Levnet og Meeninger, edited by Jens Aage Doctor (Copenhagen: Dansklærerforeningen/Gyldendal, 1969);

Vingesus. Udvalgte Digte, foreword and notes by Keld Zeruneith (Copenhagen: H. Reitzel, 1985);

Levnet og Meeninger, afterword by Zeruneith, notes by Christensen (Copenhagen: Gyldendal, 1986);

Herr Panthakaks Historie; Levnet og Meeninger, afterword and notes by Johnny Kondrup (Copenhagen: Danske Sprog- og Litteraturselskab/Borgen, 1988);

Digte, edited by Asger Schnack (Copenhagen: H. Reitzel, 1990);

Udvalgte Digte, afterword and notes by Esther Kielberg (Copenhagen: Danske Sprog- og Litteraturselskab/Borgen, 1998).

TRANSLATIONS: Gottlieb Konrad Pfeffel, *Philemon og Baucis. Et Skuespil med Sang, i en Handling* (Copenhagen: L. N. Svare, 1772);

Christian Friedrich Sintenis, *Max Vind og Consorter, eller, Maaske de blive tilsidst endnu alle Kloge. Et Bidrag til Narrenes Historie* (Copenhagen: C. G. Proft, 1782).

Regardless of the literary genre in which he wrote, Johannes Ewald renewed it from within. He liberated Danish lyric poetry from the constraints of classicism and was the first Danish author to write prose that expressed the complex, poignant emotional life of its characters–and he did so with acumen and humor. Ewald's background was complex: raised in an evangelical Christian environment, he was a central figure but also a critic of the Enlightenment; he was classically educated but also well read in the latest contemporary literature. With sensitivity he recorded how the new came into being out of the old. In this sense Ewald was the first modern poet in Danish literature. He published occasional poetry, personal poems, and dramas and wrote several prose works, including the autobiographical *Levnet og Meeninger* (Life and Opinions, serialized in *Den danske Tilskuer* and *Ny Minerva,* 1804–1808), published posthumously and considered his major work.

Johannes Ewald was born on 18 November 1743 in Copenhagen into a pietistic milieu. Pietism was a widespread eighteenth-century Protestant movement in Lutheran Northern Europe stressing emotional piety, tolerance, and a pure Christian life. Ewald's father, Enevold Ewald, was a minister in Det Kongelige Vajsenhuset (The Royal Orphanage) in Copenhagen and one of the foremost Pietists in Denmark. Johannes Ewald's mother, Marie Wulff Ewald, came from the community of Moravian Brethren (in Danish called *Herrnhuterne,* after the German village where Moravians fleeing religious persecution had settled in 1722), followers of the German pietistic pastor Nikolaus Ludwig von Zinzendorf.

Ewald did not have a good relationship with either of his parents. At the age of eleven, on the day his father died, he was sent away from home to grammar school in Schleswig, and throughout his life his relationship with his mother was riddled with conflict. In 1758, at the age of fifteen, he passed the university entrance exam and enrolled at the University of Copenhagen to study theology. In *Levnet og Meeninger* Ewald writes that he fell in love with Arendse Huulegaard that same year. According to his own statements, he cut short his theology studies to win her. In the spring of 1759 he traveled to Hamburg with his older brother,

Mathias. They wanted to join the Prussian military, but the Prussians did not want them, and Ewald ended up on the losing side of the Seven Years' War with the Austrians, under whom he served as a drummer. In October 1760 he returned home from Prague in poor health. He took up his studies in Copenhagen again and in 1762 received a degree in theology. That same year Ewald was offered a free residency in Valkendorf's dormitory at the University of Copenhagen, where he wrote treatises on theology and aesthetics, as well as several poems.

Ewald made his literary debut in 1764 with the allegorical *Lykkens Tempel* (The Temple of Fortune), which was written according to all the formulas of the aesthetics of reason. The work is a dream vision that builds on a contrast between temporal joy (the joy of Fortune) and eternal joy–Eusebia (piety) and Aretes (virtue). In keeping with the author's allegorical tendencies, the young narrator naturally opts for eternal joy. One of Ewald's aesthetic treatises from this period is *De poëseos natura et indole* (On the Nature and Character of Poetry, 1767). He based his thesis on a classical understanding of poetry in an extension of Jean François Marmontel's *Poétique françoise* (French Poetry, 1763) and Charles Batteux's *Les Beaux-arts réduits à un même principe* (The Fine Arts Reduced to a Common Principle, 1746)–that is, the aesthetics of reason and tradition. The writer is defined according to the rhetorical triad: *natura* (innate abilities), *usus* (practice at writing), and *ars* (knowledge of the authorial craft). Ewald still understood the author as *ingenium* (a man of genius). Certain passages in the treatise, however, suggest a more modern aesthetic horizon.

Ewald's literary breakthrough came with his text for a cantata on the death of King Frederik V in 1766, *Sørge-Sang i Christianborgs Slots-Kirke* (Mourning Song in Christianborg Chapel, 1766), with music by Johann Adolf Scheibe, which opens with "Hold Taare op at trille" (Cease, tears, to flow), a line that evoked admiration. Ewald's classical tendencies flavor this important cantata. In 1767 he wrote the text for another cantata, on the occasion of the inauguration of Christian VII, and, in 1769, the text for a Passion cantata.

At the University of Copenhagen, Ewald chiefly studied Latin and French classics. Pierre Corneille became his greatest teacher in the field of drama. At this time Ewald was reading English literature in German translation. He also quickly became familiar with the German milieu in Copenhagen, which at the time included authors such as Heinrich Wilhelm von Gerstenberg and Friedrich Gottlieb Klopstock. Ewald also picked up new doctrines on the poetic arts from the Germans and from Denis Diderot and Edward Young. In the works of these writers Ewald encountered the notion of the poet as genius: the poet as an inspired individual, the poetic work as a personal expression, and poetic creation as an individual effort–in other words, *poiesis* (creation) as opposed to *imitatio* (imitation). Indeed, his evolution away from the idea of mimesis had been foreshadowed in his treatise on the nature of poetry.

In 1769 Ewald published a drama about the Fall, *Adam og Ewa eller Den ulykkelige Prøve* (Adam and Eve; or, The Ill-Fated Test). The play draws on works by Corneille, John Milton, and Klopstock. Ewald based his drama on a scene, which he had written a few years earlier for a competition, dealing with one of the characteristics of God. In particular, the character of Eve reflects the new aesthetic doctrine of the time and foreshadows aspects of Ewald's later authorship. During these years he began reading Christoph Martin Wieland's prose translations of William Shakespeare and studying the poems attributed to Ossian in James Macpherson's *Fragments of Ancient Poetry, Collected in the Highlands of Scotland, and Translated from the Galic or Erse Language* (1760). Both Wieland's and Macpherson's works marked a move away from the aesthetics of reason and classicism. Reading them convinced Ewald to study the English language: "Jeg lærte det, og hvilket bundløst Væld af Digterrigdom aabnede sig nu for mig" (I learned it, and what an unfathomable wealth of poetic riches opened up before me), as he later wrote in the "Fortale" (Preface) to the first volume of his *Samtlige Skrifter* (Collected Writings, 1780–1791). His acquaintance with Klopstock was leading him in the same direction. In the five-act tragedy *Rolf Krage* (1770), Ewald tried using a Shakespearean style. He put aside his French alexandrines and instead wrote in a lyrical prose that was highly reminiscent of the Ossian poetry and Klopstock's *Der Messias* (The Messiah, 1749). Denis Diderot's emotional prose dramas also influenced the diction of Ewald's play. *Rolf Krage* is a somewhat uneven piece, but it can be viewed as a laboratory for Ewald's development of new aesthetic doctrines.

The acting Danish prime minister, J. H. E. Bernsdorff, wanted to send Ewald to Scotland to collect Celtic folk songs–the community of German scholars in Copenhagen was searching for the roots of Germanic poetry–but Ewald's hopes for a secure future disappeared with Bernsdorff's fall from power. Ewald expressed his sorrow over this occurrence in *Philet, en Fortælning* (Philet, a Tale, 1770). At the same time, his health was seriously affected by arthritis and alcoholism.

Ewald continued throughout his career to make a name for himself as a playwright. After *Adam og Ewa* and *Rolf Krage* he wrote a grotesque comedy in alexandrines, *Harlequin Patriot eller den uægte Patriotisme. En*

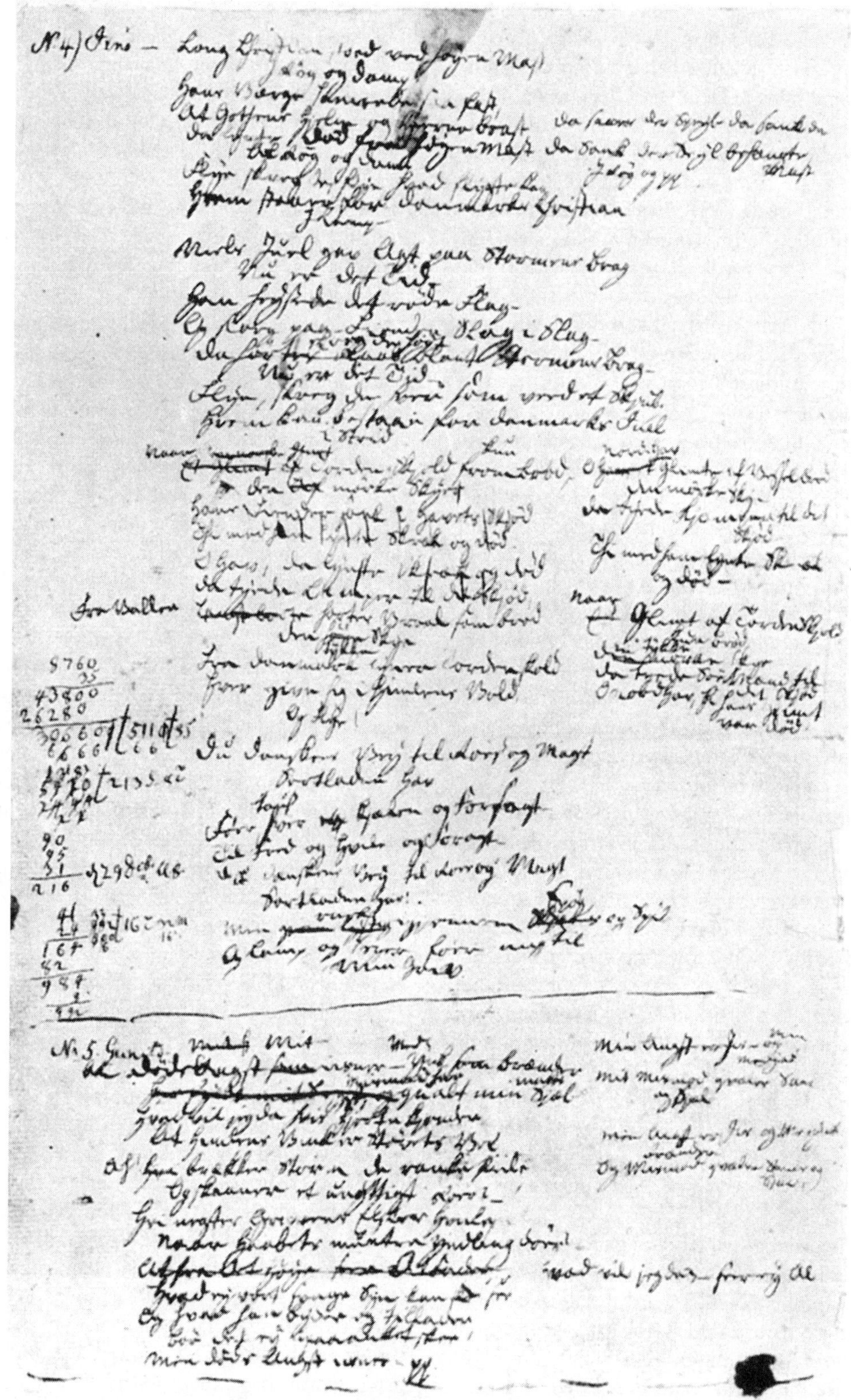

Manuscript for "Kong Kristian stod ved højen Mast" (King Christian Stood by the Lofty Mast), written by Ewald in 1778 for his ballad opera Fiskerne *(The Fishermen, 1779). Set to new music by D. F. R. Kuhlau in 1828, it was adopted as the Danish royal anthem in 1830 (courtesy of the Danish Royal Library, Copenhagen).*

comisk Comoedie i tre Handlinger paa Vers (Harlequin Patriot; or, The False Patriotism: A Comical Comedy in Three Acts in Verse, 1772), a harsh commentary on the repressive conditions in Denmark after the 28 April 1772 execution of Johann Friedrich Struensee, the German physician who had wielded considerable political power for two years through his influence over the mentally unstable Christian VII. Ewald's comedic writing, which, in addition to the Harlequin play, includes *De brutale Klappere* (The Brutal Clappers, 1771), employs both classical and commedia dell'arte elements, but as comedies they are overly contrived and develop into a critique of the comedic foundation of classical comedy: the world is a ruin in Ewald's comedies.

During the early 1770s Ewald also wrote a series of personal poems that are considered to rank among the most significant in all of Danish literature. The best are his odes, which combined inspirations from the classical odes of Pindar and Horace and from neoclassical odes that he encountered primarily in Klopstock's poetry and, later, in English lyric poetry by James Thomson and Young. Ewald blended these patterns together with unprecedented linguistic energy and a resonant richness that transformed Danish poetry. "Da jeg var syg" (When I Was Sick, 1771) marked the birth of first-person poetry in Danish literature. The following year he published the reflective poem "Haab og Erindring" (Hope and Remembrance).

To ensure his economic survival, Ewald also wrote many occasional poems for members of the bourgeoisie, nobility, and royalty. He wrote for the sake of money, but he never gave in to the platitudes that have generally plagued the genre over the ages. Ewald was highly esteemed for his occasional verse, which he wrote with an awareness of the conventions of the genre but with great artistic strength. These poems, most dating from 1767 to about 1775, were written for funerals, weddings, and baptisms. He also wrote texts for mourning cantatas and settings of the Passion of Christ *(Passionstekster)*. His occasional verse included several poems for friends and acquaintances. Of Ewald's ninety poems, seventy deal with events in other people's lives.

Ewald's occasional poems are exemplum poems in the classical sense, in which the life of the deceased or the newlywed is embellished by general reflections of a Christian or moral nature. The particular and the general are always reconciled into a unified cosmic whole. Precisely because the world could be viewed as a cosmos, Ewald was able to use the rhetorical technique of the exemplum: the particular, when viewed in a spiritual light, includes common experience. The world is complete–that is the fundamental comfort in the funeral poems. This harmonious worldview collapses in specific poems, especially in one written for the funeral of his friend Frederik von Arnsbach, "Taarer ved Herr Frederik von Arnsbachs Grav" (Tears at Mr. Frederik von Arnsbach's Grave, 1772). Pain dismantles the structures of the rhetorical genre in acknowledgment of the fact that the classical exemplum technique, and thereby the classical cosmology, can no longer be upheld. In this poem Ewald separates the individual from the common experience, thereby creating a new poetic situation. He wrote from this perspective for most of the rest of his career.

In the early 1770s Ewald also found the time to experiment with a new prose genre; he wrote periodical essays aimed at improving morals and manners, based on the model of the English essayists Joseph Addison and Richard Steele. Ewald's thirteen-issue series of periodical works was published posthumously as *De Fremmede* (The Foreigners, 1805). The series includes the draft of a novel, called *Frankhuysens Historie* (Frankhuysen's Story, 1805), as well as other short-story and novel fragments and sketches. The essays of *De Fremmede* mimics those of Addison and Steele's *The Tatler* (1709–1711) and *The Spectator* (1711–1712, 1714) and other periodicals of the day that criticized contemporary mores, but at the same time they dismantle the moral idealism and faith in common sense that was typical of such publications. Ewald experimented his way to a more complex form, one that he found in the contemporary novel. The dissolution of the periodical essay, in other words, gave way to the novel. This change is apparent in the stories and novel sketches included in the series, such as *Mester Synaals Fortelling* (Master Sewing Needle's Tale, 1780), *Herr Panthakaks Historie* (Mr. Panthakak's Story, 1805), and *Frankhuysens Historie*. Ewald likely began *Herr Panthakaks Historie* in 1771; it remained the fragment of a novel when published posthumously in 1805. The Greek *pantakak* means "everything is bad." *Panthakak* is a counterweight to the optimistic Pangloss in Voltaire's *Candide* (1759). The text is a parody that touches on both Voltaire's philosophy and Gottfried Wilhelm Leibniz's metaphysics. Another side of the work deals with Ewald's preoccupation with the novels of Henry Fielding, primarily *Joseph Andrews* (1742) and *Tom Jones* (1749). In contrast to Liebniz's speculation and Voltaire's cynicism, Ewald latches onto Fielding's trust in the primacy of experience and his naive faith that "the good heart" will triumph in the world. The combination of these two aspects probably explains why Ewald was not able to finish the work.

Frankhuysens Historie demonstrates that experience and a good heart do not automatically lead to happiness. It is structured around two main characters, who are opposites. The overall format comes from Fielding's

Tom Jones. Tom Jones and his rival, Blifil, have been turned into the good-hearted Frankhuysen and the evil Schliker. At every turn Frankhuysen confronts a series of middle-class stereotypes, after which it is expected that he will fashion himself: financial discretion, avarice, egotism, and hypocrisy. Modeling oneself after such a world would be tantamount to doing away with one's sense of decency, which is precisely what Schliker does. Thanks to his violence, deceit, hypocrisy, and, above all, his extraordinary egotism, everything goes wonderfully for Schliker's career. By consistently following his good and helpful heart, on the other hand, Frankhuysen's life becomes a catastrophe. His critical perspective sets him apart from good society, while Schliker deliberately models himself after the powerful. *Frankhuysens Historie* is critical of the entire bourgeois world and its self-righteousness. The contrasting figures of Frankhuysen and Schliker embody a fundamental dichotomy in middle-class society related not only to the opposition between nature and culture but also to the juxtaposition of art and money. In this way, inspired by the characters in Fielding's novel, the story is structured as a contrastive balancing act between constraint, control, discomfort, and discipline on the one hand and inclination, spontaneity, passion, and ease on the other. While Schliker's phlegmatic temperament suits the "nu brugelige Klogskab" (now common wisdom) like a hand in a glove, Frankhuysen's fiery soul is poetic. In this way Ewald shows that there was actually quite a sizable difference between art and the practice of life. Frankhuysen's expulsion from the middle-class environment is at the same time what liberates his art. In his innermost nature–also in his role as "citizen"–lies the source of his art. His art is an attempt to remind the corrupt of what is going wrong in the world of the powerful. The work of art is not a tribute to pure, unspoiled internal forces or a genuflection to external ones; Ewald's art insists on the necessity of discussing both. Frankhuysen struggles to act upon his internal feelings, but every time he asserts himself, he is caught by society's punitive measures. This experience turns him into a poet, Ewald contends. Poetry becomes simultaneously a location for insight and a boundless, nonintegrated space.

In an effort to remove Ewald from the capital city and its excesses, his domineering mother and Minister Johan Christian Schønheyder persuaded the thirty-year-old writer to move north to Rungsted, where he lived through 1775 in a sort of exile. Together, the two attempted to make the unruly poet live a proper Christian life. They forced him to exist on a meager income, to live under meticulous supervision, and to endure a steady stream of admonitions, lectures, and threats of internment. With Ewald's mother and Schønheyder on one side and Ewald himself on the other, there was a battle for who would make decisions for him. He was forced to return to the pietistic Christian community that he had left earlier in his life. In Rungsted Ewald wrote some of his most significant literary work, including his most famous poem, "Rungsteds Lyksaligheder. En Ode" (An Ode to the Joys of Rungsted, 1775). He resided at the inn that later became the home of twentieth- century Danish writer Karen Blixen. "Rungsteds Lyksaligheder" is a virtuoso rendition of the classical elements of a pastoral poem, but at the same time it surpasses the classical poetic form. In the poem Ewald employs rhetoric to new ends. It marks the birth of Romantic poetry in Denmark, depicting the poet as an enthusiastic genius who is inspired by nature, love, and–not least of all–the loss of love.

Ewald wrote his principal work, *Levnet og Meeninger,* during this repressive period in Rungsted, engaging in a subtle and indirect dialogue with the religious zealots who surrounded him. His autobiographical work is mentioned for the first time in a letter by Schønheyder to the poet on 16 October 1774. Gradually, as Ewald wrote the various sections of the manuscript, he forwarded them to Schønheyder and a few other readers. Ewald likely stopped working on the text in 1775 and picked it up again briefly in 1778.

Levnet og Meeninger comprises twelve chapters. Ewald first describes his and his brother's journey to Prussia and their involvement in the Seven Years' War. The opening chapter depicts the two young men during a stop along the way in Hamburg. At the end of the chapter Ewald enlists as a soldier, serving under the Prussian privy councillor. In the next chapter he leaves his brother, who has given up and wants to return home, and sails down the Elbe toward the war. When he runs out of money at one point on his journey, he steals a bottle of wine, lies down on a hillside, and gives himself over to the pleasures of the wine, imagining countless war exploits. In the meantime, the boat sails off without him, and the rest of his journey toward the battlefield is described only through innuendo and with significant gaps. Ewald does not describe the battlefield at all. On the other hand, he details his reflections–the "opinions" of the title–at great length, and the plot loses most of its narrative force. Starting with his love for Arendse, the narrator gives his imagination free rein on the subject of sex, primarily in flashbacks to the erotic fantasies of his youth. These memories culminate in the first sublime, but also comical, meeting with the object of his desire, Arendse. The meeting inspires him to go off and earn a fortune as a soldier rather than live as a diligent theologian at home in Copenhagen. The account concludes with a loosely drafted chapter, "Magdeborg," which hints at the rest of Ewald's fate until he reaches the war theater. The work ends with a reflective chapter, "Min Ærlighed" (My Honesty), in which he discusses the many aspects of honesty. It is intended as a defense for a life lived outside the framework of respectability.

Similar to Laurence Sterne's *Tristram Shandy* (1759–1767), *Levnet og Meeninger* revolves around its many narrative associations and digressions, which give the work its energy. Hence, the adult narrator, who sits propped up amid a pile of pillows in his armchair at his desk and indulges his imagination, is the focal point of the work. The text exists somewhere between the experienced past and the written present; it is patterned after the narrative styles of the novels of the period. The text includes a wealth of references to other works of European literature, a private canon of works stretching from Augustine's *Confessiones* (Confessions, circa 397–401) to the latest English novels. At no point is the presentation collected into a neatly organized whole. It is made up of fragments written down, just as the many opinions the narrator continuously interjects do not crystallize into a coherent life history with one telos–quite the contrary. Therefore, when considered as an autobiography or a confession, *Levnet og Meeninger* has quite a few shortcomings. Despite its many loose ends, however, there is a discernible overall plan of composition, and Ewald's own manuscript still exists.

In the first five chapters Ewald depicts the wholesome effects of wine and nature, with love as the subtext. In the following chapters love takes the spotlight, and wine and nature become the subtexts. The individual sections are arranged in an ascending pattern, which culminates with the composite image of the first meeting with Arendse–the sublime experience in the book. But this elevated depiction and the rise up to it are juxtaposed at every turn by a falling pattern, until these two movements–the rising and the falling–finally meet in the last chapter about Arendse, where the elevated poet is well on his way to falling down the stairs and losing his joy. The pathetic and the laughable run together; this complexity permeates all the other chapters. These paradoxical aspects and Ewald's sardonic sense of humor flavor the work. *Levnet og Meeninger* was an odd text for Ewald to send to a Christian minister who was concerned about his spiritual state.

In *Levnet og Meeninger* Ewald emphasizes his self-assurance and desire for adventure in his youth. He wonderingly calls himself a "Borger af en anden Verden" (citizen of another world), another pietistic expression that Ewald imbues with a worldly connotation. He is a person for whom the "sædvanlige og daglige" (ordinary and everyday) has become "modbydeligt" (repulsive), and who therefore strives to distinguish himself from his "snevrere Kreds" (intimate circle). Societal institutions have lost their hold on the individual in *Levnet og Meeninger,* in which the individual comes into existence by breaking with the authorities–both the internal and the external. The protagonist sets out into the world, leaving behind what he comes from. The book tells the story of this journey, but at the same time it is a story about the irrevocability of the journey. Half of the protagonist's destiny is in that which he destroys and liberates himself from, and the other half is in the fleeting nature of the moment.

While eighteenth-century literature often pays homage to the middle class, depicting its mercantile self-understanding as grounded in the nature of the cosmos, the narrator of *Levnet og Meeninger* objects to this tendency. Instead, the nobleman functions as a leitmotiv. *Homo oeconomicus* is not the hero of the story, nor is he the head of the family in the intimate sphere. Quite the contrary, the family limits his horizons and potential without fulfilling the promise of happiness. Thus, in the book Ewald says goodbye to his family. Similarly, he is not sentimental about himself or his fate. The reader who expects sensitivity or the rhetoric or cult of virtue will come away from *Levnet og Meeninger* empty-handed. Everything that is the basis for eighteenth-century sentimentality is the object of criticism, parody, and laughter. Ewald wants to escape from the everyday life of the middle class. He is not a middle-class hero; he is a chivalric hero.

Ewald models his youthful alter ego on literary heroes, making him a composite version of other novelistic characters. *Levnet og Meeninger* is modeled after Miguel de Cervantes's *Don Quixote* (1605, 1615). The young Ewald is the hidalgo; his brother is Sancho Panza; and Arendse is Ewald's Dulcinea. Just as that renowned Spanish bookworm set out into the world to make the literature he had studied into reality, so too does Ewald. About his reading and his life, he writes, "var det mig som Barn, den største Vellyst at høre Eventyr, da jeg blev Dreng at læse Romaner, og da jeg blev ældre, at spille dem selv" (as a child, my greatest pleasure was to listen to fairy tales, when I was a boy it was reading novels, and when I got older, playing the roles in them myself). Thus, he establishes the parodic progression of his own historical development: hearing, then reading, and finally living what he has heard and read, as if he were Don Quixote. The young hero embodies the progressive orientation of both the new novel and the new society. Overt and hidden references to European literature run throughout the journey. Ewald's interest in the novel genre had something to do with its suitability for expressing a person's preoccupation with experiencing things he has not yet experienced. In this wide-open universe he puts his attitudes, perceptions, and sensitivity to the test. The patterns that dominate eighteenth-century novels are transformed into imaginary forms in *Levnet og Meeninger,* where reality is made problematic. The book does not move forward in time, following the protagonist and his actions. It is written instead with an awareness that the odyssey has already been completed. Its epic past is past. A particularly important model for the intricate play with chronology is the English author Sterne, whose novels Ewald had studied.

Ewald's intent was to contribute to knowledge of the human heart by presenting his own. For the most part this aim is a cover for other interests. His exploration of his own life is not an attempt to describe the course of a life but a penetrating depiction of the seductive and fragile radiance of internal images. This problem is most clearly presented in the love story. It is still less about Arendse, however, than about "min Arendse" (my Arendse). The Arendse that he conjures up as an older narrator amid his armchair pillows is an attempt to hold onto a fragile fantasy image, one that is threatened by the many new images that the intervening years have yielded.

Ewald's writing for the theater culminated in two ballad operas, the tragedy *Balders Død* (1775; translated as *The Death of Balder,* 1886) and *Fiskerne* (The Fishermen, 1779). *Balders Død* brought Ewald his first theatrical success, and *Fiskerne* marked the long-awaited pinnacle of his theatrical career. Prior to *Balders Død,* which premiered on 7 February 1778, albeit without musical accompaniment, none of his works for the stage had been performed. Ewald's road to the stage and success as a dramatist was difficult. He was somewhat ahead of his time with his blend of Nordic Renaissance elements, English Restoration drama, and democratic humanism, with a universal appeal that reached beyond the traditional ethos of privileged society.

In January 1779 *Balders Død,* which had been published in 1775, was performed, with music by Johann Hartmann, at the Royal Danish Theater on the birthday of Christian VII. With this performance of *Balders Død,* Ewald had finally accomplished the theatrical breakthrough he had been seeking. It meant that for the last few years of his life, he was able to live in financial security.

In the early 1770s Ewald had moved away from the dominant rationalist Enlightenment tastes and aesthetics. In *Balders Død* he explores the border regions between reason, passion, and madness and asserts the notion of the creativity of madness. He combines the new opera and French ballad-opera styles in the play with characteristics of both Shakespearean and classical tragedies. Balder's passion becomes his fate, and his love leads to his perdition. Balder is a zealot. His fate demonstrates that he has made himself blind to everything other than his own passion. He refuses to let go of his impossible love, give up, and adapt; as the play demonstrates, this refusal leads to madness. The social and the emotional collide disastrously in *Balders Død,* as in many other European literary works from the latter half of the eighteenth century. Balder is an incarnation of the cultural misery of Johann Wolfgang von Goethe's *Die Leiden des jungen Werthers* (The Sorrows of Young Werther, 1773) or Jean-Jacques Rousseau's *La nouvelle Héloïse* (The New Heloise, 1761). The incongruity between emotional and social life is lethal. When Balder's ill-fated love simultaneously opens the way for Loki's entrance onto the stage, Ewald combines the emotional catastrophes with an eschatological perspective that joins Nordic depictions of Ragnarok (in Scandinavian mythology, the final battle between the good and evil gods) with Christian doomsday visions. In Ewald's play Balder is a rebellious Jesus figure who does not follow the will of his father, Odin, but instead chooses his humanity and his passion and as a result must die. *Balders Død* ends in a catastrophe without rebirth.

Ewald wrote *Fiskerne* at the request of the director of the Royal Theater. The play, performed on the birthday of Christian VII in 1780, is a tribute to the new nationality law adopted in 1776, which was a reaction to the oppressive, illegitimate "reign" of Struensee. The purpose of this law was to ensure that the citizens and nobility of Denmark, Norway, and Holstein had priority for government positions. Ewald also paid homage to the law in the ode "Indføds-Retten" (The Citizens' Law) in 1778.

Fiskerne is set in the Renaissance, during the reign of Denmark's renowned King Christian IV. It opens with a terrible storm that threatens to destroy the fishermen's pound nets. After fruitless attempts to save the fishing gear, desperation gives way to the approaching ruin. At the same time, an English ship runs aground, and its crew is on the verge of being lost. Against all odds, the fishermen succeed in rescuing the captain of the ship, who is the sole survivor. But after this magnificent effort, the fishermen still lack the means to subsist. Their unhappy situation is finally remedied by a generous, noble patriot who gives them money and a lifelong pension. The conclusion of the play is purely idyllic.

The brave fishermen are hardened by their circumstances to great virtue. The deus ex machina of the play, with the noble name Odelheim (ancestral home), demonstrates through his monetary gift that virtue is rewarded. In this way the ocean drowns the free patriotic idyll on land, just as Christian IV in the national song of the play tames the ocean waves while standing on the high mast. The message is that in such an unpre-

Monument to Ewald and his contemporary, the poet Johan Herman Wessel, beside Trinitatis Church, which adjoins the Round Tower in Copenhagen (courtesy of the Danish Royal Library, Copenhagen)

dictable existence, as symbolized by the ocean and the storm, one needs law and order. Throughout the play thunder rumbles and the waves roll dangerously and unpredictably, and the men must be daring. Once again Ewald celebrates the heroic, and with the fishermen's words he scoffs at the oppressive comfort of the farmers on shore. Their security does not fascinate him, not even in the idyll *Fiskerne.*

Ewald died on 17 March 1781. The year before his death, while living in Copenhagen, he produced several significant religious odes: "Til Sielen. En Ode" (An Ode to the Soul, 1780), "Død og Dom" (Death and Judgment, 1780), "Hellige, Hellige" (Holy, Holy, 1780), "Poenitenten. En Ode" (The Penitent: An Ode, 1780), and "Følelser ved den hellige Nadvere" (Feelings at the Holy Communion, 1780). The last of these works was dedicated to Ewald's spiritual mentor, Schønheyder. Even if Ewald's later Christian poetry evokes Pietism, it distinguishes itself from pietistic confessional literature, in which salvation is assured, by focusing on a moment of crisis–that is, Ewald's verse focuses on the hope of salvation but not the assurance of it.

Ewald's contributions to Danish literature are normally discussed in connection with the breakthrough of Romantic literature in Europe at the end of the eighteenth century. To be sure, Ewald wrote Romantic poetry, but his connection with Enlightenment literature and thought are remarkably strong at the same time, such that his work can be understood only in the context of its interaction with the classical literary canon and conventions. The latter elements mean that Ewald was open to irony, parody, and intellectual interests that extended well beyond the scope of the emotional literature of the Romantics. His own work was clearly influenced by his love of Sterne's ironic and parodic novels and Cervantes's *Don Quixote.* Ewald's texts reflect an ongoing dialogue with other works, both with the classical (Virgil and Horace) and the contemporary (Sterne and Klopstock). This dialogue means that Ewald's authorship is more dissonant than harmonious: he sets the Enlightenment's intellectual doubt and emotional split into dramatic relief in his texts.

From the character of Eve in his first play, *Adam og Ewa,* to Balder in *Balders Død,* a specific theme is at the core of Johannes Ewald's poetics and authorship. The real and active center of his poetics is his loyalty to an intuitive illumination–the sublime elevation, the impact of the sudden–that can never become a cultural norm. The power that comes from this illumination makes it impossible to summarize neatly or succinctly Ewald's authorial development. His textual universe is characterized by the absence of reconciliation or unity. But at the same time, an ardent energy, an immense linguistic force, and the intense will of his monumental effort emanate from his work. Ewald wrote at a time when art was becoming autonomous and classicism was in crisis. For him, as for many of the authors after whom he modeled himself, time is the opposite of order; existence is hopeless, and every attempt is a new foray into the unarticulated. Thus, the best of Ewald's texts hover around the norms of the day and surpass those norms. They deal with ruptures that cannot be mended and wounds that cannot be healed–and they do so with a great deal of cheerfulness, a burning pathos, and a keen sense of irony. In this process Ewald gave voice to eighteenth-century doubts about civilization and its public morality and theories.

Biographies:

Christian Molbech, *Johannes Evalds Levnet* (Copenhagen: C. A. Reitzel, 1831);

Frederik Christian Olsen, *Digteren Johannes Ewalds Liv og Forholde i Aarene 1774–77* (Copenhagen: J. H. Schubothe, 1835);

Ludvig Schrøder, *Ewald og Baggesen, deres Læremestre og deres Velyndere* (Kolding: K. Jørgensen, 1884);

Adolf Ditlev Jørgensen, *Johannes Evald* (Copenhagen: Gyldendal, 1888);

Louis Bobé, *Johannes Ewald. Biografiske Studier* (Copenhagen: H. Hagerup, 1943);

Louis E. Grandjean, *Johannes Ewald og Birthe i Rungsted* (Copenhagen: Høst, 1960);

Keld Zeruneith, *Soldigteren. En biografi om Johannes Ewald* (Copenhagen: Gyldendal, 1985).

References:

Thomas Bredsdorff, "Da vi blev syge," in *Danske digtanalyser. Digte fra folkevisen til det tyvende århundrede læst af digtere, forskere, lærere, kritikere,* edited by Bredsdorff (Copenhagen: Arena, 1969), pp. 49–59;

Bredsdorff, *Digternes natur. En idés historie i 1700-tallets danske poesi* (Copenhagen: Gyldendal, 1975);

Hans Brix, *Johannes Ewald. En Række kritiske Undersøgelser* (Copenhagen: Gyldendal, 1913);

Brix, "Til Johannes Ewalds *Levnet og Meeninger,*" in his *Analyser og Problemer,* volume 4 (Copenhagen: Gyldendal, 1933), pp. 107–162;

Brix, ed., *Johannes Ewald-Manuskripter* (Copenhagen: Danske Sprog- og Litteraturselskab/E. Munksgaard, 1944);

Mogens Brøndsted, "Fantaster i dansk og fremmed Digtning," *Edda,* 48 (1948): 1–57;

Jens Aage Doctor, "Ewalds Levnedsbog," in *Guldalderstudier. Festskrift til Gustav Albeck den 5. juni 1966,* edited by Henning Høirup, Aage Jørgensen, and Peter Skautrup (Århus: Universitetsforlaget, 1966), pp. 47–73;

Doctor, *Herrens Billeder* (Copenhagen: Berlingske, 1976);

Ernst Frandsen, *Johannes Ewald. Et stykke dansk åndshistorie,* second edition (Copenhagen: Gyldendal, 1968);

John Greenway, "The Two Worlds of Johannes Ewald: Dyd vs. Myth in *Balders Død,*" *Scandinavian Studies,* 42, no. 3 (1970): 394–410;

Alf Henriques, *Shakespeare og Danmark indtil 1840. Vurdering, Opførelse, Oversaettelse, Efterligning* (Copenhagen: E. Munksgaard, 1941);

Marianne Horsdal, *Konkordans over digte af Johannes Ewald* (Odense: Odense Universitetsforlag, 1976);

Edvin Kau, *Den ewaldske tekst mellem himmel og jord. En analyse af grundtemaer i Ewalds forfatterskab–som scene for sammenstødet mellem feudal og borgerlig ideologi i overgangsprocessen mellem feudalt og kapitalistisk samfund* (Copenhagen: Medusa, 1977);

Jette Lundbo Levy, "Mennesket som romanhelt," in *Tekstanalyser. Ideologikritiske tekster,* edited by Jørgen Holmgaard (Copenhagen: E. Munksgaard, 1971), pp. 35–48;

Hans Møller, *Beiträge zur Charakteristik der Dichtungen Johs. Ewalds* (Kiel: Lüdtke & Martens, 1906);

Erik A. Nielsen, "Pietismens genstridige søn–Johannes Ewalds visdom," in his *Solens fødsel. Seks tekster om kristendommens hemmeligheder* (Frederiksberg: Anis, 1998), pp. 115–179;

Adam Oehlenschläger, *Om Ewald og Schiller. Forelæsninger holdte ved Kjøbenhavns Universitet i Aarene 1810 og 11,* volume 1 (Copenhagen: Lohse & Delbanco, 1854);

Erik Oksbjerg, *Empirisme i Ewalds digtning, 1769–72. Gnisten* (Værløse, [1986]);

B. Rasmussen, "Adskilligt om Johannes Ewalds teater," *Orbis Litterarum,* 5 (1947): 10–18;

Lars Peter Rømhild, "Det rigtige i det forkerte. Johannes Ewalds Mester Synaals Fortelling," in *Analyser af dansk kortprosa,* volume 1, edited by Jørgen Dines Johansen (Copenhagen: Borgen, 1971), pp. 92–109;

F. C. Rosen, "Et Par Ord om Johannes Ewalds Disputatser," *Nyt dansk Aftenblad* (1826);

Doery Smith, *Johannes Ewald, 1743–1943* (Oslo: Norden, 1943);

Peer E. Sørensen, *Håb og erindring. Johannes Ewald i oplysningen* (Copenhagen: Gyldendal, 1989);

Sørensen, *Johannes Ewalds digtning og poetik* (Trieste: Parnaso, 1997);

Sørensen, "Poesiens inversion. Ewald, Rifbjerg og Højholt," in *Mere lys! Indblik i oplysningstiden i dansk litteratur og kultur,* edited by Mads Julius Elf and Lasse Horne Kjældgaard (Hellerup: Spring, 2002), pp. 129–147;

Haakon Stangerup, *Romanen i Danmark i det attende Aarhundrede. En komparativ Undersøgelse* (Copenhagen: Levin & Munksgaard, 1936);

Ejnar Thomsen, "Per Langes Ewald-digt," in his *Digteren og Kaldet. Efterladte Studier,* edited by Else Dalhoff Thomsen, Erik Dal, and Aage Henriksen (Copenhagen: Gyldendal, 1957), pp. 57–86;

Helge Toldberg, *Det nordiske Element i Johs. Ewalds Digtning* (Copenhagen: P. Branner, 1944);

Knud Wentzel, "Manøvrer i det episke, udført i Ewalds *Levnet og Meeninger,*" *Kritik,* 18 (1971): 63–99.

Papers:

Johannes Ewald's manuscripts and letters are at the Danish Royal Library in Copenhagen.

Mathilde Fibiger

(13 December 1830 - 17 June 1872)

Marina Allemano
University of Alberta

BOOKS: *Clara Raphael. Tolv Breve,* anonymous, foreword by Johan Ludvig Heiberg (Copenhagen: C. A. Reitzel, 1851 [i.e., 1850]);

Et Besøg. Nye Breve, af Forfatterinden til Clara Raphael (Copenhagen: C. A. Reitzel, 1851);

Hvad er Emancipation? as Sophie A**** (Copenhagen: C. A. Reitzel, 1851);

En Skizze efter det virkelige Liv, af Forfatterinden til Clara Raphael (Copenhagen: C. A. Reitzel, 1853 [i.e. 1852]);

Minona. Fortælling, af Forf. til Clara Raphaels Breve (Copenhagen: A. F. Høst, 1854 [i.e. 1853]).

Editions: *Clara Raphael. Tolv breve,* afterword by Eva Bendix (Copenhagen: Linghardt & Ringhof, 1976);

Clara Raphael–Minona, edited by Lise Busk-Jensen (Copenhagen: Det Danske Sprog- og Litteraturselskab/Borgen, 1994).

OTHER: E. T. A. Hoffmann, *Nøddeknækkeren og Musekongen og Det fremmede Barn: To Eventyr,* translated by the author of *Clara Raphael* [Fibiger] (Copenhagen: Hagerup, 1856);

Hoffmann, *Brudevalget og Guldskaalen: To Eventyr,* translated, with an introduction, by the author of *Clara Raphael* [Fibiger] (Copenhagen: Schönberg, 1858);

Bertholdt Auerbach, *Stedmoderen,* translated by the author of *Clara Raphael* [Fibiger] (Haderslev: Folkeskriftselskabet i Haderslev, 1858);

Auerbach, *Udvalgte Skrifter,* translated, with an introduction, by the author of *Clara Raphael* [Fibiger] (Copenhagen: Schønberg, 1861–1862)–comprises *Barbene, Ivo, den lille Theolog, Alpeblomsten,* and *Professorinden;*

Ilia Fibiger, *Digtninger* (Copenhagen: Gyldendal, 1867)–includes "En biografisk Skizze," by Mathilde Fibiger.

SELECTED PERIODICAL PUBLICATIONS–UNCOLLECTED: "Kunst og Videnskab," review of Ilia Fibiger's *Rettroende Eventyr, Berlingske Tidende* (25 January 1859);

Mathilde Fibiger (courtesy of the Danish Royal Library, Copenhagen)

"Den Ensommes Hjem," *Tidsskrift för hemmet, tillegnad den svenska qvinnan,* 11 (1869): 366–375;

Commentary on Leonora Christina Ulfeldt's *Jammersminde, Tidsskrift för hemmet, tillegnad den svenska qvinnan,* 12 (1870): 108–110;

"Nytaarsnat 1870," *For Ide og Virkelighed,* 1 (1870): 71;

"Lidt om Kvindelighed," *Jyllandsposten* (21 January 1872).

The emancipation of women was not a new topic in mid-nineteenth-century Europe. Mary Wollstonecraft had, with her *A Vindication of the Rights of Women* in 1792, articulated the many concerns of inequality that the bourgeois revolution in France had placed on its agenda, and she had criticized Jean-Jacques Rousseau's Romantic ideals of womanhood and femininity that situated women in a gendered and complementary sphere. However, with the spread of Romanticism in Europe, the Enlightenment ideals of sexual equality receded in favor of an ideology that emphasized differences between men and women in their biology and inner lives. Women's liberation was not necessarily perceived as a battle for social, political, and legal rights in society, but more as a desire for spiritual and intellectual freedom on a par with men's personal imaginative freedom.

In Denmark, Mathilde Lucie Fibiger embraced some of these Romantic ideas and wrote in response to them an extraordinary novel, published anonymously in 1851 with the title *Clara Raphael. Tolv Breve* (Clara Raphael: Twelve Letters). Fibiger was only twenty years old and employed as a governess at that time, but in spite of her age and station, she gained immediate recognition, and her novel caused a stir–"Clara Raphael-fejden" (the Clara Raphael Feud)–among the literati. Feminists of the twentieth century still regard Fibiger's book as the first manifestation of the women's movement in Denmark, even if some of the author's idealistic pronouncements appear odd and unfeasible.

Fibiger was the youngest of nine children born to Johan Adolf Fibiger and Margrethe Cecilie Nielsen Aasen. Fibiger's father was an officer and an author of military publications, and in 1830 he became the director of Den militære Højskole (The Military College), where Johan Ludvig Heiberg was employed at the same time to teach logic and literature. The college and the official residence provided for the family were located in the old Gjet-house at Kongens Nytorv in Copenhagen, where the Royal Theatre (built in 1874) is now situated. Fibiger was born in the residential house on 13 December 1830, and the first five years of her life were some of her happiest. The house was bright and modern according to sanitary standards of the day, and the family entertained many important cultural and political guests. But in 1835 Adolf Fibiger suffered a severe setback and was dismissed from his position at the college. Internal politics at the institution were cited as the cause of his dismissal, but the director's openly democratic ideas and encouragement of societal reform similar to those begun in France after the July Revolution in 1830 were probably contributing factors. The family moved to Vejle in Jutland, where it did not thrive, either economically or emotionally. As a result, the parents separated in 1837 and were legally divorced in 1843, after which the mother returned to Copenhagen with the elder daughter, Ilia Marie Fibiger, and the three youngest children.

Margrethe Fibiger was a beautiful, caring, and emotional woman, but she lacked formal education and strong skills in domestic affairs. Ilia Fibiger, who was twenty years old at the time of the separation and already the lively center of the family, took charge of the household until her mother's death in 1844, when the home dissolved. As a teenager, Ilia Fibiger fell in love with a young officer, Oswald Marstrand (brother of the famous painter Wilhelm Marstrand), who did not return her affections, and after his death at the Battle of Eckernförde in 1849 during the Three Years' War of 1848–1851, the young woman's unrequited love turned inward and found its expression in fiction. Both Ilia and Mathilde became writers around this time, but the younger sister became inspired by the new political conflicts and democratic movements that translated into youthful ideas regarding women's emancipation.

Unlike the Fibiger boys, the girls in the family received little formal instruction beyond reading and writing. Most of their education came from the reading of contemporary poetry and fiction by such foreign authors as Sir Walter Scott, James Fenimore Cooper, Friedrich Schiller, Johann Wolfgang von Goethe, Novalis (pseudonym of Friederich von Hardenberg), and E. T. A. Hoffmann, and the Danish poets Adam Oehlenschläger, B. S. Ingemann, and Christian Winther. By the time she was eight years old, Fibiger demonstrated already in her letters to family members and girlfriends an unusual talent for writing, but the family's precarious financial situation eventually forced the unmarried sisters to find employment as governesses. After three years of private instruction in order to qualify as a teacher of younger children, the nineteen-year-old Fibiger took a position as governess in 1849 at Maltrupgård, near the town of Sakskøbing on the southern island of Lolland. During her stay there, she wrote the manuscript for her first novel, *Clara Raphael. Tolv Breve,* an epistolary novel that presents twelve letters by Clara Raphel to her friend Mathilde. The author subsequently sent the manuscript to Heiberg in Copenhagen at the end of October 1850. Fibiger's hope was that Heiberg, who was by then the director of the Royal Theatre and one of the leading critics in Denmark, would help her with the publication of her work. Not only did Heiberg facilitate the publication of the novel with C. A. Reitzel, but he also wrote a laudatory preface, and by Christmas 1850 (the title page reads 1851) the slim volume appeared in the bookstores.

Like the author, the young Clara leaves the capital to take employment as a governess on an estate in the provinces, but unlike Fibiger, Clara eventually becomes engaged to the young baron, Axel, with whom she plans to have a platonic marital arrangement. Upon her arrival at the estate, she begins to write a series of letters to her friend Mathilde in which she describes her new environment. Eleven of the letters are composed by Clara; one other letter is written by her friend Anna while Clara lies ill with a nervous attack. Clara's tone is generally critical, but her diction is lively and articulate, and her characterizations are credible and often humorous.

Clara Raphael is a novel of manners with concrete, realistic descriptions of daily life. At the same time, it is a romantic narrative similar to those written by the Brontë sisters in England. But *Clara Raphael* is more than an imitation of an established genre; it also includes philosophical reflections on such topics as the differences between affectation and ordinariness, the emptiness of polite conversation, the advantages of solitary life, and the disadvantages of traditional education. Questions concerning women's emancipation form a central part of the novel as do theological queries into the letter writer's personal relationship to God. Clara also conveys her idealistic views of nationalism, and most importantly she renounces worldly love. In her eighth letter to Mathilde, Clara writes about her allegiance to the pure Maid of Orléans, Joan of Arc, who in Schiller's version of the story, *Die Jungfrau von Orleans* (1801), is able to achieve wonderful things on earth by resisting all earthly love.

The feminist sensibility of Clara Raphael is complex. In her afterword to the 1994 edition of *Clara Raphael–Minona,* Lise Busk-Jensen analyzes Clara's position in regard to women's emancipation and points out that Clara's polarized worldview is not represented by the different sexes but by God's Idea (the good) versus the World's Idea (the bad). While Heiberg's romantic view of the sexes is hierarchical–that is, man represents mankind in front of God, and woman is only connected to mankind by association with man, Clara's romantic idealism rejects the notion that woman is different in kind. As observed by Busk-Jensen, Clara's insight that woman does not constitute the "other" in the triad God-man-woman is a forerunner to theories of alterity developed nearly a hundred years later by Simone de Beauvoir in *Le deuxième sexe* (1949). In Fibiger's novel, Clara articulates Fibiger's view that both sexes are capable of having a direct, personal relationship with God. Hence, the agenda of the novel is not aimed at social and political equality but rather at "aandelig" (spiritual and intellectual) freedom. Clara's weapon in the battle for spiritual equality is typically her use of language and writing; in other words, she renounces Motherhood and embraces the Word.

The reception of *Clara Raphael* was exceptional and gave rise to the Clara Raphael Feud, a public debate that lasted for more than six months. A total of eleven pamphlets and twenty-five articles were written in newspapers and journals in defense of or in opposition to the emancipatory ideals proposed in Fibiger's book. Proponents of both the extreme right and the extreme left wings of the political spectrum were highly critical of Fibiger's idealism and in particular of the unusual ending of the book. The conservative group headed by author Meïr Goldschmidt was of the opinion that women's liberation meant the freedom for females to follow their nature–that is, their destiny as wives and mothers; everything else would be unnatural. The socialist Frederik Dreier saw Fibiger's project as only relevant to salon ladies and not to society at large. Reform-friendly liberals and feminists supported some of Fibiger's ideas, but such women teachers as Pauline Worm and Athalia Schwartz stressed the importance of education and employment over abstract idealism. Many liberal men, including Heiberg, adhered essentially to a traditional notion of gender and were critical of Fibiger's idealized figure of the virgin-warrior Joan of Arc. Only teacher Fanny Normand de Bretteville agreed with Fibiger that women should first and foremost be able to act as themselves, motivated by their own inner strength.

In May 1851 Fibiger joined the debate with a pamphlet, *Hvad er Emancipation?* (What Is Emancipation?), written under a pseudonym. In the three letters written alternately by Sophie and Bertha, the author reconsiders the rather vague notions of "erkendelse" (consciousness) and "aand" (spirit or mind) and reiterates her arguments from *Clara Raphael* that women must know inner freedom before pursuing social and political change. In the last letter, Sophie suggests an interesting interpretation of Genesis, in which she sees the infamous Fall as a progressive step for mankind and the serpent as a falsely accused tempter. By gaining knowledge of good and evil, she argues, humanity rose from a state of unmediated spontaneity to independence and self-reliability. In Sophie's words, emancipation is spiritual reform or enlightenment; in modern terms, she calls for consciousness-raising.

In September of the same year, twenty-year-old Fibiger published yet another defense of her views in a longer pamphlet, *Et Besøg* (A Visit). In the eight letters addressed to "mine Læserinder" (my women readers), Fibiger seeks to correct previous misunderstandings and to add new arguments. She remains the idealist but modifies her opinion that worldly renunciation is necessary. In the seventh letter she suggests that God's Idea is supranatural, that it includes nature and hence also human sensuality. Fibiger also denies being myopic; *hyperopic* is the term she chooses for herself, and in returning to the topic of Eve's role in Paradise as a raiser of consciousness for mankind, Fibiger shows, in fact, farsightedness in her articulation of woman's nature. On the theme of "Kvindelighed" (womanliness or femininity) in her fifth letter, Fibiger distances herself from the conventions dictating proper ladylike behavior–for example, that to take long strides, to walk in public without a chaperone, to speak frankly to a man, or to defend one's opinion with passion is unfeminine. To Fibiger the entire notion of "Kvindelighed" is alternately a straitjacket, a veil, a leash, a tether, and a blindfold. To free oneself from the straitjacket has a hefty price tag: if a woman flouts the expected ladylike manners, she will be considered an outsider; if she conforms, she will lose her freedom to be a person. As the reader would expect, Fibiger opts for personhood.

In the summer of 1851 Fibiger moved back to Copenhagen to live with her family. Ilia and the Fibiger brothers disapproved of her public visibility during and after the scandalous debate, and she spent a couple of quiet years during which she and Ilia supported themselves by teaching, sewing, and doing literary translations and porcelain painting. In late 1851 Fibiger stayed at Rønnebæksholm near Ringsted, where she was a guest at the home of N. F. S. Grundtvig and his wife, Marie Toft. Here she began working on her second novel, *En Skizze efter det virkelige Liv* (A Sketch Taken From Real Life), which was released at Christmas 1852, although the date on the title page is 1853.

Fibiger's prose was still elegant and well crafted, but she stopped using the epistolary form in favor of an omniscient third-person narrative. However, *En Skizze efter det virkelige Liv* is much more conventional than *Clara Raphael,* with an ending that did not upset the readers and critics. The plot involves two young and beautiful sisters and their suitors. Margrethe becomes disillusioned with the follies of mankind and ceases to demand happiness for herself–that is, marriage–while her younger sister, Victoria, cannot live without it. At the end of the novel, Fibiger makes the two lovers, Victoria and her suitor, declare their commitment to each other in a surprisingly conventional manner. Victoria says, "Lov mig Din mandige Beskyttelse i Sorg og Glæde" (Promise me your manly protection in happiness and sorrow), to which Frederik responds, "Jeg lover Dig for Gud, der har gjort mig saa usigelig lykkelig, at jeg vil vogte og beskærme den Skat, som nu er min Ejendom, imod alt det Onde, der truer den . . ." (I promise you in the name of God, who has made me so profoundly happy, that I will guard and shelter the treasure that now belongs to me, against all evil that threatens it . . .). Still, several minor thematic concerns are of interest to the modern reader, especially as represented by the character Mrs. Staal, who is liberal-minded and tolerant, except of boredom. Echoing Fibiger's previous opinion on life in society, Mrs. Staal criticizes social discourse and conversation as empty, arty forms of rhetoric, while she prefers dialogue (in Danish, "Samtale") as an honest exchange of opinions.

In September 1853, Fibiger had the manuscript of her third and last novel, *Minona. Fortælling,* ready for submission but had to look for a new publisher, as Reitzel had died. Feeling insecure about managing the business end of authorship, she turned this time to Goldschmidt for help. Although he had been critical of *Clara Raphael,* he and Fibiger had since met at Grundtvig's house and were now on friendly terms. With Goldschmidt's assistance, the book was published by A. F. Høst in December 1853, although the title page bears the date 1854.

The novel was received with much disdain, and according to Busk-Jensen, the critics used every means to silence the young writer. Even Hans Christian Andersen, who had followed the Fibiger sisters' writing careers with interest, wrote to Ingemann that he found *Minona. Fortælling* horrid and likened it to a poisonous water plant, slimy and disgusting. The novel is well written and carefully plotted, but the central theme of incestuous love between brother and sister was too much for the critical readers to bear. In a way, the character of Minona is the other side of Clara Raphael. They are both idealists, but whereas Clara remains celibate and follows her ideal upward toward Heaven, Minona idealizes her own desire as a manifestation of God and nature that by her definition is without sin and hence guilt-free. Viggo, the older brother from whom she has been separated since childhood, reciprocates her feelings but is soon overcome by guilt and finds the forbidden love dark and painful. He eventually becomes a pastor, and Minona dies a Christian after having first repented her unnatural love for her brother.

In spite of the melodramatic ending, the novel deals with some interesting themes that reflect different philosophical thoughts on the moral codes concerning love in middle-class Denmark at that time. Minona, and to an extent her young stepmother, Helene, follow the desires of their hearts without reflecting on the moral standards of society. A minor character, Tyra, also flouts the rules of society, enters an illicit relationship, and becomes a single, self-supporting mother. Viggo, on the other hand, overcomes his desires and follows the call of duty, while another secondary character, Vir-

1) Nu er min Fortælling endt, og jeg beder Dem undskylde dens forvirrede Fremstilling, i Betragtning af at den er skreven i et Sygeværelse, hvor en kjær Patient bestandig gjorde Fordring paa min Opmærksomhed. Deres

Tolv Breve

Anna H××.

Den 7de Juli 1849.

Min elskede Mathilde!

Slutning

Saa uundværlig er Du mig, saa uadskillelig er Tanken om Dig, fra mine bedste og dybeste Følelser, at ingen Glæde er fuldkommen for mig, før jeg har meddeelt Dig den. Derfor maa jeg ogsaa idag nedlægge min Lyksalighed i Dit kjærlige Hjerte.

Vi have seiret og han lever, som jeg elsker. Jo, jeg elsker ham endnu, ligesaa høit, men paa en bedre Maade end før. Fra ham fik jeg Efterretningen om Slaget ved Frederits. Mine Følelser overvældede mig næsten, og Mathilde! jeg tør lade Himlen see disse Følelser. Det var ikke alene Qvindens Tak til Forsynet, for hendes Elskedes Frelse. det var ogsaa den danske Piges Jubel over Fædrelandets Seir. ~~Derpaa kjender jeg mig selv igjen~~ Danmark var min første Tanke, Axel den anden, derpaa kjender jeg mig selv igjen! Jeg føler mig selv i hvert Aandedrag og Gud i mig! O Mathilde! Saa god, saa mageløs kjærlig er Gud, at den jordiske Lykke, som jeg forskjød da Fristeren derfor vilde kjøbe min evige Sjæl den bereder Gud mig nu selv, og jeg tør glad modtage den, som en Gave af hans faderlige Haand. Hvor sandt er ikke hans Ord: Søger først mit Rige da skal ogsaa det Øvrige Fornødne blive Eder tildeelt!

Hør selv, hvad Axel skriver: „Min elskede Clara! Tør jeg, der allerede skylder Dem saa meget, vove en Bøn endnu? – Der stod i det Brev, hvis mindste Stavelse jeg gjemmer i mit Hjerte: „Havde jeg elsket ham paa samme Maade som jeg elsker Gud da kunde jeg blevet hans Hustru uden derved at bryde mit Løfte." – Jeg er overbeviist, at Deres Følelser allerede ere luttrede til en søsterlig Kjærlighed

Manuscript pages for Fibiger's epistolary novel Clara Raphael. Tolv Breve *(Clara Raphael: Twelve Letters), published in 1850 (courtesy of the Danish Royal Library, Copenhagen)*

t) rene Flamme, og jeg lover Dem, ved Deres eget, for mig
helligste Navn, at al min Stræben skal gaae ud paa
at forædle min Lidenskab for Dem, og befrie den fra
enhver Blanding af Egenkjærlighed. Men hertil maa
De hjælpe mig, Clara! Giv mig ikke alene en Broders Plads i Deres Hjerte, men en Broders dyrebare
Ret til at leve for Dem, og hos Dem. Det kan kun
skee, hvis De vil blive min Hustru, for Verden;
for Gud x og hinanden ville vi leve sammen x som
kjærlige Søskende. Ingen Lidenskab skal fra min
Side forstyrre Deres Fred, thi De skal ikke see
mig igjen, før mine Følelser for Dem, ere blev-
ne til en Broders, kun stærkere, og endnu uegen-
nyttigere. — (Ingen afsæt)
Som min Forlovede vil De finde den moder-
ligste Modtagelse hos min kjære Tante, og i
hendes og Annas Selskab, et behageligt Hjem
i vort Huus. Skjænk mig den Trøst, at vide Dem der!"
Er han ikke ædel, stor? Han svarer til det I-
deal af en Mand, som jeg undertiden forestillede mig i mine Drømme, men aldrig ventede
at træffe i Livet. Og han vil være min Broder!
Anna er næsten ligesaa lykkelig, som jeg, den
søde Pige! — Nu paastaaer hun, at jeg skal hol-
de op at skrive, da hun mener det anstrænger
mig for meget, og det er vel ogsaa bedst, om
ikke for andet saa for at føie hende. Men
nu er jeg snart ganske rask, og Du faaer da
et længere Brev fra

Din

Clara Raphael.

Clara Raphael.

Tolv Breve,

udgivne

af

Johan Ludvig Heiberg.

Kjøbenhavn.

Forlagt af Universitetsboghandler C. A. Reitzel.

Trykt hos Kgl. Hofbogtrykker Bianco Luno.

1851.

Title page for Fibiger's first novel. The book was published in December 1850 for sale at Christmas, and–as was the practice at the time–the following year appears on the title page (from Clara Raphael–Minona, *edited by Lise Busk-Jensen, 1994; Knight Library, University of Oregon).*

ginie, is the ultimate self-sacrificing woman, who lives with her heartache without any bitterness and commits herself to altruistic love. Interestingly, both Minona and Tyra die prematurely, as does Tyra's child, while Viggo and Virginie are survivors. Viggo, however, loses himself to the memory of his beloved sister, and as far as Virginie is concerned, her quiet Christian life, which, according to the narrator, gives her more joy than anything the world could give, is, in the narrator's opinion, not fit for storytelling ("egner sig ikke til Stof for en Fortælling"). The apparent moral of the story is that bad girls perish and good girls and boys live on. However, Fibiger's subtext tells a different story–that transgressive love is a dangerous but exciting force worth reckoning with, and that repressive love is boring and leads to nothing but monotony. Not until later in the century, after 1870 and the Modern Breakthrough, did women writers such as Agnes Henningsen develop the theme of women's erotic love in an overt fashion and idealize such passionate female figures as J. P. Jacobsen's eponymous character in *Fru Marie Grubbe* (1876). In an indirect way *Minona. Fortælling* is an example of Fibiger's hyperopic vision.

After *Minona. Fortælling,* Fibiger gave up on writing fiction, but in 1856 she was nevertheless awarded an annual pension from Queen Caroline Amalie. Fibiger supplemented her income during the years 1856–1861 by sewing shirts and translating stories and novels by E. T. A. Hoffmann and Bertholdt Auerbach. In 1859 she wrote a review of her sister Ilia Fibiger's collection of tales, *Rettroende Eventyr* (Right-Minded Fairy Tales, 1859), titled "Kunst og Videnskab" (Art and Science) in the daily *Berlingske Tidende,* and after her sister's death in 1867, she also wrote Ilia's biography as an introduction to the posthumous volume *Digtninger* (Poetry, 1867).

In 1863, thirty-three-year-old Fibiger embarked on a new career that eventually brought as much fame to her name as *Clara Raphael* had. With the help of C. E. Fenger, who was finance minister at that time, she began an apprenticeship as a telegraph operator, and after three years of training, she obtained a position as Extraordinary Assistant at Den danske Statstelegraf (The Danish Telegraph Service). The position was extraordinary because she was the first woman in Denmark to hold public office. She was stationed in Helsingör the first four years, after which time she worked as a supervisor at the telegraph station in Nysted on Lolland before finally moving on to Århus.

During her last years, she found time to write a couple of nonfiction pieces for the Swedish journal for women, *Tidsskrift för hemmet.* In 1869, she submitted an essay, "Den Ensommes Hjem" (The Home of the Solitary), which is not as depressing as the title suggests. Fibiger, who remained unmarried, argued strongly against the institution of the extended family and spoke up for women's right to live as single individuals without other family members or chaperones. The fate of many women was to move from their childhood homes to their marriage homes, while everything outside these homes was akin to a foreign land. Even women who worked as tutors or governesses essentially lived within protected homes, and widows and spinsters often spent their lives looking after other family members. Fibiger encourages single individuals to found new families of spiritual kin. In fact, the article is a plea for human rights and individual rights and demonstrates more than anything both her fierce independence and her far-sightedness.

That same year she read with interest Georg Brandes's translation of John Stuart Mill's *The Subjection of Women* (1869; translated into Danish as *Kvindernes Underkuelse,* 1869), and in 1870 she wrote a letter to *Tidsskrift för hemmet* upon the release of Leonora Christina Ulfeldt's *Jammers-Minde* (1869; translated as "A Record of the Sufferings of the Imprisoned Countess," in *Memoirs of Leonora Christina, Daughter of Christian IV of Denmark,* 1872). Although written during the seventeenth century, the memoir was first published in 1869. Not surprisingly, Fibiger saw the imprisoned princess as a free individual with an inner strength that overshadowed the shame of her husband's treason. At the beginning of 1871, Fibiger had a four-stanza poem, "Nytaarsnat 1870" (New Year's Eve 1870), published in a literary magazine, and the following January she sent a pseudonymous letter about "womanliness" to the newspaper *Jyllandsposten.*

In 1871, Dansk Kvindesamfund (Danish Women's Society) was founded, and Fibiger became a member the same year, although she was too weak to be active. She died of pneumonia in June 1872, only forty-one years old. In 1891 her niece Margrethe Fibiger wrote her biography, *Clara Raphael–Mathilde Fibiger–et Livsbillede* (Clara Raphael–Mathilde Fibiger: A Life Portrait), which is still the main source of information for Fibiger scholars.

In spite of Mathilde Fibiger's modest literary production, her importance as a writer and thinker is significant. Her three novels and at least three of her nonfiction works–*Hvad er Emancipation? Et Besøg,* and "Den Ensommes Hjem"–challenge ideas prevalent during her lifetime concerning womanly behavior and the nature of woman, vis-à-vis human nature. Her thoughts on women's emancipation as a process for each individual woman to raise her self-consciousness have also proved to be important for the history of the women's movement–whether in the 1850s or in the 1970s–important enough, in fact, for Dansk Kvindesamfund to create a prize in 1970, *Mathildeprisen,* in her name and in her honor.

Biography:

Margrethe Fibiger, *Clara Raphael–Mathilde Fibiger–et Livsbillede* (Copenhagen: Philipsen, 1891).

References:

Tine Andersen and Lise Busk-Jensen, *Mathilde Fibiger–Clara Raphael. Kvindekamp og kvindebevidsthed i Danmark 1830–1870* (Copenhagen: Medusa, 1979);

Lise Busk-Jensen, "Fibiger, Mathilde Lucie," in *Dansk kvindebiografisk leksikon,* volume 1, edited by Jytte Larsen (Copenhagen: Rosinante, 2000), pp. 477–479;

Busk-Jensen, "Intimsfærekulturen," in *Dansk litteraturhistorie,* third edition, volume 6, edited by Busk-Jensen and others (Copenhagen: Gyldendal, 2000), pp. 117–142;

Busk-Jensen, "Kvindebevægelsens første manifest: Om Mathilde Fibigers *Clara Raphael,*" in *Nordisk kvindelitteraturhistorie,* volume 2, edited by Elisabeth Møller Jensen and others (Copenhagen: Rosinante, 1993), pp. 313–318;

Carl S. Petersen and Vilhelm Andersen, *Illustreret dansk Litteraturhistorie,* volume 4: *Den danske litteratur i det nittende Aarhundredes anden Halvdel* (Copenhagen: Gyldendal, 1925), pp. 109–112;

Lise Sørensen, *Den nødvendige nedtur. Besyv om Mathilde Fibiger og kvindernes gamle sag* (Copenhagen: Gyldendal, 1977).

Papers:

Mathilde Fibiger's manuscripts, ninety-six of her letters, and other papers are at the Danish Royal Library in Copenhagen.

Karl Gjellerup

(2 June 1857 – 11 October 1919)

Poul Houe
University of Minnesota

BOOKS: *En Idealist: Skildring,* as Epigonos (Copenhagen: C. A. Reitzel, 1878);

"Det unge Danmark": En Fortælling fra vore Dage (Copenhagen: C. A. Reitzel, 1879);

Antigonos: En Fortælling fra det andet Aarhundrede (Copenhagen: Schou, 1880);

Rødtjørn: Sange og Fantasier (Copenhagen: Schou, 1881);

Arvelighed og Moral: En Undersøgelse tilkjendt Universitetets Guldmedaille (Copenhagen: Schou, 1881);

Aander og Tider: Et Rekviem over Charles Darwin (Copenhagen: Schou, 1882);

Germanernes Lærling: Et Livsafsnit fra vore Dage (Copenhagen: Schou, 1882);

Romulus: En Novelle (Copenhagen: Schou, 1883; revised, 1889);

G-Dur: En Kammer-Novelle (Copenhagen: Schou, 1883);

Brynhild: En Tragedie (Copenhagen: Schou, 1884; revised edition, Copenhagen: Lybecker, 1910);

En klassisk Maaned: Billeder og Stemninger fra en Grækenlandsrejse (Copenhagen: Schou, 1884);

Vandreaaret: Skildringer og Betragtninger (Copenhagen: Schou, 1885);

Saint-Just: Historisk Sørgespil i fem Handlinger (Copenhagen: Schou, 1886);

En arkadisk Legende (Copenhagen: Schou, 1887);

Kampen med Muserne: Dramatisk Digt (*Thamyris* 1) (Copenhagen: Schou, 1887);

Helikon: Et dramatisk Digt (*Thamyris* 2) (Copenhagen: Schou, 1887);

Hagbard og Signe: En erotisk Tragedie i fem Handlinger (Copenhagen: P. G. Philipsen, 1888);

Bryllupsgaven: Rococo-Komedie fra det galante Sachsen i fem Handlinger (Copenhagen: Schou, 1888);

Min Kjærligheds Bog (Copenhagen: P. G. Philipsen, 1889);

Minna (Copenhagen: P. G. Philipsen, 1889); translated by C. L. Nielsen as *Minna: A Novel from the Danish* (London: Heinemann, 1913); revised German edition, *"Seit ich zuerst sie sah"* (Leipzig: Quelle & Meyer, 1918);

Karl Gjellerup (courtesy of the Danish Royal Library, Copenhagen)

Richard Wagner i hans Hovedværk "Niebelungens Ring" (Copenhagen: P. G. Philipsen, 1890); enlarged as *Richard Wagner i hans Hovedværker* (Copenhagen: Gyldendal, 1915);

Herman Vandel: Sørgespil i tre Handlinger (Copenhagen: P. G. Philipsen, 1891);

Ti Kroner og andre Fortællinger (Copenhagen: Gyldendal, 1893);

Kong Hjarne Skjald: Tragedie i fem Handlinger (Copenhagen: Gyldendal, 1893);

Wuthhorn: Sørgespil i fem Handlinger (Copenhagen: Schou, 1893);

Pastor Mors: Eine seltsame Geschichte (Dresden: Minden, 1894); republished in Danish as *Pastor Mors: En underlig Historie* (Copenhagen: Gyldendal, 1894);

Eine Million: Schauspiel, by Gjellerup and Wilhelm Wolters (Dresden: E. Pierson, 1894); translated into Danish by Gjellerup as *En Million: Skuespil i tre Handlinger. Efter Nikolaus Pawlows Novelle* (Copenhagen: Gyldendal, 1894);

Hans Excellence: Skuespil indledet ved en Efterskrift til mine Dramer (Copenhagen: Gyldendal, 1895);

Møllen: Roman i fem Bøger (Copenhagen: Gyldendal, 1896; revised, 1911);

Mit formentlige Høiforræderi mod det danske Folk: En Redegjørelse i Anledning af Denunciationerne i Flensborg Avis (Copenhagen: Gyldendal, 1897);

Konvolutten: En graphologisk Studie (Copenhagen: Schubothe, 1897);

Ved Grænsen: Roman (Copenhagen: Gyldendal, 1897);

Fabler (Copenhagen: Gyldendal, 1898);

Gift og Modgift: Komedie i fem Akter og paa Vers (Copenhagen: Gyldendal, 1898);

Tankelæserinden: Sjællandsk Præstegaardsidyl (Copenhagen: Gyldendal, 1901);

Die Opferfeuer: Ein Legenden-Stück, illustrated by Walther Witting (Leipzig: Hermann Seemann, 1903); translated into Danish by Gjellerup as *Offerildene: Et Legendestykke,* illustrated by Witting (Copenhagen: Schubothe, 1903);

Elskovsprøven: En Borgscene i Niebelungenvers (Copenhagen: Gyldendal, 1906);

Pilgrimen Kamanita (Copenhagen: Gyldendal, 1906); translated by John E. Logie as *The Pilgrim Kamanita: A Legendary Romance* (London: Heinemann, 1911; New York: Dutton, 1912);

Den fuldendtes Hustru: Et Legendedrama (Copenhagen: Gyldendal, 1907);

Verdensvandrerne: Romandigtning i tre Bøger (Copenhagen: Gyldendal, 1910);

Fra Vaar til Høst, illustrated by Hans Tegner (Copenhagen: Gyldendal, 1910);

Villaen ved Havet/Judas: To Fragmenter (Copenhagen: Gyldendal, 1910);

Rudolph Stens Landpraksis, 2 volumes (Copenhagen: Gyldendal, 1913);

Guds Venner (Copenhagen: Gyldendal, 1916);

Den gyldne Gren (Copenhagen: Gyldendal, 1917);

Das heiligste Tier: Ein Elysisches Fabelbuch, illustrated by Paul Hartmann (Leipzig: Quelle & Meyer, 1919);

Madonna della laguna: Eine venezianische Künstlergeschichte, illustrated by Paul Hartmann (Leipzig: Quelle & Meyer, 1920).

Edition and Collection: *Karl Gjellerup, der Dichter und Denker: Sein Leben in Selbsterzeugnissen und Briefen,* 2 volumes, with an introduction by P. A. Rosenberg (Leipzig: Quelle & Meyer, 1921, 1922);

Romulus, with an introduction by Svend Erichsen (Copenhagen: Westermann, 1942).

PLAY PRODUCTIONS: *Herman Vandel: Sørgespil i tre Handlinger,* Copenhagen, Folketeatret (Studentersamfundets fri Teater), 14 May 1892;

Wuthhorn: Sørgespil i fem Handlinger, Copenhagen, Dagmarteatret, 2 March 1893;

Kong Hjarne Skjald: Tragedie i fem Handlinger, Copenhagen, Dagmarteatret, 1 December 1893;

En Million: Skuespil i 3 Handlinger, by Gjellerup and Wilhelm Wolters, Copenhagen, Dagmarteatret, 20 February 1894;

Hans Excellence: Skuespil, Copenhagen, Folketeatret (Studentersamfundets fri Teater), 27 April 1895;

Gift og Modgift: Komedie i fem Akter og paa Vers, Copenhagen, Dagmarteatret, 1 September 1898;

Møllen, Copenhagen, Casino, 12 April 1901;

Offerildene: Et Legendestykke, Copenhagen, Kongelige Teater, 3 September 1904;

Kampen med Muserne (Thamyris, 1–2): Dramatisk Digt, Copenhagen, Kongelige Teater, 9 February 1908.

OTHER: *Nyere dansk Lyrik,* edited by contributing authors, contributions by Gjellerup (Copenhagen: Stochholm, 1883), pp. 353–370;

Tusindfryd: Udvalgte Digte af nyere Forfattere, contributions by Gjellerup (Copenhagen: Schou, 1893), pp. 37–50;

Den ældre Eddas Gudesange, introduced, translated, and explained by Gjellerup (Copenhagen: P. G. Philipsen, 1895);

Johannes Fibiger, *Mit Liv og Levned, som jeg selv har forstaaet det,* edited by Gjellerup (Copenhagen: Gyldendal, 1898);

Nutids-Lyrik: En Samling danske Digte fra Aarhundredets Slutning–1872–1900, edited by Aage Matthison-Hansen, with an introduction by Alfred Ipsen, contributions by Gjellerup (Copenhagen: Bergmann, 1899), pp. 71–76;

Danske Kærlighedsdigte, edited by Kai Hoffmann, contributions by Gjellerup (Copenhagen: Gyldendal, 1916), pp. 167–169 and (Copenhagen, 1923), pp. 162–164;

Dansk Poesi 1880–1920, edited by Dansk Forfatterforening, contributions by Gjellerup (Copenhagen,

Christiania, London & Berlin: Gyldendal, 1922), pp. 8–13;

Digternes Danmark, edited by Frederik Nygaard, contribution by Gjellerup (Copenhagen: Schultz, 1941), pp. 41–42;

Danske lyriske Digte, edited by Mogens Brøndsted and Marie-Louise Paludan, contributions by Gjellerup (Copenhagen: Politiken, 1953), pp. 130–131.

TRANSLATIONS: Richard Wagner, *Valkyrjen, Første Dag af Trilogien "Niebelungens Ring"* (Copenhagen: P. G. Philipsen, 1891);

Otto Weininger, *Kjøn og Character: En principiel Undersøgelse* (Copenhagen: Christiansen, 1905);

Wagner, *Tristan og Isolde* (Copenhagen: Gyldendal, 1912).

While the Nobel Prize in literature in most instances confirms the career of an author already prominent, in the case of Karl Gjellerup it marked the end of a lifelong struggle for artistic recognition. In spite of his prolific output in many genres and on many subjects, Gjellerup was both an anachronistic and a disharmonious writer, whose high-flown style, passionate abstractions, and indirect language failed to reconcile him with most audiences. An erudite freethinker in most of his poetry, drama, and fiction, his peculiar versatility betrays a moral and religious claim to core convictions that he never found within the confines of Danish culture. Gjellerup's irrepressible idealistic drive led him into various uneasy relations with modern forms of realism. To the extent his personality found rest, it was in private idyllic settings or in otherworldly aesthetics.

While his collected work may never achieve classical status, its formal and artistic incoherence–in part acknowledged by the author himself, in part established by leading scholars and critics–is sufficiently interesting to qualify Gjellerup as an intermediary between the modern and the traditional. His remarkably cultured background and upbringing, and his voluntary residence in Dresden during the last half of his life, contribute to a "cross-cultural" literary production that illuminates the intersections between Danish and German traditions.

Karl Adolph Gjellerup was born in Roholte in Zealand on 2 June 1857 to a clergyman, Carl Adolph Gjellerup, and his second wife, Anna Johanne Elisabeth Gjellerup, née Fibiger. Karl had two sisters, Margrethe and Elisabeth, and seven half siblings from his father's first marriage, one of whom was historian Sophus Gjellerup. When Karl's father, who had moved from Roholte to the vicarage of Landet-Lyde in Lolland in 1858, died in 1860, his son Karl was sent to be raised by another clergyman, his mother's cousin Johannes Fibiger, who was perpetual curate of the Copenhagen Garrison Church, and his wife, Amalie.

While keeping in touch with his biological mother and sisters, Karl found in the home of his foster parents both emotional devotion and intellectual inspiration. Fibiger was a high-strung and able theologian with deep philological and aesthetic interests, whose own literary ambitions never met with general approval but whose linguistic aptitude and spiritual influence did not leave young Karl untouched. Among the visitors to the Fibiger home were Mathilde Fibiger, his mother's sister and his foster father's cousin, who founded the modern women's movement in Denmark and was a writer in her own right, and historian Edvard Holm, who was married to Amalie's sister, Karl's beloved "aunt" Edle.

Karl favored the traditional values of his uncle Edvard over his aunt Mathilde's novelties, and despite his own later ventures into secular modernism and freethinking, his emotional ties to the Fibigers and their old-world universe were never severed. Initially, they secured him good preparatory schooling in Copenhagen, where he was taught by émigré teachers from the formerly Danish duchy in South Jutland. After Fibiger's appointment to the provincial vicarages of Vallensved by Næstved and later Ønslev-Eskildstrup in Falster, the Fibigers gave Karl a hospitable foothold in the pleasurable parsonage culture and nature of Denmark's southern island kingdom, to which he repeatedly returned in later years.

On a superficial level, his departure from home to study theology, with aesthetics and moral philosophy on the side, at the University of Copenhagen seemed to be a pursuit of the same intellectual course that his foster father had followed. Gjellerup, however, had no intention to prepare himself for the ministry. Both the German Bible criticism that attracted his attention and his dissertation on Darwinian evolution and morals, for which he won a gold medal at the university, make evident that the impulses of his upbringing were far from uncontested.

In his many early attempts at poetry, drama, and fiction, Gjellerup had essentially sought to process the cultural stimuli he had absorbed in his home. Its staples were heroic ideals composed of ingredients from Percy Bysshe Shelley, Algernon Charles Swinburne, and German Romantic music and literature, interspersed with the elements of free spirit known from Greek antiquity, Johann Wolfgang von Goethe, and Friedrich von Schiller, and a variety of clichés picked up from slightly younger Danish Romantics. Between graduation in 1878 and the prizewinning dissertation of 1880, Gjellerup became a published writer with a stridently modern agenda implanted into a body of immaturely received idealistic norms and values.

As Poul Houe has argued, the way Gjellerup's career began presaged the outcome. Chronologically, Gjellerup debuted with *En Idealist: Skildring* (An Idealist: A Depiction, 1878) under the pen name Epigonos, while the first title under his own name was *"Det unge Danmark": En Fortælling fra vore Dage* (The Young Denmark: A Contemporary Narrative, 1879). While Epigonos was meant to suggest the author's belonging to the classical tradition, it has been misconstrued to mean an inappropriate imitator. Critics from Herman Bang to Houe, however, have pointed out that idealistic tradition and empirical modernity were conflated from the outset and have remained the mixed blessing of Karl Gjellerup's artistic legacy. His early radicalism was strained and tendentious, and he never managed to silence a different and deeper-seated idealism.

Gjellerup himself later admitted as much in an exchange with poet Holger Drachmann, who had welcomed Epigonos as a young disciple of critic Georg Brandes. In his memorial preface to an anniversary edition of *En Idealist* (1903), Gjellerup justifiably took issue with Drachmann's verdict. While the protagonist of the novel, an idealistic young aesthete with the German name Max Stauff, insists he is a realist, his more realistic counterpart in the sequel to *En Idealist, "Det unge Danmark,"* is an unsuccessful young poetic writer with the unmistakably Danish name Knud Vinge, who has reason to consider himself an idealist. In the final analysis, Max and Knud are characters of a kind–fragmented Romantic heroes (in the tradition of heroes in the works of George Gordon, Lord Byron), yet deprived of romantic fortunes in real life.

Title page for Gjellerup's 1881 poetry collection. It is dedicated to the critic Georg Brandes, who supervised the composition of the book and suggested the title (from Georg Nørregård, Karl Gjellerup–en biografi, *1988; Main Library, Indiana University).*

For his depictions of such idealistic characters, Gjellerup found inspiration in the realism of Ivan Turgenev's Russian novels. The Danish German Max Stauff is his version of Turgenev's prototype Rudin, and the tragic destiny Max shares with Knud Vinge typifies Gjellerup's reception of his Russian artistic role model. Johan Fjord Jensen has argued that Turgenev's poetic realism was a revelation to Gjellerup and that, while Schiller satisfied Gjellerup's bent for high poetry and grand style, Turgenev influenced his realistic fiction without compromising his virtuous idealism. Throughout the initial phase of his work, Gjellerup found in Turgenev's characters, dramatic compositions, and descriptive impressionism a spiritual alternative to the virtual monopoly of French naturalism on the realistic doctrine of the "Modern Breakthrough" in Nordic literature.

Even more characteristic of Turgenev's influence are the virtuous female characters and the homey situations that frame and subdue them. Turgenev's Helena, the principal character of his novel *On the Eve* (1860) and one of his prototypal women, is related to Helene of *En Idealist,* whose philosophy of love further anticipates Arthur Schopenhauer's philosophy of death, which becomes noticeable in Gjellerup's later work. In like manner, the motif of lost love in the early novels, connoted by the tragic beauty of a setting sun, is at once a reflection of Turgenev and a possible premonition of the total dissolution of individual personality that most scholars find prevalent in the later, Indian phase of Gjellerup's work. As Georg Buchreitz states, Gjellerup's "sympathies for the far East date far back."

During the same period, Gjellerup continued to be involved in more immediate concerns. *Antigonos: En Fortælling fra det andet Aarhundrede* (Antigonos: A Tale from the Second Century, 1880) is a narrative, dedicated to radical intellectual Edvard Brandes, about a second-century Christian convert who ends up reverting to the gods of antiquity. Gjellerup appears still to be waging theological war on his own heritage, thinly and abstractly veiling his radical heresies as tributes to classical paganism.

Even less veiled is the cultural radicalism in *Rødtjørn: Sange og Fantasier* (Red Hawthorn: Songs and Fantasies, 1881), a collection of lyrical poetry dedicated to Georg Brandes, who gave the work its title and under whose supervision it was composed. Brandes and his brother Edvard had earlier served as mentors to the young writer, correcting his manuscripts and reviewing his books, and in *Rødtjørn* the Brandesian spirit was credited in explicitly sacred terms. In a 7 August 1880 letter to J. P. Jacobsen, Edvard openly concedes that he and his brother were united in deliberate efforts to prepare "the little Gjellerup" for service in their army of true radicals. But apart from achieving status as the enfant terrible of this camp and frequently attracting the ire of staunch conservatives, little came of Gjellerup's radicalism.

Swedish playwright August Strindberg, in a 26 June 1882 letter to Edvard Brandes, wrote of his delight in *Rødtjørn,* but such prominent modern novelists as Jacobsen were unconvinced of Gjellerup's literary talent, and eventually Edvard and Georg Brandes, too, gave up on Gjellerup's abstractions and anti-Semitic slurs. Gjellerup's absence in Georg Brandes's *Det moderne Gjennembruds Mænd* (The Men of the Modern Breakthrough, 1883) is no less conspicuous than his presence in Herman Bang's *Realisme og Realister* (Realism and Realists, 1879) with its less partisan and more artistically inclined view of modern realism.

The uneven mix of classical poetic forms in *Rødtjørn* was but one object of Jacobsen's harsh critique; in addition, its author's thematic exercises in anti-Christian freethinking were pronounced more stridently than Jacobsen could tolerate. Niels Møller, as paraphrased by Claus Jensen, opines that Gjellerup's idealistic search for meaning attracted him to such radicals as Brandes, with whom he had in common only the rejection of conventional Christendom. In the end, says P. A. Rosenberg, Gjellerup's "anti-religious radicalism proved merely a point of transition on his way to an absolute Arian and religious idealism." An ideological gap was opening at this point in his life between his adopted radical view and his own intellectual history, and as the chasm widened, his search for personal balance suggests why he later was inclined toward Buddhist thinking.

In his prizewinning dissertation *Arvelighed og Moral: En Undersøgelse tilkjendt Universitetets Guldmedaille* (Heredity and Morality: An Investigation Awarded the Gold Medal of the University, 1881), Gjellerup's detailed history of Darwinism foreshadowed his own naturalism, and he made a particularly radical turn by adding a section on the moral right to suicide, a move that provoked a reprimand from the university. Nevertheless, as Fjord Jensen points out, Gjellerup's dissertation did not initiate any systematic appropriation of naturalism; instead, Gjellerup turned to the art of Turgenev and the thoughts of Schopenhauer. What appealed to Gjellerup in Darwin's theory of heredity was its transindividual implications, which set it apart from earlier theories of individualism.

Gjellerup's position was not scientific, and in his next book, *Aander og Tider: Et Rekviem over Charles Darwin* (Spirits and Times: A Requiem over Charles Darwin, 1882), the title alone professes that positivistic naturalism was a lesser priority than spirituality and musicality. In *Germanernes Lærling: Et Livsafsnit fra vore Dage* (The Teutons' Apprentice: A Period of Life from Our Own Time, 1882) the author's radical period was nearing its conclusion. As the narrator battles–on Gjellerup's behalf–with both theology and an actual theologian in fictional disguise, he exposes the tumultuous history of his radicalism. Influenced by the anti-German sentiments of his southern Jutland relatives, the narrator is still attracted to the spirits of Gotthold Ephraim Lessing, Goethe, and Schiller and even fails his divinity-school exam for voicing tenets of German Bible criticism in which he barely believes.

In many respects this Teutons' apprentice is his author's alter ego and so portrays Gjellerup's personal and authorial leanings toward German culture, at least as the cultural alternative to French culture. Danish critic Hakon Stangerup mentions how the social dimension supplants the poetic in this literary work, and his German colleague Heinrich Anz adds that the epochal clash between radical realism and classical idealism, which dominated the cultural scene in Denmark, was transposed by Gjellerup to a strife between undesirable Danish modernity and desirable German classicism. In the same vein, the preferential treatment in the novel of the German woman Johanna foreshadows both protagonists in a manner similar to the title figure in *Minna* (1889) and Eugenia Anna Caroline Heusinger Bendix, a woman Gjellerup had recently met.

Eugenia was married to Fritz Bendix, a musician and Brandes's cousin. Gjellerup found her a liberating soul mate and kindred spirit of his other chosen affinities of German origin. Awaiting the outcome of a lengthy divorce procedure, Eugenia, who suffered from both the physical and the spiritual climate in Denmark, relocated temporarily to Dresden; Gjellerup joined her there intermittently between 1885 and 24 October 1887, when the couple married. After five years' residence in suburban Copenhagen, they and Eugenia's young daughter, Margrethe, moved to Dresden, where they appear to have led a modest and reclusive life.

Preceding his German self-exile, Gjellerup in 1883 went abroad on his principal *Bildungsreise* (journey of spiritual education) to Germany, Switzerland, Italy, Greece, and Russia. In Venice he proofread his novel *Romulus: En Novelle* (Romulus: A Novel, 1883) and wrote defensive letters home (for example, on 14 March 1883, in response to Otto Borchsenius, who had reviewed the book) about his use of factual material behind the dramatic story. A fine psychological treatment of a horse subjected to military abuse, the novel extends its humaneness to the human experience of love. Its female protagonist comes to self-realization as she learns to reach beyond the protective barrier of her social class by identifying with the suffering animal, and her reticent male counterpart comes to her defense as she stands up to the creature's tormentor. Her practical ethics becomes his source of inspiration, and in siding with her, he comes to realize how to reclaim an innocent past as part of a dual responsibility. Meanwhile, as the suffering horse finally succumbs to its mortal destiny, the modern world barely takes notice.

The uplifting dimension of this novel is its compelling plea for community–between individuals and between their community and the larger world. It defies the more radical Brandesian notion of social responsibility, and Georg Brandes, who otherwise constructively suggested condensation of the narrative (adopted in its subsequent editions), failed to appreciate its venture into a social realism that is both formal and thematic, both tragic and poetic. When the images of virtuous womanhood modeled on Eugenia and the import of Turgenev on Gjellerup's style and characterization are added to this mix, the allegiance of the book to the modern movement is ambiguous. Its literal juxtaposition of Darwin the scientific naturalist and Richard Wagner the musical monumentalist further suggests that Gjellerup is both ahead of and behind the times.

In his subsequent novel, *G-Dur: En Kammer-Novelle* (G-Major: A Chamber Story, 1883), the musical title and looser atmospheric composition point to an attenuated Russian influence. The tragedy *Brynhild* (1884), finally, shows the departure from Brandes's artistic prescriptions to be nearly complete. While *Brynhild* may seem a drama about problems debated in the 1870s, it is rather, by Paul V. Rubow's account, a problematic case of superhumans battling society in the mode of Wagner's theatrical aesthetics. Hans Brix calls *Brynhild* a post-Romantic drama of ideals, for which Drachmann had paved the way, and Brix claims that its complexity encompasses characterization, pictorial language, dialogue, the role of the choir, and many other technical and substantive elements. While its composition tends to defy logic, the central struggle between Brynhild and Gudrun–to the detriment of their male counterparts Gunnar and Sigurd–is powerful and revealing of a love so uncompromisingly ideal that only death can see it through. Compared to the heroic sternness of the Norse source material, Gjellerup's version, according to C. E. Jensen, emphasizes romantic passion; but it also brings the philosophical state of Nirvana to the fore. Ultimately, the will to live succumbs to nothingness, and the individual personality ceases to exist, as Schopenhauer envisioned.

Brynhild is dedicated to Eugenia, and critics agree that it celebrates both the author's struggle to win her hand in marriage and the virtuous and monogamous sanctification of holy matrimony to which she (like so many of his female characters) bears witness. The embracement of eternal values and rejection of instant gratification in *Brynhild* made it "the most significant dramatic work in the grand style by century's end," according to Vilhelm Andersen, and Gjellerup never achieved anything else similar to it. The critical reception, by such critics as Carl Behrens, Julius Clausen, and later Rubow, was favorable, although no theatrical performance ever ensued.

While his break with naturalistic realism was now complete, Gjellerup's formal denouncement of his former associates came upon his return from his 1883 European journey. In *En klassisk Maaned: Billeder og Stemninger fra en Grækenlandsrejse* (A Classical Month: Images and Poetic Descriptions from a Journey to Greece, 1884) he deals rather straightforwardly with the Grecian leg of the trip, whereas in *Vandreaaret: Skildringer og Betragtninger* (The Year of Wandering: Depictions and Reflections, 1885), in which he treats the remaining sites of his tour, he admits to having lacked a personal center of gravity and a natural sense of balance between conflicting attractions in his intellectual environment. His formal resolution confirms his earlier experience–that his future lies with stylistic monumentality and with actual reality only insofar as it informs a style of this nature. The artistic goal is not an aesthetic affirmation of the momentary, but an ethical-religious striving to move beyond this world and its partisan bickering. Accordingly, he is less enthusiastic about the Italian Renaissance than about idyllic scenes in Switzerland, not to mention the tastes of a pessimism he enjoys in Russia and the near Orient.

In *Saint-Just: Historisk Sørgespil i fem Handlinger* (Saint-Just: Historical Tragedy in Five Acts, 1886), a tragedy about Maximilien Robespierre's incorrigible match in revolutionary zeal, Louis Saint-Just, Gjellerup attempted to dress his supreme idealism in historical costume. His failure to do so to the satisfaction of any theater director caused him deeper distress than any of his many other aborted bids for a career as playwright. A similar fate befell his dramatic poem *Thamyris* (1887).

d 13de Dec 1886.
Dresden.

Kjære Moder!

First page of a letter from Gjellerup to Eugenia Anna Caroline Heusinger Bendix, whom he married in 1887 (courtesy of the Danish Royal Library, Copenhagen)

Like its precursor, it obstructed the alleged purpose in *Vandreaaret* to serve art before (cultural) politics. It, too, was art of a second order–literature about literature–and with an incoherent fusion of Nordic Germanic and classical idioms underneath its high and learned style.

Rosenberg sees the hero's blindness as signifying a denial of this world and insight into one beyond finitude. Buddhist-like elusiveness attached itself to Greek particulars. The sequel to the poem, called *Helikon: Et dramatisk Digt* (Helikon: A Dramatic Poem, 1887), with ingredients of Friedrich Wilhelm Nietzsche and Goethe, and mythological figures Marsyas and Midas as parts of its erudition, affords an even more imaginative confrontation of idealism and realism. No less ambitious than *Thamyris, Helikon* met with authorial disappointment, as documented by Georg Nørregård, although an abbreviated version was eventually performed at the Kongelige Teater (Royal Theater) in Copenhagen in 1908.

Gjellerup's next work, *En arkadisk Legende* (A Legend from Arkadia, 1887), is a prose narrative situated in the same Greek antiquity as *Thamyris*. In *Hagbard og Signe: En erotisk Tragedie i fem Handlinger* (Hagbard and Signe: An Erotic Tragedy in Five Acts, 1888), written after his marriage to Eugenia and dedicated to her, Gjellerup returns to drama and to the kind of Nordic source material that inspired his *Brynhild*. But his effort to incorporate literary impulses from a "non-historical early Medieval" into difficult ancient and medieval meters failed. And in *Bryllupsgaven: Rococo-Komedie fra det galante Sachsen i fem Handlinger* (The Wedding Gift: A Rococo Comedy from Gallant Saxony in Five Acts, 1888), set in Dresden, he fails to make the rococo elegant and the comedy humorous.

The novel *Minna,* on the other hand, marks one of Gjellerup's few popular successes. It, too, takes place in the Dresden area, and its title character is cast in the same mold as Eugenia and the fictive females in her wake. In a conflict between her physical desire for one man and an ethical affinity to the narrator of the novel, Minna's weakness for the former leads to insanity and death, albeit with the empathy of both narrator and author. Minna may be an anachronism, but the world in which she is doomed is a contemporary one. The work includes clear references to Goethe and Schiller, though the poetic side of the text is not mired in cliché.

In 1889 Gjellerup wrote an essay titled "Schiller, Flaubert, Schandorph, Rudolf Schmidt," a harsh polemic in defense of Schiller against charges by critic Rudolf Schmidt that Schiller's later dramas sacrifice quotidian realism for an indistinct idealism. Gjellerup retorted that Schiller always sought to express the general in the individual, but then he went on to say that in Schiller's work the individual at its best is the typical–or the most deeply humane. The claim to realism is precisely what makes a text by Schiller a valid idealistic construction, according to Gjellerup, who views a text by himself in the same light.

In *Min Kjærligheds Bog* (My Love Book, 1889), a Danish version of Heinrich Heine's *Buch der Lieder* (The Book of the Songs, 1827), Gjellerup gathered older and new poems around his recurrent love motif. Critic C. E. Jensen compares the collection, with its intended classicism, to "a bouquet of wilted violets." Most of Gjellerup's anthologized poems are from this volume, including four lines titled "Et Par" (A Couple). Bordering on the chaotic, love in this poem remains part of a conflicted harmony that gives nightly birth to an ever-recurrent world. The unity of real and ideal, eternal and dynamic is consistent with Gjellerup's growing interest in Indian philosophy. "Et Par" also alludes to the ideas and feelings associated with music that he explored in 1889 in the leitmotivs of Wagner's principal work, *Der Ring Des Niebelungen* (The Ring of the Niebelung, 1874). His extensive work on Wagner, which was honored by his being extended an invitation to the Wagner festival in Bayreuth in 1914, includes translations of the Valkyrie parts of *Der Ring Des Niebelungen* and later of *Tristan and Isolde* (1912). It is a work related to Gjellerup's general interest in Norse lore, as demonstrated later in his 1895 translations from the elder *Edda*.

Like *Minna, Herman Vandel: Sørgespil i tre Handlinger* (Herman Vandel: Tragedy in Three Acts, 1891; first performed, 1892) is about the catastrophic consequences of love gone astray. Herman's commitment to marry the girl he has seduced at the expense of the choice of his heart is considered immoral and is paid for with suicide. C. E. Jensen compares Gjellerup's charges against conventional marriage to Søren Kierkegaard's assault upon the state church. One betrays the absolute idea of marriage; the other, the idea of self-sacrificing Christianity. In *Wuthhorn: Sørgespil i fem Handlinger* (Wuthhorn: A Tragedy in Five Acts, 1893; first performed, 1893) another triangular love drama unfolds on a Swiss mountaintop, whereas *Kong Hjarne Skjald: Tragedie i fem Handlinger* (King Hjarne Scald: Tragedy in Five Acts, 1893; first performed, 1893) is a play about love and war in the mythic past of Denmark; its scaldic rhetoric in iambic verse is both powerful and cumbersome. In *En Million: Skuespil i tre Handlinger. Efter Nikolaus Pawlows Novelle* (A Million: A Play in Three Acts. Based on Nikolaus Pawlow's Short Story, 1894; first performed in Danish as *En Million: Skuespil i 3 Handlinger,* 1894), initially written in German by Gjellerup with Wilhelm Wolters to earn money and premiered in Berlin, the theme is love and money, while the novel *Pastor Mors: En underlig Historie* (Pastor Mors: A Strange Story, 1894) is a peculiar tale about young love resurrected in the imagination of an old divinity professor. Unlike the Christian resurrection of the flesh, the professor's love story is reborn in an incorporeal sphere above and beyond the mundane world of human vanity. An allegorical dissolution of individual mortality, Gjellerup's learned theological and philosophical text is written on the border between neo-Danish and neo-German spiritual life with an unmistakable leaning away from Lutheran doctrine toward the Buddhistic teachings about Nirvana.

The love triangle in *Hans Excellence: Skuespil indledet ved en Efterskrift til mine Dramer* (His Excellency: A Play Introduced by a Postscript to My Dramas, 1895; first performed, 1895) includes a prominent politician who bestows marital sentiments upon his wife and erotic

Eugenia Gjellerup (photograph by Schiffter & Genscheidt; courtesy of the Danish Royal Library, Copenhagen)

passion upon his mistress in accordance with Nietzsche's moral code for the superhuman. Human affairs are once again depicted in high style, yet with realistic settings, and the experimental text is prefaced by a "postscript to my dramas," in which Gjellerup praises Schopenhauer, whose thinking led him to the Indian and Buddhist teachings for final clarification of his innermost spiritual needs. Moral superiority is not individualism but religious self-abrogation, as illustrated by Wagner's musical dramas. C. E. Jensen finds Gjellerup's moral code religious in spite of all his rebellion and calls it Buddhism interspersed with Christian redemption. Self-assertion and self-denial become one–above the heads of common crowds. And, as Rosenberg writes, with the guidance of Schopenhauer's philosophy of will as the core principle of life, of suffering as the common state of life, of compassion as the foundation of ethics, and of self-annihilation as liberation, Gjellerup definitively found his way out of the spheres of influence of radical Copenhagen and out of the shadows of Darwin and his philosophical counterpart, Herbert Spencer.

In 1896 Gjellerup published another dramatic love story in prose, *Møllen: Roman i fem Bøger* (The Mill: A Novel in Five Books; first performed, 1901), written in Dresden but set in the Danish island environment of his youth. The newly widowed miller contemplates marriage to the sister of a religious forester; yet, both the miller and his journeyman are infatuated with the maid of the mill. Suddenly the miller proposes to the maid, but while he is in town to secure royal permission to marry the young girl, she enters the mill to flirt and conspire against him with the journeyman. Later he catches them unawares and is able unnoticed to arrange for the machinery of the mill to crush them. He then marries the forester's sister, but, tormented by guilt, he confesses to his crime and dies in prison.

Gjellerup's combination of Christian and Indian thought is here extended with elements of superstition. Yet, the author still endeavors to reconcile the metaphysical aspects of the novel with its realistic environment, specifically verisimilitude in mill design. The psychological analysis is intimate; the composition is clear and atmospheric; and the mix of natural and supernatural is both mythical and symbolic. While Edvard Brandes rejected the irrational features, Andersen valued that even domestic animals function within the mythological universe in place of gods and demons. *Møllen* is one of Gjellerup's memorable accomplishments; it was adapted for both stage and screen productions.

Gjellerup's many years in Dresden were marked by solitude and health problems, vacations in the surrounding areas and abroad, and occasional professional visits to Denmark. A few Danish friends and family members dropped by now and then, but the unremarkable daily routines prevailed. Musical events were his preferred entertainment, and he continued with mixed results to pursue the theatrical career he felt he had been denied in Denmark. Yet, his output as a German writer was limited chiefly to newspaper articles and German versions of his books, and the kudos he received came from a few critics and academics. Meanwhile, his personal ties to Denmark remained vivid even as his professional and intellectual attachments gradually vanished or soured. An occasional recipient of the Ancherske Travel Stipend, he was awarded a Civil List Pension in 1889. All the same, his finances were never opulent.

Mit formentlige Høiforræderi mod det danske Folk (My Alleged High Treason against the Danish People, 1897) is an indication of his ambiguous feelings for Denmark; it is a booklet in which he rejects charges leveled against him that he has betrayed his Danish language and culture. While gladly conceding an admiration for such Germans as Otto von Bismarck, he holds the Danish national-liberals responsible for loss of the southern provinces of Denmark and for alienating her German roots.

After the well-crafted story *Konvolutten: En grapholog isk Studie* (The Envelope: A Study in Graphology, 1897) came the novel *Ved Grænsen* (At the Border, 1897), which refers in its title not to the contested southern frontier but to the sea border farther east, south of the island of Falster, where *Møllen* was also set. Idyllic provincial towns and landscapes, viewed through the exilic writer's nostalgic lens, constitute ties otherwise severed by the contested political border. A drama performed in Copenhagen and called *Gift og Modgift: Komedie i fem Akter og paa Vers* (Poison and Antidote: A Comedy in Five Acts and in Verse, 1898; first performed, 1898) continues Gjellerup's depictions of love as both confusing and tragic, and a collection of *Fabler* (Fables, 1898) includes a versified story told by Buddha. In *Tankelæserinden: Sjællandsk Præstegaardsidyl* (The Female Thought-Reader: A Zealand Vicarage Idyll, 1901), the author returns to his foster father's idyllic vicarage of Vallensved for yet another love intrigue and yet another exilic reflection on the land of his youth.

With the exception of the short *Elskovsprøven: En Borgscene i Niebelungenvers* (The Love Trial: A Castle Scene in Niebelungen Verse, 1906), a play in one act and medieval meter set in a castle on the Rhine, the first decade of the 1900s is dominated by Gjellerup's major Indian works, of which *Fabler* gave but a simple taste. *Offerildene: Et Legendestykke* (The Sacrificial Pyres: A Play of Legend, 1903; first performed, 1904), based on passages from the Upanishads (treatises that deal with Brahma-knowledge), was performed by the Kongelige Teater in Copenhagen and at different locations in Germany. Its lead character is a Vedic-Age Brahman who is summoned by his king in northern India to join a speech competition and who comes out of the contest as the winner; meanwhile, one of his apprentices, left behind in the master's house, has won the love of the Brahman's daughter and eventually obtains the returning Brahman's position and prize of one thousand white cows as well. Rosenberg mentions how the confrontation of self-worship and worship of the world god in the play maps the only way to redemption, while Rubow more specifically notes that the play remains at the stage of the Upanishads, where it develops the pessimism of late Brahmanism and reminds one of Schopenhauer's thought, to which Gjellerup had been guided by his German friend Paul Deussen.

In *Pilgrimen Kamanita* (translated as *The Pilgrim Kamanita: A Legendary Romance,* 1911), in particular, Gjellerup articulates his Buddhist subject matter in the style of late Jugend or Art Nouveau, the flowery ornamental style typical of the fin de siècle period and its search for artistic freedom. Fritz Paul has demonstrated how this decorative, precious, and heavily symbolic style and esoteric arrangement is in perfect concert with the content of the novel and its combined spirit of Schopenhauer, Nietzsche, and Wagner. In the first part, Kamanita, in his search for the Buddha, meets the elevated one himself but fails to recognize him. Yet, in the process of telling his unfulfilled life story to the goldsmith's lovable daughter Vasithi, he experiences Buddha's philosophy. This exuberant and exotic narrative is then deciphered in the pseudophilosophical appendix to the second part in the manner of Nietzsche's Zarathustra. Here the reader learns of Kamanita's cosmic existence after death; his re-encounter on the beaches of the divine Ganges with Vasithi, from whose affection circumstances of life had tragically estranged him; and finally his disappearance into the endless Brahma world of night and grayness.

Gjellerup in 1898 (drawing by Knud Søborg; from Georg Nørregård, Karl Gjellerup–en biografi, *1988; Main Library, Indiana University)*

As opposed to Rubow, who saw Gjellerup's Indian phase as a self-absorbed abstraction immune to outside influences, Paul points to a process of transformation in which Nietzsche is turned into a Buddhist with a bent for neo-Romantic biology. Incompatible stylistic elements are brought together to render rationally comprehensible a universe composed of esoteric mythology and idioms of decadence. On the one hand, many of these influences are subject to Gjellerup's biases about the Orient; on the other hand, his appropriations do foreshadow fin de siècle and later stylistic movements. His pseudoscientific Jugend style and various exotic forms lend themselves to kitsch but also to modernistic constructs and radical revisions. The reality they elicit lies in the power of an imaginative will whose verbal expression is suggestive rather than referential.

While Gjellerup's biographer Nørregård deems the Danish version of *Kamanita* "exceptionally well-written," Paul considers the German version less disruptive of the aesthetic illusion. But linguistics aside, the core of the story is indisputably the creative nihilism included in the narrator's dictum that comprehending the downfall of creation enables comprehension of the uncreated. In *Den fuldendtes Hustru: Et Legendedrama* (The Perfect One's Wife: A Legend Drama, 1907) and the cognate novel *Verdensvandrerne: Romandigtning i tre Bøger* (The World Wanderers: Novelistic Fiction in Three Books, 1910), the soul continues its wanderings toward Nirvana through mystical stages and levels. Rubow finds this drama life-denying in the extreme, like "the idea of life as smoke from a fire that has never burnt," a nihilism less creative than pure. Rosenberg, by contrast, stresses Gjellerup's ability to evoke such exotic Indian environs solely on the basis of his imagination.

Subsequent to the Indian decade, Gjellerup returned with new insights to cultural settings closer to home. A small selection of his poetry, *Fra Vaar til Høst* (From Spring to Autumn), and two epic fragments, *Villaen ved Havet/Judas: To Fragmenter* (The Villa by the Sea/Judas: Two Fragments), are both from 1910, but his first major attempt to integrate the Nirvana-thought into a familiar milieu is the novel *Rudolph Stens Landpraksis* (Rudolph Sten's Country Practice, 1913), another intricate love story endowed with an atmosphere of the country culture the author knew from his youth and laden with the philosophizing his readers had come to expect from his later years. Eventually, realism gives way to an impersonal escape from time and space. In the allegedly historical novel *Guds Venner* (God's Friends, 1916), the Buddhist trend has yielded to Christian sentiments. Finally, in his last book in Danish, *Den gyldne Gren* (The Golden Bough, 1917), Gjellerup, following in the footsteps of James Frazer's work with the same title, depicts characters and events in classical Rome.

In 1919 and 1920 two more books by Gjellerup appeared in Germany. *Das Heiligste Tier: Ein Elysisches Fabelbuch* (The Holiest Animal: An Elysian Book of Fables) is built on animal legends and myths with tributes to Buddha, and the posthumous *Madonna della laguna: Eine venezianische Künstlergeschichte* (Madonna of the Lagoon: The Story of a Venezian Artist) is a narrative with traits of comedy and Venezian atmosphere. These late works of fiction were followed by yet another publication in German, Gjellerup's autobiography as artist and thinker, supplemented with a selection of his letters and an introduction by his Danish friend Rosenberg.

This finale is quite indicative of Gjellerup's development. He always relished strains of German culture, but after moving to Dresden, his immersion approached identification. Most of his books were written in both languages, often in German first, if not in German only. During World War I he even wrote the bulk of his large correspondence in German in order to accommodate his censors. Meanwhile, the war broke his spirit, and when in 1917 he shared the Nobel Prize in literature with Henrik Pontoppidan, the award came too late to assuage his many physical and financial problems. By the end of his life, his defiance had merged with despair, and he often wrote home to Denmark that his authorial ambitions had come to naught. The thought of death became increasingly comforting to his pride, and it arrived at his door on 11 October 1919, about a year after armistice. His grave is in Dresden.

In a letter from 1880 pastor Fibiger predicted that his adopted son would return to Christianity after his radical experiments. The pastor was proven both right and wrong. Religious fervor did fill his son's personality, but it filled it with thoughts and sentiments that tended toward eliminating the notion of personhood as an integral whole. Gjellerup's artistic gifts and priorities have been debated by critics, as have his political attitudes; yet, there is no denying that as a writer he crossed cultural borders and served as an intermediary between the traditional and the modern. From his position at the margins of modern letters in both Denmark and Germany, he made his mark on a few notable Scandinavians at center stage–for example, Swedish Nobel laureate Verner von Heidenstam and Danish Nobel nominee Valdemar Rørdam.

Letters:

"Karl Gjellerup: Nogle Breve [to William Behrend]," *Tilskueren,* 2, no. 36 (1919): 407–420.

Biography:

Georg Nørregård, *Karl Gjellerup–en biografi* (Copenhagen: C.A. Reitzel, 1988).

References:

Claes Ahlund, "Karl Gjellerup: *Germanernes Lærling* (1882)," in *Den skandinaviska universitetsromanen*

1877–1890 (Stockholm: Almqvist & Wiksell International, 1990), pp. 74–85;

Knut Ahnlund, "Ett delat Nobelpris," in *Diktarliv i Norden: Litterära essäer* (Stockholm: Brombergs, 1981), pp. 248–279;

Vilhelm Andersen, "Firsernes Folk," in *Illustreret dansk Litteraturhistorie,* 4, no. 2 (Copenhagen: Gyldendal, 1925), pp. 376–393;

Heinrich Anz, "Ein Literarischer Grenzgänger im Fin de siècle: Karl Gjellerup zwischen dänischer und deutscher Literatur," in *Kulturelle Identitäten in der deutschen Literatur des 20. Jahrhunderts,* edited by Heinrich Detering and Herbert Krämer (Frankfurt am Main: Peter Lang, 1998), pp. 21–33;

Anz, "'Rastloses Schaffen in zwei Sprachen': Karl Gjellerup (1857–1919) im interkulturellen Kontext," in *Blickwinkel: Kulturelle Optik und interkulturelle Gegenstandskonstitution,* edited by Alois Wierlacher and Georg Stötzel (Munich: Iudicium, 1996), pp. 489–502;

Herman Bang, "Karl Gjellerup," in his *Realisme og Realister* (Copenhagen: Schubothe, 1879), pp. 97–113;

Edvard Brandes and Georg Brandes, *Brevveksling med nordiske Forfattere og Videnskabsmænd,* volumes 1–6, 8, edited by Morten Borup, with the assistance of Francis Bull and John Landquist (Copenhagen: Gyldendal, 1939–1942);

Hans Brix, "Karl Gjellerup," in his *Danmarks Digtere* (Copenhagen: Aschehoug, 1951), pp. 441–445;

Georg Buchreitz, "Europæiske paavirkninger paa Karl Gjellerups forfatterskab til 1900," *Edda,* 30 (1930): 400–433;

Johan Fjord Jensen, "Karl Gjellerup–poetisk realisme," in his *Turgenjev i dansk åndsliv* (Copenhagen: Gyldendal, 1961), pp. 222–223, 235–252;

Vridhagiri Ganeshan, *Das Indienbild deutscher Dichter um 1900: Dauthendey, Bonsels, Mauthner, Gjellerup, Hermann Keyserling und Stefan Zweig: Ein Kapitel deutsch-indischer Geistesbeziehungen im frühen 20. Jahrhundert* (Bonn: Bouvier Verlag Herbert Grundmann, 1975), pp. 188–233;

Constantin Grossman, "Karl Gjellerup: Ein Gedankenblatt," *Dreiundzwanzigstes Jahrbuch der Schopenhauer-Gesellschaft,* 23 (1936): 249–268;

Poul Houe, "Begyndelsen på enden: Karl Gjellerups debutroman(er)," in *On the Threshold: New Studies in Nordic Literature,* edited by Janet Garton and Michael Robinson (Norwich: Norvik Press, 2002), pp. 144–151;

Houe, "Det epokaltypiske grænsetilfælde [Review of Olaf C. Nybo, *Karl Gjellerup*]," *Nordica,* 20 (2003): 344–350;

C. E. Jensen, "Karl Gjellerup," in *Vore Dages Digtere: Karakteristiker* (Copenhagen: Det nordiske Forlag, 1898), pp. 1–16;

Claus Jensen, "Karl Gjellerup and Henrik Pontoppidan (Literature 1917): An Odd Couple," in *Neighbouring Nobel: The History of the Nobel Prizes,* edited by Henry Nielsen and Keld Nielsen (Aarhus: Aarhus University Press, 2001), pp. 147–206;

Marius Kristensen, "Karl Gjellerup," in *Hovedtræk af nordisk Digtning i Nutiden,* edited by Ejnar Skovrup (Copenhagen: Aschehoug, 1920), pp. 103–109;

Sven Møller Kristensen, *Impressionismen i dansk prosa 1870–1900* (Copenhagen: Gyldendal, 1965);

Olaf C. Nybo, *Karl Gjellerup–ein literarischer Grenzgänger des Fin-de-siècle* (Hamburg: Verlag Dr. Kovac, 2002);

Fritz Paul, "Gjellerup und die Aufwertung des Jugendstils," *Danske Studier,* 66 (1971): 81–90;

P. A. Rosenberg, "Karl Gjellerup," *Ord och Bild,* 27 (1918): 218–226;

Paul V. Rubow, "Herman Bangs Samtidige: Karl Gjellerup," in his *Herman Bang og flere kritiske Studier* (Copenhagen: Gyldendal, 1958), pp. 79–86;

Rudolf Schmidt, "Et Gjensyn," *Literatur og Kritik,* 1 (1889): 288–296;

Kalle Sorainen, "Gjellerup och Höffding," *Orbis Litterarum,* 6 (1948): 115–132;

Hakon Stangerup, "Karl Gjellerup," in *Danmarks store Digtere,* volume 2, edited by Stangerup (Odense: Skandinavisk Bogforlag, 1944), pp. 73–82;

Stangerup, *Kulturkampen,* 2 volumes (Copenhagen: Gyldendal, 1946);

Nicolae Zberae, "K. Gjellerup: A Master of Expression of Indian Thought," *Indo-Asian Culture,* 19, no. 1 (1970): 30–33.

Papers:

The major collections of Karl Gjellerup's letters and manuscripts are at the Danish Royal Library in Copenhagen and at the *Sächsischen Landesbibliothek* in Dresden.

Meïr Goldschmidt

(26 October 1819 - 15 August 1887)

Mogens Brøndsted
University of Southern Denmark

(Translated by Mark Mussari)

BOOKS: *En Jøde. Novelle,* as Adolph Meyer (Copenhagen: M. Goldschmidt, 1845); translated by Mary Howitt as *Jacob Bendixen, the Jew* (London: Colburn, 1852); by Anna S. Bushby as *The Jew of Denmark: A Tale* (London: Routledge, 1852); and by Kenneth H. Ober as *A Jew* (New York: Garland, 1990);

Fortællinger, as Meyer (Copenhagen: C. A. Reitzel, 1846)–includes "Erindringer fra min Onkels Hus," translated by Goldschmidt as "My Uncle and His House: A Story of Danish Life," *Macmillan's Magazine,* 7 (1863): 461-476; and "Aron og Esther," translated by Goldschmidt as "Aaron and Esther; or, Three Days of Rabbi Nathan Clausener's Life," *Chambers's Journal* (24 January 1863): 53-61;

Das illustrirte Schleswig-Holstein und Dänemark. Humoristisches Taschenbuch vom Herausgeber des Corsaren (Leipzig: W. Jurany, 1847);

Hjemløs. En Fortælling, 3 volumes (Copenhagen: A. F. Høst, 1853-1857); translated by Goldschmidt as *Homeless; or, A Poet's Inner Life,* 3 volumes (London: Hurst & Blackett, 1861);

Blandede Skrifter, 4 volumes (Copenhagen: O. B. Wroblewsky, 1859-1860)–includes "Don Cleophas," translated and adapted by Goldschmidt as "The Elf Ring," *Victoria Magazine,* 2 (October 1864): 508-531; (November 1864): 26-44; (December 1864): 129-137; and "Rabbi Meirs Hustru," "Rabbi Joschuah og Prindsessen," "En græsk Philosoph og en Rabbi," and "Rabbi Raschi," translated by Goldschmidt as "Rabbi Meir's Wife," "Rabbi Joschuah and the Princess," "A Greek Philosopher and a Rabbi," and "Rabbi Raschi," in *Chambers's Journal* (4 October 1862): 212-216;

Rabbi Eliezer. Dramatisk Digtning (Copenhagen: O. B. Wroblewsky, 1861);

Meïr Goldschmidt (photograph by Hansen & Weller; courtesy of the Danish Royal Library, Copenhagen)

Svedenborgs Ungdom. Dramatiseret Skildring (Copenhagen: A. F. Høst, 1863);

Fortællinger og Skildringer, 3 volumes (Copenhagen: C. Steen, 1863-1865)–includes *Arvingen,* translated and abridged (probably by Goldschmidt) as *The Heir* (London: W. Bunker, 1865); "Den sidste Svovlstik," "Photographierne og Mephistopheles," and "Ved St. Donofrio," translated by Goldschmidt as "The Last Lucifer Match," "The Photographs and Mephistopheles," and "At St. Onofrio–Tasso's Life," in his *The Society of Virtue at Rome* (London: Victoria Press, 1868);

Nogle politiske Bemærkninger og Notitser (Copenhagen: C. Steen, 1864);

Breve fra Choleratiden. Indeholdende en lille Begivenhed (Copenhagen: C. Steen, 1865); republished as *En Roman i Breve* (Copenhagen: C. Steen, 1867);

Dagbog fra en Reise paa Vestkysten af Vendsyssel og Thy (Copenhagen: Forlagsbureauet, 1865);

En Hedereise i Viborg-Egnen (Copenhagen: C. Steen, 1867);

Kærlighedshistorier fra mange Lande (Copenhagen: C. Steen, 1867);

Ravnen. Fortælling (Copenhagen: C. Steen, 1867);

En Skavank. Skuespil i tre Acter og med et Forspil (Copenhagen: C. Steen, 1867);

Den Vægelsindede paa Graahede. Fortælling (Copenhagen: C. Steen, 1867);

Smaa Fortællinger (Copenhagen: C. Steen, 1868)–comprises "Maser," "Den flyvende Post," "Hævnen," "Bjergtagen" (parts 1 and 2), "I en Postvogn," and "Ekko'et"; "Den flyvende Post" translated by Carl Larsen as "The Flying Mail," in *The Flying Mail,* by Goldschmidt and others (Boston: Sever, Francis, 1870), and in *Stories by Foreign Authors: Scandinavian* (New York: Scribners, 1898);

I den anden Verden. Komedie i to Acter (Copenhagen: C. Steen, 1869);

Rabbi'en og Ridderen. Drama i tre Acter (Copenhagen: C. Steen, 1869);

Avrohmche Nattergal (Copenhagen: C. Steen, 1871); translated by Lida Siboni Hanson as "Avrohmche Nightingale," in *Denmark's Best Stories: An Introduction to Danish Fiction,* edited by Hanna Astrup Larsen (New York: American-Scandinavian Foundation/Norton, 1928), pp. 71–116;

Fortællinger og Virkelighedsbilleder, ældre og nye, 2 volumes (Copenhagen: Gyldendal, 1877);

Livs Erindringer og Resultater, 2 volumes (Copenhagen: Gyldendal, 1877);

Fortællinger og Virkelighedsbilleder. Ny Samling (Copenhagen: Gyldendal, 1883);

Smaa Skildringer fra Fantasi og Virkelighed (Copenhagen: Gyldendal, 1887).

Editions and Collections: *Den flyvende Post; Hævnen. To Fortællinger* (Copenhagen: P. Hauberg, 1888);

Poetiske Skrifter, 8 volumes (Copenhagen: Gyldendal, 1896–1898);

Udvalgte Arbejder (Copenhagen: Gyldendal, 1906);

M. Goldschmidt i Folkeudgave, 8 volumes, edited by Julius Salomon (Copenhagen: Gyldendal, 1908–1910);

Udvalgte Skrifter. Romaner, Fortællinger og Skildringer, 6 volumes, edited by Salomon (Copenhagen: Gyldendal, 1908–1916);

Udvalgte Fortællinger, 2 volumes (Copenhagen: Gyldendal, 1910);

En Hedereise i Viborg-Egnen, edited, with an introduction, by Valdemar Andersen (Kolding: K. Jørgensen, 1954);

Ravnen, edited, with an afterword, by Jørgen Gustava Brandt (Copenhagen: Gyldendal, 1963);

Livs Erindringer og Resultater, 2 volumes, edited by Morten Borup (Copenhagen: Rosenkilde & Bagger, 1965);

En Jøde, afterword by Brandt (Copenhagen: Gyldendal, 1986);

M. A. Goldschmidts Dagbøger, 2 volumes, edited by Kenneth H. Ober, Uffe Andreasen, and Merete K. Jørgensen (Copenhagen: Danske Sprog- og Litteraturselskab/C. A. Reitzel, 1987);

Arvingen, edited, with an afterword, by Johnny Kondrup (Copenhagen: Danske Sprog- og Litteraturselskab / Valby: Borgen, 1988);

Noveller og andre Fortællinger, edited, with an afterword, by Thomas Bredsdorff (Valby: Borgen, 1994);

Hjemløs. En Fortælling, edited, with an afterword, by Mogens Brøndsted, notes by Brøndsted and Harald Jørgensen (Copenhagen: Danske Sprog- og Litteraturselskab / Valby: Borgen, 1999).

OTHER: *Sjællandsposten* (1839), edited by Goldschmidt;

Corsaren (October 1840 - September 1846), edited by Goldschmidt; reprinted, edited by Uffe Andreasen, 6 volumes (Copenhagen: Danske Sprog- og Litteraturselskab/C. A. Reitzel, 1977–1979);

Nord og Syd (1847–1859), edited by Goldschmidt;

Alfred Assollant, *Acacia. En Berättelse från Förente Staterne,* translated by Goldschmidt (Stockholm: P. G. Berg, 1859);

Ragnhild Goldschmidt, *En Kvindehistorie,* anonymous, foreword by Meïr Goldschmidt (Copenhagen: Gyldendal, 1875);

Bret Harte, *Gabriel Conroy,* translated by Goldschmidt (Stockholm: Seligmann, 1876).

SELECTED PERIODICAL PUBLICATIONS–UNCOLLECTED: "A Norwegian Musician," *Cornhill Magazine,* 6 (1862): 514–527;

"On the Danube, and Among the Mountains," *Chambers's Journal* (2 August 1862): 65–70.

Meïr Aron Goldschmidt secured his place in the literary history of Denmark as the first author to address the problem of being Jewish in nineteenth-century Danish society. His general literary contribution was even greater. In several novels and short stories with myriad settings, Goldschmidt united psychological realism with an idealistic worldview; even his most realistic depictions assume a metaphysical perspective. As he once commented to Georg Brandes while they were viewing an exhibition of Dutch portrait paintings, "Hos mig er der altid noget bagved" (With me, there is always something deeper).

Goldschmidt's central problem, which he faced throughout his life, was his struggle to belong, a search that started in his youth and was characterized by several painful separations. He was born Meyer Aron Goldschmidt on 26 October 1819 in the market town of Vordingborg on the island of Sjælland. He was the firstborn son of Aaron Goldschmidt and Lea Levin Rothschild Goldschmidt. His Jewish childhood home also functioned as a merchant's business, equipped with both a brewery and a distillery. Thus, keeping an Orthodox Jewish home was out of the question. In fact, several illegalities took place in the household, which was rife with smuggling and bribery (as was an uncle's farm and lumberyard in Kalundborg). Goldschmidt believed that this disregard for the law may well have influenced the social criticism that marked his later journalistic efforts.

To learn the proper rites of Judaism, the six-year-old Goldschmidt was sent to another uncle in Copenhagen, where he encountered Orthodox rituals as a mystical initiation. As his father's firstborn son "of the tribe of Levi," he moved ahead of his uncle's eldest son and felt, from that moment on, that it was always his duty to be the first. After a year he returned to his own parents, who, following a fire at their home, acquired a farm in Valby. At that time market conditions were unfavorable; three years later the family moved to Copenhagen, and the boy lost his rural paradise. Goldschmidt's father's business suffered in the city. Aaron Goldschmidt became a partner in a ship that wrecked at sea and was swindled out of his share of the insurance claim (an event that Meïr Goldschmidt later depicted in his 1867 novel *Ravnen* [The Raven]). Despite the economic difficulties, nothing was spared on this son. After his father moved to Næstved in a final attempt at making it as a brewer and distiller, Goldschmidt was placed in one of the best schools in Copenhagen and housed among Orthodox relatives.

As a youth Goldschmidt was ambitious. When he failed–against all expectation–to graduate with honors (thanks mostly to some questions involving Christian doctrine), he considered himself a failure. He soon abandoned the medical studies he had long decided to pursue. Even his Mosaic foundation was about to be shattered after he witnessed his beloved headmaster offering a nature-worshiping morning prayer. In addition, Goldschmidt suffered an unhappy infatuation with a cousin. All this inner chaos finally found expression in prose writing. Following on the heels of the poetry and drama favored by the older Danish Romantics, prose gained ground in the 1830s with writers such as Steen Steensen Blicher, Thomasine Gyllembourg, and Hans Christian Andersen. Short-story magazines became increasingly popular, and Goldschmidt submitted his first efforts, only to be rejected. While visiting his uncle in Kalundborg, he accidentally stumbled upon a newly published local magazine and decided to make a similar effort in his father's town. Before his eighteenth birthday he had signed up subscribers to a new magazine, *Næstved Ugeblad* (Naestved Weekly), edited in Copenhagen. Goldschmidt's first short story, "Friheden og Kvinden" (Freedom and the Woman), soon appeared in the magazine. It told the story of a young count who, following the French Revolution, searches for comfort from a hopeless love by fighting in Napoleon's armies. The first word in the title is also notable: an enthusiasm for freedom eventually served as Goldschmidt's main political device.

Even as a child at his home in Valby, where his family had delivered butter to the royal court, Goldschmidt had become irritated with his mother for fretting over the smallest possible speck of dirt. He enjoyed hearing his father criticize the politics of Frederik VI. In school Goldschmidt read with enthusiasm about the great republicans of the past. The French Revolutions in 1789 and 1830, along with the Polish rebellion of 1830, lit fires of liberalism and justice that inspired him. When an anonymous reader requested useful information for townspeople and farmers instead of bad short stories, Goldschmidt crafted a program for citing injustices and for defending citizens' interests in the face of the authorities. He also addressed problems in specific cases, thus drawing so much attention that the magazine eventually merged with one in Kalundborg to become *Sjællandsposten* (The Sjælland Post), thus garnering a wider audience–including Sjælland's assembly of the States General. Under the influence of the July Revolution of 1830, the States Generals for Denmark's islands, the Jutland Peninsula, and the area of Slesvig-Holsten had been established in 1834 as the king's advisory bodies, with membership to be chosen by the propertied classes. Goldschmidt responded with commentary in the liberal spirit.

After the death of Frederik VI in 1839, the republicans sensed the dawning of a new day, and Goldschmidt, disposing of the provincial organ, set his sights on Copenhagen. Together with a band of like-minded souls from the newly established Academic Book Club (a counterpoint to the conservative student organization) he launched an oppositional and satiric weekly magazine, *Corsaren* (The Corsair), named for its French model. The new king, Christian VIII, who as a vice-regent had been instrumental in the signing of the Norwegian Constitution of 1814, nevertheless maintained absolute monarchy. The monarchy also retained the right of censorship, and the police confiscated one issue of *Corsaren* after the other. Although Goldschmidt tried to hide behind editorial straw men, he was eventually imprisoned, fined, and permanently censored.

Goldschmidt faced his sentence after returning from Sweden, where he had taken part in a Nordic student meeting in Uppsala in 1843, at a time when Scandinavianism was in vogue. He was persecuted politically but embraced by academic youth. When the newly established Scandinavian Society arranged an open-air assembly at Skamlingsbanken, a meeting ground in southern Jutland, Goldschmidt resurfaced. When society members arranged for his lodging in a Jewish household, however, it opened old wounds. He began the meeting with these words: "Jeg er Jøde, hvad vil jeg imellem jer?" (I am a Jew. What am I doing among you?). Although he was welcomed among them, the opposition remained seated throughout his speech. Thus, Goldschmidt spoke more pugilistically to the Slesvig-Holsteners than he had planned. Similarly, he was dragged, half against his will, into a polemical debate with Søren Kierkegaard, whom he actually admired. Finally, Goldschmidt abandoned *Corsaren* so that he could travel throughout Europe and "blive af med Skarpheden og Bitterheden" (dispose of harshness and bitterness). One day, in the midst of the debate over the magazine, he expressed his bitter feelings to a literary friend, who replied that from such feelings one writes a novel. Thus, Goldschmidt composed his first novel, *En Jøde* (1845; translated as *Jacob Bendixen, the Jew,* 1852), the story of a young, idealistic Jew who, because of Christian prejudices, is forced back into the ghetto. Jews had first immigrated to Denmark in the 1600s and, by 1814, had acquired both citizenship and freedom of trade. Animosity toward them among commoners remained, however, and in 1819 it exploded into riots in Copenhagen. Jewish houses and stores were vandalized.

In *En Jøde* Jacob Bendixen experiences at the age of ten the repercussions of persecution in his father's merchant house on the island of Funen. Despite his Orthodox upbringing, when the boy is sent to attend grammar school in Copenhagen, he is swept up into the headmaster's enlightened humanism and breaks with the faith of his ancestors. He refuses to be baptized, though, professing instead an undogmatic belief in God that alienates him from both Jewish and Christian acquaintances. His engagement to the blonde-haired Thora is soon broken. In desperation Jacob decides to fight for societal revolution and volunteers to serve with French troops in Algeria. He then receives word of his father's death and regrets their falling-out. As the Arabs in their white burnooses attack, he thinks he sees his parents in religious garb and cannot defend himself. When he decides to participate in the Poles' fruitless fight for freedom, he discovers that his beloved has married his rival. Bound to his past, Jacob is reduced to a life of hatred and vengeance. After his return home he takes a job, partially against his will, as a pawnbroker in order to gain pecuniary power over his rivals. The final chapter depicts his burial and his legacy in the ghetto, where he worked to get Jewish boys apprenticed to Jewish masters, in opposition to the assimilation he once believed in. The final words of the novel are spoken by his old classmate: "Han troede engang paa den evige Poesi og det evige Liv" (He once believed in eternal Poetry and eternal Life). This friend, a Jewish physician, lacks Jacob's violent and irritable nature; he is therefore spared a life of sharp conflicts.

Goldschmidt distanced himself somewhat from his aggressive literary debut by publishing *En Jøde* under a pseudonym, Adolph Meyer. (He had given the same first name to a son he had had with a humble non-Jewish woman while he was still living with his family.) The following year, 1846, Goldschmidt published the more neutral *Fortællinger* (Tales) under the same pseudonym. The collection opens with "Erindringer fra min Onkels Hus" (translated as "My Uncle and His House: A Story of Danish Life," 1863), a series of reflections on his uncle's home in Kalundborg. In "For otte Skilling Hvedebrød" (Wheat Bread for Eight Pence) one can clearly detect the magical significance of the number three and the reliance on good fortune found in fairy tales. Three young friends are swimming one morning in Copenhagen when one of them, Richard, finds the courage to accept a wager. Out of sheer appetite he has foolishly purchased too much bread, and his friends dare him to offer one of the extra rolls to the next person who happens to walk by. His daring is rewarded as the next stranger turns out to be an elder legal counselor, and Richard reminds him of his lost son. He decides to use Richard in a personal case. As a foreign diplomat the older man once fathered a child with a Creole woman, who has since died; therefore, he wants to travel to her South American homeland to care for the child. He calls upon Richard to follow him as soon as the young man has passed his medical exams. When Richard finally arrives after graduation, the old man is dead. Richard then accidentally acquires the wealthiest woman in the country as his patient. Even more fortuitously, he stumbles upon his patron's daughter, whom he marries. He has become fortune's child, especially when one considers the fate of his comrades, who have suffered while he has prospered, one while seeking fame in the Foreign Legion and the other as an unlucky dreamer and fantasist. Goldschmidt's story, with its echoes of the great fantasy hero of Danish Romanticism, Adam Oehlenschläger's Aladdin, also anticipates the antifantasy hero in Hans Egede Schack's realist *Phantasterne* (The Fantasts, 1857).

The next story in *Fortællinger,* "Aron og Esther" (translated as "Aaron and Esther; or, Three Days of Rabbi Nathan Clausener's Life," 1863), offers insight into pious Old World Judaism, a world in which scriptural interpretation serves as the basis for all business deals. After having violated ceremonial rites, young Aron wonders whether he can ever marry Rabbi Nathan's daughter. Nathan is scrupulous not because he opposes having Aron as a son-in-law but because he is paid by the religious community as an expert in interpreting Holy Scripture. In the concluding story, "En Majfest" (A May Party), Goldschmidt employs a compositional form borrowed from Blicher: the frame story, introduced in Blicher's "E Bindstouw" (1842; translated as "In the Spinning Room," 1945), which summarizes and supplies themes from previous stories. The frame tale surrounding "En Majfest" involves an excursion to Esrom Lake in conjunction with the yearly rally celebrating the ordinance granting the right of assembly for the States General. Held on 28 May, this day of freedom recalls Norwegians' 17 May independence celebrations. The first piece, "Drømmene" (The Dream), alludes directly to the opening tale of the collection, "Erindringer fra min Onkels Hus," and the notion that childhood memory determines meaning. The next piece, "Watteaus Maleri" (Watteau's Painting), is a disillusioned counterpart to the love story in "For otte Skilling Hvedebrød." "Fortælling om en Flue" (The Story of a Fly) takes an ironic look at the religious problem introduced in "Aron and Esther." Goldschmidt also uses his narrative as a social platform in the political fable "Kejser Napoleon" (Emperor Napoleon), in which the emperor finally betrays the notion of freedom, and freedom's fairy extinguishes the lucky star above his palace. She offers to relight it, but he realizes that he is too late. The merging of pathos and politics recalls Goldschmidt's magazine *Corsaren.*

Goldschmidt's plans for a European excursion turned into a two-year stay (1846–1847) in countries filled with political unrest: Germany, Austria, Italy, and Switzerland. The last of these countries, with its amalgamation of free cantons despite linguistic differences, made a strong impression on him. After he returned home, Goldschmidt used his various travel impressions for a new monthly journal, *Nord og Syd* (North and South, 1847–1859). The objective reporting and political summaries in the periodical garnered Goldschmidt the distinction of becoming Denmark's first modern journalist.

Nord og Syd also included literary works, and later issues featured Goldschmidt's bildungsroman, the trilogy *Hjemløs* (1853–1857; translated as *Homeless; or, A Poet's Inner Life,* 1861), based partially on the author's travel experiences. The novel, depicting the development of a personality, is composed as a circle, with the protagonist returning to his original point of departure. Thus, its three volumes are *Hjemme, Hjemløs,* and *Hjem* (At Home, Homeless, and Home). The story begins in the milieu that Goldschmidt first experienced in his provincial merchant home. In the garden, a kind of Eden, Otto Krøyer plays with his childhood sweetheart, Emilie; they are reenacting the Fall into sin with the forbidden fruit, which he eats "fordi der var en Magt over ham" (because there was some power over him). Otto is an idealist, however, and after Emilie allows another to flirt with her, he breaks off their relationship and is bedazzled by a famous actress. He has rendered himself spiritually homeless, and in the second volume, which bears that title, he has become a wandering soul. As a student he moves in the intellectual circles of the time and, along with an aesthete friend, cultivates Greek ideals. From these literary and political circles Otto gradually acquires insights into the intrigue lying behind societal facades, and so he decides to travel abroad.

In Europe, Otto encounters religious and broad political currents, debates with Catholics, and takes part in a freedom movement during the revolutionary year of 1848. But the decisive encounters recall events in his childhood home. In Rome he meets a fellow Jewish townsman who introduces him to a Jewish Englishman, a philanthropist who trains Otto in the art of Shekinah, the divine manifestation of justice that provides for moral balance. Traces of this concept surface throughout the various threads in the novel. After Otto's ensuing military adventures in the Alps and France, which only result in further disillusionment, he returns home.

Hjem, the third and final volume, consists mainly of sad and bitter reunions. All of Otto's friends, now married and settled down, have long abandoned their ideals and resigned themselves to furthering their careers. Finally, Otto finds Emilie. Although she too has settled down (with the local minister), Otto cannot help himself: he must once again take the apple from her hand. At the last minute their attempted relapse into sin is prevented by her husband's unexpected arrival, but it is too late for Otto. In his mind it has happened, and as punishment and atonement, a fire rises in which he is burned. Now he finds his life's calling: to become a teacher at a factory school, run by his childhood friend Peter Krøll and financed by the rich Jewish Englishman. Otto has made amends with his existence; he has rediscovered his inner child by the time death surfaces.

Because the protagonist of *Hjemløs* dies at the age of thirty-five, Goldschmidt's great bildungsroman does not actually cover a wide time period. According to an afterword in *Nord og Syd,* the novel also discloses the author in constant play with one of the central concepts of his writing, Nemesis, "den Side af Guddommen der er virksom i Jordelivet" (that side of Divinity at work in our earthly lives). It is a force that sooner or later demands justice.

Hjemløs also reflects Goldschmidt's own personal crisis at this time. In 1848 he had entered into a pro-forma marriage with the mother of his son after she had a daughter whom he knew was not his. Four years later they divorced. When his own father died, Goldschmidt moved in with his mother and sister. There were also moral accounts that needed to be settled. Political entanglements surfaced in 1849, the year the Danish constitution was adopted. For a short time he became a member of certain political organizations, but he remained, basically, an independent whose main interests included social concerns, boarding schools, and employment laws. In foreign matters Goldschmidt supported forcing a showdown with Prussia over the ill-fated question of Slesvig-Holsten. Yet, for the most part, he stood alone, becoming the target of grotesque attacks, and he felt his literary inspiration fading. He also suffered from both ill health after a bout of typhus and growing debt following some aborted publishing efforts. In 1861 Goldschmidt decided to move to London, where he had frequently visited his well-heeled cousin, Benjamin Rothschild. Since many of his books had been translated into English, Goldschmidt hoped he could carve out a career for himself as an author and correspondent.

Success came slowly, however, and Goldschmidt clashed with the Orthodox London congregation (reflected in rough drafts for a reworking of *Hjemløs* with a Jewish protagonist). When Rothschild, who now viewed his cousin as a burden, offered to pay for a stay in Rome, it awakened in Goldschmidt a deep longing for the Eternal City. From January to May 1863 he experienced an artistic breakthrough–partially because he rediscovered an old flame, the half-Jewish Christiane Kirchhoff Stilling, vacationing in Rome with her consumptive husband, the philosopher P. M. Stilling. During their platonic time together Christiane reawakened Goldschmidt's calling as a Danish writer and also served as the inspiration for several selections in his three-volume *Fortællinger og Skildringer* (Tales and Descriptions, 1863–1865). As in his first volume of tales, *Fortællinger,* he set a frame around this new story cycle. "Hvorledes man fortæller i Rom" (How You Tell Stories in Rome, 1863) reflects Goldschmidt's own experiences with fellow countrymen, Englishmen, and Scandinavian artists and literati in Rome. Women and romance play central roles in these tales, which run the gamut from the poet Torquato Tasso's legendary love for Princess Eleonore to the story of the Danish farmwife Ane, rumored to have made two suitors happy. Although Ane loves Erik, she is compelled to marry Jørgen, who has an inheritance. Her energy revitalizes his farm and turns the lazy husband into a local deputy. Meanwhile, Erik takes up the bottle. One Sunday, hymnbook in hand, she parades into Erik's room and yells at him: "Skammer du dig ikke, du Svin? Drikker jeg?" (Have you no shame, you pig? Do I drink?). From that moment on he becomes industrious, takes a clever wife (in a marriage arranged by Ane), and is soon able to measure up against Jørgen. Goldschmidt's affair with

Goldschmidt in 1862 (courtesy of the Danish Royal Library, Copenhagen)

Christiane, along with her challenge to his duty as a Danish writer, surfaces within the tale.

The central work of *Fortællinger og Skildringer,* which takes up the entire third volume, is the novel *Arvingen* (1865; translated as *The Heir,* 1865). The narrator Axel's father has lost the family estate through fraud; like Goldschmidt, the son dreams of rehabilitating his family's good name. The injustice eventually costs Axel's father his life. On his deathbed he pleads with Axel to bring the swindler to justice and calls on heaven's blessing for his son. He tells the boy it will come "som Dug den Aften du mindst venter det" (like dew that evening you least expect it).

When Axel becomes a traveling companion to a count's son, he tries, like his counterpart, to hold his own in warrior escapades and gambling in foreign countries. Recognizing the error of his ways, he accepts a research position at an Italian royal library. At this point destiny seems to reward Axel and his late father when a message informs him that the swindler is now dead and has left him the estate as his proper inheritance.

Other forces, however, are at work. While in school Axel fell in love with Astrid, but the loss of the estate cost them their relationship. She later entered into a marriage of convenience to take care of her deceased sister's children, and Axel sought comfort with a young woman whom he married (only to protect her reputation) and then immediately divorced. Now, when he meets Astrid in Rome, her husband is already about to leave her and take the children with him to convert them to Catholicism. Axel manages both to save the children and save Astrid from his royal traveling companion's amorous advances. The couple can finally reunite and experience a little bit of paradise, symbolically enough, in Ehden, near the Lebanese port city of Tripoli. Still, they have offended each other with their degrading marriages, and Nemesis will not allow their happiness. A traumatic turn of events destroys Astrid's health, and she dies after leaving Axel the adopted children as a special inheritance. The sorrow is so encompassing that he decides to remain among foreigners. But after an old Arab's evening greeting–"nu kommer Duggen" (here comes the dew)–Axel recalls his father's blessing, and he decides to return home to his inherited estate.

Goldschmidt, too, was able to return home to his Danish family. His son graduated with highest marks (though still not with honors), and his younger sister, Ragnhild, developed a fine literary sense and became his constant adviser. Goldschmidt also explored new areas of his homeland. Through a previous marriage P. M. Stilling had become the owner of an estate south of Hjørring, which provided the opportunity for many visits to northern Jutland. The first, in the summer of 1865, is described in Goldschmidt's *Dagbog fra en Reise paa Vestkysten af Vendsyssel og Thy* (Diary of a Trip along the West Coast of Vendsyssel and Thy, 1865). A visit undertaken the following year is recounted in *En Hedereise i Viborg-Egnen* (A Journey on the Heath in the Viborg District, 1867).

Goldschmidt's experiences in Jutland found further expression in short stories building on local oral traditions. *Den Vægelsindede fra Graahede* (The Waverer from Graahede, 1867) involves a proud farmer's daughter named Katrine Graa who marries the son of a crofter. Because she is so determined to take the lead, her husband harnesses her to the plow (along with their only cow). The story offers psychological insight into the Jutlanders' contrarian temperament. "Ekko'et" (The Echo), published in *Smaa Fortællinger* (Short Tales, 1868), builds on a local legend about a hill by a church tower where sounds reverberate in a deeper tone–supposedly because a young man was burned to death there as punishment for having seduced a knight's lady. Goldschmidt inserts this plot device into a modern love story. A legend from the island of Fur, where Stilling owned a farm, drives "Bjergtagen" (Bewitched), also published in *Smaa Fortællinger.* A noblewoman's attraction to a legendary young man in a hill and repulsion for her prosaic husband function as a clear projection of her deep inner longing. When her husband decides to excavate the hill, a fire breaks out, first as a brushfire in the heath (which seems to devour a great bird, more than likely a reference to the mythological phoenix) and then in the castle, where the flames immolate the wife. Legend claims that she started the fire, which corresponds to the flames of her inner desire.

Both folktales and legends surface in the string of literary pearls that form *Kærlighedshistorier fra mange Lande* (Love Stories from Many Lands, 1867). The stories are united by a prologue from the 1867 World Exposition in Paris. The first tale, "Senki," relates the story of a religious contrast, this time between a Mandean and a Muslim. The next tale updates the legend, popular with the Romantics, of the tempting siren Lorelei, in which bewitchment leads to disaster. A Jewish legend serves as the foundation for "Fuglen der sang" (The Bird that Sang), in which the herdsman Elijah is encouraged by his ambitious betrothed to seek the highest–that is, to become a rabbi. Later, he is tempted to ask the Lord for "blot et Glimt af det Højeste eller høre blot et kort Øjebliks Lyd fra Din Evighed!" (just a glimpse of the highest or to hear for just a brief moment sounds from your eternity!). The bird of eternity then sings two notes. When Elijah returns to his wedding feast, two generations have passed, and he collapses on his beloved's grave. In the

Christian version of the same legend, "Munken og Fuglen" (The Monk and the Bird), the glimpse of eternity is a reprieve. In the Mosaic view it becomes an impropriety–and in several of the love stories it underscores the failure to realize that love is "the highest."

"Assar og Miriam," a story without supernatural elements, comes from Israel's history under the Greek king Antiochus IV Epiphanes in the second century B.C. The hero of the tale, Assar, loves Judas Maccabeus's daughter, Miriam. To spur the people on to resistance, he advises the king to take a harsher course. Although the plan succeeds, the Maccabeans view Assar as an evil counselor. When one of their warriors strikes at him, Miriam throws herself in front of him and is run through in his place. Killing himself with his own sword, Assar cries out, "O Israel, du er dyr at frelse!" (Oh Israel, it is costly to save you!). In this series of tales, the high price is exactly this: love.

The next tale in *Kærlighedshistorier fra mange Lande,* "Guds Engel fra Rørvig" (God's Angel from Rørvig), is of Danish origin. The meek and mild maiden, to whom folk in that area have given the nickname "Guds Engel," is the daughter of the local customs officer. In their home lives a captain who seized an English merchant vessel during the 1807 bombardment of Copenhagen by the British. They fall in love and she decides to leave with him, but ten days later she dies at sea, sick with longing for her homeland. When the captain finally returns to settle along the beach–at the very spot where she arrived to leave with him–the legend soon spreads that he has a chest filled with gold and silver (his treasure from the prize vessel) but with a corpse lying on top of it (the price for his treasure: love).

Folk- and fairy-tale elements play their own strange role in Goldschmidt's most popular novel, *Ravnen,* published in 1867. Danish critic Jørgen Gustava Brandt has called *Ravnen* "periodens betydeligste danske romanværk" (the most outstanding Danish novel of the period). The title refers to a lucky raven carrying in its beak a stone that will fulfill all its owner's wishes. The owner turns out to be a short, black-garbed Jewish commissioned agent, Simon Levi. Levi's employer has cheated him out of a promised lottery agency, thereby revealing his villainy. As a joke Levi is lured up on a donkey (a symbol for the synagogue in Christian art) that kicks him off–whereby he lands, like a bird, in the arms of his employer, further proving the villain's identity. The scoundrel has already ruined another family, the Carøes. Three of the Carøe brothers are trying to reestablish themselves (a plot drawn from Goldschmidt's own life that is also used in *Arvingen* and *Hjemløs*). Vilhelm, who possesses intellectual gifts, studies medicine; Morten is a skilled craftsman who constructs machines (like Peter Krøll in *Hjemløs*);

Goldschmidt in 1887, the year of his death (drawing by Frans Henningsen; from Mogens Brøndsted, Meïr Goldschmidt, *1965; Walter Royal Davis Library, University of North Carolina at Chapel Hill)*

Ferdinand, though only a ship's boy, believes in the wish-granting raven. Their wise grandmother stresses the importance of the three commandments dealing with the treatment of one's neighbors.

The narrator delineates the winding paths that the Carøe brothers take to achieve social ascent. Vilhelm marries a young woman from high society, and her father introduces Morten to a financially powerful gentleman who wants to invest in his plans for a factory. From Levi, Ferdinand learns that the investor is actually the same man who cheated the family out of its solvency. The investment equals the sum he swindled. In the happy ending the plans for the factory include profit sharing and proper housing and schools for the workers, recalling Krøll's industrial facilities in *Hjemløs* (in which Otto finds his life's calling as a teacher). Goldschmidt had studied social conditions for workers, especially in England. In other works he depicts the wretched conditions of farmhands. In *Arvingen,* for example, he stresses the importance of the landowner's obligation to his workers to, in the words of Astrid, "leve med dem som Familie, man havde faaet anbetroet" (live with them as if they were family with whom one had become entrusted). Once again, the story reflects the grandmother's three commandments.

Goldschmidt based Levi, the character of the Jewish agent, on a real person in contemporary Copenhagen; he seemed so real that reviewers and readers asked to learn more about him. The author granted their requests and wrote "Maser," published in *Smaa Fortællinger,* in which the shrewd Levi faces a trial by fire. After he receives an unexpected inheritance, he is required to pay one-tenth to the destitute; his unmarried sister suggests that he give the money to their brother, who is always in financial need. The brother, Levi's foil, has casually started a family and adopted Christian manners. Levi attempts to dodge his sister's suggestion, but when the conflict makes her dangerously ill, he promises to give in to her wishes so that she can become well. Goldschmidt relates the story with priceless humor.

The final story about Levi, "Levi og Ibald" (Levi and Ibald, 1883), is tragicomic. He meets another minor character from *Ravnen,* the writer-fantasist Ibald (who had tricked him onto the donkey). Ibald alarms Levi by recounting that he heard some socialists singing anti-Semitic songs and saw some ministers attacking Judaism as a capitalistic threat against the people. Levi is now a house owner and decides to protect himself by renting to Ibald. At a tenant party, however, a hard-boiled naturalist and Darwinist praises Levi as a representative of old Judaism's "social hatred," a necessary link in the societal chain. Although Levi treasures the commandment to love one's neighbor, he sees himself proclaimed a new Nathan, fighting the Christian church, in a poem by Ibald. When a pair of ministers uses the occasion to visit Ibald's landlord, Levi assumes it is a sign of the return of pogroms; he faints and dies shortly thereafter. The current ideological war, along with its social and religious unrest, creates a crisis for Jewish culture.

A stronger sense of empathy characterizes *Avrohmche Nattergal* (1871; translated as "Avrohmche Nightingale," 1928), the title character of which is also based on a real person, a known Copenhagen scalper. Avrohmche (Little Abraham) falls in love with a Christian girl (Goldschmidt's infatuation with Christiane Stilling flared up again after her husband's death). Avrohmche is a failed singer with the sobriquet of "Nightingale." Similarly, Goldschmidt had recently suffered a defeat at the Royal Theater with his drama *Rabbi'en og Ridderen* (The Rabbi and the Knight, 1869), the story of a Jewish knight who, after being expelled from his ancestral society, seeks refuge in Christian circles. Avrohmche, in contrast, is only disowned by his father and now lives with another Jewish family on the island of Lolland, where the family's servant girl, Emilie, is the object of his affection. At the theater Emilie socializes with a young man, provoking jealousy in Avrohmche. When the man offers her his arm as they exit, Avrohmche yells, "Stop, han ta'r min Kone!" (Stop, he's taking my wife!), thus scandalizing both her and himself. He later tries to hang himself, but his landlady arranges a marriage for him with an older sister in the family (who has also suffered an unhappy love affair with a Christian). Now, Avrohmche "hangs right."

Feeling his own career in decline, Goldschmidt decided the time had come to settle all accounts. Friends prompted him to write his memoirs, including the story of his work on *Corsaren,* and to view that time in light of his main theme of Nemesis. To pursue the historical concepts of religion in the Judaic and Egyptological traditions, he frequented libraries in Paris and London. Seeing a young woman, a communard, on her way to being executed in Paris revealed the weight of living and dying for an ideal. As Goldschmidt posits in *Fortællinger og Virkelighedsbilleder* (Tales and Pictures of Reality, 1877), "Paa sin Maade har hun betalt sin Gjæld, og hvad der saa gjøres ved hende, kan hun ikke være fortabt. Hvad skal der blive af mig?" (In her own way she has paid her debt. Whatever they do to her, she can never be lost. What shall become of me?). He found the strength to endure all attacks on his heritage; he began to see his Jewish and Danish identities as compatible, as part of a greater whole. This realization also characterizes his final stories, a group of which he titled "Nemesis Billeder" (Pictures of Nemesis, 1870–1877). Goldschmidt concludes the first part of his *Livs Erindringer og Resultater* (Recollections and Results, 1877) with an explanation of his point of view; the second part is an attempt to trace the origins of this viewpoint in antiquity and its broader historical manifestations. He finally achieved something of a reconciliation between his two worlds, both of which were spiritual, but he remained unsympathetic toward the materialism and naturalism of the new era–including its Jewish harbinger in Denmark, Brandes.

Meïr Aron Goldschmidt died on 15 August 1887 in Copenhagen. He had long struggled to find an audience for his writings. As a Jew he was always partially alien, as a republican he remained an outsider, and he constructed his own religion. To make matters worse, Brandes fostered contempt for his fellow Jew, because he did not approve of Goldschmidt's crypto-Romanticism. Goldschmidt's writing was a poor fit with the naturalistic climate prevailing at that time. Still, his social and psychological insights, in conjunction with his sterling narrative skills, eventually won him a broad public and a secure place in Danish literary history. Outside of Denmark he inspired a specific literary genre in the German language, *die Ghettogeschichte* (the Ghetto story).

Letters:

Goldschmidt and Otto B. Wroblewsky, *Oplysninger om hvorledes Hr. M.A. Goldschmidt har handlet med "Rabbien og Ridderen." En Brevvexling* (Copenhagen: O. B. Wroblewsky, 1869);

Breve fra og til Meïr Goldschmidt, 3 volumes, edited by Morten Borup (Copenhagen: Rosenkilde & Bagger, 1963);

Meïr Goldschmidts breve til hans familie, 2 volumes, edited by Borup (Copenhagen: Rosenkilde & Bagger, 1964);

Goldschmidt and Lodovica de Bretteville, *En brevveksling om kvindens stilling i samfundet,* edited by Gotfred Appel (Copenhagen: Futura, 1979).

Bibliography:

Aage Jørgensen, *Dansk litteraturhistorisk bibliografi, 1967–1986* (Copenhagen: Dansklærerforeningen, 1989), pp. 211–212.

References:

Vilhelm Andersen, "Bjergtagen: Et Motiv hos Goldschmidt," *Edda,* 1 (1914): 75–87;

Andersen, *Illustreret dansk Litteraturhistorie,* volume 3 (Copenhagen: Gyldendal, 1924), pp. 638–656;

Uffe Andreasen, in *Dansk biografisk leksikon,* volume 5, edited by Svend Cedergreen Bech (Copenhagen: Gyldendal, 1980), pp. 233–237;

Andreasen, in *Dansk litteraturhistorie,* volume 3, edited by P. H. Traustedt (Copenhagen: Politiken, 1976), pp. 420–424, 448–460;

Ib Bondebjerg, "Den hjemløse myte–en ideologikritisk analyse. Om dannelsesromanen og Goldschmidts 'Hjemløs,'" *Kritik,* 23 (1972): 5–24;

Morten Borup, "Goldschmidtiana," *Danske Studier,* 61 (1966): 106–118;

Georg Brandes, "M. Goldschmidt," in his *Samlede Skrifter,* volume 2 (Copenhagen: Gyldendal, 1899), pp. 447–468;

Jørgen Gustava Brandt, afterword to *Ravnen* (Copenhagen: Gyldendal, 1963), pp. 255–270;

Brandt, ed., *Meïr Goldschmidt. Digteren og journalisten* (Odense: Danmarks Radio, 1974);

Elias Bredsdorff, *Goldschmidts "Corsaren." Med en udførlig redegørelse for striden mellem Søren Kierkegaard og "Corsaren"* (Aarhus: Sirius, 1962); revised as *Corsaren, Goldschmidt og Kierkegaard* (Copenhagen: Corsaren, 1977);

Mogens Brøndsted, *Goldschmidts fortællekunst* (Copenhagen: Gyldendal, 1967);

Brøndsted, *Meïr Goldschmidt* (Copenhagen: Gyldendal, 1965);

Jørgen Egebak, "Alting og forstanden: Meïr Goldschmidt, Bjergtagen I," in *Analyser af dansk kortprosa,* volume 1, edited by Jørgen Dines Johansen (Copenhagen: Borgen, 1971), pp. 204–225;

Jørgen Gleerup, *Den borgerlige katastrofe og romanen i det 19. århundrede* (Odense: Odense Universitetsforlag, 1976), pp. 36–62;

Vivian Greene-Gantzberg, "En Jøde og samtidige jødiske skildringer," *Danske Studier* (1980): 133–143;

Aage Lærke Hansen, "Fra dannelsesroman til udviklingsroman," *Kritik,* 8 (1968): 20–24;

John C. Jørgensen, *Den sande kunst. Studier i dansk 1800-tals realisme* (Copenhagen: Borgen, 1980), pp. 155–162;

Johnny Kondrup, *Levned og tolkninger. Studier i nordisk selvbiografi* (Odense: Odense Universitetsforlag, 1982), pp. 158–189;

Lars Kruse-Blinkenberg, *Assimilationens (u)mulighed i M. Goldschmidts roman En Jøde. En religionshistorisk skitse* (Copenhagen: C. A. Reitzel, 2000);

Kruse-Blinkenberg, *Jøden Simon Levi i M. Goldschmidts roman Ravnen. En religionshistorisk studie* (Copenhagen: C. A. Reitzel, 1998);

Hans Kyrre, *M. Goldschmidt,* 2 volumes (Copenhagen: H. Hagerup, 1919);

P. M. Mitchell, *A History of Danish Literature* (Copenhagen: Glydendal, 1957), pp. 144, 161, 165–167, 197;

Kenneth H. Ober, *Die Ghettogeschichte* (Göttingen: Wallstein, 2001);

Ober, "Goldschmidt's English Novel 'Homeless,'" *Orbis Litterarum,* 34 (1979): 113–123;

Ober, *Meïr Goldschmidt* (Boston: Twayne, 1976);

Paul V. Rubow, *Goldschmidt og Nemesis* (Copenhagen: Munksgaard, 1968);

Søren Schou, "Kærlighedens Babelstårn. Meïr Aron Goldschmidt: Kjærlighedshistorier fra mange Lande," in *Læsninger i dansk litteratur,* volume 2 (1820–1900), edited by Povl Schmidt and Ulrik Lehrman (Odense: Odense Universitetsforlag, 1998), pp. 198–214, 350–351;

Knud Sørensen, ed., *Goldschmidt, en fortrolig fremmed* (Risskov: Hovedland, 1985);

Knud Wentzel, *Fortolkning og Skæbne. Otte danske romaner fra romantismen og naturalismen* (Copenhagen: Fremad, 1970);

Wentzel, "Udvikling og påvirkning: Goldschmidts vej fra korsar til skriftklog," *Kritik,* 10 (1969): 52–89.

Papers:

Meïr Goldschmidt's papers and letters are at the Danish Royal Library in Copenhagen.

N. F. S. Grundtvig

(8 September 1783 – 2 September 1872)

Sune Auken
University of Copenhagen

(Translated by Carol Gold)

SELECTED BOOKS: *Maskeradeballet i Dannemark 1808. Et Syn* (Copenhagen: J. H. Schubothe, 1808);

Nordens Mytologi eller Udsigt over Eddalæren for dannede Mænd der ei selv ere Mytologer (Copenhagen: J. H. Schubothe, 1808);

Optrin af Kæmpelivets Undergang i Nord (Copenhagen: J. H. Schubothe, 1809);

Idunna. En Nytaarsgave for 1811 (Copenhagen: G. Bonnier, 1810);

Nytaarsnat eller Blik paa Kristendom og Historie (Copenhagen: A. Seidelin, 1810);

Optrin af Norners og Asers Kamp (Copenhagen: J. H. Schubothe, 1811);

Saga. Nytaarsgave for 1812 (Copenhagen: A. Seidelin, 1811);

Kort Begreb af Verdens Krønike i Sammenhæng (Copenhagen: A. Seidelin, 1812);

Kort Begreb af Verdens Krønike, betragtet i Sammenhæng (Copenhagen: A. Seidelin, 1814);

Roskilde-Riim (Copenhagen: A. Seidelin, 1814);

Roskilde-Saga, til Oplysning af Roskilde-Riim (Copenhagen: A. Seidelin, 1814);

Europa, Frankrig og Napoleon, en dansk historisk Betragtning (Copenhagen: A. Seidelin, 1815);

Heimdall. Dansk Nytaars-Gave for 1816 (Copenhagen: A. Seidelin, 1815);

Imod den lille Anklager, det er Prof. H. C. Ørsted. Med Beviis for at Schellings Philosophie er uchristelig, ugudelig og løgnagtig (Copenhagen: A. Seidelin, 1815);

Kvædlinger eller Smaakvad (Copenhagen: A. Seidelin, 1815);

Danne-Virke. Et Tids-Skrift, 4 volumes (Copenhagen: A. Schmidts, 1816–1819)–volume 2 includes "Paaske-Liljen," translated by Alexander Marlowe as *The Easter-Lily* (Blair, Neb.: Danish Lutheran Publishing House, 1919);

Lithograph (1848) based on an 1831 painting by Christian Albrecht Jensen; courtesy of the Danish Royal Library, Copenhagen

Udsigt over Verdens-Króniken fornemmelig i det Lutherske Tidsrum (Copenhagen: A. Seidelin, 1817);

Nyaars-Morgen. Et Rim (Copenhagen: J. H. Schultz, 1824);

Kirkens Gienmæle imod Professor Theologiae Dr. H. N. Clausen (Copenhagen: Wahl, 1825);

Danske Høitids-Psalmer til Tusindaars-Festen (Copenhagen: Wahl, 1826);

Kong Harald og Ansgar. Rim-Blade af Danmarks Kirke-Bog til Jubel-Aaret (Copenhagen: Wahl, 1826);

Skribenten Nik. Fred. Sev. Grundtvigs Literaire Testamente (Copenhagen: Wahl, 1827);

Christelige Prædikener eller Søndags-Bog, 3 volumes (Copenhagen: Wahl, 1827–1830);

Krønike-Riim til Børne-Lærdom med Indledning og Anmærkninger (Copenhagen: Wahl, 1829);

Nordens Mythologi eller Sindbilled-Sprog historisk-poetisk udviklet og oplyst (Copenhagen: J. H. Schubothe, 1832);

Haandbog i Verdens-Historien efter de Bedste Kilder, volumes 1–2 (Copenhagen: Wahl, 1833, 1835–1836), volume 3 (Copenhagen: J. H. Schubothe, 1843 [i.e., 1856]);

Sang-Værk til den Danske Kirke (Copenhagen: Wahl, 1837);

Til Nordmænd om en Norsk Høi-Skole (Christiania [Oslo]: C. Grøndahl, 1837);

Nordiske Smaadigte (Christiania [Oslo]: C. Grøndahl, 1838);

Skolen for Livet og Academiet i Soer (Copenhagen: Wahl, 1838);

Bøn og Begreb om en dansk Høiskole i Soer (Copenhagen: Wahl, 1840);

Brage-Snak om græske og nordiske Myther og Oldsagn for Damer og Herrer (Copenhagen: C. A. Reitzel, 1844);

Danske Ordsprog og Mundheld (Copenhagen: C. A. Reitzel, 1845);

Danske Kæmpeviser til Skole-Brug (Copenhagen: C. A. Reitzel, 1847);

Græsk og Nordisk Mythologi for Ungdommen (Copenhagen: J. H. Bing, 1847);

Danskeren, et Ugeblad, 4 volumes (Copenhagen: Privately printed, 1848–1851);

Fest-Psalmer (Copenhagen: C. G. Iversen, 1850);

Christenhedens Syvstjerne. Et kirkeligt Sagakvad (Copenhagen: T. Michaelsen & Tillge, 1860);

Den Christelige Børnelærdom (Copenhagen: K. Schønberg, 1868);

Sang-Værk til den Danske Kirke-Skole (Copenhagen: C. G. Iversen, 1870);

Kirke-Speil, eller, Udsigt over den Christne Menigheds (Copenhagen: K. Schønberg, 1871);

Mands Minde, 1788–1838. Foredrag over det sidste halve aarhundredes Historie, holdte 1838 (Copenhagen: K. Schønberg, 1877).

Editions and Collections: *Prædikener i Frederiks-Kirken, 1832–39,* edited by C. J. Brandt (Copenhagen: K. Schønberg, 1875);

Sidste Prædikener i Vartov Kirke, 1861–72, edited by Brandt, 2 volumes (Copenhagen: K. Schønberg, 1880);

N. F. S. Grundtvigs poetiske Skrifter, volumes 1–7, edited by Svend Grundtvig; volumes 8–9, edited by Georg Christensen (Copenhagen: K. Schønberg, 1880–1930);

Nik. Fred. Sev. Grundtvigs udvalgte Skrifter, 10 volumes, edited by Holger Begtrup (Copenhagen: Gyldendal, 1904–1909);

Digte i Udvalg, edited by Frederik Rønning (Copenhagen: K. Schønberg, 1916);

Udvalg af N. F. S. Grundtvigs selvbiografiske Digtning, edited by Ida Falbe-Hansen (Copenhagen: Gyldendal, 1921);

Vartovs-Prædikener, 1839–1860, selected and edited by Begtrup (Copenhagen: Gyldendal, 1924);

Haandbog i N. F. S. Grundtvigs Skrifter, edited by Ernst J. Borup and Frederik Schrøder (Copenhagen: H. Hagerup, 1929–1931);

Et lille Udvalg af Nicolai Frederik Severin Grundtvig's Skrifter og Sange i Tidsfølge, edited, with an introduction, by Begtrup (Copenhagen: Gyldendal, 1930);

Udvalgte Værker, 10 volumes, edited by P. A. Rosenberg (Copenhagen: Danmark, 1930);

Digte af N. F. S. Grundtvig, edited, with an introduction and notes, by Carl S. Petersen, illustrated by Joakim Skovgaard (Copenhagen: Foreningen "Fremtiden," 1933);

Værker i Udvalg, 10 volumes, edited by Christensen and Hal Koch, (Copenhagen: Gyldendal, 1940–1949);

Grundtvigs Sang-Værk, 6 volumes, edited by Thorvald Balslev and others (Copenhagen: Danske Forlag, 1944–1964; reprinted, Copenhagen: Gad, 1982–1984);

Udvalgte Digte, edited, with an introduction and notes, by Steen Johansen (Copenhagen: H. Reitzel, 1963);

Skrifter i Udvalg, edited, with an afterword, by Kaj Thaning (Copenhagen: Gyldendal, 1965);

Grundtvig. Tekstudvalg, edited by K. E. Bugge (Copenhagen: Nyt nordisk Forlag, 1980);

Historie og Kristendom. En Grundtvig-Antologi, edited by Erik Høegh-Andersen, Joakim Garff, and Jørgen I. Jensen (Haarby, 1983);

N. F. S. Grundtvigs Prædikener, 1822–26 og 1832–39, 12 volumes, edited by Christian Thodberg (Copenhagen: Gad, 1983–1986);

N. F. S. Grundtvigs Præstø-Prædikener, 2 volumes, edited by Thodberg (Copenhagen: Gad, 1988);

Prædikener i Vartov, 4 volumes, edited by Jette Holm and others (Copenhagen: Forlaget Vartov, 2003).

Editions in English: *Selected Writings,* edited, with an introduction, by Johannes Knudsen; translated by Knudsen, Enok Mortensen, and Ernest D. Nielsen (Philadelphia: Fortress Press, 1976);

A Grundtvig Anthology: Selections from the Writings of N. F. S. Grundtvig, edited, with an introduction, by Niels Lyhne Jensen; translated by Edward Broadbridge and Jensen (Cambridge: J. Clarke / Viby, Denmark: Centrum, 1984; Greenwood, S.C.: Attic Press, 1984);

Selected Educational Writings, edited by Max Lawson (N.p.: International People's College/Association of Folk High Schools in Denmark, 1991).

OTHER: Snorri Sturluson and Saxo Grammaticus, *Prøver af Snorros og Saxos Krøniker,* translated by Grundtvig (Copenhagen: A. Seidelin, 1815);

Saxo Grammaticus, *Danmarks Krønike,* 3 volumes, translated by Grundtvig (Copenhagen: Privately printed, 1818–1823);

Snorri Sturluson, *Norges Konge-Krønike,* 3 volumes, translated by Grundtvig (Copenhagen: Privately printed, 1818–1823);

Bjowulfs Drape. Et gothisk Helte-Digt fra forrige Aar-Tusinde, af angel-saxisk paa danske Riim, translated by Grundtvig (Copenhagen: A. Seidelin, 1820);

Theologisk Maanedsskrift (1825–1826), co-edited by Grundtvig;

Beowulfes Beorh eller Bjovulfs-Drapen, det old-angelske Heltedigt, edited and translated by Grundtvig (Copenhagen: K. Schønberg, 1861; London: J. R. Smith, 1861).

N. F. S. Grundtvig was active in many fields and is remembered in Denmark as a clergyman, poet, theologian, mythologist, critic, philologist, philosopher, educational reformer, politician, and debater. His writing constitutes the largest known body of authorship in Danish, with a bibliography numbering 1,479 items, including a large number of longer works. The register of his unpublished manuscripts fills twenty-eight volumes (with one item per page). Grundtvig's influence on Danish cultural and intellectual history was extensive. In Denmark he is most famous for his hymns and hymn adaptations, which account for roughly one-third of the Danish Lutheran hymnal, and for his work with adult education. Although he wrote only a few texts on adult education, they nonetheless lay the groundwork for the creation of *folkehøjskoler* (literally, "folk high schools," also sometimes translated as "people's colleges"). These are exam-free schools that people can attend for periods stretching from four months to one year, purely for enlightenment, without the goal of obtaining a formal degree.

Grundtvig was perhaps the single most influential person in Danish intellectual history and has, as have few in Denmark, an organized movement named after him, "Grundtvigianism," which even today influences the cultural landscape in Denmark, although perhaps less now than formerly. Grundtvig was one of the most self-willed thinkers and poets in Danish literature. His status as Denmark's unofficial religious and national father figure gives him a special standing, positive as well as negative, in cultural debates. He was feared for his temper and is still both admired and disliked for his visionary thinking and writing style. His capacity for work was amazing; he practically never slept, and his ability to absorb and synthesize great amounts of material was legendary.

Grundtvig's international reputation is more modest and does not measure up to that of his younger contemporaries, Hans Christian Andersen and Søren Kierkegaard. Grundtvig's educational theories have had the greatest international influence, and *folkehøjskoler* around the world draw inspiration from his ideas. In 1999 the European Union's adult-education program was named after him. Within the field of Old English literature, Grundtvig's work with *Beowulf* and the Exeter Book is well known and considered to be pioneering scholarship. His influence beyond these areas is mostly local.

Nikolai Frederik Severin Grundtvig was born on 8 September 1783, the youngest child of clergyman Johan Grundtvig and Cathrine Marie Bang Grundtvig. Two of his brothers and his one sister died while he was still young. The only surviving sibling was his oldest brother, Otto, who was also a clergyman and later became a rural dean but led a more secluded life.

In the middle of the first decade of the nineteenth century, after a long series of unpublished juvenilia, N. F. S. Grundtvig found in Old Norse literature the material that was to unleash his poetic abilities. One element in this release was his intensely unhappy love for Constance Leth, the mistress of the manor where he was a tutor for some years. Grundtvig's interpretation of the Old Norse material in his earliest published works (1806–1810) was inspired by several contemporaneous German thinkers, among whom were Friedrich Wilhelm Joseph von Schelling, Johann Gottlieb Fichte, and Johann Gottfried Herder. Grundtvig's first published work, "Lidet om Sangene i Edda" (On the Songs in the Edda, 1806), is an attack on a comic rendition of the Old Nordic poem *Skírnismál* (The Lay of Skirnir), which Grundtvig claimed was misunderstood. His two most important works of this period, *Nordens Mytologi* (Mythology of the North, 1808) and *Optrin af Kæmpelivets Undergang i Nord* (Scenes from the Downfall of the Heroic Life in the North, 1809), both deal with Old

Norse subjects. The latter was intended to be the concluding volume in the rewriting of the history of the pagan North. It describes the Christianization of Denmark and the tragic attempt by the last heathen chieftain, Palnatoke, to save paganism.

Nordens Mytologi is presented as an introduction to Nordic mythology but is actually a comprehensive and independent interpretation of the myths. After an introduction, in which Grundtvig discusses previous interpretations and the sources of Nordic mythology, the book has three sections. The first deals with "the number, names and conditions of the gods" and identifies a god over the Aesir (the collective name by which some of the gods were known) called Allfather, who rules the Aesir and the course of history through the Norn (goddesses of fate). The second section, "The Aesir Doctrine," is the most important part of the book. In it Grundtvig discusses the course of Nordic mythology, beginning with the creation of the world. He describes the Aesir's fall from grace and their fight against the giants throughout history up to Ragnarok (Doom of the Gods), the event in which their offenses against Allfather are wiped clean with their death, whereupon a new, pure world appears. In the third section, "The Teaching of the Fable," Grundtvig discusses the connection between the history of the gods and the life of humanity. At decisive points in the book he includes his own poems and a passage from Adam Oehlenschläger's play *Baldur hin Gode* (Balder the Good, 1807).

Nordens Mytologi is a pioneering scholarly and artistic work. It is the most significant book in the first period of Grundtvig's writing career and an important work of Danish Romanticism. In it he makes use of many elements of Schelling's historical philosophy, which are presented in the guise of mythology. For this reason Grundtvig's mythology is highly abstract; the figures of Nordic mythology are stripped of their individuality and act almost exclusively as characters in the young writer's system of historical philosophy. The book is radically different from Grundtvig's later work, in part because of its creative aesthetics and its undefined attitude toward Christianity, which appears only once in the discussion of mythology. When Christianity is mentioned, however, it has such an intense impact that it shatters the deeper meaning of the book.

During the 1810 Christmas season, as Grundtvig was finishing a second volume in his revision of Old Nordic history, *Optrin af Norners og Asers Kamp* (Scenes from the Struggles of the Norn and the Aesir, 1811), he was struck by a serious religious crisis (and probably the first of four mental breakdowns), which resulted in a Christian conversion. The crisis and the conversion are discussed in two collections of poetry. *Idunna* (titled after the goddess who keeps the apples of youth), published in 1810, demonstrates Grundtvig's departure from Nordic paganism. *Nytaarsnat eller Blik paa Kristendom og Historie* (New Year's Eve or a View of Christianity and History, 1810) details his arrival at Christianity. Grundtvig's first important hymn, "De hellige tre Konger" (The Three Wise Men), dates from this crisis period. (It is better known in Denmark as "Dejlig er den himmel blå" [Lovely Is the Blue Sky], from the first line.) It was published in 1811, together with a programmatic introduction in which Grundtvig announced his intention of writing an entire sequence of hymns, a promise he was first able to fulfill in the mid 1830s. After this crisis he resolutely regarded himself as a traditional Lutheran and rejected his earlier work on Old Nordic history as ungodly. He added several scenes of Christian refutations to *Optrin af Norners og Asers Kamp,* in a conscious break with the original plan of that work. The planned retelling of the Old Nordic tales was aban-

Grundtvig's first wife, Lise Blicher Grundtvig, whom he married in 1817 (from Finn Abrahamowitz, Grundtvig. Danmark til lykke, *2000; Wilson Library, University of Minnesota)*

doned. Grundtvig worked through his remaining interest in Nordic mythology with the poetry collection *Saga* (1811).

Grundtvig's new religious convictions were expressed in *Kort Begreb af Verdens Krønike i Sammenhæng* (A Short Consecutive Account of the Chronicle of the World, 1812). The book is a sweeping survey of history in which Grundtvig judges historical and–especially–contemporary individuals using his Lutheran biblical interpretation as the absolute standard. His judgment of figures from German intellectual history who had previously influenced him was particularly harsh. Grundtvig's world history was a succès de scandale. It won him fame but it also isolated him within Danish cultural life and hindered him from receiving both the pastoral position and the historical professorship to which he felt entitled. This isolation only ended in the 1830s, when his popularity grew enormously among the public.

Grundtvig's newfound Christianity went hand in hand with his unflagging interest in history. The long *Roskilde-Riim* (Roskilde Rhyme, 1814), which is the primary poem from this period, is fashioned as a journey from grave to grave at the cathedral in Roskilde, where the Danish kings are buried. The speaker of the poem, who (as is often the case with Grundtvig) is the poet himself, stops at each grave, recounts the fate of the buried monarch and of the country during his reign, and passes judgment on him. Grundtvig's attempt to write a commentary on the many paths and byways in *Roskilde-Riim* grew into an entire book, *Roskilde-Saga* (The Roskilde Saga, 1814), which covers the same time frame but is an independent work. This book is his only history of Denmark. At the same time, he sought in articles, books, and poems to convert his ostensibly ungodly contemporaries.

During this period Grundtvig was also formulating new interests and ideas. In 1814 he decided to translate Snorri Sturluson's saga of the Norwegian kings, *Heimskringla* (circa 1225). Although Grundtvig's new attempt to write a history of the world, *Kort Begreb af Verdens Krønike, betragtet i Sammenhæng* (A Short Account of the Chronicle of the World, Considered Consecutively, 1814), never made it past the Old Testament period, the book pointed in the direction of a new breakthrough. The narrow focus on the present, which had led to the debate surrounding his first world history, was gone, and the polemic was toned down. The book was more academic, with notes and literary references, and exhibited a renewed interest in questions of poetry and language that went beyond the tendencies in *Kort Begreb af Verdens Krønike i Sammenhæng.*

In 1815 the change in Grundtvig's writing became unmistakable. His fierce religious advocacy had isolated him so much that his opportunities for independent preaching were almost exhausted. He was tired from a series of unpleasant controversies, and his preaching had not resulted in the Christian conversion of Danes that he sought. The tone of his writing now calmed down considerably. *Imod den lille Anklager* (Against the Little Accuser, 1815), Grundtvig's last work in connection with the disputes about his world history, is more humorous than his earlier efforts in the debate. The poetry collection *Kvædlinger eller Smaakvad* (Small Songs, 1815) renewed his writing in two ways. It reprinted a series of poems dating from before his conversion, which were now included in his work again, even though Grundtvig criticized their religious deviations in a series of appendices. The collection also included, for the first time since *Saga,* a new poem with a subject from Nordic mythology. The poem "Thryms-Kvide" (The Song of Thrym) is a free rendition of the Old Nordic lay *Þrymskviða* (The Song of Thrym), in which Grundtvig, through reorganization and revision, proposes a hidden Christian revelation, concealed beneath several layers of irony.

Another important change in Grundtvig's work took place at this time. With his orientation toward the Old Norse, he had long hoped for spiritual renewal in Norway. But when Denmark and Norway were split up in 1814, following the Napoleonic Wars, and Norway did not react with sorrow at the demise of the dual monarchy, Grundtvig was disappointed. In response he became an enthusiast for Danish identity. This new interest was first expressed in *Europa, Frankrig og Napoleon* (Europe, France and Napoleon, 1815), a prophecy about the importance of Napoleon Bonaparte's future role in Europe, which was wrong even as it was being published. From this time on, the issue of Danish identity was a constant theme in Grundtvig's writings. It led him to long discussions about the character of Danes, to dreams about the spiritual meaning of the country in a coming renewal of world history, and to an entire cascade of songs for Danes, who seemed unworthy of their considerable historical heritage and role. As a consequence of the split between Denmark and Norway, Grundtvig took it upon himself also to translate Saxo Grammaticus's early-thirteenth-century *Gesta Danorum* (History of the Danes) from Latin into Danish.

As part of this new breakthrough, Grundtvig added yet another subject to his scholarship. In 1815 Grímur Jónsson Thorkelin published in Copenhagen the first edition of the Anglo-Saxon epic poem *Beowulf.* Grundtvig was much taken with the poem but also aware of the problems with Thorkelin's faulty Latin translation. The result was a bitter debate with Thorkelin but also a lifelong interest in *Beowulf* and Old

English poetry. As a result, Grundtvig decided to translate the poem himself.

Grundtvig's new preaching and enthusiasm for Danish cultural identity are repeated and deepened in the poems from his last work of 1815, *Heimdall* (titled after the watchman of the gods). Here he removed his ironic mask, but he did not return to the aggressive preaching of his earlier years or give up his renewed interest in paganism. The main piece in the collection is the epic poem "Et Blad af Jyllands Rimkrønike" (A Page from Jutland's Rhyming Chronicle). It moves from a free rendition of Denmark's pagan history to the introduction of Christianity by Archbishop Ebbo of Rheims and by St. Ansgar. Along the way, a series of prophetic visions is presented, expressing the basic historic conditions of Denmark and reaching forward to Judgment Day. Grundtvig is now interpreting paganism through the perspective of Redemption. By itself, paganism cannot withstand the pressure from the devil's various associates, but through the saving grace of Christianity it can receive its permanent worth. The poem demonstrates this idea by introducing pictures from paganism into the important Christian prophecies.

The breakthrough in 1815 also marks a delineation of decisive features in Grundtvig's poetic writing style. His juvenilia was pretentious and affected the style of the Old Nordic literature. From 1810 to 1815 he was dominated by a desire for simple sermons and a justification of Christianity, so he kept his style plain and sparse, with restrained imagery and a simplicity of syntax and composition. After 1815 Grundtvig began writing in a complex, synthesizing, and metaphoric style that valued connotation as highly as denotation and that focused on the ability of pictures and text to connect meanings and to allow insight into the deepest meaning of existence.

Over the course of the following years, Grundtvig expanded and deepened his work with this breakthrough as a background. In the periodical *Danne-Virke* (1816–1819), titled after the earthen defense system at the German border built in the early Middle Ages by Queen Thyra Dannebod, he tried to carry through his rebellion against German idealism. The four volumes of the journal (about sixteen hundred pages) were written almost entirely by Grundtvig himself. At the same time, through his poems and essays he developed an epistemology based on Christianity. Especially noteworthy in this connection is the extensive article "Om Aabenbaring, Konst og Vidskab" (On Revelation, Art and Understanding), from the third volume of the magazine, in which Grundtvig discusses different possibilities for the recognition and expression of the human soul, starting with a polemic against Immanuel Kant's epistemology.

Grundtvig in 1827, the year he lost a libel suit and was sentenced to lifetime prepublication censorship (engraving by C. W. Eckerberg; from Finn Abrahamowitz, Grundtvig: Danmark til lykke, *2000; Wilson Library, University of Minnesota)*

The most significant literary work in *Danne-Virke* is "Paaske-Liljen" (1817; translated as *The Easter-Lily,* 1919), which consists of a framing poem and a dramatic scene. The Easter hymn "Påskeblomst, hvad vil du her?" (Easter Flower, What Do You Want?) is taken from the two parts of the framing poem. In the first part the poet turns questioningly to the Easter lily, the symbol of the Resurrection, asking what it symbolizes and the meaning of its symbol. The answer can be given only historically. The poet is carried back to Christ's grave the night before Easter morning, and a dramatic scene, with clear inspiration from William Shakespeare, is enacted. A series of figures discusses the identity of the man who lies buried behind the stone. Several theories are suggested. Two soldiers do not understand the meaning of the event and treat the affair as a ghost story. A Roman chieftain insists condescendingly and unsympathetically that Jesus was a Jewish philosopher and nothing more. A Pharisee understands that there is more at stake here but purposefully leaves the grave site early so as not to have his own faith challenged by the new faith about to appear. Finally, the tough veteran Tacitus has seen signs that have convinced him that the dead man really is God's son. The angel's arrival decides the discussion, and only Tacitus is able to remain standing to see it. The poet's original question is answered, and the resurrection he asked for turns out to have taken place in his own breast, so that at the end of the poem he can stand as a sign of the Resurrection.

Other poems in *Danne-Virke* include a series titled "Efterklange" (Echoes), which features Grundtvig's current reflections on and continuations of what he has heard in poetic texts of the past. Another poem, "Ragna-Roke, et dansk Æmter" (Ragnarok, a Danish Tale), was written in 1817 on the occasion of the three-hundredth anniversary of the Reformation. In it Grundtvig uses a combination of Old Nordic and Old English material, together with Lutheran poetry and theology, to challenge the soulless present and to suggest hope for an historical renewal of Danish cultural, religious, and public life.

The argument in *Danne-Virke* against German idealism is also found in Grundtvig's third world history, *Udsigt over Verdens-Krøniken fornemmelig i det Lutherske Tidsrum* (A View of the History of the World, Mostly During the Lutheran Period, 1817). This book repeats the review of ancient times from the earliest recorded history, but Grundtvig rewrote and expanded the account of the modern period, concentrating on movements in recent German intellectual life.

In 1817 Grundtvig married Lise Blicher, to whom he had been engaged since 1811. They remained married until her death in 1851 and had three children: Johan (1822), Svend (1824), and Meta (1827). Their marriage was not the result of a deep love, and Grundtvig's great passions were for other women, especially his first love, Constance, and his second wife, Marie Toft. But by the standards of the time, the marriage was a good one for many years, and Lise, in keeping with the wifely ideal of the time, was his faithful support through the many vicissitudes of his life.

The third important work of this period was the completion of three translation projects. Work on them covered the entire period from 1814 to 1823. The first volumes of the Saxo and Snorri translations were published in 1818, and the final volumes appeared in 1823 (although both say 1822 on the title page). The translation of the shorter *Beowulf* was published separately as *Bjowulfs Drape* (The Song of Beowulf) in 1820. Grundtvig adjusted the titles of the two Nordic works of history to make them similar. Saxo's *Gesta Danorum* was titled *Danmarks Krønike* (The Chronicle of Denmark) and Snorri's *Heimskringla* became *Norges Konge-Krønike* (The Chronicle of Norway's Kings). Thus, Grundtvig included the two medieval authors in the same historical tradition in which he placed himself, since he called his world histories "chronicles." He also made the two works, quite different in their original versions, stylistically similar, so that they appear as an organic whole. In his translations he attempted to make the works more popular and reader friendly. Both Saxo's Silver Age Latin, which matched Grundtvig's joy with its oratorical swings, and Snorri's more measured northern rhetoric were rewritten as a comprehensive account, with frequent use of proverbs and occasional variegated expressions. The more-or-less conscious goal of Grundtvig's rhetorical strategy was to emphasize the continued connection between the two Nordic countries after their separation.

The translation of *Beowulf* had a different purpose. It was the first translation of the poem into any modern language. In agreement with the publisher, Grundtvig rendered *Beowulf* entirely as a poem, although not all in the same meter and with the inclusion of poems that can be sung. This edition has a more academic orientation than the Saxo and Snorri translations. Because Grundtvig was publishing a work that was largely unknown in learned circles at that time, he tried to stimulate interest in the forgotten epic by including it in an intellectual tradition through the use of extensive notes and a detailed, scholarly introduction.

The culmination of this extensive broadening of Grundtvig's literary production was *Nyaars-Morgen* (New Year's Morning, 1824). Next to the hymns, it is his most important poetic work. The poem consists of 312 eleven-line stanzas divided into ten cantos. In the first canto, the speaker of the poem sends a blessing of "God's Peace" throughout the Nordic world; he points back to a struggle played out at night and forward to a victory that the day will bring. The world described in the first canto is characterized by the speaker's unification with his surroundings, by fellowship, life, and the warmth of a living connection with the past, present, and future. At the beginning of the second canto, the poem jumps back to the beginning of the night, to a condition that, in direct opposition to the first canto, is characterized by cold, dark, death, isolation, and defeat. The second through the ninth cantos describe the journey of the speaker through the night toward morning. Through a gradual connection with the history of the Nordic people and a series of remarkable events, Grundtvig moves forward to the breakthrough of light and warmth that greeted the reader in the first canto. The tenth canto begins with a repetition of the first three stanzas from the first canto, thereby indicating that the cycle is completed. The rest of the canto, the final twelve stanzas in the poem, are spoken by "the Spirit," who prophesies about what will happen next.

Nyaars-Morgen is autobiographical, although not in the usual sense. It describes Grundtvig's own development, but the events in his life are woven into a complicated pattern of interpretation that differs greatly from a traditional autobiography. The pattern takes elements from the movements of the day and the year (as is indicated by the title), with emphasis on the struggle between the various elements (light versus dark, warmth versus cold, and so on). The poem is also interspersed with references to Old Norse literature and the Bible. Grundtvig interprets his own development in connection with these stories and at the same time stresses that his development has a decisive significance for the triumph of light and warmth in the world. Only long after it was published did *Nyaars-Morgen* achieve status as a major work in Grundtvig's writing and in Danish literature. Originally, it was ignored by the public, and the first edition did not sell out for many years. Together with *Nyaars-Morgen* Grundtvig wrote a related hymn, "De Levendes Land" (The Land of the Living), which was first published in 1832 in a revised version but which, in its original form, is a central summary of his poetry and theology.

Grundtvig's decisive religious breakthrough happened shortly after, and in close connection with, the publication of *Nyaars-Morgen*. This breakthrough is usually called *den mageløse Opdagelse* (the unparalleled discovery), and the interpretation of Christianity that accompanied it is called *den kirkelige Anskuelse* (the ecclesiastic understanding). Grundtvig abandoned his belief that the Bible is the foundation of true faith and substituted an emphasis on the two sacraments of baptism and Holy Communion. He stressed that the Apostles' Creed is the only true article of faith. This view followed from his conviction that the Bible arose from Christianity, not the reverse. The Bible is to be understood as a work that will enlighten Christians.

This new understanding was first announced in a sermon but received its first noticeable expression in *Kirkens Gienmæle* (The Church's Reply, 1825). This work was an attack on the young professor Henrik Nicolai Clausen's *Catholicismens og Protestantismens Kirkeforfatning, Lære og Ritus* (The State Rites and Doctrine of Catholicism and of Protestantism, 1825). In *Kirkens Gienmæle* Grundtvig speaks on behalf of the Christian Church against the heretic Clausen, accusing him of wanting to destroy Christianity, demanding his dismissal as professor, and subjecting his interpretation of the Bible to scathing criticism. Grundtvig's "ecclesiastic understanding" is put forward as an alternative. This work, which was his second succès de scandale, did not achieve the desired effect. Clausen did not acknowledge that Grundtvig spoke as a representative for the Christian Church and instead, to Grundtvig's surprise and indignation, brought a civil libel suit against him. Grundtvig lost the case in 1826 and as a result was placed under lifetime prepublication censorship. The censorship was, however, revoked in the late 1830s.

Partly as a result of the "unparalleled discovery" and of the libel suit, Grundtvig did not produce much literary work in the period after the publication of *Kirkens Gienmæle*. He concentrated on debates and on the further interpretation of the consequences of his religious views. This focus is particularly evident in the treatises "Om den sande Christendom" (About the True Christianity, 1826) and "Om Christendommens Sandhed" (About the Truth of Christianity, 1826–1827), which were published serially in *Theologisk Maanedsskrift* (Theological Monthly). Grundtvig had been co-editor of the periodical until the imposition of censorship.

There was, however, more literary work. In 1826, on the occasion of the celebration marking the millennium of the introduction of Christianity to Denmark, Grundtvig published a small hymnal, *Danske Høitids-Psalmer til Tusindaars-Festen* (Danish Festival Hymns for the Millennial Celebration). The most interesting selection is the revision of an old Danish hymn that, in Grundtvig's version, "Den signede Dag" (The Blessed Day), became one of the central hymns for services in the Danish Lutheran Church. Grundtvig, however, did not receive permission to use the new hymns for the anniversary service.

For the millennial celebration Grundtvig also wrote *Kong Harald og Ansgar* (King Harald and Ansgar, 1826), which consists of a tribute to King Frederik VI; three monologues in rhyming chronicle style spoken, respectively, by the ninth-century King Harald Klak, St. Ansgar, and Rimbert, Ansgar's disciple and hagiographer; and a poem about the relationship between country and faith, "Christi Kirke (Til Dana)" (The Christian Church [for Denmark]). In the monologues the three figures recount their roles in the introduction of Christianity to Denmark. The most distinctive of these is probably Harald's monologue, which was inspired by Ermold Nigellus's ninth-century account of the baptism of the pagan king but freely expands the story. Grundtvig invents a court poet who explains several times how the old Danish religion, Nordic mythology, can be interpreted as a precursor of the Christianity that Harald and his people accepted.

Grundtvig reacted to his censorship with a work that was almost playful, *Skribenten Nik. Fred. Sev. Grundtvigs Literaire Testamente* (The Literary Testament of Writer Nik. Fred. Sev. Grundtvig, 1827). In it he takes stock of his writings and defends himself against the various criticisms and accusations that had been leveled at him. The censorship was a catalyst for new ideas, and in another treatise, "Om Religions-Frihed" (On Freedom of Religion, 1827), the third part of which was the only one of his works to be suppressed by the censor, he presents a new and lasting religious under-

Vartov Church in central Copenhagen, where Grundtvig became pastor in 1839 (from Finn Abrahamowitz, Grundtvig. Danmark til lykke, *2000; Wilson Library, University of Minnesota)*

standing. He places freedom on all levels at the center and stresses both freedom of belief and the right of the faithful freely to choose their own ministers.

In continuation of his historic interests and as a break from his polemics, Grundtvig published *Krønike-Riim til Børne-Lærdom* (The Rhyming Chronicle of Elementary Doctrine, 1829). In fifty-two poems he moves between geography and history in an account in which countries, peoples, phenomena, and individuals use simple rhyme to talk about themselves in the first person.

In *Nordens Mythologi eller Sindbilled-Sprog* (Nordic Mythology or Symbolic Language, 1832) Grundtvig returns to broader areas of interest after the focus of the previous years on apologetics and moralizing. Many see this work as yet another breakthrough in his writing. It serves as an entry to his later work because of its broad, inclusive narrative style and its grandiose purpose. None of these characteristics is foreign to Grundtvig's earlier work, but they receive their classic form in *Nordens Mythologi.* Following an introductory poem and a preface, there are two parts to this work: an introduction (almost two hundred pages), which covers several different topics, and an even longer section consisting of the actual discussion of Nordic mythology. Because of its general interest and its form as a cultural program, the introduction is often discussed separately from the whole work, but the two parts really belong together. Both contribute to a poetic historical anthropology, which is theoretically portrayed in the introduction and figuratively expressed as a story in the longer section.

Instead of viewing Nordic mythology as a religious system competing with Christianity, Grundtvig interprets it as the Nordic pagans' understanding of humanity. The gods are understood as a sort of positive projection. In the mythology the pagans depicted their own highest concepts of humanity in the form of gods and thereby expressed their understanding of the world and the place of humans in it. This view is presented through a series of single-minded interpretations of mythological stories and characters. Spiritual implications are attributed to the stories and characters, which together create the many-faceted anthropology of the work. The essence of this work is an historical understanding of humanity, which sees possibilities in an active participation in the struggle between life and death that gives shape to history. *Nordens Mythologi* has a definite contemporaneous perspective and includes a general interest in the creation of understanding and consciousness on all levels, from the individual to the institutional, from youth to old age.

These two interests, an understanding of history and the creation of an historical perspective, were prominent in Grundtvig's writing of the 1830s. His interest in history was demonstrated by the extensive work he did in composing yet another world history. The first volume of *Haandbog i Verdens-Historien* (A Handbook of World History), which covered ancient history, was published in 1833. The second volume, on the Middle Ages, was published in 1835–1836. Work on the last volume on modern history was begun in 1842 and not finished until 1856, and even then Grundtvig got no farther than the year 1700. A fifteen-page appendix on the period from 1700 to 1869 appeared in 1869 in conjunction with the second edition of the work. *Haandbog i Verdens-Historien* was not meant as an actual world history but rather as a resource for teaching. Nevertheless, the result is a seamless interpretation, portraying history as a collective movement in which various peoples occupy center stage by turns and carry history forward. Grundtvig conceives of world history in the character of a single person, so that there is a parallel between the development of the individual person and that of humanity. At the same time he sees history as a movement in which the center shifts from the lands around the Mediterranean to those around the Baltic, including Denmark. This and other interpretations in the work do not, however, hinder the concrete description and interpretation of people and events. As with *Nordens Mythologi,* this book is also broad in its conception; it includes many notes and literary references. Grundtvig also engages in reflections and considerations on several different subjects.

In the 1830s Grundtvig's hymn writing finally gained momentum. He had written hymns off and on since his religious crisis in 1810, and several of his most important ones were written before 1830, but from now on they dominated his poetry. In the middle of the decade his good friend Gunni Busck gave him the resources that enabled him to concentrate on writing hymns. The result was *Sang-Værk til den Danske Kirke* (Song Work for the Danish Church, 1837). With 401 hymns, it is one of the most important collections of hymns in Danish literature, together with Thomas Kingo's *Vinter-Parten* (The Winter Part, 1689) and Hans Adolph Brorson's *Troens Rare Klenodie* (Faith's Rare Jewel, 1739). After "Forspil" (Prelude), which is an excerpt from *Nyaars-Morgen,* the hymns divide into two untitled parts. The composition of the first part is subject to debate, but the structure of the second part is well known. It includes hymns for all the principal holy days in the Christian calendar, organized historically according to Grundtvig's views about the existence of seven major churches in Christian history–Hebrew, Greek, Roman, Anglo-Saxon, German, Nordic, and an as-yet-unknown seventh church. Since it is still unknown, there are no hymns from this seventh group.

Grundtvig includes his own original hymns in the section on the Nordic church. He also includes revisions of Kingo's and Brorson's hymns as well, along with those of his friend B. S. Ingemann, who was not happy about having his own hymns rewritten. Grundtvig treated his predecessors with both reverence and disrespect. He admired them, but he changed everything with which he did not agree. The revisions are thus strongly personal, and many of them became a central expression of his understanding of Christianity. They are regarded in Denmark, and rightly so, more as original hymns by Grundtvig than as translations.

Grundtvig's understanding of Christianity and his imagery in the hymns is, as in the rest of his works, historically oriented. In revising hymns from the different historical churches, his purpose was to turn religious history into a living, active force in the present, so that contemporary churchgoers could experience their own Christianity in light of the past and the historic could appear in a spirit that speaks to the present. Thus, the congregant was included in an historical process that began with Jesus himself and was carried forward through eighteen hundred years of Christianity, forming a link in history that leads to the revelation of Judgment Day.

Sang-Værk til den Danske Kirke is, like most of Grundtvig's poetry, extremely mixed. He combines prophecies with bad puns and hymns of praise with abstruse, didactic poems. Some hymns are intimate or mild, while others are dominated by grandiose images and expressive rhetoric. Central to Grundtvig's hymns, as to his understanding of Christianity, is his belief that the world as created and redeemed by God and inscribed in the Bible must not be understood exclusively as a place of sin and death. It is the already existing world and the already existing person who are saved through Redemption. The image of God in which humans were created was certainly polluted and concealed in the Fall, but it is still present as the highest element of humanity. It is also the most authentic aspect of humanity, because, according to Grundtvig, God had originally made humans in this way. Salvation takes place as a holy transfiguration of the human world. Grundtvig does not deny Original Sin and does not believe man is capable of contributing to his own redemption, but in the end he values humanity positively, despite the Fall. This belief had a decisive influence on his hymn writing. Again and again, the connection between the mortal and the heavenly worlds is illustrated and stressed. Redemption creates awareness of this connection and makes it possible for

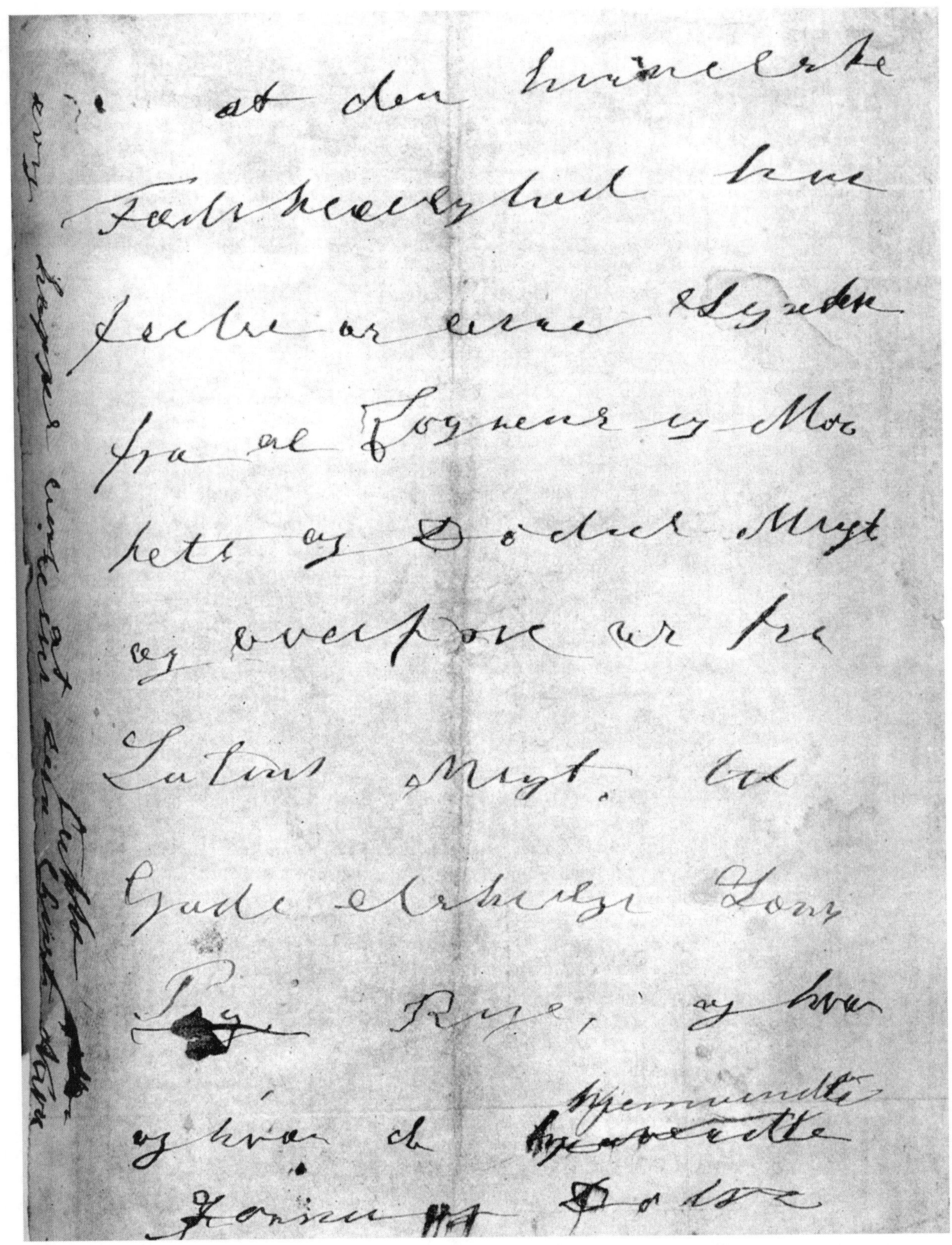

Page from the manuscript for a sermon by Grundtvig (from Carl S. Petersen and Vilhelm Andersen, Illustreret dansk Litteraturhistorie, *volume 3:* Litteratur i det nittende Aarhundredes første Halvdel, *1924; Suzzallo Library, University of Washington)*

humans to function as Christians rather than, as in much other Lutheran theology, to turn away from the connection. This strong worldliness does not mean that Grundtvig's hymns lack a heavenly or eschatological perspective. Precisely because his understanding of Christianity is historical, the Creation, Redemption, and eternal life are always present in his hymns as a manifest or implied deeper reality.

Grundtvig's hymn writing continued until his death in 1872. In 1839, after finishing *Sang-Værk til den Danske Kirke,* he began work on *Sang-Værk til Den Danske Kirke-Skole* (Song Work for the Danish Church Schools, 1870), which was to be a series of biblical and historic songs from the Creation to the present. The book was not finished until 1870. After Grundtvig's death the rest of his hymns were published in several collections, and the title *Sang-Værk* today refers to *Grundtvigs Sang-Værk* (Grundtvig's Song Work, 1944–1964), the six-volume edition of all his hymns. *Sang-Værk til den Danske Kirke* is the first volume in the collection, and *Sang-Værk til Den Danske Kirke-Skole* is the second volume. The three following volumes present the remainder of Grundtvig's hymns in chronological order. The last volume includes notes, variations, and an index.

At the same time that he was working with world history and writing hymns, Grundtvig began the publication of some of his most influential work–his writing on *folkehøjskoler.* The first essay on this subject, "Det Danske Firkløver eller Danskheden partisk betragtet" (The Danish Four-Leaf Clover; or, A Biased Account of Danish Identity), appeared in 1836. In the following years he wrote *Til Nordmænd om en Norsk Høi-Skole* (To Norwegians, about a Norwegian Folk High School, 1837), *Skolen for Livet og Academiet i Soer* (The School for Life and the Academy in Sorø, 1838), "Om Nordens videnskabelige Forening" (On the Scientific Union of the North, 1839), and *Bøn og Begreb om en dansk Høiskole i Soer* (A Petition and Idea for a Danish Folk High School in Sorø, 1840).

Skolen for Livet og Academiet i Soer is perhaps the most important of these works and is typical of Grundtvig's efforts. In it he levels a scathing critique at the current school system, from primary schools through the university. The system of classical education, with its emphasis on Latin culture and the importance of Latin, is attacked as a glorification of the dead, soul-destroying, and thoroughly harmful relic of the Roman spirit, which, in its time, by means of the Roman Empire and the Papacy, had spread its fatal domination across the globe. Even in Grundtvig's time, the classical-education model held the school system and those who had to go through it in its grasp. Even worse was the fact that students were subjected to an examination system that forced them in only one direction.

According to Grundtvig, this school system made people unfit for life because it educated them for participation in a transnational, transhistorical, and erudite world instead of teaching them to be civil servants and citizens in a particular society at a specific time. This approach was fine for those few who constituted the learned in society, but it was useless for everyone else. There was thus a need for a school system that could deliver higher education based on different premises. Grundtvig suggested that the ailing Sorø Academy be converted into an institution of higher education that could educate citizens and civil servants with consideration for their role in society and their participation in life, and not with the acquisition of a dead doctrine. Similarly, he stressed the necessity for teaching that was directed toward students' acquisition of specific subjects rather than focused on passing exams. Grundtvig refused to specify the curriculum for the new academy, but it was obvious that Danish history, demography, social studies, literature, and language should be at the center.

The latter half of the 1830s was characterized by an important change in Grundtvig's relation to the public. In 1837 the prepublication censorship was rescinded, to his great relief, although it had not hindered him much. From June to November 1838, with royal approval, he gave fifty-one public history lectures at Borchs Collegium. They were a great success but were not published until after his death, with the title *Mands Minde* (In Living Memory, 1877). It was at one of these lectures that the Danish tradition of singing at public meetings was started. In 1839 Grundtvig was appointed pastor at Vartov Church in central Copenhagen. The church was attached to a retirement home for elderly female civil servants. It was thought that this post would be a leisurely retirement position for him since he was close to sixty, but it turned into much more. Grundtvig held the position until his death more than thirty years later.

Since there were only limited duties connected with this position, Grundtvig had energy for extensive outreach activities. His work with the Danske Samfund (Danish Society) was central. He founded this society in reaction to the elite, philological, nationalist orientation of the Danish Historical Society, out of whose founding meeting he stormed. In the Danske Samfund, which served as a forerunner for the *folkehøjskole* movement, Grundtvig and his supporters (including Kierkegaard's brother, Bishop Peter Christian Kierkegaard) lectured on all of his favorite topics. These lectures were aimed at both the elite of the organization and a broader public. At the same time Grundtvig also achieved an impor-

Grundtvig in 1847 (drawing by Peter Christian Skovgaards; from Finn Abrahamowitz, Grundtvig. Danmark til lykke, *2000; Wilson Library, University of Minnesota)*

tant place in the consciousness of contemporary Pan-Scandinavianists. His sermons attracted a growing, independent congregation of enthusiastic, almost fanatical supporters.

The death of King Frederik VI and the ascension of Christian VIII in 1839 were of great significance to Grundtvig. Frederik had been relatively friendly toward Grundtvig, and the writer's devotion to the king was almost without bounds, but Frederik's decisions had often gone against Grundtvig. This situation improved with the change of kings. Christian's wife, Caroline Amalie, was one of Grundtvig's earliest and most enthusiastic supporters. He thus achieved an influence that gave him considerable political importance up to the death of Christian in 1848. As a part of his ongoing struggle within the Danish Church and the fight for religious freedom, Grundtvig opposed the powerful Bishop Jakob Peter Mynster's proposed new altar book. Partially owing to Grundtvig's influence, the new book was never introduced.

With Christian VIII on the throne, the plans for the *folkehøjskole* in Sorø moved an important step closer to realization. In *Bøn og Begreb om en dansk Høiskole i Soer* and "Om Indretningen af Sorø Academi til en folkelig Høiskole" (On the Organization of Sorø Academy as a Folk High School, 1843–not published during Grundtvig's lifetime but presented directly to Christian), Grundtvig set out concrete plans and presented suggestions for which subjects should be taught and how. The choice of subjects and ideology was determined by his purpose for the school–to train civil servants for the royal Danish government. Weight was therefore given to Danish history, geography, social conditions, and culture, particularly poetry and folk songs.

Grundtvig's last collection of secular poetry, *Nordiske Smaadigte* (Short Nordic Poems), was published in 1838. It is an anthology of his poetry up to 1824. A planned second volume never appeared. He continued to write many poems in addition to his hymns, but they were published in newspapers, periodicals, and private editions. Only the hymns were collected in larger book publications. By this time in his life Grundtvig had long since given up the literary scene as such. He did not engage in the daily literary debates or in the lively theater life of the period. The majority of his prose writing dealt with subjects that were not, on the surface, literary. The specifically and recognizably literary aspects of the latter part of his career were limited to his hymn writing–which poured forth during the rest of his life as a stream of new hymns and revisions of others' works–and a series of other poems, most of which were addressed to a specific situation and time. But there was considerable overlap between the poetry and prose. The ideas and the style of the prose works have poetic features, with a lively and extensive illustrative form that is central to the presentation and the argument, and with an intricate and elaborately balanced syntax that allows Grundtvig to blend broadly provocative and descriptive prose with sudden sharp formulations.

The secular poetry of Grundtvig's later years consisted mostly of occasional poems. He wrote on the occasion of events in the royal house or other national events or political situations, for public and private parties, and for events in his own family or circle of friends. This kind of writing was not a sign of decline in his work, but rather a logical extension of the tendency of his writing. None, or almost none, of Grundtvig's texts were written without some form of relationship to the present. His engagement in the present grew more and more pronounced throughout his life, but the immense historic-poetic universe that he developed in his thought and other writing was always present in his poems. Therefore, the perspective of his poetry was never limited only to the present but allowed him to place the present within larger historic, theological, and poetic contexts. At the same time, his passionate nature prevented the poems from degenerating into repetition and petty conventionality.

Grundtvig's elegies are a good example. Some of the most important of these were written in the 1840s, including "Povel Dons" (1843; published, 1867), for a childhood friend who died after many years of insanity (an illness perhaps brought on by Grundtvig's own first intense mental crisis); "Albert Thorvaldsen" (1844; published, 1848), written for the sculptor Bertel Thorvaldsen; and "Henrich Steffens" (1845), for a cousin and inspiration of that name. These poems mirror Grundtvig's complex relationships and growing degrees of intimacy with the three men. At the same time, nuanced portraits of each of the men are drawn, with sharp attacks against the soulless times. The different fates of the three subjects are reflected in Grundtvig's summative judgment in each case. But despite their differences, he nonetheless placed all three within the larger context of the period of which they were a part. He reflects particularly on their attitudes toward the cultural breakthrough that he believed took place in Denmark at the beginning of the nineteenth century. Their different fates are reflected in their relationships to this breakthrough. The two older contemporaries, Steffens and Thorvaldsen, appear as the messengers and bearers of this change, while the younger Dons is seen as one who, although he lived through it, was too fragile and therefore snapped under the violent visions.

In 1843 and 1844 Grundtvig gave a series of lectures on Nordic and Greek mythology. They were published in 1844 with the title *Brage-Snak* (Bragi Talk), named for the Old Icelandic "Bragaræður" (Speeches of Bragi), the false early-modern name for the first part of "Skaldskaparmál" (On Poetic Diction), from Snorri's *Edda* (circa 1200 A.D.). These lectures were just as popular as the *Mands Minde* lectures and were strongly influenced by the fact that, for the first time in Grundtvig's experience, women were present in the audience, and he flirted persistently with them. *Brage-Snak* was broad in its presentation format; despite the fact that the titles and topics were taken from the two mythologies, frequently discussion of mythology did not begin until several pages into the lectures. They were characterized by an appeal to the audience's common sense and by descriptions from and references to everyday reality. Grundtvig's attempt in *Nordens Mythologi* to use mythology as a springboard for the creation of a modern anthropology and worldview is further developed here to show the variety of ways in which mythology can be used to illustrate a series of psychological, historical, anthropological, literary, and scientific problems. Grundtvig does this without losing the lighthearted style that is characteristic of these lectures.

In the spring of 1844 Grundtvig suffered his second serious mental breakdown. The result was a severe depression that lasted for several months but had only limited impact on his writing or his public position.

Even though Grundtvig had left the literary scene, he retained an active interest in literature, especially historic and popular poetry. In the 1840s this interest resulted in a collection of proverbs, *Danske Ordsprog og Mundheld* (Danish Proverbs and Sayings, 1845), and a collection of folk songs, *Danske Kæmpeviser til Skole-Brug* (Danish Ballads for Use in Schools, 1847). Popular interpretation of ancient literature continued to hold Grundtvig's interest; *Græsk og Nordisk Mythologi for Ungdommen* (Greek and Nordic Mythology for Youth, 1847) is a short account of the two mythologies. Written probably on commission, it was his only book since *Idunna* to be illustrated (with drawings from the two mythologies). Grundtvig wrote it with a true pedagogical intent, attempting to tone down his own interpretations in order to leave as much room as possible for material on the two mythologies.

On 20 January 1848 Christian VIII died after a short illness and unsuccessful bloodletting. With the king's death, Grundtvig's hopes for a popular *højskole* in Sorø were finally ended, and his plans for a school for royal Danish civil servants were never implemented. During the 1840s, however, *folkehøjskoler* were built in Denmark on private initiative. The object was to train and educate the rural population in accordance with Grundtvig's educational ideas. The movement grew throughout his lifetime and continued to grow after his death. *Folkehøjskoler* are even today a striking and characteristic element of the Danish school system.

The year 1848 was in many ways an important one in Danish history. No sooner was Christian's successor, Frederik VII, on the throne than two crises erupted–the struggle for a constitution and the Slesvig-Holsten conflict. Both crises had been escalating during the 1840s, and they both reached a climax in March 1848. On 21 March the king agreed to a popular manifesto demanding that he fire his ministers and appoint new, responsible ministers from the National Liberal Party.

Throughout his life Grundtvig had been a convinced supporter of absolute monarchy. According to contemporary accounts, he behaved like a lion in a cage during the struggle for a democratic constitution. Nevertheless, he allowed himself to be appointed to the constituent assembly (1848–1849), on which he served as an energetic and colorful but not particularly influential member. A few elements in the Danish constitution can, however, be traced back to Grundtvig. He also held a seat in parliament (1849–1858), where he played a similar role. He always spoke longer than allowed

Grundtvig's second wife, Marie Toft, née Carlsen, whom he married in 1851 (from Finn Abrahamowitz, Grundtvigz: Danmark til lykke, *2000; Wilson Library, University of Minnesota)*

and introduced bill after bill, all of which were voted down. None of this seemed to bother him.

Two days after Frederik's establishment of constitutional monarchy, a civil war broke out in Slesvig and Holsten. During the 1840s there had been growing tension in these duchies between the large German minority (who were the majority of the population in the territories) and the Danish central government. On the one side were the duchies, supported in their bid for independence by the German Confederation, and on the other side was the Danish army, supported by Norwegian volunteers. What is today regarded as a civil war was viewed by the Danish at the time as an attempt by Prussia to conquer part of Denmark. Danish nationalism reached new heights during the war. Grundtvig's two sons, Johan and Svend, fought on the Danish side.

Grundtvig's own participation in the war had two parts. In parliament he advocated a consistent policy of attack in carrying out the war. At the same time, from 1848 to 1851, he published the weekly *Danskeren* (The Dane), which featured contributions from more writers than *Danne-Virke* had, but which was, like the earlier periodical, written mostly by him. The first edition of *Danskeren* was published symbolically on 22 March 1848–between the day of the king's acceptance of the demand for a responsible government and the day on which the war in Slesvig-Holsten started. *Danskeren,* although not as varied a publication as *Danne-Virke,* nonetheless was quite broad in its coverage. The periodical functioned mostly as a political and ideological mouthpiece for Grundtvig. He campaigned for the idea that to be Danish was something independent and valuable in relation to being German, and he tried to promote a Danish defensive, and occasionally even offensive, spirit.

Grundtvig took a middle position on the territorial question. He argued for a division of the duchies (the so-called Ejder policy, named after the Ejder River, which divides the two territories), so that only the northernmost duchy, Slesvig, which had a Danish majority and culturally belonged with Denmark, would remain with the country. He warned against the so-called unitary-state policy, which sought to retain both duchies as part of Denmark.

In *Danskeren* Grundtvig published a long series of speeches he had given, particularly in the Danske Samfund and in parliament, as well as several more-comprehensive articles written especially for the weekly. Even though the magazine was dominated by political articles, there was also room for several of his favorite topics, which could now, possibly because of his seat in the legislative assembly, more clearly than before be dealt with as political issues. At the same time *Danskeren* published a series of Grundtvig's poems that also dealt with the contemporary situation and within which his imagery and poetic universe were obviously still alive. With the conclusion of the war, he closed down *Danskeren.* In the final article he expressed concern about the unitary-state policy as well as the political and military victory, but also his hope for a rebirth of a true Danish identity. After the end of fighting in 1850, Prussia was pressured into accepting the terms of the London Convention of 1852, under which Slesvig-Holsten was to remain with Denmark.

For many years Grundtvig had been printing individual hymns for the Vartov congregation. In March 1850 these were collected for the first time in a work titled *Fest-Psalmer* (Festival Hymns). This collection originally had only thirty hymns, numbered consecutively following the official hymnal, but it was expanded during Grundtvig's lifetime into successively longer editions and eventually comprised more than three hundred hymns. He lived to see ten editions of the book; the last one was published in 1870.

In January 1851 Grundtvig's wife died. Their marriage had cooled considerably during the preceding decade, and in the final years there had been no real personal contact between the spouses. Grundtvig's public reaction and his speech at her funeral were markedly subdued, almost formal, with no strong expression of feelings. He did not write a poem for her funeral, which was uncharacteristic of him. An important backdrop for the cool relationship between the two, and possibly also a partial cause of Lise's death, was Grundtvig's growing attraction to another woman, the widow and landowner Marie Toft, who was thirty years his junior. Their personal acquaintance started in 1845, when Toft, who was involved with a religious revivalist congregation in Southern Zealand, visited Grundtvig in order to challenge his negative opinion about her congregation. Despite the fact that the first meeting resulted in a confrontation, the relationship between the two developed during the following years, first into friendship and then–even during Lise's life–into an intense love. Although Grundtvig was not directly unfaithful, his interest in Toft put a serious burden on the already cooling relationship with his wife. On 24 October 1851 Grundtvig married Toft. In the beginning there was serious indignation in Copenhagen, and his remarriage gave rise to a confrontation with his sons. Nonetheless, the marriage was happy, albeit short.

At this time, close to Grundtvig's seventieth birthday, his production tempo and general activity level were still amazingly high. A mild mental crisis in 1853 did not impair his productivity. There were considerably longer periods between the large, collected works, but a stream of individual poems and articles still flowed from his hand. The articles were largely contributions to the current political debate, of a political, religious, or popular nature. The poems were also primarily directed at specific situations, with the exception of the hymns, which continued in an unbroken stream throughout the entire course of Grundtvig's writing and were regularly published in hymnals and periodicals. In 1853 he wrote a free rendition of the poem "The Phoenix," from the Exeter Book.

Marie died in childbirth on 9 July 1854 at age forty, after having delivered the couple's first and only child, Frederik Lange. On the occasion of Marie's death, Grundtvig wrote a long series of elegiac poems, only a few of which were published during his lifetime.

On 5 November 1854, only four months after Marie's death, Grundtvig published the first part of yet another wide-ranging project–a poetic rewriting of Christian history in seven songs. They were published in *Dansk Kirketidende* (The Danish Church News), one song at a time, at irregular intervals up to 15 July 1855. The songs were collected as *Christenhedens Syvstjerne* (The Sevenfold Star of Christianity), published in 1860. By then Grundtvig had a third wife, the much younger Asta Tugendreich Adelheid Reedtz, Countess Krag-Juel-Vind-Frijs, widow of Privy Councilor Holger Christian Reedtz. She was one of Grundtvig's faithful parishioners and a supporter of his views of Christianity. They were married on 14 April 1858 and remained together until Grundtvig's death. Asta never had the spiritual importance for Grundtvig that Marie had had, but she remained an unfailing support for him during his long old age. Together they had a daughter, Asta Marie, born in 1860.

Christenhedens Syvstjerne describes the development of Christianity in seven songs. Each describes a "major congregation" in the history of Christianity; the movement through the seven churches is meant to constitute the entirety of Christian religious history. Grundtvig's point of departure was the seven letters in the introduction to the Book of Revelation, each of which addresses a congregation. The seven churches, as in *Sang-Værk til den Danske Kirke,* are the Hebrew, Greek, Roman, Anglo-Saxon, German, Nordic, and the as-yet-unknown seventh church, which Grundtvig places in India. The transition through Christian history has the form of a *V.* There is a fall from the Hebrews to the Greeks and then down to the Romans. The Anglo-Saxon church is the low point but is also the point at which Christianity turns and starts back up again toward the German, through the Nordic, and finally to the seventh church. The first and last churches are so close to God that there is a kind of godly "heat" hanging over them, which means that they are judged more sternly than the other churches. This proximity explains, for instance, the harsh speech in Revelation to the seventh church, in Laodicea.

Christenhedens Syvstjerne is written with the seven-line stanzas of which Grundtvig was fond and ranges from confessional polemics through mild ardor to prophetic visions. Stylistically, the text is somewhat uneven and is marked by a less-coherent metaphoric structure and less-precise composition than is *Nyaars-Morgen.* Christian history is understood as the interaction between a universal Christianity and the different human conditions of the individual churches. The focus of the poem is Grundtvig's own time. He attempts to compel the members of the congregation of the sixth church, the Nordic, to understand their historic mission and to see their church in light of Christianity as a whole. Thus, the earlier churches are interpreted with frequent use of Nordic mythology, which, for Grundtvig, creates the metaphors in which it is most natural for people of the North to understand their world.

The posthumously published "Dansk Ravne-Galder" (Danish Raven-Song) was written in 1860. The title is from the disputed Edda poem "Hrafnagaldr Oðins" (The Song of Odin's Ravens), to which Grundtvig attributes neither weight nor authenticity in his theoretical works on mythology. In this poem

Grundtvig's third wife, Asta Tugendreich Adelheid Reedtz, Countess Krag-Juel-Vind-Frijs, in 1880. They were married in 1858 (photograph by J. Petersen & Søn; courtesy of the Danish Royal Library, Copenhagen).

Grundtvig first describes how he is received as the third of Odin's ravens and initiated as prophet and poet. He then tells how, with the help of the Holy Spirit, he is able to overcome the boundaries set for Odin and his ravens and can fly freely throughout God's created history. This freedom carries him forward in time, until he lands on the mast of a ship that sails from Denmark. He overhears representatives from a series of countries discussing the country they are leaving and its fate.

In May 1861, as the culmination of many years of work on the subject, Grundtvig published an Old English edition of the Beowulf cycle, *Beowulfes Beorh* (Beowulf's Barrow). It includes an introductory poem in Old English, written by Grundtvig, many extensive notes, and an index of characters. That same month he celebrated the fiftieth anniversary of his ordination. For this occasion the minister of church affairs delivered notification that, as the country's third-greatest writer of hymns, Grundtvig was being granted rank on a par with the bishop of Zealand. (Both Kingo and Brorson, the two greatest hymn writers, had held the rank of bishop.)

One of the best-known events in Grundtvig's later years was a mental breakdown that took place during Easter services in 1867. He performed a peculiar service in which he proclaimed several newly discovered revelations, among them that the more than seventy-year-old dowager queen, Caroline Amalie, would give birth to Holger Danske, a mythological figure who was supposed to wake up and save Denmark in time of emergency. Grundtvig was isolated by his family and friends and slowly improved.

Only in the 1860s, when Grundtvig was in his seventies and eighties, was there a slowing of his manic productivity, and even then he wrote many works. Beginning in 1855 he had published a series of articles with theological subjects in *Kirkelig Samler* (Church Collector). The series concluded in 1861 and was published as a collection in 1868 with the title *Den Christelige Børnelærdom* (Elementary Christian Doctrine). It brings together his understanding of Christianity and is central in theological research on Grundtvig because it is the closest that he came to writing a unified statement of dogma.

Grundtvig wrote several long poems during the 1860s, particularly with subjects or inspiration drawn from Nordic mythology and ancient history: "Nordens Myther" (Nordic Myths, 1864), "Havamaal" (Sayings of the High One, 1866), and "Højnordens Rimkrønike. Hundedagene 1867" (The High North Rhyming Chronicle: Dog Days 1867). These poems remained unpublished during his lifetime, and there is still no definitive critical edition of them. In 1870 Grundtvig published *Sang-Værk til den Danske Kirke-Skole,* a collection consisting mostly of poems written earlier but also including some new works. The book carried through with the original plan conceived when he first began work on it in 1839, and its 134 poems move from the Creation, through a series of biblical and religious intermediate stages, and forward to Grundtvig's own time. The reader stands finally with a poetic account of the entire history of Christianity. The historical-religious account *Kirke-Speil* (Mirror of the Church, 1871) is based on a series of lectures Grundtvig delivered at his home from 1860 to 1863. The publication was based on his lectures but was not collected by Grundtvig himself, so there was a series of minor errors in the first edition.

Grundtvig's final poem, "Gammel nok jeg nu er blevet" (Now I Am Old Enough, 1872), describes his experience of approaching death with fear of loss but also with confidence that, with God's help, he will cross over the sea of death to "the harbor of heaven." He died peacefully on 2 September 1872, the week before his eighty-ninth birthday. He had preached at Vartov Church just a few days earlier. His casket was carried in a procession through Copenhagen, and he was buried in southern Zealand, near Rønnebæksholm, next to his second wife, Marie.

The history of N. F. S. Grundtvig's work is not limited to the strictly literary but stretches through wide areas of Danish social and cultural life. Large segments of Danish culture, education, and religion identify with him. The significance of the Grundtvigian movement is far-reaching. Research into his life and writing started early but first took off and became systematized with the establishment of the Grundtvig Society in 1947. The society has since published the yearly journal *Grundtvig-Studier* (Grundtvig Studies), with scholarly articles in Danish, English, German, and several other languages. At the same time, the society has authorized the publication of a series of important scholarly works on the author. The journal and the publication series are the cornerstones of the modern and varied research on Grundtvig. During this period, international research with important books and monographs in English and German, among other languages, has emerged. A collective effort to translate Grundtvig's body of works into one or more major languages has still not been realized.

Grundtvig in 1869 (photograph by Budtz Müller & Co.; courtesy of the Danish Royal Library, Copenhagen)

Letters:

Grundtvig og Ingemann. Brevvexling, 1821–1859, edited, with an introduction, by Svend Grundtvig (Copenhagen: Samfundet til den Danske Litteraturs Fremme, 1882);

Christian Molbech og Nikolai Frederik Severin Grundtvig. En Brevvexling, edited by Ludvig Schrøder (Copenhagen: Gyldendal, 1888);

N. F. S. Grundtvigs Breve fra England til Dronning Karoline Amalie, 1843, edited by Frederik Lange Grundtvig (Kolding, 1891);

N. F. S. Grundtvigs Breve til hans Hustru under Englandsrejserne, 1829–1831, edited, with an introduction, by Stener Grundtvig (Copenhagen: A. Marcus, 1920);

Breve fra og til N. F. S. Grundtvig, 2 volumes, edited by Georg Christensen and Stener Grundtvig (Copenhagen: Gyldendal, 1924, 1926);

N. F. S. Grundtvig og hans nærmeste Slægt under Treaarskrigen. En Brevveksling, edited by Ingeborg Simesen (Copenhagen: Gad, 1933).

Bibliography:

Steen Johansen, *Bibliografi over N. F. S. Grundtvigs Skrifter,* 4 volumes, foreword by Georg Christensen (Copenhagen: Gyldendal, 1948–1954).

Biographies:

Hans Brun, *Biskop N. F. S. Grundtvigs Levnetsløb, udførligst fortalt fra 1839,* 2 volumes (Kolding: K. Jørgensen, 1879, 1882);

Frederik Rønning, *N. F. S. Grundtvig. Et Bidrag til Skildring af dansk Åndsliv i det 19. Århundrede,* 8 volumes in 4 (Copenhagen: Schønberg, 1907–1914);

Hal Koch, *Grundtvig* (Copenhagen: Gyldendal, 1944); translated, with an introduction and notes, by Llewellyn Jones (Yellow Springs, Ohio: Antioch Press, 1952);

Johannes Knudsen, *Danish Rebel: A Study of N. F. S. Grundtvig* (Philadelphia: Muhlenberg Press, 1955);

Finn Abrahamowitz, *Grundtvig. Danmark til lykke* (Copenhagen: Høst, 2000).

References:

Sigurd Aage Aarnes, *Historieskrivning og livssyn hos Grundtvig* (Bergen: Universitetsforlaget, 1961);

Gustav Albeck and others, *Registrant over Grundtvigs Papirer,* 30 volumes (Copenhagen: Danske Sprog- og Litteraturselskab, 1957–1964);

Arthur Macdonald Allchin, *N. F. S. Grundtvig: An Introduction to his Life and Work* (London: Darton, Longman & Todd / Aarhus: Aarhus University Press, 1997);

Allchin and others, eds., *Grundtvig in International Perspective: Studies in the Creativity of Interaction* (Aarhus: Aarhus Universitetsforlag, 2000);

Allchin and others, eds., *Heritage and Prophecy: Grundtvig and the English-Speaking World* (Aarhus: Aarhus Universitetsforlag, 1993);

S. A. J. Bradley, *N. F. S. Grundtvig's Transcriptions of the Exeter Book: Grundtvig Archive Fascicle 316, nrs 1–8, in the Royal Library Copenhagen: An Analysis* (Aarhus: Grundtvig-Selskabet, 1998);

Knud Eyvin Bugge, *Skolen for livet. Studier over N. F. S. Grundtvigs pædagogiske tanker* (Copenhagen: Gad, 1965);

Bent Christensen, *Omkring Grundtvigs Vidskab* (Copenhagen: Gad, 1998);

Henning Høirup, *Grundtvigs Syn paa Tro og Erkendelse* (Copenhagen: Gyldendal, 1949);

Anders Holm, *Historie og Efterklang. En studie i N. F. S. Grundtvigs tidsskrift Danne-Virke* (Odense: Odense Universitetsforlag, 2001);

Flemming Lundgreen-Nielsen, *Det handlende ord. N. F. S. Grundtvigs digtning, litteraturkritik og poetik, 1798–1819* (Copenhagen: Gad, 1980);

William Michelsen, *Tilblivelsen af Grundtvigs historiesyn* (Copenhagen: Gyldendal, 1954);

Donald. J. Sneen, "The Hermeneutics of N. F. S. Grundtvig," dissertation, Princeton University, 1968;

Kaj Thaning, *Menneske først. Grundtvigs opgør med sig selv* (Copenhagen: Gyldendal, 1963);

Thaning, *N. F. S. Grundtvig,* translated by David Hohnen (Copenhagen: Danske Selskab, 1972);

Christian Thodberg and Anders Pontoppidan Thyssen, eds., *N. F. S. Grundtvig, Tradition and Renewal: Grundtvig's Vision of Man and People, Education, and the Church, in Relation to World Issues Today,* translated by Edward Broadbridge (Copenhagen: Danske Selskab, 1983);

Helge Toldberg, *Grundtvigs symbolverden* (Copenhagen: Gyldendal, 1950);

Ole Vind, *Grundtvigs historiefilosofi* (Copenhagen: Gyldendal, 1999).

Papers:

N. F. S. Grundtvig's extensive manuscript collection is in the Grundtvig Archives at the Danish Royal Library in Copenhagen.

Thomasine Gyllembourg

(9 November 1773 - 2 July 1856)

Helle Mathiasen
University of Arizona

BOOKS: *Familien Polonius,* anonymous, in *Kjøbenhavns flyvende Post,* 1827; republished in *Noveller, gamle og nye,* anonymous, 3 volumes (Copenhagen: C. A. Reitzel, 1833–1834);

En Hverdags-Historie, anonymous, in *Kjøbenhavns flyvende Post,* 1828; republished in *Noveller, gamle og nye,* anonymous, 3 volumes (Copenhagen: C. A. Reitzel, 1833–1834);

Noveller, gamle og nye, anonymous, 3 volumes (Copenhagen: C. A. Reitzel, 1833–1834)–comprises *En Hverdags-Historie, Drøm og Virkelighed, Den magiske Nøgle, Kong Hjort, Slægtskab og Djævelskab, Mesalliance, Familien Polonius, Den lille Karen,* and *De lyse Nætter;*

Nye Fortællinger, anonymous, 3 volumes (Copenhagen: C. A. Reitzel, 1835–1836)–comprises *Ægtestand, En Episode, Extremerne, Jøden,* and *Hvidkappen;*

To Noveller, anonymous (Copenhagen: C. A. Reitzel, 1837)–comprises *Montanus den Yngre* and *Nisida;*

Maria, Novelle, anonymous (Copenhagen: C. A. Reitzel, 1839);

Een i Alle, anonymous (Copenhagen: C. A. Reitzel, 1840);

Nær og Fjern, anonymous (Copenhagen: C. A. Reitzel, 1841);

En Brevvexling, anonymous (Copenhagen: C. A. Reitzel, 1843);

Korsveien, anonymous (Copenhagen: C. A. Reitzel, 1844);

To Tidsaldre, anonymous (Copenhagen: C. A. Reitzel, 1845).

Editions and Collections: *Skrifter af Forfatteren til "En Hverdags-Historie,"* anonymous, 12 volumes (Copenhagen: C. A. Reitzel, 1849–1851)–includes *En Hverdags-Historie, Drøm og Virkelighed, Mesalliance, Montanus den Yngre, Slægtskab og Djævelskab, Ægtestand, En Brevvexling, Extremerne, De lyse Nætter, Een i Alle, Nær og Fjern, Hvidkappen, Maria, Sproglæreren, Kong Hjort, Jøden, Magt og List, Castor og Pollux, Den lille Karen, Nisida, En Episode, Fregatskibet Svanen, Korsveien, De Forlovede, To Tidsaldre, Den magiske Nøgle, Familien Polonius, Jens Drabelig, Findeløn, Smaaskrifter af blandet Indhold,* and *Udvalg af Forfatterens og Udgiverens Fortaler;*

Thomasine Gyllembourg (engraving by J. M. Petersen from a painting by Jens Juel; courtesy of the Danish Royal Library, Copenhagen)

Familien Polonius og En Hverdags-Historie og Fru Gyllembourgs Litterære Testamente (Copenhagen: Gyldendal, 1868);

Fru Gyllembourgs samlede Romaner og Noveller, 4 volumes, edited by Borchsenius (Copenhagen: Kunstforlaget Danmark, 1912);

Ægtestand, edited by Margrethe Møller (Copenhagen: Westermann, 1942);

Ægtestand, edited by Vibeke Blaksteen (Copenhagen: Dansklærerforeningen/Skov, 1982);

Drøm og Virkelighed; To Tidsaldre, edited by Anni Broue and Anne-Marie Mai (Copenhagen: Borgen, 1986);

Ægtestand, translated into modern Danish and edited by Sten Hansen (Hørsholm: Sten Hansen Forlag, 1996);

De Lyse Nætter, excerpts, in *Min Yndlingshistorie* (Copenhagen: Aschehoug, 1999).

The Golden Age of Denmark, roughly the first half of the nineteenth century, was an era of political and economic upheaval. This era also produced one of the first successful professional Danish woman writers, Thomasine Gyllembourg. Between her debut in 1827 and 1845, the year of her last published work, Gyllembourg wrote twenty-six novels, novellas, and stories, and four plays. Her works were published and republished in Danish during her lifetime, and they were translated into Dutch, German, French, Italian, and Swedish.

In her life and in her work, Gyllembourg confronted the limitations imposed on women of the Copenhagen bourgeoisie. Her upbringing gave her an insider's view of the moral failings of wealthy Danes. Her social criticism made her a precursor of the authors of the Modern Breakthrough. Gyllembourg was hardly a radical social reformer, however. Her fiction upholds a conservative morality, and her heroines are usually meek, neat, and self-disciplined. Her heroes may behave badly for a time, but they usually improve and become good husbands. Courtship forms the plot and marriage the happy ending in the majority of her literary works. Gyllembourg's vision is essentially comic.

Before her literary debut, Gyllembourg had already created a name for herself in Copenhagen. Her divorce from her first husband, writer Peter Andreas Heiberg, and her quick remarriage to Swedish officer and baron Carl Frederik Gyllembourg-Ehrensvärd had created a well-known scandal. "Fru Gyllembourg," as she was known, flouted convention in her personal life, but she was a conventional writer. In *Litterære Testamente* (Literary Testament, 1868) she explained the contradiction as follows: "At jeg gjør 'min ydmygste Afbigt til den quindelige Beskedenhed' er vist mit Hjertes oprigtigste Mening. Jeg har ofte 'med ret eller Uret' tænkt, at jeg havde krænket eller fornærmet den ved at vove mig ud paa en Forfatters mandige Bane" (It is truly the sincere intention of my heart to pay homage to female modesty. I have often thought, whether rightly or wrongly, that I might have injured or insulted it by daring to take the manly course of becoming a writer).

Thomasine Christine Buntzen was born in Nyhavn on 9 November 1773, the eldest of four daughters of Johan Buntzen and his second wife, Anna Bolette Sangaard. Her family resided in the same Nyhavn house that Hans Christian Andersen later occupied. When she was eight years old, Thomasine suffered the loss of her mother; however, her father exerted himself to provide for Thomasine and her sisters a loving home and the best tutors in singing, dancing, music, English, French, German, and Italian. In 1785 her father hired Peter Andreas Heiberg, a translator and tutor who was fluent in several European languages, as the girls' teacher. On 7 May 1790 Thomasine Buntzen married the thirty-year-old Heiberg. He soon alienated his young wife, and they grew apart. She found emotional solace in her son, Johan Ludvig Heiberg, born in 1791. Her husband, meanwhile, sought pleasures outside the home. Peter Heiberg's extravagant lifestyle and the government fines provoked by his political satires drove him into debt. The couple spent less and less time together. Thomasine devoted herself to her child, studied European literature past and present, and developed into a well-educated, independent thinker.

Three years after their marriage, the Heibergs took Carl Frederik Gyllembourg-Ehrensvärd into their home as a guest. He had been exiled from Sweden because he knew about the conspiracy to assassinate the Swedish king Gustav III. Gyllembourg had an amiable and gentle nature, and his noble Swedish manners enchanted his friend's young wife.

In 1799 Peter Andreas Heiberg published "Politisk Dispache" (Political Dispatch), which included a statistical calculation of how much the monarchs of the different European countries cost their populations. At a time when both France and Sweden had seen recent regicides, the king of Denmark did not take kindly to such humor. After a lengthy court case, Heiberg was sentenced to exile. He chose Paris, with the understanding that he would send for his wife and son when he had established himself in France.

At twenty-six, Thomasine Heiberg was left with debts, which she paid by selling off her property and asking her father for help. She moved back into her father's Nyhavn home with Johan Ludvig. As evidenced by her letters addressed to her exiled husband and printed in Johanne Luise Heiberg's edition of the Heiberg and Gyllembourg correspondence, Thomasine Heiberg consulted her husband about her romantic feelings for their mutual friend. Heiberg advised her, "Gjør i den Henseende, som om jeg ikke var til" (Act in that regard, as if I did not exist). She interpreted this response to mean that he did not love her. That summer she began her relationship with Gyllembourg. For this adulterous affair, she was condemned by family and friends and by the Copenhagen public. Deeply in love with Gyllembourg, Thomasine asked her husband for a divorce in writing in Danish, appealing to Heiberg's love of freedom and truth and his friendship for her. Heiberg was stunned. His reply from Paris in four separate letters expressed anguish at this sudden blow and rage at the seducer, Gyllembourg. Heiberg believed that his wife was innocent of having encouraged her lover. He was willing to forgive her, even if she had committed adultery. Unmoved by her husband's expressions of love, Thomasine replied with an application for divorce. Heiberg responded by informing her that divorce would mean losing custody of her son. He also sent her an application for a royal pardon for himself. She signed the divorce application for both of them, giving as a reason for the divorce his exile and her inability to leave Denmark to join him abroad. The divorce was granted by royal decree on 4 December 1801; and on 17 December, Thomasine married Gyllembourg. Heiberg's application for a royal pardon was unsuccessful. He was a political exile for life, and Johan Ludvig was raised by family friends.

In 1806, after their estate in the country burned down, the Gyllembourgs moved back to Copenhagen, where they could visit Johan Ludvig more frequently. In 1807 Thomasine's father died. Soon after, Carl Frederik Gyllembourg was implicated in a plan to elect a Dane to the Swedish throne. This plan failed, causing Gyllembourg to fall into a major depression. He never got over being exiled from his home country and died from a mastoid infection at age forty-eight.

Devastated and in debt after the death of her second husband, Thomasine Gyllembourg sold her furnishings and moved once more. She turned again to her family, this time to her cousin Andreas Buntzen. She became his children's tutor. Around this time her son had an affair with Buntzen's wife, Camilla. This liaison produced a son, Georg Buntzen, and probably a daughter, as well. Though Johan Ludvig Heiberg never acknowledged Georg as his child, Gyllembourg always showed a special fondness for Georg, caring for him until his death from tuberculosis in 1847.

Gyllembourg's life before her debut as an author in 1827 comprised several moves, serious financial concerns, two marriages, a divorce, the death of her second husband, and caring for her only son's illegitimate child. "Fru Gyllembourg," the name by which she was known in the Danish literary world, later wrote in her literary testament that her turbulent life became the source of much of her fiction. She published her first two novels, *Familien Polonius* (The Polonius Family, 1827) and *En Hverdags-Historie* (A Story of Everyday Life, 1828) in the periodical *Kjøbenhavns flyvende Post.* Johan Ludvig Heiberg was the editor, and Søren Kierkegaard, Adam Oehlenschläger, and Andersen were contributors. At this time, Gyllembourg found a

Gyllembourg's second husband, Carl Frederik Gyllembourg-Ehrensvärd (gouache by A. U. Berndes, circa 1790; courtesy of the Danish Royal Library, Copenhagen).

protégé, Johanne Luise Pätges, a young actress with whom Johan Ludvig Heiberg was in love. She invited Pätges to live in her home, where she treated her like a daughter. Pätges and Heiberg were married in 1831. Gyllembourg, Johanne Luise, and Johan Ludvig Heiberg then developed a family relationship that lasted for twenty-five years. The extraordinary friendship of the two women resulted in Johanne Luise Heiberg's publishing the letters of Peter Heiberg and Thomasine Gyllembourg, which became the chief source of Gyllembourg's biography.

Familien Polonius was published anonymously, serialized in *Kjøbenhavns flyvende Post* beginning 12 January 1827. It is an epistolary novel with a clever twist that made it instantly popular. The premise is that the editor has agreed to publish a young lieutenant's "besynderlige Historie" (strange story). The lieutenant feels embarrassed about using *Kjøbenhavns flyvende Post* as a forum to reveal the secrets of his heart but feels he has no other choice. The lieutenant is returning to Denmark from Germany. He visits Polonius's house and falls in love with Polonius's daughter, Lydia.

The plot moves through courtship to marriage along circuitous routes. The lovers meet such obstacles as Lydia's oppressive father and a madwoman carrying a kidnapped baby. But in the end, Gyllembourg finds her theme in a paean to love, "Hvor salig er Kjærlighed! . . . kun den allene giver os Forsmag paa Evigheden, thi kun den lever paa eengang i det Forbigangne, det Nærværende og det tilkommende, som i eet saligt øieblik" (How blissful is love! . . . only it alone gives us a foretaste of eternity, for only love lives at once in the past, the present, and the future, as if in one blissful moment). In this story, Gyllembourg appeals to her audience, well acquainted with William Shakespeare, by choosing names from *Hamlet* and creating a plot that echoes Shakespeare's tragedy. She enhances her Danish love story by alluding to works by many other European artists, including writers Petrarch, Samuel Richardson, and Ludvig Holberg, and composer Wolfgang Amadeus Mozart (and his opera *Don Giovanni*). This manner of incorporating her humanistic education appears often in Gyllembourg's later works. *Familien Polonius* is especially permeated by Gyllembourg's impressions of the Romanticism of Jean-Jacques Rousseau, François-René de Chateaubriand, and Johann Wolfgang von Goethe. The work impressed Gyllembourg's readers, many of whom thought the story was true.

Gyllembourg's choice of a plot with a happy ending and noble and good characters is nothing new, but what was new in Danish prose was her delineation of the double life of the Copenhagen bourgeoisie. She describes them at play–performing charades, dancing, and playing music–but also depicts the underside of bourgeois life. She raises such issues as paternalism, adultery, female depression, madness in women, violent death, single motherhood, and illegitimacy. She penetrates the respectable Biedermeier facade of the Copenhagen bourgeoisie in order to reveal oppression and unhappiness, especially for women. Children, too, are depicted as victims, but the suffering of a child can redeem an erring adult. This theme of child as redeemer became central to Gyllembourg's later work. Other themes from *Familien Polonius* are repeated later–for example, the pairing of opposite characters to illustrate passion and reason, and the association of human love with religious feeling.

Her second effort, *En Hverdags-Historie,* was also serialized in *Kjøbenhavns flyvende Post,* again anonymously. This story became the author's signature: she used "By the Author of *En Hverdags-Historie*" as a byline for all of her subsequent works. The setting of this novella is Mecklenborg, in northern Germany. Anton, the young Danish narrator, falls in love with Jette, who is passionate but uncultured. Disillusioned with Jette, Anton turns to the Swedish Maja, a cultivated and quiet woman and a good housekeeper. Complications arise when Henning, Maja's former fiancé, turns up to claim her. But Henning is happy with Jette, a circumstance that allows Anton to marry Maja. The diction and tenor of this story reflect Continental Romanticism; however, in this work as elsewhere, Gyllembourg cautions against excessive indulgence in emotion. Characters grow sick, and women have seizures from strong emotions. The female and male ideals combine feeling with intelligence, judgment, and proper piety. Maja has soul as well as a firm grip on reality. Gyllembourg was perhaps acquainted with the work of Jane Austen. She shares Austen's valuation of moderation and order.

Gyllembourg's next story, *Drøm og Virkelighed* (Dream and Reality), published in *Noveller, gamle og nye* (1833–1834), portrays her Copenhagen birthplace, Nyhavn. On a somber December evening, the narrator, twenty-three-year-old Julius B., a lawyer and ward of his lawyer uncle, hurries into Nyhavn on a secret visit to his pregnant mistress, working-class girl Lise. The plot echoes that of *En Hverdags-Historie:* A young man must learn to appreciate true femininity by choosing between an inferior, but sexually vibrant woman, and a socially superior, ascetic woman. Julius faces a serious choice between financial ruin if he chooses his lover, or financial security if he marries the daughter of his sponsor. Gyllembourg realistically depicts the Dickensian squalor of Lise's Nyhavn dwelling and her decline as she bears Julius two sons. She becomes aggressive and sloppy, and she finally dies of consumption. Laura, the uncle's daughter and Julius's cousin, appears to Julius in a vision, wearing angel's wings. She becomes Julius's savior, adopts Lise's two boys, and marries Julius. *Drøm og Virkelighed* describes an illegitimate sexual relationship that transgresses class barriers and that leads to domestic cruelty, sickness, and death. The author cautions against marrying a bad housekeeper and mother. Unlike working-class Lise, who is punished by death, Julius B. outgrows his youthful passion; he learns to control his desire with Laura's help. In Gyllembourg's fictional universe, a sloppy and resentful working-class woman redeems neither herself nor her lover. The angelic, bourgeois Laura is needed to teach Julius his duty as a father and husband.

The plot of *Montanus den Yngre* (Montanus the Younger), published in *To Noveller* (1837), is inspired by Holberg's *Erasmus Montanus* (1723). In Holberg's comedy, Rasmus Berg is a conceited university student returning to his childhood home in the country to shame his parents. However, his Latin learning falls short when contrasted with the common sense of his country family. Gyllembourg's protagonist, Conrad Valberg, has been to America, where he has learned modern industrial methods that he wishes to introduce in his homeland. However, Conrad has to be properly humbled and educated before he understands how to integrate the new technology into his Danish milieu.

In *Slægtskab og Djævelskab* (Kinship and Devilry), published in *Noveller, gamle og nye,* Gyllembourg again contrasts good and evil characters in order to expose the materialistic and oppressive patriarchy of the bourgeoisie. The story takes place in Copenhagen, among the wealthy Haldorf family. This family shelters terrible secrets of embezzlement, suicide, forced marriage, gambling, and dissipation. An evil mother-in-law foments devilry with the aid of her German friend, but kinship resolves the family's wounds as a daughter forgives and a child dies to redeem the sins of the fathers. According to Gothic convention, Gyllembourg stages her reconciliation on the grave of a child. The story is an explicit and implicit indictment of the merchant class, in which domestic tyrants victimize women and children. Yet, no outrage is expressed, only sadness.

Ægtestand (Matrimony), published as volume one of *Nye Fortællinger* (1835–1836), is one of three Gyllembourg novels still in print. In 1996, this story appeared in a modern Danish translation with commentary by Sten Hansen, who compares Gyllembourg to Jane Austen. The critic points out that both Austen and Gyllembourg present entertaining and action-filled stories of everyday life buttressed by each author's rich experience of human nature: "Latteren ligger nærmere end fordømmelsen" (Laughter lies closer than condemnation). The comparison to Austen is especially apt when one considers that the authors use many of the same techniques–for example, pairing for contrast of characters. In *Ægtestand,* Gyllembourg creates a sensible character, Sofie, and an emotional character, Annette, as Austen does in *Sense and Sensibility* (1811). Both authors also set their stories in their own time and use plots that turn on courtship and marriage.

With *Ægtestand,* Gyllembourg reached a new level of realism. The plot centers on a meeting on the Lindal estate. Sofie Lindal, married to a cold and arrogant husband, is tempted by the passionate but demonic Frenchman Sardes. She almost gives in to him and is only saved by her child, Anton. Lindal notices Sardes's fascination with his wife, and jealousy revives his own passion for Sofie. The Frenchman impresses Sofie as her soul mate, but then he turns threatening. He suggests they have an affair, since her husband does not love her. On the brink of adultery, Sofie is saved with the aid of the Virgin Mary. Sofie's two sisters, Annette and Caroline, act as foils to Sofie. The narrator ends the story with an admonition to her female reader as modernized in Sten Hansen's edition: "Min kære unge læserinde! Du, som maaske har taget denne bog i haanden for at adsprede dig fra tanker, som du næppe tør tilstaa dig selv: dig især være denne simple fortælling helliget med en ukendt vens varme ønsker for din sejr" (My dear young reader! Perhaps you have picked up this book to distract yourself from thoughts that you hardly dare to confess to yourself: may this simple tale be especially dedicated to you with an unknown friend's warm wishes for your victory).

With her novella *Jøden* (The Jew), published as volume three of *Nye Fortællinger,* Gyllembourg addresses a controversial issue, anti-Semitism in Denmark. The publication of *Jøden* was preceded by the Jewish Feud of 1819, an uprising that took place in Copenhagen on 5 September. The novella is set in Denmark in 1801, thirteen years before Danish Jews were granted civil rights. The protagonist, Joseph Branco, is the foster father of Frederik Volmer. Branco has become a successful wholesaler, scholar, and philosopher. However, he grieves about his misfortune in being born Jewish. His friend Dr. Bille counsels Branco to convert to Christianity, but Branco refuses, claiming that the Christian community will never accept a convert. Branco's distrust of Christian acceptance of Jews drives the plot, determining its conclusion. Branco's Jewish wife has died giving birth to a son. With Dr. Bille's help, Branco buries as his own son the corpse of a boy Dr. Bille had acquired for dissection and adopts his real son as his foster son. This family secret comes to light at the end, when Frederik Volmer, Branco's real son, wants to marry. As Branco's love for Frederik had caused him to conceal Frederik's Jewish parentage, so now his love motivates Branco to reveal Frederik's Jewish birth. Frederik accepts his origins, marries his beloved, and inherits his father's estate.

This extraordinary story demonstrates Gyllembourg's favorite plot of courtship with the added theme of child as redeemer and the taboo of incest. Most significantly, Gyllembourg tackles the issue of anti-Semitism in Denmark with realism. The title of the story refers to Frederik, who does not know he is a Jew, and to Joseph Branco, his father. In delineating Branco's sufferings as a Jew, Gyllembourg creates sympathy for him, as Meïr Aron Goldschmidt did for the protagonist in his novel *En Jøde* (1845).

Gyllembourg was a contemporary of Steen Steensen Blicher and Andersen. These writers often included among their women characters the neat, pious, and reserved mother figure exemplified by the protagonist of Gyllembourg's story *Maria* (1839). However, Gyllembourg takes her study of the female psyche in a Freudian direction as she attributes Maria's sexual reticence to childhood abuse. Maria is a widow living in Copenhagen with her two adopted children, supporting herself by sewing. Her domestic situation is well ordered; her children little paragons. Adolph, her childhood friend, falls in love with her and wants to marry, but Maria cannot marry: because of incestuous sexual abuse suffered in her childhood, she can no longer love a man. She is happy in her role as mother; however, Adolph

Kjøbenhavns

flyvende Post.

1827.

Kjöbenhavn.

Trykt hos Directeur Jens Hostrup Schultz,

Kongelig og Universitets-Bogtrykker.

Cover for the periodical in which Gyllembourg published her first novel, Familien Polonius *(The Polonius Family). Her son, Johan Ludvig Heiberg, was the editor of the journal (courtesy of the Danish Royal Library, Copenhagen).*

pines away and finally dies from unrequited passion. The outcome of this excellent story indicates that women can be content with mother love whereas men crave sexual passion. Maria explains its dangers, "Denne Følelse, man kalder Elskov, synes ofte at ligne en dæmonisk Indskydelse, der for en Tid berøver Mennesket den moralske Frihed, . . . og skjøndt den kalder sig Elskov egenlig kun elsker sig selv og viser sig ofte haard og grusom, selv mod sin Gjenstand" (This feeling called passion often seems to resemble a demonic caprice that temporarily deprives humans of their moral freedom . . . and though it calls itself passion, actually only loves itself and often appears hard and cruel, even toward its object).

Gyllembourg's four plays–*Hvidkappen* (The White Robe), collected in *Nye Fortællinger; Sproglæreren* (The Language Tutor), collected in *Skrifter af Forfatteren til "En Hverdags-Historie"* (1849–1851); *Magt og List* (Power and Deviousness), collected in *Skrifter af Forfatteren til "En Hverdags-Historie";* and *Fregatskibet Svanen* (The Frigate Swan), collected in *Skrifter af Forfatteren til "En Hverdags-Historie"*–were not well received. *Sproglæreren* was performed at the Royal Theater in 1832. *Fregatskibet Svanen,* based on an article from *The Spectator,* was rejected by the Royal Theater. *Magt og List* was accepted with reservations and performed in 1832. Its reception was lukewarm.

Gyllembourg abandoned playwriting to return to prose fiction with her last and best novel, *To Tidsaldre* (Two Ages, 1845). She garnered lavish praise for this work from Kierkegaard. Her novel inspired the philosopher to devote a book-length manuscript to an evaluation of her fiction, and especially to an analysis of this last work. Kierkegaard's enthusiastic review was published in 1846 as *En literair Anmeldelse. To Tidsaldre, Novelle af Forfatteren til 'en Hverdags-Historie'* (translated as *Two Ages. The Age of Revolution and the Present Age,* 1978).

To Tidsaldre remains in print as a Danish classic and is taught in schools and universities. The novel contrasts the era of Gyllembourg's own youth, the time of the French Revolution, with the contemporary era, the 1840s. A young Danish woman, Claudine, meets and falls in love with a dashing French officer, Lusard. They consummate their passion, and a son, Charles, is born. The patriotic lover returns to France. Mother and child spend several years in seclusion before Lusard returns to Denmark to assume an estate and reunite in marriage with Claudine. Part 2 begins in 1844, fifty years later. Claudine and Lusard have died. Charles returns from France to his father's estate. He is childless and seeking an heir. He finds a suitable heir in a poet and distant relative, Ferdinand Valler.

Gyllembourg differentiates between the two ages structurally and stylistically. In part 1, the beautiful Danish countryside forms the backdrop for Lusard and Claudine's affair. Part 2 takes place in a house in Copenhagen. In both parts, the artist presents a bourgeois milieu of wealthy merchants similar to the one in which she grew up. In part 1, she shows how the idealistic enthusiasm about freedom, equality, and fraternity, originating in the slogan of the French Revolution, fires young Danish spirits; in part 2, she illustrates the cheapening into domestic materialism and narcissism of this pure inspiration from revolutionary France. In part 1, Gyllembourg integrates the gentleness, intelligence, and faithfulness portrayed in different heroines in her other stories into the heroine of *To Tidsaldre,* Claudine. This female ideal unites sexual passion with altruistic mother love by virtue of her strong personality. Claudine thus resolves the dialectic of Gyllembourg's previous contrasting characters–for instance, Jette and Maja, and Lise and Laura. Lusard, the male protagonist, also integrates passion with reason, and he contributes the courtly manners of a French nobleman. In addition to presenting these well-tempered personalities, in part 2 of *To Tidsaldre,* Gyllembourg demonstrates her talent for humorous satire of the bourgeois class. She ridicules the decline in domestic relations, the misbehavior of naughty children, and the snobbery and materialism of her own age, the 1840s. However, she also shows this period as bringing forth such new and useful scientific discoveries as railroads and steamships. She approves of the changing social structures that allow for the mingling of different social classes in Georg Carstensen's Tivoli, founded in 1843. Her work ends on an optimistic note: humanity, always capable of improvement, will progress toward perfection. Meanwhile, love should regulate the individual and the family, and female refinement should guide social intercourse.

Like her most famous novel, Thomasine Gyllembourg's life had two parts. Part 1 consisted of her two marriages and the birth of her son. Part 2 became her writing career. In her later years she reflected on her dealings with Peter Heiberg and regretted having caused him pain. They remained on friendly terms for the rest of their lives. The death of her grandson, Georg Buntzen, in 1847, caused her to grow old suddenly. Johanne Luise Heiberg relates that Gyllembourg ceased to laugh as heartily as she had done before. In 1854 she fell at home and broke her hip. She never walked again. Johan Ludvig and Johanne Luise Heiberg were present at her death in their home on 2 July 1856.

As an artist Gyllembourg stands alone among early women authors in Denmark. In a difficult time for her nation and herself, she showed the impact of world history, especially the French Revolution, on family life in Denmark. She described the refined conversation and entertainment of bourgeois life but also exposed the immorality behind middle-class respectability and the subordinate position of women and children in this society. Her reputation rests on *Ægtestand, Drøm og Virkelighed,* and *To Tidsaldre*–novels that continue to deserve close scholarly scrutiny.

References:

Benedicte Arnesen-Kall, *Fru Gyllembourg og hendes Værker i Forhold til vor Tid* (Copenhagen: Rudolph Klein, 1875);

Steffen Auring and others, "Thomasine Gyllembourg. En Hverdags-Historie 1827," *Litteratur and Samfund,* 31 May 1980;

F. J. Billeskov Jansen, *Thomasine Gyllembourg. Et mindeportræt* (Copenhagen: Gaea, 1977);

Stig Dalager, *En aften i Hamborg* (Aarhus: Arkona, 1983);

Birgitte Dalsgård and Ole Riber Christensen, *Lidenskabens masker. Fire forfatterskaber. Thomasine Gyllembourg. Herman Bang. Tove Ditlevsen. Ib Michael* (Copenhagen: Gyldendal, 1991);

Johan de Mylius, "Billeddannelsens historik," in *Nordisk litteraturhistorie* (Odense: Odense University Press, 1978), pp. 76–88;

de Mylius, "Thomasine Gyllembourg: The Golden Age Confronted," in *Female Voices of the North,* edited by Inger M. Olsen, Sven Rossel, and Robert Nedoma (Vienna: Edition Praesens, 2002), I: 183–207;

Anne Marie Ejrnæs, *Som svalen* (Copenhagen: Rosinante, 1986);

Henning Fenger, *Familjen Heiberg* (Copenhagen: Museum Tusculanum, 1992);

Åge Friis and Just Rahbek, eds., *Johanne Luise Heiberg, Peter Andreas Heiberg og Thomasine Gyllembourg,* 2 volumes (Copenhagen: Gyldendal, 1947);

Johannes Grønborg, *P. A. Heiberg og hans Hustru* (Aarhus: Albert Bayer, 1915);

Tiina Hamilton-Nunnally, *Kvindelige danske forfattere. Bibliografi over prosa i bogform 1820–1910* (Copenhagen: Bibliotekscentralens forlag, 1979);

Johanne Luise Heiberg, *Peter Andreas Heiberg og Thomasine Gyllembourg,* 2 volumes (Copenhagen: Gyldendal, 1947);

Lis Helmer Larsen and Jannie Roed, "The Art of Womanhood and Wedlock. Thomasine Gyllembourg. A Writer in Spite of Herself," *New Comparison,* 4 (Autumn 1987): 92–106;

Elisabeth Hude, *Thomasine Gyllembourg og hverdagshistorierne* (Copenhagen: Rosenkilde & Bagger, 1951);

Anni Broue Jensen, "Penge og kærlighed. Religion og socialitet i Thomasine Gyllembourgs forfatterskab," *Odense University Studies in Literature,* 14 (Odense: Odense University Press, 1983);

Søren Kierkegaard, *Two Ages. The Age of Revolution and the Present Age. A Literary Review,* edited and translated by Howard V. Hong and Edna H. Hong (Princeton: Princeton University Press, 1978);

L. Kornelius-Kybel, *Nogle bemærkninger om P. A. Heiberg og fru Gyllembourg* (Copenhagen: U. F. Levison, 1883);

Jan Møller, *Borger i guldalderens København* (Viborg: Sesam, 1999);

Poul Møller, *Efterladte Skrifter,* volume 5 (Copenhagen: C. A. Reitzel, 1856);

Klaus P. Mortensen, *Thomasines oprør* (Copenhagen: Gad, 1986);

Inge Nørballe, *Guldalderdigtere. Portrætter og poesi* (Copenhagen: Høst, 1999);

Vibeke Schroeder, *Tankens våben. Johan Ludvig Heiberg* (Copenhagen: Gyldendal, 2001).

Papers:

Thomasine Gyllembourg's letters, portraits, and manuscripts are housed in the Danish Royal Library in Copenhagen. Jens Juel's portraits of Thomasine Gyllembourg and Peter Andreas Heiberg are at Frederiksborg Castle, Hillerød, Denmark.

Carsten Hauch

(12 May 1790 - 4 March 1872)

Finn Hauberg Mortensen
University of Southern Denmark

(Translated by Mark Mussari)

BOOKS: *Contrasterne. To dramatiske Digte* (Copenhagen: Gyldendal, 1816);

Castor og Pollux eller endnu et Par Ord om Tvillingforkasterne af Freias Alter, as Ludvig Jakobsen (Copenhagen: Privately printed, C. Græbe, 1817);

Rosaura. Et lyrisk Drama (Copenhagen: Privately printed, 1817);

Om første Deel af J. J. Baggesens Breve til Oehlenschläger. Med en Extract af Doms-Præmisserne i Sagen mellem Baggesen og Hjort, samt med et Tillæg, appendix by Adolph Engelbert Boye (Copenhagen: J. H. Schultz, 1818);

Om J. J. Baggesens Anmærkninger til de saakaldte hundrede Aphorismer og een. Med et Tillæg af P. Wegner [i.e., Boye] indeholdende nye Beviser for Baggesens Upaalidelighed og Uvidenhed (Copenhagen: Privately printed, H. F. Popp, 1818);

Degli organi imperfetti che si osservano in alcuni animali della loro destinazione nella natura, della loro utilità riguardo la storia naturale (Naples: R. Miranda, 1827); revised and translated as "Kort Oversigt over en Deel rudimentariske Organer, over deres Bestemmelse i Naturen, samt over en systematisk Udviklingsfølge, der tildeels paa disse kunde bygges," *Blandinger fra Sorøe,* 1 (1831): 16–76;

Dramatiske Værker (Copenhagen: C. A. Reitzel, 1828–1830)–comprises volume 1, *Bajazet og Tiber. To Sørgespil* (1828); volume 2, *Gregorius den Syvende og Don Juan. To Dramaer* (1829); and volume 3, *Hamadryaden. Et episk og dramatisk Digt* (1830);

Den babyloniske Taarnbygning i Mignature. Et Forsøg i den Aristophaniske Comoedie (Copenhagen: C. A. Reitzel, 1830);

Carl den Femtes Død. Sørgespil i fem Acter (Copenhagen: S. Trier, 1831);

Om de tre Organsystemer med Hensyn til Klassificationen. Indbydelsesskrift (Copenhagen: Sorø Akademi, 1831);

Lithograph by Emilius-Ditlev Bærentzen; courtesy of the Danish Royal Library, Copenhagen

Maastrichts Beleiring. Et Sørgespil i fem Handlinger (Copenhagen: S. Trier, 1832);

Vilhelm Zabern. En Autobiographie, indeholdende hidtil ubekiendte Efterretninger fra Christian den Andens Tid (Copenhagen: C. A. Reitzel, 1834); republished as *Vilhelm Zabern. En Autobiographi fra Christian den Andens Tid* (Copenhagen: Gyldendal, 1893);

Guld-mageren, en romantisk Begivenhed fra det forsvundne Aarhundrede (Copenhagen: C. A. Reitzel, 1836);

Tvende Digtninger (Copenhagen: C. A. Reitzel, 1837)–comprises "Den hjemkomne Sømand" and "De Geers Ungdomsliv, fortalt af ham selv til Theodor Hirschberger";

En polsk Familie. Roman, 2 volumes (Copenhagen: C. A. Reitzel, 1839);

Svend Grathe eller Kongemødet i Roeskilde. Tragoedie i fem Acter (Copenhagen: C. A. Reitzel, 1841);

Lyriske Digte (Copenhagen: C. Steen, 1842; revised and enlarged edition, Copenhagen: C. A. Reitzel, 1854; first edition reprinted, Copenhagen: Gyldendal, 1949);

Om Realunderviisning. En Tale holdt d. 18. Sept. 1842 paa Sorøe-Academie (Copenhagen: C. Steen, 1842);

Om flere af den ældre Verdens religiøse Myther og om deres Forhold saavel indbyrdes som til den høiere Sandhed. Indbydelsesskrift til Kongens Fødselsdag, høitideligholdt på Sorø Akademi (Copenhagen: Sorø Akademi, 1845);

Slottet ved Rhinen, eller de forskiellige Standpunkter. En Roman (Copenhagen: C. A. Reitzel, 1845);

Die nordische Mythenlehre, nach einer Reihe von Vorlesungen dargestellt (Leipzig: Baumgärtner, 1847);

Saga om Thorvald Vidførle, eller den Vidtbereiste (Copenhagen: C. A. Reitzel, 1849);

Søstrene paa Kinnekullen. Et dramatisk Eventyr i tre Akter (Copenhagen: C. A. Reitzel, 1849);

Marsk Stig. Tragødie i 5 Akter (Copenhagen: C. A. Reitzel, 1850);

Nogle Betragtninger angaaende Underviisningstiden i vore Skoler (Copenhagen: C. A. Reitzel, 1850);

Æren tabt og vunden. Skuespil i tre Handlinger (Copenhagen: C. A. Reitzel, 1851);

Tycho Brahes Ungdom. Drama i 3 Acter (Copenhagen: C. A. Reitzel, 1852);

Robert Fulton. En Fortælling (Copenhagen: C. A. Reitzel, 1853); translated by Paul C. Sinding as *Robert Fulton, an Historical Novel* (New York: Macdonald & Palmer, 1868);

Gjengjeldelsen. Romantisk Drama i tre Acter (Copenhagen: C. A. Reitzel, 1854);

Et Eventyr i Ørkenen. Drama i tre Acter (Copenhagen: C. A. Reitzel, 1855);

Æsthetiske Afhandlinger og Recensioner, 3 volumes (Copenhagen: C. A. Reitzel, 1855–1869);

Kongens Yndling. Skuespil i fire Acter (Copenhagen: C. A. Reitzel, 1858);

Charles de la Bussière. En historisk Digtning fra den franske Revolution (Copenhagen: C. A. Reitzel, 1860);

Lyriske Digte og Romancer (Copenhagen: C. A. Reitzel, 1861);

Valdemar Seier. Et romantisk Eventyr (Copenhagen: C. A. Reitzel, 1862);

Henrik af Navarra. Drama i fire Acter (Copenhagen: C. A. Reitzel, 1863);

Fortælling om Haldor (Copenhagen: C. A. Reitzel, 1864);

Bemærkninger over nogle ved Christendommen modificerede Oldtidsminder i vore Viser fra Middelalderen, med et kort Tillæg om disse Visers senere Skjæbne og Virkning (Copenhagen: C. A. Reitzel, 1866);

Julian den Frafaldne og Et Martyrium i Nutiden. To Digtninger (Copenhagen: C. A. Reitzel, 1866);

Minder fra min Barndom og min Ungdom (Copenhagen: C. A. Reitzel, 1867);

Quindehævn. Lystspil i to Acter (Copenhagen: C. A. Reitzel, 1868);

Nye Digtninger (Copenhagen: C. A. Reitzel, 1869)–includes *Bellman, en novelle;*

Minder fra min første Udenlandsreise (Copenhagen: C. A. Reitzel, 1871).

Editions and Collections: *Dramatiske Værker,* 3 volumes (Copenhagen: C. A. Reitzel, 1852–1859)–comprises volume 1, *Bajazet og Tiberius. To Sørgespil* (1852); volume 2, *Hamadryaden, et romantisk Eventyr i blandet Form* (1856); and volume 3, *Gregorius den Syvende og Don Juan* (1859);

Samlede Romaner og Fortællinger, 7 volumes (Copenhagen: C. A. Reitzel, 1873–1874)–comprises volume 1, *En polsk Familie;* volume 2, *Vilhelm Zabern; Fortælling om Haldor;* volume 3, *Guld-mageren;* volume 4, *Slottet ved Rhinen;* volume 5, *Saga om Thorvald Vidførle;* volume 6, *Robert Fulton;* and volume 7, *Charles de la Bussière; Et Martyrium i nutiden; Bellman;*

Samlede Digte, 2 volumes, edited by A. G. Ø. Hauch (Copenhagen: C. A. Reitzel, 1891);

Søstrene paa Kinnekullen. Et dramatisk Eventyr i tre Akter, edited, with an introduction, by Georg Christensen (Copenhagen: Gyldendal, 1921);

Udvalgte Skrifter, 3 volumes, edited, with an introduction, by Poul Schjærff (Copenhagen: J. Jørgensen, 1926–1929)–comprises volume 1, *En polsk familie;* volume 2, *Robert Fulton;* and volume 3, *Poetiske arbejder;*

Charles de la Bussière. En historisk Digtning fra den franske Revolution, introduction by Frederik Schyberg (Copenhagen: Westerman, 1942);

Digte, edited by Kjeld Elfelt, illustrated by Anne Fabricius (Copenhagen: C. Andersen, 1945);

Befrielsens Aand og andre digte (Copenhagen: Gyldendal, 1957);

Digte af Carsten Hauch (Copenhagen: H. Reitzel, 1988).

PLAY PRODUCTIONS: *Den hjemkomne Sømand,* Copenhagen, Royal Theater, 2 September 1844;

Søstrene paa Kinnekullen, Copenhagen, Royal Theater, 26 April 1849;

Marsk Stig, Copenhagen, Royal Theater, 15 March 1850;

Æren tabt og vunden, Copenhagen, Royal Theater, 23 September 1851; Stockholm, Royal Theater, 21 January 1852;

Tycho Brahes Ungdom, Copenhagen, Royal Theater, 27 October 1852; Stockholm, Royal Theater, 1857;

Gjengjeldelsen, Copenhagen, Royal Theater, 5 April 1854;

Et Eventyr i Ørkenen, Copenhagen, Royal Theater, 11 January 1855.

OTHER: *Iris. Nytaarsgave for 1819,* edited by Hauch (Copenhagen: B. Brünnich, 1819);

Hermes. Nytaarsgave for 1820, by Hauch and others (Copenhagen: Privately printed, C. Græbe, 1820);

Frederikke Elisabeth Hauch, *Tyrolerfamilien og de tre Haarlokker. To Digtninger,* anonymous, edited by Carsten Hauch (Copenhagen: C. A. Reitzel, 1840);

Frederikke Elisabeth Hauch, *Frue Werner. En Novelle,* anonymous, edited by Carsten Hauch (Copenhagen: C. A. Reitzel, 1844).

SELECTED PERIODICAL PUBLICATIONS–UNCOLLECTED: "Annotationes ad motum arbitrarium, cum organis ad motum pertinentibus comparatum, in animalibus, vertebris instructis," *Journal de physique* (1821);

"Om Naturvidenskabernes Værd og Øiemed (Tale ved Kongens Fødselsdag 28. Januar 1830)," *Blandinger fra Sorøe,* 1 (1831): 1–5;

"Kort Udsigt over Nervesystemet med Hensyn paa dets forskiellige Forretninger og især med Hensyn paa den dyriske Følelse," *Blandinger fra Sorøe,* 4 (1834): 126–188;

"Et Par Bemærkninger over nogle af den nærværende Tids Fordringer," *Blandinger fra Sorøe,* 5 (1835): 73–111.

Although Carsten Hauch was educated as a scientist and taught science for twenty years, he gained greater significance as the author of tragedies, novels, and poetry. As a professor of aesthetics at the University of Copenhagen, Hauch opposed Johan Ludvig Heiberg's genre-oriented aesthetics. A Romantic and an idealist, Hauch insisted on the writer's ethical and religious responsibility. Thus, he carried the Romantic tradition of Adam Oehlenschläger forward to the Modern Breakthrough in Danish literature.

Johannes Carsten Hauch was born on 12 May 1790 to Frederik Hauch and Karen Tank Hauch. As the son of a high-ranking general with close ties to the court, Frederik Hauch at a young age obtained several important posts at the king's behest. In 1779 he was made chamberlain, and in 1781 he became chief administrative officer of Østfold County (formerly known as Smaalenenes Amt) in southeastern Norway. Carsten Hauch was born in Frederikshald (now Halden, Norway) and spent his early childhood years in Bergen, where in 1789 his father was promoted to diocesan county officer and chief administrative officer of Søndre Bergenhus County. At the age of eight Carsten Hauch was sent to Malmanger to board with Niels Hertzberg, a minister who was to educate the boy. Living in the mountains and valleys of Norway's Hardanger region, the boy developed a pantheistic sensibility. His discovery that his soul was undeniably drawn to nature later served as the inspiration for his work as both writer and scientist.

In 1803 the family moved to Copenhagen because Hauch's father was once again promoted–this time to the high post of chief county officer for Copenhagen, Zealand, Bornholm, and the Faeroe Islands. Until his death in 1839, Frederik Hauch held several other offices, among them postmaster general. He was also decorated with the Grand Cross of the Order of the Dannebrog and bore the distinguished title of privy councilor.

In Copenhagen Carsten Hauch continued his schooling in the renowned Schouboske Institute. Like many other youths, he joined the Danish Voluntary Corps when England bombed Copenhagen in 1807. This patriotic act failed to bring him anywhere near the enemy, however. His urge to participate stemmed from his excitement for his country's history and for heroic tales from Nordic antiquity. Hauch matriculated in 1808, and, in line with his administrative ancestry and in keeping with his father's wishes, he chose to study law. After 1814 he changed to science, partly influenced by the scientific interests of his distinguished uncle Adam Wilhelm Hauch and partly by the physicist H. C. Ørsted, for whose Romantic natural philosophy Hauch felt an affinity. Hauch specialized in zoology and received a master's degree in 1820. The following year he earned a doctoral degree with a dissertation on organs of locomotion among the higher classes of animals.

In addition to his academic studies, Hauch was also deeply engaged in the literary debates of his day, chiefly the dispute between Jens Baggesen and Oehlenschläger. When the censors of the Royal Theater refused Oehlenschläger's drama *Freias Alter* (The Altar of Freya) in 1816, Hauch published a defense in the form of an article in the journal *Athene* and a short polemical pamphlet (under the pseudonym Ludvig Jakobsen), *Castor og Pollux eller endnu et Par Ord om Tvillingforkasterne af Freias Alter* (Castor and Pollux or Yet a Few Remarks about the Dual Rejection of The Altar of Freya, 1817). He followed up with critical writings about Baggesen and joined a group of twelve students who decided to challenge Baggesen to defend in Latin his attacks on Oehlenschläger. Reading the latter's work exposed Hauch to literature that remained dear to him: works by William Shakespeare, Johann Wolfgang von Goethe, and Ludwig Tieck. The lyrical poems of Hauch's youth were strongly influenced by German Romanticism, but in as early a work as "Rejsen til Ginnistan, et dialogiseret Æventyr" (Journey to Ginnistan, an Adventure Performed in Dialogue), from *Contrasterne* (Contrasts, 1816), he satirizes the genre and aligns himself with Jean Paul's critique of this writing as being "et tomt maleri af Æther i Æther med Æther" (an empty painting of air in air with air). Neither with this effort, however, nor with the lyrical drama *Rosaura* (1817) could Hauch win approval from Oehlenschläger, who doubted his poetic abilities. Following this criticism from the master, Hauch abandoned poetry for the world of science. After completing his dissertation, he received an official grant that provided for his journey south, part of the educational process for many intellectuals and artists at this time. He left in May 1821 with the continuation of his scientific studies as his goal.

Hauch had chosen a subject situated on the border between religion and science. Whereas nature had earlier been understood as a great mechanical work set in motion by God, pantheists after 1800 perceived it as one great connected organism that was identical with God. Consequently, faith in a personal God and any emphasis on the connection between faith and morality were forced into the background. Faith was replaced by an historical consideration of the development of this world organism. Scholars were interested in geology as the history of the earth's origin, with less emphasis on time. In place of a belief that the earth was created six thousand years earlier, as in the creation story of the Pentateuch, scientists became certain that the earth must be many millions of years old. This message led to an uncertainty about what had caused the earth's development. If not God, then humans must be the driving force, and intellectuals and scientists became preoccupied with the human being's place in the development of other species. The development of this branch of comparative botany and zoology led to the grouping of species by similarity of traits and to historical perspectivism. Before Charles Darwin's *On the Origin of Species* (1859) there was no comprehensive theory of biological evolution, although there had been many attempts to develop such a theory. One must view Hauch's studies on the limbs of vertebrates in the context of these early attempts.

Hauch first undertook a year-long residence in Paris, where he studied the collections of the botanical gardens and became familiar with the famed zoologist Georges Cuvier. In the winter of 1822–1823 Hauch traveled to Nice, where he was engrossed in studying the animals of the Mediterranean, the original goal of his travels. While there he also exacerbated an injury to his right foot. His studies had to end, and the new purpose of the journey became treating his injury. In the fall of 1824 Hauch arrived in Naples, where he settled, but neither doctors nor treatments at spas were able to save his foot. Before the amputation of his right leg below the knee, Hauch was deeply depressed. Plagued by pain and doubt, he threw himself into the writing that had lain fallow for some seven years. In the winter of 1824–1825 he wrote the natural-philosophical and Romantic adventure poem *Hamadryaden* (The Hamadryad, 1830), which depicts the great battle between good and evil in existence. Evil is symbolized by a serpent whose power can only be broken by a young man who, with help from nature's powers, can conquer it on land and at sea.

Before the amputation in March 1825, Hauch had also managed to write the first three acts of the historical play *Bajazet* (1828), which he finished after the operation. In the following winter he suffered a new depression: he lost faith in his abilities as a writer and could not find meaning in life as a cripple. He attempted suicide but failed and then interpreted this failure as a sign from God, although he had previously not been particularly religious. This experience led to a religious sensibility that came to characterize both Hauch's writing and his life. His depression vanished after he took up residence in Rome in the summer of 1826 and became part of the Danish colony there, whose central figure was the sculptor Bertel Thorvaldsen. In this world of art and antiquity Hauch composed the dramatic works *Tiber* (Tiberius, 1828) and *Gregorius den Syvende* (Gregorius VII, 1829) before traveling during the spring of 1827, north through Florence, Venice, and Munich to Dresden. There he visited Tieck, who lauded him for *Hamadryaden,* which he had read in an unpublished German translation.

Back in Denmark, Hauch was named *lektor* (senior lecturer) in the natural sciences at Sorø Academy in 1827. He was married on 18 February 1829 to the seventeen-year-old Frederikke Elisabeth Brun Juul, the only daughter of a judge in Helsingør. Because of her parents' early death, she had been raised by an uncle, Commander Peter Frederik Wulff, at that time the best-known translator of Shakespeare into Danish. Hauch's young bride was known as "Renna," and their home in Sorø became a center for good family life; their many children received a free-spirited, Rousseauian upbringing. One of the children was named Adam Gottlob Øhlenschlæger Hauch (born 1836), after Hauch's idol, Oehlenschläger. Renna caused indignation by her broad-mindedness, which inspired her to such acts as tossing off her corset and bathing in the lake. She maintained a lifelong friendship with the influential literary critic Georg Brandes, who admired her strong personality. Renna did not have a recognized career as a writer but belonged to that group of early women writers who were closely associated with literary circles and published anonymously. With her husband's support, she published a volume of short stories, *Tyrolerfamilien og de tre Haarlokker* (The Tyrolean Family and the Three Locks of Hair, 1840), and the novel *Frue Werner* (Mrs. Werner, 1844).

Sorø Academy had been reestablished after a debate dating from the turn of the century. After graduating, students now had the opportunity to pursue three semesters of education and then take an exam on the same level as the basic philological-philosophical exam at the university. Although students were still schooled in the old aristocratic sports, such as riding and fencing, as well as in the classical languages, emphasis was now placed on natural sciences and modern languages. With the encouragement of Ørsted, Hauch reworked his dissertation, which he had published in Naples in 1827, as "Kort Oversigt over en Deel rudimentariske Organer, over deres Bestemmelse i Naturen, samt over en systematisk Udviklingsfølge, der tildeels paa disse kunde bygges" (Short Survey of Some Rudimentary Organs, of Their Function in Nature, along with a Systematic Sequence of Development That Could Partially Be Based on These). It was published in *Blandinger fra Sorøe* (Miscellanies From Sorø) in 1831. Also published that year was Hauch's contribution to the study of the historical determination of species: *Om de tre Organsystemer med Hensyn til Klassificationen* (On the Three Systems of Organization of Organs with Regard to Classification). In 1834 *Blandinger fra Sorøe* published his "Kort Udsigt over Nervesystemet med Hensyn paa dets forskiellige Forretninger og især med Hensyn paa den dyriske Følelse" (Short Look at the Nerve System, with Regard to Its Different Functions and especially with Regard to Animal Sensation).

However, Hauch flourished during his nearly twenty years at Sorø Academy not as a scientist, but as a literary author. The attitude toward literature in the environment of the academy was characterized by uniformity. Whereas literary critics from Heiberg to Baggesen assumed roles as Oehlenschläger's opponents and from the 1820s–with inspiration from Georg Wilhelm Friedrich Hegel–also served as the leading critics and arbiters of taste in the theater, the aesthetic tradition of Oehlenschläger was carried on at Sorø Academy. In addition to Hauch, the writer Bernhard Severin Ingemann and the critic Peter Hjort also belonged to this milieu. In 1822 these two were named senior lecturers in Danish and German, respectively, while Hauch became lecturer in Greek; Christian Wilster, in English; and Johannes Christian Lütken, in philosophy. Close by on his farm lived the playwright Christian Hviid Bredahl, whose heavy-handed dramas were certainly not considered modern in Copenhagen. In 1846 P. L. Møller skewered "Sorø Skolen" (The School at Sorø) in an article about a fictional visit to the sleepy town: "Sorø er det eneste Sted, hvor der findes berømte Mænd i Danmark" (Sorø is the only place in Denmark where you can find famous men). Among them was Hauch.

Hauch's first effort at Sorø Academy was to collect the historical dramas from his foreign travels, *Bajazet, Tiber,* and *Gregorius den Syvende,* along with the newly composed *Don Juan,* into the three-volume *Dramatiske Værker* (Dramatic Works, 1828–1830). During his time at the academy he also published the historical dramas *Carl den Femtes Død* (The Death of Carl V, 1831) and *Maastrichts Beleiring* (The Seige of Maastricht, 1832). Like the earlier works, they were written in the tragic style of an earlier period in Danish theater and dealt with historical situations in which wills clashed with destinies. They were published around the same time that Heiberg, having success with his light vaudevilles, was deriding Oehlenschläger for lacking deference to literary form and disregarding the demands of different genres. Heiberg also attacked Hauch, whose drama he also found lacking in the same respects. Even though Hauch had at first been spared by Heiberg–who had made his acquaintance in Paris–he felt once again called upon to defend Oehlenschläger. Afterward, Heiberg elegantly satirized Hauch, along with Hjort and Wilster, describing them as "de 3 Professorer i Fægtekunsten ved Lidenskabernes Akademi i Sorø" (the three fencing professors at the Academy of Passions in Sorø). After a month Hauch responded with *Den babyloniske Taarnbygning i Mignature. Et Forsøg i den Aristophaniske Comoedie* (The Babylonian Tower in Miniature. An Experiment in Aristophanic Comedy, 1830), in which he depicts "Vaudevillemesteren" (That Master of Vaudeville) Heiberg constructing two gigantic towers on the art of writing. One tower consists of vaudevilles, the dramatic art that Heiberg actually revived in Copenhagen but that was rejected at Sorø as being too superficial, and the other tower consists of the new theoretical criticism that Heiberg practiced based on his understanding of Hegel. In the cellar of the two towers the spirit of Shakespeare rumbles, causing the entire construction to collapse.

These literary feuds inspired many harsh words. When Henrik Hertz published his anonymous *Gjengangerbreve* (Ghost Letters, 1830) and thereby extended Baggesen's epistles from paradise, Hauch received from this Heiberg supporter yet another criticism for his ponderous material and lack of concern for language. Another opponent was Christian Molbech, who reviewed Hauch's works particularly harshly. Literary feud or no, Hauch's dramatic works from his foreign travels and from Sorø never became successful.

Since the breakthrough of the novel in 1820s Denmark as an original prose form, the genre had risen from the level of frivolous entertainment. It was a challenge for most authors to develop this literary form with appeal to a broad readership so that it could address existential questions. After *Waldemar den Store og hans Mænd* (Valdemar the Great and His Men, 1824), the first volume of his great epic cycle about the age of Valdemar, Ingemann shifted from poetry to prose with *Valdemar Seier* (1826). Hauch followed suit eight years later with the novel *Vilhelm Zabern* (1834). The publisher gave the novel the subtitle *En Autobiographie, indeholdende hidtil ubekiendte Efterretninger fra Christian den Andens Tid* (An Autobiography, Containing Hitherto Unknown Information from the Age of Christian II). Like later publishers of Søren Kierkegaard, Hauch pretended to have taken the work from an old manuscript, about whose origin he could not give readers any information. *Guld-mageren* (The Alchemist, 1836) is set in the 1700s. As is often the case in Hauch's novels, the historical setting in *Guldmageren* serves as a thin foil for the theme, which in this case involves the age-old dream of great wealth produced by a mastery of nature through alchemy. It also involves the equally old idea of the necessity of controlling those powers that are thereby released, so that one does not enter into a pact with evil itself.

Hauch's two novels with contemporary settings–*En polsk Familie* (A Polish Family, 1839), about a tragic fight for freedom, and *Slottet ved Rhinen* (The Castle on the Rhine, 1845)–feature narrative traits similar to those in Ingemann's novels: direct address to readers; retrospective, authoritative first-person narrators; and speeches taken from tragedies at the Royal Theater. Hauch's decision to replace the historical setting with a contemporary one was a departure, otherwise reserved for younger novelists such as Hans Christian Andersen. As a genre the novel offered room for more material than drama, just as it was better suited to Hauch's broad descriptions and somewhat loose composition. In his contemporary novels one recognizes themes from his historical dramas, such as the treatment of existential questions from an ethical perspective that is elevated above egoism and material interests. These novels, however, frequently lack the local color and keen observations of daily life that a writer such as Andersen could procure on his journeys (and that he wisely remembered and used). The most interesting facet of Hauch's early novels is their characteristic lyrical element, especially the poems woven into the prose–for example, the lyrical poems in *En polsk Familie,* among them the beautiful "Hvorfor svulmer Weichselfloden" (Why Does the River Vistula Swell).

Hauch left Sorø in March 1846 to become professor of Nordic languages and literature at the university in Kiel. Because of rebellion in the duchies of Slesvig and Holsten, he was forced to leave his professorship in 1848, but his lectures in Nordic mythology were translated into German as *Die nordische Mythenlehre* (1847).

Hauch circa 1870 (photograph by Budtz Müller & Co.; courtesy of the Danish Royal Library, Copenhagen)

In 1851 Hauch succeeded Oehlenschläger as professor of aesthetics at the University of Copenhagen. Hauch's tenure here resulted in the three-volume *Æsthetiske Afhandlinger og Recensioner* (Aesthetic Studies and Reviews, 1855–1869). The first volume features several "Afhandlinger af blandet Indhold" (studies of miscellaneous contents). They include fundamental discussions of questions concerning *Bildung* (education) and aesthetics. The articles are, for the most part, edited reprints. Characteristically enough, the youthful polemic is absent. Instead, Hauch speaks as a humanist, at length, and with several reservations. The first volume concludes with a talk, "Om Poesiens Fremtid" (On the Future of Poetry). After having noted the current cleaving of abstract reasoning in the natural sciences from immediate perception, Hauch adds that these sciences concern themselves with practical, material questions, which is useful but insufficient. He searches for the future of poetry in the development of humanity, seen in the light of Christianity and subordinated to the general development of life from "Legemlighed til Aandelighed" (corporeality to spirituality), thus breaking through nature's own repetitive rhythms. The poet should not write about steam engines and other technical inventions, which the scientist Ørsted had encouraged in *Aanden i Naturen* (The Spirit in Nature, 1851), but "dog skal man skildre Menneskets Digten og Tragten i alle de forandrede Forhold, som Tiden og dens Opfindelser nødvendig ville medføre" (however, one should depict humanity's endeavors in all the changing conditions that time and its inventions, by necessity, would entail). Poetry is thus seen idealistically as concerning itself with the humane conditions for and consequences of the developments of the concrete life that exists as a link in the historical realization of an ideal state.

Among the noteworthy studies in the first volume of *Æsthetiske Afhandlinger og Recensioner* is the introduction to Hauch's lectures on the thirteenth-century *Njáls Saga.* With these lectures he became the first scholar to view the Icelandic sagas as a literary genre.

The last volume of *Æsthetiske Afhandlinger og Recensioner* includes articles about Hauch's two great models in the dramatic arts, Oehlenschläger and Shakespeare. As a whole the three volumes do not represent an important departure from the idealistic views on art and literature that characterized the Golden Age of Denmark (roughly the first half of the nineteenth century). Still, they are noteworthy for not having been influenced by Heiberg and his Hegelianism. Hauch was too much of a civil servant to be able to pose as a sharp literary critic. Instead, his ethically and aesthetically based understanding of a literary work became a critical method, the assumptions of which all related to his own poetic self. When he attempted to universalize his experiences as a poet, the results were often a vague sensitivity in connection with poetry in a devotional setting. In both their merits and demerits, Hauch's aesthetic studies and lectures were closely connected to his fiction. He achieved most in his literary analysis when he devoted himself to the composition of a work and the delineation of literary characters.

During his years at the University of Copenhagen, Hauch continued writing fiction. In *Saga om Thorvald Vidførle* (The Saga of Thorvald Vidførle, 1849) he successfully imitates the terse style of the sagas, which he had researched as a professor. Character traits, patterns of action, formulas, and other stylistic characteristics of the sagas are not assumed directly but are shaped by Hauch into a harmonic entity.

A similar economy also characterizes *Robert Fulton* (1853; translated as *Robert Fulton, an Historical Novel,* 1868), in which Hauch used the structure of the developmental novel, or bildungsroman, to organize the source material into a coherent plot. The story of the title character's life takes place in Pennsylvania and deals with his acceptance of his life's calling and duty. It involves inventing a steamship that he can navigate on rivers, thereby changing the rivers into waterways for transportation. Hence, wild nature is tamed by the human spirit and becomes his servant. The project of taming nature recalls that of Benjamin Franklin, whom the reader also meets in long speeches in the narrator's account. Much is said and little happens in Hauch's novels, but this tendency is typical of many Danish novelists of this period.

Charles de la Bussière (1860) takes place in Paris during the French Revolution. The narrator leads readers in and out of the settings of the novel while he describes what has happened and offers finely edited speeches. *Fortælling om Haldor* (Haldor's Tale, 1864) is set in the Norwegian royal court in the time of the sagas, a period that Danish Romanticism never wanted to abandon as a setting but to which Hauch, with his childhood experiences of nature, was able to give special weight. The plot is aptly narrated in the terse style of a chronicle, thus achieving the saga tone without appearing to be a pastiche of a saga.

As a dramatist Hauch also acquired a greater technical grasp in his mature years. His greatest successes were the lyrical *Søstrene paa Kinnekullen* (The Sisters of Kinnekullen, 1849), *Æren tabt og vunden* (Honor Lost and Won, 1851), and *Tycho Brahes Ungdom* (Tycho Brahe's Youth, 1852), about the Danish scientist who was torn between honor and truth.

In his perception of literature, however, Hauch did not change. His diligent literary activity provided a fine example of his emphasis on ethics and personal growth. His writing improved, and he continued to believe in his calling, even though he only rarely achieved public success. In 1842, after Heiberg wrote a positive review of the drama *Svend Grathe* (1841), Hauch published his *Lyriske Digte* (Lyrical Poems), which was enlarged in the second edition in 1854. In his later years Hauch's unique voice achieved a lyric breakthrough that also procured admiration from the public. His *Lyriske Digte og Romancer* (Lyrical Poems and Romances, 1861) includes the ballad cycle "Valdemar Atterdag," which was followed a year later by *Valdemar Seier.* In these texts one discovers Hauch's seriousness, his enthusiasm for nobility of spirit, and his distaste for wretched and petty things. His best poems include examples from many genres: the romance "Valdemar's anden Sang" (Valdemar's Second Song) in "Valdemar Atterdag"; commemorative poetry (for Oehlenschläger's wife, Christiane); the hymn "Solen i sin klare Glans" (The Sun in Its Clear Radiance); confessional poetry, such as "Bekendelse" (Confession); and the cosmological "Plejaderne ved Midnat" (The Pleiades at Midnight).

In 1855 Hauch became chairman for the commission that organized the internal affairs of the Royal Theater after the end of absolute monarchy in Denmark in 1849. In 1858 and 1859 he was one of the two directors of the theater, and afterward he served as censor of plays from 1860 to 1871. He concluded his writing with two volumes of memoirs: *Minder fra min Barndom og min Ungdom* (Memories from My Childhood and My Youth, 1867) and *Minder fra min første Udenlandsreise* (Memories from My First Journey Abroad, 1871). The title word "Minder" (memories) refers to the circumstance that the two volumes were written without notes or other sources as Hauch attempted to find the leitmotiv in his existence through pure memory. The old poet and public servant was anything but cocksure, but he affirmed the family tradition by laying weight on calling and duty, both in relation to king, fatherland, and family and in relation to expressing his genius. Because of weak health he had to give up his posts in the fall of 1871 and travel to Rome, where he recommended Brandes as his successor as professor of aesthetics at the University of Copenhagen. (This recommendation was not acted upon.) On 4 March of the following year, Hauch died and was buried in the Protestant graveyard in Rome.

With Carsten Hauch the Christian idealism and work ethic that characterized the official civil-servant class created by the Danish absolute monarchy were maintained and carried forth to the Modern Breakthrough. Hauch did not adhere to a scientific ideology, although he was quite familiar with science through his education. Once he had chosen his course, nihilism could gain no hold on him. The depth of obligation that characterized Hauch involved a withdrawal from the material and concrete aspects of life. This trait surfaces in his novels and plays in a manner that, to a later readership, may cause these works to seem lacking in action and sensory concreteness. Even though Hauch modernized and improved his narrative techniques, this distance from the experiential, concrete life remained important to him.

Letters:

Hauch og Ingemann. En brevveksling, edited by M. Hatting (Copenhagen: Gyldendal, 1933).

Bibliographies:

Thomas Hansen Erslew, *Almindeligt Forfatter-Lexicon for Kongeriget Danmark med tilhørende Bilande fra før 1814 til efter 1858,* volume 1 (Copenhagen: Forlagsforeningen, 1843), pp. 595–598;

Erslew, *Almindeligt Forfatter-Lexicon for Kongeriget Danmark med tilhørende Bilande fra før 1814 til 1840. Supplement indtil Udgangen af Aaret 1853,* volume 1 (Copenhagen: Forlagsforeningen, 1858), pp. 724–729.

Biographies:

F. Rønning, *Johannes Carsten Hauch. En Levnedsskildring med et Udvalg af hans Digte* (Copenhagen: Gad, 1890; second edition, 1903);

Kjeld Galster, *Carsten Hauchs Barndom og Ungdom, 1790–1827* (Kolding: K. Jørgensen, 1930);

Galster, *Carsten Hauchs Manddom og Alderdom, 1827–1872* (Kolding: K. Jørgensen, 1935).

References:

Niels Barfoed, *Don Juan. En studie i dansk litteratur* (Copenhagen: Gyldendal, 1978), pp. 135–177;

Georg Brandes, "Carsten Hauch," in *Danske Digtere. Charakterbilleder* (Copenhagen: Gyldendal, 1877), pp. 1–103;

Jørgen Breitenstein, "Carsten Hauchs romaner," *Danske Studier* (1969): 20–47;

Mogens Brøndsted, "Dansk og nordisk litteraturhistorie," in *Københavns Universitet 1479–1979,* edited by Svend Ellehøj and Leif Grane, volume 9: *Det filosofiske Fakultet,* part 2, edited by Povl Johannes Jensen (Copenhagen: University of Copenhagen, 1979), pp. 27–32;

Paul V. Rubow, "Carsten Hauch," in his *Dansk litterær Kritik i det nittende Aarhundrede indtil 1870* (Copenhagen: Levin & Munksgaard, 1921), pp. 214–219.

Papers:

Carsten Hauch's papers, manuscripts, and letters are at the Danish Royal Library in Copenhagen.

Johan Ludvig Heiberg

(14 December 1791 - 25 August 1860)

Finn Hauberg Mortensen
University of Southern Denmark

(Translated by William Banks)

BOOKS: *Marionettheater* (Copenhagen: F. Brummer, 1814)–comprises *Don Juan* and *Pottemager Walter;*

De poësos dramaticæ genere hispanico, et præsertim de Petro Calderone de la Barca, principe Dramaticorum. Dissertatio aesthetica (Copenhagen: Gyldendal, 1817);

Dristig vovet halv er vundet. Romantisk Skuespil (Copenhagen: B. Brünnich, 1817);

Julespøg og Nytaarsløier. Comødie (Copenhagen: Christensen, 1817);

Ny A-B-C-Bog i en Times Underviisning til Ære, Nytte og Fornøielse for den unge Grundtvig. Et pædagogisk Forsøg (Copenhagen: Thiele, 1817);

Psyche. Et mythologisk Skuespil (Copenhagen: B. Brünnich, 1817);

Tycho Brahes Spaadom. Skuespil i tre Acter (Copenhagen: H. F. Popp, 1819);

Formenlehre der dänischen Sprache (Altona, Germany: J. F. Hammerich, 1823);

Nina, eller den Vanvittige af Kierlighed. Skuespil i fem Acter (Copenhagen: A. Seidelin, 1823);

Om den menneskelige Frihed. I Anledning af de nyeste Stridigheder over denne Gjenstand (Kiel: Universitets-Boghandlingen, 1824);

Kong Salomon og Jørgen Hattemager. Vaudeville (Copenhagen: C. A. Reitzel, 1825);

Der Zufall, aus dem Gesichtspunkte der Logik betrachtet. Als Einleitung zu einer Theorie des Zufalls (Copenhagen: C. A. Reitzel, 1825);

Aprilsnarrene, eller Intriguen i Skolen. Vaudeville (Copenhagen: F. Prinzlau, 1826); translated by Peter Vinten-Johansen as *The April Fools; or, An Intrigue at School: A Vaudeville,* Wisconsin Introductions to Scandinavia II, no. 9 (Madison: Department of Scandinavian Studies, University of Wisconsin-Madison, 1999);

Den otte og tyvende Januar. Vaudeville (Copenhagen: F. Prinzlau, 1826);

Courtesy of the Danish Royal Library, Copenhagen

Om Vaudevillen, som dramatisk Digtart, og om dens Betydning paa den danske Skueplads. En dramaturgisk Undersøgelse (Copenhagen: F. Prinzlau, 1826);

Et Eventyr i Rosenborg Have. Operette (Copenhagen: F. Prinzlau, 1827);

Nordische Mythologie. Aus der Edda und Oehlenschlägers mythischen Dichtungen (Slesvig: Königlichen Taubstummen-Institut, 1827);

Recensenten og Dyret. Vaudeville (Copenhagen: F. Prinzlau, 1827);

De Uadskillelige. Vaudeville (Copenhagen: F. Prinzlau, 1827);

Elverhøi. Skuespil i fem Acter (Copenhagen: F. Prinzlau, 1828);

Beskrivelse over Decorationen paa den Kgl. Theaterbygning ved Stadens Illumination i Anledning af D. K. H. Prinds Ferdinands og Prindsesse Carolines Indtog den 5. Oct. 1829 (Copenhagen: J. H. Schultz, 1829);

Prindsesse Isabella, eller tre Aftner ved Hoffet. Lystspil i tre Acter (Copenhagen: F. Prinzlau, 1829);

Kjøge-Huuskors. Vaudeville (Copenhagen: F. Prinzlau, 1831);

Udsigt over den danske skjønne Litteratur. Som Ledetraad ved Forelæsninger paa den Kongelige Militaire Høiskole (Copenhagen: A. Seidelin, 1831);

Grundtræk til Philosophiens Philosophie eller den speculative Logik. Som Ledetraad ved Forelæsninger paa den Kongelige Militaire Høiskole (Copenhagen: A. Seidelin, 1832);

Et halvt Dusin udvalgte Nytaarsvers fra Theatret til Publicum forfattede af Prof. Heiberg, og fremsagte af Fru Heiberg som Prolog ved det Kongelige Theaters Søndags-Forestilling den 1ste Januar 1832 (Copenhagen: J. H. Schultz, 1832);

De Danske i Paris. Vaudeville (Copenhagen: J. H. Schubothe, 1833);

Om Philosophiens Betydning for den nuværende Tid. Et Inbydelses-Skrift til en Række af philosophiske Forelæsninger (Copenhagen: C. A. Reitzel, 1833);

Alferne. Eventyr-Comedie (Copenhagen: J. H. Schubothe, 1835);

Indlednings-Foredrag til det i November 1834 begyndte logiske Cursus paa den Kongelige Militaire Høiskole (Copenhagen: J. H. Schubothe, 1835);

Nej. Vaudeville (Copenhagen: J. H. Schubothe, 1836); translated by Michael Leverson Meyer as *No,* in *Three Danish Comedies* (London: Oberon Books, 1999);

Fata Morgana. Eventyr-Comedie (Copenhagen: J. H. Schubothe, 1838);

Ja! Vaudeville-Monolog (Copenhagen: C. C. Lose & Olsen, 1839);

Emilies Hjertebanken. Vaudeville-Monolog (Copenhagen: J. H. Schubothe, 1840);

Grethe i Sorgenfri. Vaudeville-Monolog (Copenhagen: J. H. Schubothe, 1840);

Syvsoverdag. Romantisk Comedie (Copenhagen: J. H. Schubothe, 1840);

Nye Digte (Copenhagen: C. A. Reitzel, 1841)–includes *En Sjæl efter Døden,* translated and abridged by Henry Meyer as *A Soul after Death,* edited by Sven H. Rossel (Seattle: Mermaid Press, 1991);

Danmark, et malerisk Atlas, illustrated by C. F. Christensen (Copenhagen: H. J. Bing, 1842);

Dagen før Slaget ved Marengo. Operette i een Act (Copenhagen: J. H. Schubothe, 1843);

Thorvaldsen. Prolog ved Det kongelige Theaters Mindefest (Copenhagen: C. A. Reitzel, 1844);

Ulla skal paa Bal. En bellmansk Situation (Copenhagen: J. H. Schubothe, 1845);

Valgerda. Lystspil i to Acter (Copenhagen: J. H. Schubothe, 1847);

Prolog til 1ste Forestilling efter Kong Christian VIII's Død (Copenhagen: C. A. Reitzel, 1848);

Gadeviser. Texter og Melodier (Copenhagen: C. A. Reitzel, 1849).

Editions and Collections: *J. L. Heibergs Samlede Skrifter. Skuespil,* 7 volumes (Copenhagen: J. H. Schubothe, 1833–1841);

J. L. Heibergs Samlede Skrifter. Digte og Fortællinger, 2 volumes (Copenhagen: J. H. Schubothe, 1834, 1835);

J. L. Heibergs Samlede Skrifter. Prosaiske Skrifter, 3 volumes (Copenhagen: J. H. Schubothe, 1841–1843);

Johan Ludvig Heibergs Poetiske Skrifter, 8 volumes (Copenhagen: J. H. Schubothe, 1848–1849);

Samlede Skrifter. Prosaiske Skrifter, 11 volumes (Copenhagen: C. A. Reitzel, 1861–1862)–includes *Autobiografiske Fragmenter,* volume 11;

Samlede Skrifter. Poetiske Skrifter, 11 volumes (Copenhagen: C. A. Reitzel, 1862);

En Sjæl efter Døden. En apocalyptisk Comedie, edited by Alfred Ipsen (Copenhagen: C. A. Reitzel, 1893);

Vaudeviller. Ny Samling (Copenhagen: Gyldendal, 1903);

Udvalgte Digtninger (Copenhagen: Gyldendal, 1905);

Udvalgte poetiske Skrifter. Folkeudgave (Copenhagen: Gyldendal, 1911);

En Sjæl efter Døden, edited by Oskar Schlichtkrull (Copenhagen: V. Pio, 1919);

Elverhøi. Skuespil i fem Acter, edited by Morten Borup (Copenhagen: Gyldendal, 1928);

Poetiske Skrifter, edited by Carl S. Petersen, 3 volumes (Copenhagen: Gad, 1931–1932);

Julespøg og Nytaarsløier, og andre dramatiske Digte, edited by Paul V. Rubow (Copenhagen: Gyldendal, 1950);

Elverhøi; Aprilsnarrene; De Uadskillelige, edited by Henning Fonsmark (Copenhagen: H. Reitzel, 1965);

Nye Digte, edited by Jens Kistrup (Copenhagen: Gyldendal, 1965);

En Sjæl efter Døden; Recensenten og Dyret; Nej, edited by Fonsmark (Copenhagen: H. Reitzel, 1965);

Om Vaudervillen og andre kritiske Artikler, edited by Hans Hertel (Copenhagen: Gyldendal, 1968);

Elverhøi. Skuespil i fem Acter, introduction by Carl Johan Elmquist (Copenhagen: Nordisk Bogforlag, 1978);

Nye digte, 1841. Reformationskantaten, 1839, edited by Klaus P. Mortensen (Borgen: Danske Sprog- og Litteraturselskab, 1990);

Dramatik i udvalg, edited by Jens Kristian Andersen (Borgen: Danske Sprog- og Litteraturselskab, 2000).

PLAY PRODUCTIONS: *Tycho Brahes Spaadom,* Copenhagen, Royal Theater, 29 January 1819;

Nina, eller den Vanvittige af Kierlighed, Copenhagen, Royal Theater, 20 March 1823;

Kong Salomon og Jørgen Hattemager, Copenhagen, Royal Theater, 28 November 1825;

Den otte og tyvende Januar, Copenhagen, Royal Theater, 28 January 1826;

Aprilsnarrene, eller Intriguen i Skolen, Copenhagen, Royal Theater, 22 April 1826;

Recensenten og Dyret, Copenhagen, Royal Theater, 22 October 1826;

Et Eventyr i Rosenborg Have, Copenhagen, Royal Theater, 26 May 1827; produced in German as *Ein Rendezvous im bothanischen Garten,* Hamburg, Stadttheater, 1855;

De Uadskillelige, arranged by Vaudeville-Selskabet, Copenhagen, Royal Theater, 11 June 1827;

Elverhøi, Copenhagen, Royal Theater, 6 November 1828; as *Elfjungfrun,* Stockholm, Kungliga Dramatiska Teatern, 28 January 1857;

Supplikanten, Copenhagen, Royal Theater, 16 May 1829;

Prindsesse Isabella, eller tre Aftner ved Hoffet, Copenhagen, Royal Theater, 29 October 1829;

Kjøge-Huuskors, Copenhagen, Royal Theater, 28 November 1831;

De Danske i Paris, Copenhagen, Royal Theater, 29 January 1833;

Alferne, Copenhagen, Royal Theater, 29 January 1835;

Nej, Copenhagen, Royal Theater, 1 June 1836; Hamburg, Stadttheater, 26 December 1852;

Fata Morgana, Copenhagen, Royal Theater, 29 January 1838;

Ja! Copenhagen, Royal Theater, 24 February 1839;

Emilies Hjertebanken, Copenhagen, Royal Theater, 13 May 1840;

Syvsoverdag, Copenhagen, Royal Theater, 1 July 1840;

Grethe i Sorgenfri, Copenhagen, Royal Theater, 18 September 1840;

Dagen før Slaget ved Marengo, Copenhagen, Royal Theater, 9 May 1843;

Thorvaldsen. Prolog ved Royal Theaters Mindefest, Copenhagen, Royal Theater, 9 April 1844;

Pottemager Walter, Copenhagen, Royal Theater, 28 June 1845;

Ulla skal paa Bal, Copenhagen, Royal Theater, 5 July 1845;

Valgerda, Copenhagen, Royal Theater, 5 February 1847;

Prolog til Abekatten, Copenhagen, Royal Theater, 12 May 1849.

OTHER: *Messager Français du Nord* (1825), edited by Heiberg;

Kjøbenhavns flyvende Post (1827–1828, 1830), edited by Heiberg; reprinted, 4 volumes, with an afterword by Uffe Andreasen (Copenhagen: Danske Sprog- og Litteraturselskab/C. A. Reitzel, 1980–1983);

Maanedsskrift for Litteratur (1829–1832), co-edited by Heiberg;

Thomasine Gyllembourg, *Noveller, gamle og nye,* 3 volumes, edited by Heiberg (Copenhagen: C. A. Reitzel, 1833–1834);

Gyllembourg, *Skuespil,* edited by Heiberg (Copenhagen: C. A. Reitzel, 1834);

Kjøbenhavns flyvende Post. Interimsblade, nos. 1–100 (1834–1836); nos. 101–135 (1836–1837), edited by Heiberg;

Carl Bernhard [Andreas Nicolai de Saint-Aubain], *Et Aar i Kjøbenhavn. Novelle,* 2 volumes, edited by Heiberg (Copenhagen: J. H. Schubothe, 1835);

Gyllembourg, *Nye Fortællinger,* 3 volumes, edited by Heiberg (Copenhagen: C. A. Reitzel, 1835–1836);

Gyllembourg, *To Noveller,* edited by Heiberg (Copenhagen: C. A. Reitzel, 1837);

Perseus. Journal for den spekulative Idé (1837–1838), edited by Heiberg;

Gyllembourg, *Tolv Skizzer,* edited by Heiberg (Copenhagen: C.A. Reitzel, 1838);

Gyllembourg, *Maria. Novelle,* edited by Heiberg (Copenhagen: C. A. Reitzel, 1839);

Gyllembourg, *Nær og fjern. Novelle,* edited by Heiberg (Copenhagen: C. A. Reitzel, 1841);

Eet Hundrede lyriske Digte af den danske Litteratur, edited by Heiberg (Copenhagen: H. J. Bing, 1842);

Intelligensblade (1842–1844), edited by Heiberg;

Gyllembourg, *En Brevvexling,* edited by Heiberg (Copenhagen: C. A. Reitzel, 1843);

Urania. Aarbog for 1844, edited by Heiberg (Copenhagen: H. J. Bing, 1843);

Nøddeknækkerne, in *Urania. Aarbog for 1845,* edited by Heiberg (Copenhagen: H. J. Bing, 1844);

Urania. Aarbog for 1846, edited by Heiberg (Copenhagen: C. A. Reitzel, 1845);

Gyllembourg, *Skrifter af forfatteren til "En Hverdags-Historie,"* anonymous, 12 volumes, edited by Heiberg (Copenhagen: C. A. Reitzel, 1849–1851);

Clara Raphael [Mathilde Fibiger], *Tolv Breve,* edited, with an introduction, by Heiberg (Copenhagen: C. A. Reitzel, 1851).

TRANSLATIONS: Ovid, *Skabelsen* (Copenhagen: Sebbelow, privately printed, 1806);

Heinrich von Kleist, J. K. Musäus, and E. T. A. Hoffman, *Noveller,* 2 volumes (Copenhagen: Gyldendal, 1818, 1819);

Louis Angely, *Syv militaire Piger. Vaudeville* (Copenhagen: F. Prinzlau, 1827);

Eugène Scribe and Germaine Delavigne, *Kjærligheds-Drømme. Vaudeville* (Copenhagen: F. Prinzlau, 1827);

Anonymous, *Landsby-Sangerinderne. Syngespil i to Acter,* Det Kongelige Theaters Repertoire, no. 3 (Copenhagen: F. Prinzlau, 1828);

Eugène de Planard, *Skovhuggerens Søn. Syngestykke i tre Acter,* Det Kongelige Theaters Repertoire, no. 10 (Copenhagen: F. Prinzlau, 1828);

Gioacchino Rossini, *Pigen ved Søen. Syngespil i tre Acter* (Copenhagen: F. Prinzlau, 1828);

Félix-Auguste Duvert, Armand Chapeau (as Desvergers), and Charles Voirin (as Varin), *Den fortrædelige Formiddag. Lystspil i een Act,* Det Kongelige Theaters Repertoire, no. 19 (Copenhagen: F. Prinzlau, 1829);

Scribe and Frédéric de Courcy, *Formynder og Myndling. Lystspil i een Act,* Det Kongelige Theaters Repertoire, no. 20 (Copenhagen: F. Prinzlau, 1829);

Scribe and Bruté de Nierville (as Brulay), *Snyltegjæsten. Lystspil i een Act,* Det Kongelige Theaters Repertoire, no. 21 (Copenhagen: F. Prinzlau, 1829);

Franz von Holbein, *Aloise. Syngespil i tre Acter* (Copenhagen: F. Prinzlau, 1830);

Scribe and Delavigne, *Den stumme i Portici. Opera i fem Acter,* Det Kongelige Theaters Repertoire, no. 26 (Copenhagen: F. Prinzlau, 1830);

Scribe and Jean Henri Dupin, *Christen og Christine. Dramatisk Idyl i een Act* (Copenhagen: F. Prinzlau, 1830);

Carl Töpfer, *Seer jer i Speil! Lystspil i een Act* (Copenhagen: F. Prinzlau, 1830);

Scribe and Delavigne, *Den fortræffelige Onkel. Lystspil i een Act,* Det Kongelige Theaters Repertoire, no. 34 (Copenhagen: F. Prinzlau, 1831);

Scribe, *Bruden. Syngespil i tre Acter,* Det Kongelige Theaters Repertoire, no. 35 (Copenhagen: F. Prinzlau, 1831);

Jean Nicolas Bouilly and Scribe, *Musiktexten til De to Nætter. Syngespil i tre Acter* (Copenhagen: F. Prinzlau, 1832);

Scribe and Paul Duport, *Qvækeren og Dandserinden. Lystspil i een Act,* Det Kongelige Theaters Repertoire, no. 39 (Copenhagen: F. Prinzlau, 1832);

Scribe, *Familien Riquebourg. Drama i een Act,* Det Kongelige Theaters Repertoire, no. 40 (Copenhagen: F. Prinzlau, 1832);

Scribe, Dupin, and Théophile Marion Dumersan, *Kostgængeren. Lystspil i een Act,* Det Kongelige Theaters Repertoire, no. 44 (Copenhagen: F. Prinzlau, 1832);

Scribe, *Den første Kjærlighed. Lystspil i een Act,* Det Kongelige Theaters Repertoire, no. 45 (Copenhagen: J. H. Schultz, 1832);

Scribe, Anne Honoré Joseph Duveyrier (as Mélesville), and Jean-François-Alfred Bayard, *Et Feiltrin. Drama i to Acter* (Copenhagen: C. A. Reitzel, 1832);

William Rowley, *Brødrene Foster. Lystspil i fire Acter,* Det Kongelige Theaters Repertoire, no. 50 (Copenhagen: F. Prinzlau, 1833);

Scribe and Antoine-François Varner, *Den skjønneste Dag i Livet. Vaudeville i to Acter* (Copenhagen: J. H. Schubothe, 1833);

Scribe and Duport, *Den unge Hovmesterinde. Lystspil i een Act,* Det Kongelige Theaters Repertoire, no. 60 (Copenhagen: F. Prinzlau, 1834);

Bayard, *En Time i Stervbo. Lystspil i een Act,* Det Kongelige Theaters Repertoire, no. 62 (Copenhagen: F. Prinzlau, 1834);

Felice Romani, *Den Ubekjendte. Tragisk Syngespil i to Acter,* Det Kongelige Theaters Repertoire, no. 63 (Copenhagen: F. Prinzlau, 1834);

Scribe, *Den hemmelige Lidenskab. Lystspil i tre Acter,* Det Kongelige Theaters Repertoire, no. 66 (Copenhagen: F. Prinzlau, 1834);

Adolphe d'Ennery, *Kjolen gjør ikke Manden. Lystspil i een Act* (Copenhagen: J. H. Schubothe, 1835);

Frédéric Soulié and Edmond Badon, *Et Eventyr under Carl den Niende. Lystspil i tre Acter,* Det Kongelige Theaters Repertoire, no. 72 (Copenhagen: F. Prinzlau, 1835);

Duveyrier (as Mélesville) and Nicolas Brazier, *Guldkorset. Lystspil i to Acter,* Det Kongelige Theaters Repertoire, no. 79 (Copenhagen: F. Prinzlau, 1836);

Duport and Paul Foucher, *Coliche. Lystspil i een Act,* Det Kongelige Theaters Repertoire, no. 85 (Copenhagen: F. Prinzlau, 1836);

Joseph Bernard Rosier, *En Criminalproces. Lystspil i to Acter,* Det Kongelige Theaters Repertoire, no. 87 (Copenhagen: F. Prinzlau, 1837);

Henri de Saint-Georges, Adolphe de Leuven, and Auguste de Forges, *Farinelli. Lystspil i tre Acter,* Det Kongelige Theaters Repertoire, no. 94 (Copenhagen: F. Prinzlau, 1837);

François Ancelot and François-Isaac-Hyacinthe Décomberousse, *Man kan, hvad man vil. Lystspil i to Acter,* Det Kongelige Theaters Repertoire, no. 96 (Copenhagen: F. Prinzlau, 1838);

Scribe and Philippe Dumanoir, *Enten elskes eller døe! Lystspil i een Act,* Det Kongelige Theaters Repertoire, no. 100 (Copenhagen: F. Prinzlau, 1838);

Scribe, *De Uafhængige. Comedie i tre Acter,* Det Kongelige Theaters Repertoire, no. 123 (Copenhagen: F. Prinzlau, 1840).

SELECTED PERIODICAL PUBLICATIONS–UNCOLLECTED: "Teatret. Væringerne i Miklagaard," *Kjøbenhavns flyvende Post,* nos. 99–101 (1827);

"Svar paa Hr. Prof. Oehlenschlägers Skrift: 'Om Kritiken i Kjøbenhavns flyvende Post, over Væringerne i Miklagaard,'" *Kjøbenhavns flyvende Post,* nos. 7–16 (1828).

Johan Ludvig Heiberg lived during Copenhagen's Golden Age; he was surrounded by a flourishing theater and salon culture and was influenced by the Danish Romantic movement. More cosmopolitan than the National Romantic writers, he also came to represent neoclassicism, which made its mark on the cultural revival that began around 1830 in the capital. For the next twenty years Heiberg, through his periodicals, his aesthetic criticism, and not least his plays and vaudevilles, exerted an unusually high degree of influence on the formation of literary taste in Denmark. Contributing to the scope of his influence were his adaptations of French theater–principally, the dramas of Eugène Scribe–which brought about a transformation of the repertoire of the Royal Theater. Heiberg's formal and aesthetic approach to theater and poetry received philosophical strength from Georg Wilhelm Friedrich Hegel, who with Heiberg set a new standard for contemporary idealist conceptions of culture.

Heiberg's father, the writer and satirist Peter Andreas Heiberg, was among the first to pass the new philological examination of 1777 at the University of Copenhagen, and in 1785 he was named *notarius publicus.* On 7 May 1790 Peter Andreas Heiberg married Thomasine Buntzen, his language student. Their only child, Johan Ludvig, was born in Copenhagen on 14 December 1791. Peter Andreas Heiberg had planned to follow the path of his superior as a notary official, but charges that his political satires had overstepped the bounds of press restrictions, combined with an earlier offense, resulted in his banishment from Denmark on Christmas Eve 1799. When the young writer left Copenhagen for Paris on 7 February 1800, there was much sympathy for him, and it was expected that the sentence would not be made permanent. Although Heiberg offered to accept imprisonment in the citadel in Copenhagen in exchange for the opportunity to raise his son, no compromise could be reached. Crown Prince Frederik remained bitter over the sympathetic response of the people to Heiberg's critique of the establishment, while Heiberg became furious that his wife had betrayed him in Copenhagen, where she failed to further the cause of his many requests to return home. The marriage was dissolved in 1801, and that year Thomasine married the Swedish baron Carl Frederik Ehrensvärd-Gyllembourg.

After the divorce Johan Ludvig Heiberg was, at the direction of his father, first taken into the care of his mother's sister, Lise Jürgensen, but was then placed in the care of his father's good friends Knud Lyne Rahbek and Kamma Rahbek. The couple lived at Bakkehuset (the House on the Hill), a residence located outside of central Copenhagen in Frederiksberg, but one could not have grown up closer to the center of the Danish literary world. Heiberg studied Latin with Knud Rahbek and modern languages with Kamma Rahbek. The couple also retained a young theologian, Peter Hansen, who for six years was responsible for the rest of their foster son's education.

The many guests at Bakkehuset voiced their negative opinions of Thomasine Gyllembourg, which damaged the boy's affection for his mother. After 1804 he lived again with his aunt, but he began to pass more and more time with the Gyllembourgs, who had returned to Copenhagen in 1806, after their estate in Zealand had burned down. Another theologian succeeded Hansen as Heiberg's tutor and in 1809 supervised his admission into the university. Up until his examination he received a strong education in mathematics under the tutelage of the well-known natural scientist Hans Christian Ørsted, and although after two years as a student Heiberg had ceased living with the Rahbeks, he continued to visit the childless couple. Unofficially, he lived from 1811 onward in a finely furnished room in the Gyllembourgs' flat at the corner of Amaliegade and Blancogade (now Fredericiagade), from which there was a superb view of the ships in Copenhagen's harbor, since there were at that time no buildings on the other side of Amaliegade. Here Heiberg found peace in close familial relations, feeling affection for his mother and friendship for her husband, the Swedish baron. In accordance with his mother's wishes, he studied medicine, but his talents were many and opinions on his career prospects varied widely. The Gyllembourg home was a lively gathering place. While the literati of the revolutionary age and the new Romantic poets flocked to the Rahbeks at Bakkehuset, the Gyllembourg circle was peopled by diplomats and the nobility.

Heiberg was also a guest of the wealthy merchant Konferensråd (Councillor) Constantin Brun at his country estate, Sophienholm, and in his salon on Dronningens Tværgade in Copenhagen. Brun was of German birth, and his wife, Friederike, was the daughter of the pastor of St. Petri in Lübeck, Germany (and, from 1808, the leader of the Danish State Church). She had since her youth been active in German literature. The Bruns' marriage was based on a mixture of reason and freethinking, which was in fashion among the merchant aristocracy of the revolutionary age. Brun was significantly older than his wife, and for a time he accepted her lengthy travels in Europe with her lover and the youngest of their five children, Ida, whom she had chosen for a special upbringing. At some point, however, this situation became too much to bear. Friederike chose the marriage and her child, who thus became the center of the most prominent salon for artists and intellectuals. All admired Ida's beauty and talents, which were developed through the free and sensitive upbringing her parents gave her, based on the ideas of Jean-Jacques Rousseau. Many poems were composed in praise of Ida, and it came as no surprise that Heiberg was among those who fell in love with her. For him she was to remain an unrequited love.

Among the Bruns' circle, Heiberg was known as *l'enfant,* which was quite appropriate, because in his youthful innocence he could move freely among the many dignitaries who had contributed to his education and upbringing. When, as a boy, he had once fallen ill, the composer Christoph Ernst Friedrich Weyse and the author Laurids Kruse had presented him with a puppet theater, for which he wrote his first piece, in rhymed dialogue and in the style of Ludvig Holberg. For the 1812 birthday party of Anna Taube, a Swedish countess to whom the young *bel esprit* had lost his heart, Heiberg wrote the four-act *Don Juan,* based on Molière's *Dom Juan, ou Le Festin de Pierre* (Don Juan, or The Stone Banquet, 1665), for which he was praised from all quarters. With his youth and upbringing Heiberg moved in the circles frequented by both Jens Baggesen and Adam Oehlenschläger, the principal combatants in the great Danish literary feud of the new century. At the premier of *Don Juan* he received a brotherly kiss from Oehlenschläger, who thereby repeated the gesture with which Baggesen at his 1800 departure from Copenhagen had acknowledged the genius of the young Oehlenschläger and granted him access to the Danish Parnassus. Baggesen was also enthusiastic about Heiberg, predicting that he would one day "judge through poetry the victor in the war between Baggesen and Oehlenschläger."

Heiberg's father, the writer Peter Andreas Heiberg (portrait by Lahde, 1794; courtesy of the Danish Royal Library, Copenhagen)

The Taubes invited Heiberg home with them to Stockholm, where the young medical student and dandy resided for three months in 1812. He was introduced to the highest circles, where he socialized, attended the theater, and became acquainted with the melodies of Carl Michael Bellmann, which he later often employed in his vaudevilles. This life in a whirl of pleasures suited Heiberg handsomely. His mother wrote angry letters to Countess Taube, whom she believed was in the process of seducing her son. This charge was without foundation, as Heiberg's enthusiasm for the countess vanished when she told him she was pregnant.

Back in Copenhagen, Heiberg published his debut, *Marionetteater* (Marionette Theater, 1814), which, in addition to the romantic and mystical *Don Juan,* included *Pottemager Walter* (Walter the Potter), inspired by the literary comedies of Ludvig Tieck. With the death of his stepfather in 1815, the family finances became tighter. Together with his mother, Heiberg moved in with his cousin Andreas Buntzen, who was married to Camilla (with whom Heiberg had a son in 1816 and later a daughter). Heiberg's literary breakthrough occurred in 1817, when, in continuation of

Oehlenschläger's "Sanct Hansaften Spil" (Midsummer Night's Play, 1803), he published his most original work, the literary revue *Julespøg og Nytaarsløier* (Christmas Jests and New Year Tricks). In it he poked fun at the sentimental and dreadfully Romantic youthful poetry of B. S. Ingemann, an act that was not without consequences, as N. F. S. Grundtvig rushed to the rescue of his colleague Ingemann. From this riposte there emerged still more parody, as in the same year Heiberg answered with the flippantly titled *Ny A-B-C-Bog i en Times Underviisning til Ære, Nytte og Fornøielse for den unge Grundtvig. Et pædagogisk Forsøg* (New ABC Book, an Hour's Instruction for the Edification, Use, and Pleasure of the Young Grundtvig: A Pedagogical Essay). The polemic concluded as festively as it had begun, with a peace offering from Heiberg titled "Vaaren og Freden" (Spring and Peace).

In 1817 Heiberg managed to publish three additional works. First, he defended his dissertation in Latin on Pedro Calderón de la Barca, the seventeenth-century Spanish dramatist. The goal of this treatise, *De poësos dramaticæ genere hispanico, et præsertim de Petro Calderone de la Barca, principe Dramaticorum,* was in part historical and in part formal and aesthetic. Heiberg attempted to prove both that Calderón's dramas were typical of Spanish literature and that Spanish poetry typifies Romanticism. From this conclusion it follows that Calderón above all is the most Romantic of authors. In this argument Heiberg distinguished himself from Oehlenschläger, who preferred William Shakespeare as a model. Heiberg's dissertation builds on the Friedrich Schlegelian concept of the intimate connection between a given poetic art and a people. Although Heiberg was still unacquainted with the ideas of Hegel at this time, the chain of argumentation in this study approaches the dialectical constructions in which Heiberg's later aesthetic criticism is rooted, a tendency also evident in his series of dramatic works related to Nordic folk poetry. In 1817 he also published the comedy *Dristig vovet halv er vundet* (Well Begun Is Half Won), which is Calderónesque both in style and content. In the mythological drama *Psyche* (1817), material from antiquity receives a modern, Romantic bearing and a Nordic tone. No one could hereafter be in doubt of the young poet's energy and sense of form. The historical drama *Tycho Brahes Spaadom* (The Prophecy of Tycho Brahe), including later, much-admired poems about the sixteenth-century astronomer's observatory, Uraniborg, was also published in revised form in 1819.

At the urging of the Bruns, Heiberg had envisioned a future in diplomacy, with his dissertation serving as a kind of letter of introduction. These plans, however, fell by the wayside, and he instead obtained a travel stipend from the Royal Treasury, departing in 1819 via London for Paris, where he was to live with his father for three years. At this point Heiberg had a variety of ideas concerning his future plans, including studies in natural science, mathematics, poetry, and aesthetics. He remained largely preoccupied, however, with social activities. Prince Christian and Princess Caroline Amalie had established a salon in Paris, where he met with an assortment of future politicians and budding *beaux esprits* like himself, including Christian Molbech, Carsten Hauch, and Peter Hjort, all of whom later became Heiberg's opponents in the ongoing feud over Oehlenschläger's views of literature and the theater.

Since his arrival in Paris in 1800, Peter Heiberg had lived modestly on his income as an interpreter for the French foreign ministry. His son was long awaited and warmly received. Through his father, Heiberg was able to meet with prominent French politicians, scientists, and humanists. He studied natural science with Georges Cuvier and was, like Hauch, a frequent visitor to the Jardin des Plantes. He also studied French literature and both gave and received music lessons. More important than any other experience in Paris was his viewing of Louis Jacques Jessé Milon's ballet *Nina, ou la Folle par Amour* (Nina, or the Craziness of Love, 1813), which he adapted as a five-act play, *Nina, eller den Vanvittige af Kierlighed,* produced in Copenhagen in 1823 and published that same year. This long and widely varied journey of education engendered no further clarity regarding Heiberg's future and was in addition most costly to his father, who until his death in 1841 was forced to persist in extremely tight financial circumstances.

At the expense of the Danish prince, Heiberg returned to Copenhagen in 1822, where he unsuccessfully sought an appointment at Sorø Academy. Instead, his application for a lectureship beginning in the fall of 1822 at the University of Kiel, submitted by his mother, was accepted. Together with his mother and his illegitimate son, Georg Buntzen, whom his mother had taken in, Heiberg departed for Kiel. The transition from the enjoyment of Parisian life to the responsibilities of a breadwinner and the demands of a poorly rewarded and lowly esteemed lectureship was harsh. He nevertheless took up the challenge, benefiting from the need to concentrate his interests. Whereas natural science had been at the center of his interests in Paris, philology now became the priority. On the basis of his Kiel lectures, Heiberg published the German-language *Formenlehre der dänischen Sprache,* a Danish grammar, in 1823 and *Nordische Mythologie* (Nordic Mythology) in 1827. In the grammar there may be seen a lack of a historical understanding, as Heiberg, with no knowledge of the work of philologists such as Rasmus Rask and

Jacob Grimm, describes Icelandic suffixes as divergences from and not precursors to modern Danish.

At Kiel, Heiberg, through a colleague, became acquainted with Hegel. During a stay in Berlin he had the opportunity to meet with the master, whose pupil the lawyer Eduard Gans directed him to *Grundlinien der Philosophie des Rechts; oder Naturrecht und Staatswissenschaft im Grundrisse* (The Philosophy of Right, or Natural Law and Political Science Outlined, 1820), the introduction to which included the dictum of the mature Hegel, which became the starting point for the "Right Hegelians" (the conservative adherents of the philosopher's ideas): "What is rational is real, and what is real is rational." In a Hamburg hotel room, according to his own account, Heiberg experienced a vision of the Hegelian system in its entirety, an account that follows to the letter the conventions for describing a religious breakthrough. The dialectic was not just abstract logic; it encompassed an understanding of every concrete phenomenon and its context. The phenomenon arises as a reaction, as an antithesis in relation to its precondition, but with the consequence that the immediate contradiction is lifted to a higher level in a synthesis. Thereby the original contradiction between thesis and antithesis is mediated, and thus it is further possible to explain why contradictions in both the larger cultural history and in individual development must be transformed over time from the immediate to the progressively more reflective.

Heiberg's first working out of these thoughts is found in *Om den menneskelige Frihed. I Anledning af de nyeste Stridigheder over denne Gjenstand* (On Human Freedom: On the Occasion of the Latest Disputes on this Subject, 1824), which constituted his contribution to the Howitz Dispute. This debate concerned free will, and the occasion was an article by Franz Gothard Howitz on sanity and insanity, which had engendered a response from the lawyer Anders Sandøe Ørsted. Heiberg argued that the debate could be resolved from the point of view of neither David Hume nor Immanuel Kant, which lay behind the views of the combatants, but only through Hegel, who did not conceive of freedom and necessity as absolutes but as dialectical opposites. *Om den menneskelige Frihed* was followed by the German-language *Der Zufall, aus dem Gesichtspunkte der Logik betrachtet. Als Einleitung zu einer Theorie des Zufalls* (On Chance, Observed from the Point of View of Logic: As an Introduction to a Theory of Chance, 1825); indeed, Heiberg would have liked to have ranked among his German colleagues, preferring an appointment at Berlin or Greifswald. His main goal, however, was a chair in philosophy at the University of Copenhagen.

None of these plans succeeded. Under the pretext of taking a holiday, Heiberg vanished from his post at Kiel in 1825, evading the creditors from whom it took him three years to secure the return of his mortgaged furniture. In spite of his insufficient attention to his duties as lecturer, he managed to force his successor to pay him severance until he obtained a new position. Back in Copenhagen after six years of failures in both France and Germany, Heiberg set himself to the task of combining his experience with French and German theater into a Danish vaudeville. He intended to place more emphasis on the music and its connection to the action and character development than in the French and German models, as well as to tie in the comedies of Holberg and the songs of Bellmann. Success came quickly with the 28 November 1825 premiere of *Kong Salomon og Jørgen Hattemager* (King Solomon and George the Hatter). Among both actors and the public there

Puppet theater given to Heiberg during a childhood illness by the composer Christoph Ernst Friedrich Weyse and the author Laurids Kruse. Heiberg wrote his first play for this theater (Theater Museum; from Morten Borup, Johan Ludvig Heiberg, *volume 1, 1947; William T. Young Library, University of Kentucky).*

Heiberg and his wife, Johanne Luise, listening as Heiberg's mother, the writer Thomasine Gyllembourg, reads to them. The painting on the wall is J. M. Petersen's well-known portrait of the young Gyllembourg (painting by Wilhelm Marstrand, 1870; courtesy of the Danish Royal Library, Copenhagen).

was support for this alternative to the many medieval-garbed tragedies of the previous generation of National Romantic poets. Now the works appeared in quick succession. After taking note of the thirteen-year-old Johanne Luise Pätges, who, together with C. N. Rosenkilde, had performed Poul Martin Møller's dialogue "Hans og Trine," Heiberg wrote a vaudeville for the couple. *Aprilsnarrene, eller Intriguen i Skolen* (translated as *The April Fools; or, An Intrigue at School,* 1999) debuted on 22 April 1826. Like Heiberg's *Et Eventyr i Rosenborg Have* (An Adventure in Rosenborg Gardens, 1827) and *De Uadskillelige* (The Inseparables, 1827), it was intended to unlock the particular talents of the young Pätges.

After receiving intense criticism for *Recensenten og Dyret* (The Critic and the Animal, 1827), Heiberg withdrew the piece and began to work out his principal statement on the new drama. *Om Vaudevillen, som dramatisk Digtart, og om dens Betydning paa den danske Skueplads. En dramaturgisk Undersøgelse* (On the Vaudeville as a Dramatic Genre and Its Significance for the Danish Stage: A Dramaturgical Investigation, 1826) was directed in part toward the general public and in part toward Knud Rahbek and others who did not find the buffoonery of the vaudeville to be suitable material for the theater. *Recensenten og Dyret* was now revived in reworked form and became a success.

Heiberg's contact with the reading public continued through *Kjøbenhavns flyvende Post* (Copenhagen's Flying Post), the first issue of which hit the streets on 1 January 1827. The popular journal was published twice a week until 1829, when, after a pause, it came out thrice weekly through the end of 1830. Heiberg resumed irregular publication of *Kjøbenhavns flyvende Post* in 1834, concluding the project in 1837, when all 235 issues were collected in two volumes. Through his journalism Heiberg revived the role of the publicist, which had been held by several members of the generation immediately preceding the Romantics, such as Peter Heiberg and Knud Rahbek. The publicity Heiberg created in his journalism provided opportunities for a new group of writers to come forward, including Christian Winther and Hans Christian Andersen. Thomasine Gyllembourg, writing in the journal as "The Author of *An Everyday Story*" (a reference to *En Hverdags-Historie,* her 1828 story serialized in *Kjøbenhavns flyvende Post*), created an entirely new genre of prose fiction.

Kjøbenhavns flyvende Post was also significant in that through its pages a newly educated public became aware of Heiberg's formal aesthetics, a fulfillment of Baggesen's prophesy that Heiberg would act as judge in the feud between himself and Oehlenschläger. In his critique of Oehlenschläger's *Væringerne i Miklagaard* (The Warriors of Miklagaard, 1827), he sided with Baggesen's view that form has primacy in relation to content. Thus was the prelude provided for the next round in this literary dispute, which was now carried out between Heiberg's formal-aesthetic camp and the followers of Oehlenschläger, who remained adherents of Shakespeare. Heiberg had in the meantime formulated something as yet unseen in Denmark: a complete aesthetics in which the concept of genre is central. He placed the principal genres of the lyric, the epic, and the drama in a triad. The establishment of a further triad within drama was highly provocative, in that he traced a development from a drama of immediacy through tragedy to comedy, thereby elevating his own vaudevilles above the tradition-rich Nordic medieval-garbed tragedy. While he readily ceded "poetic" evaluation to the public, he reserved the technical aspects of criticism for professionals. The purpose of the critic was to evaluate the single work on the basis of the ideal genres. Heiberg thought Oehlenschläger, whom he viewed as an epic-lyrical poet, should stick to the romances at which he excelled, while Heiberg saw himself as suited for the more reflective drama, which ranked high within the hierarchy of genres that he had constructed.

Heiberg wrote *Elverhøi* (Elves' Hill), featuring Christian IV as the main character with music by Friedrich Kuhlau, for a 6 November 1828 gala performance at a royal wedding. All the artistry of the theater is employed in this seamless blend of folk songs and melodies, making the piece into a national *Festspiel* (festival play), performed more than any other play at the Royal Theater on Kongens Nytorv (King's New Square). In appreciation of the success of *Elverhøi,* Heiberg was named resident playwright and translator for the Royal Theater, with a salary and the responsibility for translating several plays each year, as well as for the writing of prologues and occasional poems. One of the first results was *Prindsesse Isabella, eller tre Aftner ved Hoffet* (Princess Isabella, or Three Evenings at Court), which was staged for the first and last time on 29 October 1829. In contrast, Heiberg had a great deal of success with his dramaturgical adaptations and with his translations of many of Scribe's enormous repertoire of plays and vaudevilles.

In 1829 Heiberg received the title of professor, and the following year he was named docent in logic, aesthetics, and Danish at the newly founded Royal Military Academy. From this teaching activity, which continued until 1836, came several writings and published lectures. Although of an introductory nature, they are important for the demonstration and development of the new Hegelian forms of thinking. They include *Udsigt over den danske skjønne Litteratur. Som Ledetraad ved Forelæsninger paa den Kongelige Militaire Høiskole* (View of Danish Literature: A Guide to the Lectures at the Royal Military Academy, 1831), *Grundtræk til Philosophiens Philosophie eller den speculative Logik. Som Ledetraad ved Forelæsninger paa den Kongelige Militaire Høiskole* (Outline of the Philosophy of Philosophy, or Speculative Logic: A Guide to the Lectures at the Royal Military Academy, 1832), *Om Philosophiens Betydning for den nuværende Tid* (On the Contemporary Significance of Philosophy, 1833), and *Indlednings-Foredrag til det i November 1834 begyndte logiske Cursus paa den Kongelige Militaire Høiskole* (Introductory Lecture for the Course on Logic Beginning November 1834 at the Royal Military Academy, 1835).

After her 1826 triumph in *Aprilsnarrene,* Pätges had become a theater student, thus freeing her from dancing lessons. She had already inspired a great number of authors to write roles for her and an even larger number to court her, including Heiberg. He was at first rebuked; however, his mother intervened by taking in the young actress, who secretly became engaged to the son of the house. Heiberg married Pätges on 31 July 1831 at Slangerup Church in Slangerup, where his former teacher Hansen was pastor. The newly married couple later invited Thomasine Gyllembourg to live with them in their residence at Søkvæsthuset (the Naval Infirmary) on Christianshavn in Copenhagen.

After her marriage at the age of nineteen, Johanne Luise Heiberg always used the title "Mrs. Heiberg" at the theater, even though it was considered socially unacceptable that the wife of a gentleman should appear onstage. Her husband, however, guarded constantly against any slander. In the ensuing years Heiberg continued his extensive dramaturgical work. Some of his occasional poetry was collected in 1832 in *Et halvt Dusin udvalgte Nytaarsvers fra Theatret til Publicum* (A Half-Dozen Selected New Year's Verses from the Theater to the Public). He also wrote the vaudevilles *Kjøge-Huuskors* (The Holy Terror of Køge, 1831), *De Danske i Paris* (The Danes in Paris, 1833), and *Nej* (1836; translated as *No,* 1999); a series of monologues, including *Ja!* (Yes! 1839); and *Alferne* (The Elves, 1835), a fairy-tale comedy in the spirit of Tieck.

After a trip with his wife to Berlin and Paris, where they visited his father, Heiberg shifted from vaudevilles to speculative writing in his works of 1837 and 1838, the characteristics of which were discussed in the periodical *Perseus. Journal for den spekulative Idé* (Perseus, Journal for the Speculative Idea), which he edited. In the fairy-tale comedy *Fata Morgana* (1838), which addresses the issue of the false and illusory nature of reality, Heiberg once again gave form to a genre he himself had defined, in this case the speculative comedy, which he now placed at the top of the hierarchy of the development of literary genres, since it was now possible to take one more step further away from specific settings and topical themes and up the path toward the realization of ideas. While other literatures used content to suggest ideas, speculative literature is characterized by particular ideas referring to general or universal ideas. This same distinction is seen in the title of his 1832 guide to the lectures of the Royal Military Academy. In Heiberg's idealism, ideas are conceived as objective determinants in relation to individuals and phenomena.

Neither *Fata Morgana* nor *Syvsoverdag* (Day of the Seven Sleepers, 1840), a *Festspiel,* met with success on the stage. In 1839 Heiberg was named censor at the Royal Theater, freeing him from a portion of his translation duties. His popularity had dwindled, in part because of his many conservative commentaries in the revived *Kjøbenhavns flyvende Post* that addressed the early democratic developments related to the 1834 establishment in Denmark of four provincial consultative chambers (or assemblies). His *Nye Digte* (New Poems, 1841) was composed in the manner of Oehlenschläger's *Digte* (1803), with lyric, epic, and dramatic sections. The dra-

Administration buildings of the Royal Theater in Copenhagen, with the theater itself on the left. Heiberg was named resident playwright and translator at the theater in 1828, censor in 1839, and director in 1849 (painting by Danser, circa 1860; Theater Museum; from Morten Borup, Johan Ludvig Heiberg, *volume 1, 1947; William T. Young Library, University of Kentucky).*

matic section of *Nye Digte* consists of the apocalyptic comedy *En Sjæl efter Døden* (translated as *A Soul After Death,* 1991), in which the new politicians find themselves in a hellish state, "den slette uendelighed" (false eternity), where everything is repeated without end. As hell is on Earth, so also is heaven, of which Heiberg writes in the lyric poems. He now viewed Protestantism as a religion in which God and thought are one.

In the four issues of Heiberg's *Intelligensblade* (Intelligence Papers, 1842–1844) the reader is informed of the masses' lack of both the ability and the right to pass judgment on spiritual matters. The shift in public interest from literature and philosophy to the political and material became the object of Heiberg's contempt and the target of his satire in *Danmark, et malerisk Atlas* (Denmark, a Pictorial Atlas, 1842), and in the satyr play *Nøddeknækkerne* (The Nutcrackers, 1844). His own path became the resumption of his scientific interests, which now focused on astronomy. He shared a birthday with his role model, Tycho Brahe, and he published in three volumes the yearbook *Urania* (1843–1845), which included astronomical articles as well as longer pieces on Hven, the island site of Brahe's Uraniborg, and Sophie Brahe, the astronomer's sister. In the anonymously produced *Valgerda* (1847), Heiberg's only modern comedy, he rises above the conflicts between liberals and conservatives. In this play the woman question is put to debate, and Heiberg was later to awaken a stir when he came out in support of improving women's social status by editing Mathilde Fibiger's *Tolv Breve* (Twelve Letters, 1851), published under the pseudonym Clara Raphael.

When control of the Royal Theater was to be turned over to the state in 1849 as a consequence of the transition from absolutism to a democratic constitutional monarchy, Heiberg was named its new director. Torn between the conflicting demands of politicians, Heiberg held this position for seven stormy years. Although he gained power, his views on the theater now exerted only a meager influence. In addition, there were problems associated with his being married to the leading actress of the day. After his dismissal in June 1856, Heiberg was again named censor, but he used his final years for travel and scientific pursuits. His 1857 poem "De samle sig lig underfulde Drømme" (They Gather like Marvelous Dreams), a memorial to Ida

Brun, was published in *Adresseavisen,* a modest neighborhood paper consisting largely of advertisements, in order to mock the political press.

As a natural scientist Heiberg remained an amateur. As a philosopher his greatest effort, aside from his comprehension of the Hegelian system, was the establishment of a formalist approach to literary aesthetics, which made possible the systematic analysis and evaluation of texts. He created this approach somewhat before Hegel himself worked out such a system, and the aesthetic systems of the two philosophers are indeed distinct from one another, as their tastes differed greatly. Heiberg's second great accomplishment, achieved through his roles as playwright, translator, dramatist, censor, and director of the Royal Theater, was his development of an elegant new form of comedy, which allowed the tradition of Holberg to continue. Abstractionism is Heiberg's distinguishing mark as well as his strength, but it is also his weakness, for his interests in psychology and history remain sparsely developed, so that his assessments of poetry in certain instances seem unreasonable. In Heiberg's third major achievement, his superb taste and sense of structure, combined with Hegel's dialectic, became the standard of Danish Hegelianism, which found adherents among poets and exerted a strong influence in the academy among theologians, humanists, and lawyers in the period before and during the transition to democracy. With his wife, Johanne Luise, Heiberg's final contribution was to provide for his contemporaries the ideal image of a tasteful family life. Søren Kierkegaard called the Heiberg circle "Familen" (The Family) and stated that "Hos ham mødtes ved middagsbordet ikke færre end de tre gratier, men ikke flere end de ni muser" (At his place no fewer than the three Graces met at the dinner table, but no more than the nine Muses). With Georg Brandes and the Modern Breakthrough, Heiberg's influence in aesthetics and literary criticism came to an abrupt end, but Danish academics have owed much to his focus on form and genre.

Letters:

Breve fra og til Johan Ludvig Heiberg (Copenhagen: C. A. Reitzel, 1862);

Fra det Heibergske Hjem. Johan Ludvig og Johanne Luise Heibergs indbyrdes Brevveksling, edited by Aage Friis (Copenhagen: J. H. Schultz, 1940);

Heibergske Familiebreve, edited by Morten Borup (Copenhagen: Gyldendal, 1943);

Breve og Aktstykker vedrørende Johan Ludvig Heiberg, 5 volumes, edited by Borup (Copenhagen: Gyldendal, 1946–1950).

Bibliographies:

Thomas Hansen Erslew, *Almindeligt Forfatter-Lexicon for Kongeriget Danmark med tilhørende Bilande, 1814–1840,* volume 1 (Copenhagen: Forlagsforeningen, 1843);

Erslew, *Almindeligt Forfatter-Lexicon for Kongeriget Danmark med tilhørende Bilande fra før 1814 tuk 1840. Supplement indtil Udgangen af Aaret 1853,* volume 1 (Copenhagen: Forlagsforeningen, 1858), pp. 739–743.

Biography:

Morten Borup, *Johan Ludvig Heiberg,* 3 volumes (Copenhagen: Gyldendal, 1947–1949).

References:

Vilhelm Andersen, "Den heibergske Skoles Naturopfattelse," in his *Danske Studier* (Copenhagen: Gad, 1893), pp. 96–171;

Georg Brandes, *Samlede Skrifter,* volume 1: *Danske Personligheder* (Copenhagen: Gyldendal, 1899);

Henning Fenger, *The Heibergs,* translated and edited by Frederick J. Marker (New York: Twayne, 1971);

Johanne Luise Heiberg, *Et Liv gjenoplevet i Erindringen,* 4 volumes, edited by Adolf Ditlev Jørgensen (Copenhagen: Gyldendal, 1891–1892);

Heiberg, "Peter Andreas Heiberg og Thomasine Gyllembourg," *Museum. Tidsskrift for Historie og Geografi,* 1 (1890);

Torben Krogh, *Heibergs Vaudeviller. Studier over Motiver og Melodier* (Copenhagen: P. Branner, 1942);

Paul V. Rubow, *Dansk litterær Kritik i det nittende Aarhundrede indtil 1870* (Copenhagen: Levin & Munksgaard, 1921), pp. 150–174;

Frederik Schyberg, *Dansk Teaterkritik indtil 1914* (Copenhagen: Gyldendal, 1937), pp. 155–216;

Niels Birger Wamberg, *H. C. Andersen og Heiberg. Åndsfrænder og Åndsfjender* (Copenhagen: Politiken, 1971).

Papers:

Johan Ludvig Heiberg's manuscripts are in the Danish Royal Library and in the National Archives in Copenhagen.

Johanne Luise Heiberg

(22 November 1812 – 21 December 1890)

Lanae H. Isaacson

BOOKS: *Peter Andreas Heiberg og Thomasine Christine Gyllembourg: En Beretning støttet paa Efterladte Breve,* 2 volumes, edited by Heiberg (Copenhagen: Gyldendal, 1882); enlarged and edited by Aage Friits and Just Rahbek (Copenhagen: Gyldendal, 1947);

Et Liv gjenoplevet i Erindringen, 4 volumes, edited by A. D. Jørgensen (Copenhagen: Gyldendal, 1891–1892); *Et Liv gjenoplevet i Erindringen,* 4 volumes, enlarged and edited by Aage Friits (Copenhagen: Gyldendal, 1944); *Et Liv genoplevet i Erindringen,* 3 volumes, enlarged and edited by Niels Birger Wamberg (Copenhagen: Gyldendal, 1973–1974); "Memories of Taglioni and Elssler," from *Et Liv gjenoplevet i Erindringen,* pp. 276–280, translated by Patricia McAndrew in *Dance Chronicle,* 14, no. 1 (1918): 14–18.

Edition and Collection: *Af hendes Levnedsbog,* edited by Niels Heltberg (Copenhagen: Hasselbach, 1968).

PLAY PRODUCTIONS: *En Søndag paa Amager. Vaudeville i en Akt,* Copenhagen, Det Kongelige Teater, 5 March 1848;

Abekatten. Vaudeville i 1 Act, Copenhagen, Det Kongelige Teater, 1 May 1849;

En Sommeraften: Vaudeville i een Act, Det Kongelige Teater, 30 March 1853.

OTHER: *Johan Ludvig Heibergs Samlede Skrifter. Poetiske Skrifter,* 11 volumes, edited by Johanne Luise Heiberg (Copenhagen: C. A. Reitzel, 1862);

Digte, in Just Rahbek, *Omkring Johanne Luise Heiberg* (Copenhagen: Gyldendal, 1948);

Johanne Luise Heibergs tanker ved et slambad, edited by Niels Birger Wamburg (Fredriksberg: Jørgen Fisker, 1986).

SELECTED PERIODICAL PUBLICATIONS–UNCOLLECTED: "Mode-Artikel, Meddeelt af en Dame," *Intelligensblade,* 4 (1844): 90–96;

Lithograph by W. Tegner, 1848; courtesy of the Danish Royal Library, Copenhagen

"Resultaterne," as Anonymous, *Kjøbenhavnsposten,* 11 August 1858; republished in Rahbek, *Omkring Johanne Luise Heiberg* (Copenhagen: Gyldendal, 1948), pp. 100–102;

"Om Huusvæsenet og Pigebørns Opdragelse," as Spectatrix, *Ugentlige Blade* (1859): 188–192, 201–204;

"Quinde-Emancipation," as Oculus, in Just Rahbek, *Omkring Johanne Luise Heiberg* (Copenhagen: Gyldendal, 1948), pp. 90–99;

"Tag ikke i Huset hos dine Børn," as Oculus, in Rahbek, *Omkring Johanne Luise Heiberg* (Copenhagen: Gyldendal, 1948), pp. 103–116.

Johanne Luise Heiberg rose from obscurity, a harrowing childhood, and extreme poverty to become the preeminent actress of her day at Det Kongelige Teater (the Royal Theatre), Copenhagen. In addition to her many stage roles, Heiberg took on the role of exponent for the literary aesthetics of her husband–critic, playwright, and poet Johan Heiberg–and of his mother, Thomasine Gyllembourg, also an author. In the first decades of the nineteenth century, Thomasine Gyllembourg and Johan Heiberg set the cultural tone, and, by marrying into the tightly connected unit of mother and son, Johanne Luise Heiberg was expected to echo Heiberg taste and form, to maintain a certain reserve, and to hold her own passions in check. She consistently did so in everyday life, living an illusion of harmony that obscured her own individuality and replaced her emotional self–the self glimpsed in *Et Liv gjenoplevet i Erindringen* (A Life Relived in Memory, 1891–1892)–with an embittered woman who knew lifelong isolation within an offstage drama.

Johanne Luise Heiberg's claim to a niche in Danish literary history rests with her four-volume autobiography and memoirs, *Et Liv gjenoplevet i Erindringen,* cryptically referred to as *Et Liv genopløjet i Erindringen* (A Life Re-lied in Memory) by critics and a reading public who believed that Heiberg had lied her way through life, despite her incessant insistence on God as her witness and on the veracity of her life as she wrote (and relived) it. In her article "At være en anden og dog sig selv" (To Be Another and Oneself, 1998), about *Et Liv gjenoplevet i Erindringen,* Karin Sanders suggests that Johanne Heiberg used her extraordinary dramatic genius to create "*scenisk illusion*" (scenic illusion) and stage her own life; to perform her life story by writing; and, to have the all-important final say in the wins and losses of her long life. Written over a period of nearly thirty years (from 1855 to 1882), *Et Liv gjenoplevet i Erindringen* includes an account of a hardscrabble childhood and descriptions of the flowering of early womanhood, with notes on the *"Lys og Skygge"* (light and shadow) of her nature; depictions of the glories of Denmark's Golden Age (circa 1800–1850) and portraits of remarkable individuals; essays on dramatic art, its ethical minefields and personal perils; an unequivocal defense of Heiberg aesthetics and angry attacks on those who explored new artistic and literary possibilities; and a long look at the tragic effects of isolation and the walls of hatred and guilt that Johanne Heiberg built. *Et Liv gjenoplevet i Erindringen* serves several ends: the work conveys a deliberate image of harmony within the Gyllembourg-Heiberg circle; it allows for the performance of a drama in which Johanne either unfetters the dark side of her nature or exercises control, at her discretion; it provides a strident defense of Johan Heiberg's aesthetics while describing the difficulties he faced as director of the Royal Theatre (1849–1856); and finally, it records the tragedy of a cultural and ethnic outsider trapped by social conventions and prejudice.

Johanne Luise Pätges was born 22 November 1812 in the Nørrebro District of Copenhagen. She was the second youngest of the nine children born to humble German immigrants Christian Heinrich Pätges and Henriette Hartwig. Christian Heinrich Pätges had fled Cologne and military service for an apprenticeship to a wine merchant in Copenhagen. He did not succeed in managing a business of his own, so he turned to innkeeping for others. Henriette Hartwig was made of sterner stuff, and, because of her Jewish heritage, Johanne both revered her resourceful mother, the woman who took over when her husband failed to create order from chaos, and at the same time despised Henriette's Jewishness, the dark cloud always lingering on the horizon and forcing Johanne to play the role of outsider. Anti-Semitism was prevalent in Denmark during much of the nineteenth century, and the actress remained ambivalent about her heritage, never able to reconcile being both Jewish and Danish.

As young children, Johanne and her younger sister Amalie attended Zangenberg's Dance School in Aalborg, where Henriette Hartwig Pätges kept the family going by operating a restaurant for the Second Jutlandic Regiment. Johanne became something of a protégée, and, when the family returned to Copenhagen in 1820, she won an introduction to Carl Dahlén, a solo dancer with the Royal Danish Ballet. Dahlén quickly recognized Johanne's talent and helped both her and her sister to gain admission to the Royal Danish Ballet School. According to the account in *Et Liv gjenoplevet i Erindringen,* Johanne and Amalie were always close but different in temperament: Johanne was a shy, sensitive girl who burst into tears at the slightest criticism or even the faintest praise. Amalie, on the other hand, was less talented, less agile, and less bothered by the slights–real or imagined–of the other ballet pupils. Because of her epilepsy, Amalie lagged behind Johanne and embarrassed her older sister by frequent seizures.

As the two youngest girls grew up, the Pätges family acquired a tutor, Johan Gebhard Harboe (Herman in *Et Liv gjenoplevet i Erindringen*), and from him they received ordinary schooling and financial support. However, things got out of hand as Johanne approached young womanhood: Harboe, thirteen years Johanne's senior, transformed into a persistent suitor, much to the

Johanne Luise Pätges in 1827 (miniature by C. Petersen; Museum of National History at Frederiksborg Castle; from Bodil Wamberg, Johanne Luise Heiberg: Kærlighedens stedbarn, 1987; *Alderman Library, University of Virginia)*

young girl's dismay. The tumult caused by Harboe's relentless pursuit of Johanne eventually led to her removal from her home and her brief stay with actress Anna Wexschall and her violinist husband, F. T. Wexschall. On 29 March 1829, the despondent Harboe committed suicide. Harboe's sister Arentine, however, later proved a loyal friend to Johanne.

On 22 April 1826, Johanne Luise Pätges made her official acting debut as Trine Nar in Johan Heiberg's *Aprilsnarrene* (1826; translated as *The April Fools,* 1999). The playwright attended the initial performance, for which Pätges received critical acclaim and accolades for her role in the piece. The play led Pätges to leave the ballet and concentrate on acting, even though she remained a devoted dancer all her life. She continued to perform in Johan Heiberg's vaudevilles and comedies, in roles Heiberg created for her–Christina in *Et Eventyr i Rosenborg Have* (An Adventure in Rosenborg Gardens, 1827); Caroline in *De uadskillige* (The Inseparables, 1827); Agnete in *Elverhøi* (Elves' Hill, 1828); and, the title role in *Prindsesse Isabella* (1829). Clearly, Johanne Luise Pätges had caught Johan Ludvig Heiberg's eye, for ingenues invariably caught the eye of *l'enfant,* as Heiberg's mother called him; and, he began to court this actress twenty years his junior. Still shy of engagements and marriage, Pätges rebuffed the playwright. However, on 28 April 1830, she moved to the Christianshavn home of Heiberg's mother, Thomasine Gyllembourg. In this home, Pätges's dark side of wild passions, longings, and impulses ran counter to Heiberg reserve. Pätges was well aware of–even frightened by–her own demons; as she said in *Et Liv gjenoplevet i Erindringen,* "der på bunden af min Sjæl var Dæmoner, jeg måtte vogte mig for" (in the depths of my soul were demons I had to guard myself against).

Johan Heiberg renewed his courtship of the nineteen-year-old actress, and on 31 July 1831, Pätges married the thirty-nine-year-old playwright in Slangerup Kirke. This marriage was a challenging move for a talented, passionate young woman, because a mature artist at the pinnacle of his creative powers and an elderly woman whose strange and strong ties to her son meant that the ostensibly harmonious household of three endured with considerable tension below the surface. (Johanne Luise Heiberg's article "Tag ikke i Huset hos dine Børn" [Do Not Go to Live with Your Children, 1858] warns parents against living with their adult children. Johanne Luise Heiberg felt warm affection for her mother-in-law; however, she was also aware of a fierce competition between Thomasine and herself for the love of Heiberg.)

During the 1830s and 1840s, Johanne Heiberg's acting career blossomed, just as Johan Heiberg scored success with his plays. Johanne starred in role after role on the stage, where plays allowed a venue for her inner passions. Her triumphs quickly made her the toast of Copenhagen, as playwrights wrote leading roles just for her, and she took on greater artistic challenges; her parts included Lotte in *Amors Genistreger* (Cupid's Strokes of Genius, 1830) and Jolanthe in *Kong Renes Datter* (King René's Daughter, 1845), by Henrik Hertz; Marie in *Alferne* (The Elves, 1835), Nina in *Nej* (No, 1836), and the title role in *Valgerda* (1847), by Heiberg. These parts also included the title role in Adam Oehlenschläger's *Dina* (1842) and Juliet (opposite Michael Wiehe) in the 1847 production of William Shakespeare's *Romeo and Juliet* (written circa 1595; first printed in 1597).

On the home front, Johanne Heiberg played the refined hostess for the *læseballer* (literary dance parties) that drew artists, writers, and poets to the Gyllembourg-Heiberg home. Of course, Heiberg played the role of Pygmalion, creating plays for his young actress/wife/Muse and molding her as surely as though she were made of clay–his clay. Their relationship was entirely in Johan Heiberg's hands; increasingly, Johanne Heiberg's opinions echoed those of her husband. Scenes from *Et Liv gjenoplevet i Erindringen* suggest the temper of the times and the undercurrent of passion welling up and approaching open expression in the younger Johanne but held in check, only vetted on the stage and in a written retrospective, described by literary critic Mette Winge as "omfortolket" (re-interpreted).

By 1842, severe depression, overwork, and the loneliness of living within the Gyllembourg-Heiberg regime caught up with Johanne Heiberg. She also gave in to a real passion–for Michael Wiehe, a promising actor eight years her junior. Wiehe was beginning to make his mark as a lyrical hero, and Johanne took him on as her protégé, commending his lyrical style, his melancholy and moodiness, his appealing shyness and quiet determination. Every time she played opposite Wiehe, Johanne lived an illusion of love on the stage of the Royal Theatre; she found what Sanders terms "en forløsning for den passion, hun så skarpt må afgrænse i det virkelige liv" (a release for the passion she had to limit so sharply in real life); then, finally, years later, she reperformed the love and veiled passion in writing *Et Liv gjenoplevet i Erindringen.* Her memoirs suggest that Wiehe shared her passion, at least onstage, but that he could only respond to *her* as a stage lover. By her accounts, the pair made something special happen on the stage, and Johanne made it happen again in her illusory, reconfigured written life. In the 1850s, Wiehe joined his boyhood friend, actor F. L. Høedt, in forming a new company and resigned from the Royal Theatre; at that point, Johanne lamented the loss of Wiehe's fine acting talent to Høedt, someone she described in *Et Liv gjenoplevet i Erindringen* as wily and conniving.

By the late 1840s, Johan Heiberg's isolation within the Gyllembourg-Heiberg home was complete: he usually retreated to his study and his less than stellar work on astronomy. Once again, Johanne Heiberg lost her husband, not to Thomasine Gyllembourg, but to nightly astronomical observations–to his written thesis, *Urania* (1844–1846). To while away her own hours of leisure, Heiberg began composing songs and lighthearted vaudevilles that contrasted with her own deep despair. She duly submitted three such "duftvaudeviller" (light vaudevilles) to her husband for approval, and all three–*En Søndag paa Amager* (Sunday on Amager, 1848), *Abekatten* (The Monkey, 1849), and *En Sommeraften* (Summer Evening, 1853)–were performed and well received at the Royal Theatre. Johanne Heiberg struck an especially responsive chord with her portraits of Lisbet and Jokum from *En Søndag paa Amager.*

For many years, Johan Heiberg had been routinely passed over for the directorship of the Royal Theatre: his sterling literary pedigree and his many contributions to the theater seemed to make him the logical choice. Finally in 1849, he secured the appointment, and a seven-year nightmare, what has been referred to as "Teaterkrige" (theater wars), began. In her tortured third volume of *Et Liv gjenoplevet i Erindringen,* Johanne Heiberg makes clear that her husband was unfairly treated; her work is a refrain to that effect. But the real injustice to her husband stemmed from the delay in securing the post, for other literary lights were now shining more brightly than his. Johanne Heiberg offers a telling comment on what happened: As a boy, Johan Heiberg played with marionettes; he moved wooden (pawn) figures on a marionette stage that he controlled completely. At long last, his wife relates, his childhood dream was on the verge of becoming reality: "Dukkerne var forvandlede til levende Mennesker og Vennekredsen til et stort Publikum. Som han havde elsket sine små tavse Skuespillere, således elskede han nu de store levende" (The dolls were transformed into living people, and the circle of friends into a large audience. Just as he had loved his small, silent actors, so did he now love the large living ones). But the actors on the stage between 1849 and 1856 were not silent pawns for him to move and change at will; they were partners and artists in performances, with ideas of their own and with a new willingness to experiment with realistic drama. Both Johanne and Johan Heiberg misread the signs of the times and set themselves up for the constant dissension Johanne Heiberg describes in her work; true to Heiberg aesthetics, Johanne Heiberg launched a fierce counterattack in her memoirs: former friends such as Anna (Wexschall) Nielsen, who welcomed Wiehe into her inner circle, and C. C. Hall, who eventually sought Johan Heiberg's resignation from the Royal Theatre (finally submitted on 21 June 1856), became the focus of all Johanne Heiberg's ire. Truth be told, her husband had reached the end of his career long before he took over the directorship; he no longer set the trends as he had done in the early years of the century; he could no longer command acceptance of an outdated Romanticism in drama, what Mette Winge describes as "en ophøjet, idealiserende kunst" (a lofty, idealizing art).

As he often did, Johan Heiberg responded by turning to flirtations. In 1850, writer Mathilde Fibiger contacted the fifty-nine-year-old Heiberg with an unusual request: she proposed that Heiberg edit *Tolv Breve* (Twelve Letters), a protest work written under the pseudonym Clara Raphael; considering Fibiger's attack on the prevailing patriarchy in Denmark and her insistence on women's independence, one marvels at her approach to the reactionary Heiberg. Heiberg cautioned Fibiger concerning her incendiary ideas, but he agreed to edit the work. Fibiger struck a chord with Heiberg, just as Johanne had twenty years before, and through letters he was off again, until a meeting during Christmas 1850 ended the paper romance. With her discussion of the difficulties women faced in combining work and a relationship, Fibiger also provoked a firestorm in Johanne Heiberg, who angrily attacked *Tolv Breve* and Fibiger's advocacy of independence in an unpublished article, "Quinde-Emancipation" (Women's Liberation, 1851). Johanne Heiberg's subsequent articles, "*Ogsaa et Ord om Quindens Huuslige Dyder*" (Also a Word concerning the Domestic Virtues of Women, 1857) and "*Om Huusvæsenet og Pigebørns Opdragelse*" (On the Institution of the Home and the Education of Girls, 1859), also expressed her strikingly conservative views on the roles of women and on appropriate education for girls. (Johanne Heiberg's ideas on education had dire consequences for the three girls she later adopted, for she did nothing to help them hone their talents or find rewarding uses for their intellectual and personal skills.)

Throughout her long life Johanne Heiberg carried on extensive correspondence with mentors, colleagues, family members, and friends. Her letters to and from her associates often take on a cordial tone, and she includes letters, salutations, official commendations, and celebratory or praise poems among the pages of *Et Liv gjenoplevet i Erindringen.* During the summer of 1832, for example, the Heibergs, Thomasine Gyllembourg, and their close friend, deaf playwright Henrik Hertz, abandoned Copenhagen for a country idyll in Hirschholm. The summer proved a rainy one, but between downpours, the Heibergs and Hertz reveled in the peaceful countryside; they made the most of country evenings–singing songs by the Swedish lyricist/composer Carl Michael Bellman and composing new poems (in Hertz's case, *De Hirschholmske Digte* [The Hirschholm Poems]) and talking art, music, and poetry far into the night. Later, Hertz sent the Heibergs the poem "Hyacintherne" (The Hyacinths) in memory of the Hirschholm or Bellman Summer, and Johanne Heiberg included the poem in her chapter on Hirschholm 1832.

The correspondence between the Heibergs is another matter, an illustration of what Heiberg scholar Bodil Wamberg termed "fjernheden i nærværet, og nærværet i fjernheden" (distance in proximity, and proximity in distance). The letters between the couple, written in 1854–1855 when Johanne first visited Marienbad to receive treatment for serious illness, then continued on to further cures in Franzenbad, were included in *Fra det Heibergske Hjem: Johan Ludvig og Johanne Luise Heibergs indbyrdes Brevveksling* (From the Heiberg Home: Johan Ludvig and Johanne Luise Heiberg's Mutual Correspondence, 1940). Behind the facade of an undying union the Heibergs became what modern critics describe as distant. They faced inner and outer forces that kept pushing them together and pulling them apart, so much so that they struggled when they were apart (principally because Johan Heiberg lost control of his wife) and struggled when they were together (essentially because Johan Heiberg insisted on reserve within the relationship). Not being able to live together–or apart–is hardly equivalent to absence making the heart grow fonder or bridging distance or finding intimacy, as Johanne Heiberg discovered. The letters between the Heibergs illustrate the kind of impasse the couple constantly faced. Johan Heiberg's response was his usual retreat from the passion inherent in her artistic genius, from what he dismissed as "exaltation." His cool admonitions always won the day over his wife's search for intimacy and passion.

On 17 February 1855 Johanne Heiberg began to work on her memoirs, the work that became *Et Liv gjenoplevet i Erindringen* and occupied her until 1882. Because the work took so long to write (from 1855 to 1882) and covered an even longer time span (1812–1882), *Et Liv gjenoplevet i Erindringen* underwent many changes in style, tone, and format; these changes are especially true for the difficult–and definitely less engaging–third volume, concerning Johan Heiberg's tenure at the Royal Theatre; Johanne Heiberg kept revising the volume, even as she worked on the fourth and final book, and censors edited various tendentious, overly harsh passages out of the volume in preparation for the posthumous publication Johanne stipulated.

Johanne Heiberg began writing *Et Liv gjenoplevet i Erindringen* in an effort to understand why things had turned out as they had, why she had made the choices she had, why the "wild nature" so essential to her art and performances onstage had brought her so much pain and loneliness offstage. The self-portrait Johanne Heiberg cultivates and creates early on in her writing is of an artistic genius with a sensitive soul, an outsider deeply ambivalent about her Jewish heritage and guilty, almost afraid, of the good fortune coming her way. By joining the Gyllembourg-Heiberg family, Johanne courted disaster, giving up in real life the passion so essential to the illusory life of the theater. *Et Liv gjenoplevet i Erindringen* recovers that passion, this time as a performance of her life and its fiction, the "udprægede romantræk" (marked qualities of the novel) in a different setting, mode, and moment. Since Johanne was still active onstage when she began writing *Et Liv gjenoplevet i Erindringen,* her own performance in writing influenced the life she continued to lead as a kind of interplay between the person she had been, the one she was becoming by writing, and the fiction she was making of her life. Johanne Heiberg began writing her chef d'oeuvre when things were changing in her personal life. After a lingering illness, Thomasine Gyllembourg died on 1 July 1856, and, finally relieved of his duties for the Royal Theatre, Heiberg left, then died on 25 August 1860. Johanne Heiberg remained active on the stage, even as her husband retreated; she still won over theater critics and the public. She resigned from the Royal Theatre in July 1857 but soon discovered that she missed her work, so she returned on 5 October 1859 as Lady Teazle in Richard Brinsley Sheridan's *School for Scandal* (first performed 1777). The audience to her performance was as enthusiastic as ever, but the gala occasion was marred by Johan Heiberg's absence and ill health. Johanne Heiberg completed the first volume of *Et Liv gjenoplevet i Erindringen* (1812–1842) in August 1860, coinciding with her husband's death. A four-year break in her writing ensued; she resumed work on the second book of her memoirs (1842–1849) in 1864 and finished in 1867. In the meantime, from 1860 to 1864, she remained busy; she was motivated, never at a loss for activity. She continued her acting career with Friedrich von Schiller's *Maria Stuart* (1800), which opened on 13 January 1861; she began editing her husband's *Samlede Skrifter. Poetiske Skrifter* (Collected Writings. Poetic Writings, 1862); she moved to a new home in the Copenhagen suburbs; and, with the help of Arentine Harboe, she adopted three abandoned girls from the West Indies–Sarah, Lelia, and Anna. Johanne had always felt a special link to small children, so much so that she regretted never having had children with Johan Heiberg. She did manage to provide a close, loving home for the three girls in Copenhagen, though her views on education marred their future significantly.

Shortly after the death of her husband, Johanne Heiberg acquired a mentor and surrogate father for the girls–her neighbor, the former minister of the interior, Andreas Frederik Krieger. Krieger was Johanne's correspondent, companion, and advisor, someone who knew the actress as well or better than anyone else–perhaps even better than Johan Heiberg. The remarkable correspondence between the two neighbors, *Johanne Luise Heiberg og Andreas Frederik Krieger: En Samling Breve 1860–1889* (Johanne Luise Heiberg and Andreas Frederik Krieger: A Collection of Letters, 1860–1889) was published in 1914 and 1915.

Johanne Heiberg brought her long acting career to an end with a performance of Johan Heiberg's *Elverhøi* on 2 June 1864. Ever active and engaged, she turned to teaching for the Royal Theatre (1867–1874). In 1869 she resumed work on *Et Liv gjenoplevet i Erindringen,* specifically on the "war years" between Johan Heiberg's appointment to the Royal Theatre and his resignation. Johanne worked on the third volume until 1876–constantly revising, and defending Heiberg's aesthetics and decisions for the Royal Theatre. The third volume of *Et Liv gjenoplevet i Erindringen* is regrettably an endless diatribe and defense of values no longer part of Danish cultural life and an outright attack on those who dared to explore new possibilities for literature, poetry, and drama. The fourth and final volume of *Et Liv gjenoplevet i Erindringen* includes an essay questioning the moral value–if any–of such an ephemeral art as acting, "Er Skuespilkunsten en Moralsk berettiget Kunst?" (Is the Art of Acting a Morally Justified Art? 1869). (Johanne Luise Heiberg frequently questioned the lasting value of acting performances as well as the effect of acting on the morals of actors. She concluded that acting might have a more deleterious effect on men, who were usually not as accustomed to public display as women.) The final volume of her memoirs begins with the death of Thomasine Gyllembourg (1856) and concludes with her own seventieth birthday (1882).

Heiberg in 1882 (photograph by Hansen and Weller; courtesy of the Danish Royal Library, Copenhagen)

Increasingly, Johanne Luise Heiberg turned to religious redemption and signs of divine intervention and providence. She consulted Bishop Hans L. Martensen as a spiritual guide, but he never managed to influence her as deeply as Krieger. In 1882, Martensen and Johanne Heiberg both published books dealing with Thomasine Gyllembourg. Martensen's memoir, *Af mit Levnet* (From My Life), includes an angry, bitter attack on Thomasine Gyllembourg's *En Hverdags-Historie* (An Everyday Story, 1828), her worldliness, and her decision to divorce her husband. Clearly, Martensen found Thomasine guilty of unforgivable moral transgressions, beyond all hope of redemption. Johanne concluded her essay and edition of the correspondence between Peter Heiberg and Thomasine Gyllembourg, *Peter Andreas Heiberg og Thomasine Christine Gyllembourg: En Beretning støttet paa Efterladte Breve* (Peter Andreas Heiberg and Thomasine Christine Gyllembourg: An Account Supported by Surviving Letters), an effort to come to terms with the Heibergs as a family, as *her* family, with a call for the compassion Thomasine Gyllembourg had shown others. Johanne Luise Heiberg's remarkable life ended on 21 December 1890 in Copenhagen.

Et Liv gjenoplevet i Erindringen reveals all the conflicts Johanne Heiberg faced in her work as an actress and in her private life. As the last of the Heibergs, she depicts and defends the cultural values of a bygone era; she remains true to the past, but also documents the beginning of a new age.

Letters:

Johanne Luise Heiberg og Andreas Frederik Krieger: En Samling Breve 1860–1889, 2 volumes, edited by Aage Friits and P. Munch (Copenhagen: Gyldendal, 1914, 1915);

Fra det Heibergske Hjem: Johan Ludvig og Johanne Luise Heibergs indbyrdes Brevveksling, edited by Friits (Copenhagen: Schultz, 1940);

Heibergske Familiebreve, edited by Morten Borup (Copenhagen: Gyldendal/Nordisk Forlag, 1943);

Breve fra og til Johanne Luise Heiberg, edited by Just Rahbek (Copenhagen: Gyldendal, 1955).

Biographies:

Elisabeth Hude, *Johanne Luise Heiberg, 1860–1890* (Copenhagen: Gad, 1961);

Henning Fenger and Frederick J. Marker, *The Heibergs* (New York: Twayne, 1971);

Bodil Wamberg, *Johanne Luise Heiberg: Kærlighedens stedbarn* (Copenhagen: Gad, 1987);

Vibeke Schroder, *Dæmoni og dannelse: Johanne Luise Heiberg* (Copenhagen: Gyldendal, 1995).

References:

Erik Aschengren, *Fra Trina Nar til Maria Stuart: En Studie i Fru Heibergs Kunst* (Copenhagen: Gad, 1961);

Annalisa Forssberger, *Ekon och speglingar, Studier kring Victoria Benedictsson, Johanne Luise Heiberg och Herman Bang* (Stockholm: Rabén & Sjögren, 1961);

Ole A. Hedegaard, *Johanne Luise Heiberg og krigen 1864: en militær- og personalhistorisk studie* (Frederikssund: Thorsgaard, 1991);

Elisabeth Hude, *Johanne Luise Heiberg og J. C. Jacobsen* (Copenhagen: Gad, 1964);

Hude, *Johanne Luise Heiberg og Peter Simonsen* (Copenhagen: Gad, 1959);

Hude, *Johanne Luise Heiberg som brevskriver* (Copenhagen: Gad, 1964);

Jette Lundbo Levy, "Johanne Luise Heiberg: Et kvindeligt redskab i borgerskabets klassekamp," *Teaterarbejde,* 4 (1979): 63–72;

Lise-Lone Marker and Fredrick J. Marker, "Fru Heiberg: A Study of the Art of the Romantic Actor," *Theatre Research,* 13 (1973): 22–27;

Robert Neiiendam, *Johanne Luise Heiberg* (Copenhagen: Nyt Nordisk Forlag/Arnold Busck, 1960);

Neiiendam, *Rivalinder – Johanne Luise Heiberg, Anna Nielsen* (Copenhagen: Slotsholmen: Center for Music, 1955);

Just Rahbek, *Omkring Johanne Luise Heiberg* (Copenhagen: Gyldendal, 1948);

Karin Sanders, "At være en anden og dog sig selv. Johanne Luise Heiberg, *Et Liv Gjenoplevet i Erindringen,*" in *Læsninger i Dansk Litteratur (1820–1900),* 5 volumes (Odense: Odense University, 1998), II: 169–183, 347–348;

Sanders, *Fra Krop til Form. Kvindelig Imagination og den imaginerede Kvindelighed i Romantikken* (Copenhagen: Københavns Universitet, 1981);

Sanders, *Konturer. Skulptur–og Dødsbilleder fra Guldalderlitteraturen* (Copenhagen: Museum Tusculanums Forlag/Københavns Universitet, 1997);

Sanders, "Kvindelighedens skønne Positur. Om Johanne Luise Heiberg," *Nordisk Kvindelitteraturhistorie* (Copenhagen: Rosinante, 1998), pp. 125–134;

Sanders, "Staging the Invisible: From the Scene of Theatre to the Scene of Writing," in *Scandinavica: An International Journal of Scandinavian Studies* (London: Academic Press, 1993), pp. 5–23;

Else Thylstrup, *Kunsten og Kaldet–En Analyse af 3 Danske Kunstneres Selv-Biografier med særligt Henblik på den Kunstneriske Selvforståelse* (Copenhagen: Københavns Universitet, 1987);

Torben Topsøe-Jensen, *Sommeren i Hirschholm 1832* (Hørsholm: Museumsforeningen For Hørsholm og Omegn, 1982);

Mette Winge, "Forfatterportræt: Johanne Luise Heiberg," *Arkiv for Dansk Litteratur* <http://www.adl.dk>.

Papers:

Johanne Luise Heiberg's unpublished poems are in Rigsarkivet (the Royal Danish Archives), Copenhagen; manuscripts and essays, including "Ogsaa Et Ord om Quindens Huuslige Dyder" (1857) and "Er Skuespilkunsten en Moralsk. berettiget Kunst?" (1869), are in Fru Heibergs Arkiv at the Danish Royal Library in Copenhagen.

Ludvig Holberg

(3 December 1684 – 28 January 1754)

Sven Hakon Rossel
University of Vienna

Copperplate by I. M. Bernigeroth, 1757; courtesy of the Danish Royal Library, Copenhagen

BOOKS: *Introduction til de fornemste Europæiske Rigers Historier Fortsat Indtil disse sidste Tider* (Copenhagen: Printed by Johann Jacob Bornheinrich, 1711);

Anhang Til hans Historiske Introduction Eller Underretning Om de Fornemste Europæiske Rigers og Republiqvers Stater (Copenhagen: Printed by Ove Lynnow, 1713);

Moralske Kierne Eller Introduction Til Naturens og Folke-Rettens Kundskab (Copenhagen: Printed by Ove Lynnow, 1715);

Dissertatio V. de historicis Danicis (N.p., 1719);

Dissertatio juridica de nuptiis propinqvorum (N.p., 1719);

En Sandfærdig Ny Wiise Om Peder Paars, as Hans Mickelsen (N.p., [1719–1720]); revised as *Peder Paars Poema Heroico-comicum,* as Mickelsen (N.p., 1720); translated by Bergliot Stromsoe as *Peder Paars* (Lincoln: University of Nebraska Press / New York: American-Scandinavian Foundation, 1962);

Democritus og Heraclitus (N.p., 1721);

4re Skiemte-Digte Med Tvende Fortaler, Samt Zille Hans Dotters Forsvars-Skrift for Qvinde-Kiønned, as Mickelsen (N.p., 1722);

Comoedier Sammenskrevne for Den nye oprettede Danske Skue-Plads, as Mickelsen, 3 volumes (N.p., 1723); comprises *Den politiske Kandestøber,* translated by Oscar J. Campbell and Frederic Scheck as *The Political Tinker,* in *Ludvig Holberg: Comedies* (New York: American-Scandinavian Foundation, 1915); *Den Vægelsindede,* translated by Henry Alexander as *The Weathercock,* in *Four Plays by Holberg* (Princeton: Princeton University Press, 1946); *Jean de France eller Hans Frandsen,* translated by Gerald A. Argetsinger and Sven H. Rossel as *Jean de France; or, Hans Frandsen,* in *Jeppe of the Hill and Other Comedies by Ludvig Holberg* (Carbondale: Southern Illinois University Press, 1990); *Jeppe paa Bierget eller den forvandlede Bonde,* translated by Campbell and Scheck as *Jeppe of the Hill,* in *Ludvig Holberg: Comedies* (New York: American-Scandinavian Foundation, 1915); *Mester Gert Westphaler eller den meget talende Barbeer,* translated by Henry Alexander as *The Talkative Barber,* in *Seven One-Act Plays by Holberg* (Princeton: Princeton University Press, 1950); *Den 11. Juni, Barselstuen, Det arabiske Pulver,* translated by Alexander as *The Arabian Powder,* in *Seven One-Act Plays by Holberg* (Princeton: Princeton University Press, 1950); *Jule-Stue,* translated by Alexander as *The Christmas Party,* in *Seven One-Act Plays by Holberg* (Princeton: Princeton University Press, 1950); *Mascarade,* translated by Alexander as *Masquerades,* in *Four Plays by Holberg* (Princeton: Princeton University Press, 1946); *Jacob von Tyboe eller den stortalende Soldat,* translated by H. W. L. Hime as *Captain Bombastes Thunderton,* in *Ludvig*

Holberg: Three Comedies (London: Longmans, Green, 1912); *Ulysses von Ithacia eller En Tydsk Comedie,* translated by Argetsinger and Rossel as *Ulysses von Ithacia; or, A German Comedy,* in *Jeppe of the Hill and Other Comedies by Ludvig Holberg* (Carbondale: Southern Illinois University Press, 1990); *Kilde-Reysen,* translated by Reginald Spink as *The Healing Spring,* in *Ludvig Holberg: Three Comedies* (London: Heinemann, 1957); *Melampe,* and *Uden Hoved og Hale;*

Metamorphosis eller Forvandlinger, as Mickelsen (Copenhagen, 1726);

Ad virum perillustrem. Epistola (N.p., 1728); translated as *Memoirs of Lewis Holberg* (London: Hunt & Clarke, 1827);

Dannemarks og Norges Beskrivelse (Copenhagen: Printed by Johan Jørgen Høpffner, 1729); revised as *Dannemarks og Norges Geistlige og Verdslige Staat* (Copenhagen, 1749);

Den Danske Skue-Plads, 5 volumes (N.p., 1731–1754); volumes 1–3 are reprints of the 1723 edition; volumes 4–5 comprise *Henrich og Pernille,* translated by Hime as *Henry and Pernilla,* in *Ludvig Holberg: Three Comedies* (London: Longmans, Green, 1912); *Diderich Menschen-Skræk,* translated by Alexander as *Diderich the Terrible,* in *Seven One-Act Plays by Holberg* (Princeton: Princeton University Press, 1950); *Hexerie eller Blind Allarm, Den pantsatte Bonde-Dreng,* translated by Alexander as *The Peasant in Pawn,* in *Seven One-Act Plays by Holberg* (Princeton: Princeton University Press, 1950); *Erasmus Montanus eller Rasmus Berg,* translated by Campbell and Scheck as *Erasmus Montanus,* in *Ludvig Holberg: Comedies* (New York: American-Scandinavian Foundation, 1915); *Pernilles korte Frøiken-Stand,* translated by Argetsinger and Rossel as *Pernille's Brief Experience as a Lady,* in *Jeppe of the Hill and Other Comedies by Ludvig Holberg* (Carbondale: Southern Illinois University Press, 1990); *De Usynlige,* translated by Alexander as *The Masked Ladies,* in *Four Plays by Holberg* (Princeton: Princeton University Press, 1946); *Den Stundesløse,* translated by Hime as *Scatterbrains,* in *Ludvig Holberg: Three Comedies* (London: Longmans, Green, 1912); and *Den honette Ambition;*

Dannemarks Riges Historie, 3 volumes (Copenhagen: Printed by Johan Jørgen Høpffner, 1732–1735);

Synopsis historiae universalis (Copenhagen: Printed by Johan Jørgen Høpffner, 1733); translated by Gregory Sharpe as *An Introduction to Universal History* (London: Printed for A. Linde, 1755);

Compendium geographicum (Copenhagen: Printed by Johan Jørgen Høpffner, 1733); translated by Sharpe as *A Short System of Geography with Maps, etc.,* in *An Introduction to Universal History* (London: Printed for A. Miller in the Strand, J. Ward in Cornhill, and A. Linde in Catherine-Street, 1758);

Opuscula quaedam latina. Epistola I. Cujus nova haec editio prioribus est emendatior. Epistola II. Quinque libri epigrammatum. Epistola tertia. Epigrammatum liber sextus, 2 volumes (Leipzig: Printed for Hieronymus Christian Paulli's widow, 1737, 1743);

Den berømmelige Norske Handels-Stad Bergens Beskrivelse (Copenhagen: Printed by Johan Jørgen Høpffner, 1737);

Almindelig Kirke-Historie fra Christendommes første Begyndelse til Lutheri Reformation (Copenhagen: Printed by Johan Jørgen Høpffner, 1738);

Adskillige store Heltes og berømmelige Mænds, sær Orientalske og Indianske sammenlignede Historier og Bedrifter, 2 volumes (Copenhagen: Printed by Johan Jørgen Høpffner, 1739);

Nicolai Klimii iter subterraneum (Copenhagen & Leipzig: Printed for Jacob Preuss, 1741); translated as *A Journey to the World Under-Ground by Nicholas Klimius* (London: Printed for T. Astley, 1742);

Jødiske Historie fra Verdens begyndelse, fortsatt til disse Tider, 2 volumes (Copenhagen, 1742);

Moralske Tanker (Copenhagen: Privately printed, 1744);

Adskillige Heltinders og navnkundige Damers sammenlignede Historier (Copenhagen: Printed by Johan Jørgen Høpffner, 1745);

Don Ranudo de Colibrados eller Fattigdom og Hoffærdighed (Copenhagen: Christian Gottlob Mengel, 1745);

Oratio funebris in obitum augustissimi monarchae Frederici Quarti (Copenhagen: Det Berlingske Officin, 1746);

Mindre Poetiske Skrifter (Copenhagen: Ernst Henrich Berling, 1746);

Herodiani Historie (Copenhagen, 1746);

Den Danske Comoedies Ligbegængelse (Copenhagen: Printed by Johan Jørgen Høpffner, 1746); translated by Argetsinger and Rossel as *The Burial of Danish Comedy,* in *Jeppe of the Hill and Other Comedies by Ludvig Holberg* (Carbondale: Southern Illinois University Press, 1990);

Epistler, Befattende Adskillige historiske, politiske, metaphysiske, moralske, philosophiske, Item Skiemtsomme Materier, 5 volumes (Copenhagen, 1748–1754);

Epigrammatum libri septem (Copenhagen & Leipzig: Printed for Otto Christopher Wentzel, 1749);

Moralske Fabler (Copenhagen, 1751);

Lettres de Mr. le Baron de Holberg, qui contient quelques remarques sur les Memoires concernant la reine Christine nouvellement publiés (Leipzig: François Christian Mumme, 1752);

Remarques sur quelques positions, qui se trouvent dans L'esprit des Loix (Copenhagen: Otto Christopher Wentzel, 1753);

Den Danske Skue-Plads, 2 volumes (N.p., 1754); comprises *Plutus eller Proces imellem Fattigdom og Rïigdom, Huus-Spøgelse eller Abracadabra,* and *Den forvandlede Brudgom,* translated by Alexander as *The Changed Bridegroom,* in *Seven One-Act Plays by Holberg* (Princeton: Princeton University Press, 1950); *Don Ranudo de Colibrados eller Fattigdom og Hoffærdighed, Philosophus udi egen Indbildning, Republiqven eller det gemeene Beste,* and *Sganarels Reise til det philosophiske Land,* translated by Alexander as *Sganarel's Journey to the Land of the Philosophers,* in *Seven One-Act Plays by Holberg* (Princeton: Princeton University Press, 1950); and *Artaxerxes.*

Editions and Collections: *Samlede Skrifter,* 18 volumes, edited by Carl S. Petersen (Copenhagen: Gyldendal, 1913–1963);

Memoirer, edited by F. J. Billeskov Jansen (Copenhagen: Schønberg, 1943);

Moralske Tanker, edited by Billeskov Jansen (Copenhagen: H. Hagerup, 1943);

Epistler, 8 volumes, edited by Billeskov Jansen (Copenhagen: H. Hagerup, 1944–1954);

Værker i tolv Bind, 12 volumes, edited by Billeskov Jansen (Copenhagen: Rosenkilde & Bagger, 1969–1971);

Niels Klims underjordiske rejse 1741–1745, translated and edited by A. Kragelund (Copenhagen: Gad, 1970);

Seks komedier, edited by Jens Kr. Andersen (Copenhagen: Det dansk Sprog og Litteraturselskab/Borgen, 1994).

Editions in English: *Three Comedies,* translated by H. W. L. Hime (London: Longmans, Green, 1912);

Comedies, translated by Oscar J. Campbell and Frederic Schenk, introduction by Campbell (New York: American-Scandinavian Foundation, 1915);

Four Plays by Holberg, translated by Henry Alexander (Princeton: Princeton University Press, 1946);

Seven One-Act Plays by Holberg, translated by Alexander (Princeton: Princeton University Press, 1950);

Selected Essays by Ludvig Holberg, translated by P. M. Mitchell, introduction by Mitchell (Lawrence: University of Kansas Press, 1955);

Three Comedies, translated, with an introduction, by Reginald Spink (London: Heinemann, 1957);

Memoirs. An Eighteenth-Century Danish Contribution to International Understanding, edited by Stewart E. Fraser (Leiden: Brill, 1970); comprises *Ad virum perillustrem. Epistola,* volume 1; *Epistola,* volume 2; *Epistola,* volume 3; and Epistle no. 447;

Jeppe of the Hill and Other Comedies by Ludvig Holberg, translated, with an introduction, by Gerald S. Argetsinger and Sven H. Rossel (Carbondale: Southern Illinois University Press, 1990);

Moral Reflections & Epistles, translated by Mitchell (Norwich, U.K.: Norvik Press, 1991).

PLAY PRODUCTIONS: *Den politiske Kandestøber,* Copenhagen, Lille Grønnegade-teatret, 25 September 1722;

Den Vægelsindede, Copenhagen, Lille Grønnegade-teatret, 1722;

Jean de France eller Hans Frandsen, Copenhagen, Lille Grønnegade-teatret, 1722;

Jeppe paa Bierget eller den forvandlede Bonde, Copenhagen, Lille Grønnegade-teatret, 1722;

Den 11. Juni, Copenhagen, Lille Grønnegade-teatret, 11 June 1723;

Barselstuen, Copenhagen, Lille Grønnegade-teatret, October 1723;

Mester Gert Westphaler eller den meget talende Barbeer, Copenhagen, Lille Grønnegade-teatret, 1723;

Jule-Stue, Copenhagen, Lille Grønnegade-teatret, February 1724;

Mascarade, Copenhagen, Lille Grønnegade-teatret, February 1724;

Det arabiske Pulver, Copenhagen, Lille Grønnegade-teatret, 2 May 1724;

Ulysses von Ithacia eller En Tydsk Comedie, Copenhagen, Lille Grønnegade-teatret, June 1724 (?);

Kilde-Reysen, Copenhagen, Lille Grønnegade-teatret, [1 July 1724];

Henrich og Pernille, Copenhagen, Lille Grønnegade-teatret, 1724;

Diderich Menschen-Skræk, Copenhagen, Lille Grønnegade-teatret, 1724;

Jacob von Tyboe eller den stortalende Soldat, Copenhagen, Lille Grønnegade-teatret, Spring 1725;

Den pantsatte Bonde-Dreng, Copenhagen, Lille Grønnegade-teatret, 12 July 1726;

Den Stundesløse, Copenhagen, Lille Grønnegade-teatret, 25 November 1726;

Pernilles korte Frøiken-Stand, Copenhagen, Lille Grønnegade-teatret, 3 February 1727;

Den Danske Comoedies Ligbegængelse, Copenhagen, Lille Grønnegade-teatret, 25 February 1727;

Erasmus Montanus eller Rasmus Berg, Germany 1742; Copenhagen, Det lille Gethus, Kgs. Nytorv, 1747;

*De Usynlige,*Copenhagen, Det lille Gethus, Kgs. Nytorv 1747;

Den honette Ambition Copenhagen, Det lille Gethus, Kgs. Nytorv 1747;

Hexerie eller Blind Allarm, Copenhagen, 1750;

Plutus eller Proces imellem Fattigdom og Riigdom, Copenhagen, Komediehuset [Det kongelige Teater], 14 April 1751;

Sganarels Reise til det philosophiske Land, Copenhagen, Komediehuset [Det kongelige Teater], 1751;

Don Ranudo de Colibrados eller Fattigdom og Hoffærdighed, Copenhagen, Komediehuset [Det kongelige Teater], 30 August 1752;

Huus-Spøgelse eller Abracadabra, Copenhagen, Komediehuset [Det kongelige Teater], 3 November 1752;

Det lykkelige Skibbrud, Copenhagen, Komediehuset [Det kongelige Teater], 3 January 1754;

Republiqven eller det gemeene Beste, Copenhagen, Komediehuset [Det kongelige Teater], 17 April 1754;

Philosophus udi egen Indbildning, Copenhagen, Komediehuset [Det kongelige Teater], 14 August 1754;

Den forvandlede Brudgom, Copenhagen, Det kongelige Teater 1882.

At the beginning of the eighteenth century, Scandinavian literature, with a few exceptions, was almost a century behind the developments abroad. That within a few decades this literature was on par with other European literatures resulted solely from the efforts of one person, Ludvig Holberg, the most important man of letters in eighteenth-century Denmark and Norway. He is often referred to as the "Molière of the North," even though he was as productive as a satirist, historian, and essayist as he was as a playwright. As a true child of the Age of Enlightenment, Holberg advocated tolerance and moderation, but he also transgressed its parameters. He introduced several classical genres but violated their rules, pointing ahead to twentieth-century absurdist drama. He generally supported the status quo of absolute monarchy but sometimes criticized its deficiencies quite openly–in particular when he saw a chance to address the outdated educational system. He also emerged as a modern advocate of women's rights–in fact, as the first Scandinavian feminist.

Holberg never accepted the provincialism of the Dano-Norwegian society of the early 1700s. At the first opportunity, he went abroad on the first of several foreign journeys; upon his return he opened the doors at home to an international and modern cultural scene. Eventually, he became a towering cosmopolitan figure, extremely well read, not only in the classics but also in contemporary literature, fiction as well as nonfiction. He saw himself foremost as a European writer and was strongly influenced by the European intellectual tradition to which he contributed so richly through his critical and probing mind, his audacity in transgressing borders, and, above all, through the artistic quality and modernity found particularly in his comedies.

Ludvig Holberg was born on 3 December 1684 in the northwestern Norwegian town of Bergen, which at that time, with fifteen thousand inhabitants, was a busy and wealthy trade center and the most internationally oriented town in the Dano-Norwegian dual monarchy. His father, Christian Nielsen Holberg, was of peasant stock but had risen to the rank of colonel in the army. His mother, Karen Lem, belonged to a distinguished family of clergymen; she was the granddaughter of a former bishop of Bergen, Ludvig Munthe, after whom Holberg was named. Holberg's father died in 1686, leaving behind six children, of whom Ludvig was the youngest. After the death of his mother in 1695, he was brought up by a wealthy uncle, first attending the German boys' school and later Bergen Cathedral School. When in 1702 a fire broke out that ravaged most of the town, including his uncle's home and the school, Holberg finished his school education in Copenhagen; a few months later, on 20 July 1702, he matriculated–as his two older brothers had done the year before–at the University of Copenhagen, the only university of the dual monarchy.

Penniless, Holberg returned to Bergen soon thereafter and moved on to the village of Voss, earning his living as a tutor and assistant in the house of the local rural dean. In his Latin autobiography he has described how ill suited he was as a teacher and preacher because of his nervous, choleric temperament. After a year, in the fall of 1703, Holberg returned to Copenhagen via Bergen. There he studied French and Italian and in March and April 1704 received degrees in philosophy and theology. Thus, at the age of nineteen and a half he had earned the qualifications needed for a career as a schoolteacher or a clergyman in the Lutheran State Church. Holberg's experience in Voss, however, must have persuaded him not to choose such a career. Moreover, at the time a surplus of bachelors of divinity existed, so he returned instead to Bergen, spending the summer of 1704 tutoring the children of the future bishop of the town, Niels Smed. In his youth Smed had traveled extensively abroad, and Holberg had a chance to read his travel diaries. After reading them, Holberg was seized by a desire to go abroad, and in the fall of 1704, he left Bergen, traveling to the Netherlands, attracted by its international status and reputation as a safe haven for critical, dissenting spirits.

At this point, Holberg showed no interest in those areas of scholarship in which he later distinguished himself–history, natural law, and literature. He did not embark on a traditional educational journey but rather traveled as a curious tourist in order to experience the cosmopolitan and liberal atmosphere and to gain access to a much more sophisticated press than he had encountered at home. Soon he ran out of funds and left Amsterdam by ship in late September on borrowed money, going not to Bergen, where he risked his family's ridicule because of his unsuccessful journey, but to Kristianssand in southern Norway. There he earned enough during the winter of 1705–1706 from tutoring in music (Holberg was an accomplished flautist and violinist) and foreign languages to pay off his debts and put money aside for his next trip. In the spring of 1706 he went to England–never to return to Norway–not to see the tourist sights but to enroll at Oxford University in order to expand his horizon by familiarizing himself with the latest scholarship; the next step was to publish and thereby qualify for an academic career. The primitive library conditions in Denmark made a study trip abroad necessary for any ambitious student, and at that time Oxford, with its famous Bodleian Library, was the place to go. England, moreover, was admired by the philosophers of the Enlightenment because of its prevailing critical attitude toward authoritarian thinking. Holberg's memoirs and his continued fascination with England attest to his having enjoyed his two-and-a-half-year stay immensely, admired by his fellow students for his excellent command of Latin and for his musical talent. To what extent Holberg familiarized himself with English literature during his stay is unclear. After all, he was contemporary with such prolific writers as Jonathan Swift and Daniel Defoe. Clearly, however, he received no inspiration from the English drama for his own comedies, and oddly enough, Holberg never mentions William Shakespeare. At the Bodleian Library, though, he became aware of his vocation as an author of popular nonfiction.

With a manuscript for a reference work on European geography and modern history in his baggage, Holberg arrived in the summer of 1708 in Copenhagen, which now became his permanent residence. Once again he had run out of money, and he tried to earn a living by lecturing students on foreign affairs, geography, and political science, using the disciplines he had studied in Oxford as his point of departure. At this time Holberg made the acquaintance of two of the most distinguished teachers at the University of Copenhagen–Poul Vinding, professor of Greek, and Christian Reitzer, professor of law–and at their homes, he made the acquaintance of learned historian Hans Gram. Reitzer, in particular, guided Holberg's education in a more contemporary direction by pointing out to him the works of Dutch scholar Hugo Grotius, founder of modern international law; German jurist and historian Samuel Pufendorf; and the latter's most talented student, Christian Thomasius.

In October, Holberg was offered the opportunity to go abroad as Vinding's son's mentor. Together they went to Dresden, and thanks to his generous salary, Holberg was able to continue on to Leipzig. He spent a couple of months in Leipzig eagerly partaking in the local student life, just as in Oxford, and also attending lectures. In his memoirs Holberg mentions various professors, most importantly professor of history Johann Burkhard Mencke. In order to meet the founder of German Enlightenment, Thomasius, he also went to Halle. Thomasius, however, showed no interest in the young theologian, and to Holberg's annoyance, only conversed about the weather and other unimportant topics. From Halle, Holberg returned to Copenhagen via Hamburg, crossing in the bitter winter cold over to Zealand, an adventurous trip that he describes in his memoirs with gusto and humor.

On his return, Holberg once more made a living as a tutor; but in August 1709 Vinding obtained for him an annual sum of money and free lodging in a college, Borchs Kollegium, where he remained until 1714. Relieved of economic worries, Holberg set out to qualify himself for an academic career, entering on a period of immense productivity. On his return from Oxford he had discovered to his chagrin that in his absence a book similar to his manuscript had been published in 1707. Hence, Holberg divided the manuscript into two parts. In 1711 he published *Introduction til de fornemste Europæiske Rigers Historier Fortsat Indtil disse sidste Tider* (Introduction to the History of the Principal Kingdoms of Europe Down to These Latest Times), followed in 1713 by *Anhang Til hans Historiske Introduction Eller Underretning Om de Fornemste Europæiske Rigers og Republiqvers Stater* (Appendix to His Historical Introduction or Information about the Principal Kingdoms and Republics of Europe), which treats the geography of Germany, England, and Holland. The *Introduction* is based primarily on a work by Pufendorf with a similar title, *Einleitung zu der Historie der vornehmsten Reiche und Staaten, so jetziger Zeit in Europa sich befinden* (1682–1686), but Holberg had brought it up to date and expanded it; in it he focuses on current information that he largely found in contemporary German and French gazettes. The two volumes may best be characterized as a blend of popular social science and reference work, and they clearly demonstrate Holberg's inclination for what was most topical at the moment.

Holberg's history of Europe from 1711, the first of its kind in Denmark, was extremely successful, and its author was mentioned as a potential candidate for a professorship. Further to qualify himself, Holberg proceeded to update previous histories of Denmark by writing a major account of the reigns of the Danish kings Christian IV and Frederik III (1588–1670), mentioning that he was also working on the period of the present king's father, Christian V (1670–1699). This manuscript was never published but most likely secured Holberg a generous four-year scholarship in

May 1712 and an appointment by King Frederik IV as adjunct professor of philosophy in January 1714. Four months later, in May 1714, Holberg left for the journey that more than any of the previous ones became a decisive factor in his intellectual development. He sailed to Amsterdam, visiting friends there, then proceeded through Holland on a horse-drawn barge and from Brussels walked all the way to Paris. Holberg stayed in Paris for more than a year, visiting the great public libraries but not attending lectures at the university. No direct evidence exists that he read Molière's comedies or went to the theater. Either Holberg did not have the money to do so, or he refrained from mentioning any theater experience in order to stress his independence as a playwright. Nevertheless, during this time he must have acquired his knowledge of modern French, Italian, and Spanish literature while studying primarily the ancient and modern history of France and England.

In August 1715 Holberg left Paris, heading for Rome. He wrote about this decision in his memoirs, clearly stressing his wanderlust while constantly complaining about his frail health, his scanty financial means, and highway robbers. He drove by coach to Lyon, where he fell ill with malaria, continued down the Rhone to Avignon, and then on foot to Marseilles. From there he sailed to Genoa; while crossing over to Civitavecchia, the port city of Rome, his ship was threatened by Algerian pirates. When Holberg reached Rome in October 1715, however, he had forgotten all his tribulations. Rome was for him primarily a city of splendid baroque architecture with its regularity and symmetry–the ordered world of absolutism translated into architecture. He also became acquainted with the popular Italian masked comedy, the so-called commedia dell'arte. With its set characters, semi-improvised plot, and slapstick effects, this genre had a significant impact on his own plays.

Toward the end of February 1716 Holberg chose to walk back through Italy, crossing the Alps on a hinny-drawn carriage and riding down into Savoy by sledge. He continued on foot all the way to Paris and then by coach to Amsterdam. Finally rid of his malarial fever, Holberg in Amsterdam had a chance to play chamber music with his friends, and a few days later he boarded a ship for Hamburg, from where he walked to Copenhagen, arriving in the summer of 1716.

Rather than a study trip, Holberg's journey to France and Italy was a process of maturation, broadening his tastes and widening his horizons. In fact, colorful characters that he had met en route later resurfaced in several of his comedies. Upon his return, he published another reference work, *Moralske Kierne Eller Introduction Til Naturens og Folke-Rettens Kundskab* (Moral Core or Introduction to the Science of Natural Law and the Law of Nations, 1715). Holberg wrote a dedication to his benefactor, King Frederik IV, and a preface that reflects his experiences visiting centers of learning abroad. He evaluates the relevance of the sciences and, at the same time, outlines a program for modern studies. Of highest rank is moral philosophy, based on natural law and serving as man's sole guide in making ethical decisions. Next highest is medicine, and Holberg sharply attacks the curriculum of the University of Copenhagen for its emphasis on metaphysics and logical exercises. Thus, the work anticipates his satire on education in his comedy *Erasmus Montanus eller Rasmus Berg* (1731; translated as *Erasmus Montanus,* 1915). For *Moralske Kierne,* Pufendorf–and to a lesser degree, his student Thomasius–served as sources. Through Pufendorf's work, *De jure naturae et gentium* (1672), Holberg was also introduced to the pessimistic philosophy of Thomas Hobbes, and with both he shared the view that only a strong government–to Holberg that was the current absolute monarchy–can hold human passions in check.

In December 1717 Holberg was offered a professorship in metaphysics, a subject he had written against. He was met with suspicion by his colleagues, nor were the students pleased with their new teacher, who showed absolutely no enthusiasm for his new position. In May 1720, however, a position became vacant in Latin oratory, and for the next ten years, a period that coincided with his own breakthrough as a poet, Holberg taught Roman literature. In two Latin satires from 1719 Holberg had polemicized against a fellow historian, Andreas Hojer, who had criticized his *Introduction . . .* from 1711 for being a piece of plagiarism. As a stylistic model, Holberg had chosen the Roman satirist Juvenal and his sixth satire on marriage, which together with Nicolas Boileau-Despréaux's imitation of it in his tenth satire, *Les femmes* (1693), became the direct models for Holberg's first actual poetic work, a poem in alexandrine meter, "Poeten raader sin gamle Ven Jens Larsen fra at gifte sig" (The Poet Advises His Old Friend Jens Larsen against Marriage, 1722). Holberg's advice is to say no to marriage, but the reason is solely found in Jens Larsen's own personality, and Larsen can perhaps be interpreted as a self-portrait of Holberg himself, who by then must have chosen to remain a bachelor for the rest of his life.

Juvenal's works, Boileau-Despréaux's satirical epic *Le Lutrin* (1674–1683), Miguel de Cervantes's novel *Don Quixote* (1605–1615), and the classical epics by Homer and Virgil also served as models for the comic epic, also in alexandrine meter, *En Sandfærdig Ny Wiise Om Peder Paars* (A True, New Ballad about Peder Paars, 1719–1720), better known under its title from

1721, *Peder Paars Poema Heroico-comicum* (translated as *Peder Paars,* 1962). Virgil's *Aeneid* provided the structure for the parodic plot: the shopkeeper Peder (Aeneas/Don Quixote) sets out on a voyage to visit his fiancée Dorothea but is driven off course by the goddess Envy (who was to be found residing at the university) and is shipwrecked on the island of Anholt (Carthage). On Anholt, Peder falls in love with the bailiff's daughter, Nille (Dido); but on Venus's intervention, he leaves the island without her and is finally reunited with Dorothea. In spite of Holberg's many sources, *Peder Paars* is a highly original and immensely entertaining work. The broad humor, realism, and farcical situation comedy of the poem are features that clearly point to Holberg's later comedies.

Peder Paars was published under the pseudonym Hans Mickelsen, a name Holberg also used when in 1722 he published *4re Skiemte-Digte Med Tvende Fortaler, Samt Zille Hans Dotters Forsvars-Skrift for Qvinde-Kiønned* (Four Satirical Poems with Two Prefaces as well as Zille Hans's Daughter's Defense of Womankind), which also includes the satire "Poeten raader sin gamle Ven Jens Larsen fra at gifte sig." For the first poem of the volume, *Democritus og Heraclitus* (Democritus and Heraclitus), which had been printed separately in 1721, the two Greek philosophers, one of whom weeps for the follies of mankind while the other finds them ludicrous, are borrowed from Juvenal's tenth satire. In "Apologie for Sangeren Tigellio" (Apology for the Singer Tigellio), the capriciousness of the title character, who goes from one extreme to the other, is defended, since everybody is, in fact, afflicted by inconsistency. In "Critique over Peder Paars" (A Critique of Peder Paars) Holberg defends satire by stressing, in perfect accordance with the ideas of Enlightenment, its usefulness. Nevertheless, in referring to "Homeri gyldne Bog" (Homer's Golden Book), he praises imagination and poetry and thus actually points beyond his own rationalist times. So does the concluding poem, by Zille Hans Dotter, in its highly radical assertion of women's equality, not only with regard to education but also in filling public office. This poem foreshadows the highly independent female characters of Holberg's comedies. The four satires stand a little apart and are based on the same philosophy of life as the comedies: life is a madhouse, and humanity is ruled by chaos and thus deserves both to be pitied and to be laughed at. Even though God has bestowed upon humans the light of reason, they abuse it because of the various passions that control them.

Of Holberg's early fiction, *Peder Paars* in particular created a stir. It was considered not only a literary but also a social satire, and Holberg was accused of offending religion, the judiciary, and the University of Copenhagen. Thus, Holberg's former friend Gram felt offended because of the satire aimed at scholars, and the owner of Anholt, Frederik Rostgaard, complained to the king about the portrayal of the inhabitants of the island as greedy and ignorant–but the king actually enjoyed the work and repudiated the accusation.

The king, as well as Rostgaard (from 1721 chief secretary of the chancellery), may once again have interfered with Holberg's career when in 1722 the latter was asked to write comedies for the newly established Grønnegade Theater. In Holberg's time, Danish drama was languishing. From 1682 to 1721 a French theatrical troupe resided in Copenhagen, performing plays by Molière and others in French. In 1721 the French actors were replaced by a German opera company, but instead of leaving Denmark, the artistic director of the French troupe, René de Montaigu, on 1 July 1722 applied to the king for permission to produce plays in Danish. The permission was granted, and on 23 September, Montaigu premiered with Molière's *L'Avare* (1669) in Danish in a new building in the street of Lille Grønnegade. Two days later, Holberg's comedy *Den politiske Kandestøber* (1722; translated as *The Political Tinker,* 1915) premiered. The performances continued with varying success, and on 25 February 1727 Holberg's *Den Danske Comoedies Ligbegængelse* (1746; translated as *The Burial of Danish Comedy,* 1990) was performed, signaling the forthcoming closing of the theater. A devastating fire in 1728 put a stop to all entertainment, and with the accession in 1730 of Christian VI, who was deeply influenced by German Pietism, theater performances came to a virtual stop. Holberg, who had also been involved in the management of the theater, stopped writing comedies altogether. But before the theater closed, he had managed to write twenty-five plays.

Sources of inspiration for Holberg's comedies are, in ascending order of importance, works of Aristophanes, Terence, Plautus, Italian commedie dell'arte, and, first and foremost, Molière. They can be divided into the following categories, which to a certain degree also follow the order of their composition: comedies of character, of intrigue, of presentation, of parody, and of philosophy.

First, in a series of dramatic portraits of confused central characters, Holberg vied with the great comedies of character in the tradition of Molière. In contrast to the French playwright, however, he expanded the characterization to its utmost limits, adding a dimension of madness or insanity that transgressed the poetics of classicism and brought his characters closer, in fact, to Cervantes's sublime fools in *Don Quixote.* The title character of *Den politiske Kandestøber,* pewter smith Herman, suffers from the delusion that, although he is without any education or public experience, he is a great politician. Through an intrigue, he believes he is appointed mayor of Hamburg but completely loses control of the situation. He reaches a stage of desperation that takes him to the verge of suicide. Then the intrigue is revealed; Herman learns his lesson; and he is brought back to the reality of absolute monarchy with its strict social hierarchy.

Through the recognition of Herman's follies and those of others, the audience was supposed to learn and improve–a moral dimension aimed at Holberg's Copenhagen middle-class audience, which is overruled by a powerful comic vitality, frequently with a strong farcical element such as that found in Plautus's but not in Molière's plays. Thus, in *Erasmus Montanus eller Rasmus Berg,* Holberg, in his portrait of a peasant student, Rasmus Berg, offers a hilarious satire on the academic disputations in formal logic held at the University of Copenhagen. Upon returning to his village from Copenhagen with his name Latinized (that is, Rasmus Berg has become "Erasmus Montanus"), Erasmus not only treats his family with arrogance but also ridicules the local people by engaging them in academic disputes. Once again a trick is played on the title character, who only escapes punishment by renouncing his claim that the earth is round, which has so shocked the village. Holberg thus adds a tragic perspective both to his title character, who, after all, is right in his claim, and to the comedy in general, by demonstrating the protagonist's inability to communicate properly.

A similar tragic touch is found in Vielgeschrey, the title character of *Den Stundesløse* (1731; translated as *Scatterbrains,* 1912), which has much of its plot in common with Molière's *Le malade imaginaire* (1673). But once again Holberg goes beyond Molière's decorum by portraying someone brought to the brink of insanity by his own folly. When, in a pivotal scene, Vielgeschrey tries to gain control by claiming to be Alexander the Great, the confusion not only reaches a climax, but also Vielgeschrey, as a character losing his original identity, is transformed into a character of modernity. No sympathy, on the other hand, is shown toward *Jean de France eller Hans Frandsen* (1723; translated as *Jean de France; or, Hans Frandsen,* 1990), a young Copenhagener who, after a short visit to Paris, is just as full of French affectation as Erasmus is of Latin, and therefore, like Molière's Tartuffe, is chased away rather than being reformed.

Whether or not the alcoholic title character of *Jeppe paa Bierget eller den forvandlede Bonde* (1723; translated as *Jeppe of the Hill,* 1915) is being reformed is questionable. The plot goes back to an anecdote about a sleeping peasant in Jakob Biedermann's fictitious travel memoir *Utopia* (1640). After drinking himself into a stupor, Jeppe, abused by his wife and the local bailiff, wakes up–as part of the intrigue–in the local baron's bed and thus becomes another portrayal of a person losing his identity. Once again Holberg moves his protagonist into a gray zone between comedy and tragedy when he depicts with stark realism the downtrodden peasantry, a topic beyond Molière's reach. The psychological depth of the character of Jeppe is carried further in *Den Vægelsindede* (1723; translated as *The Weathercock,* 1946), in which Holberg makes a reference to the fickle title character, Tigellio, from *4re Skiemte-Digte.* In this comedy, Holberg presents a woman who overexercises her privilege to change her mind, a move that costs her the hands of two suitors, and when she finally gives her consent to the third–and this is the bittersweet twist–she suddenly changes her mind again.

Jacob von Tyboe eller den stortalende Soldat (1723; translated as *Captain Bombastes Thunderton,* 1912) is inspired by Plautus's *Miles Gloriosus* (circa 205 B.C.), but Holberg moves this Falstaff-like character of a soldier who boasts of imaginary exploits and his ironic parasite and companion to Copenhagen, adding local color and psychological complexity, and juxtaposes the braggart to a pedantic scholar. The rivalry of these two comic characters for the favors of the young woman Lucilia sets the intrigue in motion.

In *Jacob von Tyboe,* character delineation and intrigue are kept in perfect balance. In a series of comedies, however, Holberg avoids an individualized main character–at the same time downplaying the didactic element of the comedy–by using the stock characters of the commedia dell'arte, which he had seen performed in Rome, such as the cantankerous old father objecting to his children's plans, the young people in love, and the sly servant. Above all, Holberg upgrades the characters of the servants, who set the intrigue in motion, and while the servants are more or less the same, the intrigue varies from play to play. These servants, and other characters as well, frequently carry the same name from comedy to comedy–the quick-witted servant Henrich and the astute maid Pernille, who is usually the inventor of the intrigue, recruiting Henrich as her assistant. In *Henrich og Pernille* (1731; translated as *Henry and Pernilla,* 1912) Pernille even becomes one of the title characters in an elegant comedy of mistaken identity in which the intrigue, found in Alan-René Le Sage's novel *Historie de Gil Blas de Santillane* (1715–1735), tangles up the two social classes of servants and masters. A similar relation between servant and master in *De Usynlige* (1731; translated as *The Masked Ladies,* 1946), inspired by two plays by Pierre Marivaux that Holberg had seen during his second journey to Paris in 1725, *Arlequin poli par l'amour* (1720) and *Le prince travesti* (1724), turns into a parody of upper-class behavior. In the rather cynical *Pernilles korte Frøiken-Stand* (1731; translated as *Pernille's Brief Experience as a Lady,* 1990), this relation is depicted as a gulf between the lower and upper classes, which can only be bridged through an intrigue tricking a rich but rather unpleasant old gentleman into marrying the servant maid. In two comedies, *Uden Hoved og Hale* (Without Head or Tail, 1723) and *Hexerie eller Blind Allarm* (Witchcraft, or False Alarm, 1731), Holberg makes superstition the point of departure for the intrigue, less in order to moralize than to create comic relief. In the first, which is related to *Den Vægelsindede,* as Holberg takes up once again the theme of a person who goes from one extreme to the other, two brothers–one skeptical, the other superstitious–witness the devil being conjured up. The skeptical brother then becomes superstitious, and the other previously superstitious brother, who also witnesses the unmasking of the trick, is cured of his beliefs. In the second comedy, the actor Leander practices a scene in which the devil is conjured up. This scene is witnessed by a passerby, and Holberg now illustrates how such a coincidence can bring about rumors of witchcraft, creating not only an atmosphere of witch-hunting in a provincial town but also business for the actor, who pretends to be able to foresee the future.

The third type of comedy, situated between the comedy of character inspired by Molière and the comedy of intrigue inspired by the Italian commedia dell'arte, is the comedy of presentation. Holberg's main source of inspiration was the elegant and sprightly plays by one of Molière's successors, Florent-Carton Dancourt, presenting scenes from both life in the country and in the city. The comic elements in such comedies with their many walk-on parts can be found in the depiction of the milieu itself, and in Holberg's case, usually in the stultification of a certain custom, fashion, or cultural pattern, which thus becomes in a sense the main character of the play. In *Barselstuen* (The Receiving Room, 1723) Holberg aims his ridicule at the hubbub of servants, physicians, and visiting lady friends that unfolds around the exhausted young woman in confinement. Moreover, an additional comic element is being interwoven–the humiliating doubts of the aged husband concerning the paternity of the newborn baby. In the one-act play *Jule-Stue* (1723; translated as *The Christmas Party,* 1950) Holberg intertwines the Christmas preparations and festivities of a Copenhagen family with a shockingly immoral and cynical erotic intrigue, and in *Mascarade* (1723; translated as *Masquerades,* 1946), he mixes the splendor of the popular masquerade balls of the times with a traditional comedy of mistaken identity.

Of Holberg's two literary parodies, one, *Melampe* (1723), takes aim upward at the French classical tragedy; the other, *Ulysses von Ithacia eller En Tydsk Comedie* (1723; translated as *Ulysses von Ithacia; or, A German Comedy,* 1990), downward at the still popular so-called Haupt- und Staatsactionen, performed by traveling German troupes and based on dramatic events from world history but staged with exaggerated effects, farcical elements, and crude gestures. In *Ulysses von Ithacia,* Holberg condenses the contents of the entire *Iliad* and *Odyssey* by Homer, utilizes the entire stage machinery, and not only ridicules the conventions of Baroque drama but also violates the traditional unities of classical drama, and–thus pointing ahead to the twentieth century–the dramatic illusion itself. He creates a hilarious, timeless show that anticipates the great comics of the silent movie and the farces of Dario Fo. Much more subdued, and undeservedly less successful, is *Melampe,* in which the target of the parody is the high-strung treatment of psychological conflicts in the French tragedy. In this play, the conflict is between two sisters who both fight for the ownership of the same lapdog, Melampe, a conflict that is only solved through bloodshed when their brother kills the dog. By keeping a straight face and letting the main characters express their pain and hatred in exquisite alexandrine meter, Holberg creates a theatrical universe that in the final account is nonexistent; thereby, he moves the play into the realm of total absurdity.

When the new theater opened in 1748, two years after the accession of Frederik V, Holberg, after a break of approximately twenty years, resumed his playwriting. The new theater's repertoire consisted mainly of comedies by Holberg, Molière, and Jean-François Regnard, but a lighter, more contemporary comedy emerged around 1750 and found favor with the audience. Holberg fought in vain against this new, sentimental comedy, in which the focus is not on vice anymore but on virtue. Nevertheless, the six new comedies he wrote for the new theater are influenced by the new trend. The comic element has now largely been replaced by seriousness and slapstick by dialogue, but, nevertheless, Holberg subtly indicates his true allegiance by choosing more openly than ever the classical (Greek and Roman) drama as his model. Among these so-called philosophical comedies only two, *Huus-Spøgelse eller Abracadabra* (House Ghost, or Abracadabra, 1754), an adaptation of Plautus's *Mostellaria,* and *Den forvandlede Brudgom* (1754; translated as *The Changed Bridegroom,* 1950) are plays of disguise in the tradition of the earlier comedy of intrigues. The former is noteworthy as being written for an all-male cast, whereas the latter was written for an all-female cast.

The remaining four plays place abstract concepts on the stage, and Holberg unmistakably reaches back to the originator of comedy, Aristophanes. In *Plutus eller Proces imellem Fattigdom og Riigdom* (Plutus or the Process between Poverty and Riches, 1754), modeled after Aristophanes' comedy *Wealth,* the title character, the blind god of wealth, is opposed to Penia, the personification of poverty, in order to show that the gifts of wealth are distributed most successfully precisely because the god is blind. The abstraction increases with *Republiqven eller det gemeene Beste* (The Republic, or the Common Good, 1754): the title figure is a female personification of the state. She is forever being pestered by cranks with wild schemes, and thus Holberg thematically points back to *Den politiske Kandestøber;* in fact, Herman himself reappears. Even in this late work, Holberg remains a satirist. Finally, in *Philosophus udi egen Indbildning* (Philosopher in His Own Imagination, 1754) and *Sganarels Reise til det philosophiske Land* (1754; translated as *Sganarel's Journey to the Land of the Philosophers,* 1950), again finding inspiration in Aristophanes, Holberg introduces satirical portraits of pedants and philosophers, or rather, would-be philosophers. In the former, Pernille reappears to spin the intrigue that makes the title character, a self-righteous hypocrite, change his ways and repent. Whereas Holberg in this negative portrait clearly launched a severe attack at Pietism, in *Sganarels Reise* his aversion is more generally aimed at any abuse of philosophy. Leander and his servant Sganarel set out to seek wisdom, arriving in the same philosophical country that is also described in Holberg's novel from 1741 about Niels Kliim. The plot of the work is only secondary. Of sole importance is the introduction of philosophers of various schools, all of whom fail to live their lives according to their precepts. *Artaxerxes* (1754) is an insignificant reworking of a melodramatic opera libretto by Pietro Metastasio about the uncovering of a regicide in ancient Persia. Both the genre and the topic were alien to Holberg's artistic temperament.

Artaxerxes, as well as all of Holberg's last comedies, lacks dramatic force. Apart from *Plutus,* which was lavishly produced by incorporating dance and music, processions and slapstick effects, they were unsuccessful and are–though perhaps they should not be–held in low esteem by the critics. One should keep in mind that they were not based on the same dramaturgical rules as the earlier comedies, but should rather be considered philosophical soliloquies by an aging writer taking stock of a lifetime of experiences, extracting the surprisingly modern(ist) lesson already expressed in the poem about Tigellio: "Thi i hvert Menneske en selsom Chaos er" (For in every human being there is an uncanny chaos).

Holberg never felt that he was properly appreciated by his contemporaries either in Denmark or abroad. Together with the closing of the theater in 1725, which must have been a major setback for him, since at that time he was in the midst of a period of almost frantic productivity, this sense of rejection must have been a major factor in his decision to write an autobiography for the learned world abroad and hence in Latin, *Ad virum perillustrem* (To a Famous Man, 1728; translated as *Memoirs of Lewis Holberg,* 1827). This work was succeeded by two additional fictitious autobiographical letters published in the two volumes of his *Opuscula quaedam latina. Epistola I. Cujus nova haec editio prioribus est emendatior. Epistola II. Quinque libri epigrammatum. Epistola tertia. Epigrammatum liber sextus* (Small Latin Works. First Epistle. This new edition is emendated compared with the previous. Second Epistle. Five Books of Epigrams. Third Epistle. Sixth Book of Epigrams, 1737, 1743) to which should be added autobiographical letter no. 447, from 1754, which updates Holberg's vita to 1753. These letters (translated as *Memoirs. An Eighteenth-Century Danish Contribution to International Understanding,* 1970) constitute almost the sole biographical information that exists about Holberg and thus must be interpreted with great caution. They share a lively and varied style, which Holberg modeled after one of his favorite Roman authors, Pliny the Younger. His travels are treated with particular humor, but the main purpose of the letters was undoubtedly to promote their author abroad. Holberg thus summarizes his published comedies in great detail in order to attract translators and theater managers. A more direct reason for publishing the memoirs at this point can be found in the fifth (and last) journey abroad that Holberg decided to undertake, in July 1725. He took a leave of absence from the university, officially to go to the warm springs of Aachen in Germany to restore his health after, as he explains, the hectic writing of so many comedies. In fact, he went via northern Germany, Amsterdam, and Brussels to Paris. This time he did not leave home as a student in constant need of money. He traveled in comfort, well aware of his position as a university professor with a considerable production behind him. Seeing Paris again, however, was something of a disappointment. Holberg complains in his autobiography about the many beggars and the expensive prices, but he made good use of his time. Once again he visited the libraries, but above all he went to the theaters night after night, and "for tidsfordriv" (to pass the time) he translated two of his comedies into French. He tried to interest the manager of the Théâtre Italien, Luigi Riccoboni, in his comedies by sending him a copy of *Den politiske Kandestøber,* which, according to Holberg, Riccoboni found entertaining, but, because of its satire, too dangerous to perform.

Probably in March 1726, Holberg returned via Amsterdam. Back in Copenhagen he applied the finishing touch on a work he had begun before his departure, a major epic cycle, *Metamorphosis eller Forvandlinger* (Metamorphosis, or Transformation, 1726), a stylistic imitation of Ovid's work of the same title. But whereas

Ovid changes humans into animals and plants, Holberg reverses the transformation and a strong satirical purpose dominates the text. With this work, Holberg took temporary leave of fiction. Instead, he returned to his scholarly writings. In 1730 he was appointed professor of history (his favorite subject) and geography. When these subjects in 1732 became part of the curriculum for the philosophical examination at the university, Holberg was asked to compile two textbooks on world history and geography, *Synopsis historiae universalis* (translated as *An Introduction to Universal History,* 1755) and *Compendium geographicum* (translated as *A Short System of Geography with Maps, etc.* in *An Introduction to Universal History,* 1758), both published in 1733; both works demonstrate his talent for presenting complex material in a well-structured and pedagogical manner.

In 1729 Holberg had published a long-planned *Dannemarks og Norges Beskrivelse* (Description of Denmark and Norway), using material compiled as far back as his Oxford days. Its analyses of national character, economy, trade, and religion form a well-written counterpart to *The Present State of England* (1668–1671) by Edward Chamberlayne, whose journalistic style and emphasis on cultural history served as Holberg's model. Any criticism of absolute monarchy is strongly rejected, and when Holberg subsequently published his major historical work, *Dannemarks Riges Historie* (The History of the Kingdom of Denmark, 1732–1735), he made the death of King Frederik III in 1670 and the introduction of absolutism appear as a triumphant apex of Danish history. Holberg, however, was more a man of letters than a scholar of history. To him, history itself should serve a wider didactic purpose, and hence the study of history becomes part of Holberg's ethical system as the ultimate collection of exempla of good and evil. His own pride in his three volumes is both understandable and legitimate. They are unusual in Danish intellectual history, written in a lively and graphic language and achieving a perfect balance between description and interpretation. Holberg's interest in cultural and social conditions is particularly noteworthy and also lies at the center in the colorful volume *Den berømmelige Norske Handels-Stad Bergens Beskrivelse* (Description of the Famous Norwegian Commercial City of Bergen, 1737). This work is based on the manuscript of one Edvard Edvardsen, who had been assistant principal when Holberg had studied at the Cathedral School in Bergen. *Den berømmelige Norske Handels-Stad Bergens Beskrivelse* again displays Holberg's acute power of observation and unusual ability to organize unwieldy material.

Holberg had always been fascinated by psychological portrayal as evidenced through his fictional writing, and it also became a distinctive feature of his descriptions of the various monarchs in his *Dannemarks Riges Historie.* This psychological fascination increasingly dominated his following works. In 1738 he published *Almindelig Kirke-Historie fra Christendommes første Begyndelse til Lutheri Reformation* (General Church History from the Beginning of Christianity to the Lutheran Reformation), with Moses and Martin Luther as its main heroes. The sixteen chapters of the volume, each devoted to one century, are written with inspiration and enthusiasm. In particular, Holberg's spiritual and empathetic résumé of the Gospels deserves to be stressed, demonstrating as it does an unbiased attitude toward religion that sets Holberg apart from his much more radical French counterparts. Holberg finished yet another large historical work, *Jødiske Historie fra Verdens begyndelse, fortsatt til disse Tider* (Jewish History, from the Beginning of the World to the Present Time, 1742), the main source of which was Flavius Josephus's *The Antiquities of the Jews* (A.D. 90), which, however, only treats certain periods of Jewish history. Holberg, on the other hand, excels in presenting a complete overview in a lively and engaging style. He was always fascinated by the destiny of the Jewish people and their survival, which he saw as a reflection of God's love and justice.

In the two volumes of *Adskillige store Heltes og berømmelige Mænds, sær Orientalske og Indianske sammenlignede Historier og Bedrifter* (Several Comparative Histories and Deeds of Great Heroes, 1739) and *Adskillige Heltinders og navnkundige Damers sammenlignede Historier* (Several Comparative Histories of Heroines, 1745) Holberg, employing the classical portraits of the Greek historian Plutarch in his *Parallel Lives* (circa second century) as his point of departure, juxtaposes historical characters in pairs in order to shed light on their abilities and dispositions. Thus, the works are psychological rather than historical, and this orientation becomes increasingly prolific in the second volume without, however, neglecting a political and social context. Thus, in the double portrait of the Syrian-Roman queen Zenobia and the Russian empress Catherine the First, Holberg harks back to his poem about Zille Hans Dotter in the volume from 1722 in order to exemplify and promote female emancipation.

These years marked a steady advance in Holberg's academic career. The high point of this period was the awarding to Holberg in 1735 of a one-year tenure as the president of the University of Copenhagen, at the conclusion of which he delivered a speech in Latin presenting his view of academic responsibility: to strike a balance between extremes, to find solutions agreeable to all parties, and to forward one's own policies, but only if they are accepted by the majority. In 1737 Holberg became the bursar of the university, a position that probably suited him better, and he proved to be an efficient steward of finances until he resigned in 1751. In fact,

LUD. HOLBERGS

Epistler,

Befattende

Adskillige historiske, politiske, metaphysiske, moralske,
philosophiske,

Item

Skiemtsomme Materier,

Deelte udi 2de Tomer.

TOMUS I.

Kiøbenhavn, 1748.
Trykt paa Autors Bekostning.

Title page for the first volume of Holberg's five-volume collection (1748–1754) of 542 fictitious letters on "historical, political, metaphysical, moral, philosophical, and witty topics" (from Jens Hougaard, Knud Lundbæk, and Ejgil Søholm, Tre epistler til Holbergs ABC, *1984; Widener Library, Harvard University)*

Holberg was an extremely clever businessman with regard to his own economy as well. He earned good money from writing. Most often he was his own publisher, selling his works from his home. Holberg remained unmarried and lived frugally; already around 1730 he had amassed a considerable fortune, which he first invested in real estate in Copenhagen and, in 1740 and 1746, in two estates in the countryside.

The impressive output of historical works was followed by the third, and last, philosophical phase in his production. The first volume of Latin works from 1737 had included a reprint of his first autobiographical letter and its sequel, *Epistola II;* the volume also included a series of epigrams, *Epigrammata,* 758 in all, which were augmented in the second volume of his Latin works from 1743 and finally published in a single volume titled *Epigrammatum libri septem* (1749), including 937 epigrams altogether. The core of these short poems is their satirical nature, as in the work of Holberg's models, the Roman Martial and, to an even larger degree, the Englishman John Owen. Holberg often increases his epigrams to four or more lines, enlarging some of them with psychological observations and philosophical maxims, while others are snapshots based on direct experiences.

In several of Holberg's epigrams, themes and ideas are introduced that come to fruition in his philosophical science-fiction novel *Nicolai Klimii iter subterraneum* (1741; translated as *A Journey to the World Under-Ground by Nicholas Klimius,* 1742), written in Latin in yet another attempt at reaching a learned European audience. In 1742 the novel was translated into Danish as *Niels Kliims Reise under Jorden.* As the work criticizes the strict Pietism during the reign of Christian VI, Holberg, in order to guard himself against government reprisals and censorship, chose the well-established genre of utopian literature and had his novel published anonymously in Leipzig. But another reason for choosing this genre was his fascination with the fantastic and exotic, which had inspired his models, Defoe's *Robinson Crusoe* (1720), Swift's *Gulliver's Travels* (1726), and Charles-Louis de Montesquieu's *Lettres persanes* (1721), the latter exemplifying for Holberg how to satirize one's own country and get away with it. Like Swift, Holberg has his traveler narrate his experiences, and he presents the book as the memoirs of a real person. Niels's journey leads to the center of planet Earth, where he visits many different countries. Holberg makes use of the opportunity to attack religious intolerance and satirize vanity and other human follies exactly as in his comedies and with the same intriguing mix of conservative and progressive ideas. Thus, in his ideal country, Potu (Utop[ia] spelled backward), the form of government is hereditary monarchy, and the inhabitants are skeptical toward reforms; yet, religious freedom and coeducational institutions of learning exist with women holding high positions. The utopian genre offered Holberg's imagination the freest reign possible. He displays an astonishing degree of linguistic imagination and employs grotesque exaggerations and bold paradoxes, so that he adds an almost Surrealist touch to the work. The novel created a sensation. In Denmark it was almost confiscated; abroad, however, it quickly became a best-seller and was immediately translated into German, Dutch, and French; the following year into English; and later into Swedish, Russian, Hungarian, Polish, and Finnish.

In 1743 Holberg's third Latin autobiographical letter, or *epistola,* was published. It displays his concern with the trouble his novel had stirred but also reflects his increased interest in philosophical writers. During the early 1730s Holberg had acquainted himself with Cicero and Seneca and later with Michel de Montaigne's *Essais* (1580–1588). In his third letter he praises Montaigne for his candor and use of paradoxical statements in order to "angribe almindelig anerkendte Forestillinger" (attack generally acknowledged opinions), an aim that came to characterize the last part of Holberg's own writings. He then proceeded to employ Montaigne's method in the first of six essays that conclude the letter and in which he discusses the concept of godliness.

These six essays were translated into Danish by Holberg himself and became part of his next work, *Moralske Tanker* (Moral Thoughts, 1744). Each of its sixty-three chapters is headed by one of Holberg's own Latin epigrams, and in many cases the ensuing essay develops the idea of the epigram. The overall aim of the work is the realization of Montaigne's dictum of examining generally accepted opinions. The topics range from a metaphysical discussion of good versus evil and an analysis of hypochondria to analyses of literature in the post-Molière era. These and other subjects are never treated provocatively but rather with a voice of moderation and common sense. Of a different nature are the five volumes of *Epistler, Befattende Adskillige historiske, politiske, metaphysiske, moralske, philosophiske, Item Skiemtsomme Materier* (Epistles, Historical, Political, Metaphysical, Moral, Philosophical, and Witty Topics, 1748–1754). These 542 fictitious letters are generally more encyclopedic in nature, as illustrated by the subtitle. Altogether these essays offer fascinating insights both into Holberg's own personality, as in the autobiographical letter number 447, and into his cosmopolitan orientation. For factual information, he relied on a fairly small number of standard works, above all Pierre Bayle's *Dictionnaire historique et critique* (1697), with its biblical criticism, skeptical views of the church dogmas, and doubts about the justice of God; Ephraim Chambers's *Cyclopaedia* (1728); and the *Bibliothèque Britannique* (1733–1747). Without ever embracing Bayle's radicalism, Holberg demonstrated an astounding appetite for controversial issues and exotic topics, going far beyond the scope of traditional eighteenth-century middle-class education. His reaction to his reading, however, was always that of the Enlightenment–to apply the principles of moderation and reason.

These principles are also the foundation of Holberg's last literary effort, his collection of 232 *Moralske Fabler* (Moral Fables, 1751) in a rather dry prose. Holberg claims not to have used the acknowledged fabulists–such as Aesop, Jean de La Fontaine, and Christian Fürchtegott Gellert–as his models, but he nonetheless raids the entire European tradition for inspiration. The themes he deals with can also be found elsewhere in his work, but in this work they are presented with an unmistakable element of an older man's bitter wisdom if not straight pessimism.

In return for willing his estate in 1747 to Sorø Academy, an institution intended to provide the absolute monarchy with well-educated administrators and diplomats by using modern pedagogical principles, Holberg was raised the same year to the rank of baron. He then saw himself not only as a Scandinavian literary figure but also as a European writer, who could participate in international exchange on the highest level. Thus, in 1752 he responded to a biography of the Swedish seventeenth-century Queen Christina by the German-born Swedish historian Johann Arckenholtz with *Lettres de Mr. le Baron de Holberg, qui contient quelques remarques sur les Memoires concernant la reine Christine nouvellement publiés* (Letters of Baron Holberg, Containing Some Remarks about the Recently Published Memoirs Regarding Queen Christina), and in 1753 he joined others in a polemic against Montesquieu with the booklet *Remarques sur quelques positions, qui se trouvent dans L'esprit des Loix* (Remarks about Some Positions which Can Be Found in *L'esprit des Loix*), offering, as could be expected, a defense of absolutism as the ideal form of government. Until his death, Holberg remained faithful to the regime that had offered him so many opportunities. When he died on 28 January 1754, Sorø Academy showed its gratitude toward him by placing his coffin in the medieval abbey church of Sorø, the burial site of several Danish kings.

With his writings, Ludwig Holberg elevated a backward and provincial Dano-Norwegian culture and literature to a contemporary and international level. Inspired by the poetics and aesthetics of the classical writers and of French seventeenth-century authors, he consistently took it upon himself to introduce, to improve, or to find inspiration through several classical genres: the satire, the comic epic, the epigram, the fable, and–first and foremost–the comedy. His best plays open perspectives to the future with comic force. Holberg creates a many-faceted gallery of characters full of foibles and failures, portraying humans as changeable and chaotic creatures. Holberg's awareness that life is full of inexplicable happenstance and absurdity makes his literary work timeless and universal, and makes him an early and fascinating forerunner of European modernism.

Letters:

Ludvig Holbergs Breve, 2 volumes, edited by Verner Dahlerup (Copenhagen: Gad, 1926);

Ludvig Holbergs Tre Levnedsbreve 1728–1743, 3 volumes, edited by A. Kragelund (Copenhagen: Gad, 1965).

Bibliographies:

H. Ehrencron-Müller, *Forfatterlexikon omfattende Danmark, Norge og Island indtil 1814,* volumes 10–12 (Copenhagen: H. Aschehoug, 1933–1935);

Mogens Müllertz and Paul H. Hagerup, *Bøger af og om Holberg* (Copenhagen: H. Hagerup, 1944);

Jens Kr. Andersen, "Holbergiana at the Tercentary," *Scandinavica,* 24, no. 2 (1985): 127–142.

Biographies:

Georg Brandes, *Ludvig Holberg. Et Festskrift* (Copenhagen: Gyldendal, 1884);

Thomas A. Müller, *Den unge Ludvig Holberg 1684–1722* (Copenhagen: Gyldendal, 1943);

Jens Kruuse, *En poetisk kriger: Ludvig Holberg* (Copenhagen: Berlingske Forlag, 1978);

Carl Fredrik Englestad, *Ludvig Holberg: Gjøgleren. Granskeren. Gåten* (Oslo: Aschehoug, 1984);

Jens Hougaard, *Ludvig Holberg: The Playwright and His Age up to 1730* (Odense: Odense University Press, 1993);

Sven Hakon Rossel, "Ludvig Holberg: The Cosmopolitan," in *Ludvig Holberg: A European Writer. A Study in Influence and Reception,* edited by Rossel (Amsterdam & Atlanta: Rodopi, 1994), pp. 1–40;

Lars Roar Langslet, *Den store ensomme: en biografi om Ludvig Holberg* (Oslo: Press, 2001).

References:

Asger Albjerg, *Holbergs poetiske maskerade* (Copenhagen: Vinten, 1978);

Jens Kristian Andersen, *Handling og moral. En strukturel studie i elleve Holberg-komedier* (Copenhagen: Akademisk, 1992);

Andersen, *Holbergs kilder? Studier i komediedigterens mulige litterære forudsætninger* (Copenhagen: Akademisk, 1993);

Andersen, *Professor Holbergs komedier. En struktural og historisk undersøgelse* (Copenhagen: Akademisk, 1993);

Gerald S. Argetsinger, *Ludvig Holberg's Comedies* (Carbondale: Southern Illinois University Press, 1983);

Angelika Bamberger, *Ludvig Holberg und das erste dänische Nationaltheater* (Frankfurt am Main: Haag & Herchen, 1983);

F. J. Billeskov Jansen, *Holberg som Epigrammatiker og Essayist,* 2 volumes (Copenhagen: Munksgaard, 1938, 1939);

Billeskov Jansen, *Ludvig Holberg* (New York: Twayne, 1974);

Hans Brix, *Ludvig Holbergs Komedier* (Copenhagen: Gyldendal, 1942);

Francis Bull, *Ludvig Holberg som historiker* (Christiania: Aschehoug, 1913);

Oscar J. Campbell Jr., *The Comedies of Holberg* (Cambridge, Mass.: Harvard University Press, 1914);

Peter Christensen, *Lys og Mørke: Ludvig Holberg–en moderne klassiker* (Århus: Århus Universitet, 1995);

Jørgen Stender Clausen, *Holberg og Le Nouveau Théâtre Italien* (Copenhagen: Gad, 1970);

Mads Julius Elf, *Apropos smagen* (Copenhagen: Dansklærerforeningen, 2002);

Jens Hougaard, Knud Lundbæk, and Ejgil Søholm, *Tre epistler til Holbergs ABC* (Århus: Statsbiblioteket, 1984);

Anne E. Jensen, *Holberg og kvinderne* (Copenhagen: Gyldendal, 1984);

Kerrin Jensen, *Moral und Politik: Gesellschaftsbild und Komödienrezeption in Ludvig Holbergs Frühwerk* (Frankfurt am Main: Peter Lang, 1986);

Jens Kruuse, *Holbergs maske* (Copenhagen: Gyldendal, 1964);

Erik A. Nielsen, *Holbergs komik* (Copenhagen: Gyldendal, 1984);

Harald Nielsen, *Holberg i Nutidsbelysning* (Copenhagen: Aschehoug, 1923);

Viljam Olsvig, *Holberg og England* (Christiania: Aschehoug, 1913);

Sigrid Peters, *Ludvig Holbergs Menippeische Satire. Das 'Iter subteraneum' und seine Beziehung zur antiken Literatur* (Frankfurt am Main: Peter Lang, 1987);

Sven Hakon Rossel, ed., *Ludvig Holberg: A European Writer. A Study in Influence and Reception* (Amsterdam & Atlanta: Rodopi, 1994);

Olaf Skavlan, *Holberg som Komedieforfatter, Forbilleder og Eftervirkninger* (Christiania: Cammermeyer, 1872);

Dorthe Sondrup Andersen, *Om at være sig sekv bekendt. En historisk relatering af Ludvig Holbergs komedier* (Odense: Odense University Press, 1988);

Erich Chr. Werlauff, *Historiske Antegnelser til Ludvig Holbergs atten første Lystspil* (Copenhagen: Samfundet til den danske Literaturs Fremme, 1858).

Papers:

Ludvig Holberg's manuscripts and correspondence are at the Danish Royal Library in Copenhagen.

B. S. Ingemann

(28 May 1789 - 24 February 1862)

Knud Bjarne Gjesing
University of Southern Denmark

(Translated by Mark Mussari)

BOOKS: *Digte,* 2 volumes (Copenhagen: B. Brünnich, 1811–1812)–includes *Mithridat. Skuespil;*

Procne. En Samling af Digte (Copenhagen: B. Brünnich, 1813)–includes *Turnus. Skuespil* and *Varners poëtiske Vandringer. Digtkreds;*

De sorte Riddere. Et romantisk Epos i ni Sange (Copenhagen: B. Brünnich, 1814);

Blanca. Et Sørgespil (Copenhagen: B. Brünnich, 1815);

Masaniello. Et Sørgespil (Copenhagen: B. Brünnich, 1815);

Røsten i Ørkenen. Et bibelsk Drama (Copenhagen: B. Brünnich, 1815);

Confirmations-Psalmer (Copenhagen: B. Brünnich, 1816);

Hyrden af Tolosa. Tragoedie (Copenhagen: B. Brünnich, 1816);

Julegave. En Samling af Digte (Copenhagen: B. Brünnich, 1816)–includes "Til Dannebroge," translated by Charles Wharton Stork as "Dannebrog (The Danish Flag)," in *A Second Book of Danish Verse,* edited by Stork (Princeton: Princeton University Press / New York: American-Scandinavian Foundation, 1947; reprinted, Freeport, N.Y.: Books for Libraries Press, 1968), p. 10;

Løveridderen. Tragoedie (Copenhagen: B. Brünnich, 1816);

Reinald Underbarnet. Et Tryllespil i tre Eventyr (Copenhagen: B. Brünnich, 1816);

De Underjordiske. Et bornholmsk Eventyr (Copenhagen: B. Brünnich, 1817);

Tassos Befrielse. Et dramatisk Digt (Copenhagen: B. Brünnich, 1819);

Eventyr og Fortællinger (Copenhagen: B. Brünnich, 1820);

Reiselyren (Copenhagen: B. Brünnich, 1820);

Kampen for Valhal. Tragoedie (Copenhagen: C. A. Reitzel, 1821);

Magnetismen i Barbeerstuen. Comoedie i 5 Acter (Copenhagen: Privately printed, 1821);

Monies Lithography, 1830s; courtesy of the Danish Royal Library, Copenhagen

Morgenpsalmer og Cantater (Copenhagen: C. A. Reitzel, 1822);

Morgenpsalmer til Brug for Eleverne i Sorø Academies Skole (Copenhagen: Privately printed, 1822);

Grundtræk til en Nord-Slavisk og Vendisk Gudelære. Indbydelsesskrift til den offentlige Examen ved Sorø Academies Skole (Copenhagen: J. H. Schultz, 1824);

Waldemar den Store og hans Mænd. Et episk Digt (Copenhagen: A. Seidelin, 1824);

Høimesse-Psalmer til Kirkeaarets Helligdage (Copenhagen: A. Seidelin, 1825; revised and enlarged edition, Copenhagen: C. A. Reitzel, 1843)–includes "Mesteren kommer," translated by S. D. Rodholm as "The Great and Skillful Master," in *A Harvest of Song: Translations and Original Lyrics*, edited by Rodholm (Des Moines: American Evangelical Lutheran Church, 1953), p. 66;

Valdemar Seier. En historisk Roman, 3 volumes (Copenhagen: A. Seidelin, 1826); translated by Jane Frances Chapman as *Waldemar, Surnamed Seir, or the Victorious,* 3 volumes (London: Saunders & Otley, 1841);

Noveller (Copenhagen: C. A. Reitzel, 1827)–comprises "Det forbandede Huus," "Gravmælet," "Den gamle Rabbin," and "Konstberider-Familien";

Erik Menveds Barndom. En historisk Roman, 3 volumes (Copenhagen: A. Seidelin, 1828); translated by John Kesson as *The Childhood of King Erik Menved: An Historical Romance* (London: Bruce & Wyld, 1846);

Huldre-Gaverne eller Ole Navnløses Levnets-Eventyr, fortalt af ham selv (Copenhagen: A. Seidelin, 1831)–includes "I Snee staar Urt og Busk i Skjul," translated by Rodholm as "Cheer Up," in *A Harvest of Song,* p. 109; and by Johannes Knudsen as "The Snow Lies Heavy on the Hedge," in *A Heritage in Song,* edited by Knudsen (Askov, Minn.: Danish Interest Conference, Lutheran Church in America, 1978), no. 22;

Nogle Oplysninger om Huldregaverne eller Ole Navnløses Levnets-Eventyr (Copenhagen: A. Seidelin, 1831);

Opstanden i Litteraturstaden. Dramatisk Epilog til Ole Navnløses Levnets-Eventyr (Copenhagen: A. Seidelin, 1831);

Smaadigte og Reiseminder (Copenhagen: A. Seidelin, 1832);

Blade af Jerusalems Skomagers Lommebog (Copenhagen: A. Seidelin, 1833);

Kong Erik og de Fredløse. En historisk Roman (Copenhagen: A. Seidelin, 1833); translated by Chapman as *King Eric and the Outlaws; or, The Throne, the Church, and the People,* 3 volumes (London: Longman, Brown, Green & Longmans, 1843);

Prins Otto af Danmark og hans Samtid. En historisk Roman (Copenhagen: A. Seidelin, 1835);

Varulven, Den levende Døde, Corsicaneren. Tre Fortællinger (Copenhagen: A. Seidelin, 1835);

Dronning Margrete. Et historisk Digt i ti Sange (Copenhagen: A. Seidelin, 1836);

Holger Danske. Et Digt (Copenhagen: A. Seidelin, 1837)–includes "I alle de Riger og Lande," translated by Robert Silliman Hillyer as "Holger Danske's Arms," in *A Book of Danish Verse,* edited by Oluf Friis (New York: American-Scandinavian Foundation, 1922), pp. 61–62;

Morgensange for Børn (Copenhagen: Privately printed, 1837)–includes "I Østen stiger Solen op," translated by Hillyer as "The Sun at Dawning Rises Up," in *A Book of Danish Verse,* p. 58; *Morgensange for Børn,* translated by Arne Pedersen in *Morning Songs=Morgensange for Børn,* edited by Sten Høgel (N.p.: Bøgeskoven, 1997);

Renegaten. Et dramatisk Digt (Copenhagen: A. Seidelin, 1838);

Syv Aftensange (Copenhagen: C. C. Lose & Olsen, 1838)–includes "Der staaer et Slot i Vesterled," translated by R. P. Keigwin as "The Castle in the West," in *In Denmark I Was Born . . . A Little Book of Danish Verse* (Copenhagen: A. F. Høst, 1948), p. 45; "Der staaer et Slot i Vesterled," "Den skjønne Jordens Sol gik ned," and "Den store stille Nat gaaer frem," all translated by Hillyer as "Evening Song," in *A Book of Danish Verse,* pp. 59–61; and "Bliv hos os, naar Dagen helder," translated by Rodholm as "Be with Us," in *A Harvest of Song,* p. 40;

Morgen- og Aftensange (Copenhagen: A. Seidelin, 1839);

Salomons Ring. Dramatisk Eventyr, med et lyrisk Forspil (Copenhagen: A. Seidelin, 1839);

Skyhimlen eller den Luke-Howardske Skyformationslære, betragtet som Billedform for Naturpoesien (Copenhagen: Sorø Akademi, 1840);

Stjernebilledernes Symbolik. En poetisk Anskuelse (Copenhagen: A. Seidelin, 1840);

Folkedands-Viser og blandede Digte (Copenhagen: C. A. Reitzel, 1842)–includes "Sjællands Kiøbstæder," "Jyllands Kiøbstæder," "De to Dage," and "Børnenes Julesang"; "De to Dage" translated by Stork as "The Two Days" in *A Second Book of Danish Verse,* pp. 10–13; "Børnenes Julesang" translated by D. G. M. Bach as "Christmas Is Here with Joy Untold" in *A Heritage in Song,* no. 21;

Kunnuk og Naja eller Grønlænderne. En Fortælling (Copenhagen: C. A. Reitzel, 1842);

Nye Eventyr og Fortællinger eller Kakkelovnskrogs-Historier (Copenhagen: C. A. Reitzel, 1847);

Taler og Sange ved Sørgefesten i Sorø til Christian den Ottendes Minde (Copenhagen: Sorø Akademi, 1848);

De fire Rubiner. Et Eventyr (Copenhagen: C. A. Reitzel, 1849);

Fire nye Fortællinger (Copenhagen: C. A. Reitzel, 1850)–includes *Christen Bloks Ungdomsstreger;*

Den stumme Frøken. Fortælling (Copenhagen: C. A. Reitzel, 1850);

Landsbybørnene. Nytids-Roman (Copenhagen: C. A. Reitzel, 1852);

Confirmations-Gave. Følgeblade til Luthers lille Catechismus (Copenhagen: C. A. Reitzel, 1854);

Tankebreve fra en Afdød. Digt (Copenhagen: C. A. Reitzel, 1855);

Guldæblet. Et Eventyrdigt i tolv Sange (Copenhagen: C. A. Reitzel, 1856);

Psalmer med Tillæg af andre religiøse og symbolske Digte (Copenhagen: C. A. Reitzel, 1861);

Bernhard Severin Ingemanns Levnetsbog, skreven af ham selv, 2 volumes, edited by Johannes Galskjøt (Copenhagen: C. A. Reitzel, 1862; reprinted, Copenhagen: Gyldendal, 1968);

Tilbageblik paa mit Liv og min Forfattervirksomhed, 1811–1837, edited by Galskjøt (Copenhagen: C. A. Reitzel, 1863);

Efterladte Eventyr og Fortællinger (Copenhagen: C. A. Reitzel, 1864).

Editions and Collections: *Samlede Skrifter,* 41 volumes in 20 (Copenhagen: C. A. Reitzel, 1843–1865)–includes "Aftensang," translated by S. D. Rodholm as "Now Peace Descends," in *A Harvest of Song,* p. 41; "Den Miskundelige," translated by P. C. Paulsen as "As Wide as the Skies Is Thy Love, O My God," in *A Heritage in Song,* no. 30; "Pilgrimssang," translated by Stork as "Lovely the Earth Is," in *A Second Book of Danish Verse,* p. 13; and by Rodholm as "Beauty around Us," in *A Harvest of Song,* p. 95, and in *A Heritage in Song,* no. 71;

Historiske Romaner, edited by P. E. Langballe, 4 volumes (Copenhagen: Gyldendal, 1911–1912)–comprises volume 1, *Valdemar Seier;* volume 2, *Erik Menveds Barndom;* volume 3, *Kong Erik og de Fredløse;* and volume 4, *Prins Otto af Danmark;*

Udvalgte poetiske Skrifter, 2 volumes, edited by Otto Borchsenius (Copenhagen: Gyldendal, 1912)–comprises volume 1, *Valdemar den Store og hans Mænd;* and volume 2, *Eventyr og Fortællinger;*

Digte i Udvalg, edited by Frederik Rønning (Copenhagen: Gad, 1919);

Morgen- og Aftensange, edited by Søren Holm (Copenhagen: Nyt nordisk Forlag, 1944);

Valdemar Seier, edited by Marita Akhøj Nielsen (Copenhagen: Danske Sprog- og Litteraturselskab/Borgen, 1987);

Fjorten Eventyr og Fortællinger, edited by Akhøj Nielsen (Copenhagen: Danske Sprog- og Litteraturselskab/Borgen, 1989);

Lysets engel. Udvalgte digte, edited by Dan Turèll (Copenhagen: Gyldendal, 1989);

Morgensange for Børn, 1837. Syv Aftensange, 1838, edited by Knud Bjarne Gjesing (Herning: P. Kristensen, 1989);

Tankebreve fra en Afdød, edited by Gjesing, afterword by Gjesing and Elna Bækdorf (Copenhagen: C. A. Reitzel, 1995);

Dronning Margrete. Et historisk Digt i 10 Sange, edited by Niels Kofoed (Copenhagen: C. A. Reitzel, 1997);

Tassos Befrielse. Et dramatisk Digt, edited by Kofoed (Copenhagen: C. A. Reitzel, 1998);

Levnetsbog I-II og Tilbageblik paa mit Liv og min Forfatter-Periode fra 1811 til 1837, edited by Jens Keld (Copenhagen: Danske Sprog- og Litteraturselskab/C. A. Reitzel, 1998).

Four poets have left an indelible mark on the Danish hymn: Thomas Kingo, Hans Adolph Brorson, N. F. S. Grundtvig, and, despite protest from certain theologians, B. S. Ingemann. Many religious scholars deride Ingemann's hymns as characterized more by a naive natural religion than by a strictly Lutheran Christianity. Despite theologians' distrust, Ingemann's work is loved by laypeople. His fourteen short morning and evening songs, especially, are so well known that many have no idea of their authorship. Even Ingemann never thought of these simple and idyllic texts as anything special, particularly when one considers the range of his literary output: suspenseful novels, fairy tales, lachrymose tragedies, versified travel books, contemporary satire, emotionally sophisticated love poems, religious allegories, hair-raising thrillers, and heretical statements concerning the soul's continued development following bodily death. The prolific Ingemann even found time to pursue studies in astrology and natural philosophy. In fact, his collected works number forty-one volumes.

Bernhard Severin Ingemann was born on 28 May 1789 and grew up in the village of Torkildstrup on the island of Falster. His father, Søren Sørensen Ingemann, was a minister. As the youngest of nine children, B. S. Ingemann was loved, protected, and spoiled by everyone around him. In the posthumously published *Bernhard Severin Ingemanns Levnetsbog* (Bernhard Severin Ingemann's Autobiography, 1862) he paints a happy and peaceful portrait of his early childhood in which "alle Eventyr var sande og alle Sandheder Eventyr" (all fairy tales were true and all truths were fairy tales). When his father died on New Year's Eve of 1799, at the portal to the new century, his mother, Birgitte Swane Ingemann, was forced to leave the parsonage and move with the many children to Slagelse, in Zealand, where B. S. Ingemann enrolled in grammar school. The change shocked the imaginative and sensitive boy, who had never before experienced organized schooling. His distrust strengthened after he was persuaded, against

Ingemann as a young man (painting by Christian Albrecht Jensen; Museum of National History at Frederiksborg Castle)

his will, to pursue law school at the University of Copenhagen.

Ingemann's father's death and the loss of his childhood home became symbols of a transition from a peaceful and stable time to a period characterized by war, economic crisis, and political upheaval. During the first years of the 1800s, Denmark suffered the consequences of the Napoleonic Wars. The British interpreted the 1794 neutrality treaty of Denmark and Sweden (joined by Russia and Prussia in 1800) as an act of hostility. An English naval attack on the Danish capital led to the Battle of Copenhagen in 1801, and in 1807 the British seized Denmark's battle fleet after bombarding the city. Thus, Denmark entered the war on the French side–with catastrophic consequences. In 1813 the Danish state was forced to declare bankruptcy; after Napoleon's defeat the following year, the Danish-Norwegian kingdom was divided, with Denmark forced to cede Norway to Sweden. These national catastrophes weighed on the young Ingemann, who had–of his own free will–taken part in Copenhagen's defense during the 1807 bombardment. In addition, death thinned out the ranks of his family during this time, and he was especially hard hit by the loss of his beloved mother in 1809. He, too, was plagued with sickness and the expectation of an early demise. In a draft of his memoirs Ingemann relates how, as a student, he plugged the barrel on his pistol in fear that he might "faae Lyst til et pludseligt Spring ind i Aandeverdenen" (suddenly yearn to hop into the next world). This gloomy state of mind lightened, however, when in 1812 he became engaged to his future wife, Lucie Mandix, the daughter of a high-ranking official. But because he had set aside his dreaded law studies to pursue a career in writing, Ingemann had few opportunities to achieve the middle-class existence that would justify a marriage.

In 1811 Ingemann self-published the first volume of *Digte* (Poetry), a successful collection of poems. Although the poems today seem somewhat clumsy, sentimental, and naive, their often radical image of the angel of death and their expression of weltschmerz resonated during such pessimistic times. Ingemann's inspiration was the same as that found in Edward Young's *The Complaint; or, Night-Thoughts on Life, Death, & Immortality* (1742–1746), James MacPherson's poems attributed to Ossian (1762–1763), Ludwig Tieck's *Franz Sternbalds Wanderungen* (The Travels of Franz Sternbald, 1798), and Novalis's *Heinrich von Ofterdingen* (1802). The success of Ingemann's literary debut resulted in furious productivity: by the following year he produced a second volume of *Digte* that includes the play *Mithridat,* which was then followed by *Procne* (1813). The latter, a copious work, includes the lyrical and Romantic novel *Varners poëtiske Vandringer* (Warner's Poetic Wanderings), a radicalized reworking of Johann Wolfgang von Goethe's *Die Leiden des jungen Werther* (The Sorrows of Young Werther, 1774). In Goethe's epistolary novel Werther is driven to suicide by his unhappy passion for his friend's wife. In Ingemann's retelling, the lovers die not of unhappy but of happy love. Although the wandering singer Warner achieves his heart's desire, the two lovers nevertheless choose death; their bodies have become an obstacle to complete unification. Corporeal limitation contradicts love's yearning for boundless development.

At this point in his life a lung disease brought Ingemann dangerously close to the grave and sent him into a spiritual crisis resulting in a stronger Christianity and ethical conviction. In his massive, dark, and allegorical epic *De sorte Riddere* (The Black Knights, 1814), the Christian knight Viduvelt and the skald Theobald unite to set free two young women, the beautiful Seraphine, from Greece, and the saintly Balsora, from Asia. The women are being held prisoner by two characters representing sensual pleasure and cold reflection: the Red Knight and the dwarf Pystrich. Viduvelt and Theobald eventually reunite with the two women: one pair lives a happy life on earth, whereas the other meets in heaven. The world serves as a battleground for the irreconcilable struggle between the powers of light and darkness. Only the spirit of self-sacrifice, cheerful faith in God, and child-like intrepidity can lead lightness and godliness to victory; the opposing forces are doubt, sensual desire, and cold reflection. In Ingemann's adventure poem *Reinald Underbarnet* (Reinald the Wonder Child, 1816), another allegorical tale of emancipation, the young hero's pious and spontaneous naiveté both releases and ennobles the latent forces of nature.

The impetuous Ingemann also began to make his mark as a dramatist. Often influenced by the enthusiasm of his age for William Shakespeare's inventive dramas, Ingemann managed for some time to write several plays each year. His first piece accepted for a performance at the Royal Theater was the historical drama *Masaniello* (1815), set in seventeenth-century Naples. The central character of this tragedy is a poor fisherman who decides to take charge of a populist rebellion against the city's tyrannical governor, appointed by the king. Although the rebellion in the play is completely justifiable, the purpose of the drama is not to agitate for the right to revolt against all authority. On the contrary, Masaniello's revolt, despite its righteous aim, also becomes corrupted. Throughout his life Ingemann remained a steadfast supporter of an absolute–though caring and just–monarchy. His drama interprets the French Revolution as a movement that only led to a harder and bloodier dictatorship. He achieved his greatest theatrical success with the tragedy *Blanca* (1815). The tear-jerking depiction in the play of a tragic love that can find fulfillment only in the next life resonated strongly with the women in the audience. *Blanca* and other dramas, such as *Mithridat, Røsten i Ørkenen* (The Voice in the Wilderness, 1815), *Hyrden af Tolosa* (Shepherd of Tolosa, 1816), and *Løveridderen* (The Lion-Knight, 1816), illustrate the young Ingemann's penchant for emotionalism, theatrical effects, and sensational motifs such as incest, insanity, and patricide.

The pale, beguiling author with the flowing locks was feted as an idol, and female admirers nicknamed Ingemann "Dejligheds-Barnet" (Child of Delight). The critics berated him all the more for it and accused him of painting both his poems and dramas, with their hazy atmospheres and grandiloquent emotions, "i Æter, med Æter og paa Æter" (in ether, with ether, and on ether). Johan Ludvig Heiberg's satirical farce *Julespøg og Nytaarsløier* (Christmas Jests and New Year Tricks, 1817) even used Ingemann's authorship as the object of parody. In contrast, Grundtvig was enamored of Ingemann's writing, which he defended in no uncertain terms: "Han er en besynderlig duftende og sjungende Blomst i Skoven; han er sig selv en Gaade" (He is a rare, fragrant, and singing flower in the forest; he is a mystery in himself). Although Ingemann took no part in the debate, he felt deeply wounded by the time he left Denmark on a travel grant in 1818. The journey took him to Italy, where he remained for a while in Rome. Throughout his European tour he sought contact with several artists, although he consciously avoided visiting Goethe. Ingemann, rejecting Goethe's efforts toward a purely human harmony, felt more akin to radical and nontraditional Romanticism. For some time he lived with the German poet Tieck, and his meeting with the Swedish Romantic Per Daniel Amadeus Atterbom led to a lifelong friendship.

Back in Copenhagen, Mandix was shocked to hear a rumor that Ingemann had married while in Rome. It was only an exaggeration, however, of the fact that her betrothed had been deeply moved by his meeting with a young Danish girl, Maria Bügel. (Later, in *Reiselyren* [The Travel Lyre, 1820], he sang her praises under the pseudonym Valborg.) In the fall of 1819 Ingemann returned home, and in 1822 he became an upper-school teacher in Danish language and literature at the newly reestablished Sorø Academy on the island of Zealand. He and Mandix finally married on 30 July 1822.

In *Reiselyren,* Ingemann describes his foreign adventures in Homeric hexameter. The narrative ends with his arrival in Rome–just before his meeting with Maria. Twelve years later he continued his lyrical travelogue with the publication of *Smaadigte og Reiseminder* (Short Poems and Travel Memoirs, 1832). Another product of his journeys was the completion of *Tassos Befrielse* (The Liberation of Tasso, 1819), a tragedy concerning the sixteenth-century Italian poet Torquato Tasso. Unlike Goethe's *Torquato Tasso* (1790), Ingemann's play celebrates an individual who maintained his spiritual ideals in the face of secularism and societal conventions. In the years immediately following his return to Denmark, Ingemann also wrote a pair of dramatic works, *Kampen for Valhal* (The Struggle for Valhalla, 1821) and *Magnetismen i Barbeerstuen* (Magnetism at the Barber Shop, 1821). The latter work reveals an entirely different side to Ingemann. In this cheerful comedy in the style of Ludvig Holberg, he satirizes the contemporary obsession with mesmerism (or so-called animal magnetism).

From this time on, Ingemann's main literary endeavor was in neither poetry nor drama but instead in the frequently deprecated genre of prose literature. He had previously published some prose works, such as "Krønike om Hr. Helias og Jomfru Beatricia" (The Chronicle of Mr. Helias and Miss Beatricia), from *Julegave* (Christmas Present, 1816), and *De Underjordiske. Et bornholmsk Eventyr* (Subterranean Creatures: A Fairy Tale from Bornholm, 1817). In 1820 he published the collection *Eventyr og Fortællinger* (Fairy Tales and Stories), which included three of his most popular stories, "Sphinxen" (The Sphinx), "Det høie Spil" (High Stakes), and "Moster Maria" (Aunt Maria). These tales are written in the modern "demonic" or fantastic style cultivated by E. T. A. Hoffmann in German literature. Fantasy and coarse realism, beauty and caricature, terror and humor–all are united in a bizarre blend that throws the reader into a state of vague uncertainty. Ingemann continued writing in this vein in *Noveller* (Short Stories, 1827), *Varulven, Den levende Døde, Corsicaneren. Tre Fortællinger* (The Werewolf, The Living Dead, The Corsican: Three Tales, 1835), *Nye Eventyr og Fortællinger eller Kakkelovnskrogs-Historier* (New Fairy Tales or Stories by the Fireplace, 1847), and *Fire nye Fortællinger* (Four New Tales, 1850). Although his short prose works received little attention in his own time, they are now considered landmarks of Danish thriller and horror writing. Despite their throngs of spirits, specters, and werewolves, the tales also bear witness to both a new interest in the outside world and a realistic turn in Ingemann's writing.

Marriage and his position at the remote Sorø Academy brought calm into Ingemann's life. His evening song "Fred hviler over Land og By" (Peace Falls over City and Country), collected in *Morgen- og Aftensange* (Morning and Evening Songs, 1839), dates from this time:

Der er saa fredeligt, saa tyst
I Himmel og paa Jord;
Vær ogsaa stille i mit Bryst,
Du Flygtning som der boer!

(It is so peaceful and so still
In heaven and on earth;
May silence ease my heavy heart,
This searching since my birth!)

Although his students derided Ingemann for his boring lectures, he was popular for his helpful nature and goodwill. His efforts toward improving school life are apparent in the small volume of *Morgenpsalmer til Brug for Eleverne i Sorø Academies Skole* (Morning Hymns for Students at Sorø Academy, 1822). Some of these hymns are still sung, among them "Lover Herren, han er nær" (The Lord Promises, He Is Near). The teachers at Sorø Academy, somewhat removed from Copenhagen, comprised an independent intellectual milieu, one that offered both mutual inspiration and intense power struggles. Ingemann, who lacked either the desire or the ability to take part in faculty intrigues, eventually suffered the disappointment of being named the academy's principal in 1842, a post in which he served until the closure of the school in 1849. His only responsibility as principal, however, was to teach a few hours a week, thus freeing his time for his own writing.

In 1824 Ingemann began a series of books depicting the history of Denmark. The national past had become a favored literary motif in the wave of nationalism that engulfed Europe after the Napoleonic Wars. Grundtvig translated Saxo Grammaticus's Latin chronicle *Gesta Danorum* (Deeds of the Danes, circa 1200) into colloquial Danish. Like Adam Oehlenschläger, Grundtvig also turned his attention to Nordic pagan antiquity. Ingemann, however, found greater inspiration in medieval literature. Although he introduced his series with the epic poetic cycle *Waldemar den Store og hans Mænd* (Valdemar the Great and His Men, 1824), the series first gained popularity with the ensuing novels: *Valdemar Seier* (1826; translated as *Waldemar, Surnamed Seir, or the Victorious,* 1841), *Erik Menveds Barndom* (1828; translated as *The Childhood of King Erik Menved,* 1846), *Kong Erik og de Fredløse* (1833; translated as *King Eric and the Outlaws,* 1843), and *Prins Otto af Danmark og hans Samtid* (Prince Otto of Denmark and His Time, 1835). Walt Whitman tried to publish a translated, abridged edition of *The Childhood of King Erik Menved* in the United States as "The Sleeptalker" but found no publisher. The series concluded with *Dronning Margrete* (Queen Margrete, 1836); like *Waldemar den Store og hans Mænd,* it is a narrative-poem cycle composed in shifting meters. Altogether the series covers 250 years of Danish history: from a land ravaged by civil war in 1150 to a powerful and united Scandinavia under Queen Margrete I in 1398.

With these novels Ingemann turned to the popular genre of the historical novel. With books such as *Waverley* (1814) and *Ivanhoe* (1819), the Scottish author Sir Walter Scott had ushered in the era of the historical novel. Through his own medieval depictions, Ingemann created a domestic Danish series that could compete with translations of Scott's widely popular novels. Unlike Scott, Ingemann used historical figures as central characters; he also felt the responsibility to base his literary works on the serious study of folk ballads, sagas, and Saxo Grammaticus's chronicles. Another product of his historical research was his monograph *Grundtræk til en Nord-Slavisk og Vendisk Gudelære* (Outline for a Northern-Slavic and Wendic Mythology, 1824). In his novels, though, his research was driven by a lively and artistic fantasy. While composing them, Ingemann wrote excitedly to a friend: "Der vrimler en Hær af danske Mænd og Kvinder i min Stue, saa jeg næppe kan rumme dem; mange ere halv døde endnu og mange ved jeg ikke, hvad vil mig" (A swarm of Danish men and women inhabit my living room–so many I can barely contain them. Many are already half-dead, and I have no idea what many of the others want from me).

Ingemann's home at Sorø Academy, where he began teaching in 1822 (photograph by Budtz Müller & Co.; from Carl Langballe, B. S. Ingemann. Et Digterbillede i ny Belysning, *1949; William T. Young Library, University of Kentucky)*

The retelling of history in Ingemann's novels is more popular and practical than academic in scope. That the presentation is pedagogically composed is evident immediately in the introduction to the first volume in the series, *Waldemar den Store og hans Mænd:*

Stig op af Graven, du Slægt, som døde!
Forkynd dit Fald og afmal din Brøde!
Advar os for Udslettelsens Dom,
Og viis os hvorfra din Frelse kom!

(Rise up from the grave, you generations gone!
Proclaim your end and your guilt unknown!
Save us all from the destruction done,
And show us from where Salvation shall come!)

"Kongebøgerne" (The Books about Kings), as the series came to be known, function within a populist educational and societal context. Although the novels depict events of the past, their purpose is to point toward the future. Encouraged by his friend Grundtvig, Ingemann also wanted to contribute to the rebirth of his nation after the catastrophes at the beginning of the nineteenth century. He believed this national reawakening could be aided by a depiction of the kingdom's ability in the Middle Ages to raise itself to greatness after a state of subjugation and dissolution. The moral of Ingemann's conservative historical novels is that the foundation for such an upheaval rests in fear of God and a united coalition of royal power, church, and people. His series urged a combination of national and devotional revival. Through narratives about past achievements, the present time could be moved to renewed courage and industriousness: "Hvad Danmark var, kan det atter i live: / Endnu er Fædrenes Aand i Live" (What Denmark was, it can be once again: / Our forefathers' spirit is still found within).

The prose genre was not considered truly literary in intellectual circles. It is worth noting that Scott, for this reason, published all of his historical novels through 1827 anonymously. Ingemann's novels also received harsh criticism, often in the form of petty detections of error in historical details: for example, medieval citizens were actually much smaller than they are described, and characters exchange gold coins in a time when only silver was in use. Public acclaim slowly drowned out these academic objections, and the books, read by everyone from the royal family on down, reached a wide audience, which had been Ingemann's goal in turning to an often-disparaged genre. Novels in the series such as *Valdemar Seier* have been published no fewer than thirty-six times. The books had a profound influence on national self-awareness. Far into the twentieth century, his books continued to appear as both supplements to a weekly magazine and, in various adaptations, as children's books.

Ingemann was wounded by the literary criticism aimed at his popular novels. Isolated in rural Sorø, far from Copenhagen's trendsetting circles, he felt "som en saaret Snegl i sit Hus" (like a wounded snail inside its shell). In his satiric tale *Huldre-Gaverne eller Ole Navnløses Levnets-Eventyr* (The Talismans of the Forest Nymph or the Tale of Ole the Nameless, 1831) he attempted to respond to both his critics and to all the materialist and irreligious currents that he believed threatened spiritual life. A bitter debate ensued, abetted by Ingemann's contributions, *Nogle Oplysninger om Huldregaverne* (Some Information Regarding the Talismans of the Forest Nymph, 1831) and *Opstanden i Litteraturstaden* (The Rebellion in the Literary City, 1831). His polemic attempts achieved only meager success, however, and the fight only strengthened his feelings of hopelessness and depression, expressed in his poetic cycle *Blade af Jerusalems Skomagers Lommebog* (Pages from the Notebook of the Cobbler of Jerusalem, 1833), retitled *Ahasverus* in volume 6 of *Samlede Skrifter* (Collected Writings, 1845). The poet was able to depict himself, along with his depressed state of mind, in the legend of Ahasverus, "the wandering Jew," doomed to wander restlessly until the end of time. Ingemann also felt homeless and estranged from the political and materialistic tendencies in the growing liberalism and passion for freedom of his time. His dramatic poem *Renegaten* (The Renegade, 1838) reflects the revolutionary tendencies racing through Europe in the 1830s. The central character is a young, revolutionary Jew who travels to Constantinople and, for opportunistic reasons, converts to Islam. With promises of freedom and equality, he incites the masses toward rebellion; yet, the more power he usurps, the more he turns into a gruesome despot. His foil is a disinherited sultan, a true Muslim who finally returns to recapture the throne.

In *Renegaten* and many of his other works Ingemann warned against "Kødets emancipation" (the emancipation of the flesh) and "Allemandsregimentet efter Kropsflertalssystemet" (Common rule based on a system of the majority of bodies). He was also repulsed by society's increasing politicizing:

Politik er ret blevet Mode–
Gud give den nu dog holdt Munden;
Man kan faa for Meget af det Gode,
sagde Bonden–
han fik Møglæsset over sit Ho'de.

(Politics is truly in fashion–
If only you didn't have to hear it so much;
"You can get too much of a good thing,"
The farmer said–
He got a cartload of dung on his head.)

Ingemann focused, instead, on his own feelings and fantasies. In *Holger Danske* (Holger the Dane, 1837) he crafted a ballad cycle based on tales about the old legendary hero. Holger, an emanation of the Danish soul, slumbers until times of danger awaken his courage, loyalty, and honesty, inspiring him to save his country. The hero, recently become a Christian, travels all over the world in the naive hope of discovering the kingdom of God. During his many journeys he performs glorious, chivalrous deeds; yet, he soon realizes that no earthly place can fulfill his heavenly longing. Unlike Ahasverus, Holger knows where he belongs on earth, although the soul's true home can be found only in the next world. The poetic cycle expresses a bright optimism about life's constant ability to renew itself.

Ingemann's conviction that a person's deepest longing can be sated only spiritually also appears in the dark fairy-tale drama *Salomons Ring* (Solomon's Ring, 1839). Like a Faust figure, the wise old king Solomon searches for that word that can solve the mystery of life and control the forces of nature; this quest for knowledge draws him into the clutches of a necromancer who convinces him that the solution lies in the word "Nothing!" Solomon soon loses his royal power, and his kingdom lies in waste around him. Finally, he realizes that the true solution to life's mystery lies only in the prophetic word that heralds Christ's coming. This dramatic tale opens with a cycle of sensitive, passionate poems retelling the story of the love between the Shulamite woman and Solomon in the Song of Solomon from the Old Testament.

Ingemann was admired for his collection *Høimesse-Psalmer* (Hymns for Morning Service, 1825), songs filled with the Romantic elements of horror ballads. In time, though, he was remembered more for his simple and modest morning and evening songs. The first small pamphlet, with the almost apologetic title *Morgensange for Børn* (Morning Songs for Children, 1837), was mostly considered a private greeting to Ingemann's friends. The simple and innately religious expression in the songs captivated the composer C. E. F. Weyse, however, and he set them to music; thus, they achieved a lasting popularity. Weyse also challenged Ingemann to write a complimentary collection, *Syv Aftensange* (Seven Evening Songs, 1838). The lyrical tone of the poems is both familiar and heartfelt, their religious mood characterized by a strong sense of faith and joy. They proffer the portrait of a peaceful and joyous universe in which any act of violence or conflict seems impossible. In the morning song "Lysets Engel" (The Angel of Light), the angel glides majestically over the firmament and lovingly envelops the world in his luminous cloak; yet, at the same moment, he can bend gently over a cradle to awaken a child with a soft kiss. At the triumphant sight of the angel of light, the world begins its multicolored day. The fresh morning air falls across the earth as the sun glimmers in the windows of small houses, the cocks crow, and the chirping birds give thanks for the light. Flowers nod faithfully to each other, and the snail begins his peaceful wanderings. People start their tasks, many of which end unsuccessfully. Nevertheless, in the evening song "Dagen gaaer med raske Fjed" (The Day Departs with Rapid Steps) they find comfort in their deeds when the cool evening brings peace: "Viljen seer vor Herre paa" (The Lord sees our intentions). In a final display of sumptuousness the angel of light raises its glorious castle in the west before vanishing into the castle's glowing amber tower:

Der staaer et Slot i Vesterled,
Tækket med gyldne Skjolde;
Did gaaer hver Aften Solen ned
Bag Rosenskyernes Volde.

Det Slot blev ei med Hænder gjort:
Mageløst staaer det smykket;
Fra Jord til Himmel naaer dets Port;
Vor Herre selv det har bygget.

(There stands a castle in the west
Sheathed with shields of gold;
There seeks the sun his nightly rest
Within the bright stronghold.

No mortal hand has raised those high
Flame-towers richly gilded,
That portal stretched from earth to sky–
These God himself has builded.)

Still, one must not fear the night as it spreads its shadow across the sky. In the darkness of night the glittering host of stars recalls God's light.

No great distance between heaven and earth appears in this idyllic and harmonious universe. As Ingemann observes in *Holger Danske,* "Har Sjælens Liv ei Ende, saa er der ingen Død, / Og vi er dog saa godt som i Paradiset fød" (If the soul is eternal, death has no sting, / And we are born in paradise, beneath the angel's wing). Both the morning and evening songs depict this Edenic life in its earthly form. It is not Christ the suffering redeemer who stands central to the religious worldview of such songs as "Bliv hos os, naar Dagen helder" (Remain with Us at Close of Day; translated as "Be with Us," 1953) but, instead, the almighty and protecting God: "Du kjære Fader og Gud!" (Thou dear God and father!). God lays his protective hand over all living things, the separation of time and space dissolves, and the great and the small become one in equal, benevolent concern. In "Den skjønne Jordens Sol gik ned" (The Sun of the Lovely Earth Was Setting) this view expands, almost imperceptibly, into a cosmic vision:

Gud! i din Haand alt stort er smaat,
Men kjært det Mindste tillige.
Den Barnesjæl er bjerget godt,
Som skjuler sig i dit Rige.

(God, in thy hands the great are small,
The smallest loved the most:
That child's soul, most saved of all,
Within thy heavenly host.)

Literary critics have often compared the concrete religious images and joyous sensibility of Ingemann's morning and evening songs to a more primitive, primeval faith in God. Even Georg Brandes, a naturalist and atheist, found within these texts "noget lige saa skønt og enestaaende som i en Veda-hymne eller en gammel hebraisk Salme" (something just as lovely and unique as in a Vedic hymn or an old Hebraic psalm). Brandes also felt that Ingemann possessed a "Simpelhed i hans Sind, der førte ham tilbage til den kristelige Mytedannelses første Tider" (simpleness of mind that led him back to the first age of the Christian myth's creation).

The religious feeling of the morning and evening songs may well be characterized as primitive in that they express something primordial and fundamental in their author's being. Ingemann offered a fine approach to this religious worldview in his unfinished autobiography, published as *Bernhard Severin Ingemanns Levnetsbog.* Conscious that he would probably never complete it, Ingemann worked on it in the hope that he would at least be able to present his early childhood years.

Ingemann in 1861 (photograph by Georg E. Hansen; courtesy of the Danish Royal Library, Copenhagen)

Believing that the most important traits of one's personality were formed at this time, he claimed that "man behøver kun et Slags aandeligt Forstørrelsesglas, for i en udført Barndomshistorie at læse et helt Levnetsløb" (one needs only a kind of spiritual magnifying glass to read an entire lifetime within a childhood). Ingemann emphasized the importance of portraying a child's religious upbringing. The initial childhood years are the "mythical time" when the child "ligesaa godt kunde drage de store Himmellegemer som de store Mennesker ind i sine Lege" (could just as easily involve great heavenly bodies as well as great people in his pastimes). Ingemann characterizes a child's religious feeling as "den adamitiske før Udjagelsen af Paradiset" (the Edenic, before the expulsion from paradise). This idyllic and brilliant universe reappears in his morning and evening songs. In his autobiography Ingemann tells about himself as a child: "Det var ham, som det Liv, han daglig levede, var ligesaa stadig og uforgængeligt som Sol og Maane syntes ham, der Dag og Nat gik op og ned i samme Orden" (It seemed to him that his daily life was every bit as constant and eternal as the daily rising and falling of the sun and the moon).

Ingemann's religious imagery is especially characterized by symbols of rhythmic repetition and organic development, such as the movement of the celestial bodies or the budding of flowers. Therefore, he understands the human soul's union with the divine not as a dramatic resurrection from the grave but rather as a slow awakening to the spiritual world. The divine seeds have already been planted in each human's earthly form. With time, this concept of religious awakening achieved greater and greater significance for Ingemann. Through conversations with his intellectual friend, the widow Ingeborg Christiane von Rosenørn, he slowly constructed a speculative-spiritual worldview, which he expressed in his two 1840 monographs, *Stjernebilledernes Symbolik* (The Symbols of the Stars) and *Skyhimlen eller den Luke-Howardske Skyformationslære, betragtet som Billedform for Naturpoesien* (The Cloudy Sky, or the Teachings of Luke Howard on Cloud Formations, Viewed as Images for Natural Poetry). In the latter work Ingemann interprets different cloud formations as visual expressions of the soul's ascension toward God. In the didactic poem *Confirmations-Gave* (Confirmation's Gift, 1854) he rejects the standard Christian creed of bodily resurrection. Ingemann felt that this dogma constituted "en mørk Krog i Kirken" (a dark corner in the church) and that "vore Psalmer ere ikke frie for en Liglugt deraf" (our hymns are thus marked by the smell of dead bodies). He once described the concept as "Ligenes Opstandelse" (resurrection of the corpses). Ingemann replaced this death-oriented approach with the depiction of a spiritual awakening.

Ingemann, who also rejected the conventional Christian notion of eternal judgment, contended instead that following bodily death the human soul would continue to develop in "Mellemtilstanden" (an intermediate state of being) and that this ongoing awakening would eventually result in all souls' salvation. He imagined that the spiritual development would occur through a series of rebirths on other heavenly bodies. One such spiritual development after corporeal death is depicted in poetic form in *Tankebreve fra en Afdød* (Philosophical Note from One Deceased, 1855). In his earthly life the deceased was a spiritually challenged and egotistical person (a politician!), and so his soul first wanders aimlessly after his sudden death. Slowly, though, the soul comes to its senses. By viewing its previous life it acknowledges its offenses and experiences a cleansing and an ascension, slowly bringing it closer to the spirit world. The allegorical scenery the soul passes during its ascendant journey reveals that even persons such as Judas or Cain may find a better path. The final goal is all souls' ultimate unification with God. The fairy-tale poem *Guldæblet* (The Golden Apple, 1856) presents a similar story of spiritual transformation. Every person is born with an invisible golden apple that must be preserved. The golden apple decidedly prevents its owner from finding any real joy in earthly things. Still, if one is capable of preserving it, it changes into a priceless pearl from which a bright bird ultimately soars toward heaven. Ingemann offered a more theological expression of his unorthodox viewpoints in the unfinished didactic poem *Blik paa det Første og det Sidste* (View of the First and the Last, written in 1858), which was included in the forty-one-volume *Samlede Skrifter* (1843–1865). Grundtvig, who had throughout his life served as Ingemann's helper and defender, became infuriated over these heresies and formally banished his old friend from Christianity. Ingemann continued to view himself as a Christian, though, and even accepted the job of revising the established church's hymnal in 1854.

Although Ingemann sometimes felt both isolated and lonely in rural Sorø, he enjoyed a harmonious and lifelong marriage with Lucie (or "Cie," as he called her). She was a highly individual and idealistic person who cultivated the art of painting with greater zest than talent. Her florals, altar pieces, and biblical illustrations found one of their few admirers in Ingemann. Like her husband, she also wrote a memoir, *Et lille Levnetsløb til Bernhard* (A Little Life for Bernhard), which was published in 1996. The childless couple happily received into their home guests, among them Hans Christian Andersen. Over coffee and liqueurs the older Ingemann enjoyed entertaining family friends with his jovial humor, some of which surfaces in several of his writings–for example, the merry tale *Christen Bloks Ungdomsstreger* (Christen Blok's Youthful Escapades, 1850). Some of his later works are characterized by a more down-to-earth, extroverted, and realistic viewpoint than the spiritual writings of his youth. In the poetic cycles "Sjællands Kiøbstæder" (The Market Towns of Zealand) and "Jyllands Kiøbstæder" (The Market Towns of Jutland), both published in *Folkedands-Viser og blandede Digte* (Folk-Dancing Songs and Assorted Poems, 1842), he lauds the quiet, provincial idyll. *Folkedands-Viser og blandede Digte* also includes new texts on popular occasions recalled from childhood. *Kunnuk og Naja eller Grønlænderne* (Kunnuk and Naja, or the Greenlanders, 1842) is a realistic novel about the arrival of Christianity in Greenland.

In 1848 the movement for political and national freedom that was sweeping the rest of Europe took hold in Denmark. The king promised a free constitution; with support from Germany, the German-speaking population in southern Denmark demanded independence and rebelled against the monarchy. This revolt led to war (1848–1850). Ingemann distrusted such demands for political freedom and democracy. He expressed his opposition in the allegorical fairy tale *De fire Rubiner* (The Four Rubies, 1849) but in such a vague manner that he eventually had to explicate the tale in a postscript to *Fire nye Fortællinger.* Despite his peaceful and passive nature, Ingemann was nevertheless sympathetic to the nationalism–"ånden fra -48" (the spirit of '48)–building after the rebellion of the German population and the ensuing war. The main character in his novel *Den stumme Frøken* (The Silent Miss, 1850) is a young, mute girl whose tongue suddenly finds its voice when she cries out "med Gud!" (with God!) at the shock of hearing about the German revolt. She functions as a symbol of Ingemann's dream of the national spirit, Holger Danske, who also regains his speech. The novel advises circumspection and moderation toward Denmark's enemies, however, and encourages "Ydmyghed over for Gud baade i Lykke og Ulykke" (humility in the face of God–in both joy and sorrow). The war against Germany and the pro-German elements ended in Danish victory, which strengthened Ingemann's hopes for his country's future. This bright mood characterizes his last great novel, *Landsbybørnene* (Village Children, 1852), a realistic, contemporary depiction of a poor village boy who develops into a great musician. After traveling the wide world the young man returns, following the war, to his homeland. He is ready to face the challenge of leading the movement for a true national folk music.

In the exciting years after the Danish victory of 1850, Ingemann, praised as a great national poet, received on his seventieth birthday a symbolic golden horn from a group of Danish women. He also had the good fortune to die before the same national fervor led to a catastrophic war against Germany in 1864. At the time of his death on 24 February 1862, Ingemann was sleeping calmly in the warm comfort of his own optimistic teachings on spiritual development. In one of his late poems published posthumously in Carl Langballe's 1949 biography, he gently consoles Lucie with a glimpse of their impending reunion:

Den Verden, jeg forlader,
Var Sjælens første Trin
Til alle Sjæles Fader,
Som bød os til sig ind.

(The world that I am leaving
Is but the soul's first stride
To the father of all beings
Who calls us to his side.)

Letters:

Breve til og fra Bernh. Sev. Ingemann, edited by Victor Heise (Copenhagen: C. A. Reitzel, 1879);

Brevveksling mellem B. S. Ingemann og Fru I. C. v. Rosenørn, edited by Heise (Copenhagen: C. A. Reitzel, 1881);

Grundtvig og Ingemann. Brevvexling, 1821–1859, edited by Svend Grundtvig (Copenhagen: Samfundet til den danske Litteraturs Fremme, 1882);

Ingemann og Atterbom. En Brevveksling, edited by Kjeld Galster (Copenhagen: H. Hagerup, 1924);

Hauch og Ingemann. En Brevveksling, edited by M. Hatting (Copenhagen: Gyldendal, 1933).

Biographies:

Herman Schwanenflügel, *Ingemanns Liv og Digtning* (Copenhagen: C. A. Reitzel, 1886);

Richard Petersen, *Mindeskrift om Bernhard Severin Ingemann* (Copenhagen: K. Schønberg, 1889);

Frederik Rønning, *B. S. Ingemann. Liv og Digtning* (Copenhagen: Gad, 1927);

Carl Langballe, *B. S. Ingemann. Et Digterbillede i ny Belysning* (Copenhagen: Gyldendal, 1949);

Peter Balslev-Clausen, *Salmedigteren B. S. Ingemann* (Frederiksberg: Materialecentralen, Religionspædagogisk Center, 1989).

References:

Louise Arnheim and Lena Kristensen, eds., *Registrant over B. S. Ingemann og Lucie Ingemann, f. Mandix papirer og bøger i offentlige samlinger* (Copenhagen: Kongelige Bibliotek, 1992);

Kjeld Galster, *Fra Ahasverus til Landsbybørnene* (Kolding: K. Jørgensen, 1927);

Galster, *Ingemanns historiske Romaner og Digte* (Copenhagen: H. Aschehoug, 1922);

Galster, "Stadier i Ingemanns Barndom og første Ungdom," *Edda,* 17 (1922): 66–87;

Knud Bjarne Gjesing, "Den indre revolte. B. S. Ingemann: 'Sphinxen,'" in *Læsninger i dansk litteratur,* volume 2: *1820–1900,* edited by Povl Schmidt and Ulrik Lehrmann (Odense: Odense Universitetsforlag, 1998), pp. 9–25, 331–332;

Alf Henriques, *Det danske Skæbnedrama,* Studier fra Sprog- og Oldtidsforskning, no. 172 (Copenhagen: P. Branner, 1936);

Niels Kofoed, *H. C. Andersen og B. S. Ingemann. Et livsvarigt venskab* (Copenhagen: C. A. Reitzel, 1992);

Kofoed, *Den ukendte Ingemann. Intertekstuelle Problemer og arketypiske Mønstre i B. S. Ingemanns Forfatterskab* (Copenhagen: C. A. Reitzel, 1996);

Finn Stein Larsen, "'–og ingen formummet skælm.' En tekstlæsning i B. S. Ingemann: 'Erik Menveds Barndom,'" *Kritik,* 39 (1976): 68–81;

Ivy York Möller-Christensen, "Bernhard Severin Ingemann og eventyrgenren," *Nordica,* 3 (1986): 121–150;

Jens Nørregård, *Bernhard Severin Ingemanns Digterstilling og Digterværd* (Copenhagen: K. Schønberg, 1886);

Kåre Olsen and Helge Topsøe-Jensen, eds., *Ingemann-manuskripter* (Copenhagen: Danske Sprog- og Litteraturselskab/Munksgaard, 1951);

Sven H. Rossel, "Midnight Songs and Churchyard Ballads," in *Vänbok. Festgabe für Otto Gschwantler zum 60. Geburtstag,* edited by Imbi Sooman (Vienna: Verband der Wissenschaftlichen Gesellschaften Österreichs, 1990), pp. 237–264;

Erik Thygesen, "Litteraturens Rige er en aandelig Fristat," in *Analyser af dansk kortprosa,* edited by Jørgen Dines Johansen, volume 1 (Copenhagen: Borgen, 1971), pp. 109–171.

Papers:

B. S. Ingemann's papers and manuscripts are at the Danish Royal Library in Copenhagen.

J. P. Jacobsen

(7 April 1847 - 30 April 1885)

Mark Mussari
Villanova University

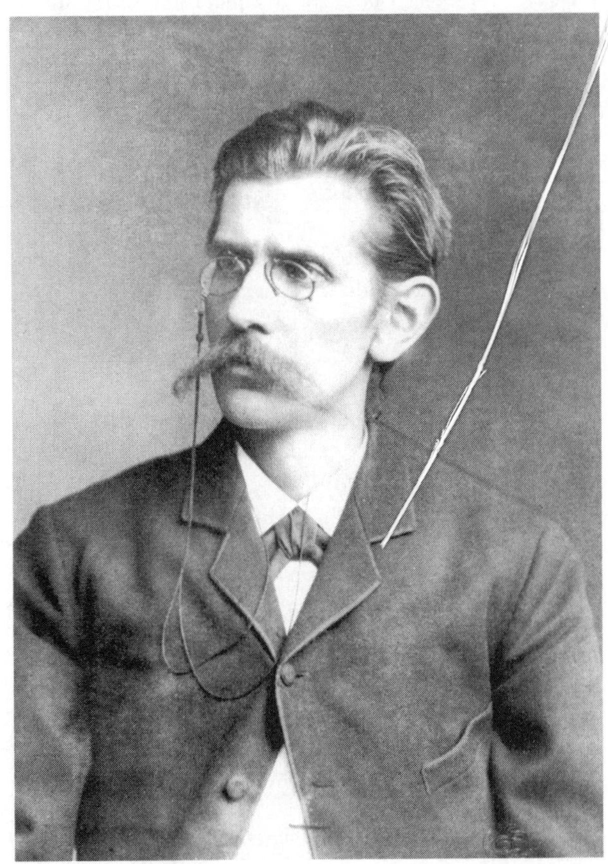

J. P. Jacobsen (photograph by J. Peterson & Søn; courtesy of the Danish Royal Library, Copenhagen)

BOOKS: *Fru Marie Grubbe. Interieurer fra det 17. Aarhundrede* (Copenhagen: Gyldendal, 1876); translated by Hanna Astrup Larsen as *Marie Grubbe. A Lady of the Seventeenth Century* (New York: American-Scandinavian Foundation, 1917);

Niels Lyhne. Roman (Copenhagen: Gyldendal, 1880); translated by Ethel F. Robertson as *Siren Voices* (London: Heinemann, 1896), and by Larsen as *Niels Lyhne* (New York: American-Scandinavian Foundation, 1919);

Mogens og andre Noveller (Copenhagen: Gyldendal, 1882); translated by Anna Grabow as *Mogens and Other Stories,* Sea Gull Library, volume 2 (New York: Nicholas L. Brown, 1921)–also includes "Fru Fønss," translated by Carl Christian Jensen as "Fru Fönss," in *Denmark's Best Stories: An Introduction to Danish Fiction,* edited by Larsen (New York: American-Scandinavian Foundation, 1928), pp. 119–148; "To Verdener," translated by H. Knudsen as "Two Worlds," in *Great Short Stories of the World,* edited by Barrett H. Clark and Maxim Leiber (Cleveland: World, 1925), pp. 766–769; and "Pesten i Bergamo," translated by Henry Meyer as "Death in Bergamo," in *Anthology of Danish Literature: Realism to Present,* edited by F. J. Billeskov Jansen and P. M. Mitchell (Carbondale: Southern Illinois University Press, 1971), pp. 289–305;

Digte og Udkast (Copenhagen: Gyldendal, 1886)–includes "I Seraillets Have," "Løft de klingre Glaspokaler," "Silkesko over gylden Læst," "Genrebillede," "Lad Vaaren komme, mens den vil," "Lys over Landet," "Har Dagen sanket al sin Sorg," "En Arabesk," "Arabesk til en Haandtegning af Michel Angelo," and "Grækenland," translated by Paul Selver as "In the Seraglio Garden," "Lift the Goblets, Loud and Glinting," "Silken Shoe upon Golden Last," "Genre-picture," "Let Spring Come Bearing, Sith He Will," "Light over the Land," "When Day Has Set its Grief Aside," "An Arabesque," "Arabesque to a Drawing by Michael Angelo," and "Greece," in *Poems by J. P. Jacobsen* (Oxford: Blackwell, 1920); "En Arabesk," "Herre, ved du hvad du gjorde," "Skoven hvisker med Toves Røst," "Nævner min Tanke dig," "Har Dagen sanket al sin Sorg," "Genrebillede," and "Det bødes der for," translated by S. Foster Damon and Robert Stillman as "An Arabesque," "Valdemar's Complaint over His Murdered Mistress," "The Wood Whispers with Tove's Voice," "Apparition," "Night Piece,"

"Genre Picture," and "Scarlet Roses," in *A Book of Danish Verse,* edited by Oluf Friis (New York: American-Scandinavian Foundation, 1922), pp. 118–125; "Nat," "Drøm," "Der hjælper ej Drømme," "Navnløs," "Silkesko over gylden Læst," and "Irmelin Rose," translated by Charles Wharton Stork as "In the Moonlight," "Dream," "No More than a Dream," "The Moment Inexpressible," "Silken Shoe upon Golden Last," and "Irmelin Rose," in *A Second Book of Danish Verse* (New York: American-Scandinavian Foundation, 1947), pp. 67–69;

Darwin, hans Liv og hans Lærer, by Jacobsen and Vilhelm Møller (Copenhagen: Gyldendal, 1893).

Editions: *Samlede Værker I–V,* edited by Morten Borup (Copenhagen: Danske Sprog- og Litteraturselskab, 1924–1929);

Niels Lyhne, edited, with an afterword, by Niels Barfoed, Gyldendals Bibliotek, no. 18 (Copenhagen: Gyldendal, 1970);

Samlede Værker I–VI, edited by Frederik Nielsen (Copenhagen: Rosenkilde & Bagger, 1972–1974);

Niels Lyhne. Roman, edited, with an afterword, by Jørn Vosmar, Danske Klassikere (Copenhagen: Borgen, 1986);

Fru Marie Grubbe, edited, with an afterword, by Jørn Erslev Andersen, Danske Klassikere (Copenhagen: Borgen, 1989);

Lyrik og prosa, edited, with an afterword, by Andersen, Danske Klassikere (Copenhagen: Borgen, 1993).

Editions in English: *Marie Grubbe. A Lady of the Seventeenth Century,* Library of Scandinavian Literature, no. 30 (New York: American-Scandinavian Foundation, 1917; revised, with an introduction and notes, by Robert Raphael, 1975);

Niels Lyhne, translated by Tiina Nunnally, with an afterword by Eric O. Johannesson (Seattle: Fjord Press, 1990);

Mogens and Other Stories, translated, with an afterword, by Nunnally (Seattle: Fjord Press, 1994).

TRANSLATIONS: Charles Darwin, *Om Arternes Oprindelse ved Kvalitetsvalg eller ved de heldigst stillede Formers Sejr i Kampen for Tilværelsen* (Copenhagen: Gyldendal, 1872);

Darwin, *Menneskets Afstamning og Parringsvalget* (Copenhagen: Gyldendal, 1874).

In 1880 Danish novelist Herman Bang was sent as a correspondent to interview J. P. Jacobsen. Jacobsen had already been fighting tuberculosis for years, and Bang was shocked at the sickly state of the famed author of *Fru Marie Grubbe. Interieurer fra det 17. Aarhundrede* (1876; translated as *Marie Grubbe. A Lady of the Seventeenth Century,* 1917). Bang was most disturbed, though, by Jacobsen's eyes. In an article appearing in the newspaper *Nutiden* (5 December 1886), Bang wrote, ". . . man syntes, det laa paa én som et Par Forskerøjne, der saa lige igennem én fra en stille Krog" (they seem to stare like the eyes of an investigator, looking straight through you from a silent corner). After some uncomfortable pauses, the two authors exchanged thoughts on the novels they were currently writing. Jacobsen told Bang that the name of his most recent protagonist was "Niels . . . Niels Lyhne."

The sickly author whom Bang encountered died five years after their meeting–but within the short span of his life, Jacobsen produced some of the most influential writing of Danish literature, affecting such world figures as Henrik Ibsen, Thomas Mann, James Joyce, August Strindberg, and Rainer Maria Rilke. Jacobsen's fame and influence are even more impressive considering the highly innovative nature of his writing. Although Jacobsen has been called a naturalist, a realist, and a Darwinist, his writing reveals that he was first and foremost a stylist whose inventive prose reflects an imagist of the highest order.

Jens Peter Jacobsen was born in Thisted, a harbor town on the Limfjord in Jutland, on 7 April 1847, the son of Christen Jacobsen, a successful merchant, and Benthe Marie Hundahl, who came from a family of educators. Jens Peter, one of four children, started school at the age of four. He was by no means a stellar student, even in the areas that interested him, natural history and Danish, but he distinguished himself with his early literary output, including poems (the first written at the age of nine), songs about school life, parodies, and a full-length play, "Kærlighed. Sørgespil i 6 Akter" (Love. A Tragedy in 6 Acts). The natural environment around Thisted harbor fed both the imaginative and the scientific sides of Jacobsen's nature. Two of his childhood friends on the beach served as inspirations for two of the main characters in *Niels Lyhne* (1880; translated, 1919), and the Limfjord's varied plant life and myriad shells sparked the scientist in Jacobsen. Botany held a special fascination for the young Jutlander, who was lauded by later professors of botany for the care and ability with which he approached plant life. On 9 April 1863, after his confirmation, Jacobsen moved to Copenhagen to pursue further studies.

In Copenhagen, Jacobsen's early prolific writing evinced itself at school in a self-produced weekly magazine called *Kvas* (Twigs). Jacobsen filled *Kvas* with poems, fairy tales (some in the style of Hans Christian Andersen), botanical essays, and lectures. On the literary front, Jacobsen had already read and been influenced by many of the great Danish authors–including Ludvig Holberg, Adam Oehlenschläger, and B. S. Ingemann–*before* he arrived in Copenhagen. By the age of eighteen, he had familiarized himself with the works of Johann

Wolfgang von Goethe and Johann Christoph Friedrich von Schiller.

As an undergraduate, Jacobsen continued both his scientific and his literary pursuits, the latter including prose pieces written in the style of Søren Kierkegaard. He referred to his diverse interests as a conflict between the lyre and the microscope. A telling hint at Jacobsen's (and many of his protagonists') detachment from religious thought also occurs in his comment that his writing "vilde ikke blive en kristelig" (would not be Christian) and that the divine, to him, meant the laws of nature. In Copenhagen he also formed a private society, Agathon, which produced a monthly magazine of the same name, many of its articles written by Jacobsen. The literary society and its publication had as their main interest "the most recent Danish literature."

As early as 1868, Jacobsen produced one of his first major works, the poetry cycle *Hervert Sperring,* which he sent to the Danish publishing house Gyldendal, where it was rejected. Two other publishing houses followed suit. It was first published posthumously in the 1886 collection *Digte og Udkast* (Poems and Sketches), edited by his friends Vilhelm Møller and Edvard Brandes. An undeniably autobiographical quality, including prescient allusions to an early death, pervades the poems of *Hervert Sperring,* in which a gifted youth is introduced to the magic of poetry by his mother. Eventually, he retreats into a dreamworld. The title also reflects Jacobsen's fondness for his youth: "Hervert" is a variant of "Havør," one of Jacobsen's nicknames as a child, and "Sperring" is the name of a village just outside of Thisted. The presence of childhood pervades much of his work. Jacobsen was primarily influenced by old Danish folklore concerning the elf maiden who appears to mortal men and seduces them into the elf hill, only to leave them transformed and unable to cope with everyday life. The elf maiden comes to represent the dream of a woman that supplants any real-life experiences for the male protagonist, a recurring erotic motif throughout Jacobsen's literary output.

That the central character of *Hervert Sperring* is an inveterate dreamer also hints at the main themes of *Niels Lyhne*. At the end of "Drøm" (Dream), one of the poems in the cycle, Jacobsen wrote on the manuscript: "Fremkaldt ved en Historie, der vil findes i 'Atheisten,' hvis jeg nogen Sinde faar denne Roman skreven" (Inspired by a story that will appear in "The Atheist," if I ever finish writing that novel). For many years "The Atheist" served as the working title for *Niels Lyhne,* the reference thus indicating how early Jacobsen was contemplating that novel.

Many critics view the poems of *Hervert Sperring* as one long monologue dealing with its author's own struggle between the joy and pain of life as a dreamer. Jacobsen once commented, "Hele mit eget Drømmerliv skulde lægges deri i alle dets Nuancer, med al dets Fryd og Smerte" (All of my own life as a dreamer would be found there, in all of its nuances, with all its joy and pain). Jacobsen's early verses also seem greatly influenced by the poetry of Edgar Allan Poe, particularly in the emphasis on fear and terror (evident in such lines as "Jeg er gal! / Men jeg kjender mit Vanvid" (I am crazy / But I know my madness). In *Hervert Sperring,* Jacobsen established many of the recurring images that came to define his later works, among them a strong reliance on colorific language, foggy scenery, distant stars, swimming clouds, and frequent references to body parts. A fine example of these techniques occurs in "Til Asali" (To Asali), later set to music by Carl Nielsen along with some of Jacobsen's other poems.

Jacobsen conceived his next work, *En Cactus springer ud* (A Cactus Blooms), though never completely finished, as a collection of both poetry and prose. Like his previous song cycle, *En Cactus springer ud* was not published until 1886. In this work, the poet once again concerns himself with the effects of madness, particularly in its relation to the erotic. Within this song cycle, Jacobsen employed his first arabesque, a name he applied to an intricate poetic endeavor that does not follow one line of progression. Jacobsen's arabesque involves the Greek mythical figure of Pan, but the narrator changes Pan from a nature figure into a love god. The imagery is a blending of madness and chromaticism as nature becomes both threatening and transformative.

In *En Cactus springer ud,* Jacobsen also included the song cycle known as "Gurresange" (Songs of Gurre), inspired by Danish medieval legends about King Valdemar and his mistress, Tove (in 1910 Arnold Schönberg set the German translation to music). Throughout the cycle Jacobsen relies heavily on contrasts of shade and light. The first poem, "Valdemar," begins in images of blue and purple, setting up a dreamscape carried throughout the poems. In a commentary to Jacobsen's *Samlede Værker* (Collected Works, 1972–1974), Frederik Nielsen observes that "Hvor *Hervert Sperring* har erosdrøm og eros-længsel har *Gurresange* eros-virkelighed" (whereas Hervert Sperring contains eros-dreaming and eros-longing, Gurresange has eros-reality). Jacobsen's finely tuned sense of the effects of natural urges on one's state of mind, inspired by his scientific leanings, is a hallmark of his writing, innovative in its honest depiction of women's as well as men's sexual instincts.

In *En Cactus springer ud,* Jacobsen also composed one of his first successful pieces of prose, "Udlændinge" (Strangers), about a disassociated couple who live on the moors outside an agrarian community: the husband is a pauper, and his wife a swarthy gypsy woman. Jens prefers to play his clarinet, and Karen would rather work at her spinning wheel than weed. When their little girl dies, a silent response to their desperate prayers for her life, they move to town, where Jens plays his music, and Karen performs a passionate gypsy dance. Finally, Karen dies, and Jens turns–for the first time in his life–to the bottle. In this brief tale, Jacobsen employs motifs he returns to throughout his writing, particularly characters who defy conventionality and prefer to live by their own instincts.

In addition to his literary output, Jacobsen continued his scientific studies and published articles on a wide range of topics in the magazine *Nyt dansk Maanedskrift* (New Danish Monthly), edited by Møller. Throughout the run of *Nyt dansk Maanedskrift,* Jacobsen published scientific articles, including "Darwins Theori" (Darwin's Theory), published in January 1871. Many scholars believe it is the first Danish article on Charles Darwin. Jacobsen's thoughts were met with resistance, including a notorious epistolary battle between Jacobsen and Danish bishop D. G. Monrad. Jacobsen's articles did, however, attract the interest of Gyldendal Publishing House, which asked Jacobsen to translate *On the Origin of Species by Means of Natural Selection; or, The Preservation of Favoured Races in the Struggle for Life* (1860). His Danish translation, *Om Arternes Oprindelse ved Kvalitetsvalg eller ved de heldigst stillede Formers Sejr i Kampen for Tilværelsen,* was published in 1872, followed in 1874 by *Menneskets Afstamning og Parringsvalget,* his translation of Darwin's *The Descent of Man, and Selection in Relation to Sex* (1871). Thus, Jacobsen introduced Darwin to Scandinavia. Anna Linck, one of Jacobsen's early biographers, observes that "Darwinismen blev Jacobsens nye Religion, og den blev han Tro resten af sit Liv" (Darwinism became Jacobsen's new religion, and he remained faithful to it for the rest of his life).

Also during this time, Jacobsen became a disciple of the teachings of Georg Brandes and the Modern Breakthrough. Brandes gave his famous lectures at the University of Copenhagen in 1871. At first, Jacobsen was joined by a small circle of Danish literati, including Møller and poet Holger Drachmann. Along with Georg and Edvard Brandes, the group founded Litteraturselskabet (The Literary Society) on 5 March 1872. Under Georg Brandes's guidance, Jacobsen committed himself to life as a writer, although his literary creations do not quite fit Brandes's specific demands for literature dealing with social debates. As Jacobsen once explained in a 30 March 1880 letter to Edvard Brandes: "jeg er for æstetisk i god slet Forstand til at kunne indlade mig paa disse direkte Prokuratorindlægs-Digtninge, hvor Problemer siges at stilles under Debat, medens de kun postuleres løste" (I am too aesthetic, in the best of the worst sense, to allow myself to get mixed up in these dictated bureaucratic writings, in which problems are supposed to be placed under debate while solutions are only postulated).

Jacobsen's first published fictional work was the short story "Mogens" (1872; translated, 1921), which also appeared, in two installments, in the February and March issues of the magazine *Nyt dansk Maanedskrift.* The arresting opening sentence of the short story–"Sommer var det; midt paa dagen" (Summer it was, in the middle of the day)–is one of the most famous in Danish literature. The sensuous nature descriptions in the tale and the author's strong reliance on color exemplify the hallmarks of Jacobsen's style: the oneiric quality of the writing, for example, is abetted by the frequent occurrence of blue moonlight. Characters "redden" in more-passionate moments, and seasons pass in the elaborately described shifting colors of leaves and changing skies. The protagonist's identification with nature, reflecting Jacobsen's own, is reinforced by repeated scenes in which Mogens is lying on the ground. Jacobsen also returns to the folkloric themes he developed earlier in his writing, mentioning trolls and elves.

In "Mogens," Jacobsen, in episodic fashion and relying heavily on the imagist sensibility already developed in his poetry, relates the cyclical tale of a young man who moves from love through despair and dissolution and finally back to a receptiveness to love. Though educated, Mogens is a rather unrefined young man, who falls in love with Kamilla, a young woman who eventually dies–in front of his eyes–in a fire. As Mogens Pahuus points out in his existential reading of Jacobsen's writing, the fire reveals to Mogens that "der også i ham selv, og i alle mennesker, i lidenskaben, findes noget, der er at ligne ved en fortærende, destruerende brand" (in passion, there exists something in himself, and in all people, similar to a consuming, destructive fire). Mogens then replaces his lost love with a life of debauchery, in which he claims that existence consists only of darkness and that "De, der gik og vare lykkelige, de vare ogsaa blinde" (Those who went around happy were also blind).

Another woman, Thora, brings Mogens back to the point of loving; as she tells him, "trolls," not people, love the darkness. Jacobsen adds an inventive twist to his story: emotionally wounded by his former tragedy, Mogens cannot pursue the physical side of their romance, but Thora's healthy sexual nature cures Mogens's paralysis. This aspect reflects one of Jacobsen's naturalist insights: the belief that states of the "soul" are frequently driven by the natural urges, not only in men but also in women. Despite the somewhat strained quality of the story, it reveals a sophisticated stylist whose imagery is driven by a deep sense of longing. Critics have for more than a century deemed "Mogens" an early example of naturalism, positivism, and realism. Like most of Jacobsen's luxuriant writing, it transcends these epithets. Rilke once commented that, when reading the story, "A whole world will envelop you, the happiness, the abundance, the inconceivable vastness of a world."

In 1872 Jacobsen also finished his dissertation, and he received the coveted Gold Medal for it in 1873. While studying nature in Jutland for his prizewinning dissertation, Jacobsen also wrote involved journal entries on such detailed observations as the red and gold colors appearing in a sunset. These careful descriptions served him well in writing his chromatically charged prose.

In 1873, during a much anticipated trip through Italy, Jacobsen suddenly began to spit up blood–the first sign, along with a noticeable tiredness expressed in his letters to his parents, of his having contracted tuberculosis. He returned home to Thisted, where he was given only two years to live. He managed to survive for twelve more, during which time he produced, slowly and with herculean effort, his most important fictional work.

In a letter of 7 March 1873 to Edvard Brandes, Jacobsen described his current research on a new novel:

> Tænk dig jeg staaer op hver Dag Kl. 11 og gaaer paa kgl. Bibliothek og læser gamle Dokumenter og Breve og Løgne og Billeder om Mord, Hor, Kapitelstakst, Skjørlevnet, Torvepriser, Havevæsen, Kjøbenhavns Belejring, Skilmisse-Processer, Barnedaab, Godsregistre, Stamtavler og Ligprædikener. Alt det skal blive til en vidunderlig Roman der skal hedde "Frue Marie Grubbe. Interieur fra det 17de Aarhundrede."
>
> (Just think–I get up every morning at eleven o'clock and go to the Royal Library where I read old documents and letters and lies and descriptions of murder, adultery, grain prices, debauchery, market prices, horticulture, the siege of Copenhagen, divorce proceedings, confirmations, estate registers, genealogical tables, and funeral sermons. All of which will become a wonderful novel to be called "Mrs. Marie Grubbe: Interior from the Seventeenth Century.")

Marie Grubbe (1643–1718) was a member of the Danish nobility who at the age of fourteen married Ulrik Frederik Gyldenløve, the viceroy of Norway and the son of King Frederik III. Begun in early 1873, the novel was not completed until December 1876. In choosing the historical figure of Marie Grubbe as the inspiration for his first novel, Jacobsen was also influenced by previous Danish writers: Marie appears as an old woman in a henyard in Andersen's tale "Hønse-Grethes Familie" (Poultry-Meg's family), and Holberg, whose eighty-ninth epistle reveals that he knew the real Marie Grubbe, surfaces as a character in the final chapter of Jacobsen's novel. Georg Brandes also contended that his own review of Andersen's "Hønse-Grethes Familie" probably sparked Jacobsen's imagination.

Many scholars view Jacobsen's *Marie Grubbe* as one of the first Danish naturalistic novels. Responding to Emile Zola's naturalism, Jacobsen–in a letter to Edvard Brandes on 14 November 1877–offered further insight into the focus of his own style when he described Zola as "ikke detailleret nok i det Psychologiske" (not detailed enough psychologically). Holberg's letters, particularly in their allusions to Marie's urge-driven and irrational nature, supplied one of the main inspirations for Jacobsen. A dreamer with a strong sense of passion, Marie is a character with steadfast loyalty to herself, for better or worse. Her erotic nature is reflected in her surroundings, as in this sensuous description of a red and pink bouquet of flowers the fourteen-year-old Marie has gathered in her skirt: ". . . den tunge søde Duft, den drivende Em af den røde Nektar, som koger i Blomsternes Bund" (the sweet, heavy fragrance rising like vapor from that red nectar that seethes in the flower-cup).

Jacobsen is also one of the first male writers to recognize that a woman's sexual nature is not limited to her youth. In many ways, the path of Marie's life is the path of her erotic existence tied, inextricably, to her dreaming nature. Sent from her father's manor in Tjele, in Jutland, to her wealthy paternal aunt's residence in Copenhagen, Marie finds herself lonely and longing until she meets Ulrik Frederik Gyldenløve, the rowdy illegitimate son of King Frederik III. Ulrik Frederik's early flirtations with the young woman are met with equal wit, another indication of Marie's strong personality and determination. Jacobsen also creates a foil for Ulrik Frederik in the figure of Ulrik Christian Gyldenløve, son of the late King Christian IV. The romantic plots of the novel are set against the historical siege of Copenhagen by the Swedes in 1658, and Marie's dreamy visions of love find brief fulfillment in the war hero Ulrik Christian. He soon dies of syphillis, however, thus shattering her romantic ideals. In his monograph on Jacobsen, Niels Lyhne Jensen describes Ulrik Christian's death scene, in which he at one point shuns all religious belief and throws the parson out of his bedchamber (only to repent later), as "perhaps the greatest tour de force in Jacobsen's work." Marie, disillusioned, finds that "Der var da ingen straalende Skikkelser at længes frem imod i tilbedende Kjærlighed" (there were no shining figures she could dream of in worshiping love).

Although Ulrik Frederik has already secretly married an older cousin, Sofie Urne, who is pregnant with his child, his father forces him to abandon the union. His eventual marriage to Marie traces the anatomy of a relationship, from passion to commitment to detachment and resentment. As with Ulrik Christian, Marie's dream notion of a lover does not mesh with reality; she lives in a world of "mournful ballads." Eventually, Ulrik Frederik's own longing takes precedence, and he leaves Marie, whose passion once again flares up in "colorful images and luring forms." When he returns, he forces himself on her and injures her hand; the next morning she attacks him unsuccessfully with a knife, for which he forgives her.

With Ulrik Frederik cavorting openly and her marriage falling apart, Marie turns her romantic attention to her thirty-year-old brother-in-law, Sti Høg, with whom she has a passionate affair that nevertheless ends in a short time. Many critics have viewed the remaining chapters of the novel as an illustration of Marie's social decline; yet, this aspect is counterpointed by a new commitment to her own sensual nature. (Herman Bang found her movement unsatisfying and claimed that the search for a man was replaced by the search for a body.) During her affair with the melancholic Sti Høg, Marie travels out of Denmark, but Sti Høg, too, proves to be a disappointment, a man who overintellectualizes existence and "hugger al Livsens Tømmer op i Tankespaaner tilhobe" (cuts the timber of life all up into thought-shavings). In Nürnberg the advances of a "golden" young nobleman seem to offer Marie further promise, but her hopes are soon dashed by his accidental death. The sadomasochism that Jacobsen is often accused of (discussed especially in Frederik Nielsen's *J. P. Jacobsen. Digteren og Mennesket* [1953]) surfaces in Marie's growing desire for "self-debasement," which she sees as "voluptuous pleasure." Her marriage to the plump, dishonorable nobleman Palle Dyre only leads to contempt, but it also results in a sensual reawakening with muscular stable boy Søren Ladefoged. Hakon Stangerup and F. J. Billeskov Jansen point out that the physical Søren, despite his brutality, is "den første mand . . . som tilfredsstiller andre behov i hende end de primitivt seksuelle: hendes offervilje, hendes tjenersind, hendes underkastelseslængsler" (the first man . . . who satisfies needs other than the primitively sexual ones: her self-sacrifice, her humbleness, her longing to surrender).

In the final scene of the novel, Marie tries to explain her personal concept of faith and human nature to an astonished Ludvig Holberg: " . . . tror I, at hun, som har levet som hun har troet, var rettelig levet, men uden Haab om Belønning hisset og uden Bøn derom, tror I, Gud vil skyde hende fra sig og kaste hende bort, endog hun aldrig bad Gud et Bønnens Ord?" (. . . do you think that she who has lived as she thought was rightly, lived but without hope of any reward hereafter and without prayer, do you think God will thrust her from Him and cast her out, even though she has never uttered a word of prayer to Him?) Marie, who has never fully abandoned the dreams of her girlhood, believes that the person who has survived life without complaining has lived her own life and will die her own death.

The chromatic sensibility Jacobsen developed in "Mogens" reached new heights in *Marie Grubbe.* At times Jacobsen all but extracted colors from their objects. His painterly description is evident in this scene of a royal procession: ". . . røde Farver bryste sig med Gule, det klare Himmelblaa lukker for det Brune, blandt Hvidt og Violblaat skjærer Søgrønt sig lysende frem, Koralrødt synker mellem Sort og Lilla, og Gulbrunt og Rosa, Staalgraat og Purpur hvirvles imellem hinanden, lyst og dunkelt, Lød paa Lød i broget Bølgen" (Reds parade with yellows; the clear sky blue envelopes brown; a luminous sea green slices through white and violet blue; coral sinks between black and lavender; tawny and rose, steel gray and purple are whirled about, light and dark, tint upon tint, in eddying pools of color). In his collection *Det moderne gjennembruds Mænd* (The Men of the Modern Breakthrough, 1883), Georg Brandes claimed that Jacobsen was the great colorist of contemporary prose: "Sikkert har der aldrig før i nordisk Litteratur været malet med Ord som hos ham. Hans Sprog er farvemættet. Hans Stil er Farvesamklang" (Certainly no one before has ever painted with words as he does. His language is saturated with color. His style is the harmony of color).

The first two chapters of *Marie Grubbe* were printed in 1874, under the title "Af Marie Grubbes Barndom" (From Marie Grubbe's Childhood), in the magazine *Det nittende Aarhundrede.* In great part because of the Brandes brothers' concerted marketing efforts, the book, which was considered somewhat "dangerous" when it was printed, still managed to become a success. First published on 15 December 1876, the novel sold out by Christmas; Jacobsen saw three printings in his own brief lifetime. Both Brandes brothers gave the book positive reviews. (Edvard even wrote an extra one anonymously in the daily newspaper *Berlingske Tidende.*) Strindberg attempted to dramatize the novel but eventually abandoned the project.

Marie Grubbe ends with the protagonist's death–as does the haunting short story "Et Skud i Taagen" (1875; translated as "A Shot in the Fog," 1923), which Jacobsen wrote while finishing his first novel. He had first researched the tale during a botanical visit to the island of Læsø in 1870; the story was printed in the January–March 1875 issue of *Det nittende Aarhundrede.* The story, a deep psychological study of vengeance, recalls some of the Poe-influenced themes of madness Jacobsen pursued in his earlier poetry. The main character, Henning, suffers from an unhealthy restlessness reflected in the author's opening use of shades of green. Henning is fixated on his wealthy cousin, Agatha, who has already rejected his advances (in great part because of his lower economic state) and who is now engaged to another man, Niels Bryde. After Henning tries to persuade her that Niels is having an affair, Agatha strikes him. Henning becomes obsessed with revenge. While hunting in the autumn fog with Niels, Henning hears the other man singing, and, filled with hatred, shoots into the direction of the song and kills Niels. Still, he convinces everyone that it was simply a shooting accident and leaves the area. When he returns a few years later, fortunes have reversed: Henning is now financially solvent enough to reclaim the manor home where he was humiliated. He successfully plots the ruin and destruction of both Agatha and her new husband. After she dies, grief-stricken after her husband's arrest, Henning can only repeat the words she spoke to him after she slapped him: ". . . jeg fortryder heller ikke hvad jeg har gjort" (. . . I too do not regret what I have done). At the end, Henning, followed by a ghostly white figure, fades into a dense white fog. Finally, the specter pursuing him wraps its "klamme, hvide Fingre" (clammy, white fingers) around his neck.

In 1878, Jacobsen won Det Anckerske Legat, a travel grant given yearly to four artists. The settings of many of his works reflect his careful observations during his travels to Germany, France, and Italy. Jacobsen's penchant for characters that are thematic foils finds further expression in the short story "To Verdener" (1879; translated as "Two Worlds," 1923), set in Austria. A hopelessly sick woman is juxtaposed with a newly married bride; in her suffering, the unhealthy woman, turning to superstition, attempts to cast her sickness onto the healthy bride. The sick woman is cured (by a doctor for the poor, Jacobsen suggests, not by any supernatural miracle) but then feels consumed, like Henning in "Et Skud i Taagen," with angst. Haunted by the picture of the bride and unable to travel from the world of pain to the world of joy, she drowns herself in the gray-black waters of the Salzach River. The story ends with an image anticipating Strindberg's imagery in *Ett drömspel* (1901; translated as *A Dream Play,* 1901). A boat soon passes carrying the bridal pair: the husband is rowing, and the still-healthy wife, wrapped in a "large gray shawl," stands and sings a nostalgic joyous song, "En Drømmeskaal" (A Toast to Dreams).

Religion as an impediment to happiness pervades "To Verdener." Early in the tale, the sickly woman overhears a conversation in a passing boat, in which a man says, "Lykke . . . er en absolut hedensk Forestilling. De kan ikke finde Ordet et eneste Sted i det nye Testamente" (Happiness . . . is a perfectly heathen notion. You will not find the word anywhere in the New Testament). In addition, the woman, suffering from guilt, makes marks of the cross in the mud along the shores of the river. Yet, to view Jacobsen's use of such images simply as an attack is myopic, and the story, with its nameless characters, has a parable-like quality heavily dependent on symbolism that is, nonetheless, religious.

Having finished *Marie Grubbe,* Jacobsen was once again ready to turn his attention to his novel about the atheist. In a letter to Georg Brandes on 12 November 1878, he describes some of his intent with his current work in progress, then titled "Niels Lyhne: En Ungdoms Historie" (Niels Lyhne: A Story of Youth). Jacobsen claimed that he was writing about the previous generation of "Fritænkere" (atheists), whom he accused of being romantically muddleheaded and incapable of applying any newfound freedom to the real world. Jacobsen's claim that his protagonist is only a representative of a previous generation has long been a point of contention, and some critics have viewed Niels Lyhne as the author's example–perhaps with a nod at Georg Brandes–of the basic impossibility of programmatic notions of thinking. Still, in his letters, Jacobsen insisted that the previous generation was his subject. The novel presents a bildungsroman dealing with the tortuous development of a lonely dreamer determined, though at times failing, to remain committed to his own ideals. Toward the end of the same letter to Brandes, Jacobsen stressed that he was focusing "specielt [paa det] Psychologiske og paa det Physiologiske med" (especially on the psychological, along with the physiological).

In the first chapters of *Niels Lyhne,* Jacobsen offers a careful overview of the hereditary forces at work on his young protagonist. Niels's mother is described as a being of a poetic, dreamy nature for whom grief is "black" and joy is "red." Niels's father, on the other hand, a man of simple pleasures, is void of zeal or desire. Eventually, he retreats from his wife's overtly romantic nature, and so she retreats into a dreamworld of disillusionment. (She later tells her grown son that she views her life as "one long, useless sigh.") As a child, Niels possesses both parents' natural inclinations, and they seem to fight over his intellectual development. Still, he is ultimately another of Jacobsen's dreamers, who, even as an adult, "skulde nu altid tænke sig Alting" (always had to imagine everything). The source of Niels's unfulfilled longings also surfaces in his mother's wistful comment that she longs for colors that the world does not possess. Jørn Vosmar contends, however, that "på alle andre områder ligger *Niels Lyhne* fjernt fra det naturalistiske program" (in all other areas *Niels Lyhne* is far removed from the naturalistic program).

When Niels's paternal aunt Edele comes to live with the Lyhnes, the young boy becomes infatuated with the idea of her. After he witnesses her verbally demolishing an unwanted suitor, the first in a series of scenes depicting women rejecting men, Niels comes face to face with the realities of shattered dreams. When Edele dies from consumption, fading into a "bluish twilight," Niels prays vehemently for her life, but his prayers are unanswered. Thus, the boy rejects God and declares himself a nonbeliever. In this early scene, Jacobsen introduces the trinity of religion, eroticism, and reality–a motif he returns to repeatedly throughout the novel.

As a student in Copenhagen, Niels encounters the world of the avant-garde along with the bohemian widow Tema Boye, his first real love. Niels hopes her love will free him from the imagined world of his childhood; yet, his emotion is an "ardent impotence." Finally, she rejects him for a socially advantageous marriage and sends him away (Georg Brandes found her character a strikingly original creation). The next woman in Niels's life is Fennimore, the wife of his closest friend and cousin, Erik, a painter manqué. Fennimore first charms Niels with her singing, thus recalling the romantic awakenings in "Mogens." Although their affair rises out of the marital detritus of Erik's drinking, Niels loves her deeply. The paralyzing forces of the past thwart their love. Even after Erik is killed in an accident, and Fennimore is free, her guilty feelings, illustrated as black ravens of thought, preclude her pursuit of happiness. She, too, sends Niels away.

In a parallel fashion, Niels's purported poetic talent also remains unfulfilled, though he tells his mother he is a poet to his "soul." Wandering through Europe, he falls in love with an Italian singer, Madame Odéro, but his own feeble attempts at being a poet pale in the face of her commitment to her art. After their affair ends, Niels abandons all hope of becoming a poet, returns to Denmark, and retreats into a pastoral setting. His marriage to Gerda, a warmhearted local girl, ends tragically when she dies young; even worse, on her deathbed she returns to Christianity, despite his efforts to wean her from religion. Tragedy is heaped upon tragedy when their young son also dies, and Niels, in lonely desperation, prays to the God he abandoned in his youth. This prayer also goes unanswered, especially as it flies in the face of the pseudoscientific acceptance of the "laws" of life Niels espouses throughout the novel. The loss plunges him into even greater despair. Finally, Niels decides to serve in the Dano-Prussian War (1864), where he meets death and accepts it without turning back to the God he has rejected. In *Omkring Niels Lyhne,* Niels Barfoed observes that "Den idé Niels ikke kunne leve for, lykkes det ham at dø for" (Niels succeeds in dying for the idea he could not live for).

Niels is trapped in a hazy view of life out of sync with his surroundings and experiences, especially the erotic ones. At one point he wonders if he has been born "et halvt Aarhundrede for sent, sommetider . . . at han var kommet alt for tidligt" (a half century too late, at other times . . . that he arrived much too early). The reader senses an undeniably Romantic quality to all of Niels's claims of being a "free-thinker." This irony reaches a zenith after Niels, who has been sitting alone in a bar at Christmas, delivers a long tirade about the new world of honest thinkers that will emerge once everyone is released from the chains of religious thought–to which his friend, the skeptical Dr. Hjerrild, can only reply, "De maa have en vidunderlig Tro paa Menneskeheden; Atheismen vil jo komme til at stille større Fordringer til den, end Kristendommen gjør" (You must have an amazing faith in humanity; atheism will make greater demands on people than Christianity does). During this scene Niels also delivers an oft-quoted outburst, his battle cry of atheism: "Der er ingen Gud, og Mennesket er hans Profet!" (There is no God, and the human being is His prophet!).

Reviewing *Niels Lyhne* in *Illustreret Tidende* (19 December 1880), H. S. Voldskov wrote that Jacobsen, with a singular talent, could "forvandle [det] Usynlige til et Anskueligt, der har hele Virkelighedens Farvespil" (change [the] imperceptible into something clear, possessing all of the play of color in reality). In his 9 February 1881 review of *Niels Lyhne,* Georg Brandes found the book "abstrakt . . . for indvendig, for lidt historisk" (abstract . . . too inwardly focused, not historical enough). Privately, the Brandes brothers were even less enthusiastic: their letters reveal that Georg thought the novel was "uvirkelig" (unreal) and that Jacobsen's style consisted of "500 Adjektiver for mange" (500 adjectives too many). Edvard also claimed that he "var ikke meget glad for Niels Lyhne" (did not care for Niels Lyhne). In his 1883 essay on Jacobsen, Georg Brandes, expressing a certain disappointment in the title character, observed that the women in the novel were "Bogens sande Hovedpersoner" (the true protagonists of the book). Jacobsen's own letters indicate that he was aware of the brothers' tepid response to the book and that he was dismayed by critics' claims that the novel was too "pessimistic."

Vosmar, who sees a markedly Kierkegaardian influence on the desperate individuality of the protagonist, points to a stylistic breakthrough in Jacobsen's writings: "En af de afgørende og nye kvaliteter ved hans digtning . . . er hans evne til at antyde, hvad der foregår i området mellem det rent kropslige og bevidstheden" (One of the crucial and new qualities about his writing . . . is his ability to indicate what transpires in the area between the purely physical and consciousness). In a comment that seems particularly suited to

Niels Lyhne, Jørn Erslev Andersen observes that Jacobsen's characters "forbliver udviklingsløst bundet til et og samme reaktionsmønster" (remain, without development, bound to the same pattern of reaction). For more than a century, *Niels Lyhne* has been a hallmark of the Modern Breakthrough in Scandinavia. In a 16 October 1895 letter, Sigmund Freud claimed that *Niels Lyhne* "has moved me more profoundly than any other reading of the last ten years."

Jacobsen's remaining short stories were all published after *Niels Lyhne*. One of his most innovative pieces is the imagist sketch "Der burde have været Roser" (circa 1880; translated as "There Should Have Been Roses," 1923). A lonely wanderer outside of Rome stops to rest by a garden wall, where he dreams of a dialogue between two pages (played by women), one dressed in blue with blond hair and an older one in yellow with dark hair. They discuss the elusiveness of happiness and the mystery of women; through their dialogue the eternal dream of love is juxtaposed with the ephemeral fulfillment of the dream of love. The reverie is interrupted for a moment by a lizard, but the wanderer then returns to his imagined dialogue.

The short story "Pesten i Bergamo" (circa 1881; translated as "The Plague in Bergamo," 1923) is a dark study of the helplessness of humanity in the face of unyielding and destructive nature. The disease-threatened inhabitants of Bergamo, Italy, move from strict piety to self-absorbed hedonism until a crusading group of flagellants, with crosses and banners, enters the city. The musical sense of crescendo and decrescendo of the prose reflects the shifting focus of the story, from the "brown, gray and black," religiously fanatic flagellants to the orgiastic citizens of Bergamo. After the flagellants' long bout of self-scourging in the town cathedral, a monk looks at the threatening crowd–demanding that he be crucified–and sees "fortrukne Ansigter, med de raabende Mundes mørke Aabninger" (contorted faces, with the dark openings of the shouting mouths). Black plays an expressionist role in the story, reflecting both the empty behavior of the hedonists and the empty crosses of the flagellants. Jacobsen's usual sympathy for the human condition is replaced by an almost nihilistic sense of despair.

In his short story "Fru Fønss" (1882; translated as "Mrs. Fönss," 1923), Jacobsen offers a strong theme of departure from life. The main character, a forty-year-old widow, must choose between her own happiness and her love for her children, who are dismayed by her return to a lover from her youth. Her joy is fleeting, however, and five years later she becomes fatally ill. Still, she accepts the evanescence of happiness and writes a letter to her children professing her love and embracing the inevitability of death. Of all Jacobsen's characters Fru Fønss seems the one most committed to herself. Upon finishing the story, Jacobsen told Møller, "Du kan tro, det er svært at skrive saadan et Afskedsbrev" (You have no idea how difficult it is to write such a farewell letter). Jacobsen's short stories were first collected and published in *Mogens og andre Noveller* (1882; translated as *Mogens and Other Stories,* 1921).

In his final, but unfinished, short story, "Doktor Faust," Jacobsen once again employed foils–two knights, one in purple and one in black–to represent the twin forces of Love and Death. Doctor Faust sits at a window and awaits their arrival. Edited by Edvard Brandes, the fragment, titled "Doktor Faust. Novelle-Fragment," was printed in the magazine *Juleroser* in December 1885. Brandes also added a note explaining Jacobsen's original plans for the development of the story: Love eventually convinces Death to grant Doctor Faust forty more years of life, but when they encounter him afterward, they discover that the extra forty years were meaningless.

J. P. Jacobsen died at his family's home in Thisted on 30 April 1885. In a letter of 2 May 1885 to Møller, William Jacobsen describes his brother's final moments: "Moder holdt hans Hovede imellem sine Hænder imod den høje Bagklædning, jeg tog hans Haand i min, men ikke den svageste Bevægelse eller Sittren i Haanden. . . . Alle beundrer vi den forfærdelige Villiekraft han udviste lige til det sidste, ved selv at rejse sig op og gaa hen, sætte sig for at dø, saa rolig for ikke at ængste nogen" (Mother held his head between her hands, supported by the high bed pillows; I took his hand in mine but there was not the slightest movement or motion in his hand. . . . We are all amazed at the incredible will power he exhibited right to the end–even to the point of getting up and walking over, sitting down to die, calmly, so as not to worry anyone). In his 1883 essay on Jacobsen, Georg Brandes wrote, ". . . dette er vor Prosas sjælfuldeste og mest digteriske Særling. Alt, hvad han sér, bliver Særsyn, Alt, hvad han skriver, faar Særpræg" (. . . this is our prose's most soulful and most poetic character. Everything he sees becomes exceptional; everything he writes is distinctive).

Letters:

Breve fra J. P. Jacobsen, edited by Edvard Brandes (Copenhagen: Gyldendal, 1899);

Georg og Edvard Brandes: Brevveksling med nordiske Forfattere og Videnskabsmænd, 8 volumes, edited by Morten Borup (Copenhagen: Gyldendal, 1939–1942), II: 237–387, III: 107–162;

J. P. Jacobsen. Samlede Værker, volumes 5 and 6, edited by Frederik Nielsen (Copenhagen: Rosenkilde & Bagger, 1974);

Et venskab. En brevveksling mellem J. P. Jacobsen og Edvard Brandes, edited by Kristian Hvidt (Copenhagen: Gyldendal, 1988).

Bibliographies:

Aage Jørgensen, *Dansk litteraturhistorisk bibliografi: 1967–1986* (Copenhagen: Dansklærerforeningen, 1989), nos. 4298–4395;

Erik Falsig, *Jens Peter Jacobsen bibliografi: fortegnelse over hans skrifter på dansk og oversat til germanske og romanske sprog* (Copenhagen: Danmarks Biblioteksskole, 1990).

Biographies:

Anna Linck, *J. P. Jacobsen. Et Levnedsløb–paa Grundlag af Digterens efterladte Papirer* (Copenhagen: Gyldendal, 1911; revised, 1947);

Søren Hallar, *J. P. Jacobsens hjem og barndom* (Copenhagen: Munksgaard, 1950);

Svend Sørensen and Niels Nielsen, *At bære livet som det er* (Thisted: Sparekassen Thy, 1997).

References:

Jørn Erslev Andersen, "En genrerytter–Marie Grubbe i dansk litteratur," *Bogens Verden: tidsskrift for dansk biblioteksvæsen,* 4 (1995): 238–241;

Andersen, "J. P. Jacobsen, kompositorisk heterogenitet og poetisk tænkning," *Spring,* 13 (1998): 81–93;

Herman Bang, "Et Møde med J. P. Jacobsen," in *Fra de unge Aar* (Copenhagen: Gyldendal, 1956), pp. 105–107;

Bang, *Realisme og Realister. Portrætstudier og Aforismer* (Copenhagen: Schubothe, 1879);

Niels Barfoed, "Efterskrift," in *Niels Lyhne,* Gyldendals Bibliotek, no. 18 (Copenhagen: Gyldendal, 1964), pp. 219–231;

Barfoed, *Omkring Niels Lyhne* (Copenhagen: Reitzels Værkserie, 1970);

F. J. Billeskov Jansen, Rolf Nyboe Nettum, Louise Vinge, and others, *J. P. Jacobsens spor i ord, billeder og toner: Tolv afhandlinger,* edited, with an introduction, by Billeskov Jansen (Copenhagen: C. A. Reitzel, 1985);

Georg Brandes, "J. P. Jacobsen," in *Det moderne gjennembruds Mænd. En række Portrætter* (Copenhagen: Gyldendal, 1883; revised, 1891), pp. 144–211;

Brandes, "J. P. Jacobsen," in *Essays. Danske Personligheder* (Copenhagen: Gyldendal, 1889), pp. 269–284;

Hans Brix, "J. P. Jacobsen," in *Danmarks Digtere* (Copenhagen: Aschehoug, 1951), pp. 417–432;

Francis Hackett, Paul Rosenfeld, Alrik Gustafson, and others, "Jens Peter Jacobsen," in *Nineteenth-Century Literature Criticism,* edited by Paula Kepos (Detroit: Gale, 1992), pp. 139–173;

Niels Ingwersen, "Problematic Protagonists: Marie Grubbe and Niels Lyhne," in *The Hero in Scandinavian Literature: From Peer Gynt to the Present,* edited, with an introduction, by John M. Weinstock and Robert T. Rovinsky (Austin: University of Texas Press, 1975), pp. 39–61;

Jørgen Bonde Jensen, "Den moderne individualitet. J. P. Jacobsen: 'Niels Lyhne,'" in *Læsninger i dansk litteratur 1820–1900,* volume 2, edited by Povl Schmidt and Ulrik Lehrmann (Odense: Odense University, 1998), pp. 232–248;

Niels Lyhne Jensen, *J. P. Jacobsen,* Twayne World Author Series, no. 573 (Boston: Twayne, 1980);

Sven Møller Kristensen, "Marie Grubbe," in his *Digtning og Livsyn. Fortolkninger af syv danske værker* (Copenhagen: Gyldendal, 1963), pp. 30–56;

Frederik Nielsen, *J. P. Jacobsen. Digteren og mennesket. En literær undersøgelse* (Copenhagen: Gyldendal, 1953);

Erik Østerud, "Unravelling the Riddle of Nature. J. P. Jacobsen's 'Mogens' in the Field of Conflict between Religion and Science," in *Theatrical and Narrative Space: Studies in Ibsen, Strindberg and J. P. Jacobsen* (Aarhus: Aarhus University Press, 1998), pp. 101–134;

Jørgen Ottesen, *J. P. Jacobsens "Mogens"* (Copenhagen: Gyldendal, 1968);

Ottesen, *Omkring Fru Marie Grubbe* (Copenhagen: Reitzels Værkserie, 1972);

Mogens Pahuus, *J. P. Jacobsens forfatterskab. En eksistentiel fortolkning* (Herning: Systime, 1986);

Carl S. Petersen and Vilhelm Andersen, *Illustreret dansk litteraturhistorie,* volume 4 (Copenhagen: Gyldendal, 1924–1934), pp. 206–225;

Bengt Algot Sørensen, "Naturalisme og naturfilosofi. Om J. P. Jacobsen, Darwin og Ernst Hæckel," *Edda,* 91 (1991): 359–367;

Hakon Stangerup and F. J. Billeskov Jansen, "J. P. Jacobsen," in *Dansk Litteratur Historie,* volume 3 (Copenhagen: Politikens Forlag, 1966), pp. 58–95;

Brita Tigerschiöld, *J. P. Jacobsen och hans roman Niels Lyhne* (Göteborg: Elanders Boktryckeri Aktiebolag, 1945);

Jørn Vosmar, *J. P. Jacobsens digtning* (Copenhagen: Gyldendal, 1984).

Papers:

Collections of J. P. Jacobsen's manuscripts and correspondences are at the Danish Royal Library in Copenhagen. Some of his papers and belongings are at the Thisted Museum.

Johannes Jørgensen

(6 November 1866 - 29 May 1956)

Jakob Stougaard-Nielsen
University of Washington

Courtesy of the Danish Royal Library, Copenhagen

BOOKS: *Vers* (Copenhagen: P. Hauberg, 1887);

Foraarssagn. Fortælling (Copenhagen: P. Hauberg, 1888);

En Fremmed (Copenhagen & Kristiania: A. Cammermeyer, 1890);

Sommer (Copenhagen: Philipsen, 1892);

Stemninger (Copenhagen: Philipsen, 1892);

Livets Træ (Copenhagen: Philipsen, 1893);

Bekendelse (Copenhagen: Philipsen, 1894)–includes "Høstdrøm," "Jeg sidder bland stille Planter," and "Bekendelse," translated by Robert Silliman Hillyer as "Autumn Dream," "The Plants Stand Silent Round Me," and "Confession," in *A Book of Danish Verse,* edited by Oluf Friis (New York: American-Scandinavian Foundation, 1922), pp. 143–146;

Hjemvee (Copenhagen: Philipsen, 1894);

Rejsebogen. Skildringer (Copenhagen: Ernst Bojesen, 1895);

Livsløgn og Livssandhed (Copenhagen: Nordiske, 1896);

Beuron (Copenhagen: Nordiske, 1897);

Den yderste Dag (Copenhagen: Nordiske, 1897);

Digte 1894–1898 (Copenhagen: Nordiske, 1898);

Helvedfjender (Copenhagen: Nordiske, 1898);

Lignelser (Copenhagen: Nordiske, 1898)–includes "Traaden ovenfra," translated by Lydia Cranfield as "The Thread from Above," *Nor,* 14, no. 4 (July–August 1956): 258–259;

Omvendelse (Copenhagen: Nordiske, 1899);

En Apostel (Copenhagen: Nordiske, 1900);

Vor Frue af Danmark (Copenhagen: Nordiske, 1900);

Eva (Copenhagen: Nordiske, 1901);

Romersk Mosaik (Copenhagen: Nordiske, 1901);

Den hellige Ild. En legende fra det gamle Siena (Copenhagen: Nordiske, 1902);

Romerske Helgenbilleder (Copenhagen: Nordiske, 1902);

Pilgrimsbogen (Copenhagen: Nordiske, 1903); translated as *Pilgrim Walks in Franciscan Italy* (Edinburgh & London: Sands, 1908);

Græs (Copenhagen: Gyldendal, 1904);

Lyrik. Udvalgte Ungdomsdigte (1885–1896) (Copenhagen: Gyldendal, 1904);

Rejsebilleder fra Nord og Syd (Copenhagen: Gyldendal, 1905); revised and republished as *Indtryk og Stemninger* (Copenhagen: Gyldendal, 1911);

Essays (Copenhagen: Gyldendal, 1906);

Blomster og Frugter (Copenhagen: Gyldendal, 1907);

Den hellige Frans af Assisi. En Levnedsskildring (Copenhagen: Gyldendal, 1907); translated by T. O'Conor Sloane as *St. Francis of Assisi, a Biography* (New York & London: Longmans, Green, 1912);

Den yndigste Rose (Copenhagen: Gyldendal, 1907);
I det Høje (Copenhagen: Gyldendal, 1908);
Af det Dybe (Copenhagen: Gyldendal, 1909);
Fra Vesuv til Skagen (Copenhagen: Gyldendal, 1909);
Lourdes (Copenhagen: Gyldendal, 1910); translated by Ingeborg Lund as *Lourdes,* with a preface by Hilaire Belloc (London: Longmans, Green, 1914);
Det Tabte Land (Copenhagen: Gyldendal, 1912);
Bag alle de blaa Bjærge (Copenhagen: Gyldendal, 1913);
Goethe-Bogen (Copenhagen: Gyldendal, 1913);
Min Livsanskuelse (Copenhagen: Gyldendal, 1913);
Cività D'Antino (Copenhagen: Gyldendal, 1915);
Den hellige Katerina af Siena (Copenhagen: Gyldendal, 1915; revised, 1927); translated by Lund as *Saint Catherine of Siena* (London & New York: Longmans, Green, 1938);
Klokke Roland (Copenhagen: Pio, 1915); translated as *False Witness. The Authorized Translation of "Klokke Roland"* (London: Hodder & Stoughton, 1916);
Udvalgte værker, 7 volumes (Copenhagen: Gyldendal, 1915);
I Det Yderste Belgien (Copenhagen: Pio, 1916); translated by Lund as *The War Pilgrim* (London: Burns & Oates, 1917);
Mit Livs Legende, 7 volumes (Copenhagen: Gyldendal, 1916–1928)–comprises *Den röde Stjærne* (1916); *Taarnet* (1916); *Vælskland* (1917); *Det usyrede Bröd* (1918); *Ved den skönne Tempeldör* (1918); *Guds Kværn* (1918); and *Over de valske Mile* (1928); translated by Lund as *Jörgensen: An Autobiography,* 2 volumes (London: Sheed & Ward, 1928, 1929);
Den Slette Tjeners Svar (Copenhagen: Pio, 1918);
Flanderns Løve (Copenhagen: Gyldendal, 1919);
Alvernerbjærget (Copenhagen: Gyldendal, 1920);
Der er en Brønd, som rinder (Copenhagen: Gyldendal, 1920);
Som en Tyv om Natten og andre lignelser (Copenhagen: Gyldendal, 1921);
Jorsalafærd, 2 volumes (Copenhagen: Gyldendal, 1923);
Breve fra Assisi (Copenhagen: Gyldendal, 1924);
Af Oliventræets Frugt. Indtryk fra Sydfrankrig (Copenhagen: Gyldendal, 1925);
Brig "Marie" af Svendborg og andre Digte (Copenhagen: Gyldendal, 1925);
Isblomster. Tolv digte i Prosa (Copenhagen: Gyldendal, 1926);
Fordi Stander Landet i Vaande (Copenhagen: Gyldendal, 1928);
Don Bosco (Copenhagen: Gyldendal, 1929); translated by Lund as *Don Bosco* (London: Burns & Oates, 1934);
Fra det ukendte Frankrig (Copenhagen: Gyldendal, 1930);
Efterslæt. Digte (Copenhagen: Gyldendal, 1931);
Som en Kærte (Copenhagen: Gyldendal, 1931);
Hr. Johansen: En Silhouet (Copenhagen: Gyldendal, 1932);
Italiensk (Copenhagen: Gyldendal, 1932);
Bibelsk (Copenhagen: Gyldendal, 1933);
Joakims Hjemkomst (Copenhagen: Gyldendal, 1933)–includes "Sanct Peder og Mardochai," translated by Ann R. Born as "St. Peter and Mordecai," in *Contemporary Danish Prose. An Anthology,* edited by Elias Bredsdorff (Copenhagen: Gyldendal, 1958), pp. 20–28;
Charles de Foucauld (Copenhagen: Gyldendal, 1934);
Omkring Axen Assisi-Salzburg (Copenhagen: Berlingske, 1938);
Den hellige Birgitta af Vadstena, 2 volumes (Copenhagen: Gyldendal, 1941, 1943); translated by Lund as *Saint Bridget of Sweden,* 2 volumes (London & New York: Longmans, Green, 1954);
Vers fra Vadstena (Copenhagen: Gyldendal, 1941);
Digte i Danmark (Copenhagen: Gyldendal, 1943);
Ti Digte (Copenhagen: Gyldendal, 1946);
Gamle Adresser (Copenhagen: Gyldendal, 1947);
Fyen og andre Digte (Copenhagen: Gyldendal, 1948);
Orion over Assisi og andre efterladte arbejder, edited by Bergstrøm-Nielsen (Copenhagen: Gyldendal, 1959).

Editions and Collections: *Tanker i Johannes Jørgensens Skrifter,* edited, with an introduction, by Oluf Elling (Copenhagen: Nyt Nordisk Forlag, 1931);
Udvalgte Digte 1884–1944, edited by Carl Bergstrøm-Nielsen and Jørgensen (Copenhagen: Gyldendal, 1944);
Johannes Jørgensen Manuskripter; Det sidste Glimt; Her vi sad ved Gribsøstranden; Døren lukkedes stille; Brevfragmenter, edited by Emil Frederiksen (Copenhagen: Munksgaard, 1946);
Taarnet. En Antologi, edited, with an introduction, by Bergstrøm-Nielsen (Copenhagen: Gyldendal, 1966);
Essays om den Tidlige Modernisme, edited, with a foreword and an afterword, by Peer E. Sørensen (Århus: Klim, 2001).

OTHER: *Taarnet. Illustreret Månedsskrift for Kunst og Litteratur,* edited by Jørgensen (1893–1894);
Katholiken, edited by Jørgensen, 1–5 (1898–1902).

TRANSLATIONS: François René de Chateaubriand, *Atala,* Dansk Folkebibliothek, no. 19 (Copenhagen: P. Hauberg, 1888);
Victor Hugo, *En Dødsdømts Sidste Dag* (Copenhagen: Dansk Folkebibliothek, 1888);
Douglas Jerrold, *Fru Caudles Gardinprædikener* (Copenhagen: Dansk Folkebibliothek, 1888);
Mark Twain, *Udvalgte Skitser I–III* (Copenhagen: Dansk Folkebibliothek, 1888–1890);

Paul Bourget, *Pasteller* (Copenhagen: Lehmann & Stage, 1891);

Edmond de Goncourt, *Paris 1870–1871* (Copenhagen: Pontoppidan, 1891);

Pierre Loti, *Lotis Giftermål* (Christiania & Copenhagen: Cammermeyer, 1891);

Loti, *Aziyadé: Østerlands-Drømmen* (Copenhagen: Lehmann & Stage, 1892);

Edgar Allan Poe, *Arthur Gordon Pyms Hændelser,* with an introduction by Jørgensen (Copenhagen: Lehmann & Stage, 1892);

J. H. Rosny, *Vamireh: Forhistorisk Roman* (Copenhagen: Lehmann & Stage, 1892);

Loti, *Matros* (Copenhagen: Lehmann & Stage, 1893);

Hugolin af Monte Giorgio, *Fioretti: Det er den hellige Frans af Assisis Smaablomster* (Copenhagen: Nordiske, 1902);

Paul Bourget, *Emigranten* (Copenhagen: Gyldendal, 1907);

Robert Hugh Benson, *Verdens Herre* (Copenhagen: Gyldendal, 1909);

Hugo von Hofmannsthal, *Komedien om Enhver* (Copenhagen: Gyldendal, 1915);

Giovanni Pascoli, *Pavl Fugl fra Firenze. Et Digt* (Copenhagen: Gyldendal, 1924);

Franz Herwig, *Den Hellige Sebastian fra Wedding* (Copenhagen: Frimodt, 1934);

Fremmed Frugt: Udvalgte Oversættelser af Europæisk Poesi, edited by Carl Bergstrøm-Nielsen and Jørgensen (Copenhagen: Gyldendal, 1945);

Giovanni Papini, *Breve til Menneskene fra Pave Celestino VI* (Copenhagen: Gyldendal, 1948).

From his elevated study in the octagonal tower on the corner of H. C. Ørstedsvej and Kastanjevej in Frederiksberg, Johannes Jørgensen began his lifelong work writing against the mediocre morals he felt were engulfing his generation in dark clouds. Any excitement had ceased to exist in modern Danish culture; even worship and faith, love and self-sacrifice were to Jørgensen long-lost virtues in the 1890s. "Derfor ruger et trist Graavejr over den moderne Kultur" (Therefore overcast clouds gloom over modern culture), Jørgensen wrote in the now well-known essay "Symbolisme" (Symbolism, published in *Taarnet,* 1893). Orthodox realism and atheism personified the darkness in the giant of Danish letters Georg Brandes. Jørgensen found life in the industrialized Danish capital unrewardingly prosaic, and he set out to deepen this life through a new and otherworldly poetic voice. His work became known as the major Danish gateway to European modernism, mainly through a new literary magazine, *Taarnet* (The Tower, 1893–1894), which he edited in his tower office, giving to the first journal of its kind in Denmark its truly modern topos.

Jørgensen's influence on the history of Danish literature has been both ill-fated and immense. In Denmark he is now best known as one of the first modernists–the ideologue of the symbolist movement, often referred to as "the poets of the nineties." He is beginning to be recognized as one of the central critical minds of modern Danish literature; after Brandes, he is perhaps the most influential critic and source of inspiration for other Danish writers. As a poet, essayist, translator, and editor, Jørgensen introduced such Modern poets as Charles Baudelaire, Stéphane Mallarmé, Paul Verlaine, and Edgar Allan Poe to the literary circles of Copenhagen. His conversion to the Catholic faith in 1896–and the denial of the same modernism he was central in promoting–expatriated him in space, time, and thought from Danish literature, and entered him instead into Catholic world literature as one of the most widely read and translated hagiographers of the twentieth century.

Jørgensen was born in Svendborg, a small town on the south coast of the Island of Fyn, on 6 November 1866, at a time when the Golden Age of Danish literature and culture was waning. He was the son of a skipper, Jørgen Christian Jørgensen, and Marie Elisabeth Johansen, and he had two younger sisters. The young Johannes was particularly under the influence of his mother because of the long absences of his seafaring father. She bestowed the religious inclination upon him. When he was a child, she had already left the Danish State Church and had become a Methodist, and Johannes was brought up in that faith, though he was never especially receptive to it. The uncomplicated faith his mother gave him was supplemented by a love of nature and a passion for literature, which his mother's brother, Jørgen Johansen, inspired in him. This uncle introduced Johannes to the German Romantics Johann Wolfgang von Goethe and Heinrich Heine with their love for nature and Romantic motifs.

In 1882 Jørgensen traveled to Copenhagen to attend grammar school (Nørrebros Latin- og Realskole). Jørgensen had to undergo much suffering in his early years. He felt different from the young people in Copenhagen, a feeling not uncommon among the young people arriving from the countryside in those years. He had a feeling of coming from an altogether different cultural background. In addition, he found himself to be ugly; in his diary he mentions his Mongol face, and wrote, after only three months in school: *Sustineo, ergo sum* (I suffer, therefore I exist). He came to hate the handsome, the privileged, and the rich–an anger he channeled into a feverish writing of revolutionary prose in his meticulously kept diary. Jørgensen's diaries reveal a portrait of the typical companion to the intellectual anarchist–the dreaming outsider and the night wanderer.

Two years later, in 1884, Jørgensen entered the University of Copenhagen as a student of classical philology, only to change his path to zoology and botany; both were popular subjects in the 1880s. Charles Darwin's *On the Origin of Species* (1860) had been translated in 1872 by Danish author J. P. Jacobsen, whose impressionistic style and Darwinist inclinations had a great influence on Jørgensen's early cycle of novels. For Jørgensen, Sophus Claussen, and Johannes V. Jensen, who all came to the capital from the provinces in this period, naturalism in science, philosophy, and literature, the sense of progress, and liberal morals were indisputably the tickets to success in academic life. Jørgensen identified himself with the skeptical intellectuals of the day, and he was adopted into the circle around professor of philosophy Harald Høffding, who opposed Brandes. At the same time, he became a member of *Studentersamfundet,* a liberal student organization established as a protest against the conservative *Studenterforening,* where he later met Viggo Stuckenberg and Claussen. These three poets formed the core of the 1890s symbolist movement.

Sparked by his opposition to the bourgeois ideals, Jørgensen soon turned his personal revolt to social revolution–from Romanticism to socialism. On Constitution Day 1886, he and a circle of friends decided to be a part of the workingmen procession, wearing their students' caps, singing "La Marseillaise," and evoking both cheers and cries of disapproval from the crowd. The result was that the patience of Jørgensen's conservative benefactors wore out. The want of industry in his studies, the aimless life, walks, and discussions instead of lectures, as he later spoke of with regret, had all been put down to his account. Those well-meaning conservative families who had supported him in Copenhagen now refused to help him, returning him to a life in the capital city verging on dissoluteness. Though Jørgensen kept his social indignation throughout his career and later struggled to keep his Catholic faith in conjunction with social ideals, he looked back on his flirtation with socialism with mixed feelings, recapitulating his engagement in poetic terms: "Den røde Stjærne havde ført mig udenfor Samfundet–og et langt Stykke nedad mod Afgrunden" (The red star had led me outside the pale of society–and a long way toward the abyss), as he later wrote in his major autobiographical work *Mit Livs Legende* (The Legend of My Life, 1916–1928; translated as *Jörgensen: An Autobiography,* 1928, 1929).

When he was twenty years old, Jørgensen finally broke with his conservative background, moved to a less expensive address on Frederiksberg, and became absorbed in studies of zoology. But still the aesthete fought the zoologist dominance. In 1887 the melancholic aesthete apparently won over the naturalist. Jørgensen's first book, a poorly bound collection of poetry titled *Vers* (Verse, 1887), was published. In these early poems the keen observer of nature walks alongside the dreaming poet, summing up the literary influences of French naturalism and German Romanticism.

But Jørgensen lived for a new kind of poetry, and his first book of poetry marked the beginning of a sizable literary production. In *Johannes Jørgensen og Symbolismen* (1975), Bo Nielsen stresses the incorporeal quality that characterizes these early poems; they signaled a new poetry that took over from the celebrated prosaic life-world of the time. The bodiless sketches of characters link the poems to impressionist paintings, but they lack the mythological motifs and religious contemplation that took a prominent place in his later works. Instead, these poems consist of unmediated observations of moods, with themes of loneliness, disgust, death, and powerlessness. The poems of *Vers* are stylistically ornate. Jørgensen experimented with compound words and phrases, as in "Fausts Ord til Foråret" (Faust's Words to Spring): "Hver sölvskællet Stjærne, der svömmer i Nathimlens sorteblaa Hav, / hvert sitrende Savn, der drömmer ved visnende Vaardages Grav" (Every silver-shelled star swimming in the black-blue ocean of the night sky, / every trembling want, dreaming at the grave of withered spring days). His style has much in common with the poetry of Mallarmé, whose poetry Edvard Brandes referred to in his review of *Vers,* and with that of Baudelaire, whose poetic works enchanted both Jørgensen and Claussen. The poems in *Vers* are highly autobiographical and give clear insight into the poet's state of mind at that time. They reflect on the lonely Promethean path he had chosen and reveal the dream-like reality of a young radical in the 1880s. The poet is left dissatisfied and frustrated, and he turns his back on life and seeks consolation in nature. Jørgensen was on target when he later called these poems eighty pages of melancholy in verse. They are imbued with a weltschmertz, a poetic hatred of everything earthly and commonplace.

In 1886 and 1887 Stuckenberg and Claussen also published their first poems, and the decadent young poets received much attention for their new poetry, even from Georg Brandes. Their mutual sensibilities brought them close together as a small group of literary revolutionaries. At times their relationship resembled that of a small family, with Stuckenberg's wife, Ingeborg, playing the parts of both ever-present mother and erotic object.

After publishing *Vers,* Jørgensen finally gave up his studies and lived as a journalist, working first at *Socialdemokraten* (The Social Democrat), then at *Kjøbenhavns Børstidende* (The Copenhagen Financial Times), the editor of which was Georg Brandes's brother Ernst, and finally in 1892 at *Politiken,* the radical newspaper established by Edvard Brandes and others in 1884. As another means of support, Jørgensen began translating the French masters: François René de Chateaubriand, Victor Hugo, and later, Pierre Loti, whose central theme of constant longing preoccupied the group in the late 1880s. Jørgensen next turned his attention to prose.

Although Jørgensen's reputation today rests mainly on his poetry, of which he wrote twelve volumes, he considered his prose works the most important part of his writings. From 1888 to 1901 he wrote nine novels. Though not particularly successful then and almost forgotten today, the novels form an important link between his early pantheistic and egotistic poems gesturing toward the apologetic works that preoccupied Jørgensen's mature life.

In the five short novels published from 1888 to 1894–*Foraarssagn* (Spring Legend, 1888), *En Fremmed* (A Stranger, 1890), *Sommer* (Summer, 1892), *Livets Træ* (The Tree of Life, 1893), and *Hjemvee* (Homesickness, 1894)–Jørgensen relates the personal experiences that formed an important background for his later conversion. The main characters in the novels are all young dreamers who have easily recognizable traits in common with the author, and though they all have different names, the protagonists form a single consciousness. The novels are stylistically reminiscent of Jacobsen's novel *Niels Lyhne* (1880) and his short story "Mogens" (1882). Jørgensen's first novel, *Foraarssagn,* takes up the thread from Jacobsen with its minute descriptions of nature and landscapes. Man is, to both writers, seen as part of nature just as the trees and the animals are. The adjectives pile up in the novels, and the complicated sentence structure is also inherited from Jacobsen. *Foraarssagn* is a series of childhood memories, youthful moods, and situations pieced together in a story about leaving home and facing degrading erotic encounters in a frame of memories and nostalgic longing. The young man Jens, the Danish name for Johannes, leads a pointless existence as a student in Copenhagen, influenced on the one hand by his physical desires and his love of nature, while on the other, he is still influenced by the sheltered upbringing and moral outlook of his home in the province. Discouraged and rejected by all the women he meets, Jens escapes to a world of dreams. In the end he is facing the hopelessness of the conflict between his natural desires and the asceticism produced by his inhibitions.

Jørgensen's early novels are traditionally seen as forming a whole, complementary, and circular system of autobiographical sketches wherein a "universal" youth is described in different stages of life. But the novels can also be seen as portraying a development in the ambivalent relationship the young man has with women and the psychological conflict that the taboo on sexuality inflicts. Whereas *Foraarssagn* treats the distance of the adolescent man to desire, *Livets Træ* is about distancing oneself from the desired object, and *Hjemvee* deals with distancing oneself from the self as a desiring subject. The protagonist of *Hjemvee,* poet and journalist Glob, catches a glimpse of his childhood love, one of the young women in *Foraarssagn;* he then leaves Copenhagen and returns to his childhood home, where he is reunited with her, realizing that what he loves in the woman is really his own homesickness.

Though Jørgensen's novels all express his loneliness, his estrangement from life around him, and an almost tormented frustration with sexuality, in 1891 he married Amalia Ewald. Soon a child was added to the family, and a happy period began in Jørgensen's life. The new home crowned by the tower became the gathering place of the younger generation of poets. Nevertheless, Jørgensen was too weak to keep entirely away from his earlier life, and gradually his happiness diminished. His wife, he said, only possessed half his heart. He got into financial difficulties, and he became so engrossed in his literary activities as to neglect everything else. At this time he also began editing the new journal *Taarnet. Illustreret Månedsskrift for Kunst og Litteratur* (The Tower. Illustrated Monthly Review of Art and Literature, 1893–1894).

As to the significance of the tower to the young poets of the 1890s, Jørgensen claims that they did not think of a church tower. By a tower they understood something solemn, something that stood by itself, not in rows like houses, and from its top one could look at the stars. From the top of Jørgensen's tower the young poets could also see through the dark, brooding clouds of modern culture. In the programmatic essay "Symbolisme," published in 1893 in *Taarnet,* he declared that a new movement would take over from Brandes and Emile Zola's naturalism. He wrote, "Dette er Symbolismen, den filosofiske og kunstneriske Symbolisme: Troen paa en Metafysik, en anden Verden, et Hinsides" (This is Symbolism, the philosophical and artistic Symbolism: The belief in metaphysics, another world, a Beyond). Like the German philosopher Arthur Schopenhauer, whose work he was reading at the time, Jørgensen truly believed in a metaphysics–a belief that had its origin in German Romanticism but eventually, through years of self-doubt and painstaking religious quarrels, led him to Italy and Catholicism.

30.

Solnedgang

Bag den fjærne Kyst
Synker Solen ned som e
Og dens gyldne Skjær
Tænder Bölgen i Blinken
Og de stille, skvulpende Var
Rulle sagte ind fra min
Og hviske med underfuld
Om gamle, kjendte Land
Og det klinger igjen i mit
I Længsel.

Thi jeg véd, thi jeg ve
Bag det matgyldne Bli
Bag det dæmrings mörk
Og bag Solfaldets Glans
Der ligger af Skove og
Om et blomnende Va
Der er du!

Manuscript for a poem by Jørgensen (from Emil Frederiksen, Johannes Jørgensens ungdom, *1946; William T. Young Library, University of Kentucky)*

31.

Og i Aftenens bløde, umodige Fred —
Du indaander tyst
Den vilde Duft
Fra den høje, aldgamle Linde,
Der suser og hvisker endnu
I den hede, tungt aandende Vind
Som hin Nat.

Men paa Himlen staar
De evige Stjærners funklende Hær
Og nikkende sé
De til dig og blinke med sølvhvidt Skjær —
Men jeg, jeg er i det fjærne,
Og Vinden er kold og raa,
Og kom jeg end did igjen,
Saa er dog min Lykkes Stjærne
Længst slukket i Skyer graa
For evig.

The transition from decadent symbolism to Catholic metaphysics is signaled by the poetry collection *Bekendelse* (Confession, 1894), a collection of poems that for the first time shows Jørgensen's personal poetic voice with its sensitive simplicity and a preoccupation with the correspondences between surrounding nature and the soul. He reflects upon his family's return to his childhood home of Svendborg, a move brought about by constant financial difficulties, in a group of poems titled "Foraarsevangelium" (Spring Gospel). *Bekendelse* shows the struggle to attain a new and positive view of life that was going on within Jørgensen's mind at this time. Two of the poems are themselves given the title of "confession"; the first, with the Danish title "Bekendelse," closes the first part of the volume and expresses a faith in an eternity, though not a Christian faith; the second bears the Latin title "Confiteor," with obvious Catholic overtones. The early poems of the volume are kept in gray nuances that depict restlessness and dissatisfaction, and the desire to escape from everyday life, its loneliness, and its isolation. In "Høstdrøm" (Autumn Dream) the poet is surrounded by a gray, rainy dreariness, and this mood encapsulates the first of many poems. Only in "Februar" (February) does a sense of hope arise, which culminates momentarily in "Bekendelse," with its growing sense of eternity and liberation: "O Evighed! Forløser og Befrier! . . . O Evighed! jeg er i Dine Hænder!" (Oh Eternity! Redeemer and Savior! . . . Oh Eternity! I am in your hands!). It captures the conflict between the two sides of the poet's personality, between his love of things earthly and his longing for things eternal. The fifteen "Kaldæa" (Chaldea) sonnets that make up the latter part of *Bekendelse* form the transition from doubt to faith, and the collection ends with the affirming "Confiteor," a piece of lyrical autobiography written from a new standpoint and with new insight.

Taarnet and the poetic transition of *Bekendelse* are both significant in understanding Jørgensen's final conversion in 1896. Though Jørgensen claimed the journal to be free of Christian ideology, imagery in the journal shows an increasing preoccupation with religion–especially through the illustrations of such young artists as Jan Verkade and Mogens Ballin, a Jewish convert to Catholicism whom Jørgensen had met in 1892. Ballin's influence on Jørgensen was decisive. In 1894 Jørgensen traveled abroad for the first time under the guidance of Verkade and Ballin, God's envoy, as Jørgensen calls Ballin in his autobiography. Jørgensen's first travel abroad took him to the cloister in Beuron in Germany, through the Italian town of Rapallo, where he met and broke with Claussen, and finally to Rome, as described in *Rejsebogen* (Book of Travels, 1895). In *Rejsebogen*–his first truly Catholic work–Jørgensen describes the early struggle between the Romantic pantheistic inclinations of his youth and the beckoning conversion to Catholicism.

Jørgensen's works from 1896 to 1900 show a writer concerned that his own story of conversion is leading his old friends to distance themselves from him. In 1894, when he had declared his new standpoint to the Stuckenbergs, Ingeborg answered by calling Jørgensen a turncoat and reproaching him for having lost the belief in the sovereign status of the individual and believing in other gods than himself. Ingeborg was concerned about the change in Jørgensen's work away from symbolist poetics to works merely concerning others–biographies and apologetic writings. Viggo Stuckenberg accused Jørgensen of turning the poet into a pastor, preaching like a Catholic. Brandes delivered the final blow to Jørgensen's reputation by calling him a small, perverted renegade–a judgment that to some extent followed the reception of Jørgensen's work in the 1900s.

In the years after 1900, Jørgensen devoted himself almost exclusively to the documentary genres of travel books and biographies. As he was drifting away from his friends, his wife, too, fell into the background. She stayed for the most part in Denmark as Jørgensen traveled Europe as a literary pilgrim.

His next book of travels was *Pilgrimsbogen* (The Book of the Pilgrim, 1903; translated as *Pilgrim Walks in Franciscan Italy,* 1908). Though Jørgensen had doubts about his future as a writer prior to this work, *Pilgrimsbogen* stands out as one of the most personal and beautiful of his works. In it Jørgensen expresses his deep love for Italy and especially the cities of Siena and Assisi, which became his home between 1914 and 1939. The travel writer himself is once again the central feature; everything is experienced directly through his eyes and imagination. He does not feel committed to any narrowly defined subject but wanders from topic to topic, indulging freely in the digressions that became a trademark of his hagiographic work. This personal trait renewed the genre of hagiography and of biographical works in general. Jørgensen published three more books of travels: *Bag alle de blaa Bjærge* (Beyond All the Blue Mountains, 1913) from Siena; *Alvernerbjærget* (Mount Alverno, 1920), taking its material from Jørgensen's travels to La Verna; and *Jorsalafærd* (Journey to Jerusalem, 1923), a detailed account of his travels to Jerusalem and also the longest of his travel books. They all figure as sketches in Jørgensen's biographies of the saints.

While he was opening this new chapter in his career, Jørgensen's financial and personal problems grew. In the autobiography, he recalls the feeling of being at a crossroads where he could choose either life or death. He felt a deep shame for his weak and egotistic nature and asked God to turn him into a new man. Ballin convinced Jørgensen that his life was unworthy of a true Christian and advised him to leave Denmark for good and live as a Catholic writer. Jørgensen was soon thereafter invited to lecture at the Catholic university in Louvain, Belgium, where he met young French painter Andrée Carof. Her presence is felt in all the works that he wrote from 1914 to 1934. In 1915 Jørgensen divorced his wife–a decision that gave him the peace he needed to produce the elaborately researched biographies of the saints.

In the hagiographies, Jørgensen combines the traditional legends of saints with modern biography: *Den hellige Frans af Assisi* (1907; translated as *St. Francis of Assisi, a Biography,* 1912) and *Den hellige Katerina af Siena* (1915; translated as *Saint Catherine of Siena,* 1938)–works that continue to appear in most languages throughout the world. The hagiographies combine thorough studies of historical sources with an engaging imagination. On the one hand, they present the lives of the saints, making them accessible to readers other than Catholics; on the other hand, they are literary works in their own right, composed around common novelistic archetypes. They all deal with "conversion" as a compositional center and make use of common literary techniques. Jørgensen presents brief surveys, as when he introduces the reader to the inner conflicts of the Catholic Church in the fourteenth century. He also dramatizes, as when he tells about Frans, who suddenly turns his back to his family, or when the six-year-old Katerina receives her first revelation. Jørgensen's work is historically correct but often emphasizes the imagination–dealing instead with "what might have taken place." Another trait that sets Jørgensen's hagiographies apart is the use of his own point of view on Catholic traditions. He quotes not only the old masters but also Percy Bysshe Shelley, Goethe, and Oscar Wilde. Jørgensen deeply identifies with both the subject and the time he describes. His hagiographies are far from unengaged, dry narratives. What Jørgensen seeks are the elements and events in the life of a saint that coincide with his own way to conversion and Catholic faith, or with his recurring experiences of religious crisis. Jørgensen writes most enthusiastically about Frans, whose departure from a bohemian life Jørgensen sees as a direct parallel to his own conversion, although, as Claussen comments, Jørgensen's youthful digressions never were so significant as might be gathered from his writings.

Having found his calling as a Catholic writer, Jørgensen, now permanently living in Italy and with a steady flow of publications that eased his financial situation but never made him rich, he found the fame of an international writer in the latter part of his career. Jørgensen moved to Assisi with his spiritual companion, Carof, to whom he began writing his autobiography, *Mit Livs Legende.* The book is a masterpiece in its genre; it refers to Augustin's *Confessions* (397), Goethes's autobiography, and even rivals Hans Christian Andersen's *The Fairy Tale of My Life* (1855). Jørgensen's autobiography is divided into seven volumes spanning his childhood in Svendborg through the separation from his wife in 1913, the year he met Carof.

In the preface, Jørgensen looks back on a turbulent life, but with the realization that it had all served a higher purpose: "hvorhen et Menneske inderst inde vil, did kommer han ogsaa. . . . Livet bestaar af en uafbrudt Række Valg, store og smaa–og Mennesket vælger uafladeligt i Følge sit inderste Væsen" (Wherever Man from his heart wants to go, there he will also arrive. . . . Life consists of an unbroken chain of choices, large as well as small–and Man chooses perpetually to follow his innermost nature). Jørgensen felt that his own life was a sacred story that took him to wherever his heart wanted him.

The first volume of the autobiography, *Den röde Stjærne* (The Red Star, 1916), describes his childhood in Svendborg and the fanatical years of studying in Copenhagen (1882–1889), all under the guiding red star. In this period from childhood to youth all authorities are overthrown while Jørgensen's own soul darkens in loneliness and terror. The pivotal scene takes place one dark night when he hears steps outside his room as from a goat's hooves. The door springs open, and the lord of darkness enters, to whom Johannes despairingly knows he belongs. The second volume, *Taarnet* (The Tower, 1916), follows the young poet from 1889 to 1894. Jørgensen relates his happy life as a married man, the bohemian life with the Stuckenbergs and Claussen, and his early religious awareness, which arose as he edited *Taarnet.* The second volume ends with Jørgensen receiving news from Ballin about the grant for European travel and a prayer thanking God for all the beauty surrounding him. *Vælskland* (Italy, 1917) follows Jørgensen's Catholic trials under the supervision of Ballin, and the fourth book, *Det usyrede Bröd* (The Unleavened Bread, 1918), relates the events occurring between 1894 and 1901. Jørgensen receives instruction in the Catholic faith at home and converts, but he only feels the joy of liberation gradually. During a stay in Assisi, Jørgensen undergoes a death-like crisis of conscience until he hears the voice of his spiritual guide, Padre Filici, beckoning him to sleep peacefully. The fifth volume, *Ved den skönne Tempeldör* (By the Beautiful Gate to the Temple, 1918), refers to the spot where Saint Peter cured the palsied; the grave of the apostle in Saint Peter's Basilica in Rome became the place where in 1903 Jørgensen knelt and sought atonement. The

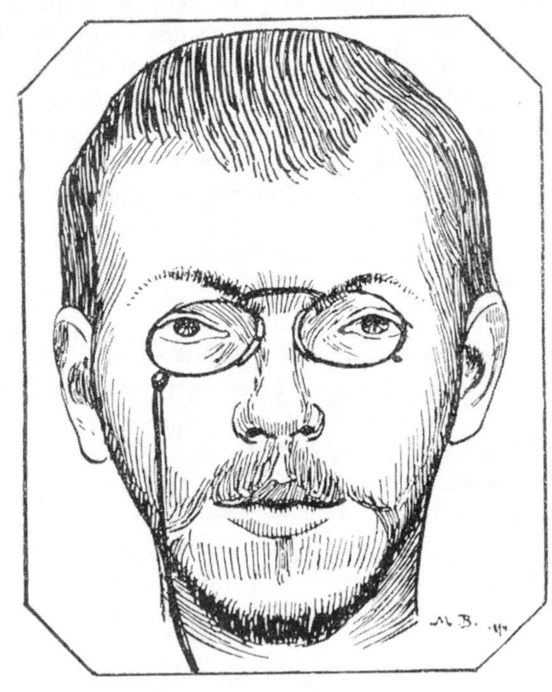

Jørgensen in 1894 (drawing by Mogens Ballin; from Emil Frederiksen, Johannes Jørgensens ungdom, *1946; William T. Young Library, University of Kentucky)*

atonement is followed by *Guds Kværn* (God's Grind, 1918), in which he dedicates much space to the tension that had built between himself and his first wife in the years 1903–1909. He comes to the realization that matters are the way they are because they cannot be otherwise. Everyone has the life he or she deserves. Each has the man or woman and the love he deserves, and he who has taken life, the man or woman, and love in vain will be punished. Considering that the autobiography is written to Carof, after Jørgensen's divorce in 1915, his realization appears double bound. For now he has the woman he deserves, which must mean that he has felt the change that happened to him after 1913, the time of his great sacrifice, his divorce. He has come to terms with his own egotism through his quest for truth and decided to correct his relations. He has realized his faults and sacrifices temporal happiness for a higher ideal. With this realization, the right love was sent to him in the guise of the most unselfish of women, Carof. Such trials and realizations convinced Jørgensen of the existence of God's providence–the governing principle in *Mit Livs Legende*. In *Over de valske Mile* (Over Italian Dunes, 1928) Jørgensen describes sending the letter from abroad that finalizes the break with his wife. By the end of 1913 in Siena, a friend can tell him, "Nu er du i dit Rige, Giovani" (Now you are in your kingdom, Giovanni). *Mit Livs Legende* is in the end the story of a poet's search for himself through self-reproach and self-assertion.

Following the last book of his autobiography came a time of both mental and literary decline for Jørgensen. He became preoccupied with his expatriation and the lack of recognition by his fellow countrymen. In 1933 Carof died and left the aging writer lonelier than ever. Not until 2 September 1937 did Jørgensen remarry. He married Helena Klein, an Austrian lady he had met in Assisi, and with the new marriage he saw an opportunity to settle down once again. He became more and more concerned with unfolding political events, especially the tensions between Italian dictator Benito Mussolini and the Catholic Church. In 1938 Jørgensen made comments in a Danish newspaper about the racial policies of Hitler and thus complicated his relations with Italian authorities. His concerns about the increasing European racism are found in articles collected in *Omkring Axen Assisi-Salzburg* (About the Axis Assisi-Salzburg, 1938). Jørgensen shows a deeply felt love for the old German culture, but the articles are also frontal attacks on the inhumanity of the new Germany. Later in the year 1938, Jørgensen visited Vadstena in Sweden to begin his work on the last major hagiography, *Den hellige Birgitta af Vadstena* (1941, 1943; translated as *Saint Bridget of Sweden,* 1954), and in 1939 he and his wife left Assisi to settle in Sweden. Jørgensen had difficulty at first collecting his thoughts on the fourteenth century when so many tragic events were unfolding in the twentieth. But enlivened by the nature of Vadstena, Jørgensen regained his strength and completed his last hagiography, which became the vastest of the biographies, an immense accomplishment for an author in his seventies. However, the reader senses a tendency to oversimplification, as found in Jørgensen's last nostalgic poems and abstractions, which diminish the work's historical value. *Den hellige Birgitta af Vadstena* embodies a vast amount of material, stemming mostly from the many quotes, but it also reveals a renewed interest in the simpler descriptions of nature without youthful ornamentations. In a letter dated 2 December 1942 to Mogen's Kai Nørregaard, Jørgensen hints at the melancholy felt in his last major work. He finds the end of the book to be near, and this fact saddens him, since Birgitta's last years remind him of himself experiencing the last creative energy as it is slowly ebbing away.

In 1953 Johannes returned to his childhood home in Svendborg, where he spent his last three years. He died on 29 May 1956, six months before his ninetieth birthday. His legacy and career have often been described as consisting of two incompatible systems of thought and philosophy, as if he belonged to two different periods in Danish literature. Underlying his growth–from a modern nihilistic poet to the great Catholic writer he became–runs a "tråd ovenfra" (thread from above [title of Jørgensen's 1898 parable]) that he himself was constantly trying to retrace. He became an honorary citizen in his beloved Svendborg in 1936–but already in 1922, the same honor had been bestowed on him in Assisi, the city whose saint became synonymous with Jørgensen's name and work throughout the world.

Letters:

Breve fra Johannes Jørgensen til Viggo Stuckenberg, edited by Jørgen Andersen (Copenhagen: Gyldendal, 1946).

Biographies:

Emil Frederiksen, *Johannes Jørgensens ungdom* (Copenhagen: Gyldendal, 1946);

W. Glyn Jones, *Johannes Jørgensens modne år* (Copenhagen: Gyldendal, 1963);

Inge Lise Rasmussen Pin, *Johannes Jørgensens Veje omkring Siena* (Copenhagen: C. A. Reitzel, 1989).

References:

Alex Garff, "Johannes Jørgensen som oversætter," in Garff and Hans Kyre, *To store oversættere* (Copenhagen: Gyldendal, 1949), pp. 9–34;

Johan Fjord Jensen, *Turgenjev i dansk åndsliv: Studier i dansk romankunst 1870–1900* (Copenhagen: Gyldendal, 1969);

W. Glyn Jones, "The Early Novels of Jørgensen," *Scandinavian Studies,* 36, no. 2 (May 1964): 103–117;

Jones, *Johannes Jörgensen* (New York: Twayne, 1969);

Jones, "Johannes Jørgensen and His Apologetics," *Scandinavian Studies,* 32, no. 1 (February 1960): 27–36;

Bo Hakon Jørgensen, *Symbolismen–eller jegets orfiske forklaring* (Odense: Odense University Press, 1993);

Bo Nielsen, *Johannes Jørgensen og Symbolismen* (Copenhagen: Akademisk, 1975);

Erik Skyum-Nielsen, "Johannes Jørgensen," in *Danske digtere i det 20. århundrede,* volume 1, edited by Torben Brostrøm and Mette Winge (Copenhagen: Gad, 1980), pp. 65–83.

Papers:

Johannes Jørgensen's diaries are at Svendborg Library, Denmark. Manuscripts and other papers are at the Danish Royal Library in Copenhagen and the Svendborg Library.

Erna Juel-Hansen

(5 March 1845 - 30 November 1922)

Nete Schmidt
University of Wisconsin–Madison

BOOKS: *Mellem 12 og 17,* as Arne Wendt (Copenhagen: Schubothe, 1881); republished as *De Smaa Piger,* as Juel-Hansen (Copenhagen: Gyldendal/ Nordisk, 1912);

Sex Noveller (Copenhagen: Philipsen, 1885);

En Ung Dames Historie (Copenhagen: Philipsen, 1888);

Da de vare unge. Skildringer af berømte Personligheders Ungdomsliv (Copenhagen: Philipsen, 1889);

Terese Kærulf. To Afsnit af en ung Kvindes Liv (Copenhagen: Philipsen, 1894; republished, Copenhagen: Gyldendal, 1914);

Kærlighedens Veje (Copenhagen: Philipsen, 1895);

Helsen & Co. (Copenhagen: Nordisk, 1900);

Holger Drachmann som Dreng. Barndomserindringer. Udg. i Anledning af Drachmanns 60-Aars Fødselsdag (Copenhagen: Gyldendal, 1906);

Henriks Mor. Fortælling (Copenhagen: Nordisk, 1917).

PLAY PRODUCTIONS: *Aftenen før–,* Copenhagen, Dagmarteatret, 29 September 1890;

Principperne leve (originally, *Hvedebrødsdage*), Copenhagen, Casino, 29 November 1894.

OTHER: *Nye Æventyr fra mange Lande,* edited by Juel-Hansen (Copenhagen: Schous, 1875);

Efter Solnedgang. Æventyr, edited by Juel-Hansen, (Copenhagen: Gyldendal, 1877);

Vore Bedsteforældres Sange, edited by Juel-Hansen (Copenhagen: Nordisk, 1897);

Hele Familien: Ugeblad for alle Hjem, edited by Juel-Hansen, 1, nos. 1–7 (1902).

TRANSLATIONS: Gottfried Keller, *Den grønne Heinrich* (Copenhagen: Schubothe, 1882);

Fyodor Dostoevsky, *Fattige Folk,* translated by Juel-Hansen and C. Sarauw (Copenhagen: Gyldendal, 1884);

Dostoevsky, *Raskolnikov* (Copenhagen: Salmonsen, 1884);

Dostoevsky, *De Forurettede og de Undertrykte* (Copenhagen: Gyldendal, 1886);

Erna Juel-Hansen (courtesy of the Danish Royal Library, Copenhagen)

Dostoevsky, *Nihilister* (Copenhagen: Gyldendal, 1886);

Dostoevsky, *Fyrst Myschkin (Idioten)* (Copenhagen: Gyldendal, 1887);

Dostoevsky, *En Hanrej* (Copenhagen: Schubothe, 1888);

Verner von Heidenstam, *Endymion* (Copenhagen: Gyldendal, 1889);

Gustave Macé, *Min Første Forbryder* (Copenhagen: Høst, 1891);

Macé, *Net Selskab* (Copenhagen: Høst, 1892);

J. Hatton, *Anna Klosstock* (Copenhagen: Pio, 1893); republished as *Ghettoens Dronning* (Copenhagen: Pio, 1916);
E. B. Duffey, *Hvad alle Kvinder bør vide* (Copenhagen: Stjernholm, 1894);
Wilkie Collins, *Maanestenen* (Aalborg: Aalborg Amtstidende, 1901);
James Ferguson, *Mørkets Gerninger* (Copenhagen: Nordisk, 1919);
Florence L. Barclay, *Den lille hvide Dame* (Copenhagen: Nordisk, 1920);
Olive Wadsley, *Johns Kærlighed* (Copenhagen: Martin, 1923);
Temple Bailey, *Tinsoldaten* (Copenhagen: Martin, 1925).

SELECTED PERIODICAL PUBLICATIONS–UNCOLLECTED:

FICTION

"En Konfirmand," *Ude og Hjemme,* 1882;
"Lille Karl. En Skitse fra Provinsen," *Ude og Hjemme,* 1883;
"De tolv smaa Profeter," *Tilskueren,* 1885;
"Kærlighed og Geografi," *Tilskueren,* 1886;
"Fristelsen," *Østsjællands Avis' Bogtrykkeri,* 1904;
"Fa'er," *Mit Hjem,* 1911.

NONFICTION

"Den Frøbelske Børnehave," *Dagens Nyheder,* 1880;
"Om en Reform af Pigeskolen," *Vor Ungdom,* 1882;
"Lidt om Gymnastik," *Dagsavisen,* 1884;
"Annie Besant. En Levnedsskildring," *Hvad vi vil,* 1890;
"Damer i Mørke," *Politiken,* 1894;
"Mand og Kone," *Kvinden og Samfundet,* 1895;
"En Dreng som blev Digter," *Juleroser,* 1896;
"Bjørnson i Hillerød," *Politiken,* 29 November 1897;
"Kvinder og Forhørsdommere," *Damernes Blad,* 1901;
"Holger Drachmann som Dreng," *Politiken,* 28 February 1906;
"Forfatterinden Fru Erna Juel-Hansen om sin Broder, Holger Drachmanns Barndom," *Hver 8. Dag,* 1906;
"Da vi gamle var unge," *Vore Damers Jul* (Copenhagen), 1920.

Erna Juel-Hansen's life cannot be separated from her literary work. The majority of her writing consists of lectures, articles, essays, and short stories published in magazines and newspapers. Her seven novels paint a vivid portrait of the women of her time, and, by reflection, of herself, as a social reformer and feminist visionary. Pil Dahlerup's published doctoral dissertation *Det Moderne Gennembruds Kvinder* (Women of the Modern Breakthrough, 1984) singles out Juel-Hansen as one of the leading women writers of her generation and aptly characterizes her as "det hele menneske" (the whole human being).

Erna Emilie Louise Vilhelmine Drachmann was born in Copenhagen on 5 March 1845, the oldest daughter of Andreas Georg Drachmann, a doctor, and his first wife, Vilhelmine Marie Stæhr. Her brother, writer Holger Drachmann, was born a year and a half later. Vilhelmine Stæhr, Erna Drachmann's mother, gave birth to five children and died from tuberculosis when Erna was thirteen years old. Her father was a doctor and public-health advocate who instituted a new kind of physical exercise for girls. He educated his sons and daughters equally, and he fostered a particularly close relationship with Erna. She became her father's trusted companion, working with and for him; his ideas about cleanliness and health formed the basis for her later work as a women's health advocate.

After her confirmation in 1861, Drachmann applied for permission to continue her studies and graduated with a *Studentereksamen* (General Certificate). Instead of seeking suitors and an eventual marriage, she wanted a medical degree, but this route was barred to women. To compensate for the disappointment, her father employed her as his secretary, and in 1866 she accompanied him to Paris in order to study a system of physical exercise for women, which she then taught professionally for the next four years.

In 1868, Drachmann began a passionate and prolific daily correspondence with Niels Juel-Hansen, a twenty-seven-year-old law student. Together with him, Drachmann found her calling in life and decided to dedicate herself to the introduction of kindergartens in Denmark. The first step on the way was getting a certificate to teach elementary school, a goal she accomplished in 1870. Later, she moved to Berlin to study the system of kindergartens built on Friedrich Frøbel's model. In 1871 Drachmann and Juel-Hansen opened the first Danish kindergarten in Copenhagen, and shortly afterward they were married. The kindergarten was not an immediate success, and throughout its existence it never completely overcame the public's initial skepticism. During the first two years of marriage, Erna Juel-Hansen had the first of four children, but her married life was not the source of fulfillment she had hoped for. Her work as a teacher in the kindergarten brought her joy and satisfaction, but she soon realized that her husband desired a more traditional wife. Nonetheless, she continued to teach physical exercise, work as a translator, and run her household. In 1873 she attended a lecture by the most influential literary critic of her era, Georg Brandes.

Erna Drachmann at age fourteen with her brother Holger, thirteen, and sisters Mimi, ten, and Johanne, eight (from Pia Sigmund, Oldemor Erna, *1991; Memorial Library, University of Wisconsin–Madison)*

Juel-Hansen's next vision was a coeducational school, but once more she was ahead of her time. The Juel-Hansens had to settle for an extension of their kindergarten with a preschool preparatory class that led to a school for girls only. Despite her challenging work, Juel-Hansen found herself increasingly unhappy, and she now realized that her marriage was a failure. The urge to write letters had never left her through the troubled years of her married life, and, consequently, she turned to writing fiction as a natural outlet for her thoughts. Her first attempt at a novel in 1880, "Gifte Folk" (Married People), was not published, but it honed her skills and confirmed her talent to herself. She had several prominent advisers, among whom were her brother Holger Drachmann and Meïr Goldschmidt. They encouraged her to write about areas in which she was knowledgeable and experienced. Thus, her first published novel, *Mellem 12 og 17* (Between 12 and 17, 1881), opens with a scene in a schoolyard at the end of recess.

Broaching many of the themes treated in Juel-Hansen's subsequent writings, the novel paints a portrait of Ellen, a young girl who loses her mother at the age of thirteen. The reader follows Ellen through her puberty, first infatuations, confirmation, and graduation. Ellen is caught between child and adult, between responsibility to her father and siblings and the desire for self-exploration. Her friend Ludovika embodies a sensual, liberal attitude toward prenuptial sexuality that both attracts and repels Ellen. In the end, however, her strong determination to succeed academically and her desire to study medicine help her attain a spiritual and physical equilibrium. The refined Kammila reflects the empty virtues of the inactive woman, and the school friend Emma represents a tendency toward lesbianism, which Ellen rejects. Ellen reaches maturity when the object of her passion returns from abroad, and she discovers that her infatuation has withered, leaving her free to pursue a healthy self-development.

In 1883 the kindergarten and school closed, and Juel-Hansen found herself at a crossroads. She was thirty-eight years old and had four children in her marriage of twelve years. Nonetheless, she joined the *Dansk Kvindesamfund* (Danish Women's Association) and the *Studentersamfundet* (Student Association). After spending many years in her husband's shadow, trying to conform to his ideas of appropriate female and wifely behavior, she was now eager to regain her prenuptial independence. Brandes, who had lauded her first novel, became one of her friends as she struck out on her own.

In addition to teaching and writing, she took classes in Russian in order to translate the works of Fyodor Dostoevsky. She eventually decided to turn to her previous sphere of interest (physical exercise), re-educated herself in the latest Swedish techniques, and in 1884 opened the first establishment for physical exercise for women in Denmark. The establishment became an immediate success, and Juel-Hansen benefited from the newly instituted law allowing married women to keep their incomes.

Alongside her other pursuits, Juel-Hansen continued to write, contributing letters to the editors of newspapers and essays and short stories for magazines. Her political involvement began in 1885 when she joined the *Københavns Liberale Vælgerforening* (Liberal Voters' Association of Copenhagen). She thrived as a participant in the political debates of the day and formed several lasting friendships with prominent cultural figures, including writers Erik and Amalie Skram. Later that year her second book was published as a collection of novellas, *Sex Noveller* (Six Novellas, 1885).

In this collection, Juel-Hansen bravely carries the depiction of youth to its controversial culmination in the story "Enlig" (Single). A young working woman is deserted by her partner after seven years of cohabitation. She chooses to follow her heart and pursues the physical relationship along with the platonic one, but she finds herself rejected by a man too heavily influenced by his family and the accepted social norms. The author's feminism is evidenced by the unwed protagonist of the story, who becomes pregnant, gives birth to a child, and finds happiness on her own terms. The final story, "Tøbrud" (Thaw), tells the story of a woman who is prevented from marrying for love. She consequently withdraws not only from her husband but also from her two sons, until a calamity brings them back into her arms.

Juel-Hansen's political involvement continued alongside her writing. She introduced a "reform-dress" for women without the corset and bustle, lectured extensively, and advocated women's suffrage. During the Scandinavian "morality feud" of the late 1880s, she was enraged at the conservative stance of the *Dansk Kvindesamfund* and canceled her membership in protest, but she did not dare to write an outright critique in support of Brandes. She did not believe in free love but rather in equal love between two equal persons, although she was unable to attain this ideal in her own private life.

Juel-Hansen courted controversy in her writing as well as her politics. *En Ung Dames Historie* (The Story of a Young Woman, 1888) tells of a young girl's developing independence. The protagonist, Margrethe Holm, is sixteen years old and ignorant about life and sexuality. Her bourgeois mother adheres to the norms of the day, and her busy father is ensconced in his own male realm. Neither addresses her growing instinctual longings and emptiness. Her experienced cousin awakens her eroticism, but he dies young. In a similarly ignorant state, her sister marries the local minister, and her subsequent childbirth appalls and horrifies Margrethe to the point of terror. Recognizing her need to learn about life, her father sends her to classes in basic botany, but the result is an infatuation with the teacher, although he is far from her ideal male. The resulting engagement does not live up to her expectations, and she has an affair with a young craftsman, who tires of her incessant demands for love and affection. Rejected by him, she marries the teacher, although the relationship no longer holds any promises for happiness or marital bliss.

Juel-Hansen's attack on the prevalent ignorance among young girls, coupled with the sexual experimentation of the protagonist, created a serious controversy. The reviews of the book reflected the scandalized and indignant reactions of the public. Her students left her physical-exercise establishment, and she was forced to close it in 1890 and rely on her translations for an income. Juel-Hansen also tried her hand as a playwright, but in this area she failed to excel. Her first play was rejected by the censor at the Danish Royal Theater in Copenhagen. Her second play, *Aftenen Før–* (The Night Before–), was performed nine times in 1890 at the Dagmar Theater in Copenhagen. Her third and last play, *Principperne leve* (Hurray for the Principles), was only performed twice in 1894 at the Casino Theater in Copenhagen.

In 1891 Juel-Hansen lost both her father and her third child, Niels. She was deeply affected by her losses and strained financial situation. Some of her friends presented her with a trip to the Mediterranean Sea, which helped her regain her strength and will to live. Finally, in 1894 she left her husband and finished her novel *Terese Kærulf. To Afsnit af en ung Kvindes Liv* (Terese Kaerulf. Two Periods in a Young Woman's Life, 1894).

The twenty-three-year-old Terese is orphaned and spends some months in Berlin getting an education in order to be independent of a husband. Coming from a background of craftsmen, Terese is an avid learner, politically influenced by her grandmother. As a "new woman," she is inquisitive and intelligent, and she likes to smoke cigars. She mingles happily in the radical circles of Berlin, where she finds intellectual stimulus and fulfillment through Heinrich von Schilden. When he proposes, she accepts, but shortly afterward she realizes that she is physically revolted by his appearance and breaks off the engagement. Back in Copenhagen, she meets a student of theology, Mogens Højer, who appeals to her physical side, but his incessant doubts and intellectual weakness finally induce a break. The social recognition of prostitution as an acceptable outlet for male lust to keep the intended bride "pure" is exposed as a hypocritical double standard. *Terese Kærulf* reflects Juel-Hansen's real-life promotion of equal and healthy love in a relationship. However, even without this union of spiritual and physical love, in the end Terese, through her work and art, finds success and her desired independence. This book was Juel-Hansen's first major success with positive reviews; it also had a subsequent translation into German.

With an unquenchable zest, she continued her campaign to reform and improve the lives of women, writing controversial letters and contributions to newspapers and magazines. She continued to advocate better hygiene, fresh air and ventilation, increased bathing and swimming, and an extension of the summer vacation for schoolchildren. She started bike riding and wrote articles about this sport, again

Drachmann in 1861 (from Pia Sigmund, Oldemor Erna, *1991; Memorial Library, University of Wisconsin–Madison)*

promoting a sensible and comfortable dress for women. She translated Eliza Bisbee Duffey's *What Women Should Know* (1873) as *Hvad alle Kvinder bør vide* (What All Women Should Know, 1894), dealing with such taboo subjects as childbirth and menstruation. She co-edited *Husmoderens Blad* (The Housewife's Magazine) and edited *Hele Familien: Ugeblad for alle Hjem* (The Whole Family: Weekly Magazine for All Homes, 1902). She even edited a collection of old songs, *Vore Bedsteforældres Sange* (Our Grandparents' Songs, 1897).

Inspired by her Mediterranean cruise, she wrote *Kærlighedens Veje* (The Paths of Love) in 1895. This novel consists of two stories exploring the various mazes in a love relationship. In the first story, a sailor, Knud, happily married in his homeland, yet restless and inquisitive, is seduced by a beautiful, sensual young mother, who is a passenger on his ship on one of his voyages. Finding to his surprise that he has sufficient love and affection for two women, Knud continues the relationship until the woman finds herself a new lover, releasing Knud back to the arms of his wife. Here he finds forgiveness and understanding. Juxtaposing divergent female and male morals, the happy ending advocates tolerance and personal space, yet does not condone hurting one's partner.

The second story explores the theme of self-fulfillment, introducing the shadow of self-doubt and repercussions of forbidden love. A single lady, liberal and educated, questions the borderline between friendship and love and finds that she has transgressed it with a married friend whose wife has become insane. The story centers, once again, on the conflict between eroticism and spiritual love, with the woman strongly attracted to the man, yet disinclined to follow her impulses out of fear of rejection. After involvement with several other suitors, she chooses a voyage to create a distance, and through her correspondence with the loved one discovers that finally their paths have met in a fulfilling, supportive, and mutually respectful love. The final line expresses a previously unknown optimism in Juel-Hansen, heralding a new era in her life and writing, "–hun rejser vist den store Lykke i Møde!" (–she seems to be traveling toward great happiness!).

Juel-Hansen promoted education to ensure that women would be well prepared to exercise their right to vote, and she lectured about a new kind of liaison between men and women, one based on equality and individual interests. She believed that the institution of marriage was salvageable only if girls and women were taught to develop lives of their own instead of considering marriage their only source of fulfillment.

Juel-Hansen's next work, *Helsen & Co.* (1900), encompassed a myriad of her own recollected dreams and experiences. In this continuation of *Terese Kærulf,* the reader follows the protagonist as she enters into a new phase of her life. The search for identity and meaning has led Terese to London, where her talents and skills make her a major success. Furthermore, she meets Erik Helsen, a cabinetmaker, and gradually realizes that she is in love with him and even contemplates confronting him with her affection. Fortunately, serendipity brings them together, and when she discovers that her feelings are reciprocated, a spontaneous engagement takes place. She brings furniture and funds into the marriage and proposes a working relationship parallel to their emotional one, in which they will combine her design with his skill. But the initial simplicity and clarity of their marriage, built on a union of physical and spiritual attraction, becomes muddled with pregnancy and childbirth. From being an equal partner and designer, Terese finds herself relegated to the role of mother, and her creative impulses are stifled. The female condition is shown as a stumbling block for women trying to reach their full potential in the workplace. The novel addresses the difficulty of reconciling the two components in a woman's life–family and personal ambitions. In the beginning, Erik Helsen is portrayed as a sympathetic and empathetic husband–hardworking, honest, and fatherly. However, with one more child and pecuniary problems, he strays into the arms of a shop assistant. This betrayal leads Terese to a final resignation of ideals when she chooses to forgive him. Terese is the one protagonist who most closely reaches the author's ultimate ideal. Juggling her self-respect and self-fulfillment, she attains a deep contentment as well as work-related success, even though she is merely the "Co." (Company).

Helsen & Co. became Juel-Hansen's biggest success. Finally, she was fully recognized as a writer and allotted a three-year state stipend that partially alleviated her chronic financial worries. In the meantime, she decided to quit her job as a translator of serialized stories for the newspaper and tried her hand as an agent selling and renewing lottery tickets. When her brother Holger Drachmann turned sixty in 1906, she published the memoir *Holger Drachmann som Dreng. Barndomserindringer* (Holger Drachmann as a Boy: Childhood Memories). Her dream, however, of staying with him in his house at Skagen was never realized. He died in 1908, and not till 1911 did Juel-Hansen spend several months at Skagen, where she was quickly accepted among the artists-in-residence and forged warm friendships. In 1911, Michael Ancher painted her portrait, and Juel-Hansen found herself drawn to the light of Skagen summers on several later occasions.

Juel-Hansen in 1896 (Courtesy of the Danish Royal Library, Copenhagen)

Juel-Hansen's final novel, *Henriks Mor* (Henrik's Mother), was begun in 1903 but not published until 1917. Her busy life and various engagements kept her fully occupied, but when she finally finished the novel, it became the only one of her literary works to receive nothing but effusive reviews. It is a sad story, echoing resignation, crushed illusions, and buried dreams. The mother of Henrik (a twenty-three-year-old woman on the path to success) has been biding her time until her son could marry and start his own life. She is secretly in love with a man residing in Borneo, with whom she has corresponded for six years. Her first husband had been cold and unemotional, and when he died, she was forced to build her own existence as a writer. Henrik's fiancée is a vivacious, intelligent, and pretty girl, and the wedding date is already set when calamity strikes. Henrik contracts tuberculosis and is sent to a sanatorium. His mother's life is put on hold once again. Although Henrik is not seriously ill, he turns into a hypochondriac, breaking off his engagement and relying solely on his mother as a lifelong companion. His former fiancée marries a sailor and finds happiness, whereas Henrik's mother resigns herself to living with an inconsiderate egotist and sacrificing her own life for him. The love of her life reconciles himself to her choice and marries, and the final line shows a calm acceptance of fate, "Fru Holt maa efterhaanden være kommen over Vanskelighederne, thi hendes Venner siger om hende, at hendes Sind vedbliver at være ungt–og nu er hun meget gammel" (By now, Mrs. Holt must have mastered her difficulties, for her friends say that her mind is still young–and now she is very old). This is, indeed, also a fitting parting image of the aging author.

Erna Juel-Hansen led a remarkable life as a woman and a writer. Finding little time and money for her writing, she still persevered, winning respect even from opponents who found her too liberal and emancipated. She was born into turbulent times, and she further attempted to test the limits, challenging the sedentary and weak lifestyle assigned to women and advocating a healthy and sensible alternative. Her physical prowess was matched and emphasized by her writing, in which she promoted freedom of speech and thought for women as well as for men. When she died 30 November 1922, her legacy proved primarily to be her unremitting pioneer spirit rather than her literary production. The themes from her novels reverberate in the writings of such other authors as Amalie Skram and Victoria Benedictsson. Seen from a contemporary perspective, however, her novels have been deemed to resemble popular literature too closely, a judgment that has made them somewhat less than artistically significant. Yet, Juel-Hansen's life, style, and accomplishments have inspired many books, articles, and theses. She portrayed women caught in a transition between the old and the new. In her depiction, she created a path toward a fulfilled and dignified existence for her protagonists, and her philosophy and accomplishments live on in modern women.

References:

Pil Dahlerup, "Den Kvindelige Naturalist," *Vinduet 2,* 29 (Oslo: Gyldendal, 1975);

Dahlerup, *Det Moderne Gennembruds Kvinder* (Copenhagen: Gyldendal, 1984), pp. 471–476, 533–536;

Dahlerup, *Gennembrudsnoveller* (Copenhagen: Gyldendal, 1984);

Adda Hilden, *Skal jeg sætte min datter i skole? Pigeopdragelse i 1800-tallets midte* (Copenhagen: Modtryk, 1987);

Lisbeth Møller-Jensen, "Erna Juel-Hansen, Helsen & Co., 1900/1980," *litteratur og samfund,* 31 (1980);

Jytte Nielsen, "Arbejde–kærlighed, konflikt eller forening? Analyse af Erna Juel-Hansens hovedværker om overgangskvinden og hendes situation," M.A. thesis, Odense University, 1984;

Nielsen, "Kvindekonflikter mellem arbejde og kærlighed omkring århundreskiftet. Tre nordiske forfattere og deres romaner," *Edda,* 86 (1986): 37–49;

Inger Rasmussen, "En teoretisk bestemmelse af begrebet kvindelitteratur, og i den forbindelse en analyse og litteraturhistorisk placering af Erna Juel-Hansens forfatterskab," M.A. thesis, University of Copenhagen, 1978;

Pia Sigmund, *Oldemor Erna* (Copenhagen: Borgen, 1991).

Papers:

The major collection of Erna Juel-Hansen's manuscripts is at the Danish Royal Library in Copenhagen.

Harald Kidde

(14 August 1878 - 23 November 1918)

Kim Andersen
Washington State University

BOOKS: *Sindbilleder* (Copenhagen: Nordisk, 1900);
Aage og Else. Døden (Copenhagen: Nordisk, 1902);
Aage og Else. Livet (Copenhagen: Nordisk, 1903);
Luftslotte (Copenhagen: Gyldendal, 1904);
De Blinde (Copenhagen: Gyldendal, 1906);
Loven (Copenhagen: Gyldendal, 1908);
Den Anden (Copenhagen: Gyldendal, 1909);
De Salige (Copenhagen: Gyldendal/Nordisk, 1910);
Helten (Copenhagen: Gyldendal, 1912);
Jærnet: Roman om Järnbäraland (Copenhagen: Aschehoug, 1918);
Vandringer (Copenhagen: Aschehoug, 1920);
Parabler, edited by Poul P. M. Pedersen (Copenhagen: Sten Hasselbach, 1948);
Parabler, edited by Cai M. Woel (Copenhagen: Nordisk, 1953).

Editions and Collections: *Aage og Else,* 2 volumes (Copenhagen: Gyldendal/Nordisk, 1924);
Jens Marinus Jensen, ed., *Harald Kidde. Artikler og Breve* (Copenhagen: Woels, 1928);
Jærnet: Roman om Järnbäraland, edited by Knud Bjarne Gjesing and Thomas Riis (Copenhagen: Det Danske Sprog- og Litteraturselskab, 1990).

Harald Kidde (courtesy of the Danish Royal Library, Copenhagen)

SELECTED PERIODICAL PUBLICATIONS–UNCOLLECTED: "Usædelig Litteratur," *Kristeligt Dagblad,* 15 May 1899;
"Det hemmelige rum," *Illustreret Tidende,* 10 December 1899, p. 172;
"Det forladte hus," *Illustreret Tidende,* 18 February 1900, pp. 335–336;
"Barnets Moder," *Illustreret Tidende,* 21 December 1902, pp. 167–168;
"Henrik Ibsen," *Verdens-Spejlet,* 3 June 1906, p. 645;
"Tusinde Aar," *Illustreret Tidende,* 26 September 1909;
"Foraaret og Ungdommen," *Rigets Krønnike,* 9 April 1911, pp. 5–6;
"Herman Bang," *Nationaltidende,* 31 January 1912;
"Georg Brandes," *Politiken,* 4 February 1912, pp. 39–41;
"I Vinterens Hjerte," *Almanaken Danmark for 1914,* 12 December 1913;
"Mine Forældre," *Bogvennen* (June 1915): 204–205;
"Hvorledes jeg blev Digter," *Nationaltidende,* 16 June 1915, pp. 12–16;
"Agnes Henningsen paa Finansloven," *Nationaltidende,* 10 March 1918, p. 3;
"Blomsten af dansk Nutidslitteratur," *Nationaltidende,* 15 March 1918, p. 3;
"Krigen og Litteraturen," *Litteraturen,* 1 August 1918, pp. 287–288.

In a 1906 interview with Christian Rimestad, Harald Kidde exclaimed, "Thi jeg elsker Livet overalt og over alt, Livet der for mig er hundrede gange mere værd end Kunsten" (Because I love life everywhere and more than anything else, life is to me a hundred times more valuable than art). In its brevity, this statement comprises three significant characteristics that surface in any portrait of Kidde. First, its pathos is a thematic pointer to the passionate landscapes of personal contemplation and interpersonal conflicts that dominate his novels. Secondly, despite its brevity, it clearly overemphasizes its point by doubly stating it, thus recalling Kidde's lengthy, wordy novels–encircling, probing, interpreting, and reassessing psychological dramas. Finally, it is paradoxical because more than any other Danish author, at least since Hans Christian Andersen, Kidde embodied the social role of the lonely, if not secluded, then somewhat mysterious, artist completely devoted to his art as if it were the essence of his existence around which life had to be accommodated. He was not tendentious in the sense that he sought complicated, individually introverted solutions to contemporary problems; consequently, he did not enjoy popular recognition from a wide readership nor the unreserved admiration of his peers, despite his friendship with many of them. His complex, demanding authorship and his post-Romantic, yet Romantic, poetic presence were at odds with a time period no longer catering to those ideals. The turn of the century, the pre–World War I years, revealed large-scale social problems in need of social solutions; in their private soul-searching, Kidde's works did not meet those requirements.

Still, Kidde's work has survived. Increasingly, his passionate digging in motifs and motivations, and his relentless pursuit of truth, honesty, and existential peace, paired with the tremendous level of research and preparation in his laborious and meticulous construction of each novel, have garnered much interest. His seven novels form a coherent body of work thematically related. His many allegorical short stories, collected in *Sindbilleder* (Images of Mind, 1900) and *Luftslotte* (Castles in the Air, 1904), and others posthumously published in three collections–*Vandringer* (Wanderings, 1920), *Parabler* (Parables, 1948), and *Parabler* (1953)–are evidence of his passionate psychological investigation of typically biblical themes mirroring both the central themes of his novels and the existential dilemmas of their protagonists. Kidde died in 1918 at the age of forty and the height of his creative powers. His untimely death caused a wave of attention to his authorship. His first novel, *Aage og Else* (Death and Life, 1902, 1903), was sympathetically reexamined and soon became much sought after while increasing in price. What had probably been his most considerable work, *Helten* (The Hero, 1912), had been published only because the author guaranteed the printing with state bonds. Four hundred copies were printed, and one hundred and ninety sold. After his death, sales skyrocketed, and in 1949 the fifth-edition sales had reached 21,250 copies, remarkable for a Danish novel in those days.

Kidde was born on 14 August 1878 outside of Vejle, a provincial town on the southeastern coast of the Jutland Peninsula. His family had for generations lived in the area connected to the Kidde Farm. As county inspector of roads, his father, Christian Henrik Kidde, was a prominent local citizen residing in Vejle in the county inspector's residence after having sold the family farm. In his early fifties Christian Kidde married the thirty-years-younger Inger Doris Corneliussen, whom he had known as a small child when he was a lodger in her troubled mother's house. As a five-year-old, Kidde's mother was sent to stay with family on the Danish island of Læsø. She grew up in loneliness on the remote island. She resorted to a world of imagination and literature, and later her recollection of these experiences had a profound influence upon her son. In his brief autobiographical sketch "Mine Forældre" (My Parents, 1915) Harald Kidde describes the importance of his mother:

> Hendes fortællinger om Livet der, dets Mørke, Barskhed og Vildskab, lod mig se end længere ud bag den Horizont, som min Faders Rejser havde gjort videre end Børns i Almindelighed. . . . Som en bleg, ung Pige, fantastisk og fordrømt og dog viljestærk og behersket, beriget og avet af Livets Hårdhed, kom hun tilbage til sit første Barndomshjem og sin første Barndomsven. Og hun blev hans Hustru og min Moder. Og Linien og Flugten i min Digtning.

> (Her stories about life there, its darkness, roughness and wildness allowed me to see even further than the horizon that my father's travels had broadened beyond what was common for children. . . . As a pale girl, imaginative, full of dreams, yet willful and controlled, enriched and fashioned by the toughness of life, she came back to her first childhood home and to her first childhood friend. And she became his wife and my mother. And the thread and flight of my poetry.)

In "Hvorledes jeg blev Digter" (How I Became a Poet, 1915), another short biographical sketch, the author describes the influence of his father. As a county inspector of roads, his father traveled constantly and widely by horse-drawn carriage and often took Harald with him. "Jeg har tilbragt Dage, Måneder, År i Vogn, jeg har inden mit fjortende År rullet hundreder af Mile. . . . Jeg har set Snese af Hjems Dagligliv og Vaner, før jeg var ude af min Barndom. Midt i Skoletiden hentede min Fader mig. . . . Og lidt efter sad jeg i Vognen og rullede ud mod den ny Horizont. 'Det er bedre end Skolen!' nikkede Fader. Og det var det" (I have spent days, months, years in a carriage, I have before my fourteenth year traveled hundreds of miles. . . . I have seen the daily life and habits of scores of homes, before I left childhood. Father picked me up while I was in school. . . . And a little later I sat in the carriage and rolled out toward new horizons. "This is better than school!" father nodded. And it was). But the boy always returned to the safety of that which was familiar. As these depictions indicate, Kidde's childhood was nurtured by caring parents. His mother introduced him to a world of imagination and literature while his father ingrained in him a sense of place and history, connecting him to the Jutlandic landscape that appears so prominently in his prose. Kidde also emphasizes his kin's connection to ancient Danish history in the Jelling Township and the burial hills of King Gorm and Queen Tyra, the original monarchs, according to tradition. This connection to the past surfaces as a significant theme throughout his novels.

His childhood would have been happy were it not for the deaths of two older brothers, who died in childhood, and his sister, who died at seventeen. Only Harald and his ten-years-younger brother Aage (who later became a politician) reached adulthood, and they both died young, Aage a month after Harald. The deaths during his childhood had a transforming effect on Kidde. His older sister, especially, meant much to him. He tells how she told him stories from her favorite books, the Bible, and Greek mythology. His mother taught her children traditional Danish songs about ancient kings and read the works of Charles Dickens and Ivan Sergeevich Turgenev aloud when his father was traveling. Kidde concludes, "–da blev jeg allestedsnærværende, da blev jeg fostret til Poet" (then I became omnipresent, then I was brought up to become a poet). "Allestedsnærværende" (omnipresent) is characteristic of Kidde's pathos, infusing a mode of divine reference; his idea must be simply that at home he became educated in a selection of the classics. Biographer Jens Marinus Jensen recounts Kidde's infatuation with a fifteen-year-old schoolmate, Jenny. She considered him a friend but did not return his deeper feelings. She was Kidde's great love of his youth and contributed to his determination to become a poet.

Twenty-year-old Kidde attracted attention to himself when he graduated from *gymnasium* (secondary school). In his final exam in Danish, his responses to the topics caused a controversy by being so decidedly poetic that extraordinary negotiations by the professors were needed to settle on a top grade. His essays dealt with the transition from rural to urban life and how modernity and industrialization corrupted–if not destroyed–the free, natural self of the farmer who sought a future in the city. He saw the city lights as "Kerter over evige Fester" (candles at eternal feasts) and not what they truly represented–"Lys, der brænde ved Sygesenge" (lights burning by sickbeds).

HARALD KIDDE

HELTEN

ROMAN

Ak, søger de ydmyge Steder —
BRORSON

KØBENHAVN OG KRISTIANIA
GYLDENDALSKE BOGHANDEL
NORDISK FORLAG 1912

Title page for Kidde's novel about a prostitute's son who becomes a schoolteacher on a remote Danish island (Alderman Library, University of Virginia)

After his father's death in 1894, Kidde and his family moved to another location in Vejle. In 1898 Kidde moved with his mother and brother to Copenhagen, where he began studying theology at the university. However, his deeply religious nature could not cope with the official institutional Christianity emanating from the university and the *Folkekirken* (Danish State Lutheran Church), and a year later he discontinued his studies. He later left the church entirely. In 1899 he showed some of his works to a distinguished professor of literary history, Valdemar Vedel, who encouraged him to pursue his prose rather than poetry. Vedel helped Kidde publish his first short stories in the journal *Illustreret Tidende* (The Illustrated Times) and recommended him to the leading Danish publisher, Nordisk Forlag, which published his first book, *Sindbilleder.*

In 1901 another incident reinforced Kidde's preoccupation with death; his friend Ivar Iversen died from tuberculosis back in Jutland, having spent four penniless years as a student in Copenhagen. Kidde wrote in a letter to a friend: "Han er død, men vi lever stedse. Hvor vanskeligt det er for mig at forstå han er død–han døde jo langt borte . . . –det er noget ganske nyt, der her møder mig, der dog ellers kender Døden ret vel. Alle de andre, som er døde fra mig, døde i mit Hjem . . ." (He is dead but we are still alive. How difficult it is for me to understand that he is dead–he died far away . . . –that is something quite new to me, who otherwise know death quite well. All the others who died from me died in my home . . .). Evidently, Kidde interprets death in emphatic personal terms in relation to painful and recent memories.

In 1907 Kidde married Astrid Ehrencrone-Muller, who was also attempting to establish herself as a writer. (After Kidde's death, she achieved some success in the mid 1920s with a series of humorous novels about life in little Swedish towns.) The couple rented rooms in the affluent northern Copenhagen suburb of Gentofte, and the years to come were productive for Kidde. He and his wife lived modestly as artists with relatively few possessions. Not until 1917 did they purchase a house in Hareskov, a forested part of Zealand, north of Copenhagen. Kidde's works did not sell well, but the respect for him as a writer earned him 500 kroner in 1913 annually in the form of a lifelong stipend awarded by the Danish government.

In 1902, 1904, and 1911 he traveled to Sweden, Germany, and Switzerland in preparation for his novels, and in 1913 he received *Det Ancherske Legat* (a grant) that required its recipient to live abroad. The outbreak of war necessitated Kidde's travel to Sweden, where he and his wife stayed for four years. In this period he prepared the novel that became his last, *Jærnet: Roman om Järnbäraland* (The Iron: A Novel about Järnbäraland, 1918). In a style often reminiscent of James Joyce's *Ulysses* (1922) and including a massive knowledge of the history of the iron-producing Swedish Värmland region, Kidde explores cultural progress through the eyes of the narrator, fifteen-year-old Steffan.

Although his novels had limited appeal, Kidde reached many readers through his many short parables, which he published in various journals and newspapers, such as *Illustreret Tidende, Vagten, Tilskueren, Verdens-Spejlet, Gads Magasin, Vor Tid, Riget,* and *Nationaltidende.* These short allegorical tales constitute an important window into Kidde's artistic mind, and in them the theme of death often recurs in legendary, biblical, or folkloric perspectives. *Sindbilleder* includes the brief one-page tale "Danebod," in which Gorm, the old king, returns home to find his hall decked in blue, the color of sorrow, by Tyra, his wife and queen. His fine white falcon, Dana-Ast, has been attacked and killed by a pack of ravens that flew over the castle walls. His people lament, and Gorm is devastated and cries, "Dana-Ast, Dana-Ast død! o, Tyre! lad os dø . . . lad os alle dø!" (Dana-Ast, Dana-Ast dead! Oh, Tyre! let us die . . . let us all die!). Tyra responds, "Nej, Gorm, nej! nu må vi just leve! . . . end lever Eders grå Falk . . . for hans Skyld må vi leve,–og om ham må vi bygge Kongsgårdens Mure højere op–Sten for Sten . . .–" (No, Gorm, no! precisely now we must live! Your grey falcon is still alive . . . for his sake we must live,–and around him we must build the walls of the Royal Court higher–stone by stone . . .). The text clearly alludes to the twenty-two-year-old Kidde's childhood traumas of family deaths. While Tyra suggests a solution, in the text Gorm does not have a response.

A more existential, philosophical, if not religious, tone is struck in "Lykke-Feen" (The Fairy of Good Fortune) in *Luftslotte.* (This collection was the only one of Kidde's works translated into a foreign language, namely German.) In "Lykke-Feen" (three pages long), two young men meet each other on a peaceful summer evening on the road leading to the good fairy's castle. One good-looking, well-dressed, splendid youth sports a potent stallion; the other, a dark, dusty cape hiding the light eyes and firm lips of his long, pale face. The first chastises the latter for being on foot: the wanderer will never reach there before he dies; the road is long. Precisely the point, the wanderer answers. The rider leaps ahead, calling the other a fool; the latter shakes his pale face. On a fall evening, the two meet again, the horseman now returning. The wanderer greets the rider, whose horse staggers along yard by yard. The rider's head is lowered; his arms crossed; the feathers in his hat broken. "Did you see the fairy?" the wanderer asks. The horseman clenches the saddle knob and says, "Gå aldrig derud, Broder, det er Løgn!" (Don't ever go there, brother, it is a lie!). The horseman is returning to stop anyone from going there, to let everyone know the story is a lie. The cape-clad youth smiles and tells the rider not to do that, because people will not believe him. Not even the wanderer will listen, because he is deliberately walking on foot to make the journey so long that he will die on the doorstep, never finding out whether the good fairy's castle is empty or not. He smiles and walks on. The rider stays behind, lost, and stares after the wanderer. Kidde addresses the limitations of human knowledge and the questionable desirability of probing those limits. The hero maintains a certain cynical outlook, as if not to know is best, as one might be disappointed. (Interestingly, he either does not believe the rider or else he chooses to ignore the man's experience and proceed against all rational instincts. Had the wanderer not met the rider, the existential path of "walking" would have made sense. Since the wanderer has met the rider, it does not.) Kidde's failed theological studies, his rejection of the church, and the deaths of his siblings are all experiences frequently mirrored in his authorship.

The loss of loved ones is perhaps most poignantly addressed in "Skriget fra Rama" from *Parabler.* On a wonderful spring day, Jesus is speaking to the people. Where they have gathered is not clear; most of the text (four pages) suggests biblical landscapes, but Jesus is leaning against a mountain boulder, supporting his hands in its moss. Kidde describes the people spread out around him, listening mesmerized; the sun-filled plain; and the city walls in the distance. Young mothers charge in around him, lifting their babies to the master to be blessed. Simon guards Jesus from them. Jesus stops him, letting the children come to him; he takes two in his arms. Suddenly, the peace is shattered by an angry woman's screaming voice damning him, calling him a child murderer. She is from Bethlehem; her children were murdered by King Herod so that he could go free: ". . . du, en Gud, lod din Fader ihjelslaa vore uskyldige Børn, for at du kunde frelses, og du kunne leve! Ud af Landet rømmede din Fader og Moder med dig; men lod os blive tilbage som Mordernes Rov!" (. . . you, a God, let your father kill our innocent children, so that you could be saved, and you could live! Your father and mother left the country with you but let us stay back as the murderers' prey!) She is then silent, breathless, shaking, yellow froth around her mouth. Everybody stares at Jesus. He sinks down, bows his head, his lips shaking. Kidde's literary work casts a different interpretation upon a familiar scene. The parable may be understood as an existentialist rejection of Christianity–the inability to accept the merciless God of the Old Testament presiding over the New Testament. Biographically, the senseless loss of children overrides the legendary meaning.

Kidde's first novel, *Aage og Else,* drew a great deal of attention. The main theme is the conflict between expressing oneself in the present while being bound to the past, as is the story of the Danish folk ballad it is named after. In Kidde's version, the boy Tue experiences the loss of a brother, of a playmate, and eventually of his parents. Kidde profoundly investigates the state of mind of someone who doggedly refuses to accept the inevitable loss of meaning and purpose in life that death represents. He equips the boy with an intellectual and emotional sensitivity much beyond his years and lets his reader experience up close the boy's attempts to make sense of life when faced with meaningless death. Staring into the abyss, the little boy doggedly but unsuccessfully pursues firm grounds on which to establish a healthy living, and the minute emotional drenching tests the reader's stamina.

"Mo'r, hvorfor skulle Alf og Anton dø?"
"Vi skal alle dø, Tue."
"Jamen, Mo'r, jeg døde jo ikke."
"Nej, ikke den Gang."
"Men hvorfor skal jeg leve, når Alf og Anton døde?"
"Fordi vi ikke kan undvære dig."
"Kan I da undvære Alf?"
"Å nej, Tue, men var også du død, hvad skulle så Fa'r og Regitze og jeg have gjort?"
"Mo'r, du kan ikke dø."
"Jo, Tue vi skal alle dø."
"Nej, Mo'r, ikke du! ikke du!" . . .
"Nej, nej, mit barn, nej."
Så var der dog noget fast.–"

("Mama, why did Alf and Anton die?"
"We are all going to die, Tue."
"But, Mom, I didn't die."
"No, not then."
"But why should I live when Alf and Anton are dead?"
"Because we cannot do without you."
"Can you do without Alf?"
"Oh, no, Tue, but if also you were dead what should Dad, Regitze and I have done?"
"Mom, you cannot die."
"Yes, Tue, we shall all die."
"No, Mom, not you, not you!" . . .
"No, no, my child, no."
Then at least something was firm.–")

Kidde's intention seems to be to transform a deep theological debate into a fictional drama between a mother and her son. Tue's existential desperation causes a penetrating insecurity. Right after the above dialogue, his thoughts continue, "Var det virkelig sommer? Tue begreb det ikke–tungere var Verden, tungere end nogensinde før, mørkere, uretfærdigere, mer fuld af Skræmsel end før–og hin svage Ild i hans Blod, hin Gnist fra Livslykkens flammende Bål, slukket var den, blæst i Aske–" (Was it really summer? Tue didn't understand–the world was heavier, heavier than ever before, darker, more unjust, more full of fear than before–and the weak fire in his blood, the spark from the flaming fire of happiness in life had been extinguished, blown into ashes–). Even the season is questioned while internalized into Tue's erratic state of mind. With an investigative tour de force, Kidde maintains the momentum on the following 621 pages as Tue grows older and encounters the other sex, an experience that offers a way out.

But Tue cannot let go of his faithfulness to the dead and refuses the advances of the vivacious Lull, who tries to seduce him and keep him focused on her and their future together. His schoolmate Sigurd's immediate, unproblematic joy of life represents the male attempt of tearing Tue away from the past. In the long run, this way is unsuccessful as well. Both Lull and Sigurd come up

Title page for Kidde's final novel, an exploration of cultural progress in the Swedish Värmland region through the eyes of a fifteen-year-old narrator (from Jærnet: Roman om Järnbäraland, *edited by Knud Bjarne Gjesing and Thomas Riis, 1990; Danish Studies Library, University of Washington)*

short against Tue's psychologically formed guilt of being the one who survived. He interprets potential new happiness as a treachery against the original happiness with those who now are dead. In his influential *Digtere og Dæmoner* (Poets and Demons, 1959) the philosophical writer Villy Sørensen calls Kidde "erindringens digter" (the poet of memories) in the most comprehensive treatment of his novels to date. Sørensen concludes, "Alle de mennesker der dør under Tues opvækst er dem han følte stærkest for i sin barndom: hans gamle fortolkning går til grunde samtidig med at en ny er ved at fødes, og i den forpinte konflikt mellem gammelt og nyt længes han tilbage mod den gamle harmoni" (All the people who die as Tue grows up are the ones he had the strongest feelings for in his childhood: his old interpretation is destroyed at the same time as a new one is being born, and in the painful conflict between old and new he longs for the old harmony). Kidde appears to have chosen the names of his three main characters carefully. "Tue" means "mound," signifying his bond with those in graves; "Sigurd" is the classical name of saga hero victors; and "Lull" brings to mind the Danish word *luder,* prostitute, denoting the sexual temptation she represents to Tue, which his faithfulness to the dead demonizes. The book includes some of the best-written, most emotionally charged sequences of Danish literature.

The four novels that followed–*De Blinde* (The Blind, 1906), *Loven* (The Law, 1908), *Den Anden* (The Other, 1909), and *De Salige* (The Blessed, 1910)–did not add much in terms of subject material or artistic quality to Kidde's work, nor did they gain him a wider readership. The two central character types in these novels–the weak, introverted male, unable to embrace life, and the disturbing female–are in these novels respun with different names and social settings. The novel that followed the four attempts, *Helten,* brought new dimensions to Kidde's work.

Helten takes place on a remote island in the Danish seas, a setting that brings to mind his mother's upbringing. A young doctor and his wife have sought the island as a refuge from their broken dreams. However, they constitute only the framework of the novel as they encounter the main character, Clemens Bek, the schoolteacher who has lived on the island for fifty-five years. As the doctor is called to his patient, a conversation develops in which Bek tells his story. It starts in Schwartzwald with a young student of theology, Eberhard, who leaves his studies to return to his parents. Twelve years later, after the death of his parents, he goes to Copenhagen to find and bring back his sister from her life in a whorehouse. As he sees her, he realizes that she cannot be saved, and he decides his calling is to stay and try to ease the prostitutes' suffering with the Lord's word. Another prostitute gives birth to a son, and Eberhard decides to bring up the boy as his own in a strongly religious manner. His aim is no less than to present the boy as a witness to the truth: "Eberhard bad . . . for dette Barn, hvis Ansigt skinnede i dette Skøgernes Hus som en Engels og ledte Synderindernes vaklende Fødder mod Lammets blodige Trone" (Eberhard prayed . . . for this child whose face shone in the whores' house like an angel and guided the stumbling feet of the sinners toward the lamb's bloody throne) and later, "Verden, der ligger i Kødet, at han skal sprænge dens Tag og løfte sin sårede Skare til dig, til dine naglestungne Fødder!" (the world that lies in the flesh that he may blow up its roof and raise his wounded flock to you, to your nail-penetrated feet!). The religious vision takes the form of an attack on official Christendom and its alliance with the established injustices of society between rich and poor. Clemens, the prostitute's son, is not able to live up to Eberhard's rigorous expectations. After Eberhard's death and an unrealized love affair, the dynamics of which are reminiscent of previous protagonists' inability to embrace life, Clemens runs away to the schoolteacher position on the remote island expecting to devote himself ascetically to his religious ideal, undisturbed by the "flesh."

In *Helten* the religious ideal thus replaces the past as the factor hindering the protagonist's ability to give himself to life. Unlike previous novels, *Helten* now unexpectedly takes a different turn. The island is populated by the same lust, hypocrisy, selfishness, injustice, and eccentric individuals as the greater culture he tried to escape. Clemens gets drawn into their universe, and through the utmost humiliation he comes to terms with himself as a human being–flawed, "sinful," yet capable of conducting his life selflessly in a manner worthy of his religious idol. In the journal *Bogvennen* (June 1915), Kidde stated, "Jeg vil i denne Bog vise, hvad, efter mit Skøn, et kristent Menneske er" (In this book I want to show what a Christian is, in my opinion). The author's own words, however, do little justice to the gallery of individuals, psychological insights, historical learning, theological scholarship, depictions of nature, and linguistic artistry with which Kidde paints this magnificent novel. *Helten* is Kidde's greatest artistic achievement. His prior novels had scared Kidde's audience away. After his death *Helten* brought them back.

Harald Kidde had just completed his most ambitious epic, *Jærnet,* the first of a planned grand tetralogy that would explore modern cultural development and human consciousness when he was suddenly taken ill during the flu epidemic. He died a week later, on 23 November 1918. Although Kidde's life was cut short, he managed to carve himself a position of the utmost respect in Danish literature through a literary production honest to himself as well as relentless and uncompromising in its search for truth.

Interview:

Christian Rimestad, "Hos Harald Kidde," in his *Digtere i Forhør* (Copenhagen: Nordisk, 1906).

Bibliography:

Cai M. Woel, *Arbejder af Harald Kidde. Bibliografisk fortegnelse* (Copenhagen: Woels Boghandel og Antikvariat, 1925).

Biographies:

Jens Marinus Jensen, *Harald Kidde. Bidrag til en biografi* (Århus: Forlaget Aros, 1948);

Astrid Ehrencron-Kidde, *Hvem kalder–fra mine erindringers lønkammer* (Copenhagen: Gyldendal, 1960).

References:

Jørgen Bonde Jensen, *Postscript to Helten* (Copenhagen: Gyldendal, 1972), pp. 429–439;

Jørgen Egebak, "Logikken i Harald Kiddes Jærnet," *Danske Studier,* 87, no. 3 (1992): 26–58;

Egebak, "Studier i Harald Kiddes Helten," *Danske Studier,* 61, no. 1 (1966): 75–95;

Knud Bjarne Gjesing, "De nedrige steder. Harald Kidde *Helten,*" in *Læsninger i dansk litteratur 1900–1940,* volume 3, edited by Inger-Lise Hjordt-Vetlesen and Finn Frederik Krarup (Odense: Odense Universitetsforlag, 1997), pp. 146–163;

Jørgen Helger, "Harald Kidde," in *Danske digtere i det 20. århundrede,* volume 1, edited by Ernst Frandsen and Niels Kaas Johansen (Copenhagen: Gad, 1951), pp. 167–178;

Alfons Höger, *Form und Gehalt der Romane und kleineren Erzählungen Harald Kiddes* (Munich: Verlag Uni-Druck, 1969);

Niels Jeppesen, *Harald Kidde og hans Digtning* (Copenhagen: Levin & Munksgaard, 1934);

Charles Kent, "Harald Kidde," *Edda,* 11 (1919): 281–308;

Christian Koch, "Harald Kidde," in *Danske digtere i det 20. århundrede,* third edition, volume 1, edited by Torben Brostrøm and Mette Winge (Copenhagen: Gad, 1980), pp. 259–274;

Koch, "Meningen med Helten. En studie i symbolik," *Danske Studier,* 71, no. 11 (1976): 49–75;

Niels Kofoed, *Den nostalgiske dimension. En værkgennemgang af Harald Kiddes Helten* (Copenhagen: Akademisk Forlag, 1980);

Johannes Møllehave, "Harald Kidde. Religiøs tydning og protest," in *Danske digtere i det 20. århundrede,* revised edition, volume 1, edited by Frederik Nielsen and Ole Restrup (Copenhagen: Gad, 1965), pp. 202–217;

Klaus Rifbjerg, "Pælen i Kødet," in his *Digtere til tiden* (Copenhagen: Spektrum, 1999), pp. 15–21;

Villy Sørensen, "Erindringens digter: Harald Kidde," in his *Digtere og Dæmoner* (Copenhagen: Gyldendal, 1959), pp. 46–96;

Otto Asmus Thomsen, "Fra Vejle til Varmland. Harald Kiddes opbrud fra fødebyen," *Vejle Amts Aarbog* (1969): 63–97;

Niels Birger Wamberg, *Digterne og Gyldendal* (Copenhagen: Gyldendal, 1970), pp. 238–243;

Cai M. Woel, *Dansk Litteraturhistorie 1900–1950,* volume 1 (Oslo: Forlaget Arnkrone, 1956), pp. 177–187.

Papers:

Harald Kidde's papers are at the Danish Royal Library in Copenhagen.

Søren Kierkegaard

(5 May 1813 – 11 November 1855)

Finn Hauberg Mortensen
University of Southern Denmark

(Translated by William Banks)

BOOKS: *Af en endnu Levendes Papirer* (Copenhagen: C. A. Reitzel, 1838); translated by Julia Watkin as "From the Papers of One Still Living," in *Kierkegaard's Writings,* edited by Howard V. Hong and Edna H. Hong, volume 1: *Early Polemical Writings* (Princeton: Princeton University Press, 1990);

Om Begrebet Ironi med stadigt Hensyn til Socrates (Copenhagen: P. G. Philipsen, 1841); translated by Lee M. Capel as *The Concept of Irony, with Constant Reference to Socrates* (New York: Harper & Row, 1965; London: Collins, 1966);

Enten-Eller. Et Livs-Fragment, as Victor Eremita, 2 volumes (Copenhagen: C. A. Reitzel, 1843)– includes "Forførerens Dagbog," translated by Knud Fick as *Diary of a Seducer* (Ithaca, N.Y.: Dragon Press, 1932); entire work translated by David F. Swenson, Lillian Marvin Swenson, and Walter Lowrie as *Either/Or: A Fragment of Life,* 2 volumes (Princeton: Princeton University Press / London: H. Milford/Oxford University Press, 1944);

To opbyggelige Taler (Copenhagen: Privately printed, 1843); translated by David F. Swenson and Lillian Marvin Swenson in *Edifying Discourses,* volume 1 (Minneapolis: Augsburg, 1943);

Frygt og Bæven. Dialektisk Lyrik, as Johannes de Silentio (Copenhagen: C. A. Reitzel, 1843); translated by Robert Payne as *Fear and Trembling: A Dialectical Lyric* (London & New York: Oxford University Press, 1939);

Gjentagelsen. Et Forsøg i den experimenterende Psychologi, as Constantin Constantius (Copenhagen: C. A. Reitzel, 1843); edited and translated by Lowrie as *Repetition: An Essay in Experimental Psychology* (Princeton: Princeton University Press, 1941; London: Oxford University Press, 1942);

Tre opbyggelige Taler (Copenhagen: P. G. Philipsen, 1843); translated by David F. Swenson and Lillian Marvin Swenson in *Edifying Discourses,* volume 1;

Søren Kierkegaard (drawing by Niels Christian Kierkegaard, 1838; courtesy of the Danish Royal Library, Copenhagen)

Fire opbyggelige Taler (Copenhagen: P. G. Philipsen, 1843); translated by David F. Swenson and Lillian Marvin Swenson in *Edifying Discourses,* volume 2 (Minneapolis: Augsburg, 1944);

To opbyggelige Taler (Copenhagen: P. G. Philipsen, 1844); translated by David F. Swenson and Lillian Marvin Swenson in *Edifying Discourses,* volume 3 (Minneapolis: Augsburg, 1945);

Tre opbyggelige Taler (Copenhagen: P. G. Philipsen, 1844); translated by David F. Swenson and Lillian Marvin Swenson in *Edifying Discourses,* volume 3;

Philosophiske Smuler eller En Smule Philosophi, as Johannes Climacus (Copenhagen: C. A. Reitzel, 1844); edited and translated by David F. Swenson as *Philosophical Fragments; or, A Fragment of Philosophy* (Princeton: Princeton University Press/American Scandinavian Foundation, 1936);

Begrebet Angest. En simpel psychologisk-paapegende Overveielse i Retning af det dogmatiske Problem om Arvesynden, as Vigilius Haufniensis (Copenhagen: C. A. Reitzel, 1844); edited and translated by Lowrie as *Kierkegaard's The Concept of Dread* (Princeton: Princeton University Press, 1944; Oxford: Oxford University Press, 1944);

Forord. Morskabslæsning for enkelte Stænder efter Tid og Leilighed, as Nicolaus Notabene (Copenhagen: C. A. Reitzel, 1844); translated by William McDonald as *Prefaces: Light Reading for Certain Classes as the Occasion May Require, by Nicolaus Notabene* (Tallahassee: Florida State University Press, 1989);

Fire opbyggelige Taler (Copenhagen: P. G. Philipsen, 1844); translated by David F. Swenson and Lillian Marvin Swenson in *Edifying Discourses,* volume 4 (Minneapolis: Augsburg, 1946);

Tre Taler ved tænkte Leiligheder (Copenhagen: C. A. Reitzel, 1845); translated by David F. Swenson and Lillian Marvin Swenson as *Thoughts on Crucial Situations in Human Life: Three Discourses on Imagined Occasions* (Minneapolis: Augsburg, 1941);

Stadier paa Livets Vei. Studier af Forskjellige, sammenbragte, befordrede til Trykken og udgivne af Hilarius Bogbinder, as Hilarius Bogbinder (Copenhagen: C. A. Reitzel, 1845); translated by Lowrie as *Stages on Life's Way* (Princeton: Princeton University Press / London: H. Milford/Oxford University Press, 1940);

Afsluttende uvidenskabelig Efterskrift til de philosophiske Smuler. Mimisk-pathetisk-dialektisk Sammenskrift, Existentielt Indlæg, as Climacus (Copenhagen: C. A. Reitzel, 1846); translated by David F. Swenson and Lowrie as *Kierkegaard's Concluding Unscientific Postscript* (Princeton: Princeton University Press/American Scandinavian Foundation, 1941; London: Oxford University Press, 1941);

En literair Anmeldelse. To Tidsaldre, Novelle af Forfatteren til "En Hverdags-Historie" (Copenhagen: C. A. Reitzel, 1846); translated by Alexander Dru and Lowrie as "The Present Age," in *The Present Age and Two Minor Ethico-Religious Treatises* (London & New York: Oxford University Press, 1940);

Opbyggelige Taler i forskjellig Aand (Copenhagen: C. A. Reitzel, 1847)–comprises "Hjertes Renhed er at ville Eet," translated by Amelia Stewart Aldworth and William Stewart Ferrie as *Purify Your Hearts! A "Discourse for a Special Occasion," the First of Three "Edifying Discourses in a Different Vein," Published in 1847 at Copenhagen* (London: C. W. Daniel, 1937); "Hvad vi lærer af Lilierne paa Marken og af Himmelens Fugle. Tre Taler," translated by Aldworth and Ferrie as *Consider the Lilies, Being the Second Part of "Edifying Discourses in a Different Vein," Published in 1847 at Copenhagen* (London: C. W. Daniel, 1940); and "Lidelsernes Evangelium. Christlige Taler," translated by David F. Swenson and Lillian Marvin Swenson as "The Gospel of Suffering," in *The Gospel of Suffering and The Lilies of the Field* (Minneapolis: Augsburg, 1947);

Kjerlighedens Gjerninger. Nogle christelige Overveielser i Talers Form, 2 volumes (Copenhagen: C. A. Reitzel, 1847); translated by David F. Swenson and Lillian Marvin Swenson as *Works of Love* (London: G. Cumberledge/Oxford University Press, 1946);

Christelige Taler (Copenhagen: C. A. Reitzel, 1848); translated by Lowrie as "Christian Discourses," in *Christian Discourses; and The Lilies of the Field and the Birds of the Air; and Three Discourses at the Communion on Fridays* (London & New York: Oxford University Press, 1939);

Lilien paa Marken og Fuglen under Himlen. Tre gudelige Taler (Copenhagen: C. A. Reitzel, 1849); translated by Lowrie as "The Lilies of the Field and the Birds of the Air," in *Christian Discourses; and The Lilies of the Field and the Birds of the Air; and Three Discourses at the Communion on Fridays;*

Tvende ethisk-religieuse Smaa-Afhandlinger, as H.H. (Copenhagen: Gyldendal, 1849); translated by Dru and Lowrie as "Two Minor Ethico-Religious Treatises," in *The Present Age and Two Minor Ethico-Religious Treatises;*

Sygdommen til Døden. En christelig psychologisk Udvikling til Opbyggelse og Opvækkelse, as Anti-Climacus (Copenhagen: C. A. Reitzel, 1849); translated by Lowrie as *The Sickness unto Death* (Princeton: Princeton University Press, 1941; London: H. Milford/Oxford University Press, 1941);

"Ypperstepræsten," "Tolderen," "Synderinden." Tre Taler ved Altergangen om Fredagen (Copenhagen: C. A. Reitzel, 1849); translated by Lowrie as "Three Discourses at the Communion on Fridays," in *Christian Discourses; and The Lilies of the Field and the Birds of the Air; and Three Discourses at the Communion on Fridays;*

Indøvelse i Christendom, as Anti-Climacus (Copenhagen: C. A. Reitzel, 1850); translated by Lowrie as *Training in Christianity, and the Edifying Discourse Which "Accompanied" It* (London: Oxford University Press, 1941; Princeton: Princeton University Press, 1944);

En opbyggelig Tale (Copenhagen: C. A. Reitzel, 1850); translated by Howard V. Hong and Edna H. Hong as "An Upbuilding Discourse," in *Kierkegaard's Writings,* volume 17: *Without Authority* (Princeton: Princeton University Press, 1997);

To Taler ved Altergangen om Fredagen (Copenhagen: C. A. Reitzel, 1851); translated by Lowrie as "Two Discourses at the Communion on Fridays," in *For Self-Examination and Judge for Yourselves! and Three Discourses, 1851* (London: Oxford University Press, 1941);

Om min Forfatter-Virksomhed (Copenhagen: C. A. Reitzel, 1851); translated by Lowrie as "On My Work as an Author," in *The Point of View: Including The Point of View for My Work as an Author, Two Notes about "The Individual," and On My Work as an Author* (London & New York: Oxford University Press, 1939);

Til Selvprøvelse, Samtiden anbefalet (Copenhagen: C. A. Reitzel, 1851); translated by Howard V. Hong and Edna H. Hong as *For Self-Examination, Recommended for the Times* (Minneapolis: Augsburg, 1940);

Dette skal siges, saa være det da sagt (Copenhagen: C. A. Reitzel, 1855); translated by Lowrie as "This Has to Be Said–So Be It Now Said," in *Kierkegaard's Attack upon "Christendom," 1854–1855* (Princeton: Princeton University Press, 1944; Oxford: Oxford University Press, 1944);

Øieblikket, nos. 1–9 (Copenhagen: C. A. Reitzel, 1855); edited and translated by Howard V. Hong and Edna H. Hong as "The Moment," in *Kierkegaard's Writings,* volume 23: *The Moment and Late Writings* (Princeton: Princeton University Press, 1998);

Hvad Christus dømmer om officiel Christendom (Copenhagen: C. A. Reitzel, 1855); edited and translated by Howard V. Hong and Edna H. Hong as "What Christ Judges of Official Christianity," in *The Moment and Late Writings;*

Guds Uforanderlighed. En Tale (Copenhagen: C. A. Reitzel, 1855); translated by Lowrie as "The Unchangeableness of God," in *For Self-Examination and Judge for Yourselves! and Three Discourses, 1851;*

Synspunktet for min Forfatter-Virksomhed. En ligefrem Meddelelse, Rapport til Historien (Copenhagen: C. A. Reitzel, 1859); edited and translated by Lowrie as "The Point of View for My Work as an Author," in *The Point of View;*

Dømmer selv! Til Selvprøvelse, Samtiden anbefalet, second series (Copenhagen: C. A. Reitzel, 1876); translated by Lowrie as "Judge for Yourselves!" in *For Self-Examination and Judge for Yourselves! and Three Discourses, 1851.*

Editions and Collections: *S. Kierkegaards Bladartikler, med Bilag samlede efter Forfatterens Død,* edited by Rasmus Nielsen (Copenhagen: C. A. Reitzel, 1857);

Af S. Kierkegaards Efterladte Papirer, 8 volumes, edited by Hans Peter Barfod and Hermann Gottsched (Copenhagen: C. A. Reitzel, 1869–1881)–volume 8 includes *Øieblikket,* no. 10, edited and translated by Howard V. Hong and Edna H. Hong as "The Moment, 10," in *Kierkegaard's Writings,* edited by Howard V. Hong and Edna H. Hong, volume 23: *The Moment and Late Writings* (Princeton: Princeton University Press, 1998);

Samlede Værker, 14 volumes, edited by Anders Björn Drachmann, Johan Ludvig Heiberg, and Hans Ostenfeldt Lange (Copenhagen: Gyldendal, 1901–1906); revised, 15 volumes (Copenhagen: Gyldendal, 1920–1931); revised, 20 volumes, edited by Peter P. Rohde (Copenhagen: Gyldendal, 1962–1964);

Søren Kierkegaards Papirer, 11 volumes, edited by Peter Andreas Heiberg, Victor Kuhr, and E. Torsting (Copenhagen: Gyldendal, 1908–1948); revised and enlarged, 16 volumes in 25, edited by Niels Thulstrup (Copenhagen: Gyldendal, 1968–1978)–volume 7, part 2, includes "Bogen om Adler," translated by Walter Lowrie as *On Authority and Revelation: The Book on Adler; or, A Cycle of Ethico-Religious Essays* (Princeton: Princeton University Press, 1955);

Værker i Udvalg, 4 volumes, edited by Frederik J. Billeskov Jansen (Copenhagen: Gyldendal, 1950);

Søren Kierkegaards Dagbøger i Udvalg, edited by Rohde (Copenhagen: Gyldendal, 1953);

Philosophiske Smuler, edited by Thulstrup (Copenhagen: Munksgaard, 1955);

Søren Kierkegaards Pressepolemik, edited by Ulf Kjær-Hansen (Copenhagen: Berling, 1955);

Begrebet Angest, edited, with an introduction and notes, by Villy Sørensen (Copenhagen: Gyldendal, 1960);

Frygt og Bæven, edited, with an introduction and notes, by Thulstrup (Copenhagen: Gyldendal, 1961);

Øieblikket, nos. 1–10, introduction by Poul Georg Lindhardt (Copenhagen: H. Reitzel, 1961);

Søren Kierkegaards Dagbøger, 4 volumes, edited by Rohde (Copenhagen: Thaning & Appel, 1961–1964);

Om min Forfatter-Virksomhed; Synspunktet for min Forfatter-Virksomhed, edited, with an introduction and notes, by Gregor Malantschuk (Copenhagen: H. Reitzel, 1963);

Fem Kierkegaard-Tekster, edited by Johannes Sløk (Copenhagen: Gyldendal, 1964);

Søren Kierkegaard. Tekster i Udvalg, edited by Paul Müller (Copenhagen: Nyt Nordisk Forlag, 1982);

Frygt og Bæven; Sygdommen til Døden; Taler, edited by Lars Petersen and Merete Jørgensen (Copenhagen: Danske Sprog- og Litteraturselskab/Borgen, 1989);

Begrebet Angest, edited by Petersen and Jørgensen (Copenhagen: Danske Sprog- og Litteraturselskab/Borgen, 1991);

Dagbøger i Udvalg, 1834–1836, edited by Jørgen Dehs and Niels Jørgen Cappelørn (Copenhagen: Danske Sprog- og Litteraturselskab/Borgen, 1992);

Søren Kierkegaards Skrifter, 55 volumes to date, edited by Cappelørn and others (Copenhagen: Gad, 1997–) –includes *Af en endnu Levendes Papirer, Om Begrebet Ironi,* and *Enten-Eller* (1997); *Gjentagelsen, Frygt og Bæven, Philosophiske Smuler, Begrebet Angest, Forord, Opbyggelige Taler [1843], Opbyggelige Taler [1844],* and *Tre Taler ved tænkte Leiligheder* (1998); *Stadier paa Livets Vei* (1999); *Journalerne AA, BB, CC, DD* (2000); *Notesbøgerne 1–15; Journalerne EE, FF, GG, HH, JJ, KK* (2001); and *Afsluttende uvidenskabelig Efterskrift* (2002).

Editions in English: *Selections from the Writings of Kierkegaard,* edited and translated by Lee Milton Hollander (Austin: University of Texas, 1923);

A Kierkegaard Anthology, edited by Robert Bretall (New York: Modern Library, 1936);

The Journals of Søren Kierkegaard: A Selection, edited and translated by Alexander Dru (London & New York: Oxford University Press, 1938);

Purity of Heart Is to Will One Thing: Spiritual Preparation for the Office of Confession, translated by Douglas V. Steers (New York & London: Harper, 1938);

The Living Thoughts of Kierkegaard, edited by W. H. Auden (New York: D. McKay, 1952);

Fear and Trembling and The Sickness unto Death, edited and translated by Walter Lowrie (Princeton: Princeton University Press, 1954);

Gospel of Sufferings: Christian Discourses, Being the Third Part of Edifying Discourses in a Different Vein, Published in 1847 at Copenhagen, translated by Amelia Stewart Aldworth and William Stewart Ferrie (London: J. Clarke, 1955);

Meditations, edited and translated by Thomas Henry Croxall (London: J. Nisbet, 1955; Philadelphia: Westminster Press, 1955);

The Prayers of Kierkegaard, edited by Perry D. LeFevre (Chicago: University of Chicago Press, 1956);

Johannes Climacus; or, De Omnibus Dubitandum Est, and A Sermon, translated by Croxall (London: A. & C. Black, 1958; Stanford: Stanford University Press, 1958);

The Diary of Søren Kierkegaard, edited by Peter P. Rohde, translated by Gerda M. Andersen (London: P. Owen, 1960; New York: Philosophical Library, 1960);

The Point of View for My Work as an Author: A Report to History, and Related Writings, translated by Lowrie, edited by Benjamin Nelson (New York: Harper, 1962);

Works of Love: Some Christian Reflections in the Form of Discourses, translated by Howard V. Hong and Edna H. Hong (New York: Harper, 1962);

The Last Years: Journals, 1853–1855, selected, edited, and translated by Ronald Gregor Smith (New York: Harper & Row, 1965; London: Collins, 1965);

Diary of a Seducer, translated by Gerd Gillhoff (New York: Ungar, 1966);

Crisis in the Life of an Actress, and Other Essays on Drama, edited and translated by Stephen Crites (New York: Harper & Row, 1967; London: Collins, 1967);

Søren Kierkegaard's Journals and Papers, 7 volumes, translated by Howard V. Hong and Edna H. Hong, edited by Gregor Malantschuk (Bloomington: Indiana University Press, 1967–1978);

Armed Neutrality and An Open Letter, with Relevant Selections from His Journals and Papers, edited and translated by Howard V. Hong and Edna H. Hong (Bloomington: Indiana University Press, 1968);

Parables of Kierkegaard, edited, with an introduction, by Thomas C. Oden (Princeton: Princeton University Press, 1978);

Kierkegaard's Writings, 26 volumes, edited by Howard V. Hong and Edna H. Hong (Princeton: Princeton University Press, 1978–2000);

Either/Or, edited and abridged by Steven L. Ross, translated by George L. Stengren (New York: Perennial Library, 1986);

A Kierkegaard Reader: Texts & Narratives, edited by Roger Poole and Henrik Stangerup (London: Fourth Estate, 1989);

The Sickness unto Death: A Christian Psychological Exposition for Edification and Awakening, edited and translated by Alastair Hannay (London & New York: Penguin, 1989);

Either/Or: A Fragment of Life, edited, abridged, and translated by Hannay (London & New York: Penguin, 1992);

Papers and Journals: A Selection, edited and translated by Hannay (London & New York: Penguin, 1996);

The Essential Kierkegaard, edited by Howard V. Hong and Edna H. Hong (Princeton: Princeton University Press, 2000);

The Kierkegaard Reader, edited by Jane Chamberlain and Jonathan Rée (Oxford & Malden, Mass.: Blackwell, 2001);

A Literary Review: Two Ages, a Novel by the Author of A Story of Everyday Life, edited and translated by Hannay (London & New York: Penguin, 2001);

Fear and Trembling, edited and translated by Hannay (London: Penguin, 2003);

The Humor of Kierkegaard: An Anthology, edited by Oden (Princeton: Princeton University Press, 2004).

Søren Kierkegaard's extensive catalogue of published and unpublished works had, both in Denmark and abroad, a profound influence on the theology, philosophy, and literature of the nineteenth and twentieth centuries. His religious philosophy, as well as his conflict-ridden relationship to the Danish State Church, not only greatly affected the Danish clergy but also served as an inspiration for Protestant and Catholic theology, as well as some Buddhist thought. Kierkegaard's existential philosophy and his break with the systematic idealism of the German philosopher Georg Wilhelm Friedrich Hegel were crucial for both German and French existentialism, as well as for the Scandinavian writers of the Modern Breakthrough, whose main figures–the critic Georg Brandes and the playwrights Henrik Ibsen and August Strindberg–influenced as they were by Kierkegaard's acute psychological analysis, took as the basis for their work his understanding of the individual, despite their rejection of his Christianity. Through his unique ability to vary language according to the various viewpoints he adopted, Kierkegaard achieved significance both at home and abroad, setting a new standard for fiction and analytical prose.

Kierkegaard's father, Michael Pedersen Kierkegaard, married Ane Sørensdatter Lund on 26 April 1797, after the death of his first wife on 23 March 1796. Although it was permissible for a widower to remarry after a period of three months, it was indeed awkward for the head of a household to be marrying his servant girl, who, by the time of the wedding, was in her fourth month of pregnancy. As a boy, Michael had traveled from the impoverished, heath-country parish of Sædding, near Ringkøbing Fjord, to be trained as a hosier in Copenhagen, where he later became a merchant. During the economic boom he had quickly amassed so large a fortune that he was able to build a house for his parents and three sisters back in Sædding. At the same time he acquired several properties in Copenhagen, all of which survived the great fire of 1795. By the time he married Ane, his holdings permitted him to retire from business and live as a rentier. Ane had, like her husband, left Jutland after her confirmation to earn a living, in her case as a domestic servant. Despite their considerable class and cultural differences, their marriage was a success. Michael Kierkegaard became increasingly concerned with religious and philosophical reading and speculation, while Ane had only a rudimentary knowledge of reading and writing.

The couple had three daughters, followed by three sons, from 1797 to 1809. After a few years as a country squire on an estate near Store Hestehave, near Hillerød, north of Copenhagen, the former hosier returned to the capital, where he purchased a home at 2 Nytorv, prominently situated on the former City Hall Square. There, on 5 May 1813, Søren Aabye Kierkegaard, the youngest in the family, was born. The family name referred to the occupation of his paternal grandfather, who was a sharecropper on one of the farms near the parish church in Sædding; the middle name came from a deceased relative, and the first name was that of his maternal grandfather, Søren Jensen Lund of Brande.

Every bit the last-born child, Søren Kierkegaard was spoiled, the two eldest children having died in 1819 and 1822. At the age of eight he matriculated at the highly regarded Borgerdydsskolen (School of Civic Virtue), located in what is now the headquarters of the Gyldendal publishing house, on Klareboderne in central Copenhagen. With his coarse clothing, he was awkward amid the children of the well-heeled. Although slight in stature, he avenged himself with a sharp tongue, with which he mocked and provoked both at school and at home. His childhood at 2 Nytorv was strongly marked by the influence of his ever-present and much-admired father, who involved his son in his philosophical and religious ponderings, as well as seeing to the development of his imagination and intellect. The young Søren walked about indoors, conjuring up pictures of what he would have seen on a real stroll around town, a talent he later employed as he went about his apartment, jotting down thoughts and concepts on one or another of his several desks. His talent for classical languages, first demonstrated at the School of Civic Virtue, earned him, upon his graduation in 1830, a position as a tutor at the same institution. It was to be the only paid employment of his life.

As a student at the University of Copenhagen, Kierkegaard entered the King's Life Guards but was discharged after only a few days because of the unequal length of his legs. He then threw himself into a broad range of subjects–aesthetics, philosophy, and theology–without, however, committing himself to any strict course of study or specific theoretical training. The goal was self-understanding, but by the mid 1830s his stud-

Nytorv (New Square), Copenhagen, 1839. Kierkegaard was born in number 2 (today number 27), the second house from the right, in 1813 (painting by C. E. Balsgaard; Royal Danish Embassy, Washington, D.C.; from Bruce H. Kirmmse, Kierkegaard in Golden Age Denmark, *1990; Thomas Cooper Library, University of South Carolina).*

ies had led him instead to a bohemian existence, in which the bills from the tailor mounted and the enticing café life of Østergade consumed more energy than his academic work. His father at first complied, but when the expenses reached unacceptable levels, Michael Kierkegaard reined in his son's spending with a contract. Shortly before his death in 1838, he indicated that Søren, who had left home in 1837, had kept his end of the bargain.

As a writer Kierkegaard made his public debut in 1834 in Johan Ludvig Heiberg's *Kjøbenhavns flyvende Post* (Copenhagen's Flying Post). Under the pseudonym "A" he contributed an article on the equality of women and, as "B," a piece on freedom of the press, for which he received a response from Orla Lehmann, the leading liberal of the day. On 10 April of that year, in the same journal, Kierkegaard published his first article under his own name, in which he demanded that political reformers be held accountable for their views.

In addition to the two siblings who had died in childhood, Kierkegaard lost a brother in 1832, a sister in 1833, and, only a year later, another sister, as well as his mother. He spent the summer of 1835 on the northern coast of Zealand in the village of Gilleleje, which he recalled from earlier family holidays at Store Hestehave. He now applied himself to studying nature through a cultural perspective. J. M. Thiele's *Danske Folkesagn* (1818–1823), a collection of Danish legends, guided him from place to place, and his observations of a family of charcoal makers in the Great Forest led him to experiment with a writing style much like that of Steen Steensen Blicher. Kierkegaard was interested in folk culture in connection with the humanist studies he pursued alongside his more fundamental academic work. He was especially concerned with the question of whether there was a common background to the stories of Don Juan, Faust, and Ahasuerus (the Wandering Jew). Although in fact unrelated, these figures have, especially in the popular tradition, served to inspire many tales–stories of seduction, self-understanding, and homelessness. Each received that which he coveted and hence became cursed. The summer in Gilleleje did not lead to a breakthrough in Kierkegaard's studies, even though he considered not only theology and the humanities but also natural science. He did, however, come a little closer to an understanding of himself.

From the elevated coastal cliff over the village, Kierkegaard could view the broad horizon of the Kattegat (the arm of the North Sea between Jutland and Sweden), where the sea borders the heavens and the heavens the sea. In this experience of infinity and abundance, he felt God near him, and at the same time he felt a connection to his deceased family members. Of the large family, only the eldest brother, Peter Christian (born in 1805), remained. After a superb performance on the theological exam at the University of Copenhagen, Peter Christian had studied in Berlin and in 1829 had defended his dissertation, for which his ability in dialectical argumentation had been recognized. He became a pastor with a sympathy for the teachings of the theologian and poet N. F. S. Grundtvig and later was made a bishop and minister of culture. Also still alive was Kierkegaard's father, who came to feel that his family was under a curse. He saw himself as the cause, the punishment being that none of his children would live longer than the thirty-three years of Christ, and that he himself would outlive them all. He made his sons aware of this belief, which was perhaps rooted in the fact that, as a young shepherd boy in poor and barren Sædding, he had once cursed God for the miserable lot to which he had been born.

When, as a consequence of his background, Michael Kierkegaard had chosen to go to the capital, he was in fact taking part in a quite extensive movement from the country to the city. His religious and philosophical pondering was in essence rooted in the pietistic Christianity that he shared with the many other Jutlanders living in Copenhagen. The Moravian Brethren community (in Danish called *Herrnhuterne,* after the German village where Moravians fleeing religious persecution had settled in 1722), followers of the teachings of the German pastor Nikolaus Ludwig von Zinzendorf, met regularly on Stormgade and claimed six hundred members, and Michael Kierkegaard was responsible for its organizational and financial matters. This brotherhood, with its fervent cultivation of "the heart of Christ, his blood and wounds," had been established in 1727 and thrived in Denmark during the eighteenth and early nineteenth centuries as a religious sect outside the State Lutheran Church.

Poul Martin Møller, Søren Kierkegaard's philosophy professor and partner in discussion, died on 13 March 1838, and Kierkegaard's father, on the eighth or ninth of August of that year. Both deaths were deeply meaningful, requiring Kierkegaard to stand–spiritually speaking–on his own feet. Between the deaths of Møller and his father, he had written a literary review that appeared on 7 September, with the curious title *Af en endnu Levendes Papirer* (translated as "From the Papers of One Still Living," 1990). Here Kierkegaard demonstrated his ability to carry out a literary analysis of the modern novel–specifically, Hans Christian Andersen's *Kun en Spillemand* (1837; translated as *Only a Fiddler,* 1845)–according to the standards that literary critic and playwright Johan Ludvig Heiberg had formulated on the basis of Hegel's philosophy. But Kierkegaard carried out this analysis in continuation of his dialogue with Lehmann, by demanding of the novelist a consistent *livsanskuelse* (view of life) if the work is to be judged as ideologically and aesthetically coherent. Neither the word *livsanskuelse* nor the demand implicit within it were common at the time, but it clearly affiliated the student with the late Møller.

In the meantime, Kierkegaard had to acknowledge that he had survived his father, whom he had promised that he would complete his theological studies, which he did in 1840. That same year he took a pilgrimage to Sædding, where he was thanked for his father's generosity, which had included support of the local school. Thereafter, Kierkegaard felt himself free enough to propose, on 1 September 1840, to the vivacious Regine Olsen, eleven years his junior, who had caught his eye when she was fifteen. For the next thirteen months he was not only occupied with Regine, his "Hjertes Herskerinde" (mistress of his heart), but also with his practical training at the Pastoral Seminary, as well as the philosophical studies that concluded with his dissertation. A few days after defending his dissertation, he broke the engagement because he felt that he could not commit to marriage, and he fled to Berlin, away from consternation and scandal. On 3 November 1847 Olsen married Frederik Schlegel.

Kierkegaard's dissertation, published as *Om Begrebet Ironi med stadigt Hensyn til Socrates* (1841; translated as *The Concept of Irony, with Constant Reference to Socrates,* 1965), is, like *Af en endnu Levendes Papirer,* a study of a figure related to an idea. In the dissertation, which formally concluded his humanistic studies, Kierkegaard employs his strong language skills in a philological uncovering of the figure of Socrates behind the various representations of him in antiquity. Without committing himself to any particular view of life, Socrates was able to reveal the blindness of others by asking questions as if to learn something, even though he already knew the answers; the actual reason for the questions was to reveal the respondent's lack of knowledge. Socrates could therefore contribute to the unmasking of emptiness and deception without himself being responsible. He could in an indirect manner induce others to ask questions of themselves in such a way that they recollected the truth, heretofore hidden by deception inside themselves. Socrates therefore became the one who revealed–and thereby purified–the heathendom of antiquity, after which Christ could deliver the grace of God as the positive message. Similarly, irony in German idealist philosophy–from Immanuel Kant to Hegel–also became the object of Kierkegaard's critique. The ironic writer is isolated from the ideal as well as concrete reality, and his existence is therefore without meaning. In contrast to the weltschmerz of the age (the term expressing Romantic pessimism used by German poets such as Heinrich Heine), which irresponsibly made a mockery of everything, Kierkegaard posited his Hegelian synthesis: "Ironi som behersket Moment" (irony which conquers the moment). Irony is controlled by the responsibility of individual existence and presents the possibility of critical liberation within Christianity. Just as doubt is the basis for science, so is irony the grasping of "det personlige Livs absolute Begyndelse" (the absolute beginning of the personal life). After this account of the maieutic method of Socrates, Kierkegaard was able to begin his own work of indirect communication.

From 1843 through 1855 Kierkegaard published under his own name a series of *opbyggelige Taler* (edifying discourses) from the Christian perspective for which he stood. At the same time, he pseudonymously published a series of literary works. In the latter he tested scenarios for various views of life, which, in the beginning, he called aesthetic, ethical, and religious, although he personally vouched neither for these experiments in psychology nor for the ways of life in question.

In the spring of 1843 Kierkegaard published, under the pseudonym Victor Eremita, the immense two-volume *Enten-Eller. Et Livs-Fragment* (translated as *Either/Or: A Fragment of Life,* 1944). The work consists of two parts, the first including the papers of the aesthete "A," the second those of the ethicist "B." The first part is a collection of works in three genres: the aphorisms of "Diapsalmata" (the term *diapsalma* stems from the Greek translation of the Psalms; Kierkegaard uses the plural form of the term, meaning "interlude" or "refrain"); six critical essays on aesthetic questions; and, finally, a novel titled "Forførerens Dagbog" (translated as *Diary of a Seducer,* 1932). In contrast to these diverse and heterogeneous offerings, the three long texts by B, the ethicist, range from an official statement of account to a personal letter. Whereas the first of the three texts considers the aesthetic from the perspective of the ethical, the second ponders the ethical in its own right, before the ethical collapses into the religious in the final piece. On the surface, *Enten-Eller* concerns two views of life from which the reader must choose, but that from which he is to choose influences the choosing. While the aesthete focuses on what it is to be chosen and the excitement of the choice itself, what is important to the ethicist is the individual's discovery of the truth through the act of choosing, as well as the ethical obligations of the manner in which he chooses. At the conclusion of the two parts, both points of view are brought together. The aesthete is forced to choose again and again. The ethicist must see his own humane point of view overcome by a sermon demonstrating that against God one is always in the wrong. The truth, therefore, is not, as Plato held, to be sought in man, but in God.

Kierkegaard as a student at the University of Copenhagen (sketch by David Jacobsen; from Walter Lowrie, Kierkegaard, *1938; Thomas Cooper Library, University of South Carolina)*

In the last of the many "Diapsalmata," the aesthete A is able to choose from all the world's glories, and he chooses always to have laughter on his side. The "Diapsalmata" may be understood as a designation of monotonous, repetitious refrain, which, similar to Hegel's "false infinity," is without movement, because the laughter is without perspective or responsibility, and because the dialectic still has not been set in motion. The "editor," Eremita, indicates that the short pieces in the "Diapsalmata" were found in no particular order, although some of them appear to be paired, so that they form a kind of dialogue. One of them expresses, through an apparently irrefutable philosophical proof, the contemporary European weltschmerz:

> Jeg gider slet ikke. Jeg gider ikke ride, det er for stærk en Bevægelse; jeg gider ikke gaae, det er for anstrængende; jeg gider ikke lægge mig ned, thi enten skulde jeg blive liggende, og det gider jeg ikke, eller jeg skulde reise mig op igen, og det gider jeg heller ikke. Summa summarum: jeg gider slet ikke.

> (I don't feel like doing anything. I don't feel like riding–the motion is too powerful; I don't feel like walking–it is too tiring; I don't feel like lying down, for either I would have to stay down, and I don't feel like

> doing that, or I would have to get up again, and I don't feel like doing that, either. *Summa Summarum:* I don't feel like doing anything.)

As a commentary on this humorous passage, "Diapsalmata" features a longer text headed "Enten-Eller," which begins with the injunction "Gift Dig, Du vil fortryde det; gift Dig ikke, Du vil ogsaa fortryde det; gift Dig eller gift Dig ikke, Du vil fortryde begge Dele" (Marry, and you will regret it. Do not marry, and you will also regret it. Whether you marry or do not marry, you will regret it either way). But the reader should neither cease to act because everything is equally regrettable, nor, in a Hegelian manner, attempt to mediate the two alternatives. They should instead be considered from the viewpoint of eternity. In other passages the aesthete comes as close as he is able to eternity, which for him exists in the sky between the clouds. He knows not the Christian heaven but plays on such words as "baptism" and "eternity." The closest he comes to eternity is in a portrait of an old man who is explaining the images of folk literature to a child, suggesting the interest in folk culture that set Kierkegaard in motion with *Enten-Eller*. Aside from such glimpses, all else is put to mockery in the passages of "Diapsalmata," which, taken together, formulate the aesthetic view of life in its most rudimentary form, precisely where the dialectic takes off from "false infinity."

If "Diapsalmata" mirrors the fashionable café life of Kierkegaard's student days, then the six aesthetic essays demonstrate that he had also received an aesthetic and philosophical schooling. In two dialectical movements the essays follow the aesthetic from its most unreflective forms to its most reflective. First is "De umiddelbare erotiske Stadier eller det Musikalsk-Erotiske" (The Immediate Erotic Stages or the Musical-Erotic), in which Wolfgang Amadeus Mozart's opera *Don Giovanni* (1787) is judged to be the supreme work in its genre, and the music in it–and music in general–is judged to be capable of expressing the aesthetic wholly unreflected, since language in itself is too reflective. Yet, the author expresses this "Musikalsk-Erotiske" in a language itself so musical that Kierkegaard contradicts his own point of view. The next essay is an examination of how the unreflective sorrow of antiquity is absorbed in the reflective anguish of modernity, an exercise corresponding to the treatment of irony in the dissertation. Last in the first series of three essays is "Skyggerids" (Silhouettes), a psychological survey of reflective sorrow, which lies beyond the possibility of artistic representation. After this demarcation of the aesthetic sphere, the next series of three essays attempts to pinpoint the aesthetic personality. First is a psychological analysis of "Den Ulykkeligste" (The Unhappiest One), who, caught between hope and recollection, is denied access to both. Next is the aesthete's examination of Eugène Scribe's reflective comedy *Les premières amours* (First Loves, 1825), which Heiberg had translated in 1832 as *Den første Kjærlighed* (The First Love) and placed in a prominent position in the repertoire of the Royal Theater. This analysis may be understood as a contrasting piece to the treatment of Mozart's opera in "De umiddelbare erotiske Stadier eller det Musikalsk-Erotiske." The final essay is "Vexeldriften" (The Rotation of Crops), subtitled "Forsøg til en social Klogskabslære" (A Venture in a Theory of Social Prudence), in which A wittily proclaims three maxims of wise counsel: beware of friendship, marriage, and the taking of any official post. This ethos–written by an aesthete for a like-minded reader–marks the distinction between the two ways of life. The aesthete does not desire friendship, sex, or productivity, but he is able in freedom to define the premises of his existence. Arbitrariness and laughter shall always be on his side.

This program is seen in action in the novel "Forførerens Dagbog." During the period in which Kierkegaard desired to end his engagement, he laid out in his diary a plan in which, by behaving repulsively, he would cause Regine herself to break it off, thereby allowing the slander to fall on him. It did not succeed. But in "Forførerens Dagbog" the diarist, Johannes, succeeds in both seducing a woman and disposing of her by conducting an experiment "saaledes at digte sig ud af en Pige, at man kunde gjøre hende saa stolt, at hun bildte sig ind, at det var hende, der var kjed af Forholdet" (in poeticizing oneself out of a girl in such a way as to make her so proud that she imagined it was she who was so bored with the relationship). Johannes fashions himself as a scientist of the erotic, an amalgam of Faust and Don Juan, and when his experiment is completed, he is, like Ahasuerus, forced to repeat it again and again, damned as he is by his triumph.

The diary consists of three courses of events. The first takes place in the cafés of Østergade and in the galleries and various other places around Copenhagen where the well-heeled maintained their semiofficial environs. The reflective flaneur Johannes, whose name suggests the unreflective Don Juan, has his hunting grounds in these places, which he surveys with the keen eye of a detective. Three girls engage his interest briefly, but they are each sent packing. Thereafter he encounters, just as accidentally, the one whom he chooses; although unreflective, she has the capacity for passion and consciousness of pain. The section concludes in her private room, into which Johannes has gained access to convince himself that she has the psychic energies required to enter into his reflection and his experiment. Cordelia is her name, and she shares all of the gentleness and faithfulness of her namesake in William Shakespeare's *King Lear.*

The second course of events takes place in a typical Biedermeier living room, in which Johannes wins over Cordelia's aunt in part for his own sake and in part so that he may impress on Cordelia an increasing measure of cold irony and higher flights of thought. He is an expert strategist, gaining the aunt's assent through rapid subterfuge and immediately afterward planting the embryo of future disgust at his and Cordelia's eventual engagement.

In the third section Johannes wages two wars against Cordelia. The first is a war of liberation, in which she will learn to triumph as he himself retreats. At the same time her mind will be formed by the letters, and her sense of the erotic by the pictures, that he sends to her. After this double movement of liberation and binding follows the war of conquest, in which, through his mockery of the engagement, he induces her to come forward as a sexual being who hunts him. The consummation will take place in a room he has arranged as a copy of the aunt's living room out of which he led Cordelia. The impending union connects Johannes to the pagan Roman myth of the power of love. The love that may be played out in bourgeois marriage he must see as a pale, passionless reflection of the attempt to unite man and woman, whom Jupiter had separated from one another because early humankind before this sundering was too powerful for the gods. This account is as close as Johannes may come to the biblical story of the Fall and Exile.

In the second part of *Enten-Eller,* B, Judge William, has the floor, and he proceeds in the exacting, logical, and tedious manner of the public official. Through his three letters he hopes to bring A out of the aesthetic and into the ethical. In contrast to the momentary impressions of the senses is offered a lasting joy; in contrast to seduction, the institution of marriage. William asserts that it is actually within the ethical that the aesthetic is realized, for it unites love and responsibility and through marriage is placed in relation to sin. When A says "either/or," it is in B's opinion the avoidance of choice. Against the nihilism expressed in A's pondering of his choices, B argues that what is of importance is the seriousness and pathos by which one chooses. B would gladly drive A to the point of despair, where it would be necessary to choose oneself as the absolute. In this case, A wants to create something that already exists. Therefore, he is not like God, who creates something new. But there emerges in the choice something new, which he has himself drawn out of the natural state of man. Whereas the aesthetic is, according to B, to be understood as "det i et Menneske, hvorved han umiddelbar er Den, han er" (that in a man whereby he immediately is the man he is), the ethical is "det hvorved et Menneske bliver det, han bliver" (that whereby a man becomes what he becomes). The individual must find the truth in himself and develop a self that is personal, social, and civic. This development occurs through friendship, marriage, and an official calling, which, precisely because of their binding nature, are capable of internalizing responsibility, so that it is not a power imposed from without.

The artistic type A falls short of the biblical account of the Creation and must remain in the paganism of Faust, Don Juan, and Ahasuerus, and in this way the public official B is developed dialectically within his limits through his letters to A. He asserts, like the Greeks, that man has the truth within himself, but this position is rejected in the final letter, which includes a sermon in which the thesis is that against God, man is always in the wrong. If the truth is with God, then it must be found through edification. The ethicist's final message to A is that "kun den Sandhed, der opbygger, er Sandheden for Dig" (only the truth which edifies is truth for you). Therefore, the choice between the aesthetic and the ethical became a neither/nor, and hence the floor was given to Kierkegaard himself as the author of *To opbyggelige Taler* (Two Edifying Discourses; translated in *Edifying Discourses,* 1943), which was published as an accompaniment to *Enten-Eller* on 16 May 1843.

The edifying discourses are written in a clear, accessible language and form a parallel series to the pseudonymous works, beginning with *Enten-Eller* and including *Øieblikket* (1855; translated as "The Moment," 1998), which was accompanied by the discourse *Guds Uforanderlighed* (translated as "The Unchangeableness of God," 1941), published on 3 September 1855, a little more than two months before Kierkegaard's death. Most of these works are untitled, or rather bear a title simply denoting the genre. Especially in the beginning, he included the number of discourses in the title, in 1843 and 1844 publishing volumes called *To-, Tre-,* and *Fire opbyggelige Taler* (Two, Three, and Four Edifying Discourses). According to Kierkegaard, these texts were called "Taler" (speeches) because, as an unordained theologian, he had no right to preach, although the use of this term also served to distance him from the teach "from above," for he preferred to edify "hiin Enkelte" (that single individual) whom he addressed in the foreword of each of the volumes. In the beginning this approach was a nod to Regine, for whose religious education he still felt responsible, but later it came to be directed at anyone who might be "that single individual," for religious edification presupposes that man is subjective.

Kierkegaard in January 1838 (sketch by Niels Christian Kierkegaard; courtesy of the Danish Royal Library, Copenhagen)

From beginning to end, Kierkegaard ritually upheld the practice of dedicating each volume in the series of edifying discourses to the solemn memory of his father. In relation to the rest of Kierkegaard's works, these texts are an expression of a surprising stability, which may well be likened to the regular churchgoing he maintained throughout all of the pressures of work and inner turmoil. Although he wished to distance his discourses from sermons proper, they have many characteristics in common with the new, psychologically oriented, and more literary and aesthetic–and effective–style that Bishop Jakob Peter Mynster had successfully introduced into the Danish State Lutheran Church.

As a young country pastor in Spjellerup, Mynster had long considered the question of how one could find authentic Christianity in a situation in which the traditional faith in the Scriptures as the truth revealed by God had been discredited by sciences such as archaeology and philology, even though efforts in these sciences to demonstrate the truth had failed. Mynster was influenced by Kant's distinction between the noumenal and phenomenal realities, which liberated religiosity from being merely an extension of the usual educational endeavors. Hereafter, the question of what this new freedom meant became the central problem of the new generation of Romantic theologians. In Mynster's account this freedom led, via Benedict de Spinoza, to a choice between conscience and faith in God. Mynster's mild Lutheranism did not much diverge from tradition, but he himself saw it as enough of a break to constitute the framework for that of which his predecessors had been incapable. The practical expression of Mynster's 1803 Spjellerup religious breakthrough was his working out of a new type of sermon. He published the first volume in 1810 and the next in 1815. In 1812 his deliberations on the genre appeared as *Om den Kunst at prædike* (On the Art of Preaching). Back in Copenhagen in 1811 as resident curate at Vor Frue Kirke (Our Lady's Church), Mynster won a large following among educated and cultivated citizens through his sermonizing, which united a carefully crafted oratorical and gestural idiom with a melodious text cleansed of heavy biblical citations. His style, furthermore, closely resembled contemporary poetry. Mynster not only provided an aesthetic awakening but also employed his psychological empathy with the congregation to support these bureaucrats and businessmen in their roles as decision makers.

Kierkegaard had learned much in both manner of expression and practical psychology from Mynster, his father's pastor and the man who confirmed him, although Kierkegaard in his writings speaks more intimately than Mynster to his readers. In his last edifying discourse, *Guds Uforanderlighed,* Kierkegaard returned to the same passage from the Epistle of James that he had used in the conclusion of the *To opbyggelige Taler* of 1843: "Al god Gave og al fuldkommen Gave er ovenfra" (Every generous act of giving, with every perfect gift, is from above). While he is gently persuasive in the early discourses, in the later works one can see Pietism more clearly. Faith in paradox likewise also appears in these texts. (Paradox is a significant concept in Kierkegaard's work, for example, in his concept of the "moment" in which time and eternity meet.) Nevertheless, the author's humble praise of God and entreating of hope and consolation for each individual remain unchanged. At the same time, these discourses markedly distinguish themselves from the understanding of the religious in the rest of Kierkegaard's work, which functions as their partner in dialogue. In his role as an edifying–rather, evangelical–author, Kierkegaard operates in a space seemingly undisturbed by what he has written elsewhere. One can choose to take his proclamation at his word or conceive of this series of discourses as the primary axis of his writing, which would place the reader in agreement with the interpretation that Kierkegaard himself delivered, first in *Afsluttende uvidenskabelig Efterskrift til de philosophiske Smuler* (Concluding Unscientific Postscript to the Philosophical Fragments, 1846; translated as *Kierkegaard's Concluding Unscientific Postscript,* 1941), then in *Om min Forfatter-Virksomhed* (1851; translated as "On My Work as an Author," 1939), and finally in the posthumously published *Synspunktet for min Forfatter-Virksomhed* (1859; translated as "The Point of View for My Work as an Author," 1939), written in 1848. Even if one agrees with this interpretation, it must be admitted that Kierkegaard is at his most original in texts other than the discourses. They are perhaps a symbol of the comfortable, peaceful position that he now and then dreamed of realizing by abandoning writing in favor of a post as a country parish pastor.

On 16 October 1843 Kierkegaard published three works: *Frygt og Bæven. Dialektisk Lyrik* (translated as *Fear and Trembling: A Dialectical Lyric,* 1939), *Gjentagelsen. Et Forsøg i den experimenterende Psychologi* (translated as *Repetition: An Essay in Experimental Psychology,* 1941), and *Tre opbyggelige Taler* (translated in *Edifying Discourses*, 1943). In *Gjentagelsen* the pseudonymous author, the cynical, stoic aesthete Constantin Constantius, seeks cohesion in his existence. In vain he searches for the aesthetic repetition of a Berlin theater experience and in so doing tells the story of "Det unge Menneske" (the young man), who, after his engagement, suddenly realizes that his betrothed is only his muse, only the occasion for the undertaking of difficult spiritual questions. To live with her in the ethical repetition of daily life would drive her to despair. He wonders whether the right thing to do in this situation is to break off the engagement. By reading the Book of Job, he comes to understand that even if what is most humane is right, it is still not in right relation to God, as man in relation to God is always in the wrong. He wants now to return to the relationship but discovers that the woman has married another; hence, in a proper understanding, the young man is free. He has, by humbling himself like Job, received everything in return, as well as the opportunity for a reconciliation with the woman on a higher, more spiritual plane. Thus, he has reached repetition in a religious sense. The whole is, however, revealed as a fiction, contrived by Constantius and conducted as "Et Forsøg i den experimenterende Psychologi" with a view to the understanding of his own existence.

Frygt og Bæven concerns the boundary between the ethical and the religious. From his interpretation of Abraham's plan to sacrifice his son Isaac, the pseudonymous Johannes de Silentio asserts that between the ethics of man and the demands of God for sacrifice, there is a radical break, a "leap." Abraham must step outside human society, which cannot tolerate the behavior demanded of him. He must surrender everything to his faith in the paradox of the "God-Man." Therefore, he may make "Bevægelsen i Kraft af det Absurde" (the movement by virtue of the absurd), or "Uendelighedens Dobbelt Bevægelse" (the double movement of infinity), and thus receive everything back again. Johannes's book is characterized as a "Dialektisk Lyrik." He remains silent in his inner submission to the paradox, but Kierkegaard distances himself both from the humanism of Johann Wolfgang von Goethe, in which the life of the individual is seen to develop harmoniously from phase to phase, and from the thought of Hegel, in which each individual concept is dialectically annulled in the next, contradictions are resolved through speculation, and radical paradoxes do not appear. In *Frygt og Bæven* Kierkegaard has replaced the choice between the aesthetic and the ethical with the choice between Christianity understood as a cultivated, higher ethic and Christianity understood as passionate faith in the absurd, which also includes the "teleologiske Suspension af det Ethiske" (teleological suspension of the ethical). Johannes remains the rational investigator in spite of the nature of the material he considers.

The breakthrough year of 1843 concluded with *Fire opbyggelige Taler* (translated in *Edifying Discourses,* 1944), which was published on 6 December. Corresponding to the structure of *Enten-Eller,* the nine discourses published in this year cohere in a dialectical composition, from "Troens Forventning" (The Expectation of Faith) and "Bekræftelsen i det indvortes Menneske" (Strengthened in the Inner Man) to "At erhverve sin Sjel i Taalmodighed" (To Acquire One's Soul in Patience), in which the ethicist's concepts of choice and personal development are challenged. Man does not own his own soul and thus cannot through personal development come to acknowledge the authentic self. This self belongs to God, and man can only acquire it through patience. In 1844 Kierkegaard published a corresponding series: *To opbyggelige Taler* (translated in *Edifying Discourses,* 1945) on 5 March, *Tre opbyggelige Taler* (translated in *Edifying Discourses,* 1945) on 8 June, and *Fire opbyggelige Taler* (translated in *Edifying Discourses,* 1946) on 31 August. The three installments may be seen as accompaniments to *Philosophiske Smuler eller En Smule Philosophi* (translated as *Philosophical Fragments; or, A Fragment of Philosophy,* 1936), which appeared on 13 June 1844; *Begrebet Angest* (translated as *Kierkegaard's The Concept of Dread,* 1944); and *Forord. Morskabslæsning for enkelte Stænder efter Tid og Leilighed* (translated as *Prefaces: Light Reading for Certain Classes as the Occasion May Require, by Nicolaus Notabene,* 1989), both published on 17 June.

In 1841 Kierkegaard had practiced preaching at the seminary, and in 1844 he gave his probational sermon. He later preached three times in Vor Frue Kirke and gave a final sermon at the Citadel Chapel, also in Copenhagen, in 1851. On 3 September 1855 he published this sermon as *Guds Uforanderlighed,* the final installment of the discourse series, thus demonstrating that the distance between the two genres was not decisive. The idea of becoming a country pastor was not only an economic but also a psychological safeguard. In the meantime, Kierkegaard's efforts were directed elsewhere.

Philosophiske Smuler was published under the pseudonym Johannes Climacus. On the title page Kierkegaard is identified as the editor, just as in the later works published under the pseudonym denoting Climacus's counterpart, Anti-Climacus. Kierkegaard's journals further demonstrate that Climacus and Anti-Climacus were new kinds of pseudonyms that were closer to his own views on existence. The name Johannes Climacus was inspired by a seventh-century monk, St. John Climacus, author of *Climax tou paradeisou* (Ladder of Divine Ascent); in *Philosophiske Smuler* Johannes Climacus, who himself takes the point of view of the Greeks–outside of Christianity–seeks through his thought to climb from the Old to the New Testament. On the title page are two questions: "Gives der et historisk Udgangspunkt for en evig Bevidsthed?" (Can an historical point of departure be given for an eternal consciousness?). Therefore, can one "bygge en evig Salighed på historisk Viden?" (build eternal happiness on historical knowledge?). The answer is no.

Philosophiske Smuler distinguishes between what can be demonstrated by historical knowledge and by eternal consciousness, which may only appear through leaps and paradoxes. Climacus thereby dismisses the relevance of the scientific efforts of historians, archaeologists, and philologists to examine the truth of the utterances in the Bible on the basis of the sources. According to the thought experiment in *Philosophiske Smuler,* the Greeks' notion that man has the truth within himself cannot be proven, because it is administered by God. But if truth is not a part of human nature, then there must be an absolute distinction between God and man, who must thus become a paradoxical entity–a "God-Man"–to be able to transgress the gulf. Man then receives the truth from a paradoxical giver in a "leap," which in itself includes both eternity and temporality, and he can therefore choose faith only through his subjective intimacy and contemporaneity with the paradoxical. On the final page Climacus must self-critically acknowledge that his own perspective sets limits to the way the problem presents itself. He purports to have gone further than "the Socratic" by substantiating "faith," its precondition of "consciousness of sin," the particular choice of faith in "the moment," and the paradoxical "new teacher: God in time." But he is prevented from evaluating the truth in the dogmatics he has established because he views Christianity from the outside.

Begrebet Angest is subtitled *En simpel psychologisk-paapegende Overveielse i Retning af det dogmatiske Problem om Arvesynden* (A Simple Psychologically Orienting Deliberation on the Dogmatic Problem of Hereditary Sin). The work involves a psychological investigation of despair as the foundation of faith. The pseudonymous author is Vigilius Haufniensis (He Who Watches over Copenhagen), and the book is dedicated to Kierkegaard's late professor, mentor, and inspiration in the philosophy of personality, Møller: "Græcitetens lykkelige Elsker, Homers Beundrer, Sokrates's Medvider, Aristotles's Fortolker" (The fortunate lover of Greek culture, the admirer of Homer, the confidant of Socrates, the interpreter of Aristotle). The examination of the psychological preconditions of faith takes place from a position outside of Christianity. Vigilius desires to be considered a layman, "der vel speculerer, men dog staaer langt udenfor Speculationen" (who certainly speculates, and yet stands far outside speculation); that is, the Hegelian speculative philosopher.

Vigilius distinguishes between fear, which has external causes and which his aesthetic colleague in psychology has described in *Frygt og Bæven,* and anxiety, which is a foundational human condition. In the state of innocence he understands man as "sjelelig bestemmet i umiddelbar Eenhed med sin Naturlighed" (psychically qualified in immediate unity with his natural condition). The spirit is still only latent or "dreaming" in this state of rest, the opposite of which is not "Ufred og Strid, thi der er jo Intet at Stride med. . . . Hvad er det da? Intet. Men hvilken Virkning har Intet? Det føder Angest" (contention and strife, for there is indeed nothing against which to strive. . . . What, then, is it? Nothing. But what effect does nothing have? It begets anxiety). Anxiety is therefore defined as a "Bestemmelse af den drømmende Aand, og hører som saadan hjemme i Psychologien" (qualification of dreaming spirit, and as such it has a place in psychology). Man is now defined as "en Synthese af det Sjelelige og det Legemlige" (a synthesis of the psychical and the physical), although Vigilius adds that "en Synthese er utænkelig, naar de Tvende ikke enes i et Tredie. Dette Tredie er Aanden" (a synthesis is unthinkable if the two are not united in a third. The third is spirit). Spirit in relation to the balance between the psychical and the physical represents something alien, which, however, is necessary for the maintenance of balance. Man relates anxiety to that ambiguous power, nothingness. Vigilius

Min Regine!

First page of a letter from Kierkegaard to his fiancée, Regine Olsen, to whom he became engaged on 1 September 1840. The sketch shows Kierkegaard looking through a telescope on Knippelsbro, a bridge in Copenhagen (courtesy of the Danish Royal Library, Copenhagen).

then discusses the concept of subjective anxiety, which has as its background the Fall and man's constant intensification of sin. It breaks forth in the life of the individual as a qualitative leap:

> Angest kan man sammenligne med Svimmelhed. Den, hvis Øie kommer til at skue ned i et svælgende Dyb, han bliver svimmel. Men hvad er Grunden, det er ligesaa meget hans Øie som Afgrunden; thi hvis han ikke havde stirret ned. Saaledes er Angest den Friheds Svimlen, der opkommer, idet Aanden vil sætte Synthesen, og Friheden nu skuer ned i sin Mulighed, og da griber Endeligheden at holde sig ved. I denne Svimlen segner Friheden. Videre kan Psychologien ikke komme og vil det ikke. I samme Øieblikk er Alt forandret, og idet Friheden igjen reiser sig op, seer den, at den er skyldig. I mellem disse tvende Øieblikke ligger Springet, som ingen Videnskab har forklaret eller kan forklare.

> (Anxiety may be compared with dizziness. He whose eye happens to look down into the yawning abyss becomes dizzy. But what is the reason for this? It is just as much in his own eye as in the abyss, for suppose he had not looked down. Hence anxiety is the dizziness of freedom, which emerges when the spirit wants to posit the synthesis and freedom looks down into possibility, laying hold of finiteness to support itself. Freedom succumbs in this dizziness. Further than this, psychology cannot and will not go. In that very moment everything is changed, and freedom, when it again rises, sees that it is guilty. Between these two moments lies the leap, which no science has explained and no science can explain.)

When spirit breaks through the gulf between soul and body in "the moment," the individual is torn out of his immediate chronology of time (past/present/future) and placed in relation to the contradiction between temporality and eternity. When, after the qualitative leap, sin enters the individual's world, anxiety changes in character from being nothing to being tied to the distinction between good and evil. The individual can then limit himself by remaining in anxiety of evil, but the anxiety can correspondingly become tied to fate or good; in the latter emerges the demonic. Yet, anxiety may also be used to approach faith. Having come as far as he is capable, the psychologist Vigilius on the last page delivers the concept of anxiety to Climacus's dogmatics.

Forord is ascribed to Nicolaus Notabene, who has had to promise his wife not to be an author, for that is, according to her understanding, the worst form of infidelity for a married man. Therefore, between the foreword and afterword he includes only a series of prefaces, which are addressed to the contemporary literary debate, and in this manner they function as an extension of the critique of Andersen in *Af en endnu Levendes Papirer.* In that work Kierkegaard had tried to qualify himself as a critic in the manner of Heiberg, but the master had refused to publish the result in his journal, *Perseus.* Thereafter Kierkegaard had, with the long, dialectically organized *Enten-Eller,* delivered a freestanding novel, "Forførerens Dagbog," and received only a cool response from Heiberg. In *Forord,* then, arrived the official prelude to the satire of Heiberg, which continued through much of Kierkegaard's writing. Along the way, Mynster's edifying sermons received similar treatment.

On 29 April 1845 Kierkegaard published, under his own name, *Tre Taler ved tænkte Leiligheder* (Three Discourses on Imagined Occasions; translated as *Thoughts on Crucial Situations in Human Life: Three Discourses on Imagined Occasions,* 1941) and a day later pseudonymously published *Stadier paa Livets Vei* (translated as *Stages on Life's Way,* 1940), subtitled *Studier af Forskjellige, sammenbragte, befordrede til Trykken og udgivne af Hilarius Bogbinder* (Studies by Various Persons, Compiled, Forwarded to the Press, and Published by Hilarius Bookbinder). This great work is an outgrowth of *Enten-Eller.* The "stages" should not be understood as steps on a ladder but as independent ways of life from which the individual must choose. The reader is instructed that although the stages appear in the same volume, they are not the work of a sole author but were collected by the bookbinder. It is, however, revealed that the stages share love as a common theme. The aesthetic is dealt with briefly, for it is presented as already experienced, for which reason "In Vino Veritas" appears as a recollection of a symposium on women. The speakers are all men, and among them are found Eremita and Johannes, the seducer from "Forførerens Dagbog," who, together with their aesthetic colleagues, offer opinions on the virtue and consciousness of women, ranging from those of the most innocent to the most cynical and reflective seducer. The ethical stage is represented by a defense of marriage, in which the married man in the meantime does not triumph. In contrast to *Enten-Eller,* the religious life is included as an independent third stage. The text is represented as the diary of Frater Taciturnus (Brother in Silence), "'Skyldig?'–'Ikke-Skyldig?'" ("Guilty?"–"Not Guilty?"), which is subtitled "En Lidelseshistorie, Psychologisk Experiment" (A Story of Suffering, a Psychological Experiment). In this text, which was originally intended to be included in *Enten-Eller* as a counterpart to "Forførerens Dagbog," the cold, intellectual Taciturnus documents a psychological experiment with a protagonist he himself invents. This Quidam is a melancholy man whose many possibilities for uniting with his beloved are demonstrated by Taciturnus. Quidam can acknowledge the religious, but he can neither grasp nor live it. With his

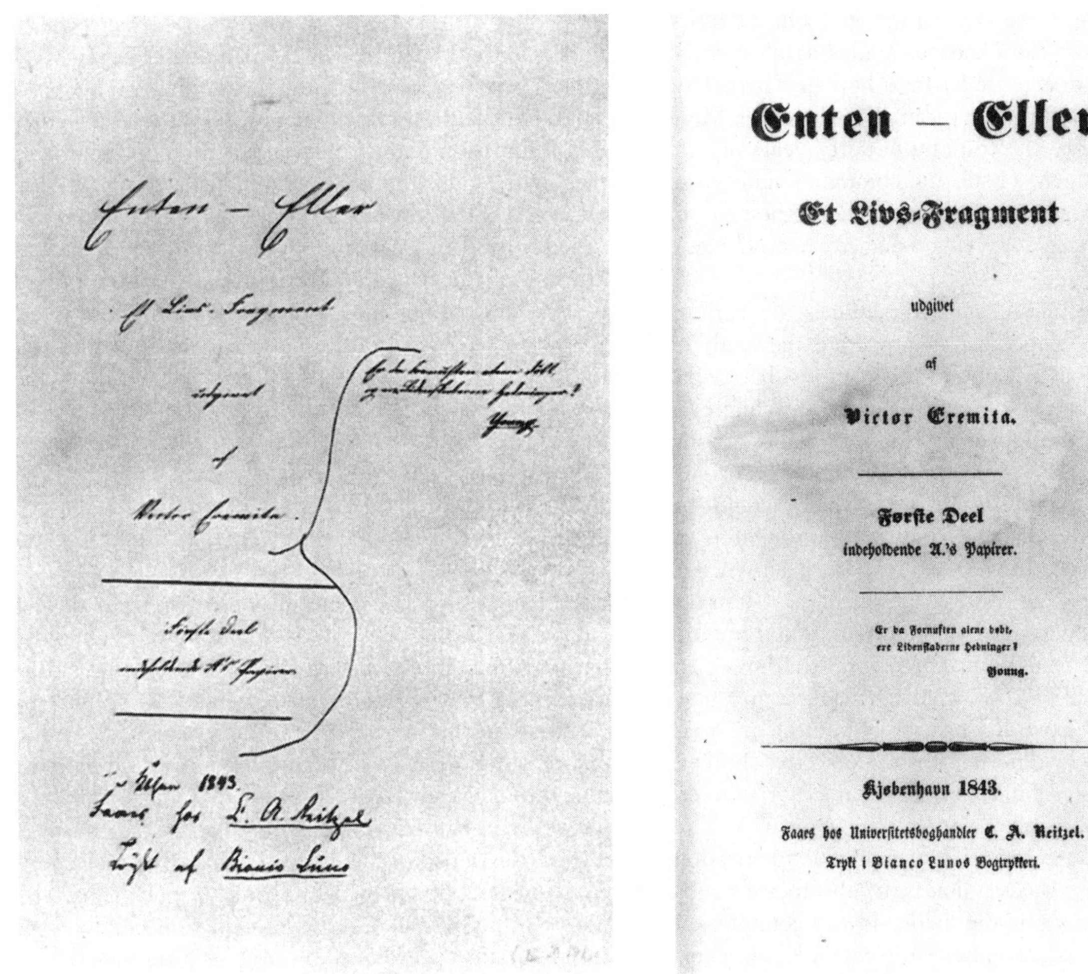

Enten – Eller.

Et Livs-Fragment

udgivet

af

Victor Eremita.

Første Deel

indeholdende A.'s Papirer.

Er da Fornuften alene døbt,
ere Lidenskaberne Hedninger?

Young.

Kjøbenhavn 1843.

Faaes hos Universitetsboghandler C. A. Reitzel.

Trykt i Bianco Lunos Bogtrykkeri.

Manuscript and printed title pages for Kierkegaard's philosophical work (translated as Either/Or: A Fragment of Life, *1944) contrasting the aesthetic and ethical viewpoints (left: P. M. Mitchell,* A History of Danish Literature, *1957, Scandinavian Studies Library, University of Washington; right: courtesy of the Danish Royal Library, Copenhagen)*

experiment Taciturnus has "lagt et Problem tilrette for det Religieuse: Syndsforladelsen" (laid out an issue for the religious: the forgiveness of sin). In this issue lies the possibility of annulling the schism between hereditary curse and marriage, which is the realization of the universal. The discussion of absolution Taciturnus must leave to the edifying discourses in *Tre Taler ved tænkte Leiligheder.* The three imagined occasions for the discourses are confession, marriage, and burial.

The greatest attention to Kierkegaard's 1846 publications was given to Climacus's extension of and eventual break with Hegel in *Afsluttende uvidenskabelig Efterskrift.* This massive volume supplemented the tenuous-appearing *Philosophiske Smuler.* The work is "Concluding" because Kierkegaard thought at this point that he would retire from writing, now that he had said all he had desired; "Unscientific" because it is a critique of contemporary science, which Heiberg had made Hegelian; and a "Postscript to the *Philosophical Fragments*" because it worked further with Climacus's problem of the subjective and the objective with respect to the acquisition of faith. The peculiar subtitle, *Mimisk-pathetisk-dialektisk Sammenskrift, Existentielt Indlæg* (A Mimetic-Pathetic-Dialectic Composition, an Existential Contribution), is a result of Kierkegaard's working behind the mask of pseudonymity and functioning as both poet and thinker from the passionate position of existence. Climacus still stands outside the religious stage. He develops the doctrine of the three stages by inserting irony as an intermediate stage in between the aesthetic and the ethical, and humor–his own position–between the ethical and the religious. While irony may conceal the ethical, humor may be understood as the humanist's mask for the religious; yet, it is the stage nearest to it. The humorist understands that suffering belongs to existence, but he does not understand its religious meaning; he "gjør den svigefulde Vending og tilbagekalder Lidelsen i Spøgens Form" (turns deceptively aside and revokes suffering in the form of the jest). On the other side lies religiosity; as Climacus writes as a potential consumer, his aim is to understand how he, "barnefødt her af Byen, nu tredive Aar gammel, et slet og ret Menneske ligesom Folk er fleest" (now thirty years of age, born in Copenhagen, a plain and common man like the run of them), may come to enjoy the highest good, which has been called "en evig Salighed" (eternal blessedness).

In the first part Climacus examines the various attempts of the sciences to demonstrate the truth of Christianity. He also examines the attempts that evoke the authority of the Scriptures, the life of the congregation, and the institution of the Church. Chief among these efforts was the Hegelians' reduction of Christianity to an historical phenomenon, which would be absorbed as a subordinate segment in the unfolding of the Absolute Spirit. In the second part, against these objective attempts to justify Christianity, Climacus poses, with the poet and thinker Gotthold Ephraim Lessing as his starting point, the question of how man can justify himself in relation to faith, and hence how subjectivity may exist, if Christianity is to be grasped. While the result is important for the objective thinker, the process is also significant for the subjective thinker, because existence is an incomplete movement. Where acquisition is the principal question, communication becomes doubly reflective; that is, it subsumes the relation between the communicated and the communicator's position of existence. In a supplement Kierkegaard allows Climacus to go through the whole of his previous work as an example of such a doubly reflective communication, after which Kierkegaard in his own name acknowledges his paternity to the pseudonyms.

The seed of Climacus's long duel with Hegel is in the observation that if there exists an all-comprehending system of existence, then it would exist not to be comprehended by man but only by the paradoxical "God-Man," who is both within and outside of existence. Climacus views Hegel's system as incomplete, in part because it lacks God and in part because it lacks the individual, and thereby each single existence, whose life is an incomplete process. Every existence finds itself in a tension between subjective existence and objective thought, and this tension may not, according to Climacus, be annulled in a higher synthesis, as Hegel had argued. Climacus says that every individual is from the beginning a subject, and that is why one's first task is, through personal development, to divest oneself of the subjective in the sense of the selfish, the incidental, and the particular. Hereafter, science asserts that the task consists in becoming objective, while the doctrine of Christianity holds that it is in a higher sense that of becoming a subject. Man should dare to be "a single individual": "At være et enkelt individ, er Verdenshistorisk slet Intet, uendelig Intet–men dog er det et Menneskes eneste sande og høieste Betydning" (to be a single individual is world-historically absolutely nothing, infinitely nothing–and yet it is the only truth and the highest meaning of the individual). While the sciences stress the truth as an object outside the acknowledged, Christianity understands truth as "Uendelighedens Lidenskab" (the passion of infinity). In this sense, subjectivity is the truth, although this position does not entail the assertion that in other, nonexistential relationships the truth is in subjectivity–a view that would make every understanding of anything equally valid and therefore equally invalid. But in the existential area defined in the *Afsluttende uvidenskabelig Efterskrift,* the absolute contrast in Christianity between good and evil and truth and falsehood applies, and not the Hegelian synthesis, which can mediate every contradiction.

Climacus distinguishes between two types of religiousness: religiousness A is found also among the pagans, for example, in Socrates. The individual in this case exists in inner consciousness of guilt, seeking to withdraw from the world through penitence or the cloister. Man believes he knows his god, who relates to him through knowledge and thought. Religiousness B builds upon the ethical-religious duty of religiousness A, but consciousness of guilt is in this case supported by consciousness of sin, which leads man out of his relation to the universal and the human. Consciousness of sin implies a rupture of the subject as a thinking being and his relation to others, for it arises from the paradox of "God in time," the paradox in which God has made himself into a man. To this paradox one may relate only through faith and in constant uncertainty, and that is why Climacus states his thesis that the truth is subjective in this way: "*den objective Uvished, fastholdt i den meest lidenskabelige Inderligheds Tilegnelse, er Sandheden,* den høieste Sandhed, der er for en *Existerende*" (*An objective uncertainty, held fast in an appropriation of the most passionate inwardness, is the truth,* the highest truth attainable for the *existing individual*). [Italics in the original.]

In 1846 Kierkegaard continued the work as literary critic that he had begun with his book on Andersen. In *Af en endnu Levendes Papirer* he had mentioned several other Danish prose writers, including "Forfatteren til *En Hverdags-Historie*" (the author of *An Everyday Story*), Thomasine Gyllembourg, whose novella *To Tidsaldre* (Two Ages, 1845) was the object of Kierkegaard's *En literair Anmeldelse* (A Literary Review; translated as "The Present Age," 1940), published under his own name on 30 March 1846. Kierkegaard's interest in Gyllembourg, Heiberg's mother, was no accident, and yet her comparison of the revolutionary 1790s of her youth with the relatively tame 1840s in *To Tidsaldre* was affirmed in

Kierkegaard's characterizations of the masses, the process of democratization, and the public. The politically engaged period of the movement in Denmark toward representative government, which in 1849 replaced absolute monarchy, had warned him that content could be boosted by form when supported by such abstractions as "the public": "Publikum er Alt og Intet, er den farligste af alle Magter og den meest intetsigende; man kan tale til en heel Nation i Publikums Navn, og dog er Publikum mindre end et eneste nok saa ringe virkeligt Menneske" (A public is everything and nothing, the most dangerous of all powers and the most insignificant; one can speak to a whole nation in the name of the public, and still the public will be less than a single real man, however unimportant). The alternative, for both Kierkegaard and Gyllembourg, was an age without passion.

Opbyggelige Taler i forskjellig Aand (Edifying Discourses in Various Spirits, 1847) is divided into three parts, each with its own title page to emphasize the distinctions. The first consists of the confessional discourse "Hjertes Renhed er at ville Eet" (Purity of Heart Is to Will One Thing; translated as *Purify Your Hearts!* 1937). God is understood as an eternity in each individual, the good, and when a person wills the good, he wills only one thing, and therefore his heart is pure. The second discourse demonstrates how one may learn to be untroubled by the temporal from the lilies of the field and the birds of the air. The final discourse is "Lidelsernes Evangelium" (translated as "The Gospel of Suffering," 1947), in which suffering is understood as a privilege that may prepare one for eternity. These discourses are referred to as Christian, and thereby Kierkegaard singled them out as expressions of the more strict understanding of Christianity he had developed over the years. The same sentiment is found in the subtitle, *Nogle christelige Overveielser i Talers Form* (Some Christian Reflections in the Form of Discourses), of *Kjerlighedens Gjerninger* (1847; translated as *Works of Love,* 1946), in which Kierkegaard, writing under his own name, offers a Christian ethics. The acts implied by love are understood as set down by God, and in the first section the Commandment on love of one's neighbor is analyzed.

In 1848 Kierkegaard published *Christelige Taler* (translated as "Christian Discourses," 1939). The following year, he published *Lilien paa Marken og Fuglen under Himlen. Tre gudelige Taler* (The Lily of the Field and the Bird beneath the Heavens: Three Devotional Discourses; translated as "The Lilies of the Field and the Birds of the Air," 1939). Here, the effort is directed at demonstrating the difference between poetry and Christianity, which, unlike the former, does not seduce through beauty. One may learn silence from the lily

Regine Olsen Schlegel in 1855, the year of Kierkegaard's death; he had broken off their engagement fifteen years earlier (courtesy of the Danish Royal Library, Copenhagen)

and the bird, who are absolutely obedient. Silence is an expression of deferential respect for that with which one cannot speak and also the beginning of the search for the kingdom of God.

Tvende ethisk-religieuse Smaa-Afhandlinger (translated in *The Present Age and Two Minor Ethico-Religious Treatises,* 1940) was published under the pseudonym H.H. on 19 May 1849. The title of the first treatise poses a question: "Har et Menneske Lov til at lade sig ihjelslaae for Sandheden?" (Does a Person Have the Right to Let Himself Be Put to Death for the Truth?). The answer is no, if it is a worldly truth, over which one could argue with another who thinks otherwise. Nor is it permissible if the action is the result of a discussion between Christians with a different understanding of the truth. But perhaps a person does have this right if Christendom is not at all Christian but in fact more heathen than heathendom. The essay also includes discussion of the question of martyrdom. In this connection Kierkegaard uses for the first time the concept of the witness for the truth. The second of the two essays, "Om Forskjellen mellem et Genie og en Apostel" (On the Difference Between a Genius and an Apostle), is a small excerpt from a large manuscript on the Bornholm pastor Adolf Peter Adler, which Kierkegaard had begun in 1846 but by and large chose to withhold from publication. The manuscript was found among his papers and was published posthumously in *Søren Kierkegaards Papirer* (1908–1948) as "Bogen om Adler" (The Book on Adler; translated as *On Authority and Revelation: The Book on Adler; or, A Cycle of Ethico-Religious Essays,* 1955). While the genius, the poetic author, receives his extraordinary ability from God, he does not write with a purpose, whereas the apostle has a calling, a commandment from God: "absolute paradox et 'for at'" (absolutely and paradoxically, an "in order that"). The apostle is a paradoxical figure, made for imitation.

Now Kierkegaard, after long deliberations, took a new pseudonym, Anti-Climacus. He defined his own position as between that of Climacus, who thought himself incapable of realizing religiousness B, and that of Anti-Climacus, who characterized himself as a Christian in the absolute sense. Because of his nearness and somewhat vacillating relationship to these two pseudonyms, Kierkegaard functioned as "editor" of the writings of both. *Sygdommen til Døden* (translated as *The Sickness unto Death,* 1941) was published as the work of Anti-Climacus in 1849; the subtitle, *En christelig psychologisk Udvikling til Opbyggelse og Opvækkelse* (A Christian Psychological Exposition for Edification and Awakening), indicates that Kierkegaard's intention was to influence readers in a Christian direction by means of a psychological investigation. Anti-Climacus takes as his starting point *Frygt og Bæven* when he defines the human self as set out by God and as "another," who appears when the relationship between soul and body is made apparent. The sickness unto death should not be understood as a sickness that leads to death but as the despair in either not willing or willing to be a self. Soul and body both belong to the mortal, but when God has set them in relation, the self is immortal. Despair is sin, and sin is the sickness that exists in a contradiction between the temporal and the eternal in the soul. This sickness may in the meantime lead to a rising acknowledgment of sin and hence to faith. In reference to Romans 14:23, Anti-Climacus emphasizes that the opposite of sin is not virtue but faith. The accompanying discourses to *Sygdommen til Døden* were published in November 1849 as *"Ypperstepræsten," "Tolderen," "Synderinden." Tre Taler ved Altergangen om Fredagen* ("The Greatest Pastor," "The Customs Official," "The Sinneress": Three Discourses at the Communion on Fridays; translated as "Three Discourses at the Communion on Fridays," 1939). In these works Kierkegaard continued the series of Communion discourses that he had begun in the final section of *Christelige Taler.*

In December 1850 Kierkegaard published Anti-Climacus's *Indøvelse i Christendom* (translated as *Training in Christianity,* 1941). This work, in which the Christian challenge is most intensified, was supplemented by *En opbyggelig Tale* (translated as "An Upbuilding Discourse," 1997), in which the ritualization of the discourse series had gone so far that the preface includes only a note referring to the preface of the *To opbyggelige Taler* of 1843. *Indøvelse i Christendom* forms the foundation of Kierkegaard's later conflict with the Danish State Lutheran Church, which had its basis in the idea that Christianity had drifted from the Christian; hence, the task was now to reintroduce Christianity to Christendom. In place of what, in his opinion, was a heathen admiration of Christianity, exemplified by the Christian art of the profound thinkers of Christianity and the sermons and analyses of theologians, Anti-Climacus argues for an understanding of Christianity as imitation. He desires not to judge, but to serve the truth; that is, Christianity in its strictest sense. He does not assert that every true Christian should follow Christ as a martyr for faith; yet, he finds it reasonable that every true Christian should "gjøre en Ydmygelsens Inddrømmelse, at han dog er sluppet lettere end de i strengeste Forstand sande Christne" (make a confession of humility, that he has gotten by more easily than they who are true Christians in the strongest sense of the word). Without naming names, Kierkegaard had already criticized the Christianity of Mynster and the theology professor Hans Lassen Martensen.

After his many problems in distinguishing his own position from that of Anti-Climacus, Kierkegaard finally abandoned indirect communication in 1851, when, under his own name, he published a summary of all the books he had written since *Enten-Eller*. *Om min Forfatter-Virksomhed* was actually only a short summary of the more in-depth *Synspunktet for min Forfatter-Virksomhed,* which, although written in 1848, did not appear until 1859, when Peter Christian Kierkegaard, his brother, published the manuscript. Neither of the two works lifts the veil on Søren Kierkegaard's authorship. Nor do they include commentary on the journals and unpublished, uncompleted manuscripts that were found in his workplace after his death. All of these papers, which, taken together, constitute far more pages than those that Kierkegaard allowed to be published during his lifetime, reveal doubt and conflict all along the way. But of this doubt the public was made aware only with the posthumous publication–and then only in part–of Kierkegaard's papers. In both *Om min Forfatter-Virksomhed* and *Synspunktet for min Forfatter-Virksomhed* his primary intention is to demonstrate that throughout he was a Christian author. In the latter work he writes that he has set forth "Christendommen, det at blive Christen, heelt og holdent ind i Reflexion" (Christianity, what it means to become a Christian, wholly and entirely within reflection). He continues spontaneously: "Hans Hjertes Reenhed var: kun at ville Eet; hvad der i levende Live var de Samtidiges Anklage mod ham, at han ikke vilde slaae af, ikke give efter, netop det Samme er Eftertidens Lovtale over ham, at han ikke slog af, ikke gave efter" (His purity of heart was to will only one thing. What his contemporaries complained of during his lifetime, that he would not abate the price, would not give in–this very thing is the eulogy pronounced upon him by after ages, that he did not abate the price, did not give in). In the end, he concludes by attributing his entire body of work to "bestyrelsen" (governance) and by describing himself as "Forfatteren, der, historisk, døde af en dødelig Sygdom, men digterisk døde af Længsel efter Evigheden, for uafbrudt ikke at bestille andet end takke Gud" (the author, who historically died of a mortal disease but poetically died of longing for eternity, where uninterruptedly he would have nothing else to do but to thank God).

On 7 August 1851, the day after *Om min Forfatter-Virksomhed* appeared, *To Taler ved Altergangen om Fredagen* (translated as "Two Discourses at the Communion on Fridays," 1941) was published; again, Kierkegaard's intention was to cease writing at this time. Yet, on 10 September he published *Til Selvprøvelse, Samtiden anbefalet* (translated as *For Self-Examination, Recommended for the Times,* 1940). In this work he was on the verge of formulating his attack on the Danish State Lutheran Church, but he held back out of concern for the aging Mynster. In 1851 and 1852 Kierkegaard worked on *Dømmer selv! Til Selvprøvelse, Samtiden anbefalet* (translated as "Judge for Yourselves!" 1941), but for the same reason it was kept back and remained unpublished until Peter Christian Kierkegaard brought it out in 1876. Both *Til Selvprøvelse* and *Dømmer selv!* are attempts at a broader, more popular formulation of the Christian message. In the former, Kierkegaard disavowed himself of the role of witness for the truth, describing himself only as "en umyndig Digter, der rører ved hjælp af Idealerne for at opnaa 'Redelighed'" (a poet without authority, who with the help of the ideal tries to achieve "honesty"). While he waited in vain for the Church, through the figure of Mynster, to admit what he later called the "Kriminal-Forbrydelse" (criminal acts) of Christendom, he wrote much in his journal but published nothing.

Mynster died on 30 January 1854. Two days before Mynster's burial, on 7 February, Martensen, who had been a tutor to the student Kierkegaard, gave a speech in Christiansborg Chapel in which he praised Mynster, referring to him as a witness for the truth. For Kierkegaard the term *witness for the truth* indicated either martyrdom or confession, and from both of these traditions Mynster had remained distant. Kierkegaard

Karikaturtegning af Søren Kierkegaard.

Caricature of Kierkegaard by Wilhelm Marstrand, circa 1870 (courtesy of the Danish Royal Library, Copenhagen)

immediately wrote a rebuttal but withheld it until 18 December of that year, in order to avoid the association of his intentions with the naming of the new bishop. The title of the article demonstrated the new, hard-edged journalistic style characteristic of his struggle against the Church: "Var Biskop Mynster et 'Sandhedsvidne,' et af 'de rette Sandhedsvidner'–er *dette* Sandhed?" (Was Bishop Mynster a "witness for the truth," one of "the genuine witnesses for the truth"–is *that* the truth?). Predictably, Martensen received the appointment as bishop. The first phase of Kierkegaard's struggle against the Church consisted of, in all, twenty-one articles published in the daily *Fædrelandet* (The Fatherland). It may be seen from the title of the last article, published on 26 May 1855, that Martensen (who continued Mynster's policy of silence toward the attack, which was otherwise loud enough) was himself the real target of Kierkegaard's polemic: "At Biskop Martensens Taushed er 1) christeligt uforsvarlig; 2) latterlig; 3) dum-klog; 4) i mere end en Henseende foragtelig" (That Bishop Martensen's Silence Is 1) Christianly

Indefensible; 2) Laughable; 3) Dumb-Clever; 4) In More Than One Respect Contemptible). Kierkegaard attacked not only Martensen's attitude but also his Hegelian theology in the salvos of satire, which he furthermore began to direct at still others: first, the "velvet-bellied pastors"; then, all of the citizens who believed themselves Christians; and finally, Christendom itself. From 24 May, Kierkegaard continued the attack in his own journal, *Øieblikket* (translated as "The Moment," 1998), the ninth issue of which appeared on 24 September 1855. He continued the critique as well in the pamphlet *Hvad Christus dømmer om officiel Christendom* (translated as "What Christ Judges of Official Christianity," 1998), published on 16 June, and in the last of the edifying discourses, *Guds Uforanderlighed.*

Common to all the issues of *Øieblikket* is the concise format and a direct, aggressive style, much closer to journalism than to the academic prose of the period. From this platform Kierkegaard came full circle in terms of genre, with the aphorisms of "Kort og Spidst" (Short and Sharp), which in form point back to the "Diapsalmata"; biblical interpretations that resemble the edifying discourses; the short story "*Først* Guds Rige" (*First* the Kingdom of God); and satirical mini-essays, which are the form most liberally represented. Many of the texts are witty to the point of mockery, just as when Kierkegaard was a boy.

The manuscript to the tenth issue of *Øieblikket* was ready for publication at the time of Kierkegaard's death. In "Min Opgave" (My Task), dated 1 September 1855, he attempted again to define his position. The world, in which all call themselves Christian, is referred to as "Vrøvlets Verden" (The World of Nonsense). In it the truth seems to be madness; hence, Kierkegaard asserts that he himself is not a Christian. He characterizes himself as a unique figure in the 1,800-year history of Christianity. His only model is Socrates, who exposed paganism and became a martyr for his thought: "Du Oldtidens ædle Eenfoldige, du er det eneste *Menneske,* jeg beundrende anerkjender som Tænker: det er kun Lidt, der er opbevaret om Dig, blandt Mennesker den eneste sande Intellectualitetens Martyr, lige saa stor *qva* Charakteer som *qva* Tænker; men dette Lidet hvor uendelig Meget!" (Thou noble simpleton of olden times, thou, the only *man* I admiringly recognize as a teacher; there is but little concerning thee that has been preserved, thou amongst men the only true martyr to intellectuality, just as great *qua* character as *qua* thinker; but this little, how infinitely much it is!). The analogy with the hero of *Om Begrebet Ironi med stadigt Hensyn til Socrates* consists in Kierkegaard's defining his task as Socratic after Christ: "at revidere Bestemmelsen af det at være Christen: selv kalder jeg mig ikke en Christen (holdende Idealet frit), men jeg kan gjøre aabenbart, at de Andre ere det endnu mindre" (to revise the definition of what it is to be a Christian: I do not call myself a "Christian" [thus keeping the ideal free], but I am able to make it evident that the others are that still less than I).

Søren Kierkegaard died at Frederik's Hospital (now the Museum of Applied Arts) on Bredgade in Copenhagen at nine o'clock on the night of 11 November 1855. His funeral service was performed at Vor Frue Kirke on the eighteenth of the month. He was buried at the family plot in Assistens Kirkegaard. In accordance with his wishes, his gravestone bears a verse from the Danish hymn writer Hans Adolph Brorson–a final nod to Kierkegaard's connection to the pietistic tradition, to which his father also belonged:

Det er en liden Tid,
Saa har jeg vundet,
Saa er den ganske Strid
Med Eet forsvunden,
Saa kan jeg hvile mig
I Rosensale,
Og uafladelig
Min Jesum Tale.

(In but a little while
Then I will have won,
Then is the entire strife
All of a sudden gone,
Then can I rest
In rose halls
And uninterruptedly
Speak with my Jesus.)

Kierkegaard's oeuvre belongs among the most significant bodies of thought in a global context. His work provided a fundamental critique of Hegel's ideas, which had dominated European philosophy during the first half of the nineteenth century, and it contributed a new concept of the individual to the Modern Breakthrough in Scandinavian literature during the second half of that century. Kierkegaard's significance for twentieth-century philosophy and theology, not to mention literature, was also decisive. He formulated an understanding of identity, relevant to Christians and non-Christians alike, that elevated the idea of the individual into the forefront of contemporary discourse. Interest in his work is continually rejuvenated by the demands of the modern age on the individual to make existential choices, especially in eras marked by violent upheaval. With the individual as his point of departure, Kierkegaard brought the basic concepts of his philosophy of personality–irony, angst, the stages, repetition, and the moment–into everyday language. By virtue of his critique of Hegelian idealism, which placed him in stark contrast to his European contemporaries,

Kierkegaard may be regarded as a poet-philosopher. Finally, he is of great significance to the Danish language as a prose stylist, a writer who understood how to draw out the rhythms and nuances of the language.

Letters:

Søren Kierkegaards og Kolderup Rosenvinges Spasereture i Breve, edited by Hans Ostenfeldt Lange (Copenhagen: Gad, 1898);

Søren Kierkegaard og Emil Boesen. Breve og Indledning, med et Tillaeg, edited by Carl Frederik Koch (Copenhagen: K. Schønberg, 1901);

Breve og Aktstykker vedrørende Søren Kierkegaard, 2 volumes, edited by Niels Thulstrup (Copenhagen: Munksgaard, 1953–1954); translated by Henrik Rosenmeier as *Letters and Documents,* volume 25 of *Kierkegaard's Writings,* edited by Howard V. Hong and Edna H. Hong (Princeton: Princeton University Press, 1978).

Bibliographies:

Thomas Hansen Erslew, *Almindeligt Forfatter-Lexicon for Kongeriget Danmark med tilhørende Bilandes, fra 1814 til 1840,* volume 2 (Copenhagen: Furlagsforeningen, 1847), pp. 24–25;

Erslew, *Almindeligt Forfatters-Lexicon for Kongeriget Danmark med tilhørende Bilande, fra før 1819 til 1840. Supplementindtil Adgangen af Aaret 1853,* volume 2 (Copenhagen: Forlagsforeningen, 1864), pp. 34–42;

Jens Himmelstrup, *Søren Kierkegaard. International Bibliografi* (Copenhagen: Nyt Nordisk Forlag/A. Busck, 1962);

Aage Jørgensen, *Søren Kierkegaard-litteratur, 1961–1970. En foreløbig bibliografi* (Aarhus: Akademisk Boghandel, 1971);

Franca Castagnino, *Gli studi italiani su Kierkegaard, 1906–1966* (Rome: Edizioni dell'Ateneo, 1972);

François H. Lapointe, *Sören Kierkegaard and His Critics: An International Bibliography of Criticism* (Westport, Conn.: Greenwood Press, 1980);

Karol Toeplitz, "Bibliografia opracowan pogladów S. A. Kierkegaarda," *Studia Filozoficzne,* 3 (1981): 157–176;

Jørgensen, *Søren Kierkegaard-litteratur, 1971–1980. En bibliografi* (Aarhus: Privately printed, 1983);

Jørgensen, *Dansk litteraturhistorisk bibliografi, 1967–1986* (Copenhagen: Dansklærerforeningen, 1989), pp. 238–273;

Calvin D. Evans, *Søren Kierkegaard Bibliographies: Remnants, 1944–1980, and Multi-Media, 1925–1991* (Montreal: McGill University Libraries, 1993);

Jun Hashimoto, Michimune Madenokoji, and Takahiro Hirabayashi, *Søren Kierkegaard litteratur i Japan, 1906–1979* (N.p.: Kwansei Gakuin University, 1995).

Biographies:

Georg Brandes, *Søren Kierkegaard. En kritisk Fremstilling i Grundrids* (Copenhagen: Gyldendal, 1877); revised in his *Samlede Skrifter,* volume 2 (Copenhagen: Gyldendal, 1899); reprinted as *Søren Kierkegaard. En kritisk Fremstilling i Grundrids* (Copenhagen: Gyldendal, 1967);

Walter Lowrie, *Kierkegaard* (London & New York: Oxford University Press, 1938);

Johannes Hohlenberg, *Søren Kierkegaard* (Copenhagen: H. Hagerup, 1940); translated by Thomas Henry Croxall (New York: Pantheon, 1954);

Josiah Thompson, *Kierkegaard* (New York: Knopf, 1973);

Joakim Garff, *SAK, Søren Aabye Kierkegaard. En biografi* (Copenhagen: Gad, 2000);

Alastair Hannay, *Kierkegaard: A Biography* (Cambridge & New York: Cambridge University Press, 2001).

References:

Theodor W. Adorno, *Kierkegaard. Konstruktion des Äesthetischen,* Beiträge zur Philosophie und ihrer Geschichte, no. 2 (Tübingen: Mohr, 1933; revised edition, Frankfurt am Main: Suhrkamp, 1962);

Heinrich Anz, Poul Lübke, and Friedrich Schmöe, eds., *Die Rezeption Søren Kierkegaards in der deutschen und dänischen Philosophie und Theologie: Vorträge des Kolloquiums am 22. und 23. März 1982,* Text und Kontext, Sonderreihe, no. 15 (Copenhagen: W. Fink, 1983);

Frederik J. Billeskov Jansen, *Hvordan skal vi studere Søren Kierkegaard?* (Copenhagen: Munksgaard, 1949);

Billeskov Jansen, *Studier i Søren Kierkegaards litterære Kunst* (Copenhagen: Rosenkilde & Bagger, 1951);

Torsten Bohlin, *Kierkegaards dogmatiska Åskådning i dess historiska Sammanhang* (Stockholm: Svenska Kyrkans Diakonistyrelses Bokförlag, 1925);

Bohlin, *Søren Kierkegaards etiska Åskådning, med särskild Hänsyn till Begreppet 'Den Enskilde'* (Stockholm: Svenska Kyrkans Diakonistyrelses Bokförlag, 1918);

Jørgen Bonde Jensen, *Jeg er kun en digter. Om Søren Kierkegaard som skribent* (Copenhagen: Babette, 1996);

Frithiof Brandt, *Den unge Søren Kierkegaard* (Copenhagen: Levin & Munksgaard, 1929);

Brandt and Else Rammel, *Søren Kierkegaard og Pengene* (Copenhagen: Levin & Munksgaard, 1935);

Jørgen K. Bukdahl, ed., *Kierkegaard and Dialectics: Lectures, Originally Delivered at a Symposium, in the Series of Scientific Symposia, Arranged to Celebrate the 50th Anniversary of the University of Aarhus, Held September 13th–16th, 1978 in Aarhus* (Aarhus: University of Aarhus/Institute for Ethics and the Philosophy of Religion, 1979);

Niels Jørgen Cappelørn and Hermann Deuser, eds., *Kierkegaard Studies: Yearbook 1996* (Berlin & New York: De Gruyter, 1997);

Arnold B. Come, *Kierkegaard as Humanist: Discovering My Self* (Montreal: McGill-Queen's University Press, 1995);

Come, *Kierkegaard as Theologian: Recovering My Self* (Montreal: McGill-Queen's University Press, 1997);

Hermann Diem, *Die Existenzdialektik von Sören Kierkegaard* (Zollikon-Zürich: Evangelischer Verlag, 1950); translated by Harold Knight as *Kierkegaard's Dialectic of Existence* (Edinburgh: Oliver & Boyd, 1959);

Diem, *Sören Kierkegaard: Spion in Dienste Gottes* (Frankfurt am Main: S. Fischer, 1957);

Frank Eberhard-Wilde, Niels Thulstrup, and Wolfdietrich von Kloeden, *Kierkegaard and Speculative Idealism,* edited by Thulstrup, Bibliotheca Kierkegaardiana, no. 4 (Copenhagen: C. A. Reitzel, 1979);

C. Stephen Evans, *Kierkegaard's "Fragments" and "Postscript": The Religious Philosophy of Johannes Climacus* (Atlantic Highlands, N.J.: Humanities Press, 1983);

Henning Fenger, *Kierkegaard-Myter og Kierkegaard-Kilder. 9 kildekritiske studier i de Kierkegaardske papirer, breve og aktstykker* (Odense: Odense University Press, 1976); translated by George C. Schoolfield as *Kierkegaard, the Myths and their Origins: Studies in the Kierkegaardian Papers and Letters* (New Haven: Yale University Press, 1980);

Joakim Garff, *"Den Søvnløse." Kierkegaard læst æstetisk/biografisk* (Copenhagen: C. A. Reitzel, 1995);

Eduard Geismar, *Søren Kierkegaard. Hans Livsudvikling og Forfattervirksomhed,* 2 volumes (Copenhagen: Gad, 1927, 1928);

Arne Grøn, *Begrebet Angst hos Søren Kierkegaard* (Copenhagen: Gyldendal, 1993);

Grøn, *Subjektivitet og negativitet. Kierkegaard* (Copenhagen: Gyldendal, 1997);

Leif Bork Hansen, *Søren Kierkegaards hemmelighed og eksistensdialektik* (Copenhagen: C. A. Reitzel, 1994);

Hjalmar Helweg, *Søren Kierkegaard. En psykiatrisk-psykologisk Studie* (Copenhagen: H. Hagerup, 1933);

Aage Henriksen, *Kierkegaards Romaner* (Copenhagen: Gyldendal, 1954);

Emanuel Hirsch, *Kierkegaard-Studien,* 2 volumes (Gütersloh: C. Bertelsmann, 1930, 1933);

Hirsch, *Wege zu Kierkegaard* (Berlin: Die Spur, 1968);

Johannes Hohlenberg, *Den Ensommes Vej. En Fremstilling af Søren Kierkegaards Værk* (Copenhagen: H. Hagerup, 1948);

Poul Houe, Gordon D. Marino, and Sven Hakon Rossel, eds., *Anthropology and Authority: Essays on Søren Kierkegaard,* Internationale Forschungen zur allgemeinen und vergleichenden Literaturwissenschaft, no. 44 (Amsterdam & Atlanta: Rodopi, 2000);

Merete Jørgensen, *Kierkegaard som kritiker. En undersøgelse af forholdet mellem det æstetiske og det etiske i Kierkegaards litterære kritik* (Copenhagen: Gyldendal, 1978);

Aage Kabell, *Kierkegaardstudiet i Norden* (Copenhagen: H. Hagerup, 1948);

Kierkegaardiana (1955–);

Kierkegaard-Studiet (1964–);

Anders Kingo, *Analogiens teologi. En dogmatisk studie over dialektikken i Søren Kierkegaards opbyggelige og pseudonyme forfatterskab* (Copenhagen: Gad, 1995);

Bruce H. Kirmmse, *Kierkegaard in Golden Age Denmark* (Bloomington: Indiana University Press, 1990);

Kirmmse, ed., *Encounters with Kierkegaard: A Life as Seen by His Contemporaries,* translated by Kirmmse (Princeton: Princeton University Press, 1996);

Carl Henrik Koch, *En flue på Hegels udødelige næse, eller, Om Adolph Peter Adler og om Søren Kierkegaards forhold til ham* (Copenhagen: C. A. Reitzel, 1990);

Sejer Kühle, *Søren Kierkegaards barndom og ungdom* (Copenhagen: Aschehoug, 1950);

Knud Ejler Løgstrup, *Opgør med Kierkegaard* (Copenhagen: Gyldendal, 1968);

Gregor Malantschuk, *Dialektik og Eksistens hos Søren Kierkegaard* (Copenhagen: H. Reitzel, 1968); edited and translated by Howard V. Hong and Edna H. Hong as *Kierkegaard's Thought* (Princeton: Princeton University Press, 1971);

Malantschuk, *Frihed og Eksistens. Studier i Søren Kierkegaards tænkning,* edited by Cappelørn and Paul Müller (Copenhagen: C. A. Reitzel, 1980);

P. M. Mitchell, *A History of Danish Literature* (Copenhagen: Gyldendal, 1957), pp. 115, 124, 126, 137, 142–149, 166, 175, 177, 208, 284–285, 291, 300;

Finn Hauberg Mortensen, *Kierkegaard Made in Japan* (Odense: Odense University Press, 1996);

Kresten Nordentoft, *"Hvad siger Brand-Majoren?" Kierkegaards opgør med sin samtid* (Copenhagen: Gad, 1973);

Nordentoft, *Kierkegaards psykologi* (Copenhagen: Gad, 1972); translated by Kirmmse as *Kierkegaard's Psychology* (Pittsburgh: Duquesne University Press, 1978);

Nota Bene: Quaderni di studi Kierkegaardiani (2000–);

Ib Ostenfeld, *Søren Kierkegaards psykologi. Undersøgelse og indlevelse* (Copenhagen: Rhodos, 1972);

Teddy Petersen, *Kierkegaards polemiske debut. Artikler 1834–36 i historisk sammenhæng* (Odense: Odense University Press, 1977);

Hermann Peter Rohde, ed., *Auktionsprotokol over Søren Kierkegaards bogsamling* (Copenhagen: Kongelige Bibliotek, 1967);

Johannes Sløk, *Die Anthropologie Kierkegaards* (Copenhagen: Rosenkilde & Bagger, 1954);

Sløk, *Kierkegaard. Humanismens tænker* (Copenhagen: H. Reitzel, 1978);

Joseph H. Smith, Harold A. Durfee, and Gloria H. Parloff, eds., *Kierkegaard's Truth: The Disclosure of the Self,* Psychiatry and the Humanities, no. 5 (New Haven: Yale University Press, 1981);

Mark C. Taylor, *Journeys to Selfhood, Hegel & Kierkegaard* (Berkeley: University of California Press, 1980);

Michael Theunissen and Wilfried Greve, eds., *Materialen zur Philosophie Søren Kierkegaards* (Frankfurt am Main: Suhrkamp, 1979);

Josiah Thompson, ed., *Kierkegaard: A Collection of Critical Essays* (Garden City, N.Y.: Anchor/Doubleday, 1972);

Marie Mikulová Thulstrup, *Kierkegaard i kristenlivets historie* (Copenhagen: C. A. Reitzel, 1991);

Marie Mikulová Thulstrup, ed., *Concepts and Alternatives in Kierkegaard,* Bibliotheca Kierkegaardiana, no. 3 (Copenhagen: C. A. Reitzel, 1980);

Marie Mikulová Thulstrup, ed., *Some of Kierkegaard's Main Categories,* Bibliotheca Kierkegaardiana, no. 16 (Copenhagen: C. A. Reitzel, 1988);

Niels Thulstrup, *Commentary on Kierkegaard's Concluding Unscientific Postscript,* translated by Robert J. Widenmann (Princeton: Princeton University Press, 1984);

Niels Thulstrup, *The Copenhagen of Kierkegaard,* edited by Marie Mikulová Thulstrup, Bibliotheca Kierkegaardiana, no. 11 (Copenhagen: C. A. Reitzel, 1986);

Niels Thulstrup, *Kierkegaard and the Church in Denmark,* edited by Niels Thulstrup and Marie Mikulová Thulstrup, translated by Frederick H. Cryer, Bibliotheca Kierkegaardiana, no. 13 (Copenhagen: C. A. Reitzel, 1984);

Niels Thulstrup, *Kierkegaards Forhold til Hegel og til den spekulative Idealisme indtil 1846* (Copenhagen: Gyldendal, 1967);

Niels Thulstrup and Marie Mikulová Thulstrup, eds., *Kierkegaard: Literary Miscellany,* Bibliotheca Kierkegaardiana, no. 9 (Copenhagen: C. A. Reitzel, 1981);

Niels Thulstrup and Marie Mikulová Thulstrup, eds., *Kierkegaard and Great Traditions,* Bibliotheca Kierkegaardiana, no. 6 (Copenhagen: C. A. Reitzel, 1981);

Niels Thulstrup and Marie Mikulová Thulstrup, eds., *Kierkegaard and Human Values,* Bibliotheca Kierkegaardiana, no. 7 (Copenhagen: C. A. Reitzel, 1980);

Niels Thulstrup and Marie Mikulová Thulstrup, eds., *Kierkegaard as a Person,* Bibliotheca Kierkegaardiana, no. 12 (Copenhagen: C. A. Reitzel, 1983);

Niels Thulstrup and Marie Mikulová Thulstrup, eds., *Kierkegaard Research,* Bibliotheca Kierkegaardiana, no. 15 (Copenhagen: C. A. Reitzel, 1987);

Niels Thulstrup and Marie Mikulová Thulstrup, eds., *Kierkegaard's Classical Inspiration,* Bibliotheca Kierkegaardiana, no. 14 (Copenhagen: C. A. Reitzel, 1985);

Niels Thulstrup and Marie Mikulová Thulstrup, eds., *Kierkegaard's Teachers,* Bibliotheca Kierkegaardiana, no. 10 (Copenhagen: C. A. Reitzel, 1982);

Niels Thulstrup and Marie Mikulová Thulstrup, eds., *Kierkegaard's View of Christianity,* Bibliotheca Kierkegaardiana, no. 1 (Copenhagen: C. A. Reitzel, 1978);

Niels Thulstrup and Marie Mikulová Thulstrup, eds., *The Legacy and Interpretation of Kierkegaard,* Bibliotheca Kierkegaardiana, no. 8 (Copenhagen: C. A. Reitzel, 1981);

Niels Thulstrup and Marie Mikulová Thulstrup, eds., *The Sources and Depths of Faith in Kierkegaard,* Bibliotheca Kierkegaardiana, no. 2 (Copenhagen: C. A. Reitzel, 1978);

Niels Thulstrup and Marie Mikulová Thulstrup, eds., *Theological Concepts in Kierkegaard,* Bibliotheca Kierkegaardiana, no. 5 (Copenhagen: C. A. Reitzel, 1980);

Carl Weltzer, *Grundtvig og Søren Kierkegaard* (Copenhagen: Gyldendal, 1952);

Weltzer, *Peter og Søren Kierkegaard* (Copenhagen: Gad, 1936);

Johannes Witt-Hansen, ed., *Kierkegaard and Contemporary Philosophy* (Copenhagen: Munksgaard, 1971).

Papers:

Søren Kierkegaard's papers and manuscripts are at the Danish Royal Library in Copenhagen.

Thomas Kingo

(15 December 1634 - 14 October 1703)

Niels Ingwersen
University of Wisconsin–Madison

MANUSCRIPTS (handwritten manuscripts circulated as books, later published in collections): "Næfvetuud og Knud her-ud" (Completed circa 1660s);
"Sæbye-gaards Koeklage" (Completed in 1665);
"Hosianna ved Christian V's Salvning" (Completed in 1671);
"De Fattiges udi Odensee Hospital" (Completed in 1682);
"Candida" (Completed in 1694).

Copperplate by Gerard Valck (1704) based on a painting by an unknown artist (circa 1689); courtesy of the Danish Royal Library, Copenhagen

BOOKS: *Dend viit-berømte Danmarckis Hovet-Fæstnings Kroneborgs korte Beskrifvelse* (Copenhagen: Printed by Matthias Jørgens-Søn, 1672);
Aandelige Siunge-Koors første Part, indeholdende 14 Gudelige Morgen- og Aften-Sange, tilligemed de 7 Kong Davids Poenitendse Psalmer sangviis forfattede (Copenhagen: Daniel Eichhorn, 1674);
Samsøes Korte Beskrivelse (Copenhagen: Printed by Christen Jensøn Bering, 1675);
Christian dend Femte, Konge til Danmarck etc., hans Majestæts første og Lyksalige Ledings-Tog Aar 1675 til ævig Hukommelse (Copenhagen: Printed by Matthias Jørgensen, 1676);
Aandelige Siunge-Koors Anden Part eller Sjælens Opvækkelse til allehaande Andagter i allehaande Tilfælde (Copenhagen: Daniel Paulli, 1681)–includes "Far, Verden, Farvel," partially translated by George Johnston as "Farewell, World, Farewell," in Jørgen Frantz Jacobsen, *Barbara* (Norwich: Norvik, 1993), pp. 63–66; "Hver har sin Skiebne," translated by John A. Duisinger as "Everyone Has His Destiny," in *An Anthology of Danish Literature,* edited by F. J. Billeskov Jansen and P. M. Mitchell (Carbondale: Southern Illinois University Press, 1972), pp. 86–89; and "Over Kedron Jesus træder," translated anonymously as "Over Cedron Jesus Passes," in *Songs from Denmark,* edited by Peter Balslev-Clausen (Copenhagen: Det danske Selskab, 1988), pp. 68–69;
Danmarks og Norges Kirkers forordnede Psalme-Bog. Vinter Parten: Efter sær kongel. Befalning af sal. D. Mort. Luthers, saa og andre gudfrygtige lærde Mænds Sange og gamle Kirke Psalmer sammendragen, og med en stoor Deel til Høitiderne . . . forbedret (Odense: Thomas Kingo, 1689)–includes "Som den gyldne Sool frembryder," translated by J. C. Aaberg as "Like the Golden Sun Ascending," in *Songs from Denmark,* edited by Balslev-Clausen (Copenhagen: Det danske Selskab, 1988), pp. 71–72.

Editions and Collections: *Samlede Skrifter,* 7 volumes, edited by Hans Brix, Paul Diderichsen, and F. J. Billeskov Jansen (Copenhagen: Ejnar Munksgaard, 1939–1975);
Thomas Kingos Graduale, edited by Erik Norman Svendsen and Henrik Glahn (Odense: Printed by Christian Schrøder, 1967);

Som dend gyldne Sool frembryder: salmer og digte, edited by Erik Sønderholm, graphic works by Bodil Kaalund (Herning: Poul Kristensen, 1985);

Digte (Copenhagen: Hans Reitzel, 1989);

Digtning i udvalg, edited by Marita Akhøj Nielsen (Copenhagen: Borgen, 1995).

Edition in English: "Admiral Niels Juel's Epitaph," translated by R. P. Keigwin in *In Denmark I Was Born,* edited by Keigwin (Copenhagen: Høst, 1950).

In 1995, Marita Akhøj Nielsen, a specialist on Thomas Kingo, wrote that the hymnist was the earliest Danish poet who is well known today. Kingo's hymns, even if abridged, are still sung in Danish churches and schools. One hymn in particular has gained preeminence–"Far, Verden, Farvel" (Fare, World, Farewell, 1681). That eloquent hymn must be included in any baroque anthology.

In Jørgen-Frantz Jacobsen's erotic novel *Barbara* (1939; translated, 1948), which takes place in the eighteenth century, the hymn completely dominates one chapter. The congregation of the Faroese town of Thorshavn assembles in a small church to listen to its Lutheran minister. As he preaches, he glances out a window and realizes that his wife is engaged in a tryst with a friend of the house. That discovery inspires him to preach with a vigor that surprises and impresses his congregation, whose members are then asked to sing the unscheduled hymn "Far, Verden, Farvel." Jacobsen records how various individuals respond to the stanzas they are singing, and clearly Kingo's stinging words on the vanity of this world strike home, often harshly.

Jacobsen captured a special feature of Kingo's best hymns: in them Kingo speaks to the individual rather than to the congregation. That claim may seem curious, for of course the *I* that appears in "Far, Verden, Farvel" and other hymns is the representative *I* with which the entire congregation was supposed to identify. If the congregation were singing the works of such later hymnists as Hans Adolph Brorson or N. F. S. Grundtvig, their *I* would function to give a sense of unification to all the members of the congregation, but Kingo is more modern and alive than many later hymnists. Even if Kingo's language poses a formidable barrier to the present-day reader, his focus on the turmoil of the mind of the human subject speaks to those readers who are well schooled in Modernism.

Some critics have maintained that Kingo was referring to his own life in some of his hymns, and he must have drawn on his own experience, but he was not writing confessional poetry in the Romantic sense of the word. First and foremost, Kingo was trying to create texts that would be effective in the church service or in the homes, because any user of the texts would find herself or himself in it. Kingo reveals that he knows much about the turbulent and troubled mind and naturally probes into that mind. However, Kingo knew, as well, the mind that could revel in a sense of salvation and in the wonders of the divine being's grace. Antithesis is a hallmark of Kingo's age and of his poetry.

Some features of Kingo's poetry can be understood by a consideration of the historical situation during the new Absolute Monarchy. The seventeenth century was dominated by Lutheran orthodoxy, which was partly a reaction against the Catholic Counter Reformation. A "fear and obey" attitude, spelled out by the catechism, as well as in weekly sermons, was intended to form a submissive populace not prone to question any authorities. At the same time, Renaissance impulses were entering Denmark–paintings, sculpture, and architecture testify to that–but the Renaissance idea of the human being exploring the world unfettered by authorities was censored.

An ambitious theologian such as Kingo naturally was keenly aware of the tenets of Lutheran orthodoxy and knew what hymns would please those in power, but some of his hymns seem to deviate from the humble and subservient spirit expected of the good Christian. Kingo's amazing social rise within the clerical hierarchy may explain that irregularity, for the weaver's son became a bishop, a prominent servant of Crown and Church.

Persons influenced by the Renaissance had more demands on the world than those shaped by Lutheran dogmatism, and they were less likely to see their destinies as an expression of divine will. Those two conflicting forces were on an ideological collision course, and that course was one charted by Kingo's works, although he hardly intended it to be. One feels a tension between the obedient servant of the Church and the ambitious, secular human being. Hence, a fluctuation–or a tantalizing inconsistency–is present. To interpret the changing moods from hymn to hymn by noting that Kingo is addressing various events as prescribed by the Church is easy–and surely that fact explains some fluctuations in attitude from text to text–but not that two hymns that seem to be dedicated to the same theme are remarkably different, as are "Far, Verden, Farvel" and "Hver har sin Skiebne" (translated as "Everyone Has His Destiny," 1972).

To characterize the age may be much easier than to describe the man Kingo. Although many facts are known about Kingo's life, Kingo himself remains elusive. Like some of his illustrious European contemporaries, Kingo left no memoirs or letters, and the accounts of contemporaries are skimpy. Biographical information exists, but for Kingo the kind of sources that most later authors made available are scarce.

Consequently, critics have turned to his texts to find the man, but the poetics of the day tended to shield Kingo from the curious eye. From the German-speaking world, a taste for the baroque arrived in the North. Baroque art engaged in a stylized, extravagant, hyperbolic discourse that fit hand in glove with the antithetical experience of the world in that age. Baroque texts use all possible stylistic special effects to make a strong emotional impression, but Kingo knew that those stylistic features should be controlled in order that they have the highest possible impact on the audience. Kingo used the complicated, learned, contrived baroque machinery with elegance, and, thus–unlike many baroque poets–he did not allow himself to use excessive stylistic devices, at least not in his best texts.

Kingo's family on his father's side came from Scotland; his father, Hans Thomas Kingo, was a weaver, who sent his son to a preparatory school for a university education. Oral tradition apparently claims that young Thomas impregnated a woman and had to be sent to a neighboring, but decidedly better, school. Since Kingo was embroiled in controversy and strife, and obviously attracted people's attention, distinguishing between fact and fiction about his life is difficult. In the new school, however, Kingo studied under a headmaster who took a great interest in the Renaissance endeavor of refining national languages for the sake of literary excellence. Kingo, thus, was introduced to the new aesthetics of his day.

Kingo started attending the University of Copenhagen in 1654; little is known about his life during those years, but the period could hardly have been devoted exclusively to theology, for Denmark was at war with Sweden. When Kingo graduated in 1658, in a customary step for a young theologian, he took a position as a tutor–in the countryside about thirty miles west of Copenhagen–and apparently he began writing poetry during those years. His manuscript of "Næfve-tuud og Knud her-ud" (Blow on Your Hands and Saint Canute Will Send Winter Away), dating from the early 1660s, records the speculation of the inhabitants of a farm as to whether Kingo will manage to make his way to their place through a ferocious blizzard. The poem ends with one young woman engaging in a "I wish I were" game, imagining that she would be a stove, a hot water bottle, and the linen that will warm Kingo's chilled bones when he finally arrives. This humorous, feisty poem seems to reflect young Kingo's ability to enjoy himself within a circle of good friends.

In 1661 he became a chaplain in a neighboring town, Kirke Helsinge, and once again he proved his talent as a poet. He composed a lengthy, somewhat didactic poem called "Sæbye-gaards Koeklage" (The Lament of the Cows at Sæby Farm, 1665), in which the cows eloquently praise a bull who was a benevolent ruler, a good neighbor to all, and a proud father of many calves. Late in his life, he is to be sold off without cause; he rebels and finally drowns himself. The message is clear: masters should not subject worthy friends to degrading indignities, but should be more like the bull himself. The poem calls for a humane attitude. Even if the text is allegorical, it is not an example of dry moralizing, and it offers a lively and lovely picture of life in the countryside.

In 1668 Kingo was appointed pastor in his hometown of Slangerup and married Cecilie (Sille) Balkenborg Worm, the widow of his former superior at Kirke Helsinge. The accomplished pastoral "Chrysillis" was most likely devoted to her. It is a private love poem, not intended for publication, but it reveals that Kingo had mastered yet another poetic genre. Sille Worm died in 1670. The following year, on 28 May, Kingo married a wealthy widow, Johanne Lauritsdatter Lund, several years his senior.

Kingo's career as a poet then started in earnest, for cleverly–and in tune with his times–he wrote occasional poems that were dedicated to, or requested by, influential people. In his poems in memory of the recently deceased, Kingo is a baroque realist–the destiny of the body to be consumed by worms is a common theme–and he does not minimize the effects of death. He admits that death seems unfair, for young people and good people are abruptly taken away. Life can seem meaningless, but it is not, for all that happens is the will of the Lord.

The tone is lighter in the wedding poems, but Kingo is once again the realist who knows that spouses may not always live harmoniously together. In one poem he lauds a widower who, after a period of sadness and deprivation, brings a new wife into his home. That his first wife died was a tragedy, but life had to go on. In Kingo's texts death is always at close quarters, a fact to which human beings have to resign themselves.

In 1671, an ambitious Kingo wrote "Hosianna ved Christian V's Salvning," a poem celebrating the crowning of King Christian V. The praise is full blown; flattery and hyperbole were means used shamelessly by baroque poets, and in this text, the king is seen as the sun who benevolently sends warmth to the entire nation. This poem and many to follow, nevertheless, suggest that Kingo subscribed to the ideology of the new absolute monarchy and genuinely felt that the king was the Divine Being's appointee.

The thirty-seven-year-old minister was doing well: through some poems to Peter Schumacher, he had managed to attract the attention of that future *rigskansler*–a position comparable to prime minister–who, like Kingo, was a commoner who had moved up in the social hierarchy. Schumacher was given noble rank and the name Griffenfeld.

In many of Kingo's poems, envy is mentioned as a demonic force that circumvents justice, and, of course, a powerful man such as Griffenfeld had enemies. The successful pastor of Slangerup, too, had a detractor, namely Jacob Worm–Sille Worm's stepson–who was appointed headmaster at the high school in Slangerup in 1671. Why a feud erupted between the two men is not known, but they both seemed headstrong and stubborn, and they clashed–with words. Satire was a rough weapon at that time.

Kingo's biographer Johannes Simonsen suggests that Worm, who was a bit younger than his "stepmother's spouse," might have been envious of Kingo's social rise, and in the so-called "Kalotvise" (Calotte-Ballad, 1671), Worm lashed out: he insinuated that Kingo was an arrogant and untrustworthy drunkard. Kingo replied in kind–even in the same meter–asserting that the author of the slanderous poem was a liar with an inferior mind. Worm's reply was not subtle, for he directly accused Kingo of having been "shamefully drunk" in church and for having tumbled down from the pulpit. Worm added that he would sally forth with even more damning accusations if Kingo did not keep quiet. Kingo did not respond.

The two men remained bitter enemies, and Worm, who was highly critical of the new absolute monarchy, had the daring to attack Griffenfeld. In fact, he even called him "the Antichrist." In 1676, Griffenfeld was arrested, and he spent the next twenty-three years in prison. Worm, the outsider, felt compassion for Griffenfeld, and, curiously, when Jacob Worm was arrested for treason and condemned to death–a verdict that was changed to deportation to the Danish possessions in India–Kingo pleaded for mercy for his bitter enemy.

So far, Kingo's poetry had been secular, but in 1674 he published a collection of hymns, *Aandelige Siunge-Koors første Part, indeholdende 14 Gudelige Morgen- og Aften-sange, tilligemed de 7 Kong Davids Poenitendse Psalmer sangviis forfattede* (Spiritual Song-Chorus, First Part, Containing 14 Pious Morning and Evening Songs, in addition to 7 Songs Written According to King David's Psalms of Penance). In keeping with baroque poetics, the book was rigidly structured–it had seven morning hymns, seven evening hymns, and seven adaptations of songs of penitence from "the Book of Psalms." Kingo intended the book to be used for private services in homes and thus defends his use of well-known secular tunes.

In some masterly hymns, dawn initiates a joyful victory celebration, for the devil has been defeated–life is a constant drama, but temptation is always at close quarters. Sin seems inevitable, but the birth of Christ is a glorious promise, for grace will redeem the human being. Nevertheless, for Kingo to include those hymns of penitence made sense: they also proved that he could handle the adaptation of the Old Testament texts into a modern idiom, for the forgiven, weak human being, who hardly deserves salvation, should not only be grateful but also be penitent.

Even if that is the predominant view of the human being, certain lines–through use of the pronoun *I*–suggest that the human being is capable not only of struggling against, but also of conquering the devil, and so he or she proudly and triumphantly states, "Jeg vil i Basunen støde" (I will blow the trumpet). As such scholars as Ejnar Thomsen and Oluf Friis have suggested, Kingo's works offer a glimpse of a Renaissance individual in the midst of Lutheran orthodoxy. For a person of Kingo's ilk–proud, vain, and ambitious–to accept not being able to take charge of one's own destiny might be difficult. To omit such surmises would hardly be fair, for such an omission would diminish some of Kingo's most brilliant psalms and ignore those modern readers who, although they have little use for Christian preaching, are profoundly intrigued by the old hymnist's texts.

After Griffenfeld's fall–a cataclysmic event to which Kingo never referred–Kingo continued to write poems in praise of the king and his war effort against the archenemy, Sweden, the country that had decimated Denmark a few decades earlier by annexing the provinces of Skaane, Halland, and Blekinge. Kingo's battle scenes are vivid, for the baroque poetic machinery worked well to conjure up, in graphic detail, bloody conflicts.

Undoubtedly, Kingo was appreciated at Court, for in 1677–when he turned forty-three–he was appointed as bishop over the Funen diocese. As the literary historian Vilhelm Andersen remarked, for a man who had not produced any scholarly theological work, that was a swift rise in social standing. A

Title pages for Kingo's two-volume collection of hymns. The first volume, published in 1647, marked a departure from his secular poetry (from Egil Elseth, Thomas Kingo: Veversønnen som ble salmedikter, *1985; Widener Library, Harvard University).*

bishop is, however, a bureaucrat, and Kingo became a capable and involved leader of his diocese. He also became, consequently, a less productive poet, but in 1681 he published the second part of *Aandeligt Siunge-Koors.* It included twenty hymns and seventeen "Hierte-Suk" ("sighs from the heart").

Critic Peer E. Sørensen maintains that the mood of the second part is decidedly different from the part published in 1674, for the voice narrating the texts in 1681–the *I*–is much more troubled. Once again, Kingo renders the process of repeated sin and forgiveness, and again and again he invokes antithesis to stress the immense difference between this deceitful world and heaven. In most cases the "sighs" elaborate on that main theme.

Contrast is at the heart of the eleventh hymn, "Far, Verden, Farvel." The human being rejects this world by casting himself or herself in the role of a slave who rebels against a master, and that master is this world in which nothing can be trusted. All is "vanity, vanity." The reader glimpses a person who has been passionately involved with this world, but who, after many disappointments, has realized that everything that one strives for turns out to be a sham. Consequently, this life is vehemently rejected for the next. The hymn reads like a confessional poem, one that its many users must have found painfully easy to identify with, for that superb text alludes to nearly everyone's life story.

The hymn is carefully wrought, and each stanza is eventually followed by an antistanza in which the profound disappointment of this life is replaced by a triumphant "vision" of existence in "Abraham's bosom"–the phrase that replaces "vanity, vanity" as a kind of refrain. This part of the hymn hardly expresses penance, however; on the contrary, the rebellious slave arrives in heaven, is welcomed as an honorable guest, and is granted an eminent position: Christ will greet him as a dear friend; he will stand out among the angels; and it seems he will be reimbursed for everything that was denied him on earth. No sense of sinfulness is voiced; on the contrary, the person who suffered in this life is finally reaping his just rewards. A lusty involvement in life is suggested by the subtext and inhabits this remarkable Renaissance text.

If the antithesis seemed absolute in "Far, Verden, Farvel," Kingo modified it in some of the ensuing hymns. In "Hver Har Sin Skiebne," he once again invokes the contrast between this deceitful world and the other, but instead of rejecting this world, he realizes that it is his lot. He knows that being in the world is the will of the Lord and that the next world will offer him what he is denied here and now. The main theme seems to be the same as in "Far, Verden, Farvel," but the attitude is different, for what is stressed is that life is a both/and, not the either/or of the preceding hymn: "Sorrig og Glæde de vandre tilhaabe" (Sorrow and joyfulness walk with each other).

The nineteenth hymn in the second part of *Aandeligt Siunge-Koors* is a prayer for travelers, and the journey envisioned is both a real one and a metaphorical one through life, but Kingo manages to make the traveling quite concrete, so that even the modern reader does not feel that the text is merely allegorical. The accompanying "sigh" is to be "used"–sung or prayed–before a sea voyage. That short poem may seem emblematic of the baroque worldview: it cascades forward in terms of changing moods and thoughts and never really reaches a resting point (even if it postulates that it does so). The narrator refers to the water in the sea, but that salty water–and the association is typical of baroque–reminds him of tears, and he examines his tears and finds them wanting, for they are bitter and resentful tears, not sweet tears shed in remorse. The sinful confessor realizes that he may drown, but if that happens, he should meet death in a sea of tears of penance, not in the bitter tears of anger. This brief and tightly structured text masterfully captures the idea that peace of mind did not come easily to the person who was caught in the inevitable conflicts between secular urges and a profound wish to be a dutiful Christian.

This volume of hymns consolidated Kingo's position in the Danish church, and even if, as a bishop, he was busy with many duties, he wisely found time to continue writing poems in praise of the monarch. But even if a common practice for poets of the time was to promote themselves by writing occasion poems in praise of their superiors, Kingo also composed "De Fattiges udi Odensee Hospital" (The Poor in Odense Hospital, 1682), a secular prayer to the king in an attempt to protect the hospital from financial cuts in order to support the war effort. In that poem, the plight of the poor–most inmates were destitute or insane–is graphically depicted with baroque hyperbole, but also with graphic and brutal realism.

The king understood that the bishop was a worthy and useful servant who could accomplish a major, warranted task: he could revise the outdated hymnal from 1569 to one that would be used from northern Norway to the southernmost part of the Danish realm. Kingo seems to have undertaken that job with relish, and in 1689 he had *Danmarks og Norges Kirkers forordnede Psalme-Bog. Vinter Parten: Efter sær kongel. Befalning af sal. D. Mort. Luthers, saa og andre gudfrygtige lærde Mænds Sange og gamle Kirke Psalmer sammendragen, og med en stoor Deel til Høitiderne . . . forbedret,* known simply as *Vinter Parten* (The Winter Part), published.

The hymns are dedicated to the major Christian events of the year–Advent, Christmas, Lent, and Easter–and the texts devoted to the Passion stand out and capture in detail the dramatic narrative of Christ's last days on earth, his suffering on the cross, and, briefly, his Resurrection. Kingo records Christ's having to face his fate alone, for Adam–everyone–as well as his disciples had betrayed him. When Christ was arrested, the Jews requested that he be crucified; Pontius Pilate tried to intervene on his behalf; but Pilate was forced to give in. Those texts indicate that members of the congregation–those singing the hymn–are as guilty as those who condemned Christ to be crucified. Kingo cleverly merges past and present so that those singing in the "here and now" realize–watch and feel–that they participated in the Crucifixion.

One hymn from *Vinter Parten,* namely "Over Kedron Jesus træder" (translated as "Over Cedron Jesus Passes," 1988), must suffice to summarize these tense narratives. In it Kingo initially and effectively uses war as the frame of reference: Christ is fleeing–as David once did–his enemies (the sinful Adam) are pursuing him, and all weapons are aimed at him. Christ arrives in Gethsemane, a place of rest, but he is not allowed peace of mind, for he anticipates what is to come, and, thus, subtly the congregation is transferred to Golgotha and becomes eyewitness to Christ's suffering–mental as well as physical–on the cross. Those stanzas that render Christ's slow death in excruciating detail are bound to capture the imagination–and conscience–of the congregation. The conclusion of the hymn comforts the penitent human being with the promise that Christ, through his death, granted the penitent salvation.

But as is common in Kingo's most tantalizing works, the congregation–or perhaps the troubled individual, who may not be able to share in the congregation's feeling of being forgiven–finds a subtext: Christ as a human shares the fearful individual's anticipation of death. That Christ is similar to humans is reassuring, but that Christ was steeped in anguish as death approached is disconcerting. To one member of the congregation the hymn may send a consoling message, and to the next it may be an expression of the fear of death.

Kingo dwells at length on Christ's suffering and the sinfulness of the human being, but in the final Easter hymn, the tone is unambiguously triumphant. One well-known text starts with the magnificent line "Som den gyldne Sool frembryder" (translated as "Like the Golden Sun Ascending," 1988), and clearly the sun allegorically refers to Christ's victory over death for the sake of the sinner. Kingo's versatility is remarkable, and his Christian worldview is not always easy to ascertain.

Kingo's career seemed to be heading toward its zenith, but the king abruptly withdrew his support for the project. Kingo's many comments on the untrustworthiness of patrons and on the grueling effects of envy come to mind. Clearly, the successful and temperamental bishop had managed to accrue many enemies who delighted in humiliating him. Kingo's revisions of well-known hymns may also have caused consternation, for 126 of the 267 entries in *Vinter-Parten* were written by Kingo. He used baroque techniques to the hilt–as Sørensen states, he was "the leading author of the modern"–and that may not have sat well with the conservative clergy close to the crown. Kingo was erudite, but most members of the congregations all across the Danish realm could barely read and write and had memorized the hymns from the old hymnal. The New and the Old clashed.

Kingo, who had expected a solid income from the sales of *Vinter-Parten,* the publication of which he had funded, refused to accept defeat, and when a commission was appointed to replace Kingo's aborted project, he pleaded for the inclusion of his hymns on Christ's Passion. When the new hymnal, titled *Den forordnede ny kirke-Psalmebog* (The Ordained New Church Hymnal, 1699), was published, 85 of its 297 texts were written by Kingo; he was permitted to be its publisher and to receive income from its sales, and it was for centuries called "Kingo's Hymnbook." The bishop of Funen was not easily dismissed.

An inscription written during the last period of Kingo's life is found to this day in the Holmen Church in Copenhagen; it honors the esteemed Admiral Niels Juel, who died in 1697. That poem (title added in translation, "Admiral Niels Juel's Epitaph," 1950) captures Kingo's antithetical worldview; examples of the distrustful nature of life are enumerated and, in contrast, followed by Juel's deeds, the memory of which will last. Lament is followed by joy.

Many of Kingo's occasional poems that praise a person recently deceased illustrate a problem that has always haunted Lutheranism. According to Martin Luther–and to the orthodoxy to which Kingo adhered–divine grace saves the human being. Human beings themselves are powerless and sinful, and their penitence is a sign that they understand that, but only the grace of the Lord, not penance, can save them. Nevertheless, Kingo stresses that some of the people whose lives he sums up are truly deserving, and although he does not state that good deeds are a road toward salvation, that thought whispers subversively in the subtext. Kingo was a man of this world, and he meticulously recorded human missteps and human virtues. This world was real to Kingo–even when he seemed, as in "Far, Verden, Farvel," to reject it.

Kingo's involvement with this world was clear late in his life. His second wife, who had been ailing for some years, died in 1694, and he remarried the same year. Biographical accounts speculate that, for quite some time, he had been in love with Birgitte Balslev, who was thirty-one years his junior. A poem "tying her to him" (in the form of a letter from 1689) seems to suggest that, and a passionate pastoral poem, "Candida," written in 1694, speaks of his love for a woman. The marriage seems to have been a happy one, and his young wife accompanied him on his arduous trips to inspect the many ministers who served under him. During Kingo's last years, his health was failing, and on 14 October 1703, he died. He was accused by a colleague–a former friend with whom he had fallen out–of economic mismanagement, but his widow cleared his name.

Artist Bodil Kaalund, who has illustrated Thomas Kingo's works, asserts that Kingo's texts bear witness to a tempestuous mental climate, with vistas over a large, open landscape. She sees wide horizons and fresh air in Kingo's powerful poetry. He appeals to all the senses. What Kingo created may well be allegorical, alluding to a higher world–a world that human beings, caught in this world, can only rarely glimpse, but that turbulent world of the senses is one that Kingo's age and the hymnist himself found to be both lowly and tantalizing. Antitheses remain the key to understanding one of the major poets of Denmark.

Bibliography:

Svend Esbech, *Thomas Kingo. En Bibliografi* (Frederiksberg, 1988).

Biography:

Johannes Simonsen, *Thomas Kingo. Hofpoet og salmedigter* (Copenhagen: Frimodt, 1970).

References:

Niels Dalgaard and Marita Akhøj Nielsen, "Knoglebrud og kongerøgelse, Litterære og filologiske overvejelser over Thomas Kingo: Odense Hospital," *Danske Studier* (1996): 38–61;

Eskild Due and others, "Om de fattige i Odense hospital," in *Historien i dansk,* edited by Peter Olivarius, Steen Svava Olsen, and Jens Walter (Copenhagen: Dansklærerforeningen, 1978), pp. 38–67;

Egil Elseth, *Thomas Kingo: Veversønnen som ble salmedikter* (Oslo: Verbum, 1985);

Wilhelm Friese, *Nordische Barockdichtung* (Munich: Francke, 1968);

Oluf Friis, introduction to *Litteraturen i Danmark og de Øvrige Nordiske Lande,* edited by Henning Fonsmark (Copenhagen: Politiken, 1961), pp. 30–40;

Kingos Salmebog 1699, special edition of *Hymnologiske Meddelelser* (1999);

Erik A. Nielsen, "Kingo's Passion," *Hymnologiske Meddelelser* (1987): 3–46;

Dagfinn Simonsen, *Diktet og makten* (Oslo: Aschehoug, 1984);

Peer E. Sørensen, *Dansk Litteraturhistorie,* volume 3, edited by Jens Hougaard and others (Copenhagen: Gyldendal, 1983), pp. 270–276, 314–344;

Eira Storstein and Sørensen, *Den barokke tekst* ([Frederiksberg]: Dansklærerforeningen, 1999);

Ejnar Thomsen, *Barokken i dansk digtning* (Copenhagen: Munksgaard, 1971);

Martin Wittenberg, *Thomas Kingos historisch-topographische Dichtung* (Bonn: Friederich Wilhelms Universität, 1972).

Papers:

Thomas Kingo's papers are at the Danish Royal Library and at Rigsarkivet, both in Copenhagen.

Jakob Knudsen

(14 September 1858 – 21 February 1917)

Knud Bjarne Gjesing
University of Southern Denmark

(Translated by Gillian Fellows-Jensen)

BOOKS: *Cromwells Datter. Skuespil i fem Akter,* foreword by Holger Drachmann (Copenhagen: Gyldendal, 1891);

Christelige Foredrag (Copenhagen: Gyldendal, 1893); revised and enlarged as *Kristelige Foredrag og andre Afhandlinger,* bibliography by Edith Ortmann-Nielsen (Copenhagen: Gyldendal, 1933);

Et Gjensyn. Fortælling (Copenhagen: Nordiske Forlag, 1898);

Den gamle Præst. Fortælling (Copenhagen: Nordiske Forlag, 1899);

Adelbrand og Malfred. En gammel Kjærlighedshistorie (Copenhagen: Nordiske Forlag, 1900);

Gjæring. Roman (Copenhagen: Nordiske Forlag, 1902);

Afklaring. Roman (Copenhagen: Nordiske Forlag, 1902); republished with *Gjæring* as *Gjæring–Afklaring. Roman* (Copenhagen: Gyldendal, 1918);

Sind. Fortælling (Copenhagen: Nordiske Forlag, 1903);

Jomfru Maria. Et Digt (Copenhagen: Gyldendal, 1904);

For Livets Skyld. Fortælling (Copenhagen: Gyldendal, 1905);

Inger. Roman (Copenhagen: Gyldendal, 1906);

Fremskridt. Roman (Copenhagen: Gyldendal, 1907);

Livsfilosofi. Spredte Betragtninger (Copenhagen: Gyldendal, 1908);

Varulven. En Nutidsskildring i Scener og Samtaler (Copenhagen: Gyldendal, 1908);

Lærer Urup. Roman (Copenhagen: Gyldendal, 1909);

To Slægter. Roman (Copenhagen: Gyldendal, 1910);

Rodfæstet. Roman (Copenhagen: Gyldendal, 1911);

Angst. Fortælling (Copenhagen: Gyldendal, 1912);

En Ungdom. Roman (Copenhagen: Gyldendal, 1913);

Mod. Fortælling (Copenhagen: Gyldendal, 1914); republished with *Angst* as *Martin Luther. Fortælling* (Copenhagen: Gyldendal, 1915);

Jyder. Sytten Fortællinger (Copenhagen: Gyldendal, 1915)–includes "Sejglivethed," translated by V. Elizabeth Balfour-Browne as "Indomitability," in *Contemporary Danish Prose: An Anthology,* edited by Elias Bredsdorff, introduction by Frederik J. Billeskov Jansen (Copenhagen: Gyldendal, 1958; reprinted, Westport, Conn.: Greenwood Press, 1974), pp. 9–16;

Jakob Knudsen (courtesy of the Danish Royal Library, Copenhagen)

Den Gang. Roman (Copenhagen: Gyldendal, 1916);

Jyder. Elleve Fortællinger (Copenhagen: Gyldendal, 1917);

En gammel Slægt (Copenhagen: Gyldendal, 1918).

Editions and Collections: *Romaner og Fortællinger,* 5 volumes (Copenhagen: Gyldendal, 1917);

Den gamle Præst. Fortælling, edited by Oskar Schlichtkrull (Copenhagen: Gyldendal/Dansklærerforeningen, 1932);

Digte, edited by Ejnar Thomsen (Copenhagen: Gyldendal, 1938)–includes "Aftenvers," translated by Johannes Knudsen as "Heavy Murky Clouds of Night," in *A Heritage in Song,* edited by Johannes Knudsen (Askov, Minn.: Danish Interest Conference/Lutheran Church in America, 1978), no. 7; and "Morgensang," translated by S. D. Rodholm as "Morning," in *A Harvest of Song: Translations and Original Lyrics,* edited by Rodholm (Des Moines: American Evangelical Lutheran Church, 1953), pp. 36–37;

Jyder. Fortællinger, edited by Thomsen (Copenhagen: Gyldendal, 1944);

Sind. Fortælling, edited, with an afterword, by Svend Norrild (Copenhagen: Gyldendal/Dansklærerforeningen, 1948);

Idé og Erindring. Artikler og Afhandlinger, edited by Jørgen Jensen and T. Krøgholt (Copenhagen: Gyldendal, 1949);

At være sig selv, edited by Ole Wivel (Copenhagen: Gyldendal, 1965);

Gjæring–Afklaring. Roman, edited by Poul Zerlang (Copenhagen: Danske Sprog- og Litteraturselskab / Valby: Borgen, 1988);

Sind. Fortælling, edited by Esther Kielberg (Copenhagen: Danske Sprog- og Litteraturselskab / Valby: Borgen, 1996).

TRANSLATION: Cicero, *Den först' af de Catilinarisk' Taaler af M. Tullius Cicero* (Kolding: K. Jørgensen, 1887).

"Kunsten er Lovbundethed inden for Fantasien" (Art is regularity within the imagination)–thus reads one of Jakob Knudsen's reflections on creative artistic activity. This regularity distinguishes artistic fantasy from ordinary reverie and daydreaming. Knudsen also often described how impressions from his childhood shaped his own artistic fantasy. By the time he had made his mark as an author, he was a man of forty whose mental state was firmly molded. It is therefore difficult to arrange his works according to a progressive line of development; however, underlying all his writings are the influences to which he was subjected in his childhood, influences that he was continually evaluating.

Knudsen's childhood home was deeply influenced by an understanding of life and Christianity that had originated with N. F. S. Grundtvig's teachings and shaped Danish culture and society in the last half of the nineteenth century. Through the agency of the primary schools and the *folkehøjskoler* (folk high schools), as well as through the teachings of the Lutheran Church, people were to be roused to a love of life and a new energy that would be transmitted to both secular and religious spheres. "Mennesket først, og kristen så" (Man first and Christian thus), as one of Grundtvig's doctrines proclaims. The ideal was to live within the Christian faith "Et jævnt og muntert virksomt Liv på Jord" (a plain and active joyful life on earth), as expressed in the first line of one of Grundtvig's best-known songs, published in 1839.

Jakob Christian Lindberg Knudsen was born in Rødding on 14 September 1858 to Jens Lassen Knudsen and Nanna Marie F. Adelaide Boisen Knudsen. His mother came from a family whose members held high positions in the Grundtvigian movement as pastors, teachers, and politicians. His father, in contrast, was from an old farming family but, influenced by Grundtvig's preaching, felt the call to become a pastor and *folkehøjskole* teacher. In the novel *To Slægter* (Two Generations, 1910), in which Jakob Knudsen treats his family background in fictionalized form, he describes the relationship between his parents' families as the contrast between a harsh and severe peasant culture and the more enlightened, refined, and lighthearted culture of public servants.

The eight children of the Knudsen family did not attend the local school but were privately taught, as was the fashion in the circles influenced by Grundtvig's thought with regard to education. Subjects considered of lesser significance, such as writing, reading, and arithmetic, were taught by a governess, while the really important matters–Christianity, history, and literature–were looked after by the children's parents. Later in life, Knudsen expressed his gratitude for this invigorating and personal instruction in spiritual matters; his father in particular had a lasting influence on him. At the same time, however, Jens Knudsen was a severe man who demanded absolute obedience from his children. This relationship between authority and freedom and between affectionate submission and fear was later to play a decisive role in Jakob Knudsen's novels.

After attending Askov Folkehøjskole in Jutland, the young Knudsen was permitted to go to Copenhagen, first to take the so-called students' examination that would gain him entry to the University of Copenhagen and then to study theology there, although he had no real enthusiasm or interest in the subject. He had actually wanted to study philosophy but abandoned this plan. When his first attempt to make his living as an author also proved unsuccessful, Knudsen lost heart and returned home to work as a teacher at Askov Folkehøjskole. This return home was a confirmation of his father's prejudices. The Grundtvigian movement had gained a particularly secure foothold among country people, who were rather suspicious of the big city and academic culture. Knudsen nevertheless married a young woman he had met in Copenhagen, Sophie Frederikke Plockross, in 1883. In 1890 the couple moved to the small town of Mellerup, on Randers Fiord in Jutland, where Knudsen was appointed pastor to the Grundtvigian Lutheran Church. His *Christelige Foredrag* (Christian Lectures, 1893) offers an impression of his ministry there. Like Grundtvig, Knudsen stressed the Creed and the promises made in connection with the sacraments of baptism and Holy Communion as reflecting direct communication between God and man. His time at Mellerup, however, ended in upheaval. He and his wife sought a divorce in 1893, causing consternation among the parishioners. Consternation turned to outrage when, three years later, Knudsen married Helga Bek, who was twenty years his junior and whom he had earlier prepared for confirmation. She was the daughter of the principal of Mellerup Folkehøjskole. Knudsen felt that he could not continue to function as a pastor or teacher and instead attempted to make a living as an author and lecturer. Part of his repertoire as a lecturer was collected in *Livsfilosofi. Spredte Betragtninger* (Philosophy of Life: Scattered Observations, 1908). *Jyder. Sytten Fortællinger* (Jutlanders: Seventeen Tales, 1915) and *Jyder. Elleve Fortællinger* (Jutlanders: Eleven Tales, 1917) include recollections of Knudsen's life as an itinerant lecturer.

Knudsen thus became an author out of economic necessity. He wanted to write lyrical poems and drama, but his need for income forced him instead to produce novels, a more popular genre. He wrote them in a straightforward and realistic style, often with dramatic plots involving murder, rape, and suicide. Although the books tend to be as gory as any blood-and-thunder novel, they are also characterized by penetrating psychological analyses and take their starting point in philosophical and theological reflections based on Knudsen's own life and experience.

In several of his works Knudsen emphasized the opposition between the morality of society and the individual conscience; he also laid stress on the opposition between secular areas and those belonging to religious life. It is, according to Orthodox Lutheran theology, a matter of "two regimes." Knudsen was therefore indignant when pious people wanted to formulate a special Christian morality and perhaps even to exploit the Sermon on the Mount and the Commandment to love one's neighbor as oneself as a program for social reform. In his view, to imagine that the individual was supposed to realize personally the message of the Sermon on the Mount could lead only to hypocrisy and self-delusion. Interpreting the words of Jesus as moral precepts and proposals for humane reforms of society would lead to the complete dissolution of the secular order. Secular life is of course also subject to the power of God, but in this sphere he works not through his gracious love but rather through the retributive principle that dominates nature. Knudsen therefore thought it was imperative that secular authorities combat subversive forces with a firm hand.

Knudsen's religious thought also embraced other elements. Different from depictions of almighty God the Father and his bipartite religious and secular regimes are images that express passive submission and amalgamation. In the essay "At være sig selv" (To Be Oneself, 1907), published in *Livsfilosofi,* the human self is described as "en Længsel i vort Indre efter at blive befriet ved Hengivelse" (an inner longing to be made free by submission). This longing for submission finds expression in children's games, a person's being spellbound by nature or art, and lovers' meetings. The longing, however, is never completely satisfied before submission to God, which Knudsen compares with the experience of oneness and amalgamation enjoyed by a religious mystic. In his poetry the blissful submission of self is often associated with female figures and is expressed through bright and happy pictures from nature or through a hymn of praise to day and the light. In the hymn "Aftenvers" (Evening Verse, 1890), with the first line "Tunge, mørke Natteskyer" (Heavy Murky Clouds of Night), God is described as "the Father of light," but even so, the conception of God the Father is associated with images of darkness, loneliness, and guilt:

Tung og mørk den tavse Nat
Over Jorden spænder,
Hist kun bag et Vindve mat
Vaagelys der brænder.
Du, som lindrer Sorg og Nød,
Al vor Synd forlader,
Lyser op den mørke Død,
Tak! Du Lysets Fader!

(Dark and threatening looms the night,
Heavy clouds are churning;
Through the dusk a distant light
Vigil-like is burning.
You who conquered sin and death,
Freely us to gather,
Gave us new-won life and breath,
Thank you, Father of light!)
(Translation by Johannes Knudsen)

In "Morgensang" (Morning Song, 1891), in contrast, submission, the delight in light, and rejoicing in life are associated with a feminine universe:

> O, at jeg tør favne Dig, skære Dag,
> kalde Dig med Navne, min Sjæls Behag,
> alle gode Navne, som bedst jeg véd:
> Moder, Søster, Elskte: min Kærlighed!
>
> (O that I dare open my heart to thee
> Radiant, happy day, dancing o'er the sea!
> Give thee names, the sweetest that I have known:
> Call thee mother, sister, my love, my own!)
> (Translation by S. D. Rodholm)

Thus, there are many aspects to Knudsen's views on life and his world of religious experience. His narratives are often built up around a clash of interests on the verge of paradox. He likes to stretch oppositions to a breaking point. The human being is to rest safely in the shelter of God's hand with his or her own hands free to be active in the world, but, whereas God's hand is always gracious, the conduct of human affairs often seems to be brutal.

In his first novel, *Et Gjensyn* (A Reunion, 1898), Knudsen describes the ambiguous relationship between a son and his beloved father, whose wielding of authority verges on brutality. In Knudsen's opinion the authority of parents was intended to prepare a child for complete submission to the absolute will of God. In *Et Gjensyn* the son has acquired a strong feeling of responsibility and a sensitive conscience as a result of his upbringing, but he has not subsequently completed the transition from reliance on human authority to trust in divine authority. His father, the only person who can soothe his qualms of conscience, dies suddenly, and the son's sense of duty then runs amok in a morbid and life-destroying pursuit of perfection. When his moral self-knowledge is troubled by an erotic conflict, he commits suicide. Only as a result of belief in a forgiving God would his troubled conscience have been able to find peace. The pursuit of perfection that does not thus find relief in religious hope is referred to by Knudsen as "vildfarende Idealitet" (erring idealism). The psychological portrait of the protagonist in *Et Gjensyn* shows how the author himself could have developed psychologically, had he not been a Christian.

Knudsen's desire for a more firmly based culture with fixed standards is often combined with an excessive belief in ethical individualism. In *Den gamle Præst* (The Old Clergyman, 1899) Count Trolle kills in anger a young man who has tried to violate his daughter. The count's spiritual adviser, the old clergyman of the title, first persuades him to deny the killing. When the count nevertheless comes to betray his guilt, the pastor advises him to commit suicide in order to shield his family from a humiliating court case; in addition, he gives the count his blessing and administers Holy Communion to him immediately before the suicide. *Den gamle Præst* thus presents a clergyman's blessing on falsehood, the taking of the law into one's own hands, and the commission of murder and suicide. This provocative book gave rise to a storm of outrage but nevertheless marked a pivotal point in Knudsen's literary career as it made him a well-known author.

Knudsen in 1890 (courtesy of the Danish Royal Library, Copenhagen)

In the semi-autobiographical 1902 novels *Gjæring* (Fermentation) and *Afklaring* (Clarification), republished together as *Gjæring–Afklaring* in 1918, Knudsen attempted to collect his experiences and describe his view on existence as being borne along by divine forces and yet at the same time directed by inclinations and purely natural, nonreligious laws. The main character, Karl Wintrup, has grown up on a large farm, but he has largely been brought up by a clergyman of the Grundtvigian school. The clergyman, however, distinguishes so sharply between spiritual matters and nature that Karl is horrified when he reaches the age of puberty and nature greets him in the form of his own incipient sexual urges. An even greater shock is provided by a different manifestation of the power of nature, when the wife and daughter of the clergyman are drowned while the clergyman stands on firm ground singing Grundtvig's hymn "Alt står i Guds Faderhaand" (All Things Stand in God's Paternal Hand, 1856). Under the impression of these events, Karl is attracted by naturalism, which was being promoted in the contemporary Danish intellectual environment by Georg Brandes. At the same time, Karl leaves his home region to go to Copenhagen to study at the university. He falls passionately in love with Rebekka Woltersien, a young lady belonging to the social circles of the Copenhagen bourgeoisie. Woltersien is a naturalist and atheist, and her loveliness seems actually to reflect the beauty and good fortune that a purely natural way of life ought to be able to bring with it. The two marry, but their relationship is never consummated. Karl realizes that Rebekka's belief in the naturalist ideology is in reality a secularized religion. Her demand that lovers should worship each other as gods and that they should win salvation here and now through their love actually tragically hinders her from being able to participate in life itself. Karl discovers that he is unable to abandon the Christian faith in which he was brought up as a child and where his roots are fixed. Once he is divorced from Rebekka, he returns to his home region and marries a childhood friend. He also founds a *folkehøjskole,* where both the truth of Christianity and the laws of nature are recognized. Knudsen's vision is that the two spheres should be able to coexist, without being mixed together.

In its composition *Gjæring–Afklaring* resembles a bildungsroman, which, in the traditional form of this genre, aims at the eventual amalgamation of opposing ways of life through a harmonizing movement. In *Gjæring–Afklaring* this concluding reconciliation of opposites is not reached by the eradication of earlier boundaries but, on the contrary, by drawing a new boundary. Christianity and naturalism can be united, not because of the discovery (as in the traditional bildungsroman) that the world, in spite of everything, is one, but because of the acknowledgment that the world is divided. The original aim of Grundtvig's interpretation of Christianity was to link religious faith with the experiences of daily life. *Gjæring–Afklaring,* in contrast, does not construct a bridge across a divide but rather seems to reinforce a division. Where Grundtvig made a link between the two, Knudsen set up a boundary between them.

In *Sind* (Temper, 1903) Knudsen once again presents a masterful father who, with a heavy hand, impresses his ideals of obedience and integrity on his son, Anders. In this novel, too, the son suffers from "vildfarende Idealitet," but the idealism turns inward, leading to self-destruction. He rebels against his father but at the same time takes over from him and further develops his absolute demand for integrity. Anders becomes master of his own farm, but when his rights to his property are infringed and he is at the same time denied the hand of the girl he loves, he initiates a vicious feud. The strife culminates in an orgy of violence in which Anders takes the law into his own hands, kills his rivals and opponents, and then celebrates his wedding night with his loved one. This dramatic tragedy is set in Knudsen's immediate past among the peasants of northern Jutland, but the fatal development of the plot and Anders's obdurate and angular figure are reminiscent of an Icelandic saga or a tragic ballad. Anders is a tragic hero, but, just as in a saga, he assumes his fate with a light heart. When he is shot down and killed after his one night of love, he still has "det samme muntre Smil om Munden" (the same cheerful smile on his lips). Although his inability to compromise leads to terrible consequences, this personal quality is depicted with respect by Knudsen.

Like *Den gamle Præst, For Livets Skyld* (For the Sake of Life, 1905) and *Inger* (1906) also describe the collision between the personal conscience and society's regulations. Both novels concern the moral rightness of dissolving an unhappy marriage, and it is clear that they reflect the considerations that Knudsen made before his own divorce. In *Inger* the right of the eponymous female heroine to break out of her marriage and follow her heart is supported, but at the same time it is suggested that she and her lover should leave the parish to which they belonged. It is understandable and justifiable that the couple follow the call of their hearts. It is also, however, equally justifiable and necessary that society should uphold its regulations and, for example, protect the inviolability of the sacrament of marriage. In special cases an individual can be forced to violate social regulations, but he must also be prepared to take the consequences.

Knudsen had an inveterate distrust of politicizing cranks who desired to "humanize" society through social reforms. The novel with the ironic title *Fremskridt* (Progress, 1907) presents a broad description of how an old agrarian community disintegrates once new political and philosophical ideas gain a footing in the neighborhood. In *Lærer Urup* (Teacher Urup,

1909) Knudsen attempted to become involved in contemporary pedagogical and political debates. The eponymous hero of the novel is a teacher who demands the same absolute obedience from his pupils that he had been used to rendering to his parents in his own upbringing. In his view, however, this strict rule of obedience applies only to external circumstances and the performance of practical skills. Urup believes that education in matters such as Christianity and history can be received only in freedom, and he is consequently unwilling to force his pupils to attend classes in these subjects. All that is relevant in the novel is sympathetic insight and the power of the narrative. To command and relate, to wield authority, and to meet in an atmosphere of sympathetic understanding–these are the leading principles behind Urup's pedagogical activity. The teacher notes, however, that these principles become turned upside down as society develops: freedom is respected in external and physical matters, while the spiritual life, on the contrary, is subject to limitations and restrictions. Moral laxness is coupled with spiritual narrow-mindedness. The authorities want to banish corporal punishment from schools, but Urup is forced to compel his pupils to receive education in spiritual and religious subjects. He refuses to abide by these instructions and tenders his resignation. The same retrograde development is also depicted in society on a larger scale. A young girl from the neighborhood is raped and murdered; however, led astray by a misunderstood and sloppy humanism, the authorities sentence the criminal to minor punishment because of his youth. When the young man returns to the area and shows signs of wanting to repeat his crime, a farmer shoots him down. Urup then reproaches himself for not having had the courage to take the law into his own hands in this way.

JAKOB KNUDSEN

AFKLARING

ROMAN

KJØBENHAVN
DET NORDISKE FORLAG
ERNST BOJESEN
1902

Title page for Knudsen's semi-autobiographical novel, in which he describes his view of existence as being controlled by divine forces and, at the same time, by purely natural laws (Alderman Library, University of Virginia)

In *Rodfæstet* (Deep-Rooted, 1911) Knudsen portrays a dynamic character who derives her willpower from being "deep-rooted." To be deep-rooted in Knudsen's view means to have one's existence grounded in an authority outside of oneself. The mature human being can be rooted in his own life experience, his personal associations, or his relationship with God, but the state of being deep-rooted originates in the restraint placed on children by their parents. The main character in *Rodfæstet,* Kathrine Gluud, is married to a much older parish preacher, who is described as peace loving and kindhearted but also as weak willed and incapable of making a decision. Kathrine, for her part, has inherited a much more energetic nature from her parents. Her father had made his fortune by trading in tainted meat, and it is even possible that he killed a man as a youth. Apparently, however, he carries the knowledge of these sins with his head held high. When Kathrine falls in love with her husband's curate, her conscience proves to be just as robust as her father's. She presses her lover to kill her elderly husband, but the curate does not have the moral courage to live with the knowledge of his crime, and he commits suicide. Kathrine then also kills herself, but only in order not to bring shame upon her parents, and she carefully conceals the humiliating reason why she has been obliged to take her own life. Although Kathrine has admittedly committed gross offenses against both moral and judicial laws, at heart she remains a pure and uncorrupted woman. It is often the case in Knudsen's novels that the characters demonstrate their vitality by killing others or themselves.

In Knudsen's last great pair of novels, *Angst* (Anxiety, 1912) and *Mod* (Courage, 1914), republished together as *Martin Luther* (1915), a similar rift appears in the composition of the work. The double novel is an account of the religious development of the Protestant reformer Martin Luther. The first part describes the boy's mixture of hate and love for his father, who brought him up with severity. The working titles for the novel were "The Son" and, later, "Father and Son." In the course of time the severe treatment brings the young Luther to doubt the justice of his father and therefore also of God; the two figures merge into one another for the boy. Behind his dread and doubt, however, are concealed several brighter recollections from his earliest childhood, a time when his mother shaped his imagination with songs and fairy tales and when he had a close and confident relationship with his father.

The guilt and anxiety that gradually spread through Luther's feelings are described on a deeper plane as a religious dread of damnation. As a young man he senses that his heavenly Father cannot be satisfied by his desperate attempts to live a holy and pious life as a monk. Not until after a spiritual breakdown does Luther recognize that his only hope is faith in the forgiveness and love of God. Not through acts but only through faith in God's sovereign grace can Luther achieve peace and find the strength to live his life with courage, the virtue that provides the title for the second novel. Luther manages to draw a line between his hope of salvation and his present life; the hope of salvation is directed toward God, who alone can fulfill it. This boundary between God and the world also implies a division between the inner and the outer life, which becomes prominent in the love story interwoven with the narrative of Luther's religious development. With Ursula, the woman he loves, Luther feels that earthly love and a life of bliss could be amalgamated. But just as Karl has to forsake Rebekka in *Gjæring–Afklaring,* Luther also has to abandon Ursula. She dies as a nun in a convent; afterward, Luther–again, like Karl–enters into a more commonsensical marriage. His longing for love and happiness is directed solely to God. Luther's hope of salvation is withdrawn from earthly life, but, in return, the description of this life in the second part of the novel shows a marked tendency to crumble into disconnected fragments.

One statement from *Martin Luther* exemplifies the psychology of the novel: "Angst har kun den, der elsker Livet saa højt, saa de *kunde* blive ham et Himmerig. Han frygter nemlig, at det ikke skulde blive det" (He alone suffers from anxiety who loves life so highly that it *could* become a heaven for him. He fears namely that it might not be so). The statement continues, "Naar saa Freden er der, saa er alt vundet.–Blot ikke Hjertet lukker sig om sin Fred–" (When peace is achieved, everything has been won.–As long as the heart does not close itself around its peace–). It might, however, appear that just such a closing around the inner peace of the heart happened to both the Luther character in the novel and the older Knudsen himself. While working on *Martin Luther,* he found it increasingly difficult to collect his thoughts, and in the last years of his life he was plagued by melancholy, qualms of conscience, and morbid whims; his friends and family were unable to reach him and help him. He died suddenly in his home from a cerebral hemorrhage on 21 February 1917.

Both in his own time and in posterity Jakob Knudsen's work has given rise to heated debate. His opinions on politics and society have been seen as a manifestation of a reactionary and authoritarian philosophy, but on the other hand, he was an indefatigable advocate of intellectual and religious freedom. Although his original and penetrating works have been met with vehement criticism, they have also served as a source of inspiration, particularly in a theological context.

Biographies:

Holger Begtrup, *Jakob Knudsen. En Levnedstegning* (Copenhagen: Gyldendal, 1918);

Richard Andersen, *Jakob Knudsen* (Copenhagen: Danske Forlag, 1958).

References:

Margrethe Auken, "Den pietistiske Atheisme. Jakob Knudsens kritik af naturalismen," *Kritik,* 19 (1971): 64–80;

Svend Bjerg, *Jakob Knudsen. Erfaring og fortælling* (Århus: Aros, 1982);

Jørgen Elbek, "Jakob Knudsen," in *Danske digtere i det 20. århundrede,* third edition, edited by Torben Brostrøm and Mette Winge, volume 1 (Copenhagen: Gad, 1980), pp. 149–168;

Knud Bjarne Gjesing, "Fortælling og forkyndelse–i Jakob Knudsens *Gjæring–Afklaring,*" *Nordica,* 4 (1987): 47–63;

Gjesing, "Jakob Knudsen," in *Danske digtere i det 20. århundrede,* fourth edition, edited by Anne-Marie Mai, volume 1 (Copenhagen: Gad, 2002), pp. 85–100;

Hans Halling, *Studier i Jakob Knudsens "Partikulier"* (Føllenslev: Luna, 2000);

Aage Henriksen, "Komplekset Jakob Knudsen," in his *Den intellektuelle. Artikler, 1964–74* (Copenhagen: Fremad, 1974), pp. 75–80;

Ove Jappe, "Jakob Knudsens Livsfølelse," *Edda,* 20 (1933): 257–289;

W. Glyn Jones, "'Det forjættede Land' and 'Fremskridt' as Social Novels," *Scandinavian Studies,* 37, no. 1 (1965): 77–90;

Finn Frederik Krarup, "Splittelse, angst og tro. Jakob Knudsen, *Gjæring–Afklaring,*" in *Læsninger i Dansk Litteratur,* volume 3: *1900–1940,* edited by Inger-Lise Hjordt-Vetlesen and Krarup (Odense: Odense University Press, 1997), pp. 45–61;

Sven Møller Kristensen, "Gjæring–Afklaring," in *Digtning og livssyn. Fortolkninger af syv danske værker* (Copenhagen: Gyldendal, 1959), pp. 122–149;

T. Krøgholt, "Jakob Knudsen," in *Vartovbogen* (Copenhagen: Kirkeligt Samfund, 1967), pp. 37–54;

Niels Lillelund, "Jakob Knudsen og opdragelsen," *Danmark i spejlet,* 11 (1992): 16–37;

Rie Nissen, "'Jeg er så naiv, at jeg stadig elsker livet. . . .' Digterhjemmet i Birkerød," in *Adel og borger, præster og bønder. Danske hjem i tyverne og trediverne,* edited by Margrethe Spies (Copenhagen: Vinten, 1978), pp. 24–50;

Svend Norrild, *Jakob Knudsen. En psykologisk Analyse* (Copenhagen: H. Hirschsprung, 1935);

Mogens Pahuus, "Livsfilosofisk teologi," *Dansk kirkeliv 1988–1989* (1988): 25–50;

Pahuus, *Uendelighedslængsel* (Århus: Philosophia, 1999);

Carl Roos, "Jakob Knudsen," in *Danske digtere i det 20. århundrede,* edited by Ernst Frandsen and Niels Kaas Johansen, volume 1 (Copenhagen: Gad, 1951), pp. 217–234;

Roos, *Jakob Knudsen. En Studie over en Aandspersonlighed* (Copenhagen: Lybecker, 1918);

Roos, *Jakob Knudsen. Et Forfatterskab* (Copenhagen: Gyldendal, 1954);

Povl Schmidt, *Drømmens dør. Læsninger i Jakob Knudsens forfatterskab* (Odense: Odense University Press, 1984);

Schmidt, "Kunst er kunstig fastholdt stemning. Jakob Knudsens fortælling 'Mindedrag,'" *Kritik,* 8 (1968): 5–18;

Villy Sørensen, "Det forgudede traume. Jakob Knudsens romaner," in *Hverken–eller, Kritiske betragtninger* (Copenhagen: Gyldendal, 1961), pp. 158–168;

Henrik Wigh-Poulsen, *Hjemkomsten og det åbne land. Jakob Knudsens forfatterskab og den grundtvigske realisme* (Copenhagen: Vartov, 2001).

Papers:

Jakob Knudsen's manuscripts and papers are at the Danish Royal Library in Copenhagen.

Thøger Larsen

(5 April 1875 - 29 May 1928)

Søren Baggesen
Roskilde University

(Translated by Mark Mussari)

BOOKS: *Vilde Roser. Digte,* as Thøger Underbjerg (Aarhus: Jydsk Forlag, 1895);

Jord. Digte (Lemvig: C. Sønderby, 1904)–includes "Sommer," translated by Charles Wharton Stork as "Summer" in *A Second Book of Danish Verse* (New York: American-Scandinavian Foundation, 1947), p. 108; and "Baalet," translated by Ian Smith as "The Bonfire" in *Informationsavis. Nordjyllands Kunstmuseum,* 102 (1980): 8;

Dagene. Viser og Digte (Vejle: Hvidehus, 1905)–includes "I Cirkus" and "Nabostjerner," translated by R. P. Keigwin as "At the Circus" and "Celestial Neighbours" in *The Jutland Wind, and Other Verse from the Danish Peninsula* (Oxford: Blackwell, 1944), p. 93;

Det Fjerne. Digte (Copenhagen: Gyldendal, 1907);

Bakker og Bølger. Digte (Copenhagen: Gyldendal, 1912);

Fjordbredden. Noveller (Copenhagen: Gyldendal, 1913);

Slægternes Træ (Copenhagen: Gyldendal, 1914)–includes "Danmark nu blunder den lyse Nat," translated by Keigwin as "The Danish Summer" in *The Jutland Wind, and Other Verse from the Danish Peninsula,* p. 93;

Stjerner og Tid. Afhandlinger (Lemvig: Eget, 1914);

Kværnen. Historier (Copenhagen: Gyldendal, 1915);

Jord. Digte (Copenhagen: Gyldendal, 1916);

I Danmarks Navn. Digte (Copenhagen: Gyldendal, 1920);

Vejr og Vinger. Digte (Lemvig: Atlantis, 1923);

Limfjords-Sange (Copenhagen: Gyldendal, 1925)–includes "Lemvig," translated by Sven Holm in *Viking's Wake: Cruising through Southern Scandinavian Waters,* edited by Richard John MacCullagh (London: Van Nostrand, 1958), p. 209;

Søndengalm. Digte fra Italiensrejsen, 1925–1926 (Copenhagen: Gyldendal, 1926);

Trækfuglevej. Fortællinger og Digte (Copenhagen: Gyldendal, 1927);

Frejas Rok. Roman (Copenhagen: Gyldendal, 1928).

Thøger Larsen (courtesy of the Danish Royal Library, Copenhagen)

Editions and Collections: *Udvalgte Digte* (Copenhagen: Gyldendal, 1917);

Udvalgte Digte, edited by Otto Gelsted and Erik Zahle (Copenhagen: Gyldendal, 1938; revised, 1945);

Jyske Noveller, edited by Gelsted and Zahle (Copenhagen: Gyldendal, 1946);
Under Stjerner. Udvalgte Digte, 1895–1914, edited by Gelsted and Zahle (Copenhagen: Gyldendal, 1952);
Sfærernes Musik. Udvalgte Digte, 1920–1927, edited by Gelsted and Zahle, with an afterword by Gelsted (Copenhagen: Gyldendal, 1953);
Jorden og Det Fjerne (Copenhagen: Gyldendal, 1955);
Langsomt Skæbnerne tvindes (Copenhagen: Borgen, 1957)–comprises "En Moder" and "Jens Højby";
Thøger Larsen. Et Udvalg, edited, with an introduction, by Christian N. Brodersen (Copenhagen: Gyldendal/Dansklærerforeningen, 1960);
Virkeligheden. Artikler og Foredrag, edited by Brodersen (Copenhagen: Gyldendal/Forening for Boghaandværk, 1961);
Udvalgte Digte (Copenhagen: Gyldendal, 1963);
Året i Danmark. Udvalgte Digte, edited by Erik A. Nielsen and Steen Piper, with an introduction by Nielsen (Århus: Hovedland, 1984);
Digte (Copenhagen: H. Reitzel, 1986);
Fire Digtsamlinger, 1904–1912, edited, with an afterword, by Lotte Thyrring Andersen (Copenhagen: Danske Sprog- og Litteraturselskab/Borgen, 1995)–comprises *Jord, Dagene, Det Fjerne,* and *Bakker og Bølger.*

OTHER: *Atlantis. Dansk Maanedsskrift,* edited by Larsen (1923–1925).

TRANSLATIONS: Edward FitzGerald, *Rubáiyát af Omar Khayyám* (Copenhagen: Gyldendal, 1920);
Tycho Brahe, *Matematiske Betragtning over den ny og aldrig nogensinde før sete Stjerne,* translated by Larsen and Otto Gelsted (Lemvig: Atlantis, 1923);
Her skrives Solsangen, som det siges, at Sæmund Præst den frode skal have kvædet, da han laa død paa Baaren (Lemvig: Atlantis, 1923);
Sappho, *Sapfos Digte* (Lemvig: Atlantis, 1924);
Edda-Myterne, 3 volumes (Lemvig: H. Bech, 1926–1928);
Fra andre Tungemaal, edited by Gelsted and Erik Zahle (Copenhagen: Gyldendal, 1948).

Although Thøger Larsen did not establish himself as an author until the beginning of the twentieth century, his writing is often considered a part of nineteenth- century Danish literature. His debut collection, *Vilde Roser* (Wild Roses, 1895), merely served as a precursor to the core of his viable oeuvre. Historically, Larsen's poetry reflects the Danish symbolism popular in the 1890s. Thus, he was one of the poets who bridged Romanticism and twentieth-century modernism.

Thøger Larsen was born on 5 April 1875 in Geller Odde, north of Lemvig, in western Jutland. In the style of the times, he published *Vilde Roser* under his toponym, Underbjerg, instead of his last name, but never again. Thøger was the eldest of three children in a home that was poor but not impoverished. His father, Peder Larsen, a millwright, had moved to Underbjerg to oversee a pump at a land-reclamation project. Thøger's mother, Kirsten Dalgaard Thøgersen Larsen, came originally from that area, and her father lived with the family. This maternal grandfather, who had a profound effect on the boy's later development, was a gifted storyteller in possession of an ancient, almost magical sense of Christianity, which provided fodder for many good stories. Larsen's parents, in contrast, took their religious understanding from the evangelical mission that came to the area. The hymnal, therefore, became Larsen's introduction to verse; his use of rhythm and sense of imagery indicate clearly that the hymns of Thomas Kingo, Hans Adolph Brorson, and N. F. S. Grundtvig strongly influenced the young man. Otherwise, Larsen recalled his parents' religious reawakening as a curb on his imaginative childhood.

Following his local schooling in the village, the thirteen-year-old Larsen worked for a short time, but his natural gifts seemed more literary. He was therefore allowed to start lower secondary school in Lemvig, where he took his preliminary exams in 1892. Although he wanted to continue his education at an upper school, his father's death in the same year made it impossible. Instead, Larsen took work as a private tutor, first for a proprietor in Mønsted and then in Ulsted. During these years, under the influence of the tendencies emanating from Georg Brandes and the radicalism of the Modern Breakthrough, Larsen abandoned his evangelical religious sense. In 1896 he returned as a surveyor's assistant to Lemvig, where he fell into a small circle of culturally conscious and free-minded youth. The group survived for several years and was frequently visited by such notable authors as Jeppe Aakjær and Johannes V. Jensen. Larsen also traveled often to Copenhagen, where he became a popular lecturer at the Student League. The Lemvig literary circle held its meetings at a local bakery, where Larsen met Thyra Paludan, whom he married in 1904. That same year, he self-published his true debut, the poetry collection *Jord* (Earth, 1904). Once married, Larsen needed to establish himself financially, so he also accepted a position as editor of the radical newspaper *Lemvig Dagblad* (Lemvig Daily). He worked as his family's provider by day and as a poet and researcher by night. He often sat up writing and studying into the small hours of the morning. Deeply engaged with natural sciences of his time, he was also an amateur astronomer.

For the first few years Larsen's lyrical production occupied most of his intellectual energies. *Jord* was followed by *Dagene* (The Days) in 1905 and by *Det Fjerne* (The Distant) in 1907. Although the three poetry collections do not quite comprise an actual trilogy, they are united by their similar formal and thematic sense. Taken as a whole, they represent Larsen's breakthrough as a lyricist. *Jord* includes the poem that he later referred to as his credo, "Pan." It is a hymn of faith to a divinity the author identifies as Pan. The poem, with its consistent rhyme scheme and irregular stanzas of varying meter, appears in the collection as the final version of a poem reaching far back in the author's life. Originally written as a hymn characterized by the saccharine Christianity of Larsen's evangelical childhood, "Pan" was transmogrified into an almost pantheistic paean to the universe and its creative power.

"Strandvalmue" (Horn Poppy), from *Dagene,* even more characteristic of Larsen's lyrical tone and technique, takes its metrical sense from Brorson's hymn of longing, "Her vil ties, her vil bies" (Here we will be silent, here we will wait, 1765). "Strandvalmue" indicates not only that the hymnal was Larsen's introduction to lyrical writing but also that he was most influenced by the nature poetry found in many Danish hymns. This model was far removed from his philosophical attitudes. Brorson's hymn is a Christian allegory in which the longing for summer in the middle of winter's darkness reflects the soul's yearning for redemption through grace. Larsen's poem, on the other hand, is a variant on his creed concerning nature. Taking its point of departure in the image of a small, shy flower, "Strandvalmue" then expands into a depiction of a summer day representing the yearly movement from the birth of spring to the death of winter. Thus, the poem depicts the cycle of nature, along with the flower's individual death, which is no less bitter because of its place within that natural cycle. This contradiction is as important a theme in Larsen's writing as his creed regarding the circle of life. Although he wrote many ecstatic hymns to summer, reproduction, and the universe, he composed just as many bitter poems about winter, frozen expressions of the fear of death that he viewed as the natural foil to the joy of life.

One of Larsen's most renowned poems of death is "Jens Højby," from *Dagene.* It is an impressionistic sketch of the farmer Jens Højby; lonely and dying in his room, he is visited by vague recollections of his meager life. The sketch is composed, however, of short stanzas describing the summer day outside. The poem is an homage to this luxuriant sense of life. This contradiction appears in a stanza that moves from the portrait of summer to the sketch of Højby's death:

Paa de velsignede Agre
Trives de frodige Køer.
Ensom ligger den magre
Bonde Jens Højby og dør.

(Upon this blessed acre
The fertile cows do graze.
The lean and lonely farmer
Jens Højby ends his days.)

"Jens Højby" captures the ugly side of existence. A creeping insect reflects life's swarming quality; a spider ensnares a fat fly within its web, and all kinds of beetles and centipedes descend on the dying farmer. Despite its repellent imagery, the poem nevertheless serves as a paean to the blind worms, those "hellige dyr" (holy creatures) whose life-devouring consumption transforms everything that dies into the fertile soil from which new life grows.

Det Fjerne, Larsen's only poetry collection composed so that it comprises a self-contained whole, opens with two contrapuntal poems. The first, "Drift" (Urge), is an expansive poem about the longing for distant fields of rare fertility and for eroticism. Its counterpart, "Aftensolen" (The Evening Sun), begins with an impressionist view of the nature in Lemvig's harbor and then expands its reach. Earth becomes merely a globe in the universe: seen from that perspective, even Lemvig can function as a representative for cosmic presence. The reader senses Larsen's nature studies lurking behind both poems–his reading might just as well have inspired descriptions of floods in India or solar eminence–but his ability to transform knowledge into sensation characterizes all his lyrics.

Larsen follows these two poems about the world and the homestead with a suite about time consisting of eight seasonal poems, two for each season. "Jorden" (The Earth) represents his most ecstatic and jubilant tribute to life, a hymn to summer, fecundity, and sex. Yet, winter belongs to death–and death, too, is cosmic:

Livløs Maanen
skinner os til Døde,
skinner saa inderligt
gudsforladt og øde.

(Lifeless shines the moon–
To Death we shall be taken,
Shining from so deep within,
Deserted and forsaken.)

Two poems about humanity and the human condition follow the seasonal suite. "Hvidenæs," a description of Larsen's childhood in the area of Geller Odde, deals chiefly with the generations of toiling life and meager death in this deserted area. Its foil, "Danmark," an occasional poem written for the Farmers' Union in Lemvig, is a slightly ironic but caring homage to fertile farm life on the good earth. Following "Danmark" are four quite different poems, all variations on the theme of fecundity and death. The most important among them, "Walther von der Vogelweide," commemorates the German medieval lyricist of that name. In *Dagene* Larsen had translated Walther's most popular poem, "Under der linden," as "Under Lindene paa Engen" (Under the Lindens in the Meadow). Larsen's commemorative poem is written as an apostrophe to the German poet: "O, Walther i de Dødes Land! / Nu er du Muld hvor jeg er Mand!" (Oh, Walther, in the land of the dead. / You are now earth as I am now man). In this elegy the poet laments not Walther's death but rather the fact that this homage cannot be heard by him. Thus, "Walther von der Vogelweide" functions also as a declaration that poetry, existing in its own time, consists of a timelessness outside of humanity's and the earth's cycle of life and death.

Det Fjerne closes with the philosophical poem "Tidernes Sang" (Song of the Times). Although it features some singularly beautiful verses, it fails to succeed as a whole: speculative musings unfortunately tend to override poetic inspiration. Still, the poem contributes greatly to an understanding of Larsen's poetry and other works. It addresses the duality of interdependence, despite boundaries, and the solitude essential to each individual, a fundamental duality that inspired and motivated Larsen throughout his life.

Larsen's next collection, *Bakker og Bølger* (Hills and Waves, 1912), includes some of his finest poetry. In "Tordenbygen" (The Thunder Shower), for example, the dense, precise landscape is described with markedly erotic connotations, until the poem culminates in a thunderstorm reflecting a cosmic union between heaven and earth. In "Morgenbadet" (The Morning Bath), mythical and scientific depictions of the origins of life are woven into a paean of love to a young girl cooling off in a fjord after an embrace. All the goddesses of love, sinners, and mothers are united in her youthful beauty. This collection also serves as a departure, however, as it includes Larsen's translation of Edward FitzGerald's 1859 English reworking of Omar Khayyám's eleventh-century *Rubáiyát.*

In 1914 Larsen published two collections. *Slægternes Træ* (The Family Tree) includes the summer song "Danmark nu blunder den lyse Nat" (Denmark, the Bright Night Rests; translated as "The Danish Summer," 1944), later set to music by Oluf Ring, and Larsen's first translation of Eddic poetry. *Stjerner og Tid* (Stars and Time) is an essay collection consisting of adaptations of several of his studies on the Atlantis legends, originally published in *Lemvig Dagblad.* These studies were the first fruits of the scholarship that for decades monopolized Larsen's intellectual energies and almost superseded his own creative writing. First and foremost, they are studies of pre-Christian mythologies. Larsen's interest in mythology did not constitute a break in his authorship, nor had he turned his back on the natural science that had previously occupied much of his time. His essays on Atlantis disclose his intention to research the possibility of a factual, world-historical basis for the legends about the sunken city. His research therefore involved not only worldwide myths of a great flood but also accounts of oceanographic relationships and well-documented cases of catastrophic earthquakes and volcanic eruptions.

Thøger Larsen

Vejr og Vinger

Digte

Med Tegninger og Vignetter
af Forfatteren

Lemvig
Atlantis' Forlag
1923

Title page for a collection that includes some of Larsen's poems about winter and death (Memorial Library, University of Wisconsin–Madison)

Larsen's work on Atlantis also presents the first formulation of the basic views driving his mythological studies. His studies of old legends and new knowledge run parallel. Although he clearly distinguishes between mythic and scientific thinking, he finds common ground in a similar wonder over the phenomena of the physical world–and in both their apparent and hidden connections. Larsen focused his translation work and his mythological studies on the Norse Eddas, one important result of which was his translation of all Eddic poetry. These adaptations, though not particularly idiomatic, are still highly esteemed by both experts and researchers. Larsen's versions of the Eddas unite philological accuracy with a powerful poetic language.

As a researcher of myth, Larsen addressed the tendency toward Nordism, popularized in the Grundtvigian folk-high-school movement. He harbored the same skepticism for this movement as for the Inner Mission religion of his childhood. (Inner Mission was an evangelical Lutheran movement with a strict moral code founded in the mid nineteenth century.) He soon realized that Nordic mythology must be viewed as only one link in a greater complex of mythologies, encompassing, in any case, all Indo-European myths. In order to study these connections in their sources, Larsen had to broaden his knowledge of languages; thus, he learned Latin and Greek in addition to Old Icelandic and even familiarized himself with Sanskrit. His knowledge of Greek bore special fruit: his 1924 Danish translations of Sappho are still considered among the best.

Larsen originally planned to collect all his studies into one massive work, with Ragnarok (in Scandinavian mythology, the final battle between the good and evil gods) as a unifying theme, but that project became too unwieldy. His research resulted, instead, in a wealth of articles comprising most of the contents of his journal *Atlantis. Dansk Maanedsskrift* (Atlantis: Danish Monthly) published from 1923 to 1925. Myths about the Phrygian goddess Cybele and her love for Attis held special interest for Larsen, for in them he discovered what he perceived as the center of all Indo-European myth. Although the validity of this claim is disputed, it reflects the relevance of his mythical studies to the rest of his oeuvre. The endless cycle of life and death, basic to all of nature, surfaces in such myths as that of the great mother who loses her beloved and must retrieve him from the kingdom of the dead. This notion is fundamental to Larsen's own erotically colored, godless pantheism.

In these myths Larsen also discovered a confirmation of the basis for his own philosophy of life, clearly visible in his nuanced view of the relationship between science and myth (the ultimate result of his studies). Larsen never renounced scientific explanations–which he still found better than mythical ones–because they rely methodologically on more enduring observations than those found in myth. Still, his sense of the depths of the myths grew stronger and stronger, for they confirmed for him that the laws of nature reflect nature's living forces.

Slægternes Træ and *Stjerner og Tid,* primary in Larsen's intellectual work during the 1910s, represent his most important writings from this period. Around the same time he also published two short-story collections. The first, *Fjordbredden* (The Bank of the Fjord, 1913), is an anthology of previously published tales about the peasantry and includes some written in the local Jutland dialect. *Kværnen* (The Grinding Mill, 1915) includes two of Larsen's most important prose works, "Hemmeligheden" (The Secret) and "Kroen" (The Inn). The first deals with Eros in a story of repetition, return, and loss told in a science-fiction setting, and the latter offers a raw, realistic depiction of folk life with an underlying mythical pattern. Neither of the stories is a great piece of prose writing–if anything, they underscore Larsen's artistic ability as a lyric poet–but they contribute greatly to an understanding of the effect of his studies on his artistic temperament.

One indication of Larsen's sparse poetic production during this period is his 1916 collection *Jord,* an adaptation of poems from his first two collections, *Jord* and *Dagene*. By the end of the decade, however, he had exhausted all his scholarly studies and turned once again to poetry. In 1920 he published his collection *I Danmarks Navn* (In Denmark's Name); *Vejr og Vinger* (Weather and Wings) followed in 1923 and *Limfjords-Sange* (Songs of the Limfjord) in 1925. None of these collections is as strong as the three from Larsen's first decade of work, and they include several weak poems but also many of his best. Among the best is his second popular ode to summer, "Sommervise" (Summer Song), more commonly known by its first line, "Du danske Sommer, jeg elsker dig" (Danish Summer, I love you). Most Danes are familiar with this poem, from *Vejr og Vinger,* as well as with the earlier "Danmark nu blunder den lyse Nat," from *Slægternes Træ*. Both poems have somewhat of a ritualistic character in Denmark: the summer is said not to begin until they have been sung. As a whole, the two poems show, in their own way, the scope of Larsen's poetry: "Danmark nu blunder den lyse Nat" is soft, almost a lullaby, whereas "Sommervise" is an ecstatic hymn. Although the Danish public views Larsen as the poet of summer and vitality, thanks chiefly to these two songs, *Vejr og Vinger* and *Limfjords-Sange* include some of his most wintry poems of death. For example, "Septembernat" (September Night) in *Limfjords-Sange* opens with the line "Venlig, men usalig / vandrer langsomt Maanen" (Friendly but unhappy / The Moon slowly wanders). The mood of the poem is best expressed in the plaintive chorus:

Høst er endt, og Løvfald
kommer, Nat og Løvfald,
Maaneskin og Løvfald,
Suk og Sorg og Løvfald.

(Harvest is over, and leaves
Are falling, Night and fallen leaves,
Moonshine and fallen leaves,
Sorrows and sighs, and fallen leaves.)

One of the few narrative poems in Larsen's oeuvre, "Blishønsene" (The Coots), in *Vejr og Vinger,* is a naturalistic fable about eight coots in the period from spring birth and growth until their death on the hard ice of winter's heart.

Although Larsen's journal *Atlantis. Dansk Maanedsskrift,* begun in 1923, served primarily as a means for publishing the results of his mythological studies, it also presented his poems and essays, along with those of other contributors. Among the few others who wrote for the journal were three young and then-unknown writers, his most immediate successors in Danish poetry: Otto Gelsted, who became one of Larsen's best friends in his final years; the Faeroe Islander William Heinesen; and Jens August Schade, whose first published poem appeared in Larsen's journal.

On his fiftieth birthday in 1925 Larsen received a monetary gift collected by his friends, which enabled him, for the first and only time, to undertake a long journey abroad. On 1 October 1925 he and Thyra headed for Italy. Along the way they spent a week at Lake Lucerne in Switzerland. After a month of traveling, the Larsens took up residence near Amalfi at San Cataldo, an abandoned monastery renovated as a refuge for Danish artists and intellectuals (it still functions as such). Larsen and his wife remained there for half a year, although they also used the monastery as a base to take longer trips to northern Italian cities.

Larsen's stay in Italy had a profound effect on him and deeply affected his writing. First, he finally managed to finish a project that had haunted him throughout his writing career: a novel, *Frejas Rok* (Freya's Spinning Wheel). Although he lived to see it accepted for publication by Denmark's leading publisher, he never saw it in print; the novel was published posthumously in the year of his death, 1928. Although *Frejas Rok* is not a great novel–Larsen lacked both the narrative skills and the gift for character development the genre demands–it is nevertheless interesting for the way it illuminates his lifelong interest in the relationship between paganism and Christianity.

Larsen's journey more directly inspired *Trækfuglevej* (The Way of the Migrant, 1927), a collection featuring some excellent prose sketches from his trip. Of special interest for understanding his travels is "Italiensk Juleaften" (Italian Christmas Eve), which illustrates the state of confusion the Italian winter inspired in Larsen. On Christmas Eve he strolls in the mountains around San Cataldo, where he sees green bushes and the blossoming crocus–that is, spring in the dead of winter. The experience thrills him, but it also unnerves him, for it seems to indicate an absence of season: winter as the death of summer. "Øen i Himlen" (Island in the Sky) is a sketch about a trip by cable car to the top of Rigi, a mountain north of Lake Lucerne. In this charmingly ironic piece, the poet depicts himself as a tourist among tourists (although a special tourist). "Øen i Himlen" also includes an exciting depiction of the Alpine landscape and of the experience of rising above the clouds and looking out toward the clearness above the mountains' peaks. The sketch ends lovingly in a thrilling depiction of a young girl standing at the edge of an abyss, where, unfazed, she sells postcards.

Larsen's central work after the trip to Italy was the poetry collection *Søndengalm. Digte fra Italiensrejsen, 1925–1926* (The Southerly Wind: Poems from the Italian Journey, 1926), in which the reader senses the importance the journey had for him. Most of the poems consist of landscape descriptions. Expanding clearly on Larsen's Limfjord nature poetry, they possess the same concrete sense impressions, but their perspective is cosmic. Another landscape inspired these poems, however, an alien landscape that bewilders the senses and gives rise to different reflections. The most immediately striking example of the sense of confusion in these poems is seen in the use of color. In Larsen's earlier writing colorific adjectives are clear and pure: the sea is blue, the meadow is green, the corn is yellow, and the snow is white. These colors reflect a definite chromatic symbolism: blue is the color of eternity or infinity, green represents life and rebirth, yellow is ripening and fertility, and white belongs to death. In the Italian poems the color adjectives, shifting character, become more searching and nuanced. In "Solnedgang" (Sunset), which describes the sun's descent over the bay at Amalfi, the blue bay does indeed lie in "Evigheds-farver" (colors of eternity), but it is not merely blue: it "ligger og kogler i Sindet Mystik og Musik, / dybblaa og grønblaa, violblaa og blegnende Farver" (lies in the mind, conjuring spells and music, / deep blue and green-blue, violet and fading hues).

At the same time, closer inspection reveals that a change in spatial dimensions represents the deepest characteristic of these poems. The Limfjord poetry relies heavily on horizontal and vertical imagery. Den-

Cover for Larsen's collection of poems based on his 1925–1926 trip to Italy (Dana College Library)

mark is a relatively flat land: there are hills surrounding Lemvig, and the city lies within a steep hollow, but there are no great heights anywhere. The countryside stretches horizontally in both reality and in Larsen's writing. Looking up, one sees sky and clouds. Italy proffered a different landscape. San Cataldo sits high above the bay, yet the land behind it rises in sheer mountainsides with distant peaks. That experience deeply captivated the poet. All of the poems in *Søndengalm* are mountain poems, not merely the landscape pieces but other poems as well. One, "Den gamle Kone fra Minuto" (The Old Wife from Minuto), functions as a kind of counterpart to the earlier "Jens Højby." It, too, deals with a person's death, but the old wife does not die alone following a fruitless life. She dies instead surrounded by her strong sons. The poem deals primarily, though, with her feet: how they carried her throughout her youth, running up and down steps and steep paths in and around her village, and how in her old age the same feet bore her, faithfully and carefully, up the same paths. At the end of the poem she lies, worn out and gray, in poor clothing on her deathbed; yet, her feet are covered in silk stockings and patent-leather shoes. Possibly, beyond the grave and the strife, she might be "kaldes / til en Dans paa Himlens Roser" (called / To a dance on heaven's roses).

"Den gamle Kone fra Minuto" is the first of four narrative poems that form the final section of *Søndengalm* and that, together, make up more than half the book. Two are notable for being Larsen's only poems clearly set in a definite locale (although in an indefinite past). "Byfogeden i Pontone" (The Judge in Pontone) is a medieval story with robbers and skeletons. "Bacchusbruden" (The Bride of Bacchus), set in Roman antiquity, tells the story of Aurelia, whose passion is so strong and demanding that only a god can satisfy her. The poem ends with a depiction of Aurelia on top of an erupting volcano preparing to meet her beloved in the all-consuming fire of his embrace. Although not the only one of Larsen's poems to deal with desire, ecstasy, passion, and death, it is unique in its wildness. The imagery is blatantly sadomasochistic: lash marks on Aurelia's back and bosom lead to orgasm in the holy marriage with the satyric god. The poem is, however, the only one of Larsen's not set within a lyrical framework. The poem is told from the perspective of the main character, Aurelia. No third party "sees" and relates the events–the reader sees only what Aurelia senses. The wildness of the poem is undoubtedly indebted to Larsen's visit to Pompeii, which released latent powers in the poet's own mind. More important, "Bacchusbruden," his "last" poem in the sense that it is the last in his final poetry collection, is the ultimate artistic manifestation of all he discovered in the depths of mystery. It is a poem about Eros as Thanatos; in life there is death, and in death there is life, an insight found in the ecstatic, all-devouring now.

Appearing in *Søndengalm* immediately before "Bacchusbruden" is "Floras Rejse" (Flora's Journey), a poem obviously written after Larsen's return, depicting how the poet, along with the goddess of spring, leaves Italy behind and arrives in "Danmarks / Agre, Enge og Søer" (Denmark's / Acres, meadows and lakes). A long, rambling poem, occasionally charming in its profession of love for the ancient goddess (depicted here as a modern young girl in a waving veil riding in a car), "Floras Rejse" is undeniably vague and unfocused in long passages. The poem is important, though, in that Larsen enumerates exactly what he has taken with him from Italy. Most important is the mountain that he will forever see fading into blue beyond his hillside.

The most important poem in *Søndengalm* is "Rigi Kulm" (Rigi Culm), a lyrical reworking of Larsen's cable-car ride to the top of Rigi (depicted in prose in "Øen i Himlen"). One of his finest poems, it is tightly composed and coherent in its imagery; yet, it is also one of the most difficult of his poems to interpret. Although

"Rigi Kulm" is neither abstruse nor hermetic, it includes so much that is immediately recognizable that the poem is rendered totally unrecognizable. Despite the plethora of contexts (including the prose sketch) and its place among Larsen's other mountain poems and earlier poems about the earth in the cosmos, "Rigi Kulm" is strikingly singular. It seems to turn its back on its own various contextual references, thus leaving the reader uncertain.

This uncertain quality in "Rigi Kulm" becomes especially apparent in Larsen's use of color. Quantitatively, gray, a color rarely found in his work, dominates. For example, images of the clouds, a gray sea encircling islands of mountain peaks, appear frequently. This image offers the first sign of uncertainty. Larsen usually paints his seas in sky blue, the color of life and eternity. Blue and white usually dominate the depiction of the islands of mountain peaks. Although this usage seems to recall his "old" use of heaven's eternal blue, the peaks appear in white, the whiteness of eternal ice and snow. They are not islands of death, however; they are "Salighedens Øer" (islands of the blessed), and the mystical allusion of this epithet is unmistakable. White represents the color of sublime life in this poem. Life streams down from these islands, the glaciers serving as "Kilder for Europas Floder" (springs for the rivers of Europe). The conclusion abets this interpretation as it depicts this descent, "ned, hvor Menneskene bygger / som paa Bund af Verdenshavet" (down, where people build / As on the floor of the sea).

"Rigi Kulm" is, at once, as ecstatic a sun poem as "Solsangen" (The Song of the Sun, from the 1904 collection *Jord*), which it does not resemble, and as frozen a poem of death as "Septembernat," to which it also bears no similarity. The uncertain meaning of "Rigi Kulm" rests on its thematic and Imagist similarities to all Larsen's other poems, despite the sense that it must be interpreted in light of his experiences on the peak. One may come closest to an answer by noticing that the poem stands isolated in the collection, alone in a separate section titled "Undervejs" (Along the Way). Although this section title obviously refers to the fact that the poet experienced his feelings "along the way" to San Cataldo, the term may possess a less literal meaning. "Rigi Kulm" was written in Lemvig, after Larsen returned home, and a tense shift in the final stanza clearly indicates that the poem is a memoir. The tense is present throughout the poem–until the swan song of the final stanza:

Ned mod Skyerne vi skrider,
Solskinsryg paa Skyggebølger,
ned fra Øen, hvor jeg saa mod
evig Sne og evig Klarhed.

(Down toward the clouds we glide,
On waves of shadows, sun on our backs,
Down from the island, where I could see
Eternal snow and eternal clarity.)

Larsen was already under a death sentence when he wrote the poem because he suffered from diabetes, which was difficult to treat at that time. Although his spirits were unfailing, he was physically about to succumb. The poem may be so singular because Larsen was, for the first and only time, able to reconcile himself to the prospect of his own death.

"Rigi Kulm" does not represent Larsen's spiritual testament, however; that title belongs to the essay "Digtningen og Aandslivet" (Writing and Intellectual Life), which he published in 1925 in the final issue of *Atlantis*. For the final time he wrestled with the question that had haunted him throughout his life: the relationship between science and religion–and the language of poetry in connection with this relationship. For Larsen, science served primarily as a critique of religion and religion as a critique of science. Science places its object outside of itself. The wonder that drives science, therefore, lies outside of science and the language in which it is expressed (because human wonder is not an object that can be viewed outside of itself). Religion possesses a language for that wonder in myth, but religion stiffens into a dogma that seeks to turn interpretation into explanation. That stiffening refutes science, but science threatens to harden into its own dogma, such as atheism, because it seeks to turn explanations into interpretations. Larsen concluded that the world must be explained scientifically but interpreted religiously.

Although one might believe that this reconciliation occurred in Larsen's poetry, the matter is not so simple. A poem can certainly be a profound expression of the wonder that feeds science (and myth) and that is expressed in religion. But because it also has its object outside of itself, a poem resembles science more than religion. The wonder–the "now"–that is the subject of a poem does not exist in the "now" of the creation of the poem. In "Jorden," from *Det Fjerne,* the poet writes, "Jeg synger med Sjælen af Latter saa varm" (I sing with the warm soul of laughter). Larsen, however, sat up late at night and struggled with composing the poem. Thus, the eternity of the poem is the eternity of repetition. It may be only one song, but it is sung again and again.

Thøger Larsen died on 29 May 1928 in Lemvig, where he was also buried. Thyra donated all the belongings in his study–furniture, books, telescope, pen, and inkstand–to the Lemvig Museum, where they are arranged exactly as he left them in his study. The outside exhibit consists primarily of a path of planets, a solar system of miniature models arranged in a distance proportionate to the actual planets' distance from the sun. This path runs along the creek out to Geller Odde, where Larsen was born. The landscape remains so little affected by modern industrial development that it looks almost exactly as it did in his own time.

Thanks to his two odes to summer, Larsen remains one of the most beloved poets in Denmark, although he has never acquired a particularly wide circle of readers. In his own time he was respected, and he counted among his friends such notable poets as Sophus Claussen and Aakjær. Although he has been mostly viewed as a local poet, Larsen has his natural place among the lesser classics in the Danish lyrical tradition. He receives his due in Danish literary histories, and his poems continue to appear in anthologies, both scholarly and popular. Volumes of his selected poems are still published. Although research into his writing is sporadic, Larsen's influence on later Danish lyrical poets remains clear: direct and indirect quotations from his works surface among even the youngest poets.

Bibliographies:

Agnes Als Hermann and Knud Madsen, *Thøger Larsen, en bibliografi. Litteratur af og om Thøger Larsen, 1875–1975* (Ålborg: Danmarks Biblioteksskole, 1978);

Madsen, *Thøger Larsen. En bibliografi, 1891–1988,* 2 volumes (Århus: Statsbiblioteket, 1997).

Biography:

Christian N. Brodersen, *Thøger Larsen. En Monografi,* 2 volumes (Copenhagen: Gyldendal, 1942, 1950).

References:

Harry Andersen, *Afhandlinger om Thøger Larsen* (Rødovre: Rolv, 1986);

Lotte Thyrring Andersen, *Registrant, Thøger Larsen-samlingen, Lemvig Museum* (Lemvig: Lemvig Museum, 1996);

Søren Baggesen, *Thøger Larsen. En kritisk monografi* (Odense: Odense University Press, 1994);

Christian N. Brodersen, ed., *Thøger Larsen–manuskripter* (Copenhagen: E. Munksgaard, 1943);

Torben Brostrøm, "Thøger Larsen," in *Danske digtere i det 20. århundrede,* edited by Brostrøm and Mette Winge, volume 1 (Copenhagen: Gad, 1980);

Jens Aage Doctor, *De centrale symboler i Thøger Larsens lyrik* (Århus: Universitetsforlaget, 1956);

Doctor, *Kunst og liv* (Copenhagen: S. Hasselbalch, 1955);

Otto Gelsted, "Thøger Larsen," in *Danske digtere i det 20. århundrede,* edited by Frederik Nielsen and Ole Restrup, volume 1 (Copenhagen: Gad, 1965);

Ebbe Kornerup, *Thøger Larsen og Breve fra ham* (Copenhagen: Woels, 1928);

Sven Møller Kristensen, *Den store generation* (Copenhagen: Gyldendal, 1974);

Felix Nørgaard, *Kvinden, solen og universet. Om Thøger Larsen som menneske og digter* (Herning: P. Kristensen, 1980).

Papers:

Thøger Larsen's papers are at the Danish Royal Library in Copenhagen.

Poul Martin Møller

(21 March 1794 - 13 March 1838)

Claus Elholm Andersen
Denmark's International Study Program, Copenhagen

BOOKS: *Efterladte Skrifter af Poul M. Møller,* 3 volumes, edited by Christian Thaarup, F. C. Olsen, Christian Winther, and L. V. Petersen (Copenhagen: C. A. Reitzel, 1839–1843);

Udvalgte Skrifter, 2 volumes, edited by Vilhelm Andersen (Copenhagen: Gad, 1895; revised, 1930).

Editions: *Sandfærdig Krønike om den norske Spillemand Eyvind, Skaldaspiller kaldet . . . ,* Nordiske Klassikere, no. 1 (Copenhagen, 1888);

Statistisk Skildring af Lægdsgaarden i Ølseby-Magle af en ung Geograf, Nordiske Klassikere, no. 2 (Copenhagen, 1888);

En dansk Students Eventyr. En ufuldtendt Novelle, edited by A. N. Brorson Fich (Copenhagen: Gyldendalsk/Dansklærerforeningen, 1934);

En dansk Students Eventyr og Lægdsgaarden i Ølseby-Magle, edited by Frederik Nielsen, Gyldendals Bibliotek, no. 8 (Copenhagen: Gyldendal, 1964).

TRANSLATION: *Homers Odyssees sex første Sange metrisk oversatte* (Copenhagen: Gyldendal, 1825).

Three years after the death of Poul Martin Møller, the young philosopher Søren Kierkegaard dedicated his work *Om Begrebet Ironi med stadigt Hensyn til Socrates* (1841; translated as *The Concept of Irony with Continual Reference to Socrates,* 1989) to his late professor at the University of Copenhagen with the words "Græcitetens lykkelige Elsker, Homers Beundrer, Sokrates's Medvider, Aristotles's Fortolker . . . min Beundring, mit Savn" (The fortunate lover of Greek Culture, the admirer of Homer, the confidant of Socrates, the interpreter of Aristotle . . . my admiration, my loss). During his lifetime Møller published only a translation of the first songs of *The Odyssey,* a few poems in various journals, and some reviews and minor philosophical writings. Although most of his work was published posthumously and only exists in the form of fragments and unfinished drafts, Møller was a central figure in the intellectual life of Copenhagen in the 1820s and 1830s. Today he is regarded as a major influence on Danish Romanticism, as the author of the novel *En dansk Students Eventyr* (The Tale of a Danish Student, 1843), written in 1824 and first published in *Efterladte Skrifter af Poul M. Møller* (Posthumous Works of Poul M. Møller, 1839–1843), and as Kierkegaard's professor. Møller's significant influence on Kierkegaard can be traced in several of the philosopher's early writings.

Møller was born on 21 March 1794 in Uldum, Jutland, the son of a pastor (later a bishop), Rasmus Møller, and Bodil Thaulow. When he was eight, Møller moved with his family to the island of Lolland, south of Zealand, where his father had been assigned. Møller grew up there in the presbytery of Købeløv and was educated at home by his father until the age of thirteen.

In 1810, shortly after Møller started his studies at Nykøbing Grammar School, his mother died after having been bedridden for several years. Soon after, his father remarried. His new wife was Hanne Winther, the widow of a minister in a neighboring parish and the mother of Christian Winther, Møller's best friend. Together the stepbrothers made their earliest attempts at writing poetry.

In 1812 Møller began studying theology at the University of Copenhagen. Throughout his four years at the university, he was highly engaged in student life, and he soon became the center of attention for his fellow students' many discussions on aesthetics, philosophy, and poetry. Yet, although he often discussed poetry and recited his own poems, Møller did not write much during these years. One of the few exceptions is his literary debut in 1815 in the journal *Dagen,* in which he published "Digt til N.S." (Poem to N.S.) in honor of his friend Nicolai Søtoft; it is included in his collected works.

Throughout most of his student years Møller was secretly engaged to Margrethe Bloch, the daughter of the principal from Nykøbing Grammar School; she was a young girl with whom he presumably had already fallen in love in 1811. A few months before he graduated, Margrethe suddenly broke the engagement. Møller was devastated, and after receiving his degree, he returned to Købeløv, where, trying to compensate for his loss, he wrote some of his most famous early poems (published posthumously in his collected works). He also began work on a translation of Homer's *Odyssey* into Danish, which he never completed; the translation of the first six songs was published in 1825.

Møller's writings from this period reflect his continuing grief over the broken engagement–for instance, in "Sandfærdige Krønike om Eyvind Skjaldespiller" (Truthful Chronicle on Eyvind the Bard) and in the poem "Torbisten og Fluen" (The Chafer and the Fly). The ironic and sometimes bitter tone in the latter hints at Møller's feelings as when the fly rejects the chafer's proposal, telling him to "Flyv til din Mødding derude" (Fly back to your dunghill out there). Møller also wrote such love poems as "Til Laura" (To Laura) and "Søde! Siig, hvornaar mon jeg dig finder?" (Sweet Girl! Tell Me When I Shall Find You?), which later in a slightly altered version were integrated into Møller's unfinished novel *En dansk Students Eventyr*. In the sonnet "Til Laura" the poetic *I* compares himself with a fly that flies in circles trying to catch the sunlight as it enters through a living-room window. In the last two stanzas of the sonnet, he explains that he must "i Kredse stedse svinge" (in circles ever swing) to catch his beloved's eyes, until: "Graven dækker kold min brændte Vinge" (the grave coldly covers my burned wing).

After spending the winter of 1816–1817 at the presbytery of Købeløv, Møller took a position as a private tutor at the manor Espegaard near Korsør in the spring of 1817. He stayed there until fall 1818. He then returned to Copenhagen, at a time when the biggest literary controversy of Danish Romanticism reached its peak in the debate between the authors Jens Baggesen and Adam Oehlenschläger. Baggesen had in reviews criticized Oehlenschläger's naive version of Romanticism. Oehlenschläger, however, had a large group of admirers, especially among the students, with Møller and eleven others publishing a defense of Oehlenschläger's poetry. Their defense, in turn, provoked another group of students to defend Baggesen. A few days later, Møller wrote a contribution to the debate in his own name, comparing the attack on Oehlenschläger's poetry with the attack of a bird of prey on a dove "hvergang den bringer et nyt Olieblad til Kunstnerens Krands" (each time it brings a new olive leaf to the artist's wreath).

During the debate, Møller wrote one of his most famous early poems, "Aprilsvise" (April Ballad), published in *Købehauns Morgenblad* (Copenhagen Morning Post) in 1825 but written in the spring of 1819. The poem compares blossoming nature with young girls walking on the fortifications surrounding Old Copenhagen, while they "Sende deres Blikke rundt som Pile" (pass their gazes round like arrows). While praising the beauty of spring, the ballad is also characterized by a sad tone, as are most of Møller's writings from this period. In "Aprilsvise" this sadness becomes most explicit in the last line, in which the poetic *I*, after describing the pretty young girls, concludes that "Det er tungt, man skal gaa hjem alene" (That one has to walk home alone is sad).

In June 1819 Møller took a job as a chaplain on a ship going to China and left Copenhagen for almost two years. This journey may have been motivated in part by the marriage of Margrethe Block. The trip had a huge impact on Møller's development as a writer and philosopher, and many of his best works were created or outlined during the trip. The journey eventually led to a change in his oeuvre, from the harmonic and almost uniform Biedermeier style in the early writings to what later became known as Poetic Realism.

From the beginning of the journey, Møller started organizing his ideas in small aphorisms–fragmentary, thought-provoking statements. He called these aphorisms "Strøtanker" (stray thoughts) and kept writing them throughout his life. In the first ones, he reflects a great deal on the genre of aphorisms, stating that they can be seen as "Tænkningens Culminationspuncter–en Slags Hermafroditer, halv Poesie, halv Prosa" (thinking climaxes–a kind of hermaphrodite, half poetry, half prose). He also wrote about how the aphorisms became a "Surrogat for Samtale" (substitute for conversation). Other aphorisms from the journey concern the poet Homer, human character, the use of rhetoric, and classical versus modern German poetry. In characterizing the latter, he states that its "Genstand er den selv, den er Poesi over Poesi" (object is itself, it is poetry on poetry)–a characteristic that Kierkegaard later employed in *Om Begrebet Ironi med stadigt Hensyn til Socrates*.

Aboard the ship Møller also wrote the comical *Statistisk Skildring af Lægdsgaarden i Ølseby-Magle af en ung Geograf* (Statistical Description of the Government District Farm in Ølseby-Magle by a Young Geographer), first published in his *Efterladte Skrifter*. The composition of the statistical description is that of an academic dissertation with several elaborating notes and references to essential literature. The interplay between this academic form and the subject of the dissertation, the government district farm, accounts for the comic irony. The young geographer, the author of the dissertation, describes everything on the farm as if he were making a statistical description of a hitherto unknown country.

Page from the manuscript for Poul Martin Møller's novel En dansk Students Eventyr *(The Tale of a Danish Student), written in 1824 and published posthumously in 1843 (courtesy of the Danish Royal Library, Copenhagen)*

He describes the religion of the estate, its foreign policy, its form of government, and its different art forms. For example, he sees the housemaid as the estate rhapsodist, because she knows a single dreary ballad. He also sees a clearly primitive painting by one of the residents as the most outstanding piece of art on the estate. While praising the painting, he complains that it could be a little more aesthetic. In this part, Møller indirectly makes fun of contemporary critics by letting the young geographer use language somewhat similar to theirs: "Jeg er overbevist om, at det vil gaa de fleste Kunstdommere ligesom mig. De ville finde, at Gertruds Bagdel har for megen Masse og en alt for enorm Bredde. Men efter at have set Originalen tager jeg min overilede Dom tilbage" (I am convinced that most art critics would think the same as I. They would find that Gertrud's behind has too much substance and a too enormous width. But after seeing the original, I take my hasty verdict back). In his exaggerated interpretation of the conditions at the district farm, the young geographer even sees tendencies toward civil war.

While at sea, Møller also wrote poetry. Most prominent is a cycle of six poems, called "Scener i Rosenborg Have" (Scenes in the Garden of Rosenborg). Of the six poems, only two were published while Møller was alive. The title of the cycle was the idea of Christian Winther, who published it in *Efterladte Skrifter* shortly after Møller's death. The poems can be read as reflections of Møller's homesickness for his life in Copenhagen. Each poem describes a character–for example, a beggar, a mother with her child, and a man who revisits the garden after a long illness. The last poem of the cycle, "Hans og Trine" (Hans and Trine), is about two young lovers who secretly meet in the garden. Toward the end of the poem, however, Trine breaks up the relationship. The poem ends with Hans reciting a sonnet in which he declares how he never, in his reading of entertainment literature, has met a girl like Trine.

During the journey to China, Møller also wrote the brief travel memoir *Optegnelser paa Kinarejsen* (Notes from the China Journey), first published in his *Udvalgte Skrifter* (Selected Writings, 1895), in which he dramatized the experiences onboard the ship *Christianshavn.* His description of the first part of the trip is an early example of Møller's use of poetic realism. On the one hand, the description is characterized by poetic and vivid imagery, with the suitcases and other luggage sliding around the deck during the storm. On the other hand, Møller describes realistically how the storm made him and the rest of the crew seasick. Besides the description of the storm, which was something every travel memoir at that time included, Møller describes the seaward approach to Cape Town, South Africa, and his introduction to the Orient in Manila.

On 14 July 1821 *Christianshavn* returned to the harbor of Copenhagen. Møller was excited to be back in Copenhagen and wrote to his friend Niels Bygum Krarup on 30 August that he felt "saa usigelig lyksalig" (so inexpressibly happy). In 1820, while Møller had been away on his journey, the students of Copenhagen had set up a student union, of which Møller quickly became a prominent member, contributing several student songs while teaching Greek and Latin at Metropolitanskolen, the oldest school in Copenhagen. Also, in the student union in the spring of 1824 Møller presented the first three chapters of what later became known as his principal work, *En dansk Students Eventyr.*

Møller had already worked with the idea of a student novel on his journey to China, when he listed the main characters of the novel and a few plot points. Back in Copenhagen, however, the historical novels of Sir Walter Scott had just become well known and were widely read by Møller and his friends in the student union. Inspired by Scott, Møller changed the original idea of a contemporary student novel to a student novel set during the Reformation, around 1536. From the few chapters that exist from Møller's attempt to write an historical novel, one recognizes several episodes from the final edition of *En dansk Students Eventyr.* Møller stopped working on the historical novel in late 1822 and returned to his original idea.

Christian Thaarup, one of the editors of Møller's *Efterladte Skrifter,* in which *En dansk Students Eventyr* appeared for the first time, gave the novel its title. The novel was never completed, but Møller had supposedly told some of his friends how it was to continue. After having read the first three chapters to his fellow students on 28 February and 6 March 1824, Møller worked for a short time on a fourth chapter. *En dansk Students Eventyr,* along with Steen Steensen Blicher's *En Landsbydegns Dagbog* (1824; translated as *The Diary of a Parish Clerk,* 1996), marks the breakthrough of poetic realism in Danish literature.

The fragmentary novel tends toward the genre of the bildungsroman in its composition, but Møller's allusions to other literary genres and forms lend the novel a modern character. Several poems appear throughout the novel, and the second chapter alludes to the epistolary novels of early Romanticism. In *En dansk Students Eventyr,* Møller made extensive use of his knowledge of different types of students, using even his closest friends as models for the various characters. The spontaneous protagonist, Frits Klinger, acts before he thinks and follows his heart and his first impressions. Despite multiple digressions, the novel is mainly about Frits's love stories.

At the beginning of the novel, a group of students is gathered in a summer residence outside Copenhagen. When one of the students asks why Frits has not yet joined them, the students start discussing Frits's character, describing him as a "Kamæleon, der bestandigt antager sine Omgivelsers Farver" (chameleon, who constantly takes on the colors of his surroundings). Christian, Frits's friend and stepbrother (probably modeled after Christian Winther), suddenly interrupts the discussion and tells the others about Frits's childhood. Then Bertel, another student, takes over and tells an anecdote about Frits, describing an event that took place the previous night. Thus, the reader only experiences Frits as a person spoken about, existing through the stories and discussions of his fellow students. Through hearsay, the reader finds out that Frits belongs to a certain group of Romantic lovers who "bestandig se deres elskede med en Glorie om sin Tinding, som en hellig Jomfru, der gaar paa solbeskinnede Skyer" (constantly see their beloved with a halo around their temples, as a holy virgin, who walks on sunny clouds). This characterization can be seen as taken from Møller's 1837 outline for a dissertation on three kinds of affectation, *Forberedelser til en Afhandling om Affektation* (Preparations to a Thesis on Affectation), a concept he also often wrote about during the 1820s in his aphorisms.

In the next chapter of the novel, the reader indirectly, through letters, follows Frits's experience at *Møllerkroen* (The Mill's Inn), where he has gone to pursue one of his loves. Reading the letters aloud, Bertel recognizes his cousin in Frits's description of another lodger at *Møllerkroen,* a starry-eyed academic referred to as the licentiate (title of student holding a bachelor's degree). The licentiate is Frits's complete opposite, a man unable to act at all, not just on impulse. Bertel tells the students how he once visited the licentiate and was shocked by learning that he had been working on his dissertation, "Menneskets fysiske og intellectuelle Natur" (On the Human Being's Physical and Intellectual Nature), for years without writing a single word. Asking the licentiate why his room is filled with stones, Bertel is told,

> Jeg har bemærket, at Tankerne glider bedst fra Pennen, naar man besidder aldeles hensigtsmæssige Skriveredskaber. For at faa gode Penne, maa man have gode Knive, og for at skærpe dem, maa man besidde ret udsøgte Slibesteen. Derfor har jeg (Y) maattet trænge temmelig dybt ind i Mineralogien."

> (I have noticed that the thoughts go through the quill better if you own the appropriate writing utensils. To get good quills, you need good knives, and to sharpen them, you have to possess exquisite grindstones. Hence, I needed to start studying mineralogy.)

Furthermore, the licentiate explains why he is not a man of action. Every time he considers writing, "tænker (jeg) over, at jeg tænker derover, og deler mig selv i en uendelig tilbageskridende Rad af Jer, der betragte hinanden. Jeg ved ikke, hvilket Jeg der skal standses ved som det egentlige, og i det Øjeblik jeg stander ved eet, er det jo igen et Jeg, der standser derved" (I think about that I think about it, and I divide myself into an infinite series of retrogressive I's, who watch each other. I do not know which *I* to stop at as the real one, and the moment I stop at one, it is once again an *I* who stops there). Møller is indirectly criticizing the philosophy of the German Idealistic philosopher Johann Gottfried von Fichte, who was much debated at that time and who worked with several different categories of the Self. Later, in 1835, Møller returned to this critique in an outline for an essay titled "Om Begrebet Ironie" (The Concept of Irony). This short outline inspired Kierkegaard, who in 1841 wrote a thesis with the same title, in which one also finds an extensive critique of Fichte's subjective philosophy.

While the first two chapters of *En dansk Students Eventyr* portray Frits through the students' stories, the last two chapters offer a direct description of the protagonist. The impression of his spontaneous character is confirmed along with the earlier characterization of him as the kind of lover who does not demand any specific attributes of his beloved, since he–by will–will transmit these qualities to her. This process becomes clear during a duck hunt at *Møllerkroen,* where Frits for the second time in the novel finds a new object for his love. From *Møllerkroen,* Frits moves on to the country manor Ravnshøj in an attempt to pursue his love for the aristocratic, but uneducated, girl Sophie. She can be seen in opposition to Frits's previous love, Marie, who is educated despite her simple upbringing. The novel ends at Ravnshøj, just as the lady of the house, Sophie's mother, has invited a group of intellectuals to discuss literature.

The digressions of *En dansk Students Eventyr* and the indirect characterization of Frits are reasons that the novel, despite its fragmentary and incomplete form, has canonical status in Danish literary Romanticism. In his seemingly improvised narrative style, Møller paid more attention to the single parts of the novel than to the story line, a decision that might explain why he never finished the novel. Although he worked intensively on *En dansk Students Eventyr* for about a year, Møller did not give up on poetry and published the sonnet cycle "En Elskers Fantasier over sin Elskerindes fem Fingre" (A Lover's Fantasies about His Beloved's Five Fingers) in

1823. Each of the five sonnets describes a finger, the five metaphorically representing the different stages in a relationship. Basing a sonnet on the first digit of the hand, Møller describes how the beloved with her forefinger in the days of their early love calls the poetic *I* into the forest. In subsequent sonnets, the third finger symbolizes engagement and marriage, while the pinkie represents and celebrates the everyday life of marriage, as the beloved uses the finger to caress the poetic *I:*

Det hulde Blik til hendes Elskte titter
Da rører mig saa tit den samme Lille,
Der næsten over evne sig maa strække

(The faithful glance at her lover sighs
Then touching me with the little one
Who must stretch almost as long as it can)

In 1824 Møller returned to the University of Copenhagen to study philosophy, guided by his professor, F. C. Sibbern. Taking a final university examination in philosophy in the summer of 1826, Møller was immediately recommended by Sibbern for a position as professor in philosophy at the recently founded university in Christiania (Oslo). Just before leaving Copenhagen in October 1826, Møller proposed to Betty Berg, a well-read woman whom he had met on several occasions since returning from China. On 1 July 1827, after one year in Christiania, Møller returned to Denmark; he married Berg on 30 June, visited friends in Copenhagen, and brought his bride back to Norway with him. A year later she gave birth to their first son, Christian Rasmus. They had three other children, all boys: Frits, Poul Martin, and Rasmus Johannes.

During his stay in Norway, Møller did not write much poetry. Instead, he focused on teaching his classes in philosophy and psychology, and he occasionally contributed reviews to Danish periodicals. Among these reviews, one finds ones of books by Sibbern, two tragedies by Carsten Hauch, and a translation of the *Iliad.* Møller also wrote drafts for a moral philosophy as well as for a general history of philosophy. In his letters to other writers, including Sibbern, Møller states that he is "meget glad over, at jeg er kommet til at beskjeftige mig udelukkende med Philosophie, som nu interesserer mig over alt Andet i Verden" (very happy to devote all my time to philosophy, which by now interests me more than anything else in this world).

Møller's letters to his friends back in Copenhagen also reveal how much he missed the intellectual life of the Danish capital. Writing that he probably always will "finde mig noget fremmed her" (find myself somewhat of a stranger here), he admits that he "naturligviis meget heller vilde leve i mit Fædreneland" (would much rather, of course, live in my native country) because his "norske Omgang faar aldrig den Indflydelse paa min Tankegang, som min kjøbenhavnske Vennekreds har havt" (Norwegian acquaintances will never have the same impact on my way of thinking as my circle of friends in Copenhagen already has had).

Møller's discontent with Norway can also be traced in the aphorisms from this period, in which he focuses on the negative side of human character–discontent, hypochondria, misanthropy, dissimulation, and affectation–but also on philosophy. In one of the aphorisms, he writes that "En ulykkelig gaar i sin Tænkning reflekterende baglæns" (an unhappy person moves reflectively backward in his train of thoughts).

In April 1831, after almost five years in Norway, Møller finally returned to Copenhagen, where he, once again with the help of Sibbern, had been named a professor in philosophy at the University of Copenhagen. Møller enjoyed being back in Copenhagen, devoting all his time to teaching, both at the university and at Borgerdydskolen, a grammar school in Copenhagen.

After giving birth to their fourth son in the summer of 1833, Møller's wife was bedridden until she died in May 1834. Her death left Møller mourning and unable to work for almost six months. He did, however, find time to write his omnipresent aphorisms. Most of the aphorisms from this period focus on immortality, stating for instance that "det (udødelighed) er et uundværligt Moment i en konsekvent og harmonisk Verdensanskuelse" (it [immortality] is an indispensable factor in a consistent and harmonious philosophy of life). These reflections on immortality became the foundation of Møller's important thesis "Tanker over Muligheden af Beviser for Menneskets Udødelighed" (Reflections on the Possibility of Proof of Human Immortality), published in Johan Ludvig Heiberg's journal *Maaned-skrift for Litteratur* (Monthly Magazine for Literature) in 1837.

On 24 December 1836 Møller married Eline von Bülow, a friend of his first wife and a suitable stepmother for his children. At the same time he joined the editorial board of *Maaned-skrift for Litteratur.*

In the fall of 1836 Møller published in *Maaned-skrift for Litteratur* a long review of *Extremerne* (The Extremes), a novella written and published anonymously by Heiberg's mother, Thomasine Gyllembourg. Møller knew that Gyllembourg, an old friend of his, was the author. Møller opens his review by categorizing three different types of reviews. First is the systematic, scientific review; second is the French didactic review; and third is the most common kind, which according to Møller, can be placed between the first two. After his introduction to the genre of reviews, Møller took the three groups of reviews as a point of departure for his discussion of Gyllembourg's novella. Again and again,

Møller praises the work, emphasizing "den poetiske Harmonie, der hersker i den hele Fortælling" (the poetic harmony that dominates the whole story). Further, Møller explains that Gyllembourg confirms "den Sætning, at den, der skal være en sand Digter, først maa være et sandt Menneske" (the thesis that the one who wants to become a true author first has to become a true human being). In Møller's view, one may "betragte den poetiske Harmoni som begrundet i Forfatterens Individualitet" (consider the poetic harmony as explained by the author's individuality).

Møller's view on literature and his praise for Thomasine Gyllembourg's work can also be found in the writings of Kierkegaard, who attended Møller's lectures on philosophy at the University of Copenhagen. Although Kierkegaard later told a friend that Møller's personality was what inspired him, much more than his writings, the influence of Møller's review of *Extremerne* can be traced in several of Kierkegaard's writings, most evidently in *En literair Anmeldelse. To Tidsaldre, Novelle af Forfatteren til 'En Hverdags-Historie'* (A Literary Review: Two Ages, Novella by the Author of 'An Everyday Story,' 1845) and also in Kierkegaard's debut work, *Af en endnu Levendes Papirer* (From the Papers of One Still Living, 1938). In the latter, Kierkegaard prioritizes Gyllembourg's writing over that of Hans Christian Andersen, and he praises Gyllembourg for what he considers her authentic view of life. Hence, Kierkegaard's reason for praising Gyllembourg seems almost identical to Møller's, who stressed that the harmony characterizing Gyllembourg's work could be explained by her harmonic personality.

In 1837 Møller published the thesis "Tanker over Muligheden af Beviser for Menneskets Udødelighed," also in *Maanedskrift for Litteratur*. In this essay, which can be seen as one of his most important philosophical works, Møller gives evidence of his rejection of the influential German philosopher Georg Wilhelm Friedrich Hegel, who since Møller's stay in Norway had been a major source of influence in his academic thinking. Later, the critique of Hegel was carried out to its full extent by Kierkegaard.

The work is academic in form, listing the pros and cons of a discussion on human immortality. Møller argues that scientific proof, whether logical or ontological, does not exist in any discussion of immortality. Since, according to Møller, Hegel never takes an explicit stand in the discussion, Hegel actually "antager Begrebet om den personlige Udødelighed for en Forestilling uden al Realitet" (takes the concept of personal immortality as an idea without any reality). In not leaving any room for immortality, Møller continues, Hegel gives the best indirect evidence for the existence of immortality against his will. Hegel's seemingly consistent philosophical system is therefore a false system, since he can build a system that disregards immortality.

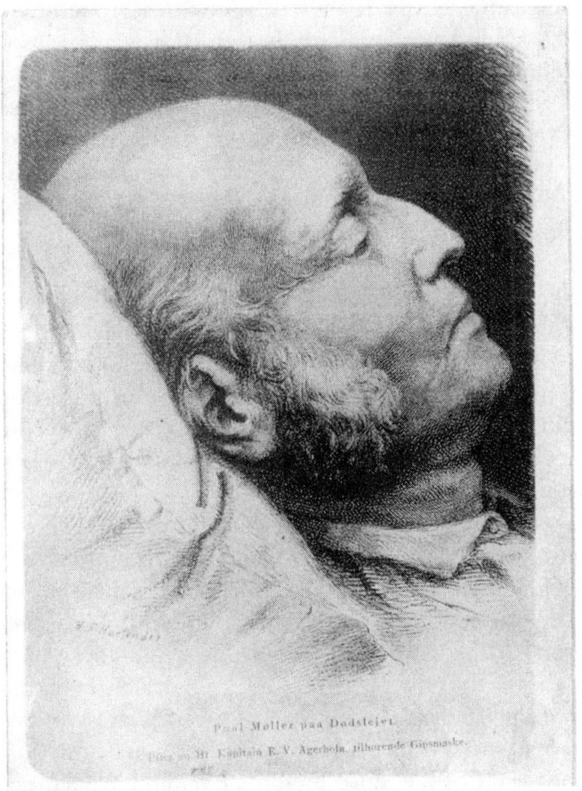

Woodcut (1844) of Møller's death mask (courtesy of the Danish Royal Library, Copenhagen)

Aiming his critique at the core of Hegel's philosophy, Møller goes on to state that "Udødelighedlæren bestandig vil gøre sig gældende som et nødvendigt Moment i Sandhedens Erkendelse" (the theory of immortality always will be present as an element in the recognition of truth). Hence, every philosophical system "hvori hint væsentlige Moment mangler, vil . . . dernæst blive fortrængt af det fuldstændigere System" (in which that essential element is missing, will . . . eventually be repressed by a system that is more complete).

The critique of Hegel's philosophical system can to some extent also be traced in Møller's uncompleted dissertation on affectation, *Forberedelser til en Afhandling om Affektation,* which he was writing in 1838, the year of his death. Møller had returned to the idea of affectation several times in his aphorisms, and in the dissertation he names three different kinds: the momentary, the fixed, and the alternated. Probably with reference to Frits in *En dansk Students Eventyr,* Møller defines the latter kind of affectation as one in which the person "som visse Dyr, skifte Farver efter dets Omgivelser" (like some animals, takes the color of his surroundings). This kind of affectation can in turn be seen as an inspiration for Kierkegaard's category of the aesthetic.

A few months before his death, Møller returned to poetry and wrote, among others, the poem "Kunstneren mellem Oprørerne" (The Artist among the Rebels). This narrative poem is about an artist who refuses to participate in a revolt but in his refusal actually takes a stand in the conflict and later regrets his behavior. The poem can be read as an allegory of Møller's own hesitation toward art. Throughout his life, he felt attracted to the idealism of the early German Romantics, but he could not combine this attraction with his knowledge of human life and society. This conflict may be one of the reasons that many of his literary writings only exist as fragments.

Prior to his death on 13 March 1838 in his home on Nytorv, in the center of Copenhagen, Poul Martin Møller asked his stepbrother to be among the publishers if a posthumous publication of his works were ever proposed. According to Møller, his stepbrother, Winther, was the only person capable at "udelade, hvad du, med dit kendskab til mig, maa formode, jeg selv ville have undertrykt" (leaving out what you with your knowledge of me, must presume I would have left out myself). Today, his *Efterladte Skrifter,* of which Winther was one of the editors, is the best source of Møller's writing.

Letters:

Poul Møller og hans Familie i Breve, 3 volumes, edited by Morten Borup (Copehagen: C. A. Reitzel, 1976).

Bibliography:

Henrik Denman, *Poul Martin Møller. En kommenteret bibliografi* (Roskilde: Denman, 1986).

References:

Vilhelm Andersen, *Poul Møller. Hans Liv og Skrifter* (Copenhagen: Gad, 1894);

Johannes Brøndum-Nielsen, *Poul Møller Studier* (Copenhagen: Gyldendal, 1940);

Oluf Friis, "Poetisk realisme og romantisme '1820–1840,'" in *Dansk litteratur historie,* edited by Oulf Friis and Uffe Andreasen, volume 3 (Copenhagen: Politiken, 1976);

Anne-Marie Mai and Mogens Davidsen, "Digtning i stykker: Poul Martin Møller–*En dansk Students Eventyr,*" in *Læsninger i dansk litteratur,* edited by Poul Schmidt and Ulrik Lehrmann (Odense: University of Odense Press, 1998), II: 35–51.

Papers:

Poul Martin Møller's papers are at the Danish Royal Library in Copenhagen.

Adam Oehlenschläger

(14 November 1779 - 20 January 1850)

Steven P. Sondrup
Brigham Young University

BOOKS: *Digte* (Copenhagen: A. Seidelin, 1803)–includes "Guldhornene," translated by George Borrow as *The Gold Horns,* edited, with an introduction, by Edmund Gosse (London: T. J. Wise, 1913);

Poetiske Skrifter, 2 volumes (Copenhagen: J. H. Schubothe, 1805)–includes *Aladdin eller Den Forunderlige Lampe. Dramatiskt Eventyr,* translated by Theodore Martin as *Aladdin; or, The Wonderful Lamp: A Dramatic Poem in Two Parts* (London: J. W. Parker, 1857); and "Vaulundurs Saga," translated by Elizabeth Kinnear as "Vaulundurs Saga: A Legend of Wayland Smith," in *Wayland Smith: A Dissertation on a Tradition of the Middle Ages,* by Georges-Bernard Depping and Francisque Michel (London: W. Pickering, 1847);

Nordiske Digte (Copenhagen: A. Seidelin, 1807)–includes *Baldur hin Gode* and *Hakon Jarl hin Rige,* translated in *Hakon Jarl: A Tragedy in Five Acts, Translated from the Danish of Oehlenschläger; and Poems after Various Authors* (London: T. Hookham, 1840);

Palnatoke. Et Sørgespil (Copenhagen: Brummer, [1809]);

Axel og Valborg. Et Sørgespil (Copenhagen: A. Seidelin, 1810); translated by Robert M. Laing in his *Hours in Norway: Poems, to Which Is Added a Version of Oehlenschläger's Axel and Valborg: A Tragedy* (London: T. Hookham, 1841);

Correggio. Tragødie (Copenhagen: B. Brünnich & E. Möller, 1811); translated by Eliza Buckminster Lee as *Correggio: A Tragedy* (Boston: Phillips & Samson, 1846);

Digtninger (Copenhagen: Forfatterens Forlag, 1811);

Faruk. Syngespil (Copenhagen: Forfatterens Forlag, 1812 [i.e., 1811]);

Stærkodder. Tragødie (Copenhagen: B. Brünnich, 1812);

Fortællinger (Copenhagen: Forfatterens Forlag, 1813);

Hugo von Rheinberg. Tragødie (Copenhagen: Forfatterens Forlag, 1813);

Kanarifuglen. Lystspil (Copenhagen: Forfatterens Forlag, 1813);

Lithograph based on a painting by J. L. Lund, 1869 (courtesy of the Danish Royal Library, Copenhagen)

Ludlams Hule. Syngespil (Copenhagen: Forfatterens Forlag, 1813);

Prolog til Kanarifuglen og Ærlighed varer længst (Copenhagen: B. Brünnich, 1813);

Helge. Et Digt (Copenhagen, 1814);

Røverborgen. Syngespil (Copenhagen: Forfatterens Forlag, 1814);

Hagbarth og Signe. Tragødie (Copenhagen: B. Brünnich, 1815);

Fiskeren. Dramatisk Eventyr (Copenhagen: B. Brünnich, 1816);

Freias Alter. Lystspil (Copenhagen: B. Brünnich, 1816);
Frederiksberg. Et Digt (Copenhagen: Forfatterens Forlag, 1817);
Fostbrødrene. Tragødie (Copenhagen: Forfatterens Forlag, 1817);
Hroars Saga (Copenhagen: H. F. Popp, 1817);
En Reise fortalt i Breve til mit Hiem, 2 volumes (Copenhagen: H. F. Popp, 1817, 1818);
Den lille Hyrdedreng. En Idyl (Copenhagen: Forfatterens Forlag, 1818); translated by I. Heath as *The Little Shepherd-Boy: An Idyll* (Copenhagen: F. de Tengnagel, 1827);
Nordens Guder. Et episk Digt af Oehlenschläger (Copenhagen: H. F. Popp, 1819); translated in part by Grenville Pigott as "The Gods of the North," in *A Manual of Scandinavian Mythology, Containing a Popular Account of the Two Eddas and of the Religion of Odin* (London: W. Pickering, 1839);
Robinson i England. Comødie (Copenhagen: Forfatterens Forlag, 1819);
Tale i Anledning af Thorvaldsens Hiemkomst til Fædrelandet. Holden ved festen den 16de October 1819 (Copenhagen: Forfatterens Forlag, 1819);
Erik og Abel. Tragødie (Copenhagen: Forfatterens Forlag, 1820);
Tordenskiold. Syngespil (Copenhagen: H. F. Popp, 1821);
Oehlenschlägers Samlede Digte, 3 volumes (Copenhagen: Forfatterens Forlag, 1823);
Øen i Sydhavet. Roman, 4 volumes (Copenhagen: Forfatterens Forlag, 1824–1825);
I Anledning af Deres Kongelige Høiheders Prinds Frederik Carl Christians og Prindsesse Vilhelmine Marias høie Forlovelse (Copenhagen, 1826);
Skuespil (Copenhagen: Forfatterens Forlag, 1827)–comprises *Flugten af Klosteret* and *Væringerne i Miklagaard;*
Hrolf Krake. Et Heltedigt (Copenhagen: H. F. Popp, 1828);
Om Kritiken i Kjøbenhavns flyvende Post, over Væringerne i Miklagaard af Oehlenschläger (Copenhagen: C. A. Reitzel, 1828);
Oehlenschlägers nye poetiske Skrifter, 3 volumes (Copenhagen: Forfatterens Forlag, 1828–1829)–comprises volume 1, *Hrolf Krake. Et Heltedigt;* volume 2, *Karl den Store. Tragødie* and *Langbarderne. Tragødie;* and volume 3, *Billedet og Busten. Syngespil* and *Overilelsen. Syngespil;*
Cantate i Anledning af Deres Kongelige Høiheder Prinds Frederik Ferdinands og Kronprindsesse Carolinas Ægteforening (Copenhagen: J. H. Schultz, 1829);
Det Gamle og det Ny. Prolog til det Dramatisk-Literaire Selskabs Halvhundredaarsfest (Copenhagen, [1830]);
Trillingbrødrene fra Damask. Lystspil (Copenhagen: Forfatterens Forlag, 1830);
Oehlenschlägers Levnet, fortalt af ham selv, 2 volumes (Copenhagen: Forfatterens Forlag, 1830, 1831);
Prolog til Evalds Mindefest, ved Forestillingen af Balders Død den 17de Marts 1831 (Copenhagen: C. A. Reitzel, 1831);
Text til Musiknummerne i Rübezahl. Et dramatisk Eventyr (Copenhagen: J. D. Qvist, 1832);
Norgesreisen. En Digtekrands (Copenhagen: Forfatterens Forlag, 1834 [i.e., 1833]);
Tordenskiold. Tragisk Drama (Copenhagen: J. D. Qvist, [1833]);
Dronning Margareta. Tragødie (Copenhagen, 1834);
De italienske Røvere. Tragødie (Copenhagen, 1835);
Fyensreisen. Digtekrands (Copenhagen, 1835);
Digterværker, 10 volumes (Copenhagen: Forfatterens Forlag, 1835–1840);
Cantate ved Universitetets Indvielsesfest, den 13. October 1836 (Copenhagen, 1836);
Nyere Digte (Copenhagen, 1836);
Sokrates. Tragødie (Copenhagen: Forfatterens Forlag, 1836);
Olaf den Hellige. Tragødie (Copenhagen: Forfatterens Forlag, 1838);
Knud den Store. Tragødie (Copenhagen, 1839);
Minde-Digt over Kong Frederik den Siette. Indbydelses-Skrift til Universitetets Sørgefest, den 28 Januar (Copenhagen, 1840);
Ørvarodds Saga. Et oldnordisk Eventyr (Copenhagen: J. D. Qvist, 1841);
Dina. Et tragisk Drama (Copenhagen: Forfatterens Forlag, 1842);
Erik Glipping. Tragødie (Copenhagen, 1844);
Gienfærdet paa Herlufsholm. Et Skuespil (Copenhagen: A. F. Høst, 1845);
Landet fundet og forsvundet: Et nordisk Heltespil (Copenhagen: A. F. Høst, 1846);
Den Rige og den Fattige. Et Lystspil i een Akt (Copenhagen, 1846);
Amleth. Tragødie (Copenhagen: A. F. Høst, 1847);
Kiartan og Gudrun: Tragødie i fem Handlinger (Copenhagen: A. F. Høst, 1848);
Mindedigt over Kong Christian den Ottende. Indbydelsesskrift til Universitetets Sørgefest (Copenhagen, [1848]);
Digtekunsten. I Poesier (Copenhagen: A. F. Høst, 1849);
Regnar Lodbrok. Et Heltedigt (Copenhagen: A. F. Høst, 1849);
Oehlenschlägers Erindringer, 4 volumes in 2, edited by Johannes Wolfgang Oehlenschläger (Copenhagen: A. F. Høst, 1850–1851).

Editions and Collections: *Oehlenschlägers Tragødier,* 8 volumes (Copenhagen: J. D. Qvist, 1841–1842);
Oehlenschlägers Digterværker og prosaiske Skrifter, 26 volumes in 13 (Copenhagen: A. F. Høst, 1851–1854);

Poetiske Skrifter, 32 volumes in 16, edited by F. L. Liebenberg (Copenhagen: Selskabet til Udgivelse af Oehlenschlägers Skrifter, 1857–1862);

Poetiske Skrifter, 5 volumes, edited by Helge Topsøe-Jensen (Copenhagen: J. Jørgensen, 1926–1930);

Langelands-Reise i Sommeren 1804, edited by Povl Ingerslev-Jensen (Copenhagen: Oehlenschläger Selskabet/Rosenkilde & Bagger, 1972);

Oehlenschlägers Levnet fortalt af ham selv, 2 volumes, foreword and commentary by Poul Linneballe and Ingerslev-Jensen (Copenhagen: Oehlenschläger Selskabet/Rosenkilde & Bagger, 1974);

Axel og Valborg. Et Sørgespil, edited by Ingerslev-Jensen (Copenhagen: Oehlenschläger Selskabet, 1975);

Helge. Et Digt, edited, with commentary, by Ingerslev-Jensen (Copenhagen: Oehlenschläger Selskabet, 1976);

Lyrik. Et Udvalg, edited by Torben Nielsen (Copenhagen: Oehlenschläger Selskabet, 1977);

Aladdin eller Den forunderlige Lampe. Et Lystspil, edited by Jens Kristian Andersen (Copenhagen: Oehlenschläger Selskabet/Rosenkilde & Bagger, 1978);

Digte, edited, with commentary, by Ingerslev-Jensen (Copenhagen: Oehlenschläger Selskabet, 1979);

Æstetiske Skrifter, 1800–1812, introduction and notes by Frederik J. Billeskov Jansen (Holte: Oehlenschläger Selskabet/Rosenkilde & Bagger, 1980);

Hakon Jarl hin Rige. Et Sørgespil, edited by Henrik Lundgren (Copenhagen: Oehlenschläger Selskabet, 1981);

Prosa. Et Udvalg, edited by Flemming Lundgreen-Nielsen and Mogens Løj (Copenhagen: Oehlenschläger Selskabet, 1987);

Helge. Et Digt, edited, with an afterword and notes, by Søren Baggesen (Valby: Danske Sprog- og Litteraturselskab/Borgen, 1996).

Editions in English: *The Gods of the North: An Epic Poem,* translated by William Edward Frye (London: W. Pickering, 1845);

Correggio: A Tragedy, translated by Theodore Martin (London: J. W. Parker, 1854);

Hakon Jarl: A Tragedy, in Five Acts, translated by John Chapman (London: R. Clarke, 1857);

Axel and Valborg: A Tragedy, translated by H. W. Freeland (London: Reeves & Turner, 1873);

Axel and Valborg: A Tragedy in Five Acts, translated by Pierce Butler (London: Trübner, 1874);

Earl Hakon, the Mighty, translated by Frank C. Lascelles (London: Chapman & Hall, 1874);

An English Version of Oehlenschlaeger's Hakon Jarl, edited and translated by James Christian Lindberg (Lincoln: University of Nebraska, 1905);

Axel and Valborg: An Historical Tragedy in Five Acts, translated by Frederick Strange Kolle (New York: Grafton Press, 1906);

Hakon Jarl: An Historical Tragedy in Five Acts, translated by Kolle (New York: F. H. Hitchcock, 1911);

Aladdin; or, The Wonderful Lamp: A Play, translated by Henry Meyer (Copenhagen: Gyldendal, 1968).

OTHER: *Forhandlinger ved Festen i Kiøbenhavn, d. 11 Decemb. 1811,* by Oehlenschläger and others (Copenhagen: Brummer, 1812);

Sange for Studenterforeningen, by Oehlenschläger and others (Copenhagen: Thiele, 1822);

Siofna for Aaret 1802, edited by Oehlenschläger (Copenhagen: G. Jacobsen, [1822]);

Bertel Thorvaldsen, *Tolv blade figurer til Tegne-øvelser,* text by Oehlenschläger, edited by G. L. Lahde (Copenhagen: A. Seidelin, [1834]);

"Juveelhandleren," in *Nye Romancer,* edited by H. P. Holst (Copenhagen: Bing & Son, 1843 [i.e., 1842]).

TRANSLATIONS: Johann Wolfgang von Goethe, *Reineke Fos. Et episk Digt af Goethe* (Copenhagen: S. Popp, 1806);

William Shakespeare, *En Skiærsommernats Drøm. Lystspil* (Copenhagen: B. Brünnich, 1816);

Joseph Meyer, *Meyers Universum, eller, Billeder og Beskrivelser af det seeværdigste og mærkværdigste i Naturen og Kunsten paa den hele Jord,* 6 volumes (Copenhagen: Bibliographiske Institut i Hildburghausen, Amsterdam og New-York/C. Steen, 1835–1840);

Ludwig Tieck, *Digtninger,* 2 volumes (Copenhagen: C. A. Reitzel, 1838, 1839);

Friedrich Schiller, *Digte,* translated by Oehlenschläger and others, edited by Frederik Schaldemose (Copenhagen: Salomon, 1842);

Shakespeare and Goethe, *Udmærkede Digterværker* (Copenhagen: Bing & Son/F. H. Eibe, 1848)–comprises Shakespeare, *En Skiærsommernats Drøm. Lystspil;* Goethe, *Götz von Berlichingen med Jernhaanden. Skuespil;* and Goethe, *Mikkel Ræv. Et episk Digt.*

Adam Oehlenschläger is typically numbered among Denmark's most appreciated and revered writers. Although not as famous internationally as his contemporaries Søren Kierkegaard and Hans Christian Andersen, he retains a continuing appeal at home. During his lifetime Oehlenschläger was celebrated for his efforts to awaken an appreciation for distinctly Nordic history and culture among his fellow Danes as well as for the original role he played in mediating between Danish literature and European Romanticism. He remains, moreover, an

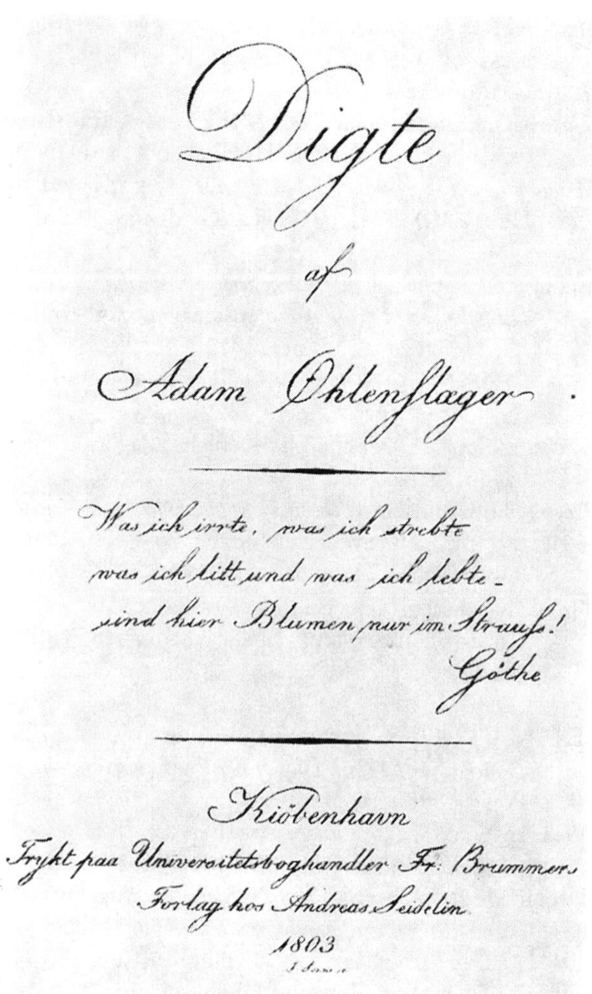
Digte
af
Adam Øhlenslæger.

Was ich irrte, was ich strebte
was ich litt und was ich lebte –
sind hier Blumen nur im Strauß!
Göthe

Kiöbenhavn
Trykt paa Universitetsboghandler Fr. Brummers
Forlag hos Andreas Seidelin.
1803

Title page for Oehlenschläger's first poetry collection. It includes "Guldhornene" (The Gold Horns), the best-known poem of Scandinavian Romanticism (from Carl S. Petersen and Vilhelm Andersen, Illustreret dansk Litteraturhistorie, *volume 3:* Litteratur i det nittende Aarhundredes første Halvdel, *1924; Suzzallo Library, University of Washington).*

important influence in contemporary cultural life whose impact has been often acknowledged by advocates of diverse positions.

Adam Gottlob Oehlenschläger (originally spelled "Øhlenschlæger") was born in the Vesterbro quarter of Copenhagen on 14 November 1779 into a middle-class family. His father, Joachim Conrad Oehlenschläger, originally from Slesvig, was the organist at Frederiksberg Church and, later, overseer at Frederiksberg Castle, where young Adam was able to witness some of the pageantry of Danish history, albeit from a distance. Adam's mother, Martha Marie Hansen Oehlenschläger, was possibly of German origin. His father would have liked to have seen him pursue a business career but recognized that his son's inclinations did not lie in that direction. During his formative years, Oehlenschläger had the opportunity to attend a school at which he received a traditional education grounded in the Greek and Roman classics. His interests soon turned, however, to the theater; setting out on his own, he took a position with Det Kongelige Teater (The Royal Theater) as an actor and performed in several minor roles during his relatively brief tenure there. Although Oehlenschläger's career as an actor was short lived, it provided him with firsthand experience in the theater that prepared him eventually to begin writing for the stage.

Oehlenschläger made his literary debut in 1799 with a ballad titled "Viisdom, Kierlighed og Venskab" (Wisdom, Love, and Friendship), which is highly reminiscent of the sentimentality of Johann Wolfgang von Goethe's *Die Leiden des jungen Werther* (1774; translated as *The Sorrows of Werther,* 1779). Oehlenschläger's youthful work manifests many characteristics of eighteenth-century rationalism and sentimentality, but, more importantly, it provides hints of the direction in which his subsequent works were to move. In Copenhagen he befriended the brothers Anders Sandøe Ørsted and H. C. Ørsted, the physicist who later discovered the relationship between electricity and magnetism. In 1800, while moving in the Ørsteds' circle of friends and acquaintances, Oehlenschläger began the study of law as well as Scandinavian history and mythology at the University of Copenhagen. That same year he submitted an essay to a competition sponsored by the university on the question of whether it would be beneficial to Scandinavian belles lettres if Old Norse mythology were introduced and generally adopted as a cultural foundation in place of classical mythology, history, and literature. He had just completed a newspaper article in which he had sought to make readers not especially familiar with Old Norse literature aware of the immense treasure available in the sagas that had been handed down from antiquity. Under the influence of Charles-Louis Montesquieu, Jean-Jacques Rousseau, and–most obviously–Johann Gottfried von Herder, as well as the cult of Ossian, Oehlenschläger argued in his prizewinning essay that the saga age was a more poetic era than the present and that the imagination of contemporary poets could be freed, stimulated, and amplified by the mythology of the indigenous past. The contemporary lack of respect for Nordic mythology, he observed, was simply a function of the widespread lack of awareness of its richness and its potential for integrating the ancient gods, the power of nature, and current human experience.

As if to illustrate his point, Oehlenschläger began work in 1801 on a novel to have been titled "Erik og Roller" (Erik and Roller). Although the work was never completed, the portrayal of Erik in terms of the Norse god Thor, of the eternal conflict between the Aesir (the more benevolent of the gods) and the powers of darkness, and of the eventual Twilight of the Gods illustrates that at an early age Oehlenschläger had a broad grasp of Nordic history and mythology and a significant commitment to their social and intellectual value.

The event that prompted Oehlenschläger to abandon work on the novel in 1802 was a forceful and completely engaging introduction to the substance of German Romantic philosophy by Henrik Steffens, who had spent time in the German university city of Jena beginning in 1798. Steffens had attended the lectures of Friedrich Wilhelm Joseph von Schelling and Johann Gottlieb Fichte and was a friend of Friedrich Schlegel, August Wilhelm Schlegel, Ludwig Tieck, and Novalis. Steffens thus had received an immediate, firsthand introduction to the principal aspects of early German Romanticism as they were articulated in Jena. In 1802 he returned to Copenhagen, where he gave a series of public lectures highly critical of the enduring strains of Enlightenment rationalism and offering ardent endorsement of the major tenets of Schelling's philosophy of nature, art, and history. Oehlenschläger must be counted among the most responsive members of the audience at these lectures, and their impact on him was profound. He was so impressed that he sought out Steffens for an extended conversation, which has become legendary in the history of Danish literature. The result of their contact was to confirm in Oehlenschläger the intellectual and aesthetic viability of his nascent interest in the Danish past and to energize his resolve to promote broader critical and social engagement with it. He accordingly reworked an ostensibly already complete manuscript, to which he added what became one of the most famous poems in Danish literature, "Guldhornene" (1803; translated as *The Gold Horns,* 1913), which relates in ecstatic terms the story of the discovery and subsequent loss of two gold drinking horns fashioned sometime around A.D. 400. The horns came to represent a call for greater attention to and appreciation of the indigenous national past.

Although the composition of "Guldhornene" is often seen as marking the beginning of Scandinavian Romanticism, the actual import of the poem is better understood in symbolic terms. Oehlenschläger's revised manuscript, including the new poem, was published in 1803 under the title *Digte* (Poems) and manifests a wide-ranging sensitivity not only to the importance of native cultural values but also to the expressive power of mixing genres that had formerly been rigorously separated. Accordingly, the volume consists of an epic section based in large measure on the tradition of late-medieval ballads and celebrating ancient Norse civilization; a more purely lyrical section, mellifluously but never naively echoing Schelling's pantheism; and a dramatic section consisting of *Sanct Hansaften Spil* (Midsummer Night's Play). Praising the bounties and beauties of a midsummer night, the play evokes nature's unity with the past, poetry, and love in a variety of meters that maintain a lightness of touch and a rollicking tempo. At the same time the play offers a critique of eighteenth-century bourgeois, Enlightenment values. Although the overall tendency of *Digte* is toward the poetic veneration of the unity of nature, history, and poetry, the failure to perceive and partake of this oneness is also portrayed in some poems that center on fragmentation, resignation, and disillusionment.

Many of the overtly Romantic initiatives undertaken in *Digte* continue into Oehlenschläger's next volume, *Poetiske Skrifter* (Poetic Texts, 1805). Like its predecessor, the volume features a diverse array of forms and philosophical arguments. There are two cycles of poems, "Langelands-Reise" (Langeland Journey) and "Jesu Christi gientagne Liv i den aarlige Nature" (The Replicated Life of Jesus Christ in Nature's Annual Cycle), in which beneficent nature is presented as a symbol of divine providence; a prose narrative, "Vaulundurs Saga" (The Saga of Vaulundur; translated as "Vaulundurs Saga: A Legend of Wayland Smith," 1847); and a five-act drama in blank verse, *Aladdin eller Den Forunderlige Lampe* (translated as *Aladdin; or, The Wonderful Lamp,* 1857), labeled a *Dramatiskt Eventyr* (dramatic fairy tale). The two poetic cycles not only illustrate Oehlenschläger's maturation and growing independence from his earlier pantheism but also are accomplished and engaging works in their own right. Based on Old Norse sources, "Vaulundurs Saga" portrays a genius in the Romantic sense of the word who is completely at one with nature. Vaulundur is depicted in relatively dark and somber hues in masterful Danish prose that echoes the cadences of its ancient sources.

Notwithstanding the effective and highly evocative tones of "Vaulundurs Saga," *Aladdin eller Den Forunderlige Lampe* is the best remembered work in *Poetiske Skrifter,* having in subsequent years become known as a masterpiece of Danish literature. The play is most obviously a free reworking from *The Thousand and One Nights* in a highly imaginative way that nonetheless shows the influence of William Shakespeare–most notably of *A Midsummer Night's Dream,* which Oehlenschläger later translated–Goethe, and Tieck. *Aladdin eller Den Forunderlige Lampe* has often been seen as Oehlenschläger's attempt to write a lighthearted counterpoint to the earliest version of Goethe's *Faust* (published as *Faust. Ein Fragment,* 1790) in the presentation of a young and spontaneous hero who circumvents the malevolent powers endeavoring to use him for their own ends and ultimately triumphs without entering into a pact with the powers of darkness. Goethe's concept of *Bildung* (education or acculturation),

Oehlenschläger in 1809 (drawing by Riepenhausen; from Carl S. Petersen and Vilhelm Andersen, Illustreret dansk Litteraturhistorie, *volume 3:* Litteratur i det nittende Aarhundredes første Halvdel, *1924; Suzzallo Library, University of Washington)*

however–formulated during the 1790s and articulated most comprehensively in his *Wilhelm Meisters Lehrjahre* (1795–1796; translated as *Wilhelm Meister's Apprenticeship,* 1824)–is probably a more fruitful context within which to frame the discussion of the relationship between the two writers. *Aladdin eller Den Forunderlige Lampe* records the intellectual, emotional, and social development of a highly intuitive and spontaneous son of nature–a figure much like Oehlenschläger himself–as he passes through vicissitudes and challenges on the way to becoming a fully integrated and responsible adult. Only in building on and perfecting his natural goodness can he become worthy of the felicity that the lamp betokens. This emphasis on the cultivation and development of personal attributes that lead to productive social integration accounts for much of the enduring value of the play and provides an early articulation of a theme that remained important to Oehlenschläger for the rest of his life. The tone, however, remains light and often ironically satirical, with an unabashedly playful treatment of misapprehensions and dramatic misunderstandings in an exotic setting. The ebullient optimism and exuberant theatricality of the play contributed to its enthusiastic reception in Denmark and an appeal that extended over much of Europe.

The publication of *Poetiske Skrifter* brought Oehlenschläger recognition as one of Denmark's foremost writers and won him fame abroad as the author of *Aladdin eller Den Forunderlige Lampe.* With a royal travel grant he set out on a journey (1805–1809) that took him to Germany, France, Switzerland, Italy, and England. The effect of his peregrination through Europe manifests itself in complementary ways: on the one hand, he came into contact with many of the intellectual and literary luminaries of the period and immersed himself in a wide range of philosophical currents, but on the other hand, he returned to his interest in Old Norse themes and Denmark's distinctive cultural birthright. Although strongly committed to this cultural patrimony, Oehlenschläger was not so naive as to presume that Norse culture could be readily transplanted so that it would take root in the modern Christian society in which he lived. He fully apprehended that a vast historical gulf divided the two worlds; yet, in such works as the plays *Baldur hin Gode* (Baldur the Good) and *Hakon Jarl hin Rige* (Earl Hakon the Mighty; translated as *Hakon Jarl,* 1840) and the poem "Thors Reise til Jotunheim" (Thor's Journey to Jotunhiem), all published in *Nordiske Digte* (Nordic Poems, 1807), he portrays the Norse gods as embodiments of eternal values that could conceivably be reconciled eventually with Christian virtue. In responding to inquiries about distinct Nordic virtues, Oehlenschläger explained that he was awaiting a time when "det hellige Kors skal smelte sammen og blive Eet med Thors vældige Hammer" (the holy cross will be fused and become one with Thor's mighty hammer).

Baldur hin Gode is a mythological drama set in Mithgarth, the realm of the ancient Norse gods, that chronicles with a grand epic sweep the descent into ruin of their once proud community. A poetic tour de force written in several evocative classical meters, the drama undertakes a penetrating psychological exploration of the circumstances surrounding Baldur's death. Although accounts of Baldur from antiquity vary, Snorri Sturluson portrays him as the most attractive, wisest, most brilliant, and best liked of all the Norse gods collectively known as the Aesir. Oehlenschläger took up Snorri's account during his summer sojourn in Weimar and Dresden in 1806, during which he sympathetically engaged the thinking of Friedrich Schleiermacher and, to a lesser extent, that of Friedrich Schiller, with both of whom various aspects of *Baldur hin Gode* can be associated. In a sequence of rapidly shifting scenes presented in a single act, the play recounts that Baldur was warned in a dream of his impending death. After he tells his mother, Frigga, of his premonition, a promise is exacted from everything in the world except the seemingly harmless mistletoe to protect Baldur's life. Loki, related to malevolent giants and ill at ease living among the Aesir, approaches Frigga disguised as an old woman and learns of Baldur's vulnerability. Loki plucks mistletoe and bestows it upon Baldur's blind brother, Hordur, whom he then entreats to shoot an arrow. Hordur's arrow hits and kills Baldur, but the disingenuous and manipulative Loki remains the principal agent of Baldur's death. Because of the high regard in which Baldur is held among the Aesir, he could be redeemed from the land of the dead if all the gods were to mourn his death. Numbed by self-contempt, Loki alone remains unmoved and unable to manifest any sorrow. Baldur's death not only represents the gods' loss of the most revered among them but also signals the end of a golden age and the beginning of their precipitous descent into ruin. This exploration of the psychology of cosmic evil invites allegorical interpretations and almost paradigmatically illustrates the Romantic conception of myths as fundamental, transhistorical patterns of human experience or particular instantiations of ideal archetypes. The mythic consciousness revealed in *Baldur hin Gode* has much in common with views of mythology held by Schlegel and Schleiermacher as well as, and perhaps more important, with those of Oehlenschläger's compatriot N. F. S. Grundtvig.

Oehlenschläger had long been attracted to the historical material upon which *Hakon Jarl hin Rige* is based and made several preparatory studies for the tragedy. Drawing on this long fascination with the historical situation, he was able to cast the work in the form of a dramatic tragedy during a period of six weeks in 1805. The play premiered in Copenhagen in 1808. Oehlenschläger's interest had been initially directed toward Olav Tryggvason, the king of Norway from 995 to 1000 who is credited with establishing Christianity in that country, but his attention soon shifted from Olav to the king's pagan antagonist, Hakon. Oehlenschläger's dramatic juxtaposition of Olav as the representative of Christianity and Christian ethics and Hakon as the embodiment of pagan valor and independence has much in common with Schiller's *Wallenstein* (1800). The encounter of the two bitter opponents representing two widely divergent ethical and political positions, moreover, dramatically echoes the climactic confrontation of Mary, Queen of Scots, and Queen Elizabeth in Schiller's *Maria Stuart* (1801). Having left his wife, Thora, for a younger woman, Hakon prepares to claim the crown of Norway but, to his dismay, finds that it is too big. The smith who fashioned the crown will not make it smaller, maintaining that it will fit the rightful heir. Just then Olav, the Norwegian king in Dublin, arrives to claim the throne. The Christian religion, with its traditional emphasis on charity and submission to God, is portrayed as characteristic of the south–foreign and hostile to the northern virtues of honor, valor, courage, independence, and strength. In their highly charged exchange Hakon portrays himself as the final spark of ancient Nordic heroism that is about to be extinguished. Olav is by no means insensitive to the great cultural patrimony that is about to slip away and is deeply moved by the account of Norse religion given by the one-eyed warrior Auden, a human analogue to the Norse god Odin. Like the rose, Christianity is a product of warmer and more congenial climes, but the rigors of life in the north require fortitude and strength. Auden's claim that Olav is an instrument of foreign cultural colonization is compelling, but the young Olav sees in Christianity the call to a higher universal morality and the necessary course of the historical process. Pursued by Olav, Hakon in the end finds refuge with Thora, the wife he had abandoned but whose love he still enjoys. Near madness, he gives his sword to one of his men, who thrusts it into Hakon's body. The play ends with Olav being proclaimed king but with Thora extolling Hakon as a great warrior and promising soon to be laid beside him. Although defeated, Hakon embodied virtues that endure and a call to awareness of a cultural history that cannot easily be ignored. In responding to the call of Montesquieu, Johann Georg Hamann, and Herder for each nation to cultivate its own particular traditions and virtues, Oehlenschläger offered a drama that at once celebrates a nearly forgotten national past but also suggests the contours of future challenges.

Again drawing on Snorri's *Prose Edda* (circa 1222), Oehlenschläger describes Thor's engagement with the giants in "Thors Reise til Jotunheim." Thor, the god of thunder and the most powerful of the gods, was widely known and venerated for his defense of the gods against giants. Oehlenschläger portrays Thor in particularly heroic terms that reflect his desire to give the Nordic region heroes who could serve as cultural points of reference, just as Homer's characters did for the Mediterranean region.

While in Paris, Oehlenschläger wrote *Axel og Valborg* (translated as *Axel and Valborg,* 1841), which was published in 1810 upon his return to Copenhagen. Something of a dramatic hybrid, the play pays respect to the classical tradition of French theater in its strict observance of the traditional unities of time, place, and action but is cast in Shakespearean blank verse rather than the classical alexandrine. The action centers on the conflict in the heart of the titular hero, Axel, between duty and inclination. The action is set in Christ's Church in Nidaros (present-day Trondheim), to which Axel returns after receiving a dispensation from the Pope to marry Valborg, a close relative. She has left a wreath signaling her continuing love for him in spite of the fact that the king, Hakon Herdebred, has been pressuring her to

Oehlenschläger reading from his works. The audience includes N. F. S. Grundtvig (resting head on hand), Hans Christian Andersen (taking snuff), and Carsten Hauch (wearing skull cap). The sculptor Bertel Thorvaldsen is asleep at right (drawing by Wilhelm Marstrand; from Carl S. Petersen and Vilhelm Andersen, Illustreret dansk Litteraturhistorie, *volume 3:* Litteratur i det nittende Aarhundredes første Halvdel, *1924; Suzzallo Library, University of Washington).*

marry him during Axel's prolonged absence. Although Axel could have rescued Valborg from the cloister into which she has fled, he responds to the call to support the king when a hostile army invades. He saves his king's life but in doing so is himself killed, a thematic development well known in the ballad tradition. Hakon's forces, though, are defeated, and Valborg dies while mourning Axel's death. *Axel og Valborg* is a tightly structured drama that lends itself exceptionally well to performance and is thus perhaps the most successful of Oehlenschläger's plays in the theater.

Correggio (1811; translated, 1846) was written during the summer of 1809, first in German, and then translated by Oehlenschläger himself into Danish. In this form it premiered in Copenhagen in 1811. Named for a small Italian city near Parma, the play relates the story of Antonio Allegri, a painter who works in obscurity far from the artistic centers of the Renaissance. On a trip through the region Michelangelo is forced to stay over in Correggio, where he eventually sees through the malevolence of Allegri's neighbor and proclaims with the gift of his ring that Allegri is one of the most accomplished painters of the time. While in Parma to sell what turns out to be his last painting, Allegri is crowned with a laurel wreath but dies under the strain of carrying his earnings, paid in copper, back home, just as word arrives that, on the recommendation of Michelangelo, the duke of Mantua has summoned him to his court. The play pays homage to Oehlenschläger's experience in Italy while more importantly raising crucial questions about the nature of art and artistic merit. The tragedy was particularly important for Denmark because of its probing inquiries into the viability of art in areas far removed from cultural centers. On a more personal level, *Correggio* interrogates the nature of Oehlenschläger's relationship to Goethe's towering genius and does so in terms of a thoughtful recapitulation of many of the issues concerning artistic genius taken up by Goethe in his *Torquato Tasso* (1790). Alhough *Correggio* was widely appreciated, the original German version did not receive its premiere until 1828.

When Oehlenschläger returned to Copenhagen from his extended sojourn abroad, he found himself to be a famous man. He was the recipient of widespread acclaim and appreciation that manifested itself most notably in his appointment as professor of aesthetics at the University of Copenhagen. In 1810 he married Christiane Heger, to whom he had been engaged since 1800. They had met at Bakkehuset (the House on the Hill), home of the prominent professor Knud Lyhne Rahbek and his wife, Kamma Rahbek, Christiane's sister and the muse for many early-nineteenth-century Danish writers. With marriage, Oehlenschläger assumed the financial responsibilities for raising a family of four children: Charlotte (1811), Johannes Wolfgang (1813), William (1814), and Marie Louise (1818). His return to Copenhagen, assumption of a faculty position, and marriage were not only accompanied by the broad acceptance of his work throughout Denmark but also by the emergence of a tone of mature moderation in his subsequent works. The energy and verve of youth gave way to the acceptance and, indeed, the advocacy of middle-class values. Oehlenschläger still retained his commitment to recouping a sense of pride and national identity from Denmark's unique literary history and cultural background, but overtones of sentimentality gradually became audible in his works. A vigorous debate between his prominent supporters and detractors occasionally became strident when the initial, generally objective tone descended into ad hominem attacks. As spontaneity yielded to discipline, and energetic commitment ceded ground to classical detachment, Oehlenschläger's artistic consistency began to wane, and the public enthusiasm for his works gradually declined.

Although Oehlenschläger's literary production during the subsequent years was somewhat uneven, works of great depth, significant literary merit, and considerable cultural import nonetheless appeared. Among the most notable is *Helge* (1814), consisting of two cycles of poems, "Frodes Drapa" (Frode's Poem) and "Helge's Eventyr" (Helge's Tale), that serve to introduce a drama, *Yrsa. Helge* centers on the fate and contrasting character of two brothers, Helge and Hroar, ancestors of the later important Danish king Hrolf Krake. Oehlenschläger knew from the beginning that this work was just the start of a much larger project that was eventually to include later works. He drew his material from the Old Norse *Hrólfs saga kraka* (Hrolf Krake's Saga, circa 1280–1350) but was formally and stylistically influenced by his reading of Sophocles' plays, especially *Oedipus Rex,* and of Schiller's *Die Braut von Messina* (1803; translated as *The Bride of Messina,* 1837), although his relation to Schiller in this case bespeaks considerably greater freedom and ingenuity than ever before. Oehlenschläger was also aware that a generation earlier Johannes Ewald, who had shared his interest in the Germanic past, had begun a tragedy to have been titled "Helge eller Den nordiske Ødip" (Helge; or, The Nordic Oedipus).

"Frodes Drapa" recounts how Frode killed his brother Halfdan and banished Halfdan's two sons, Helge and Hroar, in order to ascend the throne himself. In spite of their disguise, the brothers are eventually recognized and forced to flee into the forest. The tempestuous, aggressive, and belligerent Helge demands revenge on Frode, whereas Hroar–conciliatory, compromising, and peace loving–counsels reconciliation. Helge pursues Frode and finally kills him. "Helges Eventyr" describes Helge's adventurous travels and the humiliation he suffers when the woman to whom Frode had been engaged ridicules him in her effort to take reciprocal revenge. With Queen Oluf, Helge eventually fathers a daughter, Yrsa, who is given to a fisherman's family to rear, thus setting up the necessary situation for the subsequent Oedipal tragedy. These two poem cycles are presented in various Germanic verse forms that evoke the rich tradition of Germanic narrative poetry as well as the distinctively Scandinavian ballad tradition.

In contrast to the Nordic style of "Frodes Drapa" and "Helges Eventyr," the form of *Yrsa* is classical, as seen most obviously in Oehlenschläger's skillful and flexible deployment of iambic trimeter and trochees and in the decorum of the dramatic report of Helge's eventual heroic suicide. As an act of revenge against Helge, Queen Oluf arranges for Yrsa to be brought back to court, where Helge, upon a return visit, falls in love with and marries her. Only then does Oluf reveal that Yrsa is his daughter. Like Helge, Yrsa wants to take her life but is persuaded by Freia, the goddess of love, to go to Roskilde (*Hroars kilde* [Hroar's spring]), where she will give birth to their child, Hrolf, who will inherit Helge's throne and accomplish heroic feats. The conciliatory ending of the tragedy constitutes a bridge to its sequel, the prose narrative *Hroars Saga* (Hroar's Saga, 1817), an account of the more peaceable brother's contribution to establishing the Danish kingdom.

With the publication in 1819 of *Nordens Guder. Et episk Digt* (1819; translated in part as "The Gods of the North," 1839) Oehlenschläger signaled his return to mythology. Like Snorri, whose *Prose Edda* is a compendium of Norse mythology written at a time when widespread knowledge of Nordic pagan mythology was beginning to wane in the largely Christian Nordic world, Oehlenschläger provided his readers with a summary of Nordic mythology in a series of poems. Though clearly based on Snorri's example, Oehlenschläger's volume is neither a translation nor a paraphrase but an inventive reworking of the material in which he not only sought to do justice to the Norse sources but also to make it accessible to modern readers.

Public literary taste during the 1820s and 1830s began tending toward the presentation of inward experience and psychologically penetrating portrayals, as the

Oehlenschläger in 1846 (painting by Jørgen Roed; from Carl S. Petersen and Vilhelm Andersen, Illustreret dansk Litteraturhistorie, *volume 3:* Litteratur i det nittende Aarhundredes første Halvdel, *1924; Suzzallo Library, University of Washington)*

cultural and philosophical ideas of Johan Ludvig Heiberg, Grundtvig, and Kierkegaard suggest. Oehlenschläger's talent did not lend itself as well to detailed and nuanced portrayals as it did to wider historical panoramas executed with rather broad strokes. In 1828 he returned to the story of Hrolf Krake, of whose birth Oehlenschläger had provided an account at the end of *Yrsa.* The result, the epic poem *Hrolf Krake* (1828), brought the sequence of narratives centering on Helge and his posterity to their tragic end. Hrolf's death is depicted in a way that points to the final familial atonement for Helge's weaknesses and excesses.

During these decades Oehlenschläger continued to occupy a position of prominence as both a member of the academic community and as a writer, although public sentiment tended to be more respectful than enthusiastic. The interest in Oehlenschläger himself that had been gradually growing during the 1820s was addressed in 1829 with the publication in German of a series of his recollections. Shortly thereafter he translated them into Danish and published them as *Oehlenschlägers Levnet, fortalt af ham selv* (Oehlenschläger's Life, Related by Himself, 1830, 1831).

Oehlenschläger's literary output continued at an impressive rate, and public appreciation achieved its most concrete manifestation when he was crowned with a laurel wreath in a great celebration at the cathedral of the Swedish university city of Lund by Esaias Tegnér, a distinguished Swedish poet who had long shared many of his interests. The historical dramas that Oehlenschläger next wrote–*Karl den Store* (Charlemagne, 1829), *Tordenskiold* (1833), *Dronning Margareta* (Queen Margareta, 1834), *Sokrates* (Socrates, 1836), *Knud den Store* (Canute the Great, 1839), *Dina* (1842), *Erik Glipping* (1844), *Landet fundet og forsvundet* (The Land Discovered and Lost, 1846), *Amleth* (Hamlet, 1847), and *Kiartan og Gudrun* (Kjartan and Gudrun, 1848)–are, as a group, competent in terms of overall dramatic structure but fail to plumb psychological depths, most notably in the case of figures who particularly invite that kind of treatment. Many of these dramas play well on the stage and are occasionally still performed in Nordic theaters, but none has become a work of broadly enduring interest, internationally or in Denmark.

Although Oehlenschläger had never been able to rise to the challenge of credibly portraying deeper psychological dimensions of human experience, during the last decades of his life he nonetheless turned his attention to himself with surprising results. He wrote an autobiography, published posthumously as *Oehlenschlägers Erindringer* (Oehlenschläger's Memories, 1850–1851) and edited by his son Johannes Wolfgang. His considerable achievement in this work of portraying the development of his distinct personality and habits of mind is just beginning to be recognized. Although Oehlenschläger had long been indulging in autobiographical ruminations and had already published *Oehlenschlägers Levnet, fortalt af ham selv,* he began in earnest in the late 1840s to pull together material from the earlier volume, as well as from a copious correspondence, in an attempt to fashion an account of his life up to 1846. Particularly in the first part chronicling Oehlenschläger's youth and the years of early maturity, the autobiography stresses individualism and the dynamic process of individuation. Hearkening back to Rousseau's paradigm of self-portrayal, *Oehlenschlägers Erindringer* illustrates the way the youthful mind–particularly that of an artist–alternately engages as well as constitutes the external world. In the process of forging an individual identity, the unique inward sense of personality projects itself upon external, physical and social reality while being shaped by it. The educative role of art is stressed, as is the value of socially productive integration into society, in ways that reflect the widely influential tradition of self-cultivation of Goethe and Schiller. Oehlenschläger's important contribution to the Romantic tradition of autobiography is most evident in his description of the self's potential for endlessly generating new insight as it moves through a spiraling sequence of contractions and expansions, each in turn requiring a reconfiguration of the self in anticipations of new engagements.

Adam Oehlenschläger died on 20 January 1850, widely respected as an academic and a writer. He lies buried at Frederiksberg Cemetery. Although his later works never commanded the same enthusiastic appreciation that had been accorded those written during the earliest decades of the nineteenth century, his reputation as one of Denmark's most important writers has persisted and has been acknowledged by many writers. In recent decades, however, some critics have argued that Oehlenschläger's principle importance is historical and best understood in terms of his embodiment of the thinking of Denmark's Golden Age. Others suggest that his works may prove to be congenial to revisionist readings in terms of contemporary critical constructs. He remains, though, Denmark's major link to the broader European–and especially German–Romanticism and was an important innovator in terms of the elaboration of that tradition. He made valuable contributions to the reawakening of interest in the Nordic literary tradition and did so in ways that brought the fundamental aspects of that culture into a productive juxtaposition with contemporary sensitivities and personal, social, and religious values.

Letters:

Mindeblade om Oehlenschläger og hans Kreds hjemme og ude, i Breve fra og til ham, edited by C. L. N. Mynster (Copenhagen: Gyldendal, 1879);

Breve fra og til Adam Oehlenschläger, Januar 1798 – November 1809, 5 volumes, edited by H. A. Paludan, Daniel Preisz, and Morten Borup (Copenhagen: Gyldendal, 1945–1950);

Breve fra og til Adam Oehlenschläger, November 1809 – Oktober 1829, 6 volumes, edited by Preisz and Torben Nielsen (Copenhagen: Gyldendal, 1953–1981);

Breve fra og til Adam Oehlenschläger, Oktober 1829 – Januar 1850, 3 volumes, edited by Preisz (Copenhagen: Gyldendal, 1984–1990).

Bibliographies:

Aage Jørgensen, "Deutsche Beiträge zum Oehlenschläger-Studium. Eine Bibliographie," *Archiv für das Studium der neueren Sprachen und Literaturen,* 203 (1966): 53–57;

Jørgensen, *Oehlenschläger-litteraturen, 1850–1966. En bibliografi,* Oehlenschläger Selskabets Skriftserie, no. 6 (Copenhagen: S. Schultz, 1966);

Jørgensen, *Oehlenschläger litteraturen, 1967–1979. En bibliografi* ([Mårslet]: [A. Jørgensen], 1979);

Jørgensen, *Oehlenschläger-litteraturen, 1967–1988. En bibliografi* (Åarhus: Center for Undervisning og Kulturformidling, 1989).

Biographies:

Povl Ingerslev-Jensen, *Oehlenschläger og Wien* (Copenhagen: Oehlenschläger Selskabet, 1968);

Ingerslev-Jensen, *Den unge Oehlenschläger* (Copenhagen: Rosenkilde & Bagger, 1972).

References:

Lise Præstgaard Andersen, "Oehlenschläger, de norrøne kilder og de norrøne kvinder," *Danske Studier,* 76, no. 2 (1981): 5–31;

Thomas Bredsdorff, "Oehlenschläger's Aesthetics: Allegory and Symbolism in 'The Golden Horns'–and a Note on 20th Century Eulogy of the Allegory," *Edda,* 3 (1999): 211–221;

Svend Christiansen and Povl Ingerslev-Jensen, eds., *Til Adam Oehlenschläger, 1779–1979. Otte afhandlinger* (Copenhagen: Teatervidenskabelige Institut ved Københavns Universitet/Oehlenschläger Selskabet, 1979);

Alvhild Dvergsdal, *Adam Oehlenschlägers tragediekunst* (Copenhagen: Museum Tusculanum, 1997);

Jørgen Fafner, "Romantikkens stemme. Oehlenschläger og de romantiske læredigt," *Retorik Studier,* 4 (1979): 3–25;

Ida Falbe-Hansen, *Oehlenschlægers nordiske Digtning og andre Afhandlinger* (Copenhagen: Aschehoug, 1921);

Anker Gemzøe, "'Hakon Jarls Død.' Poetisk teknik og historiesyn hos den unge Adam Oehlenschläger," *Edda,* 2 (1989): 99–117;

Kathryn Shailer Hanson, "Adam Oehlenschläger's *Erik og Roller* and Danish Romanticism," *Scandinavian Studies,* 65, no. 2 (1993): 180–195;

Helen Høyrup, "'Som Perler paa den historiske Musas Snor': Romantic Self-Representation and Aesthetics in Adam Oehlenschlägers *Ungdomserindringer,*" *Scandinavian Studies,* 72, no. 4 (2001): 431–444;

Niels Ingwersen, "The Tragic Moment in Oehlenschläger's 'Hakon Jarl hin Rige,'" *Scandinavica,* 9, no. 1 (1970): 34–44;

Oehlenschläger Studier (1972–1979);

Gottsche Hans Olsen, *Indlæg i Anledning af Hr. Professor Oehlenschlägers Appel Til Publikum fra Theatercensorerne* (Copenhagen: Thiele, 1816).

Papers:

Adam Oehlenschläger's papers and manuscripts are at the Danish Royal Library in Copenhagen.

Frederik Paludan-Müller

(7 February 1809 – 28 December 1876)

Sven Hakon Rossel
University of Vienna

BOOKS: *Fire Romanzer* (Copenhagen: P. N. Jørgensen, 1832);

Kjærlighed ved Hoffet (Copenhagen: P. N. Jørgensen, 1832);

Dandserinden (Copenhagen: C. A. Reitzel, 1833);

Amor og Psyche (Copenhagen: C. A. Reitzel, 1834);

Zuleimas Flugt (Copenhagen: C. A. Reitzel, 1835);

Poesier. Første Deel (Copenhagen: C. A. Reitzel, 1836)–includes *Eventyr i Skoven* and *Alf og Rose;*

Trochæer og Jamber (Copenhagen: C. A. Reitzel, 1837);

Poesier. Anden Deel (Copenhagen: C. A. Reitzel, 1838)–includes *Fyrste og Page, Poetiske Fortællinger,* and *Blandede Digte;*

Venus (Copenhagen: C. A. Reitzel, 1841);

Adam Homo, 3 volumes (Copenhagen: C. A. Reitzel, 1842–1849 [i.e., 1841–1848]; first volume revised, 1849); translated by Stephen I. Klass as *Adam Homo* (New York: Twickenham Press, 1980);

Tithon (Copenhagen: C. A. Reitzel, 1844);

Dryadens Bryllup (Copenhagen: C. A. Reitzel, 1844); republished as *Dryaden* (Copenhagen: C. A. Reitzel, 1857);

Luftskipperen og Atheisten (Copenhagen: C. A. Reitzel, 1853 [i.e., 1852]);

Tre Digte (Copenhagen: C. A. Reitzel, 1854)–comprises *Abels Død, Kalanus,* and *Ahasverus, den evige Jøde;*

Nye Digte (Copenhagen: C. A. Reitzel, 1861)–comprises *Paradiset,* part 1, *Kain eller Vredens Barn,* and *Benedict fra Nursia;*

Paradiset (Copenhagen: C. A. Reitzel, 1862);

Pygmalion, in *Nye Digte af danske Digtere,* edited by Christian Winther (Copenhagen: C. A. Reitzel, 1862);

Ungdomskilden (Copenhagen: C. A. Reitzel, 1865); translated by Humphry William Freeland as *The Fountain of Youth* (London, 1867);

Ivar Lykkes Historie, 3 volumes (Copenhagen: C. A. Reitzel, 1866–1873);

Sex Digte (Copenhagen: C. A. Reitzel, 1872)–comprises *Kalanus, Abels Død, Kain eller Vredens Barn, Ahasverus, den evige Jøde, Benedict fra Nursia og hans Amme,* and *Pygmalion;*

Tiderne skifte (Copenhagen: C. A. Reitzel, 1874);

Adonis (Copenhagen: C. A. Reitzel, 1874).

Frederik Paludan-Müller (photograph by Budtz Müller & Co., 1869; courtesy of the Danish Royal Library, Copenhagen)

Editions and Collections: *Ungdomsarbeider* (Copenhagen: C. A. Reitzel, 1847)–comprises *Kjærlighed ved Hoffet, Dandserinden,* and *Amor og Psyche;* revised as *Ungdomsskrifter* (Copenhagen: C. A. Reitzel, 1854; revised again, 1861);

Mythologiske Digte (Copenhagen: C. A. Reitzel, 1854)–comprises *Venus, Dryaden,* and *Tithon;*

Poetiske Skrifter, 8 volumes (Copenhagen: C. A. Reitzel, 1878–1879);

Poetiske Skrifter i Udvalg, 8 volumes (Copenhagen: Gyldendal, 1901–1902);

Paludan-Müllers poetiske Skrifter i Udvalg, 3 volumes, edited by Carl S. Petersen (Copenhagen: Gyldendal, 1909).

Frederik Paludan-Müller is positioned between the periods of Romanticism and Naturalism at the crossroad of mid-nineteenth-century Danish literature. Keenly aware of the ongoing social and ideological changes of his time, he sharply satirized and criticized the shallow idealism and occasional sentimentality of the last offshoots of the Romantic movement as well as the smoldering materialism and atheism of the second half of the nineteenth century. At the same time, as Paludan-Müller became polemically involved in the questions of the day, he raised himself above his own time through the universality of the problems he discussed and the artistic value of his writing.

Many of Paludan-Müller's fellow writers in Denmark and abroad were vacillating between contrasting traditional and modern views, often in a dialectical process that led them to a certain degree of philosophical relativism. Some had even begun to question Christian dogmas, conservative politics, the social order, and the bourgeois concepts of morality, whereas others chose art and beauty as values that–at least on the surface–could reconcile mankind with the negative sides of existence. Paludan-Müller, on the other hand, reacted vigorously against such attempts at reconciliation and philosophical relativism, which to him foreshadowed ethical nihilism. He did so with pointed criticism and a strong demand for consistent religious commitment.

Paludan-Müller was born on 7 February 1809 in Kerteminde on the island of Fyn. His father, Jens Paludan-Müller, was of old Lutheran clerical and peasant stock; in 1819 he became archdeacon in Odense, the principal city on Fyn, and in 1830 bishop of Århus, the second-largest city of Denmark. Frederik's mother, Marie Benedicte Rosenstand-Goiske, also came from a family of clergymen. Insanity ran in this family, and she herself, when the author was still a child, became mentally ill. Paludan-Müller's childhood memories from Kerteminde are reflected in the novel of his old age, *Ivar Lykkes Historie* (The Story of Ivar Lykke, 1866–1873). From 1819 to 1828, the family lived in Odense, where Paludan-Müller passed his university entrance exams in 1828 and was considered one of the most brilliant students of that year. In the same year, he moved to Copenhagen in order to study law. He did not conclude his studies until 1835 and then decided not to enter the legal profession. Instead, he eagerly participated in the social life of Copenhagen, established a reputation as a social lion, and mingled with the trendsetting literary circles. In particular, he was influenced by the leading playwright and literary critic of the time, Johan Ludvig Heiberg. Heiberg's aesthetic views and elegant artistic style, along with the works of George Gordon, Lord Byron, became the source of inspiration for the early–somewhat sensation-seeking and beauty-worshiping–writings of Paludan-Müller. These features are not yet present in his first, separately and anonymously published, revolutionary poem, "Raab til Polen" (Cry to Poland) from 1831, inspired by the Polish fight for freedom against Russia. They are also hardly traceable in the likewise anonymously published *Fire Romanzer* (Four Romances, 1832), composed in the tradition of national Romanticism with many Gothic effects in the depictions of brutal death.

With his following works, however, Paludan-Müller developed into one of the most prolific representatives of the young Byron-inspired spleen and beauty-worshiping generation of writers in the Danish capital. His comedy *Kjærlighed ved Hoffet* (Love at the Court, 1832), the only one of his stage works performed with considerable success, was an elegant pastiche of William Shakespeare and Carlo Gozzi celebrating the victory of love and youth over courtly intrigue and snobbery. It was also interwoven with a distinct melancholy atmosphere characteristic of the author's later work. The verse epic *Dandserinden* (The Danseuse, 1833) is the first clear indication of Paludan-Müller's infatuation with Byron. It is written, as were several other works from the following years, in the Byronic, superbly executed ottava rima stanza and includes reminiscences of the love story of Don Juan and Haidée in Byron's principal work, *Don Juan* (1819–1824). In *Dandserinden,* Paludan-Müller depicts the love relationship between the celebrated ballet dancer Dione and the elegant but spineless Count Charles, framed by scenes from the fashionable life of Copenhagen high society. Charles deserts Dione when he is persuaded by his mother to marry a woman whose social rank is closer to his. Shortly before his marriage, however, Charles is killed in a duel, which he fights in order to defend Dione's honor. She consequently dies in despair after having gone insane. High points of realism are the broadly painted satirical period-pictures, but equally significant are the many reflective passages–or, rather, digressions. In this work Paludan-Müller expresses a strong awareness of transitoriness and decay, and the dissonant tone of his epic work is a genuine expression of the weltschmerz of the period and of a personal striving for some sort of eternity that is perhaps inaccessible. This tendency toward philosophical digression–also modeled after Byron–became a permanent feature in Paludan-Müller's oeuvre.

Dandserinden was an immediate success, and the following mythological drama, *Amor og Psyche* (Cupid and Psyche, 1834), was also received with enthusiasm. It is based on the folktale motif of the beauty and the beast as found in the second-century Roman prose work by Apuleius, *Metamorphoses. Amor og Psyche,* however, lacks the intensity and well-formed characters of the previous work with which it shares its basic structure: in three stages, Paludan-Müller depicts the brief moment of the elusiveness of love, one of the main character's moral failures, and his rehabilitation through remorse. *Zuleimas Flugt* (Zuleima's Flight, 1835) is a rather short, Byronesque epic poem set in Spain during the Moorish era, portraying a loving couple that flees before their enemies but are caught and killed. More significant is the first volume of *Poesier* (Poetical Works, 1836), which comprises the comedy *Eventyr i Skoven* (Fairy Tale in the Forest), a Romantic satire both on the petty bourgeoisie, inspired by Shakespeare's *A Midsummer Night's Dream* (written circa 1595 or 1596, published 1600), and on contemporary efforts to establish political democracy, and *Alf og Rose* (Elf and Rose, 1836). This short, philosophical dialogue is an allegory intended to demonstrate that earthly love is unstable and can only achieve permanence when it is transformed into an expression of the transcendent ideal of love: thus, happiness can only be achieved beyond death.

Paludan-Müller responded to a negative review of the volume with an aggressive and rude satire in verse, *Trochæer og Jamber* (Trochees and Iambi, 1837). The following year, 1838, a second volume of *Poesier* appeared. It includes Paludan-Müller's last Romantic play, *Fyrste og Page* (Prince and Page), which was performed only twice at the Royal Theater in Copenhagen in May 1838 and later was excluded by the author from his oeuvre; three Byronic epic poems, *Beatrice, Vestalinden* (The Vestal Virgin), and *Slaven* (The Slave); and other poems composed throughout the years. Among these poems one finds the most valuable texts of the volume. In it are erotic texts, which offer insights into more complex layers of the poet's psyche; however, they are all based on memory and reflection rather than on current feelings. The gripping poem "Dandsemusik" (Dance Music), on the other hand, is rooted in personal experiences and thus points ahead to the author's future conflict with his previous aesthetic attitude. This existentialist development can be traced in the poems "Nattevagt" (Nightwatch) and "Sorgen" (Grief), in which a distinct religious mood breaks through, and, particularly, in the biblical text "Lucifers Fald" (The Fall of Lucifer), which includes the first seeds of Paludan-Müller's later Christianity.

The second volume of *Poesier* concludes Paludan-Müller's youthful writings. It was met with surprise and disapproval by unsympathetic critics and readers. Another event was even more decisive. In the fall of 1837 Paludan-Müller contracted a deadly disease, which might have been typhoid fever. He was taken out of the hospital and nursed back to health by a deeply religious female relative, Charite Borch. Paludan-Müller renounced his former lifestyle and on 30 August 1838 married Borch. Under her influence, the worshiper of youth, flirtation, and spleen became a poet of commitment and sincerity, ready to write his major works. A honeymoon trip took the couple to France and Italy with extended stopovers in Paris, Rome, and Naples. After their return in September 1840, Paludan-Müller and his wife settled in Copenhagen, establishing their summer quarters in the small town of Fredensborg, north of the capital. From 1858, with permission from the royal family, they had an apartment in one of the wings of Fredensborg Castle.

The first work published after the wedding was another mythological drama, *Venus* (1841), in which the definitive transition from an aesthetic to an ethical worldview has taken place. This work also constitutes a reckoning with the self-centered, demonic, and destructive Byronic hero of the previous decade. Paludan-Müller juxtaposes sensual eroticism with spiritual love. The sexual desire of the hunter Actaeon, a true Don Juan character, drives the shepherdess Hermione to suicide. When Actaeon then pursues Diana herself, the goddess transforms him into a stag, and he is torn to pieces by his own dogs. Endymion, the bridegroom of Hermione, in contrast, is led to the land of the dead, where he will later be reunited with his beloved in Elysium. The lament about transitoriness, so pronounced in Paludan-Müller's youthful writing, has here been replaced by a strong condemnation of sensuality and a glorification of asceticism and death.

After *Venus,* which was rejected by the reading public, Paludan-Müller published in December 1841 the first part of his principal work, written in Paris, *Adam Homo,* an epic divided into six cantos. This poem combines the social criticism of *Dandserinden* with a strong demand for ethical responsibility. The life of an average human being (hence the title) is depicted from the cradle to the grave, demonstrating how this opportunist hero, or rather antihero, has committed himself

Vi gaae saa sikkre hen ad Livets Vei,
Og dybt i Slummer falder snart hveranden;
Een ved bestandig Filen med Forstanden,
Og Een fordi Forstand han bruger ei.
Vi gaae saa trygge, baade du og jeg,
Med Bind for Øiet og med Fjæl for Panden,
Og finde Alt naturligt hvad der skeer,
Og tænke aldrig paa, hvad ei vi seer.

Og Mens Underverd'nens Afgrundsdyb man skimter.

Vi vaagne op, og i vort Bryst vi sukke,
Og Verden heelt forandret nu,
vort Øie vi oplukke
For Himmel, Helvede, med Lyst og Gru.
Vel kan ei Sindet meer sig sorgløst vugge,
Vel brast som Boblen Hjertets Fred itu;
Men dog vi vaktes, om vi end med Qvaler
Vor Vækker og vor Lærer dyrt betaler.

Page from the fifth edition (1873) of Paludan-Müller's epic poem Adam Homo *(1841–1848), with revisions in his hand (courtesy of the Danish Royal Library, Copenhagen)*

to the present, pleasure, and career, constantly avoiding any moral commitment. Like a fairy-tale hero, Adam is born with rich talents, and like a Faustian character, he finally faces divine judgment for having abused these talents. His childhood in a Jutland parsonage is marked, on the one hand, by his father's pragmatic attitude and, on the other, by his pious mother's admonition to live according to the plan of God, an admonition that Adam, on his journey through life, does not follow. He moves to Copenhagen to study theology, but under the influence of a Byronic libertine, von Pahlen, he is introduced to the pleasures of a life of easy virtue in the capital. In order to be free of his debts, Adam becomes a tutor for the flirtatious countess Clara, who only plays with his feelings for her. He finds an outlet for his bitterness by seducing the maid Lotte. In vain, he seeks consolation with two prostitutes and attempts suicide. After his convalescence, Adam meets Alma, a gardener's daughter, and falls in love with her. Finally, he receives his degree, but he is overtaken by his past when he meets Lotte, now a prostitute. Nevertheless, as the topic for his first homily, Adam chooses the importance of good deeds. Then, receiving a letter from his father about his mother's fatal illness, Adam sets out on a journey home. He must depart from Alma, and in the mail coach he reads some sonnets she has given him; the rest of the work is written in Paludan-Müller's favorite meter, ottava rima, in which Alma expresses the sentiments of love Adam has stirred in her. Now Adam has a new philosophy of life: "Nu saae han som Princip i Alt kun Kjærlighed" (He saw that all lay under love's sole mastery).

The critics neither understood the stinging irony of the text nor its ultimate idealism; the negative reception was probably the main reason Paludan-Müller did not continue *Adam Homo* but instead again focused on works based on Greek legends. *Amor og Psyche* and *Venus* had been rather abstract dramas of ideas, but Paludan-Müller's next work, the dramatic poem *Tithon* (1844), developed individualized characters taken from the legends of Troy. With sublime lyricism, Paludan-Müller expresses the pain of taking leave of earthly existence and the burden of moral obligations. In the same year, 1844, *Dryadens Bryllup* (The Wedding of the Dryad), likewise a dramatic poem, was published. It expresses a somewhat positive view of life on earth and its potential values, which must nevertheless be sacrificed in order to obey the calling of transcendence. The work was written before *Tithon* and scheduled to be the first part of a planned trilogy, which, however, Paludan-Müller never finished. Its principal concept was incorporated in the biblical blank-verse poem *Abels Død* (The Death of Abel, 1854; first published in Heiberg's journal *Urania* [December 1844]); *Abels Død* is a glorification of the righteousness of God as well as man's salvation and is thus a counterpart of the previous pessimistic works, which had been based on Greek mythology.

In 1848 the second and third parts of *Adam Homo* were published (all three parts were translated into English in 1980). The reflections are more searching and the tone more authoritative than in Paludan-Müller's earlier works. Adam, on his way home to his dying mother, sees Countess Clara, now married. Once again he is attracted to her. He accompanies Clara back to her castle and, consequently, does not attend his mother's funeral. Instead, he exchanges his previous philosophy for an Epicurean view of a life guided by chance occurrence. During Adam's attempt to seduce Clara, her husband catches Adam and chases him away. Returning home to his father, Adam abandons his plan to become a clergyman. After Adam has broken off his engagement with Alma by writing her a letter, his opportunistic father arranges a marriage with the emancipated baroness Mille.

From this point on, Paludan-Müller abandons his previous coherent narrative in favor of an episodic composition. Through his marriage of convenience, Adam takes a decisive step to further his career and simultaneously shifts to an idealistic philosophy. For a time he becomes a philanthropist and establishes a speakers' club with the purpose of promoting "perfection." But Adam's opening speech is a complete failure, and thereafter he rejects his former idealism in favor of pure opportunism. While Mille commits herself wholeheartedly to the women's movement and her own short-story writing, Adam climbs the ladder of society. He is appointed privy councilor, baron, and finally manager of the Royal Theater of Copenhagen. In his inaugural speech, Adam mentions "the ideal" but banishes it to a life on the stage. After the festivities, Adam goes on a horseback ride. He catches a cold that develops into pneumonia, and he is hospitalized. At the hospital, as he is dying, he recognizes Alma keeping watch by his bed. Alma, who had remained faithful to her love for him, dies soon after from overexerting herself as Adam's nurse. After his death Adam faces judgment, and only Alma's intercessory prayers and love save him from eternal damnation. She accompanies him through purgatory toward eternal bliss.

Critics of *Adam Homo* have tended to emphasize Paludan-Müller's passing judgment on his own times at the expense of the metaphysical and mystical aspects of the work. The criticism expressed in the account of Adam's external social success develops into a pointed satire on contemporary bourgeois Danish society as an environment of mediocrity, vanity, and corruption that transcends any geographical and chronological borders. More important, however, are the inserted reflective passages, in which Paludan-Müller develops his philosophy of the personality, in many ways foreshadowing the existentialism of Søren Kierkegaard. In such a context, Paludan-Müller's ethical stance takes on a wider perspective as it becomes an analysis of responsibility versus anarchy in the life of a single human being, a life spent without preparation for its conclusion. *Adam Homo* is a grandiose religious didactic epic in which the soul, as in Dante's *Divine Comedy* (circa 1307–1321), through purification is led to salvation. But contrary to the related *Faust* drama by Johann Wolfgang von Goethe, in which Faust wins salvation through his mere striving, Adam is totally dependent on grace won through Alma's love. Like Beatrice and Gretchen, Alma represents the ideal woman becoming the strongest and quite unusual projection of the Holy Virgin that can be found in a northern, Lutheran context. In fact, in his use of purgatory and the Holy Virgin, Paludan-Müller is much closer to Catholic than Lutheran tradition. Alma's poems are testimonies of the inner richness and beauty in the life of a poor and lonely woman. They are an exquisite lyrical expression of the concept that true happiness can be found only through renunciation.

Paludan-Müller's works from the 1850s express even more strongly his doctrine of self-denial. This point of view comes to the fore less in the satirical pamphlet on atheism, *Luftskipperen og Atheisten* (The Balloonist and the Atheist, 1852), than in *Tre Digte* (Three Poems, 1854). In *Kalanus,* written in rather pale blank verse, zest for life and asceticism are juxtaposed and represented in the figures of the warrior and conqueror Alexander the Great and the Indian sage Kalanus, respectively. In the final account, Kalanus turns out to be the true victor as he seeks his death in flames on the pyre. As in *Abels Død,* Paradise is depicted as the realm of true life. Death itself, or rather eternity, is directly glorified in *Ahasverus, den evige Jøde* (Ahasuerus, the Eternal Jew), written in medieval doggerel and almost medieval in its condemnation of a decadent civilization that takes on the atmosphere of the Apocalypse. In these verses, Paludan-Müller's religious fervor as well as his defiance of the zeitgeist reaches new heights.

Ahasverus, den evige Jøde could have been a fitting conclusion of Paludan-Müller's career. Nevertheless, after some years of serious illness and depression, he resumed his writing around 1860 and published *Nye Digte* (New Poems, 1861). Whereas the somber poem *Kain eller Vredens Barn* (Cain or the Child of Wrath) portrays a human being in crippling isolation and devoid of divine grace, in the charming lyrical dialogue *Benedict af Nursia* (Benedict from Nursia) the pessimistic mood recedes in favor of a bright and delicate elaboration of a theme characteristic of Paludan-Müller–the contrast between the desire of the young title character to serve life through renunciation and his nurse's adherence to the positive and vital qualities of present life. Less successful is the dramatic poem *Paradiset* (The Paradise), which in 1862 was republished with many changes and enlarged with a second part. It includes many lyrical episodes, but the portrayal of the first man and woman and the Fall lacks intensity and dramatic vigor. The same flaws characterize the short mythological poem *Pygmalion* (1862), which, again, treats the theme (introduced with *Dryadens Bryllup*) that reconciling present life with eternity is impossible. The optimism, on the other hand, that had been expressed in *Benedict af Nursia* permeates the prose story *Ungdomskilden* (1865; translated as *The Fountain of Youth,* 1867), about a man for whom death is both beautiful and reconciling after a process of rejuvenation has brought him only anguish and misery.

More ambitious is the three-volume novel *Ivar Lykkes Historie,* written under the influence of the 1864 war between Denmark and Prussia and Austria. *Ivar Lykkes Historie* is an appeal for national regeneration and thus a sort of counterpart to *Adam Homo.* Contrary to Adam, Ivar gains inner strength through adversity. After an unjust discharge from the diplomatic service, he joins the Danish army, acquires the rank of captain, but because of misfortune and misunderstandings, loses his rank. Nevertheless, he fights on, is wounded, and loses a hand. His volunteer service during the war rehabilitates him, and he is reconciled with his early love, Filippa. Thus, the novel includes all the necessary ingredients to make it popular–excitement, romantic adventures, and an optimistic line of development of the plot in the tradition of the bildungsroman. Goethe's *Wilhelm Meisters Lehrjahre* (1795–1796; translated as *Wilhelm Meister's Apprenticeship,* 1824) is its unmistakable model. The diffuseness, colorless style, and abstract language of the novel have consigned it to obscurity. Both as a picture of mid-nineteenth-century life and manners and as a philosophical treatise aiming at reconciling the ideal with reality, it deserves to be remembered.

For the opening of the new Royal Theater in Copenhagen in 1874, Paludan-Müller wrote *Tiderne skifte* (Times Change, 1874), a rather insignificant comedy with an historical eighteenth-century setting but with many references to contemporary times. Of superb quality, on the other hand, is his farewell to his career as a writer–in fact, to life–a short epic poem written in trochees, *Adonis* (1874). For the last time, Paludan-Müller treats the motif on which his entire oeuvre is based–the zest for life contrasted with renunciation and longing for death. Adonis has always worshiped both Venus and the goddess of death, Proserpine, but to find peace of mind he finally chooses death, which alone can bring to an end the conflicts of the heart.

In his youth, Paludan-Müller was a celebrated and fashionable writer. Later he avoided all publicity and popularity. The readers of the time as well as posterity replied by ignoring his message, while the critics simultaneously stressed his mastery of form. Of Paludan-Müller's works, *Adam Homo* alone is recognized as an unusual piece of literature, but it can only be valued and interpreted exhaustively in the context of Paludan-Müller's other significant works. After a few days of sudden illness, which developed into facial erysipelas, Paludan-Müller died in Copenhagen on 28 December 1876.

Adonis's choice constitutes a crucial concept in Paludan-Müller's philosophy of life. In this respect Paludan-Müller the ethicist precedes Kierkegaard, who developed this idea further to the religious stage, salvation. Having taken an aristocratic rather than democratic stance, both sternly condemned the dilution and vulgarization of the concept of the personality. Both saw this view not only as resulting from political development but also as a result of an aesthetic outlook on life and the abstract Hegelian manipulation of philosophical terms, two phenomena rooted in Romanticism. Thus, together with the internationally recognized figures Kierkegaard and Hans Christian Andersen, Frederik Paludan-Müller marks an epoch in Danish intellectual history both by ending a preceding philosophical and aesthetic orientation and by stressing the existential commitment of the individual. All three writers are remarkable because of their innovative thoughts and approaches as well as their passionate or even polemical involvement in the questions of the day.

Letters:

Breve til Broderen Caspar og Vennen P. E. Lind, edited by H. Martensen-Larsen (Copenhagen: Frimodt, 1928).

Biographies:

Fritz Lange, *Frederik Paludan-Müller. Et Levnedsløb* (Copenhagen: Nordiske Forlag/Ernst Bojesen, 1899);

Vilhelm Andersen, *Paludan-Müller,* 2 volumes (Copenhagen: Gyldendal, 1910);

Sejer Kühle, *Frederik Paludan-Müller,* 2 volumes (Copenhagen: Aschehoug, 1941, 1942).

References:

F. J. Billeskov Jansen, *Poetik,* volume 2 (Copenhagen: Munksgaard, 1941), pp. 40–74;

Georg Brandes, "Frederik Paludan-Müller," in his *Creative Spirits of the Nineteenth Century* (New York: Crowell, 1923), pp. 267–305;

Ole Brandstrup, *Lær at behage! Otte TV-essays om "Adam Homo"* (Copenhagen: Gyldendal, 1973);

Rolf Dorset and Lisbeth Holst, "Fr. Paludan-Müller. Den tænkte evighed," in *Den erindrende Faun,* edited by Aage Henriksen (Copenhagen: Fremad, 1968), pp. 143–178;

Tue Gad and Bodil Gad, *Den gamle digter* (Copenhagen: C. A. Reitzel, 1986);

Mogens Haugsted, *Frederik Paludan-Müllers prosaiske Arbejder,* Studier fra Sprog- og Oldtidsforskning, no. 182 (Copenhagen: Povl Branner, 1940);

Aage Kabell, "Stil og Idé i Paludan-Müllers Venus," in his *To taler for kransen,* Studier fra Sprog- og Oldtidsforskning, no. 223 (Copenhagen: Branner & Korch, 1953), pp. 3–18;

Sejer Kühle, *Kilderne til Fr. Paludan-Müllers "Kalanus"* (Copenhagen: Aschehoug, 1923);

H. Martensen-Larsen, *Den virkelige Paludan-Müller. Hans Digterkald og Kristendomsform* (Copenhagen: Frimodt, 1924);

Peter Ludvig Møller, "Fr. Paludan-Müller," in his *Kritiske Skizzer fra Aarene 1840–1847* (Copenhagen: P. G. Philipsen, 1847), II: 158–191;

Sven Møller Kristensen, "Tithon," in his *Digtning og livssyn* (Copenhagen: Gyldendal, 1959), pp. 11–29;

Frederik Nielsen, "Om Paludan-Müllers dramatiske digt 'Venus,'" *Danske Studier* (1958): 46–61;

Lars Peter Rømhild, "Frederick Paludan-Müller," *Arkiv for dansk litteratur* <www.adl.dk>;

Paul V. Rubow, "Omkring Adam Homo," in his *Perspektiver* (Copenhagen: Munksgaard, 1941), pp. 7–29;

Rubow, "Paludan-Müller i historisk Belysning," in his *Reflexioner over dansk og fremmed Litteratur* (Copenhagen: Munksgaard, 1942), pp. 60–70;

Knud Wentzel, "Fr. Paludan-Müller: 'Ivar Lykkes Historie,'" in his *Fortolkning og skæbne* (Copenhagen: Fremad, 1970), pp. 65–79.

Papers:

Frederik Paludan-Müller's manuscripts and correspondence are at the Danish Royal Library in Copenhagen.

Henrik Pontoppidan

(24 July 1857 - 21 August 1943)

Flemming Behrendt

(Translated by Russell Dees)

BOOKS: *Stækkede Vinger* (Copenhagen: A. Schou, 1881)–includes "Kirkeskuden" and "Et Endeligt";

Sandinge Menighed. En Fortælling (Copenhagen: A. Schou, 1883);

Landsbybilleder (Copenhagen: Gyldendal, 1883)–includes "En Fiskerrede," translated (from an earlier magazine version) by Julianne Sarauw as "A Fisher Nest" in *American-Scandinavian Review,* 15 (1927): 476–486;

Ung Elskov. Idyl (Copenhagen: Gyldendal, 1885); revised as *Ung Elskov. Blade af en Mindekrans* (Copenhagen: Schubothe, 1906);

Mimoser. Et Familjeliv (Copenhagen: Gyldendal, 1886); translated by Gordius Nielsen as *The Apothecary's Daughters* (London: Trübner, 1890);

Fra Hytterne. Nye Landsbybilleder (Copenhagen: Gyldendal, 1887; Minneapolis: C. Rasmussen, 1888);

Isbjørnen. Et Portræt (Copenhagen: Gyldendal, 1887); translated by James Massengale as *The Polar Bear: A Portrait,* Wisconsin Introductions to Scandinavia II, no. 12 (Madison: Department of Scandinavian Studies, University of Wisconsin, 2003);

Spøgelser. En Historie (Copenhagen: Gyldendal, 1888);

Folkelivsskildringer, volume 1 (Copenhagen: P. Hauberg, 1888); volume 2 (Copenhagen: Nyt dansk Forlagskonsortium, 1890);

Krøniker (Copenhagen: P. G. Philipsen, 1890);

Natur. To smaa Romaner, 2 volumes (Copenhagen: Schubothe, 1890)–comprises *Vildt* and *En Bonde;*

Reisebilder aus Dänemark (Copenhagen: Høst & Son, 1890);

Skyer. Skildringer fra Provisoriernes Dage (Copenhagen: Gyldendal, 1890)–includes "Illum Galgebakke. En Prolog," translated by David Stoner as "Gallows Hill at Ilum" in *Anthology of Danish Literature,* edited by Frederik J. Billeskov Jansen and P. M. Mitchell (Carbondale: Southern Illinois University Press, 1972), pp. 333–359;

Henrik Pontoppidan (photograph by Frederick Riise, 1891; Collection of Flemming Behrendt)

Muld. Et Tidsbillede (Copenhagen: P. G. Philipsen, 1891); translated by Alice Lucas as *Emanuel; or, Children of the Soil* (London: Dent, 1896);

Det forjættede Land. Et Tidsbillede (Copenhagen: P. G. Philipsen, 1892); translated by Lucas as *The Promised Land* (London: Dent, 1896);

Minder (Copenhagen: P. G. Philipsen, 1893);

Den gamle Adam. Skildring fra Alfarvej (Copenhagen: P. G. Philipsen, 1894);

Nattevagt (Copenhagen: P. G. Philipsen, 1894);

Dommens Dag. Et Tidsbillede (Copenhagen: P. G. Philipsen, 1895);

Højsang. Skildring fra Alfarvej (Copenhagen: Schubothe, 1896);

Kirkeskuden. En Fortælling, second edition (Copenhagen: Schubothe, 1897);

Det forjættede Land (Copenhagen: Nordiske Forlag, 1898; revised edition, Copenhagen: Gyldendal, 1918)–comprises *Muld, Det forjættede Land,* and *Dommens Dag;*

Lykke-Per. Hans Ungdom (Copenhagen: Nordiske Forlag, 1898);

Lykke-Per finder Skatten (Copenhagen: Nordiske Forlag, 1898);

Fortællinger, 2 volumes (Copenhagen: Nordiske Forlag, 1899)–includes "Ørneflugt," translated by Lida Siboni Hanson as "Eagle's Flight" in *American-Scandinavian Review,* 17 (1929): 556–558;

Lykke-Per. Hans Kærlighed (Copenhagen: Nordiske Forlag, 1899);

Lykke-Per i det Fremmede (Copenhagen: Nordiske Forlag, 1899);

Det ideale Hjem (Aarhus: Jydsk Forlags-Forretning, 1900);

Lille Rødhætte. Et Portræt (Copenhagen: Nordiske Forlag, 1900); republished as *Thora van Deken* in *Noveller og Skitser. Et Udvalg,* volume 2 (Copenhagen: Gyldendal, 1922), pp. 269–352;

Lykke-Per. Hans store Værk (Copenhagen: Nordiske Forlag, 1901);

Lykke-Per og hans Kæreste (Copenhagen: Nordiske Forlag, 1902);

De vilde Fugle. Et Skuespil (Copenhagen: Nordiske Forlag, 1902);

Lykke-Per. Hans Rejse til Amerika (Copenhagen: Nordiske Forlag, 1903);

Et Endeligt. En Landsbyhistorie (Copenhagen: Schubothe, 1904);

Lykke-Per. Hans sidste Kamp (Copenhagen: Gyldendal, 1904);

Borgmester Hoeck og Hustru. Et Dobbeltportræt (Copenhagen: Gyldendal, 1905); translated by Martin A. David as *Burgomaster Hoeck and His Wife,* with an introduction by Flemming Behrendt, bilingual edition (Lysaker: Geelmuyden.Kiese/Scandinavian Airlines, 1999);

Lykke-Per, collected and revised edition, 3 volumes (Copenhagen: Gyldendal, 1905; revised, 2 volumes, 1918)–comprises *Lykke-Per. Hans Ungdom, Lykke-Per finder Skatten, Lykke-Per. Hans Kærlighed, Lykke-Per i det Fremmede, Lykke-Per. Hans store Værk, Lykke-Per og hans Kæreste, Lykke-Per. Hans Rejse til Amerika,* and *Lykke-Per. Hans sidste Kamp;*

Asgaardsrejen. Et Skuespil (Copenhagen: Schubothe, 1906); revised as *Asgaardsrejen. Et Forspil* (Copenhagen: Gyldendal, 1928);

Hans Kvast og Melusine (Copenhagen: Schubothe, 1907);

Det store Spøgelse (Copenhagen: Schubothe, 1907);

Den kongelige Gæst (Copenhagen: Schubothe, 1908); translated by Hanson (from 1902 periodical version) as "The Royal Guest" in *Denmark's Best Stories: An Introduction to Danish Fiction,* edited by Hanna Astrup Larsen (New York: American-Scandinavian Foundation/Norton, 1928), pp. 217–236;

Torben og Jytte, En Fortælling-Kres, no. 1 (Copenhagen: Gyldendal, 1912);

Storeholt, En Fortælling-Kres, no. 2 (Copenhagen: Gyldendal, 1913);

Kirken og dens Mænd. Et Foredrag (Copenhagen: Gyldendal, 1914);

Toldere og Syndere, En Fortælling-Kres, no. 3 (Copenhagen: Gyldendal, 1914);

Enslevs Død, En Fortælling-Kres, no. 4 (Copenhagen: Gyldendal, 1915);

Favsingholm, En Fortælling-Kres, no. 5 (Copenhagen: Gyldendal, 1916);

De Dødes Rige, 2 volumes (Copenhagen: Gyldendal, 1917)–comprises *Torben og Jytte, Storeholt, Toldere og Syndere, Enslevs Død,* and *Favsingholm;*

Et Kærlighedseventyr (Copenhagen: Gyldendal, 1918);

En Vinterrejse. Nogle Dagbogsblade (Copenhagen: Gyldendal, 1920);

Mands Himmerig (Copenhagen: Gyldendal, 1927);

Drengeaar (Copenhagen: Gyldendal, 1933);

Hamskifte (Copenhagen: Gyldendal, 1936);

Arv og Gæld (Copenhagen: Gyldendal, 1938);

Familjeliv (Copenhagen: Gyldendal, 1940);

Undervejs til mig selv. Et Tilbageblik (Copenhagen: Gyldendal, 1943)–abridgment of *Drengeaar, Hamskifte, Arv og Gæld,* and *Familjeliv.*

Editions and Collections: *Noveller og Skitser. Et Udvalg,* 3 volumes (Copenhagen: Gyldendal, 1922–1930);

Ilum Galgebakke; Den første Gendarm; Nattevagt, edited, with an introduction, by Vilhelm Øhlenschläger (Copenhagen: Gyldendal/Dansklærerforeningen, 1926);

Isbjørnen. Et Portræt, edited, with an introduction, by Svend Norrild (Copenhagen: Gyldendal/Dansklærerforeningen, 1941);

Det forjættede Land. Forkortet Udgave, edited and abridged, with an introduction and notes, by Aage Bertelsen (Copenhagen: Dansklærerforeningen, 1943);

Fra Hytterne, edited by Johannes P. Olsen (Copenhagen: Gyldendal/Dansklærerforeningen, 1953);

Mands Himmerig, edited by Esther Skjerbæk and Thorkild Skjerbæk (Copenhagen: Gyldendal, 1961);

Borgmester Hoeck og Hustru, edited by Frederik Nielsen (Copenhagen: Gyldendal/Dansklærerforeningen, 1964);

Lykke-Per, edited, with an afterword, by Thorkild Skjerbæk, 2 volumes (Copenhagen: Gyldendal, 1964);

Ung Elskov og andre Fortællinger, edited by Thorkild Skjerbæk (Copenhagen: Gyldendal, 1965);

Fra Hytterne. Skyggerids fra Landsbyen, edited by Esther Skjerbæk and Thorkild Skjerbæk, afterword by Thorkild Skjerbæk (Copenhagen: Gyldendal, 1973);

Det forjættede Land, edited, with an afterword, by Thorkild Skjerbæk, 3 volumes (Copenhagen: Gyldendal, 1979);

Magister Globs Papirer, edited, with an afterword, by Thorkild Skjerbæk (Copenhagen: Gyldendal, 1979)–comprises *Minder, Den gamle Adam,* and *Højsang;*

Mimoser. Et Familjeliv, afterword by Birgitte Hesselaa (Copenhagen: Gyldendal, 1979);

Skyer, edited, with an afterword, by Thorkild Skjerbæk (Copenhagen: Gyldendal, 1979);

Ørneflugt og andre Krøniker, edited, with an afterword, by Thorkild Skjerbæk (Copenhagen: Gyldendal, 1979)–comprises *Krøniker* and *Den kongelige Gæst;*

De Dødes Rige, 2 volumes, edited, with an afterword, by Thorkild Skjerbæk (Copenhagen: Gyldendal, 1982);

En Vinterrejse, afterword by Flemming Behrendt (Copenhagen: C. Andersen, 1982);

Det ideale Hjem, with essay by Poul Behrendt (Copenhagen: Amadeus, 1986);

Kronjyder og Molboer, afterword by Thorkild Skjerbæk (Randers: Randers Antikvariat, 1989);

Enetaler, edited by Johan de Mylius (Copenhagen: Aschehoug, 1993);

Henrik Pontoppidan, mellem Andegård og Ørnehjem, edited by Jørn Ørum Hansen (Herning: Systime, 1994);

Meninger & Holdninger. Af Urbanus' Dagbog, edited by Erik H. Madsen (Højbjerg: Hovedland, 1994);

Det forjættede Land, 2 volumes, edited by Esther Kielberg and Lars Peter Rømhild (Copenhagen: Gyldendal/Danske Sprog- og Litteraturselskab, 1997);

Henrik Pontoppidans Digte, edited by Børge Andersen (Copenhagen: C. A. Reitzel, 1999);

Smaa Romaner, 1885–1890, edited by Flemming Behrendt (Copenhagen: Danske Sprog- og Litteraturselskab / Valby: Borgen, 1999);

Smaa Romaner, 1893–1900, edited by Flemming Behrendt (Copenhagen: Danske Sprog- og Litteraturselskab / Valby: Borgen, 2004).

PLAY PRODUCTIONS: *Asgaardsrejen,* Odense, Odense Teater, 30 November 1906; revised, Copenhagen, Folketeatret, 26 January 1907; revised as *Ragna,* Copenhagen, Folketeatret, 20 November 1991;

Thora van Deken, by Pontoppidan and Hjalmar Bergman, Copenhagen, Dagmarteatret, 26 March 1914.

PRODUCED SCRIPTS: *De vilde Fugle,* Danmarks Radio, 20 August 1932;

Thora van Deken, by Pontoppidan and Hjalmar Bergman, Danmarks Radio, 18 December 1962.

When Henrik Pontoppidan turned fifteen, he was visiting the island of Bogø in southern Denmark, where his grandfather had served as the parish pastor. An older cousin took him up to the highest spot on the island and pointed across the water toward the many church spires dotting the Danish landscape. For the previous 350 years in the surrounding Danish parishes, either the pastor or his wife had belonged to the Pontoppidan family. Later in life, Pontoppidan described this experience in one of his autobiographical works, *Drengeaar* (Boyhood Years, 1933); the view of the spires made him understand that he was a sort of heir to the realm. He was descended from a long line of pastors, but he never became a clergyman himself; instead, he viewed his native Denmark as his parish. In his brief autobiography to the Nobel Foundation, written after sharing the Nobel Prize in literature with Karl Gjellerup in 1917, Pontoppidan called his three great novel sequences–*Det forjættede Land* (The Promised Land, 1891–1895), *Lykke-Per* (Lucky Per, 1898–1904), and *De Dødes Rige* (The Realm of the Dead, 1912–1916)–"et sammenhængende Billede af Nutidens Danmark" (a comprehensive picture of contemporary Denmark). Pontoppidan's literary oeuvre, one of the most voluminous and extensive in Danish literature, consists of fifty titles written over a period of more than sixty years. He lived all over Denmark, and his writings reflect his familiarity with both the Danish people and their environs. Ideologically, Pontoppidan's work reflects the new industrial era as well as the old parochial society. As a literary figure, he was both a rationalist and a Romantic, a symbolist and a linguistic puritan, a fashionable dandy and a simple wayfarer carrying only a knapsack and pen.

Henrik Pontoppidan was born on 24 July 1857 to Dines Pontoppidan and Marie Oxenböll Pontoppidan. His father, a literate, serious, and somewhat bitter man, was at this time a minister in Fredericia. His mother had a brilliant mind, but giving birth to sixteen children weakened her health. In the summer of 1863 the family moved to Randers, where the father hoped for a richer parish. The family finances remained strained, however, because of Dines Pontoppidan's duty to fund the pension of his predecessor. Throughout his life, Henrik Pontoppidan also suffered tight financial constraints. Even the Nobel Prize money he received was reduced by a bank failure in 1927. Randers became Pontoppidan's paradise on earth, particularly in his memoirs and his literary works. The Prussian occupation of Jutland from April to November 1864 made an early impression on him that did not diminish during his adult life. While his three older brothers grew up in the optimistic rush of victory after the war with Prussia (1848 to 1850) over Schleswig-Holstein, Pontoppidan, along with many of his peers, was marked for life by the Danish defeat of 1864 in the second war with Prussia.

In the early 1870s, after returning home from his visit to Bogø, Pontoppidan founded a literary group in Randers consisting of five schoolmates. The group met once a week to discuss their favorite authors, present new ideas, drink, and smoke. Outside of school, Pontoppidan led an active outdoor life: he swam and sailed in the fjord and hiked with friends, particularly north to the ocean and west to the moors and the world of his favorite author, Steen Steensen Blicher. A broad-chested, robust boy with a dark complexion, Pontoppidan was strikingly handsome, with sparkling blue eyes. He matured quickly, although he was not tall (five feet, nine inches, according to his military-service record), and he was enthusiastic on the dance floor and popular with the girls. His academic forte lay in mathematics and physics, and his father would have liked to see him become a merchant's apprentice to the childless uncle who took the boy and his cousin to Bogø. Instead, a beloved mathematics teacher helped Pontoppidan to realize his desire to become an engineer.

In the fall of 1873 Pontoppidan arrived ahead of his schoolmates in Copenhagen, where his three elder brothers already resided. Although he formed close ties with his brother Morten, his relationship to his two other brothers remained distant. After his preparatory mathematics examination, Pontoppidan was accepted in the fall semester of 1874 to the Polytechnical Institute of Denmark (later renamed the Technical University of Denmark), founded by the physicist Hans Christian Ørsted, which at that time lay in the heart of old Copenhagen. After 1875 Pontoppidan lived in the old residential quarter known as Nyboder; its village atmosphere made him feel more at home than the suburban neighborhood of Nørrebro, where he had begun his life in the capital city. He remained an outdoor person, always out trekking, and he later chose remote residences in the provinces not only because of tight finances but also because social isolation became a precondition for his writing.

In the spring of 1876, as an engineering student, Pontoppidan applied to take part in a geological expedition to Greenland. In a single sitting he plowed through Hinrich Rink's two-volume work on Greenland and its people, *Grønland, geographisk og statistisk beskrevet* (Greenland, Geographically and Statistically Described, 1852, 1857). Another student, however, was chosen for the trip. Using an inheritance from his grandfather, Pontoppidan dulled his disappointment with a trip to Switzerland. He experienced the Alps firsthand and became acquainted with mortal fear during a mountain climb. When he returned home (following a romance with a Swiss milkmaid), he threw himself into another descriptive work, Hermann Alexander von Berlepsch's *Die Alpen* (The Alps, 1861; translated into Danish as *Alperne,* 1873). Thus equipped with both firsthand and secondhand knowledge, Pontoppidan set out the following winter to write a drama drawn from his experiences, which he titled, typically for the times, "Hjemvee" (Nostalgia). At the beginning of March 1879 he sent an entirely rewritten piece to the Danish Royal Theater and received an encouraging rejection. Returning home from his father's funeral in June of the same year, he showed his brother Morten the manuscript. The manuscript was later burned, but, according to Pontoppidan's own statement in *Hamskifte* (Sloughing the Skin, 1936), it must have been "temmelig nøje kalkeret" (a rather precise painting) of his experiences in Switzerland. Despite his father's death Pontoppidan took the final examination in December 1879 but failed a major subject, hydraulics. According to contemporary statements, he could easily have taken the examination again and passed, but he did not avail himself of that option.

Pontoppidan's first story, "Kirkeskuden" (The Votive Ship), was finished in a first version in 1879. At their mother's request, Morten Pontoppidan offered his brother a job as a teacher at his *Folkehøjskole* (folk high school) in northern Zealand beginning in February 1880. At the school Henrik met Mette Marie Hansen, a farmer's daughter almost two years his elder, who was employed at his brother's house. They were engaged in the spring of 1881. During the summer of 1881 "Kirkeskuden" was rewritten and took on the stylistic color of the recently published novel *Arbejdsfolk* (Work-

Ude og Hjemme

Nordisk illustreret Ugeblad

Fjerde Aargang. — Nr. 207. Søndagen d. 18. September 1881.

Abonnement modtages i alle Nordens Boglader og Postkontorer. Prisen er overalt 3 Kr. Kvartalet. Postafgiften iberegnet.

ET ENDELIGT.

Skitse af **Henrik Pontoppidan.** Med Tegning af **Thorvald Niss.**

Ud fra den store, sorte Granskov rumlede et gammelt, gammelt Kjøretøj — som ud fra et andet Aarhundrede.

Vognen var en lille lav Fjællekarre, hvis Alder det vilde være frugtesløst at udgrunde. Men Manden maatte være mellem 90 og 300; — og at det stakkels knoklede Skind, som trippede foran i smaa, stive Hop, en Gang havde været en blankbrun Hoppe, gjættede man snart, efter at have løbet lidt rundt i Naturhistorien.

Nu vare Haarene lange og graa, især under Bugen. Hofterne stode frem som et Par Hanke, og den havde langt Skjæg under Hagen og bag Koderne.

»Du er nok kommen i Stadskarethen — Fatter Ingvor!« — raabte et rødt og grinende Ansigt, der dukkede op fra Vejgrøften.

Det var Vejmanden. Han sad og spiste sin Frokost i Skyggen af en lille Høstak, og var gjerne i godt Lune, saa længe det stod paa.

Men den gamle Mand vendte rolig Ansigtet bort, og saa' ud over Ørene paa »Stjærne« — saadan hed det urgamle Øg, formedelst en lille rund Blis i Panden.

»Snurrig gammel Tingest —«, mumlede Vejmanden, og dukkede atter ned i sit Smørrebrød, mens den gamle Vogn roligt rullede videre hen ad den støvede Landevej.

Nu kunde Stjærne atter bevæge Ørene saa frit, som den vilde. Thi det var dens Vane, naar den passerede Fremmedfolk, da at lægge Ørene tilbage og knejse med Nakken for at se rigtig frisk og fyrig ud. Og naar den dertil satte Forbenene rigtig fast i Jorden, mente den at have Anstand og Holdning som et Aarsføl.

Det var en varm Dag, og Støvet laa vistnok to Tommer tykt paa Vejen. Men Stjærne, som gjorde sig til af sin Anstændighed, flyttede de lange, krogede Ben saa jomfruelig forsigtig, at der kun stod en lillebitte Røgsky efter hver Hov. I et uhyre ærbart Løb nyslede den hen ad Vejen, og holdt sin lille Stump af en Hale saa sirligt ud fra Kroppen, som man kunde tænke sig gamle Damer gjøre, dersom de havde nogen.

Den gamle Mand lod Stjærne gaa, som den selv vilde; de vare for gode Venner til at have noget at udsætte paa hinanden. Naar undtages en underlig urolig Mimren med Munden, og en ubevidst Rokken med det lille, indskrumpede Hoved, saa' han ud, som om han sov — indtil pludselig hans smaa, farvematte Øjne fór omkring, som om de var bange for Noget. Og naar han mødte en Mand paa Vejen, vendte han Hovedet til den anden Side.

Thi Niels Ingvor var bleven menneskesky paa sine

Front page of a literary periodical with the opening of one of Pontoppidan's early short stories. The editor, Otto Borchsenius, became his mentor (from H. P. Rohde, Det lyder som et eventyr–og andre Henrik Pontoppidan-studier, *1981; Suzzallo Library, University of Washington).*

ing People, 1881) by Norwegian author Alexander Kielland. In "Kirkeskuden," a lively tale that includes the germs of a surprising number of Pontoppidan's later writings, an adolescent boy is placed in the care of a pale minister and his wife. He rebels against the couple by attempting to launch a votive ship from the church (such model ships were often displayed in churches, among other things to serve as a symbol for the Christian Church as a safe ship on the sea of the world). The ship immediately sinks, and the boy then runs off to sea. In this text sarcasm and satire are blended with the lyrical and the grotesque, particularly in the raw description of the pastor's death. Pontoppidan and Mette were married in December 1881 on the royalties of his debut book, *Stækkede Vinger* (Clipped Wings, 1881), which included "Kirkeskuden." The couple honeymooned in northern Italy.

In addition to "Kirkeskuden," which takes up two-thirds of the book, *Stækkede Vinger* also includes the story "Et Endeligt" (The End of a Life), first published in September 1881 in the literary periodical *Ude og Hjemme* (Abroad and at Home), and two short sarcastic sketches taken from Copenhagen society. *Stækkede Vinger* is neither a homogenous nor a particularly well-composed book. Whereas "Kirkeskuden" had its origin in student social excursions to the Roskilde Fjord, "Et

Endeligt" was Pontoppidan's first work about the rural proletariat. The editor of *Ude og Hjemme,* Otto Borchsenius, became his mentor. When a split developed between the "Danish" and the "European" factions of the Venstre (Liberal) political party, Borchsenius became the literary editor of the politically moderate newspaper *Morgenbladet.* In both periodicals he helped Pontoppidan along the path of his literary career, partly by accepting his contributions, often written under the pseudonym "Rusticus," and partly by reviewing his works, not uncritically and sometimes unfairly. The two severed ties in 1887.

After a satirical description of the *folkehøjskole* milieu in *Sandinge Menighed* (Sandinge Parish, 1883), Pontoppidan published his first "Skyggerids fra Landsbyen" (Silhouettes of the Village) in *Landsbybilleder* (Village Sketches, 1883). Late in 1884, along with his wife and two children, he moved to his in-laws' village, Østby, in Horns Herred. His elder daughter died in March 1885 of tubercular meningitis, which developed in the miserable and unhealthy conditions to which he had consigned his family. Meanwhile, Pontoppidan worked in a comfortable room at his sister-in-law's house on one of the larger farms in the village. In some of his writings he drew too closely upon local material, such as in "Naadsensbrød" (Alms), which was included in his next story collection, *Fra Hytterne* (From the Huts, 1887). With empathy or sarcasm he described in recognizable detail the misery and exploitation in the small, class-divided society of the village. The villagers might have tolerated this intrusion if Pontoppidan had run as a candidate for parliament and championed politically the views he had aired in his short stories. He did not take this path, however, always remaining an independent observer.

In addition to writing short stories, Pontoppidan developed a genre of his own, the "smaa Romaner" (short novels). The first one, *Ung Elskov* (Young Love, 1885), is set outside the village, in closer contact with spellbinding nature. A young girl is seduced and then abandoned by a Copenhagen student; instead of putting up with her local fiancé, she commits suicide. Pontoppidan also threw himself into several experiments with genre; with the short novel *Mimoser. Et Familjeliv* (Mimosas: A Family Life, 1886; translated as *The Apothecary's Daughters,* 1890) he discovered how easy it was to play games with the bourgeoisie. The book was acclaimed by both sides of the so-called feminist debate, but the author himself refused, as always, to take sides.

A doctor's persistent advice to move the family to healthier quarters persuaded Pontoppidan in the summer of 1886 to rent a large, abandoned manager's residence at an old paper factory on the coast of northern Zealand in Havreholm, south of Hornbæk. Here he could sit in the tower room and remain undisturbed while the family went about its business in the many half-empty rooms below. Pontoppidan's feelings for his wife are known only from a single statement in a letter dated a year after his daughter's death in 1885, prior to their final departure from Østby. At that point, his wife was pregnant with their third child, a son. Pontoppidan wrote, "Jo ældre jeg bliver, des dårligere kan jeg undvære hende. Skulde nogen nogensinde skrive min Biografi, måtte hun deri indtage den fornemste Plads" (The older I get, the more I feel I cannot do without her. If anyone ever writes my biography, she must assume the most distinguished place).

In the summer of 1887, however, at the seaside resort of Blokhus in northern Jutland, Pontoppidan met Antoinette Kofoed, five years his junior and the daughter of the widow of a ranking official in the Ministry of Justice. Later, in his old age, he described his encounter with Antoinette on a tennis court as an attraction he had tried to fight. He had already provided a convincing description of the agonies of an unfaithful husband in *Mimoser.* In the summer of 1888 his wife moved with the children from Havreholm. The couple was unable to work through the crisis of his encounter with Antoinette, and the marriage failed. Only then, according to Pontoppidan in his old age, did he renew his connection with Antoinette.

In *Ung Elskov, Spøgelser. En Historie* (Ghosts: A History, 1888), and *Vildt* (Wild Game, 1890), stories of unhappy, hard-won, and unrequited love, respectively, unfold in a spellbinding and reflective way. *Isbjørnen. Et Portræt* (1887; translated as *The Polar Bear: A Portrait,* 2003), set in Greenland, a place Pontoppidan never visited, explores the character of the priestly rebel that became so dear to his authorial spirit: pure of heart, rough in manner, and world-weary.

Nature plays an ambiguous role as both seducer and redeemer in Pontoppidan's writings. This tradition recalls the German Romanticism of Ludwig Tieck's "Der blonde Eckbert" (1797). One can also trace a melancholy from the Jutland moors, reminiscent of the work of Blicher, which unites a fairy-tale atmosphere with the earthy power of popular speech–unlike the city life of Copenhagen, with which the provincial boy from Randers was never reconciled. At the same time, however, Pontoppidan was academically schooled enough to realize how easily this natural connection could short-circuit. Not until late in his writing, in *Lykke-Per,* did he achieve mastery of nature as a religious mirror of the human soul and its labyrinths.

Pontoppidan's journalism at first consisted primarily of literary adaptations of impressions and ideas. After becoming connected to the newspaper *Politiken* in the summer of 1887 and then obtaining a job on the daily *Kjøbenhavns Børs-Tidende* (Copenhagen's Exchange-News) in August 1889, his writing acquired a more columnist-like character, although there were also reviews and literary texts among his contributions (among them, a draft version of *Vildt*).

Not until March 1884 did a personal relationship develop between Pontoppidan and the influential literary critic Georg Brandes, and even then Brandes did not become a successor to Borchsenius as a literary guide or adviser. On the contrary, he never expressed much of an opinion on Pontoppidan's writings, nor did he try to broaden European acquaintance with the younger writer's works. In his correspondence Brandes expressed a solidarity that was never reciprocated with the same warmth from Pontoppidan. In his autobiographical volume *Arv og Gæld* (Inheritance and Debt, 1938) Pontoppidan characterizes his relationship with Brandes as a fleeting acquaintance, expressing thereby its volatile character. Ideologically, Pontoppidan was closer to Brandes and his school of thought, which eventually came to be called Brandesianism, than to any other movement. Pontoppidan's personal goals, however, were higher, and, for better or for worse, his anchoring in the clerical milieu was quite alien to Brandes, who never really understood Pontoppidan's major novels, a fact that is evident in the one article Brandes wrote on Pontoppidan's works.

In April 1889 Pontoppidan and his wife officially separated. During the waiting period before he could marry Antoinette, he participated in Copenhagen's literary café life, to which August Strindberg, Edvard Brandes (Georg Brandes's younger brother), Peter Nansen, and Johannes Jørgensen also belonged, as well as the artists associated with Pontoppidan's friend Johan Rohde. Pontoppidan also became acquainted with the poet Holger Drachmann and developed a deep love-hate relationship with him with regard to literary tastes. Pontoppidan displayed a more politically oriented irony and satire in his next collection of short stories, *Skyer* (Clouds, 1890), Georg Brandes's favorite among his early books. These stories, which flay the injustices of the conservative political party Højre (Right) and the lack of political will on the part of ordinary Venstre members, were written during the period of "provisional government" from 1885, when the Højre party governed without a parliamentary basis.

In April 1892, when his divorce was finally granted, Pontoppidan married Antoinette. The couple had two children, a daughter in 1894 and a son in 1896. For many years Pontoppidan had to provide for two families, a strain that did not improve his financial situation. Both his sons immigrated (in 1905 and 1920, respectively) to the Americas: one to the United States and the other to Brazil. Neither ever returned, except for brief visits. As a father Pontoppidan was supposedly distant, not unlike his own description of the character Lykke-Per as a father. Antoinette was called "refined and sensitive" by one of the servants. Afflicted with weak health, Antoinette suffered from more than one disease, which often kept her in bed or hospitalized until her death in 1928. She was, however, a strong support for her husband in the many dark days that followed. In the poem "Sølvbruden" (The Silver Wedding Bride), Pontoppidan wrote, "Din Fryd blev min, / min Sorg blev din, / og fælles var vor Lykke" (Your joy became mine / my sorrow thine, / and united our common happiness). The literary critic Vilhelm Andersen, a close friend of the couple, wrote in his *Henrik Pontoppidan. Et nydansk Forfatterskab* (Henrik Pontoppidan: A Modern Danish Authorship, 1917) that Antoinette had "fuldt saa megen Indflydelse paa 'Stilen' i hans Personlighed som Goldschmidt paa den i hans Romaner og Noveller" (just as much influence on the "style" of his personality as [Meïr] Goldschmidt on that of his novels and short stories).

Pontoppidan's plan for his first major novel was to recall his village days. At the close of 1883 he had promised his publisher "Et stort, bredt og lyst Billede fra Landet" (a big, broad, and lighthearted picture of the country). Pontoppidan wrote that the main theme would be the breach between the followers of N. F. S. Grundtvig and the disciples of the Indre Mission (Home Mission), an evangelical sect within the Lutheran Church, between the light and the dark. The novel would also provide a vivid, painterly view of something that did not exist in Danish literature: the large popular assemblies, church meetings, election meetings, Christmas parties, and other aspects of village life with which Pontoppidan was intimately familiar. In the end the novel, planned for two volumes, came to be written in Copenhagen and changed character. Although it remained large, Pontoppidan concentrated on one main character, Pastor Emanuel Hansted, and presented an ever darkening vision of illusion and defeat. *Muld* (Soil, 1891; translated as *Emanuel; or, Children of the Soil,* 1896) was the result of approximately five years of writing.

In *Det forjættede Land* (1892; translated as *The Promised Land,* 1896), conceived and cast as a novel about a Tolstoyan idealist, Hansted is forced to resign himself to defeat in his attempt to unite his urban background with the apparently pastoral idyll with which he had fallen in love. Religious contradictions surface in the character of the weaver Hansen, a demonic seducer who undermines Hansted's illusions. The political and religious themes surface in Hansted's personal split between two women: his wife, Hansigne, from a small village, and Ragnhild, a deacon's daughter with the same cultural background as Hansted. He gives up,

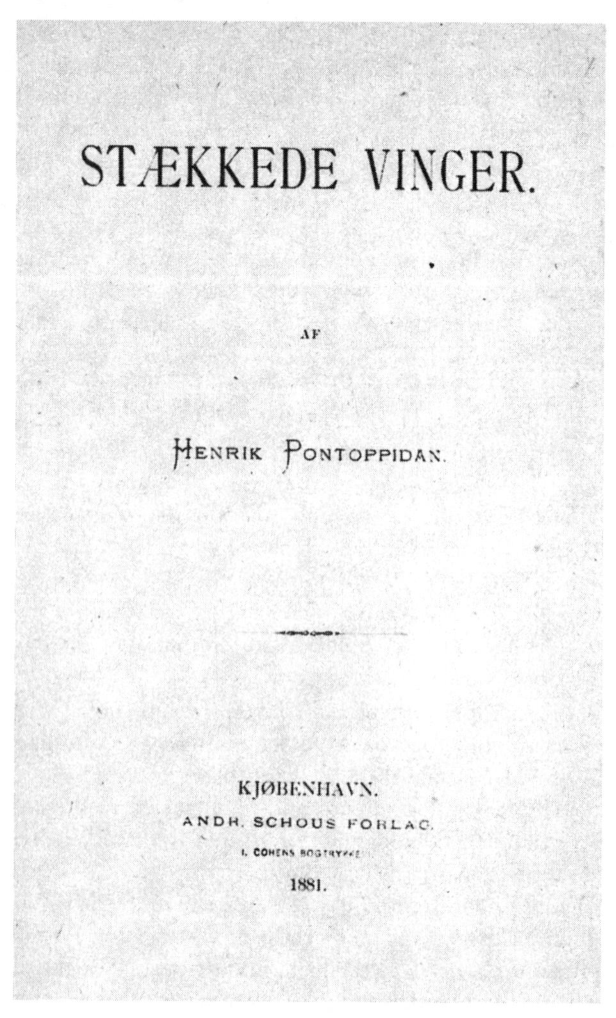

Title page for Pontoppidan's first book (Clipped Wings), which comprises the stories "Kirkeskuden" (The Votive Ship) and "Et Endeligt" (The End of a Life) and two sarcastic sketches of Copenhagen society (from H. P. Rohde, Det lyder som et eventyr–og andre Henrik Pontoppidan-studier, *1981; Suzzallo Library, University of Washington)*

leaves his wife, and, together with his children, returns to the capital city.

The year after completing the second volume of the novel sequence, Pontoppidan picked up the thread and wrote a third volume, titled *Dommens Dag* (Judgment Day, 1895), in which he places Hansted in the *folkehøjskole* environment he had already described in *Sandinge Menighed.* In the midst of far-reaching theological, cultural, and political discussions, Hansted follows his destiny into religious madness, sending him definitively into the abyss as a dreamer. The book ends with his death. This development was not a clear extension of the first two volumes and presupposed a revision of them. With some reluctance, Pontoppidan undertook this rewriting and in 1898 published an edition of the trilogy under the title *Det forjættede Land,* a version that itself proved not to be definitive.

During and after the lengthy composition of *Det forjættede Land,* Pontoppidan published a series of smaller books. Some of them were a reworking of older material. The collection *Krøniker* (Chronicles, 1890) includes short, pointed descriptions, written in an archaic–sometimes fairy-tale- or fable-like–style, which profited from Pontoppidan's deep familiarity with the language of the Bible and Danish myths. The majority of these pieces had been published, under Pontoppidan's Copenhagen pseudonym Urbanus, in the columns of *Kjøbenhavns Børs-Tidende* from September to November 1889. One of the new selections is "De Vises Sten" (The Philosopher's Stone), in which a King Lear figure, blinded and banished, teaches a downy-cheeked lad that the philosopher's stone is "a deep, silent contempt for humanity." The most bitter text in this little book, "De Vises Sten" lacks the humor that characterizes the other stories. Together with a text from 1889, "Landsbyens Dronning" (Queen of the Village), "De Vises Sten" indicates that Pontoppidan had begun to read–or at least become acquainted with–the ideas of the German philosopher Friedrich Nietzsche. In August 1889 Georg Brandes published his lectures on Nietzsche, and, like many of his Danish contemporaries, Pontoppidan derived an important impetus from them.

Vildt, one of the two short novels in *Natur* (1890), published immediately after *Krøniker,* represents Pontoppidan's initial attempt at first-person narrative in a longer format. Both books were published while he was in Berlin, where he went on his first trip to the south since his honeymoon, thanks to a much-sought-after privately funded Ancker travel grant, which he received after years of application. The grant money remained at home to support the family, and Pontoppidan cooped himself up in Berlin on an advance to continue writing *Muld.* Neither at this time nor later did he fulfill his dream, encouraged by Georg Brandes, of traveling to Paris. Pontoppidan never reached France or England.

Minder (Memories, 1893) involves a recasting of older material. The result is an original elegy upon the first-person narrator's first love, experienced early in puberty, and it unfolds in a nostalgic description of the environs, almost perfectly matching the author's childhood home and surrounding vicinity.

Pontoppidan's most famous chronicle, "Ørneflugt" (translated as "Eagle's Flight," 1929), was completed in 1893, published in a periodical in 1894, and appeared later in a new edition of *Krøniker* in volume one of *Fortællinger* (Tales, 1899). Apparently written as an inversion of Hans Christian Andersen's fairy tale "Den grimme Ælling" (The Ugly Duckling, 1843), it tells of Klaus, an eagle who grew up with "clipped wings" on a pastor's duck farm. After the pastor's death, the eagle has the chance to spread his wings into the icy wilderness of the Nietzschean mountaintops. A female eagle lures the clumsy Klaus so far away from home that he changes his mind and returns home alone, only to be shot down by a farmer as a common chicken thief and to end on the dung heap, "For det hjælper alligevel ikke, at man har ligget i et Ørneæg, når man er voxet op i Andegården" (For it is no use to come from the egg of an eagle, if one has grown up on a duck farm). The text may also be interpreted as a grim parody of the classic paradigm of the bildungsroman and the protagonist's movement from home to homelessness and then back home.

Nattevagt (Night Watch, 1894), another widely read work by Pontoppidan, became part of the canon for teachers of Danish literature. The novel takes place in a Danish colony in Rome a few years before the time when Pontoppidan himself spent his yearlong honeymoon with Antoinette in that city. His first "artist novel," part of *Nattevagt* consists of theoretical discussions between the protagonist, the painter Jørgen Hallager–a revolutionary anarchist of the social-realist school who has just married Ursula, the daughter of a patrician family–and his good friend and colleague Thorkild Drehling, who has been taken by the new sensitivity and symbolic tendencies of the times. The book includes Hallager's furious rant against the times. His final line became a familiar quotation: "Hold Galden flydende!" (Keep the wound open!). Even his name–a homonym of *halv-ager* (half-acre)–indicates that he represents only one side of the truth. Whereas Hallager intones the views of Pontoppidan's literary journalism, Drehling, for his part, repeats statements from *Spøgelser* that were interpreted as Pontoppidan's first signal of a reorientation in his writings from social to personal exploration: "Jeg véd, at man i Livet kan møde Sorger og Skuffelser, der nager langt værre end baade Sult og Kulde" (I know that, in life, one may meet sorrows and disappointments that plague one longer than either hunger or cold).

One chronicle that did not go into *Krøniker* but had been published that same year, 1890, under Pontoppidan's usual pseudonym of Urbanus in *Kjøbenhavns Børs-Tidende* was "Den gamle Adam" (The Old Adam), in which a randy Adam asks the Lord to create women for him from all his ribs. Together with his book review of a Viggo Stuckenberg novel *Messias* (The Messiah, 1889), "Den gamle Adam" resulted in a lawsuit against the newspaper. The editor of the paper, Georg Brandes's brother Ernst, was held liable for the book review, and Pontoppidan lost his state support for a year.

Less accomplished than *Minder* is *Den gamle Adam* (1894), consisting of the title work and various shorter pieces, including a brief, almost aphoristic text, a "Diary" from *Kjøbenhavns Børs-Tidende.* Like the circus girl Elvira Madigan and the Swedish count who fell madly in love and committed suicide in 1889 on Funen's southern island of Tåsinge, the vacationing older deputy judge in *Den gamle Adam* falls for a young girl, and it costs him his wife and children. Not the judge, however, but a young secondary character commits suicide over unhappy love at the end of the book. In all of these works the first-person narrator takes on increasingly individual features. He is most strongly realized in *Højsang* (Hymn, 1896). Like the narrator in *Vildt,* the philologist in *Højsang* is a rutting swain who imagines having his sexual debut with an older, married, and apparently neglected woman. In this instance the philology student has absorbed a great deal of literature in his years of study and, therefore, clothes his desire in spiritual garb.

While the narrators in *Vildt* and *Den gamle Adam* are contemporaneous with their setting, the narrators of both *Minder* and *Højsang,* the same age as their author, look back at an earlier time. In all four short novels, Pontoppidan uses these implicit elements to create ironic distance and satirical mockery, so that readers themselves are allowed to draw their own conclusions about where the "truth" of the characters–in particular, of the narrator himself–lies. Thus, the omniscient narrator who governs the major novels is suspended in many of the shorter ones for a more elegant epic game. At the time, literary critics had a difficult time understanding this game and often believed that Pontoppidan could be taken "at his word." For example, a single sentence from the parody "Preface" in *Højsang* was taken out of context to characterize the author as one who "above all loves clarity of thought and masculine mental composure." Pontoppidan did not object to this statement; from this time, he created a public mask behind which he could make his artistic faces.

Pontoppidan then turned to his next great novel, *Lykke-Per,* published in eight volumes from 1898 to 1904 and collected in 1905. Once again, he used his own life as a starting point; yet, one can understand nothing if one reads the novel as autobiography. Scholars continue to discuss the extent to which Pontoppidan knew how the course of this novel would run and how it would end. Some have seen "Ørneflugt" as the model. Peter Andreas "Per" Sidenius, son of a minister, wants to be an engineer and a modern man. He strives to surpass the limits of the environment ruthlessly to conquer the world, including Jakobe, the daughter of a

Pontoppidan in 1883 (painting by Michael Ancher; from Hakon Stangerup and F. J. Billeskov Jansen, Fra Georg Brandes til Johannes V. Jensen, *volume 4 of* Dansk litteraturhistorie, *edited by P. H. Traustedt, 1977; Suzzallo Library, University of Washington)*

wealthy Jew named Salomon. Per creates a grandiose plan for a canal system to connect the poorer parts of the country, proposes a port at the west coast of Jutland, and invents machines to collect ocean-wave energy. But when Jakobe draws him up to the thin air of freedom and demands that he choose the end over the means to finance his projects, he loses courage and flees back to Christianity and the comfortable embrace of the Danish provinces. Per then marries Inger, the daughter of a pastor, and raises his children with the same alienating distance under which he himself was raised.

It took Pontoppidan seven years to reach this point in the narrative, and now midway through he struggled with writer's block. Among other things, he used the time to edit his earlier writings and to study Nietzsche. What drew him to Nietzsche, also a pastor's son, was his individualism and his removal of "divine" judgment to the inner life of the human being. This new, modern humanism without external social duties attracted Pontoppidan, who always saw himself as an outsider. Disappointed in his political aspirations for the young Danish democracy, Pontoppidan easily absorbed Nietzsche's elitist views, which held that the strong person could master his own fate, just as one creates a work of art. The respect that must be won is self-respect.

Pontoppidan then took his character Lykke-Per down a long, tortuous road, turning the goal of his happiness from the external to the internal, from bliss in a material sense to the liberating suffering of renunciation and to an insight that goes beyond Nietzsche to Arthur Schopenhauer, back to a conception of natural religion. After separating himself from his wife and children and moving to the remotest part of the country in splendid isolation, Per–on the last page of the novel–counts himself lucky for having lived in a time that called upon the instinct "at *ville* sig selv i guddommelige Nøgenhed" (to *will* oneself in divine nakedness).

For many years *Lykke-Per* was considered part of the tradition of the Danish *fantastroman* (dreamer novel), and some scholars have interpreted the ending as an expression of Pontoppidan's irony. The conclusion has also been interpreted–for example, by Vilhelm Andersen–as an expression of Lykke-Per's inability to express and receive love. In the last few years research has focused on understanding Pontoppidan: no longer can anyone find a way around interpreting *Lykke-Per* as a deeply serious, albeit poetic, philosophical work that does not say things directly but unambiguously points in one direction. These considerations do not change the interpretation of *Lykke-Per* as a broad, multifaceted description of Denmark and Danish society in the last quarter of the nineteenth century. The humor and harsh satire in the novel are components in a tightly woven composition, using leitmotivs and symbolic icons. That Pontoppidan's struggle with the novel was difficult is also apparent from the fact that, upon completing it, he announced the new 1905 edition and asked that the novel be evaluated on the basis of the later version.

In 1900, during the pause in his work on *Lykke-Per,* Pontoppidan published two short novels, *Lille Rødhætte* (Little Red Riding Hood; republished as *Thora van Deken,* 1922) and *Det ideale Hjem* (The Ideal Home). Both are about marriage. *Lille Rødhætte* is a reworking of a story from *Landsbybilleder,* "Arv" (Inheritance); in *Det ideale Hjem* Pontoppidan plays with the idea of a matriarchy in which the children will not be affected by any incompatibility between the parents. The father remains with his sisters and helps to raise *their* children.

During these years Pontoppidan also laid the foundations for three short novels but did not complete them until later: *Borgmester Hoeck og Hustru* (1905; translated as *Burgomaster Hoeck and His Wife,* 1999), *Det store Spøgelse* (The Great Apparition, 1907), and *Den kongelige Gæst* (1908; translated as "The Royal Guest," 1928). In the first and third of these, marriage is either crippled by inner tyranny or shaken to its foundations by an external agent.

Det store Spøgelse, which is also the title of a little fable at the conclusion of *Lykke-Per,* is quantitatively the smallest of the short novels. The text fulfills the demands of the genre, presenting a novelistic mirror of the sequence of an entire life's destiny. First and foremost an emblematic text, *Det store Spøgelse* builds on the sustaining metaphor of Pontoppidan's entire body of work. "The great apparition" stands for the moral and religious prejudices from the past that should have been rejected by a modern mind. In the story a young servant girl in a village commits suicide out of fear of her master's condemnation for meeting her boyfriend.

Højsang was dramatized in 1902 as *De vilde Fugle* (The Wild Birds), but, like its successor, *Asgaardsrejen* (The Asgaard Shrimp, 1906; revised, 1928), the play enjoyed little noteworthy popularity. Neither as a dramatist nor as a poet did Pontoppidan achieve much for his efforts. *Hans Kvast og Melusine* (Hans Kvast and Melusine, 1907), another artist novel, raises the question of whether true art can be created on false premises. The surprising answer is yes. In his journalistic literary criticism Pontoppidan had earlier been preoccupied with what little meaning authenticity has for true art. Hugo Martens is a composer and as full of self-deception as Hjalmar Ekdal in Henrik Ibsen's *Vildanden* (1884; translated as *The Wild Duck,* 1890). This failing, however, does not prevent Martens from composing (after a pathetic suicide attempt) a great and successful musical work during a sea trip along the Norwegian west coast. *Hans Kvast og Melusine* is the most sarcastic of Pontoppidan's books, and he once again lent his protagonist traits of his own.

Pontoppidan later came to compare his last great novel, *De Dødes Rige* (collected edition, 1917), first published in five separate volumes from 1912 to 1916, to a musical composition, a simple atmospheric motif set for a large orchestra. Although the author does not state this motif, there can be no doubt that it is in a minor key. The melancholy in the description of the lifelong but fruitless love between the title characters in the first volume, *Torben og Jytte* (1912), is deeper than anywhere else in Pontoppidan's writings. Manor owner Torben Dihmer is not a protagonist of the same type as Hansted or Lykke-Per. His endeavors, however, lie in the same direction; despite a promising political career and an analytical mind, Torben deliberately allows a fatal but treatable metabolic disease to gain sway over his life and ends up with the same asceticism as Lykke-Per, although with the limited optimism of a broader perspective on natural religion.

Around Torben and Jytte, whose split consciousness is the primary obstacle to the couple's happiness, Pontoppidan paints a gallery of cultural fools who rush about in search of power, wealth, and honor. He drastically cut the text of the 1917 edition by a quarter, and not necessarily to its advantage, although the structure of the book became clearer. Even more than in his previous novels, Pontoppidan moves about the country and its various environs. *De Dødes Rige* is not as deep as his two previous major novels, but, with its humor, it etches a picture that does not leave much hope for the development of culture in the shadow of World War I. As Torben observes when he refuses to take over political power in the country, "Vi befinder os paa en Dødssejler, som en skøn Dag gaar tilbunds med os allesammen" (We find ourselves on a phantom ship that will one day sink with all of us on board). He describes a nation whose civilization is diseased and dares not realize itself in the divine nakedness that Lykke-Per found. With *De Dødes Rige* Pontoppidan founded, using the works of Honoré de Balzac and Emile Zola as distant models, the collective satirical novel in Denmark. Preachers, artists, politicians, doctors, businessmen, and women–even those women beloved and worshiped by Pontoppidan–do not escape being stripped of their rationalizations.

As early as *Lykke-Per,* Pontoppidan had included a portrait of Georg Brandes in his writing. In *De Dødes Rige* he included a poem for Brandes's seventieth birthday in 1912 suggesting that the ideals for which the Modern Breakthrough struggled had been deserted, not only by its descendants and camp followers but also by the originators of the movement, who were not so pure of heart that they, in Søren Kierkegaard's words, willed only one thing. The dominating politician in *De Dødes Rige,* Enslev, mirrors Brandes's misguided efforts (in Pontoppidan's eyes). Despite the deep pessimism of the novel, and despite Pontoppidan's increasing fear about the end of civilization, he has *De Dødes Rige* fade into a fragile utopia, set to the reedy tones of the panpipe.

In 1917, when Pontoppidan shared the Nobel Prize in literature with Gjellerup, he stated that it should have gone to Georg Brandes, who had been proposed for the award several times, but in vain. In

Cover for the penultimate volume (1903) of Pontoppidan's eight-volume novel (1898–1904) chronicling the life of the engineer Peter Andreas Sidenius, known as "Lucky Per" (Collection of Flemming Behrendt)

the committee's eyes, however, Brandes and Pontoppidan lacked the "idealism" that Gjellerup supposedly possessed. Therefore, the prize was shared. The award provided the occasion for new marketing, with consequent revised editions of *Det forjættede Land* and *Lykke-Per,* less thorough than previous revisions. In 1922 Pontoppidan's short novels were collected, along with his short stories, into two volumes as *Noveller og Skitser. Et Udvalg* (Novels and Sketches: A Selection), followed by a third volume in 1930.

Pontoppidan, though lacking "idealism," was not without a utopian vision. In this mental landscape, the mountaintop is the place for important decisions, and here he takes his characters in *Et Kærlighedseventyr* (An Amorous Fairy Tale, 1918). For the first time he allows a connection between a man and a woman to end happily: between the philosopher and Schopenhauer specialist Gabriel Vadum and Ingrid, the unfaithful wife of a pastor. Between these two, love becomes God. Pontoppidan changed this ending, however, in the second edition of *Et Kærlighedseventyr,* published in the third volume of *Noveller og Skitser,* after his wife's death in 1928. In the revised version Ingrid dies before she and Gabriel can fulfill their love in a lasting life together.

Pontoppidan's final novel, *Mands Himmerig* (Man's Heaven, 1927), was undoubtedly better conceived than it was executed. An echo of Enslev in *De Dødes Rige,* scholar and newspaperman Niels Thorsen, disappointed in his career, rages first against the Right and then against the Left and ends up in a blind nationalism. On the personal front, he suffers defeat in love with his neglected wife's suicide. Characters from *Asgaardsrejen* and *Et Kærlighedseventyr* reappear in *Mands Himmerig,* which never achieves the broad overview of Pontoppidan's large novels or the penetration of his short ones.

During his final thirteen years, Pontoppidan occupied himself primarily with his own life story. The four small volumes of memoirs he published from 1933 to 1940–*Drengeaar, Hamskifte, Arv og Gæld,* and *Familjeliv* (Family Life, 1940)–and the collected and abridged version, *Undervejs til mig selv* (On the Way to Myself, 1943), appear as a carefully prepared autobiography of a strong artistic character. For example, he introduces a fictional figure, called Schaff, who spiritually guides the young Pontoppidan even before he begins to create. Pontoppidan interprets and organizes his life around a fatalistic belief (Augustine's "Trahimur" [We are guided]) in a "natural" development.

Once restlessly moving around all over central Europe, Pontoppidan settled down and spent the last fifteen years of his life in a suburb of Copenhagen. He died there on 21 August 1943 after having destroyed all of the drafts, diaries, and letters he could accumulate. For many years his *Undervejs til mig selv* was the authorized version of his life. Because he was so popular in his lifetime, his works could hardly escape a decline in attention during the 1960s and 1970s, but Pontoppidan has since reemerged as a favorite among readers and critics, who appreciate him for more than his abilities as a painter of "historical" frescoes.

During his entire career Pontoppidan tended to rewrite, correct, abridge, tighten, and alter his texts. As was customary at the time, he presumed that the latest editions would automatically become the authoritative ones. After finishing the second edition of *Lykke-Per,* published in 1905, Pontoppidan addressed the distinction between the older and newer editions and claimed that the older edition related to the new in exactly the same way that a painter's nature studies relate to the finished painting. He remarked that one's preference was a matter of taste: the sketch might have a freshness of color that could not easily be preserved in a more careful composition. On the other hand, the finished painting was likely more accessible, more lucid, and thereby more strongly colored by the artist's fundamental outlook.

It was, however–and is–not simply a matter of choice with respect to either *Det forjættede Land* or *Lykke-Per:* the first editions, in each case consisting of several individual volumes, are not accessible as coherent, integrated works. One may choose the collected 1898 edition of *Det forjættede Land* and that of 1905 for *Lykke-Per,* or the further revised, collected editions of each from 1918. Today, most scholars prefer the former, but the latter are now in print in paperback. No single official policy exists among Henrik Pontoppidan's heirs and the various publishers of his works: Gyldendal, Det danske Sprog- og Litteraturselskab (The Danish Language and Literature Association), and the Pontoppidan Society. Different editions are used for different reasons. No collected, critical edition of Pontoppidan's works exists. Despite comprehensive plans, only *Det forjættede Land* has been published in a critical edition (1997) by Det danske Sprog- og Litteraturselskab. Several of the *smaa Romaner* have been reprinted (from the first editions) by Det danske Sprog- og Litteraturselskab and equipped with explanatory notes and afterwords.

Letters:

Henrik Pontoppidan og Georg Brandes, volume 1: *En dokumentarisk redegørelse for brevvekslingen og den personlige kontakt,* edited by Elias Bredsdorff (Copenhagen: Gyldendal, 1964);

Henrik Pontoppidans Breve, 2 volumes, edited by Bredsdorff and Carl Erik Bay (Copenhagen: Gyldendal, 1997).

Interviews:

C. C. Clausen, "Henrik Pontoppidan," *Hver ottende Dag,* 11 (10 September 1905): 792–794;

Anonymous, "Henrik Pontoppidan om Lykke Per," *Politiken* (19 December 1905): 4;

Carl Henrik Clemmensen, as Clerk, "Henrik Pontoppidan om Georg Brandes," *Nationaltidende,* 21 February 1927, p. 1;

Clemmensen, "Henrik Pontoppidan om sig selv," *Nationaltidende,* 23 July 1927, pp. 1–2

Bibliography:

Poul Carit Andersen, *Henrik Pontoppidan. En Biografi og Bibliografi* (Copenhagen: Levin & Munksgaard, 1934).

References:

Knut Ahnlund, *Henrik Pontoppidan. Fem huvudlinjer i författerskapet* (Stockholm: Nordstedt, 1956);

Ahnlund, ed., *Omkring Lykke-Per. En studiebog* (Copenhagen: H. Reitzel, 1971);

Vilhelm Andersen, *Henrik Pontoppidan. Et nydansk Forfatterskab* (Copenhagen: Gyldendal, 1917);

Flemming Behrendt, ed., *Undergangens angst–De Dødes Rige,* Pontoppidan Selskabets Skriftserie, 3, no. 1 (Odense: Syddansk Universitetsforlag, 2004);

Frederik J. Billeskov Jansen, *Henrik Pontoppidan. Ledetråd for læsere* (Copenhagen: Nordisk Forlag, 1978);

Georg Brandes, "Henrik Pontoppidan," in his *Fugleperspektiv* (Copenhagen: Gyldendal, 1913), pp. 1–21;

Elias Bredsdorff, *Henrik Pontoppidan og Georg Brandes,* volume 2: *En kritisk undersøgelse af Henrik Pontoppidans forhold til Georg Brandes og Brandes-linjen i dansk åndsliv* (Copenhagen: Gyldendal, 1964);

Henrik Pontoppidan–Portal for læsere, studerende, lærere og forskere <www.henrikpontoppidan.dk>;

Bent Haugaard Jeppesen, *Henrik Pontoppidans samfundskritik. Studier over den sociale debat i forfatterskabet, 1881–1927* (Copenhagen: Gad, 1962; enlarged edition, Copenhagen: Vinten, 1977);

Niels Kofoed, *Henrik Pontoppidan. Anarkismen og demokratiets tragedie* (Copenhagen: C. A. Reitzel, 1986);

P. M. Mitchell, *Henrik Pontoppidan* (Boston: Twayne, 1979);

Klaus P. Mortensen, *Ironi og utopi. En bog om Henrik Pontoppidan* (Copenhagen: Gyldendal, 1982);

H. P. Rohde, *Det lyder som et eventyr–og andre Henrik Pontoppidan-studier* (Copenhagen: C. A. Reitzel, 1981);

Hakon Stangerup and F. J. Billeskov Jansen, *Fra Georg Brandes til Johannes V. Jensen,* volume 4 of *Dansk litteraturhistorie,* edited by P. H. Traustedt (Copenhagen: Politiken, 1977);

Ejnar Thomsen, ed., *Henrik Pontoppidan til Minde* (Copenhagen: Gyldendal, 1944);

Karl V. Thomsen, *Hold galden flydende. Tanker og tendenser i Henrik Pontoppidans forfatterskab* (Århus: S. Lund, 1957);

Jørgen E. Tiemroth, *Det labyrintiske Sind. Henrik Pontoppidans forfatterskab, 1881–1904* (Odense: Odense University Press, 1986);

Tiemroth, *Maskespil* (Odense: Odense University Press, 1988).

Papers:

Henrik Pontoppidan's collected letters and manuscripts are at the Danish Royal Library in Copenhagen and at the Lokalhistorisk Arkiv in Randers.

Hieronimus Justesen Ranch

(1539 - 1607)

Leif Søndergaard

University of Southern Denmark

BOOKS: *Kong Salomons Hylding. Enn ny lystig og nyttig Comoedi* (Copenhagen: M. Vingaard, 1585);

En Ny Vjse, Om nogle Fuglis Natur oc Sang (Copenhagen: Privately printed, 1617);

Samsons Fængsel. Det er, En ynckelig Tragedi om den dræfflige stærcke Krigs Hældt Samson (Aarhus: H. H. Skonning, 1633);

Karrig Niding. Det er, En lystig Leeg eller Comedie, om en sulten og karrig Hofsbonde oc hans Hustru (Copenhagen, 1664).

Editions and Collections: *Hieronymus Justesen Ranch's Danske Skuespil og Fuglevise,* edited, with an introduction, by Sofus Birket Smith (Copenhagen: Samfundet til den danske Literaturs Fremme, 1876–1877);

Karrig Niding. En jysk Komedie fra ca. 1600, afterword and notes by Erik Dal (Copenhagen: Forening for Boghaandværk, 1962);

Karrig Niding, edited, with commentary and afterword, by Niels Lyhne Jensen (Copenhagen: Munksgaard, 1973);

Kong Salomons Hylding, edited, with commentary and afterword, by Allan Karker (Copenhagen: Munksgaard, 1973);

Samsons Fængsel, edited, with commentary and afterword, by Henrik Nyrop-Christensen (Copenhagen: Munksgaard, 1973);

Karrig Niding, afterword by Janne Risum (Copenhagen: Gyldendal, 1988).

OTHER: "Tyrkernes erobring af Raad," in *Danske Viser fra Adelsvisebøger og Flyveblade, 1530–1630,* volume 6, edited by Hakon Harald Grüner-Nielsen (Copenhagen: Gyldendal/Danske Sprog- og Litteraturselskab, 1930; reprinted, 1979), pp. 75–83.

Hieronimus Justesen Ranch is usually judged to be the best author of drama in Denmark before Ludvig Holberg, who began writing for the stage in 1722. Ranch's reputation primarily rests on the play *Karrig Niding* (Nithing the Niggard, 1664), written in the late 1590s.

Hieronimus Justesen Ranch was born to Just Lauridsen Ranch and Karen Jacobsdatter Ranch in a small village near the cathedral town of Viborg in 1539. His father served as a parson outside the town. Hieronimus attended the Latin School at the cathedral in Viborg and probably went on to Copenhagen in order to initiate his studies at the university there. From 1563 he was enrolled at the university in Martin Luther's hometown, Wittenberg, as "Hieronimus Ranch, Cymber" (that is, a Cimbrian from Northern Jutland). After he had acquired his master's degree, he returned to Viborg, where he became a parson at the Grey Friars' Church in 1572 and married the widow of the former minister. In 1591 Ranch was appointed rural dean of a church district outside Viborg and at the same time served as canon at the cathedral. Little is known about his official business and private life.

One of Ranch's functions was to serve as a schoolmaster and thus to teach at the Latin School. A church ordinance of 1537 recommended that the schools perform plays in Latin and Danish in order to train pupils in the use and understanding of rhetoric and Latin. It is known that in Odense at the beginning of the sixteenth century, schoolboys from Our Lady's School performed carnival plays in the German style, saints' plays, and school comedies (plays in the style of Plautus and Terence) at guildhalls or taverns during Shrovetide. Their schoolmaster, Christiern Hansen, collected three play manuscripts, adding his name and the year 1531 at the end.

Similar plays, as well as biblical plays with topics from the Old Testament and allegorical morality plays, were performed at the University of Copenhagen and Latin schools in other Danish towns (Aarhus, Ribe, Randers, Helsingør, and Kolding) during the sixteenth century. The most comprehensive repertoire of nine plays dates from circa 1607 in Randers. The school at the cathedral in Viborg also had an earlier play tradition. Ranch staged a Susanna play (based on the story of Susanna, considered by Catholics a canonical text of the Book of Daniel) in 1574 in the presence of King Frederik II, who rewarded the school by giving annual support to thirty pupils. In connection with the publication of Ranch's first play, *Kong Salomons Hylding* (Allegiance to King Solomon, 1585), a poem written in homage to the author mentions that "Vor

Woodcut from the printed version (1585) of Hieronimus Justesen Ranch's play Kong Salomons Hylding *(Allegiance to King Solomon) depicting four fools tied together in a chain as an allegory of the cyclical nature of the foolishness of the world (courtesy of the Danish Royal Library, Copenhagen)*

klerck' oc Schol' i Viborg bye / Haffde da opret deris spil paa nye" (Our clerk and school in the town of Viborg / Have reestablished their playing anew). The philological editor of Ranch's plays, Sofus Birket Smith, argues that a biblical play, *Tobiæ Comedie* (Play of Tobit), was written in Viborg in the late sixteenth century, and the Danish scholar Hans Brix is of the opinion that it can be attributed to Ranch.

In 1584 the king's chancellor, Niels Kaas, who was Ranch's patron, and the Viborg bishop, Peder Thøgersen, exhorted Ranch to write a play on the occasion of a coronation ceremony that Frederik II was holding for his son, the seven-year-old Prince Christian, in order to secure support from the nobility. Ranch wrote *Kong Salomons Hylding* for the occasion of this ceremony, which took place that year in Viborg. (Christian ascended the throne as Christian IV in 1588, but the country was governed by a four-member regency until 1596.)

Since the Middle Ages, Viborg had been the site of the *Thing* (assembly) of Jutland and Funen, and it was a natural place to promote the prince. From Frederik's own coronation ceremony in 1559, Christian's reaffirming coronation of 1596, and other important royal events in Denmark and Europe, it is known that enormous sums of money were spent in order to create splendid and powerful ceremonies. Tournaments, jousting, dancing, masquerades, dramatic performances, music, and fireworks were often part of the entertainment.

Frederik's diary records only that the coronation of Christian took place on 16 June 1584. The nobility had to swear allegiance to the prince; the king invited the Rigsrådet (National Council) for dinner, and the next day he invited the noblemen. The diary does not tell of the festive events, but *Kong Salomons Hylding* was performed by school pupils in a central square in Viborg during the coronation festivities. The play was published in Copenhagen in 1585.

Ranch picked the topic for *Kong Salomons Hylding* from 1 Kings and added elements from other parts of the Old Testament and references to authors from antiquity. David anoints and crowns his son Solomon before his death in order to prevent rivalry from other pretenders to the throne–in the play, one of the king's other sons, Adonia (Adonijah). The play describes David as a just king and his son Solomon as the legitimate heir of the crown in opposition to the morally corrupt Adonia. The characters are types. David is equipped with a crown, a scepter, and a harp (his attribute). Solomon often speaks in proverbs, which refer to the Book of Proverbs. *Kong Salomons Hylding* was performed on a Terentian stage, on which all locations were indicated on the stage simultaneously, and all the parts were played by schoolboys or young men.

The central allegory in *Kong Salomons Hylding* points directly to the political situation in Denmark, so that the characters of David, Berseba (Bathsheba), and Solomon represent Frederik; his queen, Sophie; and Christian. By the example of Adonia, the young prince is indirectly warned that power may corrupt and that fate may change quickly (the wheel of fortune may turn). Plays with biblical or classical topics that served as allegories of contemporary political situations were commonplace in the European drama of the sixteenth century.

In other respects Ranch was a modern playwright. He inserted episodes in *Kong Salomons Hylding* in which the fool, Krage (which means "Crow"), could represent the lower levels of society and thus give the play a broader social scope. Krage's dramaturgical function is to comment on the speeches and actions of Adonia. His scattered parodic comments serve to show the foolishness of Adonia and to subject him and his men to the laughter of the audience by means of proverbs, platitudes, and mere nonsense.

A ballad by Ranch titled "Tyrkernes erobring af Raad" (The Turkish Conquest of Raad) was written down by a scribe named Niels Børgesen around 1600 on some blank pages in a book of medical works. Another scribe added that this ballad was composed by Hieronimus Justesen in Viborg in 1595. The ballad, a complaint about the surrender of Castle Raad in Hungary to the Turks the previous year, was published in 1930 in *Danske Viser fra Adelsvisebøger og Flyveblade, 1530–1630* (Danish Ballads from Nobles' Ballad Books and Flyleaves, 1530–1630). The manuscript is in the collection of the University of Oslo Library.

In the drama of Ranch's time, farcical episodes were sometimes totally disconnected from plays and placed in interludes. In Denmark three interludes written by an unnamed colleague of Ranch (some think by Ranch himself) have survived as part of the repertoire in the Randers manuscript from circa 1607. One of the interludes, *Hercules and Omphale,* was performed in connection with Terence's *Eunuchus* (The Eunuch, 161 B.C.) as a commentary on Thrasos, who wants to marry a prostitute. These double plays in Latin and Danish were common in the sixteenth and early seventeenth centuries, as can also be seen from Ranch's next play, *Karrig Niding.*

On a single sheet of paper at the Danish Royal Library in Copenhagen, *Karrig Niding* is mentioned along with three other plays that were performed in Randers in 1606. One of them was Plautus's *Aulularia* (The Pot of Gold), which deals with the problem of stinginess. The paper notes that immediately after Plautus's play *Karrig Niding* was performed as an additional drama, a sort of local reworking of the theme of stingy husbands: "Aulularіam Plauti, et superflue Comoediam Niding" (Plautus's *Aulularia,* and, in addition, the comedy *Niding*). This relation is reflected in the prologue to *Karrig Niding:* "Her kommer Niding, en Dansk Mand, / Den anden hafd hiem i Græcken Land" (Here comes Nithing, a Danish man / The other lived in Greece). The traditional formulaic greeting is moved to the epilogue and slightly transformed: "Værer velkommen alle sammen, / Fattig, Rige med hin anden / Unge, Gamle, Store oc Smaa / Denne vor Leeg har seet oppaa" (Welcome everybody / Poor, rich together / Young, old, big and small / Who have attended this play).

Karrig Niding was probably performed for the first time by school pupils in Viborg in 1597. Ranch delivered a play to the professors at the University of Copenhagen in 1598 and asked for permission to publish it, but the professors refused to deal with it as they had "more important things to take care of." This play must have been *Karrig Niding;* it was aimed at a much broader audience than *Kong Salomons Hylding,* which might be the reason the censors turned the play down. In any case, it was not published until 1664. *Karrig Niding* is set in Viborg, as is indicated in the text by references to the tower of the cathedral, the town hall, and the local beer. Niding belongs to the upper social stratum of the town, and his neighbor, Eubulus, is said to be a senior member of the town council.

Niding has gold in his box, rich clothes in his chest, and plenty of food and drink in his larder. He has a beautiful wife, Jutta, two children, two servants, and two maids, but he does not behave according to his social status. He is extraordinarily stingy, so everybody in his household, including Niding himself, is starving. He does not fulfill his marital obligations, either in bed or in the house in general. He does not act as a proper father to his children and is not a good master to his servants. Niding even questions his own identity as a burgher in the town when he changes his clothes to those of a beggar. In the popular tradition of drama from the medieval farce onward, it is dangerous to leave one's wife unprotected, and as soon as Niding is out of sight, a real beggar shows up. When he realizes that Jutta is alone and hungry–in all respects–he introduces himself as Jep Skald (a reference to Skald, the local Viborg beer) and opens his sack of food to her. He calls the children and the servants in order to let them eat too. After the meal he makes a pass at Jutta, attempting to seduce her by using poetical phrases, but in fact, he does not need to because she has already surrendered. Everybody in the household is satisfied with the change

Woodcut of a coronation from Kong Salomons Hylding. *Although the recipient of the crown is shown as a mature man with a beard, scholars contend that Solomon was a boy when his father, David, chose him to be the next king (courtesy of the Danish Royal Library, Copenhagen).*

of husband, and they decide to play a trick on Niding. When Niding returns, they simply deny that the house is his. As a good husband Jep invites Niding into his house, giving him food and drink. Jep ends up offering him his own rags, and Niding accepts. The complete change of identities is fulfilled.

At the end Niding realizes that he has not treated his family and household in a proper way, but it is too late. He is not reinstated in his former position in the house but is expelled to live the life of a wandering vagabond. *Karrig Niding* begins with the dissonant and chaotic situation of Niding's relation to his wife, children, and household–and to society in general–but at the end harmony and order are restored. The right man is placed in the right position. In the epilogue the moral of the play is stated thus: eat, drink, and behave moderately, and give food and beer to the servants, but do not overspend, or the money will soon come to an end.

It has been debated whether *Karrig Niding* is a comedy in the classical tradition of Plautus and Terence, a farce, or a school comedy. In the 1664 edition the play is called "En lystig Leeg eller Comoedie" (A Merry Play or Comedy), reflecting the pragmatic way the authors of the period dealt with the problem of genre. The discussion of categorical genres is a later phenomenon. Elements from all three traditions seem to run together in the play. The structure of *Karrig Niding* harks back to classical comedy. The play is set in a burgher's family, as was the case with Plautus's plays. The problems are caused by a defect in the protagonist's character, and he takes such an extreme position that his family and friends are compelled to correct him. Jep incarnates the carnivalesque principle from late-medieval farces and *Fastnachtspiele* (Shrovetide plays).

While *Karrig Niding* was intended for audiences composed of common people in Danish towns, Ranch's *Samsons Fængsel* (Samson's Captivity) was written for an audience that included nobles, as is stated in the prologue. The play was published in 1633 by the well-known book printer Hans Skonning, and this text gives 1599 as the year it was first performed. An early-seventeenth-century manuscript version titled "Samsons Fengsell," now in the collection of the Danish Royal Library in Copenhagen, lacks the prologue, final scene, and epilogue; the text of the play also differs from the published version in some respects.

The topic of *Samsons Fængsel* is taken from the Book of Judges. Samson fights for God against the Philistines, who are represented in the play in a comic and parodic way. As was the case with *Kong Salomons Hylding,* there are obvious parallels in *Samsons Fængsel* to the situation of Denmark in Ranch's time. As the Philistines were God's enemies in the story from the Book of Judges, the Catholics were his enemies in the contemporary context of the play. Samson is an instrument in God's hand to punish the Philistines, but at the same time he is punished by God's anger because of his immoral life with his mistress. The moralistic repudiation of Samson's behavior is stressed already on the title page, together with the common theme of changeable fortune. This theme is further developed in the play by Samson (who is sentenced to turn the grindstone of a mill) in his miller's song, in which he compares fortune to the grindstone.

The Old Testament situation in the play is adapted to Ranch's own time; in particular, the episodes with the miller and his family offer insight into social life at the end of the sixteenth century. The play satirizes the miller's and his wife's greediness and their endeavors to press as much work out of Samson as possible. The miller's servants and maids all have parodic names in the medieval tradition, with meanings such as "Look into the grain chest," "Lick the ring," "Empty the sack," and "Fill the bag." The barber, called Hanns Sønder Bart (Southern Beard), and the fool, Krage, are stock characters from medieval farce. The episodes featuring these characters are only slightly connected with the biblical story in the play, and some of them in fact form small interludes. Eight songs are scattered throughout *Samsons Fængsel,* marking the first time in the history of Danish drama that songs formed an integral part of a play. In this respect *Samsons Fængsel* was the first Danish singspiel.

Ranch was also the author of *En Ny Vjse, Om nogle Fuglis Natur oc Sang* (A New Song: On the Nature and Song of Some Birds), also known as *Fuglevisen* (Song of Birds). The date of composition is unknown, but the work was first published in 1617. The nature and characteristics of various birds are interpreted in a moralistic manner, in which the birds are seen as representative of different virtues and vices. The dove loves his wife, and they live without marital strife; the song of the nightingale is compared to the word of Christ; the raven is seen as a tyrant and thief; the magpie expresses slander and calumniation; the crane incorporates pride; the eagle and the hawk are violent; and so forth. *Fuglevisen* draws on the tradition of the late-medieval *Dyrerim* (bestiaries).

Hieronimus Justesen Ranch died in Viborg in 1607. He was deeply embedded in the medieval tradition and influenced by the classical Roman comedies, but he was also highly innovative in some respects. His work anticipates later Danish literary developments; *Karrig Niding* is often seen as a forerunner of the comedy of character established by Holberg in the early eighteenth century. But Ranch must be evaluated in his own right. With *Karrig Niding* the early secular drama in Denmark reached a peak.

References:

Dorthe Sondrup Andersen, *Den humanistiske skolekomedie i Danmark* (Odense: Odense University Press, 1983);

Frederik J. Billeskov Jansen, "From the Reformation to the Baroque," in *A History of Danish Literature,* edited by Sven H. Rossel (Lincoln: University of Nebraska Press/American-Scandinavian Foundation, 1992), pp. 71–119;

Hans Brix, "Om Tobiæ Komedie og Karrig Niding," in his *Analyser og Problemer. Undersøgelser i den ældre danske Litteratur,* volume 3 (Copenhagen: Gyldendal, 1936), pp. 162–175;

Oluf Friis, "Skolekomedien," in his *Den danske Litteraturs Historie* (Copenhagen: Gad, 1975), pp. 450–476;

Anne E. Jensen, "Tidlig dansk dramatik," *Danske Studier* (1976): 104–114;

Torben Krogh, *Ældre dansk Teater. En teaterhistorisk Undersøgelse* (Copenhagen: Munksgaard, 1940);

Frederic J. Marker and Lise-Lone Marker, *The Scandinavian Theatre: A Short History* (Oxford: Blackwell, 1975);

Klaus Neiiendam, *Renaissanceteatret i Danmark* (Copenhagen: Teatervidenskabelige Institut, Københavns Universitet, 1988);

Erik A. Nielsen, "Skolen på komedie," *Kritik,* 11 (1969): 25–45;

Janne Risum, "Hieronimus Justesen Ranch," in *Dansk litteraturhistorie,* edited by Søren Kaspersen, volume 2 (Copenhagen: Gyldendal, 1984), pp. 339–356;

Risum, "Renaissancen og det humanistiske skoledrama," in *Dansk Teaterhistorie,* edited by Kela Kvam and others, volume 1 (Copenhagen: Gyldendal, 1992), pp. 38–45;

Sofus Birket Smith, *Studier paa det gamle danske Skuespils Omraade* (Copenhagen: Gyldendal, 1883);

Leif Søndergaard, *Fastelavnsspillet i Danmarks middelalder. Om Den utro hustru og fastelavnsspillets tradition* (Odense: Odense University Press, 1989);

Søndergaard, "Tab af identitet og social status. Hieronimus Justesen Ranch: *Karrig Niding,*" in *Læsninger i dansk litteratur,* volume 1, edited by Povl Schmidt and others (Odense: Odense University Press, 1998), pp. 95–110, 321–324;

Adolf Stender-Petersen, "Det jyske protestantisk-humanistiske Skoledrama," in *Humanister i Jylland,* edited by Gustav Albeck (Copenhagen: Munksgaard, 1959), pp. 31–115.

Adda Ravnkilde

(30 July 1862 – 30 November 1883)

Merete von Eyben
Pasadena City College

BOOKS: *Judith Fürste,* edited by M. Galsciødt, preface by Georg Brandes (Copenhagen: Gyldendal, 1884);

To Fortællinger: En Pyrrhussejr og Tantaluskvaler, edited by Erik Skram (Copenhagen: Gyldendal, 1884).

Editions: *Judith Fürste,* edited by Anne Marie Løn (Copenhagen: Hønsetryk, 1981);

Tantaluskvaler, edited by Vibeke Blaksteen (Copenhagen: Hønsetryk, 1983).

Adda Ravnkilde produced only three works before committing suicide at the age of twenty-one. She has nevertheless come to be regarded as a prominent member of the generation of pioneering women writers of the Modern Breakthrough period in Denmark, after having been rediscovered by feminist literary critics of the 1970s and 1980s. As a result, her works have been published in new editions by the alternative feminist press Hønsetryk. In her pioneering book *Det moderne gennembruds kvinder* (The Women of the Modern Breakthrough, 1983), Pil Dahlerup refers to Ravnkilde as one of the most outstanding talents of her time. Dahlerup also points out that Ravnkilde was one of the few female writers who wrote *kunstnerromaner* (novels about artists and the creative process), based on her own experiences as a writer and as a woman. Furthermore, she insisted on using her own name rather than a male pseudonym, a tradition to which many women writers still adhered.

Adda Ravnkilde (Sæby Museum; from Anne Marie Løn, Adda Ravnkilde, *1978; Walter Royal Davis Library, University of North Carolina at Chapel Hill)*

Adele Marie Ravnkilde was born on 30 July 1862 in Sakskøbing, a small provincial town on the island of Lolland, the eldest child of a high-ranking civil servant, Christian Claudius Ravnkilde, who eventually became mayor of Sæby in Vendsyssel (in Northern Jutland), and Margrethe Catinka Vilhelmine, née Bruun. Though Christian Ravnkilde's salary was modest, the family was prominent in the community. In her late teens, Adda Ravnkilde became turbulently involved with Peter Brønnum Scavenius, the squire of Voergaard and a member of the aristocracy, who seriously considered marrying her.

In spite of being a solidly conservative paterfamilias, Ravnkilde's father nevertheless recognized his daughter's precocious intellectual capabilities and enrolled her in a prestigious private girls' school in Copenhagen, Frøken Zahles Skole, the tuition for which was quite a strain on the family's finances. After successfully graduating in 1876, Ravnkilde worked as a tutor-governess and then once again moved to Copenhagen, ostensibly in order to attend a teacher-training college. She was, in fact, planning to pursue a career as a writer.

Ravnkilde was twenty-one when she approached with three manuscripts the controversial icon of the Modern Breakthrough period in Danish literature, Georg Brandes, in the hope of soliciting his opinion and support. Although Brandes received Ravnkilde favorably and offered encouragement, he advised her–because of her youth and lack of experience–to postpone attempts to publish her work. Shortly afterward, in 1883, Ravnkilde committed suicide and thus did not live to see the positive reception of her works, *Judith Fürste* and *To Fortællinger: En Pyrrhussejr og Tantaluskvaler* (Two Tales: A Pyrrhic Victory and Torments of Tantalus), published posthumously in 1884. Brandes wrote a laudatory obituary in the daily newspaper *Politiken* and was instrumental in promoting the publication of Ravnkilde's literary works by the foremost publishing house in Denmark, Gyldendal.

Brandes had suggested earlier that Ravnkilde study with his friend Julius Trier, a tutor who often gave free lessons to promising young pupils in straitened circumstances. This way she would have been able to earn her *studentereksamen,* the prestigious Danish high school diploma, which might qualify the recipient for admission at the University of Copenhagen. Ravnkilde started her lessons with Trier and did well but was haunted by Brandes's suggestion that she postpone the publication of her manuscripts. After a brief conversation with him following one of his famous lectures at the University of Copenhagen, she came to the conclusion that he had not yet read her manuscripts. She then returned to her rented room in Frederiksberg where she took poison, cut her wrists, and shot herself, a course of action she had apparently been contemplating for some time.

In her monograph on the author, Anne Marie Løn speculates that the discrepancy between the person Ravnkilde assumed Brandes to be and the vain literary icon and womanizer whom she actually met, fatally shattered her illusions. Ravnkilde seemed to have based her admiration for the literary critic solely on his translation of John Stuart Mill's *The Subjection of Women* (1869; translated into Danish as *Kvindernes Underkuelse,* 1869), in which he embraced Mill's cause in an impassioned preface to his translation; thus, Ravnkilde had perceived Brandes as a champion of women's emancipation.

The authenticity of Ravnkilde's literary texts poses vexing challenges for scholars. Because the author's works were published posthumously, they underwent extensive revisions by three different editors. *Judith Fürste,* which was published in the spring of 1884, with a preface by Brandes, was edited by M. Galsciødt, who not only shortened the manuscript radically but also rewrote many passages. Identifying Galsciødt's revisions is Dahlerup's educated guesswork, prompted by editor Erik Skram's cutting *En Pyrrhussejr* (A Pyrrhic Victory, 1884) and *Tantaluskvaler* (Torments of Tantalus, 1884) from five hundred to only two hundred pages. Neither of the original manuscripts has been found, with the exception of twenty pages of *Judith Fürste* and a poem, "Ved Havet" (By the Ocean), which Ravnkilde wrote in 1878 at the age of sixteen, both of which are at the Danish Royal Library in Copenhagen. According to Dahlerup, one is forced to conclude that the texts bearing Ravnkilde's name are not her work alone. Dahlerup also emphasizes that to determine where the texts have been altered and who made the changes is impossible. By comparing the changes made to the surviving pages of *Judith Fürste* with the published version, Dahlerup surmises that Ravnkilde made these changes herself and considers the handwritten manuscript to be of greater literary value than the heavily edited published work. Dahlerup points out that *En Pyrrhussejr* has many loose ends, but whether they were the editor's responsibility or simply the way the teenage Ravnkilde composed the work is uncertain. Ravnkilde's last book, *Tantaluskvaler,* considered by most critics to be her best work, was also edited by Erik Skram and is not marred by these problems.

Ravnkilde's autobiographical texts convey raw pain, disillusionment, and a tension between the protagonist's psychological insights and her will to overcome societal obstacles. Scholars and critics have pondered whether Ravnkilde's own overpowering desperation, conveyed by the narrator-author, caused her to commit suicide or whether she identified with her fictional alter egos to such a degree that the identification brought about her desire to take her own life.

All three texts examine different coping strategies for patriarchal oppression. In each case, the conclusion is the same, that whether the protagonist chooses to sacrifice her emancipatory principles out of love for her husband, as in *Judith Fürste,* or fights back, the female protagonists are defeated. *Judith Fürste* was probably written as early as 1880 and embodies a romantically charged conclusion, the viability of which is never tested. This happy ending is contradicted a year later in *En Pyrrhussejr,* another story about a troubled marriage, in which the wife stays, this time unhappily, pledging herself to the struggle for women's emancipation rather than seeking personal happiness and fulfillment. In Ravnkilde's last story, *Tantaluskvaler,* written in 1883, the disillusionment is complete and causes the protagonist, Elizabeth, to renounce a future with the married man she loves, instead deciding to strike out on her

Ved Havet. – 1878. Fanø

Jeg gik ved Stranden og en Tid saa lang
Jeg lyttede til Havets dybe Mumlen
saa blød og sagte som en Moders Sang,
mit Øje fulgte Bølgens lette Tumlen.
En Vemod, dyb og stille, greb mig da,
saa høj en Glæde, at jeg følte Smerte
en Aandens Flugten med de unge Vinger,
der standses af de Baand, som ned dem tvinger.

"

Og mens mit Øje søgte i det blaa
med Blikket fulgte jeg en Fugl – en Terne,
den Tanke greb mig, da jeg Fuglen saa,
og mens den atter svandt i dunkle Fjerne.
Jeg er jo selv en saadan vildsom Fugl
som flyver over Vesterhavets Bølger.
hvor skal jeg hen? Hvor skal min Færden ende
hvad skal mig fra min Flugt i Leiet hende?

"

Jeg saa et Skib paa Hav opdukke da
Jeg Skibet saa i klare Vand sig spejle
sig, hvilke fjerne Havne kom det fra?
til hvilke fjerne Kyster skal det sejle?
Jeg er jo selv et Skib fra fjerne Havn,
hvad saa der bag mig, før jeg lyst skued?
og naar mig Dødens Arm engang skal favne
i hvilket fjerne Gravland skal jeg havne?

Manuscript for a poem ("By the Ocean"), written when Ravnkilde was sixteen (courtesy of the Danish Royal Library, Copenhagen)

own to become a woman writer. The story ends with Elizabeth's friend urging her, "Bring offeret og kom til København" (make the sacrifice and come to Copenhagen), assuring her that her suffering will make her ready for her vocation as a writer. Elizabeth's reply is that this prediction may indeed prove true, but that reaching that state would take a long time.

The plots of Ravnkilde's three prose works form a multifaceted exploration of women's options at the end of the nineteenth century. Taken as a whole, the works suggest that whether a woman breaks with conventions or obeys the rules of the patriarchal society, she will ultimately be deprived of the right to an independent identity and destined to a life of suffering.

Judith Fürste examines a woman's difficult marriage. The protagonist, a young woman whose stepfather refuses to let her have the money left to her by her late father, marries the most eligible man in the community, Count Johan Banner, in order to escape the financial stranglehold of her cruel stepfather and weak mother. In keeping with the structure typical of the late-nineteenth-century bildungsroman, Judith takes most of the novel to realize that she loves her husband and that he, hampered by his class and gender, simply has not been able to express his feelings for her. In both *En Pyrrhussejr* and *Judith Fürste,* the loss of a child, or the hope of having one, is the pivotal point at which the protagonists discover the true nature of their marriages. When Elizabeth's husband will not let them adopt a child, she realizes the full extent of his selfishness and possessiveness. In Judith's case, her husband's all-consuming love for their son and devastating grief over his death finally make the couple able to communicate their feelings for one another. The happy ending, the beautiful young woman with the abusive stepfather who marries the rich and noble suitor and lives happily ever after, can be found in countless popular romance novels of the nineteenth century. What gives this story a complexity not found in the popular novels is the feminist subtext, which culminates in the death of a male child as the way to reconcile Judith with her husband. Her husband's grief brings out his vulnerability and his need for her strength, and the elimination of his heir and ally so weakens him that Judith no longer feels threatened and is able to embrace her husband with love.

In *En Pyrrhussejr,* the protagonist Elizabeth and her sister, Astrid, represent the two acceptable choices for a woman who does not wish to become a spinster or a social outcast. While still in her teens, Elizabeth marries a much older doctor whom she barely knows, and certainly is not in love with, but who envelops her in such a cloak of romantic adoration that she is unable to reject him. Elizabeth wants to become a writer, and she imagines that her husband will be proud of her when she shows him the manuscript she wishes to publish. Upon being told that he considers writing an unacceptable occupation for his wife, Elizabeth complies with his demands, hoping to channel her creative energies into being a good mother. When she learns that she cannot have children and that her husband is opposed to adoption, she realizes that he is motivated by an extreme degree of possessiveness, which he legitimizes by his determination to make her conform to the decorum of their class and social standing.

Meanwhile, Astrid has married the man she loves, a doctor and aspiring poet. When Astrid learns that her husband is in love with another woman and is beseeching the woman to have an affair with him, Astrid seeks refuge in Elizabeth's home, only to be ordered back where she belongs by her brother-in-law. Astrid eventually surrenders when she realizes–just as Elizabeth has–that trying to survive as an independent woman is a nearly impossible alternative. Rather than seeing her situation as a defeat, however, Elizabeth proclaims that she and Astrid are at just the beginning of the struggle: they are the rank-and-file soldiers who are willing to die for the cause that others after them will implement. In an impassioned statement at the end of the story Elizabeth tells her sister:

> Vi vil ikke forsage. Vi vil kæmpe for vor overbevisning. Lykken er endnu foran os, om end langt borte. . . . Nu først er vi egentlig ved begyndesen af striden, lad os tage den op. . . . Ser du, Astrid . . . vi to har alligevel ikke tabt, thi hvad vil vor ubetydelige skæbne siger; vi er forløbere for en god sag, lad os så kun have virket uendelig lidt. Og lad os kun blive trampet ned. Det er forløberens skæbne. Men kan den simple soldat i slaget trøste sig ved sin død, når kun hans land må sejre–så kan vi to det vel også.
>
> (We shall not renounce. We shall fight for our convictions. Happiness may still be in our future, albeit far away. . . . Our struggle has just really begun now, so let us fight. . . . You see, Astrid . . . we haven't really lost after all, because how important is our insignificant fate; we are the forerunners of a good cause even though we may only have been able to contribute so very little. If we are trampled on, so be it. That is the fate of the forerunner. But if a humble soldier can accept his own death in battle, so long as his country is victorious–then surely you and I can do the same.)

In an article published in *Edda,* Inger-Lise Hjordt-Vetlesen points out that Ravnkilde's prose is not only uncompromising and jarring, but also cool, sarcastic, and sharp-witted. At times, her narrative offers a bird's-eye view of the characters and their interpersonal conflicts. Occasionally, her prose becomes rhetorical and romantic when depicting passion, whether erotic or, as in the quotation from *En Pyrrhussejr,* the protagonist's realization that she will have to relinquish her dreams of becoming a writer, but that she will still pledge her commitment to the struggle for women's emancipation. Hjordt-Vetlesen's conclusion is that these seemingly contradictory elements are probably a result of Ravnkilde's youth, but that her texts nevertheless fall within the tradition of the "modern" style of realism, as defined by Brandes.

Finally, *Tantaluskvaler* deconstructs the woman's acceptance of obsessive romantic love and further analyzes female vulnerability and male dominance. The text also explores the degree to which a woman may collude in her own oppression. The protagonist, Elizabeth Due, a tutor-governess in a small provincial town, falls passionately and masochistically in love with the married, but jaded and sybaritic Count Høegh, who has vowed to engage in a series of passionate sexual affairs rather than conform to the solid family life that is expected of a man of his class. As symbolized by their names (Due means *dove,* and Høegh means *hawk*), Elizabeth is powerless to withstand the count's strategy of alternately treating her as his equal, romancing her, ridiculing her ignorance, and listening to her and taking her seriously.

Elizabeth falls into all of his traps; the more she lets him hurt her, the more passionate her love for him becomes. Her strategy is to deny her feelings for him when he finally confronts her with them and reveals his own attraction for her, asking her to run away with him and defy the conventions of society. Elizabeth wants a social revolution that will make women and men equals, but she cannot bring herself to acknowledge her sexuality or break with bourgeois conventions.

Ravnkilde and her protagonist are caught between two doctrines: the conventional belief in and advocation of women's chastity and Brandes's radical cultural program, which called for the right of both men and women to express their sexuality freely, based on the belief that "good" women are also sexual beings. All of Ravnkilde's female protagonists seem capable of sexual feelings, though they are seldom able to acknowledge them as such. Of the three protagonists, sexual desire is most obviously conveyed in the depiction of Elizabeth in *Tantaluskvaler,* who nevertheless deals with her desires in an emotionally destructive way. By making Count Høegh a married man, Ravnkilde ensures that Elizabeth does not destroy her life by acting in a socially unacceptable way. The conclusion of the novel implies, however, that lying about her feelings, to herself and to Count Høegh, takes an emotional toll, but the reader is allowed to form the hope that her sacrifice will be offset by a career as a writer.

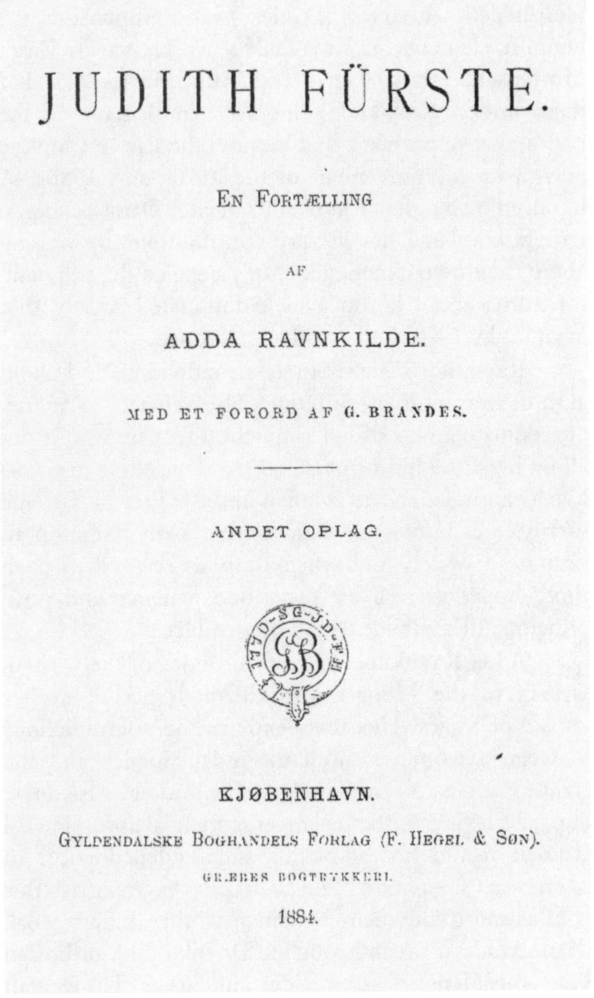

JUDITH FÜRSTE.

En Fortælling

af

ADDA RAVNKILDE.

MED ET FORORD AF G. BRANDES.

ANDET OPLAG.

KJØBENHAVN.

Gyldendalske Boghandels Forlag (F. Hegel & Søn).

Græbes Bogtrykkeri.

1884.

Title page for Ravnkilde's posthumously published novel about a woman who sacrifices her feminist principles out of love for her husband (courtesy of the Danish Royal Library, Copenhagen)

Dahlerup theorizes that Ravnkilde almost certainly showed signs of having bipolar disorder and that having a brilliant mind at a time when women were not allowed to get an education, let alone have a career or seriously pursue a vocation as an artist, further increased the stress on her as a young woman. Furthermore, Ravnkilde's involvement in a dramatic, albeit platonic, love relationship with an older man, squire Scavenius, whom she refused to marry for fear of losing control of her life, added to her frustration and disenchantment with a constrained life that demanded such impossible choices.

Not surprisingly, the early feminist critics of the 1970s and 1980s embraced Ravnkilde's works enthusiastically. According to Hjordt-Vetlesen in "Forfatterportræt: Adda Ravnkilde" (Author Biography: Adda Ravnkilde), Løn is the person who rediscovered Ravnkilde and evaluated her life and works as an early feminist's fight for women's emancipation, a view Hjordt-Vetlesen shares. Dahlerup also emphasizes the feminist elements in Ravnkilde's works, as do Birgit Mortensen, Stig Dalager, and Anne-Marie Mai. For these critics, Ravnkilde's life was emblematic of the patriarchal oppression that became the catalyst for the new women's movement of the 1970s and 1980s. A hundred years after Ravnkilde's death, Danish women writers emulated her literary contributions by writing about their own experiences: they detailed the still painful truths about life in a male-dominated society that even in the 1970s had not changed much.

Ravnkilde's life, both as an individual and as an author, was one of suffering. She refused to marry Scavenius because of her conviction that he would not allow her the kind of personal freedom she craved, to live as an independent woman and a writer. Thus, she sacrificed her love for him for her own ambition to become a writer, and when Brandes seemed to dash those hopes as well by suggesting patience and postponement, Ravnkilde took her own life.

Adda Ravnkilde was a forerunner of the women writers of the Modern Breakthrough period in her choice of topics. Her texts explore the contradictions between a woman's quest for independence and the right to be creative, often as a writer, and her passionate and perplexing erotic feelings for men, whose view of women would not allow for such independence. In Mortensen's opinion, *Tantaluskvaler* exemplifies this conflict more convincingly than any other literary work of the Modern Breakthrough in Denmark; according to Lise Busk-Jensen, Ravnkilde anticipates Norwegian writer Amalie Skram, arguably the greatest woman writer in Scandinavia during this period, with her explorations of women's sexuality and the double standard. Adda Ravnkilde not only served as a source of inspiration for women writers and critics in the 1970s, she has come to be regarded as one of the most prominent and talented pioneering women writers of late-nineteenth-century Denmark.

References:

Lise Busk-Jensen and others, *Dansk Litteraturhistorie,* volume 6 (Copenhagen: Gyldendal, 1985), pp. 451–452;

Pil Dahlerup, "Kunstnerne. Adda Ravnkilde (1862–1883)," in her *Det moderne gennembruds kvinder* (Copenhagen: Gyldendal, 1983), pp. 304–321;

Stig Dalager and Anne-Marie Mai, *Danske kvindelige forfattere–fra Adda Ravnkilde til Kirsten Thorup,* volume 2 (Copenhagen: Gyldendal, 1982), pp. 20–35;

Merete von Eyben, "Adda Ravnkilde: A Danish Feminist Pioneer," in *Female Voices of the North: An Anthology,* edited by Inger Olsen and Sven Hakon Rossel in collaboration with Robert Nedoma (Vienna: Edition Praesens, 2002), pp. 209–225;

Inger-Lise Hjordt-Vetlesen, "Forfatterportræt: Adda Ravnkilde," *Arkiv for Dansk Litteratur* <www.adl.dk>;

Hjordt-Vetlesen, "Overrumplingens æstetik–om tale og tavshed i Adda Ravnkildes forfatterskab," *Edda,* 4 (1990): 298–312;

Hjordt-Vetlesen and Birgit Mortensen, "Modernitetens vendepunkt: Om Adda Ravnkilde," in *Nordisk kvindelitteratur,* volume 2: *Faderhuset 1800-tallet,* edited by Elizabeth Møller Jensen and others (Copenhagen: Rosinante, 1983), pp. 385–390;

Anne Marie Løn, *Adda Ravnkilde* (Copenhagen: Rhodos, 1978);

Birgit Mortensen, "Adda Ravnkilde (1862–1880) Ravnkilde, Adele Marie (Adda)," in *Dansk Kvindebiografisk Leksikon,* volume 3, edited by Jytte Larsen and others (Copenhagen: Rosinante, 2001), pp. 163–164.

Papers:

A few of Adda Ravnkilde's surviving papers are at the Danish Royal Library in Copenhagen and in the City Historical Archives in Sæby.

Hans Egede Schack

(2 February 1820 - 20 July 1859)

Søren Schou
Roskilde University Center, Denmark

(Translated by Tiina Nunnally)

BOOKS: *Phantasterne,* as E.S. (Copenhagen: C. A. Reitzel, 1857 [i.e., 1858]); edition corrected by Carl Roos (Copenhagen: Holbergselskabet, 1925); edition corrected by Frederik Nielsen (Copenhagen: Hans Reitzel, 1962); edition corrected by Hans Hertel (Copenhagen: Hans Reitzel, 1970); edition corrected by Jens Kristian Andersen (Copenhagen: Det danske Sprog- og Litteraturselskab, 1986)–includes "Privat-Comedien," pp. 269–280;

Sandhed med Modifikation: En ufuldendt Roman, edited by Carl Dumreicher (Copenhagen: Dansk Kautionsforsikring, 1954); edition corrected by Hertel (Copenhagen: Hans Reitzel, 1968).

SIGNIFICANT PAMPHLETS: *Om Valgreform-Selskabets Virksomhed og Angrebene paa samme* (Copenhagen: Philipsen, 1848);

Om Slesvigs Deling (Copenhagen: Philipsen, 1849);

Nogle Oplysninger om mit Forhold til 'Bondevennerne' (Copenhagen, 1852);

Bidrag til Bedømmelse af Rigsdagens Virksomhed (Copenhagen, 1852);

Bondevennernes Virksomhed (Copenhagen, 1853);

Rigsdagen og Ministeriet 2 (Copenhagen, 1853);

Bondevennernes Parti og Forfatningsudkastet (Copenhagen: Philipsen, 1855).

Hans Egede Schack (courtesy of the Danish Royal Library, Copenhagen)

Hans Egede Schack is known almost exclusively for his only completed novel, *Phantasterne* (The Fantasts, 1857). In Danish literary history *Phantasterne* is considered the work that breaks with Romanticism and its offshoots, while at the same time heralding realism, which only later became fully developed with the advent of the Modern Breakthrough in the 1870s.

Schack was born on 2 February 1820, the youngest of the six children of Nicolai Clausen Schack and Tagea Dorothea Erasmi. Schack grew up in Sengeløse on Zealand, where his father was a pastor and later a rural dean. In 1837 Schack graduated from Borgerdyd School in Copenhagen and began studying law at the University of Copenhagen. He completed his studies in 1844. During his years at the university he became involved in the student Pan-Scandinavian movement and was an eager participant in the activities of the Studenterforeningen (Student Association). While in Uppsala in 1845–1846, he studied constitutional law and became acquainted with the new liberal currents in Swedish intellectual circles.

With the outbreak of the first Dano-Prussian War in 1848, Schack, like many other Scandinavian-minded young men, joined the army as a volunteer and served on the front lines at Als. After his return to Copenhagen, he was the youngest person elected to the assembly that convened to create the first Danish constitution, known as the June Constitution of 1849. From 1850 to 1853 Schack held a seat in the Folketing, or Parliament. He was elected as a member of the Friends of the Farmers' Party but later broke with this group, saying that he was disappointed by a type of party discipline that he characterized as "rigid." He was cofounder of a group that called itself the Detintelligente Venstre (Intelligent Left), but he ended his political career as a member of the dominant national liberal party. He then withdrew from any active role in politics, citing his failing health, although he also admitted to a certain loathing for party discipline and corruption. Henceforth, he observed the political arena from his position as administrator and government official.

In 1854 Schack became secretary of the Parliament. On 23 September of that same year he married Swedish writer Fanny Vendela Armida Hebbe, who shared his artistic and political views. In 1856 he was promoted to secretary to the Danish prime minister. He eventually achieved the rank of counselor and was awarded the title of Knight of the North Star.

From his first appearance as a politician Schack was marked by an unsentimental attitude toward the question of nationalism, a most unusual point of view in the political climate of his day. In 1849 he published the essay *Om Slesvigs Deling* (On the Partition of Schleswig), which argued that Schleswig ought to be divided between Denmark and Germany according to linguistic lines. In this sense he distanced himself from the "united monarchy" policy of the national liberal politicians, with their vision of a Denmark that would extend south to the Eider River. Schack thus anticipated the principle for drawing the boundary between Germany and Denmark that was realized in 1920. In other regards as well, he assumed the position of an independent intellectual in terms of politics, and he vigorously participated in the democratic debate, partially through the journal *1848–Ugeblad for Politik og Litteratur* (1848–Journal for Politics and Literature), which he edited from 1849 to 1850. The name of the journal demonstrated his interest in establishing a connection between politics and aesthetic concerns.

In 1857 Schack published his novel *Phantasterne* under the thinly disguised pseudonym "E.S." When he died two years later, he was at work on his next novel, *Sandhed med Modifikation: En ufuldendt Roman* (Truth With Modifications: An Unfinished Novel, 1954), which he was dictating to his wife.

Schack wrote the first draft of *Phantasterne* in 1846–1847, and he continued to work on the novel for eleven years, although with interruptions. It is a bildungsroman that, through its portrayal of the development of three young men, sternly condemns what the author regarded as a submission to Romantic daydreaming combined with a fear of facing reality that was so pervasive among his contemporaries. The story spans the period from 1831 to 1850. The protagonist is Conrad Malcolm, who in autobiographical form tells his life story from puberty until maturity. At the same time, although from a greater distance, the novel follows the careers of two friends from Malcolm's youth. The three young men represent different social groups in Denmark during that period. Conrad comes from the landed gentry, while Christian is a pastor's son, and Thomas is of peasant stock.

What originally unites them is a shared tendency toward daydreaming. The three youths spend a great deal of time together, surrendering to fantasies about power, honor, and eroticism that take them far away from their uneventful provincial milieu in Denmark. Yet, even at this point, the three boys reveal quite different personality traits. The most down-to-earth of the three is Thomas, who cannot be characterized as a fantast. On the contrary, he reacts with the pragmatic skepticism of a farm boy whenever the other two lose all grip on reality. The most flighty is Christian, who completely loses himself in fantasies about riches and magnificent acts of heroism. His far-fetched stories, which make no pretense of credibility, are clearly indebted to the melodramatic popular literature of the day and provide the author with the opportunity to satirize this type of book. Between these two extremes stands Conrad. He, too, lives in his fantasies, but they have a less egotistical and power-hungry character than Christian's.

These youthful fantasies start out innocently enough, but the boys reveal a propensity for fleeing from reality, which later becomes perilous for Conrad–and fatal for Christian. When Conrad leaves his childhood home to study for his exams to enter the university in Copenhagen, his fantasizing develops into a dangerous vice. He goes to live with his young Aunt Therese, who is a widow and a sensitive person who finds an outlet for her erotic tendencies in religious fervor. When Conrad becomes erotically attracted to his aunt, his dreams clearly acquire a compensatory nature. The awkward and insecure young man makes conquests in the world of fantasy that he cannot accomplish in real life. His pubescent daydreams about his aunt become more and more ardent. He imagines her

Om

Slesvigs Deling.

Af

H. E. Schack.

Kjøbenhavn.

Faaes hos P. G. Philipsen.

Trykt hos Directeur Jens Hostrup Schultz,
Kongelig og Universitets-Bogtrykker.

1849.

Title page for the pamphlet in which Schack argues for dividing Schleswig between Denmark and Germany on linguistic lines (from Jørgen Mathiassen, Hans Egede Schack som jurist og politiker. Dokumentation og dokumenter, *1978; Main Library, University of Illinois at Urbana-Champaign)*

in a series of erotic situations that are marked by fetishism and sadomasochism. In secrecy he also dresses up in her clothes and dreams about "at være Genstand for hendes yndige Vrede" (becoming the object of her lovely rage).

Schack portrays these pubescent fantasies with an openness that was exceedingly unusual in literary works of the time. In the real world, Conrad is far from a lady-killer–when one of the maids tries to seduce him, he flees in terror–but he suppresses his self-contempt by portraying himself in his fantasies as a great lover and conqueror.

Conrad moves out of his aunt's home and begins studying law at the university. Now that he is living an isolated existence, his fantasies take a dangerous, even pathological turn. He assumes the role of the devil himself, and in his desire to shape the world according to his own ideas, he develops hallucinations that completely seize control of him. He is about to cross the boundary to madness when he is suddenly gripped by a violent fear of death and realizes that his delusions have carried him an almost unsurmountable distance away from reality. He now has to confront all of his fantasies and illusions, and he recognizes that not God but Truth alone can help him. The cure that Conrad submits to and carries out, with no assistance from anyone else, is to a high degree an act of sheer will–self-control struggling against psychological inclinations. Conrad becomes manifestly opposed to fantasy, resumes his study of law, and eventually receives a university degree. He does not achieve the highest grades, however, for during his exams he has to use all of his mental powers to reject one last temptation to adopt a contrived identity.

For Christian, whom Conrad happens to meet again, the fantasizing becomes catastrophic and leads to insanity. Christian shapes his narcissistic dreams of prestige and omnipotence against a backdrop taken from the success stories of contemporary politics, and he has no scruples about switching from conservative to progressive role models. Christian's delusions culminate in megalomania when he begins to identify with Jesus. He is committed to an insane asylum, where he dies. In this way, Christian offers Conrad assistance–albeit indirectly–by presenting a negative example of just how wrong things might have gone for him.

A supremely prosaic Conrad wins the battle against his fantasies. But the victory has its price. He is cured, but he has also become a man who dares to live only halfway because the traumatic experiences have made him unresponsive to art and love and anything else that has the slightest tinge of fantasy about it. He becomes a government official and quickly advances, thanks to his unsentimental attitude, his diligence, and his self-discipline, and he wins wide acclaim for his work–acclaim that he had thus far found only in his daydreams. Eventually, fantasy and love enter his life again in the form of a young woman, Bianca, a Spanish princess who has immigrated to Denmark. For such an exotic figure to bring spiritual harmony to Conrad at last may seem a surprising turn of events. It also prompts Conrad to do some soul-searching: does his love for Bianca merely demonstrate that he has succumbed once again to fantasizing? His fears turn out to be unfounded. Doubt arises as to whether Bianca truly is a princess, but the question makes Conrad recognize that he loves the person Bianca, not her status as princess. When they become engaged, fantasy and reality join forces in a harmonious whole.

The career of Thomas, the farmer's son, also shows that the novel does not reject all elements of fantasy in life; rather, the overwrought fantast is the sole target of its attack. Thanks to the blossoming of his imagination during his boyhood years, Thomas has developed a sense for a world that is bigger and richer than the provincial setting in which he grew up. He manages to break away from his social inheritance. As he acknowledges, his childhood games made him regret being "a simple farmer," and he has created a good living for himself as the forester for a landowner in Jutland. Thus, for Thomas, the fantasies have been as positive a force in shaping his personality as they were destructive for Christian.

Taken as a general statement about daydreams and fantasies, the novel is quite complex. It unequivocally attacks the world of illusion that leads to an inability to perceive reality, and it condemns Schack's contemporaries who would rather dream than deal with reality. But Schack also rejects the antifantasy attitude that results from an all-out confrontation with daydreaming. Conrad's fate, which at first imprisons him in the world of illusion and later causes him to react by rejecting all activities of the imagination, demonstrates the danger of both extremes. Only when poetry and Conrad's allegiance to reality are finally united in his love for Bianca is he cured. In this novel, which is constructed in a strictly symmetrical fashion, the two friends of Conrad's youth elucidate what can happen when imagination is developed. While Christian allows himself to be overpowered by fantasies, with tragic results, Thomas experiences a positive development of his personality when he gives imagination the proper place in his life.

Phantasterne is constructed with a plot that falls into three phases: "at home," "homeless," and "back home." After the relatively harmonious home phase of childhood, the protagonist is thrown, both mentally and physically, into a state of homelessness until he reestablishes a sense of harmony on a higher level. This pattern is familiar from Johann Wolfgang von Goethe's *Wilhelm Meisters Lehrjahre* (1795, 1796; translated as *Wilhelm Meister's Apprenticeship,* 1824) and, among Schack's Danish contemporaries, from Meir Goldschmidt's *Hjemløs* (1853–1857; translated as *Homeless; or, A Poet's Inner Life,* 1861).

Schack's intention, however, is clearly anti-Romantic in that he emphasizes the close ties between overwrought idealism and a dangerous flight from reality. This theme is already indicated at the beginning of the novel when the author describes an ancient oak tree that is the symbolic expression for daydreaming. The tree, in whose shadow the three young men lounge while they surrender to their dreams, has attained a mythic status over the years. Here, ardent sweethearts have exchanged their first kiss, and here, according to legend, demonic forces have been played out. But the tree is felled by a violent November storm and ends up as firewood for the poor of the region. This little story foreshadows the course of the rest of the narrative–the destruction of the imagination, marked by crisis, and its transformation into something beneficial. The tree, with its initial negative and then positive connotations, can be traced throughout the novel; that Thomas, once so earthbound, ends up finding joy and spiritual benefits in his work as a forester is no coincidence.

The composition of the novel is at once subtle and clear as it passes through the three phases and reveals the conflicts among the life paths of the three childhood friends, with each life serving to mirror and comment on the other two. But Schack has not simply composed a bildungsroman based on contemporary conditions. As an account of people who are in the grip of their own illusions, *Phantasterne* also continues an older novelistic tradition that goes back to Miguel de Cervantes's *Don Quixote* (1605, 1615). While Schack was working on the novel, he even considered calling the book "Diary of a Modern Don Quixote." What was new for Danish literature was the detailed and almost clinical psychological portrayal of people whose dreaming led them away from reality and toward delusions.

As a psychological observer, Schack is indebted to philosopher and poet Poul Martin Møller, who had been his Danish teacher in high school. Schack later attended Møller's lectures on psychology at Copenhagen University. In his essay "Forberedelse til en Afhandling om Affektation" (Draft for a Treatise on Affectation, 1837), Møller presented a character sketch of the person who surrenders to deluded and distorted perceptions of his own identity. Affectation can be defined as pretense, or an unconscious delusion intended to make the subject look better or more powerful to both himself and others. What Møller calls affectation Schack calls fantasizing. The person who surrenders to these tendencies adorns himself with borrowed finery and rearranges everything in accordance with his inner dreamworld. Neither Møller nor Schack, however, regards this phenomenon as solely negative. Both are careful to differentiate between the type of imaginative activity that is harmless–or even enriching–and the type that is pathological and eventually breaks down the personality.

In Schack's novel the psychological portrait is given a dimension that extends beyond the individual and is presented as typical for his generation. Through the examples of Conrad and Christian, the author attempts to characterize the mentality of an entire nation that is trying to keep modern-day reality at a distance by clinging to a Romantic outlook that has lost its validity. Like Møller, Schack was a pronounced empiricist. He preferred precise psychological observation to a more speculative way of thinking and made extensive use of his observations from daily life as well as from the world of politics, which in the nationalistic zeal of the 1840s and 1850s readily mistook illusion for reality. The hypocrisy that Schack set out to expose was also reflected, in his view, in the superficial journalism of the day and the post-Romantic epigonic literature that is the source of the boys' youthful fantasies, especially in Christian's case. *Phantasterne,* in a manner similar to its model, *Don Quixote,* is a fictional work that warns against mistaking fiction for real life.

The novel caused a sensation when it was published. It was more extensively reviewed than any other Danish prose work of the 1850s, and it also received a great deal of attention in Sweden and Norway. The groundbreaking elements of the novel that were cited by the critics included its realistic setting, its detailed psychological portraits, and its depiction of fantasies as a compensation for erotic and social impotence. Few critics had any doubts that the novel should be regarded as a renunciation of the dominant academic post-Romanticism. Many were approving or outright enthusiastic.

That Schack scholars later erroneously claimed that the novel originally met with a negative reception apparently resulted from the strong reservations of prominent critic Goldschmidt. Goldschmidt published his extensive review in his own journal, *Nord og Syd* (North and South), on 20 February 1858. He said that the novel testified to "great and extraordinary talent in many respects," but he felt that the structure of the story was too loose. Goldschmidt was especially critical of the main theme, which he perceived to be "a muted but deep contempt for idealism." This analysis says more about Goldschmidt's own understanding of idealism than about Schack's novel. The depiction of Conrad, who fights for his spiritual well-being with a force of will that inspires respect, is an important, idealistically marked element of the novel. This same force of will underlies the defense in the entire novel of a way of life that creates a harmonious synthesis of realism and imagination.

In Danish literary history *Phantasterne* has been given the status of a transitional work. In terms of composition, it points back to the bildungsroman, but at the same time its realism and themes foreshadow the Breakthrough literature of the 1870s and 1880s. Schack's preference for realism as opposed to an overwrought idealism resonated with such later authors as J. P. Jacobsen, Sophus Schandorph, and Henrik Ibsen, who in various ways made a renunciation of daydreaming and delusions the main theme of their works.

Although Schack did not manage to complete his last novel, *Sandhed med Modifikation,* large sections of the manuscript do exist. These fragments of a novel were not published until 1954 (in a private edition), and the first critical edition did not appear until 1968. No one can say how the final version would have turned out, but clearly with this work Schack wanted to take yet another step in the direction of psychological realism. The fragments include a series of detailed portraits of daily life in Copenhagen. Like a reporter, Schack makes his way through various settings–marketplaces and restaurants–and describes what life is like in them. The style of the novel, in its depiction of the surroundings and its rendering of conversations among ordinary people, is marked by a realism that was new for Danish literature.

Casimir is the name of the protagonist who, like the young men in Schack's previous novel, grows up in a remote Zealand province. When the novel opens, Casimir is still a child and completely dominated by his tyrannical father, Dean Bjelke. The dean attempts to raise his son to speak the truth at all times, but the father's concept of truth is authoritarian and limited. Herein lies the central conflict of the story: Casimir is a boy being educated by his father, but his father shows a lack of insight not only regarding the child's world but also regarding himself. *Sandhed med Modifikation,* like *Phantasterne,* is a study of daydreaming and affectation, especially in its depiction of the hypocritical and deluded dean. The man's high ideals regarding truth and moral behavior are something that he puts on for the sake of appearances. His use of language reveals this trait: he usually speaks an ordinary and quite common Danish, but when he stands in the pulpit, he uses pretentious words and bombastic phrases. For him the church service is an excuse to celebrate and laud himself. On one occasion when he takes the opportunity to hail his superior, the bishop, he does so merely to promote himself as a praiseworthy individual.

This same hypocrisy manifests itself in the way he raises the resistant but not yet openly rebellious Casimir. When the dean reproaches the boy for receiving bad grades in school, he is more concerned about his own reputation than his son's future, because now people might say, "Provst Bjelkes søn er som Provst Bjelke selv" (Dean Bjelke's son is just like Dean Bjelke). And when the dean plays the role of the disappointed father, he does not flinch from comparing himself to Jehovah and his son to Cain. By portraying himself in God's image, the dean portrays God in *his* image, and thus God and his father merge into one in Casimir's consciousness. After his father's death, when he tries in

Schack circa 1855 (from Jørgen Mathiassen, Hans Egede Schack som jurist og politiker. Dokumentation og dokumenter, *1978; Main Library, University of Illinois at Urbana-Champaign)*

prayer to express his joy and relief, Casimir finds that God appears in the dean's form. As a psychological consequence of this experience, Casimir's rebellion against his father also becomes a rebellion against religion.

In addition to its criticism of a despotic father, the book presents a critique of the school system. Casimir is taught by incompetent pedagogues such as the antidemocratic history teacher, who, significantly enough, ends his lessons before the revolutionary year of 1789, and the math teacher, who is incapable of teaching his pupils anything that will prove useful later in life. But then Casimir, while the dean is still alive, comes under the influence of a humanistically inclined teacher, Professor Dirksen, who uses the Socratic method in his teaching. Dirksen considers his mission in life to be to expose all forms of affectation, a belief that leads him into conflict with the dean. With psychological astuteness, Schack shows Casimir's ambivalent attitude toward the two most important adults in his life. Emotionally he is tied to his father, but intellectually he realizes that Dirksen is in the right. Eventually, as Casimir's fear of his father's wrath takes over, the last remnant of filial loyalty disappears, and the news of his father's death arouses an instant and spontaneous feeling of happiness in the boy.

From that point on, Dirksen assumes the role of Casimir's mentor. Together they travel to Copenhagen, where Dirksen has been appointed a sort of commissioner for the citizens of the remote province. These sections of the novel had apparently not yet found their final form, and they consist of a series of loosely connected dialogues. Dirksen and Casimir talk to various tradesmen they meet in the capital, including a horse dealer, a goose dealer, and a pork dealer. Dirksen has a pedagogical motive for showing the young man how life is lived by common folks, and he concludes each episode with a few general comments about life, with the relationship between affectation and truth as a recurring theme. He hones the boy's ability to see all forms and degrees of affectation in daily life, from semiconscious delusions to the notoriously deceptive.

With several like-minded colleagues, Dirksen forms a society "for the prevention of lies" with the intention of combating all forms of falsehood and deception. The result of the association's efforts is not clear in the fragments of the novel. Schack hints that he sees a danger that the society, out of sheer self-righteousness, might end up a victim of the affectation that it seeks to combat, but the theme remains undeveloped. At this point in the story, the main characters recede into the background, and the last sections of the manuscript consist of a series of sketches. Clearly *Sandhed med Modifikation* was meant to elucidate the themes of affectation and daydreaming by angles different from those used in *Phantasterne.*

Sandhed med Modifikation, like *Phantasterne,* points ahead to the literature of the Modern Breakthrough. Schack's novels were groundbreaking in terms of theme, with his polemics against Romantic daydreaming and with his frank presentation of topics such as sexuality and criticism of religion, which had been taboo. But his work was also groundbreaking in terms of form, with his multifaceted descriptions of various milieus, his scenic style of writing, and his sensitive rendering of conversations by ordinary people, which included a higher degree of individual speech patterns than had previously been seen in Danish literature.

After a lengthy illness, Hans Egede Schack died on 20 July 1859 at Schlangenbad, a spa near Frankfurt am Main, where he was undergoing treatment for tuberculosis. Instead of offering any kind of immediate inspiration, his limited output and his polemical and anti-Romantic tendencies prevented his work from leaving its mark on the literature of his day or on authors of the next generation. Yet, he had a strong influence later, not only on the realism of the Modern Breakthrough but also in subsequent periods. In Danish literature of the twentieth century the "fantast novel" inspired by Schack became a central genre and included such notable works as Johannes V. Jensen's *Kongens Fald* (1900, 1901; translated as *The Fall of the King,* 1933), Martin A. Hansen's *Lykkelige Kristoffer* (1945; translated as *Lucky Kristoffer,* 1974), and Klaus Rifbjerg's *Lonni og Karl* (Lonni and Karl, 1968).

Letters:

Ib Ostenfeld, ed., *Breve* (Copenhagen: Hasselbalch, 1959).

References:

Jens Kristian Andersen, *Feudalistisk fantasteri og liberalistisk virkelighed. En historisk analyse af H. E. Schacks Phantasterne* (Copenhagen: Forum, 1978);

Erik M. Christensen, "Den geniale Schack og *Phantasterne,*" *Danske Studier* (1993): 28–39;

Hans Hertel, ed., *Omkring Phantasterne* (Copenhagen: Hans Reitzel, 1969);

Aage Jørgensen, "On *Phantasterne,* the Novel by Hans Egede Schack," *Scandinavica,* 5 (1966): 50–53; reprinted in *Forum for Modern Language Studies,* 6 (1970): 173–177;

John Christian Jørgensen, *Den sande kunst. Studier i dansk 1800-tals realisme: Poul Møller, Hans Egede Schack, Georg Brandes, Herman Bang* (Copenhagen: Gad, 1980);

Sven Lindahl, "H. E. Schack og antik hyrdedigtning," *Danske Studier* (1985): 123–126;

Jørgen Mathiassen, *Hans Egede Schack som jurist og politiker. Dokumentation og dokumenter* (Copenhagen: Gad, 1978);

Mathiassen, "Schack," *Ugeskrift for Retsvæsen,* 110 (1976): section B, 293–310;

Klaus P. Mortensen, "Egetræ og pindehuggeri," *Meddelelser fra Dansklærerforeningen* (1973): 262–268;

Ib Ostenfeld, "Hvad fejlede H. E. Schack?" *Medicinsk Forum,* 31 (1978): 106–113;

Frederik Tygstrup, "En usamtidig dannelsesroman. Hans Egede Schack: *Phantasterne,*" in *Læsninger i dansk litteratur,* volume 2, edited by Povl Schmidt, Anne-Marie Mai, Finn Hauberg Mortensen, and Inger-Lise Hjordt-Vetlesen (Odense: Odense Universitetsforlag, 1998), pp. 184–197.

Papers:

Hans Egede Schack's papers and manuscripts are at the Danish Royal Library in Copenhagen.

Schack Staffeldt

(28 March 1769 – 26 December 1826)

Henrik Blicher
University of Copenhagen

(Translated by Tiina Nunnally)

BOOKS: *Om den Ting, kaldet Ausrufungen o. s. v., og om andre Ting* (Copenhagen, 1789);

Digte af Schack Staffeldt. Kammerjunker og Assessor. 1ste Bind (Copenhagen: Brummer, 1804);

Nye Digte. Af Schack Staffeldt (Kiel: Den academiske Boghandling, 1808).

Editions and Collections: *Schack Staffeldts Samlede Digte,* 2 volumes, edited by F. L. Liebenberg (Copenhagen: Samfundet til den danske Litteraturs Fremme, 1843);

Samlinger til Schack Staffeldts Levnet, fornemmelig af Digterens efterladte Haandskrifter, 2 volumes, edited by Liebenberg (Copenhagen: Samfundet til den danske Litteraturs Fremme, 1847, 1851);

Schack Staffeldts Digte, edited by Liebenberg, with an introduction by Georg Brandes (Copenhagen: Philipsen, 1882);

Digte (Copenhagen: Gyldendal, 1968);

Samlede digte, 3 volumes, edited by Henrik Blicher (Copenhagen: Det Danske Sprog- og Litteraturselskab/Reitzel, 2001).

Schack Staffeldt (courtesy of the Danish Royal Library, Copenhagen)

A minor episode of deception is associated with Schack Staffeldt. When he published his first volume of poetry in 1804, it was almost identical in appearance to a work that had appeared the year before–*Digte* (Poems, 1803), by Adam Oehlenschläger, who was Staffeldt's colleague but ten years his junior. It had the same title, the same title page, the same modern typography, the same publisher, and a similar division of the contents into two separate sections. In spite of the conspicuous physical resemblance, Staffeldt included with his poems a statement that the contents had been written before Oehlenschläger's collection was published. This claim was demonstrably not true, and two years later, when the younger rival cemented his status as foremost poet of Denmark with the two-volume *Poetiske Skrifter* (Poetic Writings, 1805), Staffeldt's work was already a thing of the past. For a long time his unfortunate attempt to backdate his work made regarding his literary oeuvre as an appendix to the short-lived Oehlenschläger Romanticism far too easy. Staffeldt's work, which was devoted solely to poetry, has never become popular or initiated any sort of literary school. Yet, posterity has recognized his contribution to what he himself calls in the preface to his second and last collection, *Nye Digte* (New Poems, 1808), "Mangfoldigheden i Fædrelandets skjønne Litteratur" (the diversity of our nation's belles lettres). During Staffeldt's own century, his work was hailed by Johan Ludvig Heiberg, a contemporary of Søren Kierkegaard and the greatest authority among critics of his day. Georg Brandes, the standard-bearer of Danish Naturalism, mentioned Staffeldt's idealism with respect and preferred his work to that of Friedrich Hölderlin.

Adolph Wilhelm Schack von Staffeldt was born on the island of Rügen on 28 March 1769. When he was seven years old, he lost his mother, Maria Regina von Klingen, who came from noble German stock. His father, an unreliable military man, Major Agatus Ludwig von Staffeldt, died four years later. By that time the three brothers, of whom Schack was the youngest, had already been placed in a military preparatory school in Copenhagen for the poor and orphaned sons of officers. In a later letter to his brother August, sent from Göttingen in 1792, Staffeldt complained that although his body had certainly had parents, his heart had not. At the royal cadet academy, he was taught by German-born man of letters Werner H. F. Abrahamson, who supported the young corporal's interest in poetry. In keeping with the tastes of the time, Staffeldt made his debut with a couple of pastoral poems in 1788. The following year he became involved in a fiery debate about the privileges of German immigrants in the Danish government departments. The debate was prompted by Jens Baggesen's fairy-tale opera *Holger Danske* (1789). In the pamphlet *Om den Ting, Kaldet Ausrufungen* Staffeldt stepped forward as a self-appointed Danish citizen and declared Denmark to be "a theater for German farce." The "Holger Controversy" was also a debate about foreign–that is, German–culture versus an established Danish tradition for ballad operas. Staffeldt revealed himself to be both an indignant Danish patriot and an astonishingly well-informed man of letters who rejected the opera as "et Chaos af alle Konster" (a chaos of all arts [the point is, the opera is an unlucky mixture of different art forms]).

In 1791 Staffeldt took a leave of absence from his military career and accepted a royal grant to study at the leading university of Germany, in Göttingen. One could not train to be a poet there, nor was such training the intended purpose of his stay in Germany. The administrative burdens of the absolute monarchy of Denmark had increased, and Staffeldt became a government official. He worked compulsively, attending lectures in political science given by A. L. Schlözer, who, in a letter of recommendation, described his student as diligent, well informed, and highly talented. In the meantime, Staffeldt did not give up his literary interests, and Göttingen became the site of his first poetic breakthrough. The pride of the university was the archaeologist and philologist C. G. Heyne, who initiated Staffeldt into a whole new concept of ideal classical beauty. He encountered there the enthusiastic classicism of J. J. Winckelmann, and Staffeldt later incorporated Greek mythology into his work, although he gave its imagery a Romantic interpretation. In a letter to Baggesen from 1817, Staffeldt called Oehlenschläger's use of the Nordic gods a "Marionetspil" (marionette play), and he could not reconcile himself with these gods "der stundom have Feber og Asthma" (who occasionally suffer from fever and asthma).

During this time, which was his pre-Romantic period, Staffeldt published poems in both German (in Gottfried August Bürger's *Musen-Almanach*) and Danish. One of his most interesting poems, "Menneskhedens Bane" (The Path of Humanity), never published during his lifetime, reveals his debt to Friedrich Schiller's epochal poem of ideas, "Die Künstler" from 1789. Staffeldt's grandly scaled poem describes the development of humanity from a raw and formless barbarism to increasing degrees of perfection. As an epic showing the development of universal history, the poem covers a great expanse of time and space. Problems arise, however, when the poet uses several verses to approach the present and thus the question of whether the France of the French Revolution, then under way, could be regarded as a reborn Greece. The poem has survived in two different versions; the later version, with its many additions and omissions, bears testimony to the poet's difficulty in dealing with the tremendous expectations of an all-encompassing revolution that were present from the beginning. Among the most striking statements is Staffeldt's hymn to a justified revolution. At long last, the passage of freedom throughout the world would culminate in a total and bloody upheaval, producing the preconditions for heaven on earth:

Det Træ som nu af Blod opstiger
Snart hvælver sig til Jordens Lye
Og Himmelske fra Lysets Riger
Til Træets Rod og Skygge tye:

(The tree that now from blood arises
Soon will arc high to shelter the earth
The heavenly from the realm of light
Will take refuge in its roots and shade:)

But world history ended up overtaking the visionary Staffeldt. Upon closer reflection, he could not justify the bloody upheavals in France during the 1790s by referring to a future century. The four verses were deleted, and the poem remained unpublished. "Menneskhedens Bane," however, provided a way out for Staffeldt, who allowed tangible history to follow its own course without letting it deter his writing. He had to seek it in a new interpretation of the concept of *freedom*. For the revolutionaries, freedom was a catchword (freedom, equality, fraternity) that was to be realized in the real world. For Staffeldt (and for Schiller), freedom became another word for culture, self-education, and a regrouping of

Manuscript for a poem by Staffeldt (courtesy of the Danish Royal Library, Copenhagen)

the instincts under the direction of the goddess Venus Urania. With that usage, the reconciliation of the high and the low was postponed in earnest to the future, as evidenced in the final tribute of the poem to the approaching goddess:

> Hun selv, i salig Majesteet,
> Sin Stiernevogn fra Himlen leder
> Og Jord og Himmel vorder Eet.
>
> (She herself, in blessed majesty,
> Steers her starry coach from the firmaments
> so heaven and earth become as one.)

On his journey home to Copenhagen in the spring of 1793, Staffeldt visited Friedrich Gottlieb Klopstock, who in his youth had devised the plan for his masterpiece *Der Messias* (completed in 1773). In a lofty ode, Staffeldt vowed to accomplish something similar. Thus, a newly born poet, deeply in debt, had to seek a position in the Copenhagen administration. He had powerful benefactors, such as Ernst Schimmelmann; Friedrich Christian, the Prince of Augustenborg; and Andreas Peter Bernstorff. The latter arranged for him to receive a grant for additional extensive travels throughout Germany, Austria, Italy, and France from 1795 to 1800. Staffeldt's situation before his departure is poorly documented, as is much of his life. A solitary letter (addressed to J. E. Berger in 1794) testifies to attacks of depression; yet, in poems composed at about the same time, Staffeldt could refer with jubilation to an organizing principle of nature. In "Til den Helliganede" (To Sanctity Perceived) he reveals the mental act that will allow one to enter into speaking terms with this elusive entity. The maternal organizing principle is elsewhere called Isis; it has to be perceived because it cannot be known.

During the first years of his travels, from 1796 to 1798, Staffeldt described his impressions in a diary written in German. A major part of the diary (approximately eight hundred printed pages) was later published by F. L. Liebenberg, who was the first person to collect Staffeldt's works and revive them for Kierkegaard's generation. On the surface, the diary seems glib, abrupt, and lacking in cohesive composition, but it has rightly been described as a philosophical-aesthetic document of self-education. It includes meticulous reports from visits to galleries and parks, which occasionally form the backdrop for the sonnets that were the poetic results of Staffeldt's journey. However, no real portraits are included; instead, he presents descriptions of various types from Vienna, Venice, and Florence, where he stayed for long periods while Napoleon's republican troops kept moving the borders between countries. With a great deal of arrogance, he harshly condemns the flighty erotic life of the big cities, and yet he participates almost frantically in the merriment. Even while in Göttingen, Staffeldt attempted to learn about the new German philosophy, and in a few letters from his travels abroad, he names Immanuel Kant in association with an existential crisis regarding the borders of poetic speculation and perception. In the notes from Staffeldt's travels the later Schiller must be included: Schiller's contemporary ideas about an aesthetic education contributed to Staffeldt's high estimation of the poet's role and of himself. The well-known treatise on naive and sentimental writing, in particular, confirmed to his well-prepared reader that he, like Schiller, was sentimental–that is, a fundamentally reflective and skeptical poetic type. The sparse travel writings thus include no fewer than eight sonnets, published much later or posthumously, from gloomy stalactite caves, where the brooding poet felt he had observed the work of the cosmic spirit, with creation and destruction in all their shifting forms.

After his return to Copenhagen in the fall of 1800, Staffeldt was granted a position in the trade sector of the civil service, and for a brief time he returned to military service. When the British navy attacked Copenhagen in 1801, Staffeldt, as an officer, stood ready to participate in the defense of the city. His willingness to join in the defense was also expressed in a series of inflammatory poems written for the occasion, but that was the extent of his involvement. In the following years, up until the appearance of his debut poetry collection in 1804, he published more and more poems in journals and poetry anthologies. In this manner, Staffeldt introduced a large share of the general Romantic ideas that later were better marketed by the Danish Norwegian team of Henrich Steffens and Oehlenschläger. Around 1801 Staffeldt had already written platonic love poems with woman as pretext: "Til Eros" (To Eros), "Til Charis" (To Grace), "Til Platonismus" (To Platonism). He had hailed his role as a brilliant and bold visionary on behalf of humanity: "Tilstaaelsen" (Confession), "Opfordring" (Challenge), "Dæmonen" (The Demon). He had also composed drafts to a new perception of nature that was tied to kinship: "Til den uendelige Natur" (To Eternal Nature), "Ode til Harmonien" (Ode to Harmony). Yet, those who were interested finally recognized that Romanticism had come to Denmark only when Friedrich Schelling's pupil Steffens, in his introductory lectures from 1802, retold the development of humanity as a fall from an original ideal state to an imperfect and confused contemporary time, which, nevertheless, harbored the beginnings of a new golden age.

In literary history, Staffeldt's *Digte* is known as a collection that appeared too late. The question of how much Staffeldt's work benefited from or was indebted to Oehlenschläger's epochal poetry collection from the previous year has long played a central role in scholarship regarding Danish Romanticism. Staffeldt was attempting to catch up with and overtake his younger rival in terms of the narrative and well-conceived romance, an area for which posterity has generally agreed that he lacked the necessary qualifications. With August Wilhelm Schlegel's *Gedichte* (Poems) as his model, Oehlenschläger had divided his collection into an epic and a lyrical section, with a lively drama added on. Staffeldt created a similar division and tried to match the richness of his competitor with a discreet but self-conscious subtitle, *Part One*. The much promoted *Part Two,* which was to include Staffeldt's previously published poems, never appeared, in spite of many revisions.

Even Hakon Stangerup, in his 1940 monograph, felt compelled to address the rivalry between the two poets. Staffeldt's false statement regarding when the majority of his poems had been composed was a discredit to the nobleman. Yet, in spite of everything, Staffeldt's dependence on Oehlenschläger's work applied only to the thirty-six epic pieces in his collection. Unfortunately, the interest in this "Udhus" (annex) ended up distorting the image of "en stolt og stort anlagt Bygning" (a proud and magnificently designed edifice), meaning the twenty-two lyrical pieces in the second half of the collection.

The renewed interest in Romantic poetry, which in Denmark occurred in the 1980s, has largely relegated this conflict between the two poets to the past, along with the previously vital national perception of Staffeldt as a Danish poet with a linguistic and philosophical background that was German. Heiberg was one of the first to emphasize the lyrical-philosophical qualities of Staffeldt's work, and posterity has primarily focused on the lyrical aspect.

The collection begins with the much read and anthologized poem "Indvielsen" (Initiation), a compact anecdote of destiny about initiation into life as a Romantic poet. The four stanzas of the poem describe the way in which a vague longing finds its true, though provisional, home in the burning kiss of a muse, who is indistinguishable from a vanishing ray of the sun. After this point, anything other than a repetition is largely inadequate, although temporary consolation may be found in "Anelse, Drøm og Sang" (presentiment, dream and song). Yet, he can find no peace until he "drager Himlene ned!" (draws the heavens down!).

The main character in the remaining poems is the poet himself, someone who is equipped with equal parts longing (his mark of nobility) and imagination (his gift for creating images, which ideally coincides with a creative principle in nature). In this way he can turn to "Phantasien" (the imagination):

Ved Alaandens Barm du Kunsten drømmer,
Elskov brænder i dit Aandedræt,
Og i dit Æterblod, som Andagt, strømmer
Ud fra dig og smelter Alt til Eet

(In the spirit's embrace of art you dream,
Passion burns in your every breath
And your blood, as devotion, streams
Emanates from you, merging all in one.)

The poet confirms his "grændseløse Kald" (boundless calling) by keeping his mind calm and his poetry vein warm in a thunderingly chaotic storm "At the top of Mont Cenis." He appears in disguise as the first lover in the sweeping verse story "Lillas Minde" (In Memory of Lilla), becoming intoxicated by the image-sated joy of anticipation. But his warm-blooded Italian girlfriend refuses the role of "Alskiønheds Billedstøtte" (beauty's statue), and he has to teach her that renunciation "er Glædens Ynde, / Vort Savn er ofte Tingens Værd" (is the grace of joy / our longing often the sole essence of it all). He praises the ideal Greek condition in the elegy "Digterne" (The Poets) and follows the Italian sculptor Antonio Canova into his workshop, where the chiseled images of gods constitute "Den Eviges Selverkiendelse / I det Endelige!" (the eternal's self-knowledge / for all eternity!). And in "Genien" (The Genius) he proclaims his faith in the essential viability of the plan: "Poesie er indskrænket Evighed, Alt I det Eene, / Guddommen er Poesie, Tiden Indfatningen er" (Poetry is confined eternity, all in one / Deity is poetry, time the framework).

The epic poems of Staffeldt's collection have played a subordinate role in the most recent appraisal of his work; yet, many of them have been included in later anthologies. The poem "Snedkeren og hans Drenge, i Pestens Tid" (The Carpenter and His Lads, in Time of the Plague), with its eerie mood and the rhythmic refrain of onomatopoeic hammer strokes accompanying the production of coffins, is an ideal piece to be read aloud. In general, some resistance has arisen to the noisy tragedy of the romances, which form a link between Bürger's beloved "Lenore" and B. S. Ingemann's notorious ballads of murder and insanity. In the portrait of "Den hellige Therese" (Saint Therese), Staffeldt has inserted his own erotic dilemma and, in his own words, depicted the saint's "brændende, i individuel Elskov overgaaende Andagt" (ardent devotion, which borders on personal passion), based on her autobiography and Giovanni Bernini's baroque statue. The collection also includes a magnificently planned mythological drama of ideas, "Prometheus eller Menneskets Skabelse" (Prometheus or the Creation of Man), Staffeldt's gloomy alternative to Oehlenschläger's "Sanct Hansaften-Spil" (A Midsummer Night's Play, 1803).

Prometheus is a Titan and thus engaged in a struggle with the gods of Olympus. He creates man in his own insubordinate image, and in the first part of the play, man is equipped with everything necessary to take up the battle with the gods. Among the most promising gifts of the Titans is poetic talent, represented by the Orphic harp or lyre, from which "en Verden udskyder" (a world emerges) and "det Heele gienlyder" (all resounds).

In the second half of the poem, the proud plan is demolished, step by step, so that man ultimately remains as an ambiguous mixture of conflicting urges, an exposed presence between heaven and earth. The final programmatic poem in the collection is "Digterbekiendelse" (A Poet's Confession), which includes the poet's heroic rejection of any form of popularization. His contemporaries are wretched; his readers are uncomprehending; and the critics demand a banal correctness and facile charms. This conspiracy, attesting to Staffeldt's attentive reading of the few but injurious reviews of his work, prompted him to react with a martyr's bitter pride. *Digte* received no reviews.

In the following years Staffeldt mobilized all the personal initiative that he possessed, as well as his many influential connections. His goal was to attain a higher and better-paid position. His professional ambitions were just as great as his debts, and many times he petitioned, in vain, Prime Minister Schimmelmann and the duke of Augustenborg for a promotion within the trade department or for a chief administrator post. Staffeldt made reference to his studies in Göttingen during his travels abroad, as well as to the noble humanity he had demonstrated in his poetry. But the promotion eluded him, and his growing desperation can be read in his openhearted correspondence with Count Sigismund Schulin. Staffeldt spent the summer of 1805 with his sister, Lovise, in Jutland: "Verden har gjort mig Uret, derfor kaster jeg mig i Naturen's Skjød og glemmer den" (The world has treated me unjustly, and that is why I have thrown myself into Nature's embrace, to forget). In an unpublished birthday poem to himself (dated 1805), Staffeldt revisits several epochal events in his life, all of which share that they were full of possibilities and promising prospects, but the fog formations on this birthday in March prompt an intimate dialogue with spring:

Vil du alt en Sørgehimmel hvælve
Over mig og min Forgangenhed?
Jeg er til–dog alle Kræfter skiælve–
Du har Ret: mit bedre Selv gik ned.

(Will you raise a grief-stricken vault
Over me and my life gone by?
Here I am–though all my powers quaver–
You are right: my better self did die.)

In February 1806 Staffeldt petitioned unsuccessfully for a position as royal tutor, but in July of the same year he took matters into his own hands and traveled by ship to Kiel in present-day northern Germany. From Kiel the reigning Crown Prince Frederik oversaw his involvement in the Napoleonic Wars from 1805 to 1809. The crown prince had no scruples about promising Staffeldt a government post, but upon calculating the poet's extensive debts, he was purported to say, "De er jo Gud og Hvermand skyldig" (You are in debt to both God and the entire world). His correspondence with Schulin indicates that Staffeldt had pawned his watch and other possessions under drastic terms, but his friend intervened and provided the guarantee for a large loan from the king. With that, Staffeldt's prospects seemed brighter, and he hoped to be granted an available position. His brother Carl was serving as an officer in Holstein, and together they followed the Frenchmen's conquest of Lübeck: "Staden blev sadt under rød Viin og Blod, og der paa svømmede Liig og Boehave" (The city was filled with red wine and blood, swimming with corpses and household goods). In Kiel he met Baggesen and also proposed to the love of his life, Fredericia von der Maase. In a letter to Baggesen (dated April 1807), Staffeldt reports that his *Nye Digte* is at the printer and adds cryptically that he herewith bids farewell to "Musen for Smaaedigte, og betræder en anden Bane, hvis ikke borgerlige Forhold deri giøre Forandring" (the muse of minor poems and enters a different path, provided that domestic circumstances do not provoke a change). Presumably, he is referring to his expectations concerning both his plays and von der Maase. Staffeldt's attempts at dramas never were published or performed, and the few fragments that have survived in Liebenberg's *Samlinger til Schack Staffeldts Levnet, fornemmelig af Digterens efterladte Haandskrifter* (Collections on the Life of Schack Staffeldt, Primarily from the Poet's Remaining Manuscripts, 1847, 1851) reveal merely a fumbling with an unfamiliar medium: they are "Raphel di Urbino," "Balder hiin Gode" (Balder the Good), "Harald Haarfager" (Harald Fairhaired), "Ines de Castro," and "Romeo og Julia" (circa 1807–1810). Nevertheless, in 1820 Staffeldt could speak with undisputed self-confidence about his tentative attempts, which merely lacked "Donatellos sidste Meiselslag" (Donatello's last blow of the chisel). The expectations that Staffeldt had attached to lady-in-waiting von der Maase were denied. He makes reference to this rejection in a letter to his sister in May 1807, in which he describes himself as the unhappy brother whose most precious hopes had been dashed. Von der Maase appears again in a letter from 1810 addressed to his brother Carl, who had enjoined him to marry and establish a family: either she was unwilling or she did not dare, "Du veed hvem jeg meener og hvem jeg ikke kan glemme" (You know who I mean and who I cannot forget). The hesitations of the suitor are revealed in the manuscript of a birthday poem in which Staffeldt wavers between depicting her as "elskelig" (loving) or "tækkelig" (winsome). Von der Maase remained unmarried and died in 1823, three years before Staffeldt.

In the summer of 1807, Staffeldt was preparing his second and last poetry collection, *Nye Digte*. In June he asked Schulin, "Menneskets og Digterens Ven" (friend of poets and humanity), to find more subscribers than the already confirmed two hundred. He also mentioned suffering severe attacks of nervous fever and "tvivler paa, at selv den lykkeligste Forandring i mit Liv vil gienføde mig til Karskhed og Haab" (doubts that even the most auspicious change in my life could regenerate my health or hopes). In October he was appointed to a position at the court of the insane Peter Frederik Vilhelm of Oldenborg in nearby Plöen. Thus, the way was cleared for Staffeldt's future governmental career.

With *Nye Digte,* Staffeldt had largely completed his Danish literary works. In German, however, his other native tongue, Staffeldt achieved yet another high point in his late sonnets. He had made use of the sonnet form as early as 1792, and the new collection included a separate section consisting of fifty sonnets. Here he left behind the narrative romance in favor of a section of "Blandede Digte" (mixed poems) that included strophic poems, elegies, verse dramas, a myth, a legend, and a fairy tale. Many of the sonnets are memories from his travels in purified form; others are meditations on objets d'art, bel cantos, or such special places as ruins or stalactite caves. The verse story "Lina," the longest piece of the collection, also makes use of sonnets at moments of heightened lyricism as a means of emphasis, with an inaccessible woman at the center of the ardent visions. The six interconnected sonnets in "Sonnettkrands" (Sonnet Wreath) reveal Staffeldt as the Danish heir to Petrarch. He is less successful with his longer, epic efforts–the colorful Old Norse tale of "Kong Hadding" (King Hadding) and the verse drama "Camoens," which depicts the invented death by starvation of the Portuguese poet-king in the desert. Nevertheless, the play, which includes Staffeldt's most

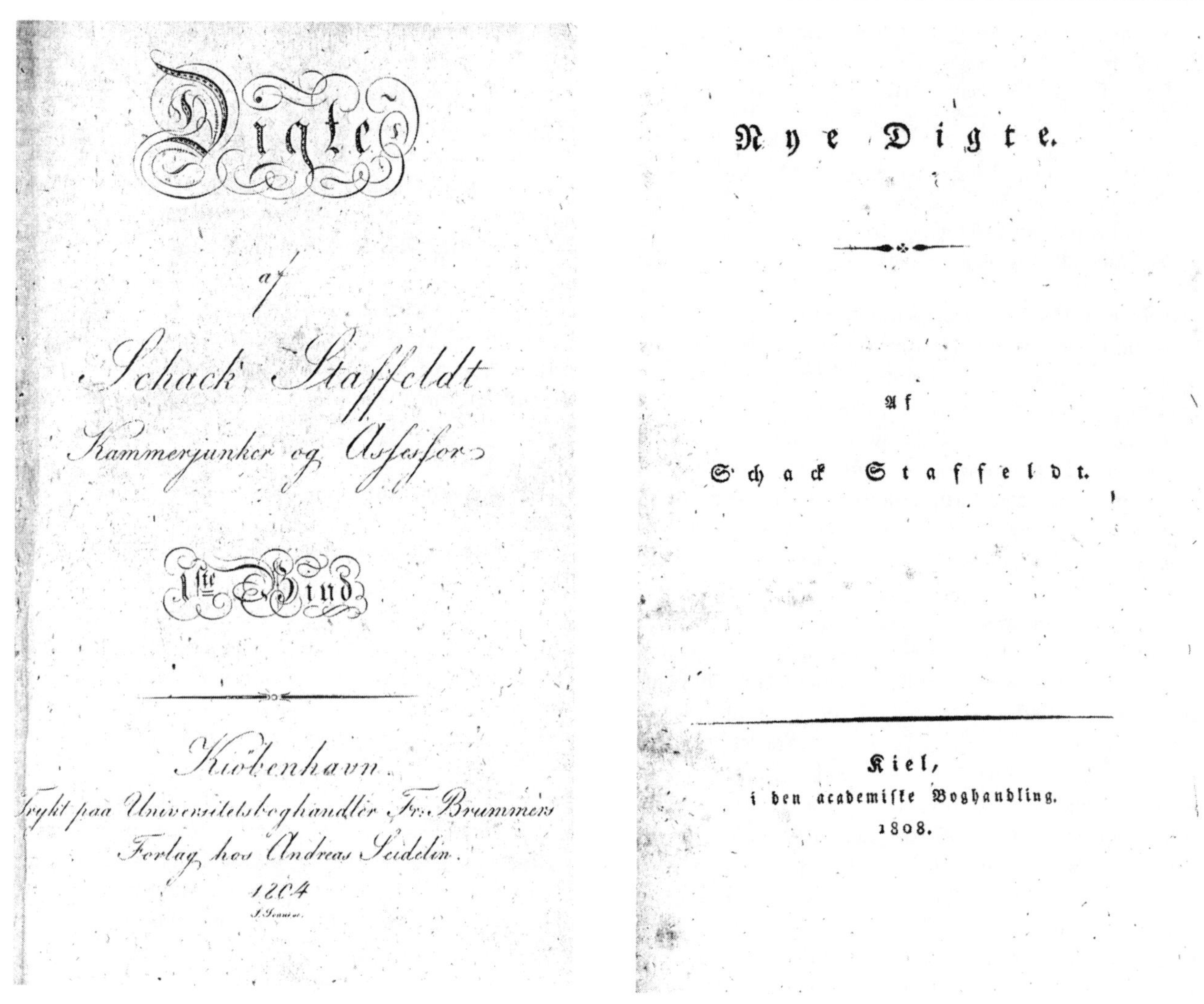

Title pages for Staffeldt's two poetry collections (Collection of Henrik Blicher)

uninhibited pathos, won favor among his contemporaries, and the exclamation "salig, salig den, som døer!" (blessed, blessed is he who dies!) resounds in many of the purest, most sorrow-laden poems of the collection. In "Til Vaaren" (To Springtime) he measures the distance to his "Sangsalige Foraar" (Song-blessed Spring) and acknowledges his lack of ability to create in poetic form what he desires.

In "Den unge Digters Klage" (The Young Poet's Lament), which is even stronger, Staffeldt speaks of being seduced by art: "Dybt i Afmagts qvalme Afgrund bunden, / Gaaer jeg levende ned i min Grav" (Deep in the sickened chasm of powerlessness / I descend into my grave alive). The basis for poetry is a fundamental distrust of the tangible world and an equally firm conviction that only in visions, borne by yearning, can humanity find a fleeting insight into god-like life. Greek mythology continues to play a central role; the collection is framed by two magnificent interpretations of the ancient myth of Orpheus and Eurydice. The separation of the couple, in service to a higher art, is played out in other impossible pairings found in the collection: "Liljen og Dugdraaben" (The Lily and the Dewdrop) and "Nattergalen og Natviolen" (The Nightingale and the Dame's Violet). In the final poem, "Til Musen" (To the Muse), the Orphic joining of heaven and earth nearly succeeds when Zeus, the god of lightning, intervenes and enjoins the poet to seek comfort and consolation from the muse.

For a long time, *Nye Digte* has stood in the shadows of the literary controversy surrounding the earlier collection *Digte;* yet, it includes some of Staffeldt's most beautiful poems. The poem "Ved et Æbletræ, som i Sept. 1804 paa eengang bar Frugter og Blomster"

(Beside an Apple Tree, which in Sept. 1804 Bore Both Flowers and Fruit) is a fascinating depiction of a miraculous exception in the rhythm of the seasons. "Forvandlingerne" (Transformation) describes a series of transformations in nature, in which "Alt er i Eet, og Eet er i Alt" (Everything is in One, and One is in Everything), first as stone, then as rose, then bird, and then the irresistible singing maiden, who will meet her bridegroom, "Evighedens salige Søn" (the blessed son of eternity).

The nature poems of the collection deserve attention. In his portrait of Staffeldt from 1882, Brandes indicates two widely differing positions in the poet's work. In a series of early poems (including *Digte* from 1804) the poet stands sovereign above nature and measures the force of his own spirit by playing it against immensely sublime scenarios of a nature in revolt. The test of strength is relegated to "Toppen af Mont-Cenis" (The Heights of Mont Cenis), where his own calm amidst chaos is proof of his "grændseløse Kald" (boundless calling).

In an ode to "Nødvendighed" (Necessity), he measures the distance to chaos with teeth-gnashing stoicism: "Uomveltet, jeg skue / Dybt Omveltningen ved min Fod!" (Immovable, I perceive / the vast upheaval at my feet!). According to Brandes, Staffeldt abandoned this position in his later poems, and this development corresponds to the movement of contemporary German philosophy toward Schelling's nature speculations, which became Staffeldt's chief source of inspiration. One of the clearest expressions of this position is "Hymne til Vandet" (Hymn to Water), which demonstrates in lyrical form Schelling's abstract determination of nature as visible spirit. Staffeldt's highest praise in speaking of water is that it has no shape or boundaries and is therefore a worthy subject for his hymnal agitation: "En Gud mig bevæger foruden Rist" (A God Doth Move Me without Ceasing). The flowing element appears in various guises, although it remains the same. The proper expression of formlessness is the sea itself, an allegorical heavenly bride with the beloved's image on its mirror-like bosom.

What humans recognize as clouds are the passionate sighs of the maiden, and what they see as rivers are her arms, yearning to embrace. Wherever the formless water encounters a barrier, the poet sides with what is formless. The obstructive shore, the defiant cliff, the poles rigid with frost–these are all expressions for the tyranny of form. In each of the forms assumed by what is formless is a built-in longing back toward formlessness. The raindrop, the teardrop, and the fount all happily leave their respective prisons to submit and surrender to "Alforeeningen" (the all-encompassing union). This type of Romantic morphology turns on end the Enlightenment perception of nature, which is admired for its ability to organize itself in increasingly sophisticated forms. Where Carl von Linné's *Systema Naturae* (1735) begins, Staffeldt would stop–if he could. That he cannot is connected to the sense of longing that he shares with the water and its formlessness. As depicted in the last verse, the unfettered and blessed world glimpsed in the rippling of the waves must be observed from the shore. Thus, the poet's state and wretchedness is to be separated from the object of his longing, both in space (standing on the shore) and in time (he comes there "saa tidt," so often). One wave will appear, and then another will recede; the water will remain the never redeemed "Pandt" (security) of the "store Forløsning" (great redemption). The other part of the poet's wretchedness is equally important: the perfectly formed verse is his only means of consorting with what is formless. By separating himself, by stepping onto the shore, the poet must acknowledge regretfully that he is not *everything,* but merely . . . a poet. Staffeldt's pantheism is sentimental.

His career, however, was progressing admirably. In 1806 he was promised a position as chief administrative officer. After several posts at court, he was appointed chief administrative officer of Cismar in 1810. From this lesser post he was promoted in 1813 to chief administrative officer of Gottorp, and his career culminated in 1814 when he was appointed head of the city of Schleswig.

Staffeldt was also honored with the title Knight of the Dannebrog in 1824. Yet, Staffeldt regarded the glorious path of his career as little more than a wandering through the desert. As becomes evident in his scanty correspondence, he felt isolated, burdened by trivial obligations, thwarted by his colleagues, and to an increasing degree cheated by fate. Just Mathias Thiele, a young admirer, described in his memoirs his encounter with the former poet at Sophienholm, north of Copenhagen in the summer of 1815. Thiele had anticipated meeting a fiery and stylish poet, but was disappointed. He found Staffeldt's attire to be rather old-fashioned, his appearance neither handsome nor spiritual, his face wizened, and his short hair powdered. But upon closer acquaintanceship, Thiele had "strax Indtrykket af en udbrændt Vulkan–en Askehob efter et deiligt Baal" (an immediate impression of a burned out volcano–an ash heap left by a lovely fire).

After *Nye Digte,* Staffeldt's lyrical production in Danish was extremely sparse. In "Erindring og Haab" (Memory and Hope), which he published in Danish in 1820, he sternly rebukes that part of the world of the imagination that, through much of his work, had pointed confidently toward the future as the time when the lofty demands of poetry would be achieved.

Addressing this false hope, he now says, "Hvad var din Gave? Digtertidsfordriv, / Blødagtigt Vanvid, ak! et hyklet Liv!" (What was your gift? A poet's time rife / With tender madness, alas! hypocritical life!). This confrontation with himself is further expanded in several of the thirteen German sonnets (published in 1823, from manuscripts written 1815–1819), in which the poet bids farewell to his youthful ideals: art, love, faith in friendship, humanity, and the fragile perceptions.

Schack Staffeldt ended his days as a rage-filled, misanthropic eccentric plagued by abdominal illness in what he regarded as a backwater of Denmark. The local populace of Schleswig regarded him, in turn, as a madman. According to one anecdote, recounted by his friend and colleague C. A. G. J. Engel in his valuable portrait of the poet, on a fall evening in 1826 the world-weary chief administrative officer was watching the sun disappear over the lake at Gottorp Castle. A passerby, wanting to share his conventional joy at the beautiful scene, received the response from Staffeldt that for him nothing was visible but "die Vernichtung," annihilation. Staffeldt died on 26 December 1826.

Staffeldt's work includes no real literary breakthroughs, but rather important shifts in emphasis. He was faithful to his poetic initiation from his years in Göttingen, but whereas in the early part of his literary career he enthusiastically renounced life and happiness in favor of the anticipatory visions of his art, his later work became a martyrdom that he was eager to escape. He never wavered from his strict idealism and its poetics but took note of the costs and decided to curtail his literary endeavors. Yet, Staffeldt has not endured as a martyr to his ideals nor because of his ability to illustrate the shifting philosophic positions of platonic or German origin. To regret the way in which Staffeldt misdirected his own life by staking all of his vital passions on his poetry is not productive. Staffeldt is first and foremost an eminent poet who achieved his poetic-philosophical high point in his last collection, which has no connection to Oehlenschläger. In this volume he shows from within what to be an idealist means. The basis for a reassessment of Staffeldt's place in Danish literary history exists in the form of a new edition of his work.

Letters:

Samlinger til Schack Staffeldts Levnet, fornemmelig af Digterens efterladte Haandskrifter, 2 volumes, edited by F. L. Liebenberg (Copenhagen: Samfundet til den danske Litteraturs Fremme, 1847, 1851), II: 371–417;

Personalhistorisk Tidsskrift, 5 (1908): 90–108; 6 (1915): 157–158; 13, no. 1 (1952): 200–202;

Henrik Blicher, "In tiefster Ehrfurcht. Ukendte breve fra Schack Staffeldt til hertugen af Augustenborg," *Danske Studier* (2002): 158–177.

References:

Vilhelm Andersen, *Illustreret dansk Litteraturhistorie,* 4 volumes, edited by Carl S. Petersen and Andersen (Copenhagen: Gyldendal, 1924-1934), III: 99-109;

Kristian Arentzen, *Baggesen og Oehlenschläger. Literaturhistorisk Studie,* 8 volumes (Copenhagen: Otto B. Wroblwsky, 1870-1878), II: 87-120, III: 64-74, VI: 328-346;

F. J. Billeskov Jansen, *Danmarks Digtekunst,* 3 volumes (Copenhagen: Munksgaard, 1944–1958), II: 31-32, III: 40–49;

Henrik Blicher, "Ånden over vandene. Om Heibergs brug af Schack v. Staffeldt," *Spring,* 3 (1992): 116-127;

Blicher, "Denne Harpe er din Brud," in *Læsninger i dansk litteratur,* 5 volumes, edited by Povl Schmidt and others (Odense: Odense Universitetsforlag, 1997–1999), II: 279–293;

Blicher, "Hvirvlen," in *Krydsfelt. Ånd og natur i Guldalderen,* edited by Mogens Bencard (Copenhagen: Gyldendal, 2000), pp. 224–235; translated as "The Vortex," in *Intersections. Art and Science in the Golden Age,* edited by Bencard (Copenhagen: Gyldendal, 2000), pp. 224–235;

Blicher, "Schack Staffeldt–die Nachtseite seiner späteren Lebensjahre. En kommenteret gengivelse af C. A. G. J. Engels optegnelser om Schack Staffeldt," *Danske Studier* (1994): 67–99;

Georg Brandes, "Adolf Wilhelm Schack von Staffeldt," in *Schack Staffeldts Digte,* edited by F. L. Liebenberg (Copenhagen: Philipsen, 1882), pp. 9–65; reprinted in *Samlede Skrifter,* 18 volumes (Copenhagen: Gyldendal, 1899–1910), I: 308–367;

Finn Brandt-Pedersen, "Det flygtige fastholdt. A. W. Schack Staffeldt: 'Sonet IV,'" in *Danske digtanalyser,* edited by Thomas Bredsdorff (Copenhagen: Arena, 1969), pp. 77–84;

Bredsdorff, "Ballonen og dragen. Om Brandes' Staffeldt," *Spring,* 14 (1999): 157–171;

Hans Brix, *Analyser og Problemer. Undersøgelser i den ældre danske Litteratur,* 7 volumes (Copenhagen: Gyldendal, 1935–1955), II: 238–244;

Brix, *Danmarks Digtere. 40 Kapitler af dansk Digtekunsts Historie* (Copenhagen, 1925); revised and enlarged as *Danmarks Digtere. Fyrretyve Kapitler af dansk Digtekunsts Historie* (Copenhagen: Aschehoug Dansk, 1951), pp. 191–198;

Mogens Davidsen, "Væbnet med romantik. Staffeldt og Strunge i sigtekornet," *Spring,* 3 (1992): 95–105;

Niels Egebak, "Den dobbelte indskrift," in *Skrift, subjekt, fiktion* (Viborg: Arena, 1980), pp. 59–75;

Ole Feldbæk, *Dansk Identitetshistorie,* 3 volumes, edited by Feldbæk (Copenhagen: C. A. Reitzel, 1991–1992), II: 57, 61–64;

Johan Fjord Jensen, "En aristokrat blandt borgere. Schack Staffeldt," in *Dansk litteraturhistorie,* 9 volumes, edited by Fjord Jensen and others (Copenhagen: Gyldendal, 1983–1985), IV: 601–606;

Bo Hakon Jørgensen, *Mastetoppe. 100 danske digte–med korte analyser* (Odense: Odense Universitetsforlag, 1997), pp. 269–271;

Flemming Harrits, *Digtning og læsning* (Århus: Aarhus Universitetsforlag, 1990), pp. 104–114;

Johan Ludvig Heiberg, "Lyrisk Poesie," in *Intelligentsblade* (1843): 26–27; reprinted in *Prosaiske Skrifter,* 11 volumes (Copenhagen: C. A. Reitzel, 1861–1862), IV: 436–444;

Vello Helk, *Dansk-norske studierejser 1661–1813,* 2 volumes (Odense: Odense Universitetsforlag, 1991), I: 96–103, II: 252;

Lisbeth Jellesen, "Om Staffeldt og Platon," *Kritik,* 27 (1973): 46–58;

Torben Jelsbak, "Staffeldts sonet-klassik," *Kritik,* 141 (1999): 34–41;

Aage Jørgensen, "Schack Staffeldts digt 'I Høsten,'" in *Kundskaben på ondt og godt. En studiebog* (Århus: Akademisk Boghandel, 1968), pp. 9–20;

Laust Kristensen, *Fantasiens ridder. En studie i Schack Staffeldts liv og digtning* (Odense: Odense Universitetsforlag, 1993);

Steffen Hejlskov Larsen, "Vers om kærligheden læst som religiøs poesi og omvendt," in *Lyriske tilværelsesmodeller. Artikler og analyser* (Copenhagen: Borgen, 1968), pp. 146–155;

Flemming Lundgreen-Nielsen, "Sjælens natside. Det ubevidste i dansk romantik," in *Kaos og Kosmos. Studier i europæisk romantik,* edited by Hans Boll-Johansen and Lundgreen-Nielsen (Copenhagen: Museum Tusculanum, 1989), pp. 75–100;

Anne-Marie Mai, "At rime 'Erde' på 'Werde'–kvindefiguren i digte af Schack Staffeldt," in *At gå til grunde. Sider af romantikkens litteratur & tænkning,* edited by Mai and Bo Kampmann Walther (Odense: Odense Universitetsforlag, 1997), pp. 45–65;

Christian Molbech, "Digteren Adolf Vilhelm Schack Staffeldt. Et biografisk Udkast," in *Samlinger til Schack Staffeldts Levnet, fornemmelig af Digterens efterladte Haandskrifter,* 2 volumes, edited by Liebenberg (Copenhagen: Samfundet til den danske Litteraturs Fremme, 1847, 1851), I: 1–224;

Klaus P. Mortensen, "Afgrundspoeten," in *Himmelstormerne. En linje i dansk naturdigtning* (Copenhagen: Gyldendal, 1993), pp. 145–148;

Erik A. Nielsen, "Fantasibegrebet hos Schack Staffeldt," in *Den erindrende Faun. Digteren og hans fantasi,* edited by Aage Henriksen, Helge Therkildsen, and Knud Wentzel (Copenhagen: Fremad, 1968), pp. 24–51; reprinted in *Kritik,* 5 (1968): 18–45; reprinted and revised in *Lyrikere. 15 udlægninger og et digt* (Copenhagen: Forlaget Spring, 2001), pp. 75–99;

Hakon Stangerup, *Schack Staffeldt* (Copenhagen: Gyldendal, 1940);

Just Mathias Thiele, *Af mit Livs Aarbøger 1795–1826* (Copenhagen, 1873), pp. 93–99, 133–136, 144, 150;

Hans Vodskov, "Schack Staffeldts Digte udgivne af F. L. Liebenberg med en Charakteristik af Digteren ved Georg Brandes," *Nordisk Tidskrift för Vetenskap, Konst och Industri,* 6 (1883): 551–562; reprinted in *Litteraturkritik i udvalg,* 2 volumes, edited by Erik Reitzel-Nielsen (Copenhagen: Det Danske Sprog- og Litteraturselskab/C. A. Reitzel, 1992), I: 383–395;

Knud Wentzel, *Utopia. Et motiv i dansk lyrik* (Copenhagen: Gyldendal, 1990), pp. 185–190.

Papers:

The main body of Schack Staffeldt's papers is at the Danish Royal Library in Copenhagen. Other papers are in the Landesarchiv Schleswig-Holstein in Schleswig and Frederiksdal slot, Sorgenfri.

Hans Christensen Sthen

(25 November 1544 - April/May 1610)

Jens Lyster

(Translated by Inger G. Tranberg)

BOOKS: *Vita Johannis Hus* (Copenhagen, 1572)–no copy survives;

En Liden Haandbog Som indeholder . . . Øffuelser vdi Gudelighed . . . Bøner oc Loffsange (Copenhagen: Matz Vingaard, 1578);

Lyckens Hiul. En kaart Vnderuisning, om Lyckens wstadighed, oc Verdens løb (Copenhagen: Andreas Gutteruitz, 1581);

En liden Trøstscrifft. For alle Christelige Forældre, naar deris Børn bliffuer siuge, eller hensoffuer i Herren . . . (Copenhagen: Andreas Gutteruitz, 1581);

Saligheds Vey. Det er: En kaart oc Enfoldig Forklaring, Offuer den Første Kong Dauids Psalme . . . ved Spørsmaal oc Giensuar vdlagt (Copenhagen: Matz Vingaard, 1584);

Geistlig Hussraad, Det er: En Christen liden nyttelig Sermon, Predicken oc Forklaring, offuer Kong Dauids 128. Psalme, vdi huilcken hand priser oc berømmer Ecteskaffs stat (Copenhagen: Hans Stockelman, 1592);

En god forfaren Persons trohiertige Formaning oc Sendebreff. I huilcken Scrifft vnge Personer finder megen smuck Vnderuisning oc Beretning, huorledis en Suend oc Tienere skal forholde sig i sin Tieniste (Copenhagen: Hans Stockelman, 1592);

En Ligpredicken Aff den 90 Psalme . . . vdi Bare Sognekircke her i Skaane, den 16 dag Maij, Anno 1602 offuer Erlig oc Velbyrdig Fru Mette Vlffstand (Copenhagen: Henrich Waldkirch, 1603);

En liden Vandrebog: Indeholdendis atskillige smucke Bøner oc trøstelige Sange, met nogle nyttige Lifs Regle, i artige Rijm befattede (circa 1589; republished, Copenhagen: Salomon Sartor, circa 1612–1615)–no copy of the first edition is known to survive;

Udvalg af Hans Chr. Sthens Salmer og aandelige Rim, edited by C. J. Brandt (Copenhagen: Karl Schønberg, 1888);

Hans Christensen Sthenius. Af hans Vandrebog, edited by Carl S. Petersen, introduction by Hans Brix (Copenhagen: Forening for Boghaandværks smaa Bøger, 1914);

Udvalgte Salmer (Aarhus: Akademisk Boghandel, 1972);

Hans Christensen Sthens Skrifter I: En liden Vandrebog, edited by Jens Lyster, assisted by Jens Højgård (Copenhagen: DSL/C. A. Reitzel, 1994);

Hans Christensen Sthens Skrifter II: Christelige oc vdkaarne Bøner and *En Liden Haandbog,* edited by Lyster, assisted by Højgård (Copenhagen: DSL/C. A. Reitzel, 2003).

OTHER: "Kortvending. Et moralsk-allegorisk Skuespil fra Frederik den Andens Tid," edited by Sophus Laurits Henrik Christian Julius Birket Smith, in *Danske Samlinger for Historie, Topographi, Personal- og Literaturhistorie,* volume 1, edited by Smith, Christian Bruun, Oluf August Nielsen, and Anton Ludvig William Petersen (Copenhagen: Gyldendal, 1865), pp. 182–288; republished as *Kort Vending,* edited by Jens Aage Doctor (Copenhagen: Tidlig dansk dramatik, 1972);

"Hans Christensøn Sthens ordsprog," in *Danmarks gamle Ordsprog,* no. 4 edited by Niels Werner Frederiksen and John Kousgård Sørensen (Copenhagen: C. A. Reitzel, 1987), pp. 231–290.

TRANSLATIONS: Johannes Avenarius, *Christelige oc vdkaarne Bøner, for alle Stater, oc for allehaande nød oc trang i den gantske Christenhed . . . paa huer besynderlig dag vdi Vgen . . . Morgen oc Afften* (1571; republished, Copenhagen: Andreas Gutterwitz, 1577)–no copy of the first edition is known to survive;

It smuct Epithalamion (Copenhagen: Laurentz Benedicht, 1572);

Cæcilius Cyprianus, *En Predicken Cæcilij Cypriani . . . i en suar Pestelentz tid, faar 1321. Aar. Item, den 91. Dauids Psalme, met . . . Vdleggelse oc Forklaring* (Copenhagen: Andreas Gutteruitz, 1578).

Thomas Kingo is generally considered the earliest of the four most important hymn writers in Denmark: Kingo, Hans Adolph Brorson, N. F. S. Grundtvig, and

B. S. Ingemann. A century before Kingo's time, however, a teacher and clergyman lived in Helsingør and Malmø who, with his obvious poetic talents, left such a lasting legacy as a hymn writer that the quartet must be considered a quintet, with Hans Christensen Sthen in fifth place, or actually in first place, as the earliest of this distinguished group of poets. The first verses of Danish hymnody are found in Sthen's work. His morning song initiates an unusual Danish hymn tradition praising nature and birds.

Sthen's fate has been to be forgotten since some of the well-known hymns he wrote were designated as "anonymous." In Kingo's hymnal from 1699, Sthen is represented by twelve hymns, but the hymnal indicates the writer of ten of these hymns as unknown, and the other two hymns are incorrectly attributed to other writers. Not until the 1840s did two scholars identify Sthen as the writer of some well-known hymns and a dozen devotional writings. Later on, his play *Kort Vending* (Abrupt Change) surfaced and was also attributed to Sthen, as was a handwritten collection of proverbs, a collection of facetiae from *Heinrich Bebels Libri Facetiarum* (1508) and *Georg Wickrams Rollwagenbüchlein* (1555), and a collection of notes with outlines for sermons and such, all with Sthen's signature. A revival of interest in Sthen's authorship in the nineteenth century made selected writings by Sthen available, and a critical edition of his collected works will be published.

Hans Christensen Sthenius Roskildensis, as he called himself, was probably born in Roskilde and attended grammar school there. An autobiographical birthday poem indicates that he was born on 25 November 1544, lost both parents as a young man, but was supported by good friends.

Nothing is known about Sthen's years of study. He probably taught at a school in Copenhagen before he was named headmaster of the grammar school in Helsingør in 1565. The following year he exchanged the headmaster position for an appointment as curate at St. Olai Church in the same town. Simultaneously, he handled his old position as headmaster during the years 1570–1574, and, as headmaster, he had the duty every Saturday afternoon to train the pupils for evensong with the church choir. He also directed the chorus at weddings, and in that context translated in 1572 a wedding song by Nicolaus Herman into Danish. With his pupils he directed games and dramatic performances at the city hall and at the cemetery for Christmas, Shrovetide, and Whitsuntide. An anonymous play, *Kort Vending,* preserved from that time is presumed to have been written by Sthen, since it includes passages found verbatim in his educational poem on the same subject, *Lyckens Hiul. En kaart Vnderuisning, om Lyckens wstadighed,*

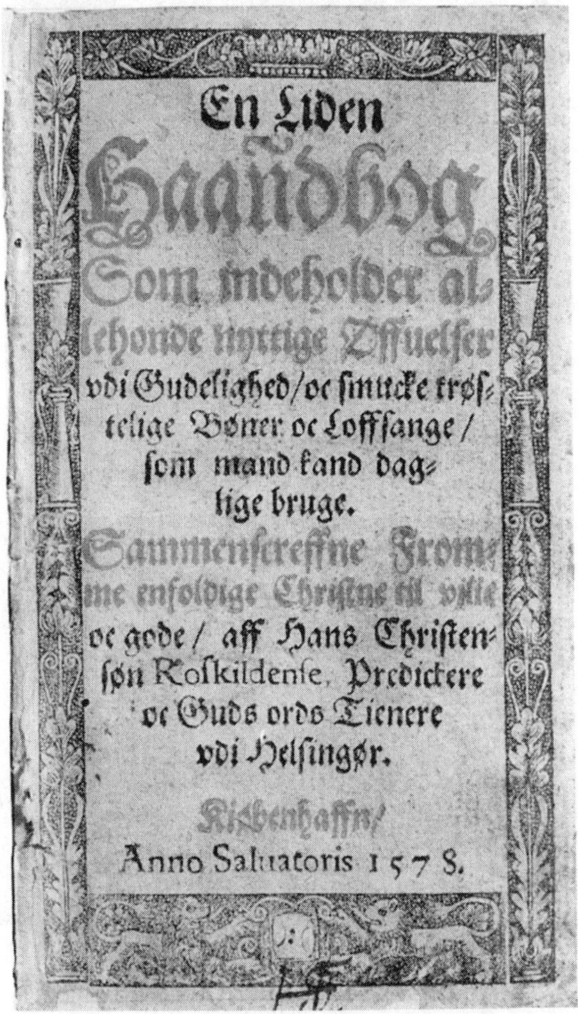

En Liden
Haandbog
Som indeholder al-
lehonde nyttige Øffuelser
vdi Gudelighed/oc smucke trøst-
telige Bøner oc Loffsange/
som mand kand dag-
lige bruge.
Sammenskreffne From-
me enfoldige Christne til villie
oc gode / aff Hans Christensøn Roskildense. Predicere
oc Guds ords Tienere
vdi Helsingør.
Kiøbenhaffn/
Anno Saluatoris 1578.

Title page for Hans Christensen Sthen's collection of prayers and hymns of thanksgiving, mostly translated from German (courtesy of the Danish Royal Library, Copenhagen)

oc Verdens løb (The Wheel of Fortune. Short Lessons about the Unsteadiness of Fortune and the Run of the World, 1581). The play adopted its main idea and central figure, Kort Vending, from Hans Sach's *Bald-anderst* (Soon Otherwise, 1534), and the main idea is developed by means of several monologues voiced by a gallery of characters who represent typical people of that period. The lost publication *Vita Johannis Hus* (On the Life of Jan Hus, 1572) may also have been a play.

Concurrent with the duties of his position, Sthen developed his talents as author, translator, and publisher of devotional books. In 1571 he made his debut with *Christelige oc vdkaarne Bøner, for alle Stater, oc for allehaande nød oc trang i den gantske Christenhed . . . paa huer besynderlig dag vdi Vgen . . . Morgen oc Afften* (Christian and Elected Prayers for All Positions of Life and for All in Need in the Whole Christianity for Every Day of the

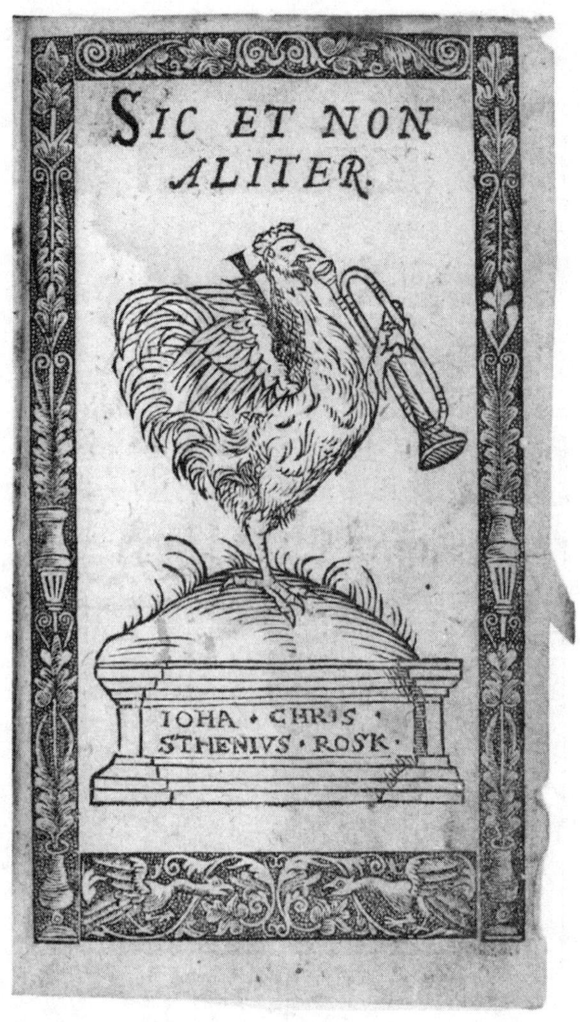

Sthen's emblem and motto, which means "Thus and not otherwise" (from Saligheds Vey, *1584; Collection of Jens Lyster)*

Week, Morning and Evening; translated as *The Enimie of Securitie,* 1579), a complete translation of Johann Habermann's (or Johannes Avenarius's) enormously popular *Christliche Gebet für alle Not und stende* (Prayers for All Needs and Stations in Life, 1565), published in a revised edition in 1567. Sthen made use of both editions. His translation became a best-seller that was reprinted up to the mid 1600s; in addition, the morning and evening prayers for each day of the week were included in other prayer books throughout the seventeenth century and were included in Kingo's hymnal as late as 1774. The framework in Avenarius's prayer book, with eight prayers for each day of the week, is based on a Jesuit model. The language of the prayers is filled with biblical allusions and quotations.

En Liden Haandbog Som indeholder . . . Øffuelser vdi Gudelighed . . . Bøner oc Loffsange (A Little Handbook Containing Exercises in Piety, Prayers, and Hymns) appeared in 1578; it consisted of prayers as well as hymns of thanksgiving, most of them translated from German, such as the still popular Christmas hymn "Nu ville wi siunge oc vere glad" (Now We Will Sing and Be Happy), based on Nicolaus Herman's "Lobt Gott jr Christen alle gleich." Several prose prayers are compiled from material from Sthen's own translation of Avenarius's work and from Nicolaus Selnecker's *Der gantze Psalter Davids ausgelegt* (The Whole Book of Psalms Interpreted, 1563–1566). Also included are casuistic instructions for *exercitia* (exercises in piety) for the daily household devotion. Sthen wished to preserve old popular piety and, by means of new interpretations, channel it into the paths of a new faith. *En Liden Haandbog* seems to have been composed of many heterogeneous parts, some of which Sthen probably tested earlier as pamphlets and broadsheet ballads, such as "En Dialogus eller Samtale imellem it Menniske oc Døden" (A Dialogue or Conversation Between a Person and Death), a longish poem of 290 doggerels, and "En trøstelig Samtale imellem Christo vor kiære Brudgom, oc en Christen Menniskes Siæl hans kiære Brud" (A Comforting Conversation Between Christ Our Dear Bridegroom and a Christian Soul, His Dear Bride).

Toward the end of 1578, a plague was the impetus for Sthen's translation of Cecil Cyprian's widely known plague sermon, *En Predicken Cæcilij Cypriani* (A Sermon by Cæcilius Cyprianus, 1578). Sthen's publication also included related topics by such German theologians as Joachim Mörlin, Johannes Gigas, Johannes Mathesius, Andreas Pouch, and Lucas Bacmeister. During the following years, the plague raged in Helsingør and claimed the lives of eight of Sthen's own children. On 9 September 1580 he erected an epitaph, which has since vanished, in memory of them in St. Olai Church. However, the moving text of the epitaph is included in his autobiographical birthday poem. The following year Sthen published–as a consolation for himself and some of his friends–*En liden Trøstscrifft. For alle Christelige Forældre, naar deris Børn bliffuer siuge, eller hensoffuer i Herren . . .* (A Little Consolation for All Christian Parents, When Their Children Are Ill or Pass Away to The Lord, 1581); its essence was *Trost der Eltern* (The Parents' Consolation) by Georg Walther, the vicar of Halle in Sachsen. However, Sthen expanded upon the German model, so that his text appears as a personal and stirring expression of his own living spiritual message. The didactic poem *Lyckens Hiul* is also dated from the same year; it elaborates on the theme of the inconstancy of happiness exemplified by figures from the Bible and Classical antiquity.

In 1581 Sthen also was granted a master's degree by the University of Copenhagen, a testament to the respect for his scholarship, preaching, and industrious productivity in publication. Another expression of respect occurred when in April 1583 the mayor of Malmø traveled to Helsingør to appoint Sthen to the position of vicar of St. Petri Church in Malmø and to the associated position as rural dean for the Oxie district in Scania. This sizable income in addition to his publishing income made possible Sthen's establishing a tasteful and well-appointed home with an impressive library.

The year after his appointment to the position in Malmø, Sthen published *Saligheds Vey. Det er: En kaart oc Enfoldig Forklaring, Offuer den Første Kong Dauids Psalme . . . ved Spørsmaal oc Giensuar vdlagt* (The Way to Salvation. That Is: A Short and Simple Explanation of the First Psalm . . . with Questions and Answers, 1584). It includes broad attacks on the Roman Pope and Antichrist, and especially on the "ny, skadelige, forgiftige jesuitiske Ukrudt" (new, damaging, poisonous Jesuit weed) that slyly works toward the seduction of youth. Sthen was inspired by a similar work by Josua Opitius, known as a fearless preacher for the large evangelical parish in Vienna during the years 1577–1581. The polemic, anti-Jesuit tone in *Saligheds Vey* is surprising, considering that a few years later Sthen allowed his sons Hans, Frans, and Gabriel to study with the Jesuits in Braunsberg, and he himself consorted with the Jesuit-minded headmaster at the grammar school in Malmø.

En liden Vandrebog: Indeholdendis atskillige smucke Bøner oc trøstelige Sange, met nogle nyttige Lifs Regle, i artige Rijm befattede (A Little Traveling Book, with Prayers and Songs for Consolation, Useful Rules of Conduct, in Pretty Rhymes) was probably published in early 1589. This unimpressive-looking book served to edify and instruct travelers for more than a hundred years and includes the majority of Sthen's hymns. The tone in these hymns is muted. They are not presented as hymns for church use but as prayers, invocations, confessions, grievances, Christian songs, and songs of thanksgiving. The prayers compensate for what is missing in the oratorical effect of the hymns with intimacy and a compassionate understanding of the debasements and degradations of human life. Sthen writes about and for the fearful human being. The only way in this world to get help, he says, is through a relationship with God and faith in Christ, the only one who can free mankind from fear and suffering; the phrases "Du er min Trøst," "Du kan mig bedst husvale," and "Du vil mig aldrig undfalde" ("You are my comfort," "You can best console me," and "You never will fail me") are repeated variously again and again, and they attest to the author's tried and tested faith in God.

In terms of form, these spiritual songs are also interesting because in several instances they borrow meter and melodies from secular songs, an aspect that apparently provoked contemporary criticism. In terms of content, some of them are so close to their secular models that they should be considered Christian counterparts to the love songs of that period. This assessment applies to the still popular "Guds Naade jeg altid prise vil" (God's Grace I Will Always Praise) and "Et trofast Hierte, O Herre min" (A Loyal Heart, O My Lord). Sthen himself calls them "kristeligt forandrede Viser" (songs revised in a Christian manner). Examples also exist of songs deliberately written as counterparts to contemporary religious songs–for instance, the song about the heavenly trial of Adam and Eve, based on a legend from the Middle Ages about God's four daughters–Justitia, Veritas, Pax, and Misericordia–who act as prosecutors and defenders of Adam and Eve at the divine court. This legend had inspired an anonymous poet in 1583 to write a song to which Sthen then produced a counterpart. This practice of writing counterparts throws light on Sthen's personal emblem, the rooster, which represents Sthen as the author of counterparts, who with his motto "Sic et non aliter" (Thus and not otherwise) wants to put theological and literary mediocrity in its place. Of especially high quality is the morning song "Den mørcke Nat forgangen er" (The Dark Night Has Passed), modeled on the medieval Christian day song. Sthen expands the morning song to a Creation song (with one stanza for each of the six days of Creation). For the corresponding evening–or night–song "Den liuse Dag forgangen er" (The Light Day Is Passed), Sthen employs a folk ballad as the melody.

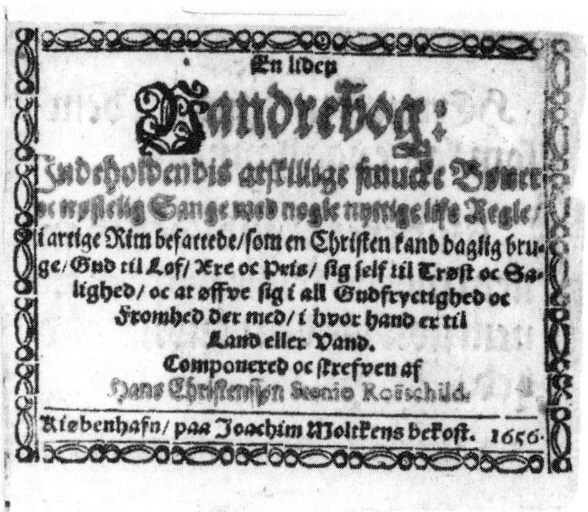

En liden
Vandrebog:
Indeholdendis atskillige smucke Bøner
oc trøstelig Sange med nogle nyttige lifs Regle/
i artige Rim befattede/som en Christen kand daglig bru-
ge/Gud til Lof/ Ære oc Pris/ sig self til Trøst oc Sa-
lighed/ oc at øffve sig i all Gudfryctighed oc
Fromhed der med/ i hvor hand er til
Land eller Vand.
Componered oc skrefven af
Hans Christensøn Stenio Roeschild.
Kiøbenhafn/ paa Joachim Moltkens bekost. 1656.

Title page for a late edition of Sthen's collection of hymns for travelers. No copy of the first edition (1589) is known to exist (Lund University Libraries).

A couple of Sthen's hymns are characterized by the eschatological notions of the last days of man and

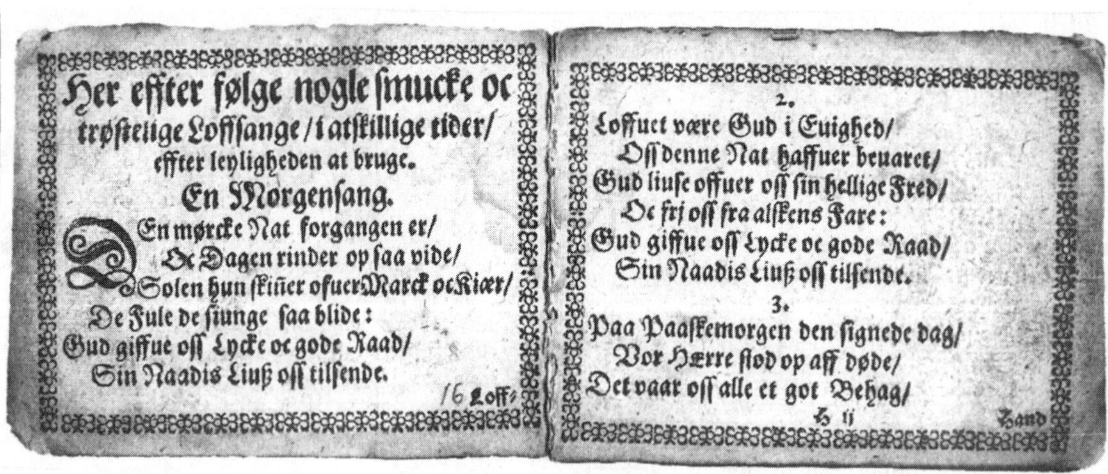

Her effter følge nogle smucke oc trøsteilige Loffsange / i atskillige tider / effter leyligheden at bruge.

En Morgensang.

Den mørcke Nat forgangen er /
Oc Dagen rinder op saa vide /
Solen hun skiñer ofuer Marck oc Kiær /
De Fule de siunge saa blide:
Gud giffue oss Lycke oc gode Raad /
Sin Naadis Liuß oss tilsende.
16 Loff-

2.
Loffuet være Gud i Euighed /
Oss denne Nat haffuer beuaret /
Gud liuse offuer oss sin hellige Fred /
Oc fri oss fra alskens Fare:
Gud giffue oss Lycke oc gode Raad /
Sin Naadis Liuß oss tilsende.

3.
Paa Paaskemorgen den signede dag /
Vor Herre stod op aff døde /
Det vaar oss alle et got Behag /
A ij Hand

Pages with the opening of the song "Den mørcke Nat forgangen er" (The Dark Night Has Passed) in the earliest surviving, fragmentary edition (circa 1612 to 1615) of En liden Vandrebog *(courtesy of the Danish Royal Library, Copenhagen)*

the imminent Day of Judgment that gave many clergymen–but not Sthen–the opportunity for moralizing, fire-and-brimstone sermons. A mediocre ballad published as a broadsheet in 1587 is typical of this tendency and became the following year, with its theologically problematic content, but also with its inciting meter and tune, Sthen's springboard for a counterpart, his masterpiece "Herre Jesu Christ, min Frelser du est" (Lord Jesus Christ, You Are My Savior) with the heading "En Christelig Supplicatz til Guds Søn" (A Christian Petition to God's Son). Whereas the moralistic precursor anticipates Christ's coming as the judge of a sinful world, Sthen's hymn expresses a longing for Christ as the Savior. He will save the world from destruction and from the catastrophes to come in the great year 1588, which according to a widespread prophecy by Johannes Regiomontanus, was to be *annus horribilis* (a horrible year). Instead, Sthen's hymn anticipates the year 1588 to be annus mirabilis, in which Christ becomes the only hope for a sinful world. That the notion of annus mirabilis plays a role in this hymn can be seen from its acrostic, since the first letters in each of the eight stanzas form the words HANS ANNO, meaning Hans (the author's first name) in the year (that is, the proverbial year 1588). Another reason for writing a prayer with the character of spiritual testament in the year 1588 might be that Sthen–who was born in 1544 and seemed to consider the number forty-four as his fateful number–celebrated his forty-fourth birthday in 1588. This birthday was the occasion for his autobiographical birthday poem. The macrocosm and personal microcosm are combined in this acrostic hymn written from the perspective of a rumbling volcano with the prospect of a coming Day of Judgment; therefore, it has served as a hymn for times of crisis from the beginning and later as a death preparation and funeral hymn; it has continued to serve the Danish people in times of crisis.

Another couple of short works from the succeeding years are preserved. In 1592 Sthen published *Geistlig Hussraad, Det er: En Christen liden nyttelig Sermon, Predicken oc Forklaring, offuer Kong Dauids 128. Psalme, vdi huilcken hand priser oc berømmer Ecteskaffs stat* (Spiritual Household Advice, That Is, a Little, Useful Christian Sermon and Explanation Regarding the 128th Psalm, in Praise of Marriage), an interpretation of David's Psalm 128, which is considered a wedding song in praise of matrimony. With *Geistlig Husraad* Sthen published *En god forfaren Persons trohiertige Formaning oc Sendebreff. I huilcken Scrifft vnge Personer finder megen smuck Vnderuisning oc Beretning, huorledis en Suend oc Tienere skal forholde sig i sin Tieniste* (A Good Experienced Person's Ingenuous Admonition and Letter, Where Young Persons Find Very Useful Education, How a Servant Shall Serve), a textbook for servants. Both writings are based on similar German works; the first one was written by the superintendent in Sorau, Petrus Streuber, while the other one is anonymous and found in a Low German publication from Greifswald in 1594. Sthen's publication was produced as a welcome greeting and New Year's present to the new lord at Malmøhus, Hak Holgersen Ulfstand, hero from the war with Sweden in 1563–1570 and now the chief steward for the young Christian IV.

While Sthen apparently had a friendly relationship with several families of the nobility on the estates in Scania, over the years a tense and at times hostile relationship developed between the zealous dean and the old established families of Malmø. In 1600 the conflict culminated in a hypocritical petition from the municipality of Malmø to the Danish king asking him to grant the senile parish vicar a newly vacant position as vicar outside of Malmø. The petition was written without Sthen's knowledge and did not result in the desired transfer, although the unsuspecting king approved the petition. Sthen was fifty-five years old but not weakened by age; when his first wife died two years later, he married the daughter of a respected canon in Lund. With her he had five children. Not until after the death of his second wife in 1607 did he apply for retirement, stating that he had now served school and church during all of forty-four years. That same year he married again, this time a young wife who gave him a child, but this third marriage also provoked the sons from his first marriage and relatives of the children of his second marriage to assert rights of inheritance. Sthen's old enemies at the municipality added fuel to the flames and now exacted a sweet revenge with the law on their side. The last years of Sthen's life were an Armageddon of repeated estate evaluations, exasperated family conflicts, writs of summons, charges of tax evasion, and spiteful defamations. During these humiliations, the poet and clergyman died in April or May 1610. He was buried in front of the altar in St. Petri Church, but his tombstone has not been found.

Biographies:

C. J. Brandt, *Salmedigteren Hans Christensen Sthen* (Copenhagen: Karl Schønberg, 1888);

Lauritz Weibull, "Anteckningar om salmförfattaren Hans Christensen Sthen i Malmö," in *Skånska Samlingar utgifna af Martin Weibull* (Lund, 1897), pp. 32–52;

Gunnar Carlquist, *Lunds Stifts Herdaminne från Reformationen till nyaste Tid,* Series 2, 2 (Lund, 1948), pp. 23–32, 393;

Jens Lyster, "Digteren og udgiveren," in *Hans Christensen Sthens skrifter: I: En liden Vandrebog* (Copenhagen: DSL/C. A. Reitzel, 1994), pp. 179–189.

References:

Carl J. Brandt and Ludvig Helweg, *Den Danske Psalmedigtning,* 2 volumes (Copenhagen, 1846), I: 171–204;

V. E. Brummer, "En liden Vandre-Bog," *Hymnologiske Meddelelser,* 22 (1993): 219–229;

Henry Bruun, "Hans Thomissøns og Sthens dagviseform," in *Den middelalderlige Dagvise,* Studier fra Sprog- og Oldtidsforskning, edited by Det Filologisk-historiske Samfund, 257 (Copenhagen: Gad, 1965), pp. 51–63;

S. Cawallin, *Lunds Stifts Herdaminne, efter mestadels otryckta källor utarbetadt,* volume 2 (Lund, 1855), pp. 5–7;

Georg Christensen, "Hans Christensen Sthens Salmer og Folkeviserne," in *Festskrift til H. F. Feilberg fra nordiske Sprog- og Folkemindeforskere* (Stockholm, Copenhagen & Kristiania, 1911), pp. 101–112;

Ernst Frandsen, *Hans Christensen Sthen. Studier i det 16. Aarhundredes danske Litteratur,* Acta Jutlandica, 4, no. 1 (Århus: Universitetsforlaget, 1932);

Krister Gierow, *Den evangeliska Bönelitteraturen i Danmark 1526–1575* (Lund: C. W. K. Gleerup, 1948), pp. 361–373;

Henrik Glahn, "Lidt mere om Hans Christensen Sthens melodibrug," *Musik & Forskning,* 6 (1980): 129–141;

Glahn, "Om Hans Christensen Sthens brudesang som musikalsk kilde," *Hymnologiske Meddelelser,* 11 (1982): 105–110;

Glahn, "Om melodien til 'Du, Herre Krist,'" *Dansk Kirkesangs Årsskrift, 1977–1978* (1980): 42–46;

P. V. Jacobsen, "Helsingørs Kæmnerregnskab for Aaret 1577 med Bemærkninger," *Danske Magazin,* 3, no. 2 (1845): 177–229;

Jacobsen, "Om Skuespil og Skuespil-Forfattere i Danmark i det 16de Aarhundrede," *Historisk Tidsskrift,* 5 (1844): 502–514, 529–534;

Chr. Ludwigs, "Hr. Hans' Navnesalme," *Salme og Sang* (Copenhagen: O. Lohse, 1915), pp. 23–30;

Jens Lyster, "Avenarii bønner i Sthens oversættelse. På sporet af den danske bønnebogs 1. udgave 1571," in *Kirkehistoriske Samlinger* (Copenhagen: Akademisk Forlag, 1976), pp. 67–83;

Lyster, "Forlæg og originalitet i Hans Christensen Sthens Trøsteskrift 1581 og Sendebrev 1592," in *Kirkehistoriske Samlinger* (Copenhagen: Gad, 1969), pp. 78–125;

Lyster, "Hans Christensen Sthen," *Arkiv for Dansk Litteratur* <www.adl.dk>;

Lyster, "Hans Christensen Sthen 1544–1994," in *Vartovbogen* (Copenhagen: Kirkeligt Samfund, 1994), pp. 56–73;

Lyster, "Hans Christensen Sthen som kontrafakturdigter," *Dansk Kirkesangs Årsskrift* (1997): 113–127;

Lyster, "Hvem har oversat 'Jeg vil din pris udsjunge'?" *Hymnologiske Meddelelser,* 22 (1993): 193–209;

Lyster, "It smuct Epithalamion fra 1572. Hans Christensen Sthens debut som salmedigter," *Hymnologiske Meddelelser,* 11 (1982): 90–104;

Lyster, "Johannes Avenarius, Johannes Mathesius und Nicolaus Selnecker als Vorbilder für Hans Christensen Sthen. Vortrag an der Jahrestagung der Johannes Mathesius Gesellschaft in Beratzhausen 1999," *Erbe und Auftrag der Reformation in den böhmischen Ländern,* 35–38 (2000): 36–49;

Lyster, "Malmøs betydning for den tidlige lutherske salmedigtning," in *Elbogen,* 63 (Malmö: Malmö Fornminnesförenings Årsskrift, 1995), pp. 79–106;

Lyster, "Om Sthens Vandrebog. Festtale i Sct. Olai på Sthens 450 års fødselsdag," *Hymnologiske Meddelelser,* 24 (1995): 54–65;

Lyster, "Skillingsviser som kilder til Sthens salmer, og Sthens egne salmer som skillingsviser," *Hymnologiske Meddelelser,* 30 (2001): 229–260;

Lyster, "Sthen og dagvisen," in *Hans Christensen Sthens Skrifter I: En liden Vandrebog* (Copenhagen: DSL/C. A. Reitzel, 1994), pp. 219–231;

Lyster, "Sthens gådefulde navnesalme. Om Du Herre Krist, dens mærkelige akrostikon og det forunderlige år, hvis lige ikke har været," *Hymnologiske Meddelelser,* 9 (1980): 71–146;

Lyster, "Synd og nåde i to salmer af Sthen. 'Jeg vil din pris udsjunge' og 'Guds nåde højt jeg prise vil,'" *Hymnologiske Meddelelser,* 26 (1997): 21–29;

Lyster, "To gange Johannes til Sct. Olai [about the hymn 'O Jesus, livsens Herre']," in *Kunsten og Kaldet. Festskrift til biskop Johannes Johansen 4. marts 1990,* edited by Inge and Søren Giversen (Herning: Poul Kristensen, 1990), pp. 17–38;

Anders Malling, "Sthens Vandrebog," *Dansk Teologisk Tidsskrift,* 15 (1952): 147–158;

Nils Schiørring, *Det 16. og 17. århundredes verdslige danske visesang,* 2 volumes (Copenhagen: Thaning & Appel, 1950), pp. 31–37;

J. N. Skaar, *Norsk Salmehistorie,* volume 1 (Bergen, 1879), pp. 232–235;

Christian Thodberg, "Om 'Du, Herre Krist,' En kendt salme af Hans Christensen Sthen i en ny bearbejdelse," *Dansk Kirkesangs Årsskrift 1977–1978* (1980): 35–41;

O. Walde, "Psalmdiktaren Hans Christensen Sthen och hans Vandrebog," *Nordisk tidskrift för bok- och biblioteksväsen,* 25 (1938): 65–72.

Papers:

Hans Christensen Sthen's manuscripts are at the Danish Royal Library, Copenhagen; Lund University Libraries, Stockholm, Sweden; and the Stralsund City Library.

Ambrosius Stub

(circa May 1705 – 15 July 1758)

Sven Hakon Rossel
University of Vienna

BOOKS: *Da hans Kongel. Majest. Vor Allernaadigste Arve Konge og Herre Den stormægtigste Monarch Kong Friderich den Femte Hans Høye Fødsels-Dag d: 31 Martii 1757 Blev celebrered med Oration og Music paa det Kongelige Gymnasio udi Odense* (Odense: Printed by Peter Wilhelm Brandt, 1757);

Arier og andre Poetiske Stykker af Ambrosius Stub, edited by Thomas Severin Heiberg (Copenhagen: Printed by H. J. Graae, 1771; revised and enlarged by Christian Stub, Odense: Printed by Kgl. Privil. Adresse-Contoirs Bogtrykkerie, 1780).

Editions and Collections: *Ambrosius Stubs samlede Digte, Tredie Udgave* (the 1773–1777 edition is considered the second edition), 2 volumes, edited and enlarged, with an introduction and notes by Frederik Barfod (Copenhagen: Samfundet til den danske Litteraturs Fremme, 1848, 1852); revised and enlarged as *Samlede Digte af Ambrosus Stub. Fjærde Udgave* (Copenhagen: Gad, 1878);

Udvalgte Digte, edited, with introduction and notes, by H. Trier (Copenhagen: Gyldendal, 1912);

Digte i Udvalg, edited by Alexander Schumacher (Copenhagen: Andr. Fred. Høst, 1918);

Digte, edited by Kjeld Elfelt, illustrated by Povl Christensen (Copenhagen: J. H. Schultz, 1941; republished, 1943);

Hvad vindes paa Verdens vidtløftige Hav og andre Digte (Copenhagen: Foreningen for Boghaandværk, 1944);

Hvad vindes paa Verdens vidtløftige Hav og andre Digte, edited by Martin N. Hansen and Kaj Hasselmann, illustrated by Axel Nygaard (Odense: Foreningen for Boghaandværk, 1947);

Samlede Digte, edited by Henning Fonsmark (Copenhagen: Hans Reitzel, 1961);

Ambrosius Stubs Digte, 2 volumes, edited, with an introduction and notes, by Erik Kroman (Copenhagen: Rosenkilde & Bagger, 1972);

Digte, edited by Asger Schnack (Copenhagen: Hans Reitzel, 1987).

OTHER: *Arier og Sange. Første Bind. Bestaaende af et par Hundrede Sange,* edited by Thomas Severin Heiberg (Copenhagen: Printed by H. J. Graae, 1773)–includes twenty-five poems by Stub;

Arier og Sange. Anden Deel. Bestaaende af to Hundrede og Firsindstyve Stykker, edited by Heiberg (Copenhagen: Printed by H. J. Graae, 1777)–includes eight poems by Stub;

Anhang til Ambrosii Stubs Poetiske Tanker, edited by Christian Stub (Odense: Printed by Kgl. Privil. Adresse-Contoirs Bogtrykkerie, 1782).

Danish literature around the mid 1750s is characterized by two currents that ran parallel to each other throughout a major part of the century. The first current is represented by rationalistic- and Classicist-oriented writers, such as Ludvig Holberg, most of them prose writers and true adherents of European Enlightenment. The second current is represented by more-emotional and religiously oriented writers, mostly lyrical poets, such as hymn writers Hans Adolph Brorson and Ambrosius Stub. Through their deep-felt Christianity these poets in many ways can be regarded as successors of the preceding German-oriented Baroque literature; through their refined and elegant style, however, they are also heralds of the more sentimental trends of around 1800 and the succeeding Romanticism.

Ambrosius Christoffersen Stub was born in 1705 in the village of Gummerup on the island of Fyn. His exact birth date is not known, but he was baptized on 17 May. His father was a tenant crofter and tailor, Christoffer Pedersen Stub, and his mother was Christense Ibsdatter. Stub is hardly mentioned in contemporary sources; until Frederik Barfod published his two-volume edition of Stub's poetry with an extensive introduction in 1848 and 1852, little was known about Stub's life. No portrait of him exists. The first editor of his poetry, Thomas Severin Heiberg (1771), mentions Stub's flighty nature, sharp tongue and quick wit, and predilection for drinking and gambling. This characterization may well be accurate, but it does not tell the

Monument marking Ambrosius Stub's birthplace in the village of Gummerup on the island of Fyn (courtesy of the Danish Royal Library, Copenhagen)

whole truth about Stub as a person and almost nothing about him as a poet. Heiberg's characterization, nevertheless, nurtured the Romantic myth about the poverty-stricken poet who lived a short and miserable life as an undisciplined and semiwretched bohemian.

Stub's father was highly respected and worked at the surrounding manor houses, whose residents showed great concern for his four children; Stub's older brother, Morten, became a leaseholder and a bailiff, and his sister, Karen, married a clergyman in the neighboring parish of Verninge. Stub's godmother was Maria Dorthea Stockfleth of Brahesholm Manor, in honor of whose deceased father Stub received his unusual first name. As a child, Stub felt at ease among the landed gentry, and he formed a close friendship with the son of his godmother, Christian Stockfleth, who in 1744 became governor of Trondheim in Norway, an appointment that Stub celebrated with a bombastic alexandrine poem. Until his death in 1750 Stockfleth was Stub's protector. In these aristocratic surroundings, Stub received a foretaste of a refined and elegant life enriched with poetry, music, and dance, and he also learned to play the piano.

In 1725 Stub passed his university entrance examinations at the grammar school of Odense, the principal town on Fyn. He spent the next ten years at the University of Copenhagen toying with the idea of studying theology without ever passing any examinations. Instead, he took an active share in the social and artistic life of the capital, found benefactors, and began to write poetry. His drinking songs, in particular, became popular, but the major part of his love poetry is also from this period, and he became a well-known and admired convivial and literary figure. For a time he worked as a secretary for high-ranking officer and civil servant Poul Vendelbo Løvenørn, whom Stub considered one of his protectors and at whose death in 1740 wrote a stately commemorative poem.

In 1734 Stub met Mette Cathrine Schousboe, a clergyman's eighteen-year-old daughter, at his sister's home in Verninge. Several of his poems from this time were written for her. Stub and Schousboe married in 1735 and moved to a farm in Langsted, near Verninge, that Mette had bought with an inheritance. Stub knew nothing about agriculture, however, and in 1738 they had to leave the farm. They moved to the town of Fåborg, where Stub's sister-in-law lived. To support his family, which grew to include five children, Stub served as a secretary to Christian Stockfleth at the manor house Brahesholm. The pay was low, however, and Stub became involved in his master's extensive smuggling activities from Germany to Denmark via the island of Ærø. Stub frequently traveled on business to Ærø, and well into the second half of the twentieth century anecdotes about his long and bibulous visits survived in popular tradition.

Stub applied for a position as deacon but was turned down. In the summer of 1741 he was appointed personal secretary to Lieutenant Colonel and Groom in Waiting Niels Juel at Valdemar Castle on the island of Tåsinge. Stub earned good money at Valdemar Castle, but he suffered from being separated from his family. He quit after half a year and was reunited with his family in Odense. Considered so poor by the authorities that he was exempt from taxation, he probably eked out a living from clerical work and the shady practice of law. As in Copenhagen, however, he was also a welcome guest in the wealthy bourgeois and aristocratic circles. In them, as well as at the manor houses in the countryside, he entertained with his sparkling wit and his musical and poetic improvisations.

But at home Stub's family had to live in two miserable rooms, and three of the children died quite young. In 1747 Stub's wife died at thirty-one, and the two surviving children were placed with relatives. Stub again became Juel's secretary, librarian, and bookkeeper. His drinking got out of control, and his life became even more irregular. Nevertheless, he was rather productive as a poet. His only pronounced love poem, "Ey saa hvi tripper du saa fast" (Oh, Why Do You Move So Fast), was written at this time and is regarded as evidence of a relationship with a maid at the castle. After a child was born, Stub was dismissed from his post. In the fall of 1752 he moved to the cathedral town of Ribe on the southwest coast of Jutland, where several of his former fellow students lived. Their admiration for Stub the poet was still alive, and in 1754 they secured him a job as schoolteacher for the town's wealthier children. The position enabled him to socialize on equal terms even with the most prominent townsmen. The other teachers complained, however, and after two years Stub had to give up this position as well. Nevertheless, the years before his death on 15 July 1758 were productive, and the major part of his religious poetry, which makes up about one-third of his entire production, was written during this period. In spite of his poverty–at his death the value of his estate amounted to 13 Rigsdaler–all of these texts express an optimistic belief that God in the final account will let "hans Vinter blive til en Vaar" (his winter turn into spring).

Stub himself never published a book; in fact, only six of his poems were printed in his own lifetime. Probably, he did not even possess copies of his own poems, but shortly after his death, a systematic collection began. Throughout the years, several of Stub's poems were recorded in manuscripts that also included texts by others–small handwritten booklets, of which one (located at the Danish Royal Library in Copenhagen) includes twenty-four poems; another (at Ribe Cathedral School Library), seventeen. In addition, several texts can be found printed in many poetry collections from the second half of the eighteenth century. A systematic collection of Stub's poems was begun by Thomas Severin Heiberg, who in 1771 published *Arier og andre Poetiske Stykker af Ambrosius Stub* (Arias and Other Lyrical Pieces by Ambrosius Stub), which made the poet broadly known by the public. This edition prompted Stub's son, Christian, to search for poems that had not yet been published. In 1780, he republished Heiberg's edition from 1771 and added twenty-five new texts, most of them previously unpublished, the major part of which he found in his father's estate. Christian Stub's edition must have been a success. Two years later, in 1782, *Anhang til Ambrosii Stubs Poetiske Tanker* (Supplement to Ambrosius Stub's Lyrical Thoughts) was published in Odense by the same printer. Undoubtedly, Christian Stub discovered most of his new material at Valdemar Castle. Later, a few new texts were found, and the entire corpus was published in 1972 in a definitive, scholarly, and annotated two-volume edition.

Stub wrote in several lyrical genres. He employed both the richly embellished occasional and commemorative poem of the seventeenth century and, above all, the elegant and singable rococo aria modeled after contemporary German texts as they were composed, for example, by Johann Christian Günther and, particularly, by Johann Sigismund Scholze, who, under the pseudonym Sperontes, published the collection *Singende Muse an der Pleiße* (1736) with convivial and cheerful songs; it gained enormous popularity. Like Günther, Stub excelled in genres ranging from religious arias and philosophical poems to drinking songs and capricious impromptu poems, often in epigrammatic form, and, finally, he composed the first actual nature poem of Danish literature, which, more than any of his other texts, points ahead toward Romanticism.

The most traditional of Stub's poems are his occasional verses, whether private, such as what is probably the oldest text by him, from 1733, "Brude-Vers til Msr. Johan Klugh og Jfr. Johanne Ehrenreich" (Wedding Poem for Mr. Johan Klugh and Miss Johanne Ehrenreich), or written for one of his many benefactors, such as his long poem on the occasion of Løvenørn's funeral in 1740, "Man har for nylig hørt Kanoners hule Torden" (Recently One Has Heard the Hollow Thunder of Cannons). A majority of these poems are written in the old-fashioned alexandrine meter and composed in the embellished, rhetorical tradition of Baroque literature and in no way, apart from displaying Stub's unusual metrical skills, artistically remarkable.

Of much greater value are Stub's philosophical poems. Among the earliest is the programmatic aria "Et Roligt Sinds fornøyelige Tilstand" (The Pleasant Condition of a Carefree Mind) with the opening lines: "Jeg lever jevnt fornøyet foruden stoere Ting, / Min Foed er Ubemøyet og frie for høye Spring" (I live quite contentedly without great things, / My foot is untroubled and without high jumps). In this poem, as everywhere in his poetry, Stub condemns vice and praises moderation and frugality, often with a touch of humor: "Jeg drikker tynd Caffe, / Frimodig alle Dage" (I drink thin coffee / Carefree every day). Nevertheless, Stub is able to endow this rather pedestrian philosophy of life–a frequent word in his vocabulary is "Dyden" (Virtue)–with artistic expressiveness by raising the contrast between unpretentiousness and splendor onto a symbolic and metaphysical level, as in "Skal Dahlens Lilie af Foragt, / Ey agtes Rosen liig?" (Why shall the lily of the valley through scorn / Not be regarded as equal to the rose?), a poem that concludes with the stern warning: "Din Herlighed omvexles, naar / Du lægges i din Grav"

Valdemar Castle on the island of Tåsinge, where Stub was employed on two occasions in the 1740s as secretary to Lieutenant Colonel and Groom in Waiting Niels Juel (courtesy of the Danish Royal Library, Copenhagen)

(Your splendor will change / When you are put to your grave).

In the poems "See Skiønhed er en Skat" (Look, Beauty Is a Treasure) and "Jeg har kun Dyden kiær" (I Only Love Virtue), beauty and passion, respectively, are characteristically rejected. This attitude did not prevent Stub from writing several love poems to his wife, but they are all strangely devoid of erotic feelings as, for example, the exquisite aria "Du deylig Rosen-Knop" (You Beautiful Rosebud), in which the beautiful young woman is warned that, like the rose, she, too, will wither and die. Only in the alluring "Ey saa hvi tripper du saa fast" does he express passion. The obligatory reference to transitoriness is only used in a crafty way to encourage the young but prudish woman to "Elsk! Elsk! Det er den rette Tiid" (Love! Love! This is the right moment).

Almost totally absent in Stub's poetry–and in this respect he is no different from other Danish poets of the time–are nature and life in nature. One noteworthy exception is the aria "Den kiedsom Vinter gik sin gang" (The Dismal Winter Has Passed). Remarkable in this poem is the way in which Stub, during a walk away from the dismal city, uses vivid imagery to make his reader see how Spring arrives–how the birds build their nests, the lambs frolic in the meadow, and the fish scurry about in the lake. In describing Spring's awakening, Stub also succeeds in merging nature with the human world, as in the lines "Ach see hvor pyntet Solen gaaer / Med lange Straaler i sit Haar" (Oh, look how dressed up the sun moves / with long beams in its hair), and finally, he lets his aria conclude in a praise of divine Providence.

On the other hand, in a series of drinking songs, Stub does not conceal his preference for alcohol. But in these songs as well he advocates a certain degree of moderation, glorifying animated intoxication rather than drinking oneself into a stupor. In this respect, the lines from the poem "Er nogen, jeg er glæde rig" (Is there Anyone Happier than Me) are almost programmatic: "Der ligger hand, jeg staaer, mig fryder Viin og Noder, / Jeg har toe Guders Gunst, men ingen Griis til Broder" (There he lies, while I stand, I enjoy wine and music, / I possess the favor of two gods, but have no pig as my brother). In all situations, Stub remains the rococo cavalier, and ease and elegance characterize his many impromptus and epigrams, which were created on the spot on festive occasions or when he met people.

Among these texts one finds Stub's self-assured statement about his importance as a poet as he counters the reproach of others for being too merry: "Jeg spiller, synger, dandser, gaaer; / Saa tit jeg det i Sinde faaer" (I play, sing, dance, walk; / as often as I like).

Almost everywhere in Stub's poetry is present a religious note that is rooted in his firm belief in Providence, a belief he shares with the other great religious poet of the time, Hans Adolph Brorson, who then was bishop in Ribe. Brorson was, in fact, Stub's next-door neighbor, but whether or not they knew each other is unknown. Together they share a fervent piety, which, in Stub's case, is totally devoid of the sentimentality that marks so much of Pietistic hymn writing. Remarkable are Stub's seven poems titled "Christi syv Ord paa Korset" (The Seven Words of Christ on the Cross) as well as a series of arias based on the contrasts between sin and grace, damnation and redemption. An expansion of the human perspective toward the universe characterizes the aria "Jeg seer dit Konstverk store Gud" (I See Your Work of Art, Great God), and the combination of such an infinite dimension with pious intimacy is precisely what characterizes Stub's religious masterpieces, reaching perfection in stanza 1 of the aria "Livet som en Seylads" (Life as Navigation):

Hvad vindes ved Verdens vidtløftige Hav!
O tusinde Farer i skummende Trav;
Man veed kuns to Havne,
Bekiendte af Navne,
Den eene vor Vugge, den anden vor Grav.

(What can be won on the world's vast ocean!
Oh thousands of dangers in the foaming waters;
we only know two ports,
by their names,
One is our cradle, the other our grave.)

By frequently employing Baroque metaphors in his religious poetry, Stub continued the rich tradition of earlier Danish hymn writing. On the other hand, the lucid and logical composition of his texts and their linguistic vigor and musicality are truly remarkable features that raise him above most of the rather conventional poets of eighteenth-century Denmark. Above all, his unconventional handling of the Danish language is the reason Stub is remembered today.

Biographies:

Thomas A. Müller, "Noget om Ambrosius Stubs Liv og Personlighed," in *Festskrift til Kristian Erslev,* edited by Poul Nørlund (Copenhagen: Den danske historiske Forening, 1927), pp. 409–448; also in his *Afhandlinger i Udvalg* (Copenhagen: Gyldendal, 1942), pp. 176–210;

Hans Brix, *Ambrosius Stub* (Copenhagen: Gyldendal, 1960);

Erik Kroman, *Ambrosius Stub og hans ærøske Forbindelser* (Copenhagen: Munksgaard, 1967).

References:

Hans Brix, "Ambrosius Stub," in his *Danmarks Digtere* (Copenhagen: Aschehoug, 1925), pp. 105–111;

Brix, "Til Ambrosius Stub," in his *Analyser og Problemer* (Copenhagen: Gyldendal, 1933), I: 281–293;

Thomas A. Müller, "Noget om Ambrosius Stubs Liv og Digtning," *Tilskueren,* 1 (1934): 73–95; also in his *Afhandlinger i Udvalg* (Copenhagen: Gyldendal, 1942), pp. 211–225;

Sven H. Rossel, "Ambrosius Stub," *Dictionary of Scandinavian Literature,* edited by Virpi Zuck and others (New York, Westport, Conn. & London: Greenwood Press, 1990), pp. 588–589;

Erik Sønderholm, "Stub og Ewald. Et par nyfundne småtekster," *Danske Studier* (1976): 114–118.

Papers:

Most of Ambrosius Stub's manuscripts are at the Danish Royal Library in Copenhagen. A few manuscripts and letters are at Universitetsbiblioteket (University Library), Oslo; Rigsarkivet (National Archives), Copenhagen; Landsarkivet (Regional Archives), Odense and Viborg; Ribe Katedralskoles Bibliotek (Ribe Cathedral School Library), Ribe; and in private ownership.

Viggo Stuckenberg

(17 September 1863 – 6 December 1905)

Sue Reindollar

BOOKS: *Digte* (Copenhagen: P. G. Philipsen, 1886);
I Gennembrud. Fortælling (Copenhagen: P. G. Philipsen, 1888);
Messias. Fortælling (Copenhagen: P. G. Philipsen, 1889);
Gylden Ungdom (Copenhagen: P. G. Philipsen, 1891);
Den vilde Jæger. Dramatisk Digt (Copenhagen: P. G. Philipsen, 1894);
Fagre Ord. En Mosaik (Copenhagen: P. G. Philipsen, 1895);
Romerske Scener (Copenhagen: P. G. Philipsen, 1895);
Valravn. To Fortællinger (Copenhagen: Nordiske Forlag, 1896);
Sol (Copenhagen: Nordiske Forlag, 1897); republished with *Valravn* as *Valravn og Sol. Smaa Romaner* (Copenhagen: Gyldendal, 1908);
Flyvende Sommer (Copenhagen: Nordiske Forlag, 1898);
Hjemfalden (Copenhagen: Nordiske Forlag, 1898);
Asmadæus. Roman (Copenhagen: Nordiske Forlag, 1899);
Vejbred. Smaa Æventyr og Legender (Copenhagen: Nordiske Forlag, 1899); translated by Una Hook as *By the Wayside: Little Tales & Legends* (London: Chatto & Windus, 1917);
Sne (Copenhagen: Gyldendal/Nordiske Forlag, 1901);
Aarsens Tid. Tolv Digte (Fredensborg: K. Kongstad, 1905);
Sidste Digte (Copenhagen: Gyldendal, 1906);
Historien om Moder. Dramatisk Digt efter H. C. Andersens Eventyr, music by Sofus Andersen (Copenhagen: Gylendal, 1910).

Editions and Collections: *Samlede Værker,* 3 volumes (Copenhagen: Gyldendal, 1910–1911);
Udvalgte Digte, edited by Carl Bergstrøm-Nielsen (Copenhagen: Gyldendal, 1954);
Vejbred, foreword by Frederik J. Billeskov Jansen (Copenhagen: Notabene, 1978).

OTHER: *Taarnet. Illustreret Månedsskrift for Kunst og Litteratur* (1893–1894), edited by Stuckenberg and Johannes Jørgensen;
Stuckenberg and others, *De Unges Bog til Holger Drachmann, den 9. Oktober 1896,* edited by Stuckenberg and Laurits Christian Nielsen (Copenhagen: Gyldendal, 1896);
Sigbjørn Obstfelder, *Efterladte Arbeider,* edited by Stuckenberg (Copenhagen: Gyldendal, 1903).

From Jørgen Andersen, Viggo Stuckenberg og hans Samtid *(1944); Suzzallo Library, University of Washington*

During the 1890s Viggo Stuckenberg was one of the young avant-garde poets who helped to bring symbolism to Danish poetry. While his early poetry and early novels in the late 1880s tended to express the gray naturalism and radicalism of the period, his later work in the 1890s was lyrical but realistic. His oeuvre earned him a position alongside Sophus Claussen and Johannes Jørgensen and continued elements found in such writers as J. P. Jacobsen and the Russian Ivan Sergeevich Turgenev. Stuckenberg was also a respected critic. His articles in major newspapers and journals and the gatherings of Danish literati at his home helped to introduce new modes of thought and expression.

Viggo Henrik Fog Stuckenberg was born on 17 September 1863 in Vridsløselille, near Copenhagen, to Johanne Georgine Fog Stuckenberg and Frederik Henrik Stuckenberg, who was a teacher at the Vridsløselille prison. The home of Viggo's youth was lively with intellectual debate. Frederik Stuckenberg was an avid atheist and a strong supporter of Georg Brandes, whose efforts to revitalize thought through the "Modern Breakthrough" of the 1870s brought naturalism and realism to Danish literature. This home environment and the cosmopolitan environment of Copenhagen undoubtedly contributed to the young poet's liberal views.

At the age of fifteen Stuckenberg went to sea on the frigate *Sjælland* in the hopes of becoming an officer in the Danish navy. He eventually changed his plans, took his university entrance exam in 1884, and began his studies at the University of Copenhagen in oriental philology, switching to zoology and botany soon afterward. In 1886 he was offered a modest teaching position at Slomann's school in Frederiksberg, a position he retained until his death.

At the age of twenty-one, during his first year at the university, Stuckenberg published his first poetry collection, *Digte* (Poems, 1886). The experimentation with verse and language in the collection of fifty-four poems gives a hint of the kinds of discourse found in his later poetry. The themes include love, happiness, freedom (or the lack of it), ego, dreams, disillusionment, and loneliness. *Digte* includes a series of five poems of special note, each titled "Vølunds Ed" (Volund's Oath), based on Norse mythology. "Frostnat" (Frosty Night) uses personification, a device that Stuckenberg later abandoned for the most part. "Stormflod" (Storm Surge) features five thought poems on the theme of the failed dream. This theme anticipates the content of many of Stuckenberg's later poems and novels. There are five love poems written to Ingeborg Pamperin, his future wife: "Elskov" (Love), "Fjældskov" (Mountain Forest), "Halvmørke" (Half-light), "Klaverstykke" (Piano Composition), and "Midnatssolen" (The Midnight Sun). These love poems are warm, affectionate, and erotic. Stuckenberg's powerful descrip-

Stuckenberg at about age five (from Jørgen Andersen, Viggo Stuckenberg og hans Samtid, *1944; Suzzallo Library, University of Washington)*

tions from nature are especially apparent in *Digte* and become even more prominent in his later writing. The collection is completed by a series of political poems reflecting his youthful radical commitments.

Ingeborg was exhibiting her artwork and writing poetry when she met Stuckenberg and sent him some of her poems. They married in 1887 and together raised two sons, Henrik and Niels Holger. The couple's ideal was to have a free relationship, living together as long as their feelings for each other endured. This attitude was shared by other young radicals of the time. By 1893 the couple had separated, with Ingeborg leaving Stuckenberg for a painter friend, Albert Gottschalk. Ten years later, in 1903, she left Denmark for New Zealand with friend and neighbor Hans Dine Madsen, never to return. A year later Ingeborg committed suicide. The tragic story of the Stuckenbergs has attracted

Stuckenberg circa 1890 (courtesy of the Danish Royal Library, Copenhagen)

many readers over the years who see aspects of their own relationships in the lives of Ingeborg and Viggo. Their story has been written about many times, fictionalized in Grete Povlsen's 1985 novel *Ingeborg. En ægteskabshistorie,* and made into a television miniseries, *To som elsker hinanden* (Two Who Love Each Other, 1988), the title taken from lines in Stuckenberg's poem sequence "Ingeborg," collected in *Sne* (Snow, 1901). Much of Stuckenberg's mature poetry and prose deals with intimate relationships between men and women and how destructive they may become.

Before their separation Stuckenberg and Ingeborg had a wonderfully rich home environment, in spite of the fact that the couple was plagued with heavy debt. In their small apartment, which served as a sort of literary salon, the prominent intellectuals of the time gathered for elegant meals, prepared at a cost far beyond the Stuckenbergs' means. Afterward, guests spent the evenings discussing Friedrich Nietzsche's ideas, the highly influential Russian writers, and the newly translated French symbolists. The excitement for intellectual renewal generated during those long evenings of discussion became the foundation for the fin de siècle move toward symbolism in Denmark.

In 1888 and 1889 Stuckenberg published in the avant-garde journal *Ny Jord* (New Earth), sharing the pages with Claussen, Brandes, August Strindberg, Herman Bang, Amalie Skram, and Ola Hansson. Along with Claussen and Jørgensen, Stuckenberg launched the avant-garde literary journal *Taarnet. Illustreret Månedsskrift for Kunst og Litteratur* (The Tower: The Illustrated Monthly Magazine for Art and Literature, 1893–1894). The tower on the frontispiece of the journal represented the artist's cloistered removal from the prosaic world in order to reflect on art. The contents included the trio's translations of works by Charles Baudelaire, Stéphane Mallarmé, Paul Verlaine, Joris-Karl Huysmans, and Maurice Maeterlinck. Jørgensen, with Stuckenberg as co-editor, formulated a new aesthetic encouraging a movement away from the gray, realistic portrayal of life and the demands of the Modern Breakthrough for the debate of current topics.

Stuckenberg, Claussen, and Jørgensen (who eventually took *Taarnet* in a more religious, Catholic direction), along with the Norwegians Sigbjørn Obstfelder and Knut Hamsun, helped to reshape literature at the end of the nineteenth century. Of the three prominent poets of the *Taarnet* group, Stuckenberg was the first to publish his poems, in his collection *Digte.* The Danish writers, especially Stuckenberg, did not take up the French symbolists' tendency toward decadence and pessimism but instead were inspired by the subtle and elusive qualities they found in French poetry and its kinship with music and the world of dreams. Their inspiration also came from Nietzsche, whose ideas had been hotly debated by Denmark's most influential critic, Brandes, and summarized in his seminal treatises "Aristokratisk Radikalisme" (1889; translated as *An Essay on Aristocratic Radicalism,* 1914) and *Dyret i Mennesket* (The Animal in the Human Being, 1890). Stuckenberg was influenced more by Nietzsche's lyricism than by his philosophical ideas. The works of Turgenev, a favorite with Danish and other European readers, often portrayed a Hamlet-like protagonist who seemed rootless and pessimistic but resigned to life. This figure especially appealed to Stuckenberg, whose protagonists were highly sensitive and responsive but resigned to the circumstances of life.

In 1888 Stuckenberg published his first novel, *I Gennembrud* (Breakthrough). The novel is in many respects an autobiographical bildungsroman. The protagonist, Jørgen Withs, is a radical student typical of the

1880s. His friend Johansen, who is studying to be a zoologist, cannot be bothered with a monogamous relationship. Jørgen is passionately in love with Emma and has proposed marriage. Johansen insists that it is not natural to be monogamous and maintains that people should love each other naturally and move on when love dies. This attitude momentarily repulses Jørgen, who feels love is more permanent. Yet, when Emma comes to his room, he rejects her because he feels she is placing him in a compromising situation. He leaves abruptly, and subsequently Emma ends the relationship. At the same time a good friend, who earlier turned to Christianity because he was diagnosed with a terminal disease, has died. Because of these two losses, Jørgen switches his studies to Darwinism and the natural sciences. He decides that his love for Emma was just a way of hiding from life and that he has been making a fool of himself over her. He has his own "breakthrough" into the mainstream and is happier living the anonymous life of the city without oppressive responsibilities.

In 1889 Stuckenberg published *Messias* (Messiah), seen by some as a sequel to *I Gennembrud.* Four fellow students, Georg Jansen among them, have high-minded ideals. They make a toast to the Messiah, the commander sergeant (Jansen himself), who will rid the temple of evil. The novel satirizes their high ideals and their inability to realize them. They establish a magazine, *Falken* (The Falcon), in which they urge their listeners not to spend time dreaming of another existence but to take action now to correct the wrongs of the world. "Valravn" (Battle Raven), published in 1893 and republished with a second part in 1896 as *Valravn. To Fortællinger* (Battle Raven: Two Stories), is based on the first split between Ingeborg and Stuckenberg. When the usually reserved Danish novelist Henrik Pontoppidan received a copy of *Valravn. To Fortællinger,* he wrote the author a congratulatory letter, which is quoted in Jørgen Andersen's *Viggo Stuckenberg og hans Samtid* (Viggo Stuckenberg and His Time, 1944). Pontoppidan noted that these two novellas were a turning point in Stuckenberg's authorship and, in particular, for the renewal of Danish poetics: "det er en i enhver Henseende unmærket Fortælling, på en Gang inderlig og gribende" (it is one excellent narrative, at once fervent and stirring). Jørgensen, who had already made his mark in the Danish literary world, sent Stuckenberg a warm letter regretting that Stuckenberg's work was slow to be appreciated, noting humbly that his own writing, which had appeared so strongly before the public, paled in comparison.

The *Valravn* novellas portray the landscapes of the mind as well as the natural landscapes, employing rich adjectives and experimental, fragmented narratives. They are intensely lyrical and gently nostalgic but violently agitated at moments. This deeply personal quality of discourse, using the first-person narrator, is also apparent in Stuckenberg's earlier work. The free flow of impressions and the silences or the ellipses become as important as the dialogue or the interior monologue, and the natural surroundings take on an active role. The exterior as well as the interior world reveal moods and depict the brooding, lonely protagonist, who was a typical figure in the literature of the 1890s. In the first novella even the walls and furniture in the room take on the emotions of the protagonist. The epigraph is from a fatalistic folk song:

> Ravnen han fløyer om Aften,
> om Dagen han ikke maa,
> den skal have den kranke Lykke,
> den gode kand ikke faa,
> Men Ravnen fløyer om Aften.
>
> (The raven he flies in the evening,
> during the day he must not,
> one shall have the sad fate
> the good one shall not have.
> But the raven flies in the evening.)

The power of fate is a theme of the novellas. Stuckenberg's protagonist does not shun fate; instead, he sensitively examines it. Johannes Prahl's wife, Hedvig, has just left him. She felt that she was wasting her life and was trapped in her marriage while time slipped away. Johannes is brutally honest with himself, trying to decipher his faults and Hedvig's needs. With a kind of tragic optimism, he sees his fate and faces it squarely, ready to live his life.

Valravn. To Fortællinger and the novel *Fagre Ord. En Mosaik* (Fair Words: A Mosaic, 1895) were written after Ingeborg had returned to Stuckenberg and the boys. The couple seems to have worked through their feelings in their art. Only Stuckenberg's name appears on the title page of *Fagre Ord,* but in 1962 manuscripts were found showing that Ingeborg worked out the basic outline for the novel and wrote the part of the female protagonist, Johanne. Critics rank these three prose works as Stuckenberg's best. *Fagre Ord* is a mosaic of the broken pieces of a couple's lives. The discourse is experimental, using fragmented dialogue, stream-of-consciousness technique, and movement from present to past memories. Johanne finds it impossible to live within the societal conventions of the times, performing as the "good wife." She reminisces about her past happiness and dreams of a better future, hoping for respect and equal treatment from her husband and his literary friends as an intelligent and creative person in her own right. In contrast, Morten, her husband, withdraws into

Frontispiece for the avant-garde literary journal founded by Stuckenberg, Sophus Claussen, and Johannes Jørgensen in 1893 (courtesy of the Danish Royal Library, Copenhagen)

his work, disregarding her dreams and memories. The Stuckenbergs were writing their lives into this novel, just as Stuckenberg had written the earlier split with Ingeborg into *Valravn.* The title *Fagre Ord* comes from a favorite folk song suggesting that honesty demands fair words, and the motto that follows the title is from Johann Wolfgang von Goethe's *Wilhelm Meisters Lehrjahre* (1795–1796; translated as *Wilhelm Meister's Apprenticeship,* 1824). It recalls that "In der liebe ist alles Wagestück . . . und der Zufall thut alles" (In love all is venture . . . and chance determines all).

The Stuckenbergs subscribed to the goals of the radical movement, but honestly living out those goals was difficult. Of Stuckenberg's works that directly treat the tensions in a love relationship, the ballad-like "Tue Bentsøns Viser" (The Ballads of Tue Bentsøn), published in *Sne,* is perhaps the most violently expressive. It was written perhaps in 1900, close to the final breakup of the marriage and Ingeborg's flight to New Zealand with Madsen. In this poem the emotions are raw and intense. There is no longer any attempt to work through the loss, no "fair words" or honest evaluations. In the fourth poem of the sequence "Ingeborg," published in *Sne* and probably written in 1896, Stuckenberg discusses the happiness and pain that couples cause each other. These lines are perhaps the most memorable and best known of any by Stuckenberg:

Thi to, som elsker hinanden,
kan volde hinanden mer' ondt
end alle de argeste Fjender,
som hævner sig Jorden rundt;

og to, som elsker hinanden,
kan læge de ondeste Saar
blot ved at se paa hinanden
og glatte hinandens Haar.

(For two who love each other
can cause each other more pain
than all the worst enemies
who take revenge the world round;

and two who love each other
can heal the most painful wound
by only looking at each other
and smoothing each other's hair.)

Here, as in Stuckenberg's other works, nature plays an important role. Reflecting the seasons in their moods, the characters are either energized by their surroundings in the natural world or comforted by nature.

Perhaps the work that earned Stuckenberg the most fame was his symbolist poetic cycle *Flyvende Sommer* (Fleeting Summer, 1898). Brandes and Claussen praised the cycle of thirty-two lyrical mood poems reflecting the seasons of the year. Stuckenberg uses nature as a symbol to express resignation, love, intimacy, tenderness, and melancholy. These poems are experimental, with no boundaries and no frames of reference other than the seasons. In *Flyvende Sommer* Stuckenberg came closest to the poetry of the symbolist school in France.

The eighteen tales collected in *Vejbred. Smaa Æventyr og Legender* (Vejbred [Plantain, a common ribgrass or ribwort]: Small Fairytales and Legends, 1899) do not often receive the attention they deserve. The title suggests that these are ordinary stories, but they are extraordinary tales told in an appealingly ordinary way. They feature a shortened form and stock characters and are sometimes referred to as modern antitales, illustrating delightfully ironic situations. Stuckenberg uses the basic structure of the tale but plays with traditional motifs and colloquial language to create an honest, realistic impression of society and gender relationships.

In many cases these antitales have the earthy quality of a fabliau. The protagonists find themselves in maddening, absurd situations and are generally disenchanted with the world around them, so they attack their conventional problems in unconventional ways. The first nine tales examine the quality of relationships between men and women. A few of these tales were written as early as 1892, not long before Ingeborg left Stuckenberg for the first time. The latter nine tales express the pain of an age disillusioned and somewhat apathetic after the energy of the Modern Breakthrough had dissipated. Even though these nine tales eschew the gender issues seen in much of Stuckenberg's writing, they still address the contrasts between what a person wants to believe and what actually is.

The 1901 collection *Sne* is probably Stuckenberg's most important and most frequently read work. It is a selection of thirty-four of his best poems from 1888 to 1901. The most memorable poems in the collection are "Ingeborg," "Min Moder" (My Mother), and "Bekendelse" (Confession), dedicated to Jørgensen. *Sne* also includes the angry "Tue Bentsøns Viser," expressing the moment of fury Stuckenberg experienced when Ingeborg first left him. Most of these poems are not experimental like those in *Flyvende Sommer* but are meticulously crafted. "Min Moder" is a poignant memorial to Stuckenberg's mother, who died in 1895. He composed it at her graveside; using imagery from nature, he recounted what she had meant to him. As is typical of Stuckenberg, he begins with memories, moves to the reality of death, and faces his loss squarely. "Bekendelse" was written in response to the deterioration of Stuckenberg's friendship with Jørgensen, who pressured him to become a Catholic and renounce the values of his youth. Stuckenberg, Claussen, and Jørgensen, who had been so instrumental in bringing symbolism to Denmark, were taking different paths at the end of the century. "Bekendelse" is important for the clear statement of Stuckenberg's attitude that the experiences and values of his youth were still part of what shaped his life and could not be renounced, for they were part of the whole.

Stuckenberg married Clara Madsen in October 1904, just a few months after Ingeborg took her life at age thirty-eight, having been abandoned in New Zealand by Clara's former husband, Hans. For perhaps the last ten years of his life Stuckenberg suffered increasing complications from kidney disease; he died on 6 December 1905 at the age of forty-two.

Viggo Stuckenberg was inspired by his reading of the French symbolists, Maeterlinck in particular, but, as the oldest member of the *Taarnet* circle of poets and as a man with domestic responsibilities and a teaching position, he eventually guided the group away from the decadence of the symbolists and their excesses, teaching them to respond instead to the world around them by reaching for a new discourse. He quickly eschewed the content of his early Modern Breakthrough novels and sought fresh ways of artistic communication. Stuckenberg drew on a rich Danish literary heritage through Jacobsen, incorporated and modified Turgenev's models, and assimilated Nietzsche's lyricism and, to a lesser extent, his philosophy.

Title page for Stuckenberg's two semi-autobiographical novellas about a man who undertakes a brutally honest self-assessment after his wife leaves him (Collection of Sue Reindollar)

Unfortunately, Stuckenberg's works have been sparingly anthologized, editors usually including a lyric or two, the *Valravn* novellas, and *Fagre Ord. Vejbred,* his collection of antitales, seems to be completely overlooked, even though much wisdom is found in these ironic tales, offered with a wry smile and a light heart. His letters to other Danish literati of his time, in a period when composing a letter was an art in itself, are also a delight to read, besides providing a transparent experience of the times.

Letters:

Breve fra Johannes Jørgensen til Viggo Stuckenberg, edited by Jørgen Andersen (Copenhagen: Gydendal, 1946);

Breve mellem Viggo Stuckenberg og L. C. Nielsen, edited by Andersen (Copenhagen: Gyldendal, 1946);

Viggo Stuckenberg–Sophus Claussen. En Brevvexling, edited by Johannes Brøndum-Nielsen, Historisk-Filosofiske Meddelelser, volume 40, no. 2 (Copenhagen: Kongelige Danske Videnskabernes Selskab/ Munksgaard, 1963).

Biography:

Jørgen Andersen, *Viggo Stuckenberg og hans Samtid,* 2 volumes (Copenhagen: Gyldendal, 1944).

References:

Jørgen Andersen, ed., *Viggo Stuckenberg-Manuskripter* (Copenhagen: Munksgaard, 1944);

Georg Brandes, "Viggo Stuckenberg" (1894), in his *Samlede Skrifter,* volume 15 (Copenhagen: Gyldendal, 1905), pp. 307–311;

Johannes Brøndum-Nielsen, *Litterærhistoriske epistler. Ludvig Bødtcher, Poul Møller, Viggo Stuckenberg* (Copenhagen: Gyldendal, 1960), pp. 54–113;

Johan Fjord Jensen, *Turgenjev i dansk åndsliv. Studier i dansk romankunst, 1870–1990* (Copenhagen: Gyldendal, 1961);

Aage Henriksen, Helge Therkildsen, and Knud Wentzel, eds., *Den erindrende Faun. Digteren og hans fantasi* (Copenhagen: Fremad, 1968);

Grete Povlsen, *Ingeborg. En ægteskabshistorie* (Copenhagen: Gyldendal, 1985);

Malene Rehr, *Afstandens mellemværende. Iscenesaettelsens udtryksformer hos Ingeborg og Viggo Stuckenberg og hos Vilhelm Hammershoi* (Odense: Odense University Press, 2001);

Sue Reindollar, "Viggo Stuckenberg: Discourse of the Fin de Siècle Intimate Sphere," dissertation, University of Wisconsin, 1992;

Ingeborg Stuckenberg, *Fagre Ord. Nyfundne Manuskripter af Ingeborg og Viggo Stuckenberg,* edited by Brøndum- Nielsen (Copenhagen: B. Luno, 1962);

Valdemar Vedel, "Dekadenter," *Tilskueren,* 11 (January 1894): 54–62;

Vedel, "Suggestion og Symbol i Digtning," *Tilskueren,* 11 (February 1894): 147–158.

Papers:

Viggo Stuckenberg's manuscripts and other papers are at the Danish Royal Library in Copenhagen and at the Library of Congress.

Birgitte Thott

(17 June 1610 - 1662)

Marianne Alenius
Museum Tusculanum Press, University of Copenhagen

(Translated by Gaye Kynoch)

MANUSCRIPTS: "Epistula ad Dominum Olaum Wormium," 19 May 1650, autograph, Danish Royal Library, Copenhagen;

"En Tractatt Om Weyen till et Lycksalligt Liff Som alle ønske sig, Faa skønne paa, Faere, ved dette Rette midell Strebe effter . . . sammenfattet aff . . . Fru Birgitte Tot Sl. Otto Giøes," ca. 1659–1660, transcription, Karen Brahe Library, Odense.

TRANSLATIONS: Philippe de Mornay, *Kort Forklaring Oc Gudelig Betenckning, offver nogle Skrifftens gylden Sprock, til Lærdom, Trøst oc Formaning, Meget nyttige . . . Fordansket,* foreword by Thott; and *Ljffvets oc Dødens Affmaling, . . . til Trøst imod Dødsens Fryct, meget Christelig forfattet* (Copenhagen: M. Marzan, 1652);

Joseph Hall, *Raad imod all Bekymring, eller, En liden Tractat om Sindetz Fornøyelse, udi hvad Tilstand mand er. Beskreffvet paa Engelsk. Udsat paa Danske. Bed oc Troe* (Copenhagen: J. Holst, 1658);

Lucius Annaeus Seneca, *Lucii Annæi Senecæ . . . Skrifter . . . om Sæderne oc et Skickligt Lefnit . . . Nu paa voris Danske Maal ofversat Af Den sin Næste dermed at tiene Begierer Trolig* (Sorø: Printed by G. Hantsch, 1658)–includes "Til det loflige Fruentimmer" and "Til Læseren," by Thott;

Epictetus, *Epicteti liden Haandbog, som vjser, huorledis mand Sindets Rolighed ved at mand om det tjmelige ret skiønner, oc det ey missbruger, kand erlange. Efter Hieronymi Wolfii version aff Græckisken paa Latine, paa Danske ofversat . . . Beder Trolig,* preface by Thott; and *Cebetis den Thebaners Taffle, ved huilcken, ligesom ved en Malning, stilles os for Øyne, huorledis Menniskerne aff Lasterne forraades, oc styrtes udi Forderfvelse. Oc Tuert imod Huorledis mand aff Dyderne, føres til en lycksalig Stand, oc frjgiøres fra alt Ont, effter Hieronymi Wolfii . . .* , anonymous (Copenhagen: J. Holst, 1661);

Thomas Fuller, *Gode Tancker udi onde oc verre Tjder, Som bestaar udi Adskillige Gudelige Betænckninger, Beskreffvid paa Engelsk aff Thomas Fuller, . . . paa Danske Sprog udsat aff Erlig oc Velb. Jomfru Sal. Elisabeth Tott,* edited by Thomas Bartholin (Copenhagen: J. Moltken, 1664)–includes "Erlig oc Velbyrdig Frue S. Birgitte Tottis til Turebye, Fortale til Læseren . . . Beder Trolig," by Thott.

Birgitte Thott (copperprint by Albrecht Haelwegh based on a painting by Abraham Wuchter, circa 1658; from Lucii Annæi Senecæ . . . Skrifter . . . om Sæderne oc et Skickligt Lefnit . . . Af Den sin Næste dermed at tiene Begierer Trolig, *translated by Thott, 1658; courtesy of the Danish Royal Library, Copenhagen)*

Birgitte Thott, a Danish noblewoman, was a scholarly author, translator, and educator; she was also a landed proprietor who personally took charge of her estate. As in southern Europe, certain intellectual Scan-

Thott, age thirty-eight (painting probably by Johan Thim, 1648; Gavnø Castle, Næstved; photograph courtesy of the Danish Royal Library, Copenhagen)

dinavian circles cultivated the phenomenon of "feminae doctae" (learned women) or "feminae illustres" (illustrious women), as they were often called in Latin. Documents record the names of about 150 Scandinavian women of the sixteenth through eighteenth centuries who were conspicuous by virtue of scholarly and artistic achievements. Of these, Thott is considered by many to be the most learned of Danish women. She was afforded great respect and was considered to be a role model and an atypical prodigy, a woman who rose "supra sexum" (above gender) and from whom men could learn a thing or two. In her learning and intelligence Thott was the Danish equivalent to her Dutch contemporary Anna Maria van Schurman, the "Tenth Muse," with whom Thott was compared and after whom she was informally given the honorary title "Nordic Tenth Muse."

Thott's erudition lay mainly in classical and modern languages, philosophy, theology, and history. Latin was the international language of scholarship, while Greek and Hebrew were the biblical languages. With a good knowledge of these languages, she was a creditable partner for discussion in scholarly circles, and with her additional expertise in modern languages as well as her extensive library, she was able to participate in learned discussions at an elevated level. She was greatly inspired by the Roman Stoic philosopher Lucius Annaeus Seneca and gave both direct and indirect prominence to this pagan philosopher at the expense of many Christian ones. Her major works were translations of Seneca's prose works and her own moral-philosophical treatise, "En Tractatt Om Weyen till et Lycksalligt Liff Som alle ønske sig, Faa skønne paa, Fære, ved dette Rette midell Strebe effter" (A Treatise on the Route to a Happy Life, which All Wish for, a Few Appreciate, and Fewer with the Right Means Aspire to), written circa 1659–1660. Although never published, manuscript copies of this influential treatise were available to contemporary scholars. Alongside her intellectual pursuits, Thott spent the last twenty years of her life as landed proprietor and manager of Thurebygård, a manor house and estate on Zealand, not far from the famous Sorø Academy. She was childless, but she brought up at least two of her nieces.

Birgitte Thott was born on 17 June 1610 at Fårupgård, a manor house and estate in southern Jutland, Denmark. Both her parents were from the aristocracy. Her father, Christen Thott, owned the estate of Boltinggård; he died when Birgitte was seven years old. Her mother, Sophie Below Thott, was, like her sister Marie Below, known for her learning. After her husband's death Sophie assumed responsibility for bringing up their three children, a son and two daughters, and made sure that they received a solid academic education. Both of Birgitte's parents were adherents of the intellectual humanism promoted in seventeenth-century northern Europe by the works of such writers as Desiderius Erasmus, Thomas More, and Juan Luis Vives.

Most likely as part of her education, Thott spent a period during her youth at Rosenholm Castle in Jutland, staying with the well-known aristocrat Holger Rosenkrantz, called "Den Lærde" (the Learned One). She became acquainted with an interesting milieu, which she later wrote about, and joined a circle of humanists who met for erudite discussions held in Latin, undoubtedly on theological and political issues. There she apparently met several of the people who remained in her circle of acquaintance throughout the following decades, including members of the noble Giøe family, one of whom, Otto Giøe, later became her husband. They were married in Odense on the island of Fyn in 1632 and moved to Thurebygård. The marriage was childless and seems to have been affected by Giøe's serious war injury, which caused his premature death just ten years after their wedding. Thott took her two nieces, Elisabeth and Sophie Thott, into her home and provided them both with a sophisticated academic education. While Giøe was still alive, she translated Rosenkrantz's controversial work *Fürstenspiegel,* as "Försters Spegel" (Mirror of Princes, 1636). Her translation was never published but was in all likelihood circulated in manuscript form among the learned milieu at Thurebygård. A fragment of Thott's correspondence, the wide-ranging scope and high quality of which is known from contemporary sources, has been preserved. It is an autograph letter in Latin, sent in 1650 to her close friend, the medical doctor and antiquarian Ole Worm. She writes about an old Norwegian shield that has come into her brother's possession and that she has been allowed to present as a gift to Worm's museum of natural and cultural history. The letter offers a glimpse of Thott's eloquent Latin.

Once widowed, Thott quickly summoned several teachers in order to resume her studies, which had ceased during her marriage. Latin was her principal subject, but she also learned Greek and Hebrew. With her knowledge of these three languages–especially Latin, which was the international language of debate for key theological discussions between Catholics, Calvinists, and Lutherans throughout Europe–she became a focal point of her intellectual circle, and Thurebygård acted as a Scandinavian variant of a French salon.

As a young girl Thott had learned several modern languages from her mother, including French and German; she also had a command of English, which was a far rarer accomplishment at the time. From contemporary accounts of her abilities, she apparently also mastered Dutch, Italian, and Spanish. There is considerable documentation for these accomplishments, and it is quite likely that she could at least read these languages, as learned women in other countries apparently could. Thott's career as a translator therefore naturally started with works translated from modern languages. When her mother died in 1650, she completed her translation from English of Daniel Dyke's oft-published *The Mystery of Self-Deceiving* (1615), under the title "Selff Bedrags Hemmelighed . . . Aff . . . Daniell Dycke, paa Engelsch beschreffuidt och ved Hans Broder Jeremiam Dycke, effter hans død til Prenten vdgiffuedt . . . fordanschidt af . . . Sophie Below" (The Secrecy of Self-deceit . . . by . . . Daniell Dyke, Written in English and Printed and Published by His Brother Jeremias Dyke, Translated by . . . Sophie Thott), and she also wrote an introduction for it. The work was not published but is extant in a manuscript written in an unknown hand.

Thott now settled down in earnest to the work of disseminating the European cultural debate to a Danish readership through her translations. Her target audience was not just learned men or men seeking greater learning but also women who were normally precluded from participating in intellectual discussions because of lack of education or because the works under discussion were not available in Danish. She chose texts for translation and wrote her own comprehensive prefaces to the works. Her subject material was chiefly of a theological or moral-philosophical nature. From French she translated excerpts from works by Philippe de Mornay, a Huguenot who was personal adviser to Henry IV of France during the period when the king was vacillating between the faith of the Huguenots and that of the Catholics. In 1652 Thott published two translations in one volume: *Kort Forklaring Oc Gudelig Betenckning, offver nogle Skrifftens gylden Sprock, til Lærdom, Trøst oc Formaning* (A Short Explanation and Faithful Consideration Concerning Some Golden Expressions in the Holy Bible Very useful for Learning, Consolation and Prescription) and *Ljffvets oc Dødens Affmaling . . . til Trøst imod Dødsens Fryct, meget Christelig forfattet* (A Discourse on Life and Death . . . as Consolation against Fear of Death, Written in a Very Christian Way). Likely during this period she also translated a French work by the Dutch-French Huguenot Pierre du Moulin that also dealt with the difficult path through life for the Christian. Her translation, "Den Christnes Strid eller Om det Kaarss och den Gienvordighed som Gudss Børn vdj dette Liff Tilslais" (The Christian's Struggle; or, On the Heavy Burden and Exertions Encountered by God's Children in this Mortal Life), was not published, but the manuscript was probably circulated. It exists in two transcriptions of the lost original.

Just two years later, in 1654, Thott is thought to have published a translation of Joseph Hall's *The Remedy Of Discontentment; or, A Treatise Of Contentation in Whatever Condition, Fit for These Sad and Troubled Times* (1645); Thott's Danish translation was titled *Raad imod all Bekymring, eller, En liden Tractat om Sindetz Fornøyelse, udi hvad Tilstand mand er*. The only extant copies, however, were published in 1658. Thott also translated Hall's *The Free Prisoner* (1644) as "Den Fri Fanges Tancker" in an undated manuscript, as well as a sermon by Hall on John 19:30, in which Jesus "gave up the ghost." She is also thought to have translated Hall's *Occasionall Meditations* (1630), probably from the original Latin version titled *Meditatiunculae subitaneae,* but no copy of this translation has survived. A work titled *Praxis Pietatis* has also been attributed to Thott, but no copy of this work exists, either. Hall, the bishop of Exeter and, later, Norwich, was known as the "English Seneca," and, like the classical philosopher by whom he was so greatly inspired, he wrote both satires and literary letters. He was an early exponent of a new genre in English, the moral epistle in the style of Seneca. Thott's interest in Hall's writings is documented by way of her translations, just as her other translations attest to her interest in moral philosophy, consolation, and the endurance of pain and grief. Like many women, she sat and watched over close relatives on their deathbeds, and, as is known from a funeral address for her niece Elisabeth in 1656, she passed time with the dying by reading and

Vir celeberrime, ac Experientissime Domine Doctor.
Quanta solertia, quantoq labore, omnia illa nostratium monumenta,
quæ de gloriosis factis Maiorum fidem faciunt, eorumq ritus vivendi,
demonstrant, è tenebris, in quibus penitùs latuêre, eruere, conatus es;
nonnulla à te præclara in lucem edita scripta satis declarant. Eande
diligentiam luculenter ostendit, illa copia rerum antiquarum ac omni
regionum selectissimarum, a te summa cum cura ex omnibus orbis
terrarum partibus congesta, et in museo tuo eâ industriâ disposita,
ut in angusto loco, multivariam, ac mirabilem naturæ operationem,
in terrestribus, aquatilibus, subterraneis, animatis, iuxta et inanimatis;
imo et populorum remotissimorum, pro ratione temporis et morum
planè diversum cultum et habitum uno intuitu aspicere liceat.
Quamobrem sanè omnes patriæ et scientiarum amantes merito grat
tibi habent maximas, & laudabili tuo, pro virili favere conatui
tenentur. Illud cum dudum animo revolverim, atq iam nuper scutum,
quod tibi per harum gerulum mitto, apud fratrem meum viderim,
nullius quidem pretii, nisi quod ipsa vetustas imposuit. Idem, quam
vis temporis diuturnitate ferè corrosum sit, non planè indignum censu
quod tuo in museo servaretur. At mihi a fratre petenti, illius tibi
offerendi potestatem faceret, læte assentiebatur, quippe cuius animus
ad meam tibi gratificandi promptissimam voluntatem lubens accedi
Sed uterq nostrum recte iudicavit, exiguum nimis esse munusculu
quod tantus vir, qui inter magna huius ævi lumina eminet, feran

Autograph letter in Latin (1650) from Thott to her friend Ole Worm about an old Norwegian shield that she is giving to Worm's museum of natural and cultural history (courtesy of the Danish Royal Library, Copenhagen)

fronte aspiceret. Spero tamen antiquitatem tibi ubiq venerabilem, vilitatē rei quodammodo supplere posse. vetustatem autem, non tantum materia quam edax rerum tempus ferè consumpsit, indicat; verumetiam forma ipsa eandem probare mihi videtur. Me iudice non multum absimilis est iis, quibus tectos, multis ab hinc retro seculis, varios populos, contra hostem pugnaturos in aciem prodiisse, Cluverus, in suo, de antiqua Germania, opere multorum probat, prisci avi authorum testimonio. Verum hoc scutum frater meus ante decennium Præses Stavangriensis Norvegorum in templo quodam eius Dioecesis, patrio sermone Röldal vocatum, propè Hardanger invenit; ubi prisci Heroïs sepulchro, inibi humo mandatis appositum fuisse ab accolis ferebatur; cuius tamen tumuli nulla apparebant vestigia, sed rumor est illud trecentos circiter annos isto in loco depositum fuisse. verum de re levissima multa verba faciens, ne tuâ abutar patientiâ, teq nugis meis a gravioribus tuis occupationibus diutius detineam, ultimam lineam afferam, sed postquam enixè terogavero, ut hoc quantulumcunq sit, tanquam pignus meæ in te benevolentiæ, benigno animo accipere velis, ratus hoc mihi esse propositum ut unamquamq tibi gratificandi occasionem avidè semper arripiam, optimè memor quanto favore agrestes meas musas amplexus es. His vale Reipubl: litterariæ præstantissimum decus, & rudem mearum quæso litterarum stylum sub singularis tuæ humanitatis velo tege. vale et salve plurimum cum iis qui tibi sunt cordi omnibus. Dabam Tureby XIV Kal: Jun: Anno ClↃlↃCL

Birgitta Tott

making translations of philosophical literature. Characteristically, Thott did not choose prayer books and devotional texts in the traditional sense, but well-written, discursive, controversial, and often even amusing works.

Quite some time had passed since 1642, when Thott had been widowed and started to study the classical languages. Now, the results of her studies began to shine through. The literary monuments of ancient Rome still retained their influential position in Europe as a model of good literature and thought. For prose writers the central focus had shifted from Cicero to Seneca. Thott devoted herself to Seneca's works from around 1650 until 1660. Justus Lipsius's major edition of Seneca of 1605 was the principal successor to Erasmus's two sixteenth-century editions. Silver Age Latin had reached northern Europe in the works of Seneca and Tacitus, and this language–dense, unpredictable, maxim charged, and at times almost affectedly concise–was much admired. "Senecæ Stil . . . er kort oc mørck" (Seneca's style . . . is concise and dark), wrote Thott. As early as 1651 it was publicly known that she was working on Seneca's writings. Thomas Bartholin wrote a letter that year, headed "de edendo Seneca" (On Editing Seneca), in which he called on Thott to publish her Danish translation, stating that she must share her knowledge of Seneca with others because there was a need for Seneca's advice on facing grief and adversity. During Thott's lifetime France produced two translations of Seneca's works, one by Matthieu de Chalvet and the other by François de Malherbe. Thomas Lodge provided England with a monumental translation in 1614.

Lipsius had provisionally put a stop to discussion as to whether Seneca the writer of tragedies and Seneca the writer of philosophical prose were one and the same person. In Lipsius's opinion he was not, and in the spirit of the times Thott concurred with this division. Her edition included only the philosophical works and not the ten tragedies attributed to Seneca, of which only one is today considered to be falsely attributed. The work used as the basis for Thott's translation was a 1626–1627 variorum edition from Martin Lasnier's printing house in Paris, with commentaries by twenty leading Seneca philologists and a text based on Lipsius's edition. Thott's own autograph copy of this Paris edition is preserved.

Thott's translation of Seneca in one thousand printed folio pages is one of the most eminent books of the seventeenth century. It is titled *Lucii Annæi Senecæ . . . Skrifter . . . om Sæderne oc et Skickligt Lefnit . . . Nu paa voris Danske Maal ofversat Af Den sin Næste dermed at tiene Begierer Trolig* (The Works of Lucius Annæus Seneca . . . about Morality and a Decent Life . . . Now in Our Danish Language Translated by One Who Wishes to Serve His Neighbor Faithfully, 1658). Thott indicated her name discreetly behind the letters *B* and *T* in "Begierer Trolig" (wishes faithfully), just as it is found on the title page in other of her works behind the motto "Bed oc Troe" (pray and believe). The Seneca edition is supplied with two prefatory copper engravings by Albrecht Haelwegh. One is an earnest portrait based on Abraham Wuchter's lost painting of Thott posed before a background of bookcases and drapes. The second depicts Seneca's suicide at the bottom and four personified virtues–Constantia, Iustitia, Sapientia, and Temperantia–standing before the entrance to a perspective view of a columned portal. At the top appears Thott, sitting atop a pile of books and dressed as the goddess of wisdom, Minerva, with a feather-bedecked helmet, flowing robes, a lance, and a shield bearing the Thott family coat of arms. The book, the first major translation of a classical text to appear in Denmark, was published in Sorø, home of the distinguished Sorø Academy, not far from Thott's estate, Thurebygård. It opens with twelve laudatory poems. The first is the finest, a Latin poem written in elegiac meter by the well-known Dutch scholar Schurman, who represented learned European women. Next is a grandiose two-part poem in Danish by the noble steward of Sorø Academy, Jørgen Rosenkrantz, son of Holger Rosenkrantz and Thott's close friend, who was responsible for the publication. Thereafter follow poems by teachers from Sorø Academy–the professor of rhetoric, Johannes Faber, who obviously wrote in Latin; the German professor of moral philosophy and Seneca expert, Heinrich Ernst; grammarian Erik Eriksen Pontoppidan; the professor of mathematics, Johann Lauremberg; the headmaster of Sorø Academy, Jesper Lauridsen Smith; Thott's friend Bartholin, professor of medicine; theologian and church minister Hans Clausen Rosing; and, possibly as a representative of her late husband's family, Marcus Giøe Falcksen, son of Thott's brother-in-law, a former headmaster of the academy. Last is a poem by the young and promising Peder Schumacher, later Count Griffenfeld, who became the most influential statesman in Denmark but ended his life in prison.

Preceding Lipsius's lengthy introduction to Seneca the philosopher and his prose writings, and before the translation itself, the book features two weighty prefaces by Thott. The second, "Til Læseren" (To the Reader), deals with the lack of translations of foreign literature into Danish and the difficulties encountered when translating into a language that does not yet have a literary written language (to the creation of which Thott hereby made a significant contribution). The preface also points out that the male readership of the book might derive benefit

Prefatory copperplate by Albrecht Haelwegh for Thott's translation of the philosophical works of Seneca (1658). Thott is depicted at the top, sitting on a stack of books dressed as Minerva, the Roman goddess of wisdom, and holding a shield with the Thott coat of arms. The virtues Constantia, Iustitia, Sapientia, and Temperentia stand before the columns. Seneca's suicide is shown at the bottom (courtesy of the Danish Royal Library, Copenhagen).

from reading Seneca's wise words in a language they understand, as Latin is not an easy language, even for those who have mastered it. The opening preface is dedicated to the female sex: "Den Danske Seneca, Kierligen tilskrefvit Det Loflige Frven-timmer, Alledennem iblant Quinde-Kiønnet, som elske Dyd oc Forstand" (The Danish Seneca, with love dedicated to The Laudable Women, all those among the female sex who love Virtue and Knowledge). This preface represents the earliest example of Danish feminism in print. Apart from encouraging women to learn to read, Thott openly disputes, as did Schurman, the arguments of that time against a woman's right to an education:

> Lader det icke afholde eder fra det at læse hvor udi Klogskab indeholdis, at I ere af det Quindelige Kiøn, hos hvilcke Lærdom actis for u-nyttig, om icke skadelig. Thi skal Visdommen holdis for farlig hos somme Menneisker, meere end hos somme, da veed jeg icke, om det kand bevisis, Vankundigheden at være gafnlig. Ere vi, som meenis, saa skrøbelige, at vi kunde icke vel bære Forstand? da kunde vi vel mindre regiere os ved u-forstand.

(You should not refrain from reading that which contains wisdom because you are of the female sex for whom learning is considered futile, if not even directly harmful. If wisdom is considered dangerous for some people more than for others, then I wonder if it can be proven that ignorance is beneficial? If we were, as supposed, so frail that we should not be able sufficiently to tolerate reason, then we would even less be able to control ourselves with lack of reason.)

Alongside her work on the Seneca translation, Thott appears to have worked on her treatise "En Tractatt Om Weyen till et Lycksalligt Liff Som alle ønske sig, Faa skønne paa,Fære, ved dette Rette midell Strebe effter." This work was never published, and the original was lost when Sorø Academy, to which Thott bequeathed her library, was destroyed by fire in 1813. But two transcriptions have been preserved in the library of her kindred spirit, Karen Brahe, in Odense. The treatise can in all probability be dated to 1659, on the basis of the mention in the introduction of devastating wars, which, although unspecified, were probably the Swedish wars. The work is unique in the annals of Danish literature; although many prayer books, hymnals, and devotional books have been preserved, there is virtually no other Danish moral philosophy from the period.

The moral-philosophy genre concerns the great questions of ethics: What are virtue and vice? Is poverty an evil? Is good health crucial? How does the understanding function? What are malice and anger? Such questions had been discussed in depth during the seventeenth century and for many centuries previously throughout the rest of Europe, first in Latin and later in national languages. An early work in the genre was Seneca's *De vita beata* (On the Happy Life, circa A.D. 58). Prominent Christian interpretations of this issue had been written by Augustine and Boethius. During the seventeenth century Church Fathers, theological polemicists, and philosophers from antiquity were quoted side by side. This practice made the moral-philosophy genre dangerous in Scandinavia. Martin Luther's Protestantism had been imposed on Denmark with a firm hand in 1536, and from then on the correct Lutheran interpretation had to be safeguarded. In this respect the Catholic Church Fathers were considered just as dangerous as the pagans of classical antiquity, even though they often debated the same issues that Luther had brought up for discussion and reached the same conclusions he did.

The strict Lutheran orthodoxy in which seventeenth-century Denmark was encapsulated left little room for interpretation. Works such as Thott's "Om Weyen till et Lycksalligt Liff" had difficulties getting past the censors of the faculty of theology at the University of Copenhagen, who had to give their imprimatur before a book could be published. Thott was doubtless consciously trying to uphold and further a type of writing that was lacking in Scandinavia: polemical works in which, as she did, the author disputed the clergy's administration of Christianity. It remains unclear as to why the treatise never went into print, but a possible reason was the brutal war with Sweden that raged across Zealand in 1658 and laid waste to Thott's manor and estate. Vast fortunes were lost, and the financial situation was unfavorable for the book market. But there was unlikely to be great enthusiasm on the part of theologians for Thott's treatise. In the course of fifty chapters she builds a work based on all the classical subjects: true blessings and false, the cardinal virtues, vices, wisdom, the power of example, and God. On her own account she included two chapters not normally found in the genre: chapter 45, "Om de nytter der er hos studeringer" (on the benefit of studying), and chapter 46, "At studeringer efter deris maade ret brugte, och er quinde Kiønnet nyttige och ingen lunde skadelige" (Studying, if used correctly, is by no means harmful, but on the contrary beneficial to women). In the latter chapter Thott refers to advocates of this view from classical antiquity, principally Seneca and Plutarch. She quotes her own translation of Seneca, the essay *Ad Helviam matrem de consolatione* (Consolation to His Mother Helvia, circa A.D. 41–49), in which Seneca encourages his mother to devote her widowhood to study, not only of account books and principles of housekeeping but also of philosophy. The chapter develops Thott's thoughts from the preface to women in her Seneca translation. Like several of her female contemporaries from further south in Europe, with whose works one can only sporadically trace her familiarity, she was fighting for women's right to study. She was not demanding access to official positions, but she argued for the right of girls to receive an education, the benefit of study to the moral status of women, and the role study could play in the realization of a happy life. It is a unique, early Danish contribution to the struggle for women's rights.

After the destruction of Thurebygård, Thott was offered free and permanent accommodation at Sorø Academy, where she lived until her death and to which she left her writings, her entire correspondence–some of which is known to have been in Latin–and her library. All of it was destroyed when the academy burned down in 1813, which is why most of her unpublished works are preserved only in transcripts. The year before her death, her translation of yet another little treatise on moral philosophy was published: the Stoic, emancipated slave Epictetus's handbook in philosophy,

Epicteti liden Haandbog (The Little Handbook of Epictetus, 1661).

Birgitte Thott died in 1662. A long, published funeral address in Latin by her friend Jørgen Rosenkrantz has been preserved. He describes the woman and the intellectual in an extravagant, glowing tribute. Manuscripts of Latin and Greek tribute poems by teachers and students at Sorø Academy, composed for her funeral, have also survived. Her contemporaries and many scholars and historians throughout the following century extolled Thott in verse and prose, including the greatest eighteenth-century Danish writer, Ludvig Holberg, as well as Peder Hansen Resen, Matthias Henriksen Schacht, Johannes Moller, Bartholin, Otto Sperling the Younger, Worm, Albert Thura, Pontoppidan, Tycho de Hofmann, Christian Juncker, and Frederik Christian Schønau. Succeeding generations looked on Thott as a model for Danish intellectual women. At the religious home for unmarried noblewomen in Odense established by two learned women, Brahe and Anne Giøe (Thott's sister-in-law), a portrait of Thott hung in the library. The two extant transcripts of "Om Weyen till et Lycksalligt Liff" are in the collection of this library. Thott was buried in Sorø Church, where a commemorative tablet is still to be found.

Bibliographies:

Albert Thura, *Gynæceum Daniæ Literatum* (Altona: Printed by Jonas Korte, 1732);

Holger Ehrencron-Müller, *Forfatterlexicon omfattende Danmark, Norge og Island indtil 1814,* volume 8 (Copenhagen: Aschehoug, 1924–1935), pp. 232–233.

References:

Marianne Alenius, "Birgitte Thotts Om et lyksaligt Liv," in *Latin og nationalsprog i Norden efter reformationen,* edited by Alenius and others, Renæssance Studier, no. 5 (Copenhagen: Museum Tusculanum, 1991), pp. 143–155;

Alenius, ". . . med den ene fod i graven ville jeg fortsat læse. Om Birgitte Thott," in *Nordisk Kvindelitteraturhistorie,* edited by Elisabeth Møller Jensen, volume 1 (Copenhagen: Rosinante, 1993), pp. 233–246;

Alenius, "Seneca-oversætteren Birgitte Thott. Et fagligt portræt," *Danske Studier* (1983): 5–47;

Erik Dal, "Birgitte Thotts Seneca, Sorø 1658," in *Levende Biblioteker, Festskrift til Palle Birkelund,* edited by Ole Hovman and others (Copenhagen: Bibliotekscentralen, 1982), pp. 41–47;

Friedrich Christian Schønau, *Lærde danske Fruentimer* (Copenhagen: N. H. Møller, 1753), pp. 1376–1431.

Papers:

Seventeenth-century transcriptions of Birgitte Thott's unpublished manuscripts are at the Danish Royal Library and the National Archive in Copenhagen and at the Karen Brahe Library in Odense.

Vilhelm Topsøe

(5 October 1840 - 11 July 1881)

Poul Houe
University of Minnesota

BOOKS: *Skizzer: Familiekarakteristikker I-IV. Vintergæk og Sommernar. To Venner eller Reflexion og Forlovelse,* as Xox (Copenhagen: Gad, 1863);
Forfatningssagen i Rigsraadet, en historisk Oversigt (Copenhagen: Gyldendal, 1865);
I Solskin. Livsanskuelser: To Fortællinger (Copenhagen: Gad, 1867);
Fra Bondeopvækkelsens Tid (Copenhagen: Gad, 1868);
"Grundejerforeningen," "Oktoberforeningen" og J. A. Hansen: Et historisk Tilbageblik (Copenhagen: Gad, 1869);
Fra Schweitz og Frankrig: Rejseskildringer af politisk og socialt Indhold (Copenhagen: Gad, 1871);
Fra Amerika (Copenhagen: Gyldendal, 1872);
Jason med det gyldne Skind (Copenhagen: Gyldendal, 1875);
Nutidsbilleder (Copenhagen: Gyldendal, 1878);
Politiske Portrætstudier (Copenhagen: Gyldendal, 1878);
Fra Studiebogen (Copenhagen: Gyldendal, 1879);
Umyndige i Kjærlighed: Skuespil i tre Akter (Copenhagen: Gyldendal, 1881);
Slagne Folk: Et efterladt Novellefragment (Copenhagen: Thieles Bogtrykkeri, 1892).

Editions and Collections: *Samlede Fortællinger,* 3 volumes (Copenhagen: Forlagsbureauet, 1891);
Jason med det gyldne Skind, illustrations by Hans Tegner, preface by Herman Bang (Copenhagen: Schubothe, 1901);
Udvalgte Skrifter, 2 volumes, edited by Vilhelm Andersen and H. Topsøe-Jensen (Copenhagen: Gad, 1923);
Nutidsbilleder, with an introduction by Niels Kaas Johansen (Copenhagen: Westermann, 1942);
Jason med det gyldne Skind, edited, with an afterword, by Finn Jensen (Copenhagen & Varde: Dansklærerforeningen/Skov, 1982).

Vilhelm Topsøe (courtesy of the Danish Royal Library, Copenhagen)

An influential political journalist and author, Vilhelm Topsøe was a transitional figure in Danish cultural life in the decades around 1870. His career coincided with the Modern Breakthrough in Nordic literature and with the protracted stalemate between progressive and conservative political, social, and cultural forces in the wake of the loss of the southern provinces of Denmark to Germany in 1864. During his short life and within his limited literary production, he came to epitomize the critical opposition to populist liberalism in parliament and to radical liberalism on the cultural scene. He was an intellectual in constant search for reasoned continuity and coherence at a time when ideological controversies dominated the national agenda. Not surprisingly, skepticism, irony, and satire penetrate several of his works.

Torn between the orderly values of a bygone Romantic-idealistic era and scientific claims grounded in modern socio-economic reality, Topsøe articulated troubling literary and historical ambiguities. Sympathetic to the modern movements per se, he felt driven by their implacable ideologues to embrace the conservative opposition. An outgoing social reformer, he sought in vain for a centrist platform. His writings, accordingly, express a realism that is both journalistic and fictional, committed to observation and portraiture rather than composition and plot. Topsøe the author is modern in his formal and technical treatment of thematic conflicts, and though issues of love permeate much of his prose and endow it with a lyric quality, his Romantic inclinations are few and far between. As critic Harald Nielsen has suggested, matters of love reveal both the skeletons left behind by outmoded Romantic idioms and the realistic sensibilities with which Topsøe repeatedly contemplated such relics of the past.

Vilhelm Christian Sigurd Topsøe, who used the initials V. C. S. for his first and middle names, was born in Skelskør on 5 October 1840 to Søren Christian Topsøe, a counselor and district judge, and his wife, Sigrid Christine Gudrun Thorgrimsen, of Icelandic descent. Topsøe was only six when his father died and his mother moved to Roskilde, where both he and his brother Haldor (later a noted chemist and civil servant) attended the Cathedral School. In 1852 the family settled in Copenhagen, where Vilhelm, delayed by a serious hip inflammation, graduated from the famed private school *Metropolitanskolen* in 1859. After graduation he enrolled in the law school at the University of Copenhagen, where he was active in student affairs. He was named president of the Student Union in 1865, the same year that he received his law degree.

In 1863, while still in law school, Topsøe co-edited and contributed to *Sværmere,* a memorable satirical magazine of national-liberal bent, and the same year he made his literary debut with some subtly tempered oppositional pieces of sociopolitical *Familiekarakteristikker* (Family Portraits), initially published as serials under the pen name Xox in *Dagbladet.* In Topsøe's 1863 book, these portraits were issued along with two other narratives, *Vintergæk og Sommernar* (Snowdrop/Jester in Winter and Fool in Summer) and *To Venner eller Reflexion og Forlovelse* (Two Friends or Reflection and Engagement) under the title *Skizzer* (Sketches).

By birth and upbringing, Topsøe was well prepared for a professional life in the circles of academics and civil servants of the mid-nineteenth-century Danish bourgeoisie. In Augusta Petersen, the daughter of a prominent wholesaler, he even found a soul mate of comparable social standing, whom he married 14 May 1868 and with whom he had a daughter, Karen (born 1872). Eventually, he embarked upon a regular career as a journalist and in 1872 became the editor in chief of *Dagbladet,* the leading national-liberal daily. In this position, he proved more sensitive than his predecessor, C. St. A. Bille, to the emerging party of the Modern Breakthrough in literature and cultural politics.

Georg Brandes, the foremost radical and naturalist critic in this movement, had launched his decisive lectures on main currents in European literature from the university lectern only a year before Topsøe was appointed editor of *Dagbladet.* Topsøe embraced Brandes's call for realism but appeared a more defensive humanist than his naturalistic counterpart. The ideas of freedom and progress that Brandes and his followers reclaimed from the Enlightenment were rather mixed blessings in Topsøe's view. While not categorically opposed to Brandes, Topsøe was considered his principal foe and, at the same time, an unreliable ally of the ultraconservative Julius Paludan, who eventually outflanked Brandes for a coveted university chair.

In his *Familiekarakteristikker,* Topsøe wraps an earnest sketch of Danish social history in irony and biting satire. For example, the piece about the naturalized German Taugenichts (No Goods) deals with an incompetent family of appointed nobility, while the story about the Danish Rige(e) (Riches) follows the bourgeoisie of trade.

Both classes are shown to have discredited their recently collapsed historical epoch, the period of absolutism, which ended 1848–1849. A progressive social view is discernible behind Topsøe's satirical exposure of the obsolete social setting around the two families; yet, in each instance the dissolution of the societal formation is described as a peaceful affair. Topsøe's treatment allows for relaxed, if not nostalgic, appraisals of this self-inflicted decline. Though socially indignant, he is too dignified to allow class warfare to be a part of his design. Instead, he implicitly advocates bourgeois humaneness and sociopolitical reform along the lines of moral reason, and his response to extremist temptations is a reticent and skeptical optimism. At the same time, his representation of true aristocrats is more forgiving than his description of bourgeois characters with new riches.

Vintergæk og Sommernar is a playful Biedermeier story that borders on a caricature of Romantic love. A young maid daydreams about a future life together with one of the student boarders in her father's pensione. But like the jester in winter and fool in summer, alluded to in the aphoristic Danish title, the liaison she hopes for comes to naught, and a bouquet of wilted flowers and sore memories is all she has left when much later she looks back upon the dreams of her youth. Yet, the spinster does her very best to make a humorous virtue of her necessity.

An understated rejection of daydreaming as a way of life, the text prefigures an important theme in Herman Bang's work, but treats it without Bang's particular sorrowful tone. Topsøe merely opts to combine his satire of false illusions with tacit compassion for their victim(s). He makes the point in his story that love is key to harmony and enrichment of human life, but he typically makes it indirectly by showing the dearth of such qualities when love is absent.

In *To Venner eller Reflexion og Forlovelse,* Topsøe also displays a travesty by demonstrating how the Romantic road to love in the post-Romantic era has become a blind alley in which fools–or caricatures of Søren Kierkegaard's caricature of the seducer–perform their acts unaffected by a perilously diminished view of reality.

The initial publication of *Familiekarakteristikker* in *Dagbladet* is typical of the persistent proximity between Topsøe's literary authorship and journalism, and the disguise of a pen name further suggests his need to separate an emerging literary persona from his more established journalistic one. His safeguard is all the more understandable considering how intertwined political themes and fictional modes actually appear to be in the texts. Topsøe saw his time as one when aesthetics was in decline and politics was on the rise. He brought to fruition a long-standing bent, honed in school compositions and student comedies, for pastische and humorous elaboration on social and political issues. Added to the mixture were techniques appropriated from such writers as Meïr Goldschmidt and Charles Dickens, both of whom were well versed in journalistic fiction and serious social satire.

A Romantic turned realist, Topsøe tended to emphasize atmosphere and situation in his portrayal of characters. Typically, case studies rather than individuals, his figures are depicted most vividly when placed off center stage. Political or not, they are mired in circumstances, love not least, that are larger than themselves and beyond their control. The setting of Topsøe's next work, *I Solskin. Livsanskuelser: To Fortællinger* (In Sunshine. Philosopies of Life: Two Stories, 1867), is no exception. In the wake of the traumatic withdrawal of Denmark from its southern border after the Danish defeat by Prussia in 1864, the idyllic setting of these stories is saturated with a fatal sense of human inferiority that foreshadows Bang's equally understated short-story art.

During his work for *Dagbladet* in the later part of the 1860s, Topsøe did not neglect the tasks of plain political reportage and commentary. Concurrently with his attempts at fiction, three series of his political articles were republished in booklets: *Forfatningssagen i Rigsraadet, en historisk Oversigt* (The Constitutional Issue in Parliament, a Historical Survey, 1865), *Fra Bondeopvækkelsens Tid* (From the Era of Peasant Revival, 1868), and *"Grundejerforeningen," "Oktoberforeningen" og J. A. Hansen: Et historisk Tilbageblik* ("The Land Owner's Society," "The October Society," and J. A. Hansen: a Historical Retrospect, 1869).

In all of these booklets, but especially the first, one senses the young lawyer's genuinely pragmatic interest in disentangling the intricate and divisive constitutional matters of his country after the loss of Slesvig and Holsten. In what sense could the truncated land still be considered or later restored to a viable nation? In the second booklet, Topsøe's balanced journalistic approach yields to a more polemic discourse against the landed gentry and in favor of the peasant farmers. The third booklet, finally, criticizes soberly the alliance between the largest landowners and a loose association of rural politicians and well-intended urban national-liberals that called itself Friends of the Peasantry. Yet, unlike Topsøe's more general social concerns, his advocacy of peasant issues was quite superficial and essentially a by-product of his national-liberal dislike of the rural upper classes.

Both his journalistic and his literary apprenticeships at *Dagbladet* culminated in trips abroad in 1870–1871. As was his later debut with an atypical bildungsroman, these formative journeys were atypical *Bildungsreisen* (educational [spiritual] journeys). They are documented in two books, which Topsøe based on his newspaper reporting, and as their titles intimate, the author was driven to modern locales and by modern motivations. *Fra Schweitz og Frankrig: Rejseskildringer af politisk og socialt Indhold* (From Switzerland and France: Travel Descriptions of Political and Social Content) and *Fra Amerika* (From America) were published in 1871 and 1872, respectively.

That Topsøe actually entered upon the former journey after an embarrassing skirmish with a Danish parliamentarian suggests a pattern noted by the author's biographer Vilhelm Andersen. While Topsøe's journalism in Denmark had been chiefly aesthetic in character, politics increasingly intruded on his style, and in France and Switzerland, the predominance of political and socio-economic concerns compelled him to alter his usual mode of reporting.

He began his journeys as the old Napoleonic empire in Europe gave way to revolution and modern republicanism and as American modernity was commanding exceptional European attention. Unlike more wholehearted moderns among his Danish contemporaries, Topsøe in his travel accounts considers the ancient and the modern to be indispensable to one another and finds his own vantage point within this delicate equilibrium. His intellectual modernity is rooted in persistent doubts about all ideologies, whether modern or historical in origin.

Whereas Brandes was modern by conviction, Topsøe was modern by default and could not withhold his apprehensions about the future. If his style seems pallid, the reason is the general skepticisim with which he honestly sought to balance conflicting perspectives, not any lack of personal engagement in the issues before him. Deprived of personal hopes by the Danish national catastrophe of 1864, Topsøe's disillusionment was perpetuated as he arrived in France in 1870 and witnessed the battle between the outmoded heroism of the dying empire and the emergent modern bourgeoisie in no less disarray. Despite his doubts about the new republic and its support for Otto von Bismarck of Germany, Topsøe realized in his reporting that France had no better role model. And though he found the belligerent revolutionaries distasteful, he reluctantly approved of their nationalistic fervor.

His most sincere misgivings about the new republic concerned its potential socialist or communist utopian excesses. As a moderate adherent of democratic freedoms who had come to acknowledge the decay of the ancien régime, he mustered a strained and dutiful evocation of solidarity with the frightening *regime moderne* (modern regime) and looked intensely for comforting signs of its leaders' moderation. When hints of violence imposed themselves all the same, he sought comfort in signs of underlying patriotism. In his writings about France, Topsøe denounces revolutionary foolhardiness but salutes the bravery of the fools.

A tribute to Swiss neutrality, Topsøe's account of his visit to Switzerland lauds the sanctuary it affords exiled members of the old French regime, whose political goals the smaller country had always despised. In its own political culture Switzerland had demonstrated how hostility against war can flow from a modern material democracy, and Topsøe approved of the result because it actually materialized in the well-intentioned theories of high-minded clergy and women in Geneva–and republicans and socialists in Germany–of whose practical sense he was otherwise not convinced. For a similar future to obtain in France, political and social morals must improve. As both the ancient and modern regimes had had their share of vices and virtues, Topsøe's conviction was that for a new order to succeed, the best of both ages must have a share in the future of the country.

In America in the early 1870s, the political outlook was not as grim as in contemporary France, and consequently, the visiting Danish journalist felt less

Topsøe in 1865 (drawing by Otto Bache; from Vilhelm Andersen, Vilhelm Topsøe: Et Bidrag til den danske Realismes Historie, *1922; Perkins Library, Duke University)*

obliged to insist on compromises between past and future. Instead, his account plainly celebrates the prospects of freedom, realism, and democracy to which the leading national cultures of Europe were merely aspiring. Andersen emphasizes once again that Topsøe, for all his gentlemanly values and traditional leanings, made his writing conform to its subject. The few poetic traits in his journalistic prose are confined to brief descriptions of landscapes, and rhetorical and philosophical elaborations are kept at a minimum in favor of his immediate sensations on location.

Typical of his balance of judgment, Topsøe argues in *Fra Amerika* that the newly completed Pacific Railway was an accomplishment shared by so many that the social health of the nation was in evidence; the social virtues of the project were likely to outweigh its political vices. American culture may have been driven by money and work, but at its best, political freedom vouchsafed both social and personal liberties, and Topsøe for once arrived at the unequivocal hope for the future that he earlier, in his book about France, labored to assert on behalf of the fledgling new European republic.

The indisputable presence of American freedoms and progress was, however, linked in Topsøe's reportage to signs of material and human degeneracy. He found the abundance of vigor and movement in the country inseparable from its shortage of rest and contemplation, and he referred to the bustling harbor of New York to illustrate his point. As he gave his endorsement to American civil liberties, he also returned to his principal theme of human love and expressed concern for the plight of the modern American family. For if the moral purity of this institution, as hailed by such writers as Alexis de Tocqueville, was decaying into a virtue of the past, how could liberties inextricably linked to the social fabric survive?

Upon his return to Denmark in 1871, Topsøe was well prepared for his promotion to editor at *Dagbladet,* which he gradually sought to expand and modernize while advancing his social and economic liberalism without breaking with the political conservatism and cultured past of the paper. His two travel books, particularly *Fra Amerika,* similarly served as background for expanding and modernizing his own realism in literary and journalistic form. First came the breakthrough novel *Jason med det gyldne Skind* (Jason and the Golden Fleece, 1875), and later, in 1878, two differently crafted yet interrelated volumes, *Politiske Portrætstudier* (Political Portrait Studies) and *Nutidsbilleder* (Pictures of the Present).

Jason med det gyldne Skind is a novel about the conversion of a Romantic idealist to realism. Jason's real name is Anton Hasting, but as Johan de Mylius points out, the existential identity suggested by his first name is secondary to his modern social identity indicated by his more frequently used last name. Indeed, most of the characters in the novel find their identity in the work life of a modern society, and Hasting in particular has accumulated his capital by curbing his desires in the modern psychological sense. As Mylius also observes, the entire psychology of the novel, so well characterized by Bang, unfolds in an atmosphere closer to that of Bang's later novel *Stuk* (1885) than to that of an earlier epochal novel by Goldschmidt, *Arvingen* (1865).

Both the presence of contemporary society and the conspicuous absence of naturalistic doctrine set Topsøe's *Jason med det gyldne Skind* apart from the novels of the Modern Breakthrough that soon followed. From the opening pages, when he returns to Denmark from entrepreneurial feats abroad, Hasting is torn between aristocratic and bourgeois characters. When he eventually sheds his misanthropy and finds his not so golden fleece in a modest personal relationship and a charitable social role as a physician for the rural poor, the model for his transition, according to de Mylius, is the composite character Ms. Rønnow, who herself once resigned from unrequited love to a social altruism and humanism. Her attitude toward life seems to reconcile the values of the bourgeoisie and aristocracy in her surroundings.

Knud Wentzel notes what makes *Jason med det gyldne Skind* a realistic novel in comparison with its predecessors: unlike Hasting, who finds some solace with a second or third girl when he cannot have his first choice, the typical hero of yesteryear opted for but one girl and lost even her because the reality of a union between the two would have compromised the idealism of his erotic desires. Compared with such contemporaries as Bang, J. P. Jacobsen, and Henrik Pontoppidan, however, Topsøe was a moderate idealist. His protagonist, according to Wentzel, has a share in their disillusioned idealism; yet, in the end he finds reasonable comfort and happiness in reality. He is not a Romantic who resigns from the sensual to the spiritual, but a sensualist who resigns to a modest reality.

Nielsen writes that no one senses reality better than a converted idealist, and Bang notes the imperceptible human emotions throbbing under the surface calm of Topsøe's love story. Wentzel even believes that these emotions are governed by the subconscious, and, according to Mylius, the development of the novel toward apparent harmony and dispassionate bliss is incomplete. In the same vein, the water that runs as a leitmotiv through the text suggests to Mylius that past passions cannot be silenced entirely, and uncompromising sentiments cannot be compromised completely. In the end, Hasting returns home, but, in contrast to the prescriptions of the bildungsroman as it is known in Danish literature since Goldschmidt and Hans Egede Schack, the home to which he returns is not the one he left.

After the years of numbing professional success overseas, Hasting has come home with the ambition to overcome his growing sense of homelessness by trumping his recent victories with domesticated love and inner happiness. But as he reconnects with Ida, the failed love of his youth, now married to his friend Bernhard, Hasting is slowly brought to realize how selfish both he and Ida have become. Their mutual attempts to control their own and each other's passions prove devastating, and no durable alternative presents itself. Ms. Rønnow, Ida's friend, is a model of unselfishness, but she can offer Hasting not an alternative partnership but merely an alternative outlook with which he must reconcile himself in relative solitude. Only thus can the restlessness and other unruly sentiments he brought home with him in the hope of dissolving them be put to productive use, although not to rest. His narrow sense of reality may finally extend into one that is truly his own.

Johan Fjord Jensen has shown that the structure of the novel comes closer to the developmental novel of French naturalism–*Madame Bovary* (1857) in particular–than it does to the indirectly revelatory and dramatic novels of Ivan Turgenev. In *Jason med det gyldne Skind* Topsøe kept the influence of Turgenev at bay with Kierkegaardian irony, a dissecting aesthetic attitude far removed from unreserved identification with the source of inspiration. In *Nutidsbilleder,* however, as he "liberates himself from the French determinism and approaches Turgenev," he accomplishes a novel that is "not about causes, but about characters." More precisely, it is about the strong-willed female character of Helene and the weaker male protagonist Flemming, who is deeply divided between the convulsions of a dying past and a disrespectful future. Fjord Jensen notes that Flemming is at odds with the cultural foundation of his own sophistication, and Hans Brix characterizes him as an aristocrat, typical of the early 1880s, who lacks will but expresses refinement and noble altruism. Like Hasting in *Jason med det gyldne Skind,* Flemming is not so much a character in his own right as he is one who is immersed in situations, and Fjord Jensen is right to say that *Nutidsbilleder* is a novel composed primarily of scenes and situations; even its atmosphere is embedded more in the latter than in stylistic descriptions.

Niels Kaas Johansen argues in his 1942 introduction to *Nutidsbilleder* that the process of transition encompasses a mix of social satire and a psychological depiction of love. A powerful polemic with atmospheric nuances, it has an ambivalent composition. While Flemming as its protagonist is meant to be a man of action, his case is one in which appearances deceive. At least initially, he is rather an escapist who seeks artistic relief from passivity and skepticism. By contrast, Helene in her escapism is less self-centered and her attitude more revealing and productively unsettling. Meanwhile, the character Harald Holst, whom the critic Nielsen sees as a symbol of the unprincipled side of Topsøe himself, relinquishes both art and tradition in favor of an aggressive agricultural and political modernity. Balancing acts–between static and dynamic forces, and between regressive and progressive modes of life–are attempted yet challenged throughout the novel as illustrated by ominous nature and weather symbols. The exception that confirms this precarious quest for equilibrium is a fourth character, Schwerin–the ultimate cynic and misanthropist, whose brutal desire for the impossible ends in nihilism.

In this novel, fictions of all sorts stand in the way of reality instead of representing it. But unlike social morals in general, Helene's ethics–like Ms. Rønnow's in *Jason med det gyldne Skind*–transcends self-interest. Her breakthrough is accompanied by Harald Holst's moral downfall, and by Schwerin's departure from the scene entirely. Flemming is then finally inspired to break out of his role of intermediary and to win Helene's respect and her hand through an unconditional commitment to the service of a disadvantaged community. In doing so, he follows in the footsteps of Hasting from *Jason med det gyldne Skind,* while Helene in the end combines the vision of Ms. Rønnow with deeper and humbler traits of other female characters in the earlier novel.

The decline of sociopolitical standards, so vividly and sarcastically depicted in *Nutidsbilleder,* resurfaces in several of Topsøe's *Politiske Portrætstudier*. This collection presents a constitutional outline in its opening chapter about the national-liberal politicians Orla Lehmann and H. N. Clausen. The structure is later detailed with few reservations in the discussion in the volume of other national-liberals. Topsøe believed the country would benefit when national prevailed over liberal in these instances of early Danish democracy, and Denmark would suffer when immoderate liberalism sought to subordinate legislative compromise to forces of popular sovereignty. He deprived the populist leaders of the peasant farmers of credit even when credit was due them.

Topsøe preferred the notion of individual civility and responsibility to the collective demands of the less cultured masses. He gave his reluctant approval to the rural aristocracy and major landowners, notably Prime Minister J. B. S. Estrup, as practical custodians of societal balance rather than to the populist partisans among the peasant farmers. Still, shortly before his death, he apparently contemplated a political takeover from Estrup, and like so many of the intermediary stances undertaken in his novels, most of the balancing acts Topsøe attempts in his political portraits fall short of stability. The national-liberals of his leaning no longer formed the strong backbone of the constitutional system but had disintegrated into single individuals sharing a gnawing skepticism about the political capacity of their own ideology. Harmonious resolutions were as elusive in Topsøe's political writings as they were, after all, in his fiction.

The virtues of the early Danish democrats, says Topsøe approvingly in his first portrait, can be summed up in Augustine's words: "Unity in the necessary, freedom in the questionable, love in everything." The adage returns the quintessence of his socio-economical and political observations and reflections to the principal theme of his artistic writings–and to the last three volumes of his oeuvre. Like his very first, *Skizzer,* both *Fra Studiebogen* (From the Study Book, 1879) and the

Paperback cover for a 1982 edition of Topsøe's 1875 novel, about a successful entrepreneur who returns to Denmark, gives up his Romantic idealism, and becomes a physician for the rural poor (Charles E. Young Research Library, University of California, Los Angeles)

two posthumous titles, *Umyndige i Kjærlighed: Skuespil i tre Akter* (Immature in Love: A Play in Three Acts, 1881) and *Slagne Folk: Et efterladt Novellefragment* (Defeated People: A Posthumous Novella Fragment, 1892), are love stories.

"En første Kærlighed" (A First Love) is the telling title of the first story in *Fra Studiebogen.* The unspoken feelings between a Gypsy musician and a newlywed Russian duchess can best be described as real yet not real. The duchess, to whom this borderline experience is more profitable than it is to the underprivileged Gypsy, is intent on keeping her distance using the stimulation the relationship provides for her own emotional purposes, much like Hasting did in *Jason med det gyldne Skind.* Meanwhile, the Gypsy takes home his own profit, albeit a more pedestrian one. He finds his memories of the noble lady quite uplifting, and his music turns more inspired than pedantic musicologists can imagine. Still, the two protagonists both benefit from one another in isolation, and save for the short-lived and elusive atmosphere between them, this first love is mutual only as an occasion for mutual self-indulgence.

The three parts of the next story, "Ved Efteraarstid" (By Fall), present further variations on novelistic themes. In "I September" (In September) a young female letter writer undergoes the same process of maturation in life and love as did the principal characters in both of Topsøe's novels. And again, the resulting harmony is not Romantic, but realistic with certain limitations. The love displayed in "I Oktober" (In October) similarly corresponds to the un-Romantic but all the more durable novelistic conclusions. In "I November" (In November), finally, the Romantic idiom is satirized by an old bachelor who prefers gout over poetry and longs for real winter in place of the perennial greyness of fall. Topsøe, according to Brix, sought to brighten the pessimistic influences from new French literature, and this story may be an example of such an attempt. An almost programmatic rejection of ideal representations of reality appears in "Daphne," in which the protagonist's spouse must remove a picture of herself before her husband can truly see her as a person. As Andersen explains, while dreams fade away in the light of reality, life is fulfilled in search of reality. As dreams must surrender to the same reality they foreshadow, a newborn dualism keeps this reality intact by keeping it from new compromises.

Umyndige i Kjærlighed proves the point. The pessimistic Dr. Brandt maturely resigns from personal claims to happiness in order to enable an attraction between his friends Cecilie and Frederik, whose mutual commitment reflects the sentiments between Flemming and Helene in *Nutidsbilleder:* only through maturation and real adversity do romantic sentiments stand a chance of becoming lasting relationships.

Topsøe's last work, the fragment *Slagne Folk,* is marked by the tension between such mature resignation and the desire to reach beyond the confines of the familiar. The gift of resignation is associated chiefly with the defeated older generation. It is their bulwark against further failures in life, love, and art. The dubious value of the gift is merely underscored by the resignation that is adopted also by a young and socially responsible doctor, who counts himself among the defeated. The fragment does not preclude that Eva, its young woman character and single opponent of its general outlook, will also succumb to its philosophy of life.

The final ambiguity of Vilhelm Topsøe's sentiments toward modernism and the ominous title of his last piece of writing are emblematic of his public work.

The fragmentary ending, which leaves the conclusion uncertain, epitomizes the impossible quest for a modern humanism that drives the novel. Topsøe was anxiously concerned with the future but did not have it ahead of him–whether as politician, journalist, or author. He died on 11 July 1881 after a short illness, survived by his wife, Augusta, and his daughter, Karen.

Hakon Stangerup claims that Brandes hated Topsøe because he was a realist who betrayed realism, to which Andersen adds that this writer of realism lost the culture war of the time. Whatever the truth, a telling letter from Edvard Brandes to his brother Georg calls Topsøe's death an occasion to celebrate, and several of the correspondences between the Brandes brothers and such leading men of Nordic letters as Holger Drachmann (in a letter from 1872) include expressions of similar disdain. Others, however, side with Georg and Edvard without sharing in the total rejection of their adversary. For instance, Bjørnstjerne Bjørnson and Alexander Kielland, two prominent Norwegian writers, testify to Topsøe's courage and liberal mind-set, and to his artistic gifts, respectively.

As such mixed reviews of his career mirror the mixed results he left behind, one is tempted to concur in Brix's assessment that Topsøe's literary work is "our classical bourgeoisie's late, indeed last, perfected bloom." Topsøe's contributions to Danish letters were noteworthy, as evidenced by the rapid decline of *Dagbladet* after his death. An inquisitive spirit in a conservative form, untimely in his own times, he warrants consideration. He patrolled the border separating a still powerful but receding aristocracy and academic bourgeoisie from an emerging middle- and farmer-class culture, blending and separating fiction and faction along the way. His experiences were situated where conflicting paradigms clash. Alloys made up of incompatible ingredients, his books are humanistic essays in syncretism.

Letters:

Vilhelm Topsøe and Godske Nielsen, *Tredive Breve fra og til en Mand uden Mening* (Copenhagen: Gad, 1885).

Biography:

Vilhelm Andersen, *Vilhelm Topsøe: Et Bidrag til den danske Realismes Historie* (Copenhagen: Gad, 1922).

References:

Herman Bang, "Forfatteren af 'Jason,'" in his *Realisme og Realister: Portrætstudier og Aforismer* (Copenhagen: Schubothe, 1879), pp. 21–40;

Edvard Brandes, "V. C. S. Topsøe," in his *Litterære tendenser: Artikler og anmeldelser,* edited by Carl Bergstrøm-Nielsen (Copenhagen: Gyldendal, 1968), pp. 43–51;

Edvard Brandes and Georg Brandes, *Brevveksling med nordiske Forfattere og Videnskabsmænd,* volumes 1–5, 8, edited by Morten Borup with the assistance of Francis Bull and John Landquist (Copenhagen: Gyldendal, 1939–1942);

Hans Brix, "Vilhelm Topsøe," in his *Danmarks Digtere: Fyrretyve Kapitler af dansk Digtekunsts Historie* (Copenhagen: Aschehoug, 1951), pp. 413–416;

Povl Engelstoft, "Topsøe, Vilhelm," in *Dansk Biografisk Leksikon,* volume 14, edited by Sv. Cedergreen Bech (Copenhagen: Gyldendal, 1983), pp. 637–639;

Marie Hvidt, "Vilhelm Topsøe's *Fra Amerika,*" in *Scandinavians in America: Literary Life,* edited by J. R. Christianson (Decorah, Iowa: Symra Literary Society, 1985), pp. 188–195;

Johan Fjord Jensen, "Vilh. Topsøe," in his *Turgenjev i dansk åndsliv* (Copenhagen: Gyldendal, 1961), pp. 165–172;

Johan de Mylius, "Fra den ny verden: 'Jason med det gyldne Skind,'" in *Læsninger i dansk litteratur 1820–1900,* edited by Povl Schmidt and Ulrik Lehrmann (Odense: Odense Universitetsforlag, 1998), pp. 215–231, 351–352;

Jørgen Johansen and Arne Jakobsen, "Det moderne gennembruds mænd," in their *Fremskridtets frontløber: Ingeniørenidansk littergtur* (Copenhagen: Teknisk Forlag, 1992), pp. 11–17;

Harald Nielsen, "Vilhelm Topsøe," in his *Moderne Litteratur* (Copenhagen: Gyldendal, 1904), pp. 83–102;

Hakon Stangerup, *Kulturkampen,* 2 volumes (Copenhagen: Gyldendal, 1946);

Knud Wentzel, "Vilhelm Topsøe: *Jason med det gyldne Skind,*" in his *Fortolkning og skæbne: Otte danske romaner fra romantismen og naturalismen* (Copenhagen: Fremad, 1970), pp. 100–110.

Papers:

Vilhelm Topsøe's papers are at the Danish Royal Library in Copenhagen.

Leonora Christina Ulfeldt

(8 July 1621 - 16 March 1698)

Marita Akhøj Nielsen
Society for Danish Language and Literature

(Translated by Tiina Nunnally)

BOOKS: *Jammers Minde,* edited by Sophus Birket Smith (Copenhagen: Gyldendal, 1869); translated by Fanny Elizabeth Bunnètt as "A Record of the Sufferings of the Imprisoned Countess," in *Memoirs of Leonora Christina. Daughter of Christian IV. of Denmark. Written During Her Imprisonment in the Blue Tower at Copenhagen 1663–1685* (London: King, 1872; corrected edition, New York: Dutton, 1929);

Jammers Minde og andre selvbiografiske Skildringer, edited by Johs. Brøndum-Nielsen and C. O. Bøggild-Andersen (Copenhagen: Society for Danish Language and Literature / Rosenkilde & Bagger, 1949);

Hæltinners Pryd, edited by Christopher Maaløe (Copenhagen: Society for Danish Language and Literature / C. A. Reitzel, 1977).

Editions: *Franske Levnedsskildring 1673,* edited by C. O. Bøggild-Andersen (Copenhagen: Forening for Boghaandværk, 1958);

Jammers Minde. Diplomatarisk udgave, edited by Poul Lindegård Hjorth and Marita Akhøj Nielsen with the cooperation of Ingelise Nielsen (Copenhagen: Reitzel, 1998).

OTHER: "Selvbiografi," edited by Sophus Birket Smith, in *Danske Samlinger for Historie, Topografi, Personal- og Literaturhistorie,* second series, 1 (1871–1872): 142–217; translated by Fanny Elizabeth Bunnètt as "Autobiography," in *Memoirs of Leonora Christina. Daughter of Christian IV. of Denmark. Written During Her Imprisonment in the Blue Tower at Copenhagen 1663–1685* (London: King, 1872).

Leonora Christina Ulfeldt (painting by Gerrit van Honthorst, 1647; Museum of National History at Frederiksborg Castle)

Leonora Christina Ulfeldt is regarded as the finest Danish prose writer of the seventeenth century. Her masterpiece is her prison memoir *Jammers Minde* (Memory of Woe, 1869; translated as "A Record of the Sufferings of the Imprisoned Countess," 1872). The work ranges in style from the polished and formal rhetoric of the baroque to an almost colloquial and sensually permeated Danish. The realistic depictions of prison life, combined with the narrator's imposing personality, have made *Jammers Minde* a popular classic work.

Leonora Christina's dramatic fate has continued to ensure her a place in Danish history books, but it took many years for her contribution as an author to be acknowledged. She published nothing during her lifetime, and many of her works are known only referentially. Not until 1869, with the publication of *Jammers Minde,* was her literary genius recognized. An autobiography written in French that has decisively colored the general perception of her persona was published as "Selvbiografi" in 1871–1872 (translated as "Autobiography," 1872). This edition was based, however, on a later copy; the original text was not published until 1958, and then only in facsimile. All of Leonora Christina's major works are autobiographical. To an exceptional degree, her life is reflected in her work in an unusually direct manner.

Leonora Christina was born at Frederiksborg Castle, north of Copenhagen, on 8 July 1621. Her father was King Christian IV, sovereign of the Dano-Norwegian Empire; her mother was the king's consort, Kirsten Munk, whom he had married after his queen's death in 1615. Since Munk was of noble but not royal birth, she was married morganatically; therefore, neither she nor her offspring had any claim to titles or estates belonging to her royal partner. Leonora Christina was their third child. As was the custom in aristocratic circles, the children were raised by their maternal grandmother. But when Denmark became embroiled in the Thirty Years' War, the king became concerned for the safety of his children and sent them to live with his niece in Friesland from 1628 to 1629. The earliest memories in Leonora Christina's autobiography stem from this time.

During the war, in which the king participated in military campaigns and was seriously wounded, Munk fell in love with a German count who was serving in Christian IV's retinue. When the king discovered the relationship, he banished Munk from his court. Although the marriage was not dissolved, they never met again, and for the rest of his life the king maintained a relationship with his mistress, noblewoman Vibeke Kruse. In his bitterness toward Munk, the king forbade his children to have any contact with their mother, who is not given a single mention in Leonora Christina's autobiographical writings. On the other hand, the king assumed responsibility for the children's further upbringing and education, which was the best the times could offer. In addition to mastering their native Danish, they were expected to learn German and French. The girls were given instruction in such traditional female pursuits as needlework, dance, and proper conduct in public. They were also given lessons in arithmetic, music, and drawing, as well as the subject that was regarded at that time as the most essential of all–religion. According to her own account in the autobiography, Leonora Christina was a talented student and became accomplished at both book learning and practical skills.

Leonora Christina's upbringing was designed for the position she was expected to take in the class-stratified Danish society. As a consequence of her mother's birth, Leonora Christina and her sisters could not become princesses; but the king granted them the title of countess of Schleswig and Holstein, thus designating their special rank–less than royal but above the rest of the nobility. At that time the king of Denmark-Norway was appointed to the throne, and his power was limited by the nobles–particularly the highest-ranking ones, who were represented in the Rigsråd (State Council). In his rivalry with Sweden, Christian IV wished to assert the place of Denmark-Norway not only as the foremost Nordic state, but also as a leader of the Protestant powers in northern Europe. The Rigsråd had reservations about such an aggressive foreign policy. In this situation the king sought to create allies among the high-ranking nobles by betrothing his daughters to promising young men from the most prominent families. He then separated the interests of his sons-in-law from those of their peers by granting them careers in state government.

For Leonora Christina the king chose Corfitz Ulfeldt, who was not wealthy but had been internationally educated and was exceedingly gifted. He was fifteen years older than his betrothed. They were promised to each other when Leonora Christina was nine. She assures the reader of her autobiography that she immediately developed a deep love for him and that she retained this feeling for the rest of her life. With great splendor and ceremony their wedding was held at Copenhagen Castle in 1636. Shortly afterward, Ulfeldt was named governor of Copenhagen, and in their lavishly furnished estate in the center of the city the couple maintained a life of elegance on an international scale. Of their happy life together, Leonora Christina writes in her autobiography: "Son Mari l'aymoit et honoroit, fit le Galand et pas le Mari. Elle passe le temps à tirer, à courir à cheval; à jouër à la paume, à apprendre tout de bon de creoner de Charle v. Mandre, sur la Viole de gambe, sur la flute, sur la Quitarres et jouit d'une vie heureuse" (Her husband loved and honored her, enacting the lover more than the husband. She spends her time in shooting, riding, tennis, in learning drawing in good earnest from Karel van Mander, in playing the viol, the flute, the guitar, and she enjoys a happy life). She did not allow pregnancy or childbirth to hamper her, even though in fourteen years she gave birth to ten children, and to a large extent she raised them all herself. While foreign guests were impressed by the couple and their home, their Danish peers regarded the Ulfeldts as extravagant, arrogant, and power hungry. Yet, many people from the lower classes, including their family doctor, Otto Sperling the Elder, became ardently devoted to the Ulfeldts and displayed a lifelong loyalty to them.

To make possible their life of splendor, Ulfeldt took on great debts, although they did not prevent him from becoming one of Europe's wealthiest aristocrats in a matter of a few years. Providently enough, his fortune was invested not only in land but also in jewels and other

Leonora Christina (far right) in 1623 with her mother, Kirsten Munk, consort of King Christian IV, and her siblings Valdemar Christian, Anna Cathrine, and Sophie Elisabeth (painting by Jacob van Doort; from Bodil Wamberg, Leonora Christina. Dronning af Blåtårn, *1991; Memorial Library, University of Wisconsin–Madison)*

valuable effects, in addition to an extensive lending enterprise. The common belief was that his wealth was built on corruption, grand in scope. Christian IV also suspected Ulfeldt of corruption but chose to overlook it at this time because of his son-in-law's undisputed brilliance. In 1643 Ulfeldt was appointed seneschal, which was the highest office in the land, and he undertook important diplomatic missions abroad, including to the Netherlands and France in 1646–1647. There the Ulfeldts, as the official emissaries of Denmark-Norway, aroused much admiration and attention, even at the discriminating French court. In Paris, Leonora Christina completely charmed the dowager queen with her loveliness, her elegance, her intelligence, and her natural self-confidence.

Back home in Copenhagen, however, the Ulfeldts were met with anger from the aging king. Besides his suspicions regarding Corfitz Ulfeldt's misuse of public funds, Christian IV harbored a deep distrust toward his son-in-law's foreign policy, which had gradually come into direct opposition with the king's own views. Added to these suspicions was that the Ulfeldts, along with Munk's other children and sons- and daughters-in-law, had been lobbying for a reconciliation between the king and his wife. About this contentious relationship with her father Leonora Christina Ulfeldt is utterly silent in her autobiography, in which she portrays herself as the king's favorite daughter. During the king's last days she and Corfitz Ulfeldt were at his side, and when he died, Leonora Christina was the one who closed the old warrior's one remaining eye. She regarded her father's death as a turning point in her life; many years later she dated one of her poems in *Jammers Minde* in this way: "1684. den 28. *Februarii,* som er 36. Aars dagen, att Høyloffligste Konning *Christian* den Fiærde, sagde Werden goede Nat, oc ieg min Wersens welfart" (Written on February 28, 1684, that is the thirty-sixth anniversary since the illustrious King Christian the Fourth bade good night to this world, and I to the prosperity of my life). Immediately after the king's death, the Ulfeldts cruelly showed the gravely ill Vibeke Kruse the door.

After Christian IV died, his son, Leonora Christina's half brother, was chosen as sovereign and became King Frederik III. His queen, Sophie Amalie, fervently hated Leonora Christina, and the feeling was mutual. By that time Ulfeldt's influence had begun to wane, even though in 1649 he was again sent on an official mission, and as usual, his wife accompanied him. During their absence his position in Danish politics was further weakened, and soon Leonora Christina suffered the humiliation of being stripped of her title of countess of Slesvig and Holstein. In the summer of 1650 inquiries were initiated into the official conduct of the seneschal, and in December a well-known prostitute, Dina Vinhofvers, caused a sensation in Copenhagen by first accusing Ulfeldt of planning to poison the king, only to claim shortly thereafter that a conspiracy was in the works to murder Ulfeldt himself. At the subsequent trial, Ulfeldt was cleared of all blame, and Vinhofvers was executed. But the inquiries into Ulfeldt's transactions continued; in his opinion, the Vinhofvers case had not been thoroughly investigated, since, through one of her lovers, she had had a direct link to the royal court.

In the summer of 1651 the Ulfeldts fled from this climate of mistrust, suspicion, and incipient disgrace. Over the next few years they developed ever stronger ties to the Swedish court, even though Leonora Christina never felt at ease in Stockholm because the Swedes did not show her the respect befitting the daughter of a king. For this reason, in 1654 she refused to attend the wedding of Karl X Gustav, the Swedish king, because she had been assigned too low a place in the entourage. Her acidly ironic account of this wedding is the oldest autobiographical entry still preserved. In 1656 she traveled to Denmark because Ulfeldt hoped that she would be able to bring about a reconciliation with Frederik III. She twice described this journey. Immediately following her return home she wrote a Danish account in which the main emphasis is placed on the exchange of words between her and the king's representatives, clearly an attempt to report the way in which the negotiations had proceeded. Many years later she gave a more dramatic and novelistic account in her autobiography. In this instance, she wrote earnestly about how her mission failed because she was stopped on her way to see the king in Copenhagen by his envoy, the son of Vibeke Kruse. The encounter between these two developed into a war of nerves in which she refused to go on foot to the meeting with him. While she awaited his reply, she surveyed her terrified escorts: "sa fille eust un accident alors, qui luy demeure encore au jourdhuy, un tremblement de teste, ces yeux ne se mouuant; Le Secretaire trembloit, que ces dents firent de bruiet. Charles estoit tout pasle" (Her female attendant was seized with an attack from which she suffers still, a trembling of the head, while her eyes remained fixed. The secretary trembled so that his teeth chattered. Charles was quite pale). She herself remained utterly composed. She was equally calm on her way back, when she had to draw her pistol in order to be rid of the king's overly zealous official.

The outcome of this journey showed Ulfeldt that he had no hope of gaining favor with the Danish king, and when war broke out between Denmark-Norway and Sweden in 1657, he was among the trusted advisers of Karl X Gustav. Ulfeldt's wife followed his lead, and both of them experienced the victorious Swedish campaign as a personal triumph. After the peace agreement of 1658, Ulfeldt dreamed of creating an aristocratic republic in the rich province of Skåne, which Denmark had been forced to relinquish to Sweden. Since Ulfeldt made no secret of his intentions, Karl X Gustav developed a deep distrust of him, and Ulfeldt did not participate in the renewed Swedish assault on Denmark later that year. The fortunes of war had turned, and in the search for a scapegoat, Ulfeldt was arrested in May 1659, accused of treasonous contact with the Danish king. Leonora Christina voluntarily shared her husband's house arrest on their estate in the Scanian city of Malmö, and because Ulfeldt was seriously ill, she handled his defense in the case. The extant documents, including her own report of an important court meeting, reveal her to be an intelligent and articulate defender who did not always adhere strictly to the truth. The case ended with Ulfeldt being convicted of high treason. In the meantime, his health had improved, and at a rumor that he and his wife were to be exiled to Finland, they each fled separately. For this reason they did not receive the message that Ulfeldt had been granted amnesty.

According to their plan, Ulfeldt was to travel to Lübeck and she to Copenhagen to seek the favor of Frederik III. Instead, Ulfeldt went to Copenhagen; when his wife arrived, both were arrested. They were imprisoned in the inaccessible fortress of Hammershus on the desolate island of Bornholm, far out in the Baltic Sea.

Leonora Christina wrote an extensive account of their seventeen-month confinement, but it has been lost; a shorter version was later included in her autobiography. Both this version and contemporary reports by officials reveal that their prison guard, Adolph Fuchs, treated them with excessive cruelty. Ulfeldt had a difficult time restraining himself whenever Fuchs provoked him, but Leonora Christina reacted with an air of cold superiority. In her autobiography she tells how she responded to one of his insults with an outright challenge: "rien ne peut effacer cette tache si non du sang. Ho; disoit il en touchant son épée et le tirant un peu hors du fourreau. Voila ce que je porte pour vous Madame. Elle en riant tire son poinçon de ces cheueux, disant, voila mes armes à present qui seront pour vous" ("nothing can efface this insult but blood." "Oh!" said he, seizing his sword, and drawing it a little out of the scabbard, "this is what I wear for you, madam." She, laughing, drew the big hair pin from her hair, saying, "Here are all the arms at present that I have for you").

The conditions became so intolerable that one March night in 1661 the couple made an attempt to escape. Using pieces of board and sheets that they had tied together, they lowered themselves and their loyal servant out of the fortress. When the moon disappeared behind some clouds, the servant fell into a ravine. Leonora Christina singlehandedly hauled him up and then carried her weakened husband down the steep cliffs. Because of his infirmity, they did not reach shore until after daylight and were apprehended by the guards.

When Fuchs inspected their escape route, he declared that only with the devil's help could Leonora Christina have rescued the servant, an accusation that she vehemently denied in her autobiography: "On peut vrayement dire que Dieu l'avoit pourvu de ces gardes, car d'échapper d'un tel danger, et en tirer un autre, ce n'est pas le seul fait d'un homme" (We can truly say that God had granted her His protection, for to escape from such a danger, and draw another out of it, could not have been done by unaided man). Subsequently, the commonly held perception was that she was a witch. After the escape attempt, Leonora Christina and Corfitz were separated until December, when they renounced nearly all of their properties in Denmark-Norway. Under humiliating circumstances, Corfitz Ulfeldt was forced to swear an oath of allegiance to the king in Copenhagen.

The background for this harsh treatment was not simply a thirst for revenge but also the political revolution that Frederik III had carried out with the support of prominent burghers. This revolt resulted in the establishment of absolute rule in the autumn of 1660, which spe-

Leonora Christina with her husband, Corfitz Ulfeldt, whom she married in 1636 (engraving based on a painting by J. Folkema; from Bodil Wamberg, Leonora Christina. Dronning af Blåtårn, *1991; Memorial Library, University of Wisconsin–Madison)*

cifically restricted the privileges and power of the nobility. During the first years of this new form of rule, the government feared rebellious propensities in noble circles, and in that connection, many thought that Ulfeldt might play a role. That was why he had to be broken. After their release, he and his family were assigned to an estate on the island of Funen, and from there they were allowed to take a trip to the Netherlands and France in 1662, for health reasons. They stayed for a long period in Brügge, where their eldest son killed Fuchs, whom they met by chance. Leonora Christina had not instigated the murder, but she thanked her son for avenging the suffering they had endured at Hammershus. Events took an even more fateful turn when Ulfeldt proposed to the electoral prince of Brandenburg that he could incite a revolt in Denmark that would win the prince the Danish monarchy. From Brandenburg the news was conveyed to Copenhagen, where the high court on 24 July 1663 condemned Ulfeldt to death in absentia. The preserved documents demonstrate that the sentence was well founded.

Before the conviction was announced, Leonora Christina traveled from Brügge to London to collect a substantial sum that Charles II, the English king, had borrowed from the couple during his exile. On behalf of the Danish government, she was arrested and sent to Copenhagen, where she arrived on 8 August and was immediately imprisoned in the Blue Tower, the prison at Copenhagen Castle. During the next few days she was subjected to lengthy interrogations by leading officials, who took it for granted that she must have been her husband's accomplice in this matter, as in all others. But she insisted that she knew nothing of Ulfeldt's plans for a coup d'état and that the accusations had to be false. Only once did the strain become too much for Leonora Christina: when she learned of Ulfeldt's death sentence, she collapsed; but she regained her composure at once. No charges were brought against Leonora Christina herself, and since she steadfastly proclaimed her husband's innocence as well as her own, any further interrogation was abandoned. Nevertheless, she remained in prison and was subjected to humiliating treatment. All of her possessions were taken away; she was bodily searched; and she was confined to a narrow, dark, and filthy cell. She was not physically tortured, but she was under constant psychological pressure.

Attempts were made to arrest not only Leonora Christina but the entire Ulfeldt circle, and with some success. In 1664 the family doctor, Sperling, was imprisoned in the Blue Tower, where he died in 1681. Ulfeldt himself eluded capture, however, and on 13 November 1663, he was executed in effigy. The couple's magnificent estate in Copenhagen was leveled to the ground, and a pillar of shame was erected on the site. All of this Leonora Christina learned about in her prison cell without being able to see what was happening. She was led to believe that her husband had actually been executed. In the meantime, he was frantically fleeing through Europe, and in February 1664 he died under a false name aboard a boat on the Rhine River. In the Blue Tower, Leonora Christina learned of his death from the palace bailiff. She wrote in *Jammers Minde:* "Ieg laae saa hen i haabet att ded saa war, att min Herre wed døden war siine Fiinder vntgaaet, oc tenkte wed mig selff, med største forundring, att ieg skulle leffwe den dag, att ynske min herre døe" (I lay there silently hoping that it might be so, that my lord had by death escaped his enemies; and I thought with the greatest astonishment that I should have lived to see the day when I should wish my lord dead).

After Ulfeldt's death, Leonora Christina posed no threat to the Danish king. Yet, in the eyes of the monarch and his queen she was no less guilty than her husband. As long as Frederik III was alive, the conditions of her imprisonment remained harsh. For a long time, any form of meaningful work was denied her, a situation that she confronted with an inventiveness worthy of Robinson Crusoe. She unraveled some of her clothing and used the yarn to embroider a rag; she made a loom from trash and, most important of all, she found a way to write: "Strøe Suckeret war i reent Papir, deraff betiente ieg mig att skriffwe paa, hwad ieg dictede, oc wille *notere;* giorde blæcket aff Lyße-Røg strøgen aff Sølffskeen oc med øll *præpareret.* Min Pen war giort aff en Hønße Winge" (Sugar came wrapped in clean paper, on which I wrote what I had composed and wished to make note of; made ink from candle soot rubbed from a silver spoon and prepared with ale. My pen was made from a chicken wing).

The conditions improved slightly after Ulfeldt's death. Leonora Christina was then allowed to read the Bible, and gradually she managed to acquire many necessities, including newspapers. She did not lack for entertainment; her fellow prisoners and the prison staff, in particular the ever-changing servant girls, were a constant source of amusement. She took an interest in their personal stories and learned from them what she could, including English. Several times she had an opportunity to escape, but she chose to stay in the Blue Tower because she wished to be formally released, partially for the sake of her children and partially for the sake of her own good name. After the death of Frederik III in 1670, for a time some people thought she would be set free. On the accession to the throne of Frederik's son and successor, Christian V, Leonora Christina received visits in prison from the new queen and later from her mother, who both attempted to intercede on behalf of the celebrated prisoner. The dowager queen, Sophie Amalie, however, opposed her release, although she could not prevent an improvement in the prison conditions. Thenceforth, Leonora Christina received a yearly allowance to use as she saw fit. The accession of a new king gave renewed hope to another prisoner from the Ulfeldt circle, Otto Sperling. His son, Otto Sperling the Younger, traveled to Copenhagen to try to win his father's release, but by the spring of 1673 he had to accept that his efforts had been in vain. Before his departure, however, he convinced both Leonora Christina and his father to write their personal memoirs, which would then be used to influence opinion in Europe and thereby put pressure on the Danish government.

With this goal in mind, Leonora Christina wrote her autobiography, and for the benefit of an international audience, she wrote it in French. The account covers her entire life, which is described chronologically, although with great leaps in time and with most of the emphasis on certain typical situations. Although the memoir was meant to be a document defending her innocence, the autobiography is filled with suspenseful episodes that are often presented with some humor. The work takes on the character of a novel, which is enhanced by the author's speaking of herself in the third person as "nostre femme" (our lady). At the same time, she acts as the first-person narrator, reflecting on and assessing what has happened in her life. She is both the actor, deeply involved in the dramatic events, and the worldly wise philosopher, viewing the vicissitudes of life from an elevated position. The theme of the work is the persecuted heroine. Time after time she becomes the victim of intrigue, harassment, and humiliation; such a position gives her the opportunity to demonstrate her courage, tenacity, detached perspective, and superior sense of calm. She finds her strength in her belief in divine dispensation and in her awareness that she is the king's beloved daughter. Her self-confidence triumphed even over Fuchs's brutal threats at Hammershus: "vous pouuez faire de moy ce que vous ne voulez au mettre, mais vous me pouuez jamais humillier de sorte, qu'il ne me souvienne, que vous auez esté le serviteur d'un serviteur du Roy mon Pere" (You may do with me whatever you will, but you can never humble me so that I shall cease to remember that you were a servant of a servant of the King my Father).

Of decisive importance throughout Leonora Christina's life was her deep and unshakable love for Ulfeldt. Considering what a central role her love for him played, Ulfeldt is depicted with remarkable detachment. While he reciprocates his wife's devotion, he is given few other positive qualities. He is consistently portrayed as weak, quick-tempered, naive, and utterly dependent on his wife. Although this portrait is not wholly misleading, it does not convey the entire truth. He was also a man of intelligence, charm, and refinement. This lopsided character sketch results from the purpose of the autobiography, which necessitated that she disassociate herself from her husband and thereby from his provable treason. The autobiography makes little attempt to explain the couple's tumultuous fate. It does not discuss the rationale behind their opponents' actions but instead claims that the animosity was an expression of jealousy.

Although the autobiography failed to achieve Leonora Christina's primary goal in writing it, it did have an impact. Sperling made use of it in his book about learned women, which may have been his intention from the beginning. At any rate, the author reports extensively on her education and knowledge. This work was well known to later historians and was disseminated in transcripts, translations, and adaptations. The original manuscript, which was smuggled out of the Blue Tower, was missing for a long time but reappeared in 1952. In 1958

Page from the manuscript for Ulfeldt's autobiography, written in French in 1673 during her twenty-one-year imprisonment in the Blue Tower at Copenhagen Castle (courtesy of the Danish Royal Library, Copenhagen)

it was published in facsimile; to date, it is the only edition of the author's own text.

Shortly after finishing her French autobiography, Leonora Christina began work on a more detailed account of her imprisonment, *Jammers Minde,* the first section of which she completed in the Blue Tower. The opening words of the preface explain the title: "Hierte Kiere Børn, billigen kand ieg med Iob sige; Der som man min Iammer weye kunde, oc mine Liidelser tilsammen i en Wect-Skaal legge, da skulle de were tyngere end Saand i Haffuet" (Beloved Children, I may indeed say with Job, "Oh, that my grief were thoroughly weighed, and my calamity laid in the balances together! For now it would be heavier than the sand of the sea"). Her motive for writing this work was twofold: She wished to remember the support she had received from God in the midst of her misfortune, and she wished to tell her children that she had a clear conscience. Just as God had saved her from misfortune on six previous occasions, he would save her from the seventh–the Blue Tower. Following the preface is an account of her first three weeks in prison. The interrogations, in particular, are described in detail, often presented in the form of a dialogue. She conducts her defense with the same self-confident and measured approach that she displayed during the trial in Malmö, and her arguments are incisive: "Cantzeler sagde; Eders Mand haffuer bøded en fremmet Herre Dannemarckis Riige til. Ieg spurte, om Dannemarckis Riige hørte min Mand til, att hand ded kunde vdbyde?" (The chancellor said, "Your husband has offered the kingdom of Denmark to a foreign lord." I inquired if the kingdom of Denmark belonged to my husband, that he could thus offer it). From the periods between interrogations, she recounts specific episodes that reveal the humiliating treatment she was forced to endure, but they also describe the few expressions of sympathy she encountered. The course of events, though, is to be considered only as the background for the essential spiritual drama that is introduced in the first words of the preface and determines the overall composition. Leonora Christina's identification with Job is the key to her own interpretation of her imprisonment. Like Job, she maintains her innocence in the face of all torments, convinced that they are trials from which God will eventually set her free. Like Job, she throws herself into an impassioned confrontation with the inscrutable will of God, struggling with her own fate.

The style of the narrative shifts considerably, ranging from the highly embellished and image-rich rhetoric of the baroque to exceedingly colloquial language, peppered with oaths and curses. Her comments are presented in a restrained and unsentimental tone. At times she allows herself to be carried away by the force of her memories, but in general the twofold purpose of the work dictates her choice of material. She probably did not envision any readers other than her own children. Many times she speaks to them directly. She enjoins them to reciprocate the good she has encountered; she explains the reasons for her actions with regard to the future of her lineage; and as for the unavoidable, though muted, criticism of their father's transactions, she emphasizes her solidarity with him: "Ieg liider for att haffue werret ælsket aff en dydig Herre oc Hoßbonde, for att ey haffue Hannem i Vlycken forlat wilt" (I suffer for having been loved by a virtuous lord and husband, and for not having abandoned him in misfortune). Another indication that she did not intend to address a larger audience is her criticism of the absolute monarchy, which in places is quite blatant.

In addition to working on her memoirs, Leonora Christina spent her time in prison reading. She was especially interested in historical books, from which she gathered material for a large collection of biographical texts on women. She also wrote some spiritual poems, although she herself did not consider them to be of professional quality. As she tells her children in *Jammers Minde:* "Giffuer intet act paa Riimene, de erre icke effter alle de Regler Poëterne sig giøre; Men giffuer act paa Materien, Meeningen oc Nytten" (Do not regard the rhymes; they are not according to all the rules which poets make; but regard the matter, the sense, and the usefulness). Yet, these poems are far from paltry; they follow the aesthetic norms of contemporary baroque hymns, but they differ from hymn writing in their content, which is often highly personal. Along with *Jammers Minde,* many of these poems have survived in various transcriptions that bear witness to their popularity among Leonora Christina's contemporaries.

Aside from her literary endeavors, Leonora Christina devoted the long years of her imprisonment to music and needlework. Even though she was kept in confinement and never allowed beyond the prison walls, she did have a certain amount of contact with life outside. She also played an exalted and active role in the little world of the Blue Tower. Even so, the passage of time could weigh heavily, as revealed in such comments in *Jammers Minde* as "Sleed saa ded Aar hen, med Læsen, Skriffwen oc dicten" (I endured the year with reading, writing, and composing).

Leonora Christina's implacable enemy, the dowager queen, during her lifetime, prevented her release from prison. Shortly after Sophie Amalie's death, Leonora Christina was finally released on 19 May 1685, after "21. Aar. 9. Maaneder oc 11. Dage" (twenty-one years, nine months, and eleven days). The government assigned her a residence in the small and remote provincial town of Maribo, where, thanks to a royal subsidy, she was able to lead a life more or less befitting her position. For the sake of her three surviving children, Leonora Christina made many attempts to reclaim the riches that she and Ulfeldt had lost, but all her attempts proved futile. In 1688 her oldest daughter came to live with her, and she also received regular visits from the youngest. Her son, who had made a brilliant career for himself in Austria, where his descendants decided to remain, was allowed to visit Leonora Christina only twice. The first time was in 1691, when he was forty years old. His mother had not seen him since he was twelve.

In general, Leonora Christina led a secluded life, although she did receive occasional visitors, including Thomas Kingo, the greatest Danish poet of the baroque era, whose work she much admired. Her most important literary work from the Maribo period was her continuation of *Jammers Minde.* She meticulously revised the old manuscript from the Blue Tower and, after several fruitless attempts, finally began writing again. The subject was now the daily life in the Blue Tower, which crystallizes around specific events and her ever-changing companions in prison–the staff, her fellow prisoners, and the domestic animals. Now at a safe distance from the events, she allowed her sense of humor, her joy of storytelling, and her interest in those around her to unfold freely, while the religious interpretation of her imprisonment, as well as the wish to show her innocence, retreated to the background. Only once does she speak directly to her children. As a consequence of this shift in focus, the style is more colloquial. The grandiloquent rhetoric has no place in this unretouched, realistic portrait of the teeming life within the walls of the Blue Tower.

When Leonora Christina reached the year 1674, the memoirs came to a standstill once again, but after a brief time she resumed work, primarily because she wanted to present her version of the prison release, which she describes in depth. On the other hand, she passes swiftly over the intervening years, depicting only a few scenes, while long periods are dealt with in cursory fashion. The period preceding her release is described from the viewpoint of the prison staff, who dread the day she is freed because they will then lose their good wages. About her own feelings Leonora Christina says nothing, a stance that lends her an almost superhuman sense of calm. When her freedom was assured, she shows no haste: "Tøtzløff spurte, om ieg wille, hand skulle lucke; efftersom ieg nu alt war frii? Ieg swarte, saa lenge ieg er inden Fængsels dørene, saa er ieg icke frii, wil oc ud med manner" (Tøtzløff asked whether I wished him to lock the doors, as I was now free. I replied, "So long as I remain within the doors of my prison, I am not free. I will moreover leave in the proper style"). She describes her actual departure from the Blue Tower as a quiet but intense triumph–God's rehabilitation at last of the proud and innocent king's daughter. Evidently, she wished to pass on this interpretation to her children, who are frequently addressed in the third section of *Jammers Minde.* In a supplement to the preface, Leonora Christina explains how many of her enemies came to an ignominious end. This death list smolders with hatred and vindictiveness.

In spite of the striking differences among the three parts of *Jammers Minde,* they are held together by the physical framework, the subject matter, the chronological narrative, and, in particular, the narrator. She is unmistakably the same throughout–patient in the face of suffering, proud in the face of humiliation, benevolently gentle toward those who are kind, coldly calculating toward those who are untrustworthy, and genuinely vindictive toward her foes. Her urge for action is indomitable, as is her will to make the best of her circumstances. Time after time, with her superior intelligence, self-control, and sense of humor, she mitigates the hardships she must endure. What carry her through the long years of imprisonment are her awareness that she has acted correctly and her unshakable faith that God is with her and will prove her innocence by allowing her to die in freedom. This point is underlined by the meticulously created illusion that all of *Jammers Minde* was written in the Blue Tower. Yet, the original manuscript reveals that it was not; two-thirds was composed and written in Maribo, probably on the basis of notes made in prison. After Leonora Christina's death, her son inherited the manuscript of *Jammers Minde,* which remained in the family's possession, unknown to anyone else until 1869 when the text was published.

Leonora Christina herself did not regard *Jammers Minde* as her masterpiece. She thought much more highly of her collection of the biographical portraits of women, *Hæltinners Pryd* (Heroines' Adornment, 1977), which she began writing in the Blue Tower but revised in Maribo. Only a fragment of this work remains, and in a poor copy. The extant section deals with wise and brave female regents, and the fundamental view is that many women have greater strength and courage than many men. She believes that to evaluate their deeds in relation to their personages instead of measuring the persons by their deeds is unreasonable. Traces of the author's own character are evident throughout the work. In the portraits of the individual women, Leonora Christina praises qualities such as courage, physical strength, well-founded pride, intelligence, patience, and piety, as well as faithful love for and obedience to a husband. At times she openly contradicts her historical sources in order to create greater similarities between herself and her heroines. In general, her presentation is marked by both a thoughtful depth and by moralizing observations, but little of sus-

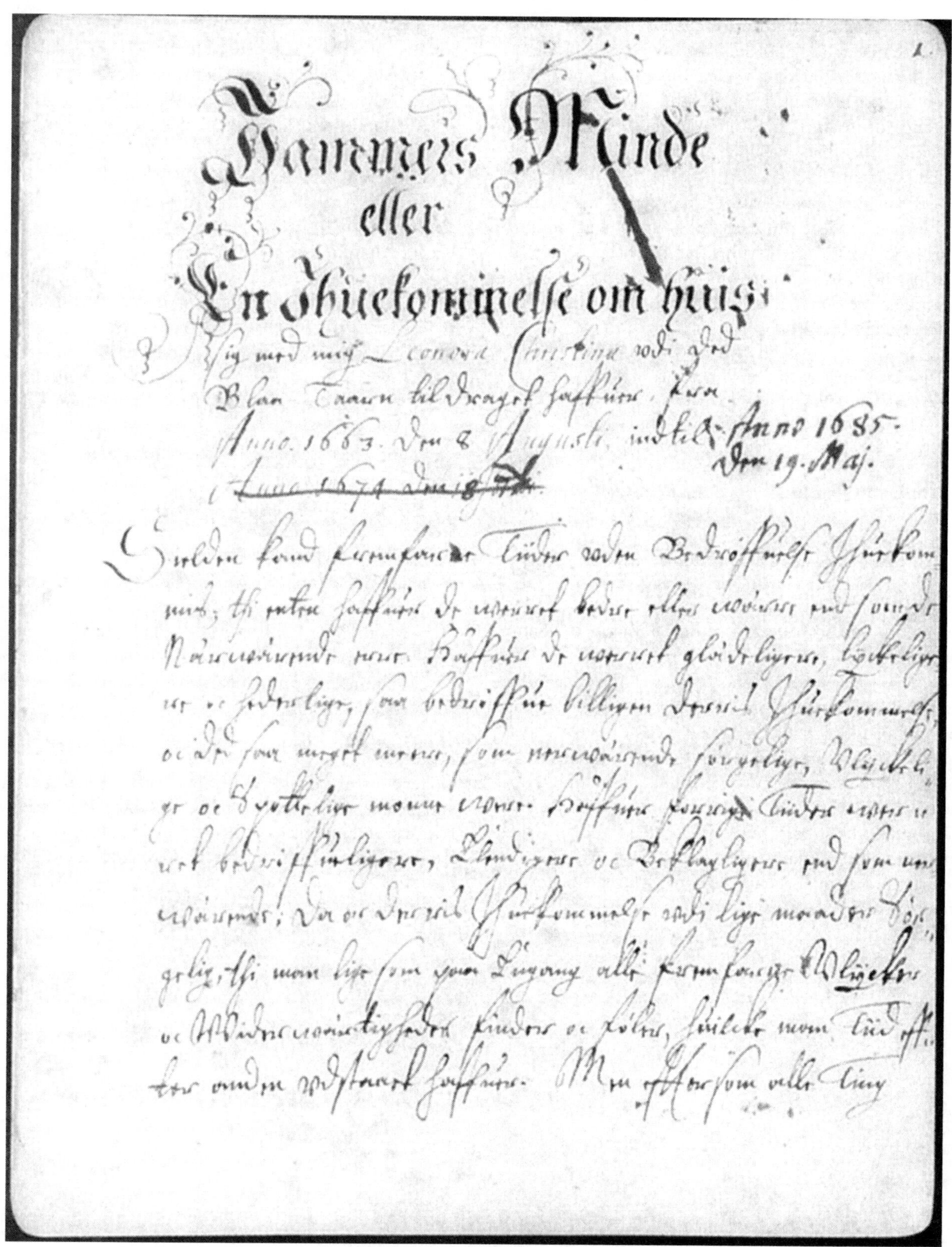

Opening page from the manuscript for Leonora Christina's memoir of her life in prison, which was not published until 1869. The dates 8 August 1663 and 19 May 1685 indicate the period of her incarceration (courtesy of the Danish Royal Library, Copenhagen).

penseful action or dramatic situations is found, even when the material might lend itself to that type of narration. Leonora Christina's contemporaries and their immediate descendants thought highly of *Hæltinners Pryd.* Sperling, for instance, praises the work in his portrait of Leonora Christina, included in his writings about learned women.

Leonora Christina also wrote poetry in Maribo. Best known is the poem from 1686 on an altar cloth in Maribo Church. The text thus far has been published only on the basis of a later, not quite accurate copy. In the original version, Leonora Christina tells her life story and mentions her marriage:

Din Haand mig ocsaa bant til Ectefellis Skæffne,
At bære Ont som Got der til gaffst du oc Aeffne.
Ey noget syntis tungt for Ecte-Kierlighed:
Troefasthed er den Dyd man ey tør bluis wed.

(Oh Lord! Your hand bound me to the fate of my husband,
You granted me strength to endure evil as well as good.
Nothing seemed hard to the devoted wife:
Fidelity is a virtue which bears no shame.)

Leonora Christina Ulfeldt died on 16 March 1698 and was buried in Maribo Church.

Ever since its publication, *Jammers Minde* has been regarded as a major work in Danish literature. It has inspired countless artists to create poems, novels, plays, operas, children's books, paintings, and sculptures. As an objective historical source, the text does not hold up. Yet, as a work of art, it is incomparable as a portrait of a proud and strong but complicated woman who endures an astounding fate and as a fresh and realistic depiction of a small group of people who, for better or worse, reflect the society at large.

Biographies:

Sophus Birket Smith, *Leonora Christina (Ulfeldt) på Maribo Kloster* (Copenhagen: Gyldendal, 1872);

Birket Smith, *Leonora Christina Grevinde Ulfeldts Historie,* 2 volumes (Copenhagen: Gyldendal, 1879–1881);

Bodil Wamberg, *Leonora Christina. Dronning af Blåtårn* (Copenhagen: Gad, 1991).

References:

Marita Akhøj Nielsen, "The Conservator's Work and Literary History: The Example of a 17th-Century Danish Autobiography," *Care and Conservation of Manuscripts,* 5 (2000): 38–47;

Akhøj Nielsen, "Leonora Christina: An Imprisoned Princess," in *Female Voices of the North I: An Anthology,* edited by Sven H. Rossel and Inger Olsen (Vienna: Wiener Texte zur Skandinavistik I, Edition Paesens, 2002), pp. 89–116;

Otto Glismann, *Om at "handle mis" med en klassiker* (Birkerød: Privately printed, 1997);

Steffen Heiberg, *Enhjørningen. Corfitz Ulfeldt* (Copenhagen: Gyldendal, 1993);

Annegret Heitmann, *Selbst Schreiben. Eine Untersuchung der dänischen Frauenautobiographik* (Frankfurt am Main: Peter Lang, 1994), pp. 138–163;

Leonora Christina, Historien om en heltinde. Acta Jutlandica, volume 58, Humanistisk series, no. 57 (Århus: Arkona, 1983).

Papers:

Collections of Leonora Christina Ulfeldt's manuscripts and correspondence are in the Museum of National History at Frederiksborg Castle in Hillerød, north of Copenhagen; in the Danish Royal Library and the State Archives in Copenhagen; and in the Swedish State Archives in Stockholm.

Anders Sørensen Vedel

(9 November 1542 - 13 February 1616)

Marita Akhøj Nielsen
Society for Danish Language and Literature

(Translated by Inger G. Tranberg)

BOOKS: *Paraphrasis psalmi CXXVII scripta Latino versu* (Copenhagen: M. Vingaard, 1569);

Antichristvs romanvs. Romske Paffuers Leffnede oc Gerninger (Copenhagen: M. Vingaard, 1571);

En Predicken som skeede vdi Erlig Velbyrdig oc Gudfryctig mands, salige Iohan Friisis begraffuelse (Copenhagen: L. Benedicht, 1571);

Oratio panegyrica, oblata serenissimo ac potentissimo Regi Daniæ, Domino Friderico II (Copenhagen: A. Gutterwitz, 1580);

Oratio de origine appellationis regni Daniae (Schlesvig: N. Wegener, 1584);

En sørgelig Ligpredicken. Salig och høylofflig ihukommelse Høybaarne Første oc Herre, Herr Frederich den Anden Danmarckis, Norgis, Vendis oc Gotthis. Konning, Hertug vdi Slesuig, Holsten, Stormarn oc Dytmersken. Greffue vdi Oldenborg oc Delmenhorst, til en Christsalig amindelse (Copenhagen: L. Benedicht, 1588);

Grundtrøst Aff S. Poffuels Epistel til de Thessalonicher i det fierde Capitel (Ribe: H. Brun & Vedel, 1591);

Guds Børns Taal oc trøst vnder Kaarsset (Ribe: H. Brun & Vedel, 1591);

Om Menniskelige liffs Kaarthed (Ribe: H. Brun & Vedel, 1592);

Den XC. Psalme: Moses Guds Mands Bøn (Ribe: H. Brun & Vedel, 1592);

Kong Svend Haraldssøn Tiuve-skæg, edited by Johannes Laverentzen (Copenhagen: J. Laverentzen, 1705);

Om den Danske Krønike at beskrive, edited by Rasmus Nyerup (Copenhagen: N. Møller & Son, 1787).

Anders Sørensen Vedel (painting by Tobias Gemperlins; Museum of National History at Frederiksborg Castle)

OTHER: Jens Grundet, *Liber posthvmvs continens similitvdines, qvibvs præcipva capita Religionis Christianæ explicantur & illustrantur,* edited by Vedel (Wittenberg: P. Seitz, 1567);

"Om merckelige Mends Død," in *Den danske Psalmebog,* edited by Hans Thomissøn (Copenhagen: L. Benedicht, 1569), fol. 342–344;

Michael, *Vita hominis. Vnderuisning Om Menniskens leffned,* edited by Vedel (Copenhagen: L. Benedicht, 1571);

Septem sapientes Græciæ. Skiøne Sprog oc merckelige Sententzer som ere faaregiffne aff de siu Naffnkundige Vise Mend, anonymous, edited by Vedel (Copenhagen: L. Benedicht, 1572);

Lauritz Bertelsen, *Vnderuisning om De tuende slags Opstandelser,* dedication by Vedel (Copenhagen: A. Gutterwitz & H. Stockelmann's Heirs, 1576);

Adam of Bremen, *Historia ecclesiastica,* edited by Vedel (Copenhagen: B. Kaus, 1579);

"En kaart Vnderuisning om Bønen," in Anders Mariager, *Fader vor oc den almindelig Lærdom om en Christen Bøn* (Copenhagen: B. Kaus, 1580), fol. T3–V3;

It Hundrede vduaalde Danske Viser Om allehaande Merckelige Krigs Bedrifft oc anden seldsom Euentyr som sig her vdi Riget ved Gamle Kemper Naffnkundige Konger oc ellers forneme Personer begiffuet haffuer aff arilds tid indtil denne nerværendis Dag, anonymous, edited by Vedel (Ribe: H. Brun & Vedel, 1591); facsimile edition, *Anders Sørensen Vedels Hundredvisebog,* introduction and notes by Karen Thuesen (Copenhagen: C. A. Reitzel, 1993);

Jens Sinning, *Oratio de stvdiis philosophicis, theologiæ stvdioso necessariis,* edited by Vedel (Ribe: H. Brun & Vedel, 1591); facsimile edition, *Tale om Nødvendigheden af filosofiske Studier for den teologiske Student, 1545=Oration on the Philosophical Studies Necessary for the Student of Theology, 1545,* translated by Christian Høgel and Peter Fischer, afterword by Frederik J. Billeskov Jansen (Copenhagen: Museum Tusculanum, 1991);

Historien om Iesu Christi vor Frelseris Pine oc Død, anonymous, edited by Vedel (Ribe: H. Brun & Vedel, 1592).

TRANSLATIONS: Niels Hemmingsen, *Via vitae* (Leipzig: A. Schneider, 1574);

Saxo Grammaticus, *Den Danske Krønicke som Saxo Grammaticvs screff halfffierde hundrede Aar forleden* (Copenhagen: B. Kaus, 1575); facsimile edition, *Anders Sørensen Vedel. Den Danske Krønicke. Saxo-oversættelse, 1575,* introduction by Allan Karker (Copenhagen: Danske Sprog- og Litteraturselskab/Gad, 1967);

Petrarch, *[Siv Gudelige Penitentze Psalmer]* (Copenhagen: A. Gutterwitz, 1577).

Anders Sørensen Vedel's significant position in Danish letters is owing to two works that are not considered originals by modern standards. He translated Saxo Grammaticus's Latin history of Denmark, *Gesta Danorum* (Story of the Danes, circa 1200), into Danish as *Den Danske Krønicke* (The Danish Chronicle, 1575), and he edited a volume of Danish ballads, *It Hundrede vduaalde Danske Viser* (One Hundred Selected Danish Ballads, 1591). In his translation of Saxo Grammaticus, Vedel displays a rich and dignified style that has always been considered a shining example of classic Danish prose. With the ballad edition he adopted the genre as aesthetically valuable literature; at the same time, he established an important precedent for the popular folk ballad. These two works are the high points in Vedel's extensive authorship in Danish as well as in Latin.

Anders Sørensen Vedel was born on 9 November 1542 in the town of Vejle on the Jutland Peninsula. In those days the town was called Vedel, and he took that name as his surname, as was common practice at that time. His father, Søren Sørensen, was a commoner but belonged to one of the most prominent families in town, as did Vedel's mother, Sidsel Andersdatter. The bright boy was a pupil at the *latinskole* (grammar school), and in 1557 he was sent to the larger "cathedral school" in Ribe, where he lived at the home of a relative, the well-known teacher Jens Grundet, who was in charge of the education of several young men. The goal of the education was partly to make the young people devout and pious Lutherans and partly to give them a thorough knowledge of Latin. Even as a boy, Vedel was interested in history, and Grundet encouraged him to study ancient and modern historical works even though they were not included in the curriculum.

In 1561 Vedel began his studies at the University of Copenhagen, where he was a pupil of Niels Hemmingsen, renowned in Europe and a pupil of the German theologian Philipp Melanchthon. The following year Vedel accepted the opportunity to study in Leipzig, made possible by his job as tutor for the young Tycho Brahe. During their three-year stay in Leipzig, Vedel had the impossible task of forcing his pupil to study law, despite Brahe's passion for astronomy. Nevertheless, the two remained friends for life. Vedel himself became a pupil of the famous philologist and historian Joachim Camerarius.

Vedel traveled home to Denmark in 1565 when his employment with Brahe ended. In the intervening years Denmark had been engaged in war with Sweden, its rival to power in Scandinavia, and at home Vedel encountered plague and death. To his sorrow he did not make it back in time to see Grundet alive. At the same time he found Wittenberg tempting: it was Martin Luther's and Melanchthon's town, and Wittenberg University was considered the most distinguished learning institution of Lutheranism. Vedel studied there for two years with such scholars as the renowned historian Caspar Peucer, and he completed his education with a *magister* (master's) degree. Before leaving Wittenberg, he published his first book, a collection of parables left by Grundet in manuscript: *Liber posthvmvs continens similitvdines* (Posthumous Collection of Parables, 1567). This Latin work represents a great effort on Vedel's part: his editing of the text was extensive, and he added to the manuscript a comprehensive biography that not only provides a handsome portrait of his old teacher but also delineates Grundet's era and background.

After his homecoming Vedel became pastor at Copenhagen Castle in 1568, a position he held for fourteen years. These years proved to be a fruitful period. He joined a group of powerful noblemen who were well educated and had cultural interests, especially in history. Although the war with Sweden ended in 1570, the rivalry between the two neighboring countries continued, and history played an important role in this rivalry. The brothers Johannes and Olaus Magnus had written descriptions of the glorious Swedish past; their works were hostile toward the Danes but won European fame after the 1550s, even though the Danish government had asked the historian Hans Svaning to refute the most preposterous assertions. It was considered a national duty to write a comprehensive national history, preferably from the biblical Flood to the present day. At the least, Saxo's *Gesta Danorum* needed to be continued. Svaning began to write, but almost nothing was published. To the old chancellor, Johan Friis, Vedel appeared to be the man able to undertake the task. Friis gave Vedel various materials, among them manuscripts by older historians. The first result of this collaboration was a rhymed papal chronicle in Danish, *Antichristvs romanvs* (1571). It is an epic poem of almost ten thousand lines consisting of monologues in which each pope tells his own story. By means of this compositional structure the work carries on the traditions of the medieval rhyming chronicles; like them, it is composed in doggerel, in which only the stressed syllables are of metric relevance. The monotony of the papal monologues is broken down by a frame story about a young Dane in Rome and his meetings with talkative locals. The poem gently combines historical narrative with a polemic Lutheran message, and in its indignant exposure of papal excesses it is often robustly humorous. Whenever an opportunity arises, Vedel gives information about Danish conditions. The poem ends in an edifying way with the young Dane having had enough and going home "til Vedel hin bolde" (to beautiful Vejle).

Alongside his historical study Vedel published several religious works, all in Danish. *Vita hominis* (The Life of Man, 1571) is a reworking of a late-medieval poem about typical human life. Vedel removed the specific Catholic elements and carefully modernized the language. He had a remarkable feeling for the aesthetic quality of medieval Danish literature and wanted to convey it to his own time. When Friis died, Vedel was at his side; Vedel's beautiful funeral sermon to his beloved patron was published in 1571 as *En Predicken som skeede vdi Erlig Velbyrdig oc Gudfryctig mands, salige Iohan Friisis begraffuelse* (A Sermon Delivered at the

Den Danske Krønicke
som SAXO GRAMMATICVS
screff/ halffierde hundrede Aar forleden:
Nu først aff Latinen vdsæt/ flitteligie
offuerseet oc forbedret/
Aff
Anders Søffrinssøn Vedel.

INSIGNIA REGIS DANIAE &c.

Cum Gratia & Priuilegio Sereniß: REGIÆ Maiest:

Anno M. D. LXXV.

Title page for Vedel's Danish translation of Saxo Grammaticus's Latin history of Denmark (from Anders Sørensen Vedel. Den Danske Krønicke. Saxo-oversættelse, 1575, *1967; Alderman Library, University of Virginia)*

Funeral of the Honorable, Well-Born, and God-Fearing Man, Blessed Johan Friis). The following year he published a collection of maxims, *Septem sapientes Græciæ* (Seven Wise Men from Greece, 1572), an original adaptation of a well-known anonymous work. In vigorous Danish, Vedel offered to a broad audience an impression of the wisdom of the ancients–at least to the extent that it harmonizes with Christianity. The work was successful and came to influence the proverb genre in Denmark.

The hope of preserving ancient culture as a central element in Protestant education was shared by Vedel and Hemmingsen, who were still close friends. In 1574 Vedel translated Hemmingsen's devotional work *Liffsens Vey* (The Path of Life) into Latin as *Via vitae;* he was not restrained by the fact that Hemmingsen had been accused of Calvinism. The esteemed professor was soon afterward discharged from his position.

In 1575, after many years of work, Vedel was able to publish *Den Danske Krønicke,* his translation of Saxo's *Gesta Danorum.* He probably used some incomplete preliminary works, but mainly he stayed with the Latin text. Vedel made use of his own knowledge of history in interjections, marginal notes, and genealogies. The translation is rather free. Saxo's poems are retold in prose, and in general Vedel's style is more ordinary than Saxo's refined Silver Age Latin; nonetheless, it does not lack rhetorical ornamentation. Variation and copiousness mark Vedel's style. His vocabulary is substantial, enriched by extensive studies of Danish and Norwegian literature, from which he had learned especially beautiful and precise expressions. Proverbs stress the moral points, and simple analogies make the presentation concrete.

Vedel also makes use of this mastery of style in his 1577 reworking of Petrarch's seven penitential psalms as *Siv Gudelige Penitentze Psalmer.* As in *Vita Hominis,* this work shows his intent to pass on the truth and literary quality that he also found in Catholic writings. That same year Vedel married his true love, Marine Svaning, the young daughter of the historian Svaning. She died after only one year of marriage, leaving no children. Vedel memorialized her with a small copper plaque featuring a double portrait of the spouses that can still be seen in the cathedral in Ribe.

To find solace, Vedel turned to the darling of his scholarship: history. In 1578 he wrote a manifesto in Latin for the needed history of Denmark, "Commentarius de Scribenda historia danica" (Commentary on the Writing of Danish History). A few years later it was rewritten in Danish as "Om den danske Krønicke at bescriffue" (To Write the Danish History). Only the Danish version was published, and not until 1787. The plan was grandiose and beautifully formulated, but it was also absolutely overwhelming. When it was presented to the government in 1578 the reaction was lukewarm. Vedel was permitted to begin the history, but the only remuneration was a promise of one day inheriting his father-in-law's clerical post. (Svaning did not die until 1584.)

Nevertheless, in 1579 Vedel edited the first edition of Adam of Bremen's *Historia ecclesiastica,* a chronicle of the archbishopric of Hamburg-Bremen. The work is an important source for Nordic history of the early Middle Ages, and the edition is absolutely equal to the international standard of that time for scholarly editions. After consultation with the government, however, Vedel left out a part of the manuscript featuring derogatory comments about Denmark.

In order to concentrate on his historical research, Vedel resigned in 1581 as pastor at Copenhagen Castle and moved to Ribe, where he married Mette, the bishop's daughter. Vedel had steady income from his clerical post, which had manageable work duties, and he also owned some capital. Imitating, among others, Brahe, who had built his castle, Uraniborg, on the island of Hven, Vedel set up his home, Liljebjerget (the Lily Hill), near the cathedral in Ribe, as a cultural center with a large library allowing some degree of public access. The marriage was harmonious, and several children were born to the Vedels.

Vedel began work on the history of Denmark, despite the halfhearted support of the government. He collected and copied documents, traveled around the kingdom to prepare a topographic description, created genealogical tables, compiled chronological outlines, completed research on various topics, and formulated drafts for individual sections. Many of these preliminary studies are preserved, most of them gradually collected by the Danish Royal Library in Copenhagen. But the road to the completed work was long. Impatient, the government put pressure on Vedel, and in 1584, as a first test, he published *Oratio de origine appellationis regni Daniae* (Speech on the Origin of the Name of the Kingdom of Denmark), the result of his etymological research on the name *Danmark.* This short text is immensely learned and especially interesting in its analysis of the second syllable, *mark.*

When Vedel was traveling, he usually visited Brahe on Hven. There, in 1586, he met Queen Sophie, who was being shown Uraniborg. A storm forced the visitors to stay for an extended time, and in order to entertain the queen, Brahe mentioned Vedel's large collection of old Danish folk ballads. Such collections had been popular since the 1550s, and the queen asked Vedel to make a copy for her. But at this point all of his time was taken up by his work on the history of Denmark.

In 1588 King Frederik II died. There were memorial church services all over the country, and Vedel gave the sermon at the cathedral in Ribe. The sermon was published that same year as *En sørgelig Ligpredicken* (A Sad Funeral Sermon). Vedel's words provide a nuanced portrait of the king, describing in powerful prose Frederik's years of governing, both politically and culturally. The carefully formulated hypothesis about the cause of his death is well known: the king could have lived many a day longer had not life at court forced him daily to imbibe large quantities of alcohol.

Frederik was succeeded by his son Christian IV, still a child. The guardian regency included several of Vedel's patrons and secured his position enough to enable him in 1591 and 1592 to expand his activities with a printing press at Liljebjerget. From there all his later works were published. First, he brought out an edition of Jens Sinning's *Oratio de stvdiis philosophicis, theologiæ stvdioso necessariis* (1591; translated as *Oration on the Philosophical Studies Necessary for the Student of Theology, 1545,* 1991). Sinning was a schoolfriend of Grundet, and the speech, like Vedel's introduction, is an expression of the humanism of Melanchthon and Hemmingsen.

The dowager queen asked for the promised copy of the folk ballads; in 1591, in order to introduce the broader public to this treasure of songs, Vedel chose to publish a selection of one hundred of the ballads, *It Hundrede vduaalde Danske Viser.* In terms of genre, the edition is the first of its kind. The book opens with a dedication to Sophie, followed by an extensive introduction in which Vedel outlines his view on the folk-ballad genre. He observes that all nations have honored the exploits of their forefathers in song, both to edify and to entertain the people. The ballads bring joy, whether they are sung at festive occasions or read in solitude. The benefits of cultivating them are manifold: although they are not historically accurate sources, they preserve memories of the past; they exemplify virtues and vices for imitation or warning; and they attest to the Danish culture of earlier days. Last but not least, Vedel states, "der som ingen anden orsag vaar til at læse disse gamle Poetiske Dict vaar denne ene nocksom for Sproget skyld: Det er for de herlige gamle Danske Gloser oc Ord for hin skøne Sprog oc runde Tale oc for den artige Compositz oc Dict i sig selff" (if there should be no other reason to read these old poems, this one would be sufficient: the language that is the wonderful old Danish words, the beautiful expressions, the rich style, the charming composition, and the plot itself).

Engraving of Vedel by Melchior Lorch, 1705 (courtesy of the Danish Royal Library, Copenhagen)

It Hundrede vduaalde Danske Viser is divided into three parts, comprising ballads about prehistoric heroes, Danish kings, and nobles. For each section and ballad Vedel provides an introduction placing the poems in an historic, literary, and moral context. Many of the introductions are small treatises on cultural history. The scholarly principles for the edition were remote from today's ascetic ideal: Vedel improved rhythm, rhyme, and composition and added new, often beautiful and touching stanzas to round off the ballads. "Kæmpebogen" (The Giant Book), as the work soon was called, has had unsurpassed significance for Danish language and literature. The complete work has been republished several times; in addition, it became the nucleus of other later ballad editions.

After this tour de force Vedel published only religious devotional books, funeral and other sermons, and reflections on the Passion of Christ. Simultaneously he continued work on the history of Denmark; for example, he wrote a section on the medieval king Sven Forkbeard, and–showing great optimism–the introduction to the entire work. In 1705 both were published by his great-grandchild Johannes Laverentzen in *Kong Svend Haraldssøn Tiuve-skæg* (King Sven Haraldson Forkbeard).

Vedel's days as a government-employed historian were numbered, however. When the last of his patrons died in 1594, his post and salary were taken away from him, and he was ordered to deliver all of his materials to his newly appointed successor. The main reason for this fall from grace was the Danish government's altered plans for the official history of the kingdom, in addition to Vedel's tardiness and the self-assured young King Christian's dislike of the whole circle of intellectuals to which Vedel belonged. Among them were Hemmingsen and Brahe, both of whom also fell into disfavor. An oversensitive posterity has later seen Vedel's comments about Frederik's excessive drinking habits as an insult to the royal dynasty, but in Vedel's time it was not considered offensive.

Vedel's attempt to succeed his father-in-law as bishop failed. For the rest of his life Vedel was reduced to an existence as a quiet scholar and clerical administrator. He had no problems as to his finances. Until his death he continued to develop his outstanding collection of books and kept up with the latest historical literature. Philology was probably his solace in his old age. Some manuscripts consisting of etymological research and collections of proverbs, proper names, and significant expressions are preserved from his later years.

Anders Sørensen Vedel died on 13 February 1616, surrounded by his wife and children. He is buried at the cathedral in Ribe, where a fragment of his tombstone can still be found.

Letters:

Bue Kaae, *Familieliv på "Liljebjerget" i Ribe omkring 1600 belyst gennem breve* (Esbjerg: Sydjysk Universitetsforlag, 1983).

Bibliography:

Gustav Henningsen, "Vedel og Syv og bogtrykkerne. En bibliografisk undersøgelse af Hundredvisebogen," *Danske Studier* (1959): 53–84.

Biography:

C. F. Wegener, "Historiske Efterretninger om Anders Sørensen Vedel," in Saxo Grammaticus, *Den Danske Krønike,* translated by Vedel, edited by Israel Levin, A. E. Boye, and Henrik Boye (Copenhagen: Samfundet til den danske Literaturs Fremme, 1851).

References:

Agnes Agerschou, "Vedels Forhold til de af ham benyttede Tekster, saaledes som det fremtræder i Hundredvisebogen," *Acta Philologica Scandinavica,* 15 (1941): 253–325;

Marita Akhøj Nielsen, *Anders Sørensen Vedels filologiske arbejder,* 2 volumes, Universitets-Jubilæets danske Samfund, no. 562 (Copenhagen: C. A. Reitzel, 2004);

Akhøj Nielsen, "Om Anders Sørensen Vedels udgivelsesprincipper," *Ord, Sprog oc artige Dict. Et overblik og 28 indblik 1500–1700. Festskrift til Poul Lindegård Hjorth,* edited by Flemming Lundgreen-Nielsen, Akhøj Nielsen, and John Kousgård Sørensen, Universitets-Jubilæets danske Samfund, no. 544 (Copenhagen: C. A. Reitzel, 1997), pp. 181–203;

Gustav Albeck, "Anders Sørensen Vedel og hans Skrift. 'Om Den Danske Krønicke at bescriffue,'" in *Humanister i Jylland,* edited by Albeck (Copenhagen: E. Munksgaard, 1959), pp. 117–152;

Karsten Friis-Jensen, *Vedels Saxo og den danske adel,* Studier fra Sprog- og Oldtidsforskning, no. 320 (Copenhagen: Museum Tusculanum, 1993);

Harald Ilsøe, "Svaning, Vedel, Huitfeldt og Krag. Omkring spørgsmålet om den første historiografudnævnelse," in *Tradition og Kritik. Festskrift til Svend Ellehøj den 8. september 1984,* edited by Grethe Christensen and others (Copenhagen: Danske Historiske Forening, 1984), pp. 235–258;

Ellen Jørgensen, *Historieforskning og Historieskrivning i Danmark indtil Aar 1800* (Copenhagen: Danske Historiske Forening, 1931), pp. 91–101;

Allan Karker, *Anders Sørensen Vedel og den danske krønike,* Studier fra Sprog- og Oldtidsforskning, no. 228 (Copenhagen: Branner & Korch, 1955);

Karker, "Kong Frederik 2.s død," *Jyske Samlinger,* new series 6 (1962–1965): 252–257;

Lundgreen-Nielsen, "Anders Sørensen Vedel og Peder Syv. To lærde folkeviseudgivere," in *Svøbt i mår. Dansk Folkevisekultur 1550–1700,* volume 4, edited by Lundgreen-Nielsen and Hanne Ruus (Copenhagen: C. A. Reitzel, 2002), pp. 153–373;

Lars Boje Mortensen, "Anders Sørensen Vedel: The Latin Writings of a Vernacular Humanist," in *A History of Nordic Neo-Latin Literature,* edited by Minna Skafte Jensen (Odense: Odense University Press, 1995), pp. 267–280.

Papers:

Anders Sørensen Vedel's papers are at the Danish Royal Library in Copenhagen.

Johan Herman Wessel

(6 October 1742 – 29 December 1785)

James Massengale
University of California, Los Angeles

BOOKS: *Kierlighed uden Strømper. Et Sørge-Spil i fem Optog,* anonymous (Copenhagen: Kongelige Universitets-Bogtrykkeri, 1772);

Lykken bedre end Forstanden. Et Lystspil i fem Optog (Copenhagen, 1776);

Til Herr Jens Baggesen (Copenhagen: Holm, [ca. 1784]);

Anno 7603 (Copenhagen: Horrebouw, 1785).

Editions and Collections: *Johan Herman Wessels samtlige Skrivter,* 2 volumes, edited by Peter Johan Monrad, Jens Baggesen, and Christen Pram (Copenhagen: A. F. Stein, 1787);

Samtlige Skrivter, 2 volumes, edited by Knud Lyhne Rahbek (Copenhagen, 1799, 1800);

Johan Herman Wessels Udvalgte Digte, 2 volumes, edited by E. H. Seidelin, with an introduction by Rahbek (Copenhagen, 1801);

Samlede Digte, edited by A. E. Boye (Copenhagen: Thiele, 1832);

Samlede Skrifter, 2 volumes (Copenhagen: B. Luno & Schneider, 1832);

J. H. Wessels Værker, edited by P. L. Møller (Copenhagen: Berling, 1848);

Johan Herman Wessels Samtlige Skrifter, 2 volumes (Copenhagen: E. L. Thaarup, 1857);

Samlede Digte, edited by Israel Levin (Copenhagen: C. A. Reitzel, 1862);

Udvalgte Digte, introduction by Jonas Lie (Copenhagen: C. Steen, 1870);

Skrifter (Copenhagen: Nyt Dansk Forlagskonsortium, 1884);

Udvalgte Skrifter (Copenhagen: P. Hauberg, 1888);

Udvalgte Skrifter, introduction by H. Schwanenflügel (Copenhagen: Schubothe, 1898);

Kærlighed uden Strømper. Sørgespil i fem Optog, edited by Axel Sørensen (Copenhagen: Gyldendal, 1911);

Kærlighed uden Strømper. Sørgespil i fem Optog, edited by T. C. Thors (Copenhagen: Dansklærerforeningen/Gyldendal, 1928);

Johan Herman Wessels Digte, foreword by Paul V. Rubow (Copenhagen: C. A. Reitzel, 1936);

Johan Herman Wessel (engraving, circa 1784, artist unknown; courtesy of the Danish Royal Library, Copenhagen)

Jeg Pigers Selskab ei kan savne. Digte, edited by Sigfred Pedersen (Copenhagen: Grafisk Forlag, 1946);

Samlede Digte (Copenhagen: H. Reitzel, 1953); revised as *Samlede Digte, samt Kærlighed uden Strømper* (Copenhagen: H. Reitzel, 1959);

Komiske Fortællinger, edited by Carl Johan Elmquist (Copenhagen: Boghallen, 1958);

Kærlighed uden Strømper. Sørgespil i fem Optog, introduction and commentary by Alf Henriques (Copenhagen: Dansklærerforeningen/Gyldendal, 1965);

For Smed at rette Bager–. Wessels komiske Fortællinger, Digte og Vers, edited by Jette Pagaard and Flemming Lundahl (Copenhagen: Apostrof, 1986);

Smeden og Bageren og andre komiske Fortellinger og Vers (Oslo: Gyldendal, 2000).

PLAY PRODUCTIONS: *Kierlighed uden Strømper,* Copenhagen, Royal Theater, 26 March 1773;

Lykken bedre end Forstanden, Copenhagen, Royal Theater, 1776.

OTHER: "Søvnen" and "Nøisomhed," in *Poetiske Samlinger,* volume 1 (Copenhagen: Et Selskab [Det norske litteraire Selskab], 1775);

"Ondt og Godt i alle Lande," in *Selskabs-Sange med Melodier,* volume 1 (Copenhagen, 1783);

"Gaffelen, en Fortælling," in *Poetiske Samlinger,* edited by Iversen (Copenhagen, 1784);

"Prologer 1780–1783," in *Lommebøger for Skuespillere,* edited by Schwartz (Copenhagen, 1784–1785);

Votre Serviteur. Otiosis. Et Ugeblad, nos. 1-54 (1784–1785), edited by Wessel;

Norske Selskabs Vers-Protokol, by Wessel and others, edited by W. P. Sommerfeldt (Oslo: Norske Selskap, 1935).

TRANSLATIONS: Antoine-François Quétant, *Grovsmeden. Et Syngestykke i to Optog,* in *Syngespil for den danske Skueplads,* volume 4 (Copenhagen, 1781);

Louis Anseaume, *Det talende Skilderie. Et Syngestykke i en Act,* in *Syngespil for den danske Skueplads,* volume 5 (Copenhagen, 1781);

Jacques-Marie Boutet de Monvel, *De tre Forpagtere. Et Syngestykke i to Acter,* in *Syngespil for den danske Skueplads,* volume 5;

Charles-Simon Favart, *Feen Ursel, eller hvad der behager Damerne. Et Syngestykke i fire Acter,* in *Syngespil for den danske Skueplads,* volume 6 (Copenhagen, 1783);

Monvel, *Julie. Et Syngestykke i tre Acter,* in *Syngespil for den danske Skueplads,* volume 6;

Thomas d'Hèle, *Den falske Formodning eller Den skinsyge Elsker. Et Syngestykke i tre Akter* (Copenhagen, 1787);

Monvel, *Stephen og Lise, eller Fortsættelse af de tre Forpagtere. Syngestykke i to Akter,* in *Syngespil for den danske Skueplads,* volume 8 (Copenhagen, 1790).

Johan Herman Wessel is recognized as a major literary figure both in the literature of Norway (since he was born a Norwegian) and in that of Denmark (since he settled permanently in Copenhagen and wrote exclusively in Danish). As Harald Beyer writes, "The [Norwegian] tradition that led from Ludvig Holberg through Johan Herman Wessel to Wergeland, Welhaven, Bjørnson, and Ibsen is inextricably bound up with Danish names like Ewald, Oehlenschläger, Heiberg, Grundtvig, and Kierkegaard." This assessment, which places Wessel squarely in the company of the elite of both literatures, would have amused the world-weary satirist, who always spoke in self-deprecating terms about his work, as in the epitaph he wrote for himself: "Han syntes fød til Bagateller, / Og noget Stort blev han ej heller" (Just bagatelles he seemed to bring, / And greatness never was his thing). This attitude may be a pose, but it is a fact that Wessel wrote only one successful play for the theater and a few dozen scattered poems during a short and mostly miserable existence on the bohemian fringe of Copenhagen's cultural life. For an explanation of this apparent anomaly, the reader must be open to the idea that great writing is not always synonymous with "serious," painful, or noble experience. Danish literature has never produced a funnier poet than Wessel, and that single fact, rather than any tacked-on critical message or modern construct of a supposed "deeper significance" to his work, is the truest and most appreciative assessment one might give him.

Johan Herman Wessel was born in Jonsrud, near Vestby in southern Norway, on 6 October 1742, the next-to-the-youngest son of an indigent curate, Jonas Wessel, and his wife, Helene Marie Schumacher Wessel. Jonas Wessel had been waiting to take over a parish from his aging and senile uncle. By the time he finally became the regular minister in the Vestby parish of Akershus, he had a family of six children to support, and his intentions to give his four sons the best possible education were permanently hindered by his small economic means. Little is known of Johan Wessel's early life in provincial Norway, but he was clearly educated at home until the age of fourteen, when his father sent him to the Latin School in Christiania (Oslo), probably intending for the boy to complete a minister's examination at the University of Copenhagen. This course of study was the accepted procedure for young men from the "double kingdom" of Denmark and Norway, since Norway at that time had no university of its own. The Christiania Latin School had a good reputation, and Wessel's instructor there, A. P. Bartholin, had a literary bent. After three years the young student was indeed matriculated at the University of Copenhagen, where he also took his next exam, the *philosophicum,* in 1762, with good results. Unlike several of his Norwegian friends and compatriots, however, Wessel neither completed his university studies nor turned his bourgeois training into a stepping-stone to a higher position back in Norway. He appears to have shown no interest in either a minister's calling or that of a lawyer or bureaucrat (the logical ends of the educational path he had begun). Undoubtedly, his family in Norway had little or no money to support his further study, and he fell back upon another eighteenth-century expedient, taking a tutor's live-in position at the house of a well-heeled Norwegian-Danish official, in this case, General Auditor Wilhelm Bornemann. Meanwhile, Wessel pursued studies in modern languages and literature (a dead-end academic venture), apparently becoming fluent in German, French, and English (and, later, Italian and Spanish).

In Copenhagen, Wessel found himself in an expatriate community of fellow Norwegians who gathered informally at local taverns or coffeehouses, where they exchanged academic opinions, drank, and whiled away evening hours after long days of study or poorly paid teaching. One of these meeting places has become famous, not least because of Wessel himself. It was run by Anne Cathrine Juel, who was not a Norwegian "emigrant" herself but rather, as Wessel expressed it, using the term "Jutland" as a joking reference to Denmark in general, "Normands Siæl logeret hos en Jyde" (Norwegian spirit found within a Jutland heart). Juel and her husband moved their pub to the address that is now Sværtegade 7 in 1774, and the Norwegian students and writers followed them, in the hopes of finding a congenial meeting place that would serve as a literary counterpart to Neergaard's coffeehouse in Badstuestræde, where admirers of Johannes Ewald assembled themselves. The Norwegians' house may still be seen at Sværtegade 7 in Copenhagen; it is now called Wessels Kro (Wessel's Tavern).

The rivalry between Danish and Norwegian-Danish writers (the latter writing in Danish, with references to their so-called homeland, Norway, or with an occasional word of dialect or a grammatical slip to identify their extraction) has, over the course of the following years, reduced itself essentially to a discussion of the personalities of two outstanding contemporaries, Ewald and Wessel. These two talented poets, growing up in the virtual cultural vacuum of original writing in Copenhagen after the death of Holberg, were quite different and yet reflected, each in his own way, the spirit of the sputtering and waning late Enlightenment. Ewald was in personality a Sturm und Drang pre-Romantic, a productive poet whose unhappy love life propelled him into self-destructive activities but also into poetic enrichment beyond the limits of his bombastic German models. Wessel quickly developed into a cool and witty classical traditionalist, an ironist specializing in absurd humor but also a poet who was ambivalent about his own talent and seemingly unambitious. His comic reluctance to improve his condition soon became the stuff of several apocryphal anecdotes, but stories of his alcoholism and unsteady lifestyle are supported by historical facts.

The conflict between Danes and Norwegians must be understood as essentially a literary one, not principally a matter of national politics. While the Danish government's central control of taxes, banking, and higher education affected the lives of Norwegians and the cultural climate in Norway, the matter of Norwegian independence or statehood was not put up for public debate at this time. What was a public issue was the brief takeover of Danish central authority by the German-born court physician Johann Friedrich Struensee. The internal palace revolution of 1770, occasioned by the mental illness of King Christian VII and complicated by a scandalous love affair between Struensee and Queen Caroline Mathilde, later received literary treatment, but it was much too sensitive a political issue to allow comment by the writers of the 1770s. The "Struensee Era," which lasted until the spring of 1772, when Struensee was tried and executed, had raised hopes among some Norwegians for the lifting of restrictions on freedom of expression, as well as the possibility for the establishment of a university in Norway. But one finds little in Wessel's poetry that reflects these concerns.

Many "integrated Norwegians," of which there were plenty in the latter half of the eighteenth century, held influential cultural positions in Copenhagen or used the relatively high profile afforded by cultural activity in the city to help them obtain prestigious jobs when they returned to live in Norway. The Trondheim native Niels Krog Bredal wrote a Nordic operetta, *Gram og Signe* (Gram and Signe), produced in 1756; his other works, *Eremiten* (The Hermit, 1761) and *Tronfølgen i Sidon* (The Royal Succession in Sidon, 1771), had solidified his position as a leading proponent of Danish imitations of French classical drama and Italian opera. As director of the Royal Danish Theater and a Norwegian, Bredal was in a position to encourage his younger compatriots to submit material for theatrical production. His call was followed by a younger Trondheimer, Johan Nordal Brun, whose *Zarine* (Zarine, 1772), a French classical tragedy in flowing (but interminable) alexandrine verse, stayed on the boards at the Royal Theater long enough to bring the author the "third-performance honorarium," resulting in a large celebration party at Madame Juel's public house. Wessel's own dramatic debut may be seen in direct conjunction with these previous dramatic successes.

Sometime between the February 1772 premiere of *Zarine* and September of the same year, Wessel wrote his own verse "tragedy," *Kierlighed uden Strømper* (Love without Stockings, 1772). It is often referred to as a parody, but there has been a good deal of unresolved critical discussion about what might be the object of the parody. Textual comparisons have been made with both Bredal's *Tronfølgen i Sidon* and Brun's *Zarine,* and

Wessel visiting the ailing poet Johannes Ewald in Rungsted (painting by Vilhelm Rosenstand, circa 1897; courtesy of the Danish Royal Library, Copenhagen)

the intertextuality is striking, but Liv Bliksrud is surely nearer the truth when she refers to *Kierlighed uden Strømper* as having a "common-parodic perspective." To use a less artificial term, the play is a farcical satire that has as its object not only the second-rank Danish imitations of Jean Racine and Pierre Corneille but also the whole tradition of tragic drama and opera, as well as the outmoded form of acting and declaiming that lingered on in European theaters in the latter half of the eighteenth century. It is not certain what Wessel set out to prove by his satire; possibly, he intended the play only as entertainment for the members of his Norwegian coffeehouse group.

Kierlighed uden Strømper was published anonymously on 2 September 1772 by the "Royal University Press." It might have had Norwegian sponsorship, for the edition could hardly have been financed by the indigent Wessel himself. The public and critical reaction was immediate, spontaneous, and overwhelmingly positive: "I det Naive og Burleske har denne Forf. vel neppe havt sin Lige siden Holberg. Alt hvad han berører, bliver under hans Haand pudseerligt" (In the naive and burlesque mode, this author has not seen his equal since the time of Holberg. Everything he touches becomes humorous), noted Jacob Baden in 1772 in Copenhagen's *Kritiske Journal.* A university student group mounted an amateur production of the play later that year, the actors probably using popular tunes for the eleven arias that are interspersed throughout the play, and by 1773 it was clear that there would have to be an official production at the Royal Theater. The Italian composer and conductor Paolo Scalabrini was commissioned to write an original score. The premiere was on 26 March 1773, and the play became the great hit of the season, with eight performances (by the standards of that theater and time, an impressive number) before the theater closed for the summer. An epilogue, added by Wessel to the text in 1774 (with a vaudeville, or finale song, also set to music by Scalabrini) is of equal quality with the rest of the play and has become a permanent part of *Kierlighed uden Strømper.*

Wessel's farce-tragedy gradually established itself as a permanent representative of the eighteenth-century Danish stage, alongside the best of Holberg's comedies. How such a perfect play could emanate from a nonprofessional playwright, who possibly considered his work a bagatelle or a nose-tweaking of his more legitimate literary Dano-Norwegian colleagues, is a mystery that later critics have pondered. The question was perhaps most eloquently expressed in 1892 by Henrik Jæger:

> I regelen overlever en parodi ikke de værker, den gjør nar af. . . . "Kierlighed uden Strømper" danner i denne henseende en mærkelig undtagelse: Ingen læser længere "Zarine" eller "Tronfølgen i Sidon," og af hundrede nordmænd eller danske, der morer sig over "Kierlighed uden Strømper," har ikke to havt en fransk tragedie i haanden. Alligevel virker stykket endnu den dag idag lige komisk.
>
> (Usually, parodies will not outlive the works they satirize. . . . "Love without Stockings" is the remarkable exception to this rule, however. No one reads "Zarine" or "The Royal Succession in Sidon" anymore, and out of any hundred Norwegians or Danes who are delighted by "Love without Stockings," not two of their number has ever had a French tragedy in their hands. This notwithstanding, [Wessel's] play is as comic today as it ever was.)

Jæger's statement is as true today as it was in 1892, but one should add that the school edition from the 1930s supplies eight pages of general introduction, twenty-four pages of excerpts from the scripts of *Zarina* and *Tronfølgen i Sidon,* fourteen pages of textual explanations, fifteen pages of musical and additional explications, and a two-page bibliography. For an English-speaking audience, the task of presenting Wessel's complex joke would be increased even more by the problem of translating his beautiful alexandrines and astonishing song texts.

The plot of *Kierlighed uden Strømper* concerns a young lady who dreams that she must be married immediately or not at all. Grete, who loves a journeyman tailor, Johan, is hard-pressed in his temporary absence to give her hand to a shoemaker, Mads, whom she had previously rejected. When Johan returns unexpectedly, Grete changes her mind on the spot and prepares for the ceremony, but Johan has no stockings to wear, and marriage in boots but no stockings is unacceptable. He is prevailed upon by Grete's maid, Mette, to steal a pair of stockings from Mads. But an inventory by Mads and his servant, Jesper, reveals the theft, and Johan stands accused of the crime in front of his bride-to-be. He commits suicide; his bride commits suicide; everybody commits suicide. In the epilogue the god Mercury as deus ex machina comes down from Olympus and revives everybody, and they all sing the vaudeville refrain "Jo galere, jo bedre" (The crazier, the better).

What a plot outline fails to reveal is the depth of tragic convention that is the central concern and the flowing dialogue, in which everyday speech and heroic poses alternate without missing an iambic beat or an alexandrine caesura. The problem of the play is that the characters are placed in a tragic framework; no matter how trivial or bourgeois their concerns might be, the framework requires that they achieve tragic status. When Johan is about to hurry away and grope into Mads's clothing chest, Mette, a sort of quality-control expert for the tragic mode of behavior, stops him short (all translations from Wessel are by James Massengale):

> Du gaaer saa snart, Johan? jeg kan dig ikke dølge,
> Jeg havde ikke tænkt, det kostede saa lidt
> For en ophøiet Siæl at giøre saadant Skridt.
> . . . .
> Bør du ei sige først, hvordan dit Hierte splittes?
> Snart sværge: at det ei ved Lyster skal besmittes?
> Snart raabe: Elskovs Gud din Gud allene er!
> Og efter elleve til tolv Omvexlinger,
> Hvormed nu Kierlighed, nu Dyden Seier vinder,
> Mag saa, at Elskov dig den tolvte Gang forbinder,
> Vræng Munden, vrie din Krop, bær dig som du var gael,
> Og naar du det har giort, bestiæl saa din Rival.
>
> (You leave so soon, Johan? I won't conceal my letdown;
> I had by no means thought, it cost so little pain
> For such a lofty soul to hurry after gain.
> . . . .
> Will you not say at first, how sore your heart is cloven?
> Then swear, by Heaven, no! No sin there, interwoven,
> Shall be! Yet–Cupid reigns, and is your only God!
> And after nine or ten such changes in your laud,
> By dint of which now love, now duty has expression,
> You fix it so that *then,* the tenth time's love's confession;
> Then make an awful face, rage like a madden'd ox,
> And when all that is done, go steal your rival's socks!)

Mette's instruction is based on her own familiarity not only with the texts of classical French drama but also with the overblown acting common in the performances of such plays. But where some scholars have emphasized the propensity for Wessel's characters to succumb to their "natural," lower-class instincts (Grete's unrestrained need to eat as well as Johan's to steal), the sustaining conflict in *Kierlighed uden Strømper* is more correctly assessed in terms of the imprisonment of five ordinary people in a verbal construct. Johan is compelled to twist his body according to Mette's instruction because he is the hero of the play. He also has to wear feathers and a tin breastplate in the fifth act for the same reason, as the conventions of the play become increasingly apparent. Johan will ultimately have to commit suicide because the play is a tragedy, and the hero commits suicide in a tragedy. The baser instincts of the characters are continually thwarted by the necessities of the "high" dramatic form in which they find themselves. One might also ask why the play needs such a drastic outcome at the end, and the answer is much the same: "Sørge-spil" (tragedy) is printed on the title page. Grete is aware from the beginning that she is part of a heroic drama, and her "tragic dream" is not only that which is bound to influence her actions but also such a part of the Aristotelian structure of drama (for example, the unity of time) that to disobey its dictum would be to step out of her own reality.

The songs in *Kierlighed uden Strømper* have a similar function. When Mads, temporarily encouraged in his attraction to Grete, sings of his passion, his principal metaphor is taken from an everyday source, but the continuation of the metaphor becomes complicated, so he has to include a pedagogic bit of explanation:

Paa mit Hiertes Skorsten brænder
En harpixet Elskovs Brand,
Som er tændt i begge Ender,
Elskovs Gud den tændte an.
Hver, som Røgen seer opstige,
(Røgen er min Aria)
Tænke maa, om ikke sige,
Det er heedt, hvor den kom fra.

(There's a kindling-stick of yearning
In my heart's own chimney-stove;
At both ends it's brightly burning,
Ignited by the God of Love.
Each one who views the smoke that rises
[My Aria's the smoke, you see],
Soon exclaims [at least, surmises]:
Where there's smoke, a fire must be.)

While the technique of addressing the audience directly was not unknown in the comic theater of the time (it is one of the tricks of standard commedia dell'arte, and was subsequently employed by Holberg), the dilemma in *Kierlighed uden Strømper* is that the characters are aware that they are participating in an artificial construct but are incapable of working free from it. There is a kind of existential angst about this problem that emerges at the end of the play–except that it is also expressed in such ridiculous terms that the audience is not expected to go along with it. When Jesper, the servant, is left alone with four corpses around him and the fatal knife (and bowl of peas) has been passed to him, he philosophizes:

Hvi skulde Mette døe? Jeg ei Aarsagen veed;
Men naar de alle døe, saa maa jeg og afsted.
(Han sætter Skaalen fra sig.)
. . . .
I Efterlevende! troer, det fra Hiertet gaaer:
Gid det ei Eder gaae, som det gik denne Stymper!
Gid Eders Kierlighed maa aldrig mangle Strømper!
(Han stikker sig.)

(Now Mette had to die? It's hard to figure why;
But when the others die, I'll have to say goodbye.
[He puts down the bowl of peas.]
. . . .
You who live on! My dictum's from the heart:
Would that your life goes well, and never ends in mocking!
Would that your love may thrive, and never lack a stocking!
[He stabs himself.])

As *Kierlighed uden Strømper* was taking shape, the informal gathering of Norwegian literati and friends had taken on a more organized form, and on 30 April 1774 Det Norske Selskab (The Norwegian Society) was officially inaugurated, with private rooms hired above Madame Juel's new cafe. The organizer of this group was one of the more bureaucratic and less talented exile Norwegians, Ole Gierløw Meyer. After the combined theatrical successes by Bredal, Brun, and Wessel, the club naturally drew attention to itself as a central location for talented writers. Prizes were established for the best prose and poetry, the winners of impromptu competitions on given subjects were rewarded with a bowl of strong punch, and volumes of poetry were planned. Three editions of poetry were eventually produced–*Poetiske Samlinger* (Poetic Collections, 1775, 1784, and 1793)–before the club began to lose inspiration and impetus. Wessel contributed two serious poems to the 1775 collection, "Nøisomhed" (On Moderation) and "Søvnen" (On Sleep), but he did not continue to cultivate the more serious aims of the Norwegian Society. After writing his epilogue to *Kierlighed uden Strømper,* he began to work as a translator for the Royal Theater, rendering the librettos of popular French comic operettas in a competent and occasionally brilliant and original style. He eventually completed seven of these translations. Wessel's second original play, a prose comedy titled *Lykken bedre end Forstanden* (Better Lucky than Rational, 1776), was also performed in 1776, but with little success. A final effort, a comic fantasy titled *Anno 7603,* based on a passage from Holberg's epic poem *Nicolai Klimii iter subterraneum* (1741; translated as *A Journey to the World Under-Ground by Nicholas Klimius,* 1742), was never deemed worthy of production and was published only in 1785, the year of the author's death.

The rest of Wessel's literary production was more or less connected with the Norwegian Society and the table songs, bantering verse, and virtuoso improvisations by several of the members. A copy of a lost *Versprotokol* (Verse Protocol) for the Norwegian Society was published in 1935 as *Norske Selskabs Vers-Protokol.* It is a copious collection of light material, representing the informal side of the society's activity. During that first half decade of the society's existence a spirit of debauchery and entertainment was matched by concerns for serious literary achievement and the correction of the flaws perceived to exist in Danish literature of the 1760s and 1770s, as Bliksrud has noted. The group had lost Brun, who left for Norway shortly after completing his most important (but politically controversial) play, *Einar Tambeskielver* (1772). But there was plenty of talent left behind in an organization that over time was to include some 250 members, including Johan Vibe, whose drinking songs still have amusing qualities; Claus Fasting, "the first one in Denmark who wrote with a journalistic consciousness"; and the serious lyrical poets P. H. Frimann and Edvard Colbjørnsen. The central figure of the group was Wessel, however, and his amoral and drastic style provided rich material for later Nordic anthologies.

In Wessel's poem "Herremanden" (The High-Born Lord, 1775) a lord meets his coachman, and a discussion ensues. Because of a profligate son who needed money for disgusting activities, the lord has overtaxed his peasants and never listened to their pleas. But the coachman has always been an accommodating fellow, and his reply gives the clue:

"Den Søn, som volder, I er her,
"Har jeg paa Halsen skaffet Jer.
"Jeg Fruen intet negte vilde.
"Og det er ilde,
"Slet ingen Ting at negte ville."
Sligt lærer hvert utugtigt Skarn,
At ikke skaffe Næsten Barn,
Skiøndt Næstens Kone gierne vilde,
Og det er ilde,
At Næstens Kone gierne vilde.

("The son that's landed you in Dutch,
I brought into the world as such,
Deny your wife, I never would,
And that's no good,
Not to deny things that one would."
The moral here is plain to see:
Don't add to neighbor's family,
Not even if his lady would,
And that's no good,
That neighbor's wife so often would.)

"Herremanden," first published in *Kiøbenhavns Aftenpost* (Copenhagen's Evening Post) on 3 January 1775 and later in Wessel's periodical weekly, *Votre Serviteur. Otiosis. Et Ugeblad* (Your Servant–for Those Who Have the Leisure: A Weekly), set the tone for the large number of versified stories that became his specialty. A defining characteristic for all of Wessel's work, and one that is impossible to render in translation, is the natural grace of his versification, together with an infallible sense of comic timing. The stories themselves, often from borrowed material, are often trivial or ribald, but the poet's voice is unlike that of any other of his time. For an English-speaking audience his particular genius is unapproachably locked into its own language idiom; for comparison's sake in the English language, his work calls to mind such later authors as W. S. Gilbert and Ogden Nash.

Wessel had by this time left the Bornemanns' house and was supporting himself in miserable quarters, receiving poor hourly wages for language tutoring. In 1776 a severe abscess and fistula in his cheek incapacitated him for the better part of two years, and, according to A. E. Boye, he never fully recovered, either physically or mentally: "Ogsaa *efter* Sygdommen var hans gode Lune forsvundet, en Følge deels af hans svækkede Helbred, deels af Mismod over hans Stilling. Allerede fra dette Tidspunkt synes det, som man maatte opgive Haabet om større Værker fra denne Digter" (Also *after* the sickness, his good humor had disappeared, partially because of his ruined health and partially because of his dissatisfaction about his circumstances. Even at that time, it appears that hope was lost that he would ever produce any more larger works). It is possible that people of influence stepped in to help stabilize his wretched finances and to assure him of a certain income from his French comedy translations, although the exact terms of the agreement are not known (possibly 100 Rix-daler per year, plus 100 Rix-daler for each completed translation). Although, given Wessel's unsystematic manner of working, the outlook for this new agreement was not especially promising, it appears to have encouraged him enough that he thought he might establish a family. In 1780 he married Anna Catharina Bukier, daughter of a Christiania official, and in 1781 they had a son, Jonas. It appears to some degree to have been a marriage of convenience: Wessel needed physical care, and his wife expected a certain degree of financial support. But he was also an alcoholic and returned to his familiar haunts, where he regained some measure of his improvisatory humor. As a last attempt to provide extra income from his pen, he began *Votre Serviteur. Otiosis. Et Ugeblad* in March 1784. The little magazine included verse fables, some of which show top Wessel quality, with a new nonstrophic, iambic verse form of varying line lengths and (as Wessel could do when writing at his best) a drastic twist and an oblique moral, such as in his well-known humorous verse fables "Gaffelen, en Fortælling" (The Fork, a Story), "Smeden og Bageren" (The Blacksmith and the Baker), and "Hundemordet" (The Dog Murder).

Votre Serviteur. Otiosis. Et Ugeblad ran for just a little more than a year in fifty-four issues. By this time, however, Wessel's lifestyle and lack of physical strength meant that he no longer had any power to withstand illness. He fell sick during the 1785 Christmas season and died on 29 December of that year. There was no one in the Norwegian Society who could carry forward Wessel's particular humorous torch, although the society itself lingered on in Copenhagen until 1813. Jens Baggesen's sentimental motto under the portrait in the first edition of Wessel's works, *Johan Herman Wessels samtlige Skrivter* (Johan Herman Wessel's Complete Writings, 1787), recorded the significance of his passing: "Graad smelted' hen i Smiil, naar Wessels Lune død, / Og Glædens Smiil forsvandt i Taarer ved hans Død" (Tears melted into smiles at what Wessel said; / Smiles then gave way to tears when he was dead).

Nineteenth-century biographers Knud Lynhe Rahbek, Boye, and Jæger emphasize Johan Herman Wessel's mild, melancholy character, his personal difficulties, and the impact on Dano-Norwegian literature of his untimely death. Early-twentieth-century criticism by Vilhelm Andersen and Frederik J. Billeskov Jansen, perhaps anticipating more-recent critical movements, dwells extensively on intertextual material, noting that most of Wessel's ideas are borrowed and that only his versification shows originality. Even such techniques as his irregular iambic lines are said to derive from Jean de La Fontaine and Wessel's compatriot Thomas Stockfleth. Later criticism centers around Wessel's radicalism, which is so well concealed in his work that it could hardly have been apparent even to his closest compatriots in the Norwegian Society; nor is it found in the fabric of their closely kept *Versprotokol.* Wessel's nihilistic and sophisticated parodic and satirical tendencies, however, appeal to postmodern critics. There may not be much difference between how his friends in the Norwegian Society perceived his poetic voice and how he may best be understood today.

References:

Gustav Albeck and Frederik J. Billeskov Jansen, *Dansk litteraturhistorie,* volume 1, edited by P. H. Traustedt (Copenhagen: Politiken, 1971), pp. 493–501, 558–567;

Billeskov Jansen, *Danmarks Digtekunst,* volume 2 (Copenhagen: Munksgaard, 1947), pp. 207–213;

Liv Bliksrud, *Den smilende makten. Norske Selskab i København og Johan Herman Wessel* (Oslo: Aschehoug, 1999);

Francis Bull, "Det Norske Selskab," in *Norsk Litteraturhistorie,* volume 2, by Bull and Fredrik Paasche (Oslo: Aschehoug, 1928), pp. 457–469;

Carl Fredrik Engelstad, *Norske Selskabs blomst og krone. Johan Herman Wessel, 1742–1785* (Oslo: Aschehoug, 1992);

Johan Fjord Jensen and others, "De nationale bevægelser" and "Johan Herman Wessel," in *Dansk litteraturhistorie,* volume 4, edited by Fjord Jensen and others (Copenhagen: Gyldendal, 1983), pp. 320–335, 336–339;

Illit Grøndahl and Ola Raknes, "Johan Herman Wessel and Det Norske Selskab," in their *Chapters in Norwegian Literature* (Copenhagen: Gyldendal, 1923), pp. 35–51;

Daniel Haakonsen, "Johan Herman Wessel," in his *Tolkning og teori* (Oslo: Aschehoug, 1987);

Jan E. Hansen, "Johan Herman Wessel," in *Norske klassikere,* edited by Peter Anker, Kjell Bækkelund, and Eilif Straume (Oslo: Tiden, 1985), pp. 600–607;

Ludvig Holm-Olsen and Kjell Heggelund, "Johan Herman Wessel," in *Norges litteraturhistorie,* edited by Edvard Beyer, volume 1 (Oslo: Cappelen, 1975), pp. 575–585;

Henrik Jæger, *Illustreret norsk Literaturhistorie* (Christiania: H. Bigler, 1892), pp. 456–484;

Harald Langberg, *Den store satire. Johan Herman Wessel og Kærlighed uden Strømper* (Copenhagen: Gyldendal, 1973);

Bjørn Linnestad, *Vesen gjennom vidd og vers. Om Johan Herman Wessel* (Vestby: Vestby Historielag, 1992);

Jørgen H. Monrad, *Den københavnske klub, 1770–1820* (Århus: Aarhus University Press, 1976);

Harald S. Naess, "Det Norske Selskab," in *A History of Norwegian Literature,* edited by Naess (Lincoln: University of Nebraska Press/American-Scandinavian Foundation, 1993), pp. 76–81;

Carl S. Petersen and Vilhelm Andersen, *Illustreret dansk Litteraturhistorie,* volume 2: *Litteratur i det nittende Aarhundredes første Halvdel* (Copenhagen: Gyldendal, 1934), pp. 543–559;

Knud Lyhne Rahbek and Rasmus Nyerup, *Bidrag til en Udsigt over dansk Digtekunst under Kong Christian den Syvende* (Copenhagen: J. H. Schultz, 1828);

Sven H. Rossel, ed., *A History of Danish Literature* (Lincoln: University of Nebraska Press/American-Scandinavian Foundation, 1992), pp. 151–152;

Sigurd Thomsen, *Kun en Digter. En Bog om Johan Herman Wessel* (Copenhagen: Jespersen & Piø, 1942);

A. H. Winsnes, *Det Norske Selskab, 1772–1812* (Christiania: Aschehoug, 1924), pp. 46–104.

Gustav Wied

(6 March 1858 - 24 October 1914)

Faith Ingwersen
University of Wisconsin–Madison

BOOKS: *Nogle Aforismer i Anledning af Interpellationen i Storehedinge og dens Følger,* as Peter Idealist (Copenhagen: M. F. Blaunfeldt, 1887);

En Hjemkomst. Sørgespil i fire Akter (Copenhagen: W. L. Wulff, 1889);

Silhuetter (Copenhagen: J. H. Mansa, 1891);

En Bryllupsnat. Skuespil i en Akt (Copenhagen: J. H. Mansa, 1892);

Barnlige Sjæle (Copenhagen: J. H. Mansa, 1893)–includes "De unge og de gamle"; *Barnlige Sjæle* revised as *Byens Stolthed. Komedie i fem Akter* (Copenhagen: Gyldendal, 1904 [i.e., 1905]);

Menneskenes Børn, 2 volumes in 1 (Aarhus: Jydsk Forlag, 1894)–volume 1 includes "Menneskernes Børn. En Akt," enlarged in *Kjærlighed. Fire Idyller* (Copenhagen: Gyldendal, 1909) and translated by Henry Steele Commager as "Children of Men" in *Denmark's Best Stories: An Introduction to Danish Fiction,* edited by Hanna Astrup Larsen (New York: American-Scandinavian Foundation/ Norton, 1928), pp. 237–247; volume 2 of *Menneskenes Børn* includes *Jægermesterinden. Skuespil i to Akter* and "Menneskernes Børn II," revised as act 1 of *Den gamle Pavillon. Skuespil i fire Akter* (Copenhagen: Gyldendal, 1902);

Ungdomshistorier. En Fortælling (Copenhagen: P. G. Philipsen, 1895)–includes "Jeg tror kun paa een gud–"; *Ungdomshistorier* revised as *Ranke Viljer. Satyrspil i fire Akter* (Copenhagen: Gyldendal, 1906 [i.e., 1907]); *Ranke Viljer* revised with Peter Fristrup as *2 x 2 = 5,* translated by Ernest Boyd and Holger Koppel as *2 x 2 = 5: A Comedy in Four Acts* (New York: N. L. Brown, 1923);

Erotik. Satyrspil i tre Akter (Copenhagen: Gyldendal, 1896);

Lystige Historier (Copenhagen: Nordiske Forlag/E. Bojesen, 1896)–includes "Livsglæde" and *Da Baby Skulde paa Hotel. En lille Komedie i tre Akter;*

Adel, Gejstlighed, Borger og Bonde. Fire Satyrspil (Copenhagen: Gyldendal, 1897)–includes *En Mindefest. Satyrspil i fire Afdelinger;*

Gustav Wied (courtesy of the Danish Royal Library, Copenhagen)

H. C. Andersen. Stemninger og Eventyr (Copenhagen: Gyldendal, 1897);

Slægten. Roman (Copenhagen: Gyldendal, 1898); revised as *Hendes gamle Naade. Skuespil i fem Akter* (Copenhagen: Gyldendal, 1904); *Slægten* translated by J. C. P. Sandeman as *The Blood-Line: A Translation of Gustav Wied's Slægten* (New York: Vantage, 1983);

Livsens Ondskab. Billeder fra Gammelkøbing (Copenhagen: Gyldendal, 1899); revised as *Thummelumsen. Komedie i fem Billeder* (Copenhagen: Gyldendal, 1901);

Det svage Køn. Fire Satyrspil (Copenhagen: Gyldendal, 1900)–includes *Fru Mimi* and *Frøken Mathilde;*

To Kroner og Halvtreds og andre Skærmydsler (Copenhagen: Schubothe, 1901)–includes *Skærmydsler,* republished (Copenhagen: Gyldendal, 1910);

Knagsted. Billeder fra Ind- og Udland (Livsens Ondskab Opus II) (Copenhagen: Gyldendal, 1902);

Et Opgør. En lille Komedie i een Akt (Copenhagen: Gyldendal, 1903);

Dansemus. Et Satyrspil (Copenhagen: Gyldendal, 1905); revised with Emma Gad as *Kærlighedens Kispus. Satyrspil i fem Akter* (1914), published in *Er vi myrdet? Omkring Emma Gad, Gustav Wied og Kærlighedens Kispus,* introduction by Ib Boye (Frederiksberg: Fisker, 1989), pp. 33–93;

Faareper. Et Liv (Copenhagen: Schubothe, 1905);

Fra Land og By. Samlede Fortællinger i Folkeudgave, 2 volumes (Copenhagen: Gyldendal, 1907);

Fædrene æder Druer–. Roman (Slægten, Opus II) (Copenhagen: Gyldendal, 1908);

Circus Mundi (Copenhagen: Gyldendal, 1909);

Kærlighed. Fire Idyller (Copenhagen: Gyldendal, 1909)–includes *Kærlighed. To Akter og en Epilog;*

Tre Satyrspil. En liden Nytaarsgave (Copenhagen: Gyldendal, 1911);

Vidunderbarnet. Satyrspil i fire Akter (Copenhagen: Gyldendal, 1911 [i.e., 1912]);

Pastor Sørensen & Co. En Redegørelse (Livsens Ondskab Opus III) (Copenhagen: Gyldendal, 1913);

Imellem Slagene (Copenhagen: Gyldendal, 1914);

Muntre Fortællinger (Copenhagen: Gyldendal, 1914);

Mindeudgave, 8 volumes (Copenhagen: Gyldendal, 1915–1916)–includes *Digt og Virkelighed,* republished as *Digt og Virkelighed. Livserindringer* (Copenhagen: Gyldendal, 1922); revised and enlarged, foreword by Henry Hellsen (Copenhagen: Gyldendal, 1950); revised and enlarged as *Digt og Virkelighed* in *Romaner, Noveller, Skuespil,* volume 1 (Copenhagen: Rosenkilde & Bagger, 1966); revised and enlarged as *Digt og Virkelighed,* afterword by Poul Carit Andersen (Bording: C. Andersen, 1969)–includes "Havanna-Udskud" and "Byer. Rejsestemninger."

Editions and Collections: *Udvalgte Skrifter,* 4 volumes (Copenhagen: Gyldendal, 1917);

Satyrspil (Copenhagen: Gyldendal, 1920)–comprises *Erotik; Adel, Gejstlighed, Borger og Bonde;* and *Det svage Køn;*

Værker i Udvalg, 5 volumes, edited, with an introduction, by Tom Kristensen (Copenhagen: Gyldendal, 1938);

En Mindefest. Et Satyrspil, foreword by Carl Erik Soya (Copenhagen: Gyldendal, 1948);

Af den gamle Vinhandlers Optegnelser, foreword by Johannes Brøndum-Nielsen (Copenhagen: Gyldendal, 1949);

Skærmydsler, og andre Satyrspil (Copenhagen: Gyldendal, 1962)–comprises *Skærmydsler, En Mindefest, Fru Mimi,* and *Døden;*

Den hellige Aand, og andre Historier (Copenhagen: Gyldendal, 1964);

Den gamle Kammerherre, og andre Historier (Copenhagen: Gyldendal, 1965);

Gustav Wied Fortæller, 3 volumes, edited by Poul Carit Andersen and Ellinor Andersen (Copenhagen: C. Andersen, 1965–1967);

Udvalgte Værker, 7 volumes (Copenhagen: Gyldendal, 1966);

Romaner; Noveller; Skuespil, 12 volumes (Copenhagen: Rosenkilde & Bagger, 1966–1968);

Ministeræderen. Fire Satyrspil (Copenhagen: Dansk Amatør Teater Samvirke, 1967);

Slægten; Fædrene æder Druer– (Copenhagen: Grafisk Forlag, 1967);

Livsens Ondskab, edited, with an afterword, by Kristensen, foreword by Ebbe Rode (Copenhagen: Lademann, 1968);

Slægten, afterword by Hans Andersen (Copenhagen: Lademann, 1979);

Pastor Sørensen & Co. (Copenhagen: C. Andersen, 1982).

PLAY PRODUCTIONS: *En Bryllupsnat. Skuespil i en Akt,* Copenhagen, Studentersamfundets fri Teater, 6 February 1892;

Erotik. Satyrspil i tre Akter, Copenhagen, Dagmarteatret, 7 April 1896;

Første Violin. Komedie i fire Akter, by Wied and Jens Petersen, Copenhagen, Folketeatret, 18 October 1898;

En Mindefest. Et Satyrspil, Copenhagen, Dagmarteatret, 3 February 1899;

Bønder, Copenhagen, Dagmarteatret, 26 September 1899;

Thummelumsen. Komedie i fem Billeder, by Wied and Peter Fristrup, Copenhagen, Folketeatret, 22 February 1901;

Skærmydsler, Copenhagen, Det Kongelige Teater, 10 May 1901;

Fru Mimi, Copenhagen, Dagmarteatret, 9 November 1901;

Atalanta, eller, Naar Piger har Penge. Komedie i tre Akter, by Wied and Petersen, Copenhagen, Dagmarteatret, 19 December 1901;

Den gamle Pavillon. Skuespil i fire Akter, Copenhagen, Det Kongelige Teater, 24 October 1902;

Kærlighed. To Akter og en Epilog, Copenhagen, Dagmarteatret, 20 February 1903;

Hendes gamle Naade. Skuespil i fem Akter, Copenhagen, Folketeatret, 29 January 1904;

Et Opgør. En lille Komedie i een Akt, Copenhagen, Det Kongelige Teater, 10 April 1904;

Byens Stolthed. Komedie i fem Akter, by Wied and Fristrup, Copenhagen, Folketeatret, 28 January 1905;

Ranke Viljer. Satyrspil i fire Akter, Copenhagen, Dagmarteatret, 12 February 1907;

Ærtehalm. Komedie i tre Akter, by Wied and Karen Adler Bramson, Copenhagen, Dagmarteatret, 12 December 1909;

Menneskenes Børn, Copenhagen, Dagmarteatret, 1 February 1910;

Vidunderbarnet. Satyrspil i fire Akter, Kristiania (Oslo), 4 May 1911; Copenhagen, Dagmarteatret, 8 November 1912;

2 x 2 = 5, by Wied and Fristrup, Copenhagen, Folketeatret, 26 December 1911;

Tanzmäuse [Dansemus], Berlin, Kleines Theater, 5 March 1912;

Kærlighedens Kispus. Satyrspil i fem Akter, by Wied and Emma Gad, Copenhagen, Folketeatret, 17 October 1914;

Da Baby Skulde paa Hotel. En lille Komedie i tre Akter, N.p., Olympia, 2 October 1923;

Frøken Mathilde, Copenhagen, Det Intime Teater, 19 September 1925.

OTHER: Caroline Catharine Wied, *Bedstemoders Manuskript. Spredte Billeder af Livet i Aarhundredets Midte,* edited by Gustav Wied (Copenhagen: Nordiske Forlag, 1897);

Første Violin. Komedie i fire Akter, by Gustav Wied and Jens Petersen (Copenhagen: Gyldendal, 1898);

Atalanta, eller, Naar Piger har Penge. Komedie i tre Akter, by Gustav Wied and Petersen (Copenhagen: Gyldendal, 1901); revised and abridged as *Kærlighed og Trøfler. Komedie i tre Akter* (Copenhagen: Gyldendal, 1912);

Ærtehalm. Komedie i tre Akter, by Gustav Wied and Karen Adler Bramson (Copenhagen: Gyldendal, 1909).

TRANSLATIONS: William Makepeace Thackeray, *Bogen om Snobberne* (Copenhagen: Schubothe, 1900);

Alexis Kivi, *Trolovelsen. Komedie i en Akt,* in Wied, *Kærlighed. Fire Idyller* (Copenhagen: Gyldendal, 1909);

Jules Laforgue, *Pierrots Giftermaal,* in Wied, *Circus Mundi* (Copenhagen: Gyldendal, 1909);

Arvid Järnfelt, "Gyngestolen" and "Dyr og Mennesker," in Wied, *Imellem Slagene* (Copenhagen: Gyldendal, 1914).

SELECTED PERIODICAL PUBLICATION–UNCOLLECTED: "Akvareller fra Land og By," *København,* 27 February 1891 - 11 December 1892–includes "De unge og de gamle" (27 December 1891), revised and republished in *Barnlige Sjæle* (Copenhagen: J. H. Mansa, 1893).

The works of Gustav Wied appeared not only in Denmark's neighboring Scandinavian countries but also as far afield as Hungary; it is said that they were better known in Germany than were the works of any other Danish writer up to his day. Wied was recognized as a humorist with a bite. Although he may have loved individuals–and he wrote warmly about a few of his characters–his oeuvre is based on misanthropy. He possessed a keen sense of human folly; in fact, his fictional characters, some of whom are eccentric to the point of the absurd, have been called Dickensian. In a long, episodic closet drama, *Dansemus. Et Satyrspil* (Dancing Mice: A Satyr Play, 1905), Wied writes of a young philosopher who kept some dancing white mice. In their cage the mice deliriously and untiringly, but rather joylessly, whirl around and around an upright stick. They stop only to copulate and eat and then begin to spin around again. Wied says that watching the mice is like viewing the doings of humankind from a high tower. An author's keeping such a distance–which can often furnish a detailed picture of a way of life–is a clever strategy, but it can be dangerous. Although distance allows the cynic free rein–and many humorists have had a cynical bent–it may also tend to separate such a person from humanity and put some strain on his use of his creative resources. Wied, who often contemplated suicide (and finally took his own life in 1914), created a literary benchmark for caustic views of the whirl of humanity in his writings on single-minded individuals, gossipy society, hypocritical clergy, and self-interested politicians.

Gustav Johannes Wied was born on 6 March 1858, the third of eleven children, three of whom died young. His parents, the kindly but often depressive Catharine Karoline Boesen Wied and the stern disciplinarian Carl August Wied, lived at Holmegaard, a farm near Nakskov. Gustav's childhood was filled with the people and doings of farm life, while his mother told him fairy tales and encouraged his writing and playacting. After his confirmation in 1873, he went into training at the Thierry Bookstore in Nakskov. The following year he joined his paternal aunt, Marie Wied, in Copenhagen, and in 1875 he became an apprentice at

Wied in 1893 (Roskilde Museum; from Frederik J. Billeskov Jansen, Gustav Wied. Den mangfoldige digter, *1997; Charles E. Young Research Library, University of California, Los Angeles)*

the Frederik Wøldike Bookstore, where he continued in training until 1879. Wied remained at his aunt's until 1883. He had received his father's permission in 1878 to study for *Studentereksamen* (the exam required for matriculation to the university), and in 1879 he passed the first part of that exam. He failed the second part three times but finally finished it in July 1886. By then he had worked at an attorney's office in Copenhagen (1881) and had been a tutor at Overgaard, a manor near Hadsund, by Mariager Fjord. There, from June 1883 to November 1884, Wied had taught the stepson of Frederik von Arenstorff, master of the royal hunt.

Holmegaard was leased out, and from the fall of 1886 Wied's parents, three of their other children, Wied himself, and his aunt Marie began residing together on Margrethevej in Copenhagen. From 1886 to 1887 Wied studied at the university for a one-year degree in philosophy.

On a visit to Overgaard Manor in 1887 Wied met the published author and actress Nathalia Larsen, who later translated two August Strindberg plays into Danish. Wied, who had begun to teach at the Sundby Realskole (a junior high school) on Amager, dedicated to her his debut in poetry, "Jeg tror kun paa en gud–og det er dig!" (I believe in but one god–and it is you! 1888). For several years Wied and "Nalle" shared an intensely erotic relationship, as well as an interest in Strindberg's works. They appeared in productions at Studentersamfundets fri Teater (the Student Society's Free Theater) and the Strindbergske Forsøgsteater (Strindbergian Experimental Theater).

In 1887 Wied published *Nogle Aforismer i Anledning af Interpellationen i Storehedinge og dens Følger* (Aphorisms with Reference to the Provocation in Storehedinge and Its Consequences), under the pseudonym Peter Idealist. A certain Ingeman-Petersen, a butter wholesaler, had accused the minister of culture, J. F. Scavenius, of frequenting a house of prostitution. Wied's twenty-five aphorisms were written against the pastors who, he felt, had demonstrated in their criticism of the wholesaler the kind of hypocrisy to which Søren Kierkegaard had earlier objected. This conflict Wied later used in *Dansemus.*

Influenced by Strindberg and Henrik Ibsen, and representing the fate of his brother Otto, Wied published the tragedy *En Hjemkomst* (A Homecoming, 1889), about the return from abroad of an emotionally ailing and hate-filled son who recognizes his rootlessness and eventually views his incarceration for mental illness as a liberation. In 1891 Wied's collection of short stories titled *Silhuetter* (Silhouettes) was published. In the guise of Johannes, a brother visiting Frørup Manor, he creates quick, harsh word portraits of the people who work or have worked at the manor. In 1892 Wied's one-act drama *En Bryllupsnat* (A Wedding Night), in which a grandmother attempts to throttle her granddaughter while awaiting the widowed father's return with his new bride, caused an uproar and was shut down. For a short period that same year he was engaged to a young actress who had appeared in the play and who was subsequently to appear in other of his plays, Anna Halberg (later Anna Larssen Bjørner). Before the year was out, however, Wied not only found himself in jail but also, through the author Agnes Henningsen, had met the woman who was to become his wife, Alice Tutein.

The meeting place of the young bohemians was the Café Bernina; the newspaper of the political opposition to the government was *København* (Copenhagen), and Wied habitually sat in the Café Bernina reading this paper. His writing for *København,* about ninety sketches published from February 1891 to December 1892, brought him the acquaintance of other Danish authors, such as Holger Drachmann, Sophus Schandorph, and Herman Bang. The brothers Helge Rode and Ove Rode, the editors of *København,* were fined or sent to prison for immoral works; that, too, was Wied's fate for his story "De Unge og de gamle" (The Young and the Old), published in the 27 December 1891 issue of *København.* Wied spent fourteen days in prison, and *København,* which was soon sold, paid his legal costs.

Ungdomshistorier (Tales of Youth, 1895) is a fictionalized memoir about Wied's early days in Copenhagen. The protagonist, Gunnar Johannes Warberg, is a student working toward a master's degree in philosophy. He becomes a victim simultaneously of his sexual passion and his misogyny. His passion is for the somewhat older Fernanda Møller, his "Sif of the Raven Guise" (in Scandinavian mythology Sif was the wife of Thor; her hair was shorn and replaced with gold by the trickster god Loki). Sif shares his artistic engagement and free spirit; though she professes her devotion to him even when rejected by him, she is never long without some young man professing devotion to her. In contrast to Warberg's view of women as sly, stupid, false, affected, and predatory, he views his young male friends as good-hearted, bright, and fun-loving but victimized by their fiancées and wives. These women usually represent the repression of society, even when, as with Sif, they appear to be breaking its code.

Alongside the story of passion between Warberg and Sif and the unfortunate lives of his supposedly promising young friends are two more accounts: that of Warberg's ineffectual and ill-fated cousin Benjamin, called Mette (as was Wied's own brother Otto), and that of an official accusation against Warberg for immorality in writing about the sexual abuse of a little boy by his religious nanny. He is told that everyone knows such abuse exists but that it is unnecessary to describe it. Warberg spends fourteen days in prison. The night before he leaves his cell, he has two dreams. In one, Sif leaves a fatherless little girl with him to raise, and–to his horror–she becomes as lustful and sly as her mother. In the next dream he and his father have a knife fight, after which his gentle mother, while tending his wounds, turns into the inescapable Sif.

Wied wrote *Ungdomshistorier* when he was thirty-seven, and nearly everyone and every event in the book has been documented as based in reality. The character who leaves the prison with Warberg was to become the best known: an imp–an inseparable companion who turns everything and everyone upside down–that, like Warberg, is identified with Wied himself. The imp says to Warberg that it is about time that they start doing "their thing" to Beauty, Goodness, and Truth.

In 1893 Wied announced his engagement to Alice and, three months later, their marriage. The latter announcement was not true, but in 1894 a son, Johan Sophus Herman, was born to the couple. The family then moved to Sæby. In April 1896, after the birth of a daughter, Inger Marie, Wied and Alice were reported by her father to the police for having had children out of wedlock. The couple were married on 1 May of that year.

During these years Wied had published three collections of short stories: *Barnlige Sjæle* (Childlike Souls, 1893), *Menneskenes Børn* (The Children of Humankind, 1894), and *Lystige Historier* (Jolly Stories, 1896). He had also seen performed his play *Erotik. Satyrspil i tre Akter* (Eroticism: Satyr Play in Three Acts, 1896), in the subtitle of which he first used his new generic term *Satyrspil.* In 1897 the Wieds' second son was born, but he died soon afterward. That same year, the family moved first to Sparresholm near Næstved and then to St. Olsgade in Roskilde.

In 1898 Wied published the novel *Slægten* (translated as *The Blood-Line,* 1983), the satiric, Darwinian story of the final decline of an old rural family, the Leunbachs. The last three heads of family have plundered the manor in order to pay debts, especially gambling debts. The present baroness, the widowed, elderly Juliane, who never completely loses command over herself–or her deaf-mute servant, Stasia–must leave the manor house when her son, Helmuth, marries Alvilda "Vilde" Raskowitz, née Rosenvinge, the new baroness. The latter is a widow with a spontaneously joyous young daughter, Karen. Hired as Karen's tutor is the easily frightened and homesick young Elise Jansen, called "Rabbit"; through the tutor's innocent letters home the reader learns of many of the happenings at the manor. Events are also commented on by others in the area, especially by Stasia and her poverty-stricken mother, the equally spiteful Maren Forlis (whose name in Danish suggests "nightmare" and "shipwreck").

The bear-like Helmuth, good-natured but easily roused to anger and violence, is a skillful overseer of his land and hopes to be able to pass it on to an heir. His wife, Vilde (whose nickname implies "wild" or "will"), is unfaithful with a neighbor: her cousin, the hypocritical ascetic and ladies' man Count von Scheele. Their punishment takes place, so to speak, offstage, and only the embers left from the destroyed belvedere, their trysting place, are described. Wied's technique is often that of recounting at second hand through accidental sightings, overheard conversation, and rumors.

One of the most despised crimes recorded in Nordic literature has been "murder by arson." Yet, one of the old-fashioned virtues of the upper class has been a stiff-necked acceptance of misfortune and the ability to overcome one's feelings (whether of guilt or grief) in order to ensure the good fortune of one's bloodline. Helmuth, however, finds his will broken, and his mother deems him to be the last hapless scion of a hopeless bloodline. Her muttered words about bad blood, spinelessness, and familial rot close *Slægten.*

If Juliane, the old baroness, is ultimately the "practical person" in the novel, she has her counterpoise in the self-loathing, idealistic, but hopelessly lustful pastor Adolf Mascani. Driven to breakdown by the contradiction between his nature and his calling, he ends by cursing God from the pulpit. Neither his Christian view nor Juliane's aristocratic determination proves to be dependable. The almost panoramic distance Wied has created between readers and the action enables them to see the absurdity of the characters' oft-disappointed beliefs and hopes. *Slægten* twice has been adapted as a motion picture: in 1912, with a screenplay by Nathalie Larsen Lippert, and in 1978, with a screenplay by Flemming Quist Møller and Anders Refn.

One of Wied's most acclaimed works, the novel *Livsens Ondskab. Billeder fra Gammelkøbing* (Life's Malice: Scenes from Gammelkøbing, 1899), is set in the fictional town of Gammelkøbing (based on Roskilde); the characters are members or would-be members of the bourgeoisie. They are people concerned with appearances, class, and scandal–whether in the form of infidelity or a simple lack of sophistication. One object of their scorn is Emanuel Thomsen, called "Thummelumsen." He has lost the family farm and lived in town for the past fifteen years, taking on various jobs, while his old mother looks after a tiny store. He continually yearns for the day when he can recover the farm and believes his dead father has appeared to give him a lottery number to ensure his repossession of the property. His father's wraith also said that two creatures–Knors, a one-eyed cat, and Mortensen, an all-but-dead rooster, which Emanuel had brought with him to town–first had to walk again on the family's land. Emanuel fulfills this obligation, wins the lottery, and is certain the Lord is with him. When he is at last the farm's proprietor, however, he discovers that his dream, like many a dream fulfilled, no longer brings joy.

Two visitors, a former customs inspector, Knagsted (called Esau), and a school principal, Clausen, discuss Emanuel's future. His wife is expecting a baby, and the romantic optimist Clausen hopes that Thummelumsen's having a son to work for will give him the purpose and energy he now lacks, whereas the pessimist Knagsted maintains that in that case, the child will surely be a girl.

Knagsted, a man covered in bristly red hair, delights in shocking, maliciously setting the record straight, and making others face their own failings and fears, but even without his help, readers may be dismayed to find that a character for whom they have entertained some sympathy is so divided that he may suddenly begin to fall into dishonesty and cruelty. Thummelumsen is just such a man. His longings and hard work are worthy of sympathy, but, in adversity, he turns into a sneering, miserly dictator toward his old mother and–his sense of justice outraged–even threatens to blackmail an old woman for taking roses from the graveyard. The double standard that nearly all the characters maintain between what they profess and what they do is the theme of *Livsens Ondskab.* To establish this theme, Wied employs contrasts, such as that between Knagsted and Clausen, and the divided selves of Thummelumsen. Knagsted is a representative of the truth and, for some, a fearsome avenger, but even this supposedly nihilistic man (like Wied himself) proves to be divided. Knagsted not only cannot bear to tell the unvarnished truth to a dying man (his later benefactor, Council Mørch), he also steps in to stop Thummelumsen from being verbally abused at a town ball.

Wied wickedly provides descriptions meant to be devoid of Romanticism. What might seem to be the start of a rather Romantic portrayal of a landscape is simply undercut by his referring back to a similar sketch on a previous page. His descriptions–whether of the ancient, almost featherless rooster, Mortensen, with his hanging wings and comb and two broken tail feathers; or of Thummelumsen, with his long right arm and crab-like sideways gait–transcend realism and reach the grotesque. If readers are startled by such descriptions, they will surely be startled into laughter by the reactions of Wied's characters. When Thummelumsen attempts to tell his mother about the wondrous vision of his father's ghost, she bursts into tears, lamenting her son's being so far gone.

After Wied's month-long stay at St. Joseph's Hospital in 1899 (possibly for a stomach ailment) and the birth of another son, Jacob Peter, in 1900, the family moved to a newly built house, Kastellet, in Roskilde. For the rest of his life Wied was to remain there except for trips to Germany (1901 and 1911), to a spa in southern France (1902), to England (1905 and 1906), and to Norway (four trips from 1909 to 1912).

In 1901 Wied rewrote *Livsens Ondskab* as the stage comedy *Thummelumsen.* In the play the protagonist is less likable, less considerate, and even more brutal in his way of talking to others. Perhaps his completely unsophisticated fiancée, Wulfdine, is the most surprising, for in embarrassment she rudely rebukes those who address her. When a count does so at a city ball, she tells him to mind his own business and leave her alone. The most astounding revision is seen in the final act. Thummelumsen has not married Wulfdine but rather the widowed Madame Svendsen, a former housekeeper who has inherited money, purchased the farm, and thereby bought Thummelumsen. The play closes with the happy man surrounded by his ready-made family. In 1941 *Thummelumsen* was adapted as a motion picture, with a screenplay by Flemming Lynge.

Knagsted. Billeder fra Ind- og Udland (Knagsted: Scenes from Home and Abroad, 1902), a travel novel, resumes the tale of *Livsens Ondskab* (as *Opus II* of that work). Knagsted, who has inherited money and moved to Copenhagen, now invites an old friend, the former headmaster Clausen, to accompany him to the spa at Karlsbad in Bohemia. Knagsted maintains that he suffers from chronic self-control. He is intelligent and distrustful of God and feels that Clausen is his better self–that Clausen is as he himself was in his innocent childhood and is in fact his reason for living. But when comparing Clausen to a child, Knagsted also likens him to women and animals in their happiness, for "human beings" are not innocently happy. A true man can be the greatest benefactor of his age–by reacting against women's talk of freedom, progress, education, optimism, and development and by suppressing culture. Knagsted sees himself as an impetus to thoughtfulness. The two friends view everything differently–nature, cultural icons, and the characters they meet along the way. These differences lend a humorous touch to the narrative, and Wied's caricatures of those they meet are superb–whether of a hen-like spa guest, a reluctantly dieting fellow Dane, or a shaky but proudly independent old man spilling food on himself. Together with *Livsens Ondskab, Knagsted* was the basis for the 1972 five-part television miniseries *Livsens Ondskab,* with a screenplay by Kjeld Larsen.

Of the many works that Wied wrote before his suicide in 1914, four are of particular interest: *Adel, Gejstlighed, Borger og Bonde. Fire Satyrspil* (Nobility, Clergy, Burgher and Peasant: Four Satyr Plays, 1897); the 1905 play *Dansemus* (first performed in Germany as *Tanzmäuse* in 1912); the novel *Fædrene æder Druer–* (The Fathers Are Eating Grapes–, 1908), subtitled *Slægten, Opus II;* and *Pastor Sørensen & Co. En Redegørelse* (Pastor Sørensen & Co.: An Account, 1913), subtitled *Livsens Ondskab Opus III.* The four satyr plays are satirically powerful portrayals of each of the traditional groups in Danish society. *Adel* depicts a dinner given in memory of a deceased wife, at which the self-absorbed widower, noble only in class, often reveals his lack of delicacy to his uneasy guest, who proves to have been his wife's lover. *Gejstlighed* and *Borger* are either casually cold or broadly comic, but in *Bonde* a farmer's wife, with icy control, legally outmaneuvers other heirs in the matter of her husband's estate. She is unwavering in assuring her child's inheritance–a child whom the other heirs know is the fruit of an ongoing affair.

The naturalistic *Fædrene æder Druer–,* which takes its title from Jer. 31:29, is a depiction with gallows humor of the widely branched Uldahl-Ege family's

Wied two months before his suicide on 24 October 1914 (photograph by Johs. Brondum-Nielsen; from Frederik J. Billeskov Jansen, Gustav Wied. Den mangfoldige digter, *1997; Charles E. Young Research Library, University of California, Los Angeles)*

degeneration and ruin through drinking, gambling, and whoring. Four main branches of the family, each with its estate farm, as well as several illegitimate branches–from families involved in the law or the ministry to the poorest female laborers with malformed or nonthriving children–all succumb to the family fate of genetic or economic ruin. The central setting is Havslundegaard, the manor of Nils Uldahl-Ege, who is extravagant, continually unfaithful, and often drunk. He lives there, somewhat apart from his wife, Line (who rejects his sexual advances), and his four teenage daughters, each, as Wied implies, evincing the degenerative family traits: drunken Anna, lying Frederikke, lesbian Charlotte, and sensitive Sofie. Like Rabbit in *Slægten,* Sophie writes about events in her correspondence–in this case, pretend letters to her admired older cousin, the district's legal principal, Isidor Seemann. The likable Isidor, a sketcher of satiric pictures, murders his newly born, malformed child, while his relative, a consumptive and mad parish clerk and schoolteacher, tries to give his disease to the children under his care.

Palle, master of the hunt and head of one of the three branches of the Uldahl-Ege family that have no heirs, bequeaths his estate to his housekeeper and her sons. They eventually acquire the three other family farms as well, including, at the last, Nils's. Once everything is lost and his daughter Sofie has drowned herself,

Nils moves to town accompanied by his ever-loyal wife. Families are said to consist of either gatherers or scatterers, but old families who have had everything have only sorrow left. Nils reaches what Wied implies is the depth of degradation: he becomes religious. Isidor has suggested a more uncommon view of God and the world: it has been created and put on stage by a great, drunken faun, who holds in his hands the strings of all his puppets. As for Wied's string pulling, *Fædrene æder Druer–* is perhaps his broadest, most satisfyingly constructed and absorbing novel.

Many of Wied's plays were not meant for the stage, and much of the background and action is revealed in the stage directions. The ultimate example is *Dansemus,* a play that, with nine acts and a conclusion, is longer than many novels. The setting is the capital city of Absalonia in the fictitious country of Rugmelie. The action takes place by seasons. Each act deals with the fates of various individuals. The work opens with a religious baker spying on the minister of culture, Maltus von Lauenburg, who is the head of the church and preaches the sanctity of marriage but visits a prostitute (a theme in Wied's *Nogle Aforismer i Anledning af Interpellationen i Storehedinge og dens Følger*). When the baker accuses the minister publicly of hypocrisy and malfeasance, the baker is arrested. Adelheide, the wife of the poet Jørgen Murer, a Don Juan, seeks consolation in, and eventually marriage to, Ejnar Hegge, a collector of authors' autographs. Ejnar's minimal sexual response is at last met by Adelheide's complete dismissal of any erotic interest on his part. A second writer's wife, Klara Halling, a lonely and exhausted mother of four, is befriended by the consoling middle-aged bachelor Hammelev. He is interested in a young genius and would-be reformer of society, the philosopher Edmund Melling, who keeps in a cage some frenziedly dancing white mice, symbolic of humankind. The ailing Melling–who is writing a book called *Dancing Mice: A World Drama in Five Acts*–defends a would-be suicide's right to die, declares himself to be Christ's twin, and ends up in an asylum.

As for the others, Murer, though now engaged, seduces his former wife, Adelheide. The baker has gotten a young woman pregnant, spent time in prison, and–the reader learns–has mistaken someone else visiting the prostitute for Lauenburg (who is nevertheless guilty of the same thing). Union workers are betrayed by their union; a silver-anniversary party ends with the wife being led to her room by a lesbian lover; and the writer Halling leaves Klara for a trip along the Mediterranean and a wealthy widow. Halling writes a play in which an unfaithful artist returns to his wife, and thus the playwright wins acclaim for making life more beautiful than it is, for making it a work of art. Art manages to seduce those–such as Klara's father–who may find the truth gravely disappointing. And so the world rolls on; the white mice stop dancing only long enough to mate and eat (often, their own young).

In *Pastor Sørensen & Co.,* Wied's last novel, Knagsted returns for a third time. He has moved from Copenhagen to the little town of Søby, in the country of Flatland. There, he becomes friends with the Meinckes, who live on Knagsted's family's former farm. Though still a bachelor, at fifty Knagsted is greatly attracted to their seventeen-year-old daughter, Line. She causes him, for a while, to trim his wild red hair and beard and to admit that he dislikes women only because they mean too much to him. He has become a kindly listener to the troubles of others, several of them women. He seems to be the sympathetic, caring person that the pastor of the title ought to be. Sørensen first appears at the end of the novel, although the reader knows a good deal about him from his former wife. Seduced at fifteen and then forced into marriage, she is untrue and unrepentant and eventually escapes her husband's grasp. Sørensen touches the lives of others negatively as well: Hother, son of the healthy, life-affirming painter Neumann, a naturist, commits suicide over his first sexual thoughts. His mother, whose sorrow over the loss of Hother turns to madness, rejects not only her husband but also her other children.

Lust and money are the cause of other tragedies, too. Treschau, the forest supervisor, has seduced many women besides Pastor Sørensen's wife and is eventually shot by a jilted mistress. A banker, Council Wæver, steals money from both the bank and his father-in-law. Upon Wæver's imprisonment and divorce, his wife, still an heiress-to-be, is consoled and courted by the pastor.

When, at last, Knagsted and Meincke sit discussing life, the former declares that youths give life its meaning. The older person must smother his longings. Knagsted is writing a comedy in five acts and a *Nachspiel* (postlude) about the tragedy of one's "best years." Meincke proudly tells Knagsted that before marrying, he and his wife, young idealists, had had children, but they were then threatened by her father with legal consequences unless they married (a situation reminiscent of Wied's own marriage). Both Meincke and Neumann would agree that sexual joy is natural and life-affirming, while Knagsted seems to represent a happy tolerance. Pastor Sørensen and his cohorts then visit Knagsted to admonish him for living with his housekeeper. The men are shown the door–the only time Knagsted truly bares his teeth–and the next day Sørensen receives from him a poem, a paean to the fulfillment of fleshly desire. It is perhaps Knagsted's *Nachspiel.*

Wied, who frequently used the dramatic technique of interspersing the disconnected and torn phrases of gossipy townspeople in short stories and novels, now turned back to the stage and, as in many cases before, revised an earlier work as a new drama. With Emma Gad, he rewrote *Dansemus* as *Kærlighedens Kispus. Satyrspil i fem Akter* (Love's Hide and Seek: Satyr Play in Five Acts), which was first performed on 17 October 1914 and published posthumously in 1989. Social criticism was removed from the drama, and it was claimed to have devolved into little more than a mating game. After its premiere, Wied sent a telegram asking, "Er vi myrdet?" (Are we murdered?), as indeed was the case, for reviews were devastating. On 24 October 1914 Wied took his life.

Twenty-six chapters of Gustav Wied's autobiographical work *Digt og Virkelighed* (Fiction and Reality) had been serialized in the newspaper *Berlingske Aftenavis* from 7 March to 22 August 1914. One final chapter appeared after his death. The full forty-five chapters, treating the years up to 1889, were not published until 1966, in the first volume of the collection of his writings titled *Romaner; Noveller; Skuespil* (Novels; Short Stories; Plays). The tone of *Digt og Virkelighed* is amusing but, owing mainly to the policy of the newspaper, fairly nonabrasive. Wied's last works seem somewhat toothless, whereas his earlier writing has kept its bite. Although the exhausted satyr left the stage, his shocked audience is still laughing.

Letters:

Gustav Wied i Breve, edited by Johannes Brøndum-Nielsen (Copenhagen: Gyldendal, 1946).

Bibliographies:

Ebbe Holten-Nielsen, *Gustav Wied. En Bibliografi over Arbejder af og om ham* (Copenhagen: J. H. Schultz, 1930);

Svend Houmøller, *Gustav Wied. En Bibliografi,* Gustav Wied Selskabets Skrifter, no. 3 (Copenhagen: Forum, 1948).

Biographies:

Ebbe Neergaard, *Peter Idealist. Studier over Gustav Wieds Ungdom,* Gustav Wied Selskabets Skrifter, no. 1 (Copenhagen: R. Naver, 1938);

Knut Ahnlund, *Den unge Gustav Wied* (Copenhagen: Gyldendal, 1964).

References:

Frederik J. Billeskov Jansen, *Gustav Wied. Den mangfoldige digter* (Copenhagen: Spektrum, 1997);

Niels Bruhn Meredin and Jan Nøhr Christensen, *Romanforfatteren Gustav Wied: En analyse med afsæt i Michail Bachtin* (Aalborg: Aalborg University Press, 2000);

Ebbe Neergaard, *Dommen og drømmen. Om "det rasende bedrøvelige" hos humoristen Gustav Wied, en psykologisk skitse,* Gustav Wied Selskabets Skrifter, no. 5 (Copenhagen: Rosenkilde & Bagger, 1951);

Axel Nielsen, *Parentesen, der voksede. Studier i Gustav Wieds Satyrspil,* Gustav Wied Selskabets Skrifter, no. 4 (Copenhagen: Forum, 1948);

Eddie Salicath, *Omkring Gustav Wied* (Copenhagen: Rosenkilde & Bagger, 1946);

Dan Turèll and Jørgen Fisker, eds., *Gustav Wied billeder. En billedbog med Gustav Wieds egne fotooptagelser* (Copenhagen: Nordiske Lande, 1985);

Turèll and Fisker, eds., *Gustav Wied i Spejlet. Gustav Wied, som sét af andre forfattere* (Copenhagen: Nordiske Lande, 1986).

Christian Winther

(29 July 1796 - 30 December 1876)

Michael Krarup

BOOKS: *Digte* (Copenhagen: C. A. Reitzel, 1828);
Digte, gamle og nye (Copenhagen: C. A. Reitzel, 1832);
Nogle Digte (Copenhagen: C. A. Reitzel, 1835)–includes "Flugten til Amerika," translated by Piet Hein as *The Flight to America* (Copenhagen: Gyldendal, 1978);
Haandtegninger (Copenhagen: C. A. Reitzel, 1840);
Sagn og Sang (Copenhagen: P. G. Philipsen, 1840);
Digtninger (Copenhagen: C. A. Reitzel, 1843);
Fire Noveller (Copenhagen: C. A. Reitzel, 1843);
Haandtegninger, gamle og nye Digte (Copenhagen: P. G. Philipsen, 1846);
Lyriske Digte (Copenhagen: C. A. Reitzel, 1849);
En morskabsbog for børn (Copenhagen: C. A. Reitzel, 1850);
Nye Digte (Copenhagen: C. A. Reitzel, 1851);
Tre Fortællinger (Copenhagen: C. A. Reitzel, 1851);
Nye Digtninger (Copenhagen: C. A. Reitzel, 1853);
Hjortens Flugt: Et Digt (Copenhagen: C. A. Reitzel, 1855);
Sang og sagn (Copenhagen: P. G. Philipsen, 1858);
Blandede Digte, 2 volumes (Copenhagen: C. A. Reitzel, 1860, 1861);
C.W.'s Samlede Digtninger (Copenhagen, 1860–1872);
Brogede Blade (Copenhagen: C. A. Reitzel, 1862);
En Samling Vers (Copenhagen: C. A. Reitzel, 1872);
Efterladte Digte (Copenhagen: C. A. Reitzel, 1879).
Edition and Collection: *Christian Winther's Samlede Digtninger,* 11 volumes (Copenhagen, 1860–1878);
Hjortens Flugt: Et Digt, with an introduction by Erik A. Nielsen (Copenhagen: Dansklærerforeningen, 1999).

OTHER: Poul Martin Møller, *Efterladte Skrifter af Poul Martin Møller,* 3 volumes, edited by Winther, Christian Thaarup, F. C. Olsen, and L. V. Petersen (Copenhagen: C. A. Reitzel, 1839–1843).

Courtesy of the Danish Royal Library, Copenhagen

The year after Christian Winther's death, Danish critic and influential thinker Georg Brandes summed up Winther's collected works in this manner: "Vore Faedre elskede dem, og de elskes af os. Vore Faedre saa dem blive til, og de leve for os. Det er Stjerner, hvis Guld ingen Rust har angrebet og hvis Ild ikke er blevet slukt" (Our fathers loved them, and they are loved by us. Our fathers saw them created, and they live for us. They are stars, whose gold no rust has attacked and whose fire has not been put out). This eulogizing tone suggests that Winther's contemporaries appreciated the landscapes Winther created in which earthly and heavenly love are united through verse. To readers of Danish poetry, Winther is best known for his major literary achievement, the epic *Hjortens Flugt* (The Flight of the Stag, 1855), generally considered the last great work of Danish Romanticism. Within the Danish literary canon, Winther–along with Emil Aarestrup and Ludwig Bødtcher–belongs to the second generation of Romantic poets, who followed Adam Oehlenschläger. The difference between the two schools of Romantic poetry of Denmark is most visible in the landscapes created by the poets. The first generation is concerned with the historical landscape, whereas the second generation is interested in the unfolding contemporary landscape.

The two vicarages where Winther spent his childhood make up the center of his poetic universe. Rasmus Villads Christian Ferdinand Winther was born on 29 July 1796 near Næstved, where his father, Hans Christian Winther, was a vicar. After his father's death, Winther's mother, Johanna Dorothea Borchsenius, married Rasmus Møller, who was also a vicar. At fifteen Winther moved in with his new family at the vicarage of Købelev, a small village on the island of Lolland, where Winther gained a stepbrother, Poul Martin Møller, who also became a poet. During the same year Winther had an opportunity to familiarize himself with Italian literature. A prominent local lawyer, Jacob Edward Colbiornsen, had stipulated in his will that his library should be given to the Danish king, Frederik VI, who thereafter had donated the collection to the newly completed university in Kristiania (subsequently, Oslo University). Because Winther had already studied some Italian literature in school and at home, he was trusted with the job of inspecting and organizing the Italian section of the library. This work was an influential experience for young Winther, who was introduced to new poets and new editions of familiar works whose varying illustrations delighted him. His love of Italian poetry and the language itself continued throughout his life. Like many Danish Romanticist writers, Winther believed that Italy was the source from which all inspiration sprang.

At the age of nineteen, Winther finished school and moved to Copenhagen, where he matriculated in the Department of Theology at the University of Copenhagen. He completed his degree in 1824. He never became a vicar, however, and made his living by tutoring the children of wealthy Copenhagen families. While teaching, Winther published his first book, *Digte* (Poems, 1828). The reception of his debut publication was a success. All critics, apart from Christian Molbech, who saw too much of an influence from Heinrich Heine in the poems, were full of praise. This critical and popular success and a considerable inheritance from his father enabled him to travel for a year in Germany and Italy in 1830–1831.

Although Winther enjoyed relative popularity among readers and critics throughout his career, he led a troubled life. He was constantly in debt to various creditors and had a problematic personal life. The two aspects of his adult life that created a sense of stability for him were the honorary title of "Professor," which he received in 1841 when he began tutoring Crown Princess Caroline, and his marriage to Julie Constantia Werliin, which took place in 1848. Despite his emotional and financial ups and downs, Winther, in his writing, often managed to create a sense of simplicity and calm, especially in his poems, which are straightforward in composition and follow the popular ideals of his time. For many years, the scholarly interest in Winther's work was minimal, but roughly one hundred years after his death, Winther's work was revisited by such Danish scholars as Bo Tao Michaelis and Lise Præstgaard Andersen. They discovered a new dimension to his writing–the presence of female erotic power, which often threatens the idyllic order of Winther's poetic universe.

Winther was never a serious student of theology. He devoted most of his time to writing and was also interested in other academic disciplines. His correspondence shows that he often needed extraordinary encouragement from friends and family to engage himself in theological writings. During his years at the university, he was popular among his fellow students and actively involved in the intellectual and political life in the dorms located around the Round Tower in Copenhagen. He was respected by other young aspiring poets, notably his stepbrother, with whom he developed an exceptionally close friendship, and during these years, he wrote most of the poems from his debut collection, *Digte* (1828), later republished in *Digte, gamle og nye* (Poems, Old and New) in 1832. The most noteworthy among these early writings are considered generally to be the group of poems referred to as "træsnit" (Woodcuts). Each of these poems has a male and a female name in the title, such as "Steffen og Anne" (Steffen and Anne) or "Hans og Grethe" (Hans and Grethe). While the male always was given the first position in the title, the female character holds a central position in the text. The poems are about young lovers in the idyllic countryside, often in conflict with their immediate surroundings or each other. During the course of each poem, the conflict is resolved and the idyll restored. An example of this pattern is "Hans og Grethe." The poem is set behind one of Winther's favorite locations, the vicarage, where the two young lovers meet at night. The time and setting for the poem follow conventional ideals of romance; nighttime suggests the dangers of the blooming eroticism of the pair, but the vicarage provides a sense of comfort and safety for them. Like his contemporary, Hans Christian Andersen, Winther was interested in anthropology and drew on the namesake of the poem, the Grimm Brothers' "Hansel and Grethel," by presenting the reader with an adult figure lurking in the dark. Instead of a witch who seduces and waylays the innocent young, as in the fairy tale, this dark figure takes the shape of a nobleman who surprises the young lovers and brings with him reminders of tradition, family, and decency.

The passion between the two lovers is thus solidified through an authority figure and their free-flowing eroticism given a purpose and directed toward the idea of unity and function. The woodcuts no longer enjoy their initial popularity but are mostly appreciated for their landscape portraits of Winther's beloved Sjælland (the Danish island of Zealand).

Winther's first collection also includes what is perhaps his most-often-cited poem, "Flyv, Fugl, Flyv" (Fly, Bird, Fly). This poem is an example of how Winther's landscape often becomes an expression of an abstract love, not necessarily personified by two young lovers as in the example above:

Flyv, fugl, flyv over Furresøens Bølger,
Stræk dine Vinger nu vel!
Ser du to elskende, dem skal du følge,
Dybt skal du spejde deres Sjæl.
Er jeg en sanger, så bør jeg jo vide
Kærligheds smigrende lyst,
Alt, hvad et Hjerte kan rumme og lide,
Burde jo tolke min Røst.

(Fly, bird, fly, over Furresøen's surges,
follow two lovers awhile.
Fashion your song from their music that merges
Laughter and sorrow and guile.
Singer I am, and my song must recapture
All of love's secret deceit;
Sing of the torment, interpret the rapture,
Conquest and bitter defeat.)

In this second stanza of the poem, the narrator addresses his monologue to the bird, a transitory being, like the singer with whom the poet identifies again and again: the poem thus becomes an expression of a universal experience of love and longing. This bittersweet declaration of love to the Danish landscape is typical of Winther's poetry during the 1830s and 1840s. The longing experienced in the text, albeit painful, also functions as a guarantee for the existence of romance. In these monologues, particularly, Winther's inspiration from Heine and George Gordon, Lord Byron, is most evident.

Winther continued to read Italian poetry while in school, often aloud to his friends, so when the publication of his first work finally allowed the poet to travel, Italy was the only logical destination. His letters reveal a poet in awe not only of the Italian landscape but also of the city of Rome. During his year in Italy, he perfected his command of the Italian language and from then on continued to read Italian poetry out loud to himself and whoever was willing to listen. After a year of traveling in Italy, Winther returned to Copenhagen in 1832 to modest but encouraging success and became engaged to Sophie Hansen, whom he had met while a student at the university. What Winther's intentions in this engagement were are unclear. The poet never contributed to his own biography, but his letters reveal a person much in love with the idea of love rather than with the actual person. He identified strongly with the idea of the demonic lover, a concept he romanticized through his readings of Byron, especially, but also through Heine. The idea of freedom, personified in a poet with no ethical or familial ties to the community, was what inspired him to write the poem "Ravnens Quide" (The Raven's Distress). In this poem, the narrator, a raven, begs to be set free from his captivity and from his engagement. The raven gets what he wants but later realizes that he made a mistake and is punished for it. The poem is satirical in tone, a fact that suggests that Winther possessed a highly developed sense of irony and yet aspired to live the life of an aesthete. He enclosed the poem in a letter he sent to Sophie Hansen, and it prompted her to break off their engagement.

In addition to the romantic musings on love and nature, Winther's poetry also includes a great deal of humor, particularly in his third book, *Nogle Digte* (Some Poems), from 1835. In this publication one finds the poem most likely to be known by Winther's English-language readers, "Flugten til Amerika" (The Flight to America). The narrator is a boy who, after getting a poor grade in school, returns home to a scolding by his mother. After being reprimanded by two authority figures, the boy steps outside–only to witness his sweetheart, "the baker's daughter, Rikke," giving a sugar cookie to another boy. The boy's sense of betrayal reaches a climax after this incident, and he resolves to flee to America and thus get back at his teacher, his mother, and Rikke. The boy's younger brother, Emil, is saddened by the prospect of losing him. The speaker invites Emil to come along with him to America; to encourage the younger brother to do so, he describes America as a land where freedom is still abundant:

Og Frihed har man endnu dertil
Fra Morgen til Aftens ende,
Man spytter på gulvet,
Hvor man vil,
Og lader Cigarerne brænde.

(Liberty is what you just are at
to whatever you desire;
You spit on the floor
when you feel like that
And play with cigars and fire.)

After this alluring description of America, the boys decide to pick up something to eat on the way. Just then their mother announces dinner through the open window. The boys obey their mother and their hunger, and during dinner the before-so-resolute boy finds comfort in the food: "Jeg drunked min Sorg og fandt min Trøst på bunden af Sagosuppen" (I drowned my worry and found my peace deep down in the sago soup). The text is thus a funny and sweet poem about a boy's longing for the promised land of the nineteenth century; the descriptions of the place serve as a comment on many contemporary conceptions about the land of plenty. The poem, however, offers more. The boy, the symbolic embodiment of the Romantic hero, obeys authority and chooses comfort over adventure. The poem mocks not just the idea of the flight to America but also the prevailing spirit of the day. At perhaps a more genuine level, the poem offers insight into how even innocent childhood romance can be heartbreaking and brutal.

In addition to poetry, Winther wrote a handful of shorter prose pieces, four of which were published in *Fire Noveller* (Four Novellas) in 1843. These four texts deal with love in its most painful aspects and were generally not well received by the Danish reading public, who were accustomed to a gentler portrait of romance. "En Hevn" (Revenge) in particular created strong dissatisfaction among Winther's readers with its portrait of destructive love in the idyllic countryside. The plot is disturbing: a young independent woman, Jeanette, is staying with her uncle, Baron B, at his country estate after her mother's death. Her circumstances are not described, only that she has been in the care of her uncle for some time. On a sunny summer afternoon she is caught in her uncle's office by her cousin, the young Baron B, Joseph. The young baron finds her going through his father's personal documents and valuables and immediately accuses her of stealing. His intention, however, is not to right a wrong but rather to use the situation to his own advantage; in exchange for his silence, Jeanette is to perform certain sexual favors. Jeanette is shocked by Joseph's proposal and refuses to take part in the exchange. In her speech to the young baron, she reveals that she had hitherto been in love with him but that the indecency of his proposal has killed her love for him. She then resolves to seek out the older baron herself and explain her situation. During this conversation between Jeanette and her foster father, a few details about her situation in life are revealed, but, more importantly, the reader learns that the young woman was in fact acting on the old baron's behalf and going through his private chambers to help prevent a document from falling into the wrong hands. During this conversation, the uncle reveals his desire to see the two young cousins get married. He is a gentle character, who during this conversation shows respect and compassion for the woman. He even indicates that she, although of lower social standing, would be better off marrying someone other than his son. To the baron's surprise, Jeanette readily accepts the idea of marriage between her and Joseph but only on the condition that nothing in their current relationship is to be changed and that the engagement is to be short. Two months later Jeanette and Joseph are married and settled in a nearby estate. After this hasty marriage, six years follow. The reader learns that Jeanette, now a baroness, is thriving in her new life. She surrounds herself with intellectuals and artists and carries on correspondences with several important thinkers. The marriage, however, has never been consummated, and the couple lead separate lives, completely isolated from each other. The only recorded detail of their interaction is that each year, on their wedding day, Joseph approaches Jeanette and humbly asks for forgiveness and a chance to atone for his sin. This approach is met with complete silence from his wife, who turns from him. The final few lines of the text portray the same procedure on their sixth anniversary, during which the young baron enters the baroness's drawing room completely insane. During this scene, Jeanette's motive in marrying Joseph, her thirst for revenge, is revealed, and after a moment of triumphant reflection, she collapses on the floor and physically disintegrates.

What offended contemporary casual readers of this text was that Winther seemed to reject love altogether in this novella, and thus the text was too clearly a break from his poetry. Passion is present, but only as the passion for revenge. The wife's complete and hateful denial of her husband is what destroys them both. This young, independent woman appears as a recognizable symbol of the future, which clashes violently with the old feudal order represented in the young baron. He is driven by insanity and she by ruthless calculation. In this text, authority and the feudal presence do nothing to aid the young couple, and thus the novella shows a departure from Winther's poetry. The text is humorous in its descriptions, especially that of the old baroness, who plays an inconsequential part in the plot.

That love could be a source not only of delight but also of devastation makes sense when Winther's own love life is taken into account. In 1836 he met the already married Julie Constantia Werliin, née Lütthans. As the wife of a vicar, she was not within his reach. The two developed and cultivated a friendship for more than a decade, and during the early 1840s, the friendship took on a more romantic tone and Winther realized that his romantic feelings were reciprocated. After a lengthy and emotionally straining divorce in 1843, the two married on 21 February 1848. Winther thereby became stepfather to her two children, Henri and Ida. Winther was delighted to have a family, but Julie's daughter, Ida, was a source for concern because of her diagnosed "hysteria," which made living in the city of Copenhagen problematic.

During his growing attachment to Julie, the nature of which was kept hidden from even close friends, Winther worked on a series of poems organized under the title "Til Een" (To One), first published in *Digtninger* (Poetic Works) in 1843. These poems, later published in

Winther in 1843 (lithograph by Em. Bærentzen & Co.; from Carl S. Petersen and Vilhelm Andersen, Illustreret dansk Litteraturhistorie, *volume 3:* Litteratur i det nittende Aarhundredes første Halvdel, *1924; Suzzallo Library, University of Washington)*

Samlede Digtninger (Collected Poems, 1960–1972), titled by numbers, are generally considered Winther's finest love poems. These poems differ from Winther's earlier Romantic writings by being clearly addressed to one particular person, and the "one" written about is clearly Julie. Love is no longer an abstraction or part of a plot in a landscape dedication. Unlike Winther's earlier works, these poems do not portray a situation but only the feelings for the "one." The landscape therefore disappears, only to appear again if integral to the feeling portrayed. With the publication of *Lyriske Digte* (Lyrical Poems) in 1849, the speaker of the poems begins to show not only love but also gratitude to the "one," and the poems become a celebration of her strength rather than just declarations of love. In the years following their wedding, these poems begin to look back and reflect upon the development of the relationship. The relationship is metaphorically compared to a journey, and their union its destination. These poems were published in 1851 as *Nye Digte* (New Poems). Winther continued to write poems to Julie for the rest of his life, some of which were found among his manuscripts after his death. What separates this segment of Winther's love poems from the earlier ones is that while the erotic tone is always present, it is now solidified through the union between the lovers rather than by the outside world.

By the 1850s, Winther was husband, father, and lover. He was an accomplished and widely read poet in addition to being a professor and had won many prizes and grants. Still, his lifelong ambition to write an epic medieval poem remained unfulfilled. During his years at the university, he had studied the kings of the Middle Ages, pagan rituals, and Danish history. His many sketches and notes were published posthumously and reveal a mind dedicated to detail and careful planning from early childhood to midlife. His thorough study of the Middle Ages culminated with his epic masterpiece, *Hjortens Flugt.* The writing of the poem was difficult. Despite his success as a poet and his grants and awards, Winther was never a wealthy man but instead constantly in debt and constantly avoiding debtors in Copenhagen.

In the summer and fall of 1854, Winther and his family rented a house in the woods north of Copenhagen. July and August were happy and productive months, and Winther made progress on the epic poem. His letters from this period are carefree and mostly concerned with work. The records at the Danish Royal Library in Copenhagen indicate that he, among other sources, borrowed and brought to the summer house books on Wendish religion. In September, problems arose. Ida's mental condition worsened, and the family decided to depart for Rome as a cure for her hysteria. Winther was anxious and afraid that he would not get back into the right tone and rhythm after the break. He also knew that he would not be able to work on the poem while in Italy and deposited his manuscript in Copenhagen when the family departed at the end of October 1854. Finally, at the end of July 1855, the family returned to Denmark. The summer was spent on the island of Møn, where Winther was delighted to start working on the poem again. During the middle of fall, the poem was finally completed. On 9 October the family returned to Copenhagen, where they had rented a new apartment, and on 28 November 1855 the epic poem *Hjortens Flugt* was published to instant popularity.

Despite the magnitude of the poem, the plot can easily be summarized. The story takes place during the course of a year, from September to September under the reign of the Danish king Erik af Pommerns (1382–1459). The poem begins in medias res. A young nobleman, Strange, is dragged out of a dungeon where he has been held in captivity and tied to the back of a frightened stag. The scream of a woman is heard in the background and hovers over the medieval fortress. The poem thus follows the recipe for true, Gothic romance. After this dramatic opening, the poem continues in the present tense but simultaneously offers the background of the conflict and of the main characters. Strange is in love with Ellen, a favorite of the queen. The king's mistress, Rhitra, also has her eye on Strange. Through her erotic power over the king, Rhitra persuades him to break up the young couple by separating and placing them in captivity–Strange in the dungeons and Ellen in a remote ruin. In twenty-two parts, the poem narrates Strange's liberation from the stag, the rescue of Ellen, and the union between the two lovers. Through the story, the reader becomes familiar with the characters that populate the medieval Danish landscape: the singer, Folmer; the king and his mistress; the loving queen; and Rhitra's mother, Gulitze.

The conflict in the story is also simple: the kingdom is endangered as dark, erotic powers have divided the king and queen. The king is ensnared by the beautiful Rhitra, the daughter of a pagan god. Rhitra, like the title character in Hans Christian Andersen's "Den lille Havfrue" (The Little Mermaid, 1837), is demonized through the obvious emphasis on her sexuality and contrasted with the fair, innocent Ellen, whom the young nobleman fights to rescue, thus ensuring not only the future of the kingdom but also the future of purity and family. The structure of the poem blends the lyrical tradition with elements from the oral fairy-tale genre and is generally regarded by critics today as one of the absolute high points of the Danish Golden Age.

After the completion of his magnum opus, Winther published two more books of poems–*Brogede Blade* (Variegated Leaves) in 1862 and *En Samling Vers* (A Collection of Verse) in 1872, along with various minor publications. Toward the end of his life, Winther was drawn more and more to southern Europe and moved to Paris, where he died on 30 December 1876.

Although *Flugten til Amerika* has remained a classic in children's literature for more than a hundred years, Winther's masterpiece *Hjortens Flugt* is the work upon which his reputation rests. This epic poem has remained a classic in Denmark, especially among young women, during most of the twentieth century, and his other poetry is still represented in anthologies today. To ascribe a specific literary influence to Winther is difficult; he is widely regarded as one of the last great poets of the Danish Romantic period and an important figure in the development of secular literature in the nineteenth century.

Letters:

Breve til og fra Christian Winther, 4 volumes, edited by Morten Borup (Copenhagen: Danske Sprog- og Litteraturselskab, 1974).

Biography:

Nicolai Bøgh, *Christian Winther: Et digterbillede,* 3 volumes (Copenhagen, 1893–1901).

References:

Lise Præstgaard Andersen, "Kunsten at være naiv," in *Læsninger i dansk litteratur,* volume 1, edited by Andersen and Ulrik Lehrmann (Odense: Odense Universitetsforlag, 2001), pp. 152–168;

Søren Baggesen, "Christian Winther," *Arkiv for Dansk Litteratur* <www.adl.dk/Winther>;

Georg Brandes, *Danske Digtere* (Copenhagen: Gyldendal, 1896), pp. 108–182;

Elias Bredsdorff, Brita Mortensen, and Ronald Popperwell, eds., *An Introduction to Scandinavian Literature* (Copenhagen: Munksgaard, 1951), pp. 95–96;

Christian Winther: Paa 150 Aarsdagen for Digterens Fødsel i Fensmark Præstegaard den 29. Juli 1796 (Fensmark, 1946);

Oluf Friis, *Hjortens Flugt: Bidrag til studiet af Chr. Winthers digtning* (Copenhagen: H. Hirschsprung, 1961);

Bo Tao Michaelis and Erik Svendsen, *Perioden det 19. århundrede* (Copenhagen: Munksgaard, 1995).

Papers:

Christian Winther's papers are at the Danish Royal Library in Copenhagen and in the Bakkehus collection in Frederiksberg.

Checklist of Further Readings

Andreasen, Uffe, ed. *Romantismen, 1824–1840.* Copenhagen: Gyldendal, 1974.

Arkiv for dansk litteratur <http://www.adl.dk>.

Balslev-Clausen, Peter, ed. *Songs from Denmark.* Copenhagen: Danish Cultural Institute, 1988.

Bernd, Clifford Albrecht. *Poetic Realism in Scandinavia and Central Europe, 1820–1895.* Columbia, S.C.: Camden House, 1995.

Billeskov Jansen, Frederik J. *Den danske lyrik,* third edition, 5 volumes. Copenhagen: Hans Reitzel, 1985–1987.

Billeskov Jansen, ed. *Et hundrede danske digte. En lyrisk antologi.* Copenhagen: A. F. Høst, 1947.

Billeskov Jansen and P. M. Mitchell, eds. *Anthology of Danish Literature,* 2 volumes. Carbondale: Southern Illinois University Press, 1971.

Borum, Poul. *Danish Literature: A Short Critical Survey.* Copenhagen: Danske Selskab, 1979.

Borum and Bente Scavenius, eds. *Malernes og forfatternes Danmark–dansk natur.* Viborg: Borgen, 1986.

Bredsdorff, Elias. *Danish Literature in English.* Copenhagen: Munksgaard, 1950; reprinted, Westport, Conn.: Greenwood Press, 1973.

Bredsdorff, Thomas. *Den brogede oplysning. Om følelsernes fornuft og fornuftens følelse i 1700-tallets nordisk litteratur.* Copenhagen: Gyldendal, 2003.

Bredsdorff. *Digternes natur. En idés historie i 1700-tallets danske poesi.* Copenhagen: Gyldendal, 1975.

Bredsdorff and Anne-Marie Mai, eds. *1000 danske digte.* Copenhagen: Rosinante, 2000.

Brøndsted, Mogens, and Sven Møller Kristensen. *Danmarks litteratur,* 2 volumes. Copenhagen: Gyldendal, 1963.

Clareus, Ingrid, ed. *Scandinavian Women Writers: An Anthology from the 1880s to the 1980s.* New York: Greenwood Press, 1989.

Dahlerup, Pil. *Dansk litteratur. Middelalder,* 2 volumes. Copenhagen: Gyldendal, 1998.

Dahlerup. *Det moderne gennembruds kvinder.* Copenhagen: Gyldendal, 1983.

Dansk Litteraturcenter. *Litteraturnet=Literaturenet* <http://www.litteraturnet.dk>.

Friis, Oluf, ed. *A Book of Danish Verse,* translated by S. Foster Damon and Robert Silliman Hillyer. New York: American-Scandinavian Foundation, 1922.

Hansen, Ib Fischer, and others, eds. *Litteraturhåndbogen,* fourth edition. Copenhagen: Gyldendal, 1995.

Hav, Niels, and Svend Bøgh Nielsen, eds. *Samlerens lyrikkanon. Danske digte i 800 år.* Viborg: Samleren, 1996.

Jensen, Elisabeth Møller, Eva Hættner Aurelius, and Mai, eds. *Nordisk kvindelitteraturhistorie,* 5 volumes. Copenhagen: Rosinante, 1993–1999.

Jørgensen, Aage. *Dansk litteraturhistorisk bibliografi 1967–1986.* Copenhagen: Dansklærerforeningen, 1989.

Jørgensen. *Dansk litteraturhistorisk bibliografi, 1967–* <http://www.dlb.dansklf.dk>.

Jørgensen, John Christian, and Thomas Bredsdorff. *Dansk forfatterleksikon,* 2 volumes. Copenhagen: Rosinante, 2001.

Jørgensen. *Den sande kunst. Studier i dansk 1800-tals realisme.* Copenhagen: Borgen, 1980.

Kaspersen, Søren, and others, eds. *Dansk litteraturhistorie,* 9 volumes. Copenhagen: Gyldendal, 1983–1985.

Kieler, Benedicte, and Klaus P. Mortensen, eds. *Litteraturens stemmer–Gads Danske Forfatterleksikon.* Copenhagen: Gad, 1999.

Kristensen. *Den dobbelte eros. Studier i den danske romantik.* Copenhagen: Gyldendal, 1966.

Kristensen. *Impressionismen i dansk prosa, 1870–1900,* second edition. Copenhagen: Gyldendal, 1955.

Larsen, Hanna Astrup, ed. *Denmark's Best Stories, an Introduction to Danish Fiction.* New York: American-Scandinavian Foundation/Norton, 1928.

Lauring, Palle. *A History of the Kingdom of Denmark,* translated by David Hohnen, second edition. Copenhagen: Høst & Søn, 1962.

Mai and Bo Kampmann Walther. *At gå til grunde. Sider af romantikkens litteratur og tænkning.* Odense: Odense University Press, 1997.

Mitchell. *A Bibliographical Guide to Danish Literature.* Copenhagen: Munksgaard, 1951.

Mitchell. *A History of Danish Literature.* Copenhagen: Gyldendal, 1957.

Mitchell and Kenneth H. Ober, eds. *The Royal Guest and Other Classical Danish Narrative,* translated by Mitchell and Ober. Chicago: University of Chicago Press, 1977.

Neiiendam, Klaus. *Renaissanceteatret i Danmark.* Copenhagen: Nyt Nordisk Forlag, 1988.

Nielsen, Erik A. *Digtere.* Copenhagen: Tiderne Skifter, 2001.

Nordstrom, Byron J. *Scandinavia since 1500.* Minneapolis: University of Minnesota Press, 2000.

Petersen, Carl S., and Vilhelm Andersen. *Illustreret dansk Litteraturhistorie,* 4 volumes. Copenhagen: Gyldendal, 1924–1934.

Rodholm, S. D. *A Harvest of Song: Translations and Original Lyrics.* Des Moines, Iowa: American Evangelical Lutheran Church, 1953.

Rossel, Sven H. *Mellem Holberg og Ewald, 1730–1766.* Copenhagen: Gyldendal, 1975.

Rossel, ed. *A History of Danish Literature.* Lincoln: University of Nebraska Press/American-Scandinavian Foundation, 1992.

Schmidt, Povl, and others, eds. *Læsninger i dansk litteratur,* 5 volumes. Odense: Odense University Press, 1997–1999.

Schroeder, Carol L. *A Bibliography of Danish Literature in English Translation, 1950–1980.* Copenhagen: Danske Selskab, 1982.

Sønderholm, Erik. *Dansk barok, 1630–1700. En versantologi.* Copenhagen: Gyldendal, 1974.

Stork, Charles W., trans. *A Second Book of Danish Verse.* Princeton: Princeton University Press/American-Scandinavian Foundation, 1947.

Thomsen, Ejnar. *Barokken i dansk digtning.* Copenhagen: Munksgaard, 1971.

Traustedt, P. H., ed. *Dansk litteraturhistorie,* 6 volumes, second edition. Copenhagen: Politikens Forlag, 1976–1977.

Wentzel, Knud. *Utopia. Et motiv i dansk lyrik.* Copenhagen: Munksgaard, 1990.

Zuck, Virpi, Niels Ingwersen, and Harald S. Naess, eds. *Dictionary of Scandinavian Literature.* Westport, Conn.: Greenwood Press, 1990.

Contributors

Marianne Alenius . . . . *Museum Tusculanum Press, University of Copenhagen*
Marina Allemano. . . . . *University of Alberta*
Claus Elholm Andersen . . . . *Denmark's International Study Program, Copenhagen*
Kim Andersen . . . . *Washington State University*
Lise Præstgaard Andersen . . . . *University of Southern Denmark*
Sune Auken . . . . *University of Copenhagen*
Søren Baggesen . . . . *Roskilde University*
Flemming Behrendt . . . .
Henrik Blicher . . . . *University of Copenhagen*
Mogens Brøndsted . . . . *University of Southern Denmark*
Merete von Eyben . . . . *Pasadena City College*
Knud Bjarne Gjesing . . . . *University of Southern Denmark*
Poul Houe . . . . *University of Minnesota*
Faith Ingwersen . . . . *University of Wisconsin–Madison*
Niels Ingwersen . . . . *University of Wisconsin–Madison*
Lanae H. Isaacson . . . .
Michael Krarup . . . .
Henk van der Liet . . . . *Universiteit van Amsterdam*
Jens Lyster . . . .
James Massengale . . . . *University of California, Los Angeles*
Helle Mathiasen. . . . . *University of Arizona*
Finn Hauberg Mortensen . . . . *University of Southern Denmark*
Mark Mussari . . . . *Villanova University*
Johan de Mylius . . . . *University of Southern Denmark, Odense*
Marita Akhøj Nielsen . . . . *Society for Danish Language and Literature*
Neil Christian Pages . . . . *State University of New York, Binghamton*
Sue Reindollar . . . .
Paul Ries . . . . *Darwin College, University of Cambridge*
Sven Hakon Rossel . . . . *University of Vienna*
Nete Schmidt . . . . *University of Wisconsin–Madison*
George C. Schoolfield . . . . *Yale University*
Søren Schou . . . . *Roskilde University Center, Denmark*
Leif Søndergaard . . . . *University of Southern Denmark*
Steven P. Sondrup . . . . *Brigham Young University*
Peer E. Sørensen . . . . *University of Aarhus*

Marianne Stecher-Hansen . . . . *University of Washington*
Jakob Stougaard-Nielsen . . . . *University of Washington*
Bo Kampmann Walther . . . . *University of Southern Denmark*
Peter Zeeberg . . . .*Society for Danish Language and Literature*
Keld Zeruneith . . . . *University of Copenhagen*

Cumulative Index

Dictionary of Literary Biography, Volumes 1-300
Dictionary of Literary Biography Yearbook, 1980-2002
Dictionary of Literary Biography Documentary Series, Volumes 1-19
Concise Dictionary of American Literary Biography, Volumes 1-7
Concise Dictionary of British Literary Biography, Volumes 1-8
Concise Dictionary of World Literary Biography, Volumes 1-4

Cumulative Index

DLB before number: *Dictionary of Literary Biography,* Volumes 1-300
Y before number: *Dictionary of Literary Biography Yearbook,* 1980-2002
DS before number: *Dictionary of Literary Biography Documentary Series,* Volumes 1-19
CDALB before number: *Concise Dictionary of American Literary Biography,* Volumes 1-7
CDBLB before number: *Concise Dictionary of British Literary Biography,* Volumes 1-8
CDWLB before number: *Concise Dictionary of World Literary Biography,* Volumes 1-4

A

B

C

D

E

F

G

H

J

K

L

M

N

O

P

Q

R

S

T

U

V

X

Y

Z

Ø

ISBN 0-7876-6837-0